Creo Parametric 13 Black Book

By

Gaurav Verma
Matt Weber
(CADCAMCAE Works)

Edited by

Kristen

ISBN # 978-1-77459-224-3

NOTICE TO THE READER

Publisher does not warrant or guarantee any of the products described in the text or perform any independent analysis in connection with any of the product information contained in the text. Publisher does not assume, and expressly disclaims, any obligation to obtain and include information other than that provided to it by the manufacturer.

The reader is expressly warned to consider and adopt all safety precautions that might be indicated by the activities herein and to avoid all potential hazards. By following the instructions contained herein, the reader willingly assumes all risks in connection with such instructions.

The Publisher makes no representation or warranties of any kind, including but not limited to, the warranties of fitness for a particular purpose or merchantability, nor are any such representations implied with respect to the material set forth herein, and the publisher takes no responsibility with respect to such material. The publisher shall not be liable for any special, consequential, or exemplary damages resulting, in whole or part, from the reader's use of, or reliance upon, this material.

DEDICATION

To teachers, who make it possible to disseminate knowledge
to enlighten the young and curious minds
of our future generations

To students, who are the future of the world

THANKS

To my friends and colleagues

To my family for their love and support

Training and Consultant Services

At CADCAMCAE WORKS, we provide effective and affordable one to one online training on various software packages in Computer Aided Design(CAD), Computer Aided Manufacturing(CAM), Computer Aided Engineering (CAE), and Computer programming languages(C/C++, Java, .NET, Android, Javascript, HTML and so on). The training is delivered through remote access to your system and voice chat via Internet at any time, any place, and at any pace to individuals, groups, students of colleges/universities, and CAD/CAM/CAE training centers. The main features of this program are:

Training as per your need

Highly experienced Engineers and Technician conduct the classes on the software applications used in the industries. The methodology adopted to teach the software is totally practical based, so that the learner can adapt to the design and development industries in almost no time. The efforts are to make the training process cost effective and time saving while you have the comfort of your time and place, thereby relieving you from the hassles of traveling to training centers or rearranging your time table.

Software Packages on which we provide basic and advanced training are:

CAD/CAM/CAE: CATIA, Creo Parametric, Creo Direct, SolidWorks, Autodesk Inventor, Solid Edge, UG NX, AutoCAD, AutoCAD LT, EdgeCAM, MasterCAM, SolidCAM, DelCAM, BOBCAM, UG NX Manufacturing, UG Mold Wizard, UG Progressive Die, UG Die Design, SolidWorks Mold, Creo Manufacturing, Creo Expert Machinist, NX Nastran, Hypermesh, SolidWorks Simulation, Autodesk Simulation Mechanical, Creo Simulate, Gambit, ANSYS and many others.

Computer Programming Languages: C++, VB.NET, HTML, Android, Javascript and so on.

Game Designing: Unity.

Civil Engineering: AutoCAD MEP, Revit Structure, Revit Architecture, AutoCAD Map 3D and so on.

We also provide consultant services for Design and development on the above mentioned software packages

For more information you can mail us at:
cadcamcaeworks@gmail.com

Table of Contents

Chapter 3 : Advanced Sketching and Practical

Chapter 4 : 3D Modeling Basics

Chapter 5 : 3D Modeling Practical and Practice

Chapter 6 : 3D Modeling Advanced

Chapter 7 : 3D Modeling Advanced Practical and Practice

Chapter 8 : 3D Modeling Advanced-II

Chapter 9 : Assembly and Practical

Chapter 10 : Advanced Assembly and Introduction to Mechanism

Chapter 11 : Sheetmetal Design

Chapter 12 : Surface Design

Chapter 13 : Drawing

Chapter 14 : Model Based Definition (MBD) and 3D Printing

Chapter 15 : Introduction to Sheetmetal Manufacturing

Chapter 16 : Simulation Studies in Creo Parametric

Preface

Creo Parametric 13 is a parametric, feature-based solid modeling tool that not only unites the three-dimensional (3D) parametric features with two-dimensional (2D) tools, but also addresses every design-through-manufacturing process. The continuous enhancements in the software has made it a complete PLM software. The software is capable of performing analysis with an ease. Its compatibility with CAM software is remarkable. Latest enhancement in the software include composite designing.

To support education, PTC gives free educational version of the Creo Parametric to students with a license of 1 year. You can get your free copy of education version of software by visiting the following link:

https://www.ptc.com/en/products/education/free-software

The **Creo Parametric 13 Black Book** is the 11th edition of our series on Creo Parametric. With lots of additions and thorough review, we present a book to help professionals as well as learners in creating some of the most complex solid models. The book follows a step by step methodology. In this book, we have tried to give real-world examples with real challenges in designing. We have tried to reduce the gap between university use of Creo Parametric and industrial use of Creo Parametric. In this edition of book, we have included new enhancements of Creo Parametric 13.4 interface. We have included topics on composite designing. The book covers almost all the information required by a learner to master Creo Parametric. The book starts with sketching and ends at advanced topics like Sheetmetal, Surface Design, 3D Printing, MBD, Sheet metal NC manufacturing, and Live Simulation. Some of the salient features of this book are :

In-Depth explanation of concepts

Every new topic of this book starts with the explanation of basic concepts. In this way, the user becomes capable of relating the things with real world.

Topics Covered

Every chapter starts with a list of topics being covered in that chapter. In this way, the users can easy find the topic of their interest easily.

Instruction through illustration

The instructions to perform any action are provided by maximum number of illustrations so that the user can perform the actions discussed in the book easily and effectively. There are about 1620 small and large illustrations that make the learning process effective.

Tutorial point of view

At the end of concept's explanation, the tutorial make the understanding of users firm and long lasting. Almost each chapter of the book has tutorials that are real world projects. Most of the tools in this book are discussed in the form of tutorials.

Project

Projects and exercises are provided to students for practicing.

For Faculty

If you are a faculty member, then you can ask for video tutorials on any of the topic, exercise, tutorial, or concept. As faculty, you can register on our website to get electronic desk copies of our latest books, self-assessment, and solution of practical. Faculty resources are available in the **Faculty Member** page of our website (**www.cadcamcaeworks.com**) once you login. Note that faculty registration approval is manual and it may take two days for approval before you can access the faculty website.

Formatting Conventions Used in the Text

All the key terms like name of button, tool, drop-down etc. are kept bold.

Free Resources

Link to the resources used in this book are provided to the users via e-mail. To get the resources, mail us at ***cadcamcaeworks@gmail.com*** with your contact information. With your contact record with us, you will be provided latest updates and informations regarding various technologies. The format to write us mail for resources is as follows:

Subject of E-mail as ***Application for resources of _______ book***.
Also, given your information like
Name:
Course pursuing/Profession:
Contact Address:
E-mail ID:

Note: We respect your privacy and value it. If you do not want to give your personal informations then you can ask for resources without giving your information.

About Authors

The author of this book, Gaurav Verma, has written and assisted in more than 20 titles in CAD/CAM/CAE which are already available in market. He has authored **AutoCAD Electrical Black Books** which are available in both **English** and **Russian** language. He has also authored **Creo Manufacturing 13 Black Book** which covers Expert Machinist and NC Assembly modules of Creo Parametric. He has provided consultant services to many industries in US, Greece, Canada, and UK.

The author of this book, Matt Weber, has authored many books on CAD/CAM/CAE available already in market. **SolidWorks Simulation Black Books** are one of the most selling books in SolidWorks Simulation field. The author has hands on experience on most of the CAD/CAM/CAE packages. If you have any query/doubt in any CAD/CAM/CAE package, then you can contact the author by writing at cadcamcaeworks@gmail.com

For Any query or suggestion

If you have any query or suggestion, please let us know by mailing us on ***cadcamcaeworks@gmail.com***. Your valuable constructive suggestions will be incorporated in our books and your name will be addressed in special thanks area of our books on your confirmation.

Chapter 1

Starting with Creo Parametric

Topics Covered

The major topics covered in this chapter are:

- ***Installing Creo Parametric 13***
- ***Starting Creo Parametric***
- ***Starting a new document***
- ***Terminology used in Creo Parametric***
- ***Opening a document***
- ***Closing documents***
- ***Basic Settings for Creo Parametric***
- ***Model Properties in Creo Parametric***
- ***Keyboard shortcuts and Mouse Functions***

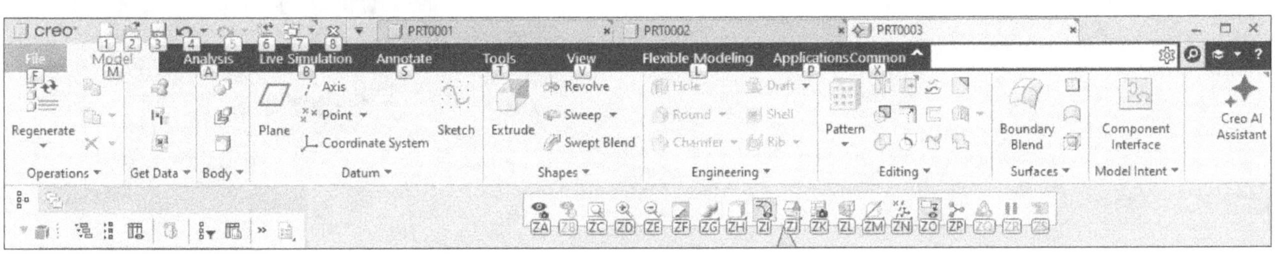

INSTALLING CREO PARAMETRIC 13

- If you are installing using the CD/DVD provided by PTC then go to the folder containing **setup.exe** file and then right-click on **setup.exe** in the folder. A shortcut menu is displayed on the screen; refer to Figure-1.

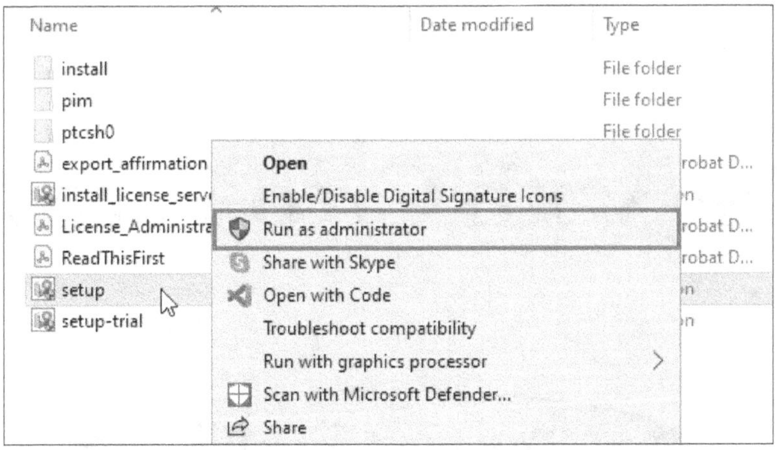

Figure-1. Shortcut menu for installation

- Click on the **Run as administrator** option from the shortcut menu. The **User Account Control** dialog box will be displayed.
- Click on the **Yes** button from the dialog box. The **Creo Installation Assistant** dialog box will be displayed; refer to Figure-2.

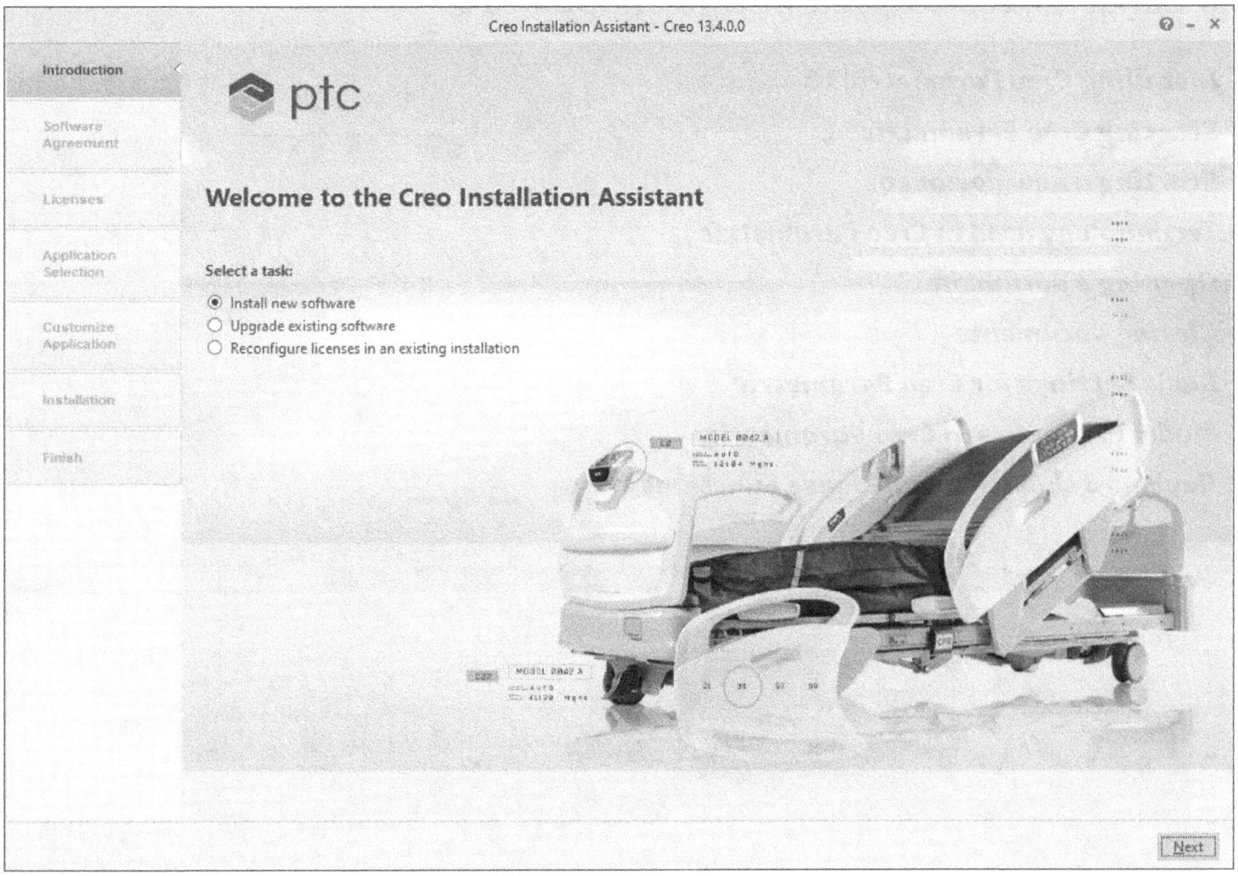

Figure-2. Creo Installation Assistant dialog box

- Click on the **Next** button from the dialog box. The **License Agreement** page will be displayed. Accept the agreement and select the check box below the agreement.

- Click on the **Next** button from the dialog box. The license page will be displayed; refer to Figure-3.

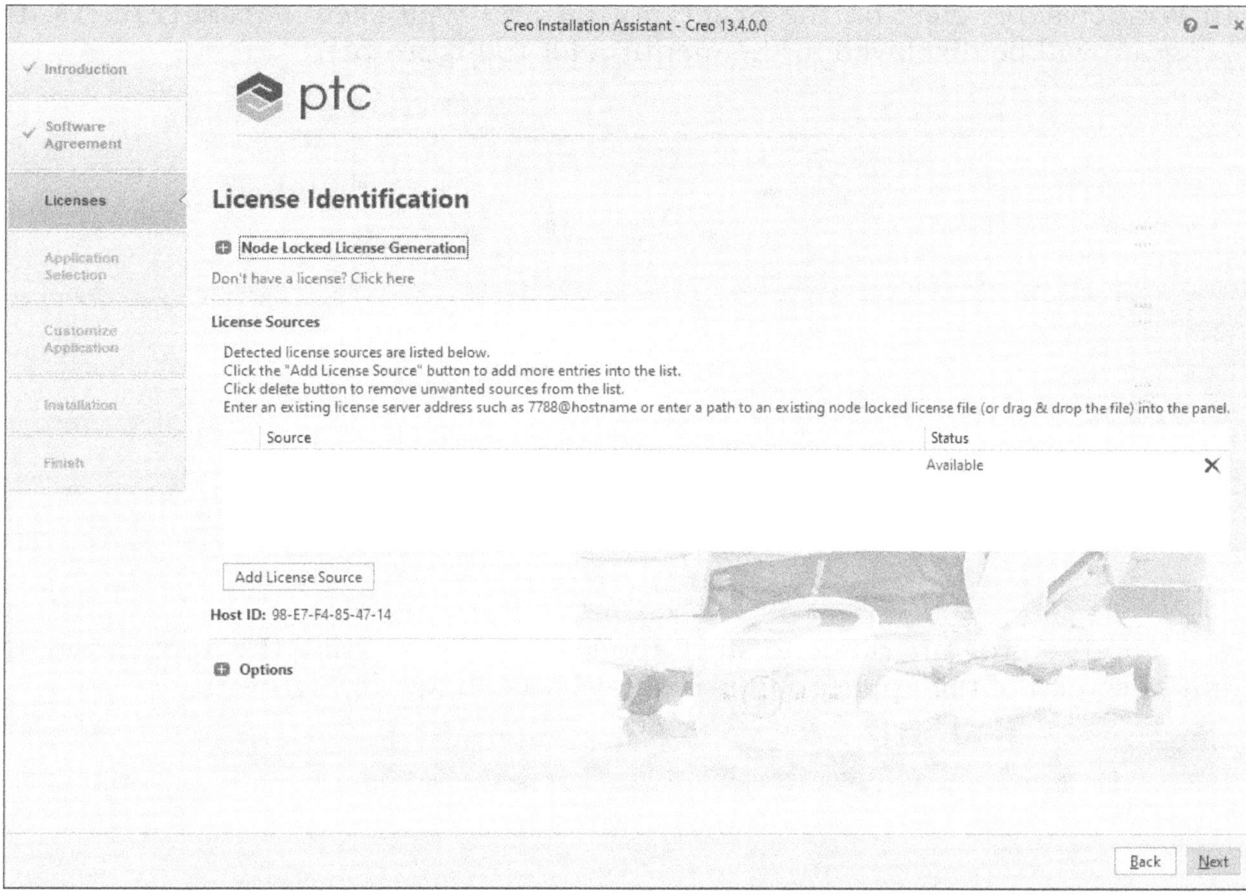

Figure-3. License page of Creo Installation

- Enter the license file location in the edit box under **Source** column in the **License Sources** area; refer to Figure-4.

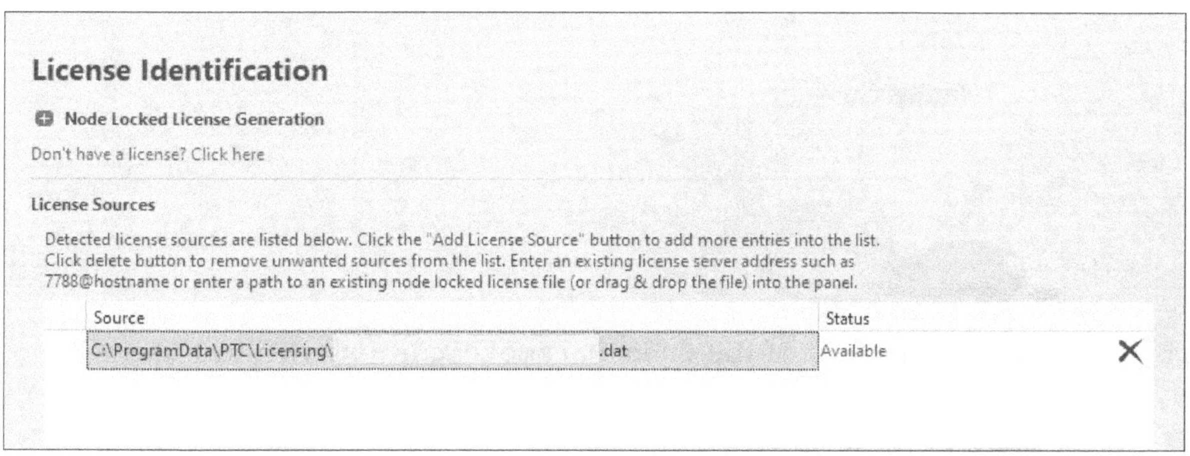

Figure-4. License file location

- Click on the **Next** button from the dialog box. Select the check boxes for the applications that you are licensed to install and click on the **Install** button. The software will be installed.
- After the installation is finished, click on the **Finish** button to exit.

STARTING CREO PARAMETRIC

- Click on the **Start** button from the **Taskbar** to open the **Start** menu.
- In Windows 10, click on the **Start** button and type **Creo Parametric 13**, the program will be displayed in the menu; refer to Figure-5.

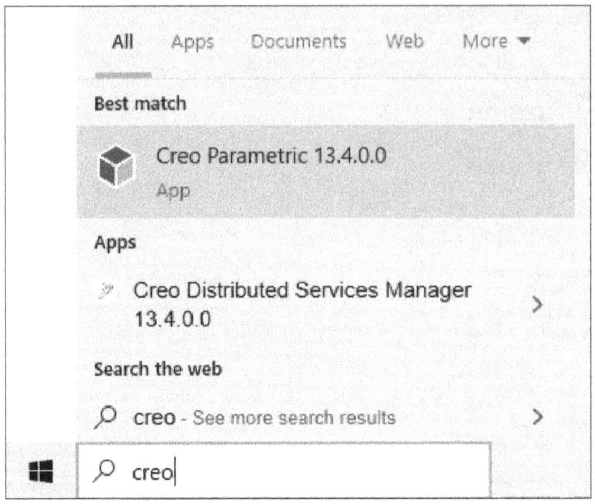

Figure-5. Start menu

- Click on the program name to start application. On starting the application, the initial screen of the application is displayed as shown in Figure-6.

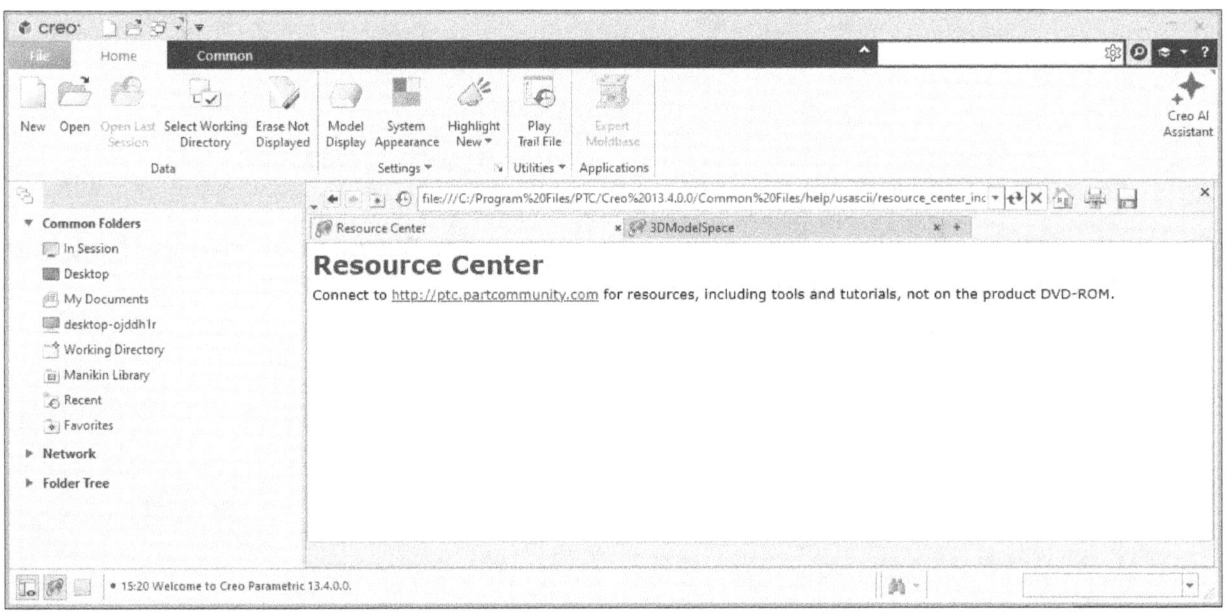

Figure-6. Initial screen of Creo Parametric

- The elements of interface of the **Creo Parametric** are shown in Figure-7.

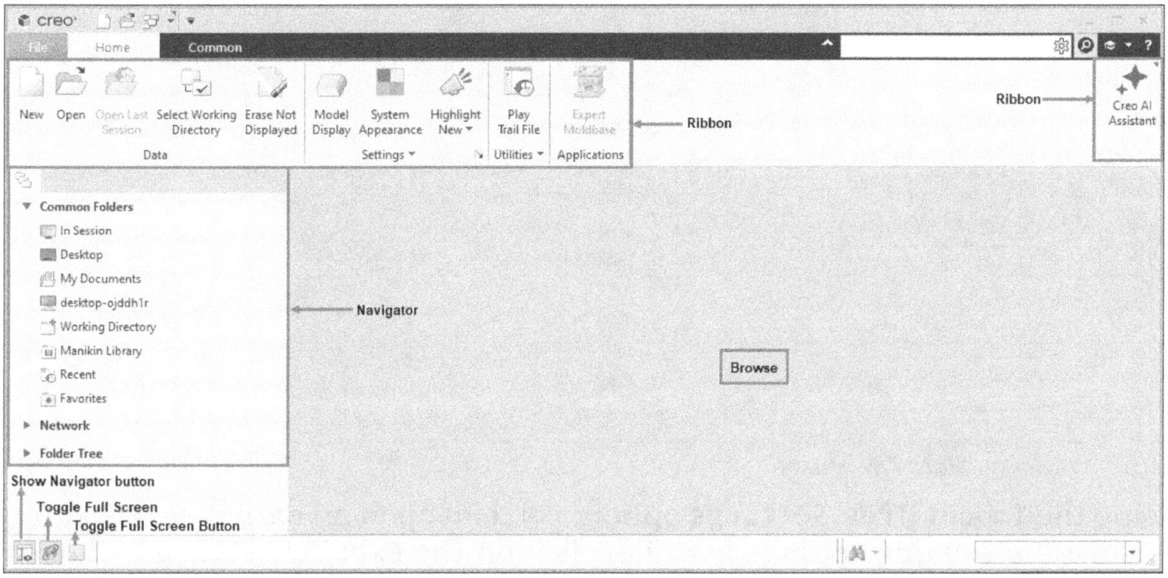

Figure-7. Creo Parametric interface

The elements in the interface are discussed next.

CREO PARAMETRIC INTERFACE

The interface of Creo Parametric comprises of various elements like Navigator panel, Browser, Ribbon, File menu, and so on. These elements are discussed next.

Navigator panel

The **Navigator** panel is used to navigate through folders and features. This panel has three tabs named: **Model Tree**, **Folder Browser**, and **Favorites**. The **Model Tree** tab will be active only when you have opened a model/assembly file; refer to Figure-8.

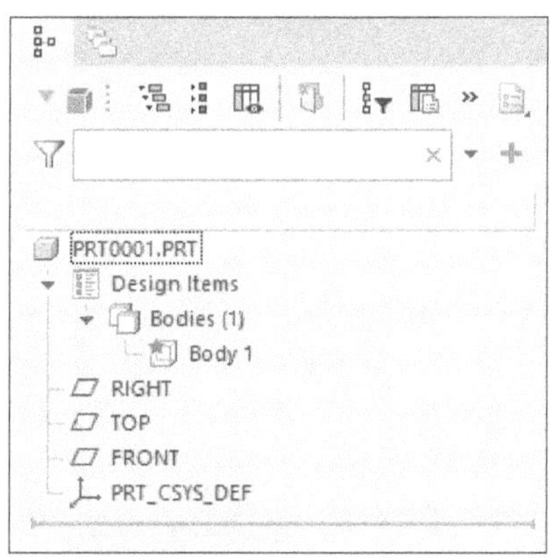

Figure-8. Model Tree

Model Tree

- The **Model Tree** contains all the features that are created automatically or manually while creating model or assembly.
- The green line in the **Model Tree** represents the position where the next feature will be inserted. You can drag this line up or down to create or suppress features.
- Click on the **Settings** button to display the menu related to settings; refer to Figure-9.

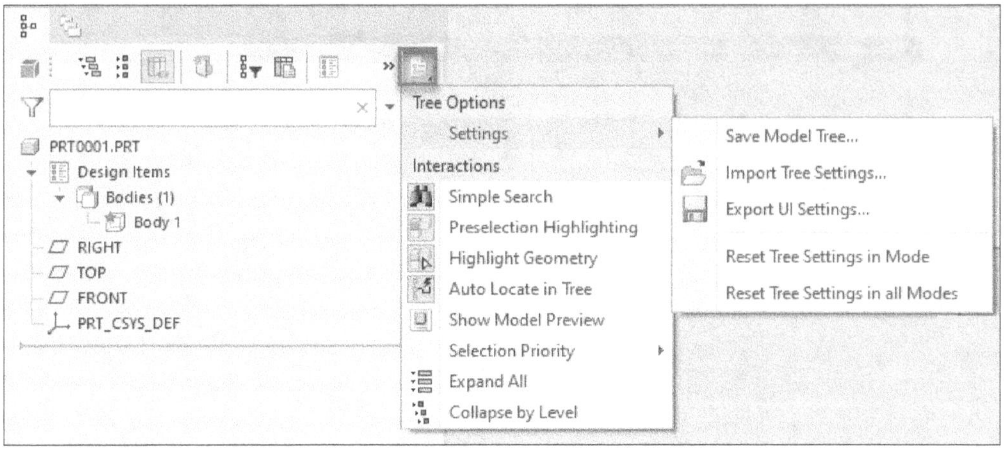

Figure-9. Model Tree settings

- Using the **Import Tree Settings** option, you can open an earlier saved setting file.
- To save the existing settings in a file, click on the **Export Settings File** option. The **Save Model Tree Configuration** dialog box will be displayed. Specify desired file name and click on the **Save** button. The settings will be saved in **.cfg** file.
- Click on the **Tree Filters** button from the **Model Tree** toolbar to add or remove the entities to be displayed in **Model Tree**. The **Tree Filters** dialog box will be displayed; refer to Figure-10.

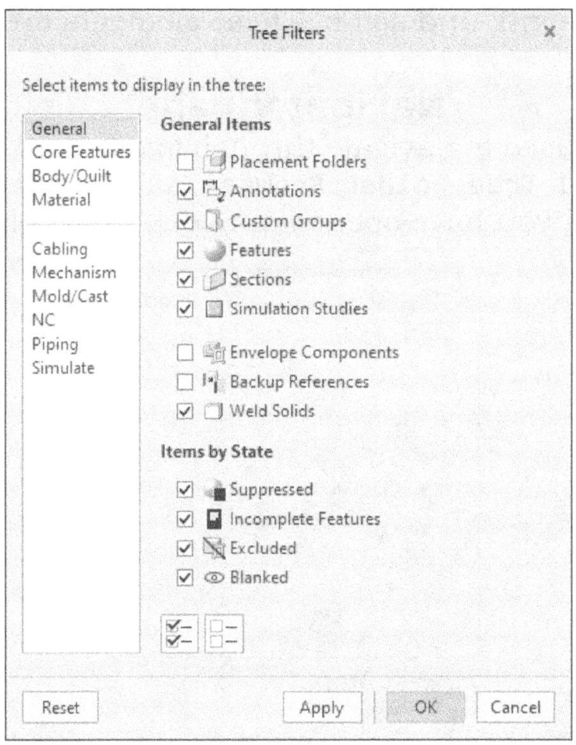

Figure-10. Tree Filters dialog box

- Select the check boxes that you want to display in the **Model Tree** and click on the **OK** button from the dialog box.

Folder Browser

- Click on the **Folder Browser** button to display the **Folder Browser**; refer to Figure-11.

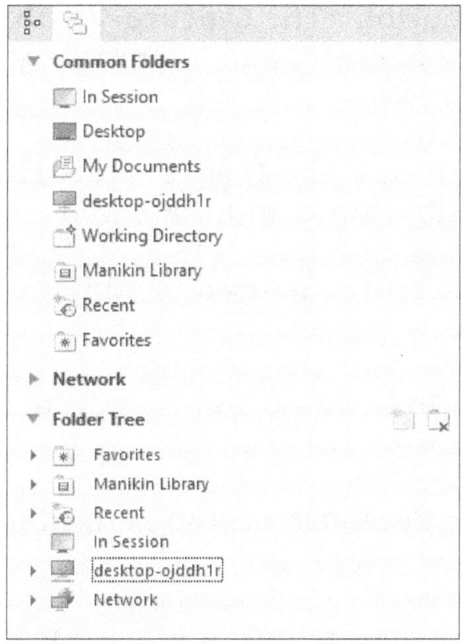

Figure-11. Folder Browser

- Using the **Folder Browser**, you can quickly browse through the folders to get desired files.

Favorites Tab

- The **Favorites** tab is used to display the locations saved as favorite.
- To display or hide the **Navigation** panel, click on the **Show Navigator** toggle button in the Status bar; refer to Figure-12.

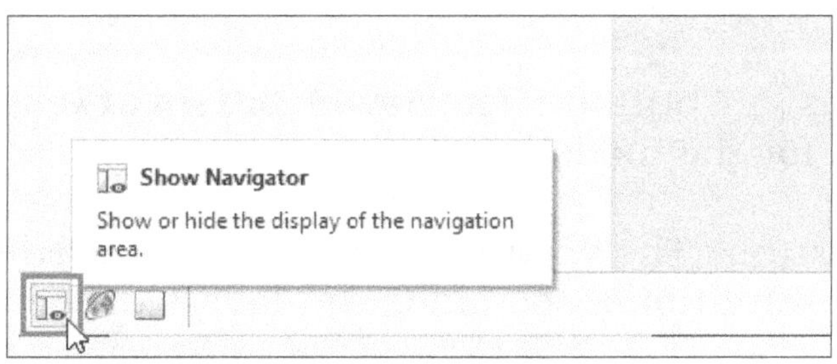

Figure-12. Show Navigator button

In-Graphics Toolbar

The **In-Graphics** toolbar is embedded at the top of the graphics window; refer to Figure-13. The buttons on the toolbar control the display of graphics. Various options available in the **In-Graphics** toolbar are discussed next.

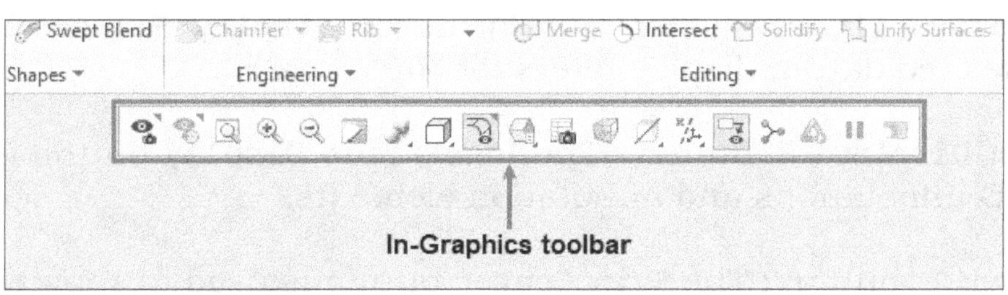

Figure-13. In Graphics toolbar

- **Capture Visibility** button : The **Capture Visibility** button is used to save the currently visible state of objects as a temporary view so that you can use it again later.
- **Toggle Visibility** button : The **Toggle Visibility** button is used to switch between the currently visible state and the saved view state of objects.
- **Refit** button : The **Refit** button is used to adjust the zoom level to fully display the object on the screen.
- **Zoom In** button : The **Zoom In** button is used to zoom in the target geometry to view in greater detail.
- **Zoom Out** button : The **Zoom Out** button is used to gain a wider perspective of the geometrical context.
- **Repaint** button : The **Repaint** button is used to redraw the current view.
- **Rendering Options** button : Click on the **Rendering Options** button to toggle the ambient occlusion effect and scene background on or off.
- **Display Style** button : Click on the **Display Style** button to set desired display style for the model.
- **Tangent Edges** button : The **Tangent Edges** button is used to toggle the display of edges between tangent surfaces.
- **Saved Orientations** button : The **Saved Orientations** button is used to set desired orientation for the model.
- **View Manager** button : The **View Manager** button is used to set the orientations, appearances, representations, sections, and layers of the model.
- **Perspective View** button : The **Perspective View** button is used to toggle the perspective view.
- **Transparency Control** button : The **Transparency Control** button is used to set transparency for bodies, quilts, and tessellated geometry in the model.
- **Datum Display Filters** button : The **Datum Display Filters** button is used to define desired datum display filters for the model.
- **Annotation Display** button : The **Annotation Display** button is used to turn on or off 3D annotations and annotation elements.
- **Spin Center** button : The **Spin Center** button is used to show the spin center and use it in the default locaton, or hide the spin center to use the pointer location as the spin center.

- **Simulate** button : Click on the **Simulate** button to toggle the simulation on or off.

- **Pause Simulation** button : Click on the **Pause Simulation** button to pause or resume the simulation.

- **Animation Options** button : The **Animation Options** button is used to display the animated deformation result and to toggle the color bands/color band animation in the deformation display.

RIBBON

Ribbon is the area of the application window that holds all the tools for designing and editing; refer to Figure-14.

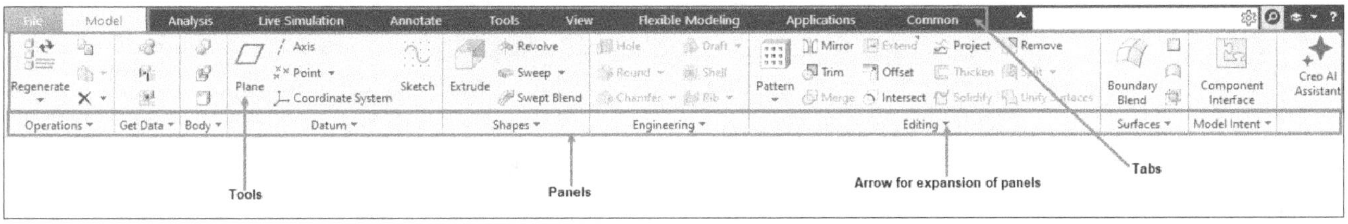

Figure-14. Ribbon

The tools in the **Ribbon** will be discussed later in the book as per their need in designing.

FILE MENU

The options in the **File** menu are used to perform operations related to files; refer to Figure-15.

Figure-15. File Menu

The options in the **File** menu are discussed next.

New Tool

The **New** tool is available in the **Ribbon** and **Quick Access Toolbar**; refer to Figure-16. This tool is used to create a new file. The procedure to use this tool is given next.

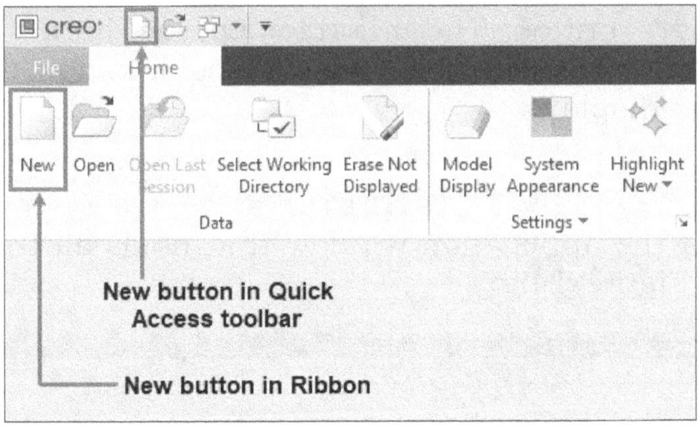

Figure-16. New button

- Click on the **New** tool from desired location. The **New** dialog box will be displayed; refer to Figure-17.

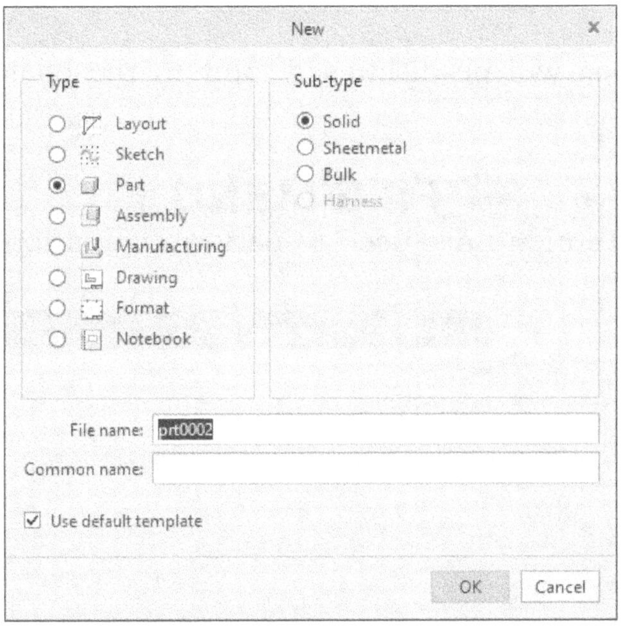

Figure-17. New dialog box

- Select desired radio button from the **Type** area of the dialog box. The related sub-types will be displayed in the **Sub-type** area.
- Select desired sub-type and specify the name in the **File name** edit box.
- For most of the file types, the **Use default template** check box is displayed. If this check box is selected then the default template is used for creating new files. The unit system for default templates is **IPS**.
- Clear this check box if you want to select any other template.
- Click on the **OK** button from the dialog box. The file will be created and environment related to selected type will be displayed.
- If you have cleared the **Use default template** check box then the **New File Options** dialog box will be displayed; refer to Figure-18.

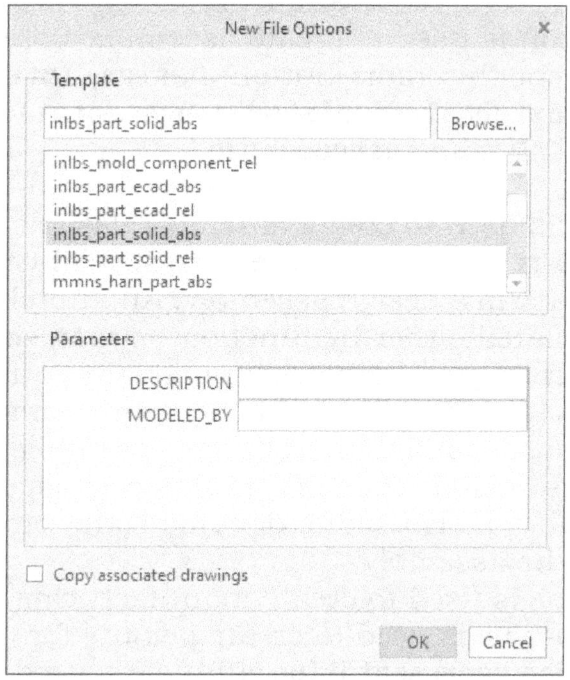

Figure-18. New File Options dialog box

- Select desired template and click on the **OK** button to create the file.

The description of various file types displayed in the **New** dialog box is given next.

Layout

The **Layout** radio button in the **New** dialog box is used to create new layout files. Layout files are used to create layouts based on the ideas. In the layout environment, you can create 2D sketches, import images, import and edit other layouts, and so on.

Sketch

The **Sketch** radio button is used to activate sketching environment where you can create sketches.

Part

The **Part** radio button is used to create 3D models. There are four sub-types for this radio button; **Solid**, **Sheetmetal**, **Bulk**, and **Harness**.

- The **Solid** sub-type is used to create solid/surface 3D models.
- The **Sheetmetal** sub-type is used to create sheetmetal models.
- The **Bulk** sub-type is used to create representation of model elements in assembly. For example, you need a generator of specific kind in your assembly but you do not want to model it then you can save generator in the bill of material (BOM) by making it a bulk part.
- The **Harness** sub-type is used to create wiring in the model. This radio button is active when you are working in an assembly and from within the assembly, you need wire harness or pipe harness.

Assembly

The **Assembly** radio button is used to create assemblies of solid/sheet metal parts. There are 10 sub-types for this radio button; **Design**, **Interchange**, **Process Plan**, **NC Model**, **Mold layout**, **External simplified representation**, **Configurable Module**, **Configurable product**, **ECAD**, and **Instrumented**.

- The **Design** sub-type is used to create assembly designs.
- The **Interchange** sub-type is used to create a special type of assembly that you can create and then use in a design assembly. An interchange assembly consists of models that are related either by function or representation. You can create both functional interchanges (to replace functionally equivalent components) and simplify interchanges (to substitute components in a simplified representation) in the same interchange assembly. Interchange assemblies, like family tables and layouts, provide a powerful method of automatic replacement.
- The **Process Plan** sub-type is used to document the process of assembling/dis-assembling parts in the assembly.
- The **NC Model** sub-type is used to create manufacturing model of the assembly.
- The **Mold layout** sub-type is used to create layouts for molds.
- The **External simplified representation** sub-type is used to create representations of the assembly. These representations can be saved independent of the parent assembly file.
- The **Configurable module** sub-type is used to create modules that consist of parts and assemblies interrelated to each other by some relation. The module can be configured with the help of variables.
- The **Configurable product** sub-type is used to create configurable assemblies.
- The **ECAD** sub-type is used to create electronic board design.
- The **Instrumented** sub-type is used to create instrumented assembly that maintains one-way associativity of parts in the assembly. In instrumented assembly, if you modify a part outside the assembly environment then it will be updated in Instrumented assembly. But, if you modify part in assembly environment then it will not be updated at source.

Manufacturing

The **Manufacturing** radio button is used to create manufacturing models for generating CNC codes. There are 9 sub-types available for this radio button; **NC assembly**, **Expert Machinist**, **CMM**, **Sheetmetal**, **Cast cavity**, **Mold cavity**, **Harness**, **Process plan**, and **Additive Manufacturing**.

- The **NC assembly** sub-type is used to create assembly model for manufacturing a component on nc machine like turning centers and milling centers.
- The **Expert Machinist** sub-type is used to perform the same work as done in NC assembly sub-type. But, the Expert Machinist is a lite version of NC assembly and is having limited tools to perform action. The **Creo Manufacturing 13 Black Book** is already available in the market on this topic from same author.
- The **CMM** sub-type is used to create programs for Coordinate Measuring Machines.
- The **Sheetmetal** sub-type is used to generate NC codes for sheet metal forming machines.
- The **Cast cavity** sub-type is used to create cavity for casting the model part.
- The **Mold cavity** sub-type is used to create mold for the model part.
- The **Harness** sub-type is used to create wiring/piping for manufacturing/layouting.

- The **Process plan** sub-type is used to generate manufacturing process plan.
- The **Additive Manufacturing** sub-type is used to create products by 3D printing and other additive manufacturing techniques.

Drawing

The **Drawing** radio button is used to create 2D drawings from models and assemblies. The drawings are the paper representations of models and assemblies for manufacturing.

Format

The **Format** radio button is used to create format for drawings. These formats are later used in multiple drawings as templates.

Notebook

The **Notebook** radio button is used to create notes of ideas regarding the design.

Open Tool

The **Open** tool is used to open Creo Parametric files and import files of other CAD applications. The procedure to use this tool is given next.

- Click on the **Open** tool from the **File** menu, **Ribbon**, or **Quick Access Bar**. The **File Open** dialog box will be displayed; refer to Figure-19.

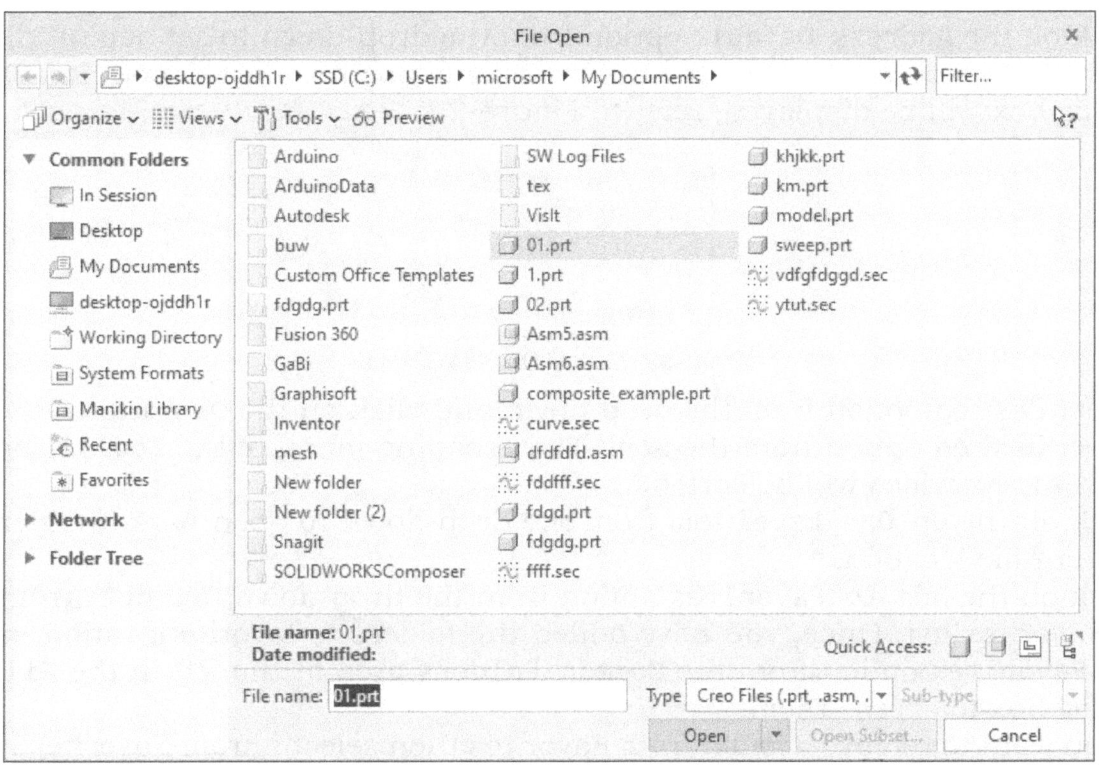

Figure-19. File Open dialog box

- The left pane of the dialog box is used to access the common folders. Note that the files that are not saved yet but are in current session can be accessed by clicking on the **In Session** link from the **Common Folders** area in the left pane.
- Click on the **Views** tool in the toolbar of the dialog box. The drop-down will be displayed as shown in Figure-20.

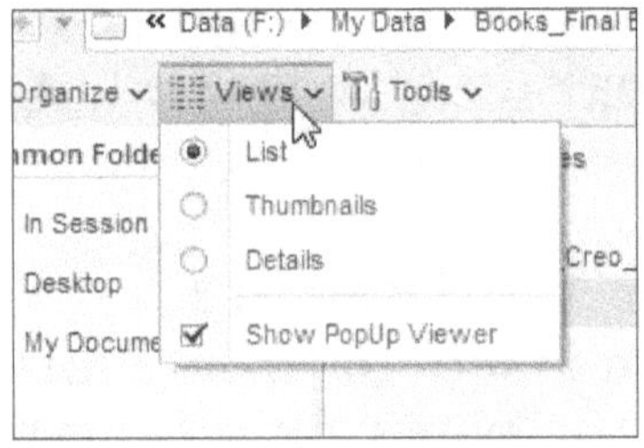

Figure-20. Views drop-down

- Select desired radio button to display the files in desired manner.
- Click on the **Tools** option in toolbar to modify parameters related to **File Open** dialog box. The drop-down will be displayed as shown in Figure-21.

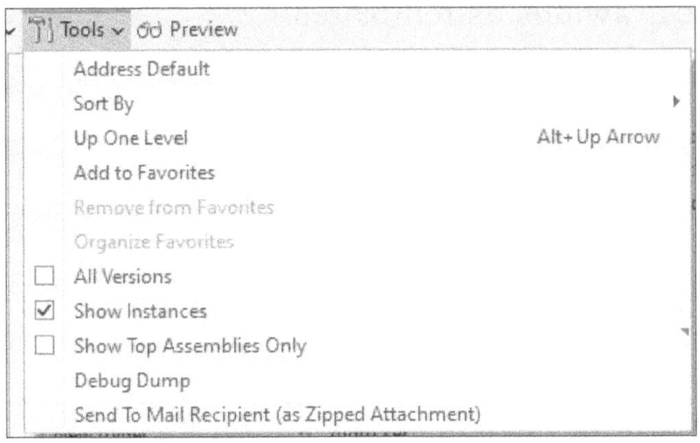

Figure-21. Tools drop down

- Click on the **Address Default** option from the drop-down to set default directory which will open automatically in **File Open** dialog box. The **'Look In' Default** dialog box will be displayed; refer to Figure-22.

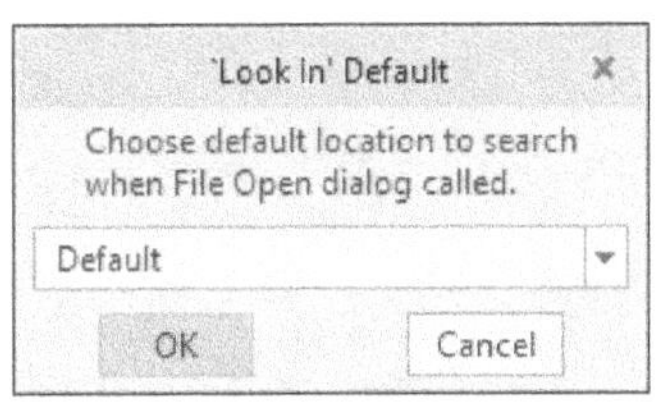

Figure-22. 'Look in' Default dialog box

- Select desired option from the drop-down and click on the **OK** button.
- Select desired option from the **Sort By** cascading menu of the **Tools** drop-down to define how files will be sorted.
- Click on the **Up One Level** tool from the drop-down to open parent folder of the current file location.
- Click on the **Add to Favorites** option from the drop-down to add current folder in Favorites list. Once, you have added the folders to favorite location, click on the **Favorites** option from the **Common Folders** area at the left in the **File Open** dialog box to access them.
- If you want to remove a folder from Favorites then select it from Favorites location and click on the **Remove from Favorites** tool in the **Tools** drop-down.
- Select the **All Versions** tool from the drop-down to check all the versions of files.
- Click in the **Type** drop-down to specify the file type; refer to Figure-23.

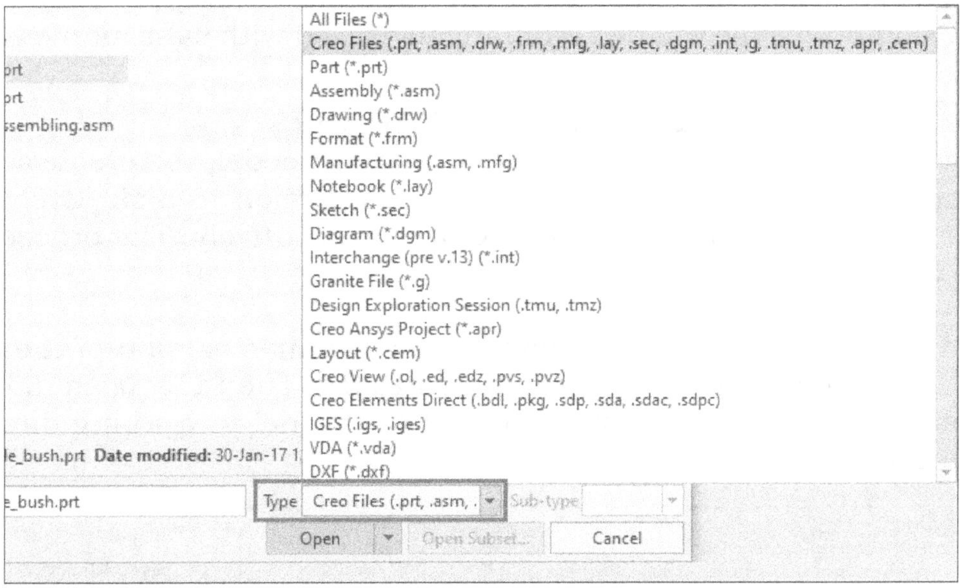

Figure-23. Type drop-down

- Double-click on the file under the **Name** column of the dialog box. The file will open.

Save Tool

The **Save** tool in the **File** menu is used to save the files. If you are saving a file for the first time then the **Save Object** dialog box will be displayed otherwise the file will be save automatically. The procedure to use this tool is given next.

- Click on the **Save** tool from the **File** menu, **Ribbon**, or **Quick Access Toolbar**. If you are saving a new file for the first time then the **Save Object** dialog box will be displayed; refer to Figure-24.

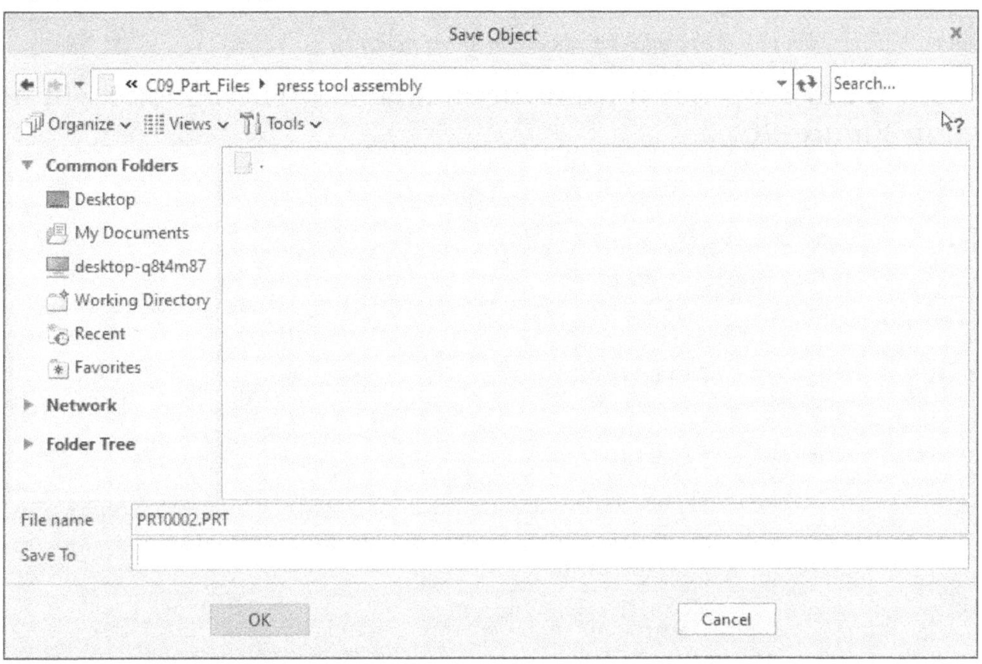

Figure-24. Save Object dialog box

- Specify the location of the file and click on the **OK** button from the dialog box to save it.

- Now, if you again click on the **Save** button then the **Save Object** dialog box will not be displayed and the file will be automatically saved with same name and settings.

Loading backup files

Every time when you save an object while creating the model, you create a new version of the object in memory, and write the previous version to disk. Creo Parametric numbers each version of an object storage file consecutively. The procedure to load all versions of the file is discussed next.

- If you want to get to previous version or last modified version of the model then click on the **Open** tool from **File** menu or **Ribbon**. The **File Open** dialog box will be displayed showing the latest version of the model in working directory; refer to Figure-25.

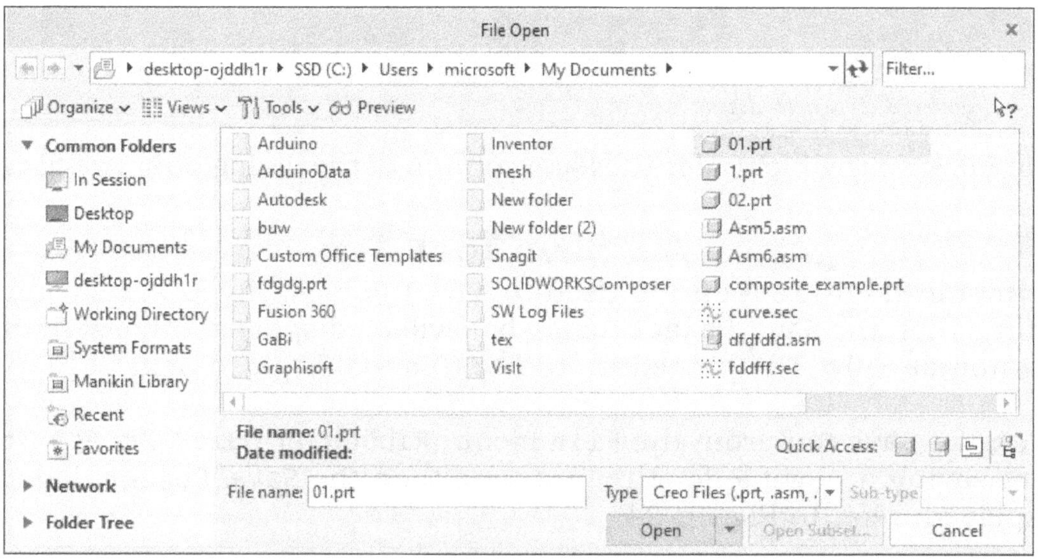

Figure-25. File Open dialog box with latest version of the model

- Click on the **Tools** drop-down from the dialog box. The options will be displayed as shown in Figure-26.

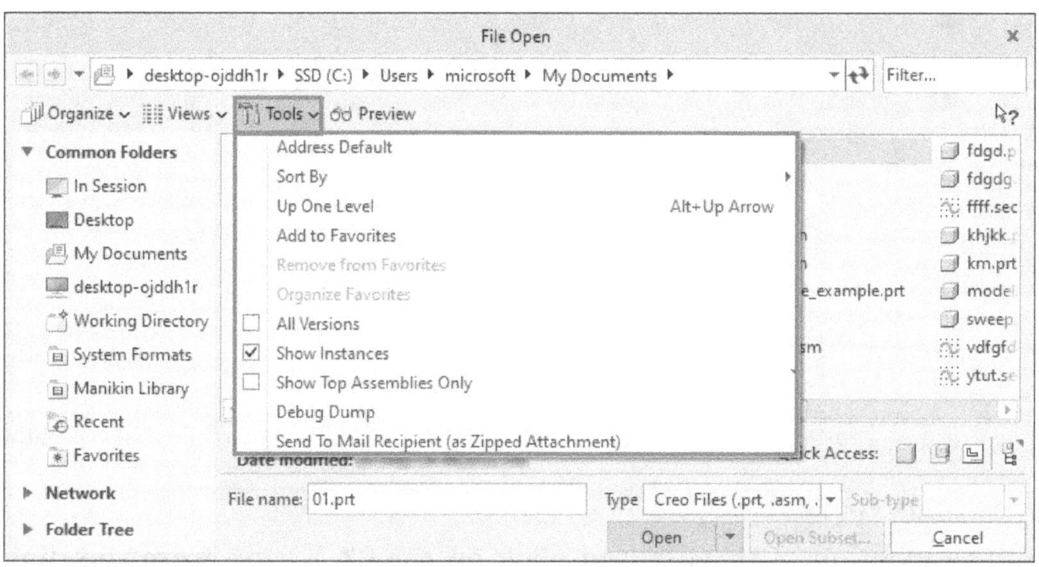

Figure-26. Tools drop-down

- Select **All Versions** check box from the drop-down. All versions of the model will be displayed in the dialog box; refer to Figure-27.

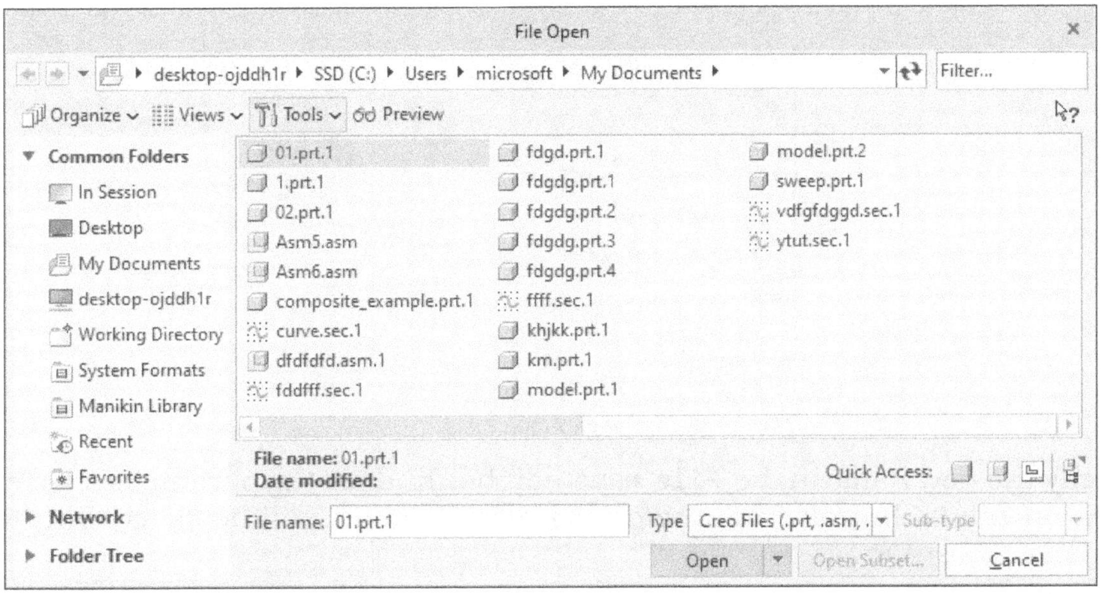

Figure-27. All versions of the model

- Select desired version of the model which you want to use and click on **Open** button. The file will be opened.

Save As

There are three options in the **File** menu for **Save As** tool; refer to Figure-28. The **Save a Copy** option is used to create a copy of the file with new name. The **Save a Backup** tool is used to create a backup copy of the current file in the same directory. The **Mirror Part** tool is used to save a mirror copy of the current file. Note that the files saved by this tool automatically synchronize with the original file. The procedure to use this tool is given next.

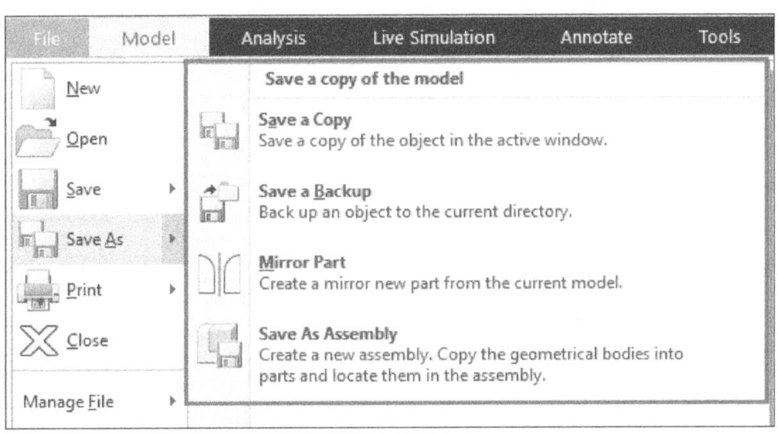

Figure-28. Save As options

- Click on desired tool from the **Save As** cascading menu; refer to Figure-28. (**Mirror Part** in our case).
- The related dialog box will be displayed; refer to Figure-29.

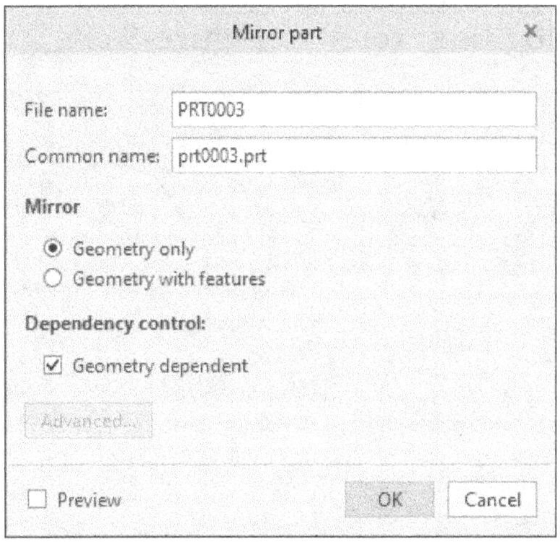

Figure-29. Mirror part dialog box

- Specify the new name in the **File name** edit box and set the parameters as required.
- Click on the **OK** button from the dialog box. The part will be saved with the new name.

Print

The **Print** tool is used to take printouts of the drawings/models for shop floor use. There are three options for printing; refer to Figure-30. The **Print** option is used to take print out of the object currently displayed in the drawing area. In this case, you can configure the printer as per your requirement. The **Quick Print** option is used to take quick prints of the objects. In this case, you can only select a printer. You cannot change the settings of the printer. The **Quick Drawing** option is displayed for models and assemblies. Using this option, you can quickly create drawings from the model/assembly and take print outs. The **Prepare for 3D Printing** option is used to prepare the model 3D Printing. You will learn more about this option later in the book. The procedures to use these tools are given next.

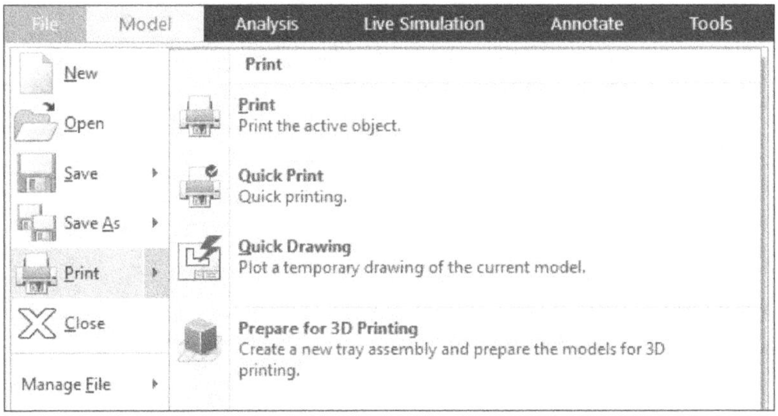

Figure-30. Print options

Print Tool

- Click on the **Print** option from the **Print** cascading menu; refer to Figure-30. The **Printer Configuration** dialog box will be displayed; refer to Figure-31.
- Click on the button and add desired printer.
- Click on the **Page** tab from the dialog box and specify desired parameters in the dialog box displayed; refer to Figure-32.

Figure-31. Printer Configuration dialog box

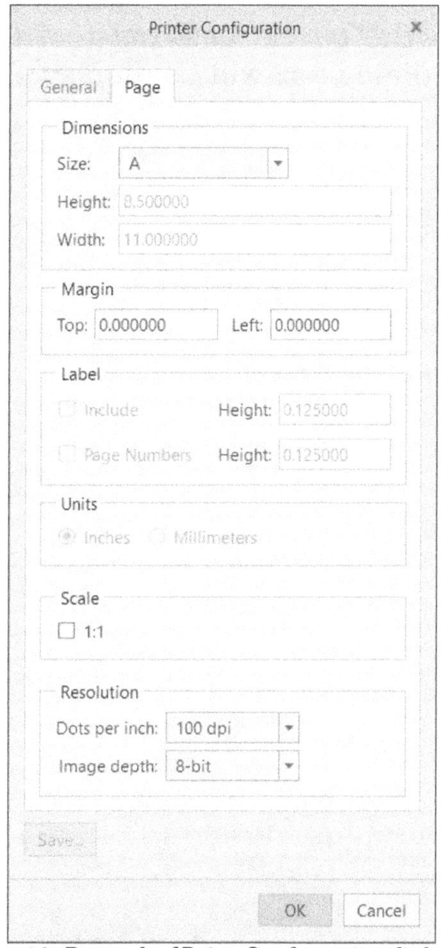

Figure-32. Page tab of Print Configuration dialog box

- Click on the **OK** button from the dialog box to print the object.

Quick Print tool

- Click on the **Quick Print** tool from the **Print** cascading menu. The **Print** dialog box will be displayed as shown in Figure-33.

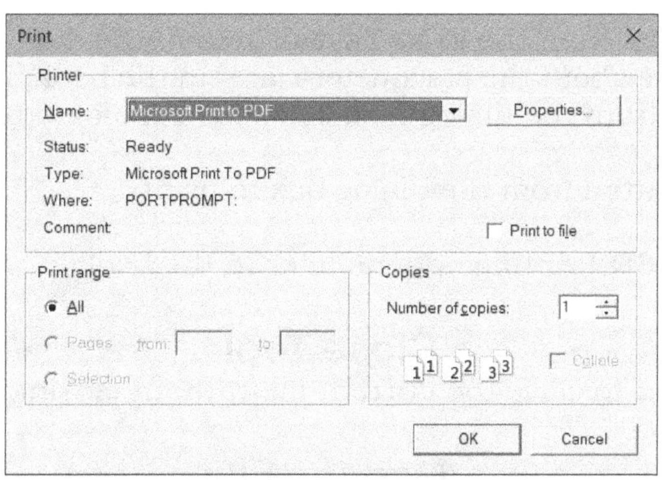

Figure-33. Print dialog box

- Select desired printer from the **Name** drop-down in the dialog box.
- Set desired parameters and then click on the **OK** button from the dialog box to print the objects.

Quick Drawing tool

- Click on the **Quick Drawing** tool from the **Print** cascading menu. The **Quick Drawing** dialog box will be displayed; refer to Figure-34.

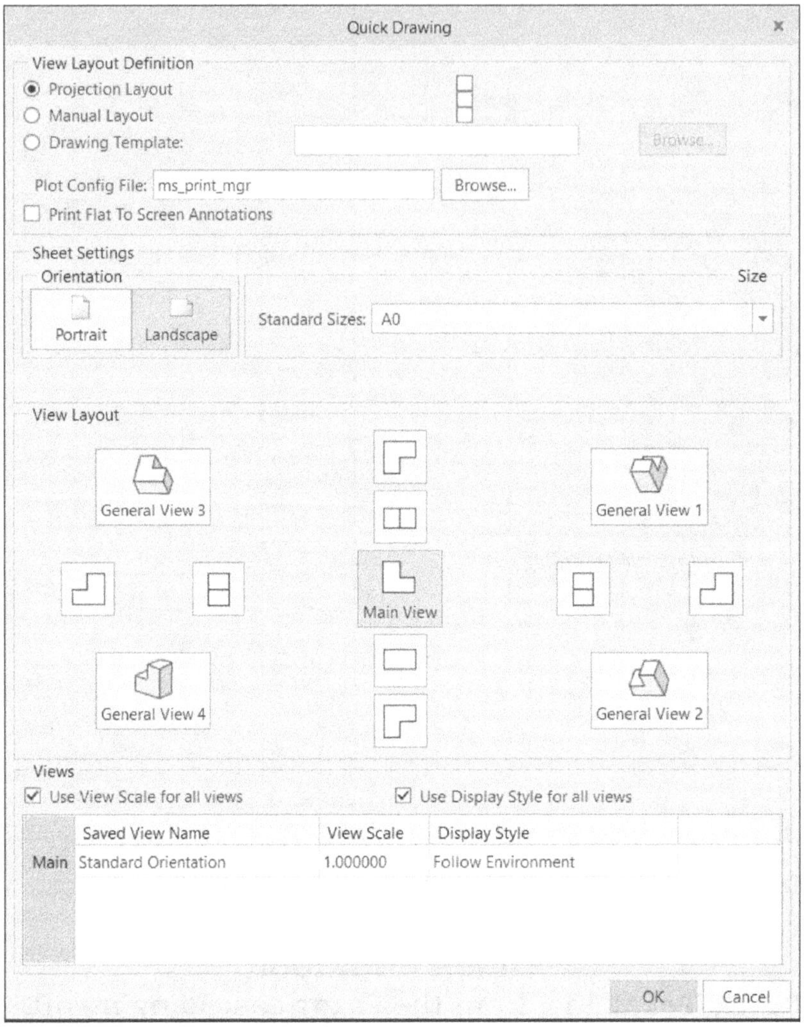

Figure-34. Quick Drawing dialog box

- Select desired views from the **View Layout** area of the dialog box.
- You will learn more about the parameters later in the book. For the moment, click on the **OK** button from the dialog box. The **Print** dialog box will be displayed as discussed earlier.
- Click on the **OK** button from the dialog box to print.

You will learn about 3D Printing options later in the book.

Close Tool

The **Close** tool is used to close the current file without closing the application.

Manage File

The **Manage File** options are used to manage files of Creo Parametric. There are five options available in this cascading menu; **Rename**, **Delete Old Versions**, **Delete All Versions**, **Declare**, and **Instance Accelerator**; refer to Figure-35.

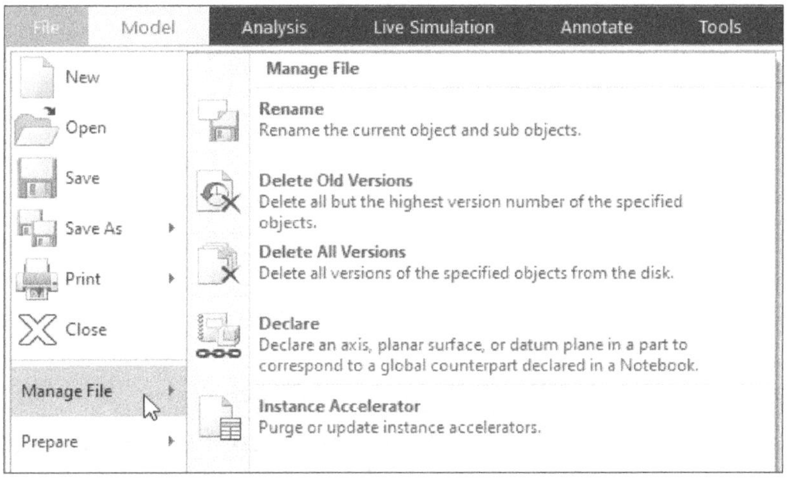

Figure-35. Manage File options

- The **Rename** tool in the **Manage File** cascading menu is used to rename the current file. To rename the file, click on this tool. The **Rename** dialog box will be displayed; refer to Figure-36. Specify desired name and click on the **OK** button from the dialog box.

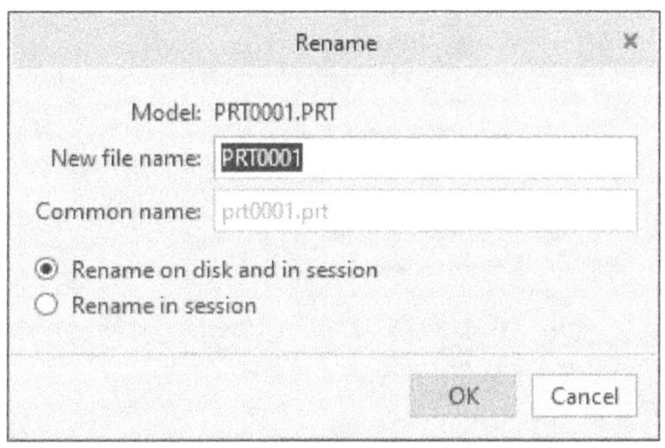

Figure-36. Rename dialog box

- The **Delete Old Versions** tool is used to delete all the previous versions of the file but to keep the latest version of the file. Note that whenever you save the file in Creo Parametric, it creates a new version of file so that anytime you can go back to previous versions. But more versions take more space on disk. So, the **Delete Old Versions** tool is used to delete the older versions. To delete the older versions of the file, click on the **Delete Old Versions** tool from the **File** menu. The **Delete Old Versions** dialog box will be displayed. Click on the **Yes** button from the dialog box to delete the older versions of the file.
- The **Delete All Versions** tool is used to delete the file and its history from session as well as working directory. This tool works in the same way as the previous tool works but it also removes the current version of file.
- The **Declare** tool is used to declare any axis or datum as global for assembly purpose. For using this tool, you must have a notebook active in session. You can create a notebook by using the **New** dialog box. Once you have declared a datum as global, each part of assembly can use it for locating itself.
- The **Instance Accelerator** tool is used to delete all the useless data of the current file so that the work can be done more efficiently on the file. Using this tool, you can delete the previous versions of the file that are of no use now. On selecting this tool, the **Instance Accelerator** dialog box will be displayed; refer to Figure-37. Click on the **Purge** button to accelerate the system processing.

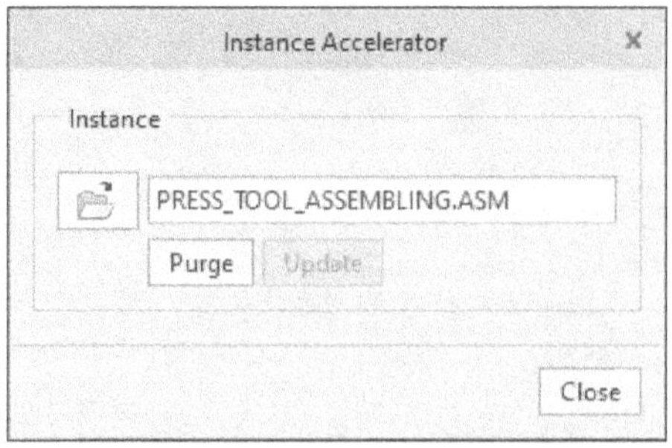

Figure-37. Instance Accelerator dialog box

Model Properties

The **Model Properties** option is available in the **Prepare** cascading menu of the **File** menu; refer to Figure-38. This tool is used to change the properties of the model. The procedure to do so is given next.

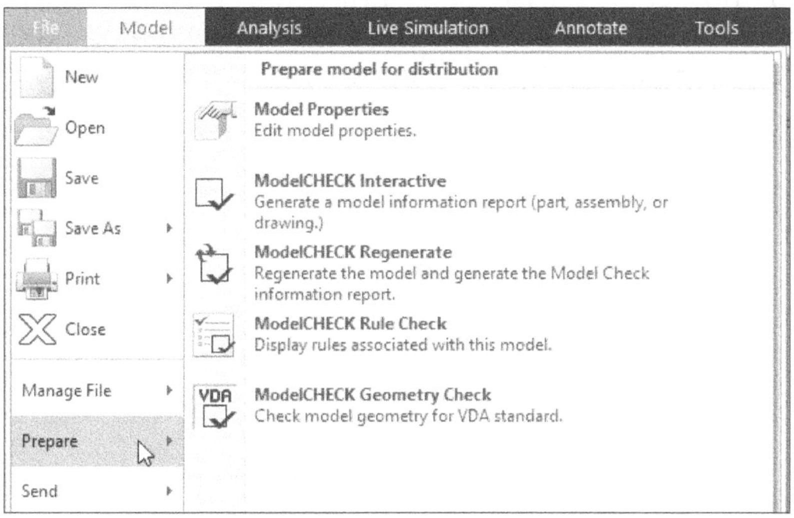

Figure-38. Model Properties option

- Click on the **Model Properties** option from the **Prepare** cascading menu. The **Model Properties** dialog box will be displayed; refer to Figure-39.

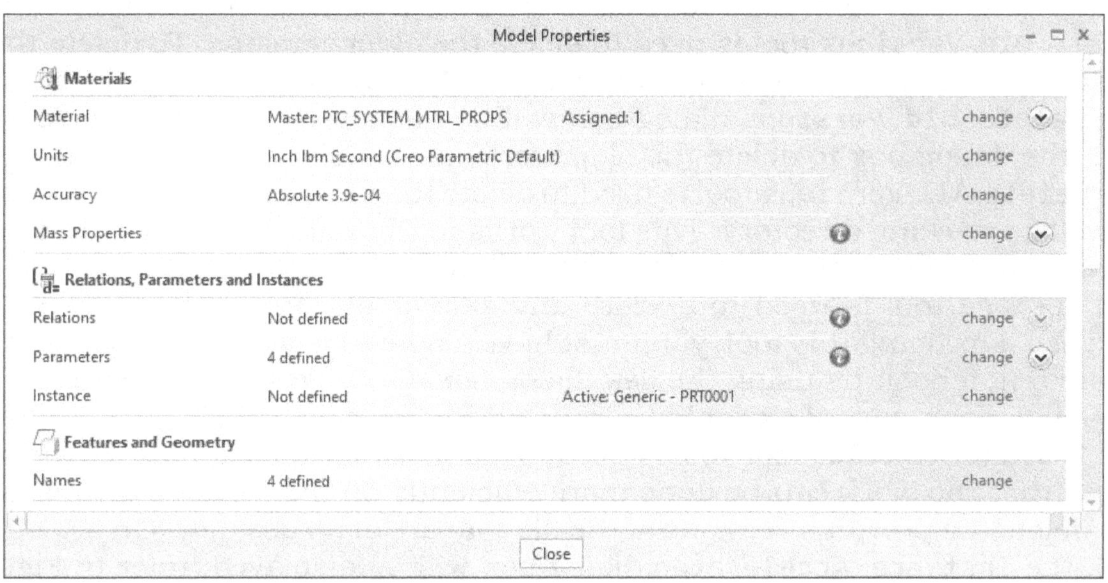

Figure-39. Model Properties dialog box

Material Selection

Using the options available in the **Materials** area of the dialog box, you can change the properties of the model related to material. The steps are given next.

- Click on the **Change** link button next to **Material** in the **Materials** area of the dialog box. The **Materials** dialog box will be displayed; refer to Figure-40.

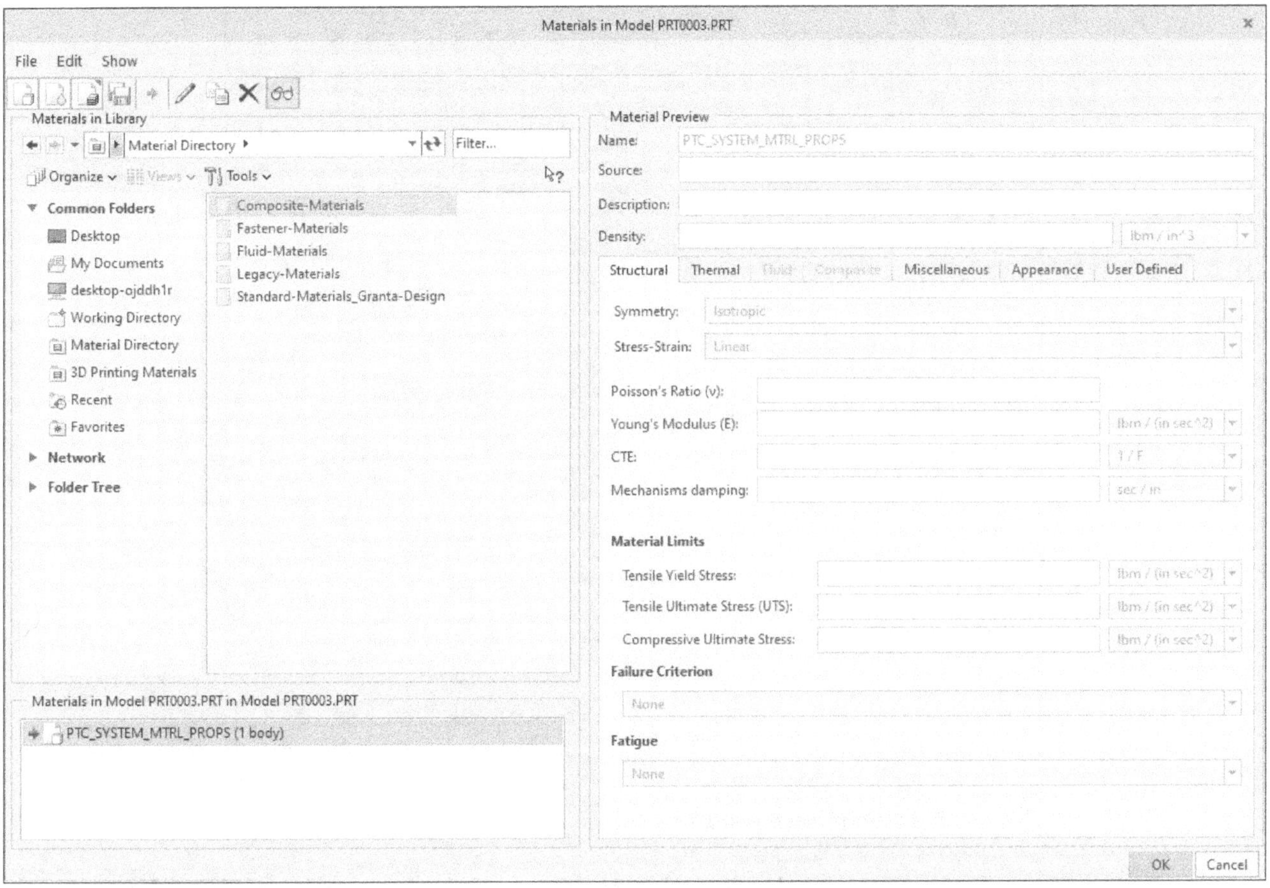

Figure-40. Materials dialog box

- Open desired directory and double-click on desired material from the list of materials to add it to the list of materials used for the current model. The material will be added in the list at the bottom as shown in Figure-41.

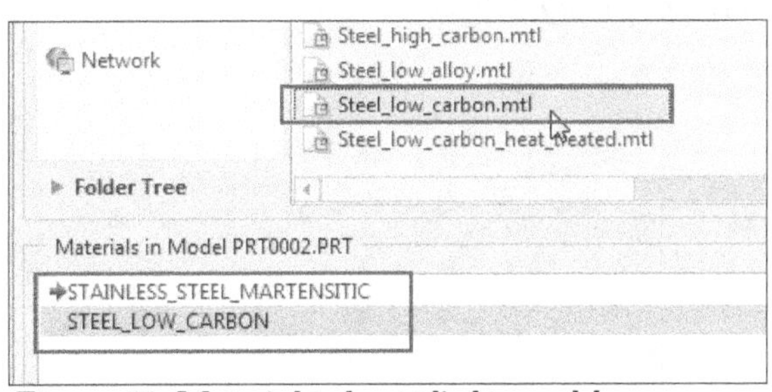

Figure-41. Material to be applied to model

- If you want to edit the parameters of the material before applying it to model then double-click on the material in the **Materials in Model** area of the dialog box. The **Material Definition** dialog box will be displayed; refer to Figure-42.

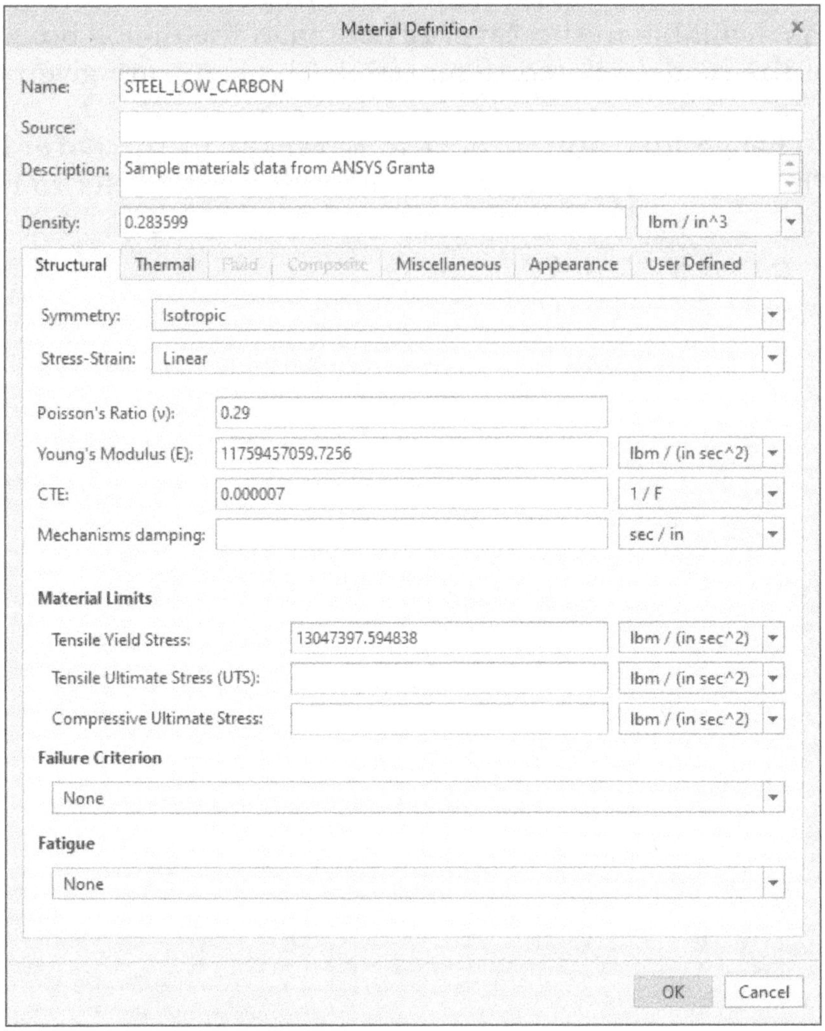

Figure-42. Material Definition dialog box

- The dialog box allows you to change the mechanical, thermal, and fluid properties by using the **Structural**, **Thermal**, and **Fluid** tabs, respectively. Similarly, you can change the **Miscellaneous** properties and appearance of the material.
- After setting desired properties, click on the **OK** button from the dialog box.
- Make sure that desired material is selected in the **Materials in Model** area of the dialog box as assigned; refer to Figure-43 and then click on the **OK** button from the dialog box.

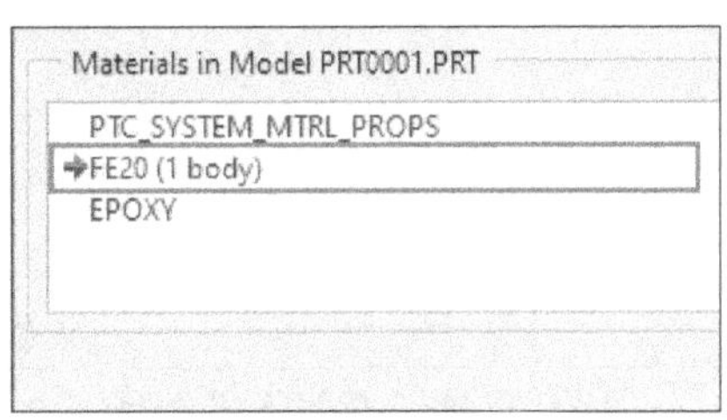

Figure-43. Material assigned

- If desired material is not assigned then right-click on desired material from the **Materials in Model** area. A shortcut menu will be displayed; refer to Figure-44.

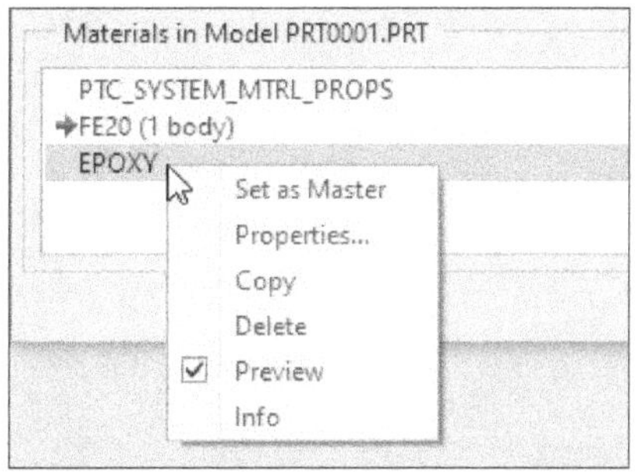

Figure-44. Shortcut menu for material

- Click on the **Set as Master** option from the menu to assign the material and then click on the **OK** button from **Question** dialog box displayed. Click on the **OK** button from the **Materials** dialog box.

Unit System

The **Units** option in the **Model Properties** dialog box is used to change the unit system for modeling. The procedure to change the unit system is given next.

- Click on the **Change** link button for **Units** in the **Materials** area of the dialog box. The **Units Manager** dialog box will be displayed; refer to Figure-45.

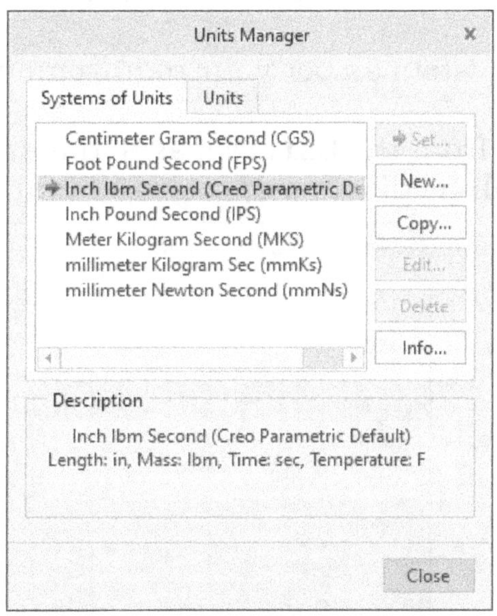

Figure-45. Units Manager dialog box

- Select desired unit system from the list in the dialog box and click on the **Set** button to apply the units. The **Changing Model Units** dialog box will be displayed; refer to Figure-46.

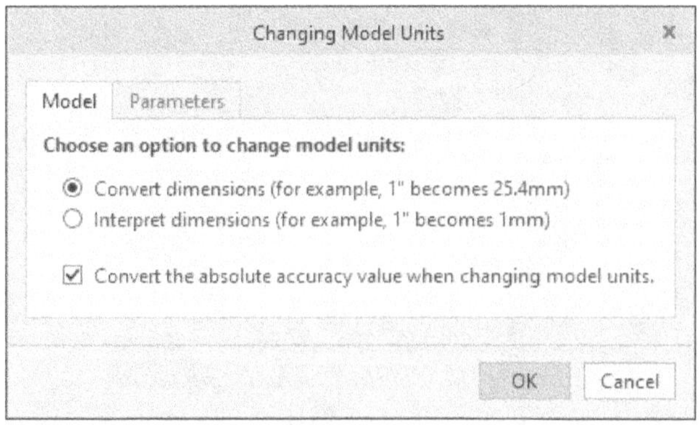

Figure-46. Changing Model Units dialog box

- If by mistake you have designed your model in inches or mm and you want the system to interpret 1" as 1 mm or 1 mm as 1" then click on the **Interpret dimensions** radio button.
- If you want to convert your model unit system from inch to mm or vice-versa, then click on the **Convert dimensions** radio button.
- Select the check box in the **Model** tab of the dialog box to convert the dimension value in the absolute accuracy while changing model units.
- After selecting desired radio button, click on the **OK** button from the dialog box. The selected unit system will be applied for the model.

You can also create a unit system as per your requirement. The steps are given next.

- Click on the **New** button from the **Unit Manager** dialog box. The **System of Units Definition** dialog box will be displayed; refer to Figure-47.

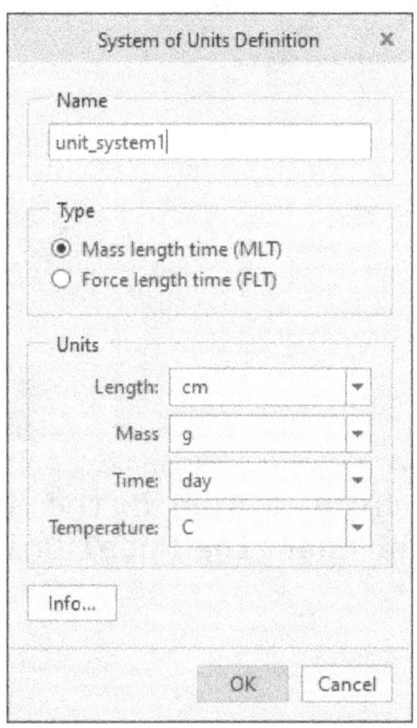

Figure-47. System of Units Definition dialog box

- Click in the edit box of **Name** area and specify desired name in it.
- Select desired radio button from the **Type** area of the dialog box.
- From the **Units** area, select the units for each property.
- Click on the **OK** button from the dialog box. The unit system will be created with the specified name.
- You can set the newly created unit system as discussed earlier.

Mass Properties

Using the **Mass Properties** option, you can change the density, inertia, and other mass properties of the model. The procedure to change the mass properties is given next.

- Click on the **Change** button next to **Mass Properties** in the **Model Properties** dialog box. The **Mass Properties** dialog box will be displayed; refer to Figure-48.

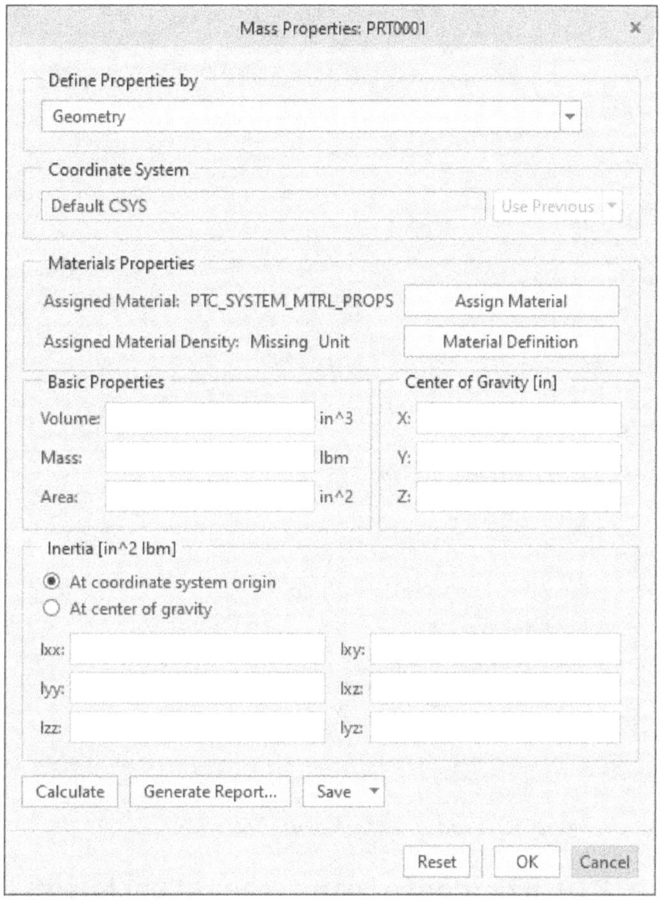

Figure-48. Mass Properties dialog box

- Specify desired value for density in the **Density** edit box.
- Click on the **Calculate** button. Based on the specified density, the other properties are calculated and displayed in the dialog box.
- You can generate report of the properties by using the **Generate Report** button.
- Now, close the dialog box by clicking on the **OK** button.

You will learn about other options of the **Model Properties** dialog box and **ModelCHECK** options in **Prepare** cascading menu of the **File** menu later in the book.

Send Options

The **Send** options in the **File** menu are used to share the model files with peers. There are two options available for sending a file to peers; **Mail Recipient (As Attachment)** and **Mail Recipient (As Link)**. The procedure for both the options is similar. The procedure is given next.

- Click on the **Mail Recipient (As Attachment)** option from the **Send** cascading menu in the **File** menu; refer to Figure-49. The **Send As Attachment** dialog box will be displayed; refer to Figure-50.

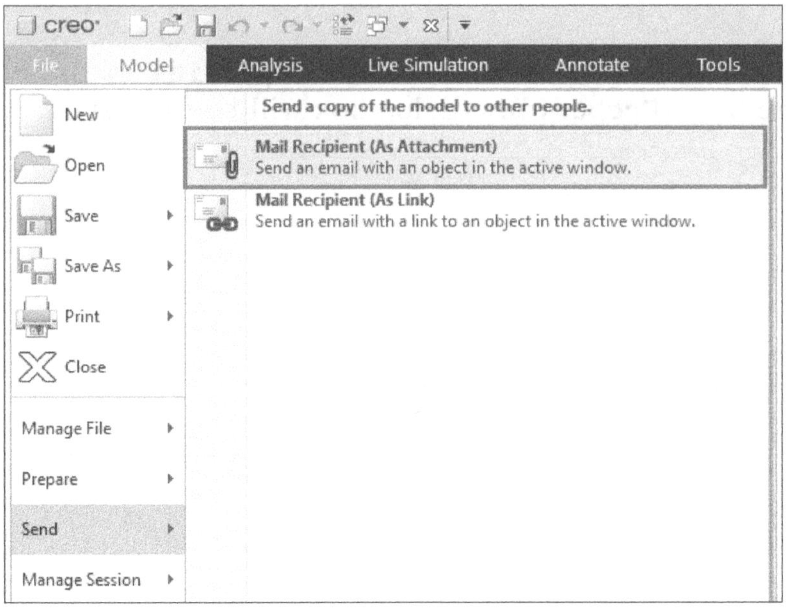

Figure-49. Mail Recipient option

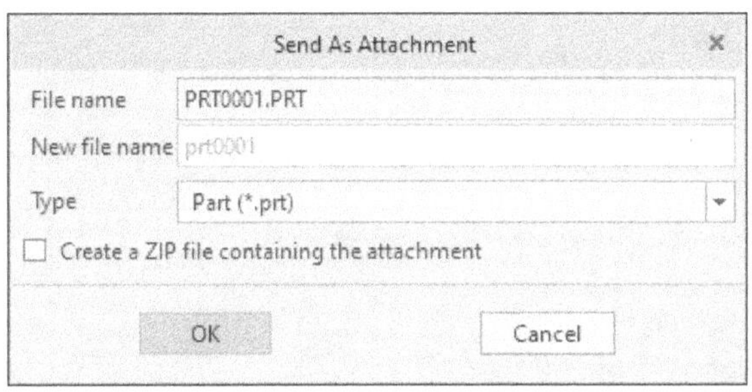

Figure-50. Send As Attachment dialog box

- Select the **Create a ZIP file containing the attachment** check box if you want to compress the file before sending it as attachment.
- Click on the **OK** button from the dialog box to send it. The default messenger will be displayed.
- Type the e-mail address of your peer and send it.
- Similarly, you can use the **Mail Recipient (As Link)** tool.

Manage Session

The tools in the **Manage Session** cascading menu are used to manage session of modeling. There are about 10 tools available in the **Manage Session** cascading menu; refer to Figure-51. Some of the options are discussed next.

Figure-51. Manage Session cascading menu

Erase

The **Erase** options are used to remove the files saved in the temporary memory. Any file that is not saved by using the **Save** button are saved in the temporary memory while working. We need to free up this memory for good performance of Creo. There are three options available in **Manage Session** cascading menu for erasing session data; **Erase Current**, **Erase Not Displayed**, and **Erase Unused Model Reps**. The procedure for all the three tools is similar; click on the tool and then click on the **OK** button from the dialog box displayed.

Erase Current: The **Erase Current** option is used to erase the current part files from the memory.

Erase Not Displayed: The **Erase Not Displayed** option is used to erase the components that are not displaying but are in the session.

Erase Unused Model Reps: The **Erase Unused Model Reps** option is used to erase the representation of the model (part/assembly). You will learn more about representations later in the book.

Select Working Directory

The **Select Working Directory** option in the **Manage Session** cascading menu is used to set desired directory as working directory. The procedure is given next.

- Click on the **Select Working Directory** option from the **Manage Session** cascading menu of the **File** menu. The **Select Working Directory** dialog box will be displayed; refer to Figure-52.

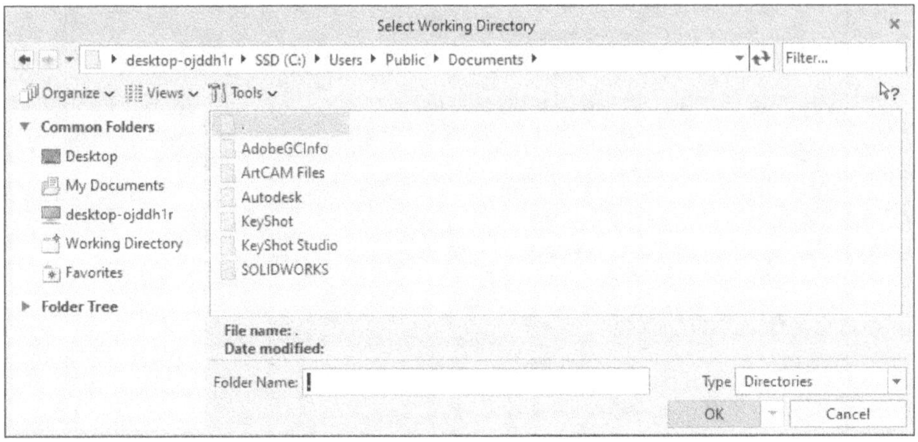

Figure-52. Select Working Directory dialog box

- Select desired directory icon and click on the **OK** button from the dialog box. The selected directory will be set as working directory.

Options

The **Options** tool in **Options** cascading menu of the **File** menu is used to access the options to configure Creo Parametric; refer to Figure-53. There are lots of options for configuration but we will discuss some important options only. The procedure to use the options is given next.

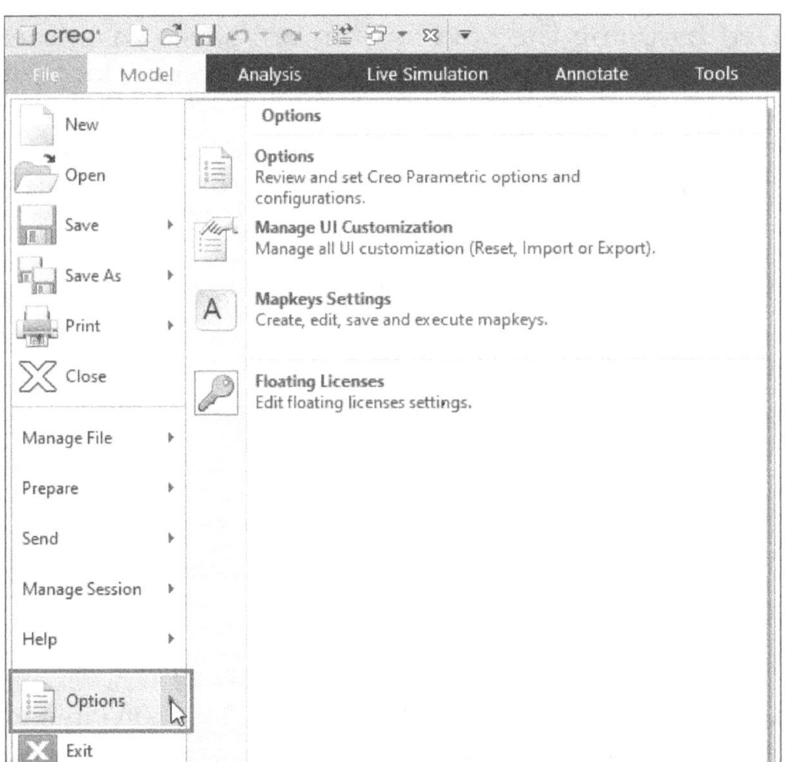

Figure-53. Options cascading menu

- Click on the **Options** tool from the **File** menu; the **Creo parametric Options** dialog box will be displayed; refer to Figure-54.

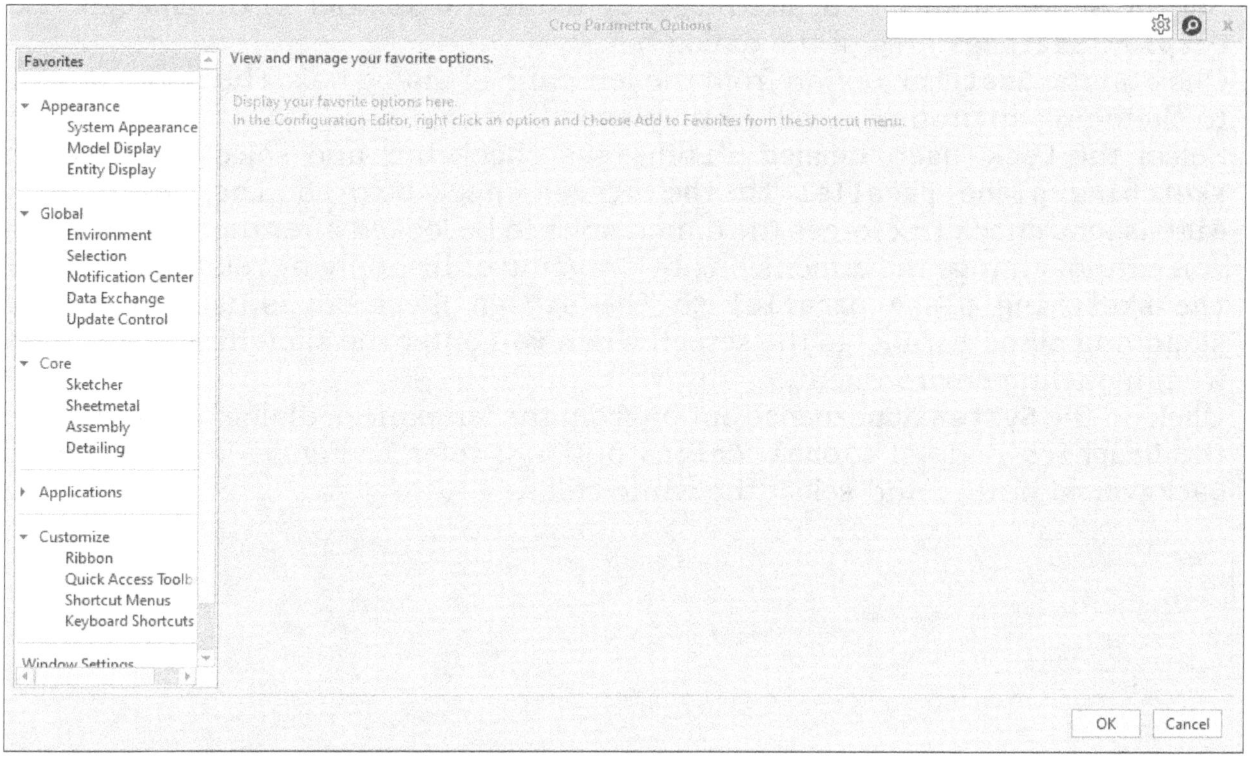

Figure-54. PTC Creo Parametric Options dialog box

- Click on the **Model Display** option from left area of the dialog box. The dialog box will be displayed as shown in Figure-55.

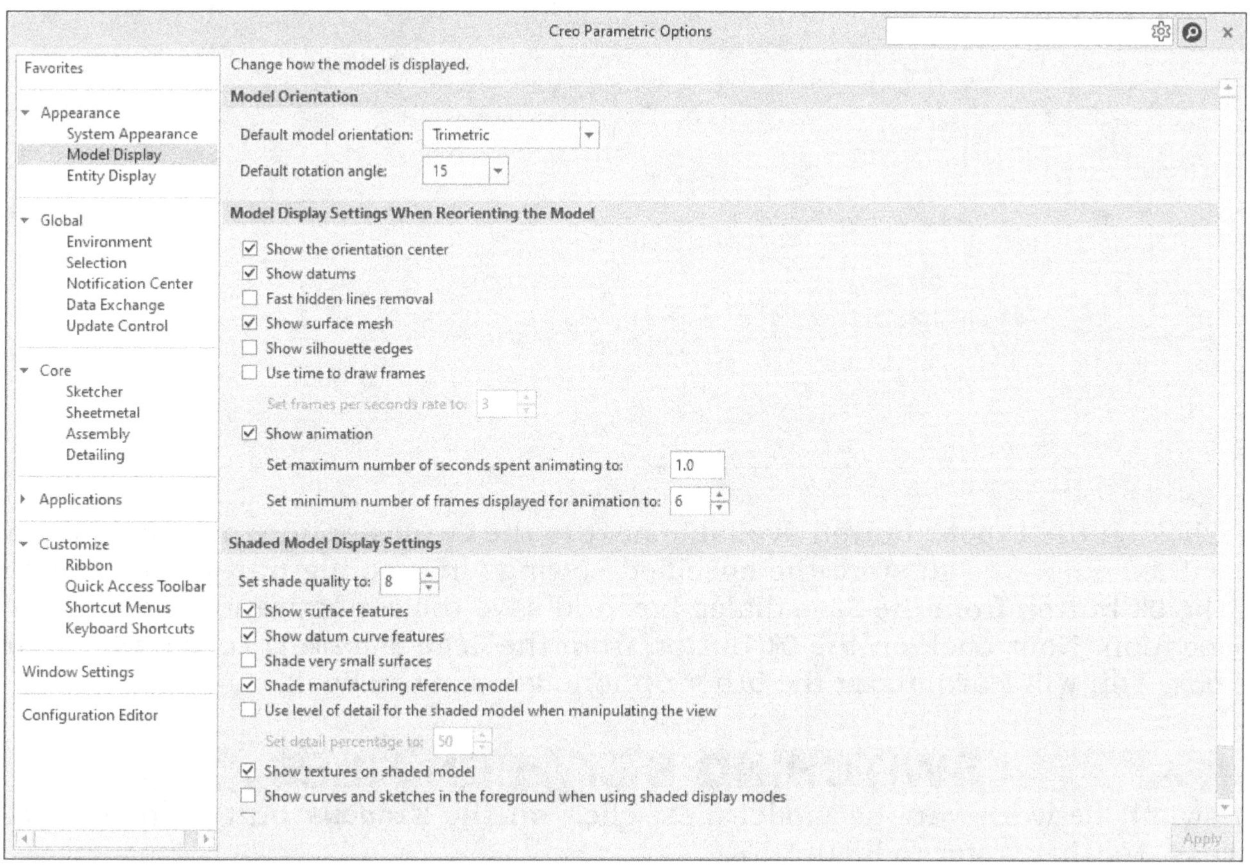

Figure-55. Model Display page of Creo Parametric Options dialog box

- Click on the drop-down for **Default model orientation** and select desired orientation. Some of the designers prefer to use **Isometric** as default orientation.
- Set the shade quality to desired level by using the spinner in the **Shaded Model Display Settings** area of the dialog box.
- Click on the **Sketcher** option from the left pane of dialog box. The options related to sketching environment will be displayed.
- Select the **Lock user defined dimensions** check box and select the **Make the sketching plane parallel to the screen** check box. The **Lock user defined dimensions** check box forces the dimensions to be locked after the user input and you cannot change the dimensions by dragging or by applying relations. The **Make the sketching plane parallel to the screen** check box is used to make the sketching plane parallel to the screen when you enter the sketching environment from modeling environment.
- Click on the **System Appearance** option from the left pane of dialog box and expand the **Graphics** node of **Global Colors** options; refer to Figure-56. Click on the **Background** button and select the white color.

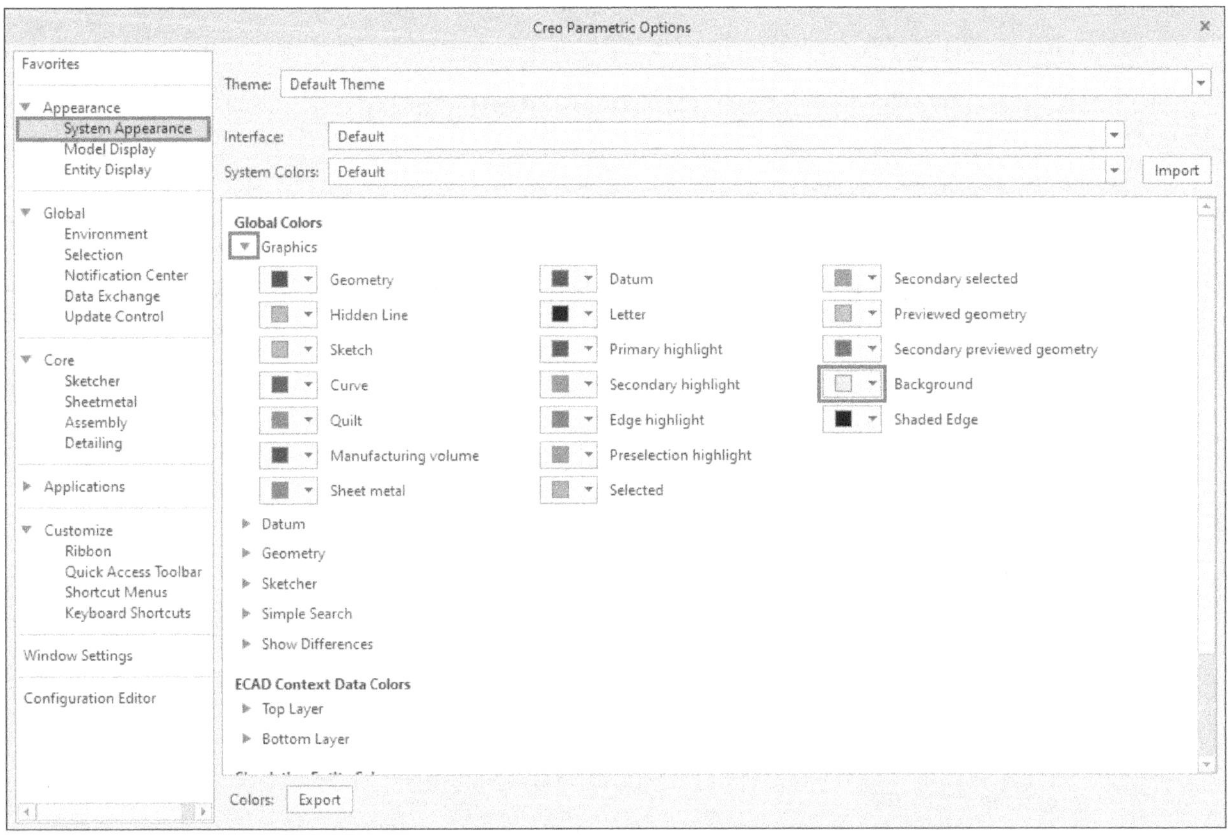

Figure-56. Graphics Colors Options

- Click on the **Export** button available next to the **Colors** option, a **Save** dialog box will be displayed to store the specified settings in a configuration file. Click on the **OK** button from the **Save** dialog box and save the configuration file at desired location. Now, click on the **OK** button from the **Creo Parametric Options** dialog box. You will learn about the other options later in the book.

SWITCHING BETWEEN FILES

To switch between various model files, click on the **Windows** button in the **Quick Access Toolbar**; refer to Figure-57.

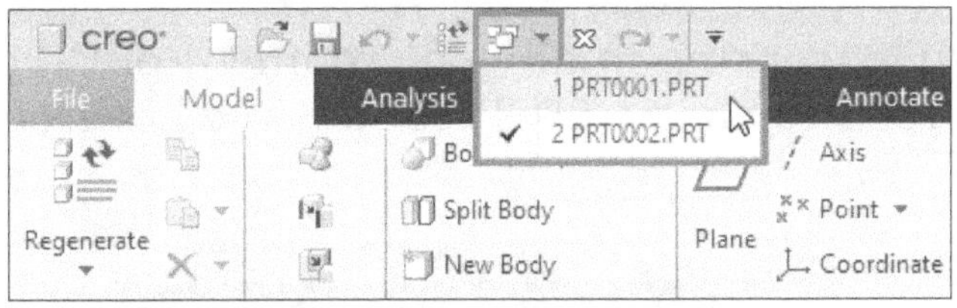

Figure-57. Windows button in the Quick Access Toolbar

Select the part file that you want to work with.

SHORTCUT KEYS AND MOUSE FUNCTIONS IN CREO PARAMETRIC

There are various ways to use tools of Creo Parametric, like you can click on the tool directly, you can use ALT+key to select a tool, you can use CTRL+key to activate a tool, or you can use right-click shortcut menu. Some of the most common shortcuts and mouse functions are discussed next.

Keyboard Shortcuts

Press the combination of **CTRL** and other key to activate the respective function as shown in Figure-58.

Figure-58. Keyboard Shortcuts

ALT Key Menu

Press **ALT** key once while working in any environment of Creo Parametric. The key tips will be displayed; refer to Figure-59. Press desired key from keyboard to activate the respective option.

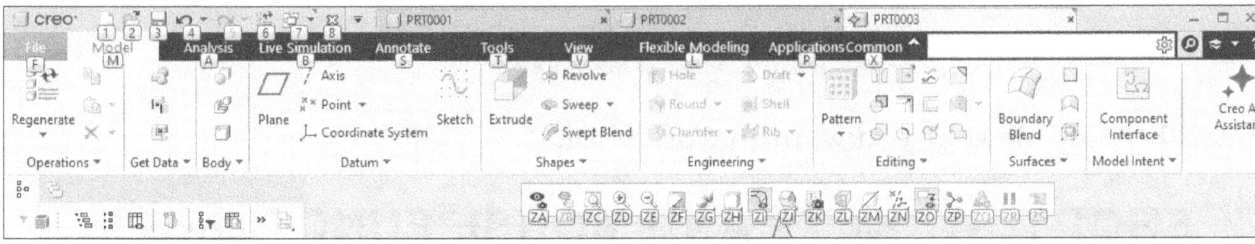

Figure-59. ALT key tips

Mouse Functions

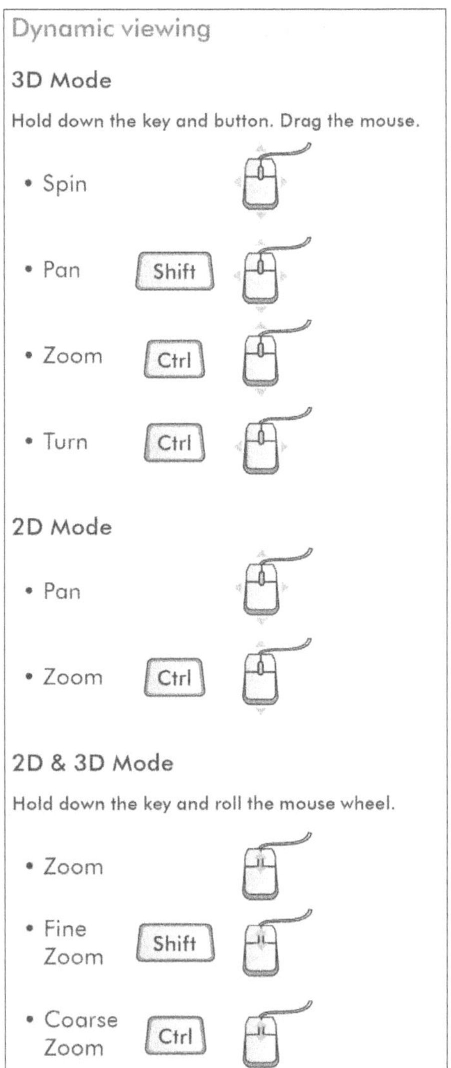

Figure-60. Mouse functions

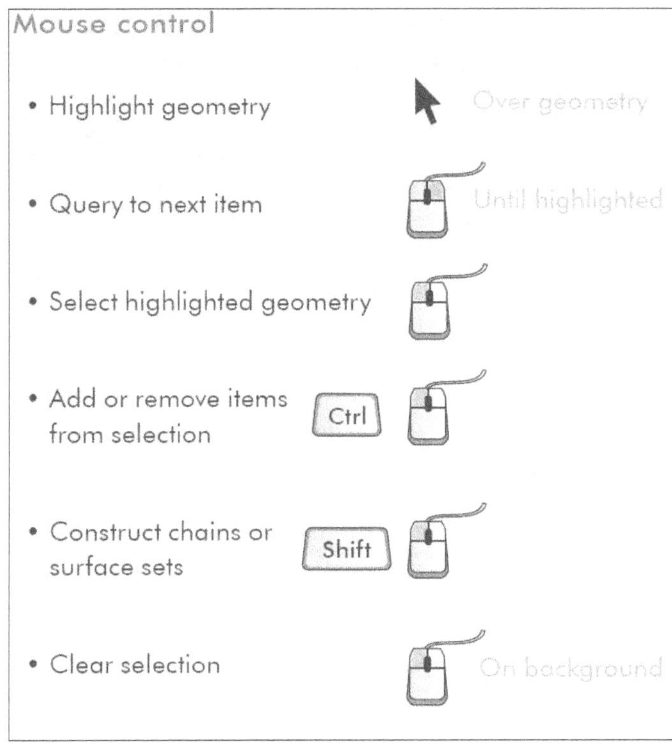

Figure-61. Mouse Control

CREO AI ASSISTANT

Creo AI Assistant is CAD embedded AI assistant model to help you during designing process with customized help topics, tips, and good design practices. Since the model is trained on help and other official data from PTC, there are fewer chances of error in response but still it is your call in the end as a design engineer.

If you are running Creo Parametric 13 and **Creo AI Assistant** tool is not available in the **Ribbon** by default, then select the **Enable Creo AI Assistant** check box from **Creo AI Assistant** page **Creo Parametric Options** dialog box; refer to Figure-62. The procedure to use this assistant is given next.

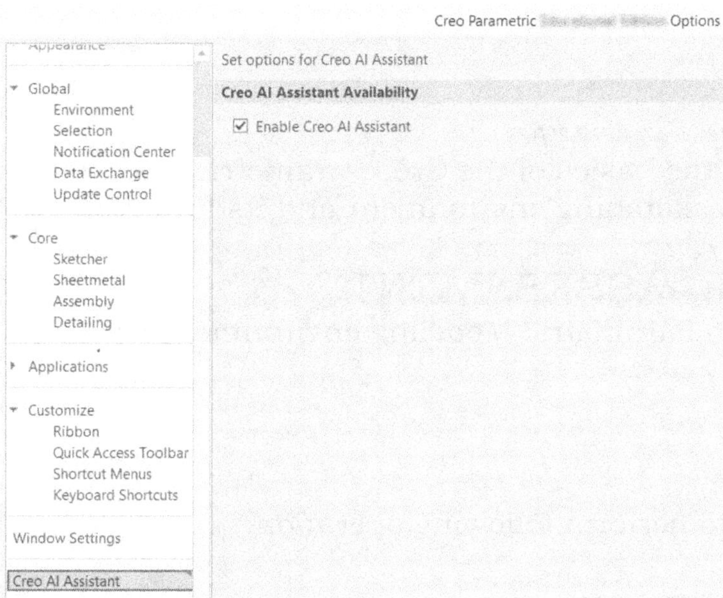

Figure-62. Creo AI Assistant page

- Click on the **Creo AI Assistant** tool from right in the **Ribbon**. The Creo AI Assistant window will be displayed; refer to Figure-63. Note that you might need to create separate account to login into Creo AI Assistant even if you have already login into PTC account.
- After login, Type your query in the edit box and click on the **Send message** button. After processing for a moment depending on internet connection and complexity of your query, Creo AI Assistant will provide advice on query.

Figure-63. Creo AI Assistant window

Note that by default, **Creo Advice** option is active in the **Assistant** which provides general tools related help and tip but if you are a commercial version user then you can also use Creo Assist mode of the AI assistant by selecting the **Creo Assist** option from **New Chat** flyout; refer to Figure-64. In Creo Assist mode, the AI assistant will be aware of your current design in graphics area and give you relevant help. This mode might not be available in educational version of software.

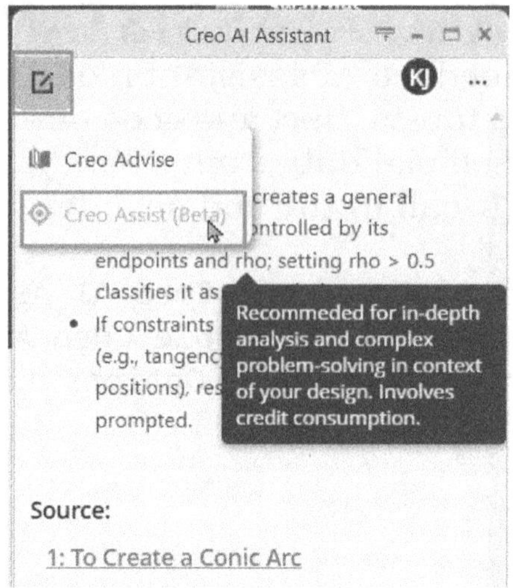

Figure-64. Creo Assist option

In this chapter, we learned about the basics of the Creo Parametric Interface. In the next chapter, we will work on the sketching environment and its function.

SELF ASSESSMENT

1. The default unit system of Creo Parametric Modeling environment is:

(a) IPS (b) MKS
(c) CGS (d) FPS

2. CTRL+G shortcut key is used to perform following operation:

(a) New file (b) Repaint
(c) Regenerate (d) Find

3. CTRL+D shortcut key is used to perform following operation:

(a) New file (b) Repaint
(c) Regenerate (d) Standard View

4. The .... tab in **Navigator** panel contains all the features that are created automatically or manually while creating model or assembly.

5. In Creo Parametric, ... is the area of the application window that holds all the tools for designing and editing.

6. The .... radio button in **New** dialog box is used to create 3D models.

7. The .... radio button in **New** dialog box is used to create notes of ideas regarding the design.

8. The files that are not saved yet but are in current session can be accessed by clicking on the .... link from the **Common Folders** area in the left pane of **File Open** dialog box.

9. The .... option of **File** menu is used to prepare the model 3D Printing.

10. The .... option in **Prepare** cascading menu of **File** menu is used to change the properties of the model like material, accuracy, units, and so on.

11. The **Process Plan** sub-type of **Assembly** type in **New** dialog box is used to document the process of assembling/disassembling parts in the assembly. (T/F)

12. The **Instance Accelerator** tool is used to clear ram to speed up function of Creo Parametric. (T/F)

13. What does the Navigator panel in Creo Parametric help with?

a) Managing animations
b) Navigating folders and features
c) Accessing simulation tools
d) Controlling material properties

14. What does the green line in the Model Tree indicate?

a) Highlighted feature
b) Suppressed element
c) Next feature insertion position
d) Model error location

15. Which file extension is used when saving Model Tree settings?

a) .mtl
b) .stp
c) .cfg
d) .set

16. What is the function of the Tree Filters button in the Model Tree?

a) To show the feature settings
b) To change model color
c) To add or remove entities in the Model Tree
d) To save the model

17. What does the Folder Browser allow you to do?

a) Open simulations
b) Run manufacturing sequences
c) Browse folders for files
d) Edit drawing layouts

18. What does the Capture Visibility button do?

a) Captures screenshots
b) Saves current visibility state
c) Enables motion view
d) Hides all features

19. Which button adjusts zoom to fully display an object?

a) Zoom In
b) Zoom Out
c) Refit
d) Rendering Options

20. What is the purpose of the Display Style button?

a) To save file format
b) To toggle display filters
c) To set model display style
d) To simulate motion

21. What does the Transparency Control button allow?

a) Change file name
b) View model in wireframe
c) Set transparency of model parts
d) Adjust rendering quality

22. Which Assembly sub-type maintains one-way associativity of parts?

a) Configurable product
b) ECAD
c) Mold layout
d) Instrumented

23. Which Manufacturing sub-type is used for 3D printing?

a) Additive Manufacturing
b) Mold cavity
c) Expert Machinist
d) NC assembly

24. Which Print option allows fast printing without settings modification?

a) Print
b) Quick Drawing
c) Quick Print
d) Order 3D Print

25. What does the Unit Manager dialog box allow?

a) Erase model features
b) Change material
c) Modify file name
d) Change unit system

26. Which dialog box is used to define density and calculate other model mass properties?

a) Materials
b) Material Definition
c) Mass Properties
d) Unit Manager

27. What does the Mail Recipient (As Attachment) tool do?

a) Stores model to local storage
b) Sends compressed model as email
c) Saves a copy
d) Opens the email client only

28. Which tool in Manage Session erases files not displayed but still in memory?

a) Erase Current
b) Erase Not Displayed
c) Delete All Versions
d) Instance Accelerator

29. What is the use of the Select Working Directory tool?

a) Rename current folder
b) Change model color
c) Set default directory
d) Modify active file

30. Which shortcut key activates menu tips in Creo Parametric?

a) CTRL
b) ALT
c) SHIFT
d) TAB

Q31. What is the primary purpose of the Creo AI Assistant?
A. Creating CNC toolpaths automatically
B. Assisting users during the design process with customized help, tips, and good design practices
C. Performing finite element analysis automatically
D. Generating manufacturing drawings automatically

Q32. If the Creo AI Assistant tool is not available in the Ribbon of Creo Parametric 13, what should you do?
A. Reinstall Creo Parametric
B. Enable the Enable Creo AI Assistant check box in the Creo Parametric Options dialog box
C. Reset the Ribbon interface
D. Update the graphics driver

Q33. Which statement correctly describes the Creo Assist mode?
A. It provides only general help topics and tips.
B. It works only in offline mode.
C. It is aware of the current design in the graphics area and provides context-aware assistance.
D. It automatically modifies the CAD model without user input.

Answer to Self Assessment Questions:

1. (a) **2.** (c) **3.** (d) **4.** Model Tree **5.** Ribbon **6.** Part **7.** Notebook **8.** In-Session **9.** Prepare for 3D Printing **10.** Model Properties **11.** T **12.** F

Chapter 2

Sketching

Topics Covered

The major topics covered in this chapter are:

- ***Starting Sketching environment***
- ***Setting Grid and other parameters***
- ***Sketching tools***
- ***Sketch editing tools***
- ***Dimensioning tools***
- ***Geometric Constraints***

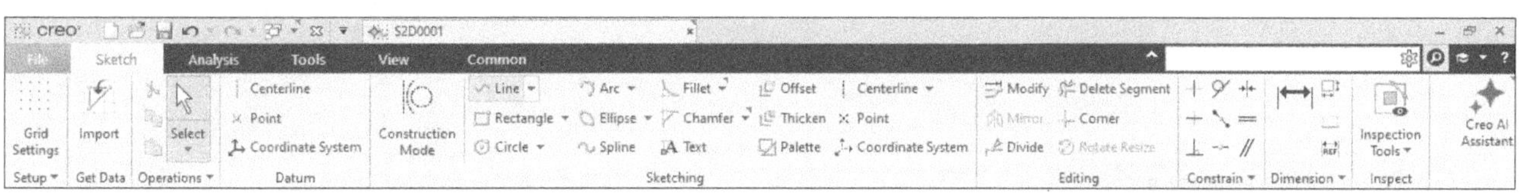

STARTING SKETCHING ENVIRONMENT

The Sketching environment is used to draw or manipulate sketches. The procedure to start sketching environment is given next.

- Click on the **New** button from the **File** menu, **Ribbon**, or **Quick Access Toolbar**. The **New** dialog box will be displayed; refer to Figure-1.

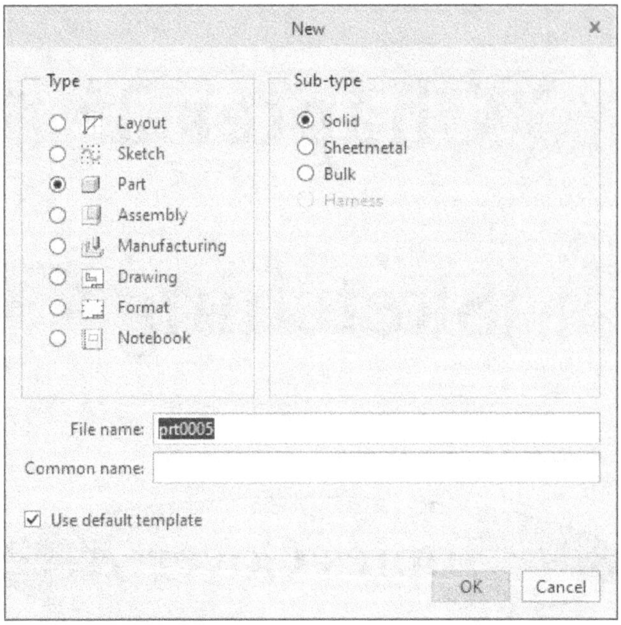

Figure-1. New dialog box

- Select the **Sketch** radio button from the dialog box and specify the name of the file in the **File name** edit box.
- Click on the **OK** button from the dialog box. The sketching environment will be displayed; refer to Figure-2.

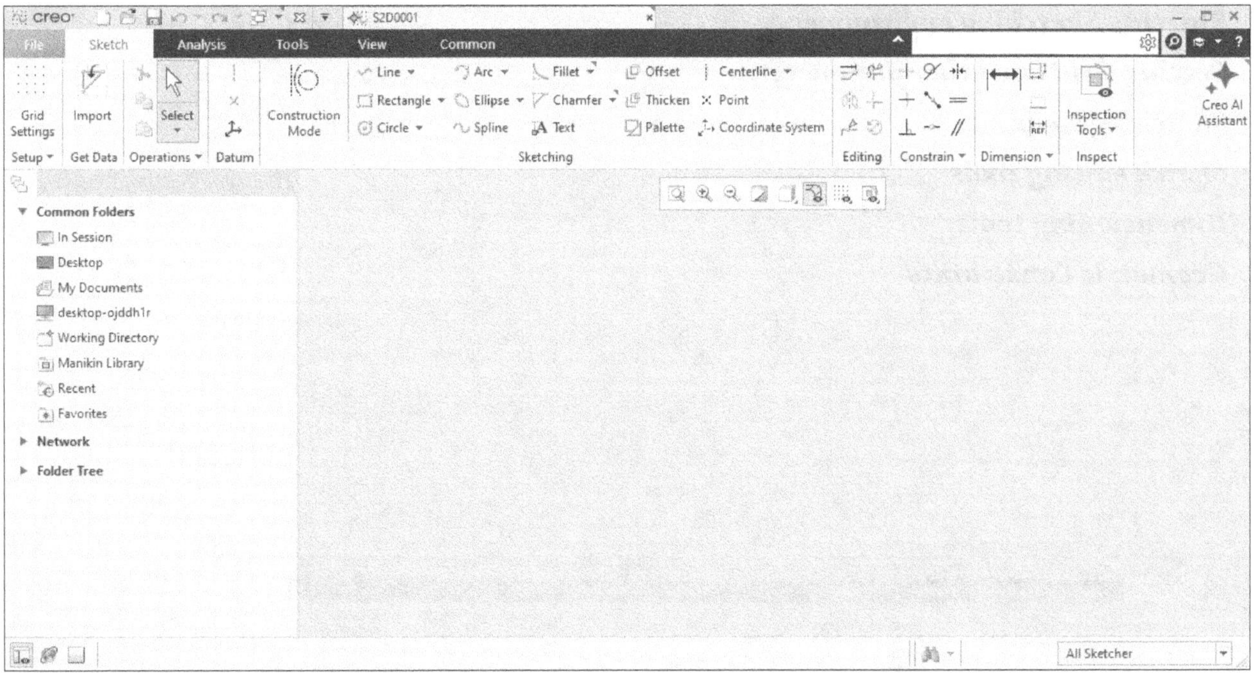

Figure-2. Sketching environment

SETTING UP GRID

The **Grid** is used to help the designer in creating sketches. It is not always necessary to use the grid, it's more often up to the designer. The procedure to setup and display the grid is given next.

- Click on the **Grid Settings** button from the **Setup** panel in the **Ribbon**. The **Grid Settings** dialog box will be displayed; refer to Figure-3.

- Specify desired values for the grid and then click on the **OK** button from the dialog box. The values for the grid will be saved in the configuration.
- To display the grid, click on the **Sketcher Display Filters** drop-down in the **In-Graphics** toolbar; refer to Figure-4. The list of options will be displayed.

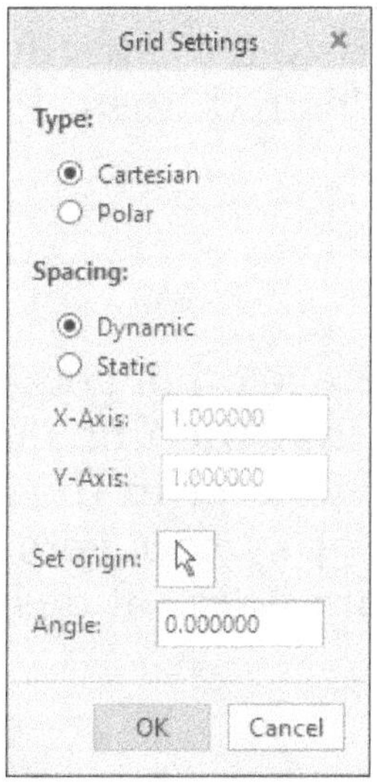

Figure-3. Grid Settings dialog box

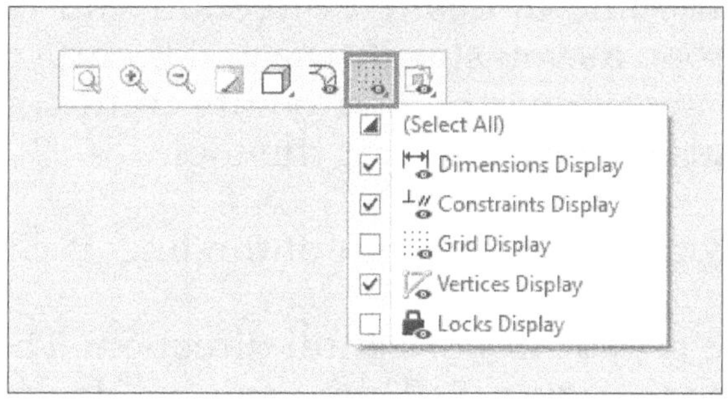

Figure-4. Sketcher Display Filters

- Select the **Grid Display** check box to display the grid. To hide the grid, you need to clear the check box.

SKETCHING TOOLS

There are various sketching tools available in the **Sketching** panel of the **Sketch** tab in the **Ribbon**; refer to Figure-5.

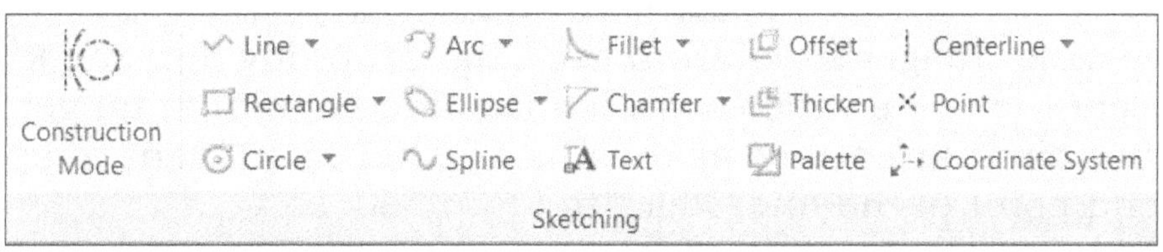

Figure-5. Sketching Tools

We will discuss one by one the procedures to use the tools in the **Sketching** panel.

Line Tools

There are three tools in Creo Parametric to create lines in the drawing; **Line Chain**, **Line Tangent**, and **Line Mid-point**. The **Line Chain** tool is used to create a chain of lines. The procedure to create the line chains is given next.

Line Chain tool

- Click on the down arrow next to **Line** tool. The list of the tools will be displayed as shown in Figure-6.

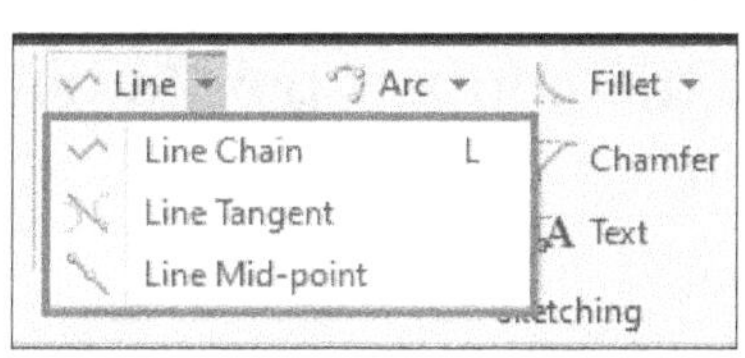

Figure-6. Line tools

- Click on the **Line Chain** tool from the list of tools. An end point will get attached to the cursor and you will be asked to specify a point on the screen.
- Click at desired location to specify the start point of the line. A rubber band line will get attached to the cursor.
- Stretch the line in desired direction and click at desired location to create the line. As soon as you specify the end point, you are asked to specify the next point.
- Keep on specifying the end points until you get desired lines. Press the **Middle Mouse Button (MMB)** to exit the tool.

After specifying the start point of the line, if you:

- Move the cursor in horizontal direction. Then the **-** symbol gets attached to the line; refer to Figure-7. This **-** symbol designates that the line is constrained as Horizontal line. You will learn about the constraints later in the chapter.
- Move the cursor in the vertical direction. Then the **|** symbol gets attached to the line; refer to Figure-8. Similar to the Horizontal constraint, it designates Vertical constraint.

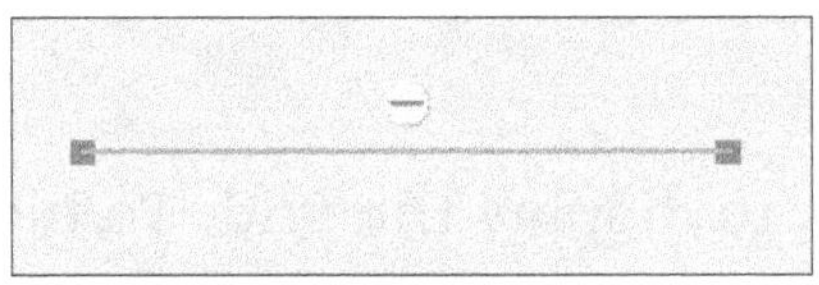

Figure-7. Horizontal line

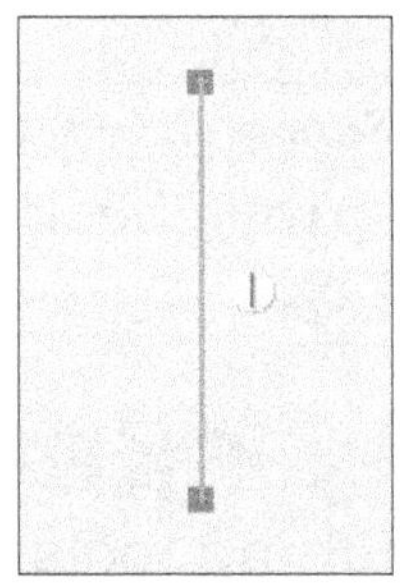

Figure-8. Vertical line

Line Tangent

- Click on the **Line Tangent** tool from the **Line** drop-down in the **Ribbon**. You are asked to select the two entities to which the line should be tangent.
- Select the two circular entities at the places where you want to specify the start point and end point of the line. Refer to Figure-9.

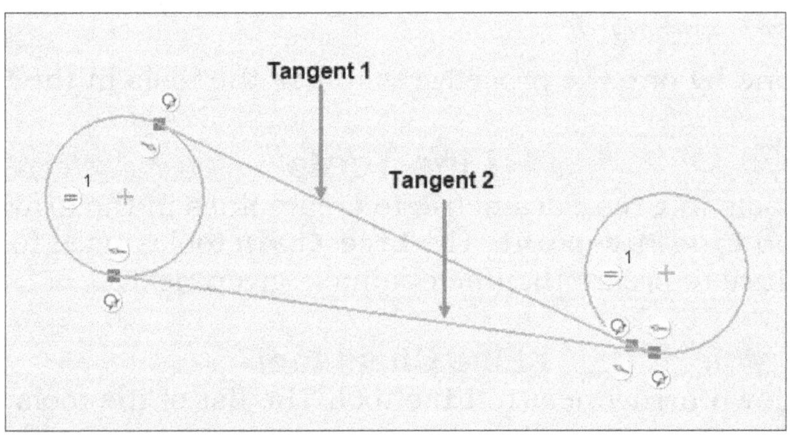

Figure-9. Tangent lines

- Note that the tangent symbol is displayed at the contact points between circles and lines. The tangent symbol refers to Tangent constraint.

Line Mid-point

- Click on the **Line Mid-point** tool from the **Line** drop-down in the **Ribbon**. You will be asked to specify a midpoint on the screen.
- Click at desired location to specify the mid-point of the line. A rubber band line will get attached to the cursor.
- Stretch the line in desired direction and click at desired location to create the line. The mid-point line will be created; refer to Figure-10.

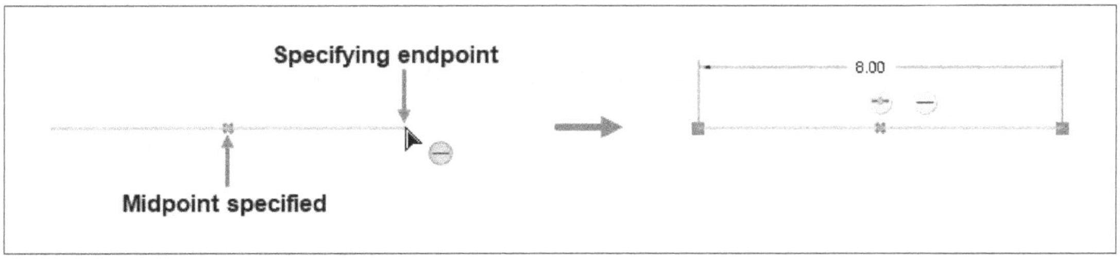

Figure-10. Midpoint line created

- Press the **Middle Mouse Button (MMB)** to exit the tool.

Rectangle Tools

There is a list of four tools in Creo Parametric that are used to create rectangles; **Corner Rectangle**, **Slanted Rectangle**, **Center Rectangle**, and **Parallelogram**. The procedure to create rectangles by using these tools is given next.

Corner Rectangle

The **Corner Rectangle** tool is used to create rectangle by using the corner points of the rectangle. The procedure is given next.

- Click on the **Corner Rectangle** tool from the **Rectangle** drop-down; refer to Figure-11. You are asked to specify the first corner point.
- Click in the drawing area to specify the first point of the rectangle. The other corner point will get attached to the cursor.
- Click to specify the other corner point. The rectangle will be created.
- Press the middle mouse button to exit the tool. The rectangle will be displayed; refer to Figure-12.

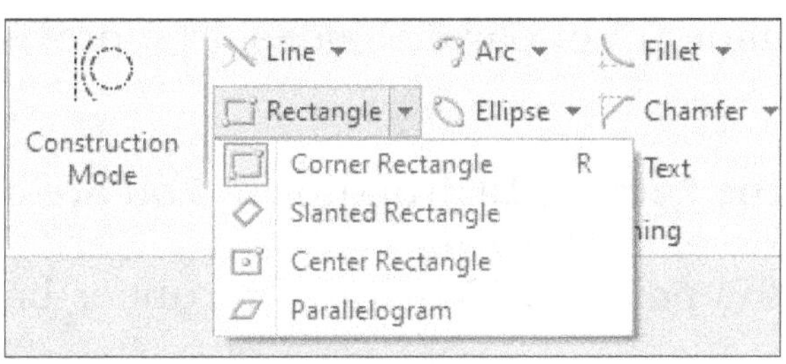

Figure-11. Rectangle drop down

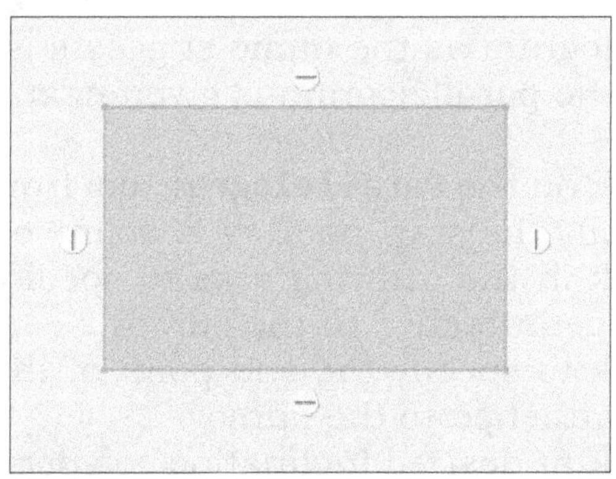

Figure-12. Rectangle created

Slanted Rectangle

The **Slanted Rectangle** tool is used to create rectangles aligned at some defined angle. The procedure is given next.

- Click on the **Slanted Rectangle** tool from the **Rectangle** drop-down. You are asked to specify the first point of the rectangle.
- Click to specify the first point of the rectangle. End point of a rubber-band line will get attached to the cursor.
- Click to specify the end point of the line at desired inclination. The adjacent side of the rectangle will get attached to the cursor.
- Click at desired distance to create the rectangle.
- Press the middle mouse button to exit the tool.

Center Rectangle

The **Center Rectangle** tool is used to create a rectangle using the center point of the rectangle and a corner point of the rectangle. The procedure to create a rectangle by this tool is given next.

- Click on the **Center Rectangle** tool from the **Rectangle** drop-down. You are asked to specify the center point of the rectangle.
- Click in the drawing area to specify the center point. The corner point of the rectangle will get attached to the cursor; refer to Figure-13.

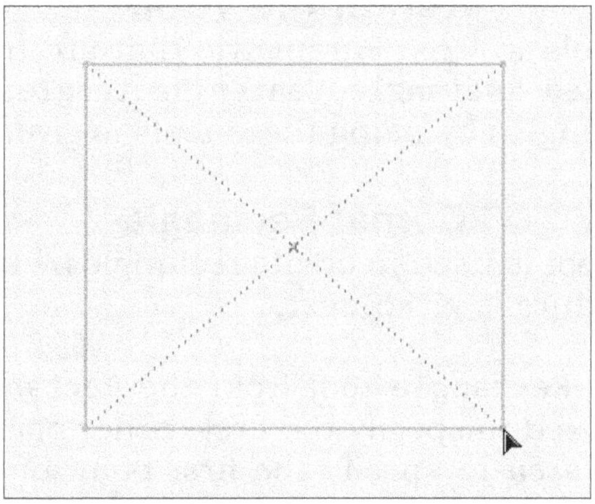

Figure-13. Corner point of center rectangle attached to cursor

- Click to specify the corner point of the rectangle.

Parallelogram

Parallelogram as the name suggests is made up of parallel sides. The procedure to create the parallelogram is given next.

- Click on the **Parallelogram** tool from the **Rectangle** drop-down. You are asked to specify the start point of baseline of the parallelogram.
- Click in the drawing area to specify the point. End point of a rubber band line will get attached to the cursor.
- Click to specify the end point of the line. Corner point of the parallelogram will get attached to the cursor.
- Click at desired inclination to specify the corner point of the parallelogram. The parallelogram will be created.
- Press the middle mouse button to exit the tool.

Note that now onwards, we will not write the step to exit the tool. By default, you need to press the middle mouse button to exit the tool.

Circle Tools

The tools available in the **Circle** drop-down are used to create circle with various methods. There are four tools available in the **Circle** drop-down; **Center and Point**, **Concentric**, **3 Point**, and **3 Tangent**. The procedures to create circles by these tools are given next.

Center and Point tool

The **Center and Point** tool is used to create circle by specifying center point and one point on its circumference. The procedure to use this tool is given next.

- Click on the **Center and Point** tool from the **Circle** drop-down; refer to Figure-14. You are asked to specify the center point of the circle.

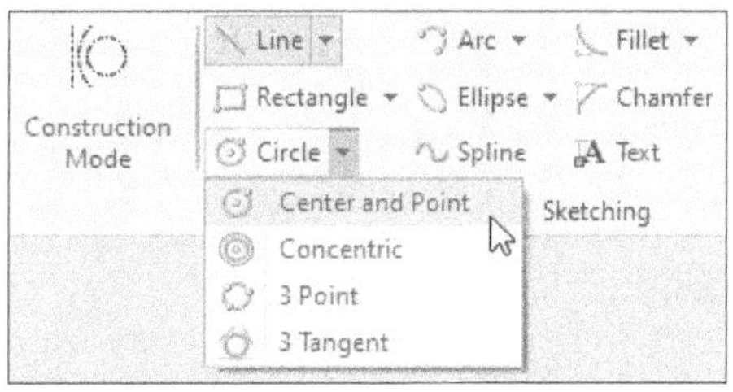

Figure-14. Circle drop down

- Click in the drawing area to specify the center point of the circle. The cursor gets attached to a point on the circumference of the circle.
- Click at desired distance to specify the radius of the circle. The circle will be created.
- Press the middle mouse button to exit the tool.

Concentric tool

The **Concentric** tool is used to create circle concentric to earlier created circles/arcs. The procedure is given next.

- Click on the **Concentric** tool from the **Circle** drop-down. You are asked to select an arc or circle.
- Select the arc/circle, a point on circumference of circle will get attached to the cursor with center of the circle coinciding with selected arc/circle's center; refer to Figure-15.
- Click to specify the radius of the circle.

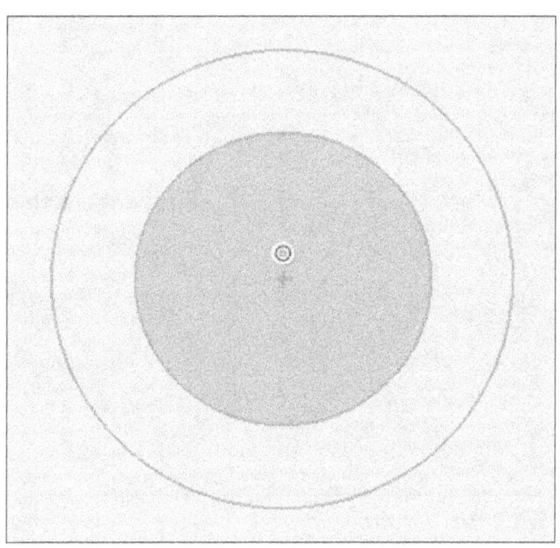

Figure-15. Concentric circle

3 Point tool

The **3 Point** tool is used to create a circle with the help of three circumferential points. The procedure is given next.

- Click on the **3 Point** tool from the **Circle** drop-down. You are asked to specify the first circumferential point.
- Click in the drawing area to specify the first point of the circle. You are asked to specify the second point on the circumference of circle.
- Click to specify the second point of circumference. You are asked to specify the last point of the circumference to completely define the circle; refer to Figure-16.

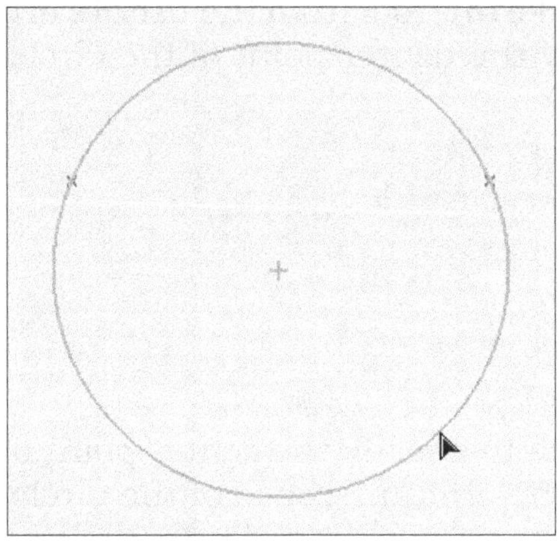

Figure-16. Three point circle

- Click to specify the last point of the circle.

3 Tangent tool

The **3 Tangent** tool is used to create circle tangent to three entities as per the possibilities. The procedure to use this tool is given next.

- Click on the **3 Tangent** tool from the **Circle** drop-down. You are asked to select first entity to which you want to make the circle tangent to.
- Click on desired entity. You are asked to specify the second entity to be tangent; refer to Figure-17.

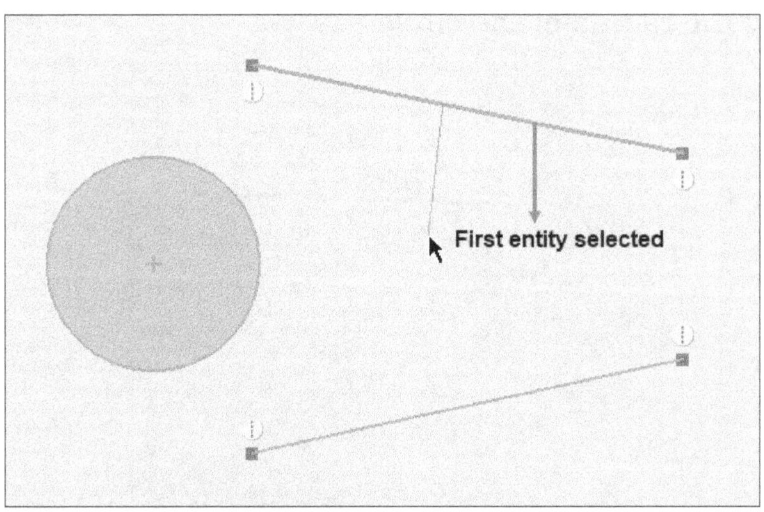

Figure-17. First entity for tangency

- Click on the second entity for tangency and then click on the next entity; refer to Figure-18.

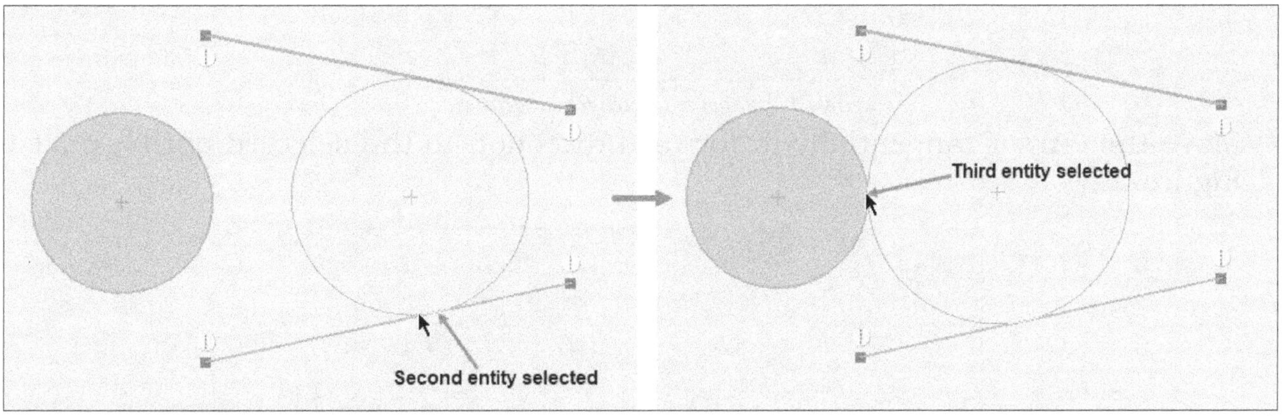

Figure-18. Tangent circle

Arcs

The tools to create arcs are available in the **Arc** drop-down. There are five tools available in the **Arc** drop-down; **3-Point/Tangent End**, **Center and Ends**, **3 Tangent**, **Concentric**, and **Conic**. The procedures to use these tools are given next.

3-Point/Tangent End

The **3-Point/Tangent End** tool is used to create arc with the help of specifying three points. You can also create an arc tangent to the entity at its one of the endpoint by using this tool. The procedure is given next.

- Click on the **3-Point/Tangent End** tool from the **Arc** drop-down; refer to Figure-19. You are asked to specify the start point of the arc.
- Click in the drawing area to specify the start point. You are asked to specify the end point of the arc.
- Click to specify the end point, you are asked to specify a point of circumference of arc to define the radius of arc; refer to Figure-20.

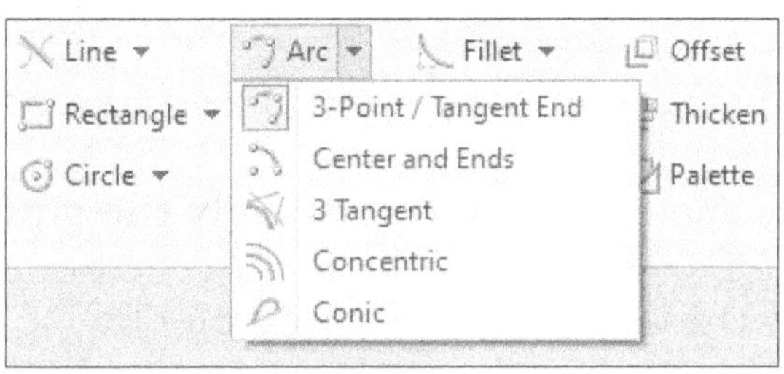

Figure-19. Arc drop down

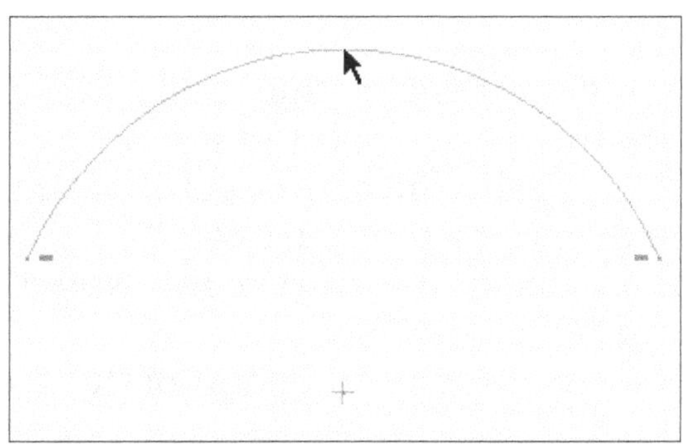

Figure-20. Specifying circumferential point of arc

- Click to specify the circumferential point of the arc. The arc will be created.

If you want to create an arc tangent to a line/arc then follow the steps given next.

- Click on the **3-Point/Tangent End** tool from the **Arc** drop-down. You will be asked to specify the start point of arc as discussed earlier.
- Click on the end point of the arc/line to which you want to make the arc tangent to; refer to Figure-21.

Figure-21. Endpoint selected for tangent arc

- Move the cursor tangentially in forward direction to the selected entity; refer to Figure-22.

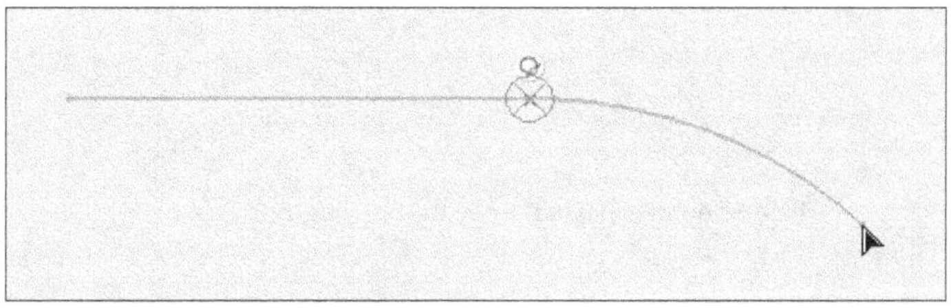

Figure-22. Cursor moved tangentially

- Click at desired point to specify the end point of the arc and press middle mouse button; refer to Figure-23.

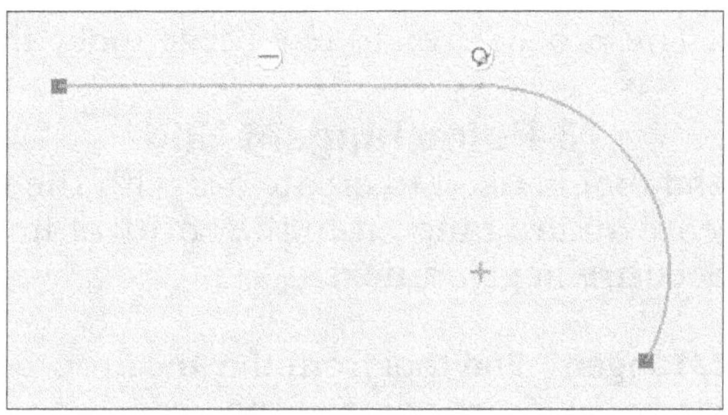

Figure-23. Arc created tangentially

Center and Ends

The **Center and Ends** tool, as the name suggests, is used to create an arc by specifying the center point of the arc and then the end points of the arc. The procedure to use this tool is given next.

- Click on the **Center and Ends** tool from the **Arc** drop-down. You are asked to specify the center point of the arc.
- Click to specify the center point of the arc. You are asked to specify the start point of the arc; refer to Figure-24.
- Click to specify the start point. Note that the arc can be created clockwise as well as counter-clockwise.
- Click to specify the end point of the arc. The arc will be created; refer to Figure-25.

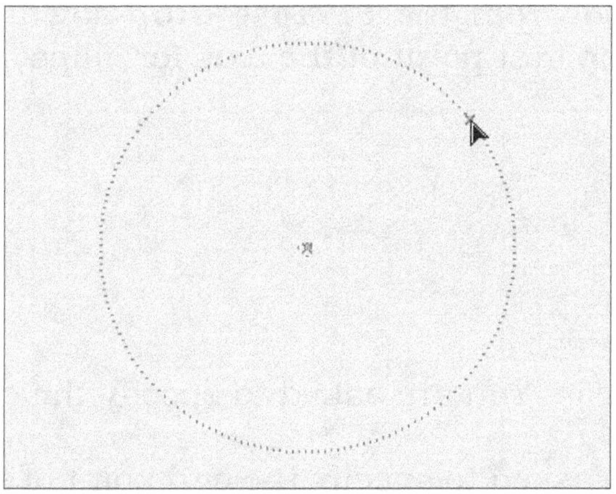

Figure-24. Start point of arc

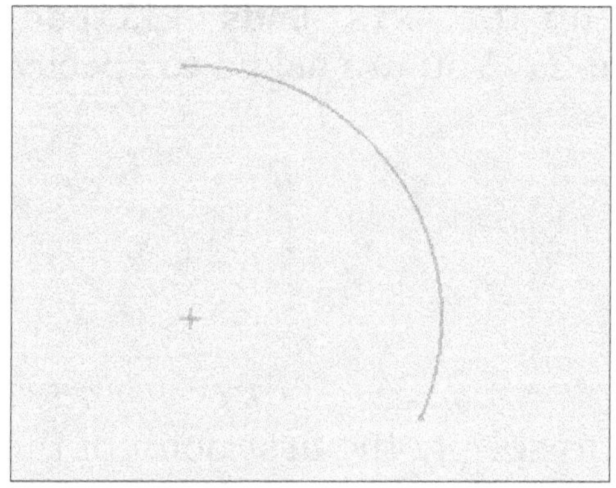

Figure-25. Arc created

3 Tangent and Concentric Arc

The **3 Tangent** and **Concentric Arc** tools work similar to **3 Tangent circle** and **Concentric circle** tools.

Conic Arc

The **Conic** tool is used to create conical arcs. Conical arcs are used in some geometries where we design the front section of boats, aeroplanes, and automotive. The procedure to create conic arc is given next.

- Click on the **Conic** tool from the **Arc** drop-down. You are asked to specify the first point of the arc.
- Click in the drawing area to specify the first point of the arc. You are asked to specify the end point of the arc.
- Click to specify the end point of the arc. Cursor will get attached to a point on the circumference of the arc.
- Click to specify the circumferential point. On the basis of this point, the **rho** value for the conic curve will be decided. After specifying the point, the conical arc will be created; refer to Figure-26.

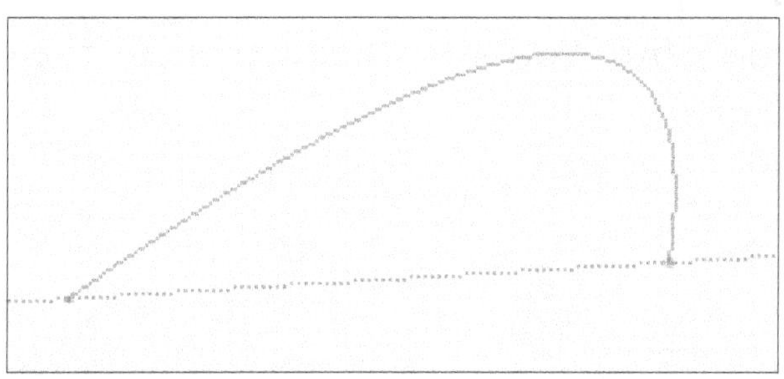

Figure-26. Conical arc

Ellipse

There are two ways to create ellipses in Creo Parametric; by using axis ends and by using center and axis. The procedures to create ellipses by both the methods are given next.

Axis Ends Ellipse

The **Axis Ends Ellipse** tool is used to create ellipses by using the axis end points. The procedure to use this tool is given next.

- Click on the **Axis Ends Ellipse** tool from the **Ellipse** drop-down; refer to Figure-27. You are asked to specify the first point of the axis for ellipse.

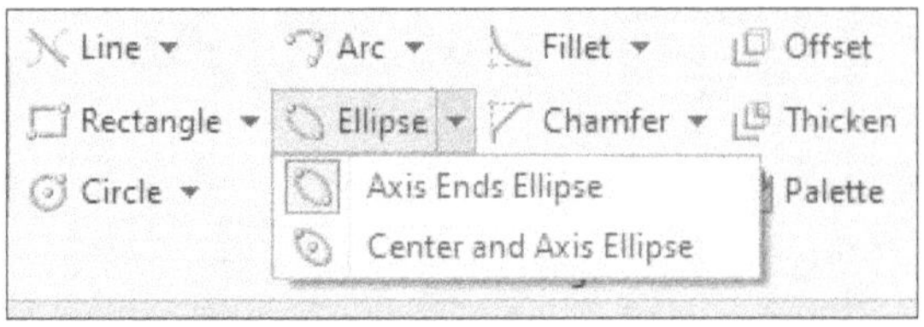

Figure-27. Ellipse drop down

- Click to specify the first point of the axis. You are asked to specify the end point of the axis.
- Click to specify the end point. You are asked to specify the end point of the other axis; refer to Figure-28.

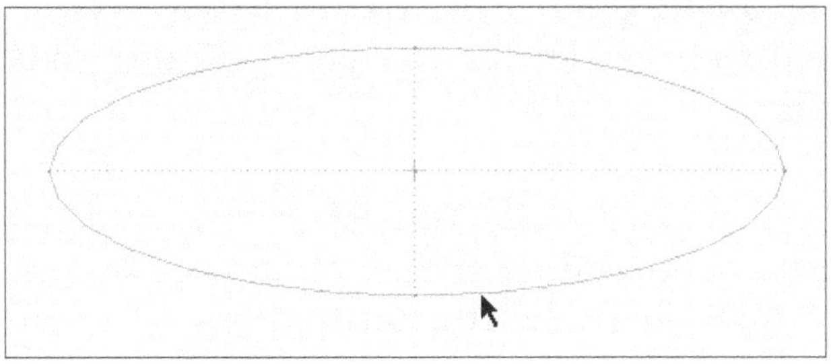

Figure-28. End point to be specified for other axis

- Click to specify the end point. The ellipse will be created.

Center and Axis Ellipse

Using the **Center and Axis Ellipse** tool, we can create an ellipse by specifying center and axis end point of the ellipse. The procedure to use this tool is given next.

- Click on the **Center and Axis Ellipse** tool from the **Ellipse** drop-down. You are asked to specify the center point for the ellipse.
- Click to specify the center point. You are asked to specify end point of the axis for ellipse; refer to Figure-29.
- Click to specify the end point. You are asked to specify the end point of the another axis; refer to Figure-30.

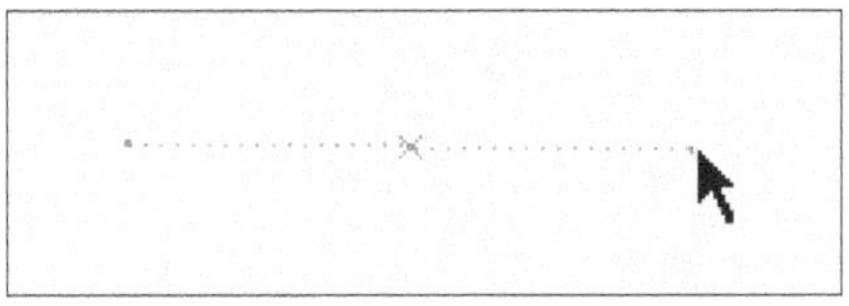

Figure-29. End point selected for axis

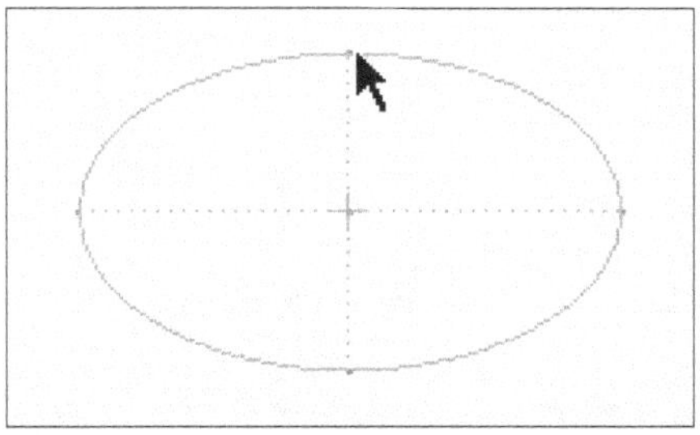

Figure-30. Axis end point for creating ellipse

- Click to specify the end point of the other axis. The ellipse will be created.

Spline

The spline is a special geometry that can be modified to smoothen the curvature. We can use spline to design aerodynamic bodies of automotive. The procedure to create spline is given next.

- Click on the **Spline** tool from the **Ribbon**. You are asked to specify the first point of the spline.
- Click to specify the point. You are asked to specify the next point.
- Click to specify the next point and keep on specifying the points until you get desired spline.
- To exit the tool and create the spline, press the middle mouse button twice. Refer to Figure-31.

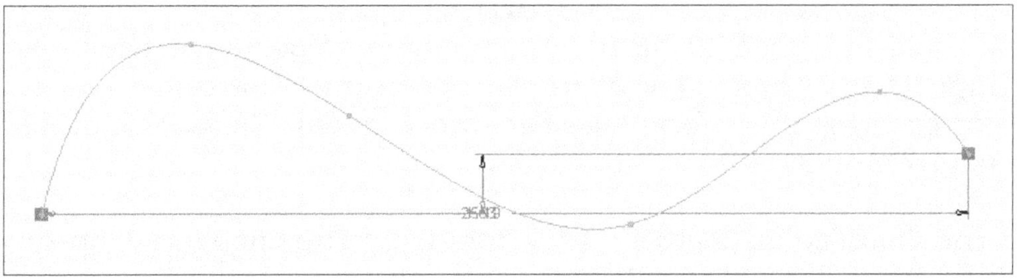

Figure-31. Spline created

Fillet

Fillet is removal of material at the sharp edges. It is used to smoothen the edges and reduce the stress at the edges. There are four tools in Creo Parametric to create fillets; **Circular**, **Circular Trim**, **Elliptical**, and **Elliptical Trim**. The procedure to create fillets by these four tools is same but the output is different. The procedure to use these tools is given next.

- Click on desired tool from the **Fillet** drop-down; refer to Figure-32. You are asked to select two entities.

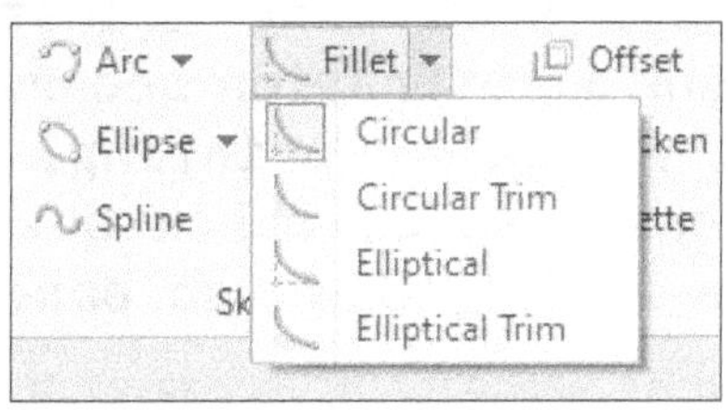

Figure-32. Fillet drop down

- Select the first entity and then select the second entity. Note that the entities must be consecutive. The fillet will be created with random values; refer to Figure-33.

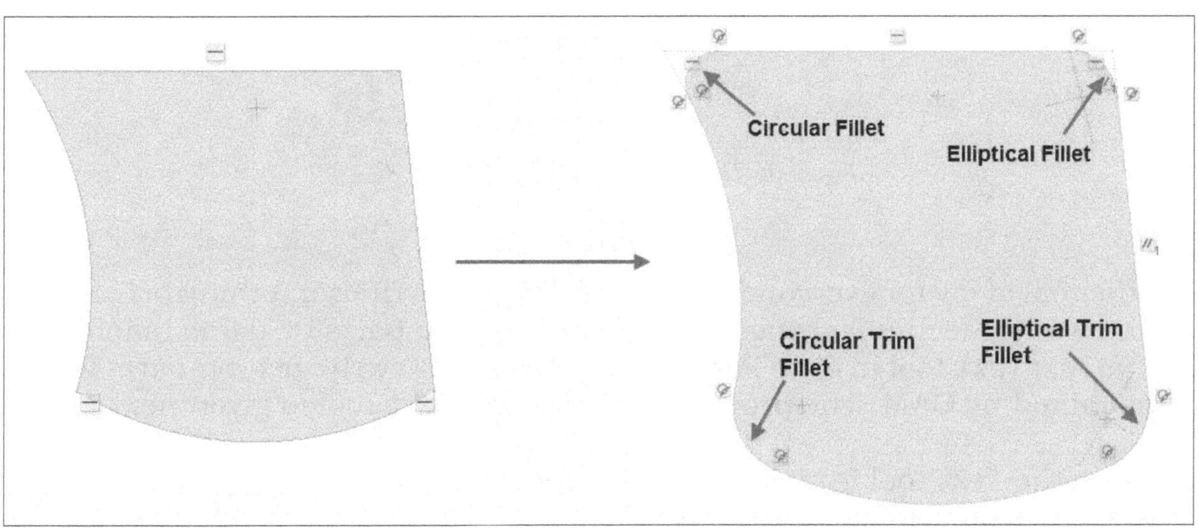

Figure-33. Fillets created

- This figure shows the difference between four type of fillets. Note that on creating the circular fillet, a reference point is created whereas on creating the circular trim fillet, no reference point is created. Similarly, the elliptical fillet and elliptical trim fillet work.
- Press **MMB** to exit the tool and double-click on the value to change it. After specifying new value, press **MMB** to apply it.

Chamfer

The **Chamfer** tools are used to blunt sharp edges of parts for their easy handling and more importantly their easy fitting in assembly. There are two tools in Creo Parametric for creating chamfers; **Chamfer** and **Chamfer Trim**. The procedure to use these tools is given next.

- Click on the **Chamfer** or **Chamfer Trim** tool from the **Chamfer** drop-down; refer to Figure-34. You are asked to select the two entities.
- Click on the first entity and then the second entity. Note that the entity must be consecutive. On doing so, the chamfer will be created; refer to Figure-35.

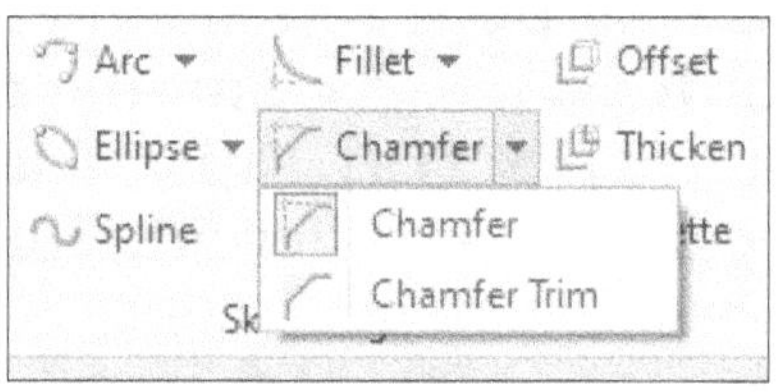

Figure-34. Chamfer drop down

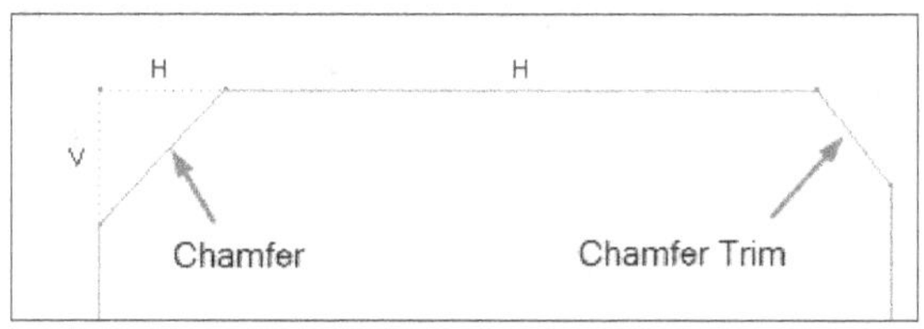

Figure-35. Chamfers created

- Press the middle button of the mouse to exit the tool.
Till this point, you have seen many illustrations but there are no dimensions displayed in our illustration because we want the illustrations to be neat and clean in the Book for printing. You can hide the dimensions by clearing the Dimensions Display check box from the Sketcher Display Filters drop-down in the In-Graphics toolbar; refer to Figure-36.

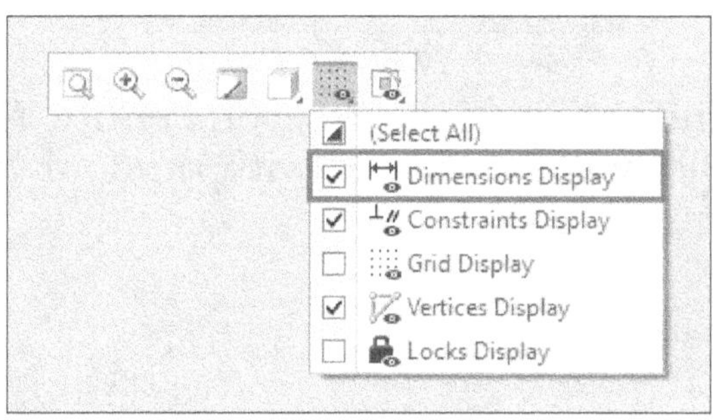

Figure-36. Dimensions Display check box

Text

This is the tool of joy for everyone. Everybody likes to write something on paper, tree, desk, and walls. Mechanical engineers like to write on parts by using machines, like brand names. **Text** tool in Creo Parametric allows us to write text on parts which are later machined by CAM. The procedure to use the **Text** tool is given next.

- Click on the **Text** tool from **Ribbon**. You are asked to specify the start point of line that will determine the height of the text.

- Click to specify the start point. You are asked to specify the end point of the line. Note that the orientation of line will determine orientation of the text.
- Click to specify the end point of the line. The **Text** dialog box will be displayed; refer to Figure-37.

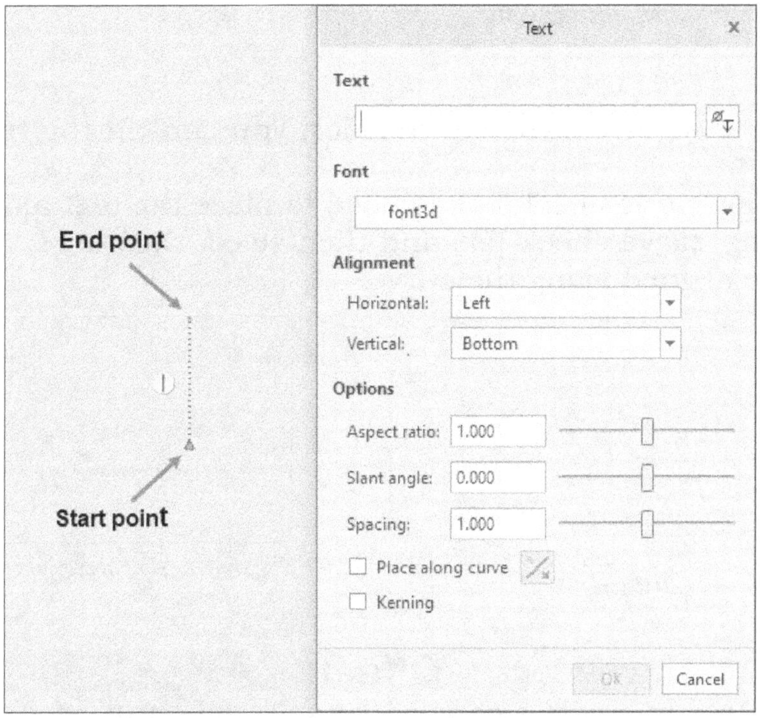

Figure-37. Text dialog box

- Click in the **Text** edit box and type desired text.
- Click on the **Text Symbol** button to add symbols. The **Text Symbol** dialog box will be displayed; refer to Figure-38.

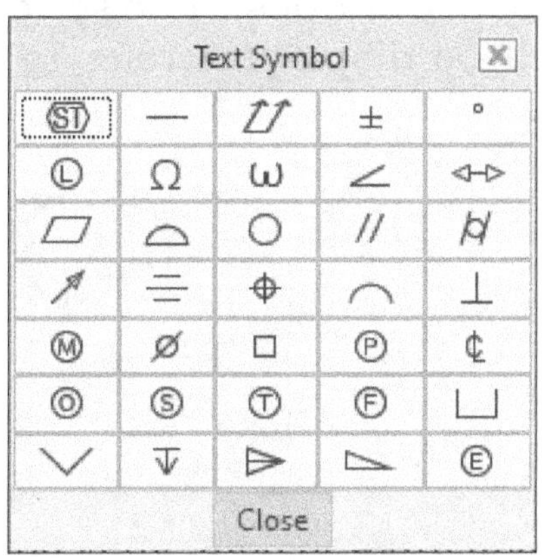

Figure-38. Text Symbol dialog box

- Select desired symbols from the dialog box and then click on the **Close** button from the dialog box to exit. The **Text** dialog box will become active again.
- In the **Alignment** area, select the horizontal and vertical justification for the text by using the **Horizontal** and **Vertical** drop-downs.
- Using the **Aspect ratio** slider and edit box, you can change the aspect ratio of the text. Aspect ratio is the ratio of width and height of the text. If you increase the aspect ratio, the text will occupy wider area; refer to Figure-39.

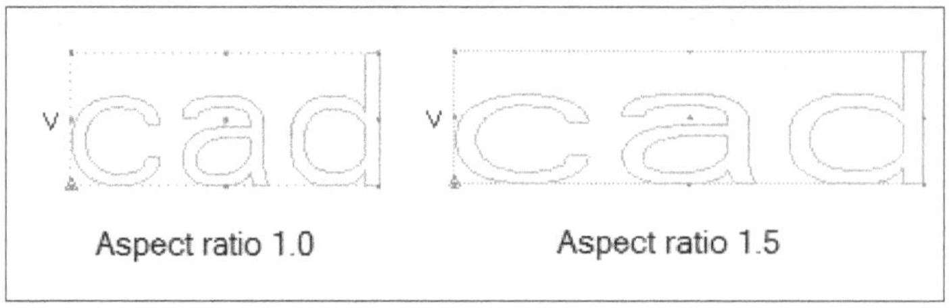

Figure-39. Aspect ratio

- Using the **Slant angle** edit box and slider, you can tilt the text at its position; refer to Figure-40.
- The **Place along curve** check box is used to place the text along a curve. Select the **Place along curve** check box and then select the curve; refer to Figure-41. The text will be aligned along the curve.

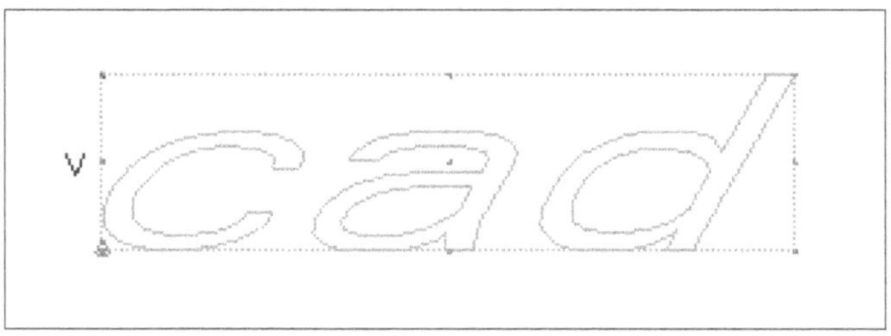

Figure-40. Slant angle set to 30 degree

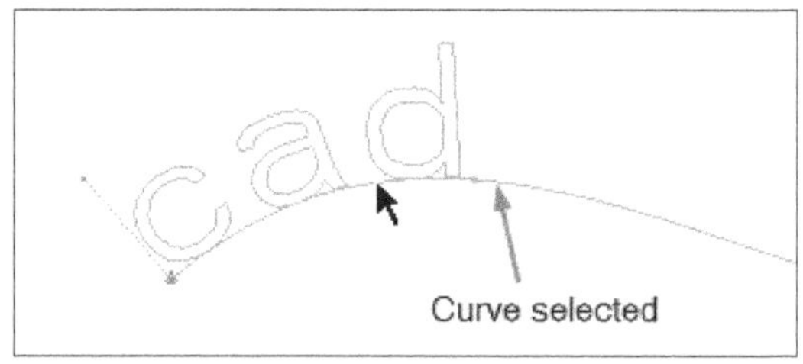

Figure-41. Text along curve

Offset

The **Offset** tool is used to create a copy of the selected entity at a specified distance. The procedure to create offset entities is given next.

- Click on the **Offset** tool from the **Ribbon**. The **Offset** dialog box will be displayed; refer to Figure-42. You are asked to select a sketch entity.
- Select an entity, chain, or loop of entities while selecting **Shift** button as required. Preview of offset entity will be displayed; refer to Figure-43. You are asked to specify the offset distance.

Figure-42. Offset dialog box

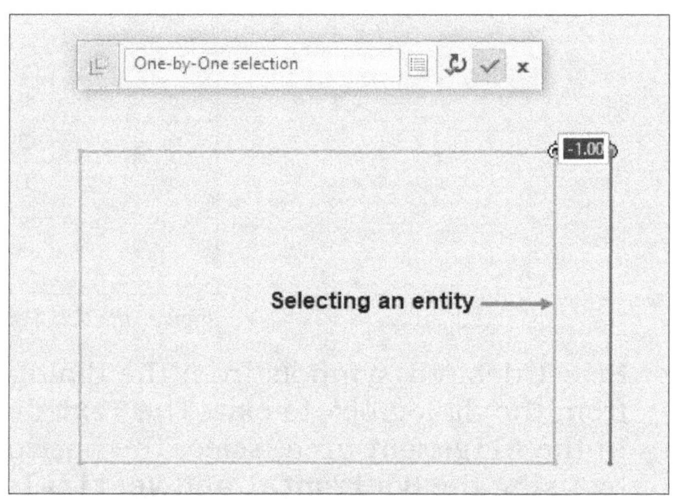

Figure-43. Selecting an entity to offset

- Specify desired distance in the edit box displayed in the drawing area. You can specify negative value for creating offset in opposite direction. Click on the **OK** button from the edit box. The offset entity/entities will be created; refer to Figure-44.

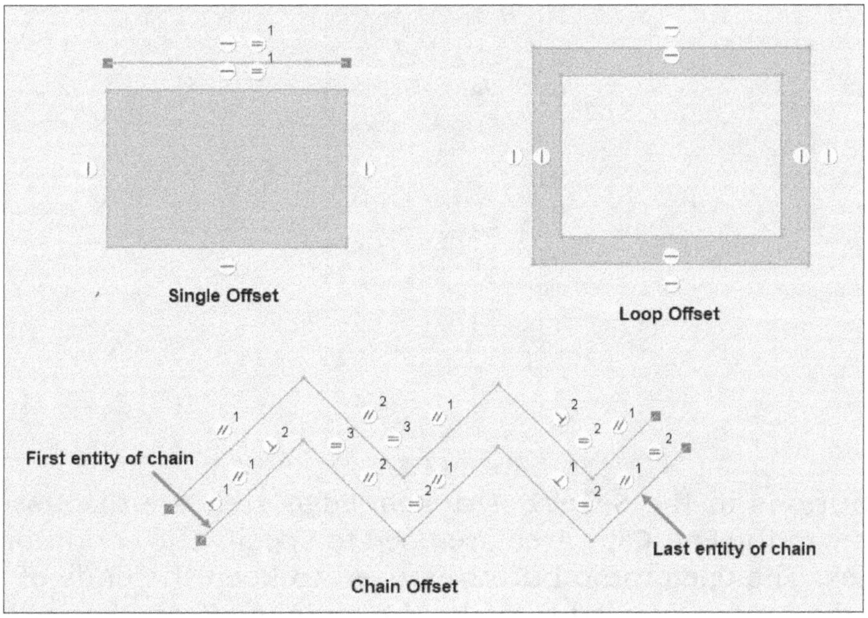

Figure-44. Offset entities

- Click on the button from the dialog box to create offset geometry from the collected references and keep the tab open.
- Click on the button to review and edit chain properties. The **Chain** dialog box will be displayed; refer to Figure-45.

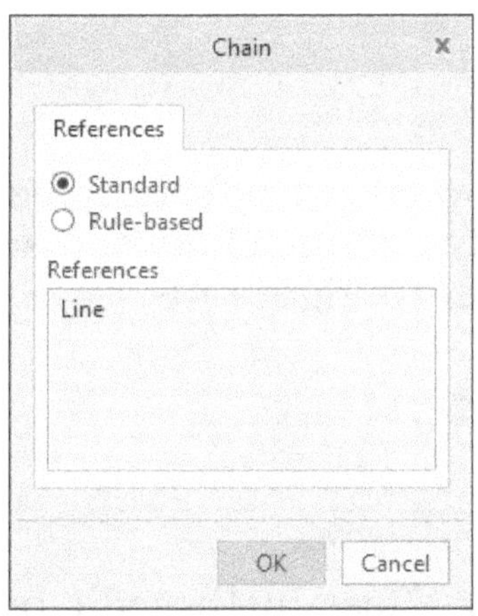

Figure-45. Chain dialog box

- Select the **Standard** radio button to individually gather all segments of the chain. Select the **Rule-based** radio button to define a rule that gathers chain segments.
- After specifying desired parameters, click on the **OK** button from the dialog box.

Thicken

The **Thicken** tool is used to create offset copy on the both sides of the selected entity. The procedure to use this tool is similar to the **Offset** tool. The procedure is given next.

- Click on the **Thicken** tool from the **Ribbon**. The **Type** dialog box will be displayed; refer to Figure-46.

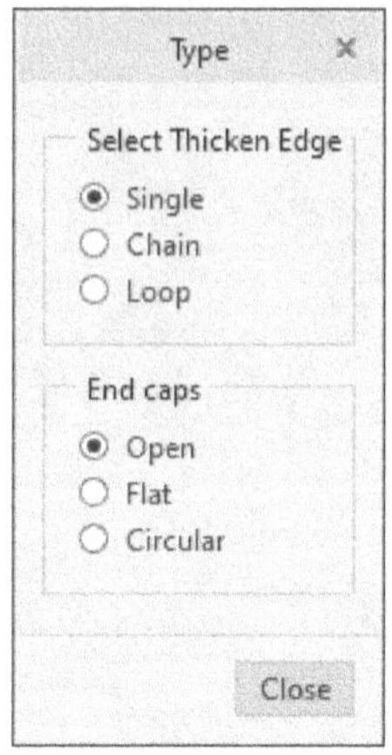

Figure-46. Type dialog box for Thicken tool

- The radio buttons in the **Select Thicken Edge** area are discussed earlier. The radio buttons in the **End Caps** area are used to specify the condition of ends of the offset entities. The **Open** radio button is used to keep the ends of offset as open. The **Flat** radio button is used to make the ends of offset entities joined by lines. The **Circular** radio button is used to make the ends of offset entities joined by semi-circles.
- Select desired radio buttons from the **Type** dialog box and click on the entity in the drawing area. The **Enter thickness** edit box will be displayed; refer to Figure-47.

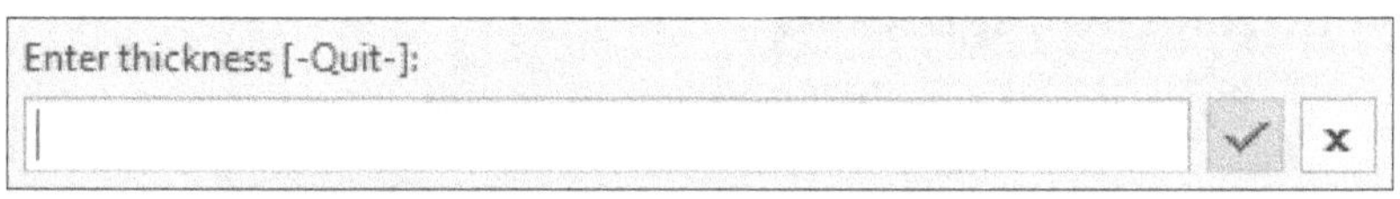

Figure-47. Enter thickness edit box

- Specify desired distance between two offset copies of the selected entity and press **ENTER**. The edit box to specify distance between selected entity and created offset copies will be displayed; refer to Figure-48.

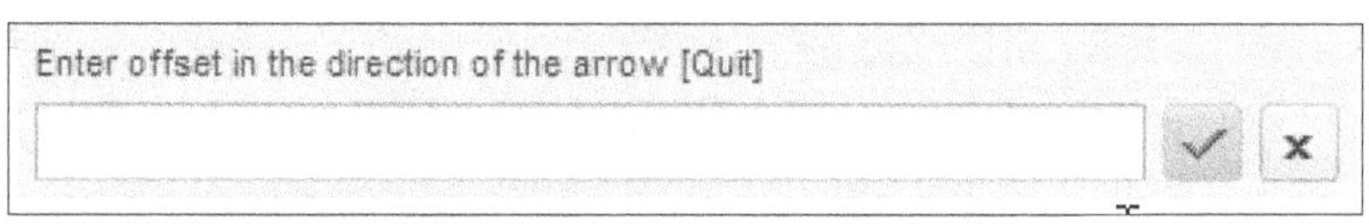

Figure-48. Offset distance edit box

- Specify desired distance for offset in the edit box and press **ENTER**. The offset entities will be created; refer to Figure-49.

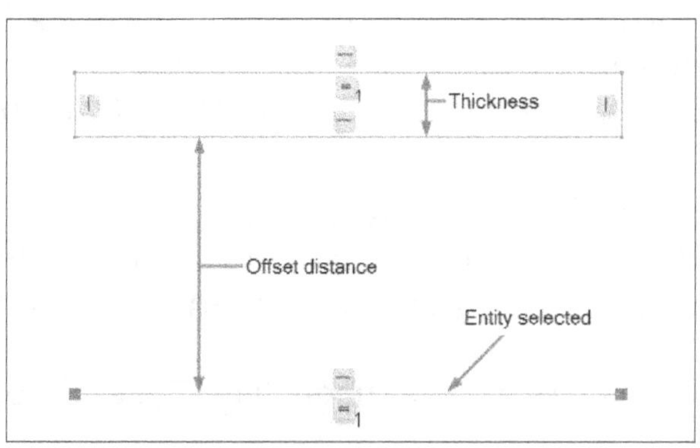

Figure-49. Thickness entities created

Palette

The **Palette** tool is used to import or use already created entities. The procedure to use this tool is given next.

- Click on the **Palette** tool from **Insert** panel of the **Ribbon**. The **Sketcher Palette** dialog box will be displayed; refer to Figure-50.

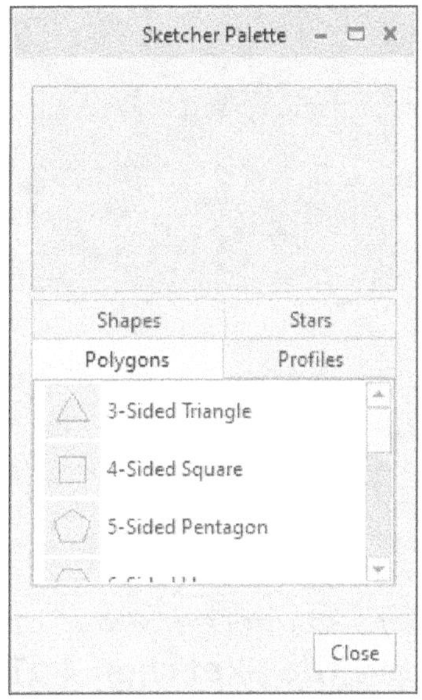

Figure-50. Sketcher Palette dialog box

- Switch between various categories by using the tabs. Double-click on the object that you want to use in the sketch. A plus sign will get attached to the cursor.
- Click in the drawing area to place the selected object. The object will be placed at the location you clicked and the **Import Section** tab is displayed; refer to Figure-51.

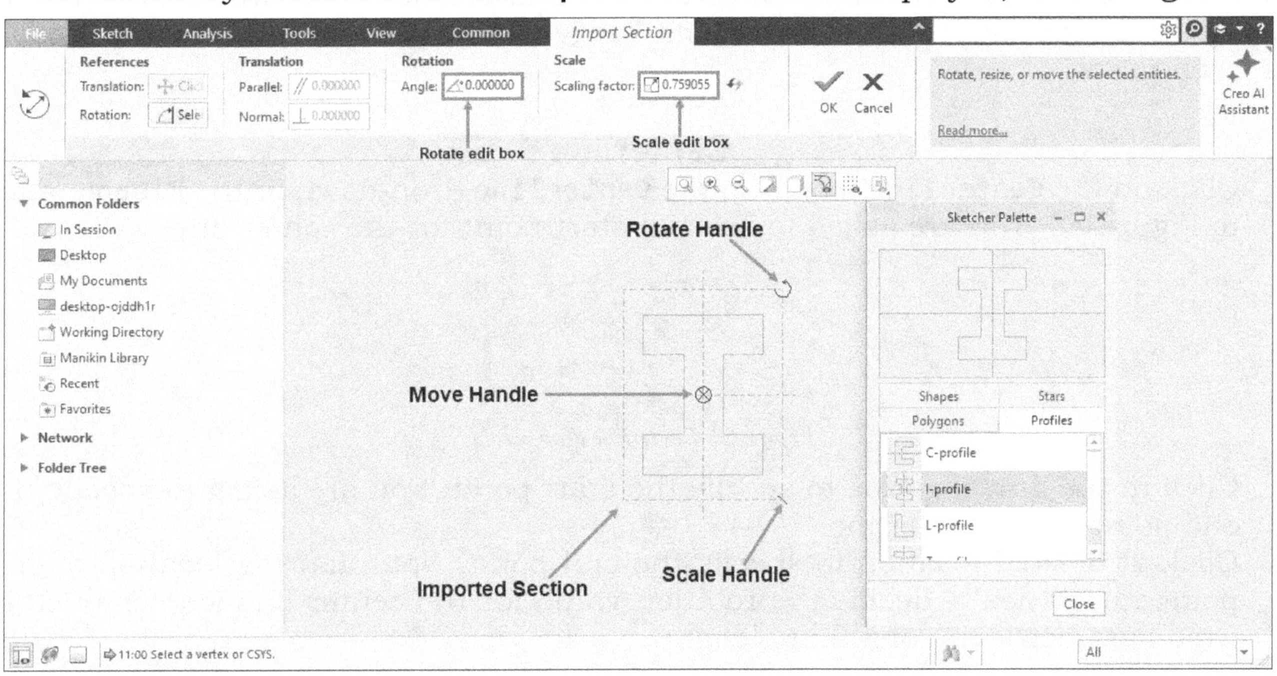

Figure-51. Imported Section

- Using the Rotate handle, Move handle, and Scale handle; you can rotate, move, and scale the imported section/object. To use the handles, click and hold the **LMB** on the handle icon, and drag the mouse to increase or decrease the value.

- You can also use the **Rotate** edit box and **Scale** edit box to specify the rotate and scale values, respectively.
- After specifying desired values, click on the **OK** button from the **Import Section** contextual tab. The section will be placed; refer to Figure-52.

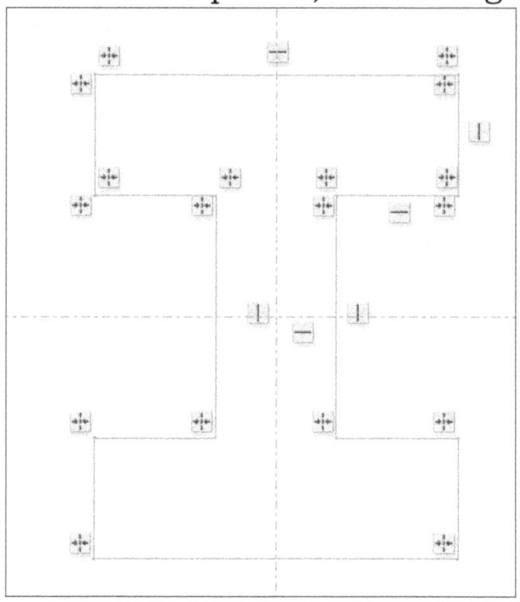

Figure-52. Imported section after placing in drawing area

- Click on the **Close** button from the **Sketcher Palette** dialog box to exit.

Centerline

Center line are the entities in Creo Parametric that are used to define a reference for creating sketch entities. When you will be creating solid models later in the book, you will get to know the importance of center line. There are two tools to create center lines; **Centerline** and **Centerline Tangent**. The procedure to use these tools is given next.

Centerline

- Click on the **Centerline** tool from the **Centerline** drop-down in the **Ribbon**; refer to Figure-53. You are asked to select a start point for the center line.

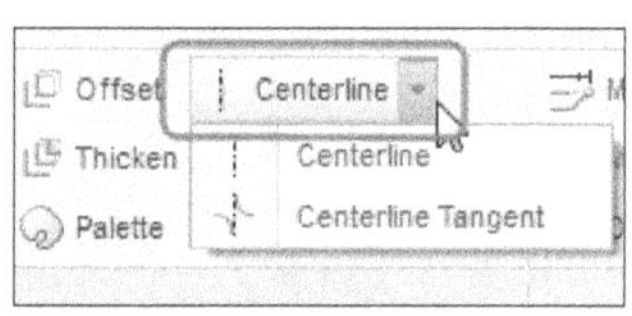

Figure-53. Centerline drop-down

- Click in the drawing area to specify the start point. You are asked to specify the end point of the centerline.
- Click at desired location to specify the end point. Note that the location of end point will basically decide the rotation value for the center line (center lines in Creo Parametric are of infinite length).

Centerline Tangent

The **Centerline Tangent** tool works in the same way as the **Centerline** tool works. The only difference is in the selection of entities. For **Centerline** tool, we need to specify points but for the **Centerline Tangent** tool, we need to select two curves to which the centerline will be tangent. Rest of the procedure is same; refer to Figure-54.

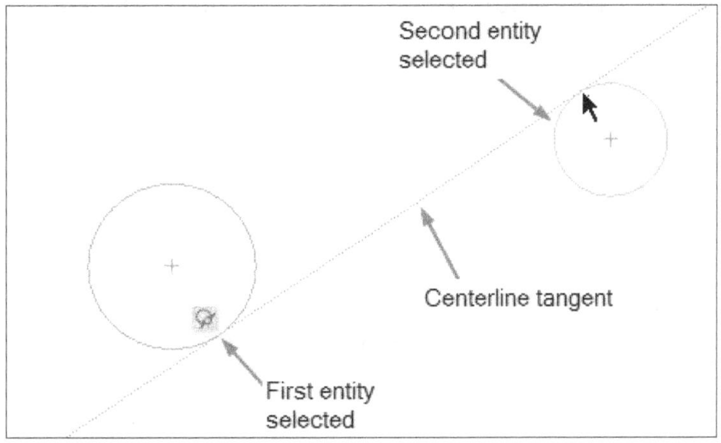

Figure-54. Tangent centerline

Point

The **Point** tool as the name suggests is used to create points in the drawing area. These points can later be used to reference other sketch entities. The procedure to create points is given next.

- Click on the **Point** tool from the **Ribbon**. You are asked to specify the position of the point.
- Click at desired location to specify the point. You can keep on clicking at desired location until you get the required number of points.
- Press the middle button of mouse to exit the tool.

Coordinate System

Coordinate system is a reference for all the entities sketched in Creo Parametric. All the base dimensions are measured from coordinate system; refer to Figure-55. The procedure to place coordinate system is similar to **Point** tool. Click on the **Coordinate System** tool from the **Ribbon** and click at desired location in the drawing area to place it.

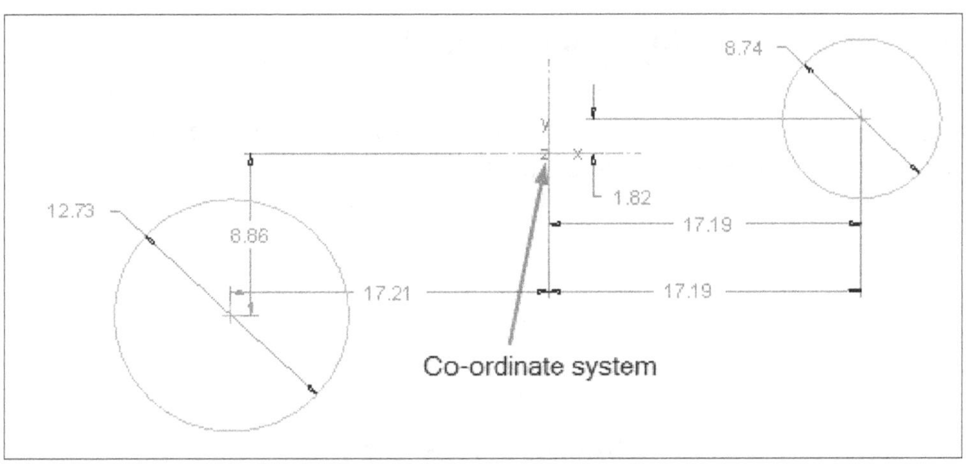

Figure-55. Coordinate system placed

Construction Mode

Sometimes while creating the sketch entities, you may require some construction entities that can support in creating sketches. The procedure to create construction entities is given next.

- Click on the **Construction Mode** toggle button from the **Ribbon**; refer to Figure-56.

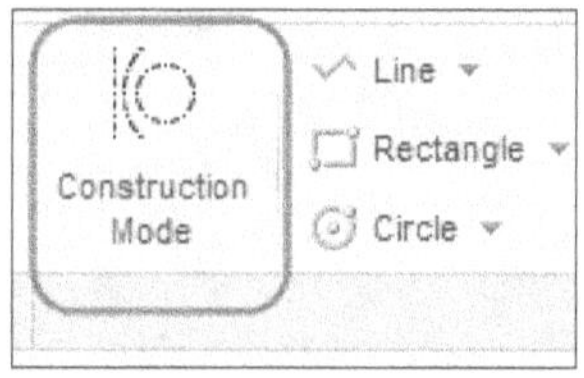

Figure-56. Construction Mode button

- Now, you can create desired construction entity by using the sketching tools discussed earlier. Figure-57 shows some construction entities created by using sketching tools.

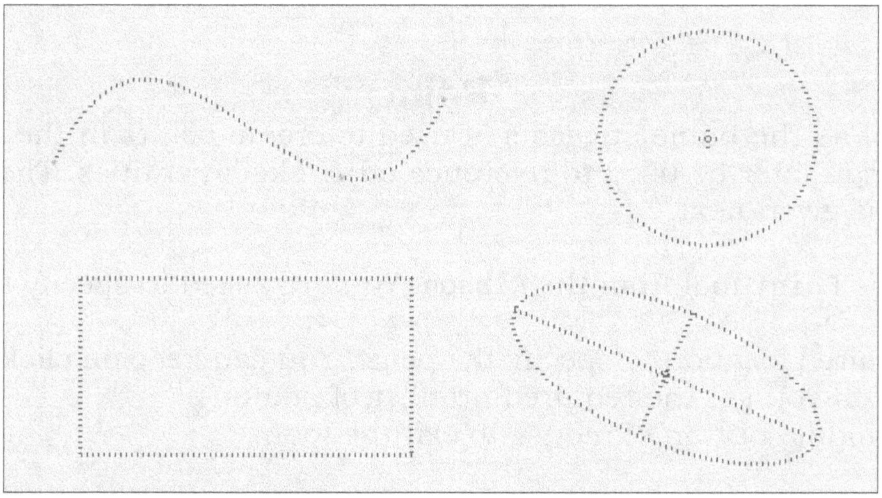

Figure-57. Construction entities

- Click on the **Construction Mode** toggle button to exit the construction mode.

There is no benefit in creating sketches without dimensions in Creo Parametric. So, we will discuss the procedures to apply dimensions to the sketches.

DIMENSION TOOLS

Unlike other CAD packages, Creo Parametric has very compact tool box for dimensioning. There are only four tools to apply dimensions to entities; refer to Figure-58. These tools are discussed next.

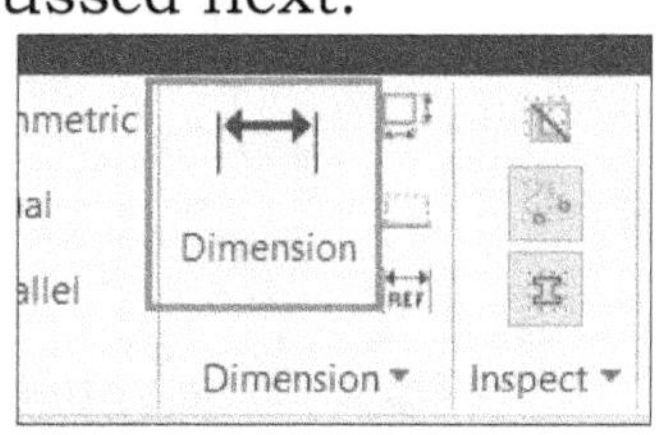

Figure-58. Dimension panel

Dimension tool

The **Dimension** tool is single tool with multiple functionality. Using the **Dimension** tool, you can dimension any type of object in Creo Parametric. There are no separate tools for dimensioning different type of entities like line, circle, spline, and so on. After creating sketches, you need to apply dimension to them for design purpose. The procedure to use this tool is given next.

- Click on the **Dimension** tool from the **Dimension** panel in the **Ribbon**. You will be asked to select entities to be dimensioned. We have different selection patterns for different entities to be dimensioned. These patterns are discussed next.

Dimensioning Line

There are two ways to dimension a line.

- After selecting the **Dimension** tool, click on the line and press the middle mouse button at the location where you want to place the dimension; refer to Figure-59. Now, you can change the value of dimension and press **ENTER**.

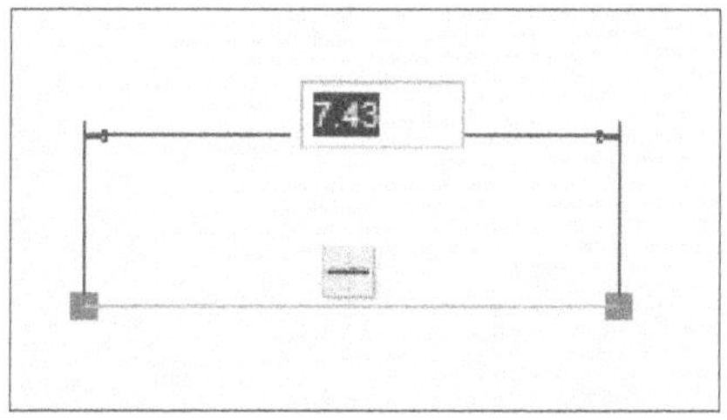

Figure-59. Line dimensioned

- After selecting the **Dimension** tool, one by one click on both the end points of the line and then place the dimension by pressing the middle mouse button; refer to Figure-59. Now, you can change the value of dimension and press **ENTER**.

Dimensioning Circle

- After selecting the **Dimension** tool, click on the circumference of circle and press the middle button of mouse to place the dimension.
- By default, the radius dimension is applied to the circle. To convert it to diameter dimension, select the dimension text by clicking on it and hold the right click button of mouse. A shortcut menu will be displayed; refer to Figure-60.

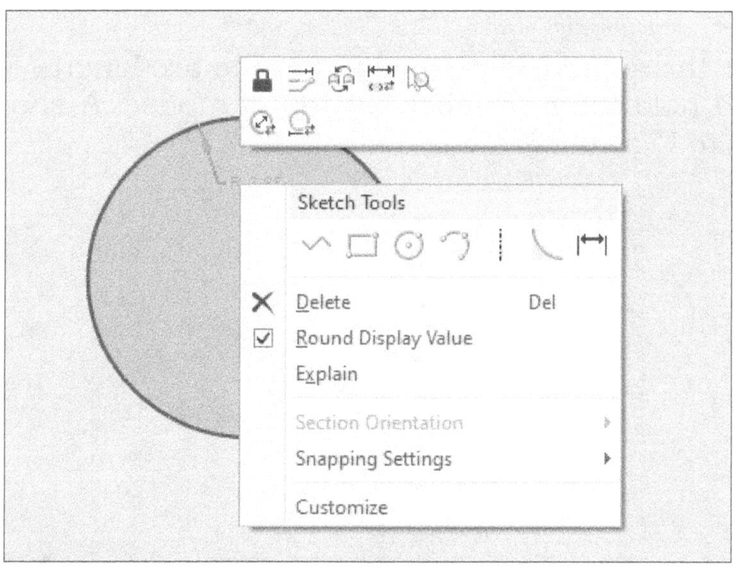

Figure-60. Shortcut menu for dimensioning of circle

- Click on the **Diameter** button from the shortcut menu. The dimension will be converted to diameter. You can do the vice-versa by following the same procedure.

Dimensioning Arc

- After selecting the **Dimension** tool, click on the circumference of circle and press the middle button of mouse to place the dimension. The radius of arc will be specified.
- Now, you need to specify the span angle of the arc. Make sure the **Dimension** tool is selected. Click on the first point of the arc, then center of the arc, and then click on the end point of the arc.
- Press the Middle mouse button at desired location to place the dimension. Angle dimension of the arc will be specified; refer to Figure-61.

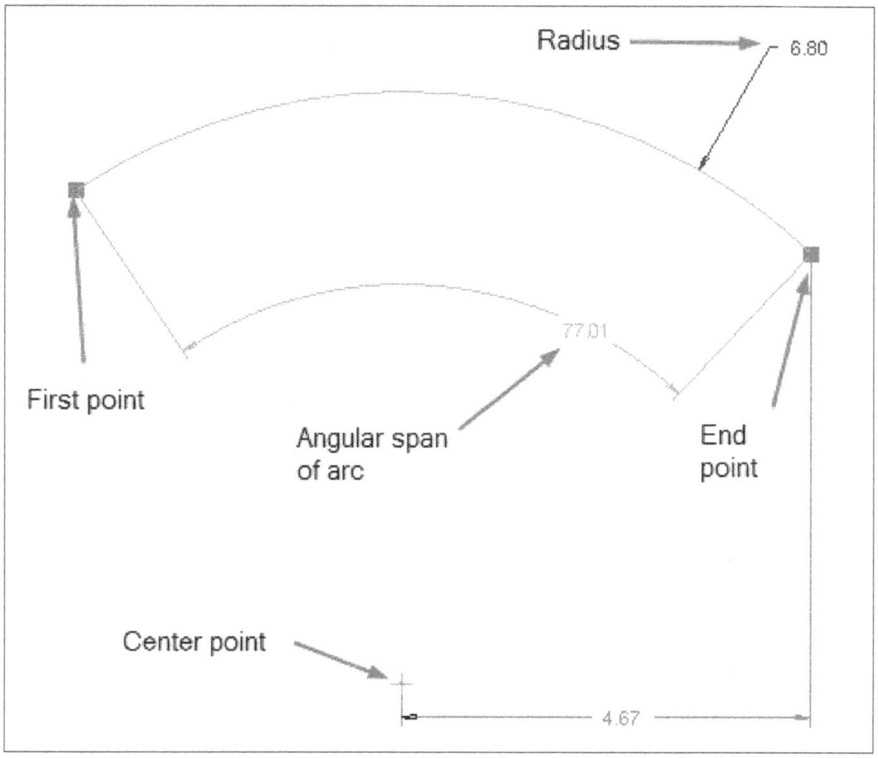

Figure-61. Dimensioning of arc

- You can change the angular dimension of arc to arc length. To do so, select the angle of arc and hold the right-click button of mouse. A shortcut menu will be displayed; refer to Figure-62.

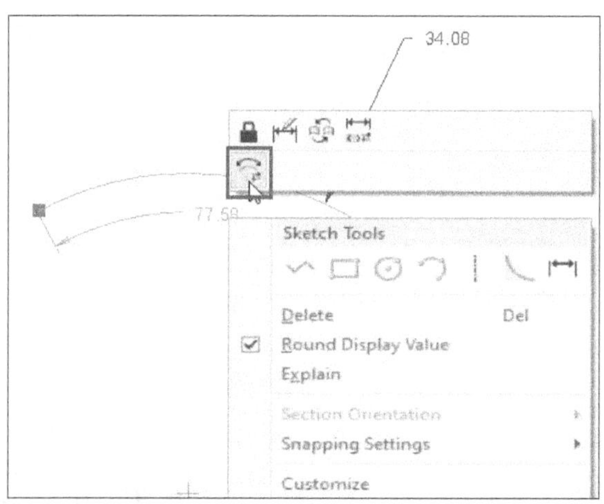

Figure-62. Convert to length option

- Select the **Length** button from the menu. The dimension will be changed to arc length.

Angular dimensions

One type of angular dimension was explained in dimensioning arcs. If you have two line for which you want to specify the angle, follow the steps given next.

- Click on the **Dimension** tool.
- Select the first line and then select the second line.
- Press the middle button of mouse in the region bound by two line; refer to Figure-63.

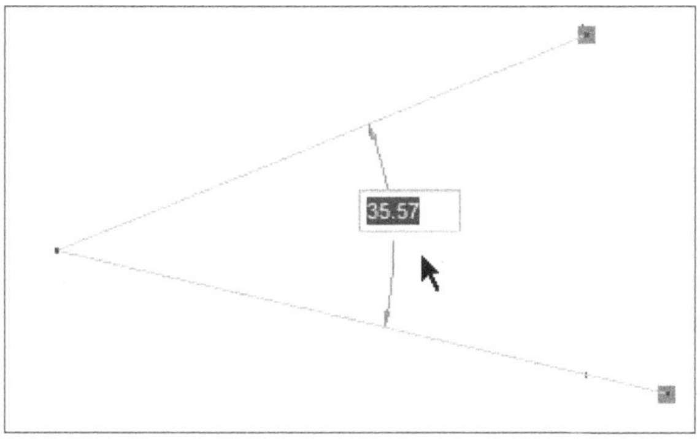

Figure-63. Angle between lines

- Note that the dimension value changes on the basis of location selected for placing the dimension. For example, if we press the **MMB** at the location outside the area bound by two lines then the obtuse angle will be displayed; refer to Figure-64.

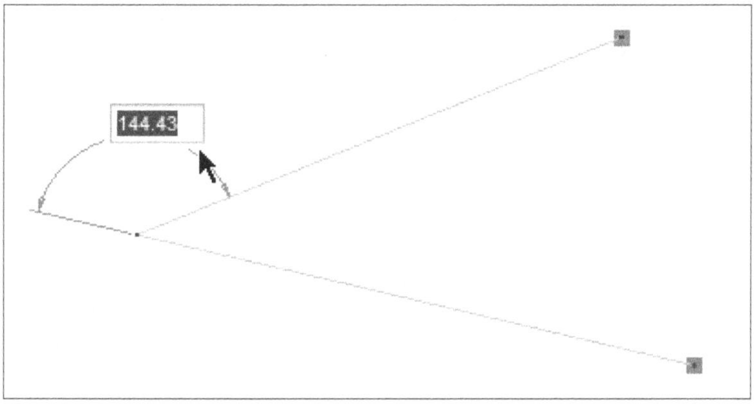

Figure-64. Obtuse angle dimension

You can move the text of any dimension by dragging it to desired place.

Dimensioning Points

Rest of the sketching entities are dimensioned with the help of their reference points. We will now discuss about dimensioning an ellipse and on the basis of that you can dimension all the other entities which are dimensioned by their points.

- Click on the **Dimension** tool if not active. Next, click one by one on the two quadrant points adjacent to each other; refer to Figure-65.

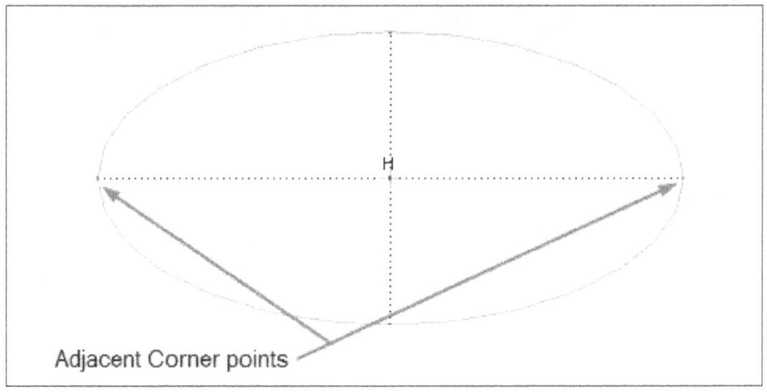

Figure-65. Points of ellipse

- Press the middle button of mouse at desired location to place the dimension. Similarly, you can use the other points to specify the dimensions.

Perimeter

Sometimes, we need to manipulate the perimeter of circle, rectangles, and other sketched entities. For those cases, we need the perimeter dimension. The steps to create and manipulate the perimeter dimension are given next.

- Select the geometry by using window selection for which you want to create the perimeter dimension and click on the **Perimeter** tool from the **Dimension** panel in the **Ribbon**. You are asked to select the varying dimension which will be manipulated to get desired perimeter.
- Select desired dimension (Note that the dimension selected must not be locked one). Refer to Figure-66.

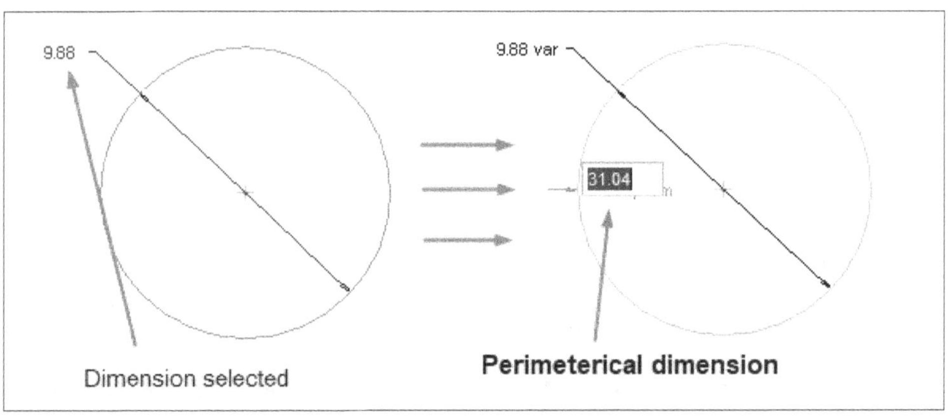

Figure-66. Perimeterical Dimension

- Double-click on the perimeterical dimension and change the value as desired.

Baseline Dimensioning

Sometimes, our sketch becomes so much complex that we are forced to remove arrows of dimension to make the sketch appear neat. In such cases, we use the Baseline dimensioning. The Baseline dimensioning is also called Ordinate dimensioning. This dimensioning also help programmers who are using NC machines for machining the parts. The procedure to dimension with baseline is given next.

- Click on **Baseline** tool from the **Dimension** panel in the **Ribbon**. You are asked to specify a reference for ordinate dimension.

- Select desired point or line to specify the origin for ordinate dimension; refer to Figure-67.
- Press the middle mouse button at location approximately collinear to the selected line; refer to Figure-68.

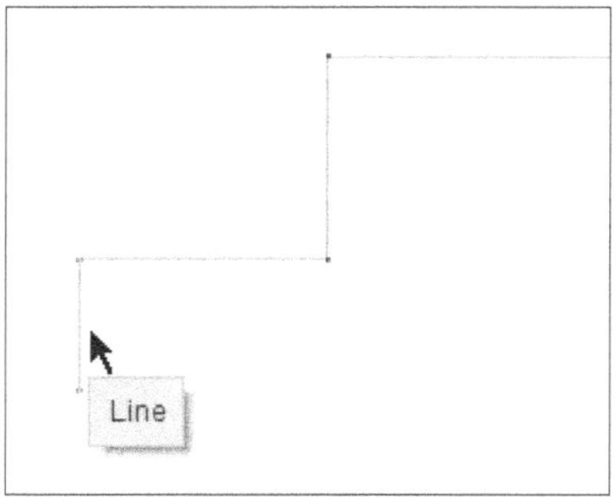

Figure-67. Line selected

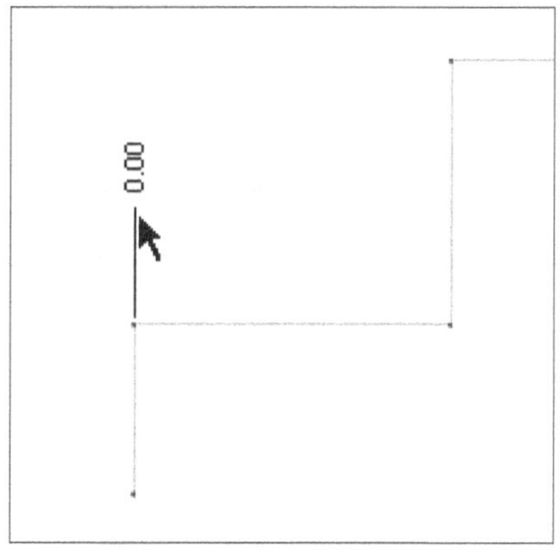

Figure-68. Ordinate dimension

- Now, click on the **Dimension** tool from the **Dimension** panel in the **Ribbon** and then click on the ordinate dimension just created.
- Next, click on the line that you want to dimension and press the middle button of mouse to place the dimension; refer to Figure-69.
- Similarly, you can specify the ordinate in vertical direction; refer to Figure-70.

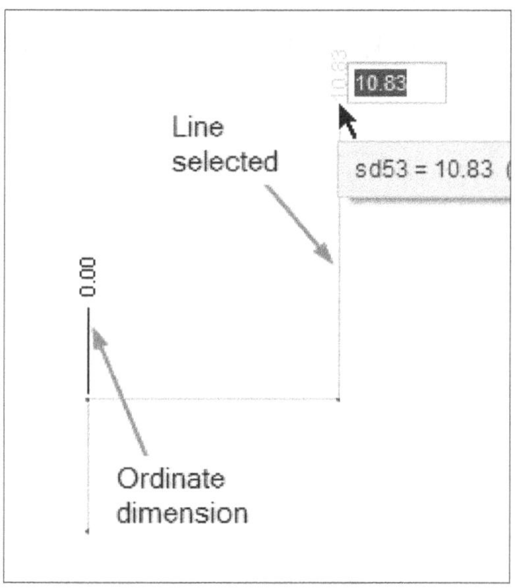

Figure-69. Ordinate dimensioning

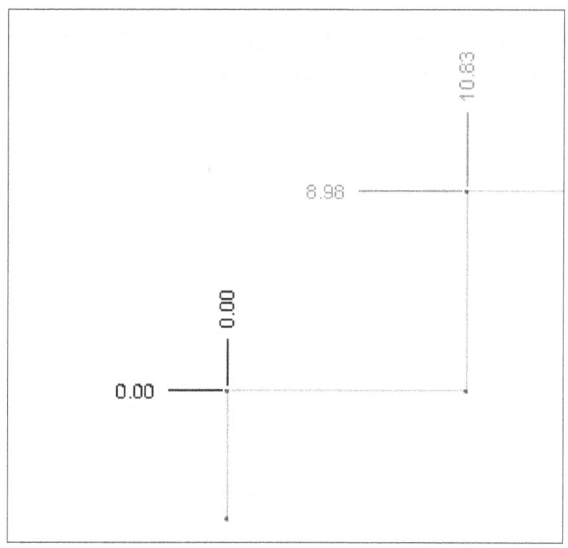

Figure-70. Vertical ordinate dimension

Reference Dimension

In some of the sketches, the applied dimensions are enough to fully constrain the sketch but still we need some more dimensions for quality check purposes. These dimensions are called Reference dimensions. Now, we will do an activity for reference dimensioning.

- Click on the **Dimension** tool from the **Dimension** panel in the **Ribbon**. You are asked to select the reference for dimensioning.
- Create a sketch of rectangles and line as shown in Figure-71.

Figure-71. Sketch to be dimensioned

- Dimension the sketch as shown in Figure-72.

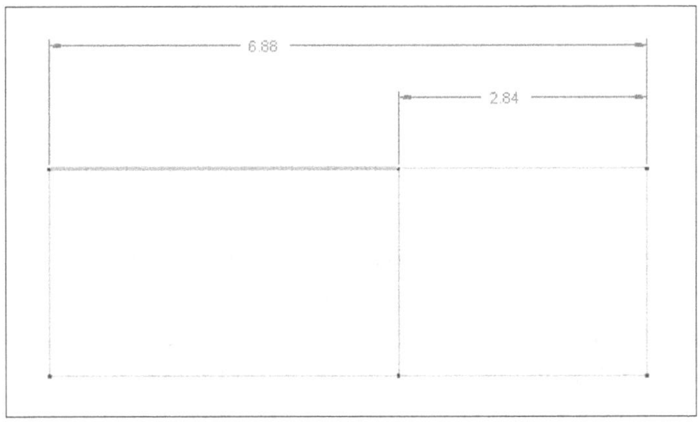

Figure-72. Sketch after dimensioning

- Now, using the **Dimension** tool, try to dimension the thick line. You will get the **Resolve Sketch** dialog box; refer to Figure-73.

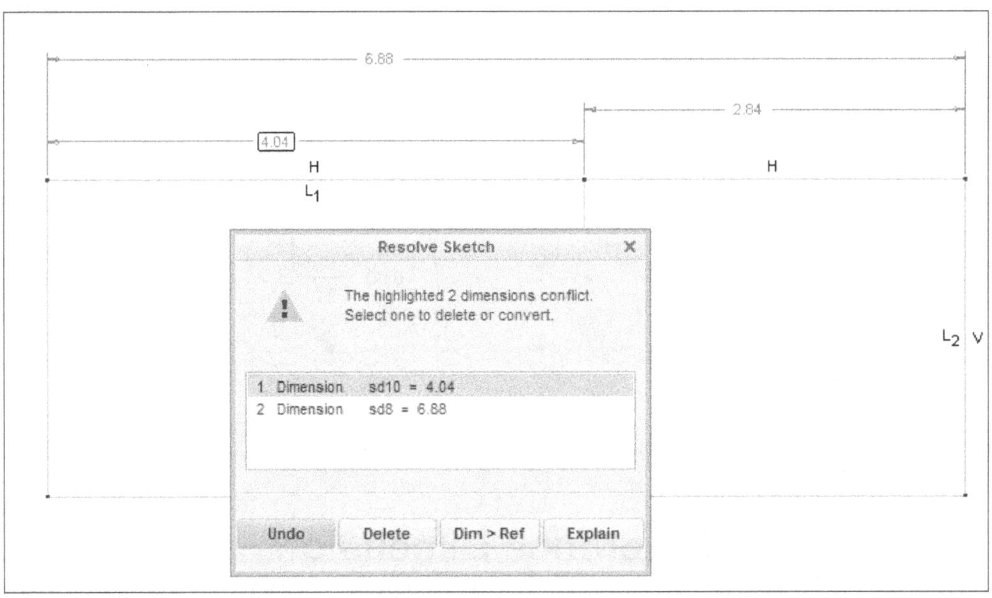

Figure-73. Resolve Sketch

- This dialog box shows that the sketch is going to be over defined i.e. dimensioned more than required. Now, we have two options; either delete the extra dimension which is **4.04** in this case, or make it reference dimension.
- If you still want the dimension to be displayed for whatever purpose then click on the **Dim>Ref** button from the **Resolve Sketch** dialog box. The dimension will be displayed as shown in Figure-74.

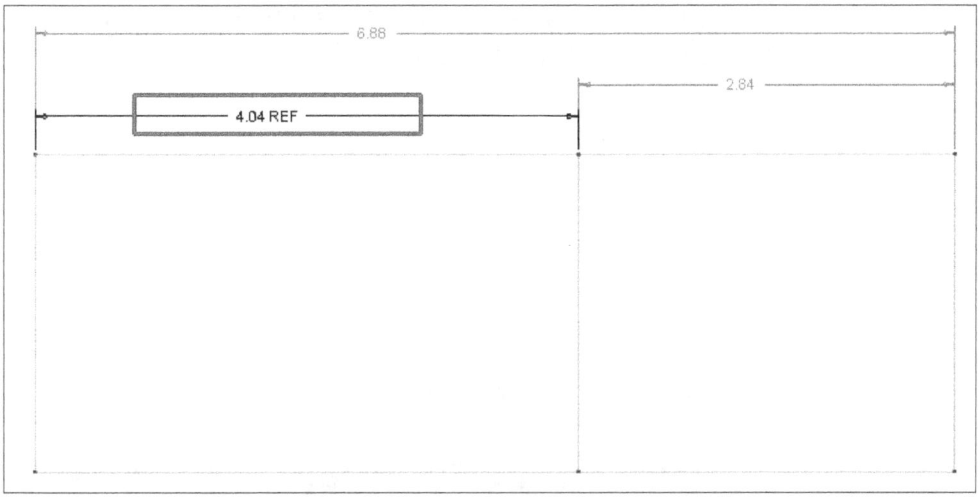

Figure-74. Reference dimension applied

- You can apply this reference dimension by using the **Reference** tool in the **Dimension** panel of the **Ribbon**.

GEOMETRIC CONSTRAINTS

Besides the dimensions, we also constrain sketches by using the Geometric Constraints. Geometric constraints are the restrictions on the sketches like, two selected lines will be of equal length, the two selected circles will be of equal diameter, and so on. Various geometric constraints available in Creo Parametric are discussed next.

Vertical Constrain

This constraint is used to make selected line vertical. You can also make two points to share same horizontal level from a reference point. The procedure to use this tool is given next.

- Click on the **Vertical** button from the **Constrain** panel in the **Ribbon**. You are asked to select entities to be constrained.
- Click on the line that you want to be vertical; refer to Figure-75. The line will be aligned vertically as shown in Figure-76.

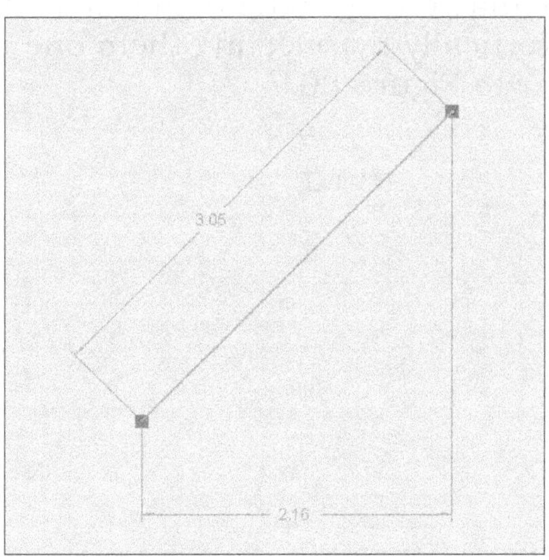

Figure-75. Inclined line

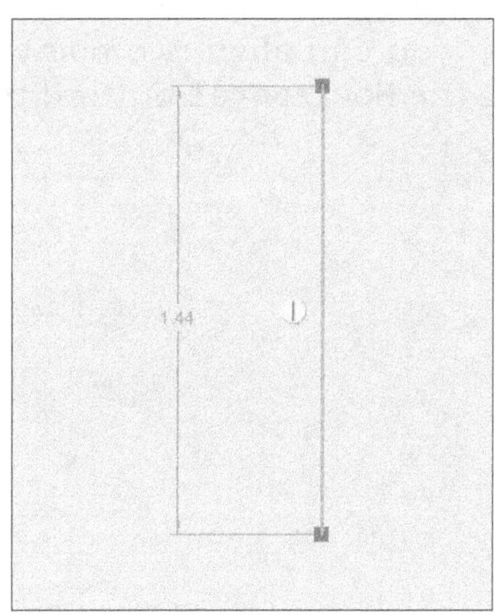

Figure-76. Vertical line created

- Similarly, you can align two points vertically by selecting them one by one after choosing the **Vertical** button; refer to Figure-77.

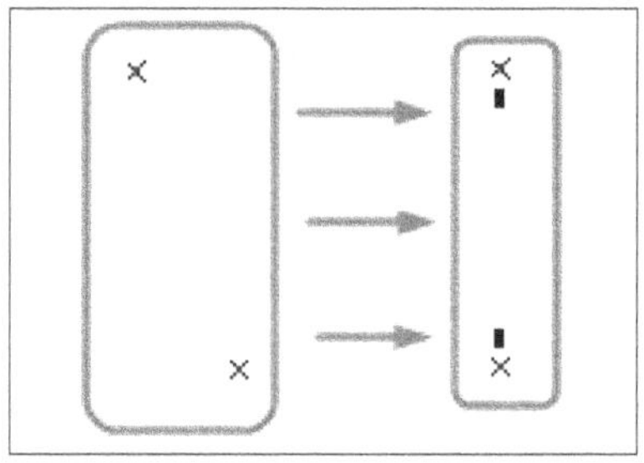

Figure-77. Points constrained vertically

Horizontal Constrain

This constraint is used to make selected line horizontal. You can also make two points aligned horizontally. The procedure to use this tool is given next.

- Click on the **Horizontal** button from the **Constrain** panel in the **Ribbon**. You are asked to select entities to be constrained.
- Click on the line that you want to be horizontal; refer to Figure-78. The line will be aligned horizontally as shown in Figure-79.

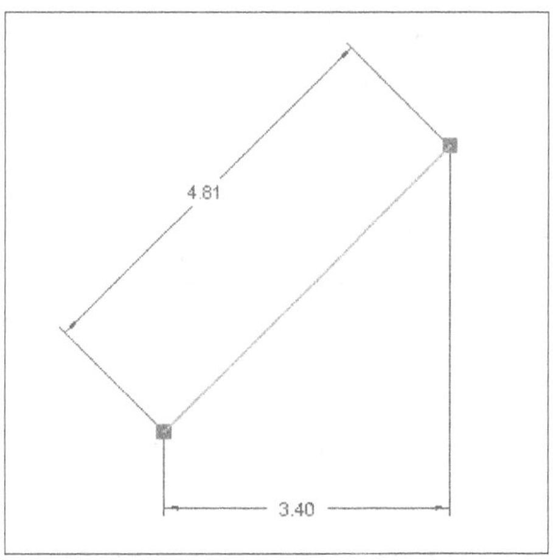

Figure-78. Inclined line

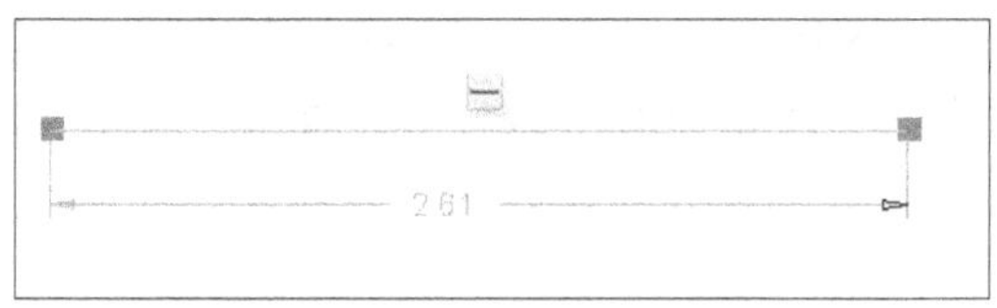

Figure-79. Horizontal line created

- Note that the length of the line is calculated as per the Pythagorus theorem.
- Similarly, you can align two points vertically by selecting them one by one after choosing the **Horizontal** button; refer to Figure-80.

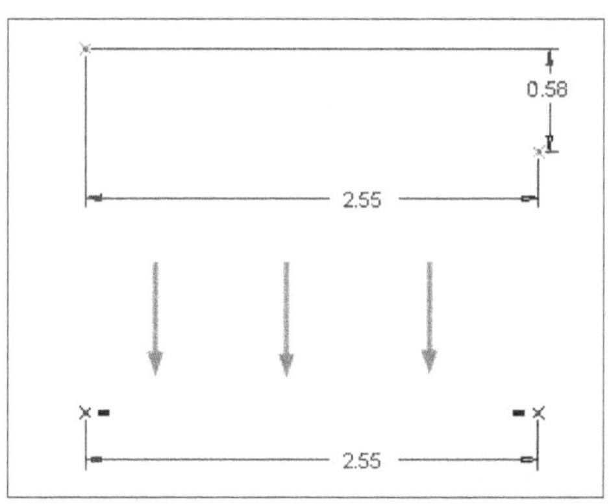

Figure-80. Points constrained horizontally

Perpendicular Constrain

The Perpendicular constrain is used to make a line/entity perpendicular to the other entity. The procedure to apply the constrain is given next.

- Click on the **Perpendicular** button from the **Constrain** panel in the **Ribbon**. You are asked to select entities to be constrained.
- Select the first entity and then select the second entity. The lines will be constrained perpendicularly; refer to Figure-81.
- Similarly, you can make an arc perpendicular to the other entity; refer to Figure-82.

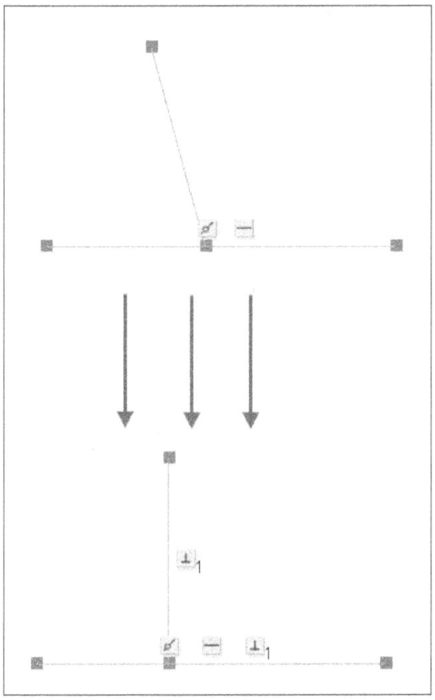

Figure-81. Lines constrained perpendicularly

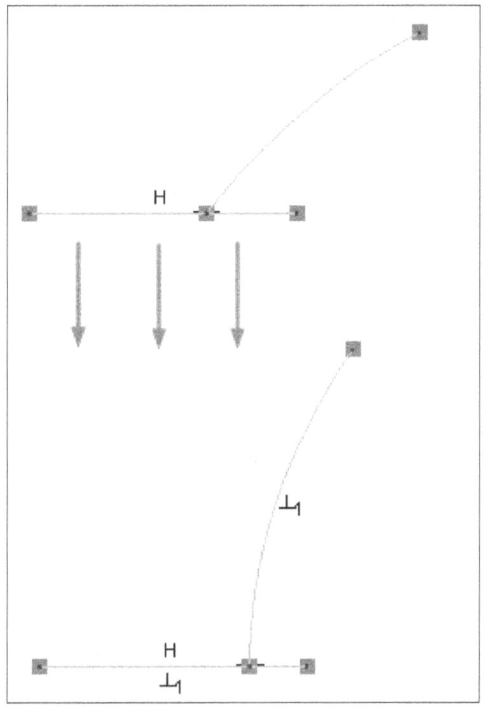

Figure-82. Entities perpendiculary constrained

Tangent Constrain

The Tangent constrain is used to make two entities tangent to each other. The entities can be combination of line and arc, arc and arc, arc and circle, circle and circle, ellipse with arc, line, or circle, and so on. The procedure to apply this constrain is given next.

- Click on the **Tangent** button from the **Dimension** panel in the **Ribbon**. You are asked to select two entities that you want to be tangent to each other.
- Select the two entities one by one. The selected entities will become tangent to each other; refer to Figure-83.

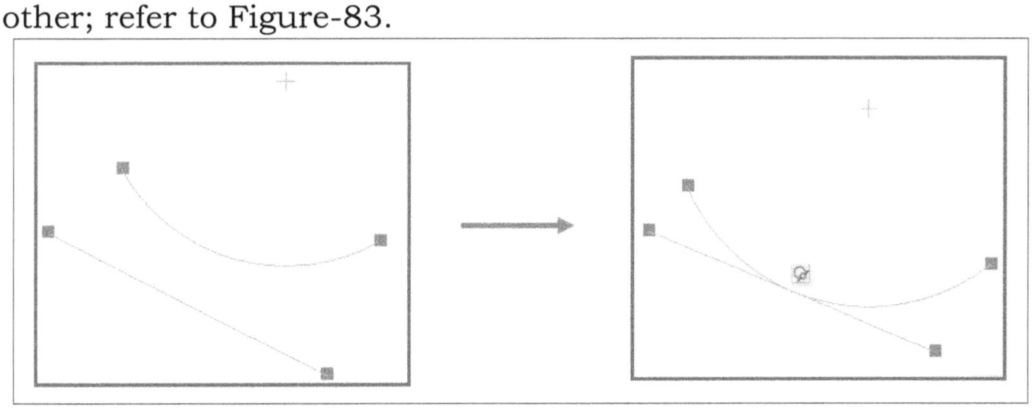

Figure-83. Tangent entities

Mid-point Constrain

The **Mid-point** button is used to place the selected point at the middle of the other selected entity. The procedure to apply the Mid-point constrain using this tool is given next.

- Click on the **Mid-Point** tool from the **Dimension** panel in the **Ribbon**. You are asked to select a point.
- Select a point (it can be of any sketch entity also). Then, select the entity on whose mid-point you want to place the selected point. The point will be placed at the mid point of the selected entity; refer to Figure-84.

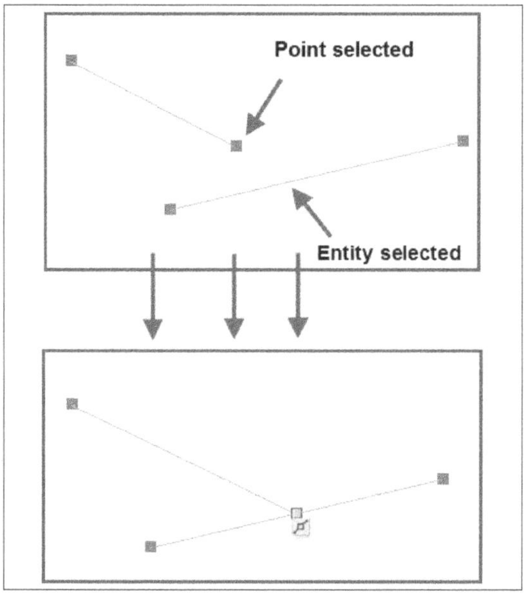

Figure-84. Lines after mid-point constrain

- In the same way, you can place selected point at the mid-point of arc, circle, ellipse, and so on.

Coincident Constrain

The Coincident constrain is used to make selected entities share the same location. The procedure to apply the coincident constrain is given next.

- Click on the **Coincident** button from the **Dimension** panel in the **Ribbon**. You are asked to select the entities to be coincident. Figure-85 shows four line with different orientations. We will make a close sketch from these lines by using this constrain.

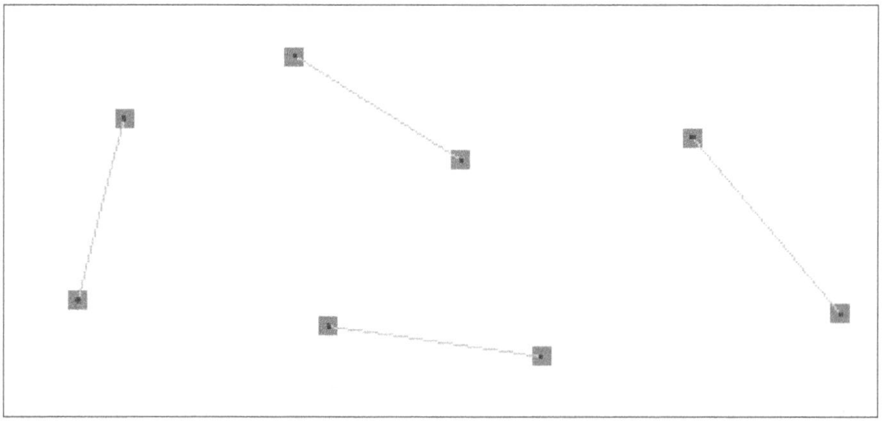

Figure-85. Lines for coincident constrain application

- Select one by one points as per their group; refer to Figure-86. Like, points in Group 1 should be selected together.

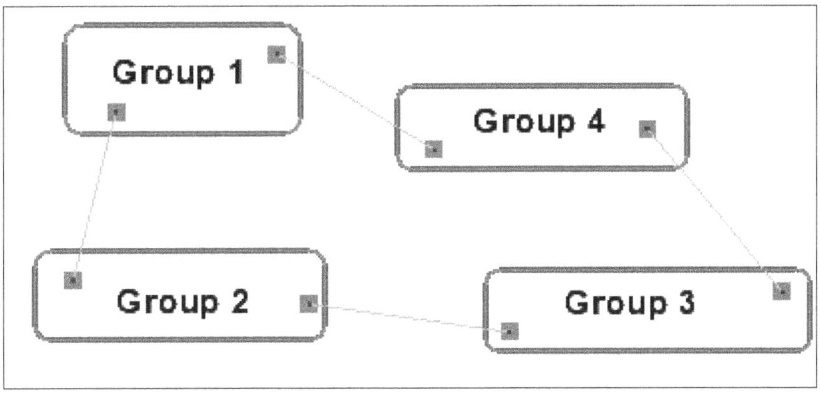

Figure-86. Groupwise points to be selected

- After selecting the points as per the group, the points will be connected as shown in Figure-87.
- If you select two lines distant from each other and at different orientation then the coincident constrain will make them collinear; refer to Figure-88.

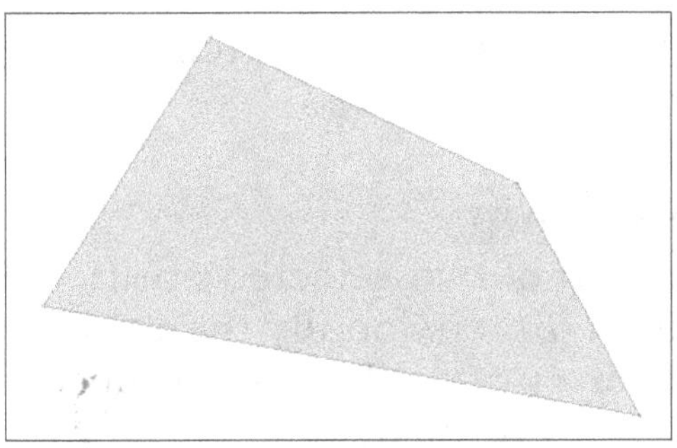

Figure-87. Lines after coincident constraining

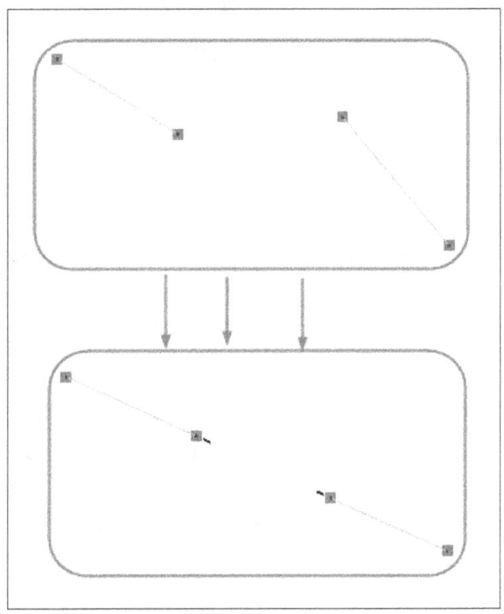

Figure-88. Lines coincident

Symmetric Constrain

The Symmetric constrain, as the name suggests, is used to make entities symmetric about a center line. The procedure to apply Symmetric constrain is given next.

- Click on the **Symmetric** button from the **Constrain** panel in the **Ribbon**. You are asked to select a centerline and then the two vertices that you want symmetric about the centerline.
- Click on the center line. You are asked to select two vertices.
- One by one select the vertices that you want to make symmetric. On selecting the points, they will become symmetric; refer to Figure-89.

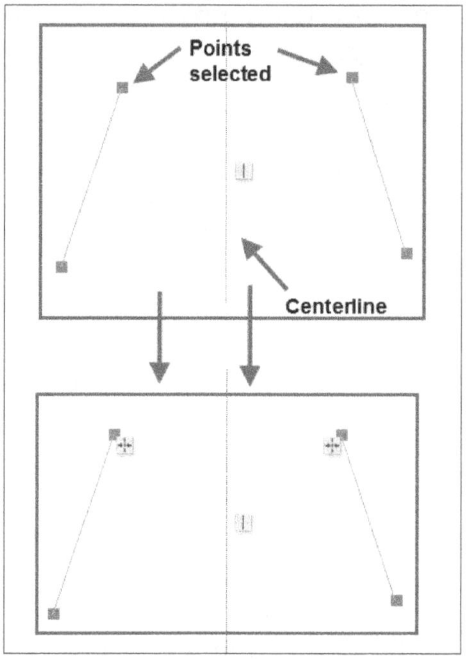

Figure-89. Applying symmetric constrain

- You can apply the symmetric constrain to points of any sketch entity like, circle, ellipse, spline, and so on.

Equal Constrain

The Equal constrain is used to make dimension of two selected entities equal. Note that if one of the two entities is not constrained dimensionally then the first selected entity will be taken as reference and the other entity will be sized according to the first. The procedure to apply this constrain is given next.

- Click on the **Equal** button from the **Constrain** panel in the **Ribbon**. You are asked to select the two entities that you want to make equal.
- Click on the first entity and then click on the second entity. The entities will become equal in dimensions; refer to Figure-90.

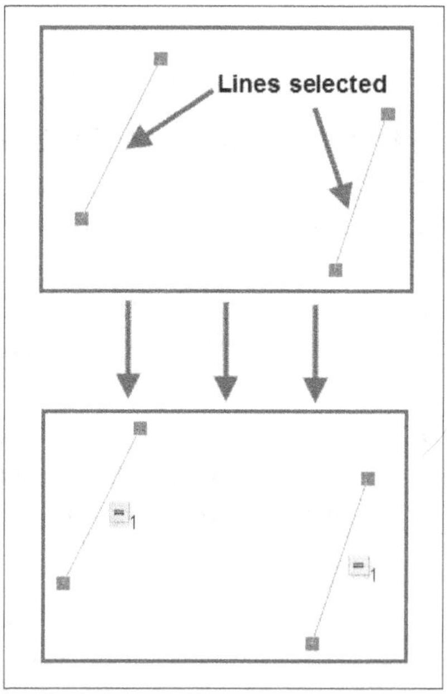

Figure-90. Applying equal constrain

Parallel Constrain

The Parallel constrain is used to make selected two lines parallel to each other. Note that if one of the two entities is not constrained dimensionally then the first selected entity will be taken as reference and the other entity will become parallel to the first entity. The procedure to apply this constrain is given next.

- Click on the **Parallel** button from the **Constrain** panel in the **Ribbon**. You are asked to select two or more line entities.
- Select the lines that you want to make parallel. The lines will be aligned parallel to each other; refer to Figure-91.

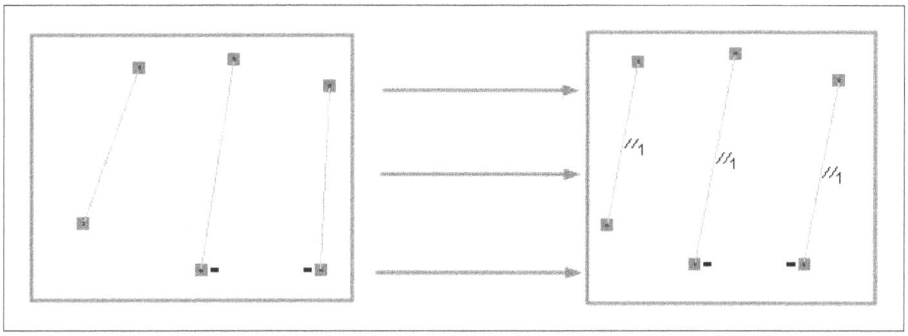

Figure-91. Lines made parallel

EDITING TOOLS

Till this point, we have learned about the sketching tools, dimensioning sketches, and applying geometrical constraints to the sketches. Now, we will learn to edit the sketch entities. The tools to perform editing are available in the **Editing** panel of the **Ribbon**; refer to Figure-92.

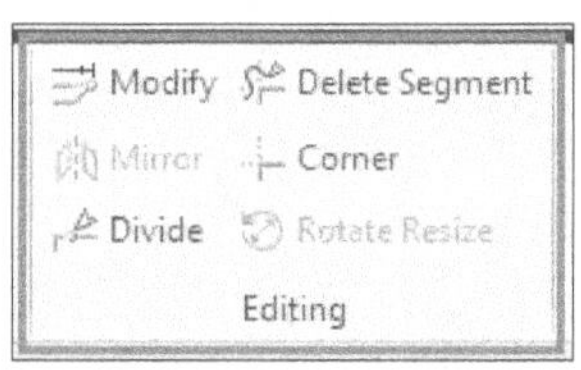

Figure-92. Editing panel

Modify tool

We have earlier modified the dimensions by double-clicking on the dimension text. But there might be a scenario where you need to modify various dimension together. To modify multiple dimensions together, we use **Modify** tool. The steps to use this tool are given next.

- Click on the **Modify** tool from the **Editing** panel in the **Ribbon**. You are asked to select the dimensions.
- One by one click on the dimensions that you want to edit. The **Modify Dimensions** dialog box will be displayed; refer to Figure-93. You can select multiple dimensions by using windows selection before activating the **Modify** tool to do the same job.

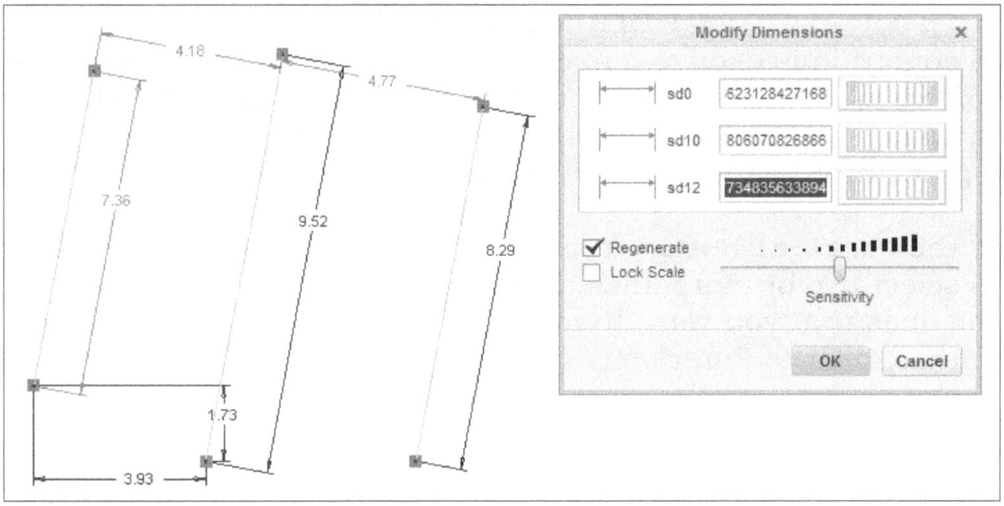

Figure-93. Modify dimensions dialog box

- Click in an edit box in the **Modify Dimensions** dialog box to change the dimension value. The dimension in the drawing area will be enclosed in a box; refer to Figure-94.

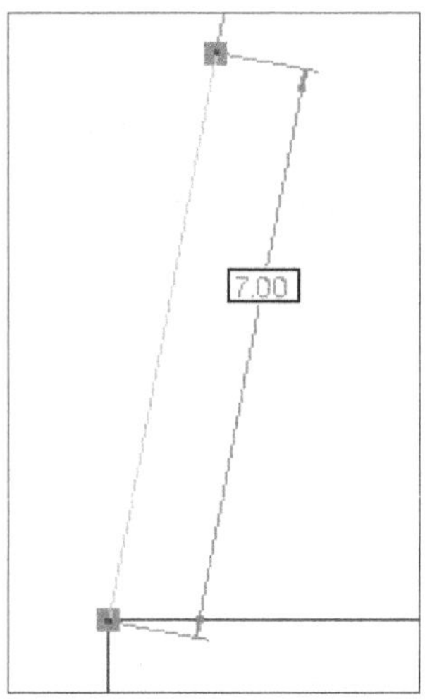

Figure-94. Dimension enclosed in box

- Specify desired value for the dimension in the edit box in **Modify Dimensions** dialog box. You can also use the slider next to the edit box to change the value of dimension.
- Similarly, you can change the value of other dimensions.
- Select the **Lock Scale** check box, if you want to change all the selected dimensions in same proportion. Now, move the slider or specify value for one dimension, the others will be modified automatically.
- Using the **Sensitivity** slider, you can change the sensitivity of sliders for dimension change.
- Clear the **Regenerate** check box from the dialog box.
- Click on the **OK** button from the dialog box to apply the changed dimensions.

Mirror Tool

The **Mirror** tool is used to create a mirror copy of the selected entity. The procedure to use this tool is given next.

- Select the entity/entities whose mirror copy is to be created. The **Mirror** tool will become active.
- Click on the **Mirror** tool from the **Editing** panel. You are asked to select a center line.
- Select the center line. The mirror copy will be created; refer to Figure-95.

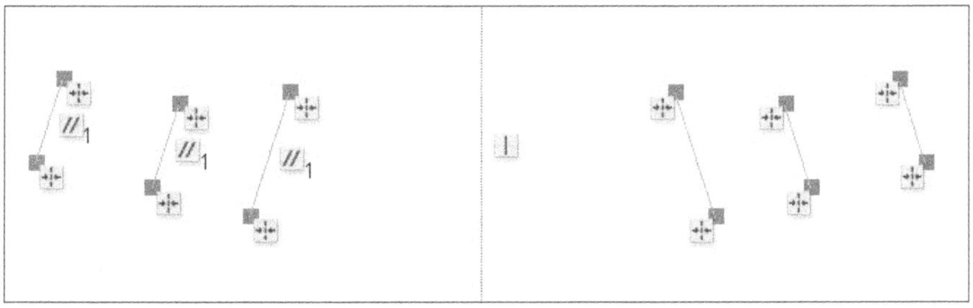

Figure-95. Mirror copy

Divide Tool

The **Divide** tool is used to break the entity at the selected position. We will need this tool later when we will be creating 3D features. The procedure to use this tool is given next.

- Click on the **Divide** tool from the **Editing** panel. You are asked to click on a sketch entity.
- Click at desired point on the entity. The entity will be broken at the clicked point; refer to Figure-96.

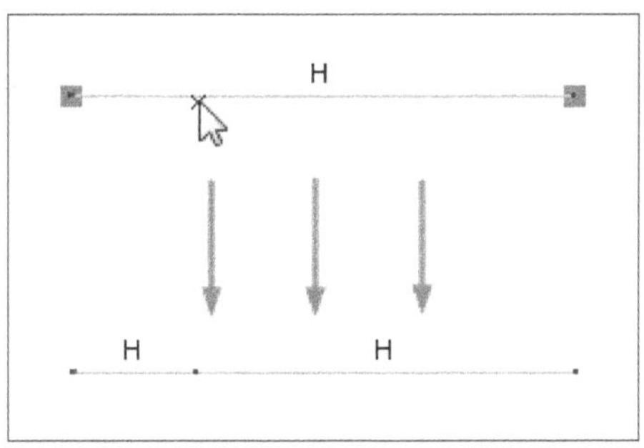

Figure-96. Line divided

Delete Segment Tool

The **Delete Segment** tool is an intelligent eraser used to delete extra portion of the sketch entity. There are many situations in sketching when we get extra length of the sketch entity being created. In such cases, we can use this tool to remove the extra portion. The procedure to use this tool is given next.

- Click on the **Delete Segment** tool from the **Editing** panel in the **Ribbon**. You are asked to select or drag over the entity that you want to remove.
- Click on the entities one by one or drag over the entities that you want to delete; refer to Figure-97.

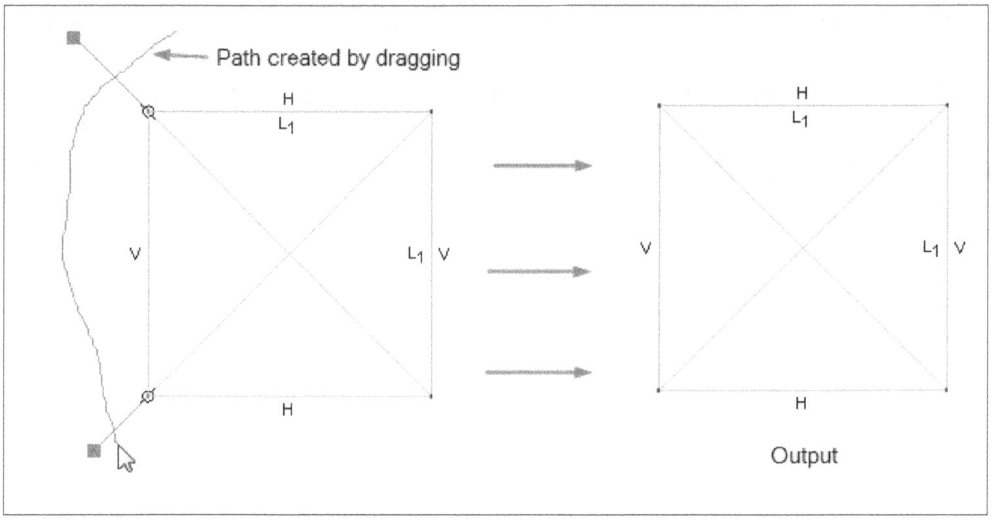

Figure-97. Delete segment tool operation

Corner Tool

The **Corner** tool is used to create corner from two entities by either trimming them and/or by extending them. The procedure is given next.

- Click on the **Corner** tool from the **Editing** panel in the **Ribbon**. You are asked to select entities to be cornered.
- Select the entities which you want to trim to form corner. Refer to Figure-98.

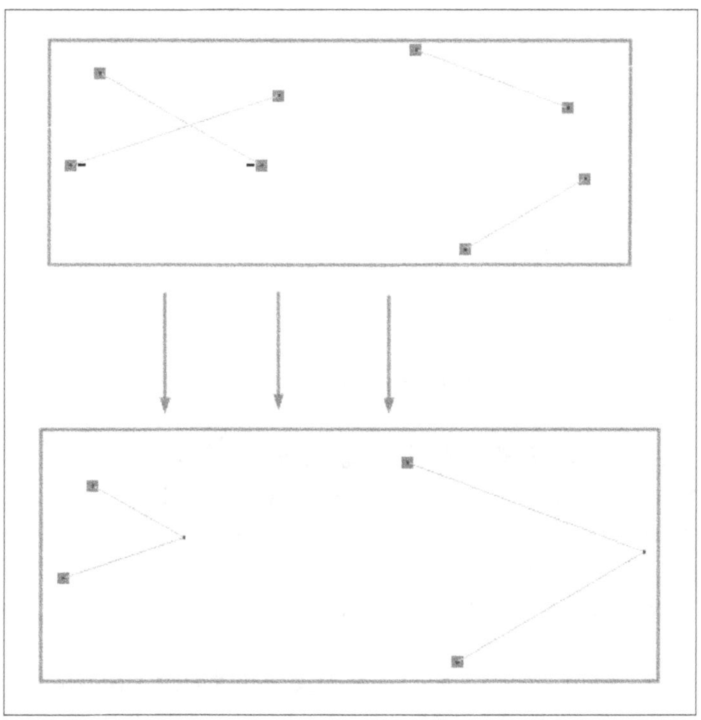

Figure-98. Cornered entities

Rotate Resize Tool

The **Rotate Resize** tool, as the name suggests, is used to rotate and re-size selected sketched entities. The procedure to use this tool is given next.

- Select the entities that you want to rotate and re-size.

- Click on the **Rotate Resize** tool from the **Editing** panel in the **Ribbon**. The **Rotate Resize** dashboard will be displayed. Also, the drag handles will be displayed with the selected sketch entities; refer to Figure-99.

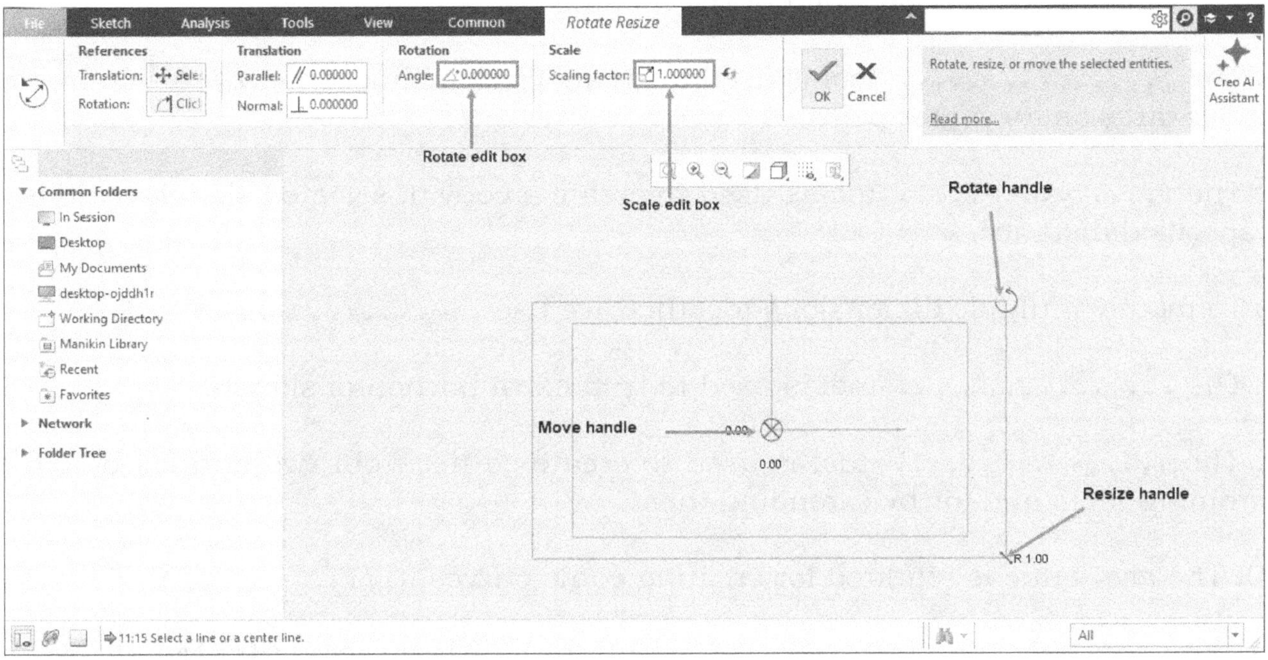

Figure-99. Rotate Resize options

- Click on the Move handle of the sketch and drag it to desired location.
- Similarly, using the Rotate handle and Resize handle, you can rotate and resize the sketch, respectively.
- You can also specify desired value in the **Rotate** edit box and **Scale** edit box. In the **Rotate** edit box, specify the angle value by which you want to rotate the sketch (You can specify a negative value to rotate in reverse direction). In the **Resize** edit box, specify desired value of scale by which you want to enlarge or diminish the sketch.

In this chapter, we learned about the basic tools required for sketching. On the basis of these tools, we can draw any kind of Sketch in Creo. But there are some advanced tools in sketching which we will discuss in next chapter and then we will work on practical examples and exercises.

SELF ASSESSMENT

1. The Sketching environment is used to

(a) draw sketches (b) manipulate sketches
(c) both (d) none

2. Which of the following tools is used to create offset copies of selected sketch entities on both sides of it?

(a) Offset (b) Thicken
(c) Chamfer (d) Palette

3. Select the .... check box in **In-Graphics toolbar** to display the grid.

4. The .... tool is used to create a rectangle using the center point of the rectangle and a corner point of the rectangle.

5. The .... tool is used to create circle using center of earlier created circles/arcs as its center point.

6. The .... tool is used to create a copy of selected sketch entities at a specified distance.

7. To modify multiple dimensions together, we use .... tool.

8. The .... tool is used to trim extra portion of sketch.

9. The .... tool is used to create corner from two entities by either trimming them and/or by extending them.

10. The **rho** value is required for creating conic curves. (T/F)

11. You can hide the dimensions by selecting the **Dimensions Display** check box from the **Sketcher Display Filters** drop-down in the **In-Graphics toolbar**. (T/F)

12. In case of texts in Creo Parametric, aspect ratio is the ratio of width and height of the text. (T/F)

13. Using the **Dimension** tool, you can dimension all types of objects in Creo Parametric. (T/F)

14. What is the function of the Grid in the sketching environment?

a) To apply constraints
b) To help in dimensioning
c) To assist the designer in creating sketches
d) To display measurement tools

15. The 3 Tangent circle tool requires selection of how many entities?

a) One
b) Two
c) Three
d) Four

16. Which Arc tool allows creating an arc tangent to another entity?

a) 3-Point/Tangent End
b) Center and Ends
c) Concentric
d) Conic

17. What is the use of the Conic Arc tool?

a) Create elliptical arcs only
b) Create arcs using three tangent points
c) Create conical arcs used in designs like boat fronts
d) Create spirals

18. How does Elliptical Trim fillet differ from Circular fillet?

a) It removes extra reference points
b) It has a different exit method
c) It works only on vertical lines
d) It creates fillet with dimension annotations

19. What is the main purpose of the Chamfer tool?

a) Make sketches round
b) Convert rectangles to polygons
c) Blunt sharp edges for handling and assembly
d) Add threads to edges

20. How can you hide dimensions in the sketching environment?

a) Deselect the Show Dimensions checkbox in Properties
b) Delete all dimensions
c) Clear Dimensions Display checkbox from Sketcher Display Filters
d) Select Hide Dimensions from File menu

21. What is Aspect Ratio in the Text tool used for?

a) Change text font
b) Align text to arc
c) Adjust width to height ratio of text
d) Set text boldness

22. What is the function of the Place along curve option in the Text tool?

a) Place text randomly
b) Stretch text to fit area
c) Align text along a selected curve
d) Convert text into geometry

23. What is the Offset tool used for?

a) Draw concentric circles
b) Create symmetrical sketches
c) Create a copy of selected entity at a defined distance
d) Create rounded corners

24. In the Offset tool, what is the function of the Chain dialog box?

a) Assign thickness to text
b) Display dimensions
c) Define standard or rule-based segment collection
d) Modify font size

25. What is the Thicken tool used for?

a) Create rounded arcs
b) Create symmetric lines
c) Create offset copies on both sides of selected entity
d) Add text annotations

26. Which end cap option in the Thicken tool joins ends of offset with semicircles?

a) Open
b) Flat
c) Circular
d) Curve

27. What is the Palette tool used for?

a) Add colors to sketch
b) Create section views
c) Import or reuse pre-created entities
d) Animate the sketch

28. Which tool allows rotating and scaling imported sections from the Palette?

a) Text tool
b) Insert Symbol
c) Import Section tab
d) Display Filters

29. What is the primary purpose of center lines in Creo Parametric sketches?

a) To apply color to sketch entities
b) To create dimensions for circles
c) To define a reference for creating sketch entities
d) To delete construction geometry

30. How is a Centerline Tangent different from a regular Centerline?

a) It uses two points instead of curves
b) It creates curved lines
c) It requires selecting two curves for tangency
d) It is used only in 3D modeling

31. What is the function of the Point tool in Creo Parametric?

a) To divide lines into equal parts
b) To create construction lines
c) To place points used for referencing sketch entities
d) To rotate sketches

32. What is true about the Coordinate System in sketches?

a) It is used for applying constraints
b) It defines the origin for dimensions
c) It cannot be moved after placement
d) It automatically creates centerlines

33. What does the Construction Mode toggle button do?

a) Activates the 3D view
b) Starts dimensioning mode
c) Allows creating construction entities
d) Deletes sketch entities

34. Which tool is used to apply any type of dimension in Creo Parametric?

a) Angle Tool
b) Circle Dimension Tool
c) Dimension Tool
d) Length Tool

35. How can you convert a radius dimension to a diameter for a circle?

a) By dragging the dimension text
b) Through the Ribbon menu
c) By clicking the Diameter option in the shortcut menu
d) By double-clicking the circle

36. What type of dimensioning is also known as Ordinate dimensioning?

a) Reference
b) Angular
c) Baseline
d) Linear

37. What happens if a sketch is fully constrained but more dimensions are added?

a) It shows an under-defined sketch warning
b) Extra dimensions get ignored
c) A dialog box appears to resolve the over-definition
d) The software auto-adjusts dimensions

38. What type of dimension is applied for inspection or verification, not for constraining sketches?

a) Baseline
b) Reference
c) Perimeter
d) Arc

39. What does the Perpendicular constraint do?

a) Aligns lines parallel to each other
b) Constrains entities at 90 degrees
c) Deletes angle constraints
d) Creates new circles

40. What is required to apply a Symmetric constraint?

a) Two arcs
b) A centerline and two vertices
c) One midpoint
d) Two rectangles

41. What does the Equal constraint do?

a) Makes two entities same color
b) Makes lines perpendicular
c) Makes dimensions of two entities equal
d) Copies geometry

42. Which constraint aligns two lines in the same direction?

a) Symmetric
b) Coincident
c) Tangent
d) Parallel

43. What does the Divide tool do?

a) Combines two entities
b) Splits an entity at a selected point
c) Changes an arc to a line
d) Deletes sketch entities

44. What does the Corner tool allow you to do?

a) Join sketches
b) Round corners
c) Trim or extend two entities to form a corner
d) Add a hole

45. What is the Rotate Resize tool used for?

a) Editing constraints
b) Changing sketch colors
c) Rotating and scaling sketch entities
d) Placing center points

FOR STUDENT NOTES

For Student Notes

Answers to Assessment Questions:

1. (c) **2.** (b) **3.** Disp Grid **4.** Center Rectangle **5.** Concentric **6.** Offset **7.** Modify **8.** Delete Segment **9.** Corner **10.** T **11.** F **12.** T **13.** T

Chapter 3

Advanced Sketching and Practical

Topics Covered

The major topics covered in this chapter are:

- ***Sketch Inspection options***
- ***Applying relations***
- ***Practical 1***
- ***Practical 2***
- ***Practical 3***
- ***Practical 4***
- ***Practices***

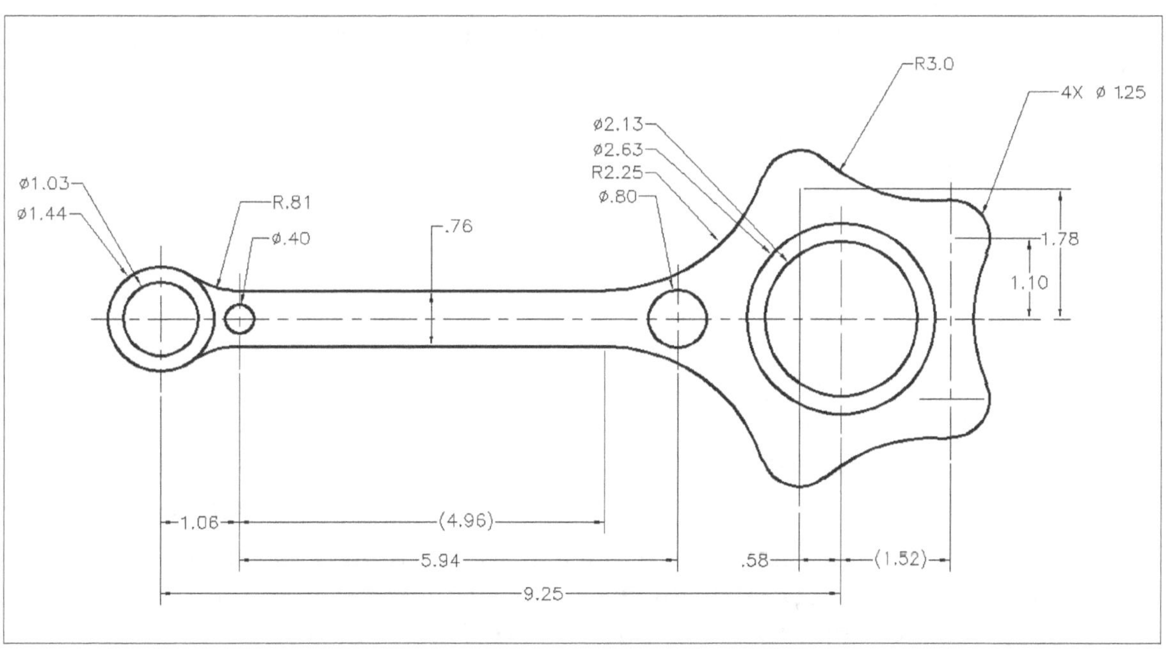

INTRODUCTION

In the previous chapter, we have learned about various sketching tools. In this chapter, we will learn about some advanced tools that help us in sketching efficiently.

INSPECT OPTIONS

There are six tools available in the sketching environment of Creo Parametric that are used to perform inspection on sketches for their suitability in modeling. The tools are available in the **Inspection Tools** drop-down of **Inspect** panel; refer to Figure-1.

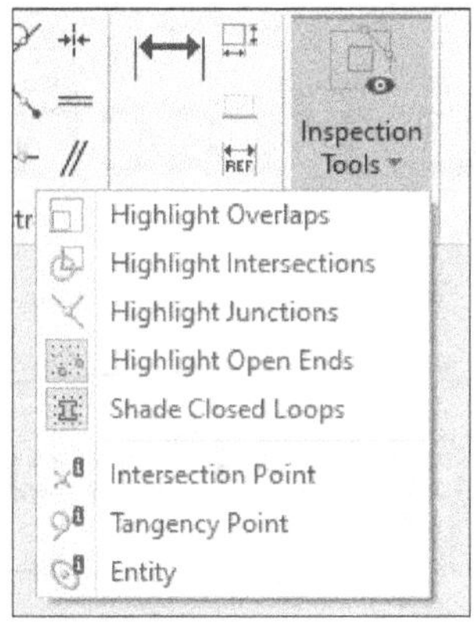

Figure-1. Inspection Tools drop-down

Highlight Overlaps

The **Highlight Overlaps** button is used to identify the overlapping sketched entities. When we will convert the sketches into 3D features, there will be various instances when the sketch will be rejected. One of the possible cause for that might be overlapping geometries. So, we need to make sure that there are no overlapping geometries in the sketch. The procedure to identify the overlapping geometries is given next.

- Click on the **Highlight Overlaps** button to activate it. All the geometries that are overlapping will be displayed in red.
- Hover the cursor on the entity highlighted and hold right mouse button on it. A shortcut menu will be displayed; refer to Figure-2.
- Click on the **Pick From List** button. The **Pick From List** dialog box will be displayed; refer to Figure-3.

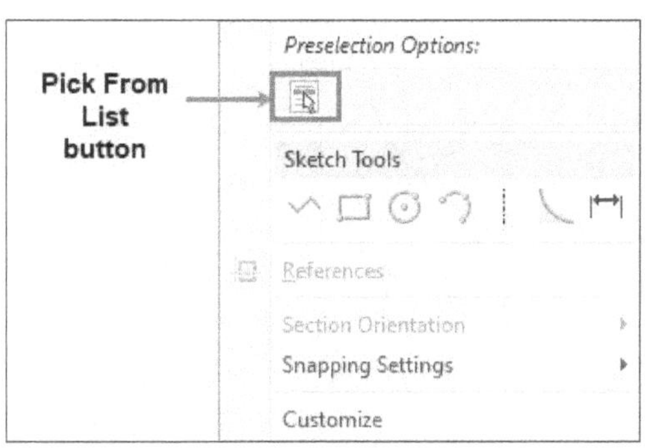

Figure-2. Entity overlapping

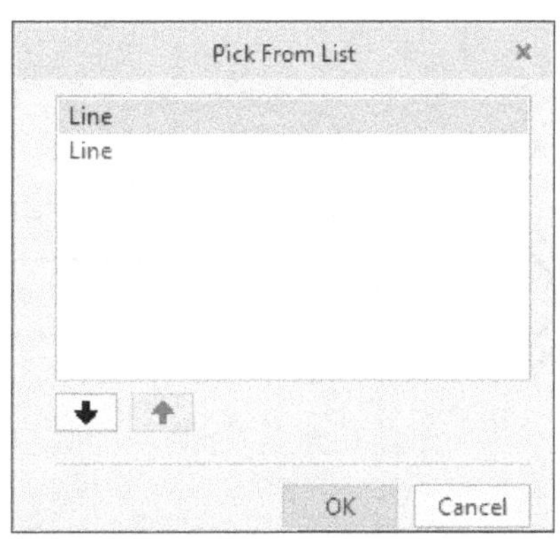

Figure-3. Pick From List dialog box

- Select the entity from the list that you want to delete and press the **DELETE** button from keyboard. Note that preview of selected entity is displayed in the drawing area.
- You can repeat the steps to delete all the overlapping entities.

Highlight Intersections

The **Highlight Intersections** toggle button is used to highlight the intersecting sketched entities. The procedure to identify the intersecting geometries is given next.

- Click on the **Highlight Intersections** toggle button to activate it. All the sketch entities that are intersecting will be displayed with the red boxes at their intersection points; refer to Figure-4.

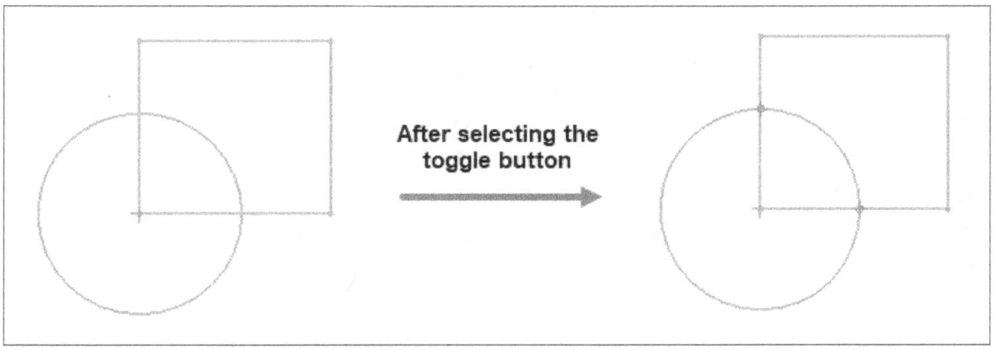

Figure-4. Intersecting entities highlighted

Highlight Junctions

The **Highlight Junctions** toggle button is used to highlight the junctions at the sketched entities. The procedure to identify the junctions geometries is given next.

- Click on the **Highlight Junctions** toggle button to activate it. All the junctions in the sketched entities will be displayed with the red boxes; refer to Figure-5.

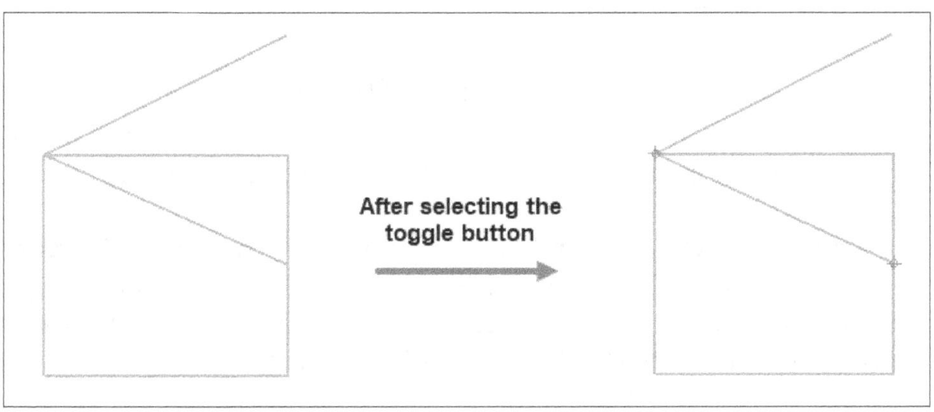

Figure-5. Junctions highlighted

Highlight Open Ends

The **Highlight Open Ends** toggle button is used to highlight the open ends of the sketch by red color boxes. Later on, we will need closed sketches to create features like extruded feature, revolved features, and so on. To make sure that the sketch is closed, we will need this inspection option. The procedure to identify the open ends is given next.

- Click on the **Highlight Open Ends** toggle button to activate it. All the sketches that are open will be displayed with red boxes at their open end points; refer to Figure-6.

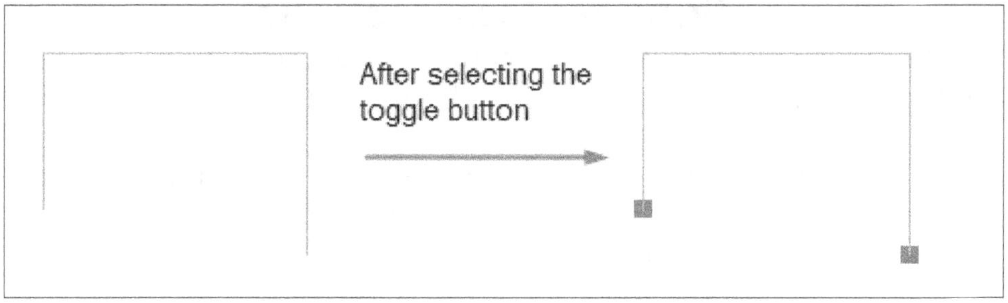

Figure-6. Open ends highlighted

Shade Closed Loops

The **Shade Closed Loops** toggle button is used to shade the closed loops in the sketch by orange color (by default). Later on, when we will need closed sketches to create features like extruded feature, revolved features, and so on. To make sure that the sketch is closed, we will need this inspection option. The procedure to identify the open ends is given next.

- Click on the **Shade Closed Loops** toggle button to activate it. All the closed loops in the sketch will be displayed as shaded by color; refer to Figure-7.

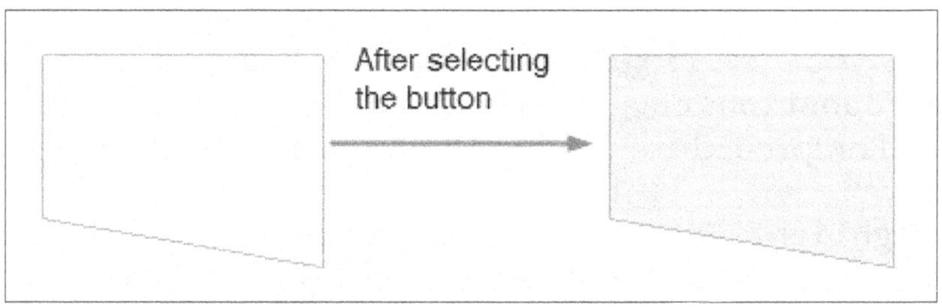

Figure-7. Closed loop shaded

Intersection Point

The **Intersection Point** button is used to identify the intersection points between the selected entities. The procedure to use this button is given next.

- Click on the **Intersection Point** button from the expanded **Inspect** panel. You are asked to select two entities from identifying their intersection points.
- One by one select the two intersecting entities. The intersection point will be displayed along with the **INFORMATION WINDOW**; refer to Figure-8.

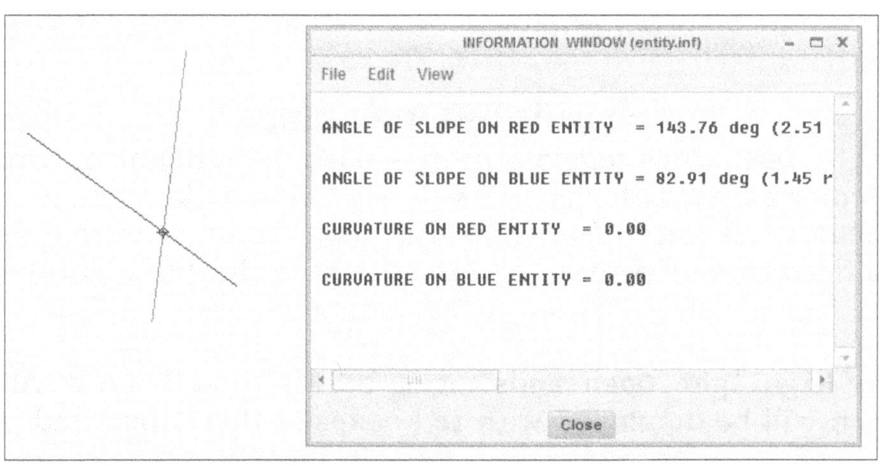

Figure-8. Intersection points with INFORMATION WINDOW

Tangency Point

The **Tangency Point** button is used to identify the tangency point of a sketch entity with respect to an arc/circle. The procedure to use this tool is given next.

- Click on the **Tangency Point** button from the **Inspect** panel in the **Ribbon**. You are asked to select the two entities.
- Select the line and circle/arc. The tangency point, if possible, will be displayed along with the **INFORMATION WINDOW**; refer to Figure-9.

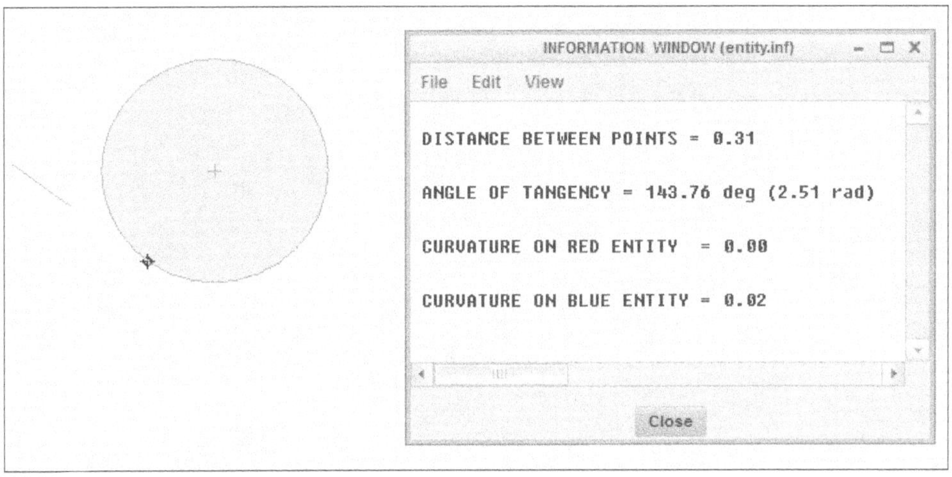

Figure-9. Tangency point created

Entity

The **Entity** tool is used to find out all the information about the selected entity. For example, if you select a line then its length, angle, and other information will be displayed. Similarly, if you select a circle then the radius, area, and other information of the circle will be displayed. The procedure to use this tool is given next.

- Click on the **Entity** tool from the expanded **Inspect** panel. You are asked to select an entity.
- Select desired entity. The **INFORMATION WINDOW** will be displayed with the information related to the selected entity; refer to Figure-10.

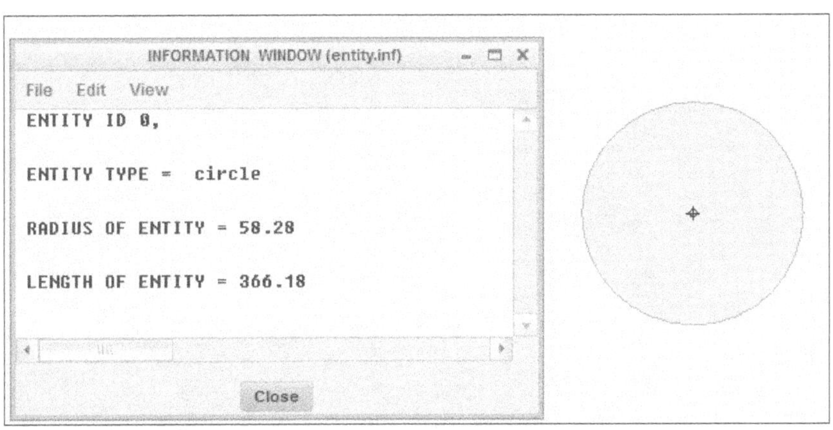

Figure-10. Entity information

APPLYING RELATIONS TO DIMENSIONS

If you are working on the geometries that need mathematical relations then you can do so by using the **Relations** tool from the **Relation** panel in the **Tools** tab of the **Ribbon**. The procedure to use this tool is given next.

- Click on the **Switch Dimensions** tool from the **Relation** panel. All the dimensions will be displayed with their designated names in place of their dimension values in the sketch; refer to Figure-11.

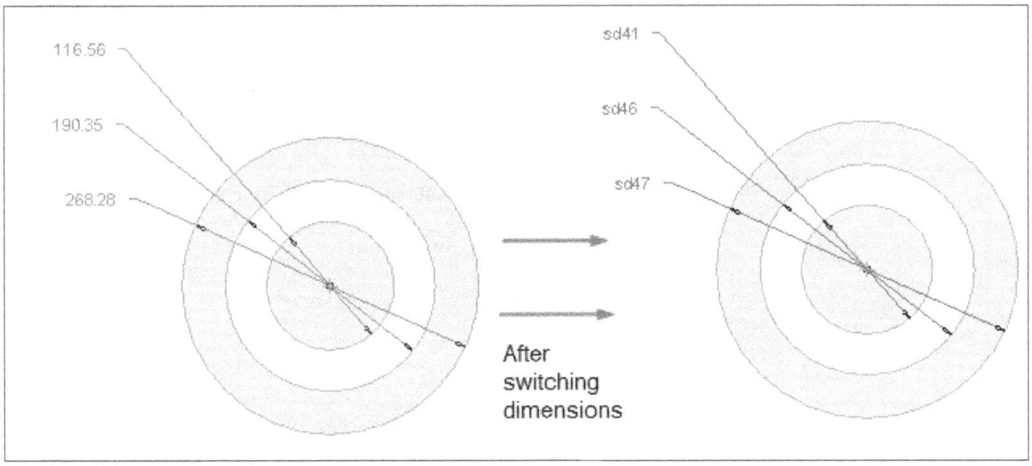

Figure-11. Switching dimensions

- Click on the **Relations** button from the **Relation** panel in the **Tools** tab of the **Ribbon**. The **Relations** dialog box will be displayed; refer to Figure-12.

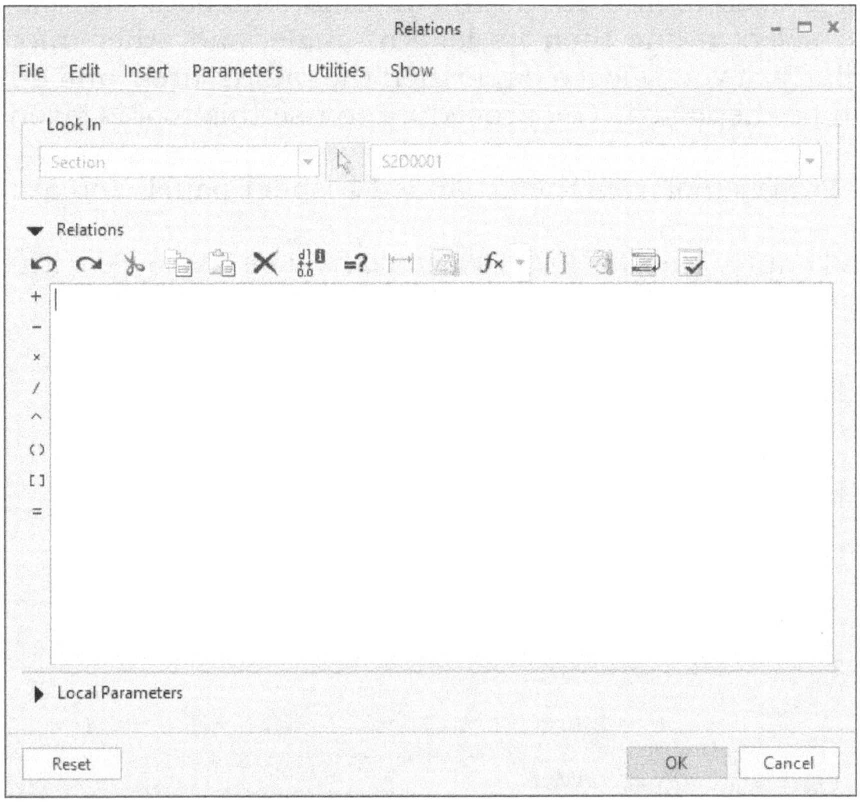

Figure-12. Relations dialog box

- Click on the dimension for/by which you want to make the mathematical relations. For example, the diameter of bigger circle is half of the multiplication of diameters of smaller circles; refer to Figure-13.

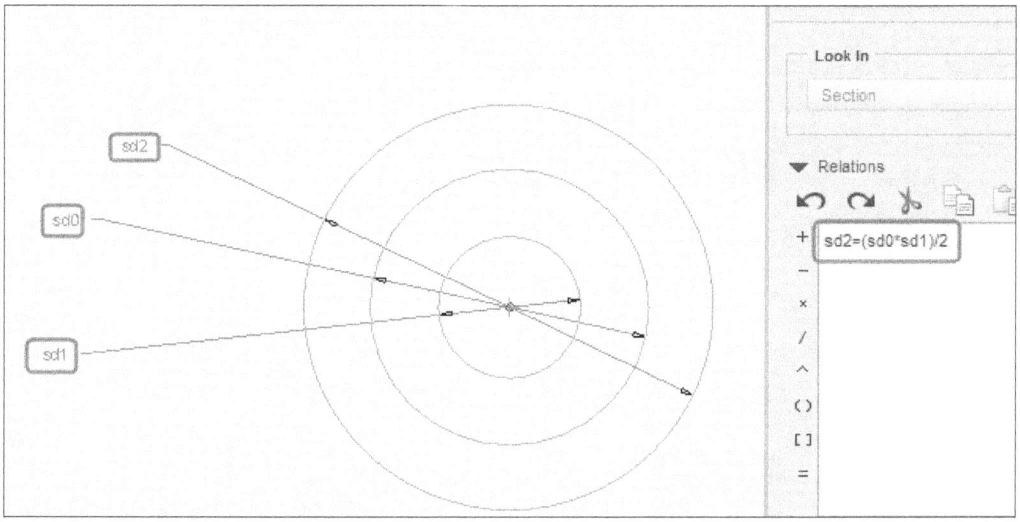

Figure-13. Mathematical relations in the sketch

- The output of the formula will be as shown in Figure-14.

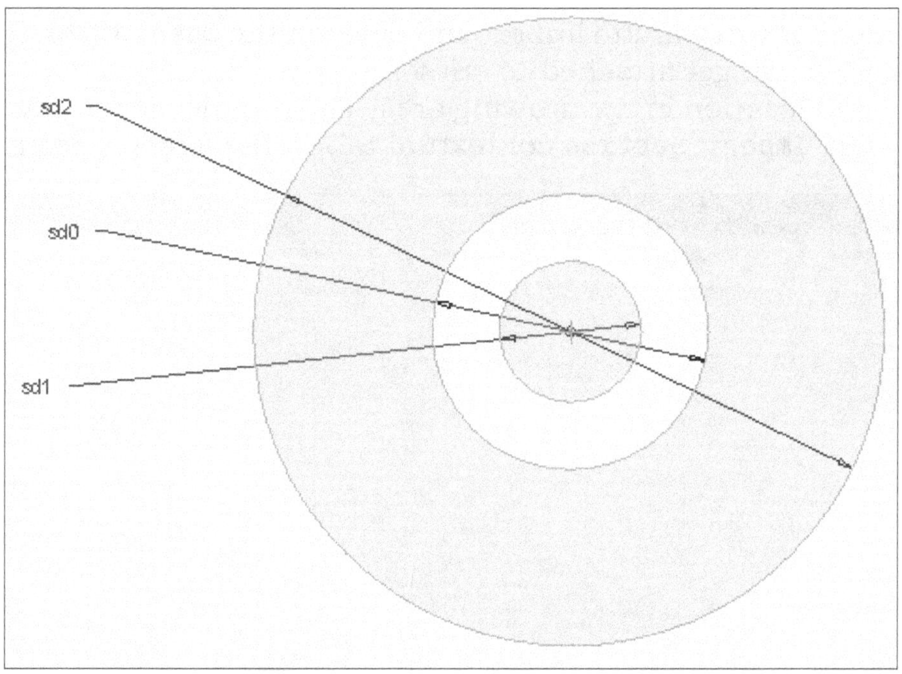

Figure-14. Output of relations

- If you try changing the value of dimension **sd2** then it will not change. But, you can change the values of **sd0** and **sd1**, and on the basis of that the value of **sd2** will automatically change.

IMPORTING SKETCHES IN CURRENT SKETCH

The **File System** tool is used to import sketches or drawing files in the sketch you are working on. The common file types that are available for importing are *.sec, *.drw, *.igs, *.iges, *.dxf, *.dwg, and *.ai. The procedure to use this tool is given next.

- Click on the **Import** tool from the **Get Data** panel in the **Sketch** tab of the **Ribbon**. The **Open** dialog box will be displayed; refer to Figure-15.

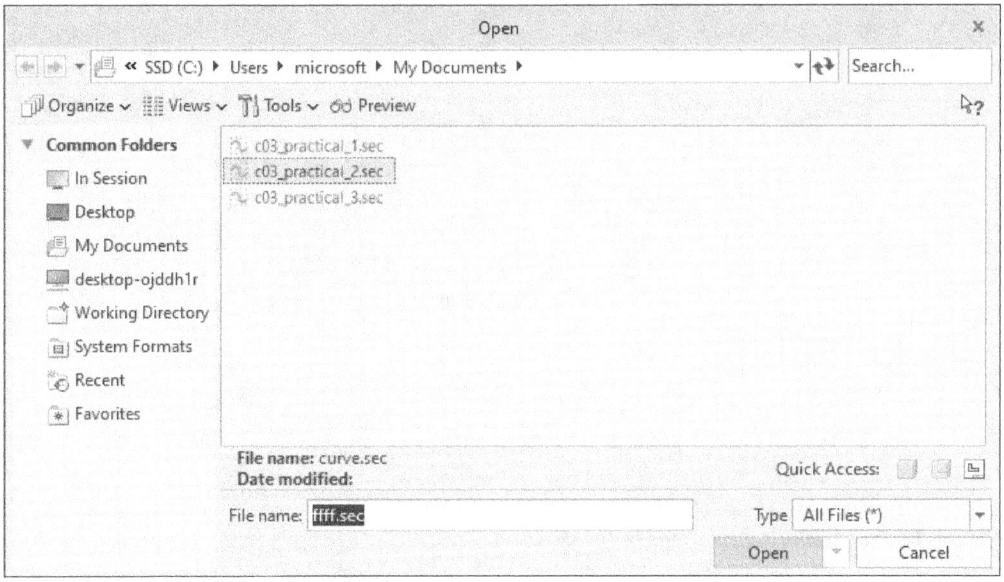

Figure-15. Open dialog box

- Select the file that you want to import and click on the **Open** button from the dialog box. The sketch will get attached to cursor.
- Click at desired location in the drawing area. The handles to modify sketch will be displayed with **Import Section** contextual tab in the **Ribbon**; refer to Figure-16.

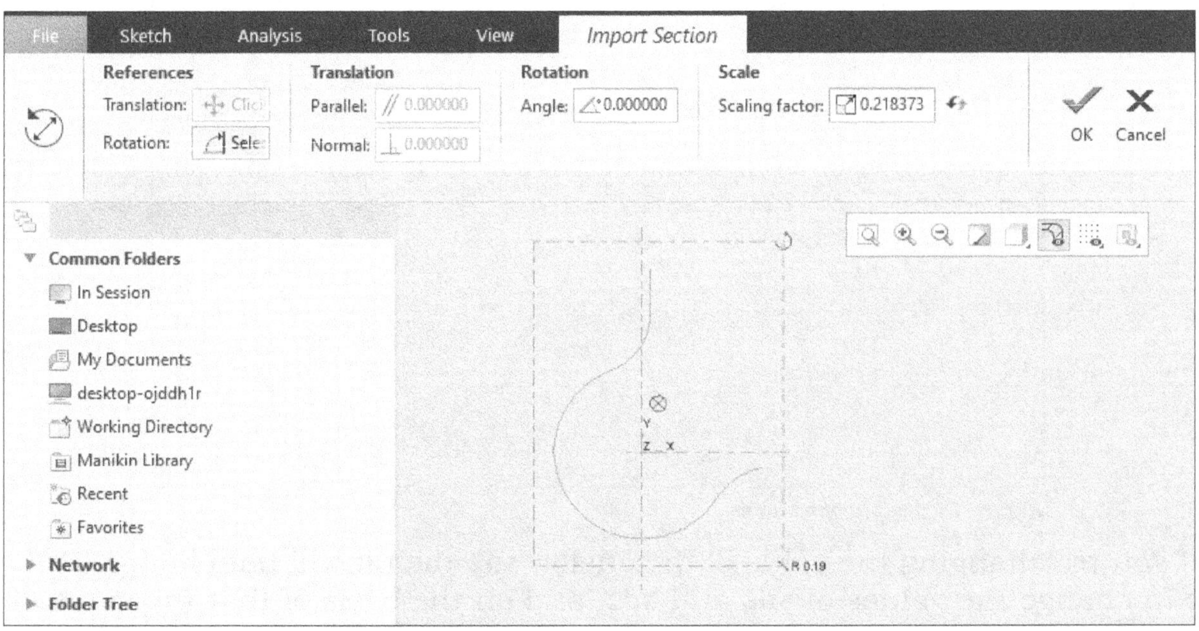

Figure-16. Handles on imported sketch

- Drag the center handle of sketch section to position it at desired location.
- Using the scale and rotate handles, you can scale up/down and rotate the section. You can also specify desired value for scale and rotation in their respective edit boxes in the **Ribbon**.
- Click on the **OK** button to create the section.

After long sessions of practicing on tools, now we will work on some drawings. Some of the practical that can be performed now are given next.

PRACTICAL 1

In this practical, we will create a sketch for the drawing given in Figure-17.

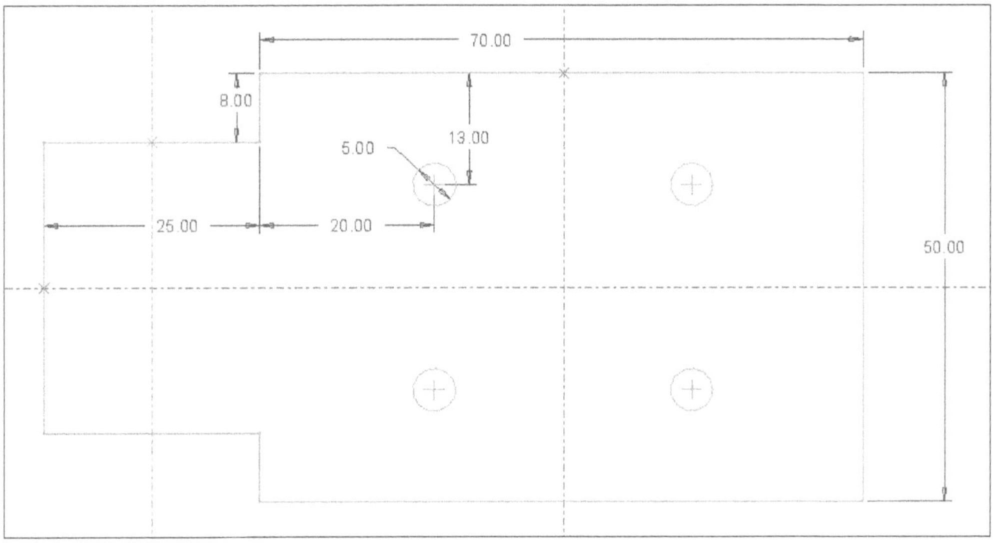

Figure-17. Practical 1

Starting Sketch

- Start Creo Parametric by double-clicking on the Creo Parametric 13.0 icon from the desktop.
- Click on the **New** button from the **Quick Access Toolbar**. The **New** dialog box will be displayed.
- Select the **Sketch** radio button from the dialog box and specify desired name in the **File name** edit box.
- Click on the **OK** button from the **New** dialog box. The sketching environment will be displayed.

Creating outer loop

- Click on the **Line Chain** tool from the **Line** drop-down in the **Sketching** panel of the **Ribbon**. You are asked to specify the start point of the line chain.
- Create a line sketch with the shape as given in Figure-18. Note that in this figure, the dimensions are hidden. After creating this loop, we need to display the dimensions again.

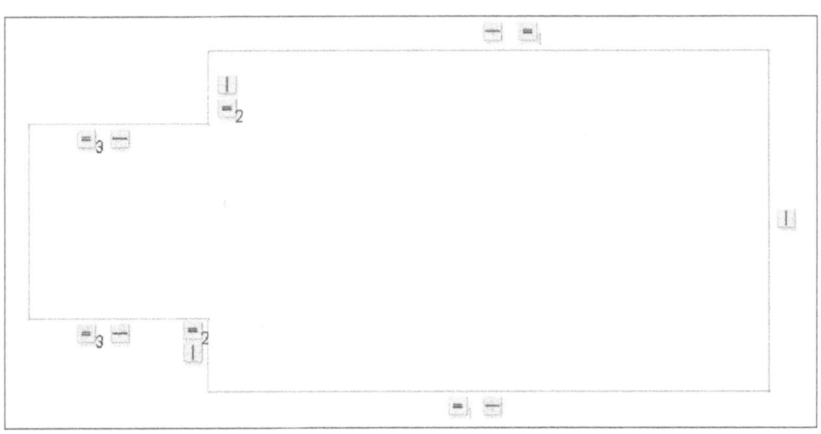

Figure-18. Sketched loop

Modifying Dimensions

- Select the whole sketch by box selection and then click on the **Modify** tool from the **Editing** panel. The **Modify Dimensions** dialog box will be displayed; refer to Figure-19.

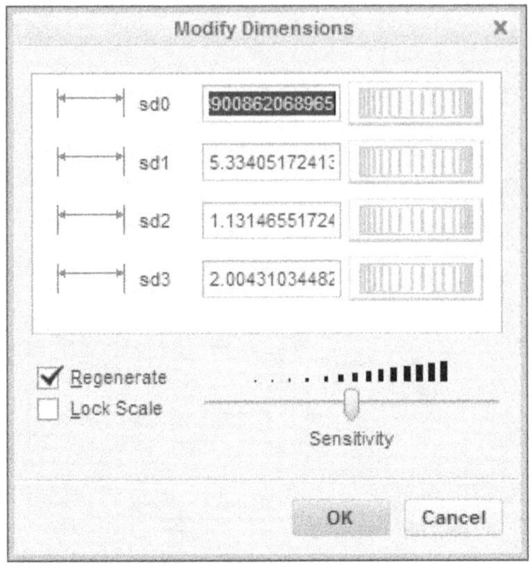

Figure-19. Modify Dimensions dialog box

- Specify the values in the edit boxes of the dialog box as per the drawing. Make sure you have cleared the **Regenerate** check box. Note that when you click in an edit box in the dialog box, the respective dimension in the drawing is enclosed in a blue box.
- Click on the **OK** button from the dialog box to apply the dimensions.

Drawing Circle

- Click on the **Center and Point** tool from the **Circle** drop-down. Click in the sketch at a position as shown in Figure-20.
- Double-click on the dimension values of the circle and change them as given in Figure-21.

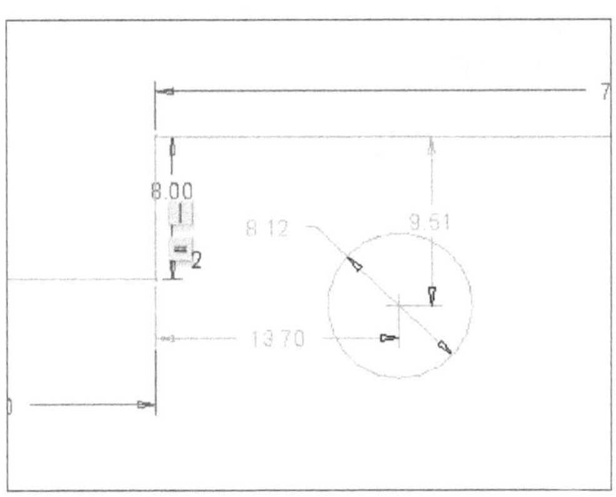

Figure-20. Placing circle

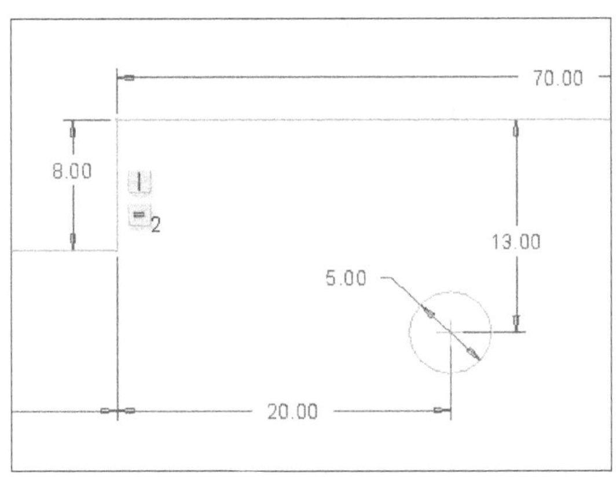

Figure-21. Circle after specifying dimensions

Creating Mirror copies of Circle

- Click on the **Centerline** tool from the **Centerline** drop-down. You are asked to specify start point for the centerline.
- Click at the mid point of the vertical line and draw a horizontal center line; refer to Figure-22.

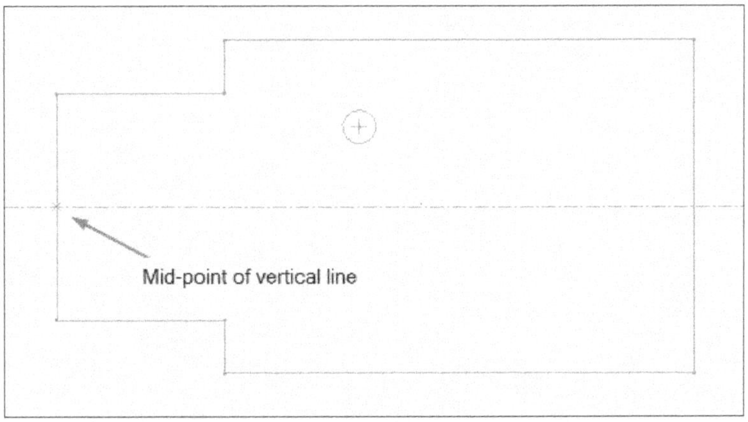

Figure-22. Horizontal centerline created

- Similarly, create the vertical centerline at the mid-point of longer horizontal line; refer to Figure-23.

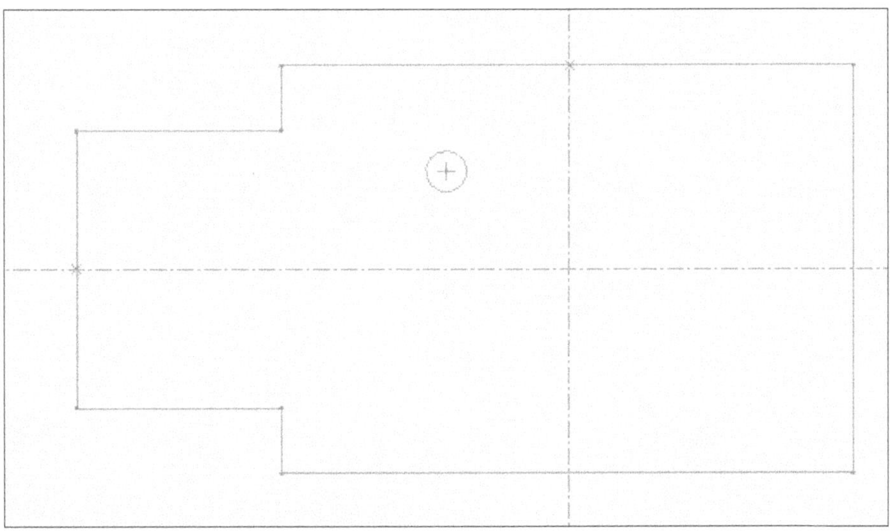

Figure-23. Sketch after create center lines

Creating Mirror Copy

- Select the circle and click on the **Mirror** tool from the **Editing** panel in the **Ribbon**. You are asked to select the centerline.
- Click on the vertical centerline. The mirror copy will be created; refer to Figure-24.

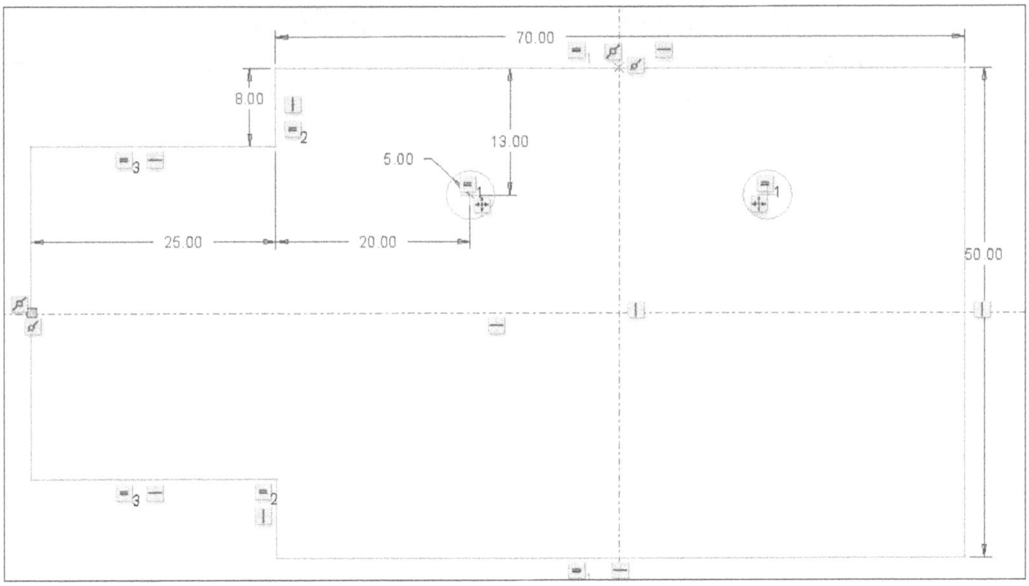

Figure-24. Mirror copy of circle created

- Similarly, create mirror copy of the two circles with respect to horizontal center line; refer to Figure-25.

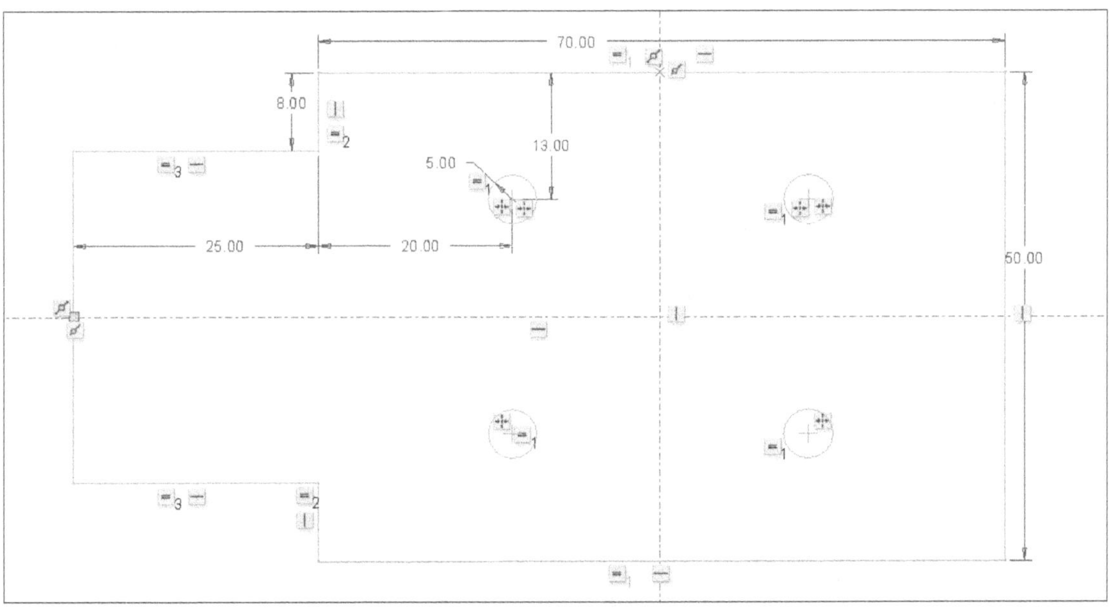

Figure-25. Sketch after creating mirror copies

- Create the last center line and complete the sketch.

In the previous practical, we created a sketch based on the dimensioned sketch. But, in real world, we will be having an engineering drawing. So now onwards, we will create sketches from the engineering drawings.

Practical 2

In this practical, we will create sketch from the drawing given in Figure-26.

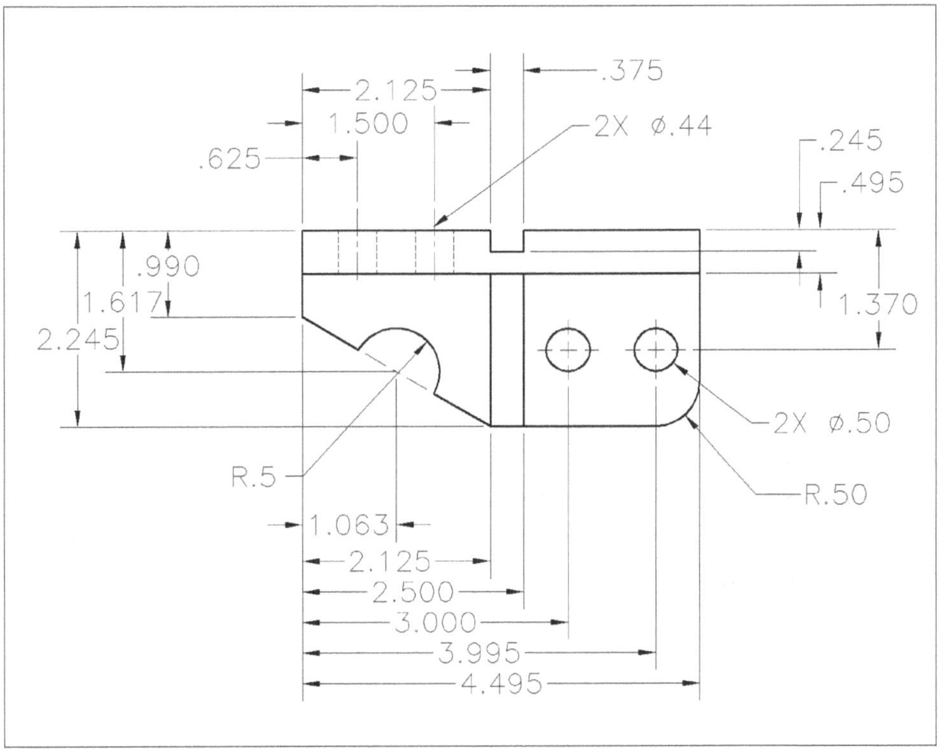

Figure-26. Practical 2

Starting Sketch

- Start Creo Parametric by double-clicking on the Creo Parametric 13.0 icon from the desktop.
- Click on the **New** button from the **Quick Access Toolbar**. The **New** dialog box will be displayed.
- Select the **Sketch** radio button from the dialog box and specify desired name in the **File name** edit box.
- Click on the **OK** button from the **New** dialog box. The sketching environment will be displayed.

Drawing the line sketch

- Click on the **Line Chain** tool from the **Line** drop-down. You are asked to specify the start point of the line.
- Create a line sketch as shown in Figure-27.

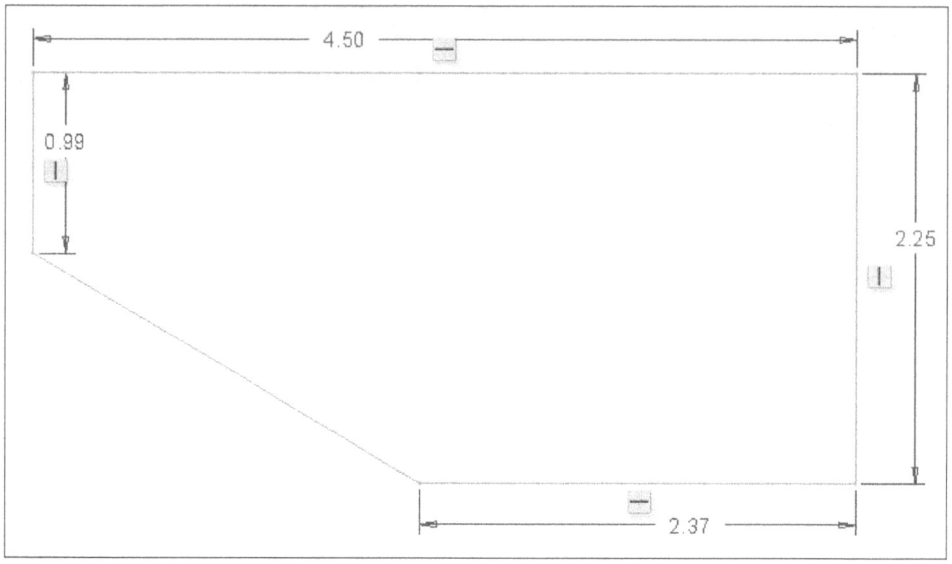

Figure-27. Line sketch

- Click on the **Offset** tool from the **Sketching** panel.
- Click on the line with dimension value **4.50**. You are asked to specify the offset distance; refer to Figure-28.

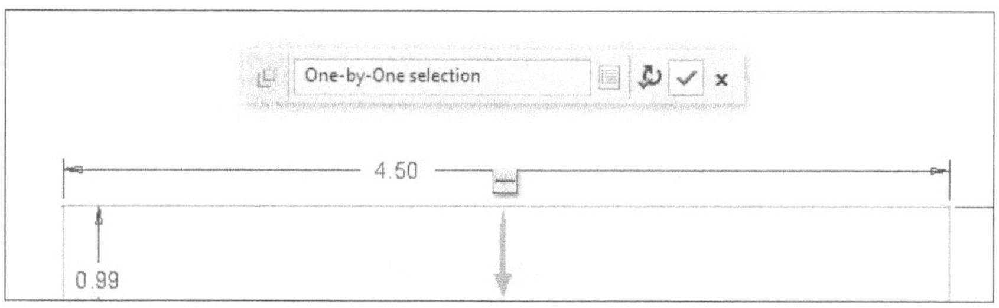

Figure-28. Offsetting line

- Specify the offset distance as **0.495** and press **ENTER**. The offset copy of the line will be created; refer to Figure-29.

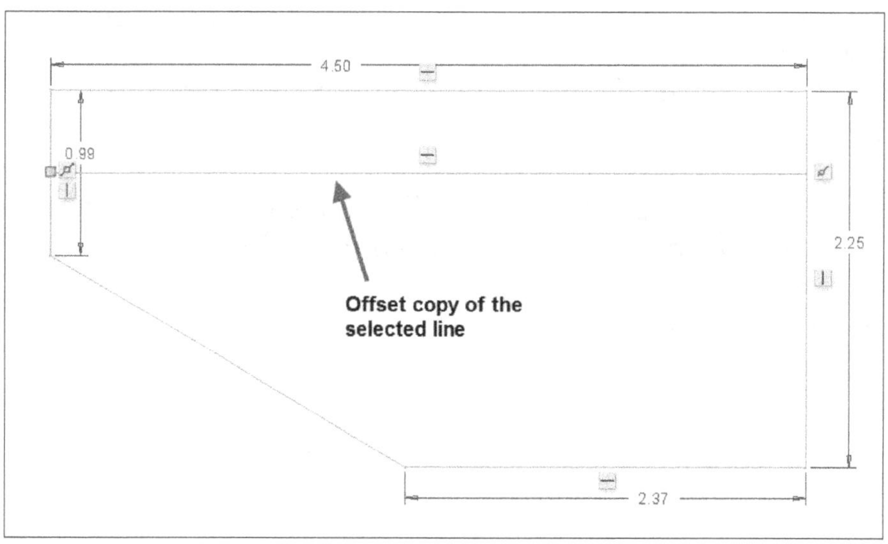

Figure-29. Offseted line

- Press the Middle button of mouse to exit the tool.
- Click on the **Line Chain** tool from the **Line** drop-down and draw a line starting from intersection point of inclined line and horizontal line to the line of length **4.50**; refer to Figure-30.

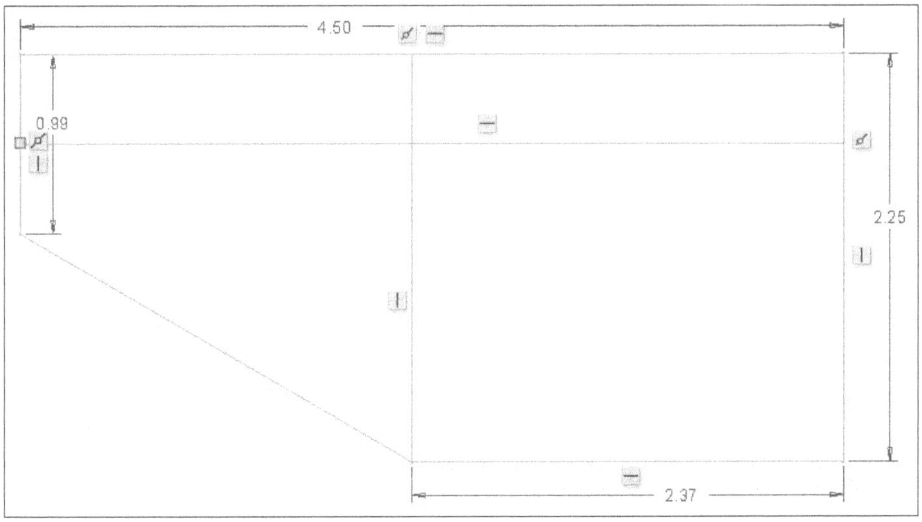

Figure-30. Sketch after creating joining line

- Click on the **Offset** tool from the **Sketching** panel in the **Ribbon** and select the line created recently.
- Specify the offset distance value as **0.375**. Make sure that the offset direction arrow is towards right otherwise you will have to specify **-0.375**. On doing so, an offset copy of the line will be created; refer to Figure-31.

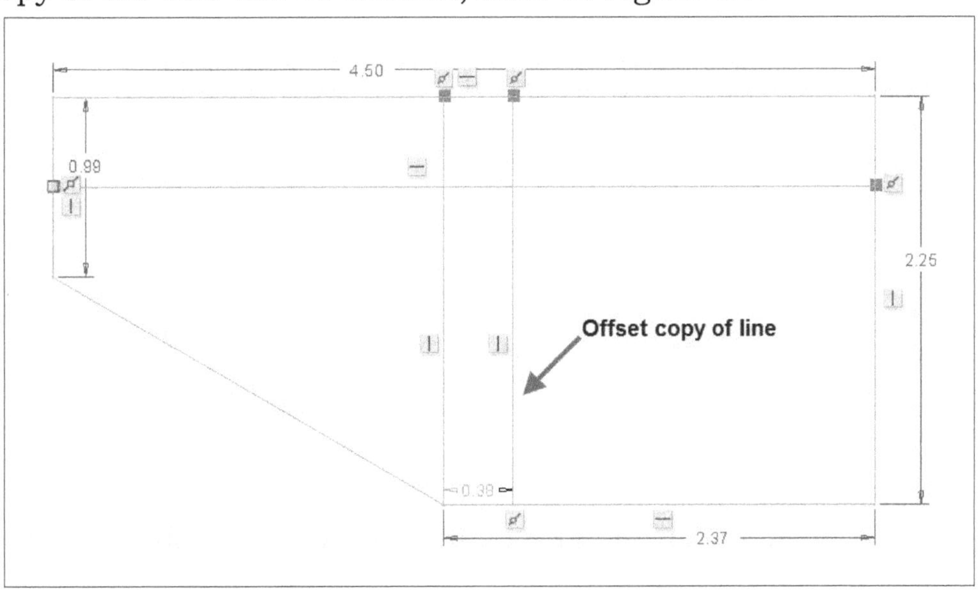

Figure-31. Offset copy of line created

- Click on the horizontal line of dimension **4.50** and offset it at a distance of **0.245** downward; refer to Figure-32.

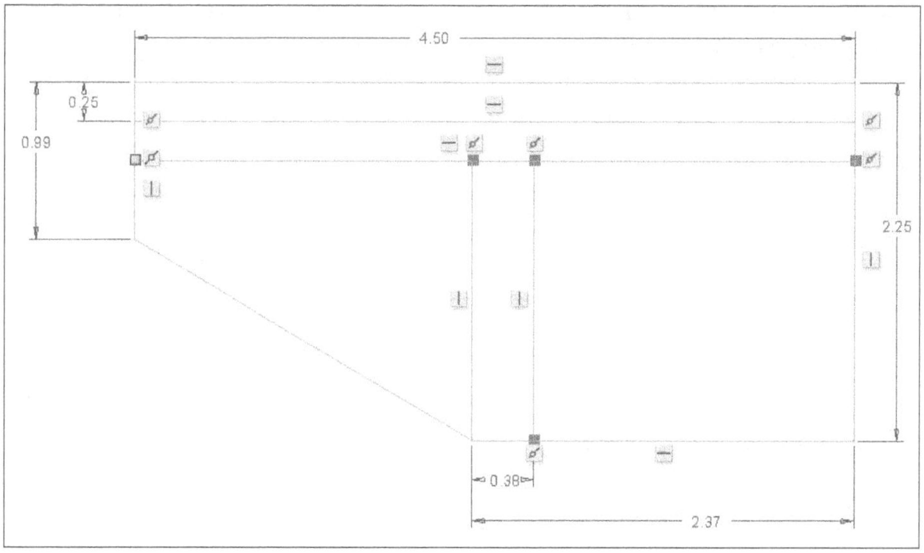

Figure-32. Sketch after offsetting line

Creating Circle

- Click on the **Center and Point** tool from the **Circle** drop-down. You are asked to specify the center point for the circle.
- Draw a circle at the location similar to the one shown in Figure-33.

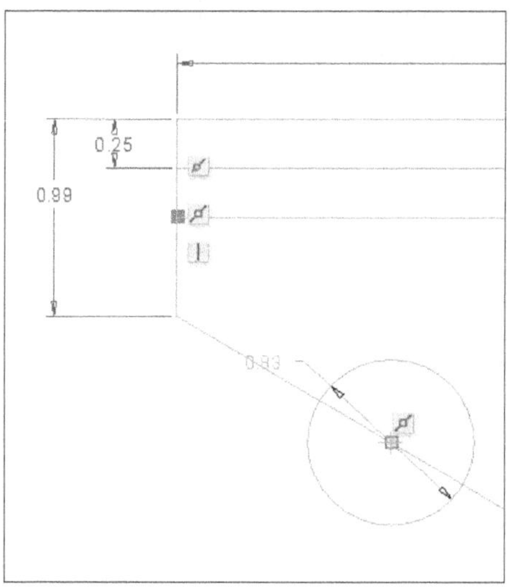

Figure-33. Circle to be drawn

- Double-click on the dimensions and change the value as shown in Figure-34.

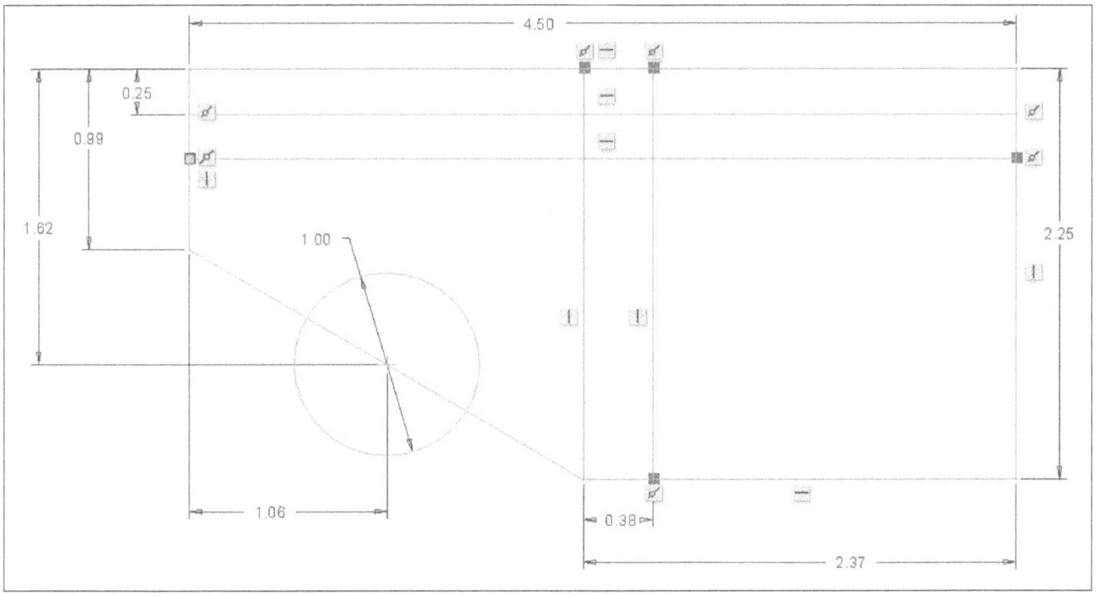

Figure-34. Circle after dimensioning

- Click on the **Center and Point** tool again and create the circle with dimensions as shown in Figure-35.

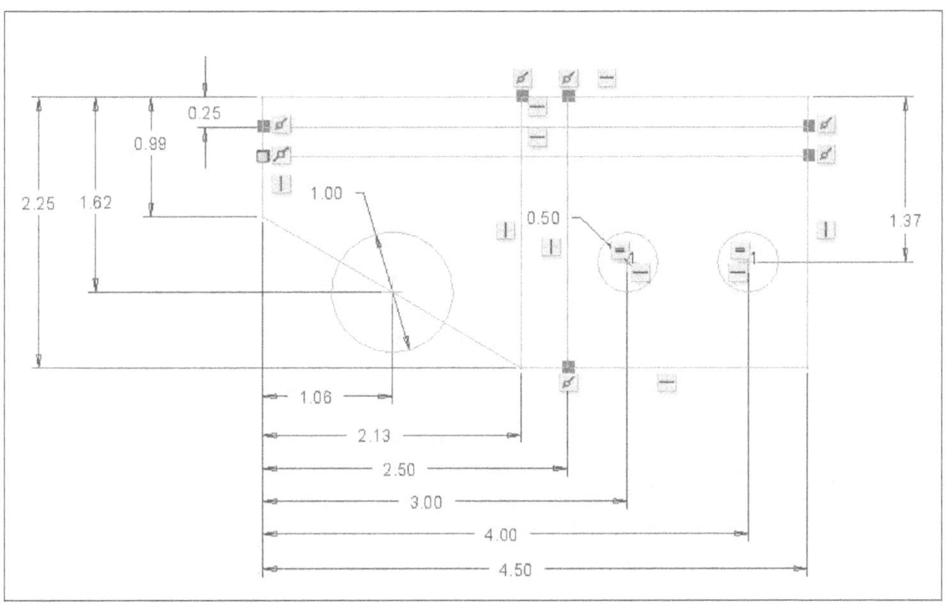

Figure-35. After creating circle

Trimming extra part of sketch

- Click on the **Delete Segment** tool from the **Editing** panel of the **Ribbon**. You are asked to select the entities that you want to trim.
- Delete the extra geometries from the sketch; refer to Figure-36.

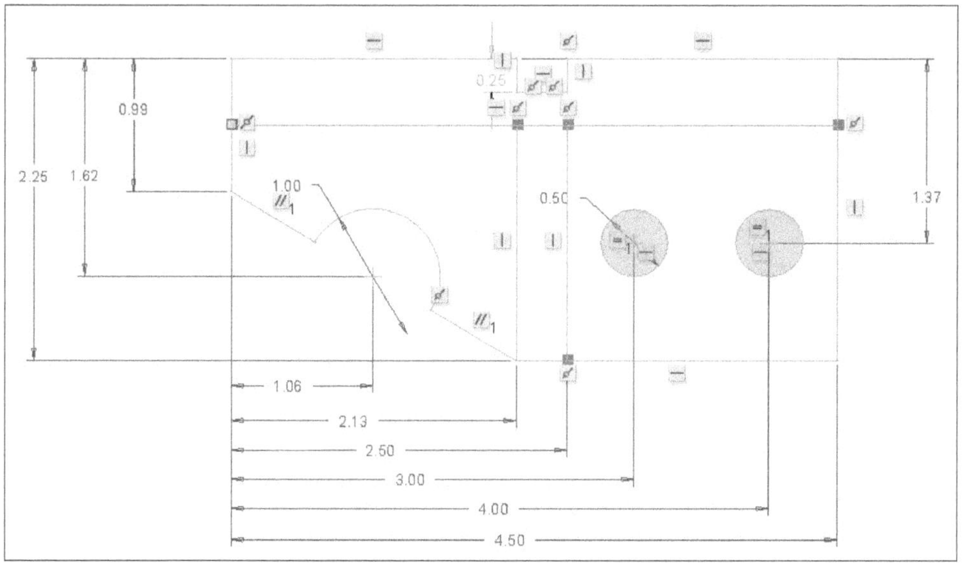

Figure-36. After trimming entities

Filleting

- Click on the **Circular** tool from the **Fillet** drop-down. You are asked to select two entities.
- Select the two lines as shown in Figure-37. The fillet will be created; refer to Figure-38.

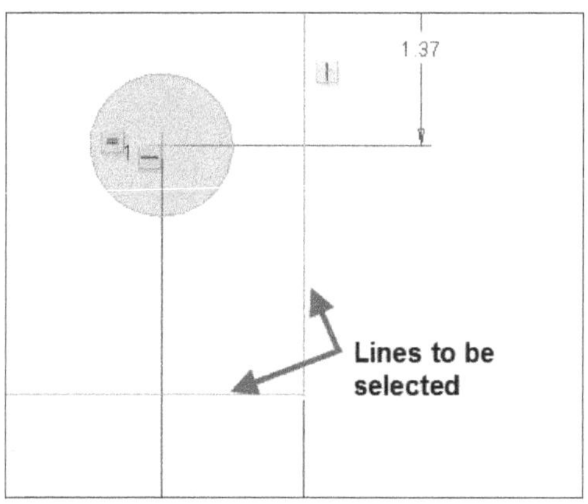

Figure-37. Lines selected for filleting

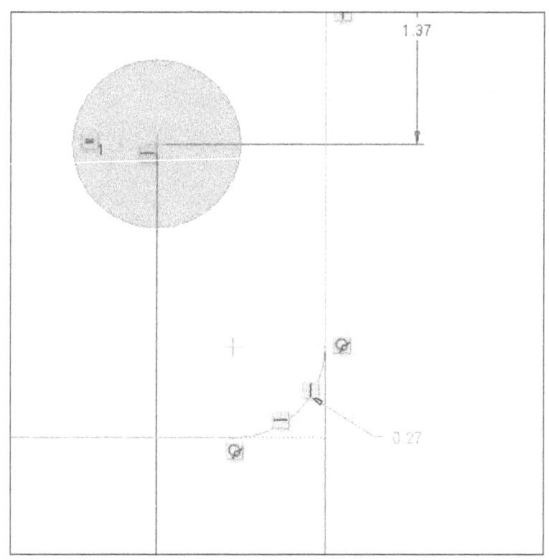

Figure-38. Sketch after filleting

- Double-click on the dimension value of the fillet and specify the value as **0.50**.

Apply rest of the dimensions as per the drawing by using the **Dimension** tool from the **Dimension** panel of the **Ribbon**.

PRACTICAL 3

In this practical, we will create a sketch as shown in Figure-39.

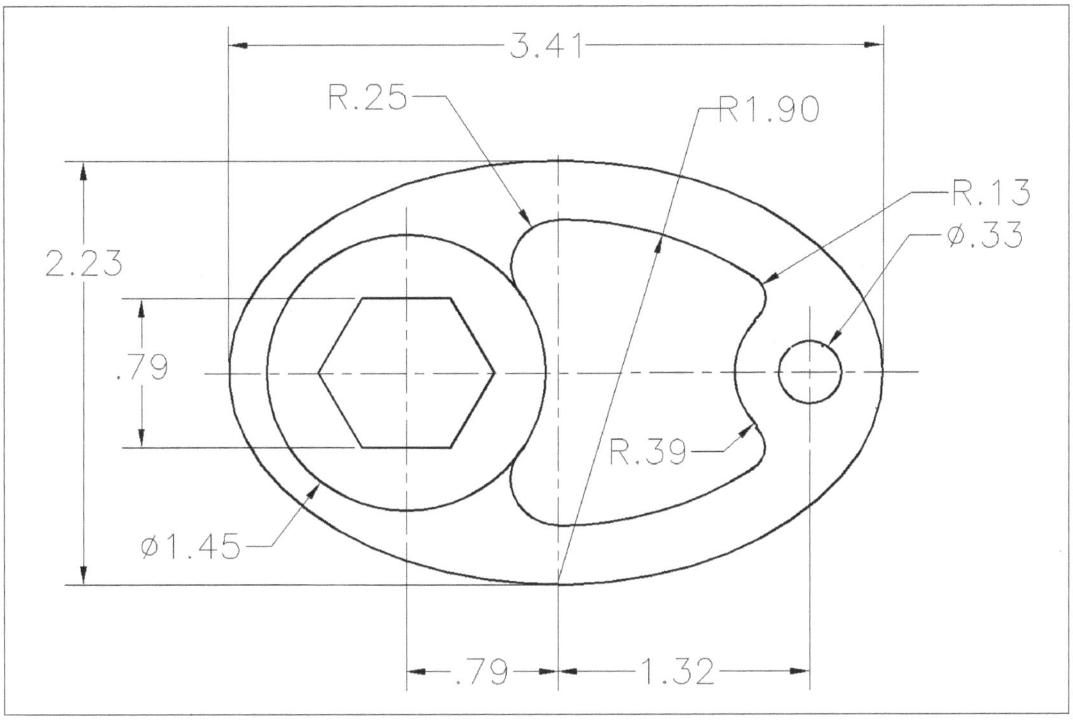

Figure-39. Practical 3

Starting Sketch

- Start Creo Parametric by double-clicking on the Creo Parametric 13.0 icon from the desktop.
- Click on the **New** button from the **Quick Access Toolbar**. The **New** dialog box will be displayed.
- Select the **Sketch** radio button from the dialog box and specify desired name in the **File name** edit box.
- Click on the **OK** button from the **New** dialog box. The sketching environment will be displayed.

Drawing the ellipse

- Click on the **Axis Ends Ellipse** tool from the **Ellipse** drop-down. You are asked to specify the start point of the ellipse.
- Click in the drawing area to specify the start point of the ellipse. You are asked to specify the end point of the major axis of the ellipse.
- Click in the drawing area to create horizontal major axis of the ellipse; refer to Figure-40. You are asked to specify the end point for the minor axis of the ellipse; refer to Figure-41.

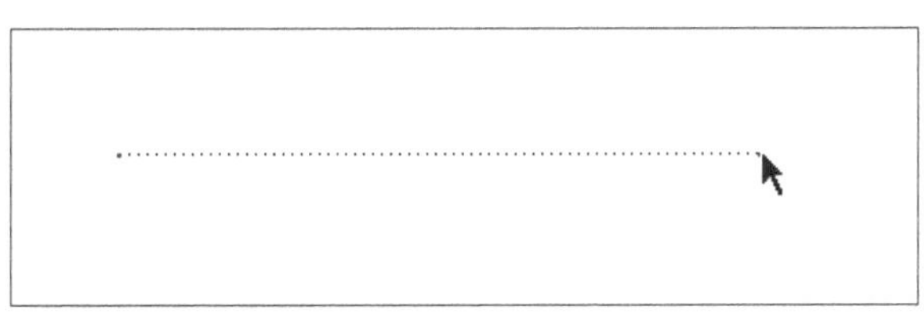

Figure-40. Major axis of ellipse

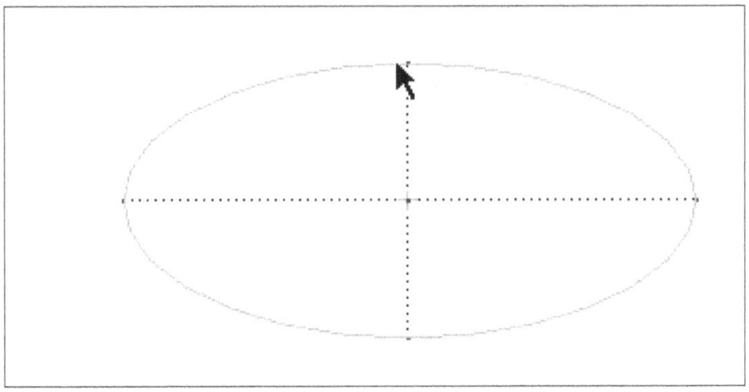

Figure-41. Minor axis of ellipse

- Click to specify the end point of the minor axis of ellipse and press the middle mouse button to exit the tool.
- Double-click on the dimensions of the ellipse one by one and specify the required values; refer to Figure-42.

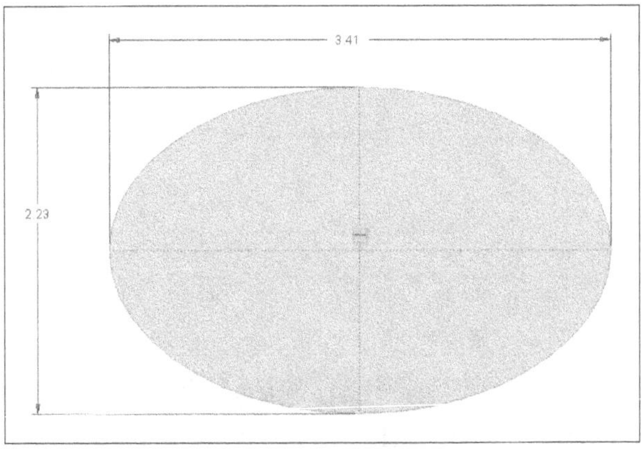

Figure-42. Ellipse after specifying dimensions

- Create a horizontal and vertical centerline from the center of the ellipse by using the **Centerline** tool.

Drawing Circles

- Click on the **Center and Point** tool from the **Circle** drop-down and draw a circle of diameter **1.45** at a distance of **0.79** to the left of the centerline of the ellipse.
- Similarly, draw a circle of diameter **0.33** to the right of the centerline at a distance of **1.32**; refer to Figure-43.

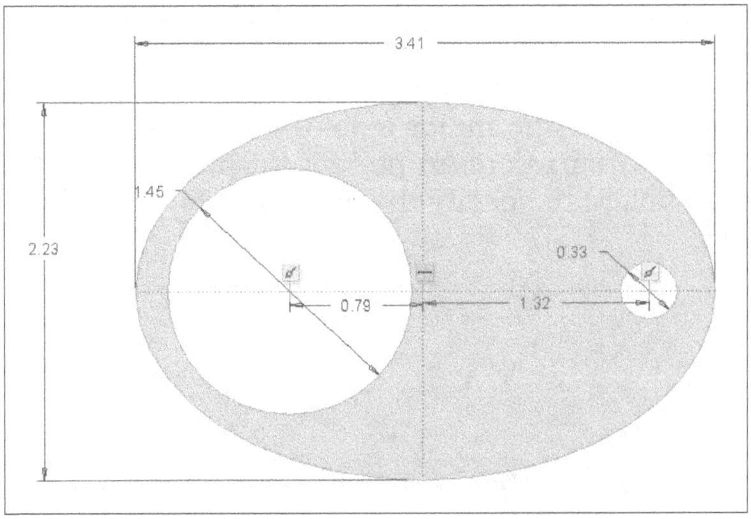

Figure-43. Sketch after drawing circles

- Create a circle of radius **0.39** concentric to the circle with diameter **0.33**; refer to Figure-44.
- Click on the **Center and Ends** tool from the **Arc** drop-down and draw an arc of radius **1.90** as shown in Figure-45.

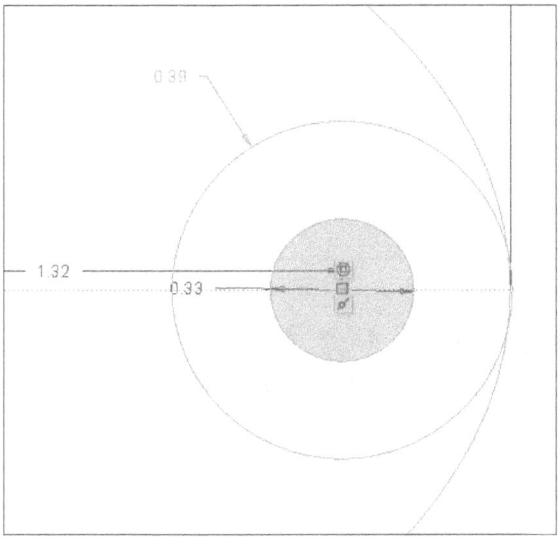

Figure-44. Creating circle of radius 0.39

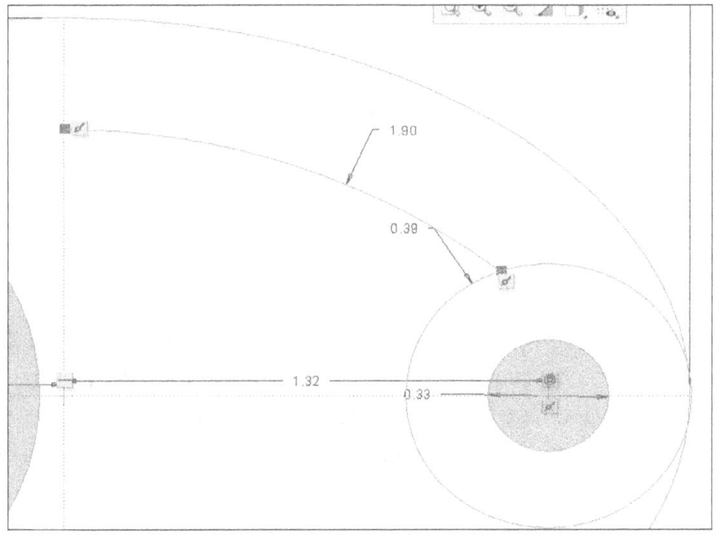

Figure-45. Arc created

Filleting the Sketch

- Click on the **Circular** tool from the **Fillet** drop-down. You are asked to select two entities for creating fillet.
- One by one select the circle and arc as shown in Figure-46. Note that you need to select the arc and circle at the positions pointed by red arrows in the figure.

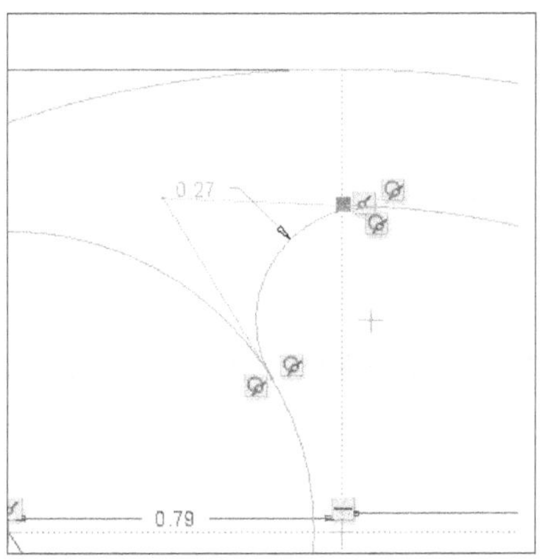

Figure-46. Selection for creating fillet

- Press the middle button of the mouse to exit the **Fillet** tool and double-click on the radius value of the fillet.
- Specify the value of the fillet as **0.25**.
- Click on the **Circular** tool from the **Fillet** drop-down and create the fillet of radius **0.13** as shown in Figure-47.

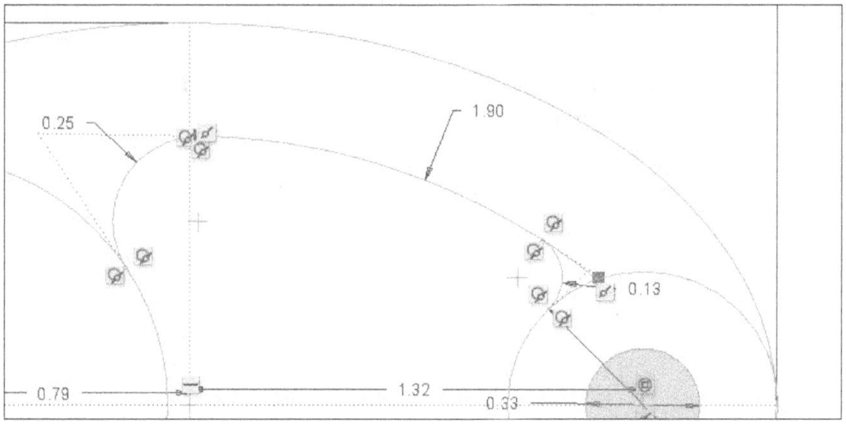

Figure-47. Fillet of radius

Trimming extra geometry

- Click on the **Delete Segment** tool from the **Editing** panel in the **Ribbon**. You are asked to select the extra entities from the sketch.
- Click on the entities as shown in Figure-48.

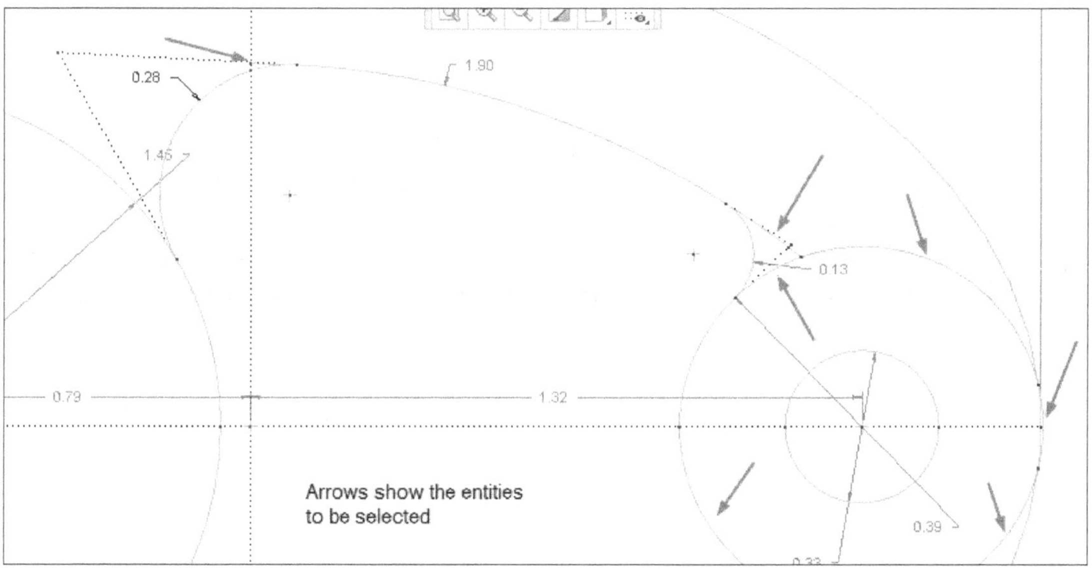

Figure-48. Entities selected for trimming

- After selecting these entities, the sketch will be displayed as shown in Figure-49.

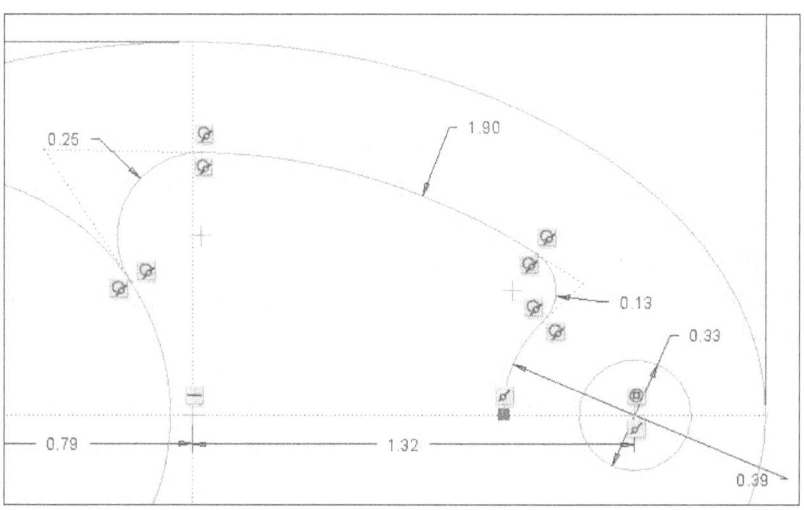

Figure-49. Sketch after trimming

Mirroring entities

- Select the entities as shown in Figure-50 by holding the **CTRL** key from keyboard.

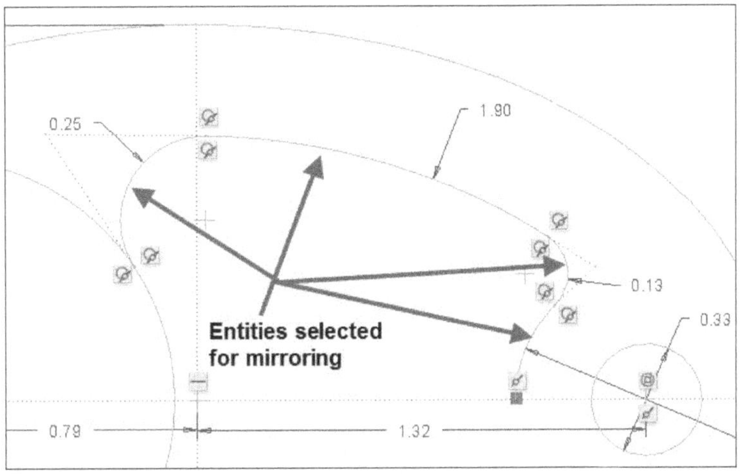

Figure-50. Entities selected for mirroring

- Click on the **Mirror** tool from the **Editing** panel. You are asked to select a centerline.
- Click on the horizontal centerline. The mirror copy of the selected entities will be created; refer to Figure-51. Note that dimension are hidden for clarity purpose.

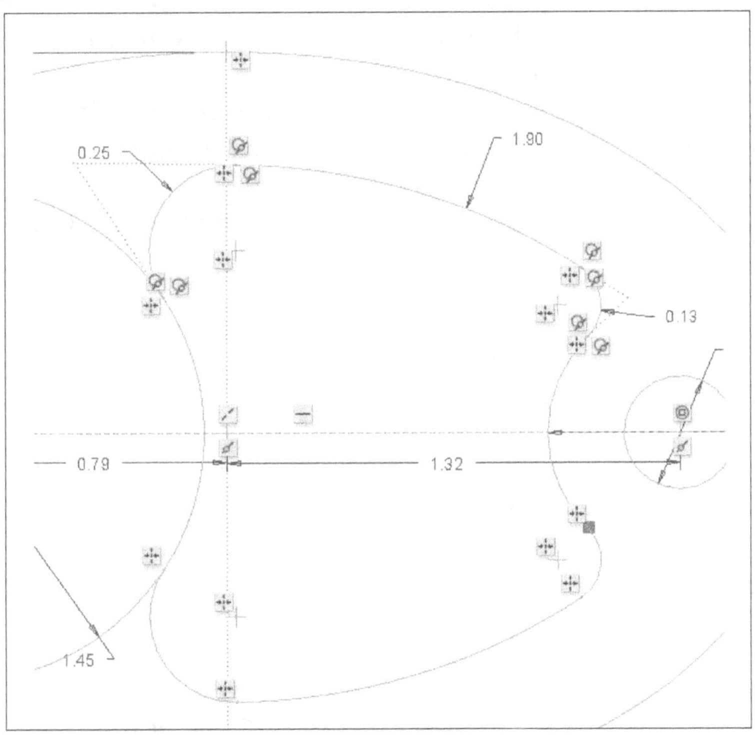

Figure-51. Creating mirror copy of entities

Creating Hexagon

- Click on the **Centerline** tool from the **Sketching** panel of the **Ribbon** and create a centerline at the center of the circle on the left.
- Click on the **Palette** tool from the **Sketching** panel. The **Sketcher Palette** dialog box will be displayed; refer to Figure-52.

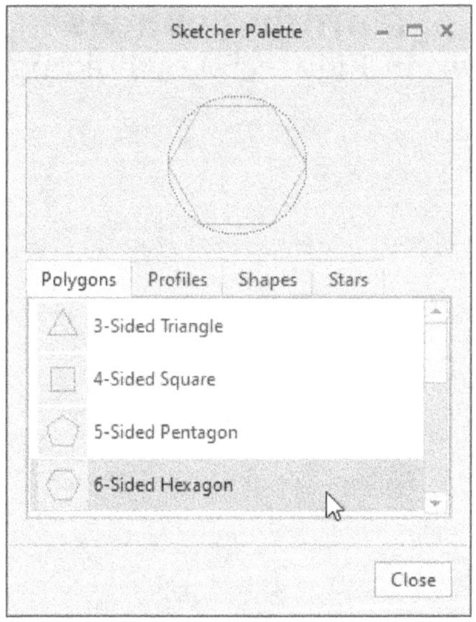

Figure-52. Sketcher Palette dialog box

- Double-click on the **6-Sided Hexagon** option from the **Polygons** tab in the dialog box. You are asked to specify the insertion point for the hexagon.
- Click on the center of the circle having diameter of **1.45**. The hexagon will be placed near the center of the circle.
- Click on the move handle of the hexagon and drag it to the center of the circle. You may need to zoom in by scrolling down for locating the center clearly.
- Click on the **OK** button from the dashboard in the **Ribbon** and click on the **Close** button from the dialog box to exit.
- Now, we need to specify dimension of the hexagon. Click on the **Dimension** tool from the **Dimension** panel in the **Ribbon**. You are asked to select the entities.
- One by one click on the two lines shown in Figure-53 and press the middle button of mouse to place the dimension. The **Resolve Sketch** dialog box will be displayed; refer to Figure-54.

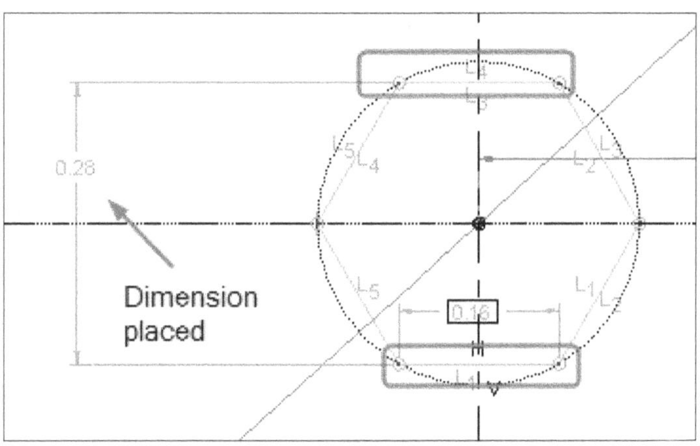

Figure-53. Dimensioning hexagon

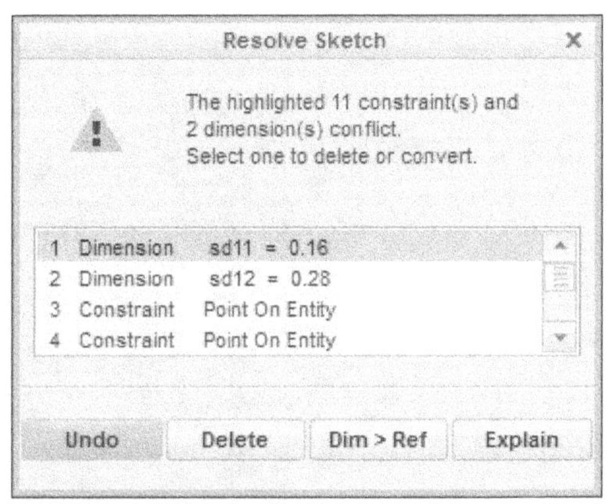

Figure-54. Resolve Sketch dialog box

- Select the dimension that is contradicting with our newly created dimension (In our case its **sd11 = 0.16**, highlighted in box; refer to Figure-53). Click on the **Delete** button from the **Resolve Sketch** dialog box. You are asked to specify value of the created dimension.
- Specify the value as **0.79** and press **ENTER** from the Keyboard. We get the sketch for drawing.

PRACTICAL 4

In this practical, we will create a sketch for the drawing given in Figure-55.

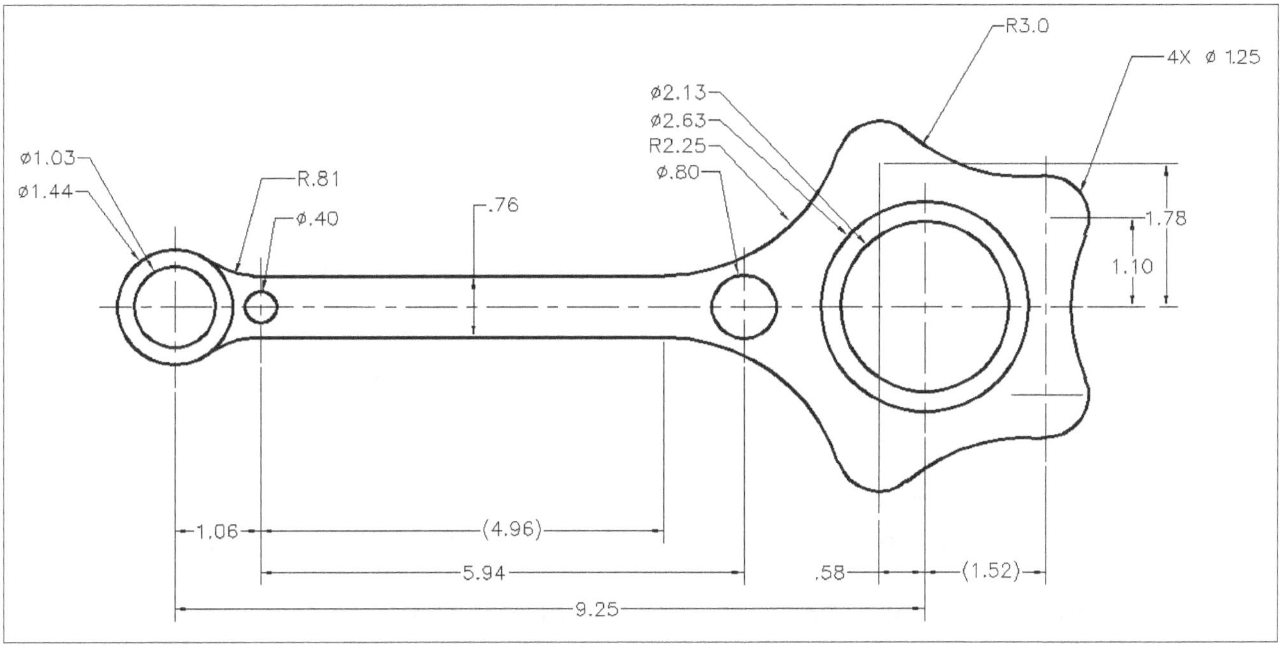

Figure-55. Practical 4

Starting Sketch

- Start Creo Parametric by double-clicking on the Creo Parametric 13.0 icon from the desktop.
- Click on the **New** button from the **Quick Access Toolbar**. The **New** dialog box will be displayed.
- Select the **Sketch** radio button from the dialog box and specify desired name in the **File name** edit box.
- Click on the **OK** button from the **New** dialog box. The sketching environment will be displayed.

Drawing Circles

- Click on the **Center and Point** tool from the **Circle** drop-down in the **Ribbon**. You are asked to specify the position of the center of circle.
- Click in the drawing area and then click to specify the size of the circle.
- Create one more circle at the same center and make it bigger than the previous one; refer to Figure-56.

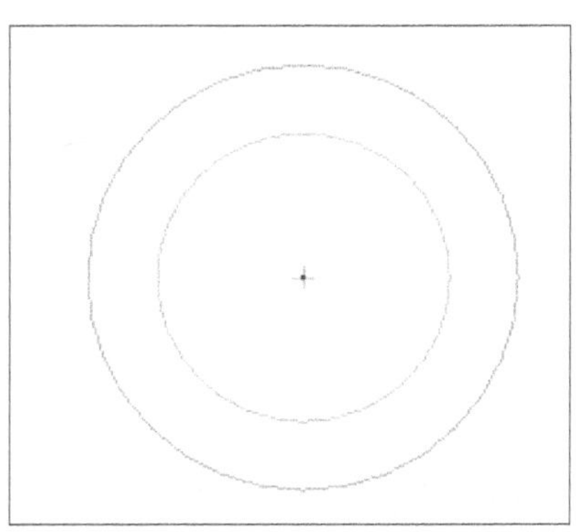

Figure-56. Concentric circles created

- Press the middle mouse button to exit the **Circle** tool and modify the dimension of the sketch as shown in Figure-57.

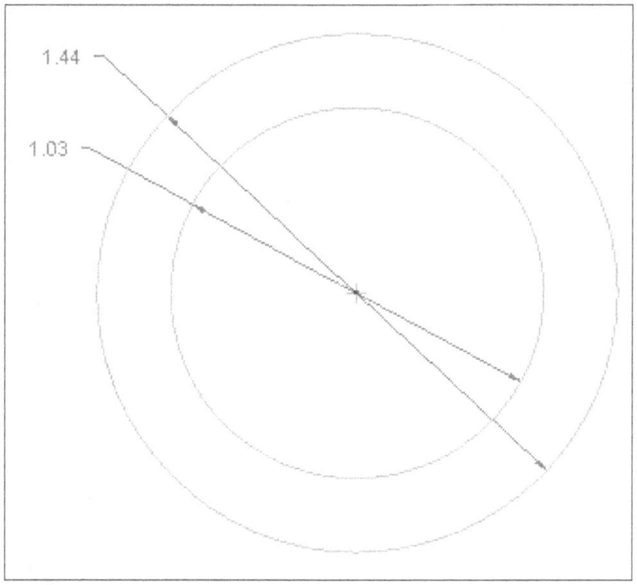

Figure-57. Circles after dimensioning

- Click on the **Centerline** tool from the **Sketching** panel and create a horizontal centerline.
- Click on the **Center and Point** tool from the **Circle** drop-down and create the circles on the horizontal centerline; refer to Figure-58. Press the middle mouse button to exit the tool.

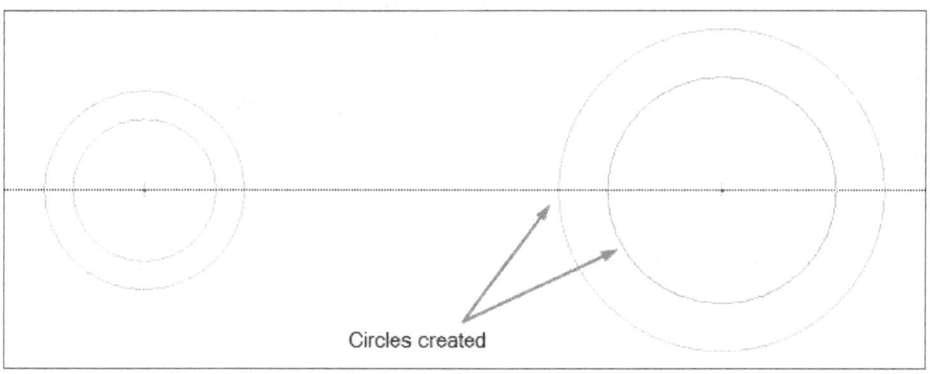

Figure-58. Circles created along centerline

- Change the dimensions as shown in Figure-59.

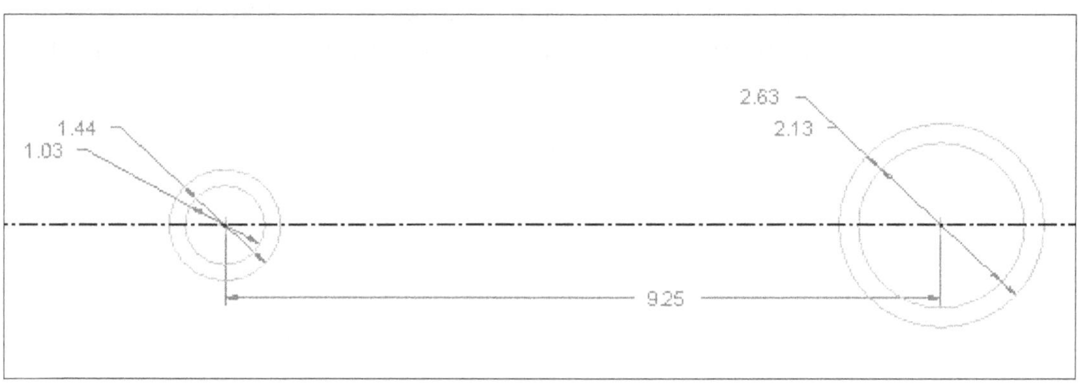

Figure-59. Sketch after dimensioning

- Create smaller circles as shown in Figure-60.

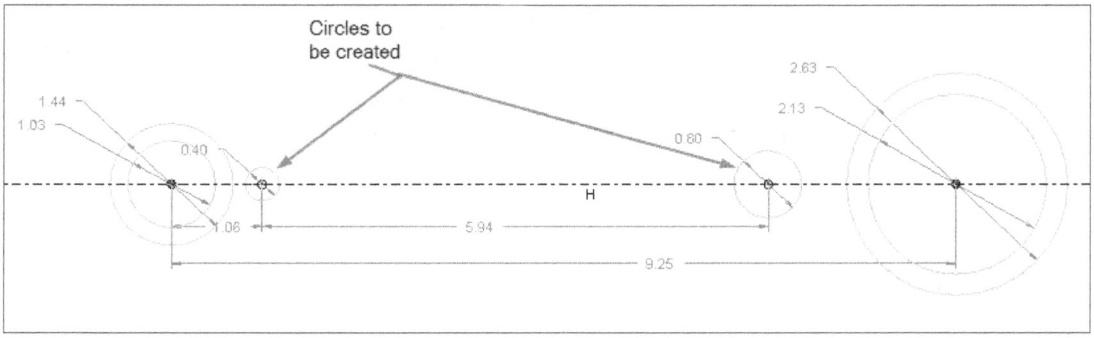

Figure-60. Circles to be drawn

- Create the circles as given in Figure-61. Note that the two circles are of same diameter.

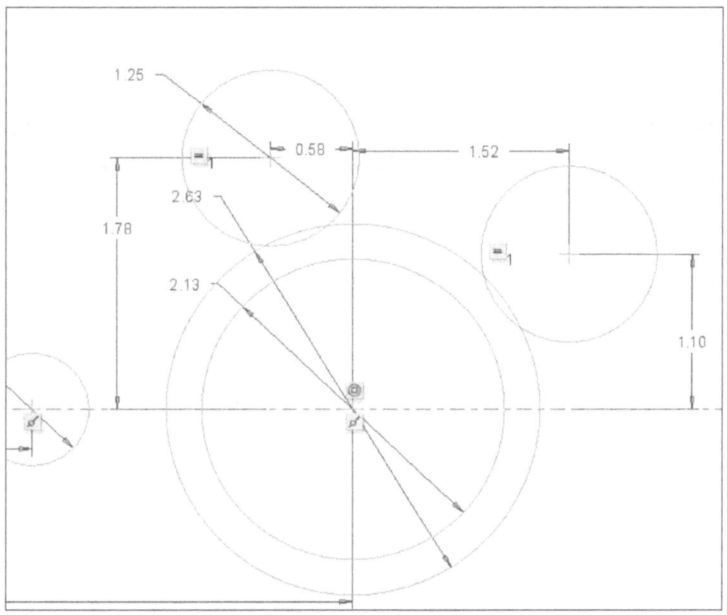

Figure-61. Circles created on the right portion

Creating Mirror copy of circles

- Select the two circles created in the previous step and click on the **Mirror** tool from the **Editing** panel. You are asked to select the centerline.
- Click on the horizontal centerline created earlier. The mirror copy of the circles will be created; refer to Figure-62.

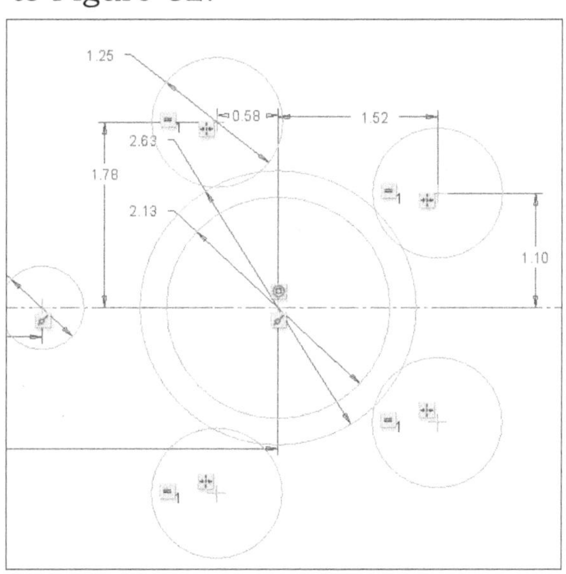

Figure-62. Mirror copy of circles created

Creating Lines

- Click on the **Line Chain** tool from the **Line** drop-down in the **Sketching** panel. You are asked to specify the start point of the line.
- Create a line connecting the two circles; refer to Figure-63.

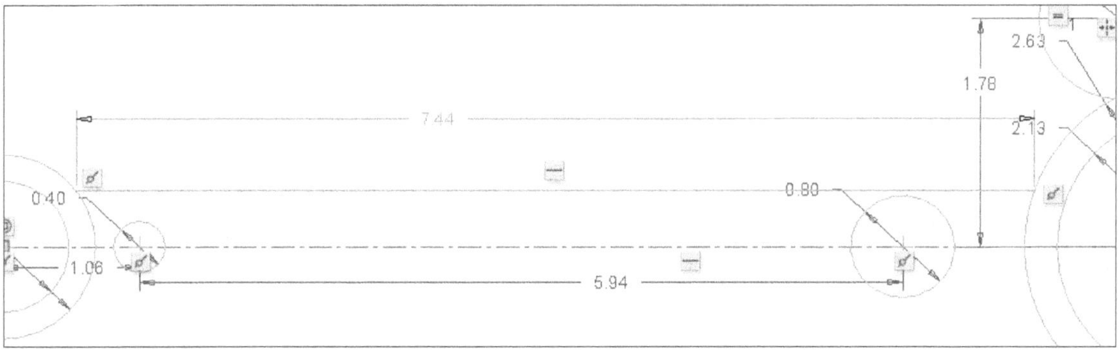

Figure-63. Line to be sketched

- Select the line and create a mirror copy of the line with respect to the horizontal centerline. Specify distance between the two lines as **0.79** by using the **Dimension** tool.

Creating Fillet

- Click on the **Circular** tool from the **Fillet** drop-down. You are asked to select two entities.
- Select the entities as shown in Figure-64 to create the fillet.

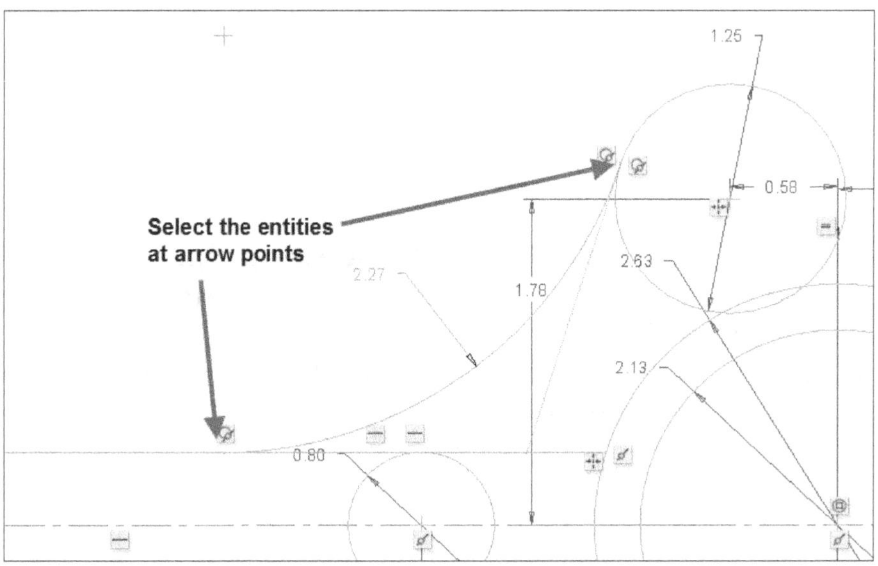

Figure-64. Entities selected for filleting

- Now, click on the two circles as shown in Figure-65 to create fillet between the circles.

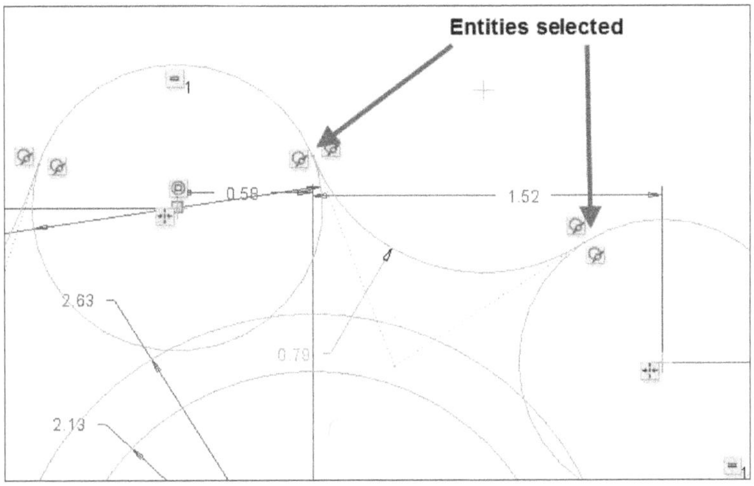

Figure-65. Circles to be selected

- Similarly, create other fillets; refer to Figure-66.

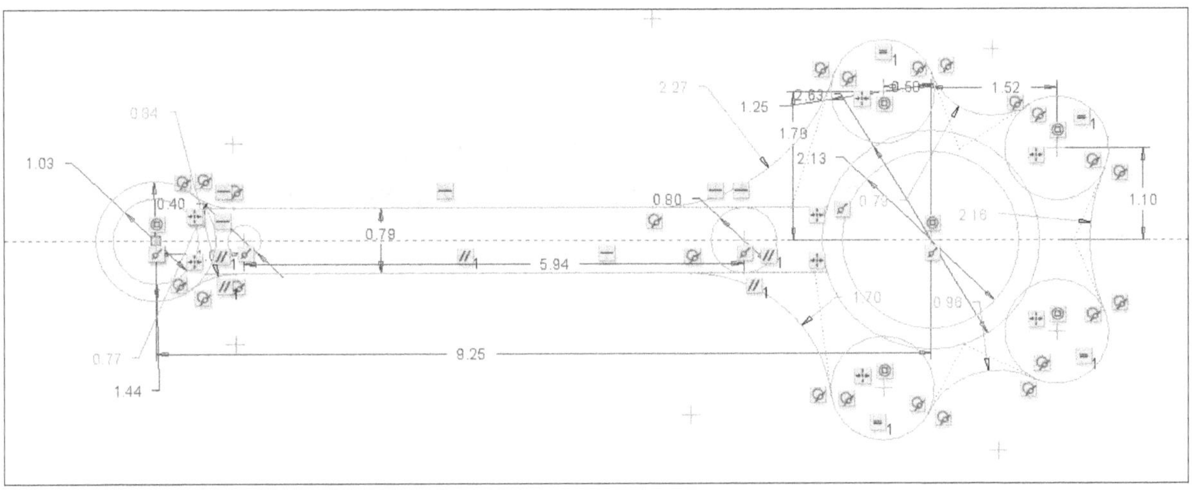

Figure-66. Sketch after creating fillets

- Double-click on the dimension values and change the values as per the drawing; refer to Figure-67. In place of dimensioning all the fillets, you can dimension one of the similar fillets and can make all the other fillets equally constrained by using the **Equal** constraint; refer to Figure-68. Note that in Figure-68, fillet radius of 3 is denoted by E1 at all the places.

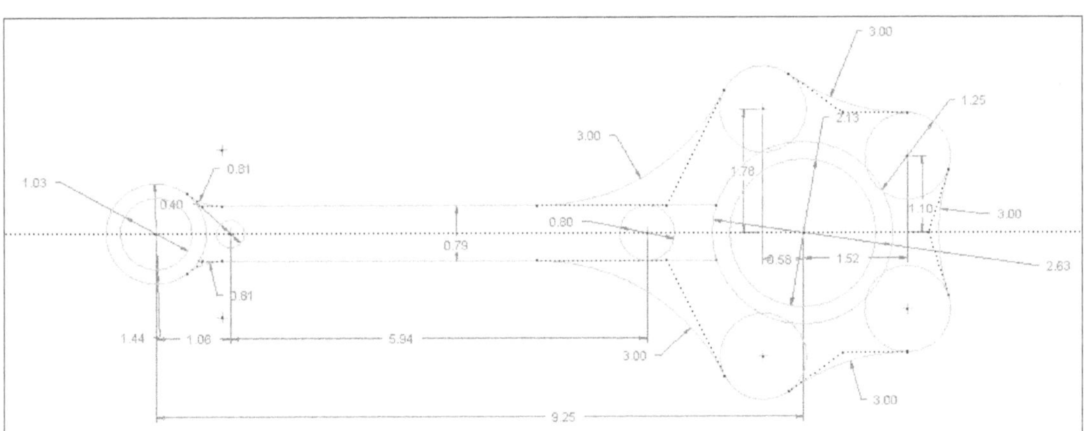

Figure-67. After dimensioning the fillets

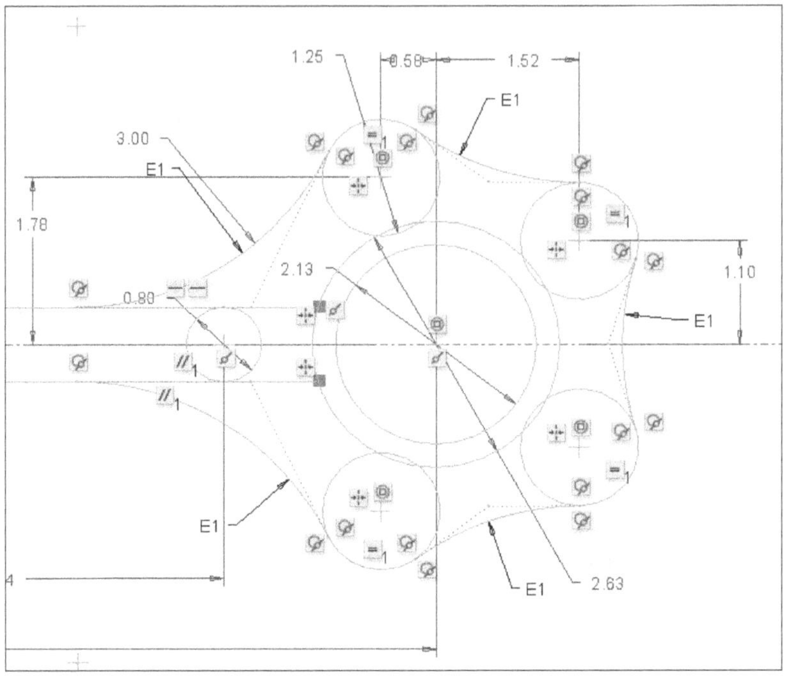

Figure-68. Fillet constrained as equal

Trimming the Extra geometries

- Click on the **Delete Segment** tool from the **Editing** panel. You are asked to select the segments that you want to delete.
- Select all the extra segments to delete them. The sketch after trimming will be displayed as shown in Figure-69.

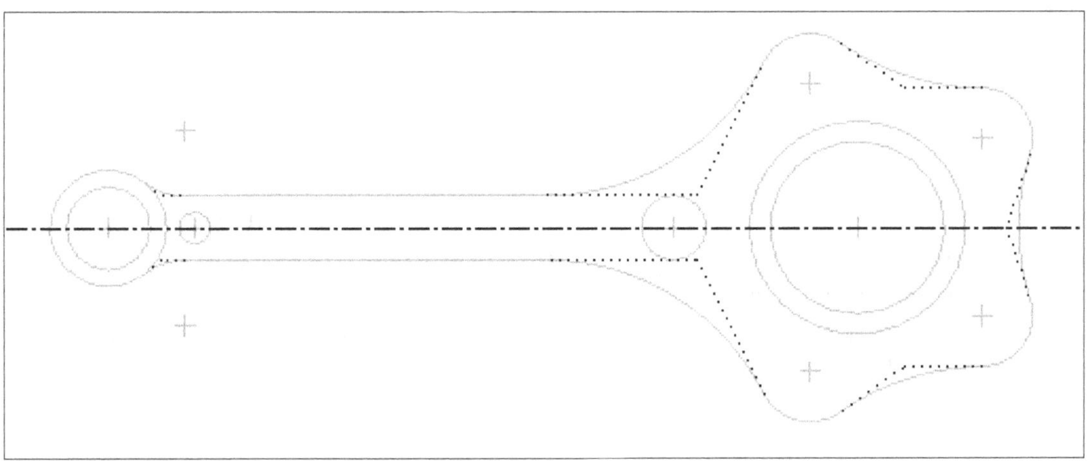

Figure-69. Sketch for Practical 4

PRACTICE 1

In this practice session, we will create a sketch for the drawing given in Figure-70.

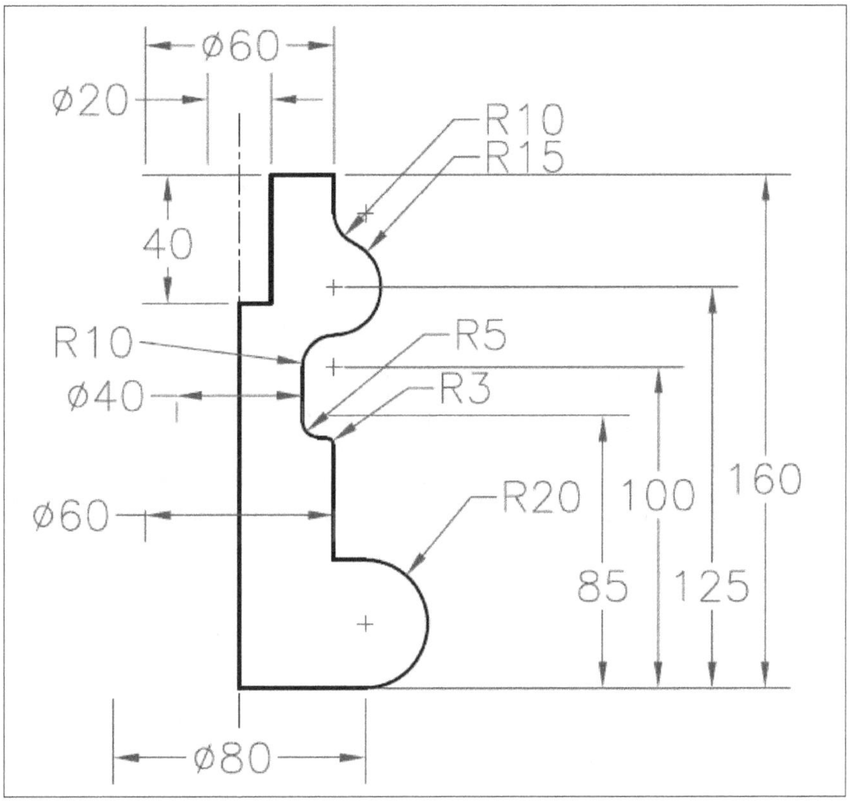

Figure-70. Practice 1

PRACTICE 2

In this practice session, we will create a sketch for the drawing given in Figure-71.

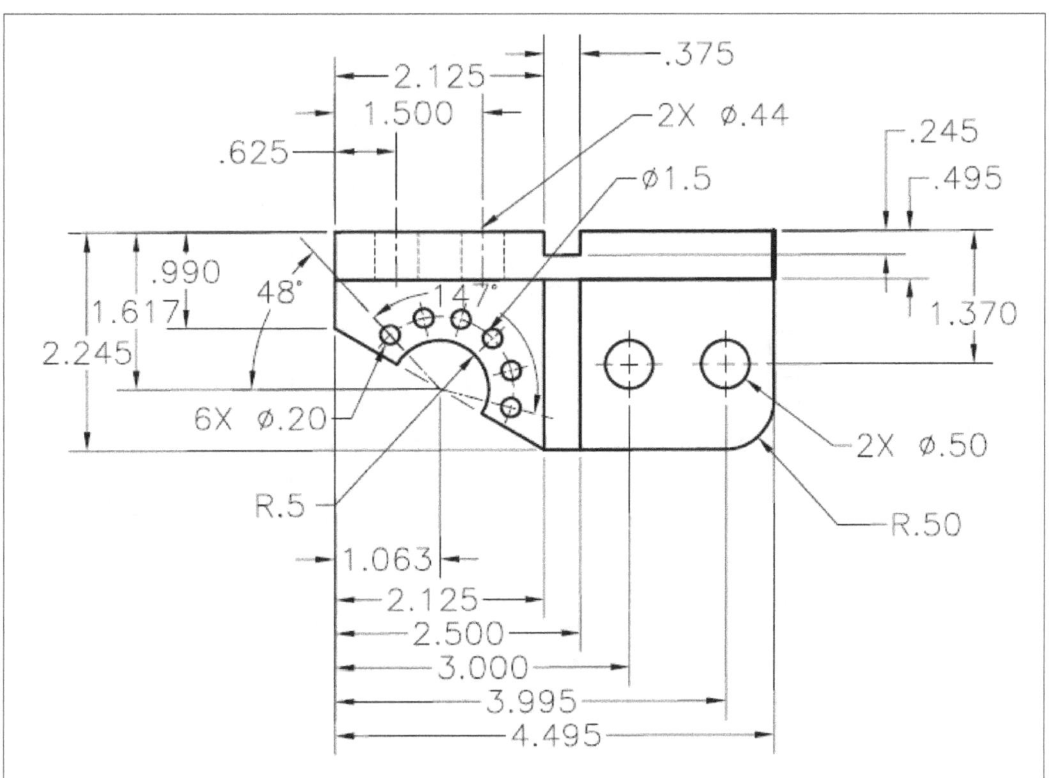

Figure-71. Practice 2

PRACTICE 3

In this practice session, we will create a sketch for the drawing given in Figure-72.

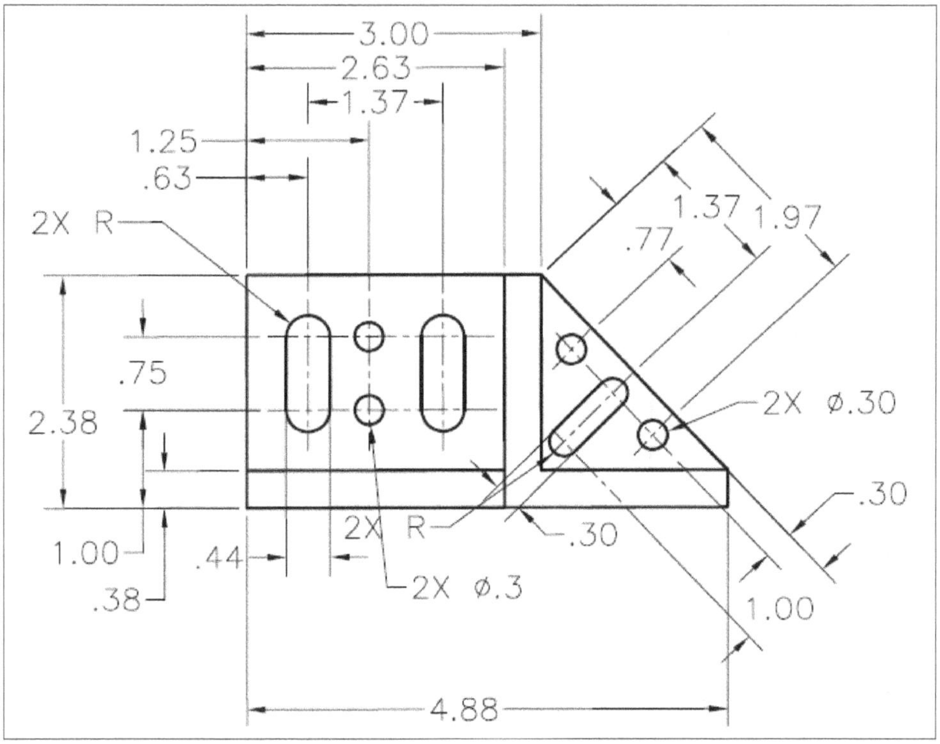

Figure-72. Practice 3

PRACTICE 4

In this practice session, we will create a sketch for the drawing given in Figure-73.

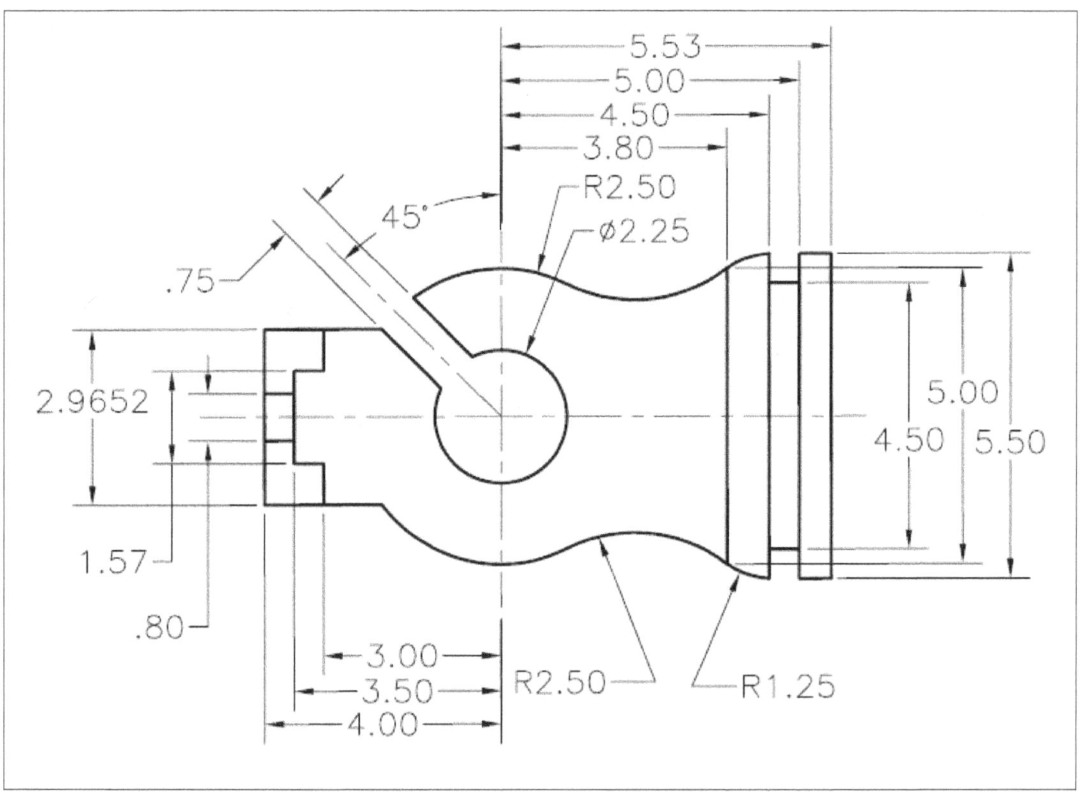

Figure-73. Practice 4

Practice 5

In this practice session, we will create a sketch for the drawing given in Figure-74.

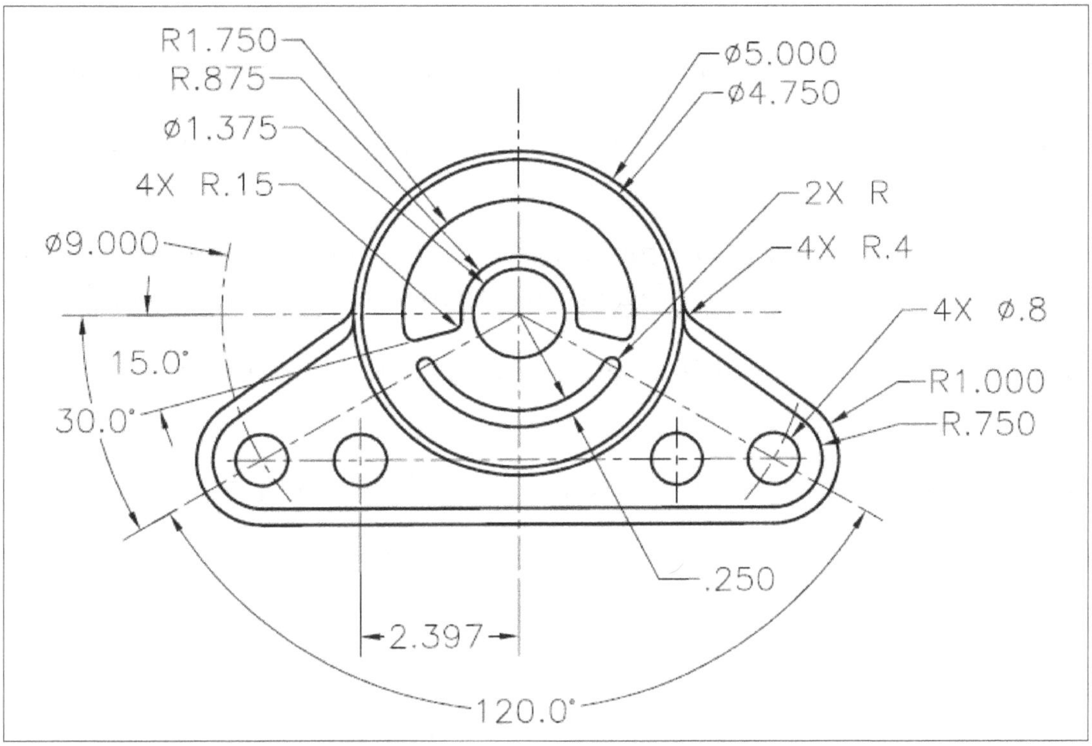

Figure-74. Practice 5

Practice 6

In this practice session, we will create a sketch for the drawing given in Figure-75.

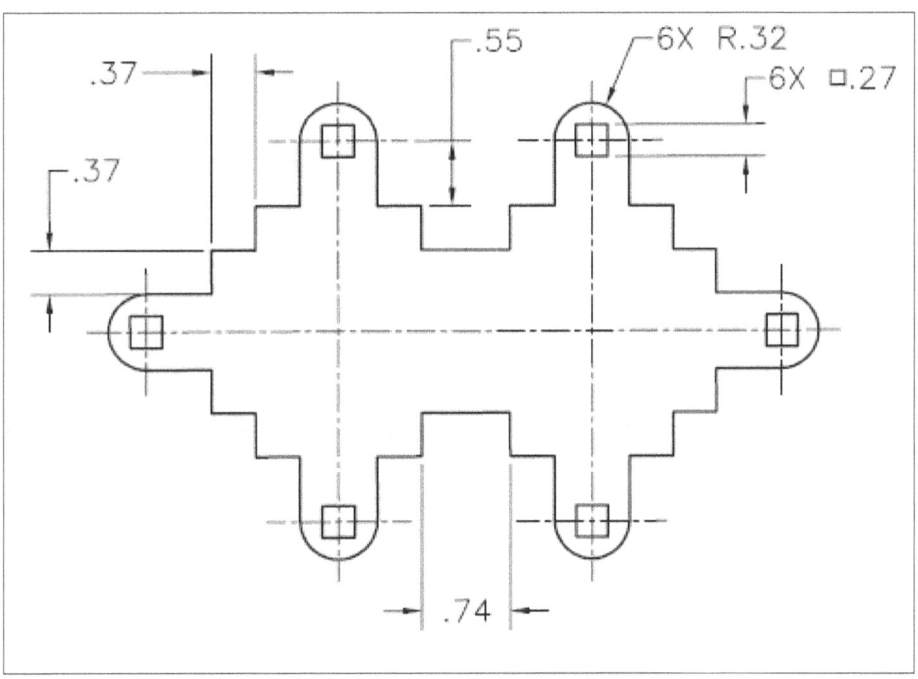

Figure-75. Practice 6

Hint: You can use the copy paste tool in sketch to create multiple copies of a sketch section. You can also use Pattern with specified points to create multiple copies.

SELF ASSESSMENT

1. The tools in .... panel are used to perform inspection on sketches for their suitability in modeling.

2. The .... button is used to identify the overlapping sketched entities.

3. The **Entity** tool is used to find out all the information about the selected entity. (T/F)

4. The .... tool in the **Relation** panel is used to display dimensions by their designated names in place of their dimension values in the sketch.

5. The .... tool is used to import sketches or drawing files in the sketch you are working on.

6. Which tool in Creo Parametric is used to identify overlapping sketch entities?

a) Highlight Intersections
b) Highlight Junctions
c) Highlight Overlaps
d) Highlight Open Ends

7. What visual cue does Creo Parametric use to show intersecting sketch entities when using the Highlight Intersections tool?

a) Blue lines
b) Green boxes
c) Red boxes at intersection points
d) Shaded regions

8. What does the Highlight Open Ends tool in Creo Parametric help identify?

a) Overlapping lines
b) Redundant constraints
c) Unconnected sketch endpoints
d) Tangent arcs

9. What color is used by default to shade closed loops using the Shade Closed Loops tool?

a) Red
b) Blue
c) Green
d) Orange

10. What does the Tangency Point tool help you identify?

a) Intersection between two lines
b) Point where line touches circle/arc tangentially
c) Center of a circle
d) Midpoint of a line

11. What is the purpose of the Relations tool in Creo Parametric?

a) To trim sketches
b) To import external geometry
c) To apply mathematical relations between dimensions
d) To highlight dimension constraints

12. What happens when you try to change the value of dimension sd2, which is dependent on sd0 and sd1 via a relation?

a) It changes independently
b) It changes randomly
c) It remains fixed
d) It becomes hidden

13. Which tool is used to bring external sketch files into your current sketch?

a) Entity tool
b) Import tool
c) Highlight Junctions
d) Relations tool

14. What is the function of the "Pick From List" option after identifying overlapping entities?

a) To zoom into the selected entity
b) To save the sketch
c) To select and delete specific overlapping entities
d) To convert sketch to 3D

FOR STUDENT NOTES

Answers to Self Assessment Questions:

1. Inspect **2.** Overlapping Geometry **3.** T **4.** Switch Dimensions **5.** File System

Chapter 4

3D Modeling Basics

Topics Covered

The major topics covered in this chapter are:

- ***Starting Part Modeling environment***
- ***Basics of Planes***
- ***Datum Features***
- ***Curves and Sketches***
- ***Importing Sketches***
- ***3D Modeling tools***

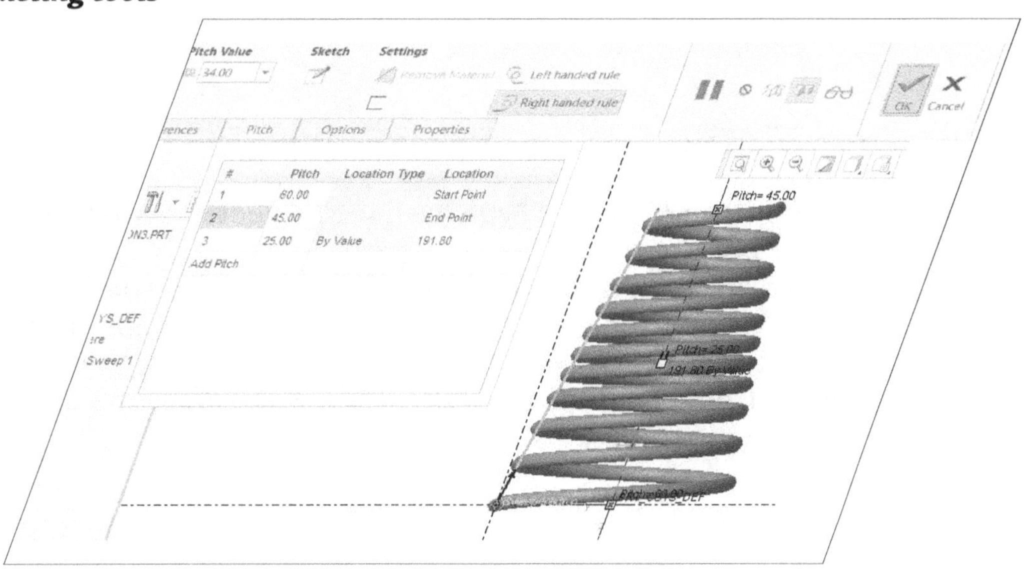

INTRODUCTION

Till now, you have learned about creating 2D sketches. But, the purpose of creating 2D sketches is, to create 3D models that can contain the features of a real model. The tools and options to create 3D models are available in the Part mode of Creo Parametric. The method of starting Part mode is given next.

STARTING PART MODE

This is the first step in the world of 3D Modeling using Creo Parametric. The steps to start Part mode are given next.

- Start Creo Parametric by using the icon from desktop.
- Click on the **New** button from the **Data** panel in the **Ribbon** or **Quick Access Toolbar**. The **New** dialog box will be displayed; refer to Figure-1.

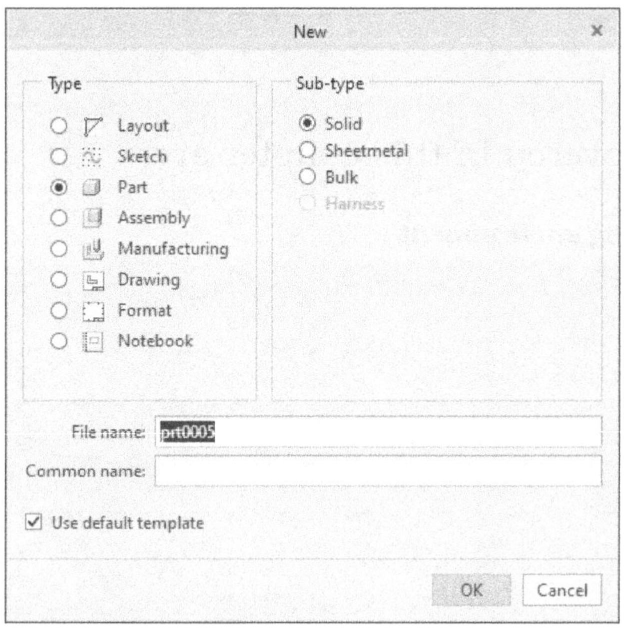

Figure-1. New dialog box

- Select the **Part** radio button from the **Type** area and select the **Solid** radio button from the **Sub-type** area of the dialog box.
- Click in the **File name** edit box and specify desired name for the file.
- Clear the **Use default template** check box because we might be working on different units in real-time.
- Click on the **OK** button from the dialog box. The **New File Options** dialog box will be displayed; refer to Figure-2.

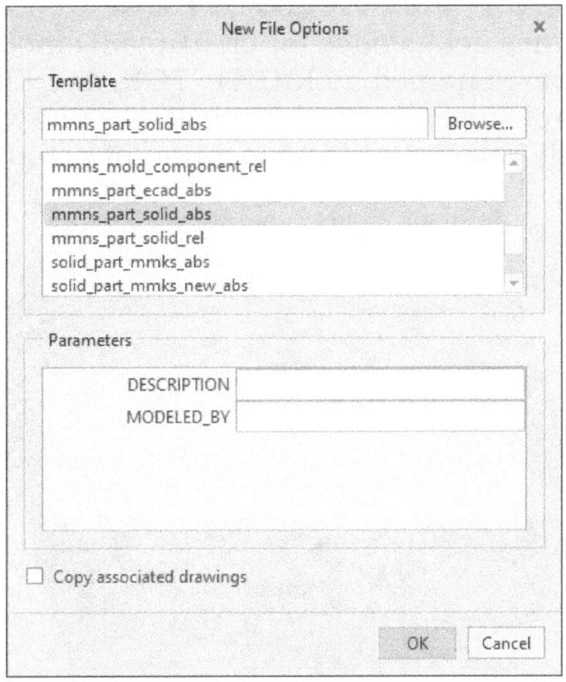

Figure-2. New File Options dialog box

- Select desired template from the list box (in our case mmns part solid). The meaning of various templates have already been discussed in Chapter 1.
- Click on the **OK** button from the dialog box. The **Part** mode of Creo Parametric will be displayed; refer to Figure-3.

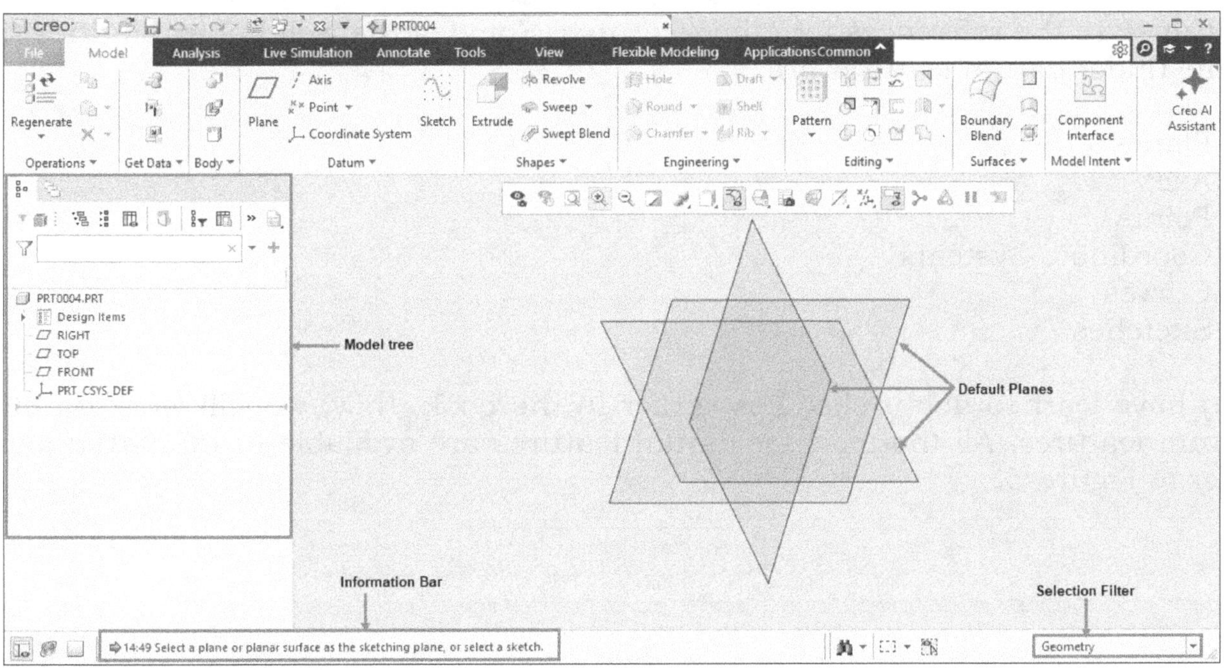

Figure-3. Part mode of Creo Parametric

Note that there are three default planes displayed in the Part mode of the Creo Parametric. These planes act as base for other features. Before stepping into 3D Modeling, you need to understand Planes and then Datum Features.

PLANES IN 3D

As discussed earlier, planes act as base for creating 3D models. In Creo Parametric, we have three default planes named as RIGHT, TOP, and FRONT. The selection of a plane for creating features depends on the orientation in which you want to create the model. You can easily understand the location of default planes from Figure-4.

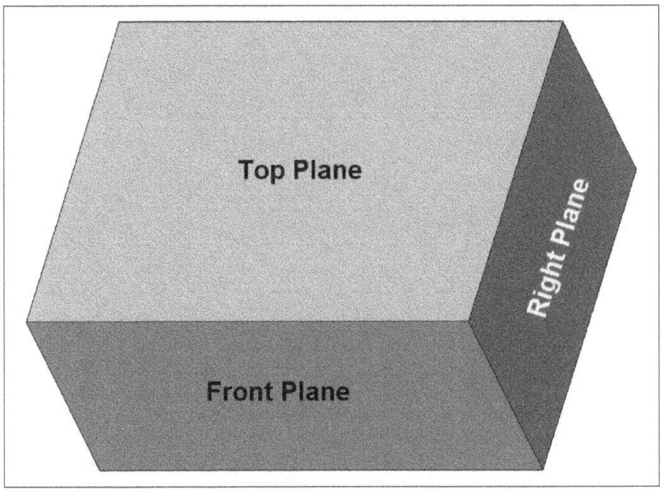

Figure-4. Planes

Note that this box is oriented in the same way as the planes are oriented by default in Creo Parametric. You can select a plane by clicking on its name in the **Model Tree**.

DATUMS

Datums are the references for other features. Some of the well known entities that come under datum features are:

- Planes
- Axes
- Points
- Coordinate Systems
- Curves
- Sketches

You have learned about sketches earlier in the book. Now, we will work on other datum features. All the tools for datum features are available in the **Datum** panel; refer to Figure-5.

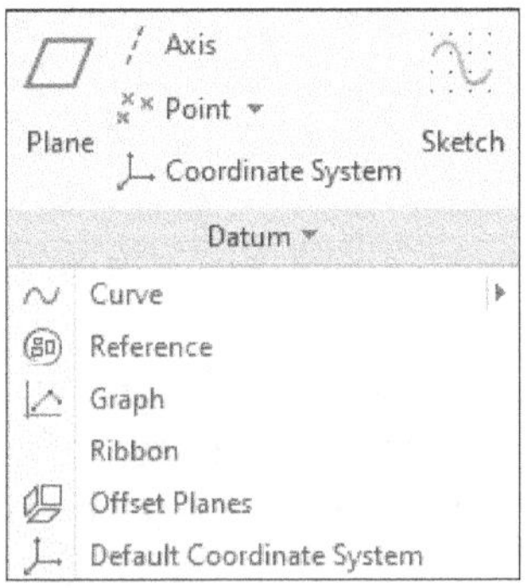

Figure-5. Datum panel

The tools in this panel are discussed next.

We will first learn to create datum axis, points, and Coordinate System. Later, we will work on the **Plane** tool.

Datum Axis

The **Axis** tool is used to create an axis in the model. The axis can be used to make reference for planes or can be used to revolve the sketch for creating revolve feature. The steps to create datum axis are given next.

- Click on the **Axis** tool from the **Datum** panel. The **Datum Axis** dialog box will be displayed; refer to Figure-6 and you are asked to select the entities for creating axis.

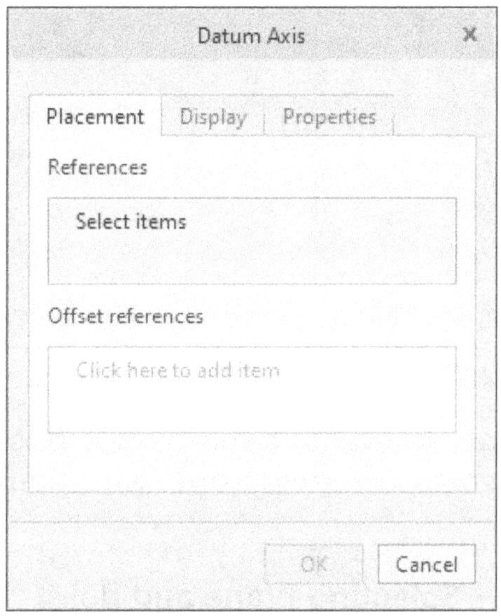

Figure-6. Datum Axis dialog box

- Select a plane perpendicular to which you want to create the axis. An axis perpendicular to the selected plane will be displayed; refer to Figure-7.

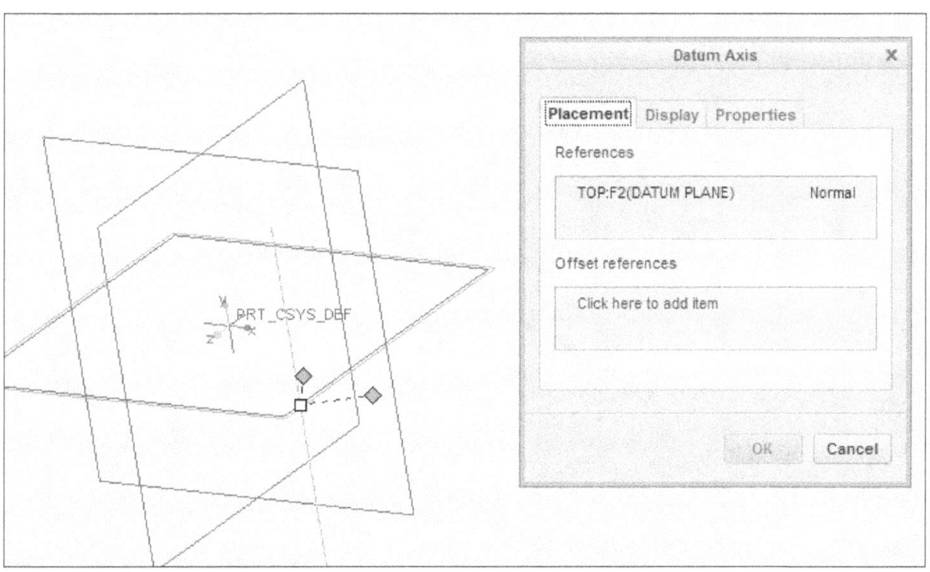

Figure-7. Perpendicular axis

- The green handles displayed are used to select the references for locating the axis with respect to the other planes.

- Drag the green handles to the plane or entity to which you want to reference the axis. You can also use the **Offset references** selection box in the dialog box to make reference selection. To do so, click in the **Offset references** selection box and select the two planes/entities while holding the **CTRL** key; refer to Figure-8.

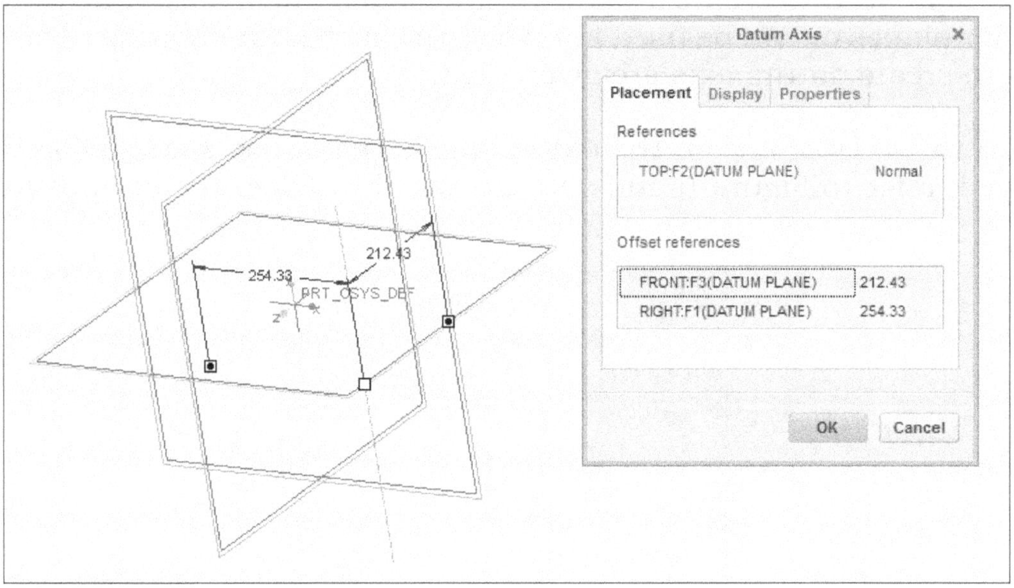

Figure-8. Axis after selecting references

Now, we will use datum points to create axes. You will learn about the datum points in the next topic. You can go to the next topic and come back to practice the axis creation using points.

Selecting plane and point

- If you select a plane and a point for creating the axis while holding the **CTRL** key then an axis perpendicular to the plane will be created which passes through the selected point; refer to Figure-9.

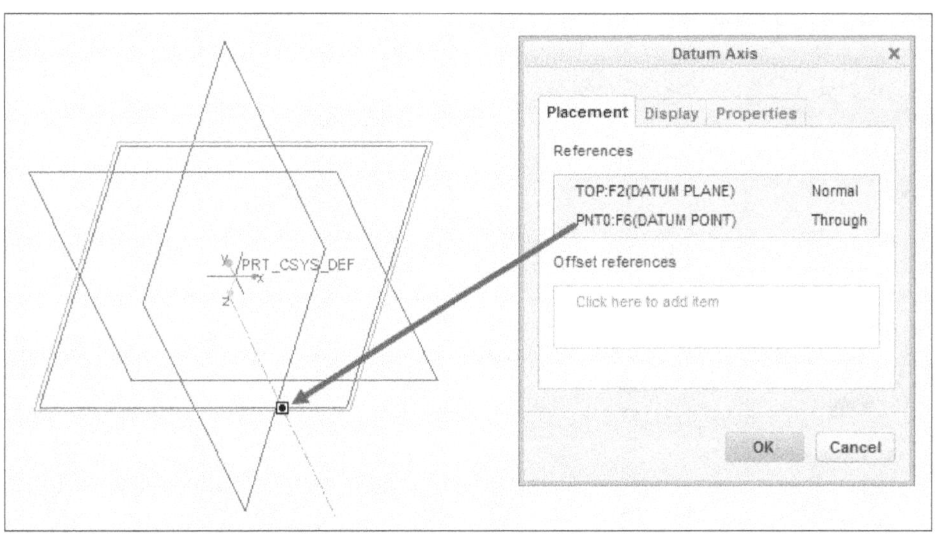

Figure-9. Axis through point and plane

Selecting point and axis

- If you select a point and an axis while holding the **CTRL** key then an axis passing through the point and normal/parallel to the selected axis will be created; refer to Figure-10. Note that if you select an edge of a solid model then an axis through the edge will be created in the same way.

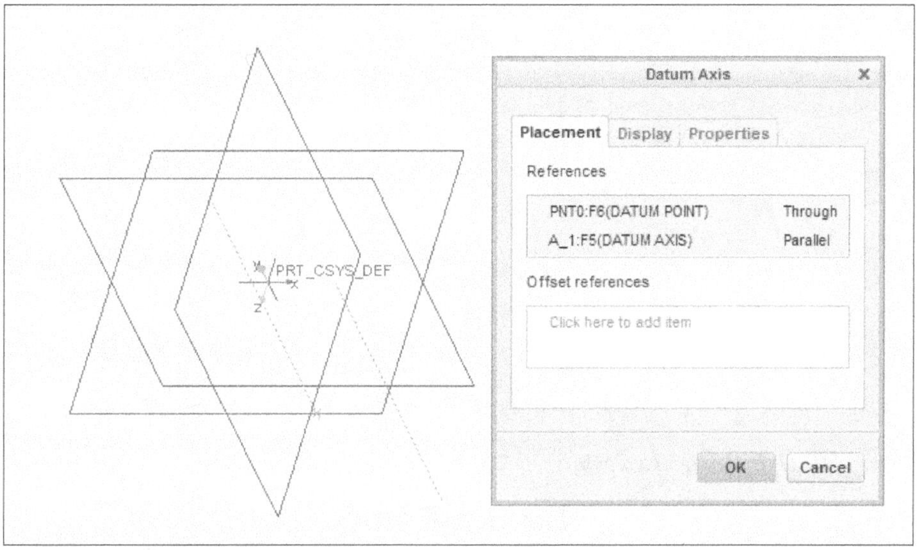

Figure-10. Axis parallel to other axis

- To make this axis normal to the selected axis, click on the **Parallel** option next to the axis in the **References** area of the **Datum Axis** dialog box. A drop-down will be displayed.
- Click on the **Normal** option from the drop-down. The axis will become normal to the selected axis; refer to Figure-11.

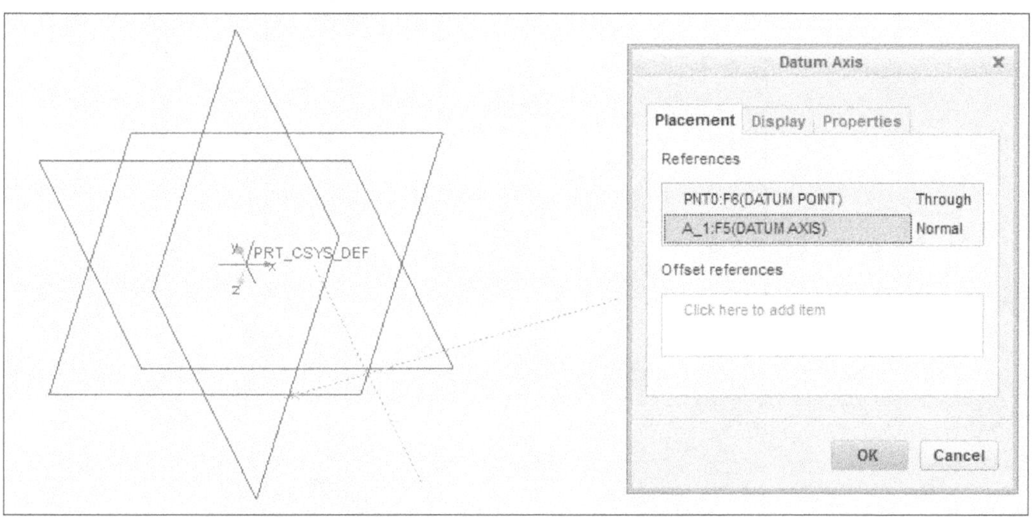

Figure-11. Axis normal to selected axis

Selecting 2 Points

- If you select two points while holding the **CTRL** key then an axis passing through both the points will be created; refer to Figure-12.

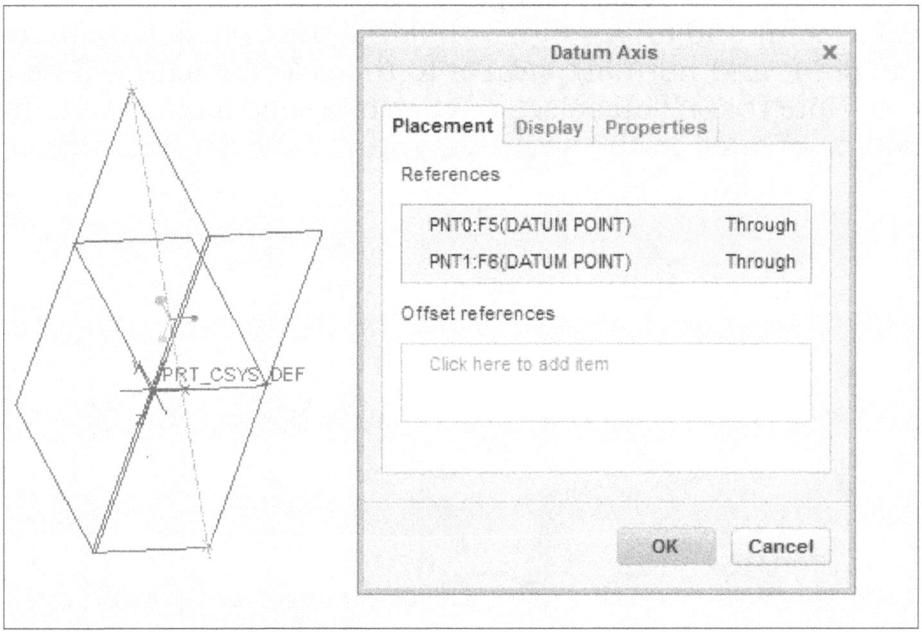

Figure-12. Axis through two points

Datum Point

The **Point** tool is used to create datum points in the model. The point can be used to make reference for planes, axes, curves, and so on. The steps to create datum point are given next.

- Click on the **Point** tool from the **Datum** panel. The **Datum Point** dialog box is displayed; refer to Figure-13 and you are asked to select entities for creating point.

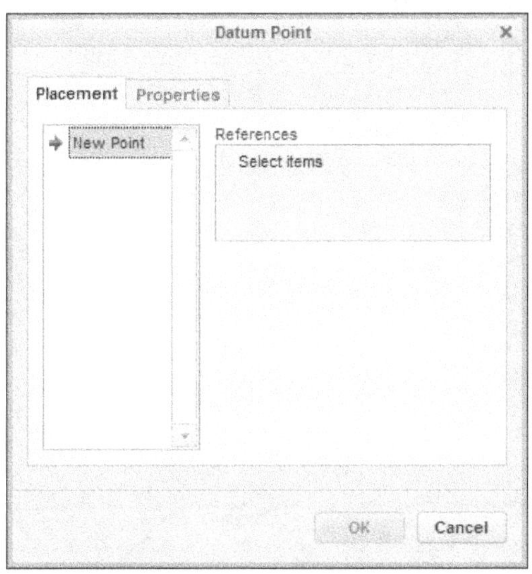

Figure-13. Datum Point dialog box

- Click on a plane. The point will be placed and you are asked to specify references for the point; refer to Figure-14.

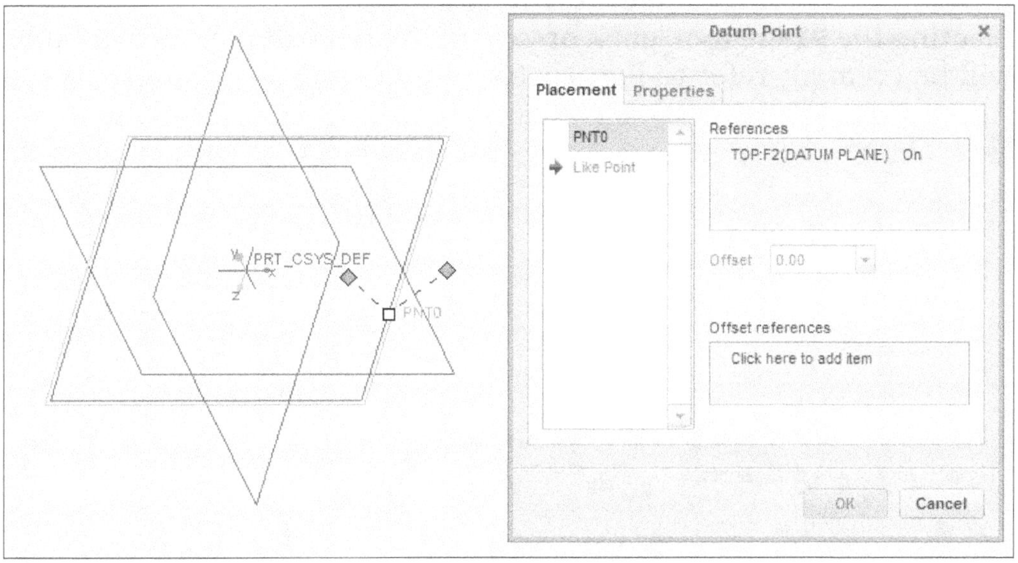

Figure-14. Datum Point placed

- Drag the handles or use the Offset references to select the references for locating the point.
- You can also select vertex of a solid model. The datum point will be created on the selected vertex.

Plane

Plane acts as a transparent floor for any feature. All the sketches that we made in earlier chapters are made on top planes. If we bring those sketches in the part environment then you can easily find it. By default, three planes are displayed in part environment named; TOP, FRONT, and RIGHT. These planes also act as reference for the planes that we are going to create in the next steps:

- Click on the **Plane** tool from the **Datum** panel in the **Model** tab of the **Ribbon**. The **Datum Plane** dialog box will be displayed; refer to Figure-15. Also, you are asked to select the entities.

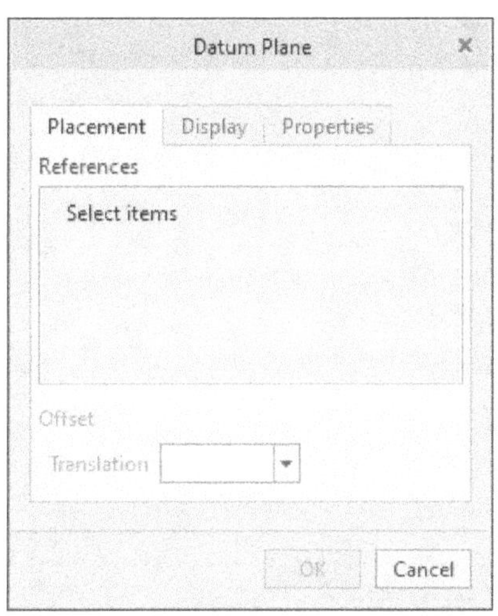

Figure-15. Datum Plane dialog box

Selecting a Plane

- After selecting the **Plane** tool, click on one of the default planes available. An offset plane will be created; refer to Figure-16.

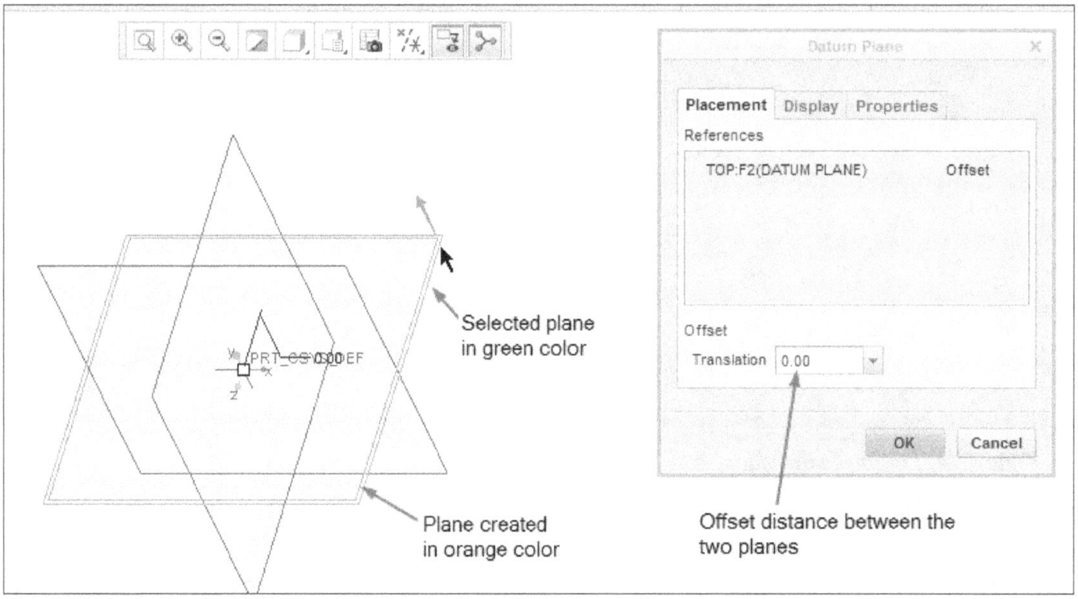

Figure-16. Offset plane created

- Specify desired offset distance in the edit box of the **Datum Plane** dialog box.
- After specifying desired distance, click on the **OK** button from the dialog box to create the plane.

Selecting Axis and Plane

- After selecting the **Plane** tool from **Datum** panel, select an axis and a plane parallel to the selected axis while holding the **CTRL** key. The plane will be displayed as shown in Figure-17.

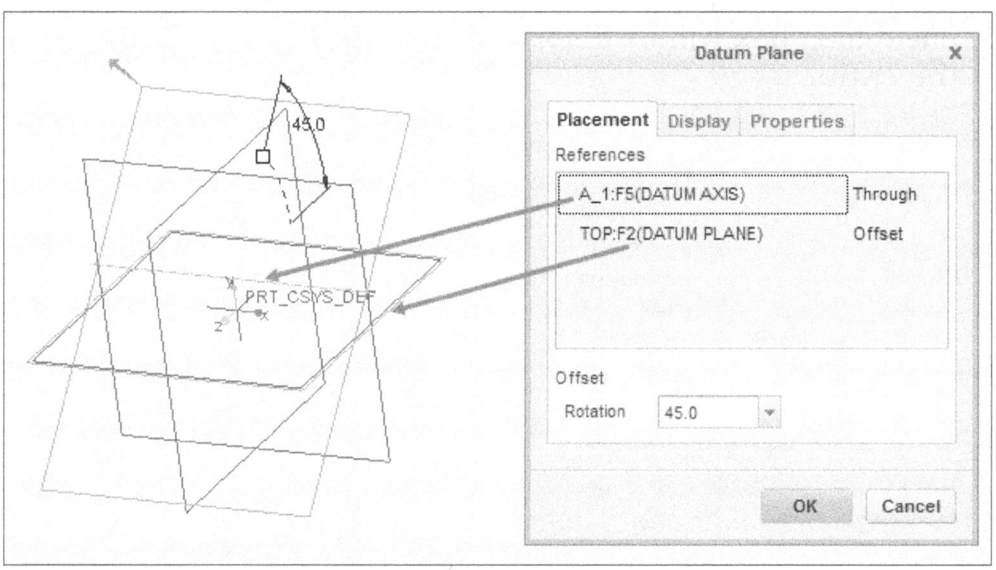

Figure-17. Datum plane with axis selected

- Double-click on the angle value to change it.
- You can also create a plane by selecting two parallel axes; refer to Figure-18.

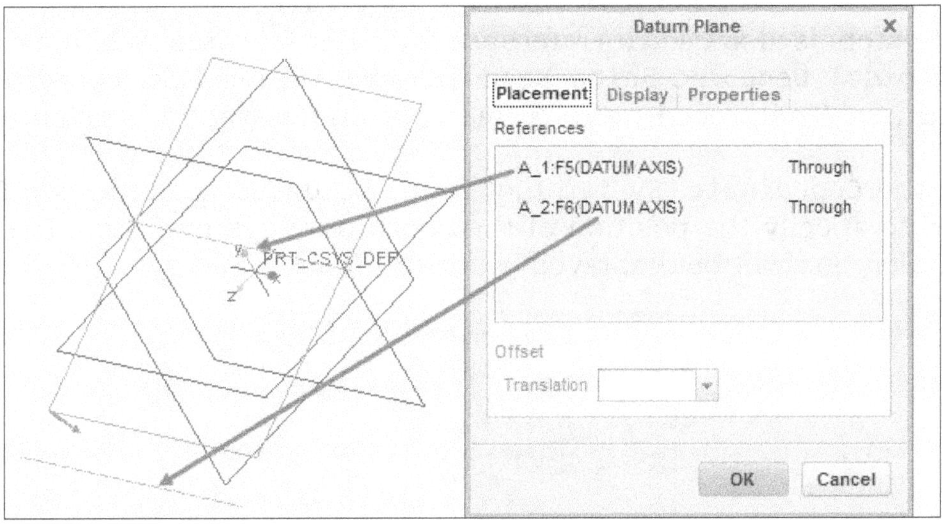

Figure-18. Datum plane by two axes

- Similarly, you can create a plane by selecting an axis and a point; refer to Figure-19.

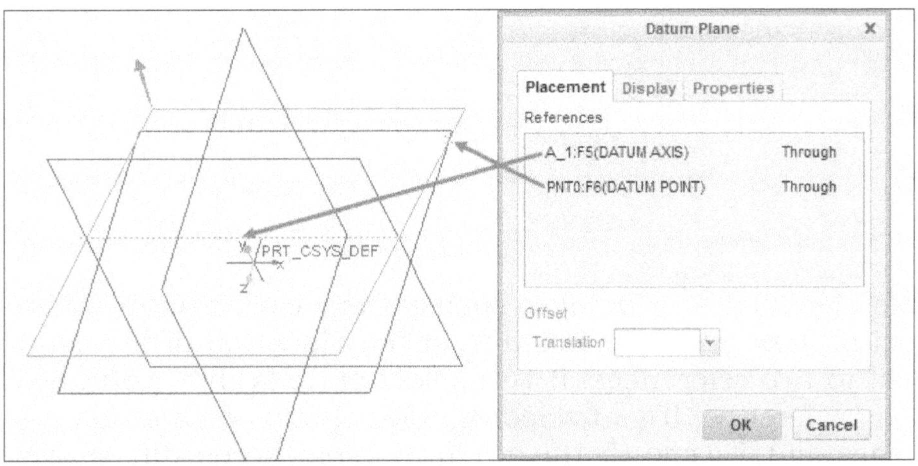

Figure-19. Plane by axis and point

Selecting Points

- After selecting the **Plane** tool, one by one select the datum points while holding the **CTRL** key to create a plane. The plane will be created passing through the selected points; refer to Figure-20.

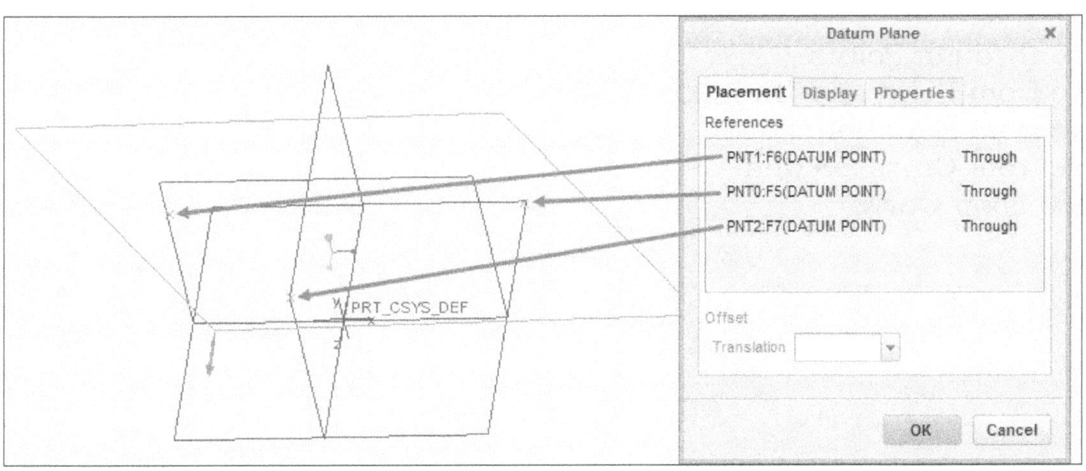

Figure-20. Datum plane created by points

Coordinate System

Coordinate System is also used as reference for other features. When we will work on tools like **Toroidal Bend** and **Spine Bend** then we will need the coordinate systems to create features. The procedure to create coordinate system is given next.

- Click on the **Coordinate System** tool from the **Datum** panel in the **Ribbon**. You are asked to specify the position of the coordinate system. Also, the **Coordinate System** dialog box will be displayed; refer to Figure-21.

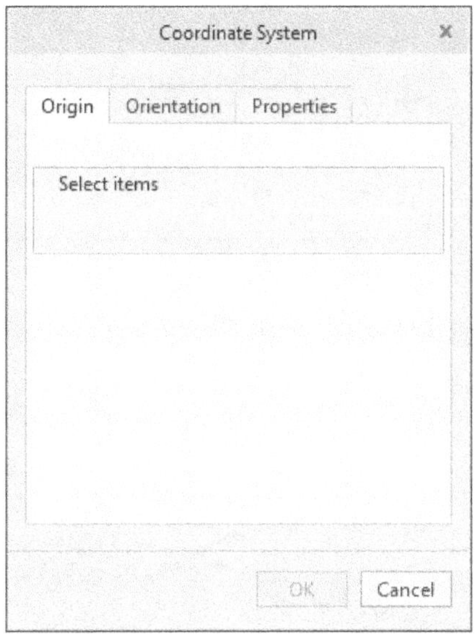

Figure-21. Coordinate System dialog box

- Click on the plane, axis, or point to specify the location of the coordinate system. If you select a plane, you are asked to specify location of the coordinate system with respect to two references. If you select an axis then you need to select one more axis as reference. If you select a point then the coordinate system will be placed on the point. To specify the orientation of the coordinate system, you need to select edges. We will learn more about them in practical sessions.

Curves

Curves are used to reference features that need path for their creation like, sweep, swept blend, and so on. There are three tools available to create datum curves: refer to Figure-22.

1. Curve through Points
2. Curve from Point and Direction
3. Curve from Equation
4. Curve from Cross Section
5. Closed Loop Curve

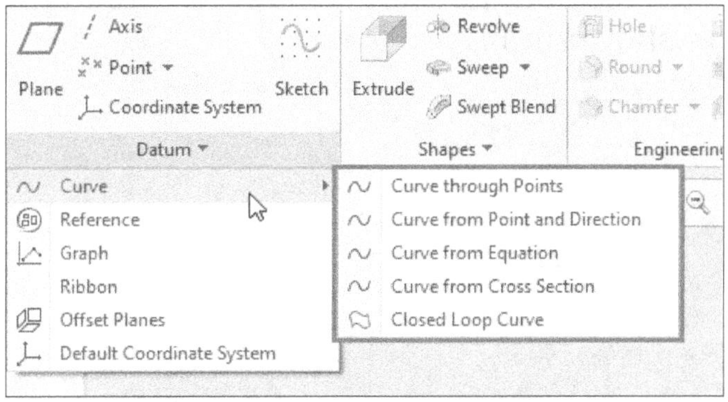

Figure-22. Tools for Datum Curves

Curve Through Points

The **Curve through Points** tool, as the name suggests, is used to create datum curve passing through the selected points. The procedure to create curves by using this tool is given next.

- Select the **Curve through Points** tool from the **Curve** menu in the expanded **Datum** panel of the **Ribbon**; refer to Figure-22. The **CURVE: Through Points** contextual tab will be displayed in the **Ribbon**; refer to Figure-23.

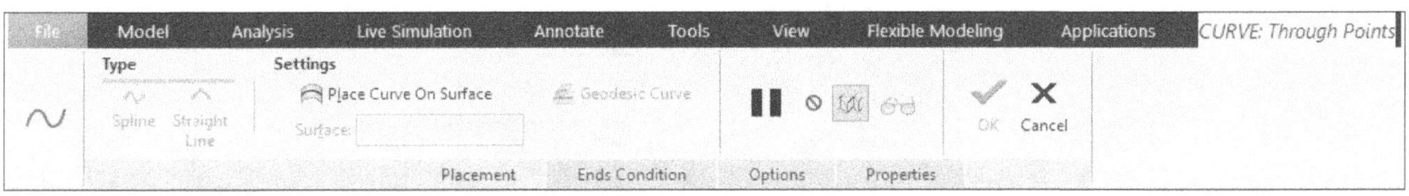

Figure-23. Curve Through Points dashboard

- One by one select the datum point while holding the **CTRL** key. The datum curve will be generated; refer to Figure-24.

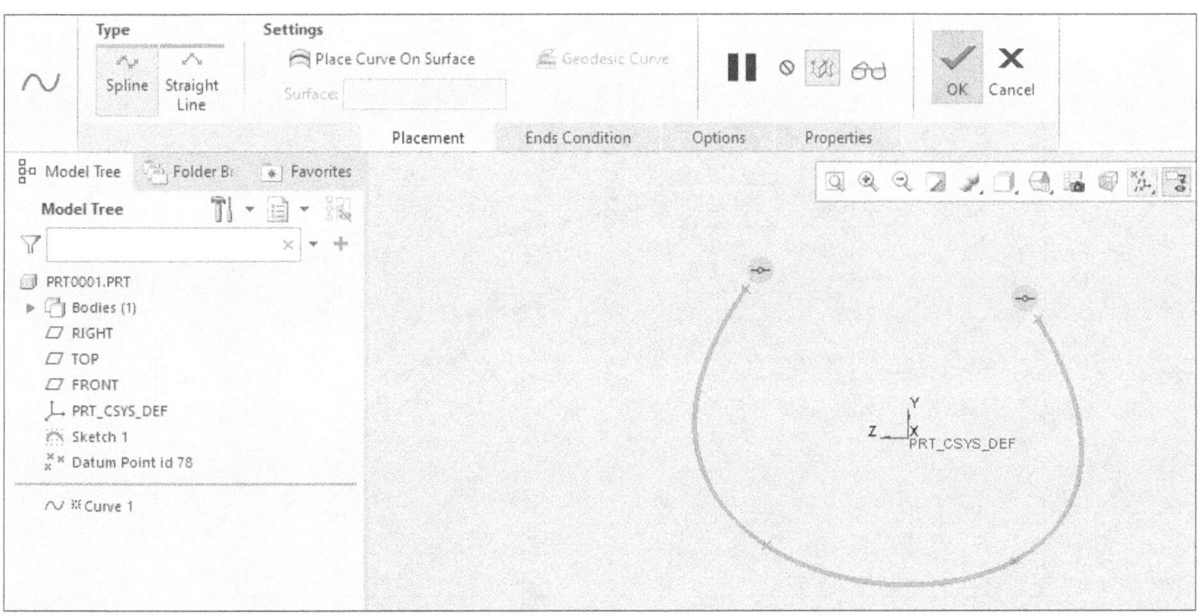

Figure-24. Datum curve through points

- You can change the curvature of the curve by selecting the two buttons highlighted in the box shown in Figure-24 after selecting each curve point.

- After selecting points, click on the **Ends Condition** tab in the **Ribbon**. The options will be displayed as shown in Figure-25.

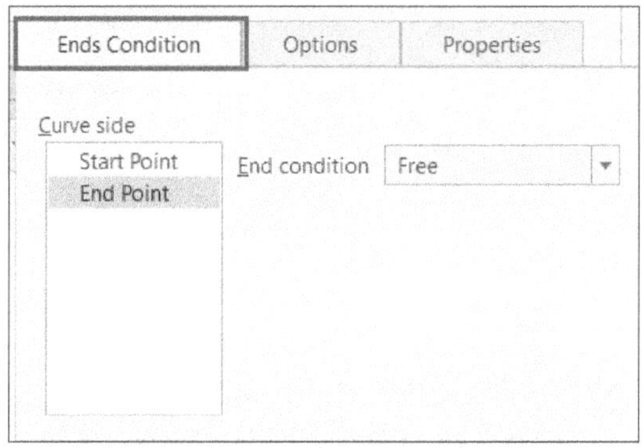

Figure-25. Ends Condition tab

- Using the options, you can change the start and end point conditions of the curve; like you can make the curve tangent to plane/edge/axis at the start point or end points.
- For example, to make the curve tangent to selected axis at end point, click on the **End condition** drop-down and select the **Tangent** option; refer to Figure-26. You are asked to select the entity to which the curve should be tangent.

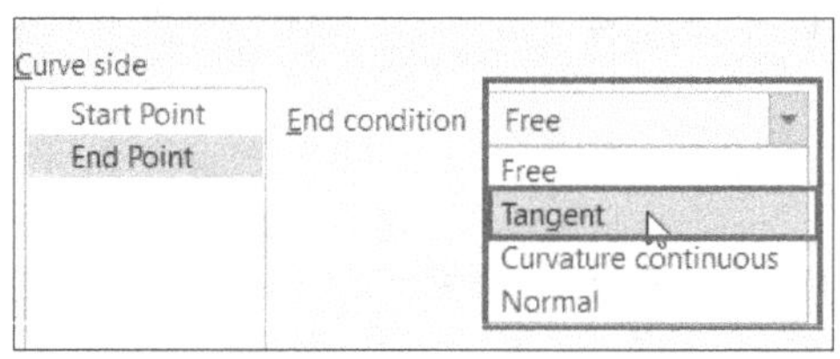

Figure-26. Tangent option for End condition

- Select the axis/edge/plane as reference. Preview of the curve will be displayed; refer to Figure-27.

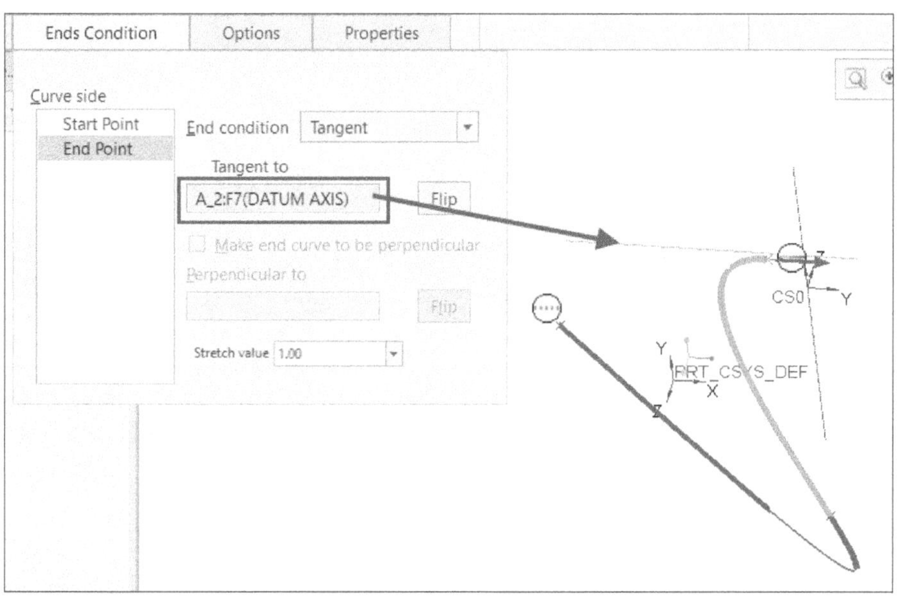

Figure-27. Preview of tangent curve

- Similarly, you can use the other options in the drop-down.

Curve From Point and Direction

The **Curve From Point and Direction** tool is used to create a geodesic curve (shortest path/arc between two points) on a surface by defining a start point and a direction. The procedure to create curves by using this tool is discussed next.

- Select the **Curve From Point and Direction** tool from the **Curve** menu in the expanded **Datum** panel of the **Ribbon**; refer to Figure-22. The **Curve: From Point and Direction** contextual tab will be displayed in the **Ribbon**; refer to Figure-28. You are asked to select the datum point.

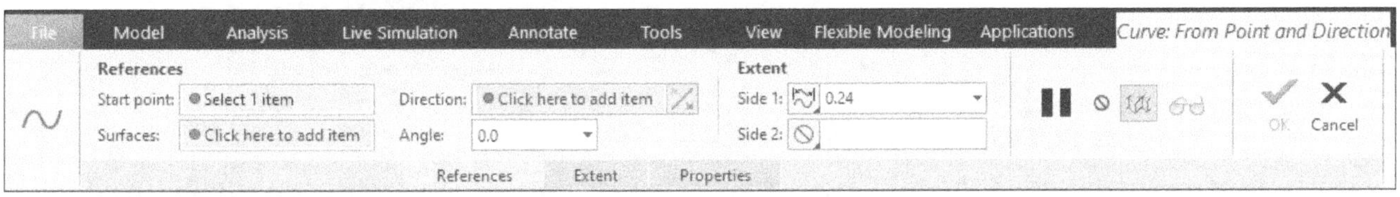

Figure-28. Curve From Point and Direction dashboard

- Select the datum point to define the start point of the curve; refer to Figure-29. You are asked to select the surface.

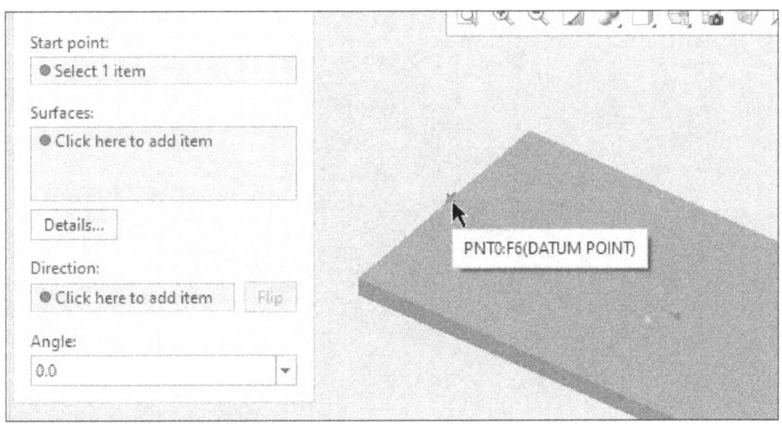

Figure-29. Selecting the point

- Select the surface on which you want to place the curve; refer to Figure-30. You will be asked to define the direction.

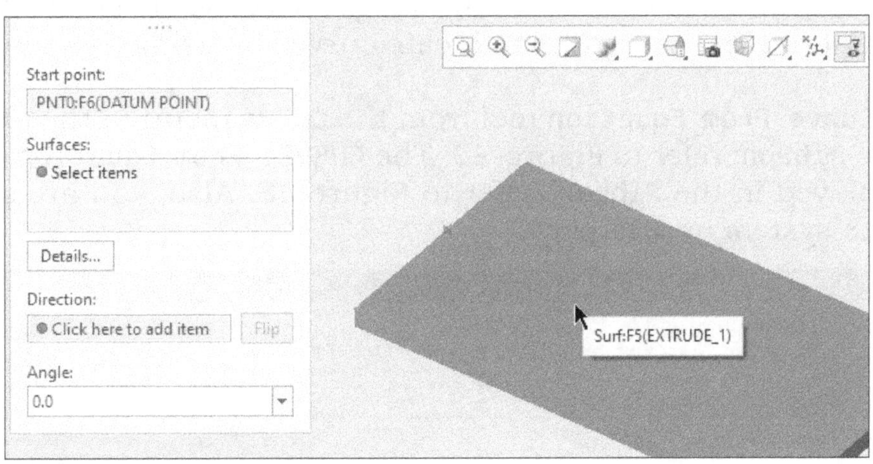

Figure-30. Selecting the surface

- Select an edge or a surface to define the direction of the curve; refer to Figure-31.

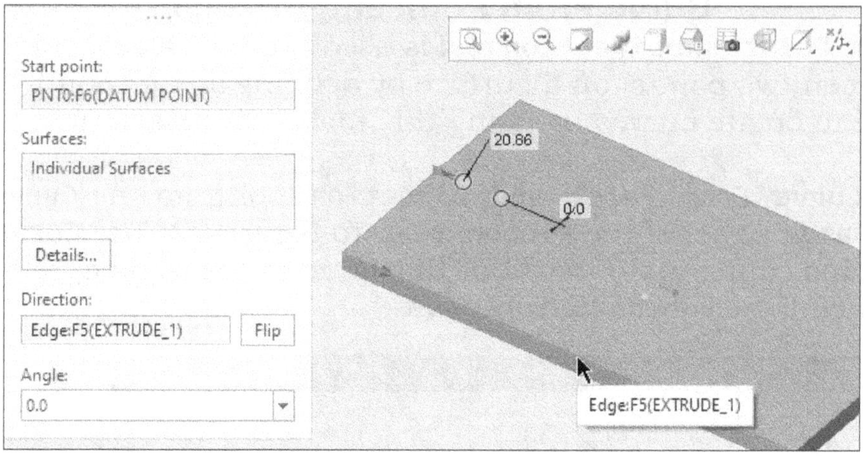

Figure-31. Defining the direction

- Specify desired angle between the curve and the given direction and specify desired length of the curve in their respective edit boxes.
- After specifying desired parameters, click on the **OK** button from the contextual tab. The curve will be created; refer to Figure-32.

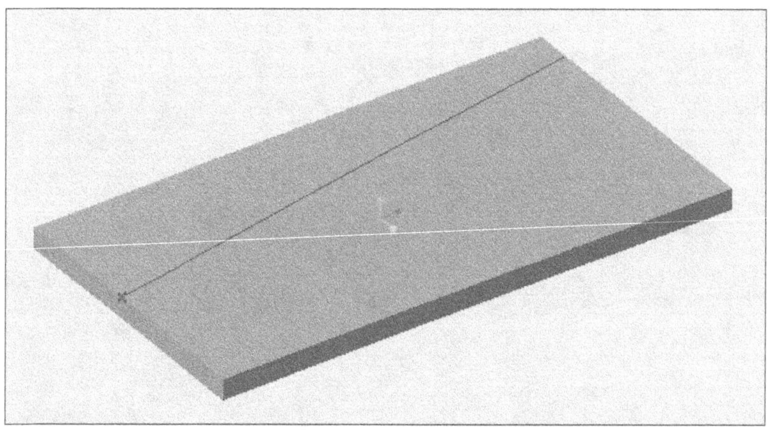

Figure-32. Curve from point and direction created

Curve From Equation

The **Curve From Equation** tool, as the name suggests, is used to create datum curve by solving the equation. The procedure to create curves by using this tool is given next.

- Select the **Curve From Equation** tool from the **Curve** menu in the expanded **Datum** panel of the **Ribbon**; refer to Figure-22. The **CURVE: From Equation** contextual tab will be displayed in the **Ribbon**; refer to Figure-33. Also, you are asked to select a coordinate system as reference.

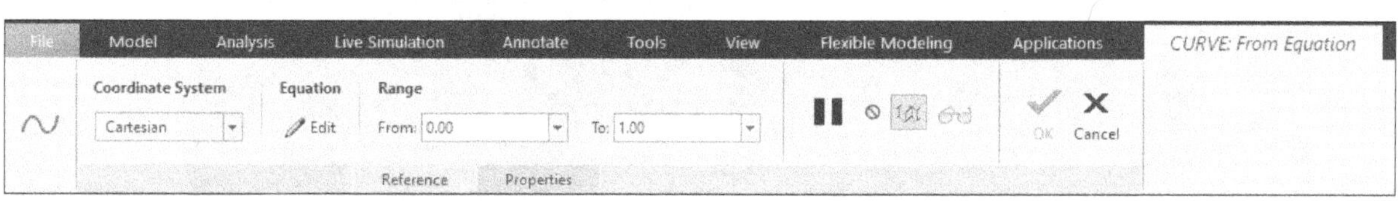

Figure-33. Curve From Equation dashboard

- Select the coordinate system from the modeling area.
- Click on the **Edit** button from **Equation** area of the dashboard. The **Equation** dialog box will be displayed; refer to Figure-34.

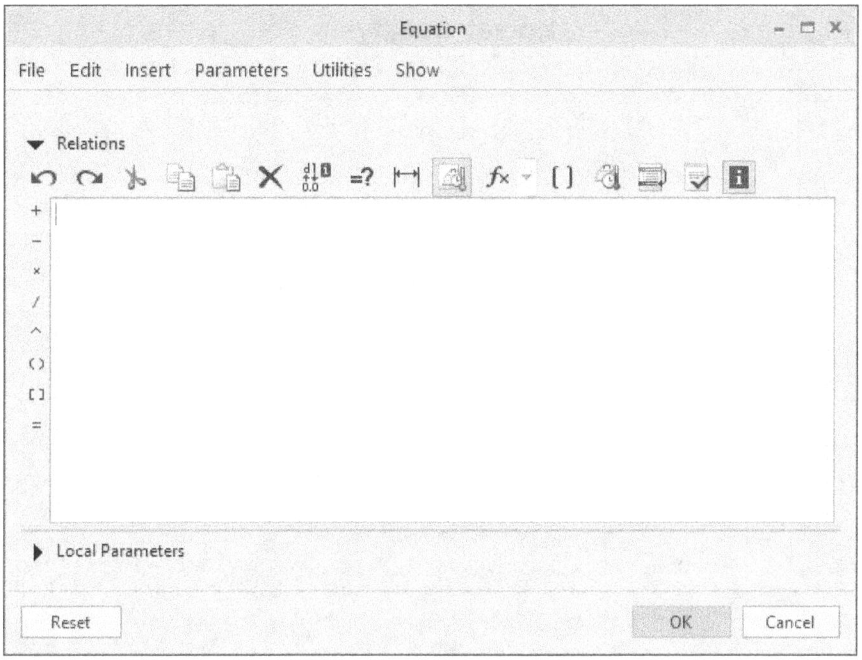

Figure-34. Equation dialog box

- Specify desired equation in the dialog box, for example:

X=t*2+t^2+cos(t)
Y=sin(t)
Z=50*sin(t/2)

- Click on the **OK** button from the dialog box and then click on the **OK** button from the dashboard. The curve will be created; refer to Figure-35.

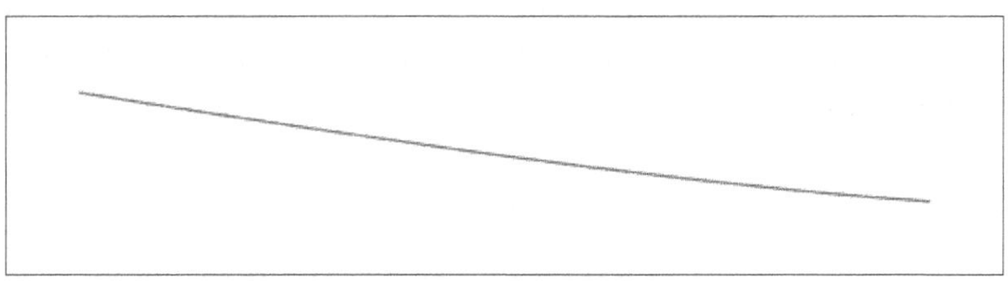

Figure-35. Curve by equation

Note that if you want higher display quality of edges as shown in Figure-36, then click on the **Options** tool from the **File** menu. The **Creo Parametric Options** dialog box will be displayed. Click on the **Entity Display** option from left area of the dialog box and select desired edge display quality from **Edge display quality** drop-down and turn **On** the **Lines Anti-Aliasing** option in the **Geometry display settings** area; refer to Figure-37. Although display quality of curves is improved by these teps, you will find major quality improvements in 3D model edges.

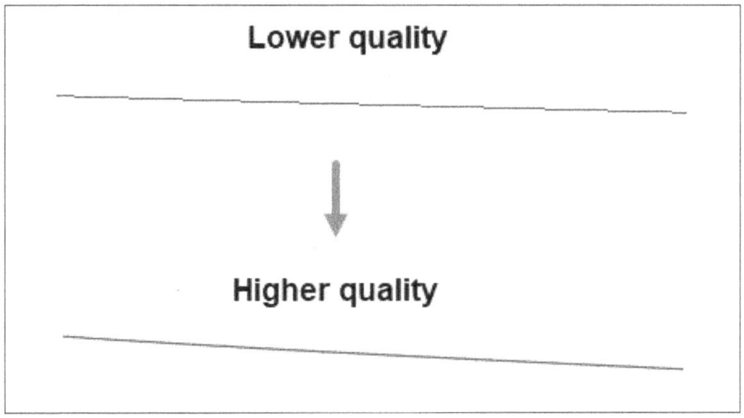

Figure-36. Display quality of edges

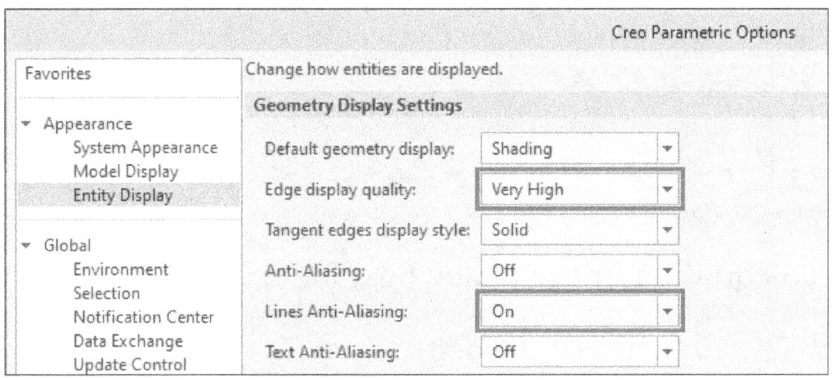

Figure-37. Entity Display options

Curve From Cross-section

The **Curve From Cross-section** tool, as the name suggests, is used to create datum curve by using the cross-section of a solid model. Note that for using this tool, you must have a solid/surface cross-section in the drawing area like the one shown in Figure-38. (You will learn about creating cross-sections later in this book) The procedure to use this tool is given next.

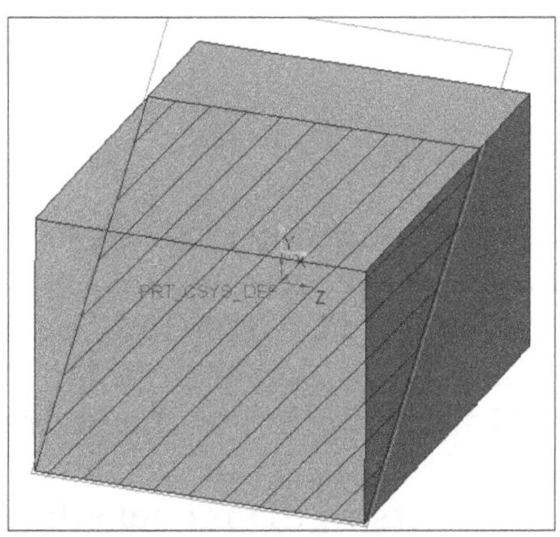
Figure-38. Cross-section created

- Click on the **Curve From Cross-section** tool from the **Curve** menu in the expanded **Datum** panel of the **Ribbon**. If there are more than one cross-section in the drawing area then the **CURVE** contextual tab will be displayed in the **Ribbon**; refer to Figure-39. If there is only one cross-section in the drawing area then the curve will be generated at the boundaries of cross-section.

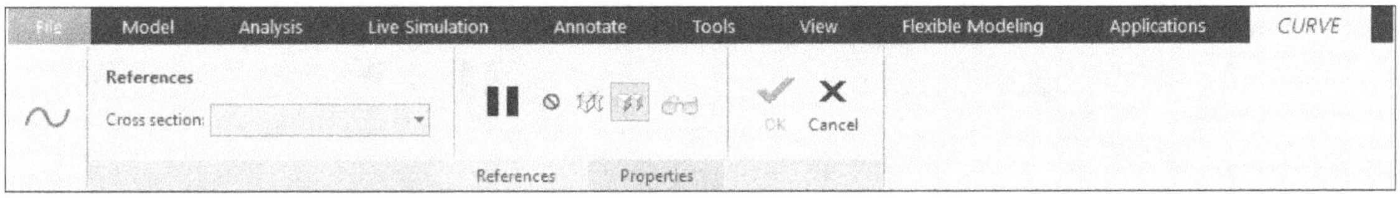

Figure-39. CURVE contextual tab

- If you have two or more cross-sections to select from then click in the **Cross-section** drop-down from **References** area of the **Ribbon** and select desired cross-section. Preview of the curve will be displayed; refer to Figure-40.

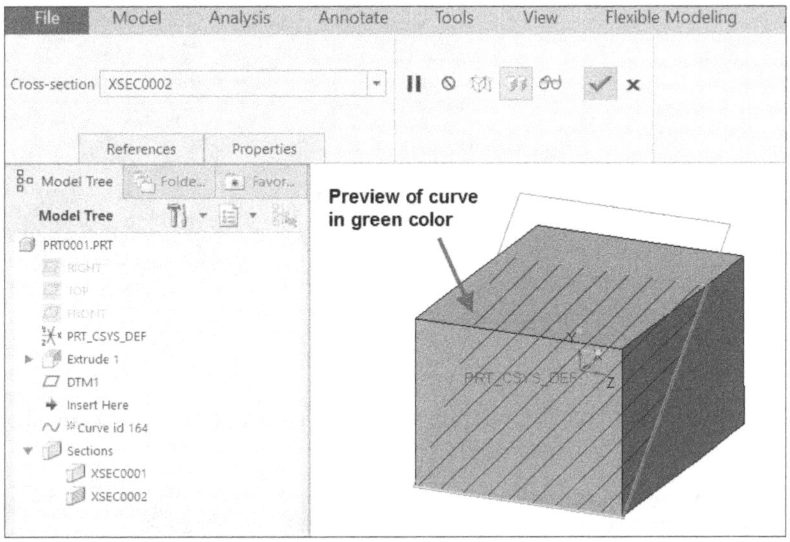

Figure-40. Preview of cross-section curve

- Click on the **OK** button from the **Ribbon** to create the curve.

Closed Loop Curve

The **Closed Loop Curve** tool is used to create a closed loop curve on a surface, quilt, plane, or body. The procedure to use this tool is discussed next.

- Click on the **Closed Loop Curve** tool from the **Curve** menu in the expanded **Datum** panel of the **Ribbon**. The **CURVE: Closed Loop** contextual tab will be displayed; refer to Figure-41. You are asked to select the placement reference.

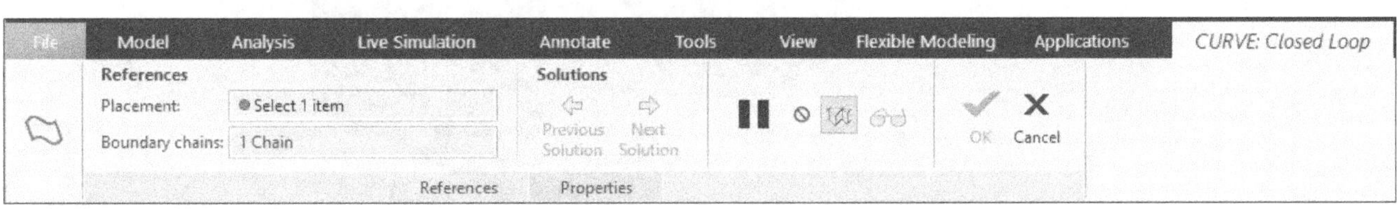

Figure-41. Curve Closed Loop contextual tab

- Select face of the model on which you want to place the loop curve; refer to Figure-42. You are asked to select the curve.

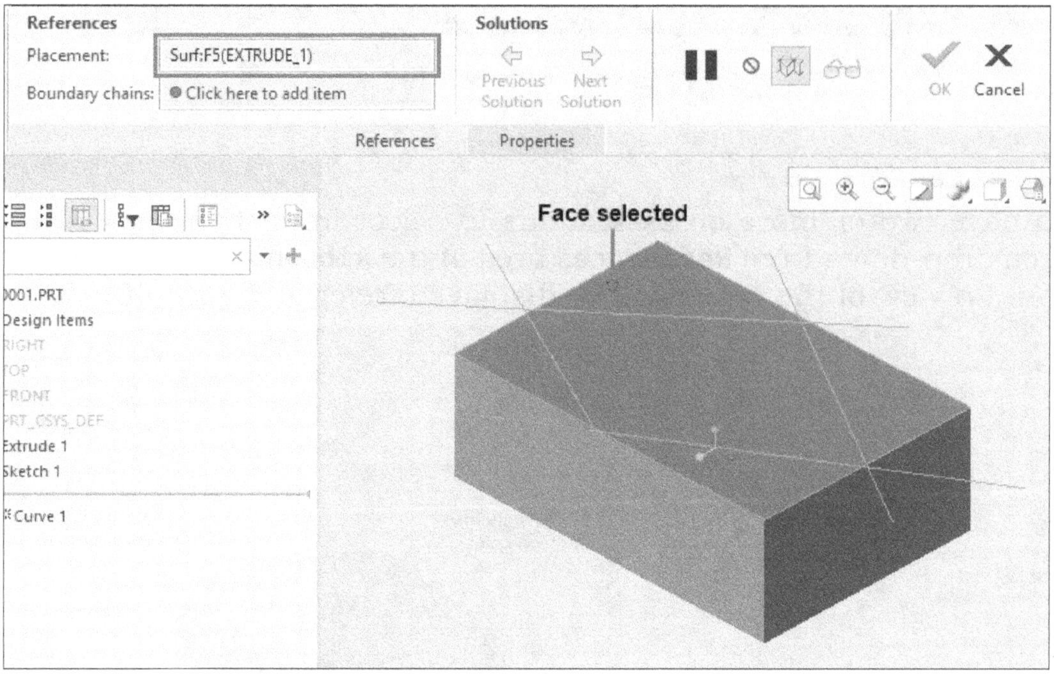

Figure-42. Face selected for placement

- Select desired curves in the drawing area to create the closed loop curve; refer to Figure-43.

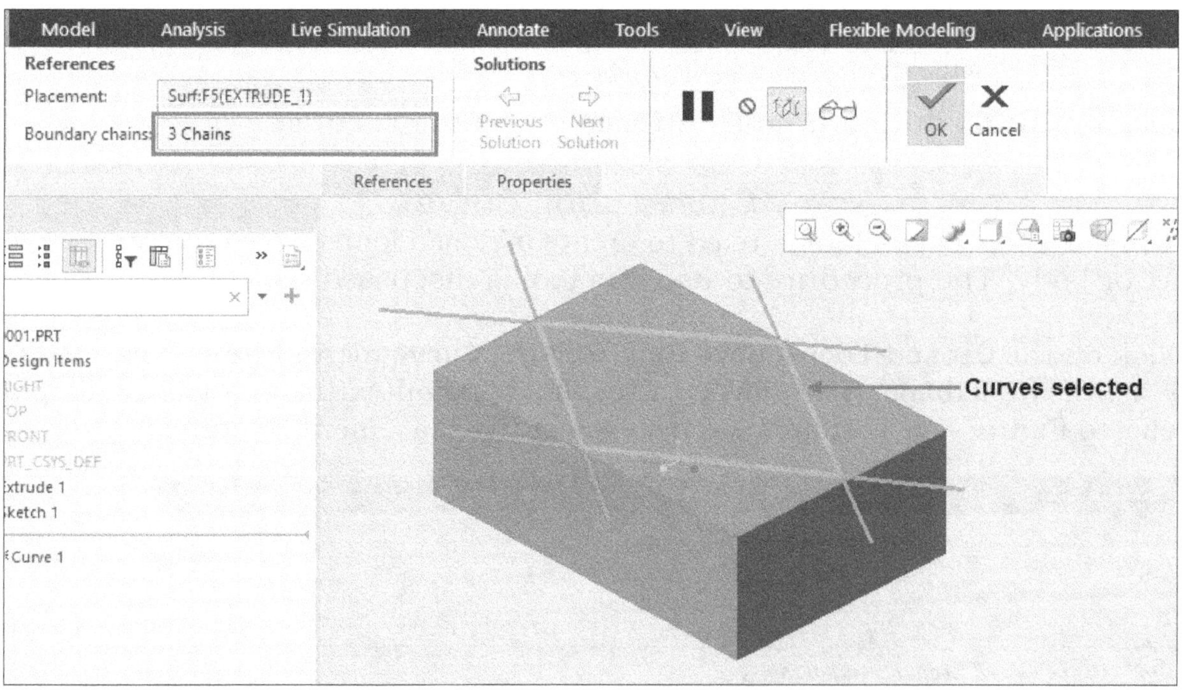

Figure-43. Curves selected

- After specifying desired parameters, click on the **OK** button from the contextual tab. The closed loop curve will be created; refer to Figure-44.

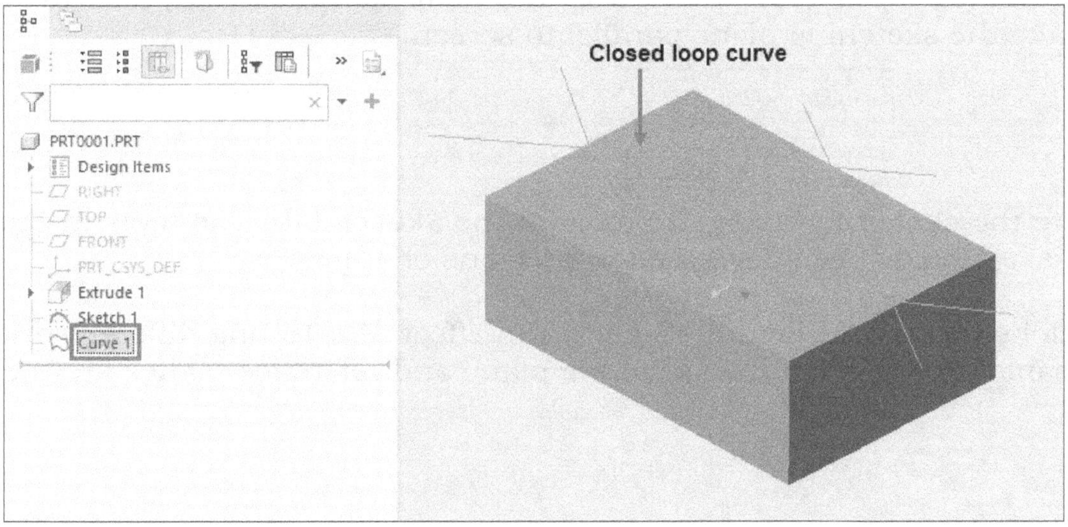

Figure-44. Closed loop curve created

You will learn about other tools of the **Datum** panel later in the book.

CREATING SKETCHES ON PLANES

We have created many sketches in previous chapter. Now, we will start creating sketches on planes. The procedure to create a sketch on a plane is given next.

- Click on the **Sketch** button from the **Datum** panel in the **Ribbon**. The **Sketch** dialog box will be displayed; refer to Figure-45. Also, you are asked to select a sketching plane.
- Select desired plane from the planes available. The sketch will be created on the selected plane.
- On selecting a plane, the references are automatically selected in the **Reference** selection box; refer to Figure-46.
- Note that the orientation of the sketch in 3D environment is based on the selected reference plane and the options selected in the reference plane. Also, without specifying the reference plane and orientation, you can not start sketching.
- After selecting desired planes, click on the **Sketch** button from the dialog box. The sketching plane will be displayed as shown in Figure-47. Also, the tools related to sketching will be displayed in the **Sketch** tab of the **Ribbon**.

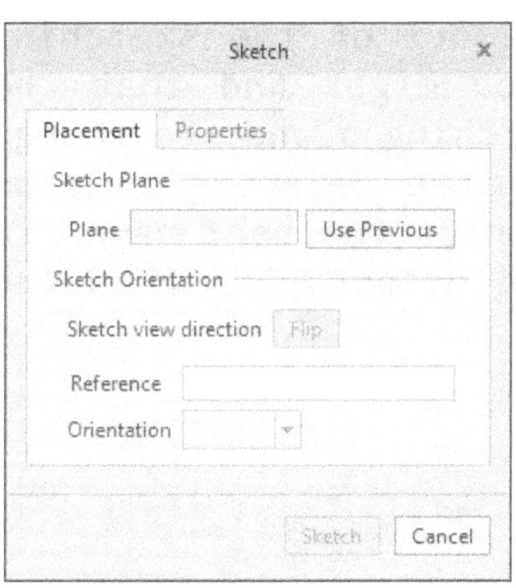

Figure-45. Sketch dialog box

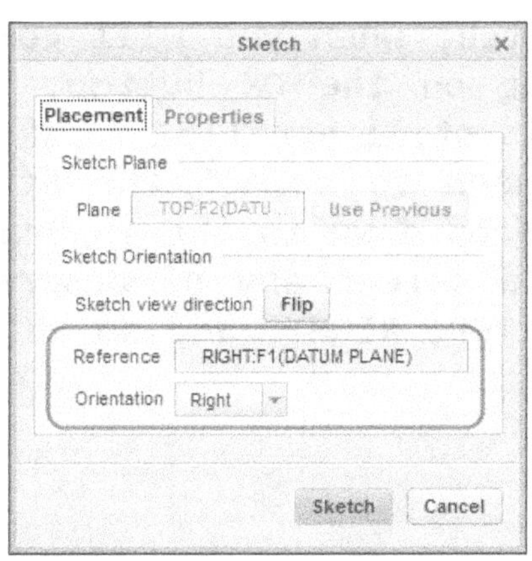

Figure-46. Reference selection box in Sketch dialog box

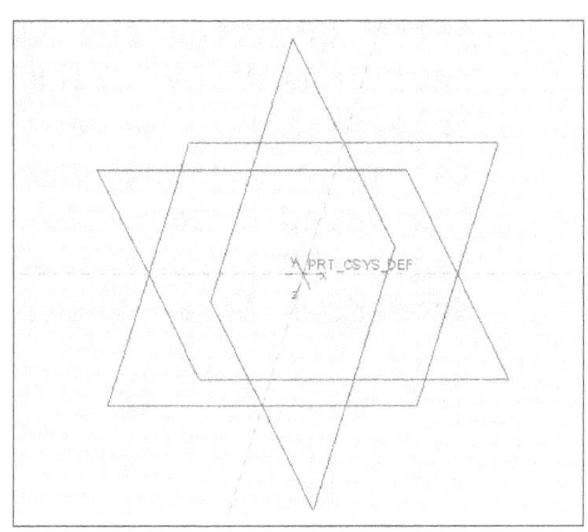

Figure-47. Sketching plane

- Click on the **Sketch View** button from the **In-Graphics** toolbar; refer to Figure-48 to make the sketching plane parallel to screen.

Figure-48. Sketch View button

- Create the sketch by using the tools in the **Sketch** tab. The tools in the **Sketch** tab have already been discussed in previous chapters.

The sketches shown in Figure-49 show the effect of selecting different orientation for the same sketch when the sketching plane and reference planes are the same.

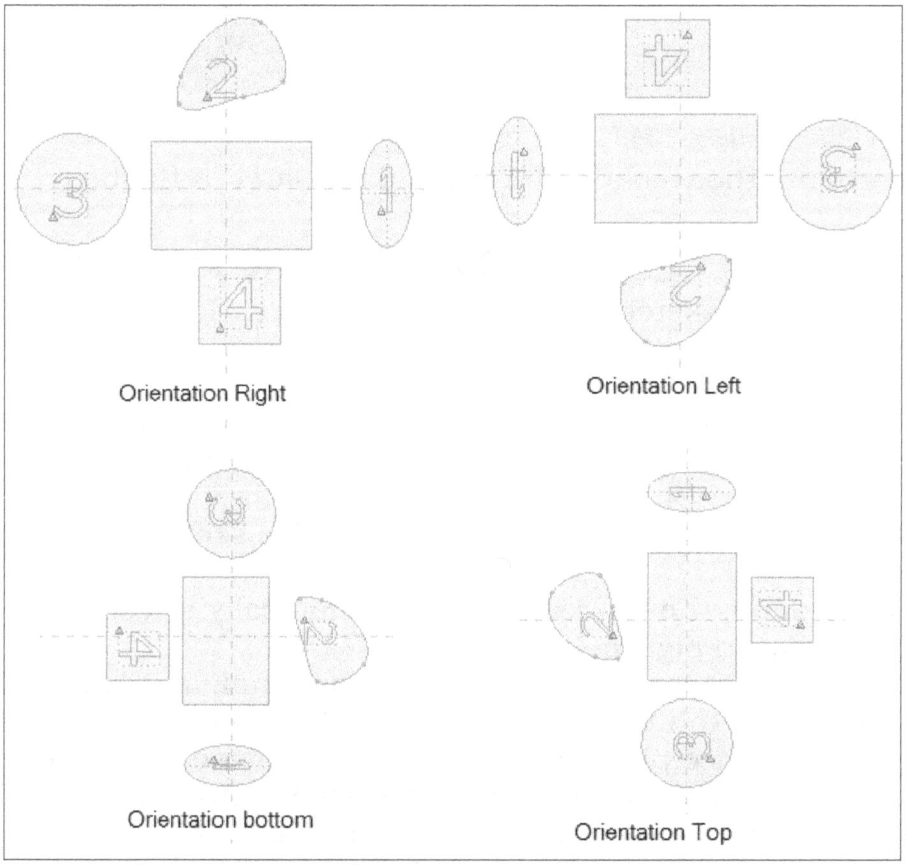

Figure-49. Effect of orientation on sketch

After creating the sketch, when you will come out of the sketching environment by clicking on the OK button, you might find that the orientation of screen is still parallel to sketching plane. To change the orientation, you need to select the Standard Orientation from the Saved Orientation drop-down in the In-Graphics toolbar; refer to Figure-50. You can also select any of desired orientation from the drop-down like, FRONT, TOP, RIGHT, and so on.

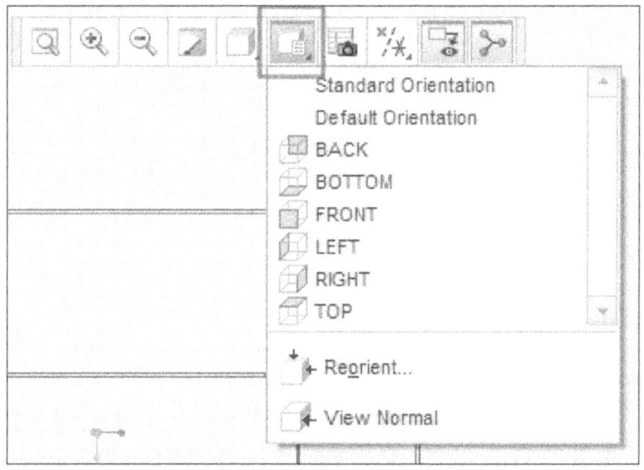

Figure-50. Saved Orientation drop-down

CREATING 3D FEATURES

Creo Parametric is a compact software with tools to create 3D features of any type. Each 3D feature tool is able to perform in many ways with combination to geometric constraints to create very simple to most complex 3D models. Tools to create 3D features are available in the **Shapes** panel of the **Model** tab in the **Ribbon**; refer to Figure-51. These tools are discussed next.

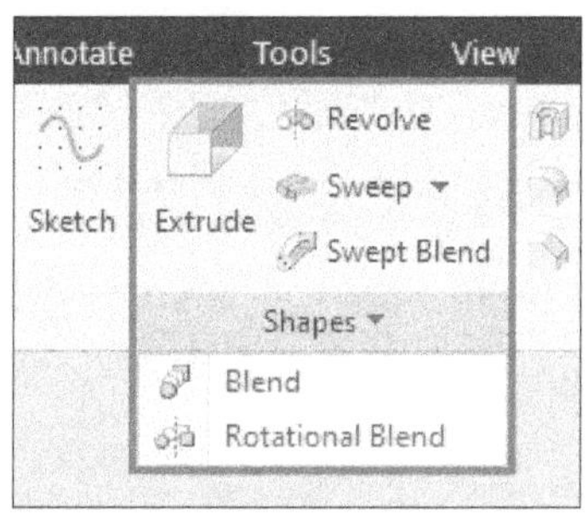

Figure-51. Shapes panel

EXTRUDE

The **Extrude** tool is used to create solids by using the volume swept by a close sketch while moving along perpendicular direction. The perpendicular movement is called the height of extrusion. It is somewhat similar to extrusion process in mechanical engineering. The procedure to create extrude feature is given next.

- Click on the **Extrude** tool from the **Shapes** panel in the **Ribbon**. The **Extrude** contextual tab will be displayed; refer to Figure-52.

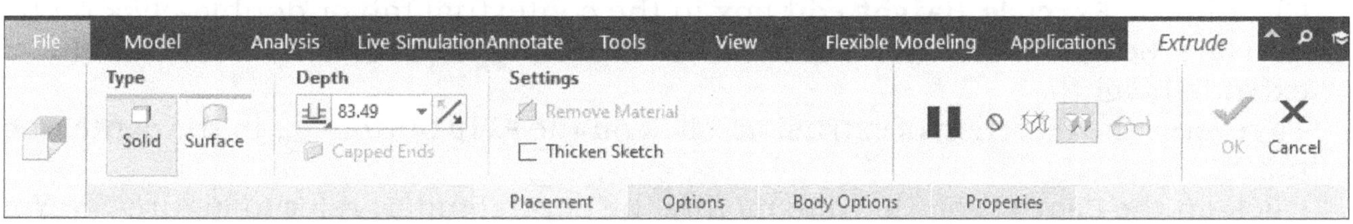

Figure-52. Extrude contextual tab

- Click on the **Placement** tab from the contextual tab. The **Placement** options will be displayed; refer to Figure-53.
- If you have a sketch already created then select the sketch. Otherwise, click on the **Define** button from the **Sketch** area of **Placement** tab. The **Sketch** dialog box will be displayed as discussed earlier.

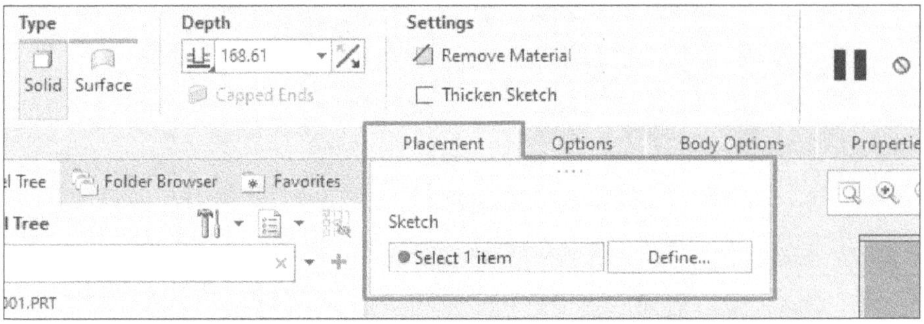

Figure-53. Placement options

- Select desired planes and create the sketch. Note that sketch for extrude feature need to fulfill some requirements. You can check the requirements of the feature by clicking on the **Feature Requirements** button from the **Inspect** panel in the contextual **Sketch** tab. On selecting this button, the **Feature Requirements** dialog box will be displayed showing the feature requirements; refer to Figure-54.

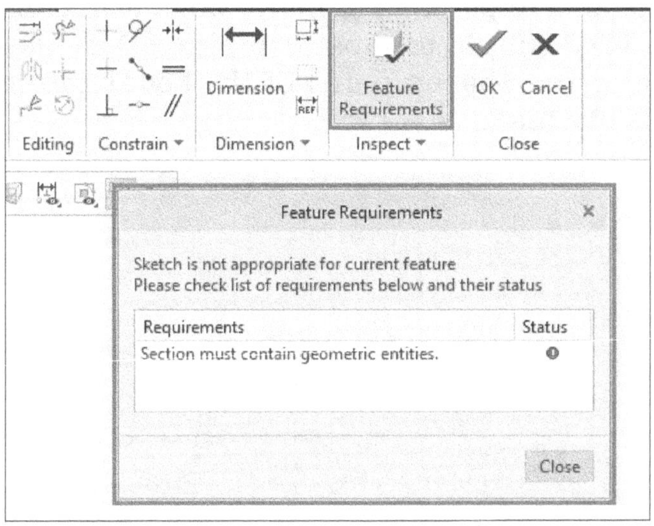

Figure-54. Feature requirements

- So, make sure you have geometric entities in sketch. After creating geometric entities again check the feature requirement. You will find some more requirements. Fulfill them all. **To summarize, we need a sketch with geometric entities in the form of single or multiple closed loops not intersecting or overlapping each other**.
- On selecting a closed sketch, the preview of extrude feature is displayed in the modeling area; refer to Figure-55.
- Click in the **Extrude Height** edit box in the contextual tab or double-click on the **Extrude Height** dimension value in the modeling area. Specify desired value of extrude height.
- To reverse the direction of extrusion, click on the **Flip** button  in the contextual tab.
- Click on the **Depth** drop-down to modify the depth limiter; refer to Figure-56. You can also use the **Depth** button in **Mini toolbar** displayed on hovering cursor on the depth value in dimension.

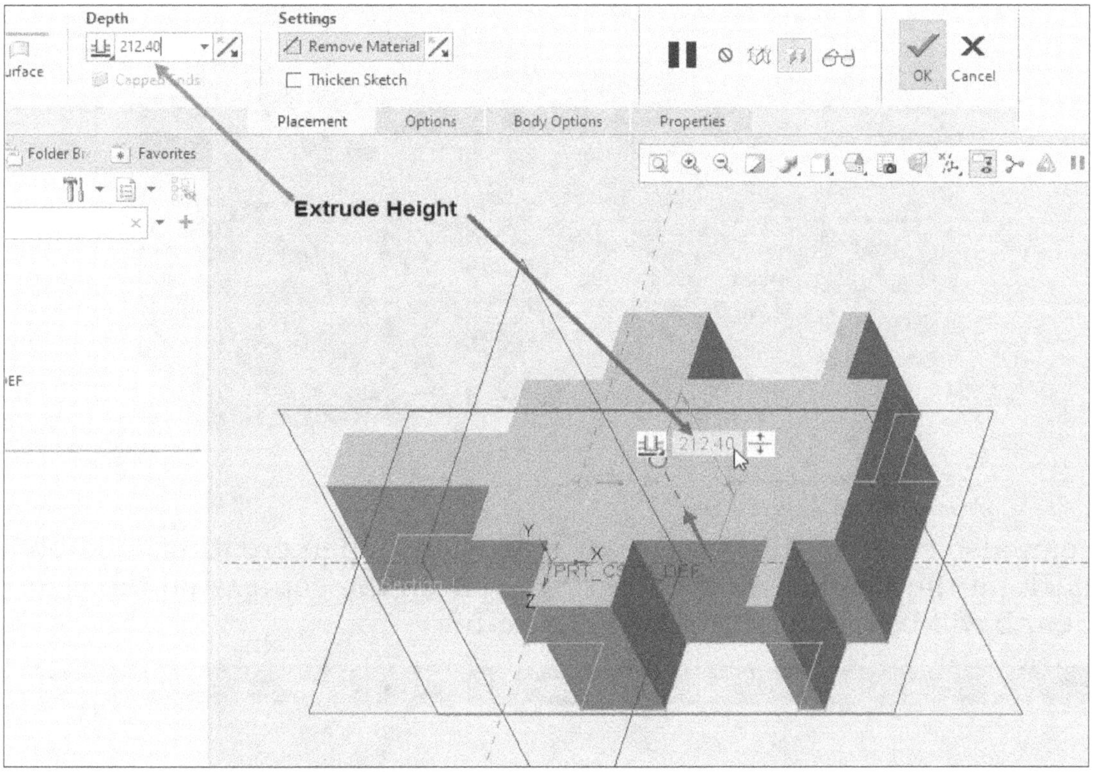

Figure-55. Preview of extrude feature

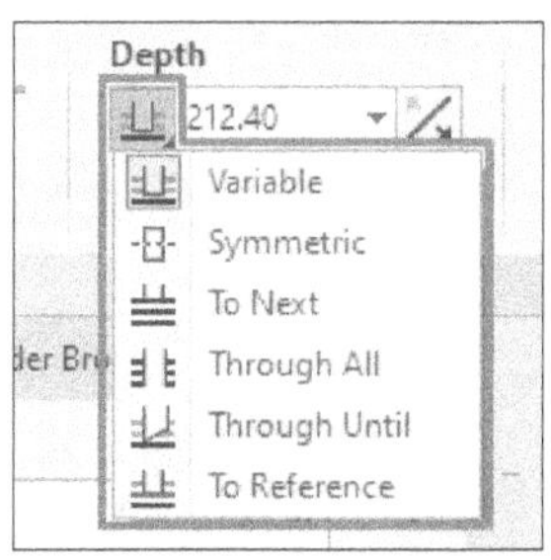

Figure-56. Depth drop-down

- Select desired limiter from the drop-down. If you have selected the **Variable** option from the drop-down, then you need to specify the depth value for each side of extrusion. If you have selected the **Symmetric** button, then the extrusion will be on both sides of the selected plane by specified extrusion height; refer to Figure-57. If you have selected the **To Next** button, then the sketch will be extrude upto the next surface in its extrusion path. If you have selected the **Through All** button, then the sketch will be extrude to intersect with all surfaces in its path. If you have selected the **Through Until** button, then the sketch will be extrude to intersect with selected surface. If you have selected the **To Reference** button, then you will be asked to select a point, edge, or face upto which you want to extrude the sketch.
- Select the **Capped Ends** button from **Depth** area of the contextual tab to create closing surfaces at both ends. Note that this button is active only if **Surface** button is selected from **Type** section of the **Ribbon**. You will learn about surfaces later.

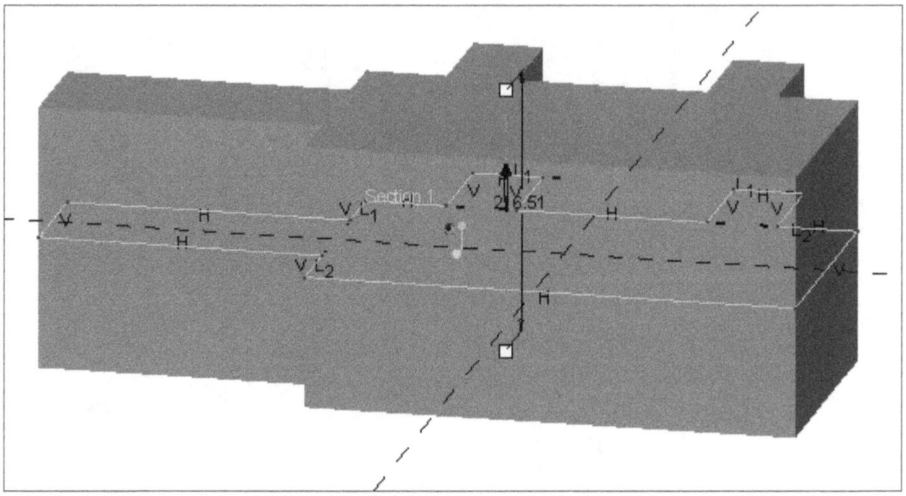

Figure-57. Extrusion both side

- You can also create a thin feature by extrusion. When creating solid body, to do so, click on the **Thicken Sketch** button from the contextual tab. The options in the tab will be modified; refer to Figure-58.

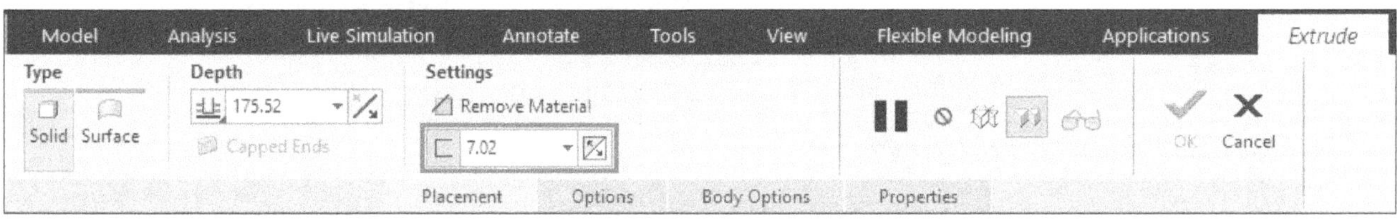

Figure-58. Thicken Sketch options

- Specify desired thickness for the section. The preview of thin feature will be displayed; refer to Figure-59.

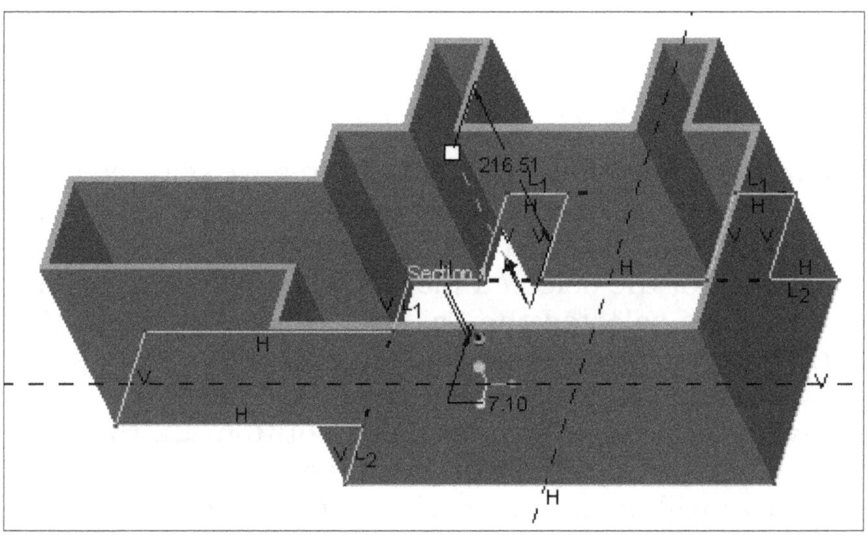

Figure-59. Thin feature preview

- The flip button next to the thickness edit box is used to switch between one side, other side, or both side thickness with respect to the sketch.
- The modifications in the extrude feature that you specified by using the tools in the contextual tab can also be specified by using the options in the **Options** tab; refer to Figure-60.

- The **Remove material** button is used to subtract material from earlier created solid. This button is active only if there is a solid feature available in the modeling area. Also, the extrusion of sketch must intersect with the solid feature for removing material; refer to Figure-61.

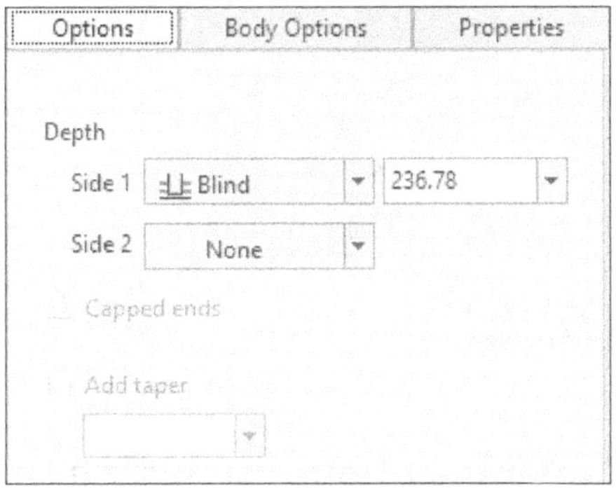

Figure-60. Options tab

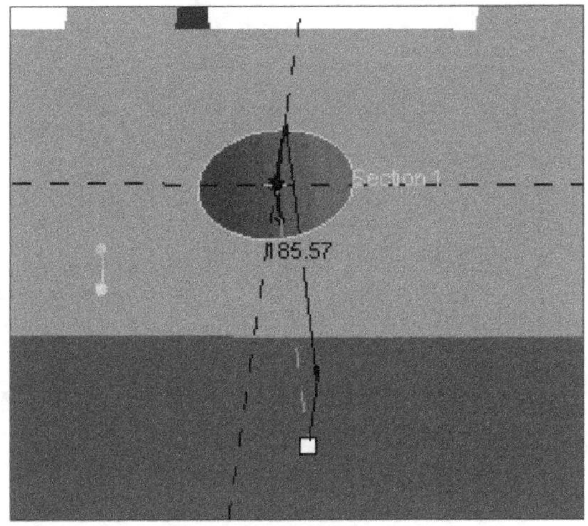

Figure-61. Material removal

- There is one more button **Extrude as surface**. This button is used to create extruded surfaces. We will learn about this button later in the book when we will be discussing about surfaces.

Note that you can use **Sketch region** selection filter if you want to extrude a specific region of intersecting sketches; refer to Figure-62. Make sure you select the sketch region before activating the protrusion tools (extrude tool, revolve tool, etc.).

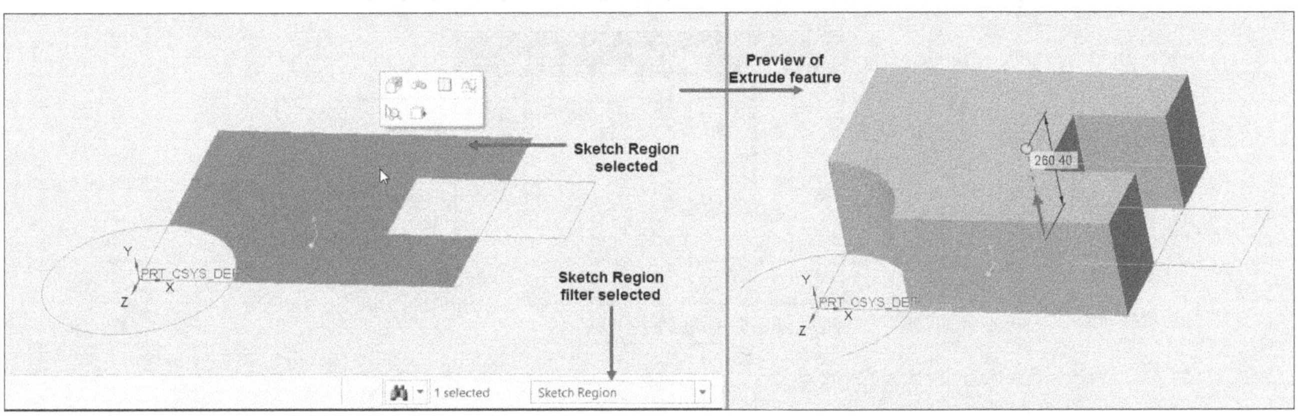

Figure-62. Extruding sketch region

- If you want to create an extrude feature as a new body then select the **Create new body** check box from **Add geometry to body** area in the **Body Options** tab of the contextual tab; refer to Figure-63. The model will be displayed as shown in Figure-64.

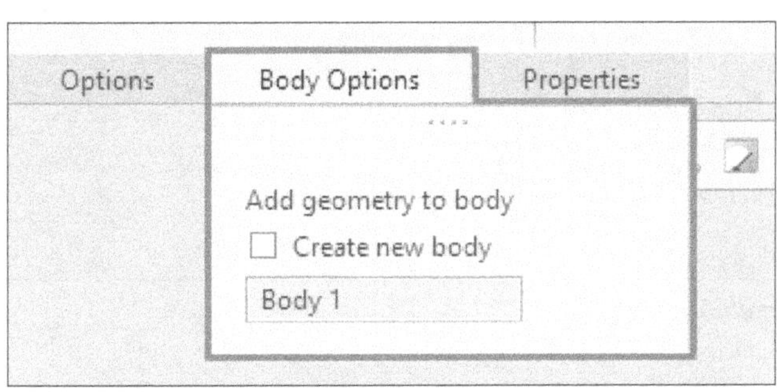

Figure-63. Body Options tab in Extrude contextual tab

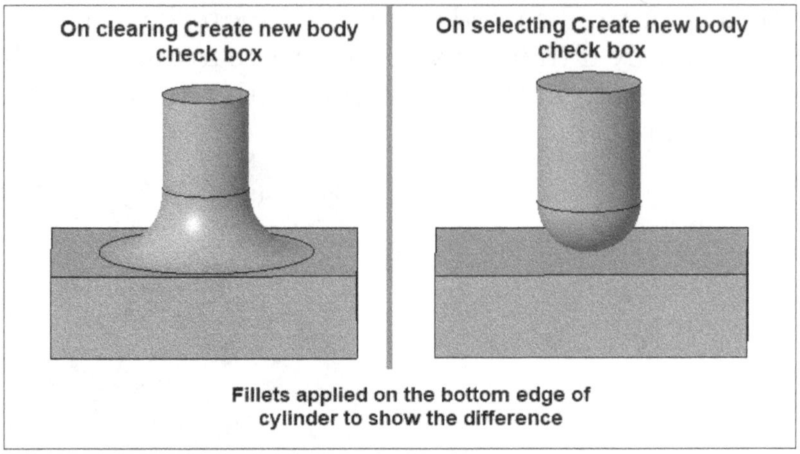

Figure-64. Use of Create new body check box

Before we move further in the modeling, we will discuss about importing the sketches so that you can practice on **Extrude** tool by using the sketches created in previous chapter.

IMPORTING SKETCHES

- Click on the **Sketch** button from the **Datum** panel. The **Sketch** dialog box will be displayed as discussed earlier.
- Select the plane on which you want to place the imported sketch and click on the **Sketch** button from the dialog box. The sketching environment will be displayed as discussed earlier.
- Click on the **Import** button from **Insert** panel in the **Ribbon**; refer to Figure-65. The **Open** dialog box will be displayed; refer to Figure-66.

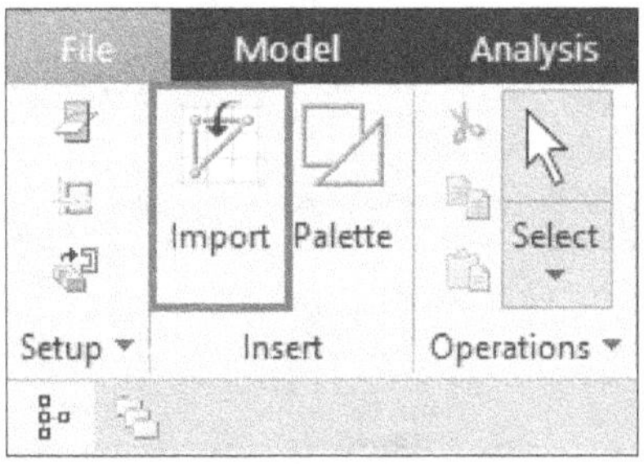

Figure-65. Import button

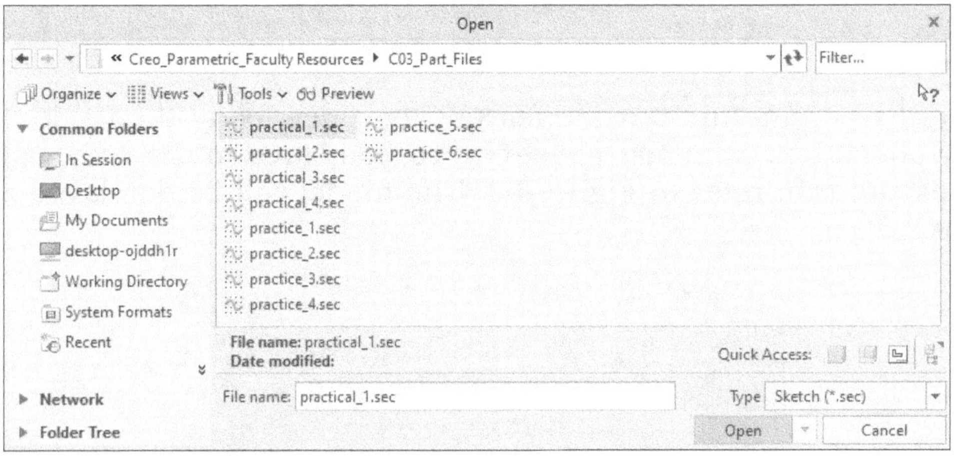

Figure-66. Open dialog box

- Select desired sketch and click on the **Open** button from the dialog box. A plus sign will get attached to the cursor.
- Click at desired place to specify the insertion point for the sketch. The **Import Section** contextual tab will be displayed along with the sketch places at the specified point; refer to Figure-67.

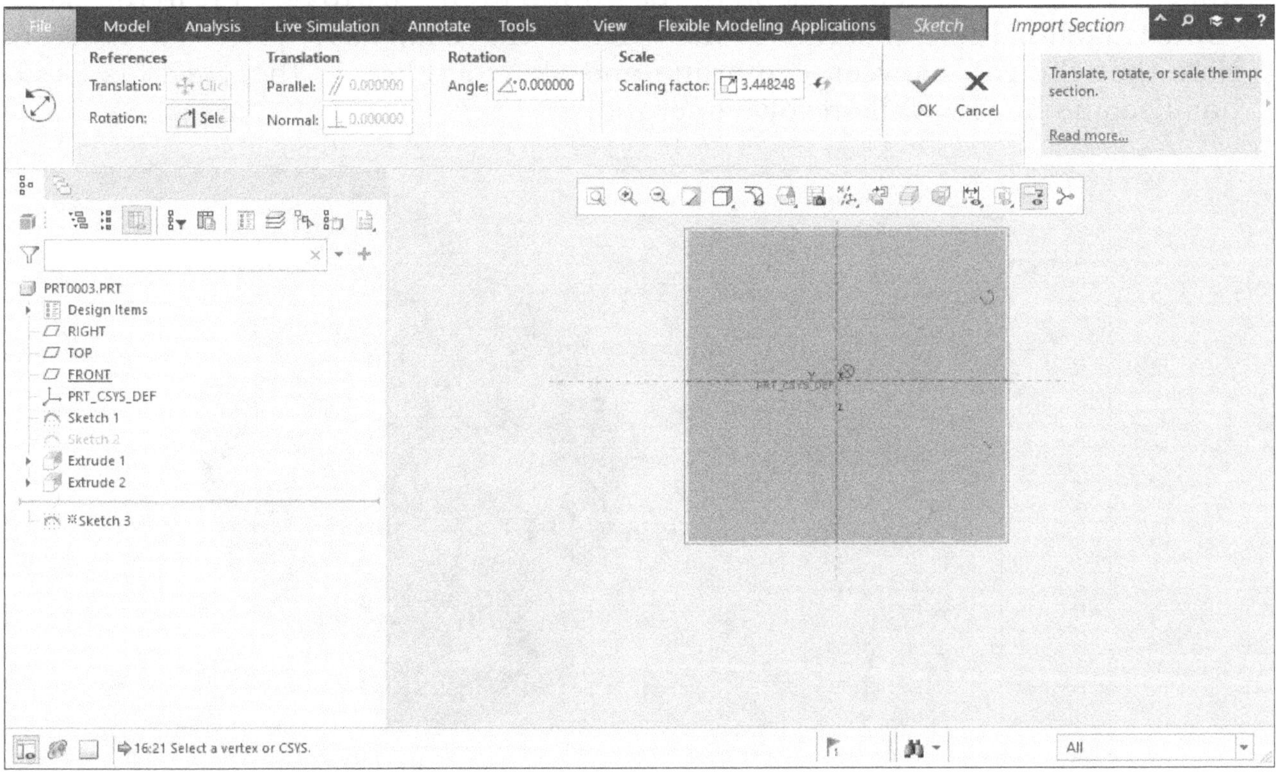

Figure-67. Import Section contextual tab

- The options in the contextual tab are similar to **Rotate Resize** tab discussed earlier. Specify the scale, rotation, and position of the sketch and then click on the **OK** button from the tab. The sketch will be placed.

REVOLVE

The **Revolve** tool is used to create cylindrical features. You can also use the **Revolve** tool to remove material from a solid in cylindrical fashion. At most of the places, where we need cylindrical features like in modeling a pen, a shaft, and so on; we can use the **Revolve** tool to reduce the modeling time. The procedure to use this tool is given next.

- Click on the **Revolve** tool from the **Shapes** panel in the **Model** tab of **Ribbon**. The **Revolve** contextual tab will be displayed; refer to Figure-68.

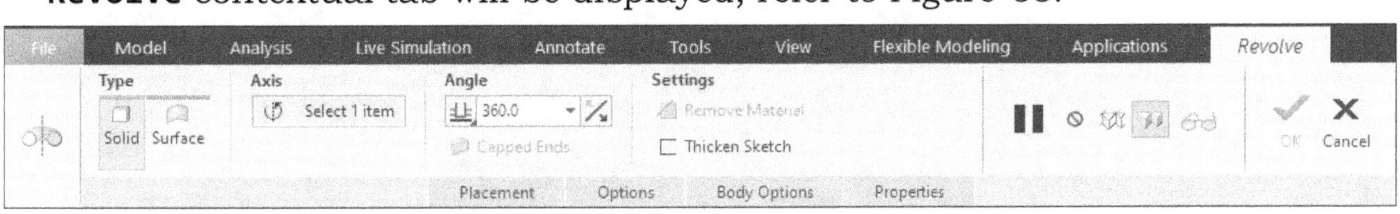

Figure-68. Revolve contextual tab

- Click on the **Placement** tab in the contextual tab as discussed earlier and click on the **Define** button. The **Sketch** dialog box will be displayed.

- Select desired plane from the modeling area and click on the **Sketch** button from the dialog box. The sketching environment will be displayed.
- Create a closed loop sketch with a center line not intersecting the closed loop; refer to Figure-69. Note that you need to select the **Centerline** tool from the **Datum** panel in the **Sketch** tab for creating the revolve feature.
- After creating the sketch, click on the **OK** button from the **Close** panel in the **Sketch** contextual tab. Preview of the revolve feature will be displayed; refer to Figure-70. Note that the gap between centerline and sketched line in the previous sketch has become hollow while revolve operation.

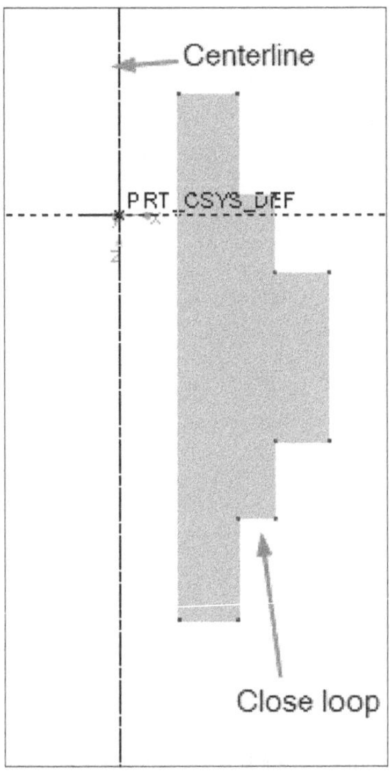

Figure-69. Sketch for revolve feature

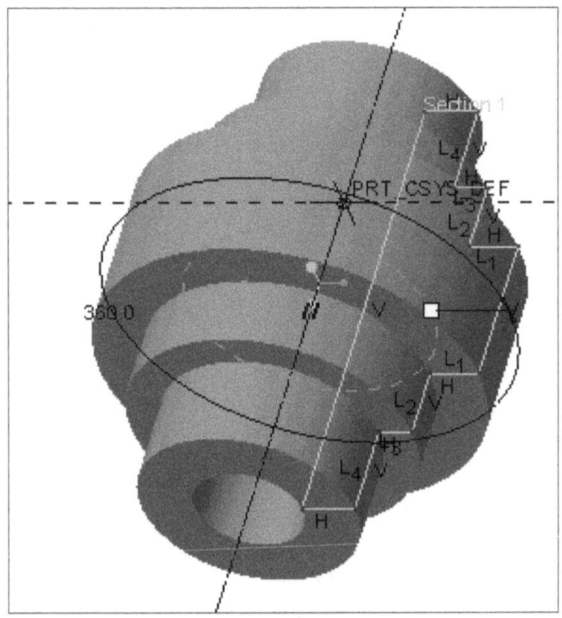

Figure-70. Preview of revolve feature

- Double-click on the dimension of 360 value displayed on the revolve feature and specify desired value for the revolution of the sketch. Figure-71 shows the same feature with revolution angle specified as 90 degree.
- If you want to select any other centerline (axis) present in the modeling area to create the revolve feature then click on the **Placement** tab and click on the **Internal CL** button from the tab options. You are asked to select an axis from the modeling area.
- Click on desired axis like Z axis of coordinate system in our case; refer to Figure-72.
- Rest of the options in the contextual tab work in the same way as the options work in **Extrude** contextual tab discussed earlier.

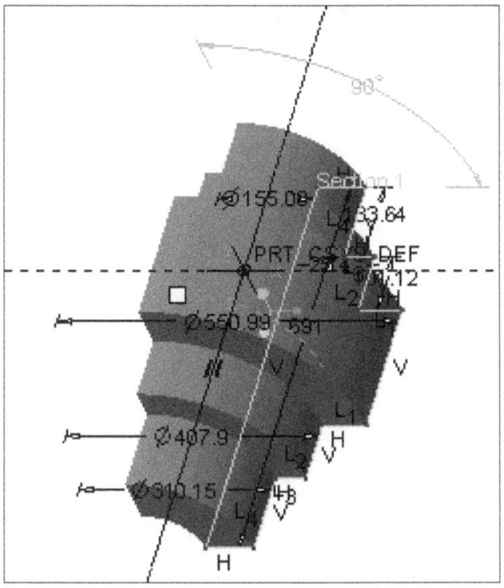

Figure-71. Revolve feature with angle set as 90 degree

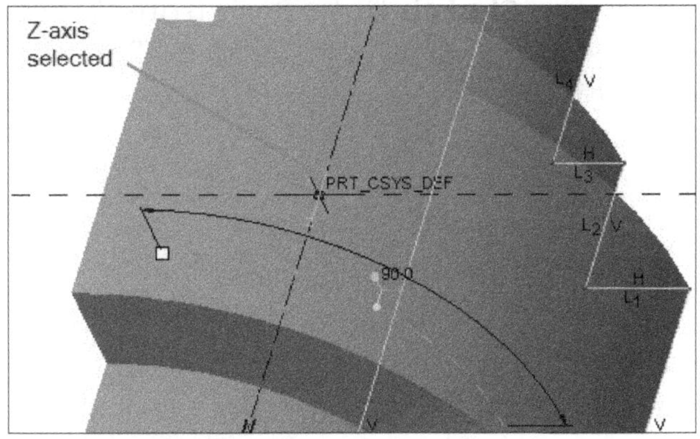

Figure-72. Revolve feature by Z axis

SWEEP

The **Sweep** tool is used to create solid/surface feature by sweeping closed loop sketch along the selected trajectory. This tool is generally used when we need to create tubes/ bars following a curvature. The procedure to use this tool is given next.

- Click on the **Sweep** tool from the **Sweep** drop-down in the **Shapes** panel. The **Sweep** contextual tab will be displayed in the **Ribbon**; refer to Figure-73. Also, you are asked to select a trajectory.

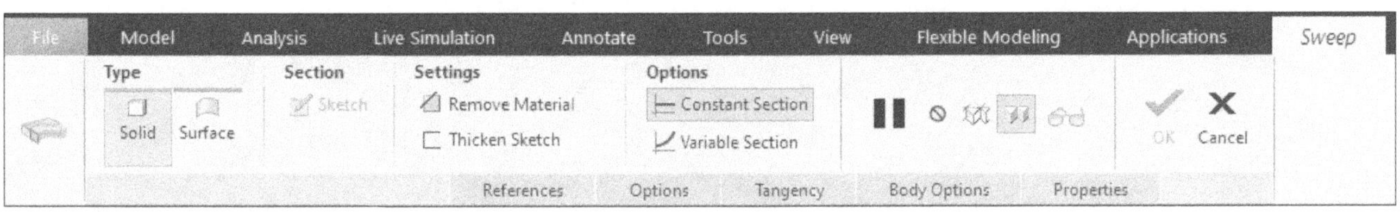

Figure-73. Sweep contextual tab

- Click on a sketch trajectory along which you want to sweep the closed loop; refer to Figure-74.

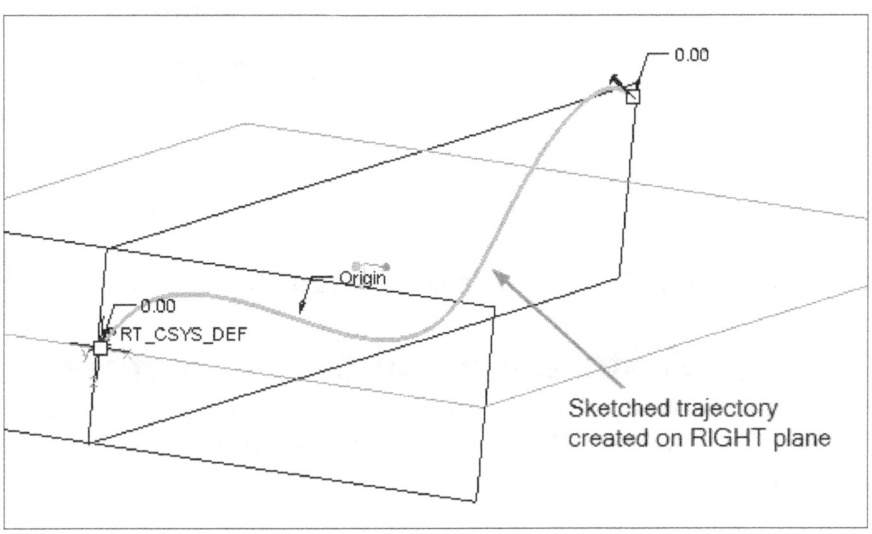

Figure-74. Sketched trajectory for sweep feature

- Click on the **Sketch** button from **Section** area in **Ribbon** to create the closed loop or section of sweep feature. The sketching environment will be activated; refer to Figure-75.

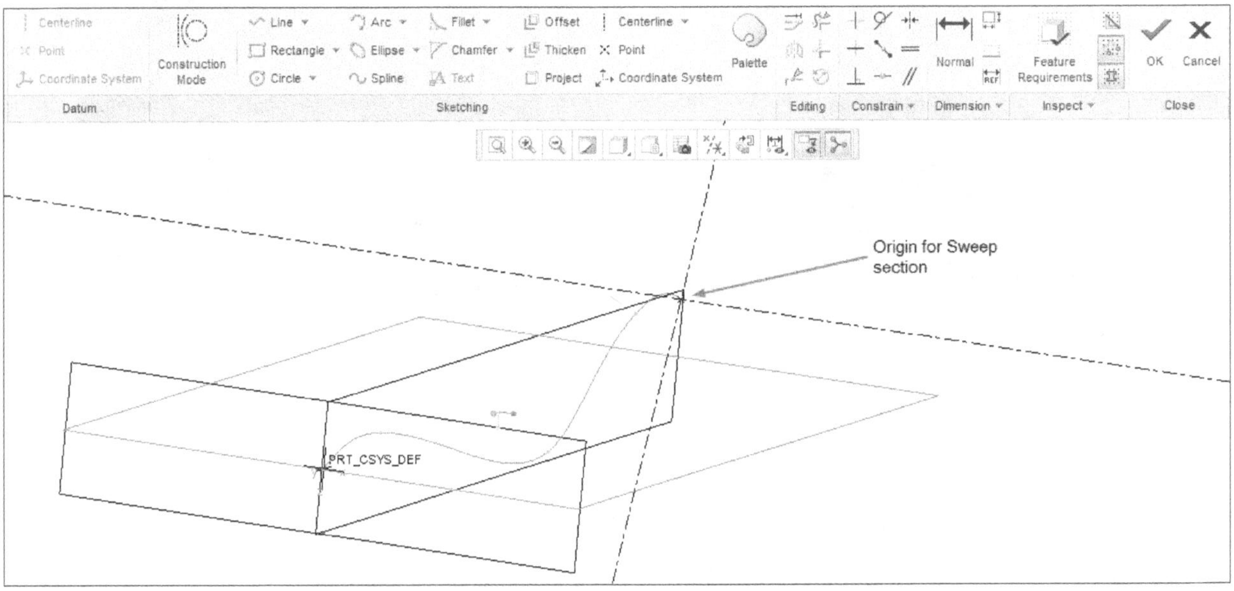

Figure-75. Sketching environment sweep section

- Create a close loop like circle/rectangle/polygon and then click on the **OK** button from the **Sketch** contextual tab. Preview of the **Sweep** feature will be displayed; refer to Figure-76.

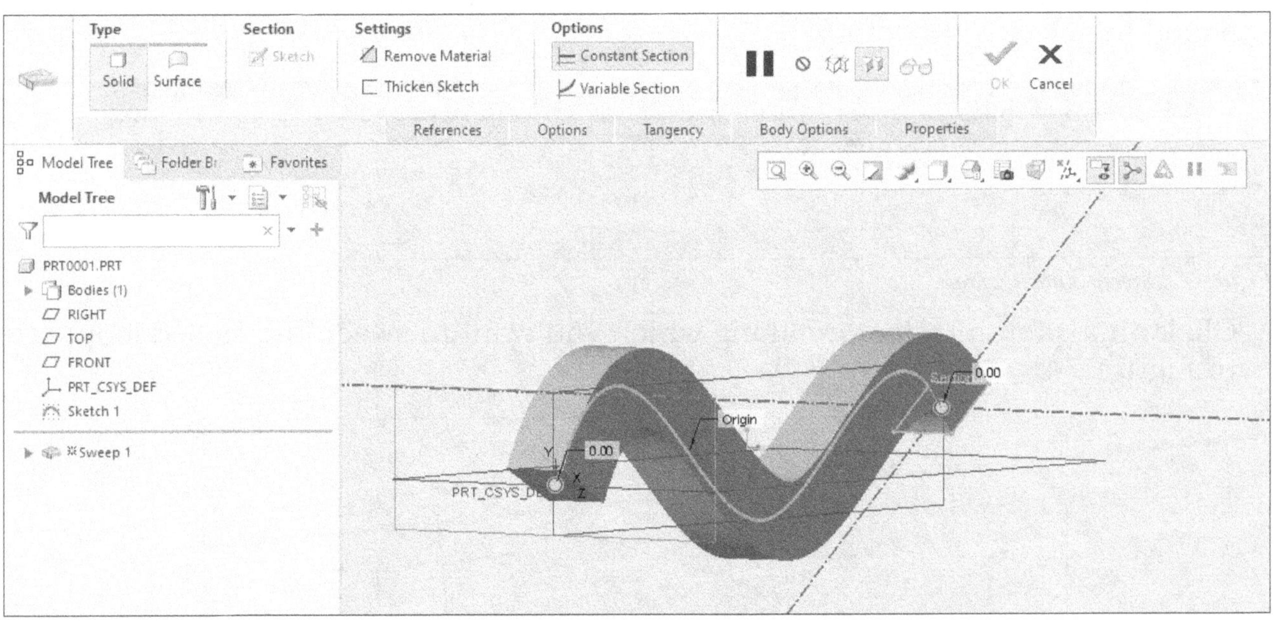

Figure-76. Preview of sweep feature

- Click on the **Constant Section** or **Variable Section** button as per your requirement.

Sweep Feature with Multiple trajectories

- You can also create a sweep feature following more than one trajectory as shown in Figure-77. To do so, select all the trajectories one by one while holding the **CTRL** key after selecting the **Sweep** tool.

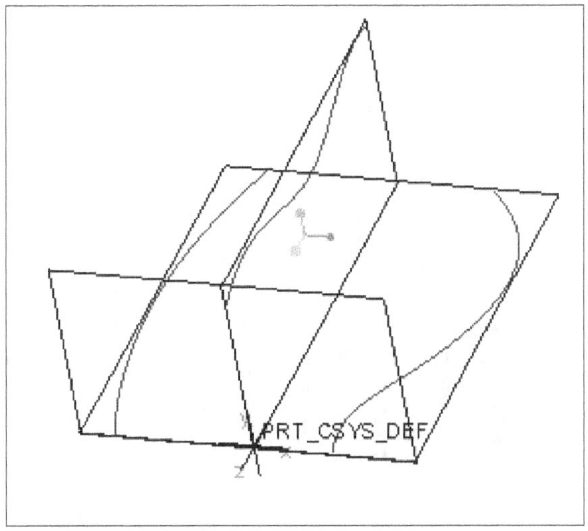

Figure-77. Trajectories for sweep feature

- Create a sketch which is coincident with all the trajectories; refer to Figure-78. You can use the **Coincident** button from **Constrain** panel in the **Sketch** tab of the **Ribbon** to make the sketch coincident.

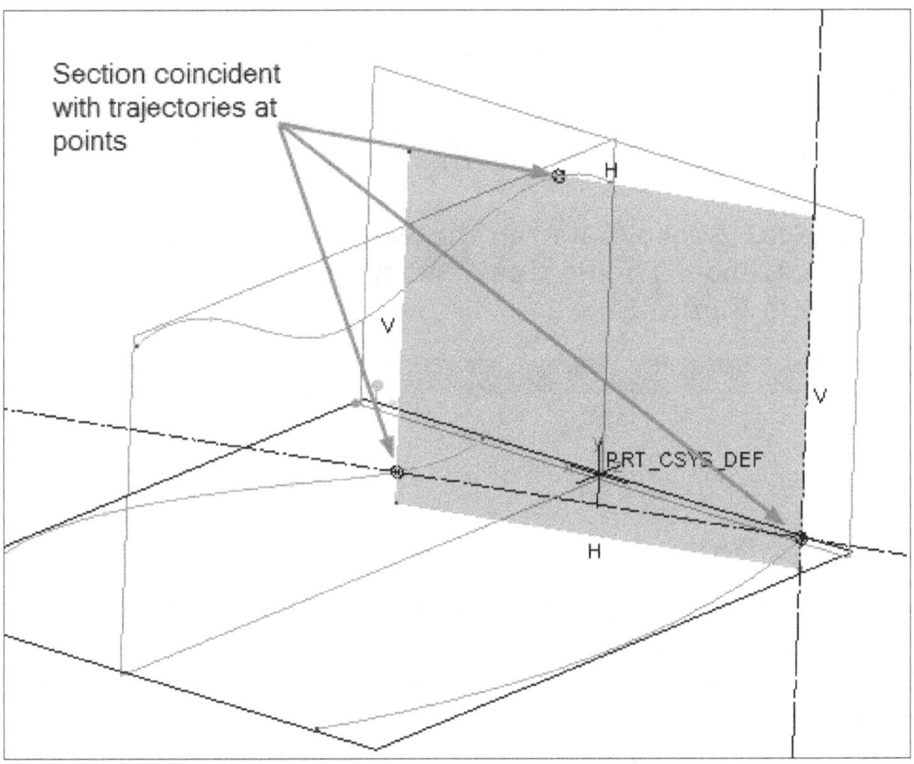

Figure-78. Section coincident with points

- After creating the section, click on the **OK** button from the **Sketch** contextual tab. Preview of the sweep features will be displayed; refer to Figure-79.

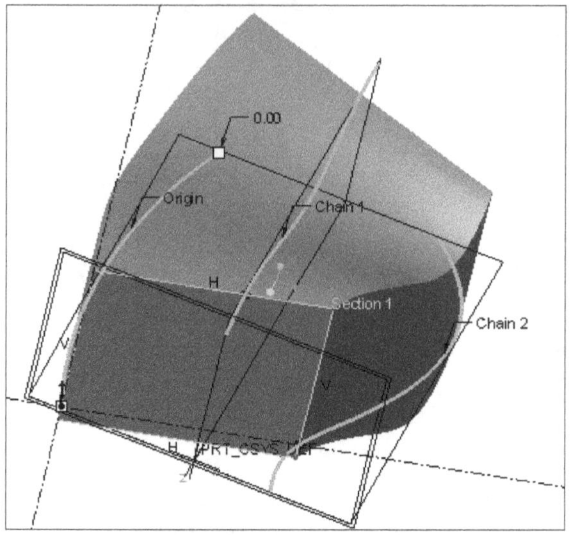

Figure-79. Sweep feature with multiple trajectory

- Note that the rest of the options like **Thin feature** button, **Surface** button, etc. are similar to **Extrude** and **Revolve**.

HELICAL SWEEP

The **Helical Sweep** tool is used to sweep a closed loop sketch along a helical path. You can use this tool to create model of spring or you can create threads on solids by using this tool. The procedure to use this tool is given next.

- Click on the **Helical Sweep** tool from the **Sweep** drop-down in the **Shapes** panel of **Model** tab in the **Ribbon**. The **Helical Sweep** contextual tab will be displayed in the **Ribbon**; refer to Figure-80.

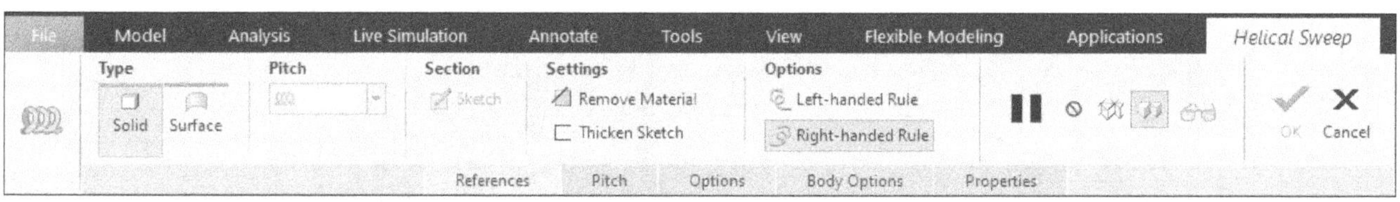

Figure-80. Helical Sweep tab in Ribbon

- Click on the **References** tab in the **Ribbon**. The options of **References** tab will be displayed as shown in Figure-81.
- Click on the **Define** button from the tab. The **Sketch** dialog box will be displayed as discussed earlier.
- Select desired plane (RIGHT plane in our case) and click on the **Sketch** button to start the sketching environment.
- Create sketch of path (You can use line, arc, and spline tools to create open sketch) and a centerline; refer to Figure-82.
- After creating the sketch, click on the **OK** button from the **Sketch** contextual tab. The path of helical sweep will be displayed with its pitch value; refer to Figure-83.

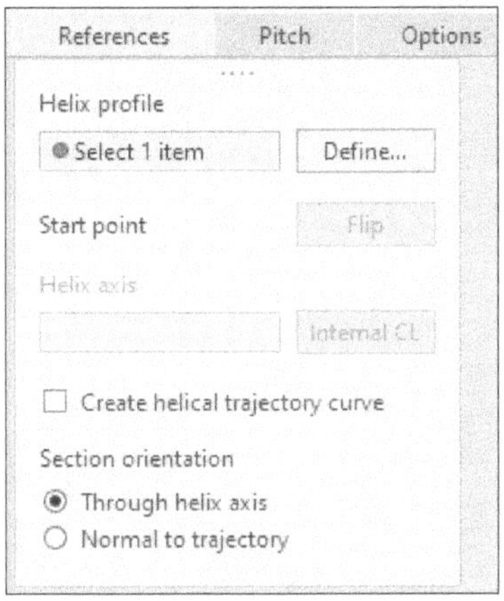

Figure-81. References options

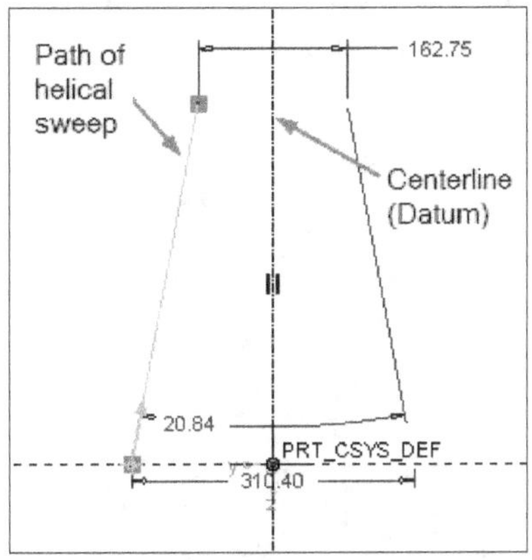

Figure-82. Sketch for path of helical sweep

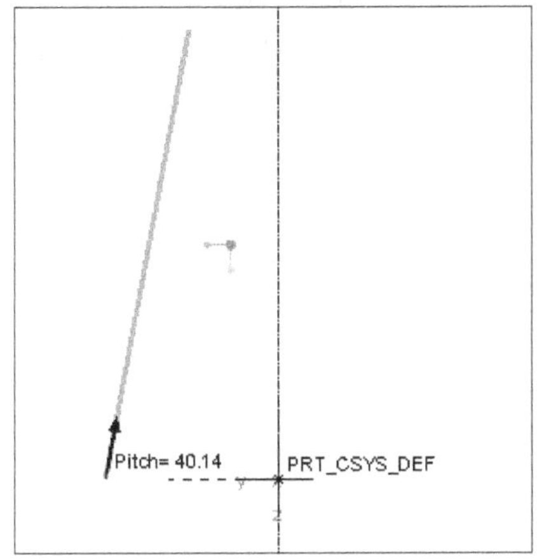

Figure-83. Path of helical sweep

- Click on the **`Create or edit sweep section`** button to create profile of section for sweeping. You will enter into the sketching environment again. Note that two intersecting center lines will be displayed in the sketch denoting the starting point of the path; refer to Figure-84.

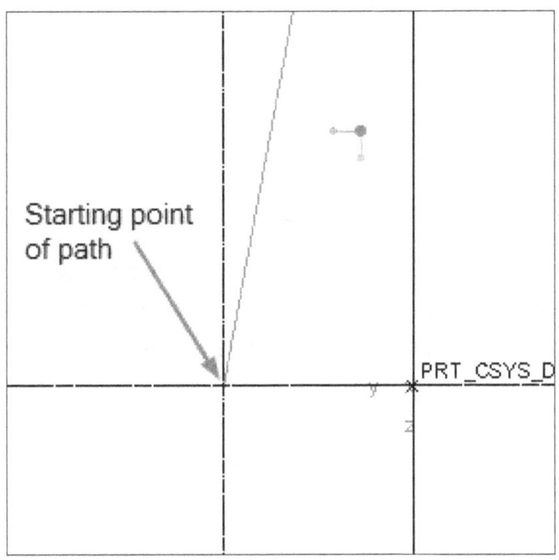

Figure-84. Starting point of path

- Create the closed loop sketch of the section; refer to Figure-85. Note that the maximum vertical span of loop must be lower than the pitch, otherwise the helical sweep will not be created due to internal overlapping.

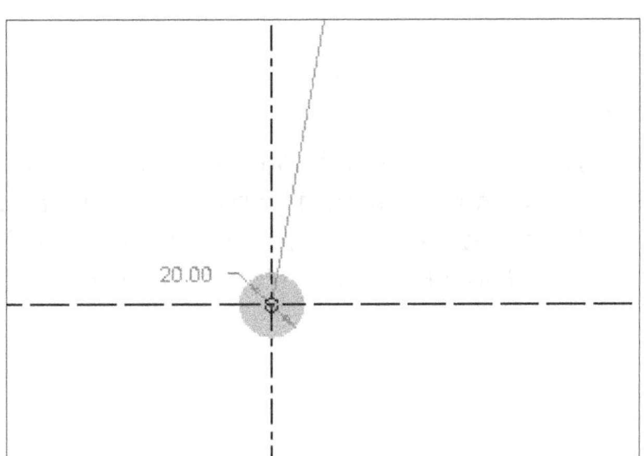

Figure-85. Sketch for section

- Click on the **OK** button from the **Sketch** contextual tab. Preview of the helical sweep feature will be displayed; refer to Figure-86.

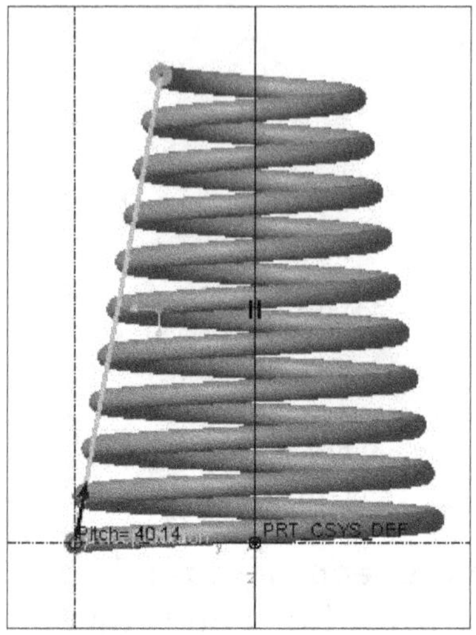

Figure-86. Preview of helical sweep

- To reverse the direction of helical sweep, select one of the two buttons shown in Figure-87.

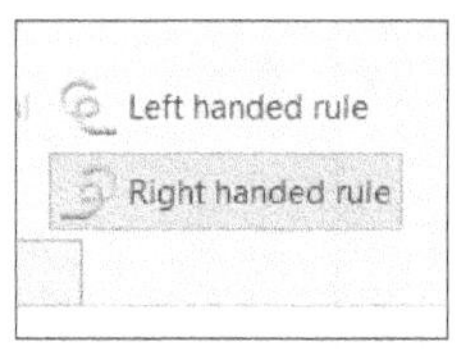

Figure-87. Rules of sweeping

- Change the pitch value from the **Pitch Value** edit box  in the **Ribbon**.
- If you need multiple pitch for the helical sweep or say spring then click on the **Pitch** tab in the **Ribbon**. The options will be displayed as shown in Figure-88.

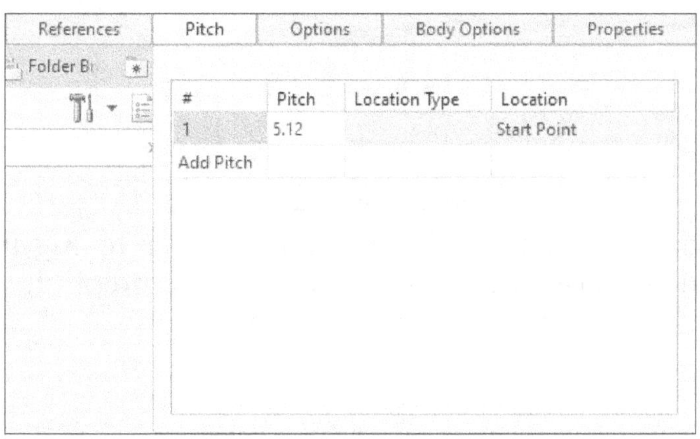

Figure-88. Pitch options

- Click on the **Add Pitch** button from the table. A new pitch will be applied to the end point of the path. Specify desired value for the new pitch in its relevant edit box.
- Click again on the **Add Pitch** button and you will be able to specify pitch at a desired point on the helical sweep path. Refer to Figure-89.

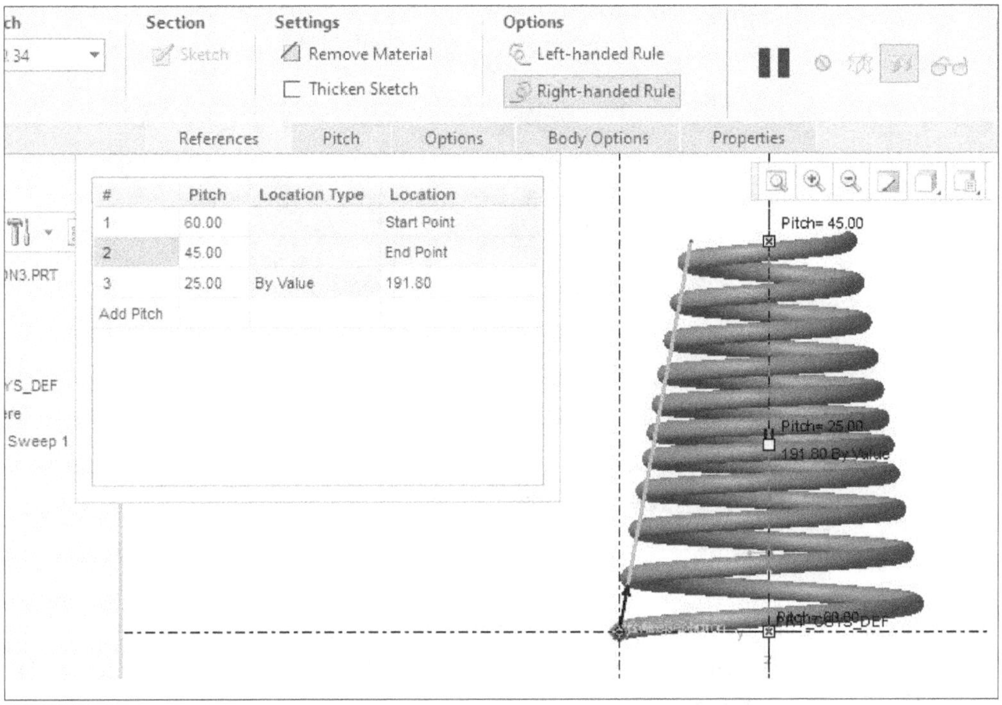

Figure-89. Helical sweep with variable pitch

- To create a tube from the solid helical sweep, click on the **Thin feature** button and specify desired thickness of the tube.
- Click on the **OK** button from the **Ribbon** to create the feature.

VOLUME HELICAL SWEEP

The **Volume Helical Sweep** tool is a tool similar to helical sweep, used to remove material by revolving sketch section along helix. The result of volume Helical sweep resembles cutting a cylindrical part on lathe machine. The procedure to use this tool is given next.

- Click on the **Volume Helical Sweep** tool from the **Sweep** drop-down in **Shapes** panel of **Model** tab in the **Ribbon**. The **Volume Helical Sweep** contextual tab will be displayed in the **Ribbon**; refer to Figure-90.

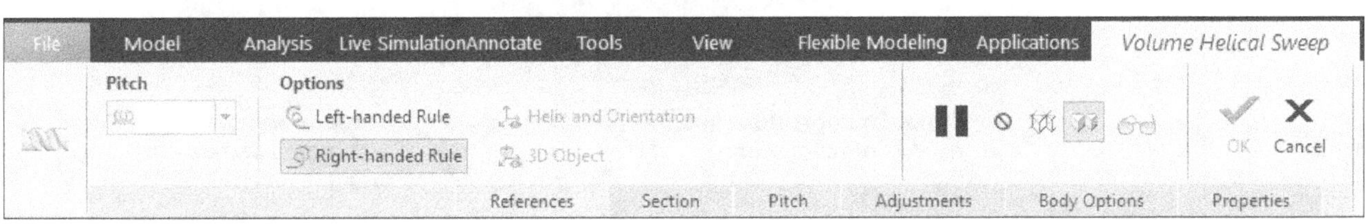

Figure-90. Volume Helical Sweep contextual tab

- Click on the **References** tab and then select sketch for helix profile (a line and centerline in sketch). If you have not created any sketch for profile then click on the **Define** button. The **Sketch** dialog box will be displayed asking you to select the sketching plane.
- Select desired sketching plane and draw a line & centerline in the sketch near solid body to be cut; refer to Figure-91. Click on the **OK** button from **Sketch** contextual tab to exit sketch environment.

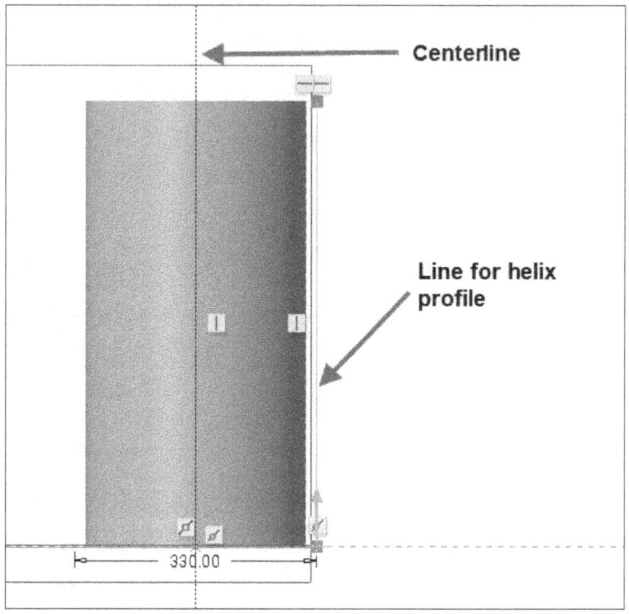

Figure-91. Sketch for helix profile

- If you have created a sketch earlier for revolved section then select the **Selected section** radio button from the **Section** tab and select the sketch with a close section. Click in the **Axis of revolution** selection box of **Section** tab and select the axis about which you want to revolve the section. Click in the **Origin** selection box and select a point on the close section to be used as origin; refer to Figure-92. Preview of volume helical sweep will be displayed.

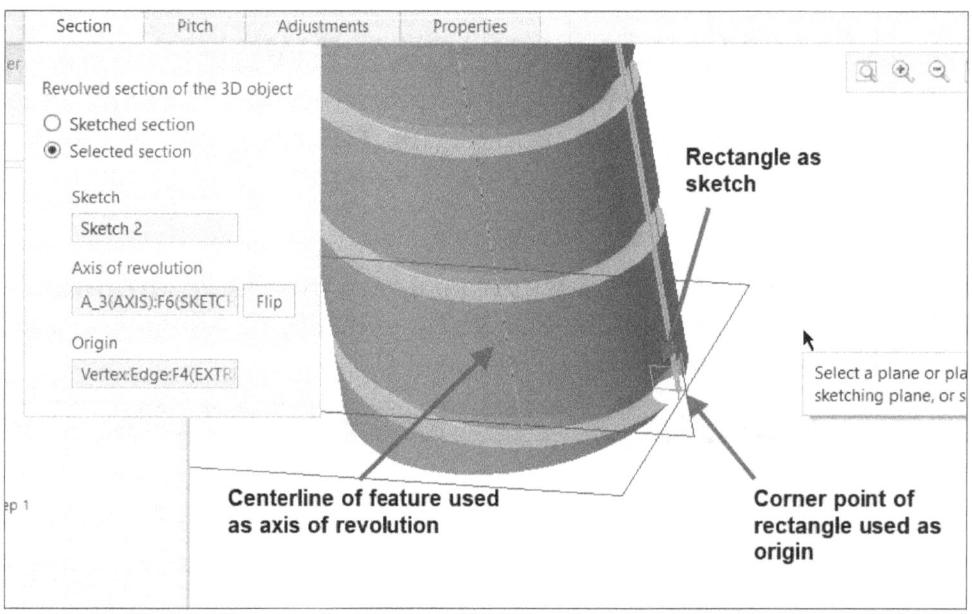

Figure-92. Selecting profile for volume helical sweep

- If you have not created a sketch for section then select the **Sketched section** radio button from the **Section** tab and click on the **Create/Edit section** button; refer to Figure-93. The sketching environment will become active automatically.
- Create the sketch of section with one line of sketch aligned to helix profile sketch earlier created; refer to Figure-94. Click on the **OK** button from **Sketch** tab after creating the sketch. Preview of volume helical sweep will be displayed; refer to Figure-95.

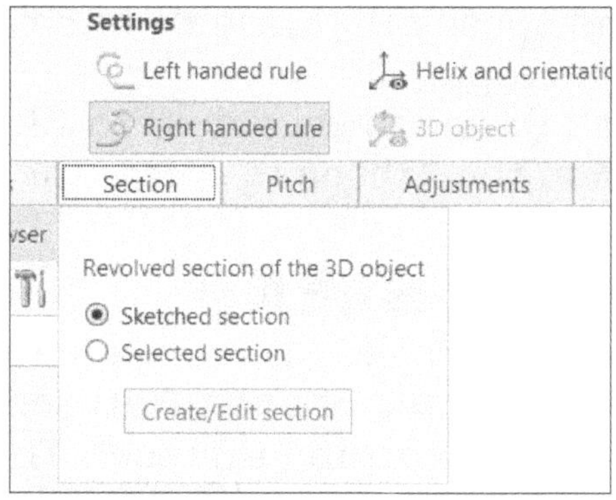

Figure-93. Create/Edit section button

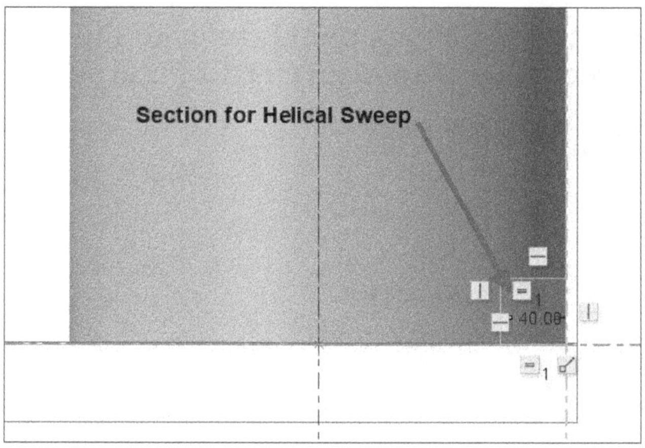

Figure-94. Section for volume helical sweep

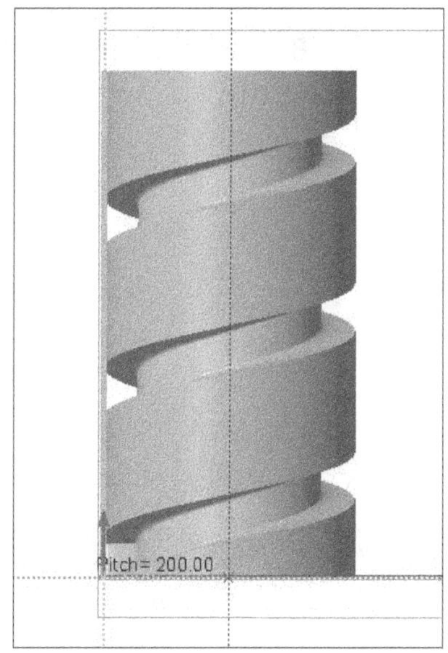

Figure-95. Volume helical sweep preview

- Click in the **Pitch** edit box at the top-left in the **Volume Helical Sweep** contextual tab and specify desired value of pitch.
- Select the **Left handed rule** or **Right handed rule** button from the **Ribbon** to define orientation of helical sweep.
- Select the **Helix and orientation** button to display helical path.
- Select the **Show the 3D object** button to display 3D section revolving on the part while cutting; refer to Figure-96.

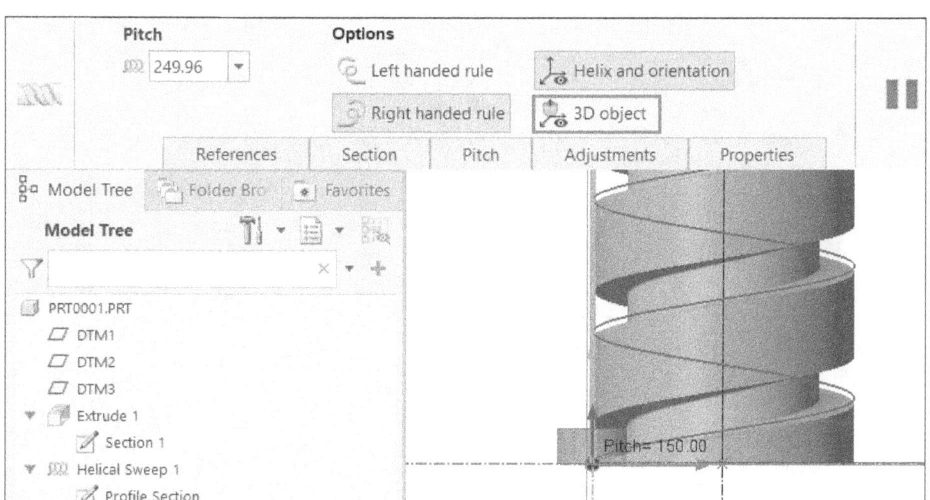

Figure-96. Show 3D object button

- Click on the **Pitch** tab and specify the variable pitch as required. This option has been discussed in previous topic.
- Click on the **Adjustments** tab and specify desired tilting angle for section.
- Click on the **OK** button from the **Ribbon** to create the feature.

BLEND

As the name suggests, **Blend** tool is used to create a feature by blending two or more different sections. One of the example of such feature is a flower vase. So, we will use flower vase as an example for learning this tool. The procedure to use this tool is given next.

- Click on the **Blend** tool from the expanded **Shapes** panel; refer to Figure-97. The **Blend** contextual tab will be displayed in the **Ribbon**; refer to Figure-98.

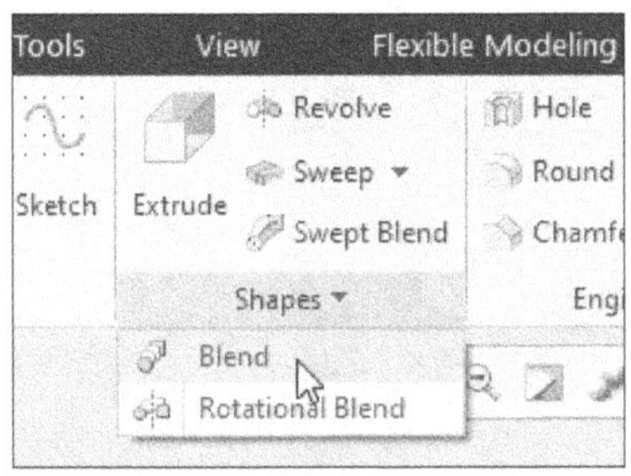

Figure-97. Blend tool

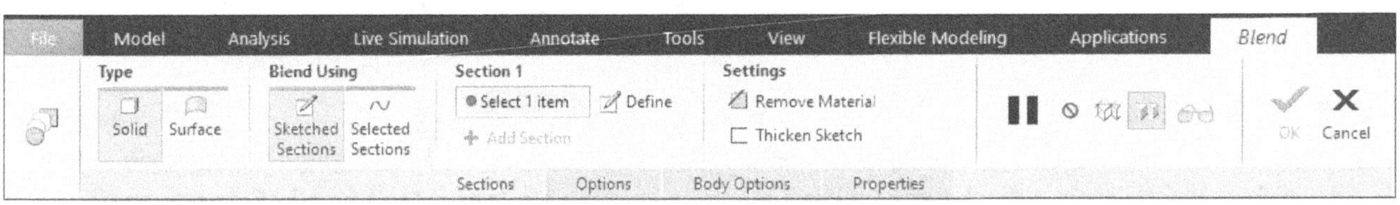

Figure-98. Blend contextual tab

- Click on the **Sections** tab. The options for selecting and sketching the sections will be displayed; refer to Figure-99.

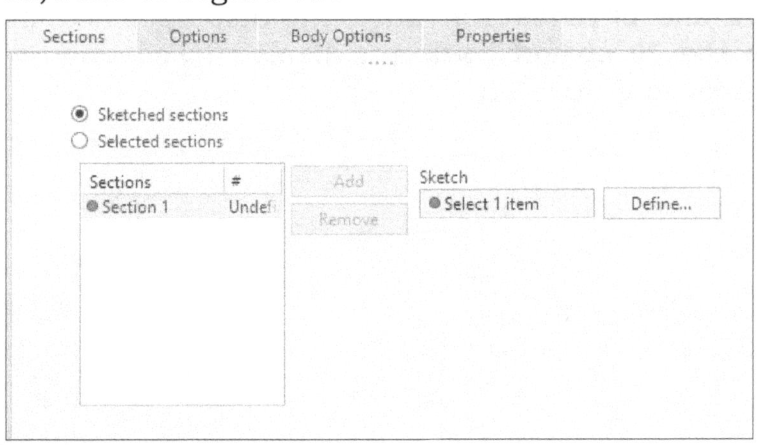

Figure-99. Options in Sections tab

- If you have a sketched section already in modeling area then click on the **Selected sections** radio button and select the sketched section. Otherwise, select the **Sketched sections** radio button and click on the **Define** button. The **Sketch** dialog box will be displayed as discussed earlier.
- Create a close loop and note down the vertices that are there in the sketch; refer to Figure-100. In this figure, there are four vertices. Also, note that there is an arrow attached to a vertex. The vertex with which the arrow is attached is the starting point of the sketch for blending.

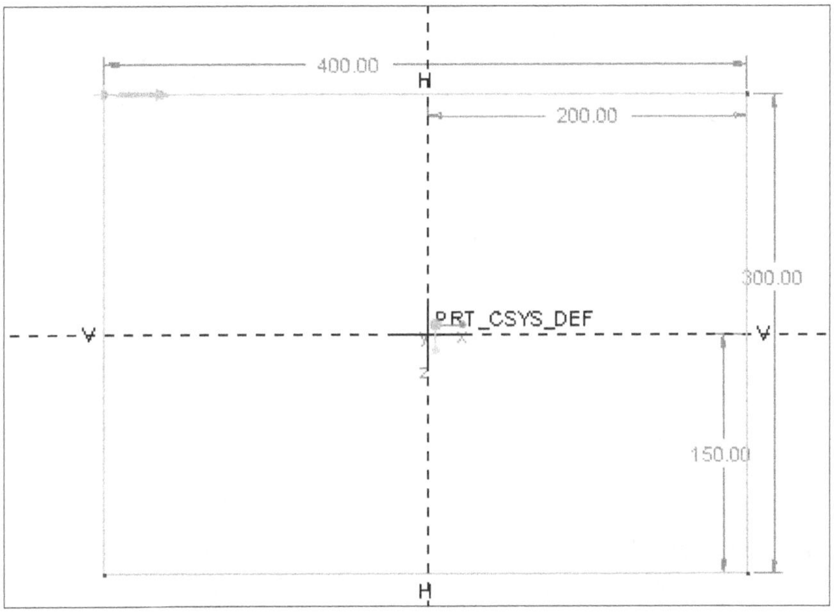

Figure-100. Sketch for blend

- Click on the **OK** button from the **Sketch** contextual tab to exit. You will move back to the **Sections** options; refer to Figure-101.

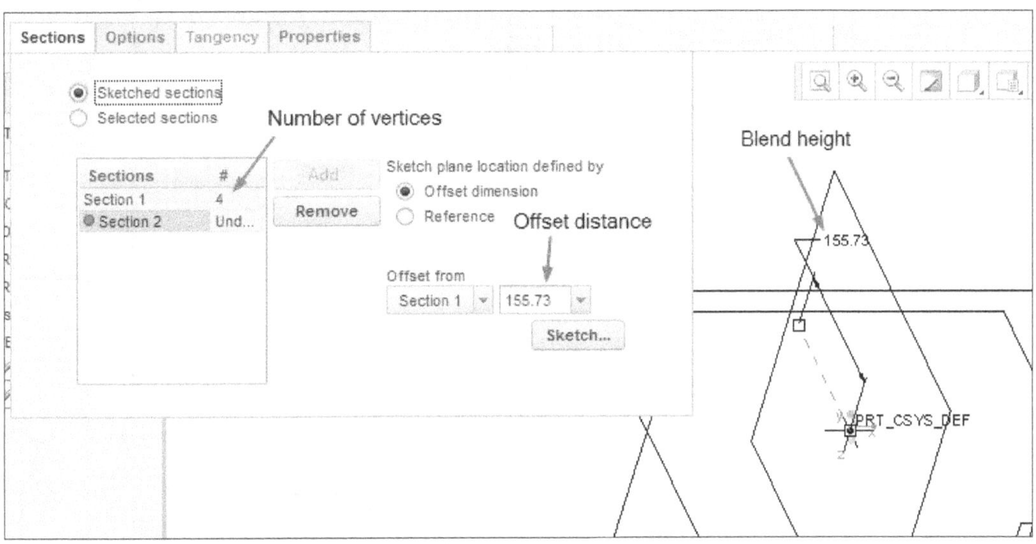

Figure-101. Blend height between two sections

- Specify desired height value by using the blend height dimension or **Offset** edit box in the **Sections** tab.
- Click on the **Sketch** button from the **Sections** tab. The sketching environment will be displayed with a hypothetical plane selected; refer to Figure-102.

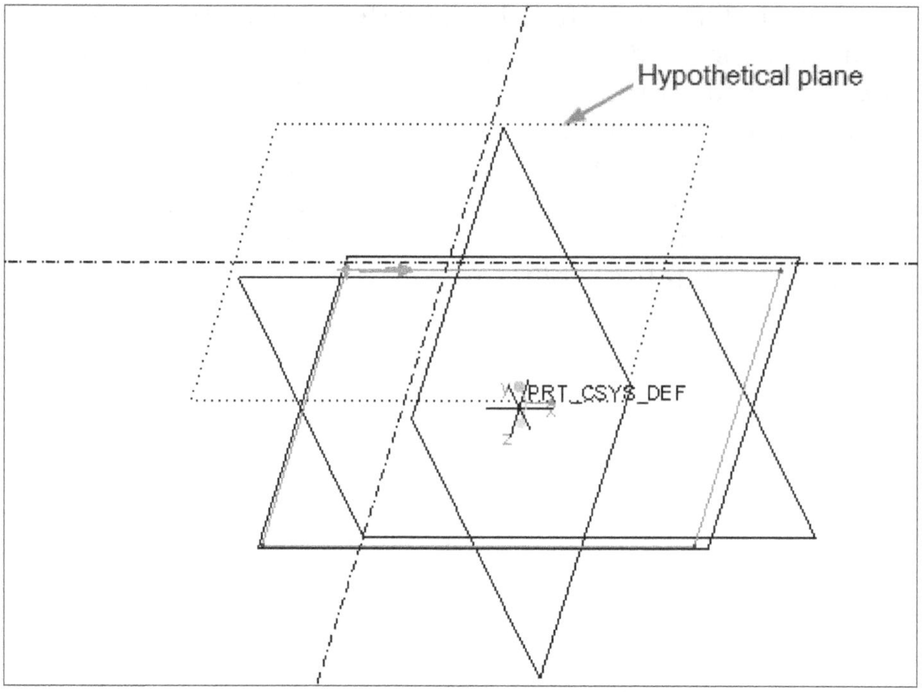

Figure-102. Hypothetical plane for blend

- Create a closed loop as per your requirement. Note that the number of vertices should be the same in all the section sketches.
- In our case, we have created a circle as other section; refer to Figure-103. But since, circle do not qualify our condition of equal number of vertices, we need to use the **Divide** tool from the **Editing** panel of **Sketch** tab to make four vertices of circle.

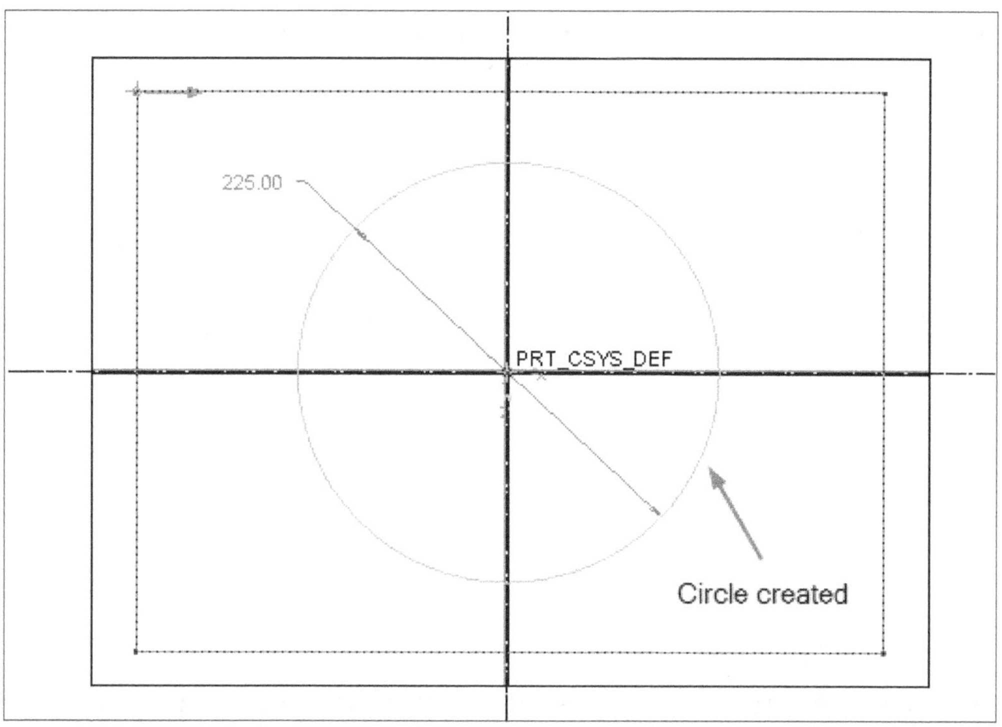

Figure-103. Section for blend

- Click on the **Divide** tool and divide the circle at the points shown in Figure-104. Now, check the direction of arrow in case of circle. It is actually opposite to the arrow direction of rectangle displaying in the background. So, we need to change the direction of arrow.

- Select the vertex of circle with the arrow and hold the right-click. A shortcut menu will be displayed; refer to Figure-105.

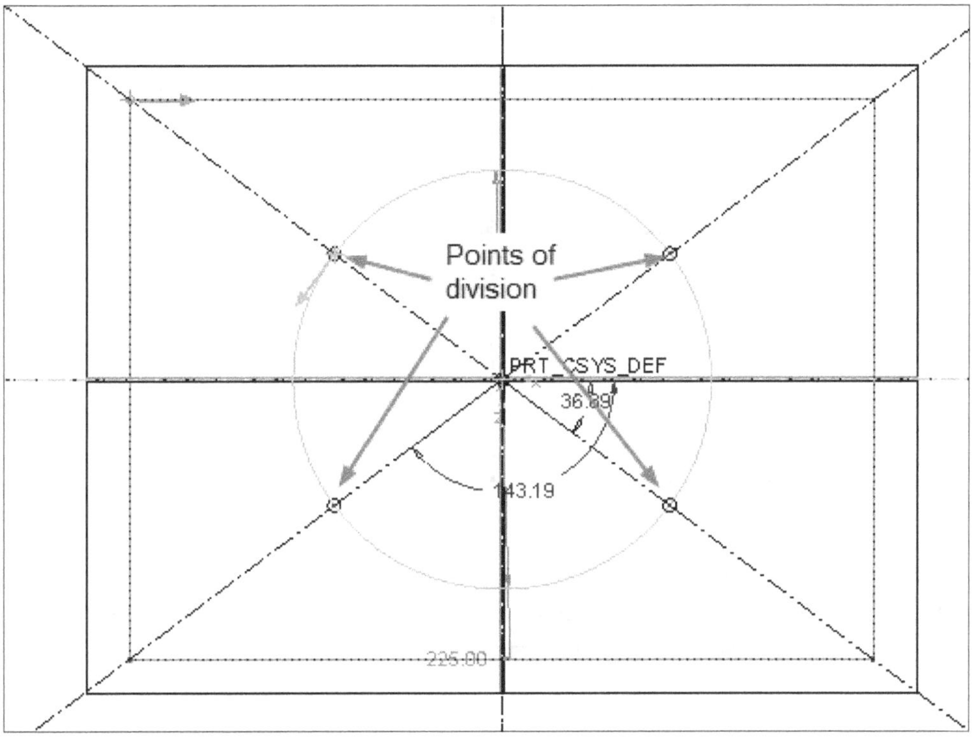

Figure-104. Division points of circle

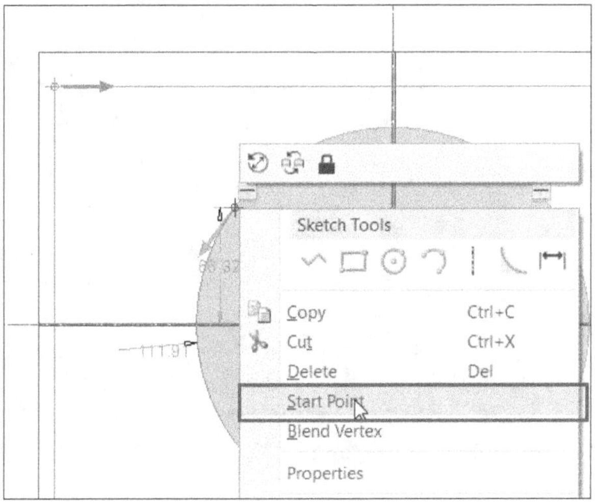

Figure-105. Shortcut menu for vertex

- Click on the **Start Point** option from the shortcut menu, the direction will get reversed; refer to Figure-106.

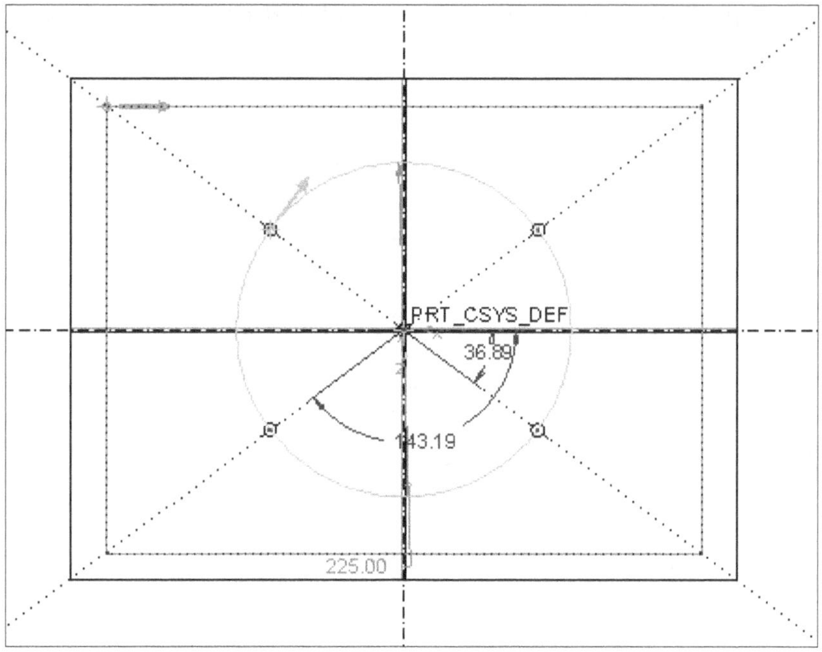

Figure-106. Reversed arrow

- Click on the **OK** button from the **Sketch** contextual tab. The preview of the blend feature will be displayed; refer to Figure-107.

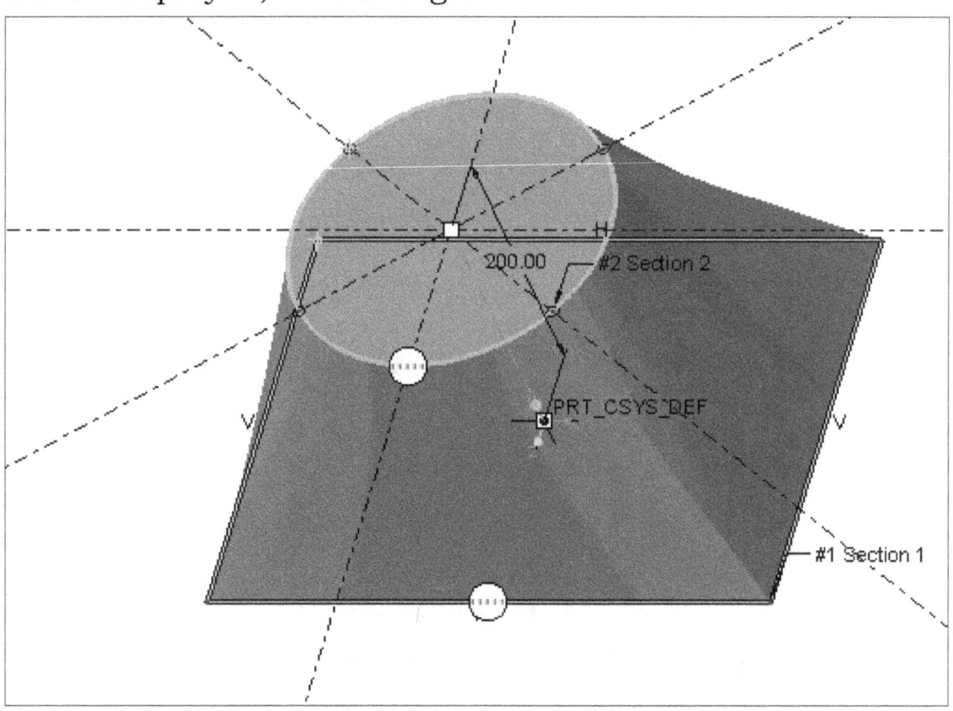

Figure-107. Preview of blend feature

- If you want to add one more section for the blend feature, click on the **Add** button from the **Sections** tab. A new section will be added and you will be prompted to specify the offset distance from the previous section; refer to Figure-108.

Figure-108. Adding section for blend feature

- Specify desired offset distance and click on the **Sketch** button from the tab to create the section.
- Create the section with same number of vertices and then click **OK** button from the **Sketch** contextual tab. Preview of the feature will be displayed; refer to Figure-109. Note that by default, the smooth blend is created but if you want to create a straight blend then click on the **Straight** radio button from the **Options** tab in the **Ribbon**; refer to Figure-110.

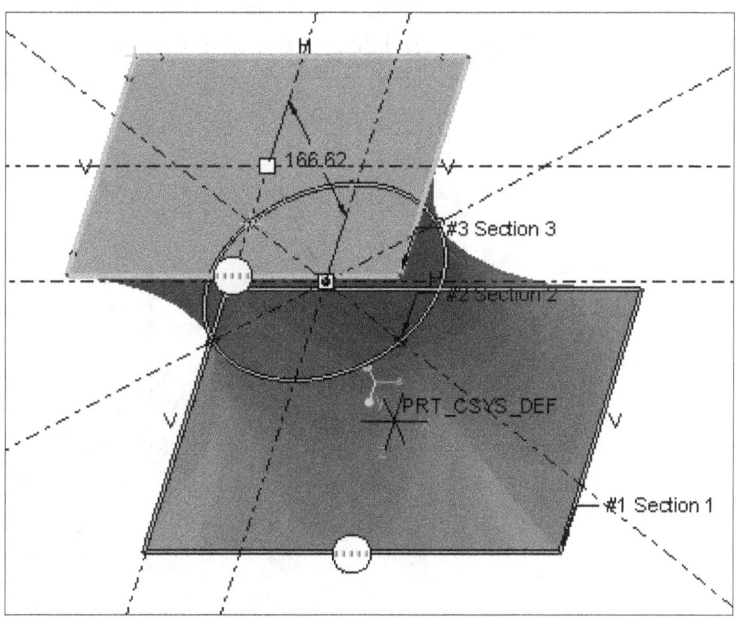

Figure-109. Preview of the blend feature

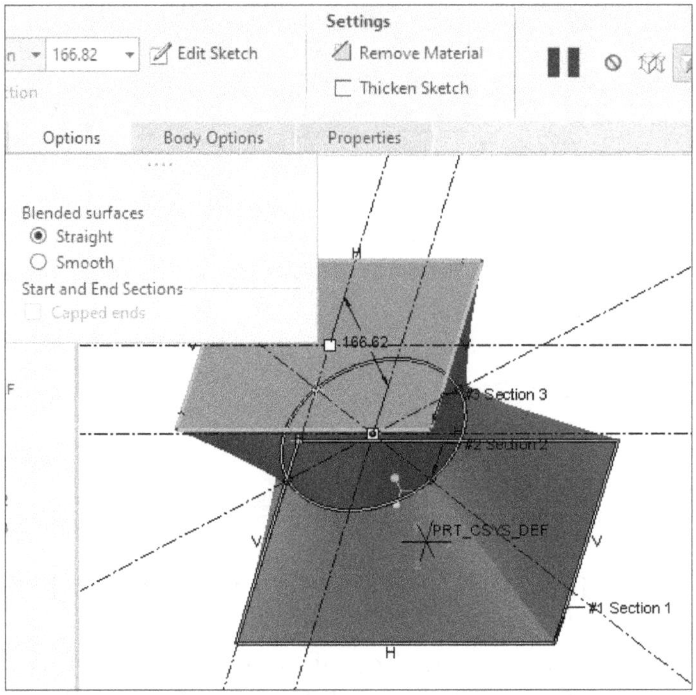

Figure-110. Preview of blend feature with straight feature

- If you have selected the **Smooth** radio button from the **Options** tab then the options in the **Tangency** tab are active. Using these options, you can specify the tangency conditions at the sections. For example, on selecting the **Normal** option from both start section and end section gives a blend as shown in Figure-111.

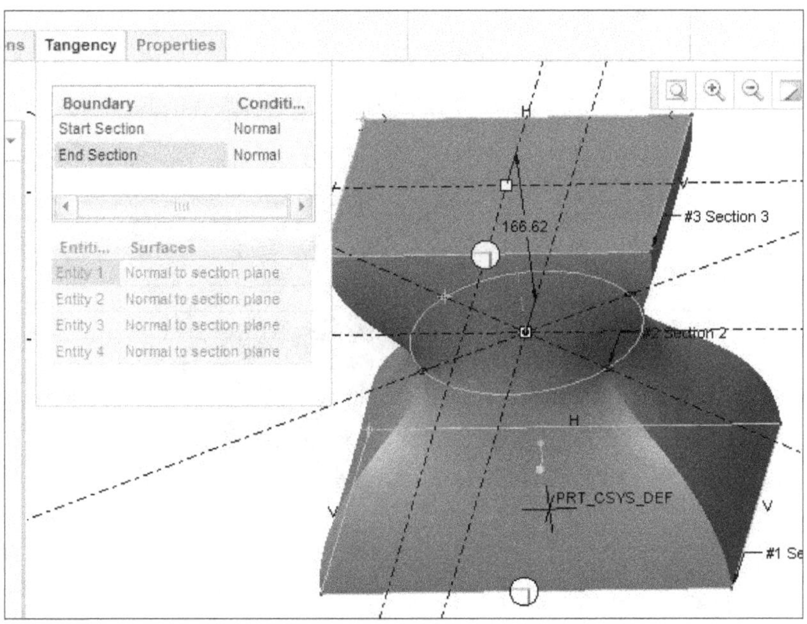

Figure-111. Blend with normal tengency

- Rest of the options in the **Ribbon** are same as discussed earlier.

ROTATIONAL BLEND

The **Rotational Blend** tool is used to create solid feature by joining two or more sections placed at different angles to each other. In the previous tool, we have specified offset distance but if we specify offset angle then we need the **Rotational Blend** tool. The procedure to use this tool is given next.

- Click on the **Rotational Blend** tool from the expanded **Shapes** panel in the **Model** tab of the **Ribbon**. The **Rotational Blend** contextual tab will be displayed; refer to Figure-112.

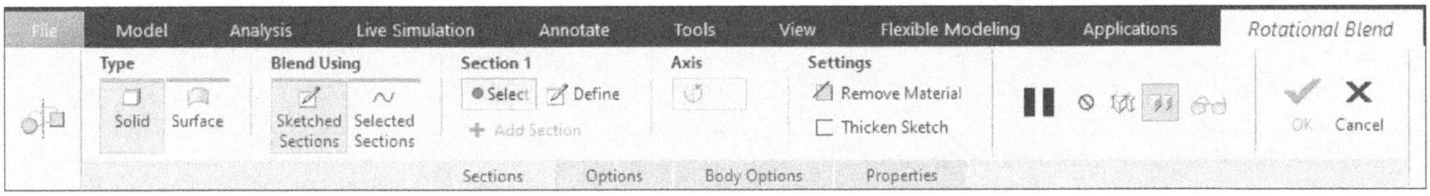

Figure-112. Rotational Blend contextual tab

- Click on the **Sections** tab and then click on the **Define** button from the tab. The **Sketch** dialog box will be displayed as discussed earlier.
- Select desired sketching plane and create a closed loop sketch.
- Create a datum center line at desired distance from the sketch created; refer to Figure-113.

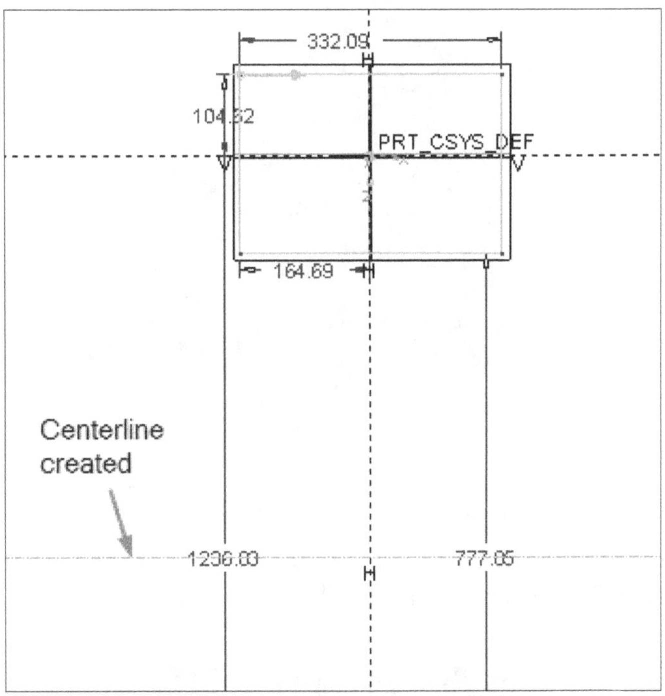

Figure-113. Sketch for rotational blend

- Click on the **OK** button from the **Sketch** contextual tab to exit the sketching environment.
- Open the **Sections** tab again and then click on the **Add** button from the tab. The options in the tab will be displayed as shown in Figure-114.

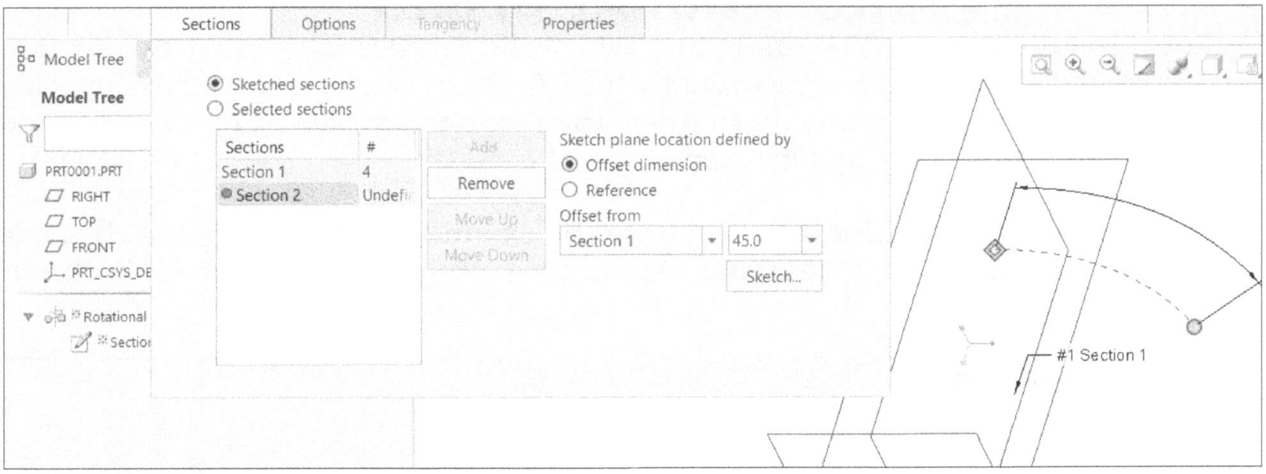

Figure-114. Inserting sections in rotational blend

- Specify desired value of angle and click on the **Sketch** button.
- Create a closed loop sketch with same starting point and direction.
- Click on the **OK** button from the **Ribbon** to exit the sketching environment. Preview of the rotational blend will be displayed; refer to Figure-115.

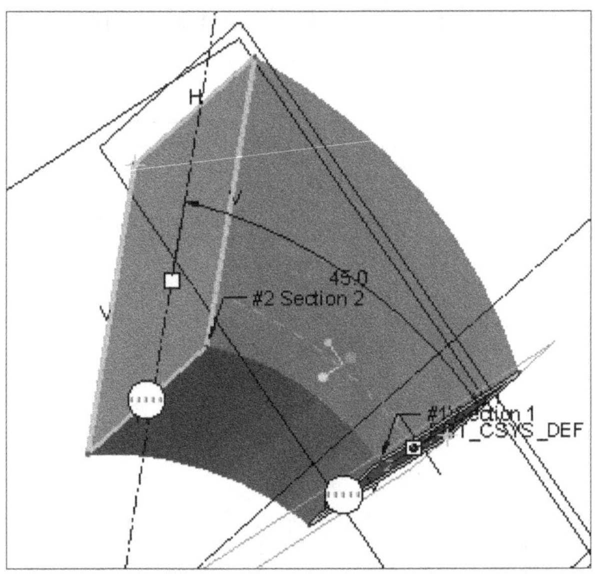

Figure-115. Preview of rotational blend

- You can create more sections in the same way as we did for **Blend** tool.
- Other options in the **Ribbon** are same as we discussed earlier.

SWEPT BLEND

The **Swept Blend** tool is used to blend two or more sections along a path. In other words, its a combination of **Sweep** tool and **Blend** tool.

- Click on the **Swept Blend** tool from the **Shapes** panel in the **Model** tab of the **Ribbon**. The **Swept Blend** contextual tab will be displayed; refer to Figure-116.

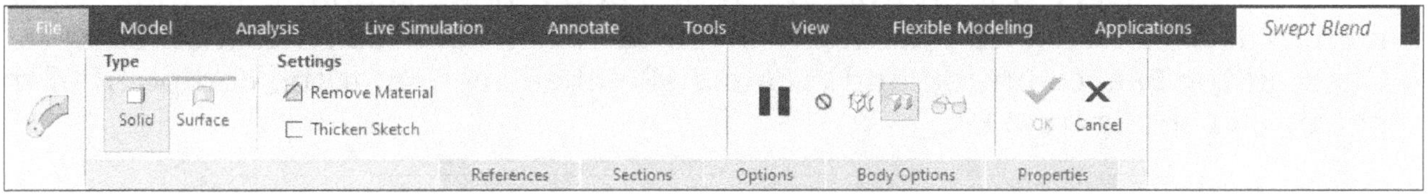

Figure-116. Swept Blend contextual tab

- Select a trajectories with points on trajectory equal to number of sections to be drawn. For example, in the path given in Figure-117, there are four number of points and hence we can create four sections on this path for swept blend feature.

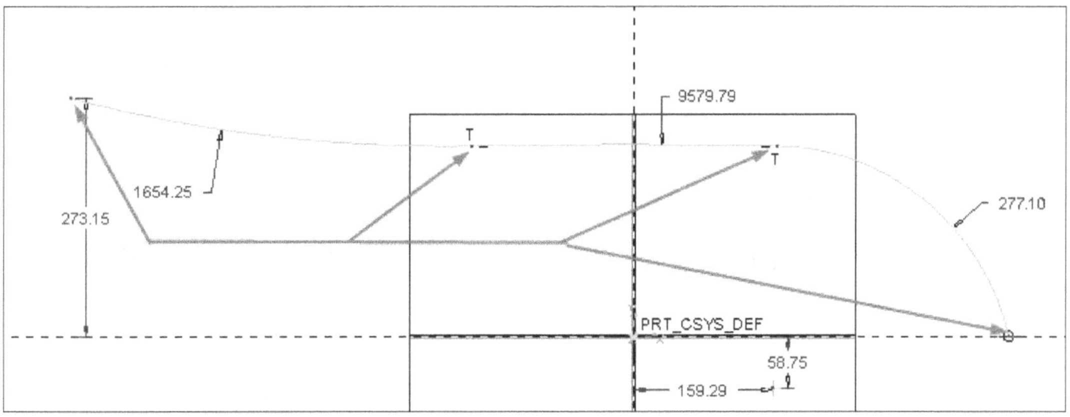

Figure-117. Points on path

- Click on the **Sections** tab in the **Ribbon**. The options will be displayed as shown in Figure-118.

Figure-118. Sections tab

- Note that in the **Section Location** selection box, **Start** is selected. This **Start** means starting point of the selected curve. Click on the **Sketch** button from the tab to create the first section.
- Click on the **Sketch View** button from the **In-Graphics toolbar** to make the sketching plane parallel to screen. Create a sketch and note down the number of vertices in the section. Click on the **OK** button from the **Sketch** contextual tab to exit.

- Click on the **Insert** button from the tab to add a new section. Note that the **End** point will be selected automatically in the **Section Location** selection box.
- Click on the **Sketch** button and create a sketched section at the end point of the path; refer to Figure-119.

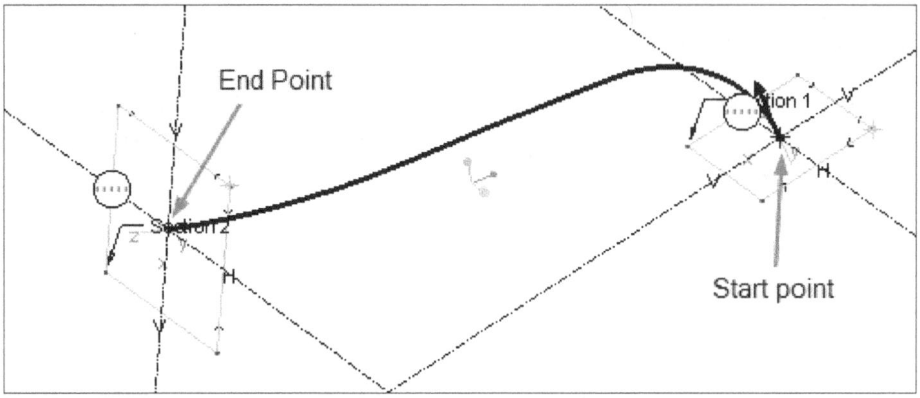

Figure-119. Sections for swept blend

- Click on the **Insert** button again and select one of the curve end point to create section; refer to Figure-120.

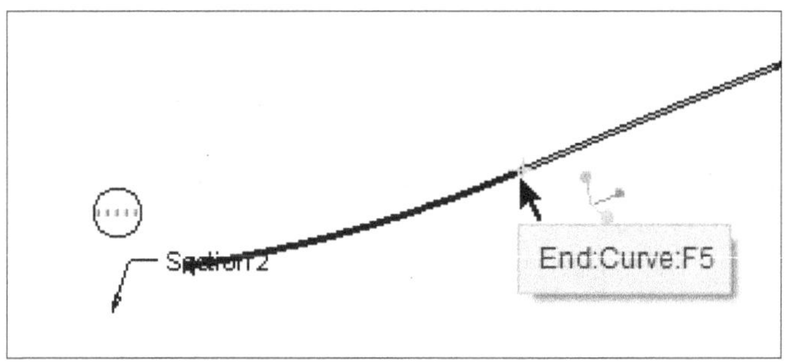

Figure-120. Point to be selected

- Click on the **Sketch** button and create a closed section with number of vertices equal to previous sections and same direction of start point as in the previous sections.

Note that if the starting points of the sections are not aligned then swept blend can be created as twisted; refer to Figure-121. After changing the start point of the middle section, the feature will be created as shown in Figure-122.

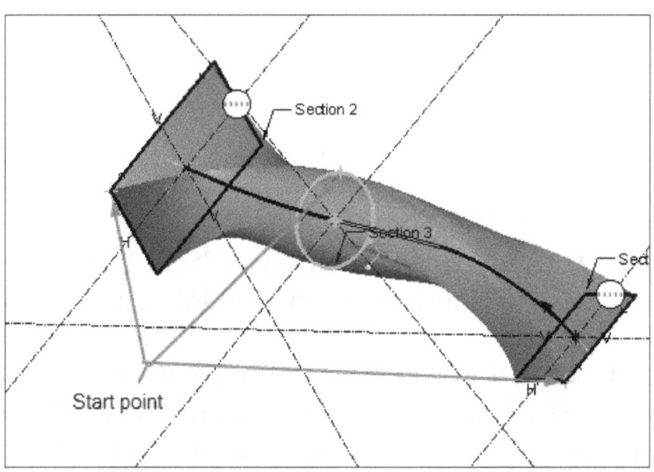

Figure-121. Swept blend twisted due to start point locations

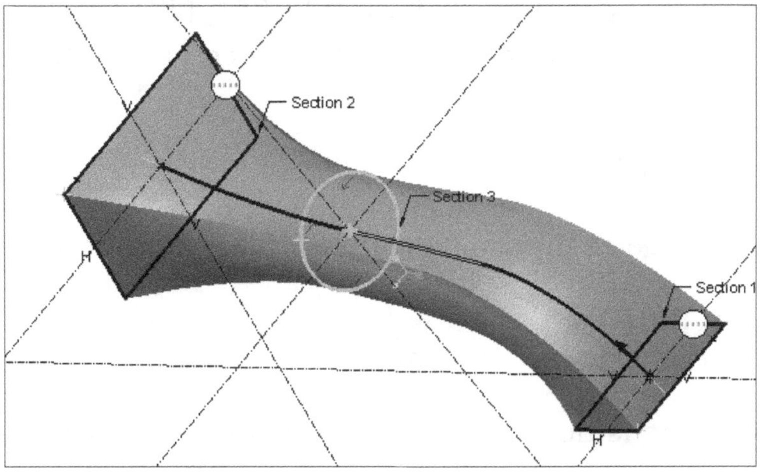

Figure-122. Swept blend feature

- Click on the **Insert** button from the **Sections** tab and create the closed loop section on the remaining point on the curve. Preview of the swept blend feature will be displayed; refer to Figure-123.

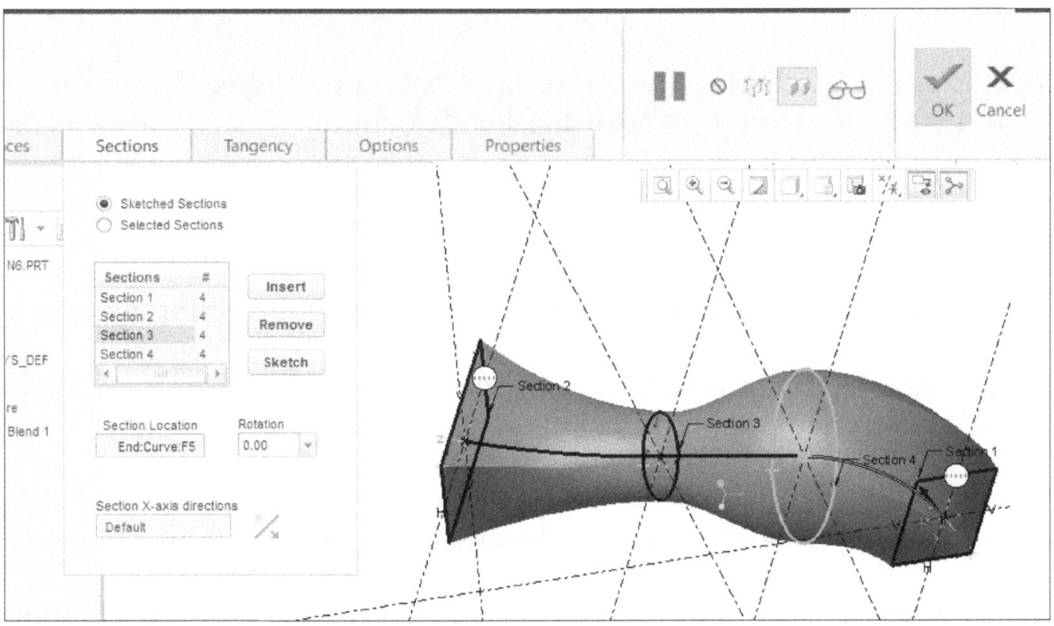

Figure-123. Preview of swept blend

- Using the options in the **Tangency** tab, you can specify the tangency condition for the feature at the start and the end points.
- Click on the **Options** tab to further refine the shape of the feature and specify desired parameters. Rest of the options in the **Swept Blend** contextual tab are same as discussed earlier.

Now, we are comfortable to create solid models with the help of solid modeling tools. But, there are some other tools that assist in creating 3D models. We will learn about them later in the book. In the next chapter, we will work on practical to create 3D models with the help of tools discussed till now.

Self Assessment

1. Which of the following is not default plane in Creo Parametric:

(a) RIGHT (b) TOP
(c) FRONT (d) LEFT

2. Which of the following are datum features in Creo Parametric:

(a) Face (b) Surface
(c) Sketch (d) Coordinate System

3. Which of the following is not a valid selection set for creating datum axis:

(a) a plane and a point (b) an axis and a point
(c) two points (d) 2 axes

4. The .... tool is used to create datum curve based on solution of equation.

5. The .... tool is used to create solids by using the volume swept by a close sketch while moving in perpendicular direction.

6. The .... tool is generally used when we need to create tubes/bars following a curvature.

7. The .... tool is used to blend two or more sections along a path.

8. In Creo Parametric, the orientation of the sketch in 3D environment is dependent on the selected reference planes. (T/F)

9. For creating solid extrude feature, we need a sketch with geometric entities in the form of single or multiple closed loops not intersecting or overlapping each other. (T/F)

10. For creating blend feature, number of corner points in the joining sketches should be same. (T/F)

11. Why should the "Use default template" checkbox be cleared while creating a new part?

a) To make Creo run faster
b) Because template selection is not required
c) To work with different units
d) To avoid saving the file automatically

12. What are datum features primarily used for?

a) To store files
b) To decorate models
c) To create references for other features
d) To add colors

13. Which of the following is not a datum feature in Creo Parametric?

a) Sketch
b) Point
c) Axis
d) Texture

14. What is the function of the Axis tool in Creo Parametric?

a) To delete an axis
b) To create a new part
c) To create an axis for reference or revolve features
d) To export the sketch

15. What happens when you select a plane and a point while holding the CTRL key to create an axis?

a) Axis is created at the origin
b) Axis is created perpendicular to the plane and passes through the point
c) Axis is created at random
d) Axis is deleted

16. What will be the result of selecting two points while holding the CTRL key for axis creation?

a) No axis is created
b) Axis perpendicular to one point is created
c) Axis is created through both points
d) Axis is parallel to the first point

17. When selecting a plane to create a coordinate system, how many references must you define the location with respect to?

a) One
b) Two
c) Three
d) None

18. What can be changed using the Ends Condition tab in the Curve Through Points tool?

a) Curve type
b) Point size
c) Tangency of the curve at endpoints
d) Curve color

19. What does the Curve From Point and Direction tool primarily create?

a) Tangent curves
b) Spline curves
c) Geodesic curves
d) Open loops

20. What input is required first when using the Curve From Point and Direction tool?

a) An axis
b) A surface
c) A datum point
d) A plane

21. What is used to define the orientation of a Curve From Point and Direction?

a) Datum point
b) Sketch
c) Direction and length
d) Coordinate system

22. In Curve From Equation, what must be selected before entering the equation?

a) A solid model
b) A sketch plane
c) A coordinate system
d) A curve type

23. Which tool is used to make the sketching plane parallel to the screen?

a) View Orientation
b) Zoom Fit
c) Sketch View
d) Align Tool

24. What is required to start sketching on a plane?

a) Color settings
b) Reference plane and orientation
c) Grid size
d) Dimensions

25. What is used to create 3D features in Creo?

a) Curve tools
b) Sketch tools
c) Shapes panel in the Model tab
d) Datum panel

26. What condition must a sketch meet to be used in the Extrude tool?

a) Only one closed loop
b) Any set of lines
c) Closed loops that do not intersect or overlap
d) Curves only

27. Which depth option allows the sketch to extrude until the next surface in its path?

a) To Reference
b) Through All
c) To Next
d) Symmetric

28. Which feature allows creation of a thin wall extrusion?

a) Thicken Sketch
b) Flip
c) Capped Ends
d) Sketch Region

29. Which tool allows for importing sketches in Creo?

a) Insert Geometry
b) Import Tool
c) External File
d) Import from Insert panel

30. What is the essential condition for the sketch used in the Revolve tool?

a) Open loop with axis
b) Closed loop with intersecting lines
c) Closed loop with a non-intersecting centerline
d) Spline curve only

31. What defines the amount of rotation for a Revolve feature?

a) Surface area
b) Rotation height
c) Revolution angle
d) Center axis

32. What must be created before using the Sweep tool?

a) An open loop sketch
b) A sketch with fillets
c) A closed loop sketch and a trajectory
d) A straight line

33. What key must be held to select multiple trajectories for a sweep?

a) Shift
b) Alt
c) Ctrl
d) Tab

34. What happens if the vertical span of a loop exceeds the pitch in a helical sweep?

a) The sweep becomes variable
b) The section gets flattened
c) The helical sweep fails due to internal overlapping
d) The sweep becomes hollow

35. What is the Volume Helical Sweep tool primarily used for?

a) Adding material along a helical path
b) Mirroring sections
c) Removing material by revolving sketch section along helix
d) Creating a solid helical shaft

36. Which tab contains the "Add Pitch" option in a helical sweep?

a) Options tab
b) Sketch tab
c) Pitch tab
d) Shape tab

37. What is the purpose of the Blend tool?

a) To blend colors
b) To create patterns
c) To create features by blending two or more sections
d) To hollow a model

38. What must be same in all sections for a proper blend feature?

a) Length of each edge
b) Number of vertices
c) Area
d) Shape

39. What is the function of the Divide tool during Blend creation?

a) Converts open loop into closed loop
b) Adds centerlines
c) Divides a circle into multiple vertices
d) Makes sketches symmetrical

40. What does the Rotational Blend tool use instead of offset distances?

a) Variable angles
b) Revolved sections
c) Offset angles
d) Mirror planes

41. In Rotational Blend, what element must be created at a desired distance?

a) Datum axis
b) Coordinate system
c) Datum centerline
d) Sweep profile

42. What is required in Swept Blend to match the number of sections with the trajectory?

a) Tangency
b) Straight segments
c) Equal number of points on the trajectory
d) Closed outer loop

43. What happens if section starting points are misaligned in Swept Blend?

a) The blend feature fails
b) The feature becomes twisted
c) Extra loops are added
d) The sketch is mirrored

44. Which tab helps define tangency conditions in Swept Blend?

a) Pitch tab
b) Sections tab
c) Tangency tab
d) References tab

45. Which feature in Volume Helical Sweep allows you to see the 3D cutting section?

a) Show path
b) Show axis
c) Show 3D object
d) Show volume

FOR STUDENT NOTES

Answer to Self Assessment Questions:

1. (d) **2.** (c) and (d) **3.** (d) **4.** Curve From Equation **5.** Extrude **6.** Sweep **7.** Swept Blend **8.** T **9.** T **10.** T

Chapter 5

3D Modeling Practical and Practice

Topics Covered

The major topics covered in this chapter are:

- ***Brief note about drawing***
- ***Practical 1 to Practical 6***
- ***Practice***

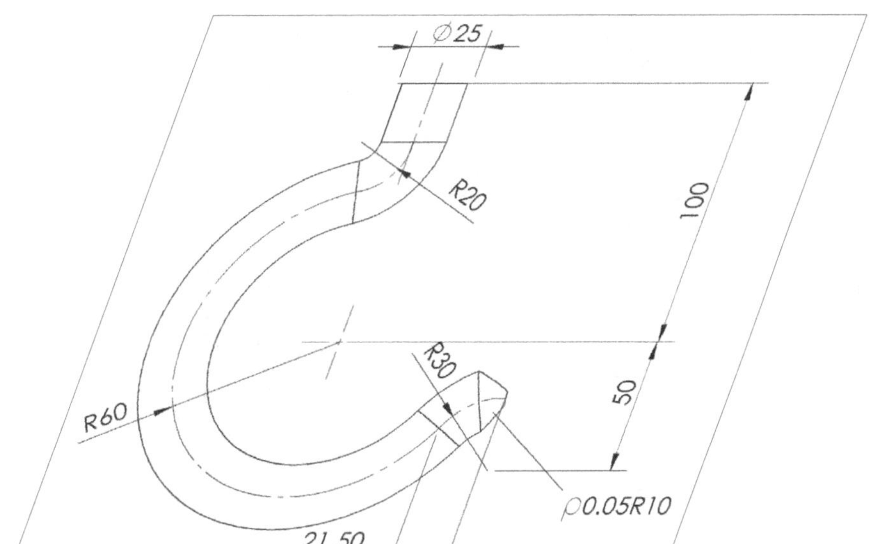

BRIEF NOTES ABOUT DRAWINGS

Till this point, we were creating sketches and then we were creating solid features like extrude, revolve, sweep, and so on with the help of those sketches. But, in real-world conditions, we are not going to have sketches. We will be finding our sketches from the engineering drawings. Being an engineer, you should be knowing about the engineering drawings and how to read them. A brief note on this topic is given next.

Engineering Drawing is the exact representation of an engineered component on the paper. There are a few qualities in Engineering Drawing given as:

- It is a clear and unmistakable representation of engineering component.
- It shows all the shapes and sizes of the engineering component.
- After reading the drawing, we get only one interpretation and there is no scope of confusion.

The Engineering Drawings are broadly classified into four categories:

Machine Drawing

It is pertaining to machine parts or components. It is presented through a number of orthographic views, so that the size and shape of the component is fully understood. Part drawings and assembly drawings belong to this classification. An example of a machine drawing is given in Figure-1.

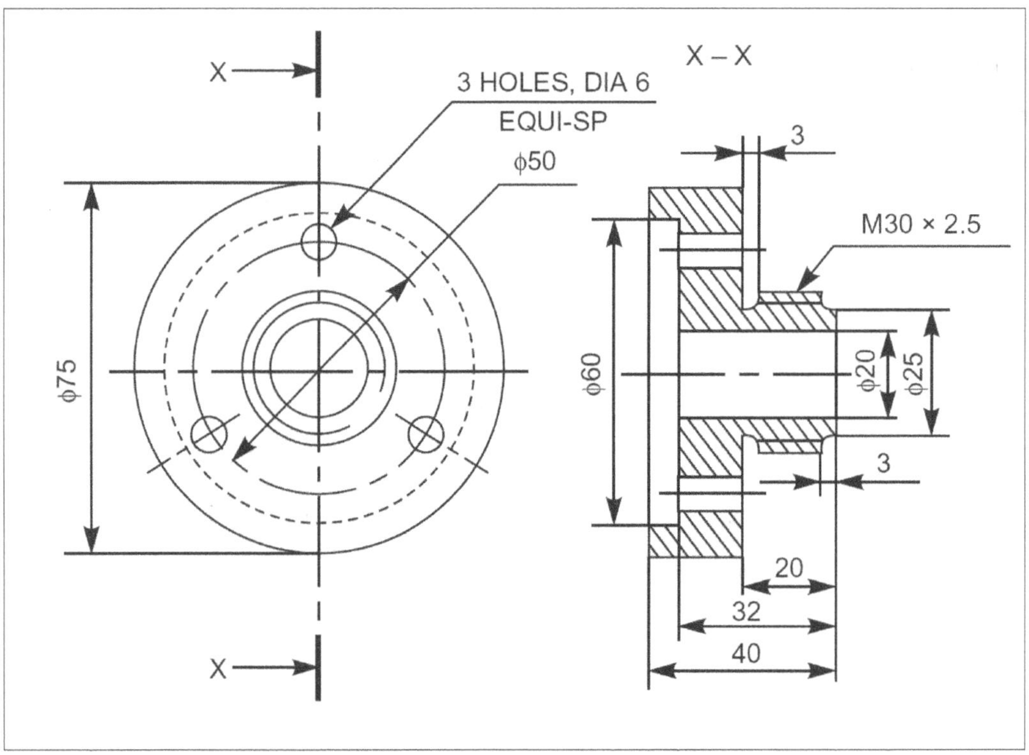

Figure-1. Machine drawing

Production Drawing

A production drawing, also referred to as working drawing, should furnish all the dimensions, limits, and special finishing processes such as heat treatment, honing, lapping, and surface finish to guide the craftsman on the shop floor in producing the component. The title should also mention the material used for the product, number of parts required for the assembled unit, and so on. Figure-2 shows an example of production drawing.

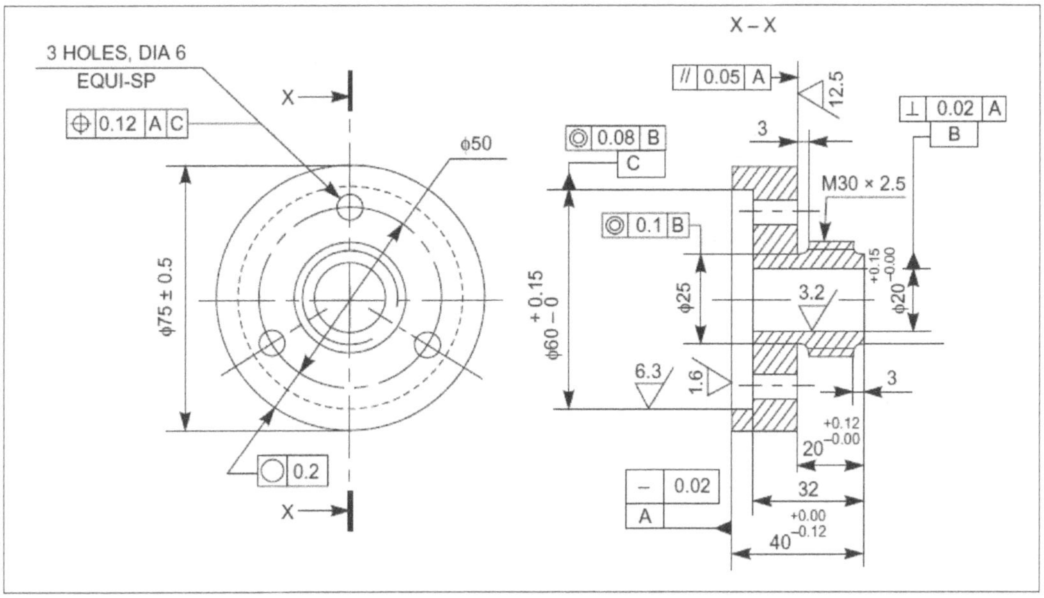

Figure-2. Production drawing

Part Drawing

Component or part drawing is a detailed drawing of a component to facilitate its manufacture. All the principles of orthographic projection and the technique of graphic representation must be followed to communicate the details in a part drawing. A part drawing with production details is rightly called as a production drawing or working drawing.

Assembly Drawing

A drawing that shows various parts of a machine in their correct working locations is an assembly drawing; refer to Figure-3.

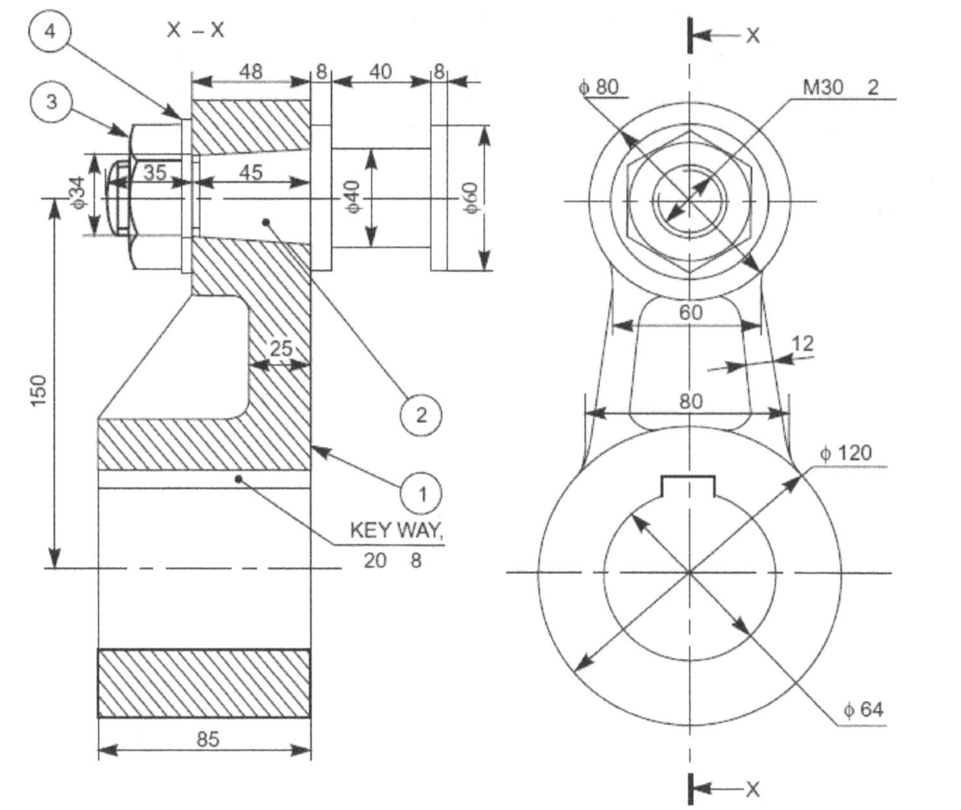

Parts List

Part No.	Name	Material	Qty
1	Crank	Forged Steel	1
2	Crank Pin	45C	1
3	Nut	MS	1
4	Washer	MS	1

Figure-3. Assembly drawing

COMPONENT REPRESENTATION METHODS

Broadly, there are two ways to present a component in engineering drawing; **Orthographic representation** and **Isometric representation**.

The orthographic representation is the method in which component is placed in the form of various views to completely define its shape and size. These orthographic views can be Front view, Right view, Top view, and so on. Refer to Figure-4.

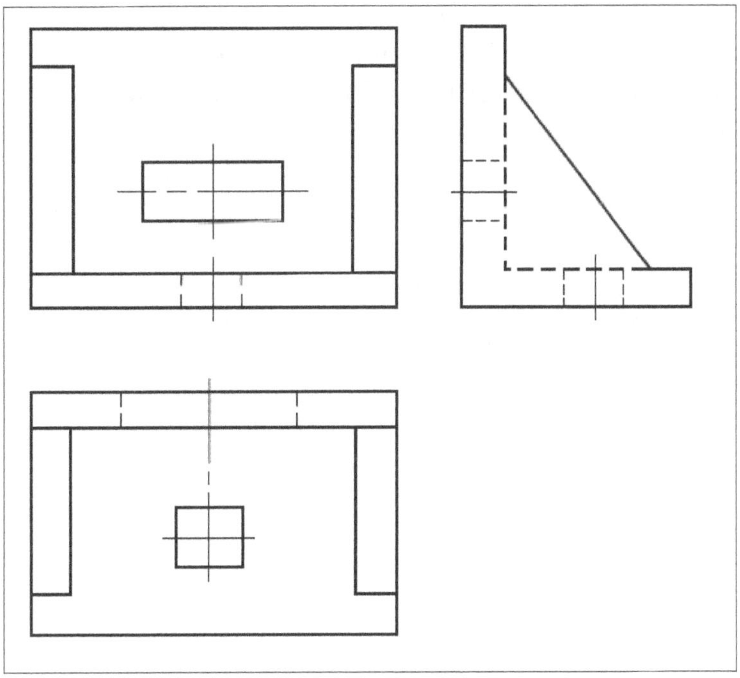

Figure-4. Orthographic views

The isometric representation is the method to display wire frame model of the object with its dimensions at standard angles from base planes. Note that all the objects can not be completely defined by this representation. So, it is useful to include Isometric view when we need to represent the shape of the object with some highly needed dimensions; refer to Figure-5.

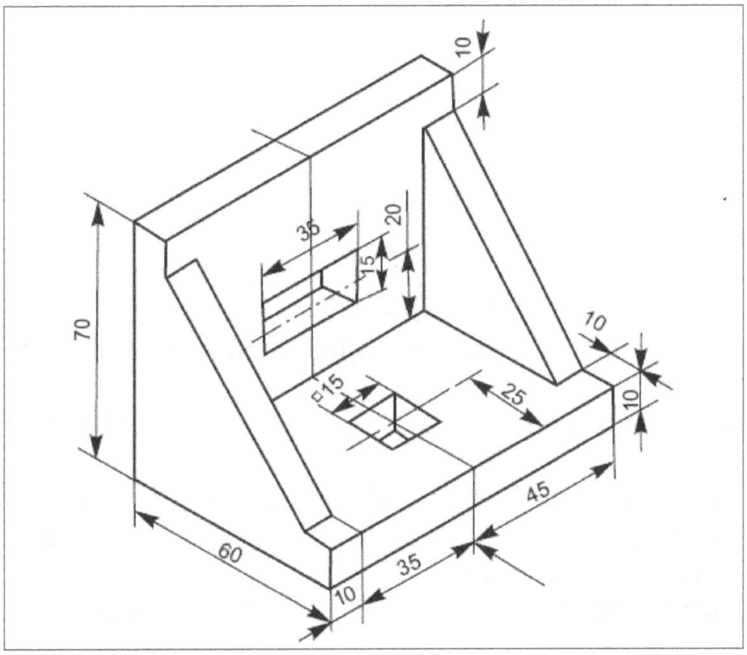

Figure-5. Isometric view

We will be using both the representations to create our models for practice.

PRACTICAL 1

In this practical, we will create a 3D model from the drawing given in Figure-6. The drawing has both isometric as well as orthographic views. You can use any of the two to create the model.

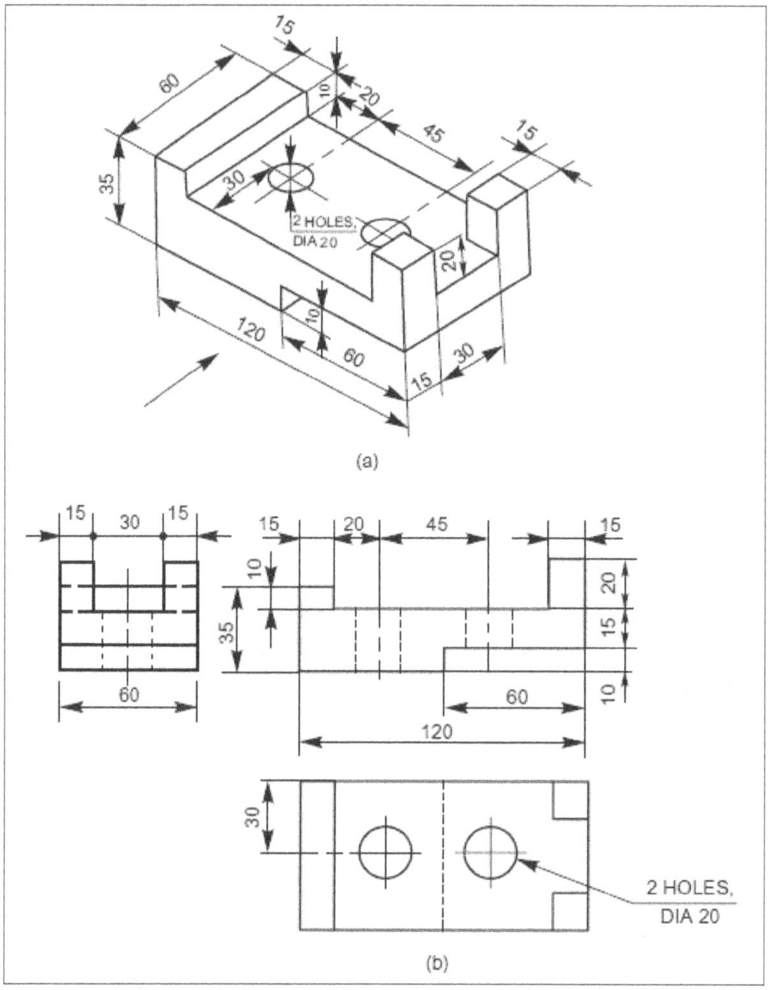

Figure-6. Practical 1

Starting Part Modeling

- Double-click on the Creo Parametric icon from the desktop to start Creo Parametric if not started already.
- Click on the **New** button from the **Data** panel in the **Ribbon**. The **New** dialog box will be displayed.
- Specify desired name for the file and clear the **Use default template** check box.
- Click on the **OK** button from the dialog box. The **New File Options** dialog box will be displayed as discussed earlier.
- Select the **mmns part solid** option from the dialog box and click on the **OK** button.

Creating base sketch

- Click on the **Sketch** button from the **Datum** panel in the **Ribbon**. The **Sketch** dialog box will be displayed.
- Select the **FRONT** plane from the **Model Tree** and click on the **Sketch** button from the **Sketch** dialog box. The sketching environment will be displayed.

- Click on the **Sketch View** button from the **In-Graphics** toolbar and create the sketch as shown in Figure-7.

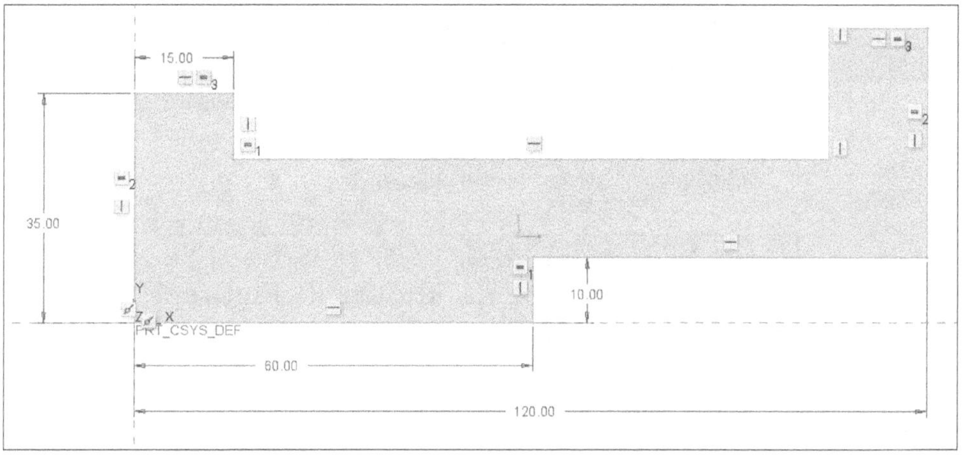

Figure-7. Sketch for base

- Click on the **OK** button from the **Sketch** contextual tab.

Creating Extrude feature

- Click on the **Extrude** tool from the **Shapes** panel in the **Model** tab of the **Ribbon**. The **Extrude** contextual tab will be displayed.
- Select the sketch earlier created. Preview of the extrude feature will be displayed; refer to Figure-8.

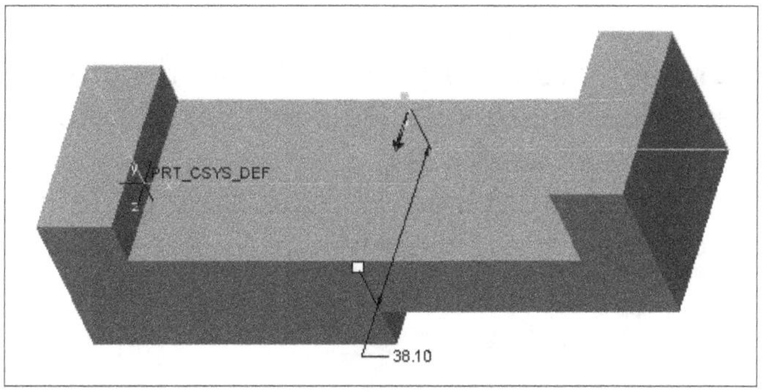

Figure-8. Preview of extrude feature

- Specify the value of height for extrusion as **60**; refer to Figure-6 for dimension.
- Click on the **OK** button from the **Extrude** contextual tab to create the feature.

Creating Extrude cut feature

- Click on the **Extrude** tool from the **Shapes** panel in the **Ribbon**. You are asked to select a sketching plane or sketch.
- Select the face as shown in Figure-9. The sketching environment will become active.
- Click on the **Sketch View** button from the **In-Graphics** toolbar to make the sketching plane parallel to the screen.
- Click on the **Project** tool from the **Sketching** panel. You are asked to select the entities to be projected on the sketching plane.

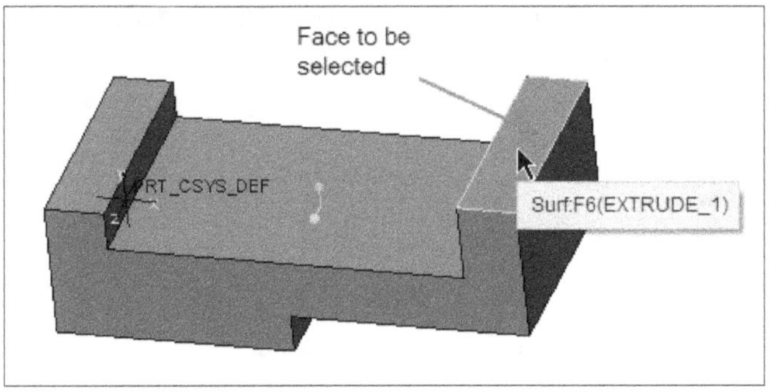

Figure-9. Face to be selected for cut

- Select the edges of the selected face as shown in Figure-10. The edges will be projected on the sketching plane; refer to Figure-11.

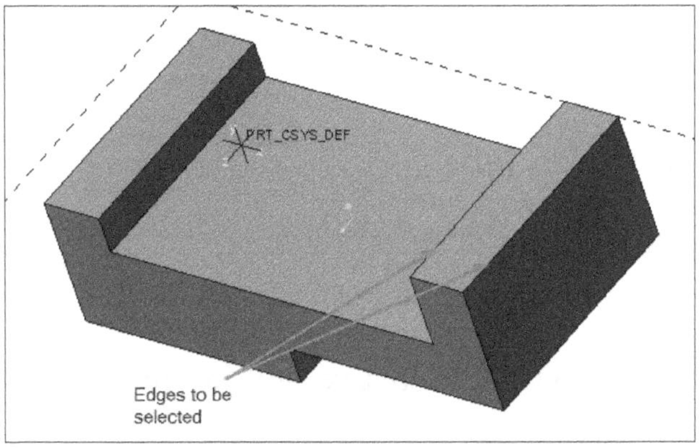

Figure-10. Edges selected for projection

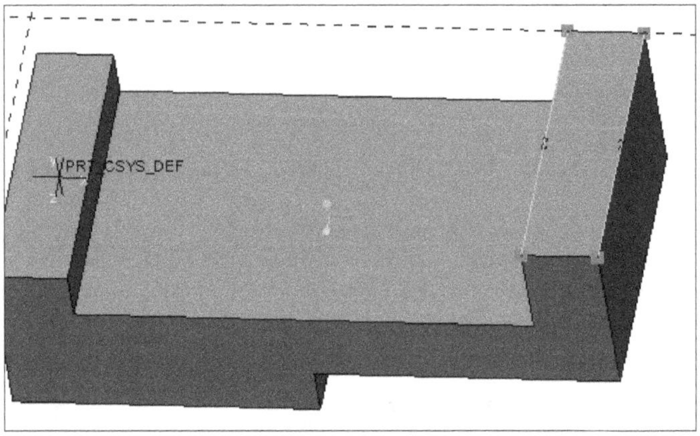

Figure-11. Edges projected

- Using the **Line Chain** tool, create the two intersecting lines and dimension them as in Figure-12. Note that dimensions that are in red color are strong dimensions (i.e. dimension with value 15 and 30).
- Click on the **Delete Segment** tool from the **Editing** panel in the **Ribbon**. Drag the cursor and create a cutter curve as shown in Figure-13. The box will be created as shown in Figure-14.

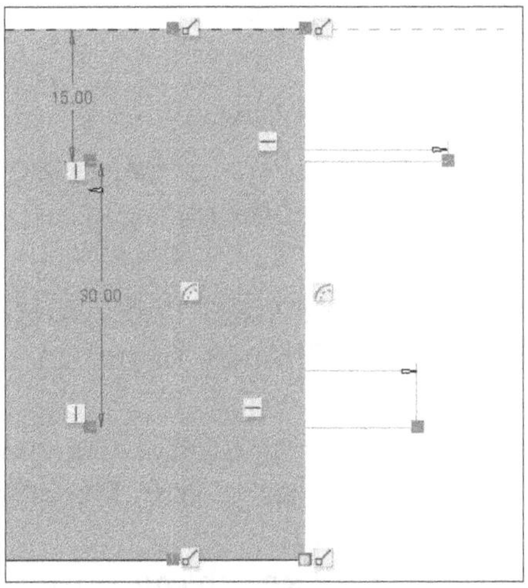

Figure-12. Lines after dimensioning

- Click on the **OK** button from the **Sketch** contextual tab. Preview of the extrude feature will be displayed.
- Click on the **Remove Material** button from the **Extrude** contextual tab displayed and then click on the **Flip depth direction** button. The preview of the extrude cut feature will be displayed; refer to Figure-15.

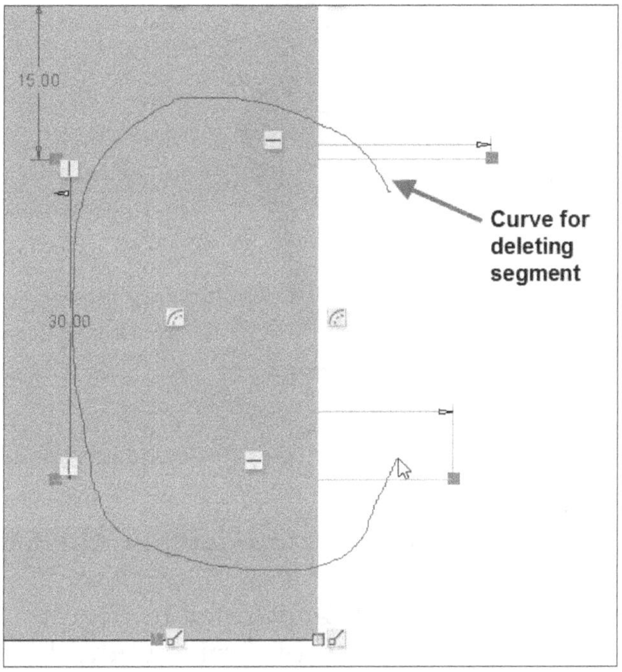

Figure-13. Segment deletion

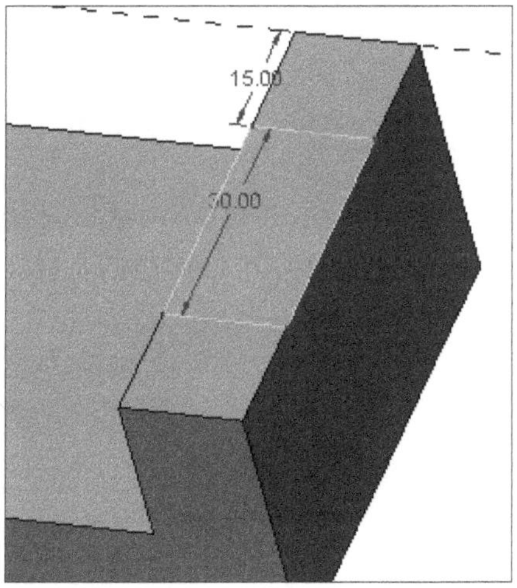

Figure-14. Box created after trimming

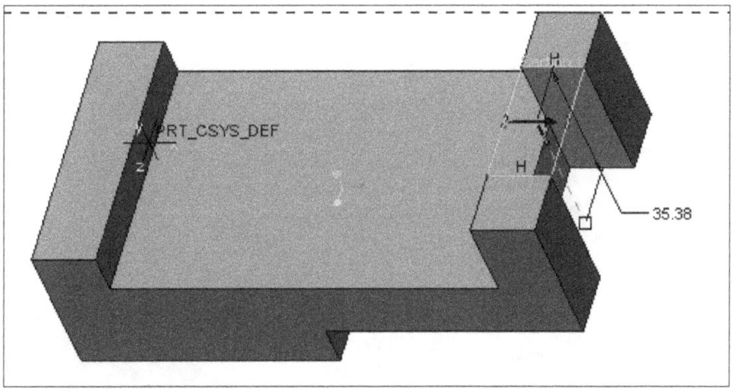

Figure-15. Preview of extrude cut feature

- Click in the **Depth** value edit box of the **Extrude** contextual tab and specify the value as **20**. Preview of the feature will be displayed as shown in Figure-16.

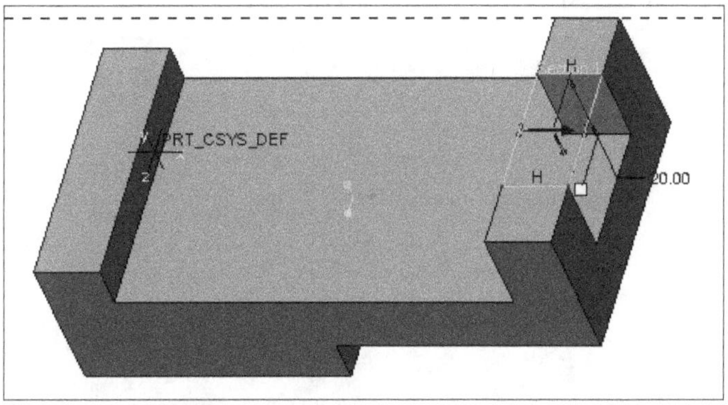

Figure-16. Preview of the cut feature

- Click on the **OK** button from the **Extrude** contextual tab to create the cut feature.

Creating Holes

- Click on the **Extrude** tool again and select the face as shown in Figure-17. The sketching environment will become active.

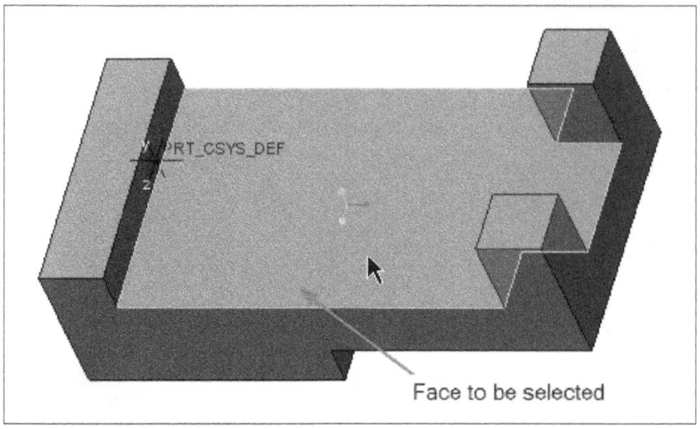

Figure-17. Face to be selected for holes

- Click on the **Sketch View** button from the **In-Graphics** toolbar to make the sketching plane parallel to the screen.
- Click on the **Center and Point** tool from the **Circle** drop-down in the **Sketching** panel of the **Sketch** contextual tab in the **Ribbon**.
- Create two circles of same radius on the selected face; refer to Figure-18. Note that dimension need not to be the same but location of circles should be similar to as shown in Figure-18.

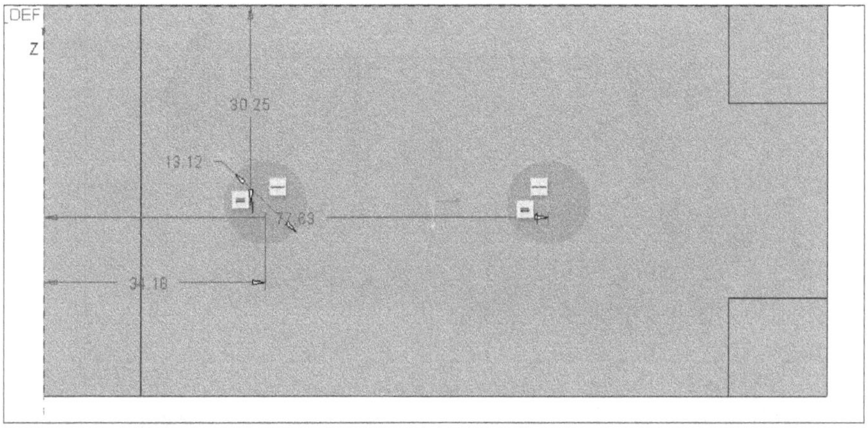

Figure-18. Circles created for hole

- Dimension the circles as shown in Figure-19.

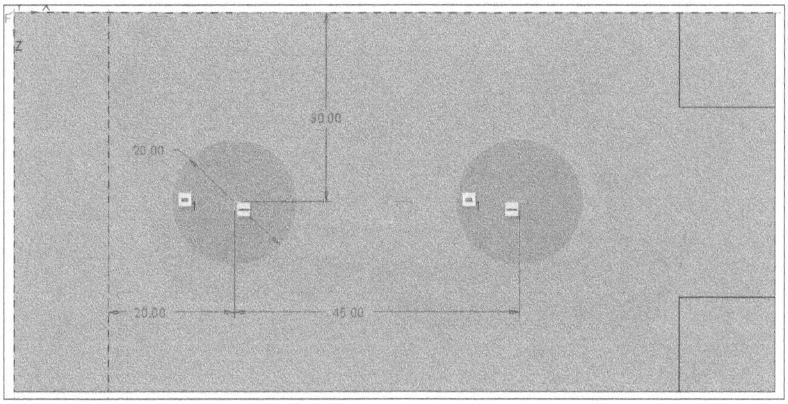

Figure-19. Circles after dimensioning

- Click on the **OK** button from the **Sketch** contextual tab. Preview of the extrude feature will be displayed.
- Click on the **Remove Material** button and then **Flip depth** button from the **Extrude** contextual tab.
- Click on the down arrow in the **Depth** area of the contextual tab and select the **Extrude to intersect with all surface** option.

- Click on the **OK** button from the **Extrude** contextual tab. The model will be displayed as shown in Figure-20.

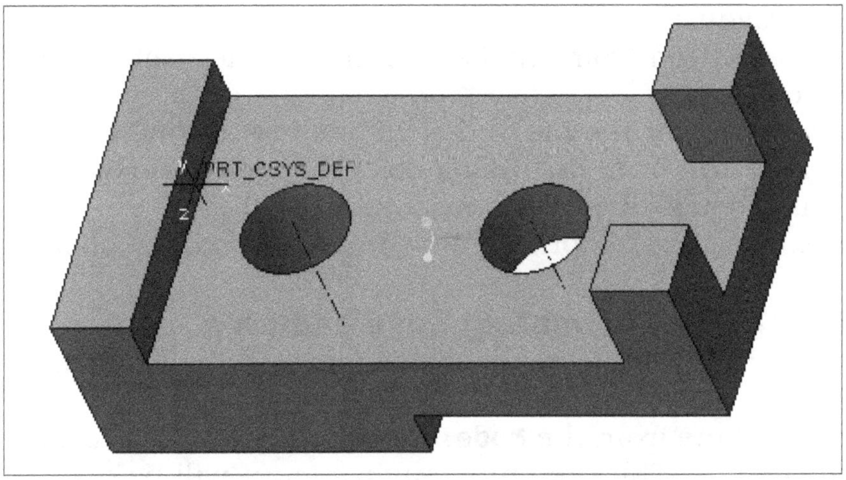

Figure-20. Model after creating holes

PRACTICAL 2

Create a solid model by using the drawing given in Figure-21.

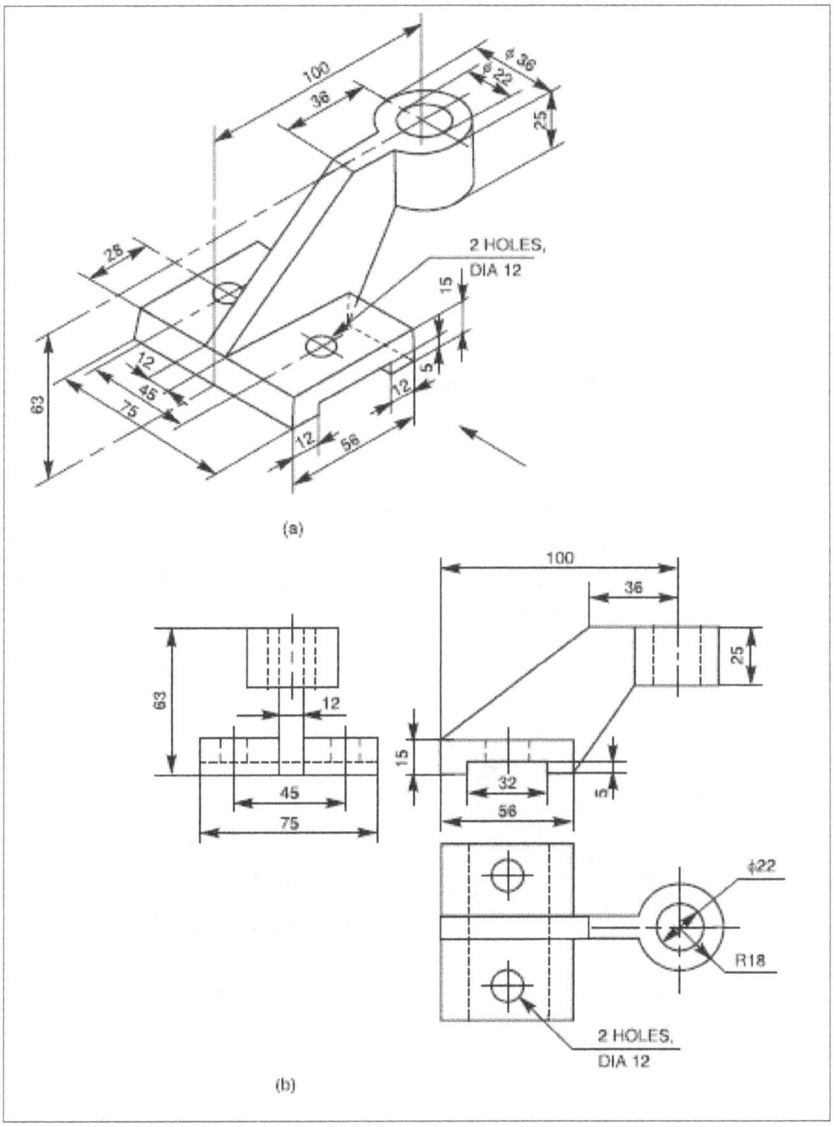

Figure-21. Practical 2

Starting Part Modeling

- Double-click on the Creo Parametric icon from the desktop to start Creo Parametric if not started already.
- Click on the **New** button from the **Data** panel in the **Ribbon**. The **New** dialog box will be displayed.
- Specify desired name for the file and clear the **Use default template** check box.
- Click on the **OK** button from the dialog box. The **New File Options** dialog box will be displayed as discussed earlier.
- Select the **mmns part solid** option from the dialog box and click on the **OK** button.

Creating base sketch

- Click on the **Sketch** button from the **Datum** panel in the **Ribbon**. The **Sketch** dialog box will be displayed.
- Select the **RIGHT** plane from the **Model Tree** and click on the **Sketch** button from the **Sketch** dialog box. The sketching environment will be displayed.
- Click on the **Sketch View** button from the **In-Graphics** toolbar and create the sketch as shown in Figure-22.

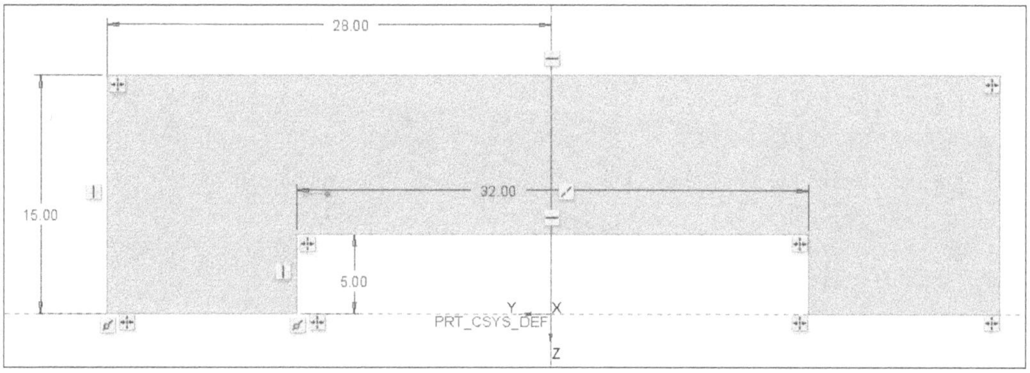

Figure-22. Sketch to be created

- Click on the **OK** button from the **Sketch** contextual tab to exit the sketching environment.

Creating Base feature

- Click on the **Extrude** tool from the **Shapes** panel in the **Ribbon**.
- Select the sketch recently created, if not selected by default. Preview of the extrude feature will be displayed; refer to Figure-23.

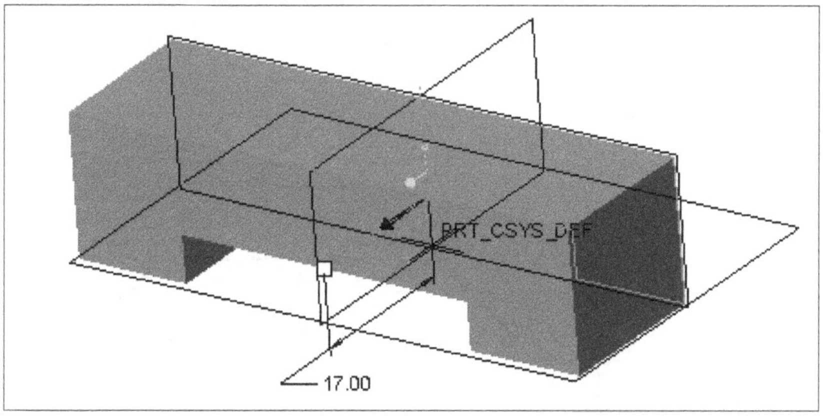

Figure-23. Preview of extrude

- Click on the down arrow from **Depth** area of the contextual tab and select the **Symmetric** option; refer to Figure-24.
- Click in the **Extrude depth** edit box and specify the value as **75**. Preview of the feature will be displayed as shown in Figure-25.

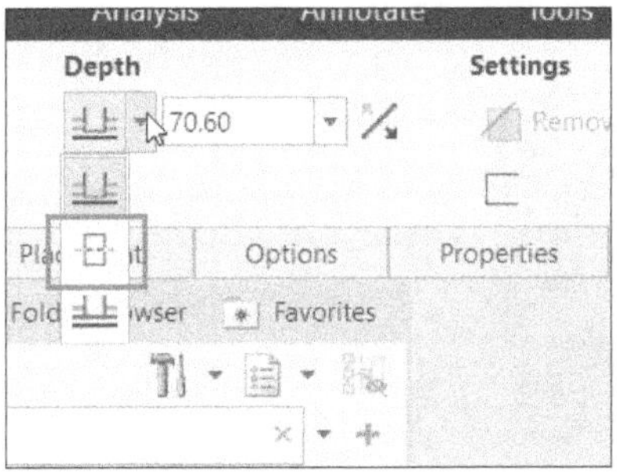

Figure-24. Extrude on both sides

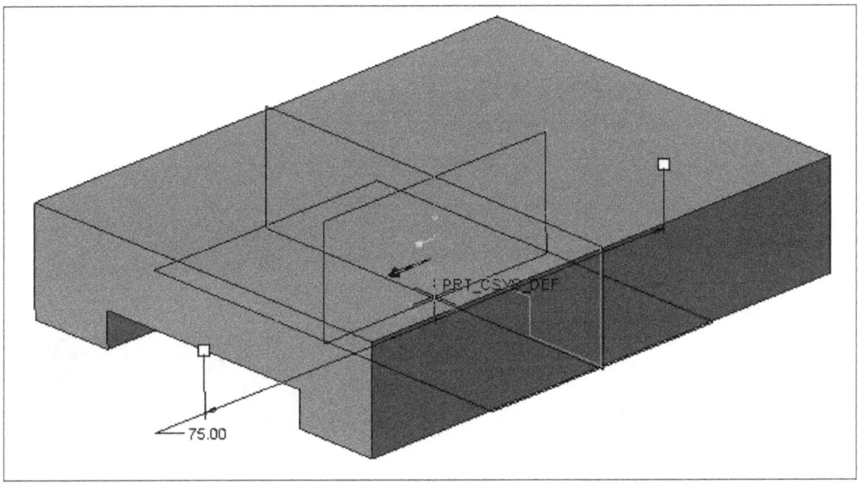

Figure-25. Extrude feature

- Click on the **OK** button from the contextual tab to create the feature.

Creating second feature

Now, we will create the rib like structure for the model. The procedure to do so is given next.

- Click on the **Sketch** tool from the **Datum** panel in the **Ribbon** and select the **RIGHT** plane as sketching plane.
- Make sure that **TOP** plane is selected in the **Reference** selection box and **Top** is selected in the **Orientation** drop-down.
- Create the sketch as shown in Figure-26.

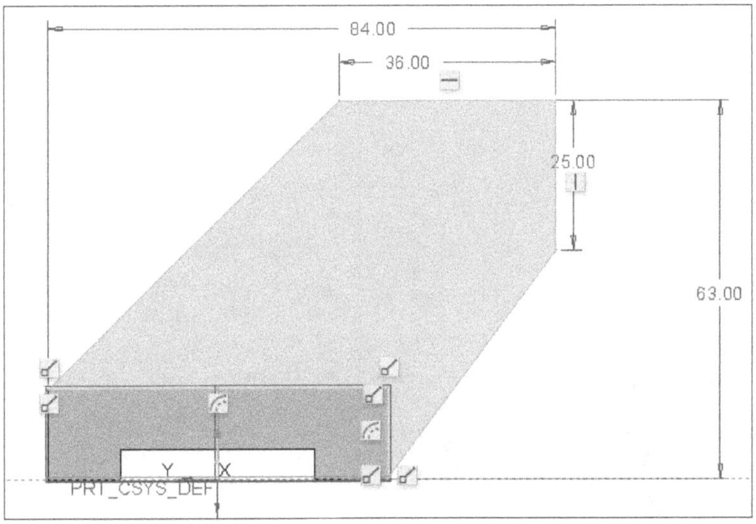

Figure-26. Sketch for rib

- Click on the **OK** button from the **Sketch** contextual tab and click on the **Extrude** tool from the **Ribbon**.
- The preview of extrude feature will be displayed. Select the **Symmetric** option from drop-down in the **Depth** area and specify the extrude depth as **12**; refer to Figure-27.

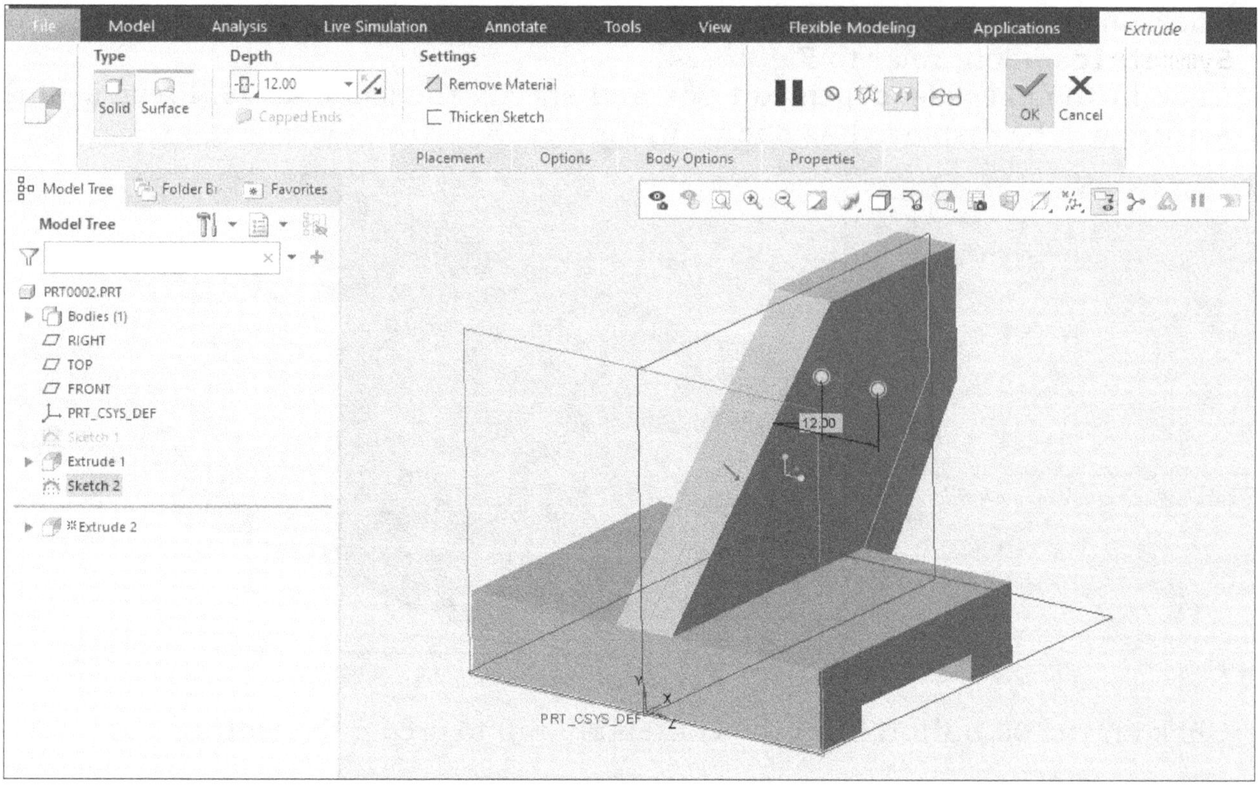

Figure-27. Extruding the rib

- Click on the **OK** button from the **Extrude** contextual tab to create the feature.

Create the third feature

- Click on the **Sketch** tool from the **Datum** panel in the **Ribbon**. The **Sketch** dialog box is displayed.
- Select the top face of the second feature as sketching plane, **RIGHT** plane as reference with **Right** as orientation, and click on the **Sketch** button from the dialog box. Refer to Figure-28.

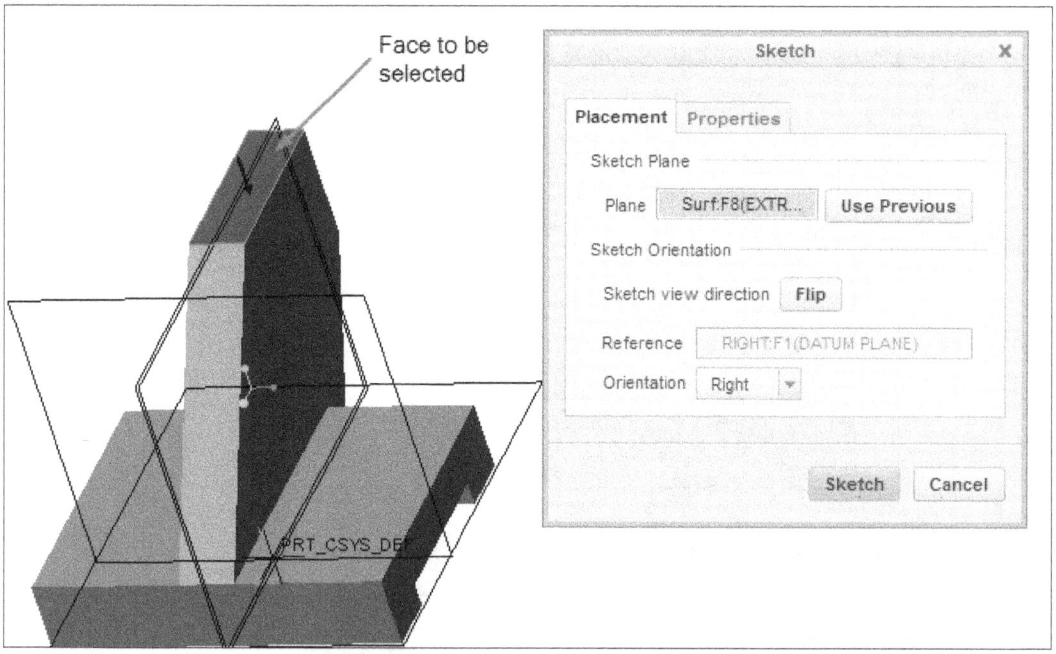

Figure-28. Sketching face to be selected

- Create the sketch as shown in Figure-29.

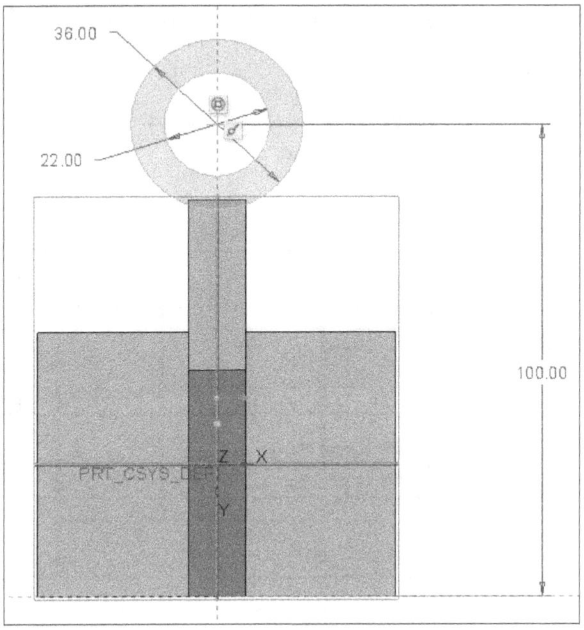

Figure-29. Sketch for third feature

- Click on the **OK** button from the **Sketch** contextual tab.
- Click on the **Extrude** button from the **Shapes** panel in the **Ribbon** and extrude the sketch by depth of **25**; refer to Figure-30.

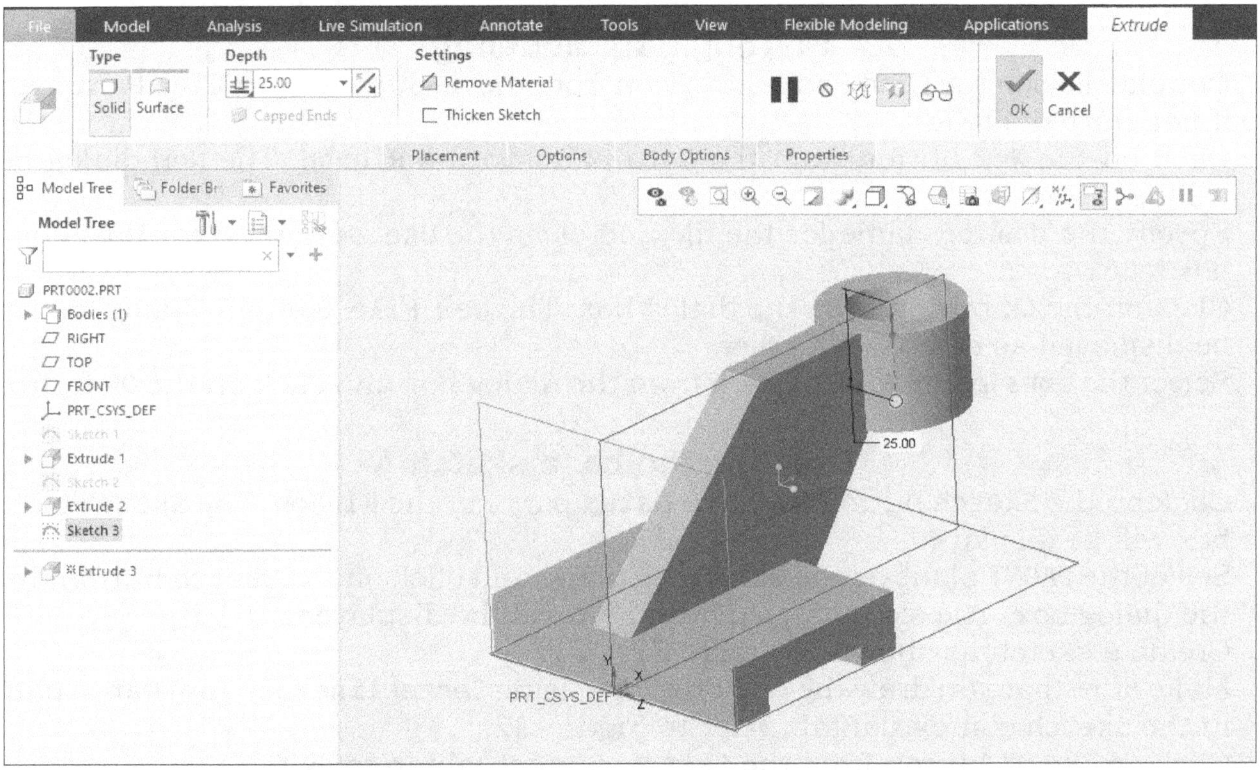

Figure-30. Preview of the third feature

- Click on the **OK** button from the **Extrude** contextual tab to create the feature.

PRACTICAL 3

Create a solid model by using the drawing given in Figure-31.

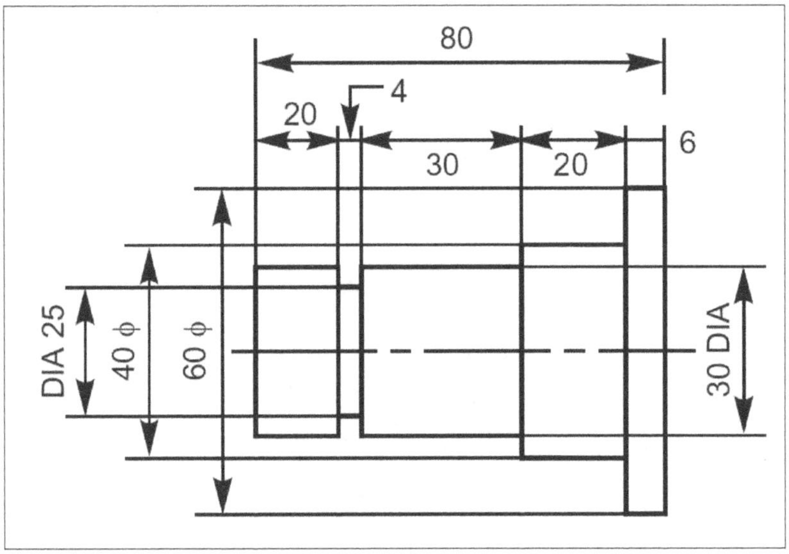

Figure-31. Practical 3

From the above drawing, we can clearly understand that we need to create a model of a round shaft with different diameters at different locations. Here, we can use the **Revolve** tool to create the model efficiently.

Starting Part Modeling

- Double-click on the Creo Parametric icon from the desktop to start Creo Parametric if not started already.
- Click on the **New** button from the **Data** panel in the **Ribbon**. The **New** dialog box will be displayed.
- Specify the desired name for the file and clear the **Use default template** check box.
- Click on the **OK** button from the dialog box. The **New File Options** dialog box will be displayed as discussed earlier.
- Select the **mmns part solid** option from the dialog box and click on the **OK** button.

Creating the base sketch

- Click on the **Sketch** button from the **Datum** panel in the **Ribbon**. The **Sketch** dialog box will be displayed.
- Select the **FRONT** plane as the sketching plane and click on the **Sketch** button from the dialog box. The sketching environment will be displayed.
- Create a sketch as shown in Figure-32.
- Make sure that you draw the centerline by using **Centerline** tool from **Datum** panel in the **Sketch** contextual tab; refer to Figure-32.
- Click on the **OK** button from the **Sketch** contextual tab to exit.

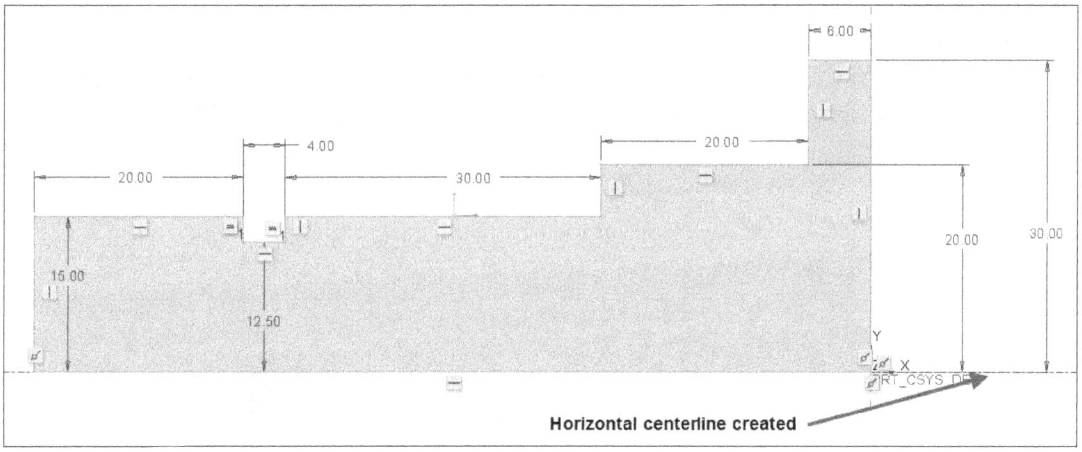

Figure-32. Sketch for base feature

Creating Revolve feature

- Click on the **Revolve** tool from the **Shapes** panel in the **Ribbon**. The **Revolve** contextual tab will be displayed.
- Select the sketch earlier created. Preview of the revolve feature will be displayed; refer to Figure-33.

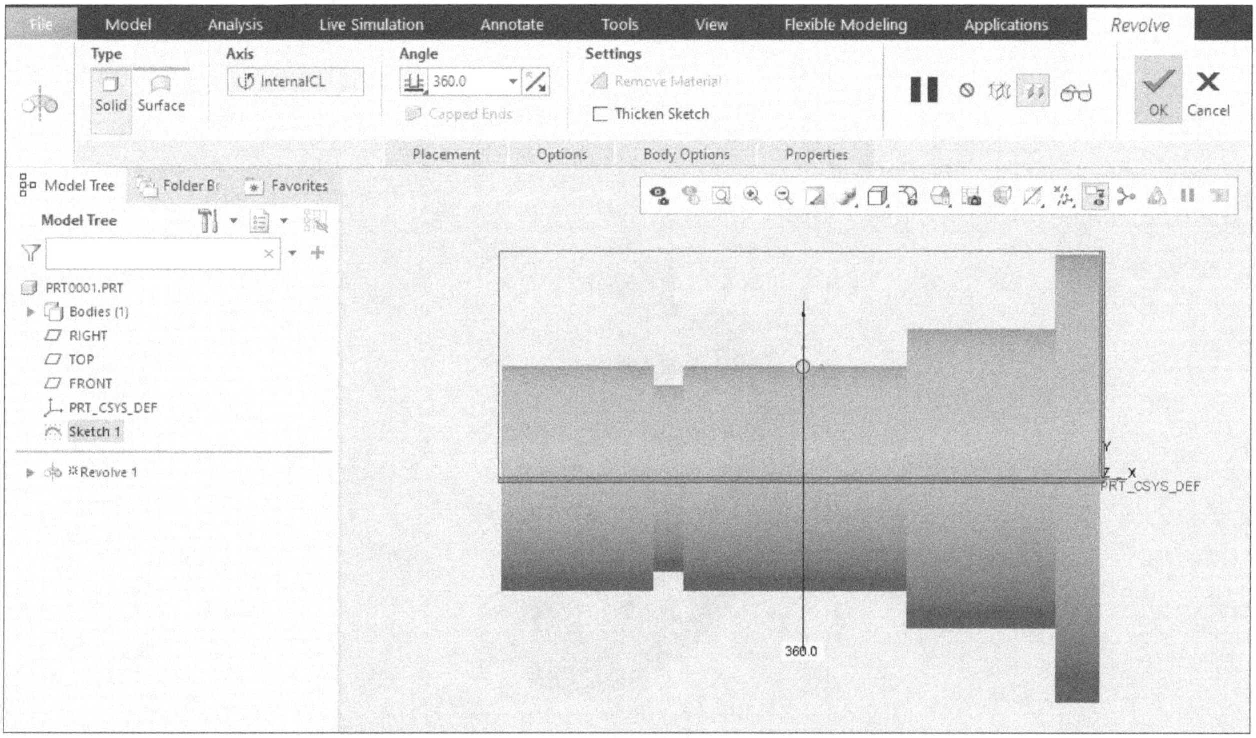

Figure-33. Preview of the revolve feature

- Make sure that **360** is specified as revolution angle and then click on the **OK** button from the **Revolve** contextual tab to create the feature.

PRACTICAL 4

In this practical, we will create a model as per the drawing given in Figure-34. The model after creation should be displayed as shown in Figure-35.

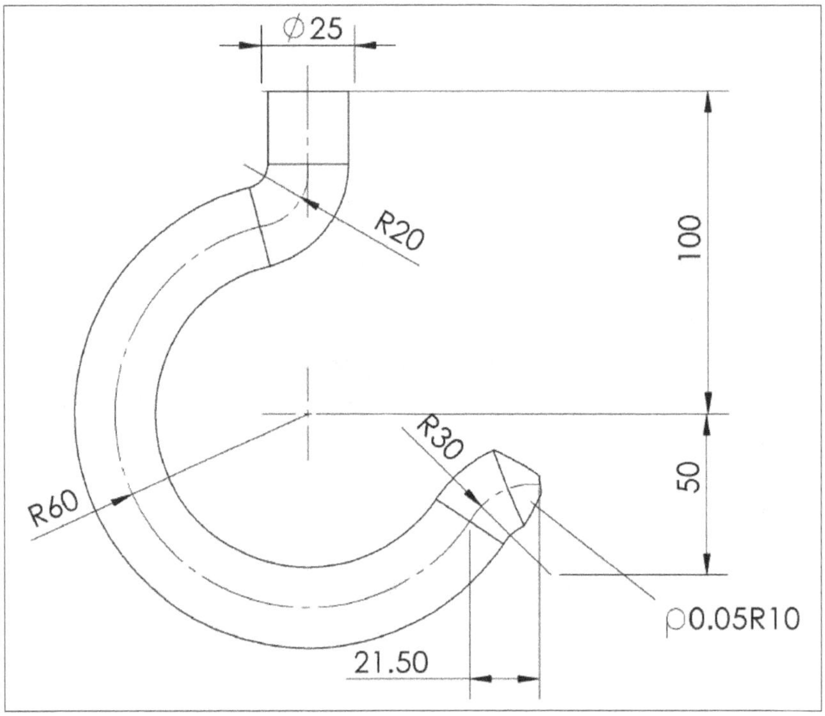

Figure-34. Practical 4

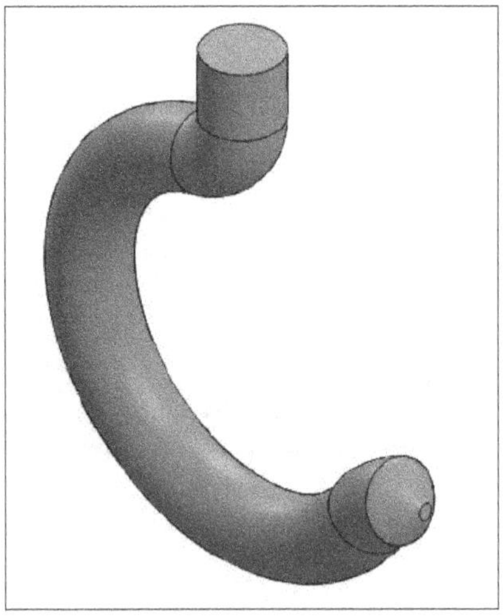

Figure-35. Model for practical 4

Starting Part Modeling

- Double-click on the Creo Parametric icon from the desktop to start Creo Parametric, if not started already.
- Click on the **New** button from the **Data** panel in the **Ribbon**. The **New** dialog box will be displayed.
- Specify desired name for the file and clear the **Use default template** check box.
- Click on the **OK** button from the dialog box. The **New File Options** dialog box will be displayed as discussed earlier.
- Select the **mmns part solid** option from the dialog box and click on the **OK** button.

Creating the base sketch

- Click on the **Sketch** button from the **Datum** panel in the **Ribbon**. The **Sketch** dialog box will be displayed.
- Select the **RIGHT** plane as the sketching plane and click on the **Sketch** button from the dialog box. The sketching environment will be displayed.
- Create a circle of diameter **120 mm** connected with line and arc as shown in Figure-36.

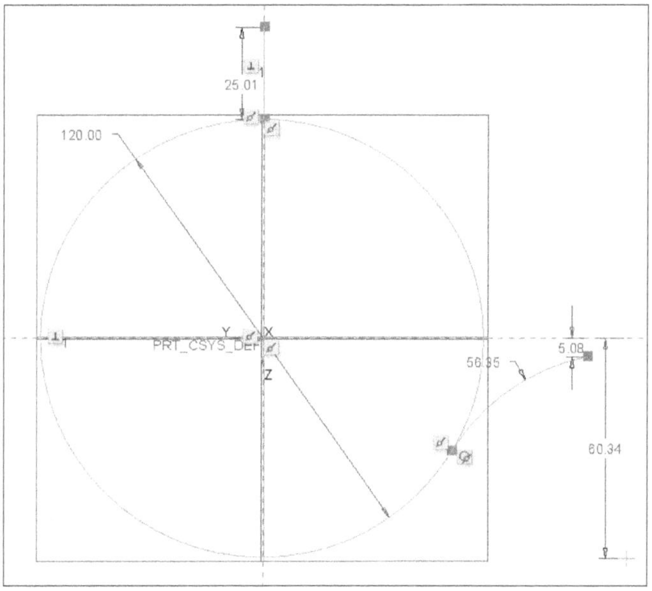

Figure-36. Sketch for path

- Change the dimensions of the sketch as shown in Figure-37.

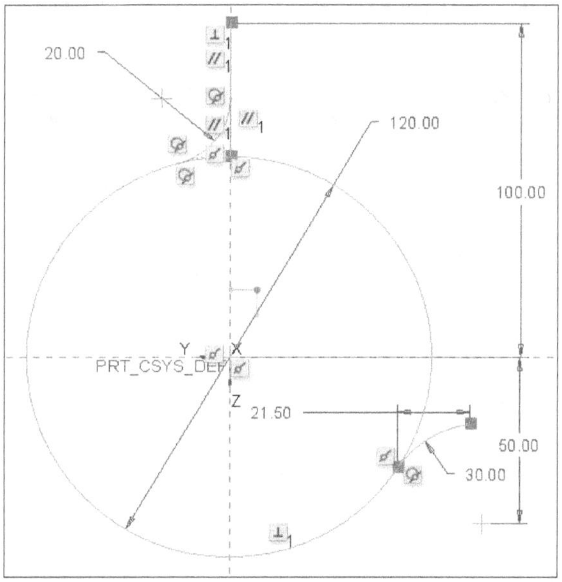

Figure-37. Sketch after dimensioning

- Trim the unwanted portion of the path so that the path is displayed as shown in Figure-38.

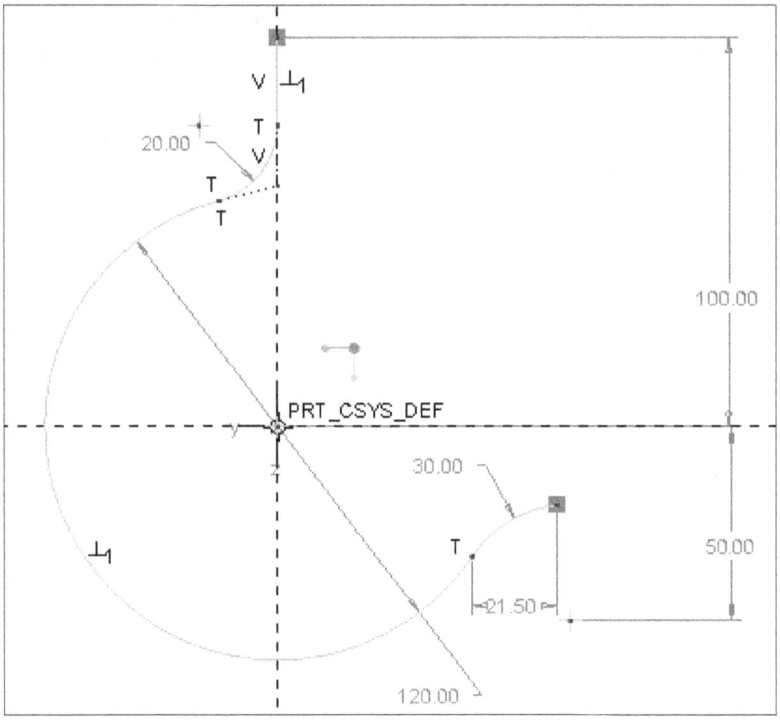

Figure-38. Sketch after trimming

- Click on the **OK** button from the **Sketch** contextual tab to exit the sketching environment.

Creating Sweep feature

- Click on the **Sweep** tool from the **Sweep** drop-down in the **Shapes** panel of the **Ribbon**. The **Sweep** contextual tab will be displayed with sketch selected as trajectory; refer to Figure-39.

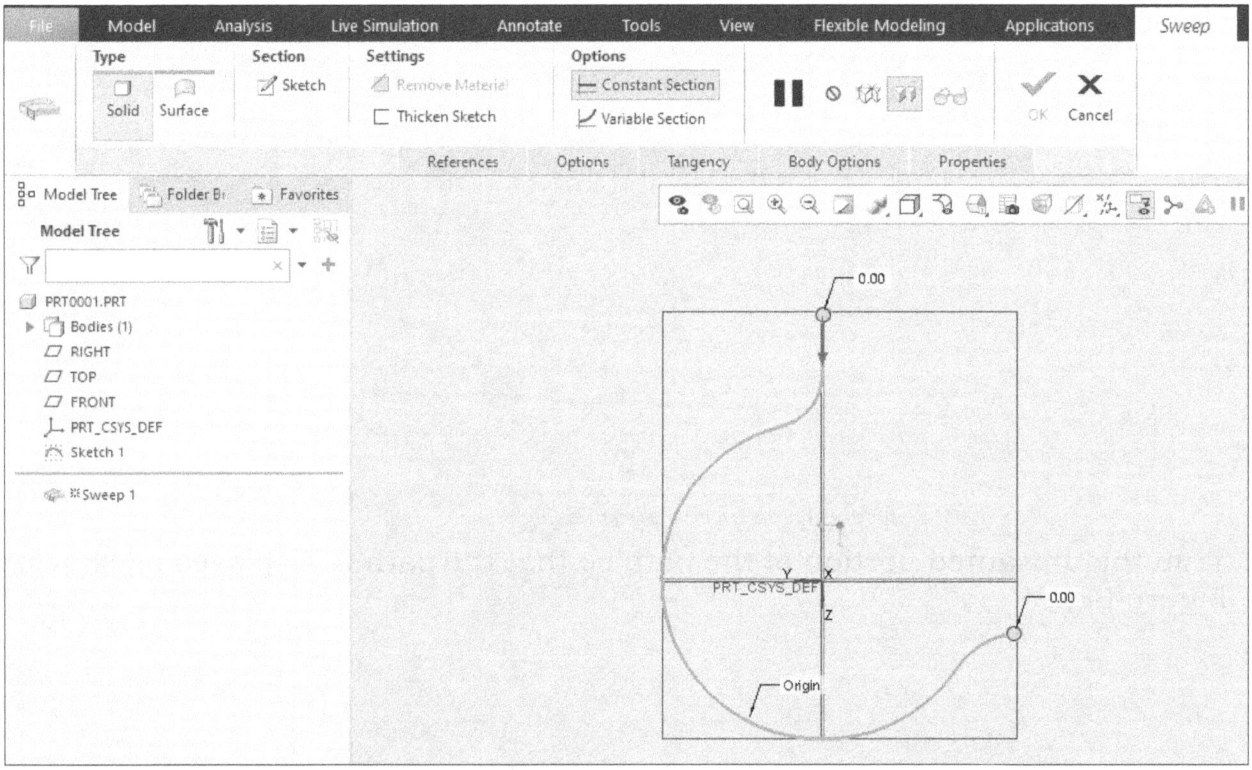

Figure-39. Sweep contextual tab

- Click on the **Sketch** button from **Section** area of the contextual tab. The sketching environment will be displayed.
- Click on the **Sketch View** button from the **In-Graphics toolbar** and draw the sketch as shown in Figure-40.
- Click on the **OK** button from the **Sketch** contextual tab. Preview of the sweep feature will be displayed; refer to Figure-41.

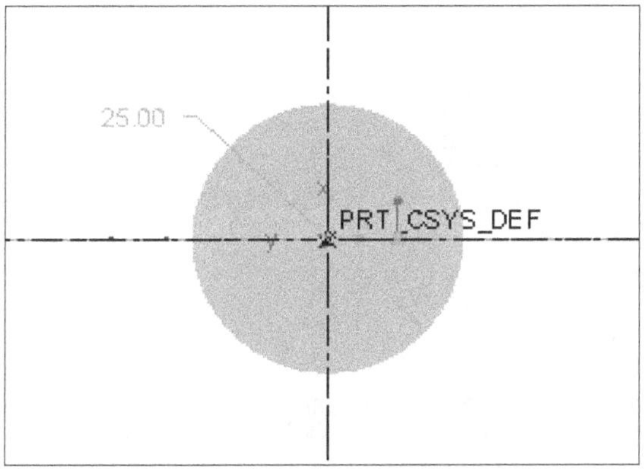

Figure-40. Sketch to create

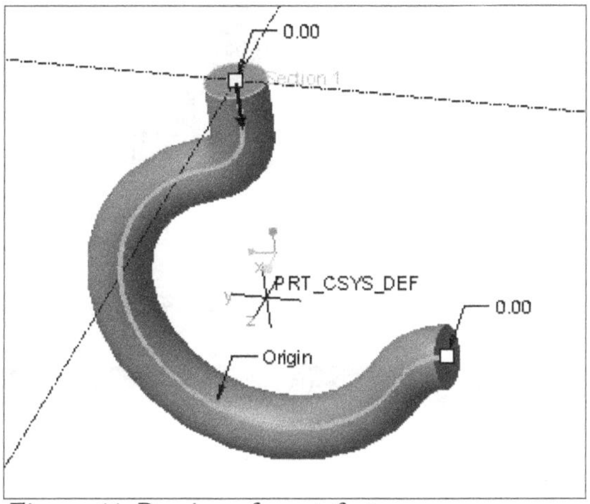

Figure-41. Preview of sweep feature

- Click on the **OK** button from the **Sweep** contextual tab to create the feature.

Now, we will apply a conic fillet on the end edge of sweep feature. You will learn more about this tool in the next chapter.

- Click on the **Round** tool from the **Round** drop-down in the **Engineering** panel of the **Ribbon**; refer to Figure-42. The **Round** contextual tab will be displayed in the **Ribbon**; refer to Figure-43.

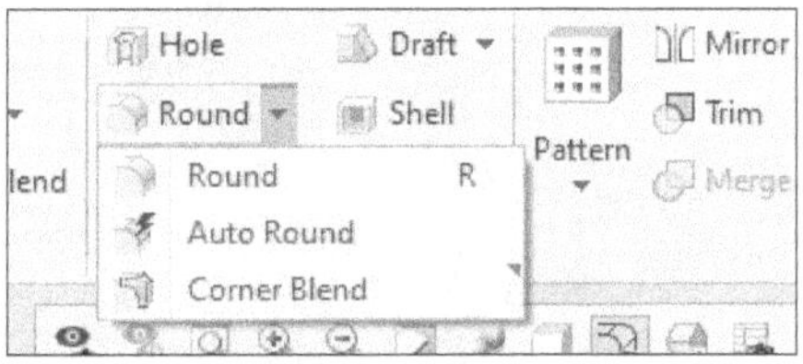

Figure-42. Round drop-down

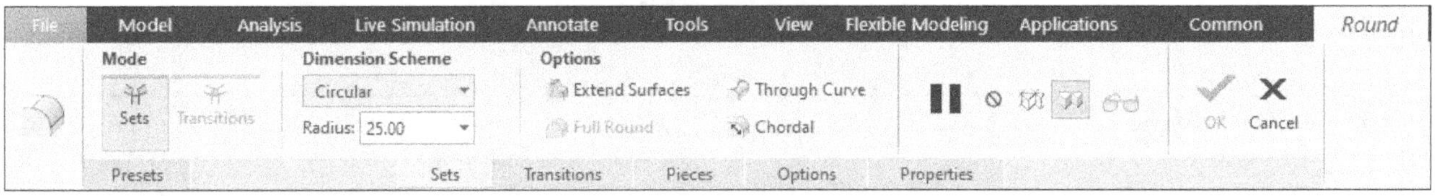

Figure-43. Round contextual tab

- Select the end edge of the sweep feature as shown in Figure-44. Preview of the round will be displayed; refer to Figure-45.
- Select **Conic** option from the **Cross-sectional shape** drop-down in the **Dimension Scheme** area of the contextual tab; refer to Figure-46. Two values will be displayed on the preview of round; refer to Figure-47.
- Change the **Rho** value i.e. 0.50 to 0.05 and change the **D** value i.e. 2.70 to 10. Preview of the round after changing the values will be displayed as shown in Figure-48.
- Click on the **OK** button from the **Round** contextual tab to create the feature.

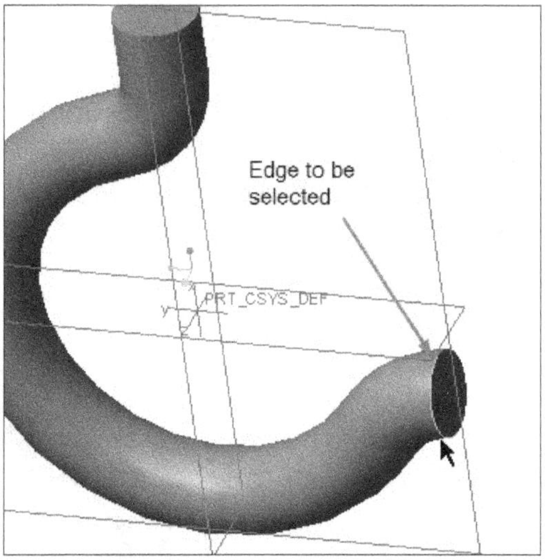

Figure-44. Edge to be selected

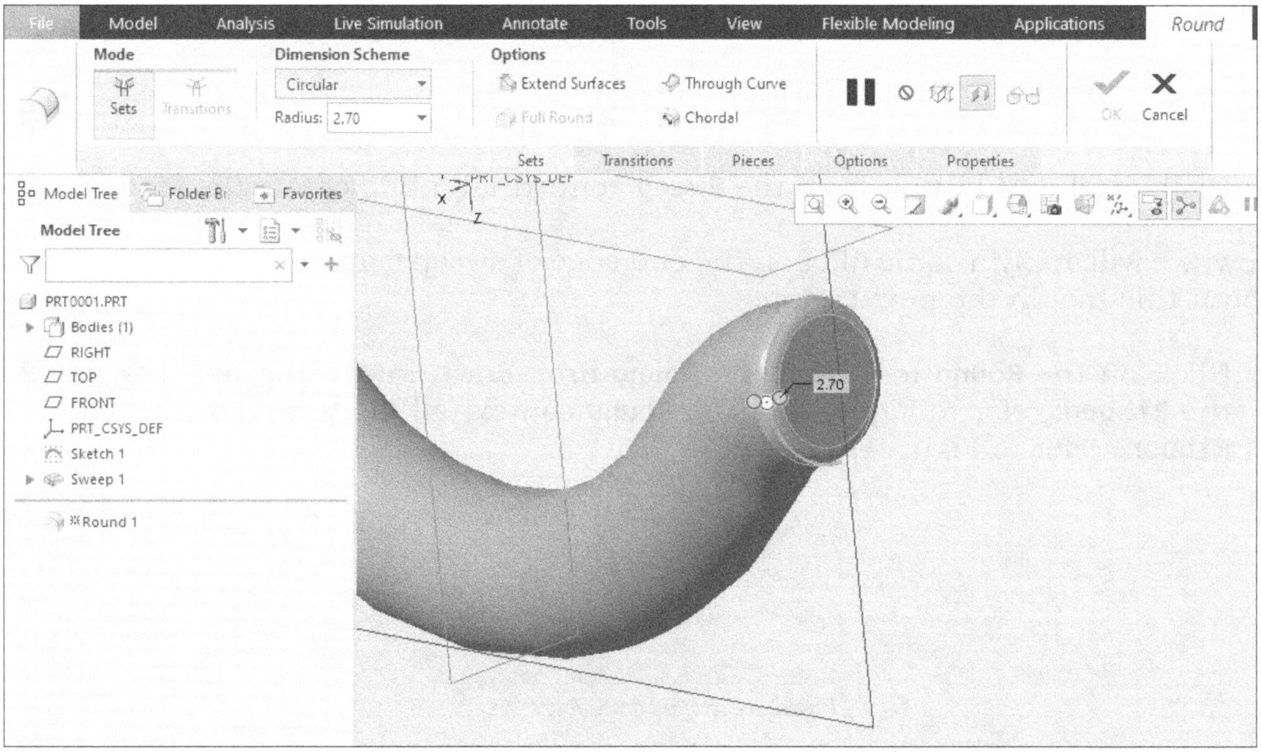

Figure-45. Preview of round

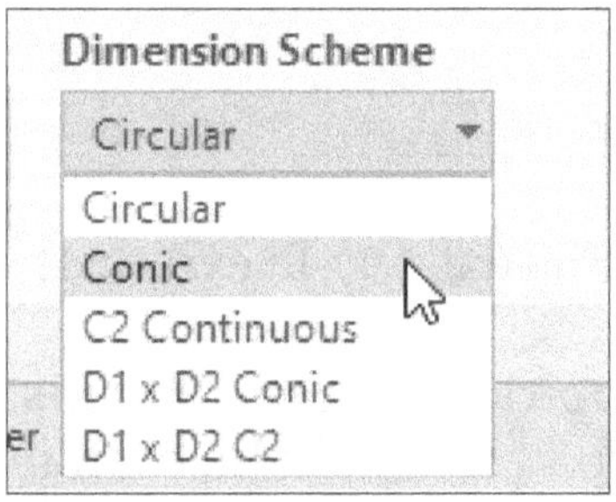

Figure-46. Drop-down in Dimension Scheme area

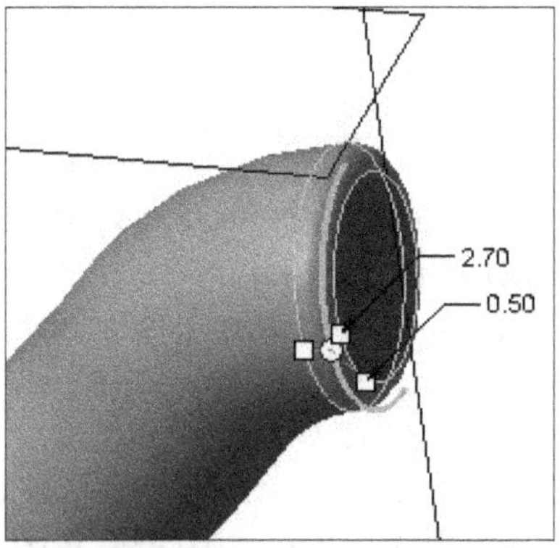

Figure-47. Preview of conic round

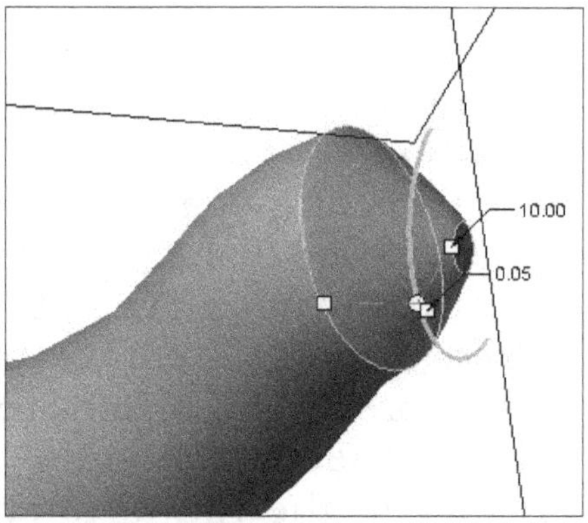

Figure-48. Preview of round after changing values

PRACTICAL 5

In this practical, we will create a model shown in Figure-49 as per the drawing given in Figure-50. The model is of a pipe with varying section and it will require the use of datum curve.

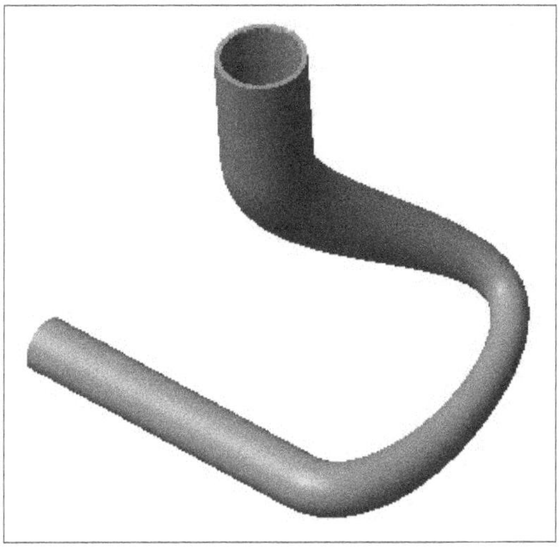

Figure-49. Practical 5 model

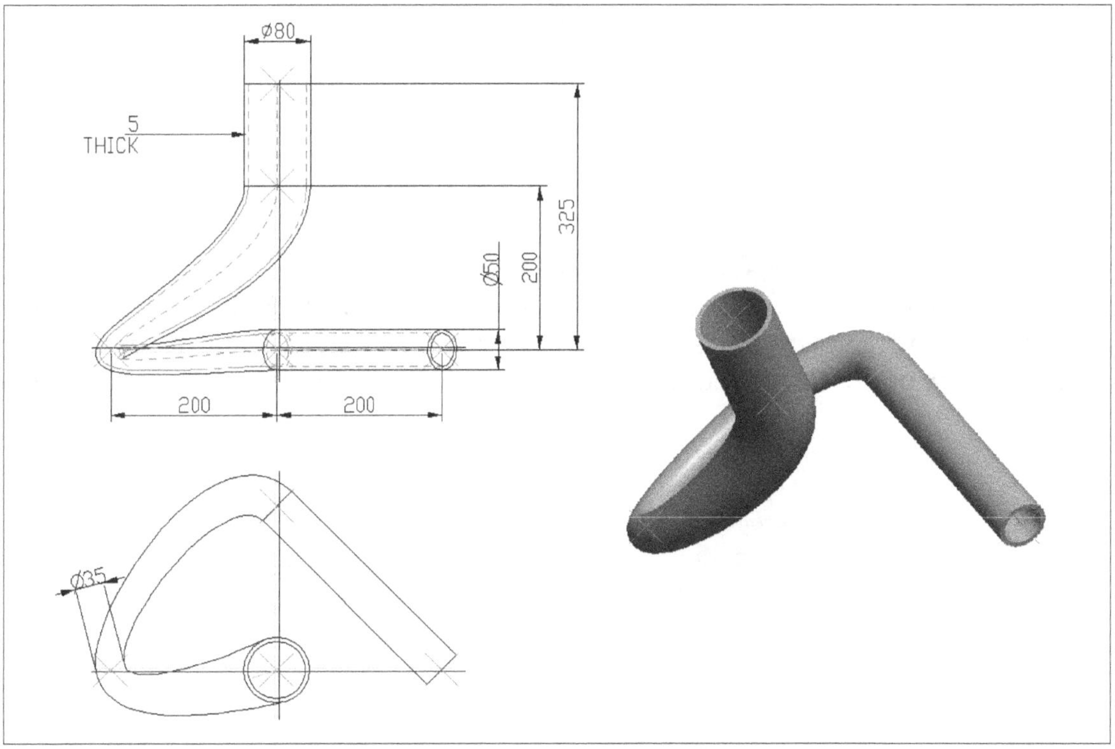

Figure-50. Practical 5

Starting Part Modeling

- Double-click on the Creo Parametric icon from the desktop to start Creo Parametric if not started already.
- Click on the **New** button from the **Data** panel in the **Ribbon**. The **New** dialog box will be displayed.
- Specify desired name for the file and clear the **Use default template** check box.
- Click on the **OK** button from the dialog box. The **New File Options** dialog box will be displayed as discussed earlier.
- Select the **mmns part solid** option from the dialog box and click on the **OK** button.

Creating the base sketches

- Click on the **Sketch** button from the **Datum** panel in the **Ribbon**. The **Sketch** dialog box will be displayed.
- Select the **FRONT** plane as the sketching plane and click on the **Sketch** button from the dialog box. The sketching environment will be displayed.
- Create datum points as shown in Figure-51.
- Similarly, create a sketch with datum point on the **TOP** plane; refer to Figure-52.

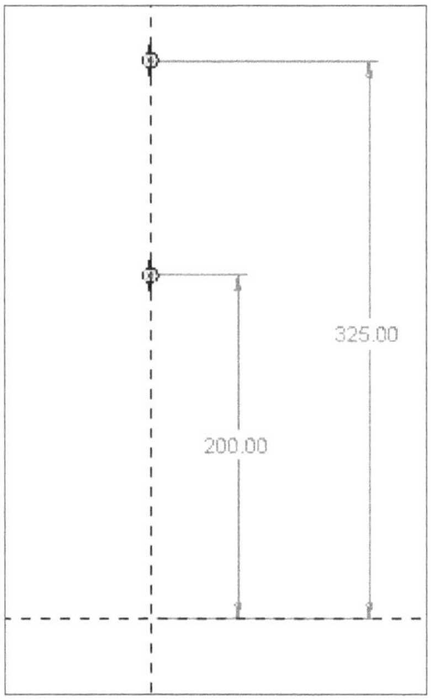

Figure-51. First sketch

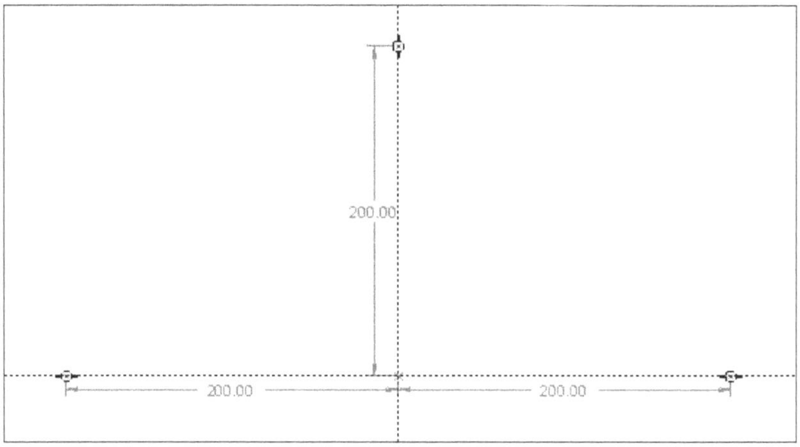

Figure-52. Second sketch

Creating Datum curve

- After creating the sketches, click on the **Curve through Points** tool in the **Curve** cascading menu from the expanded **Datum** panel in the **Ribbon**; refer to Figure-53. The **CURVE: Through Points** contextual tab will be displayed; refer to Figure-54.

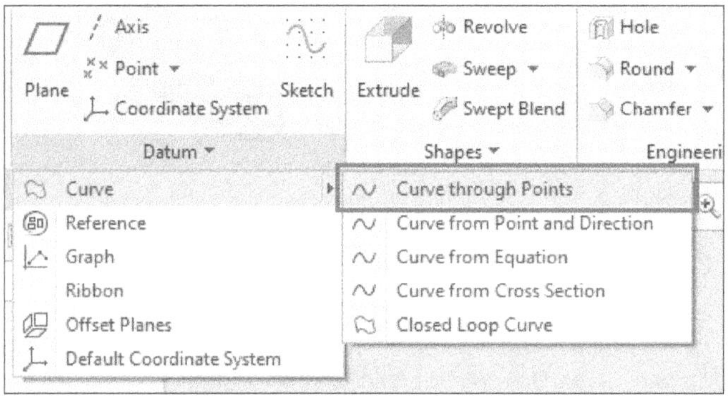

Figure-53. Curve through Points tool

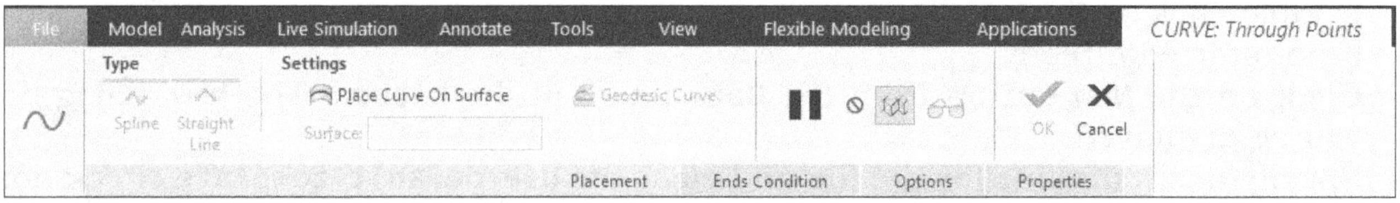

Figure-54. CURVE Through Points contextual tab

- Select the points one by one in the order given in Figure-55. For example, point denoted by 1 will be selected first, then 2, 3, 4, and so on.

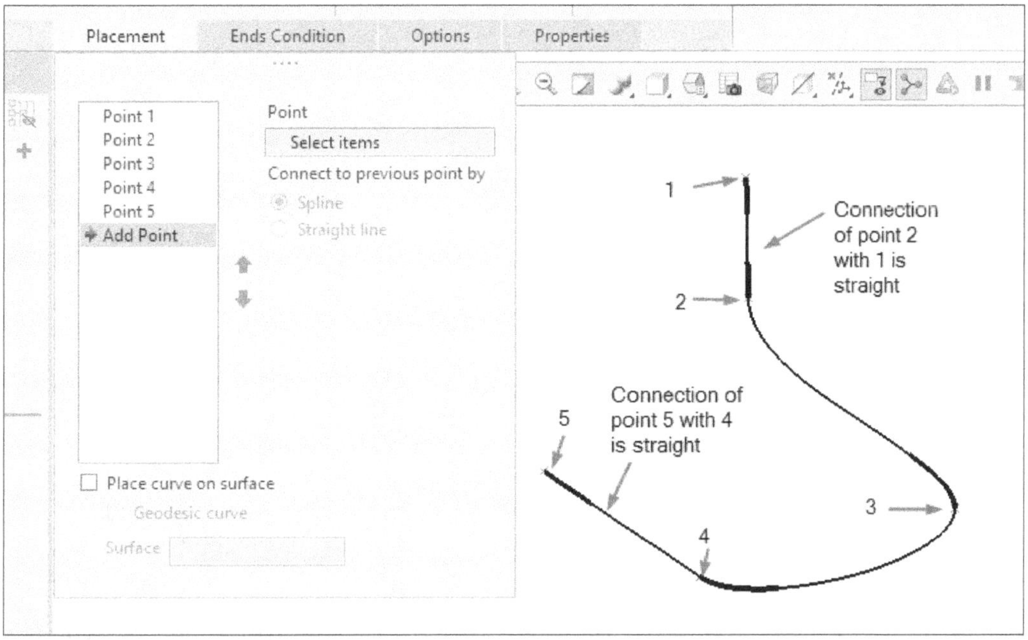

Figure-55. Preview of curve

- To make a straight connection between the two points, select the later point from the **Placement** tab and select the **Straight line** radio button; refer to Figure-56.

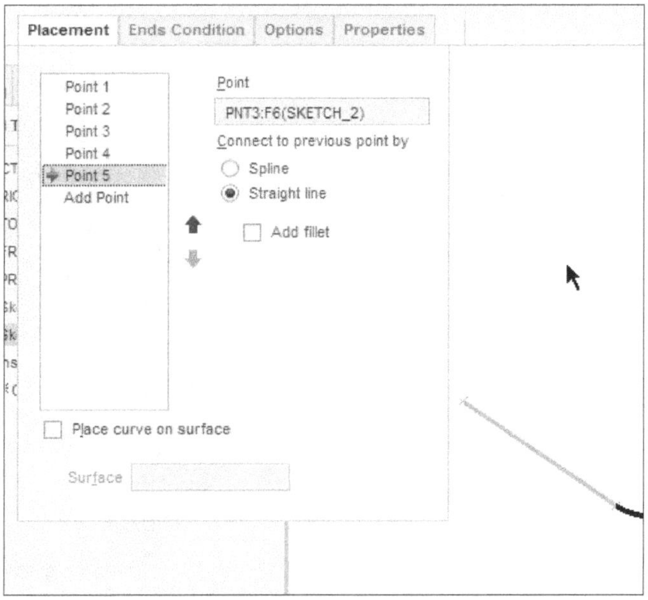

Figure-56. Straight line connection

- Click on the **OK** button from the **CURVE: Through Points** contextual tab to create the curve.

Creating Swept Blend feature

- Click on the **Swept Blend** tool from the **Shapes** panel in the **Ribbon**. The **Swept Blend** contextual tab will be displayed with the curve selected.
- Click on the **Sections** tab and then click on the **Insert** button from the tab.
- A new section will be added with its location at the start point of the curve; refer to Figure-57.

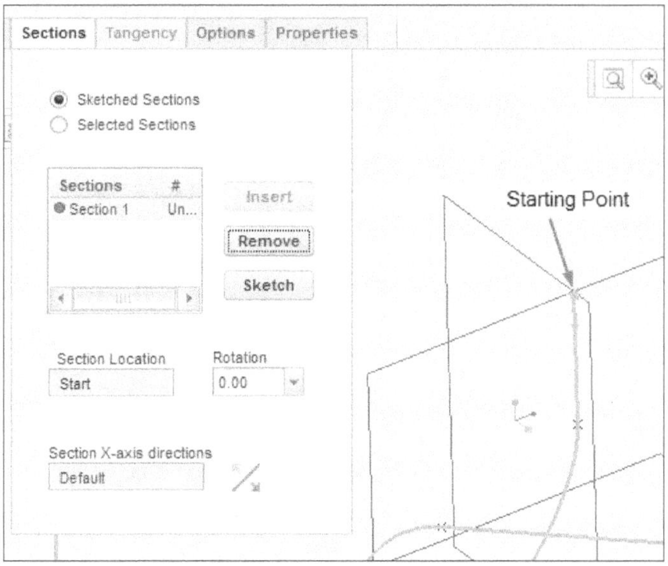

Figure-57. Starting point of profile

- Click on the **Sketch** button and create a circle of diameter **80** at the intersection point of reference planes; refer to Figure-58.
- Click on the **OK** button from the **Sketch** contextual tab.
- Similarly, create sketches on other points as per Figure-50. Preview of the Swept blend feature will be displayed as shown in Figure-59.

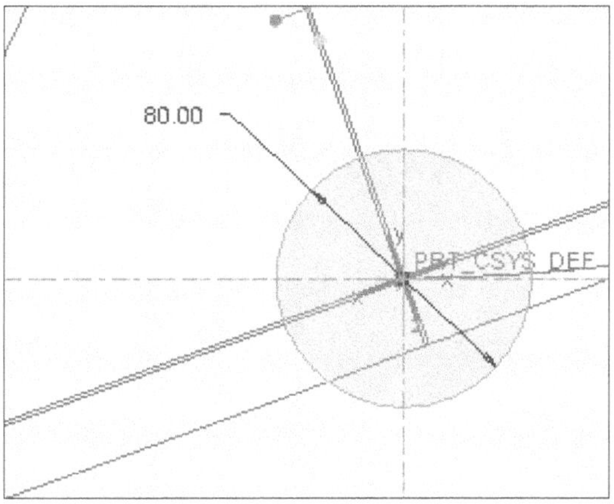

Figure-58. Sketch at first point

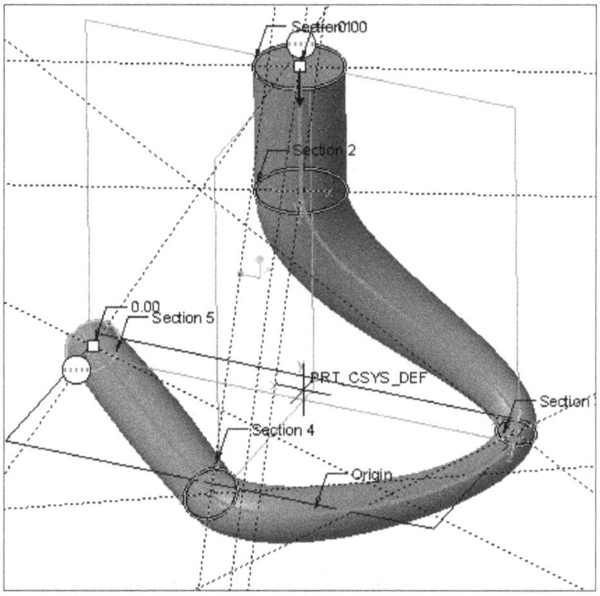

Figure-59. Preview of swept blend

- Click on the **Thicken Sketch** button from **Settings** area of the **Swept Blend** contextual tab. You are asked to specify the thickness value of walls in the swept blend feature; refer to Figure-60.

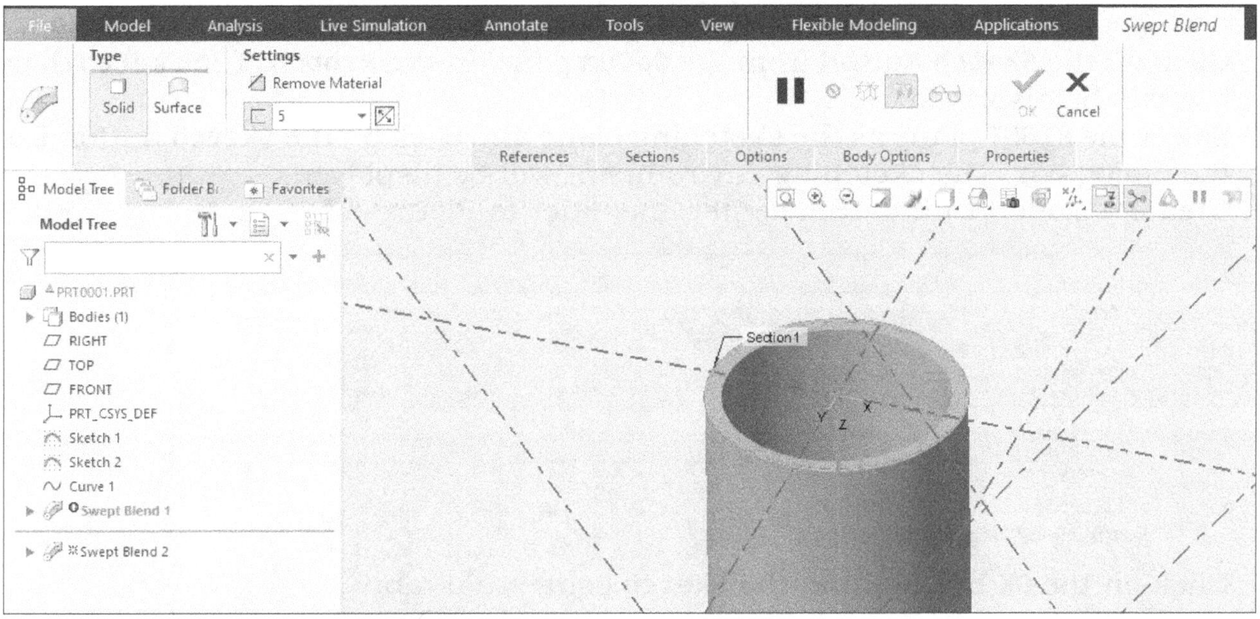

Figure-60. Thickness of swept blend feature

- Specify the thickness value as **5** in the edit box and then click on the **OK** button from the contextual tab to create the feature.

PRACTICAL 6

In this practical, we will create model of a bolt; refer to Figure-61. Note that relations are to be applied in the dimensions to get bolts of various sizes.

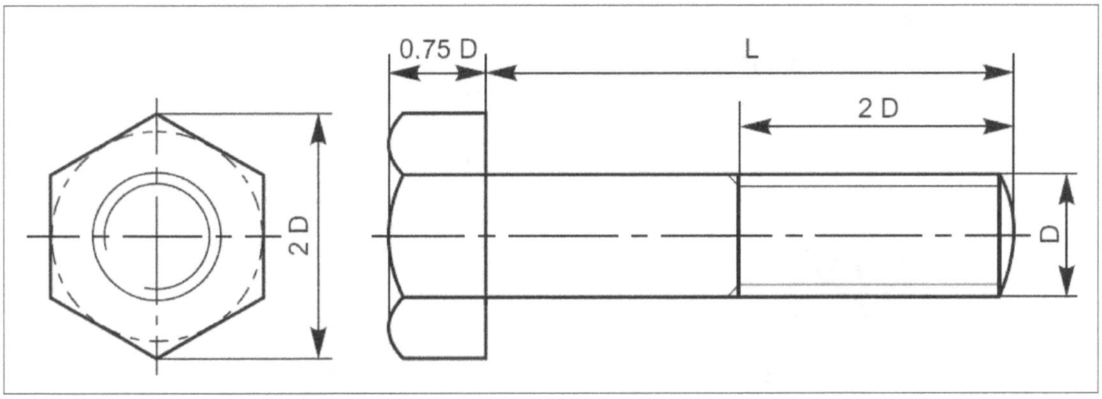

Figure-61. Practical 6

In this practical, we will assume the value of **D** as **30** and **L** as **100**.

Starting Part Modeling

- Double-click on the Creo Parametric icon from the desktop to start Creo Parametric if not started already.
- Click on the **New** button from the **Data** panel in the **Ribbon**. The **New** dialog box will be displayed.
- Specify desired name for the file and clear the **Use default template** check box.
- Click on the **OK** button from the dialog box. The **New File Options** dialog box will be displayed as discussed earlier.
- Select the **mmns part solid** option from the dialog box and click on the **OK** button.

Creating the base sketches

- Click on the **Sketch** button from the **Datum** panel in the **Ribbon**. The **Sketch** dialog box will be displayed.
- Select the **RIGHT** plane as the sketching plane and click on the **Sketch** button from the dialog box. The sketching environment will be displayed.
- Create a sketch with datum center line; refer to Figure-62.

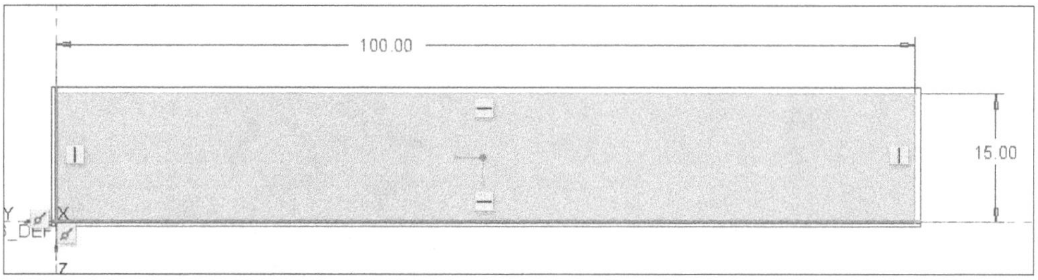

Figure-62. Sketch for Practical 6

- Click on the **OK** button from the **Sketch** contextual tab.

Creating the Revolve Feature

- Click on the **Revolve** tool from the **Shapes** panel in the **Ribbon**. The **Revolve** contextual tab will be displayed.
- Select the sketch and then click on the **OK** button from the contextual tab. The revolve feature will be created; refer to Figure-63.

Creating Extrude feature

- Click on the **Extrude** tool from the **Shapes** panel in the **Ribbon**. The **Extrude** contextual tab will be displayed.
- Select the top face of the model; refer to Figure-64.

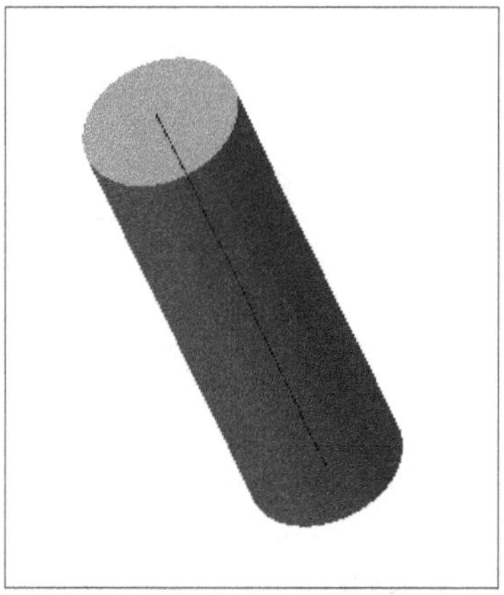

Figure-63. Revolve feature created

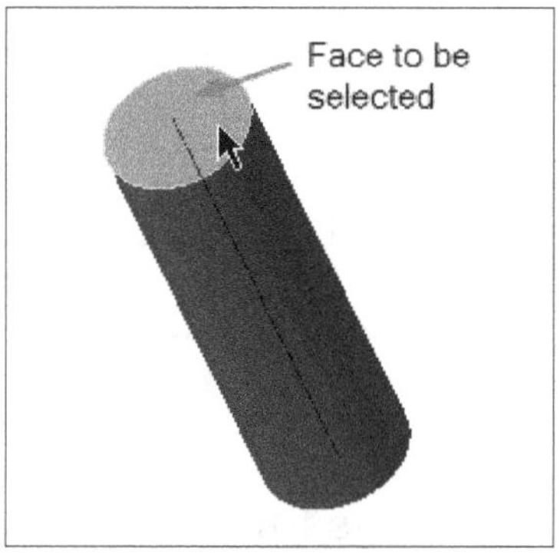

Figure-64. Face to be selected for extrude feature

- On doing so, the sketching environment will be displayed. Click on the **Palette** tool from **Sketching** panel in the **Ribbon**. The **Sketcher Palette** dialog box will be displayed; refer to Figure-65.

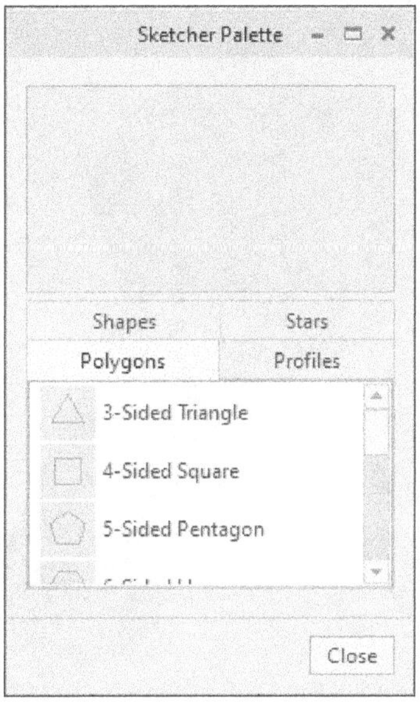

Figure-65. Sketcher Palette dialog box

- Double-click on the **6-Sided Hexagon** option from dialog box. Place the hexagon at the center of the circle; refer to Figure-66.
- Change the dimension of the hexagon as shown in Figure-67.

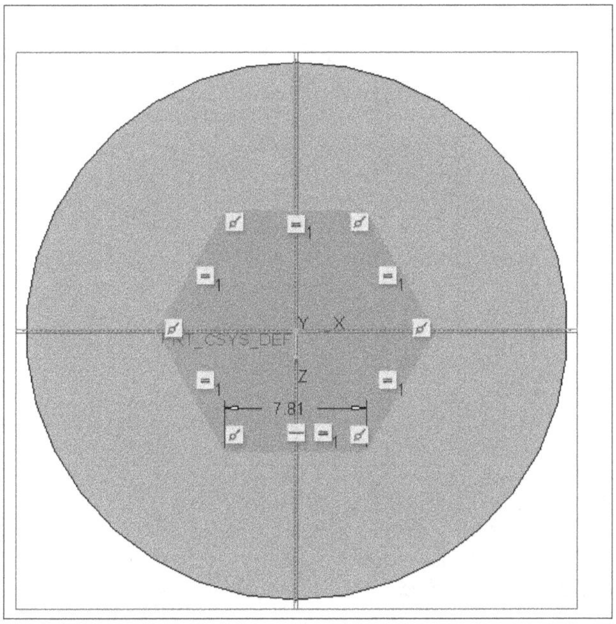

Figure-66. Hexagon placed at center of circle

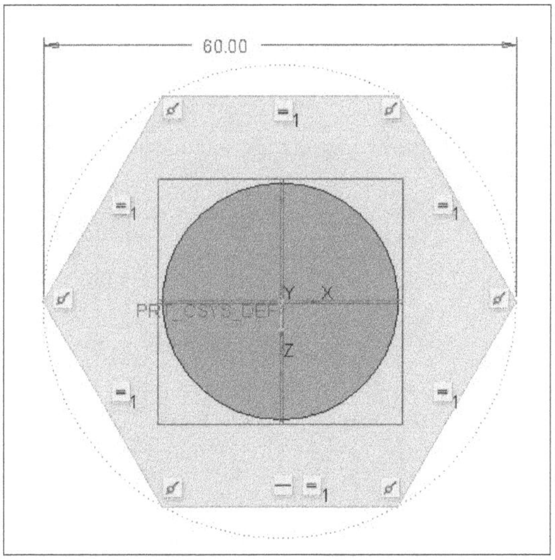

Figure-67. Dimensioned hexagon

- Click on the **OK** button from the **Sketch** contextual tab. Preview of extrude feature will be displayed.
- Change the extrude depth value to **22.5** and click on the **OK** button from the **Extrude** contextual tab. The extruded bolt head will be displayed; refer to Figure-68.

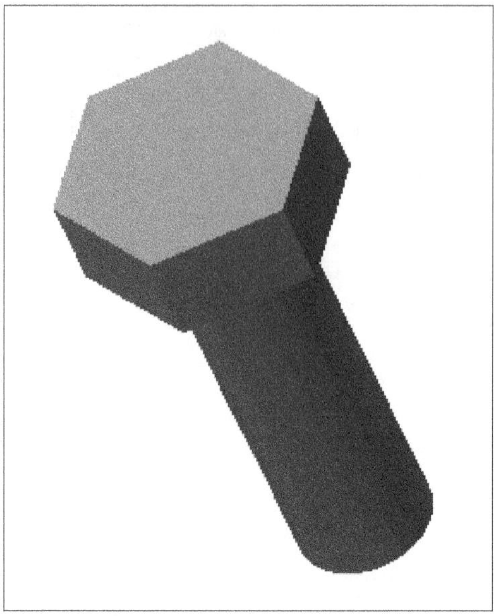

Figure-68. Extruded bolt head

Applying Relations

- Click on the **Annotate** tab and click on the **Show Annotations** button from **Manage Annotations** panel. The **Show Annotations** dialog box will be displayed; refer to Figure-69.

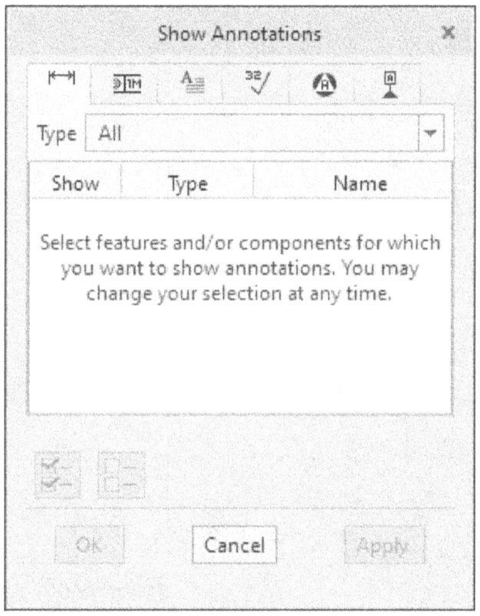

Figure-69. Show Annotations dialog box

- Select the model features while holding the **CTRL** key. The annotations will be displayed; refer to Figure-70.
- Select all the check boxes under the **Show** column in the dialog box to display the annotations.
- Click on the **OK** button from the **Show Annotations** dialog box. Drag the dimensions out of the model for clear view.
- Click on the **Relations** tool from the expanded **Model Intent** panel in the **Model** tab of the **Ribbon**; refer to Figure-71.

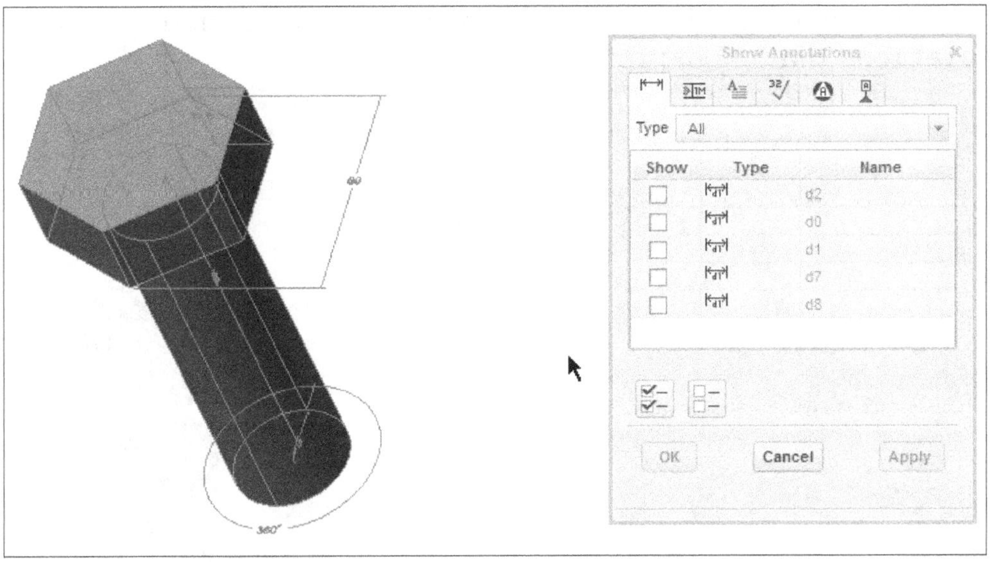

Figure-70. Model with annotations

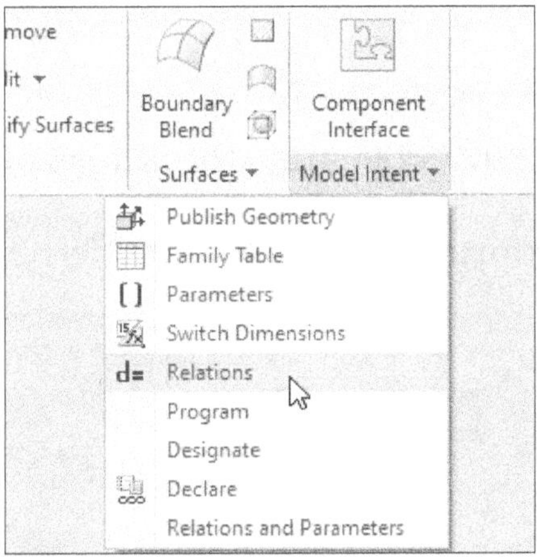

Figure-71. Relations tool

- On selecting this tool, the **Relations** dialog box will be displayed; refer to Figure-72.

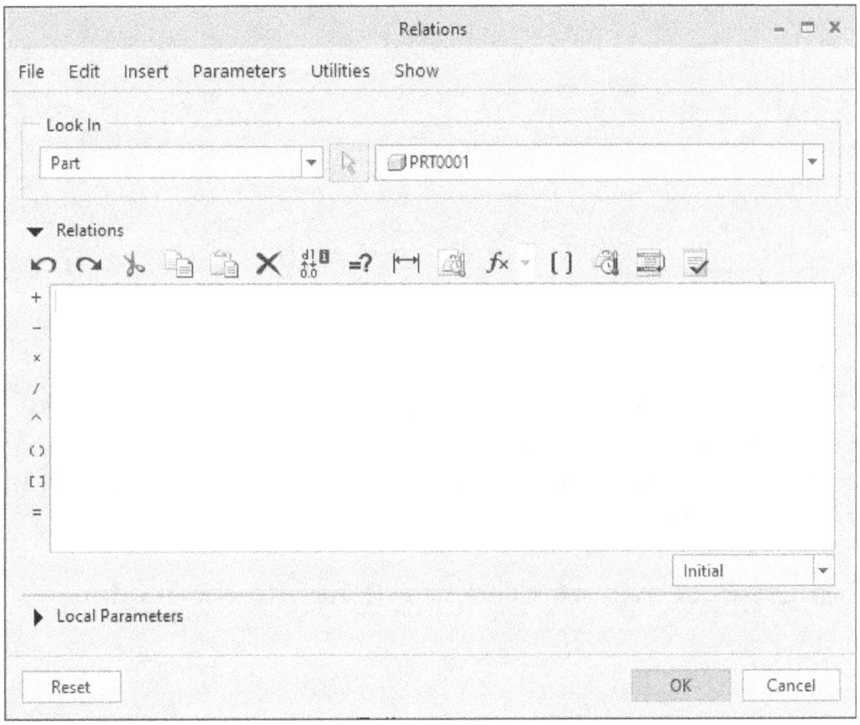

Figure-72. Relations dialog box

- Select the dimension for thickness of the bolt head. The dimension will be displayed in the **Relations** dialog box; refer to Figure-73.

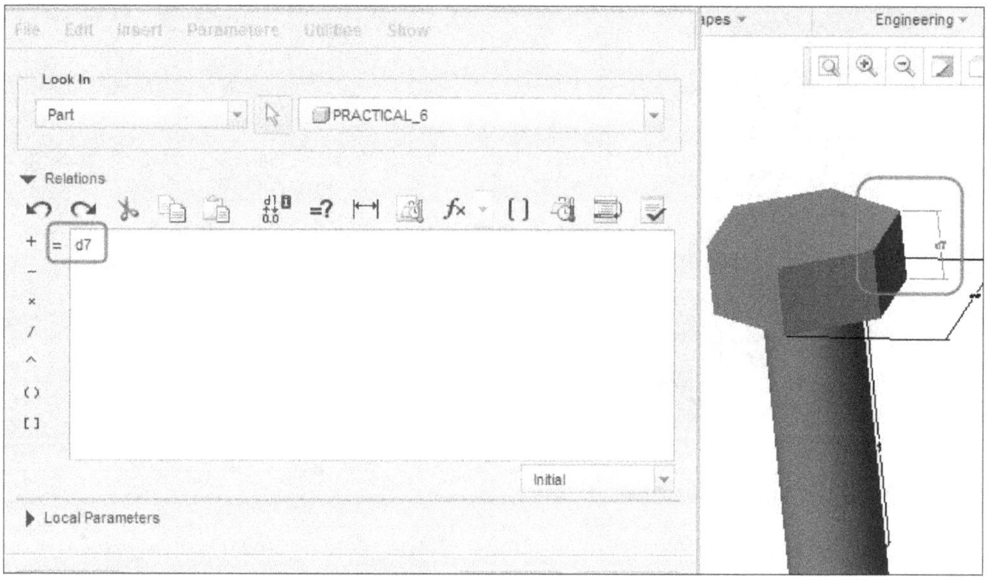

Figure-73. Dimension selected for relation

- Write the formula **d7=d0*2*0.75** because thickness of bolt head is **0.75** of diameter of the bolt shank.
- Similarly, write the other formula **d8=d0*4** in the next line; refer to Figure-74.

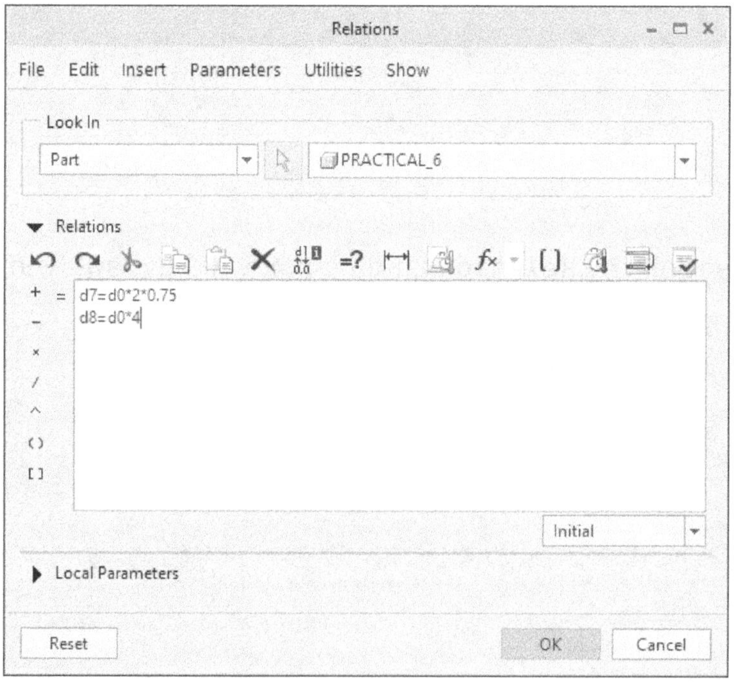

Figure-74. Relations dialog box with formulae

- Click on the **OK** button from the dialog box.
- Now, change the value of shank diameter to **20** by double clicking on it while holding the **ALT** key; refer to Figure-75.

To make the changes effective, we need to regenerate the model.

- Click on the **Regenerate** button from the **Quick Access** toolbar; refer to Figure-76. The value of bolt head thickness and bolt head width will change automatically as per the formula.

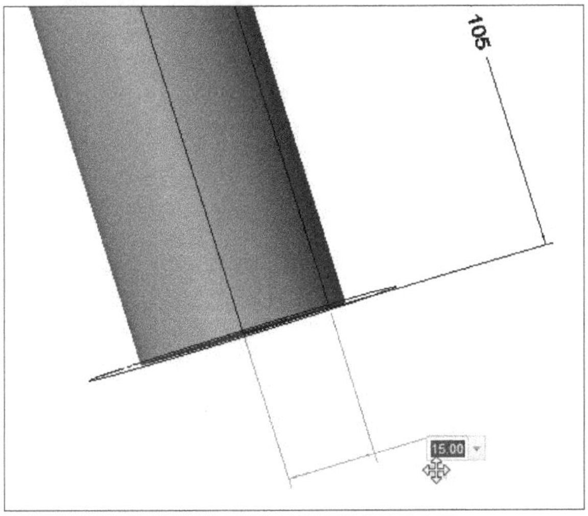

Figure-75. Diameter value to be changed

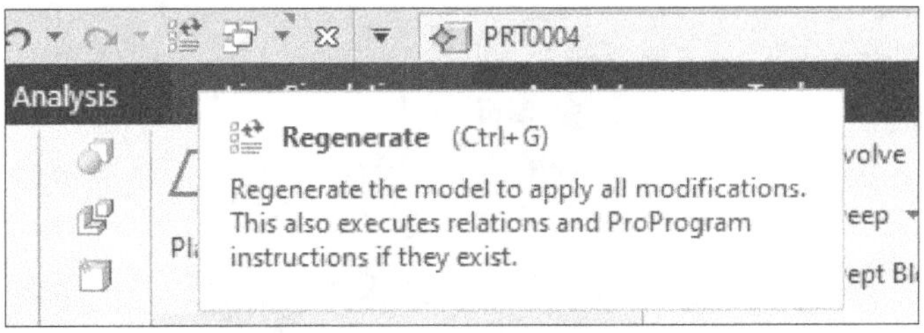

Figure-76. Regenerate button

PRACTICE 1

Create the model shown in Figure-77.

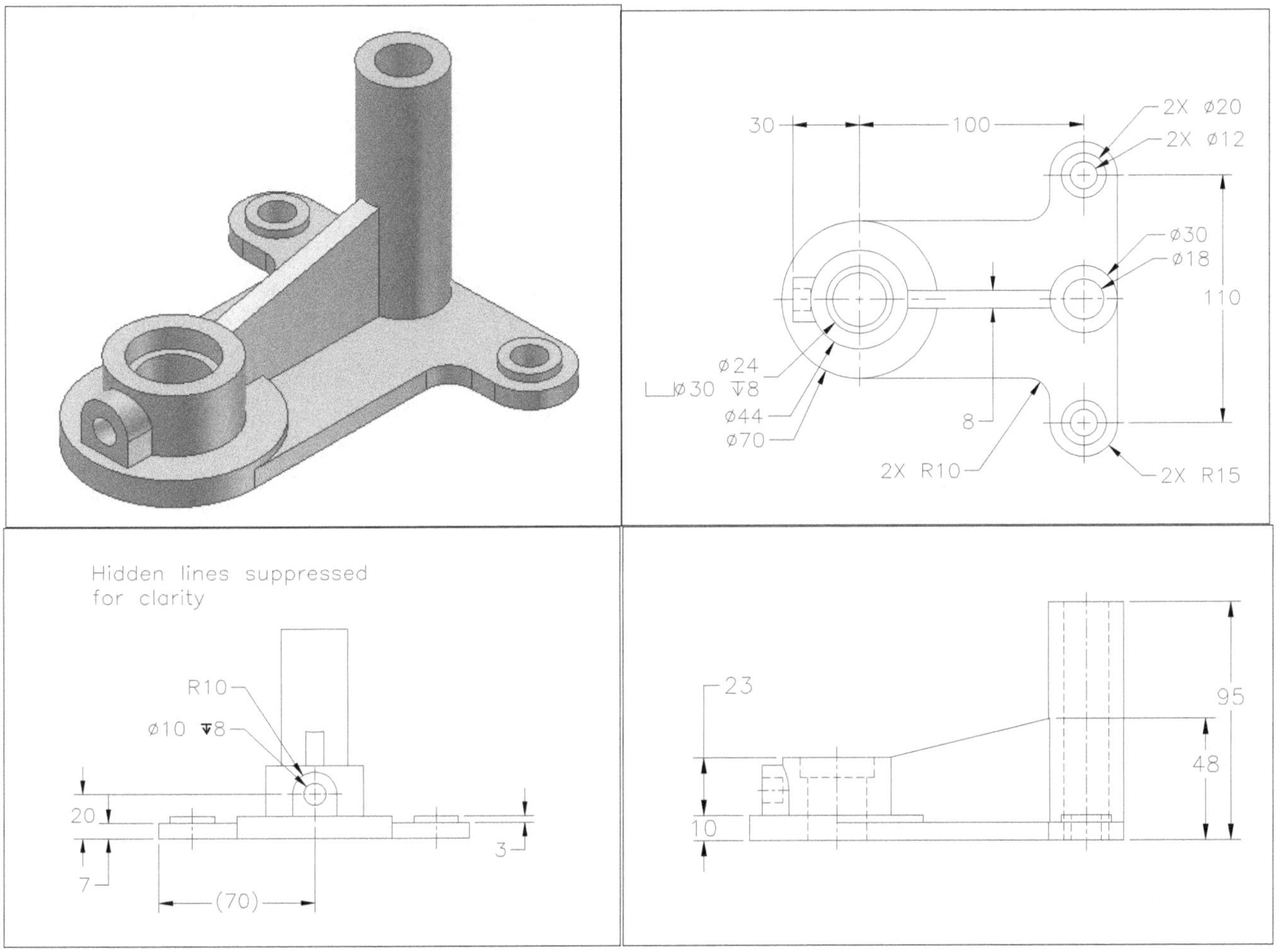

Figure-77. Views and dimensions of the model

PRACTICE 2

Create the model shown in Figure-78.

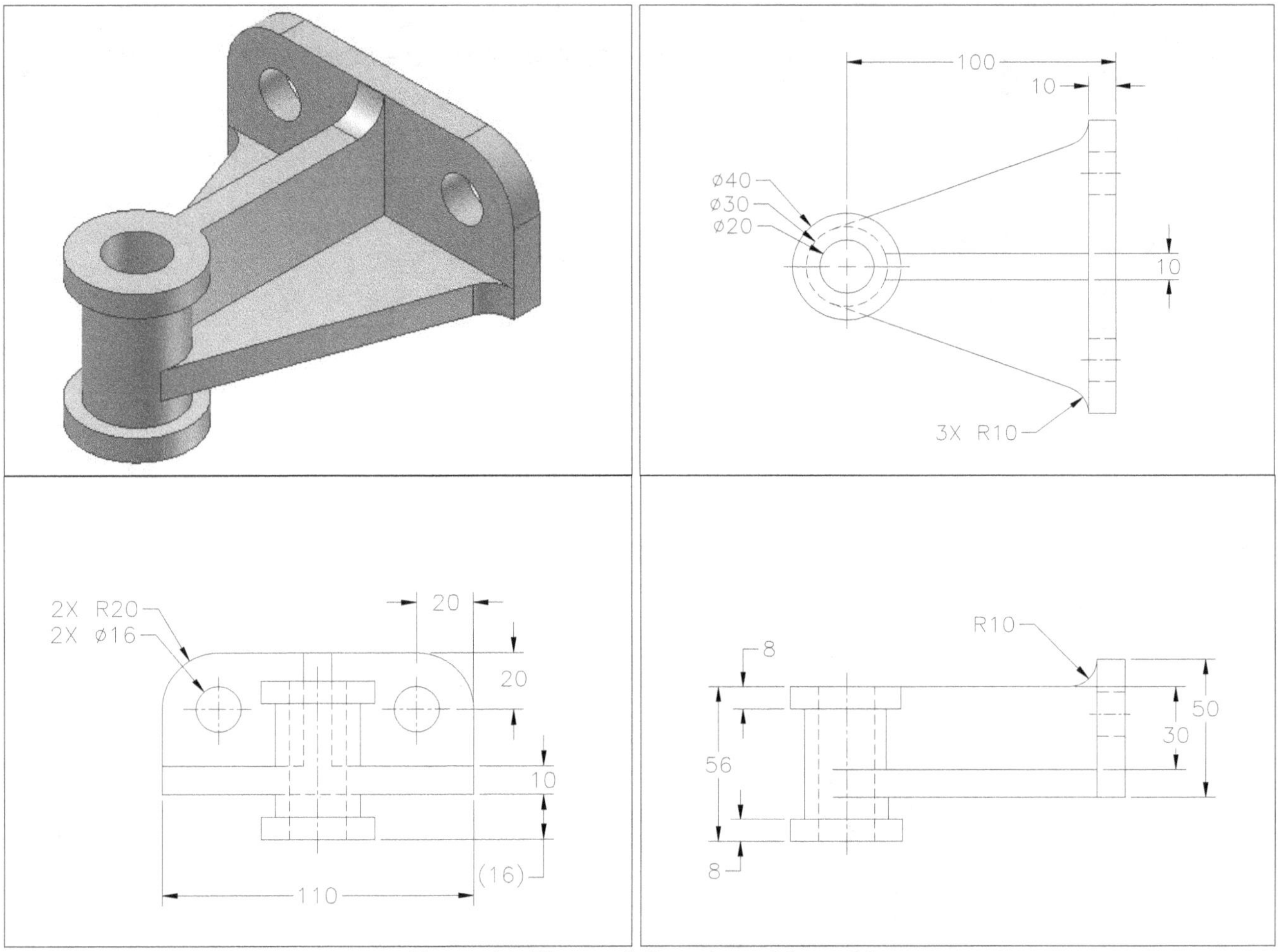

Figure-78. Views and dimensions of the model

PRACTICE 3

Create the model shown in Figure-79.

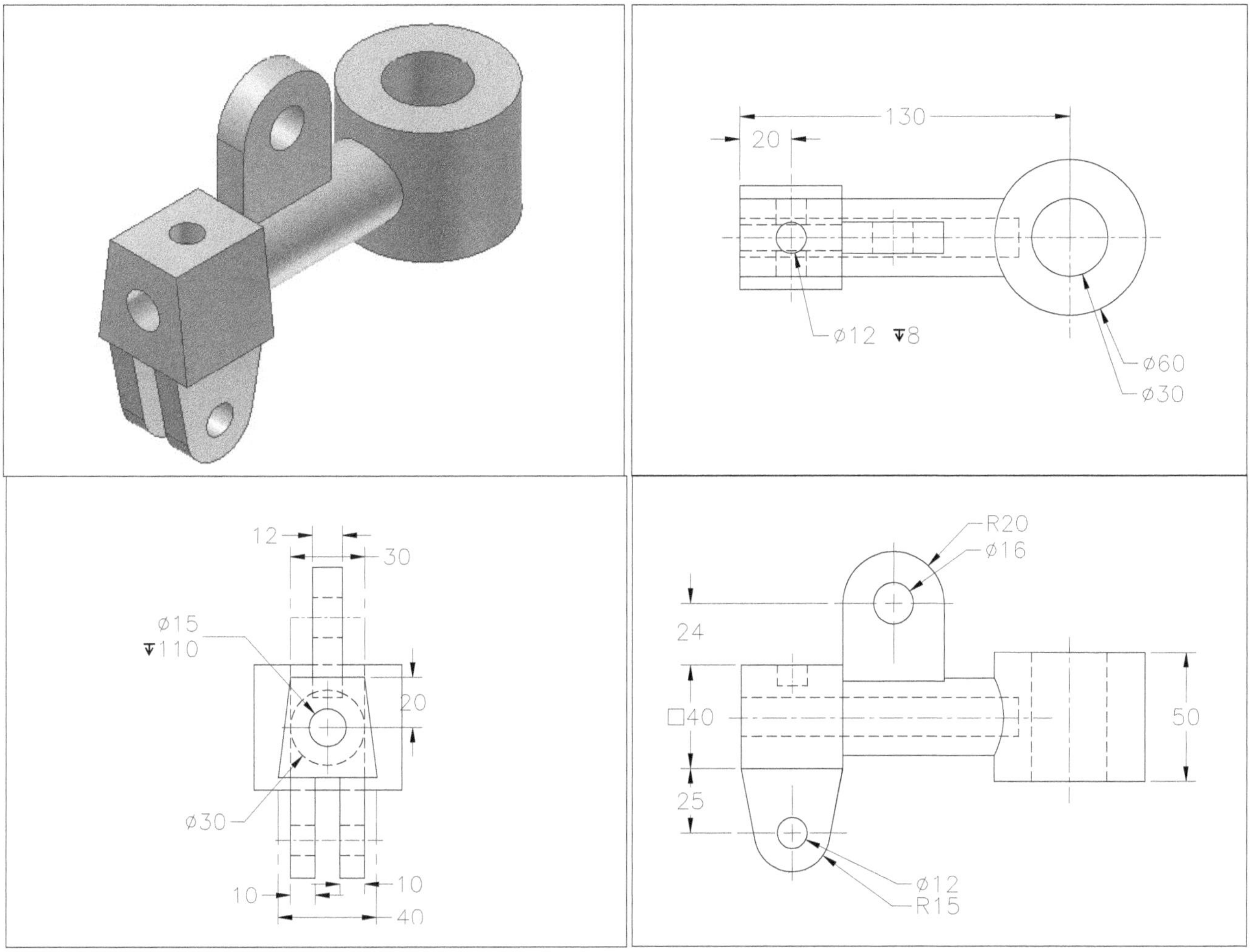

Figure-79. Views and dimensions of the model

FOR STUDENT NOTES

Chapter 6

3D Modeling Advanced

Topics Covered

The major topics covered in this chapter are:

- ***Engineering Features like Hole, Round, Chamfer, Draft, and so on***
- ***Shell, Rib, Pattern, Project, Wrap, and Warp tools***

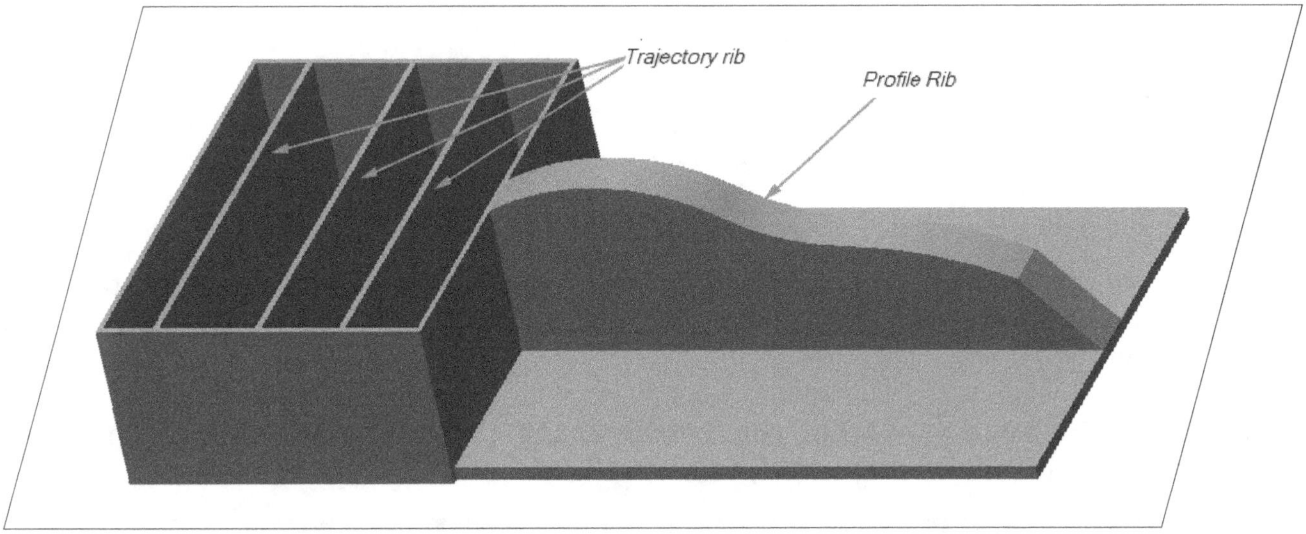

INTRODUCTION

In the previous chapters, we have worked on the basic tools for creating 3D models. Now, we will learn about the tools that are used to add or modify the features of a base 3D model. These tools are discussed next.

ENGINEERING FEATURES

The engineering features are the 3D model features that get their parameters from the engineering tables and act as add-on to the model. Some of the engineering features to name are: Hole, round, chamfer, rib, and so on. The tools to create these features are available in the **Engineering** panel of the **Ribbon**; refer to Figure-1. Now, we will discuss these features one by one.

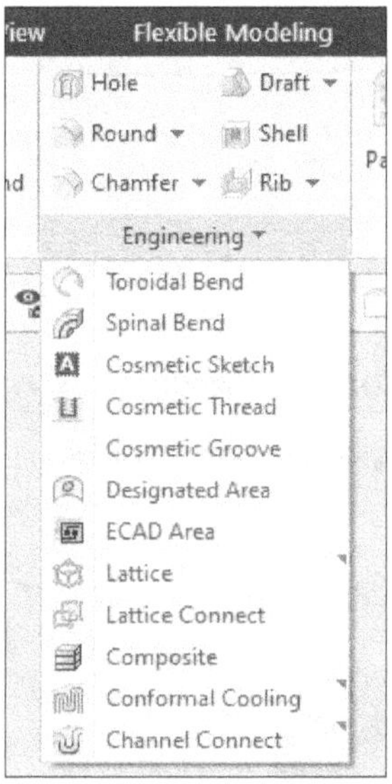

Figure-1. Engineering panel

Hole

The **Hole** tool is used to create holes with standard sizes or custom sizes. The standard holes can be of metric standard or unified standard. The procedure to use this tool is given next.

- Click on the **Hole** tool from the **Engineering** panel of the **Ribbon**. The **Hole** contextual tab will be displayed; refer to Figure-2.

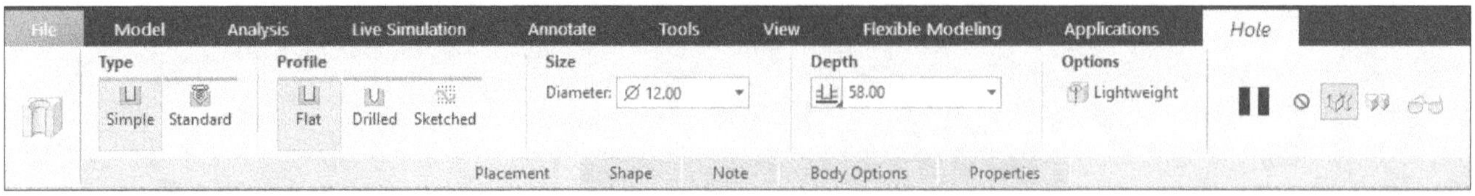

Figure-2. Hole contextual tab

- Click on the **Placement** tab and select the face on which you want to place the hole; refer to Figure-3.

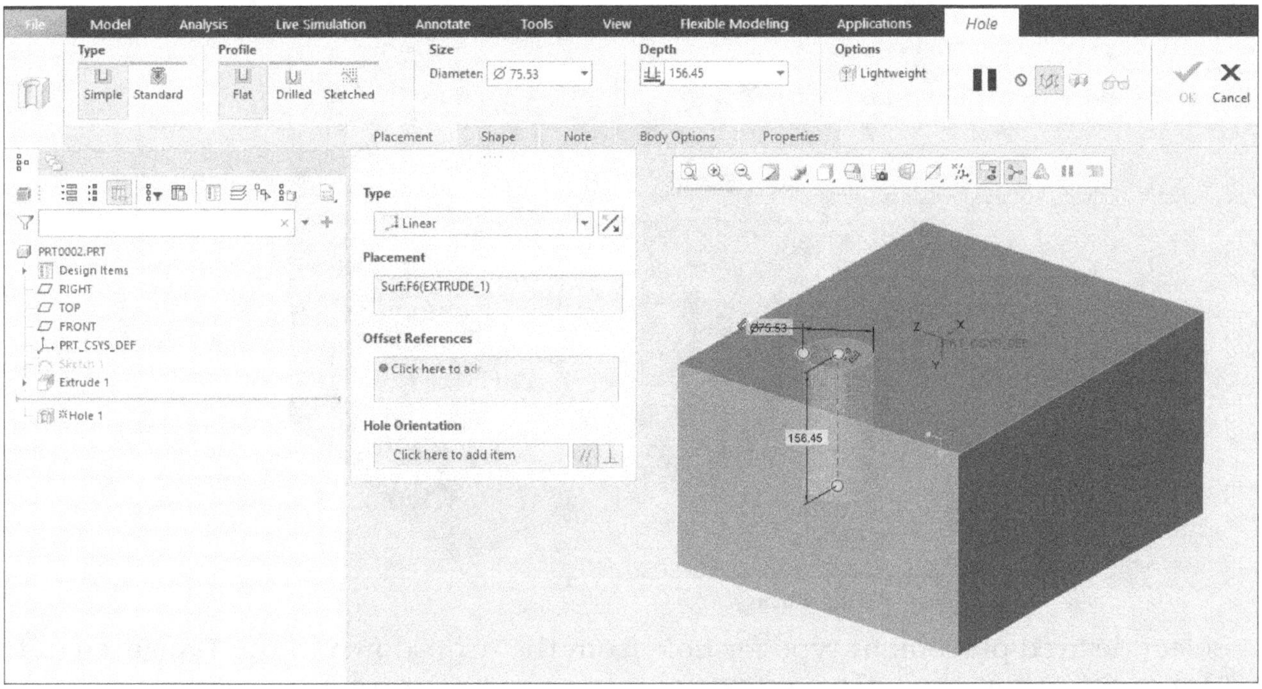

Figure-3. Hole placed on a face

- Drag the two reference handles to desired location references one by one; refer to Figure-4.

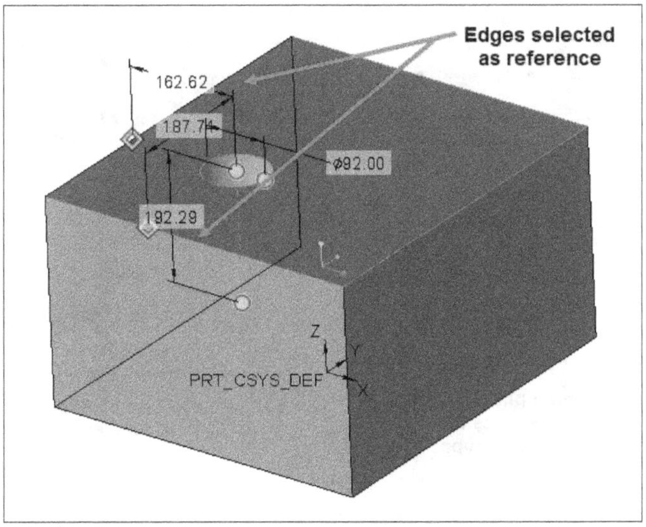

Figure-4. References to be selected for hole

- Change the dimensions of the hole as required. Various dimensions of hole in the model are given by Figure-5.

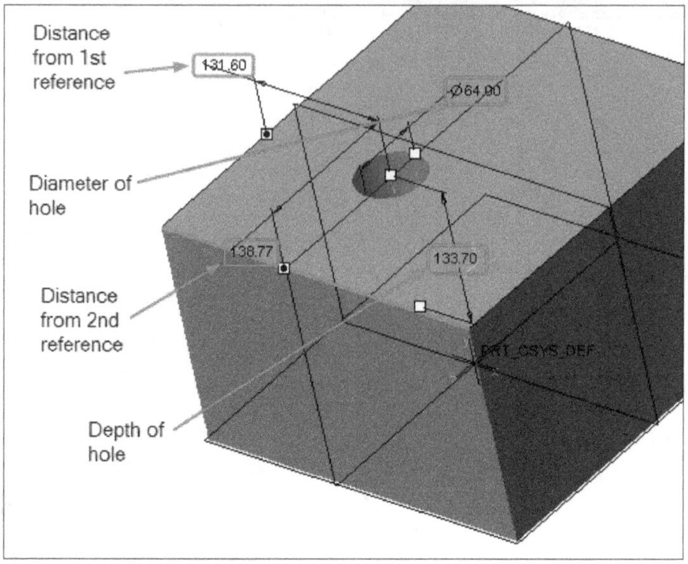

Figure-5. Dimensions for hole

- Select desired placement type for hole from the drop-down in the **Type** area of the **Placement** tab in the **Hole** contextual tab; refer to Figure-6.

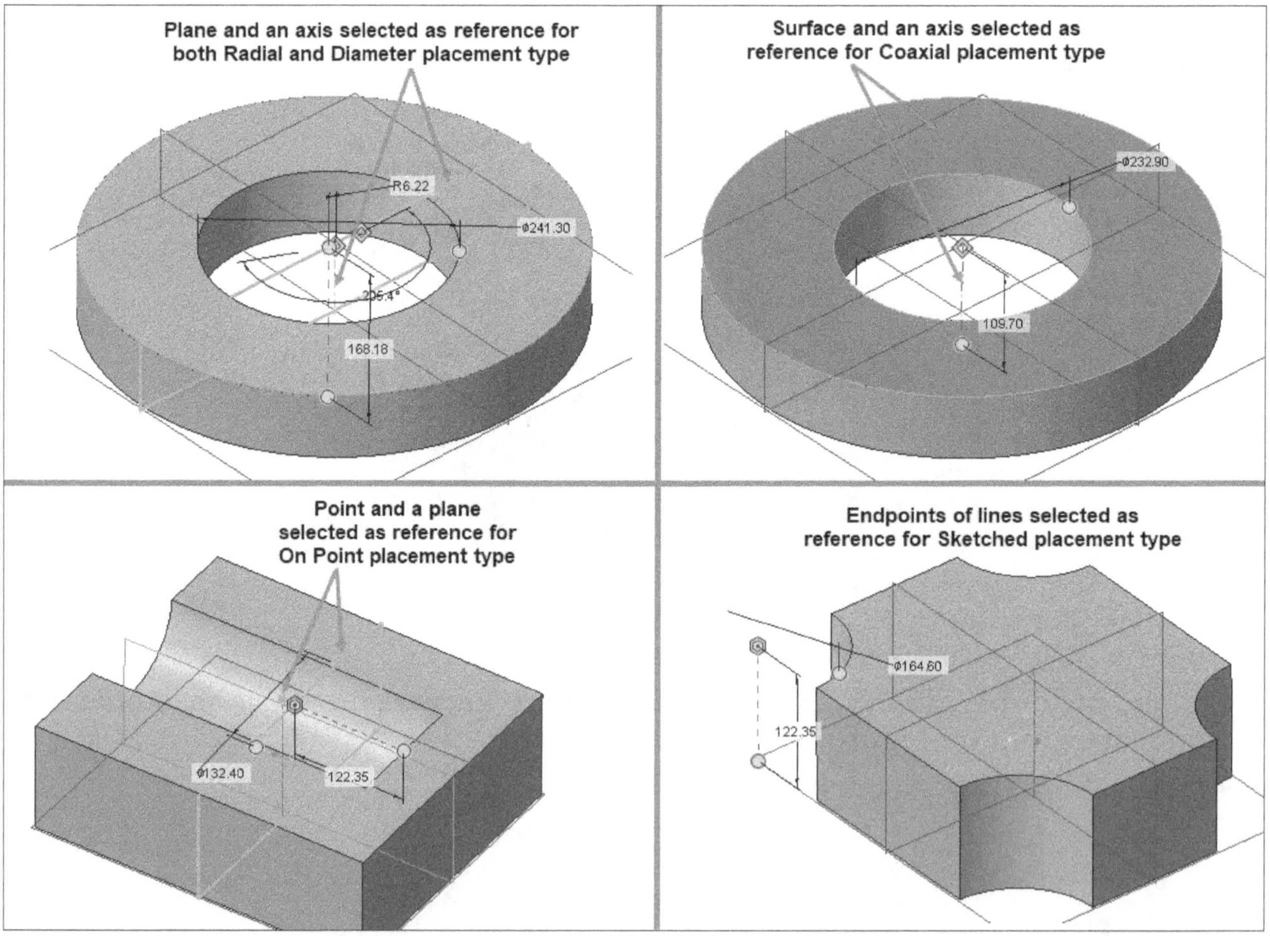

Figure-6. Placement types for hole

- Select the **Linear** option from the drop-down when you reference two linear dimensions. Select the **Radial** option from the drop-down when you reference a linear and an angular dimension. Select the **Diameter** option from the drop-down when you reference a planar solid surface or a datum plane. Select the **Coaxial** option from the drop-down when you reference a surface, datum plane, or axis. Select the **On Point** option from the drop-down when you reference a datum point. Select the **Sketched** option from the drop-down when you sketch datum points, and endpoints and midpoints of sketched straight lines in an external or internal sketch.

Sketched Hole

- If you want to create a custom shaped hole then click on the **Sketched** button from **Profile** area in the **Hole** contextual tab. The options in contextual tab will change as shown in Figure-7.

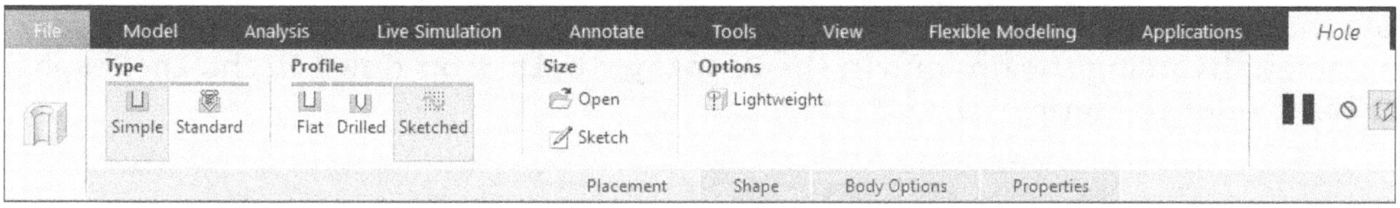

Figure-7. Options for sketching hole profile

- Click on the **Open** button from **Size** area of contextual tab and select desired profile sketch earlier created or click on the **Sketch** button from **Size** area. On selecting the **Sketch** button, another application window with sketching environment will be displayed. Create the sketch of the hole profile; refer to Figure-8.

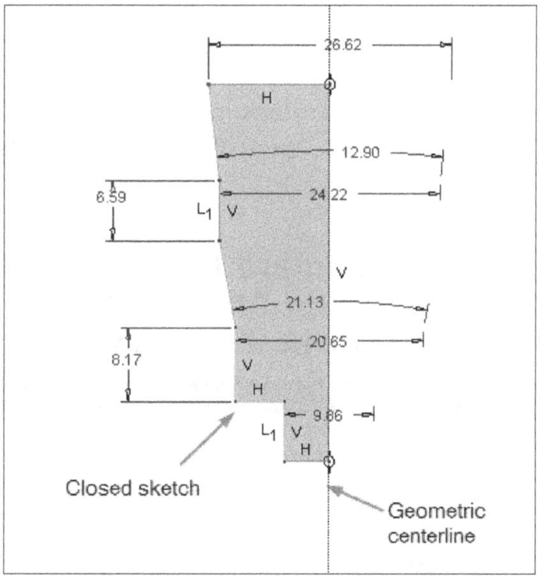

Figure-8. Profile of the hole

- After creating the profile, click on the **OK** button from the **Ribbon**. Preview of the hole will be displayed; refer to Figure-9.

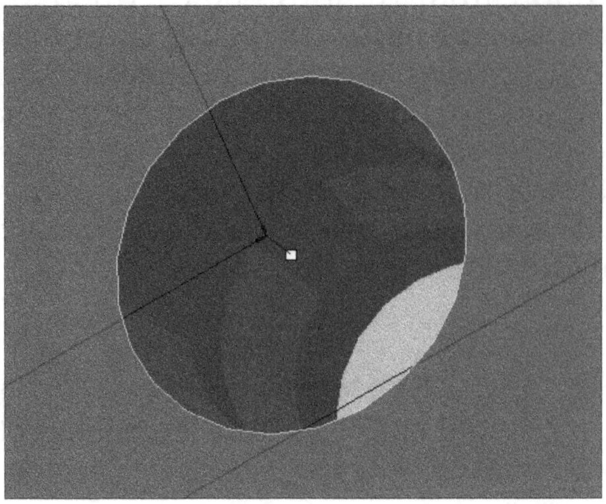

Figure-9. Preview of the hole

Note that you can change the view style of the model to hidden, wire frame, no hidden, and so on; by using the options in the **Display Style** drop-down in the **In-Graphics toolbar**; refer to Figure-10.

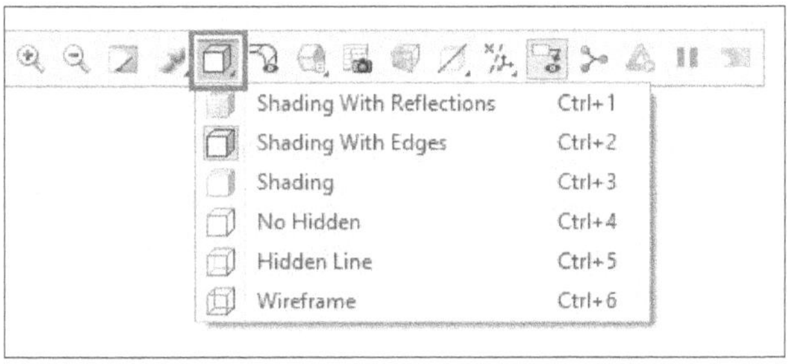

Figure-10. Display Style drop-down

The dimensions that are shown in the previous figure are for simple holes. But in real industry, we have drills of specific sizes to create holes. So, we need to create standard holes for easy machinability.

Standard Hole

- To create standard holes, click on the **Standard** button from **Type** area in the **Hole** contextual tab. The options in the dashboard will change; refer to Figure-11.

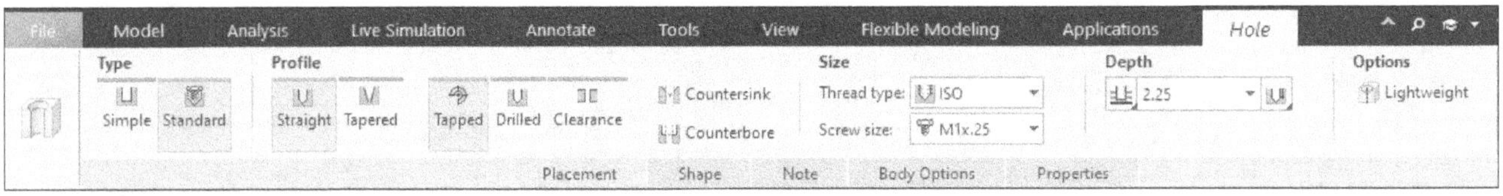

Figure-11. Hole contextual tab for standard holes

- On selecting the **Straight** option from **Profile** area of the contextual tab, the three options will be displayed, viz., **Tapped**, **Drilled**, and **Clearance**. Select **Tapped** button if you want to display the cosmetic tapping marks in the drawing. You will learn about creating drawings from model later in the book. Select **Drilled** button if you want to create drilled hole. Select **Clearance** button if you want to create clearance hole.
- If you want to create tapered holes then select the **Tapered** option from **Profile** area of the contextual tab. The sizes of hole will be displayed accordingly in the hole size drop-down.

- Select desired standard from **ISO**, **UNC**, and **UNF** standards by using the **Standard** drop-down. If you have selected the **Tapped** button then specify desired type of thread from the **Thread type** drop-down in the **Size** area of the **Ribbon**.
- Select desired size from the **Screw size** drop-down in the **Size** area of the **Ribbon**.
- Similarly, you can change the hole to a counter-sink or counter-bore hole. After selecting desired button, you need to specify the parameters for counter-bore/counter-sink in the **Shape** tab of **Hole** contextual tab in the **Ribbon**.
- Select the **Lightweight** button from the **Options** area of the contextual tab to set a lightweight representation of the hole to improve performance.
- After setting desired parameters, click on the **OK** button from the **Ribbon**. The hole will be created and an annotation of hole will be added to the model; refer to Figure-12.

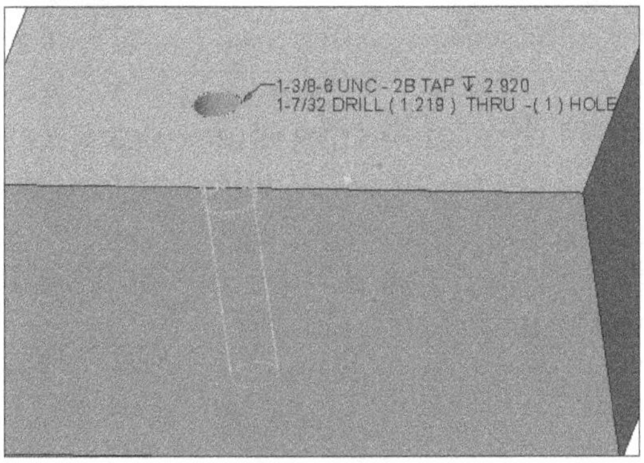

Figure-12. Standard hole with callout

Round

The **Round** tool is used to create rounds and fillet at the sharp edges. Creating a round at the sharp edges helps in two ways:

1. It helps in reducing stress at the edges.
2. It helps in easy handling.

The procedure to create fillets by using **Round** tool is given next.

- Click on the **Round** tool from the **Round** drop-down in the **Engineering** panel of the **Ribbon**; refer to Figure-13. The **Round** contextual tab will display; refer to Figure-14.

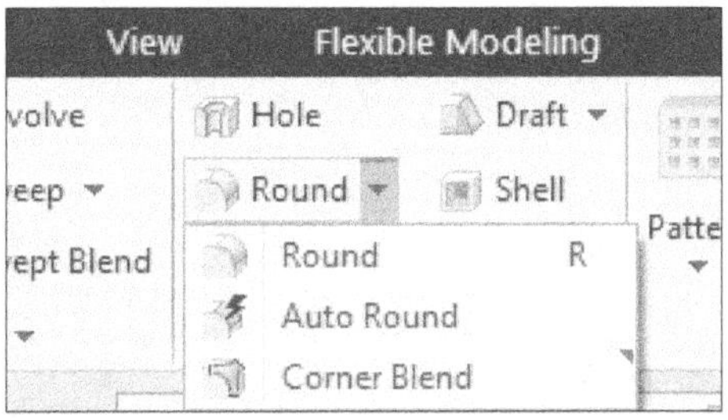

Figure-13. Round tool

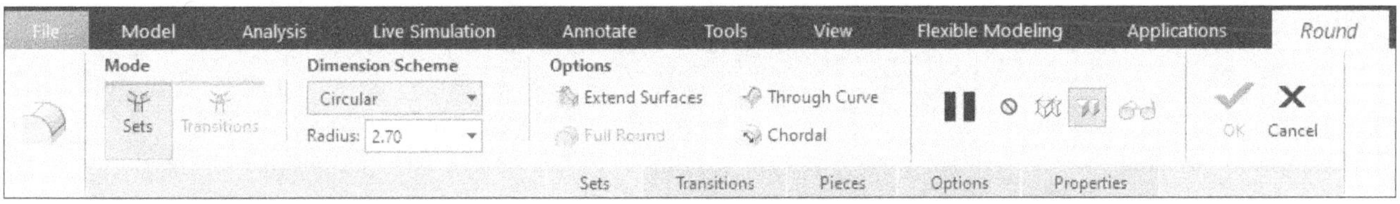

Figure-14. Round contextual tab

- Select an edge of the model or two intersecting faces. Preview of the round will be displayed; refer to Figure-15.

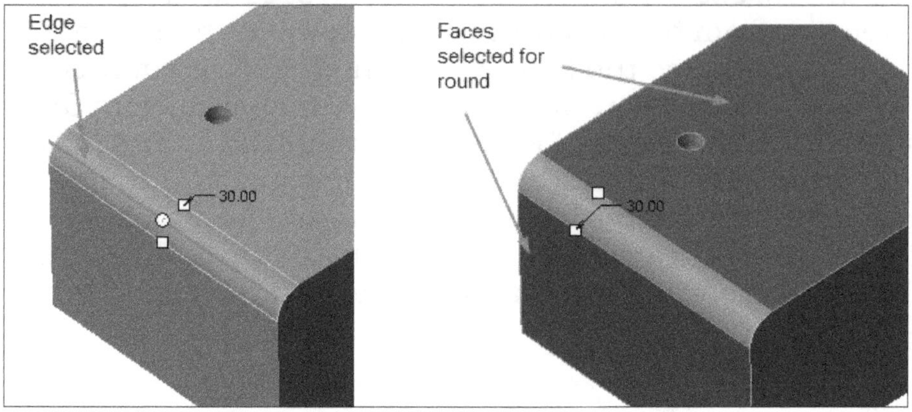

Figure-15. Edge and faces selected for round

- Double-click on the radius dimension in the modeling area or click in the **Radius** edit box from **Dimension Scheme** area of the contextual tab to change the value of radius.
- Click on the **Sets** tab to change the shape of the round. The expanded **Sets** tab will be displayed as shown in Figure-16.

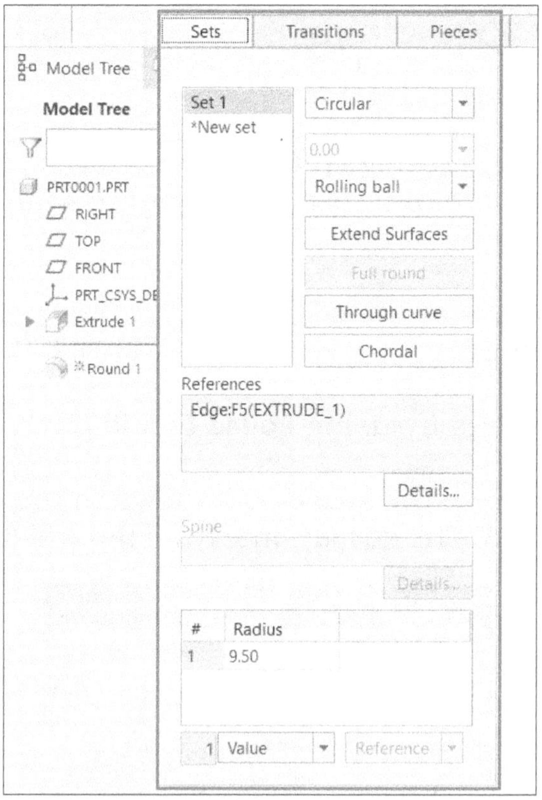

Figure-16. Sets tab

- Click on the **Cross-sectional shape** drop-down from **Dimension Scheme** area of the contextual tab or from the **Sets** tab of the **Ribbon**. A drop-down list will be displayed; refer to Figure-17.

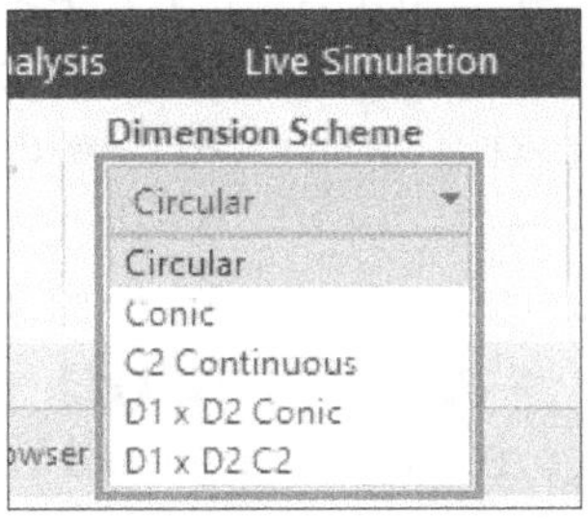

Figure-17. Cross sectional shape drop-down

- Using the options in the drop-down, you can create a round with Circular or conic shapes. You have used this option in practical of previous chapter.
- If you are creating a round by using three edges that are meeting at the same vertex as shown in Figure-18, then you can control the shape of round at the intersecting vertex by selecting the **Transitions** option from **Mode** area of the contextual tab.

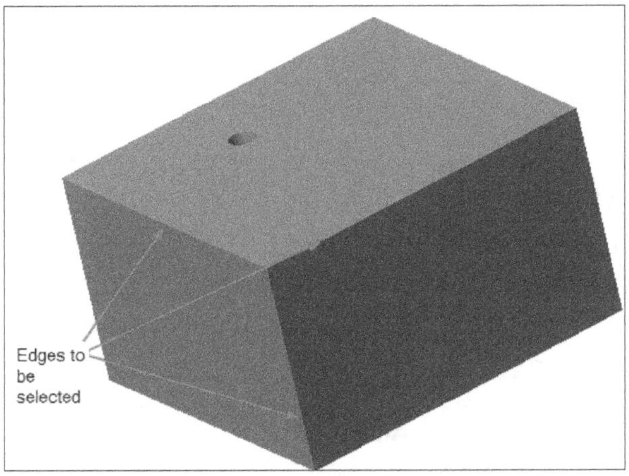

Figure-18. Edges for creating round

- After clicking on the button, select the portion that is created at the intersection vertex. The options to modify the transition will be displayed in the contextual tab; refer to Figure-19.

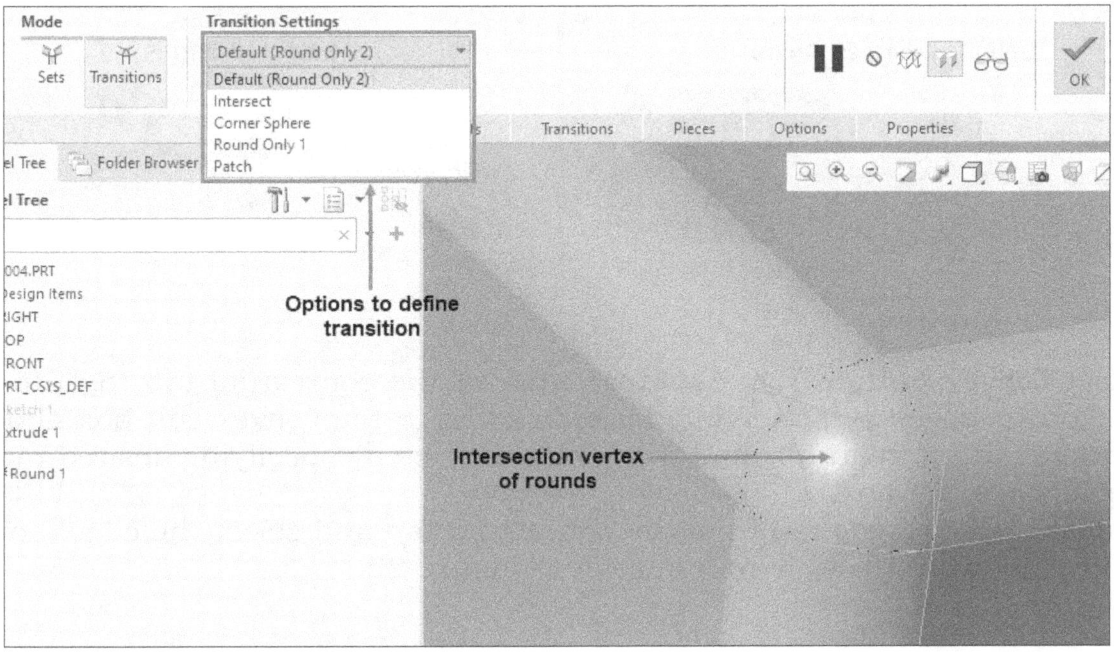

Figure-19. Options to change transition

- Similarly, you can modify other options for creating round (fillet).
- After specifying desired options, click on the **OK** button from the contextual tab to create the round feature. Note that you can select multiple faces/edges to create a fillet/fillets.

Auto Round

The **Auto Round** tool is used to create round at all sharp edges of the model at once. The procedure to use this tool is given next.

- Click on the **Auto Round** tool from the **Round** drop-down. The **Auto Round** contextual tab will be displayed; refer to Figure-20.

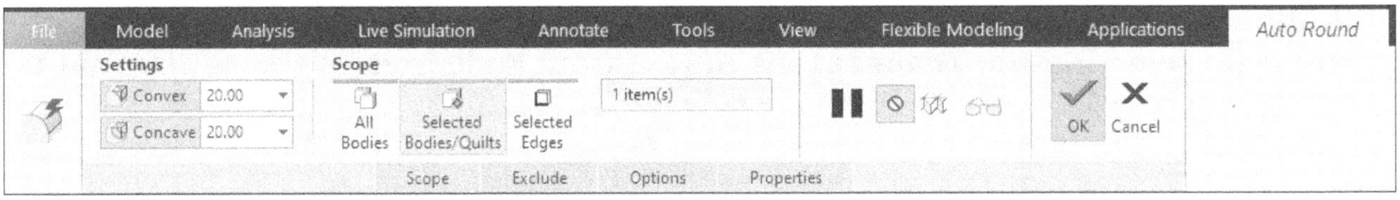

Figure-20. Auto Round contextual tab

- Select desired option from **Scope** area of the contextual tab to auto-round the features. Select the **All Bodies** option to create auto-round features on the edges of all solid bodies in the model. Select the **Selected Bodies/Quilts** option to auto-round features on the edges of the selected quilts and bodies. Select the **Selected Edges** option to create an auto-round feature on selected edges or intent chains; refer to Figure-21.

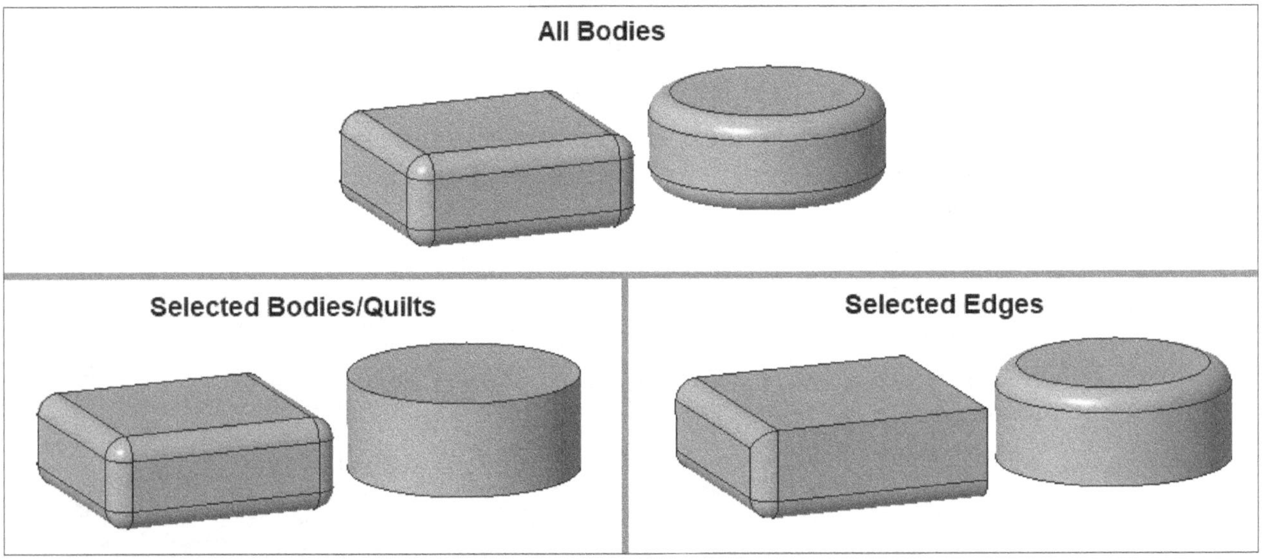

Figure-21. Auto round features

- Select **Convex** button from **Settings** area of the contextual tab to auto-round the convex edges by specifying desired radius in the **Convex** edit box and select **Concave** button to auto-round the concave edges by specifying desired radius in the **Concave** edit box.
- Click on the **Exclude** tab from the contextual tab and select the edges to which you do not want to apply round; refer to Figure-22.

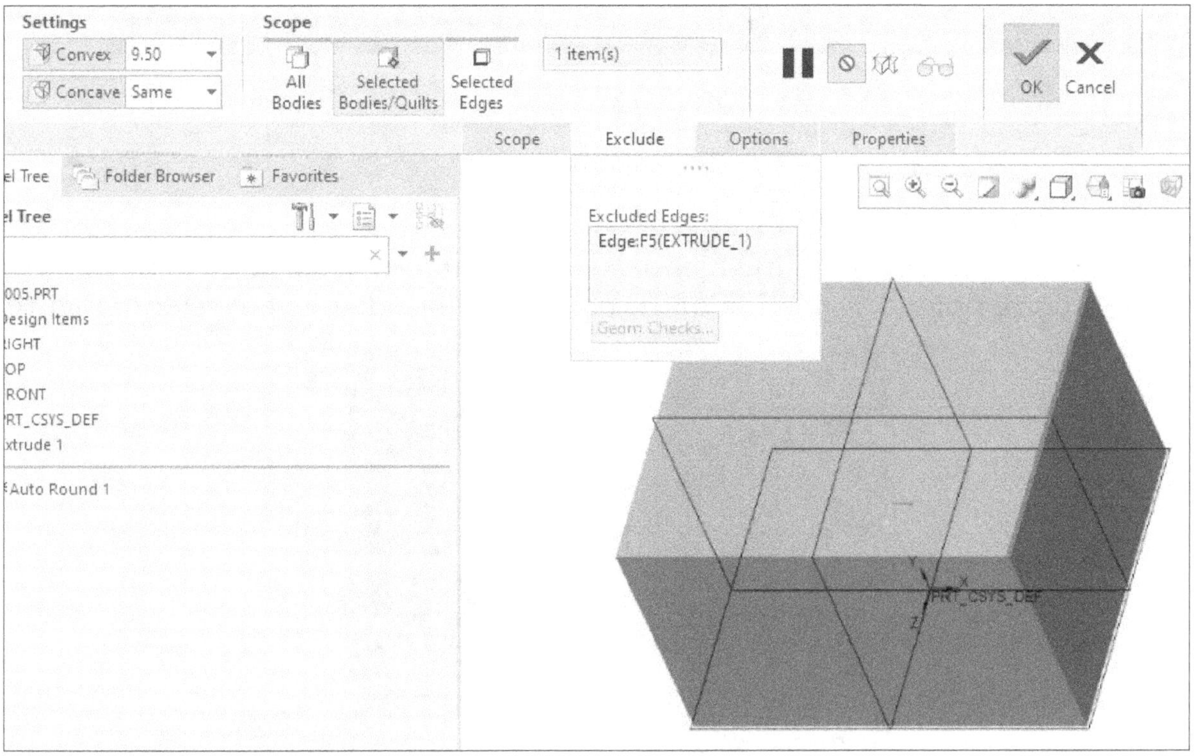

Figure-22. Edge not included for auto round feature

- Specify desired value of radius in the contextual tab and click on the **OK** button. The model will be displayed as shown in Figure-23.

Figure-23. Model after applying auto round

Corner Blend

The **Corner Blend** tool is used to create a smooth, rounded corner at the intersection of two or more blended (rounded) edges. The procedure to use this tool is discussed next.

- Click on the **Corner Blend** tool from the **Round** drop-down. The **Corner Blend** contextual tab will be displayed; refer to Figure-24.

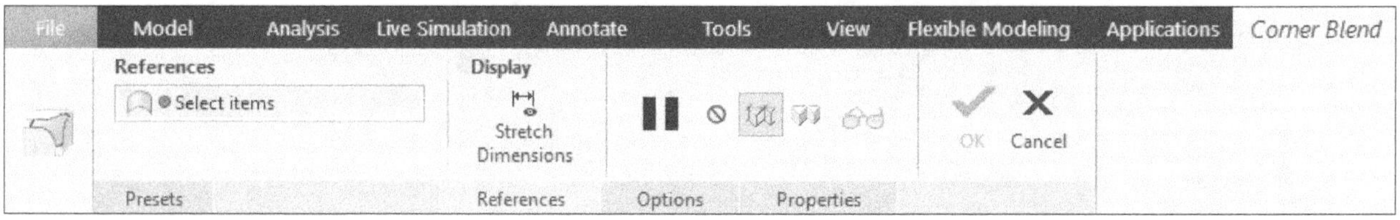

Figure-24. Corner Blend contextual tab

- Select two or more intersecting blended edges that form a corner where you want to create a corner blend. A preview of the corners will be displayed; refer to Figure-25.

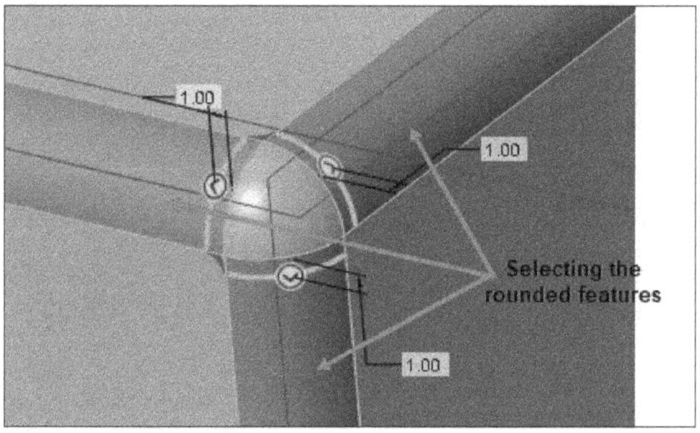

Figure-25. Selecting the featured corners

- Click on the **References** tab. The options in the tab will be displayed as shown in Figure-26.

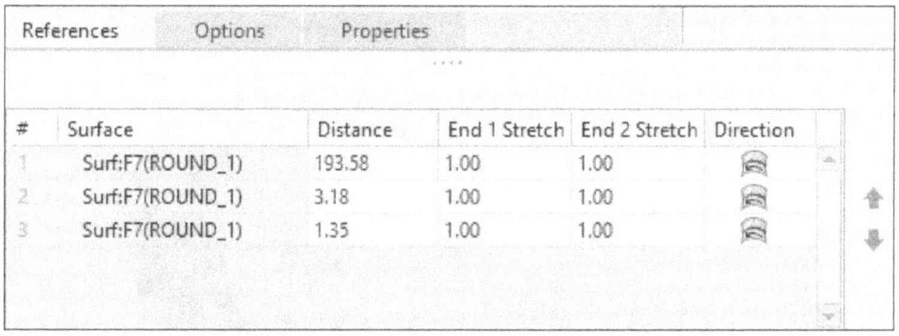

Figure-26. References tab

- Click in the **Distance** edit box and specify desired value to define the distance of the isoline from the corner.
- Click in the **End 1 Stretch** and **End 2 Stretch** edit box, and specify desired values to extend the blend curve along the surface edge.
- Click on the button to specify the direction of the isoline.
- Click on the **Stretch Dimensions** button to show the stretch dimension on the model.
- After specifying desired options, click on the **OK** button from the contextual tab. The corner blend will be created; refer to Figure-27.

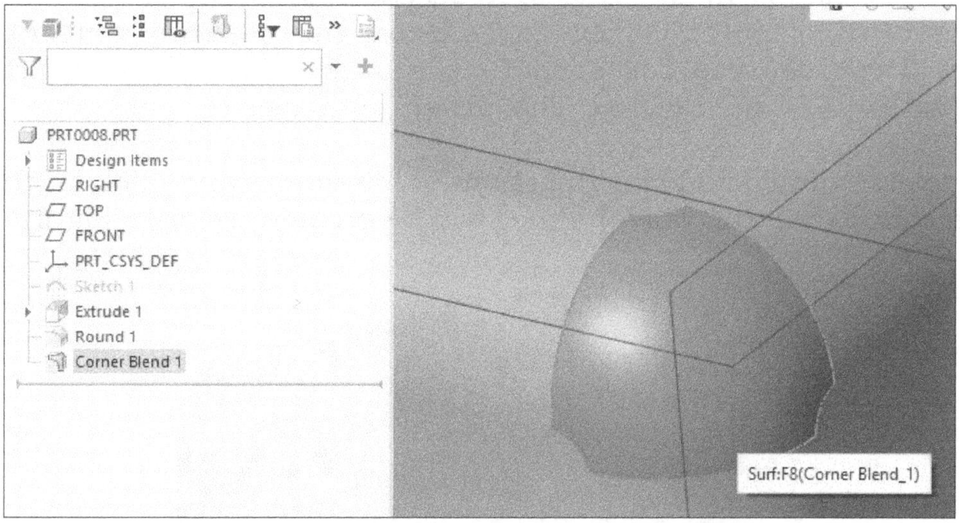

Figure-27. Creating the corner blend

Edge Chamfer

The **Edge Chamfer** tool is used to blunt the edges so that the stress is reduced at the edges and parts can be assembled easily. The procedure to use this tool is given next.

- Click on the **Edge Chamfer** tool from the **Chamfer** drop-down in the **Ribbon**; refer to Figure-28. The **Edge Chamfer** contextual tab will be displayed; refer to Figure-29.

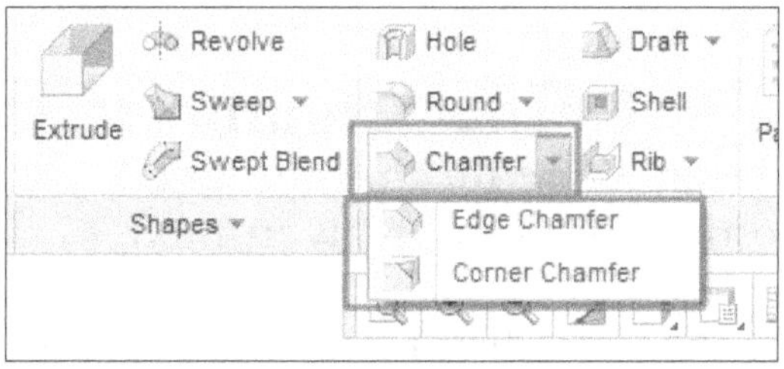

Figure-28. Chamfer tools

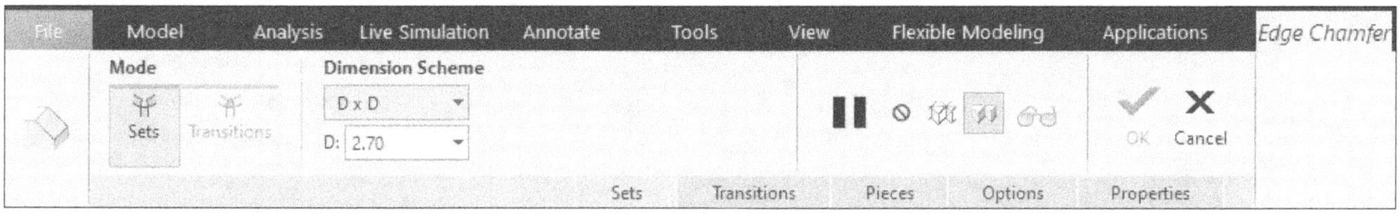

Figure-29. Edge Chamfer contextual tab

- Select the edges which you want to chamfer.
- Click on the **Dimension Scheme** drop-down and select desired option; refer to Figure-30.

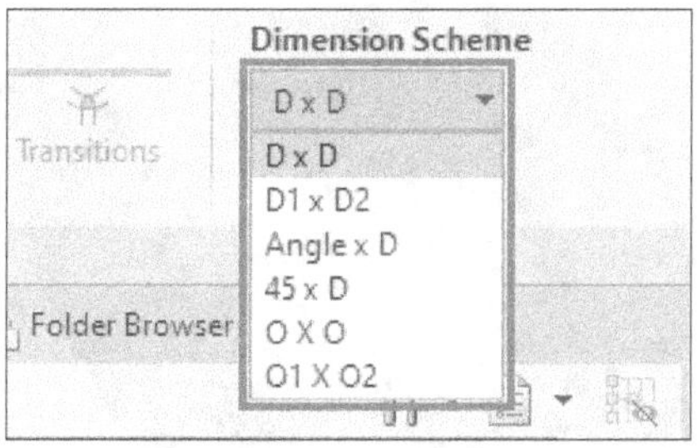

Figure-30. Dimension Scheme drop-down

Using the D1 x D2 option in the Dimension Scheme drop-down, you can independently specify the distance of chamfer edges from the chamfer centerline. Using the Angle x D option, you can specify the angle and distance value for the chamfer. Similarly, you can use the other options.

- Specify desired dimensions for the chamfer/chamfers and click on the **OK** button from the contextual tab. The chamfer will be created; refer to Figure-31.

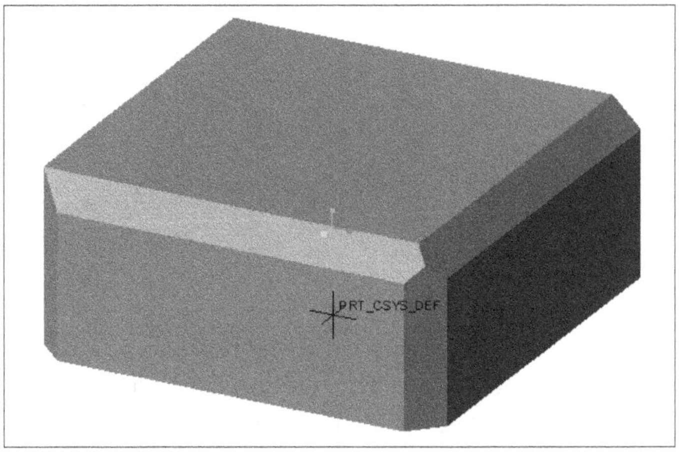

Figure-31. Chamfered model

Note that the options like transition will work in the same way as they work for **Round** tool.

Corner Chamfer

The **Corner Chamfer** tool is used to create chamfer at the corner created by intersection of edges. The procedure to use this tool is given next.

- Click on the **Corner Chamfer** tool from the **Chamfer** drop-down in the **Ribbon**. The **Corner Chamfer** contextual tab will be displayed; refer to Figure-32.

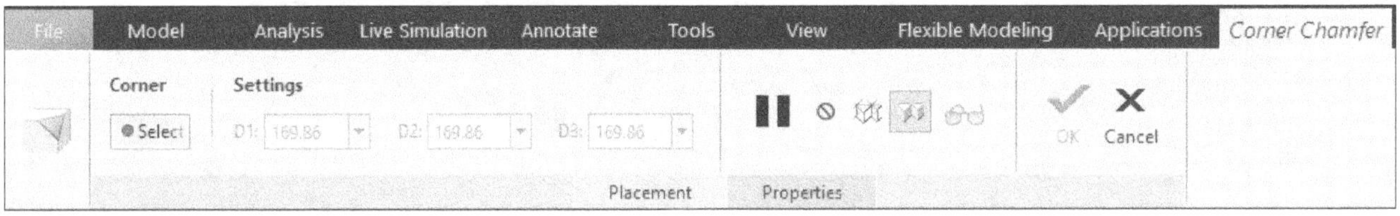

Figure-32. Corner Chamfer contextual tab

- Select a vertex, created by intersecting edges, on which you want to create corner chamfer. Preview of the chamfer will be displayed; refer to Figure-33.

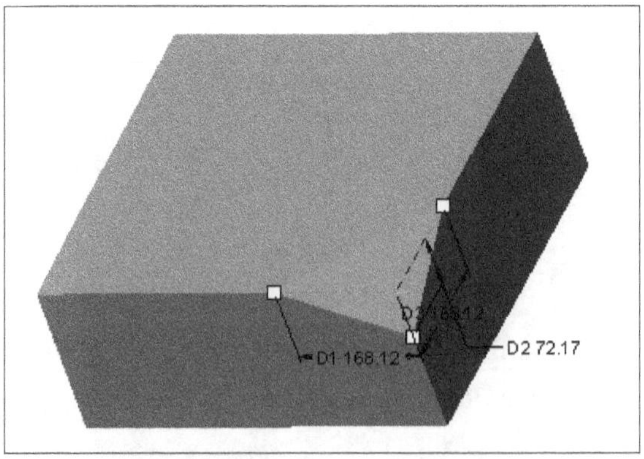

Figure-33. Preview of corner chamfer

- Change the distance values of the chamfer as desired, by using the dimension values displayed in the modeling area.

Draft

The **Draft** tool is used to apply taper to the faces. Draft is mostly used in mold designing, where you need to extract the molded part from the cavity. You will learn more about molding later in the book. The procedure to use this tool is given next.

- Click on the **Draft** tool from the **Draft** drop-down in the **Ribbon**. The **Draft** contextual tab will be displayed; refer to Figure-34.

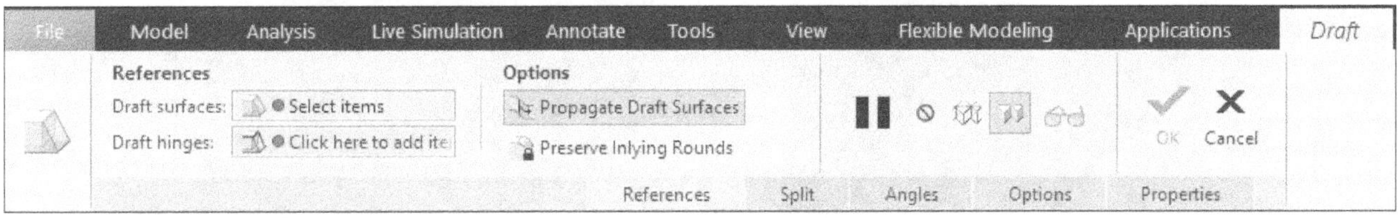

Figure-34. Draft contextual tab

- Click on the **References** tab. The options in the tab will be displayed as shown in Figure-35.
- Click in the **Draft surfaces** selection box and select the face that you want to make tapered; refer to Figure-36.

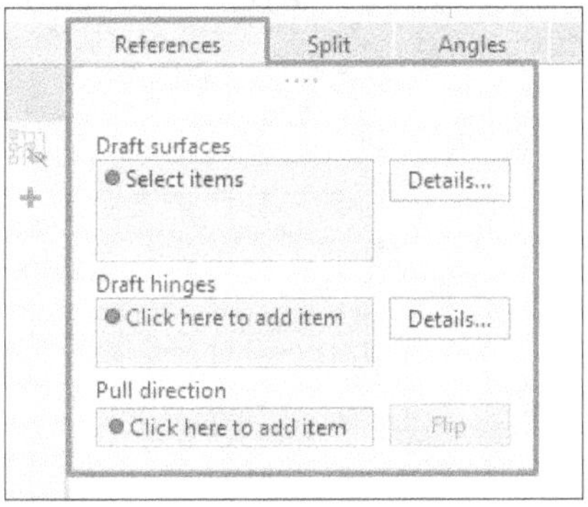

Figure-35. References tab

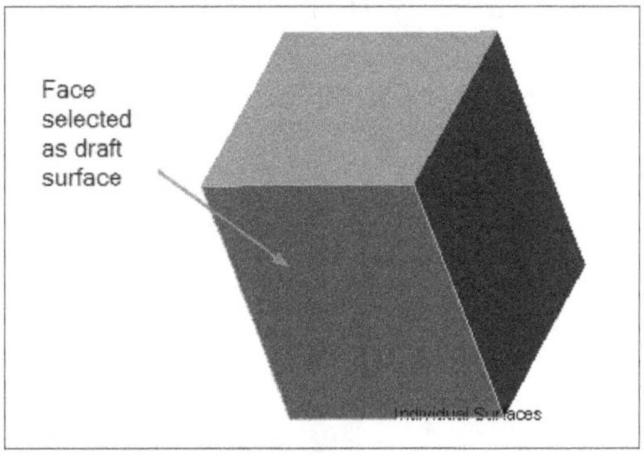

Figure-36. Face selected as draft surface

- Click in the **Draft hinges** selection box and select the edge about which you want to rotate the face for applying draft; refer to Figure-37.
- Click in the **Pull direction** selection box and select a reference (face, edge, or axis) to define the pull direction for the draft; refer to Figure-38.

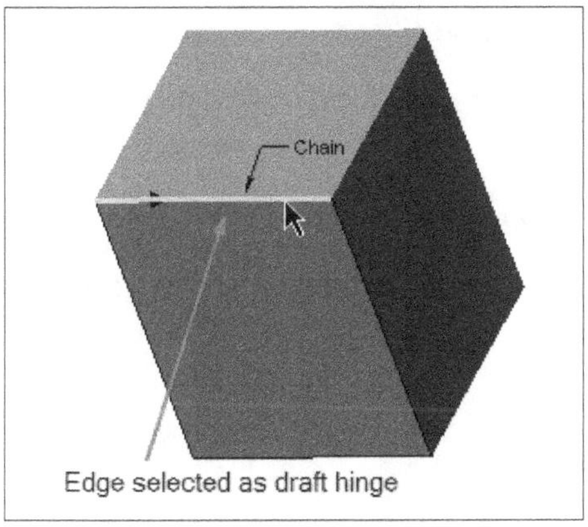

Figure-37. Edge selected as draft hinge

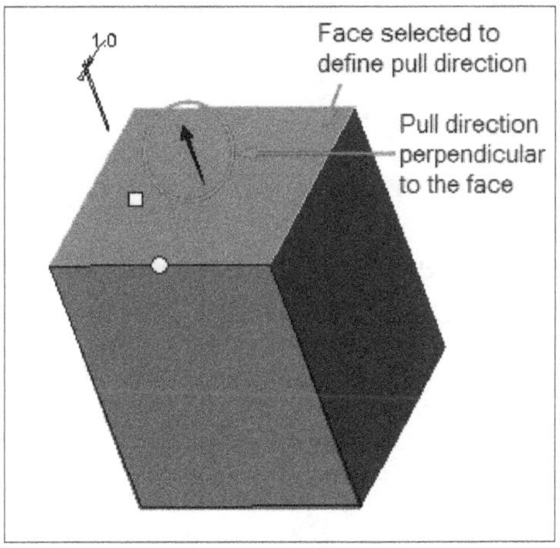

Figure-38. Face selected to define pull direction

- Double-click on the angle value and specify desired draft angle. You can specify a negative value to draft in opposite direction or you can click on the **Flip** button next to **Pull direction** selection box to reverse the direction.
- Creo Parametric 5.0 onwards, you can now apply draft to faces which have round or chamfer applied on their edges; refer to Figure-39.

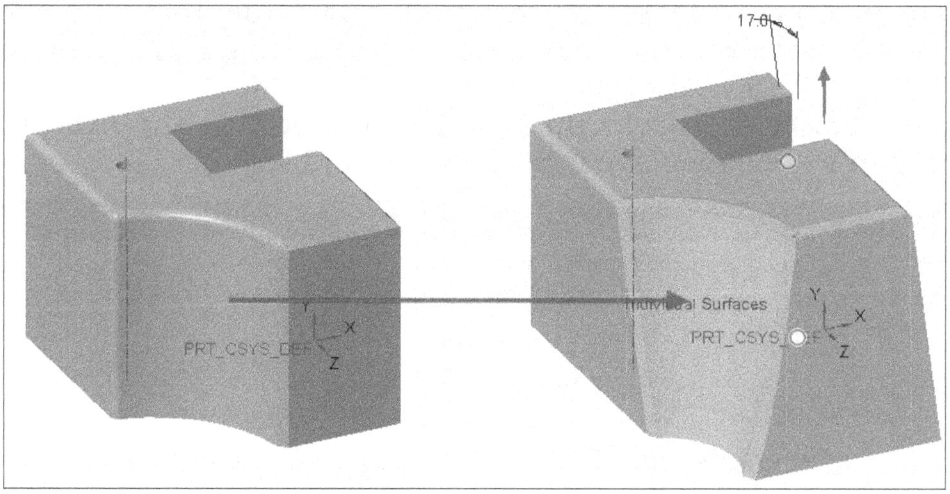

Figure-39. Applying draft to faces with chamfer and round

- Select the **Propagate Draft Surfaces** button from **Options** area of the contextual tab to include nearby tangent faces automatically in draft; refer to Figure-40.

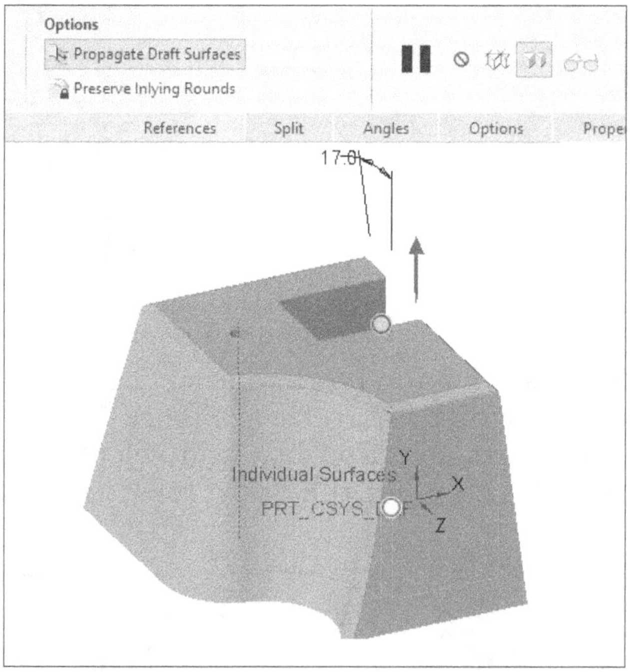

Figure-40. Including tangent faces in draft

- Select the **Preserve Inlying Rounds** button from **Options** area to exclude rounds at the transition faces; refer to Figure-41.

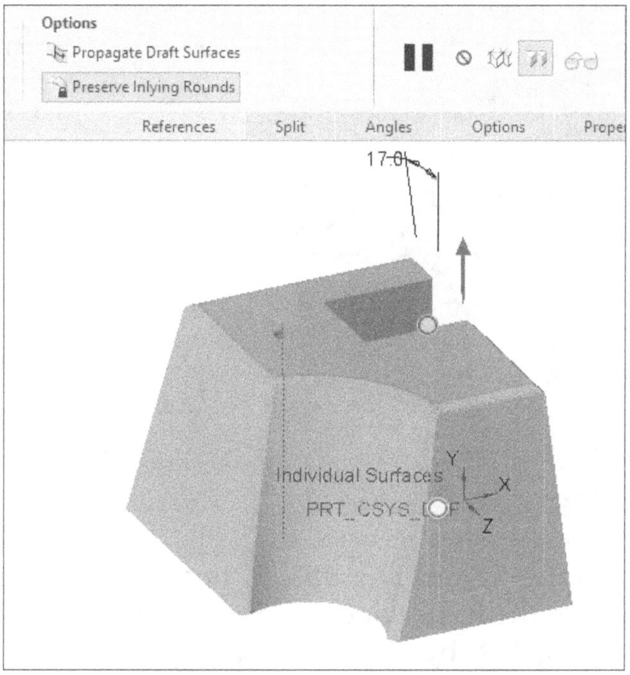

Figure-41. Excluding round at transition faces

- If you want to apply multiple angled draft to the face then press and hold **RMB** on the white dot displayed on the edge selected as hinge; refer to Figure-42.
- Select the **Add Angle** option displayed in the shortcut menu; refer to Figure-43.

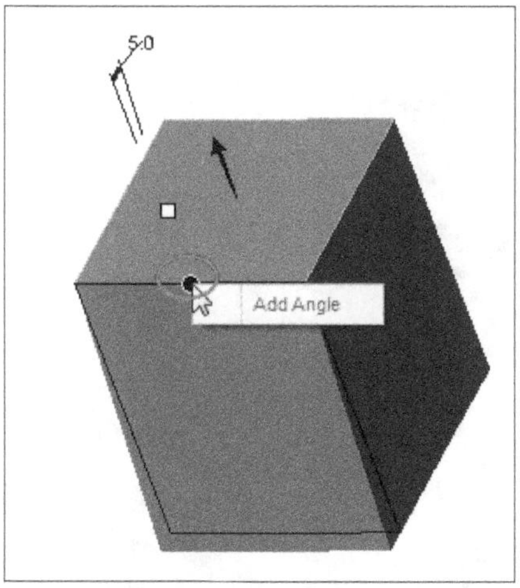

Figure-42. Shortcut menu for multiple angle draft

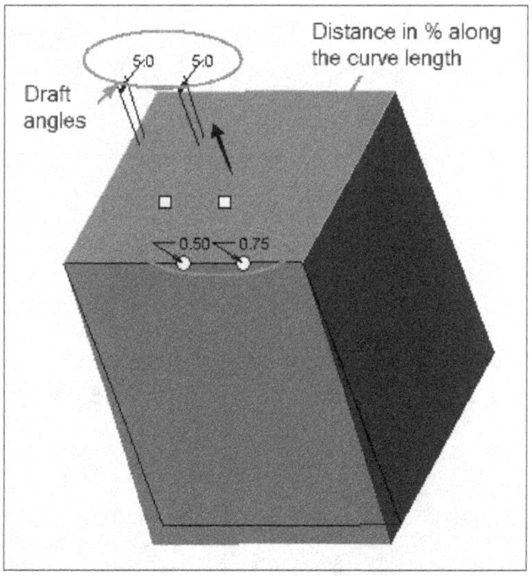

Figure-43. Preview of multiple angle draft

- You can add more angle values by pressing and holding **RMB** on the white dot and following the same procedure.
- Change the distance values and draft angle values as desired; refer to Figure-44.
- Click on the **Split** tab. The options in the tab will be displayed as shown in Figure-45.

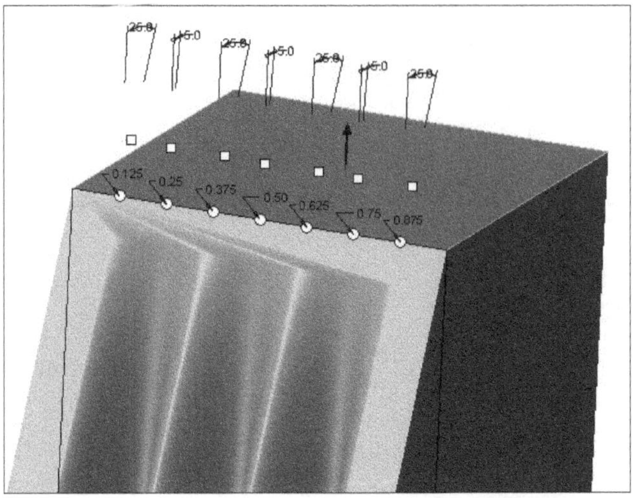

Figure-44. Preview of draft after applying multiple drafts

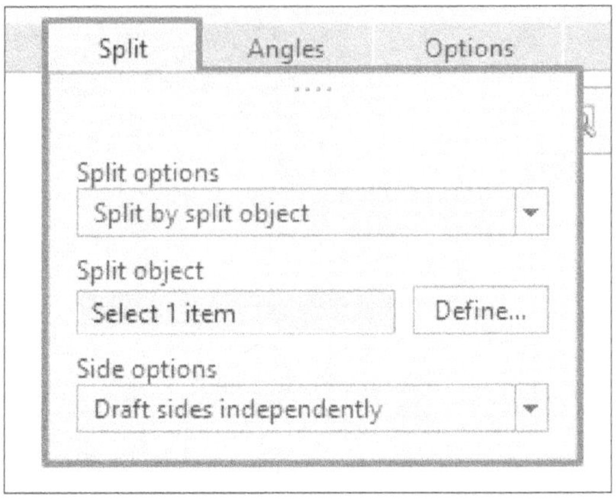

Figure-45. Split tab

- Select the **No split** option from the **Split options** drop-down in the tab if you do not want to split the draft surfaces. Note that whole surface pivots about the draft hinge. Select the **Split by draft hinge** option from the drop-down to split the draft surfaces along the draft hinge. Select the **Split by split object** option from the drop-down to split the draft surfaces by using a quilt or sketch; refer to Figure-46.

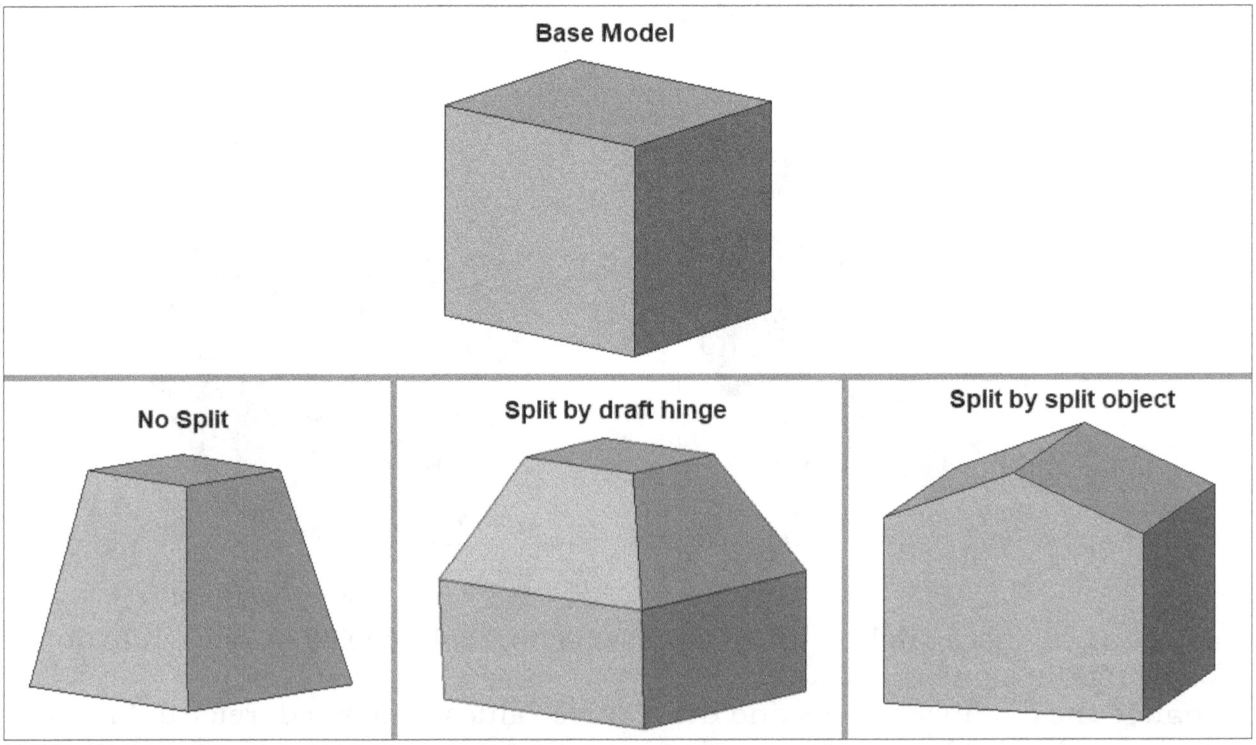

Figure-46. Split options

- Select desired option from **Side options** drop-down in the **Split** tab to draft one side of the split or both, dependently or independently.
- Click on the **OK** button from the **Draft** contextual tab to create the feature.
- Similarly, you can the **Variable Pull Direction Draft** tool to create tapered faces with varying angles.

Shell

The **Shell** tool is used to scoop out the material from the model. The procedure to use the **Shell** tool is given next.

- Click on the **Shell** tool from thc **Engineering** panel in the **Ribbon**. The **Shell** contextual tab will be displayed; refer to Figure-47.

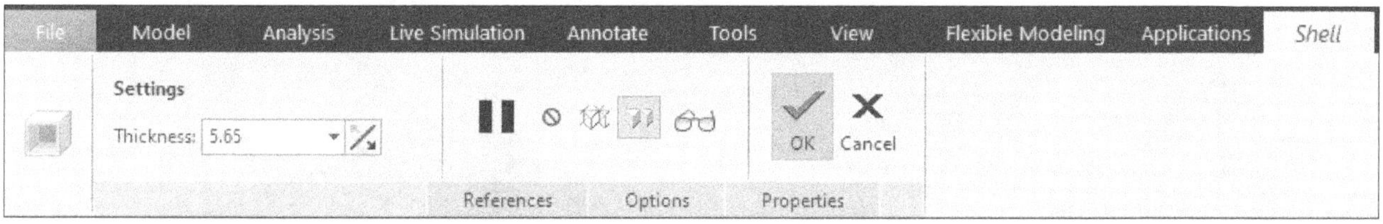

Figure-47. Shell contextual tab

- Click on the **References** tab. The options will be displayed as shown in Figure-48.

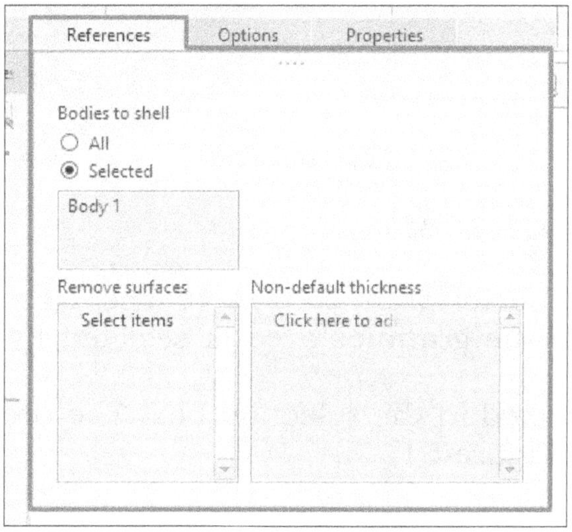

Figure-48. References tab of Shell tool

- Select **All** radio button from **Bodies to shell** area of the **References** tab. You are asked to select the surfaces to be removed.
- Select the face of the model that you want to remove completely. The preview of shell feature will be displayed; refer to Figure-49.

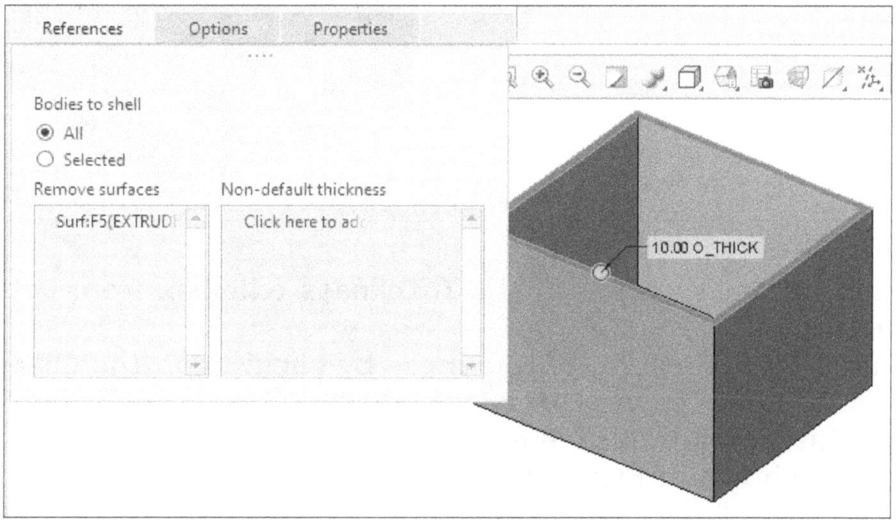

Figure-49. Preview of shell feature

- Click in the **Non-default thickness** selection box from **References** tab. You are asked to select the face to which you want to assign a different thickness value.
- Select desired face or multiple faces of the model. An edit box will be displayed in the **Non-default thickness** selection box.
- Specify desired thickness value for the face in the edit box and press **Enter**. The preview of different thickness will be displayed; refer to Figure-50.

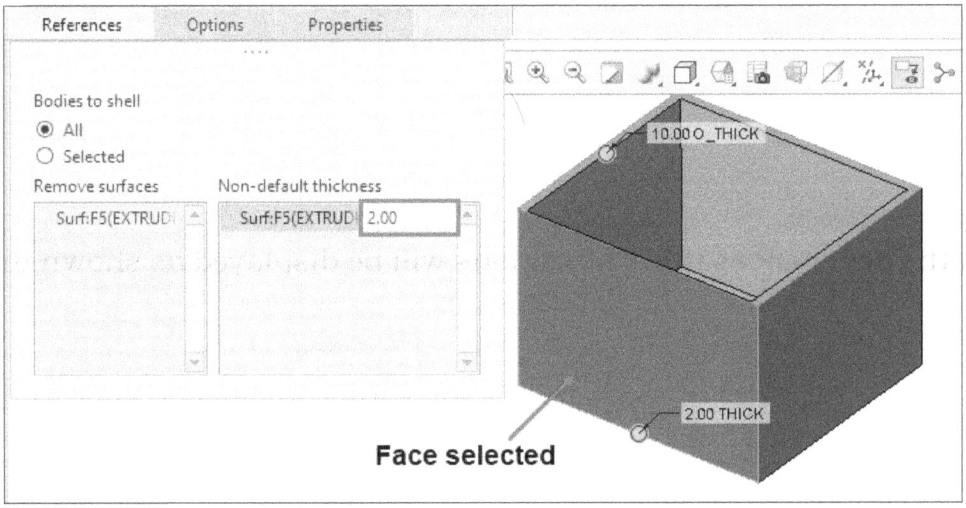

Figure-50. Preview of different thickness

- Select **Selected** radio button from **Bodies to shell** area of the **References** tab. The bodies present in the graphics area is selected by default in the **Selected body** selection box.
- Click on the body selected in the selection box. The preview of shell feature will be displayed; refer to Figure-51.

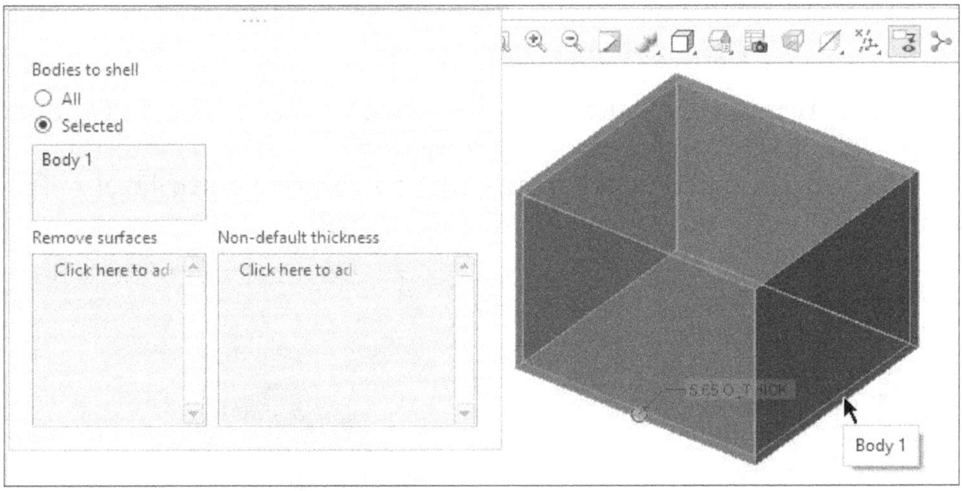

Figure-51. Preview of shell feature

- Enter desired thickness value in the **Thickness** edit box from **Settings** area of the contextual tab.
- You can change the direction of thickness by clicking on the **Change thickness direction** button next to the **Thickness** edit box.
- Click on the **Options** tab from **Shell** contextual tab. The options in the tab will be displayed as shown in Figure-52.

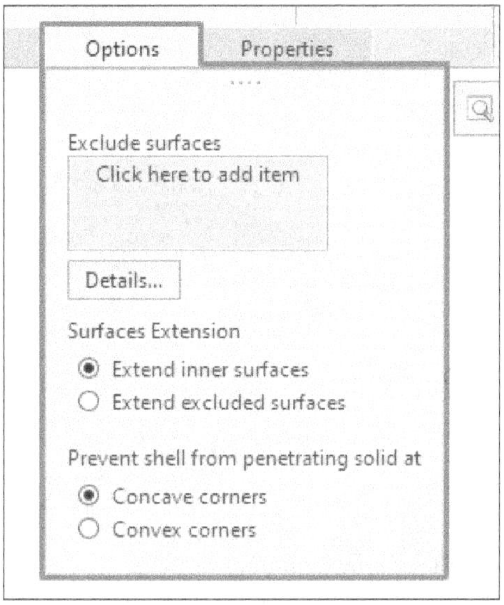

Figure-52. Options tab of Shell contextual tab

- Click on the **Exclude surfaces** selection box. You are asked to select the faces to be excluded from shell.
- Select desired faces of the model you want to exclude from shell; refer to Figure-53.

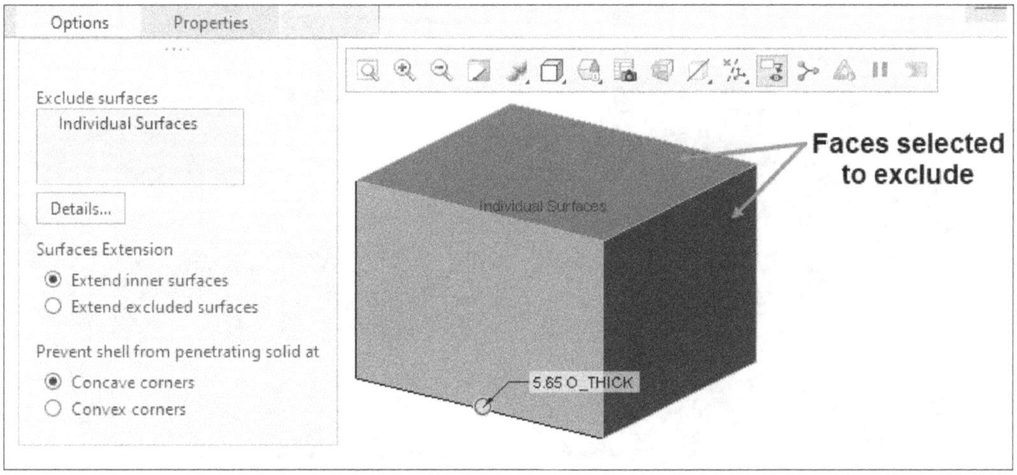

Figure-53. Faces selected to exclude

- Select desired option from the **Surfaces Extension** area of the **Options** tab. Select the **Extend inner surfaces** radio button to extend the inner surfaces of the shell. Select the **Extend excluded surfaces** radio button to extend the excluded surfaces.
- Select desired option from the **Prevent shell from penetrating solid at** area of the **Options** tab. Select the **Concave corners** radio button to prevent the shell from cutting through the solid at concave corners. Select the **Convex corners** radio button to prevent the shell from cutting through the solid at convex corners.
- After specifying desired parameters, preview of shell will be displayed; refer to Figure-54.
- Enter desired thickness value in the **Thickness** edit box from the **Settings** area of the contextual tab and click on **OK** button. The shell feature will be created.

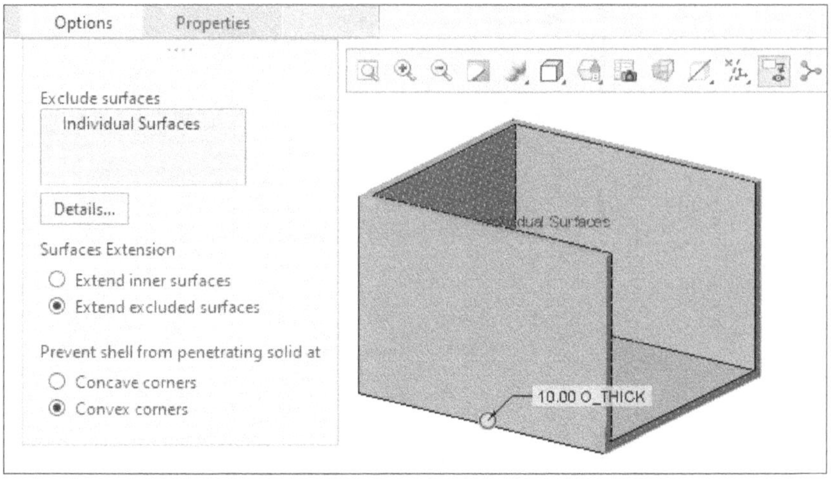

Figure-54. Preview of shell after excluding surfaces

Rib

There are two types of rib features available in Creo Parametric; **Trajectory Rib** and **Profile Rib**. The Trajectory ribs are created in a location bounded by walls; refer to Figure-55. The Profile rib allows to use the selected profile while creating the rib; refer to Figure-55. The procedures to create these ribs are given next.

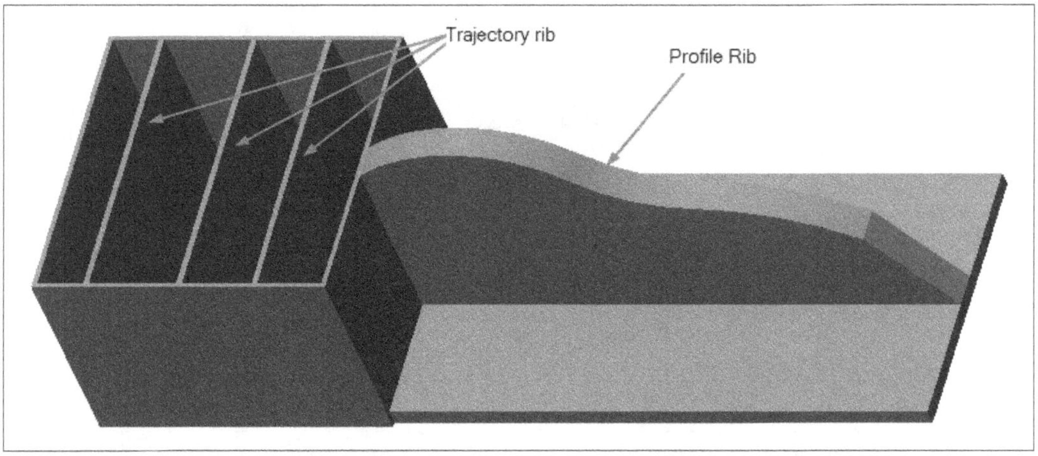

Figure-55. Trajectory ribs and Profile rib

Trajectory Rib

- Click on the **Trajectory Rib** tool from the **Rib** drop-down in the **Engineering** panel of the **Ribbon**. The **Trajectory Rib** contextual tab will be displayed; refer to Figure-56.

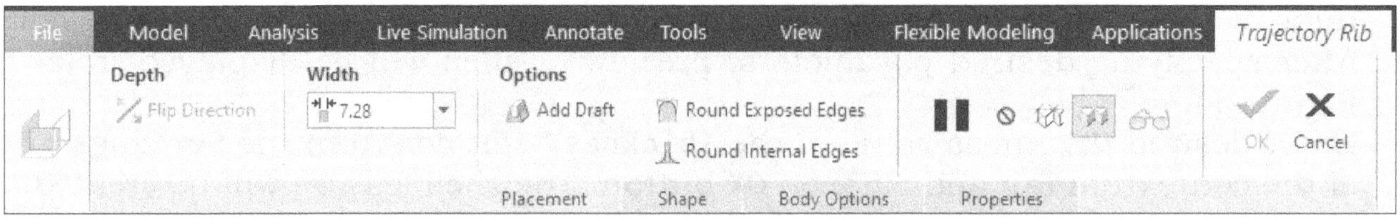

Figure-56. Trajectory Rib contextual tab

- Click on the **Placement** tab and select the top face of the model; refer to Figure-57.

Figure-57. Top face of the model

- Create the sketch as shown in Figure-58.
- Click on the **OK** button from the **Sketch** contextual tab. Preview of the trajectory rib will be displayed; refer to Figure-59.

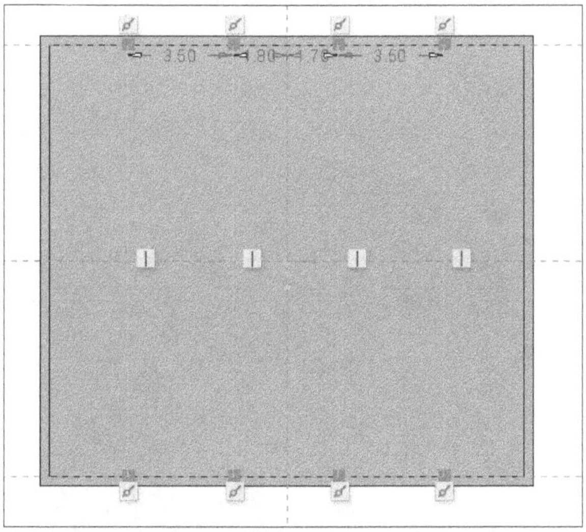

Figure-58. Sketch for trajectory rib

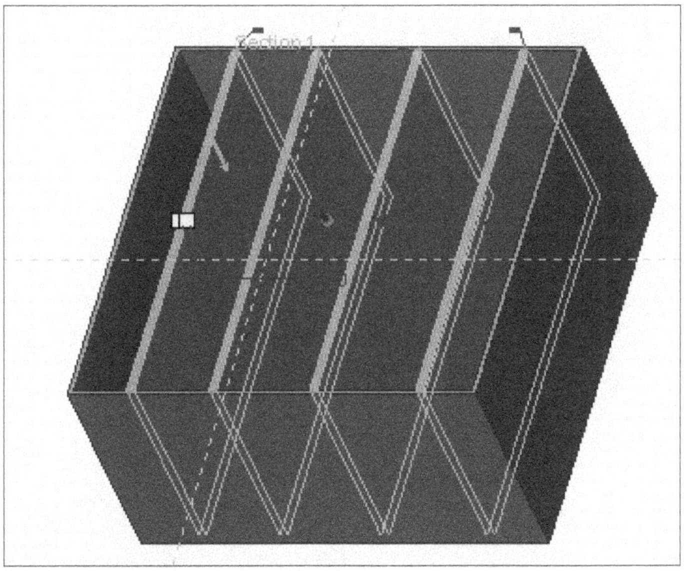

Figure-59. Preview of trajectory rib

- Click on the **Shape** tab from the **Trajectory Rib** contextual tab to define rounds and a draft angle and to preview a cross-section of the rib. The options will be displayed as shown in Figure-60.
- Select the **Add Draft** option from the **Options** area in the **Ribbon** to add drafts to the side surfaces. The preview of rib feature with add draft option will be displayed as shown in Figure-61.

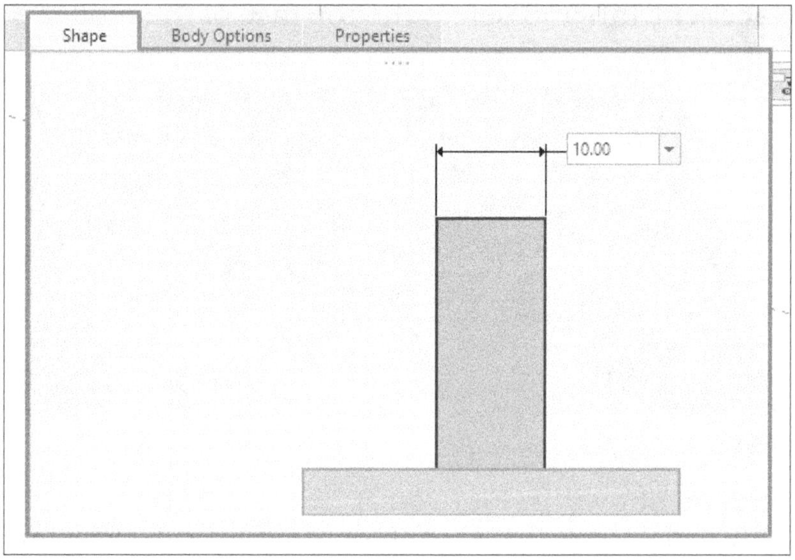

Figure-60. Shape tab of Trajectory Rib tool

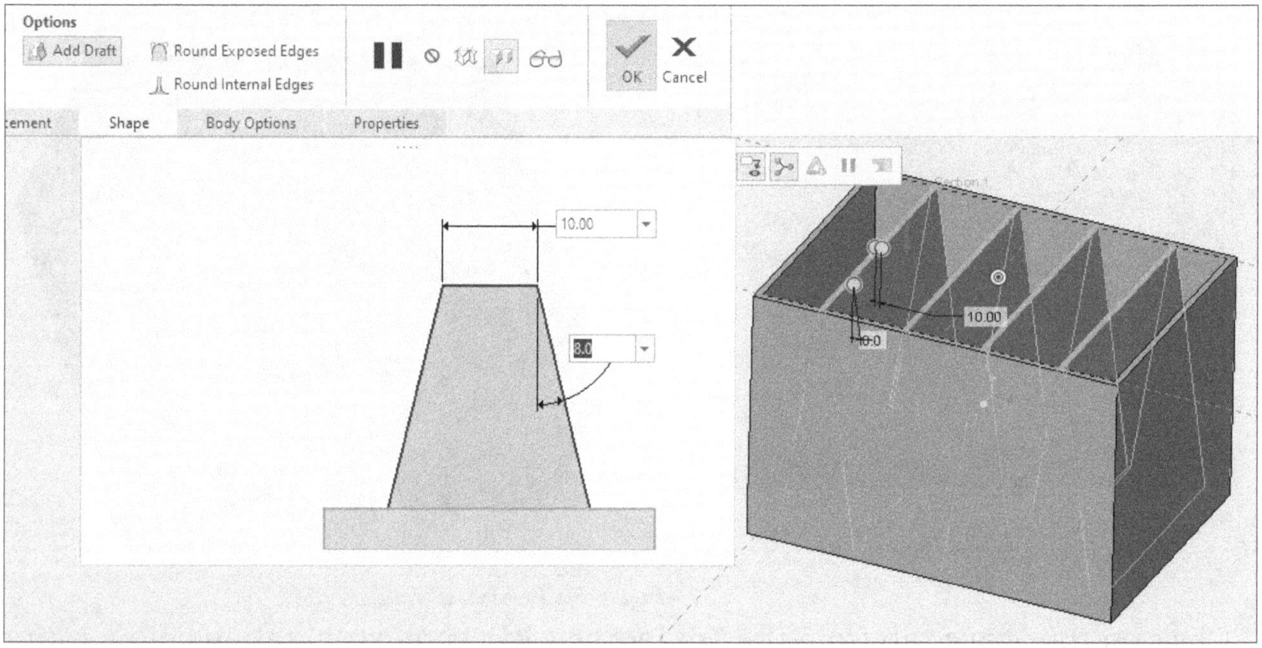

Figure-61. Preview of rib with draft feature

- Specify desired values for the **Add Draft** option in the edit boxes displayed in the **Shape** tab.
- Select the **Round Exposed Edges** option from the **Options** area in the **Ribbon** to add rounds on the exposed edges. The preview of rib feature with rounds on the edges will be displayed; refer to Figure-62.
- Specify desired values for the **Round Exposed Edges** option in the edit boxes displayed in the **Shape** tab.
- Select the **Round Internal Edges** option from the **Options** area in the **Ribbon** to add rounds on the internal edges. The preview of rib feature with rounds on the edges will be displayed; refer to Figure-63.

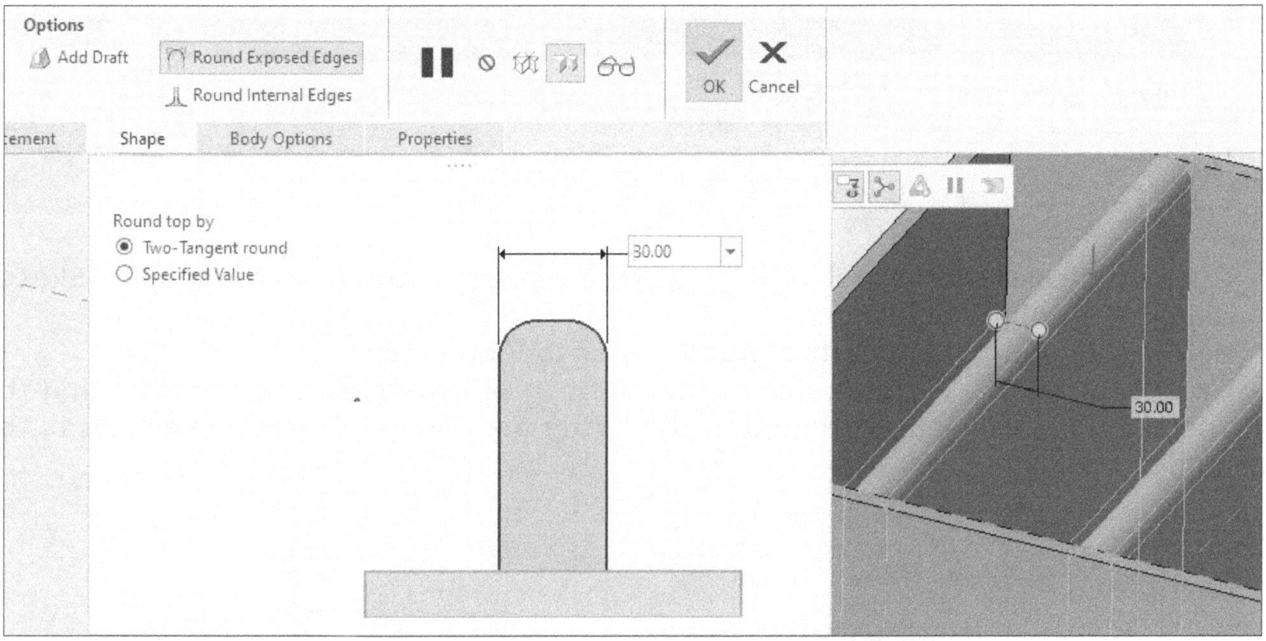

Figure-62. Preview of rib feature with rounds on exposed edges

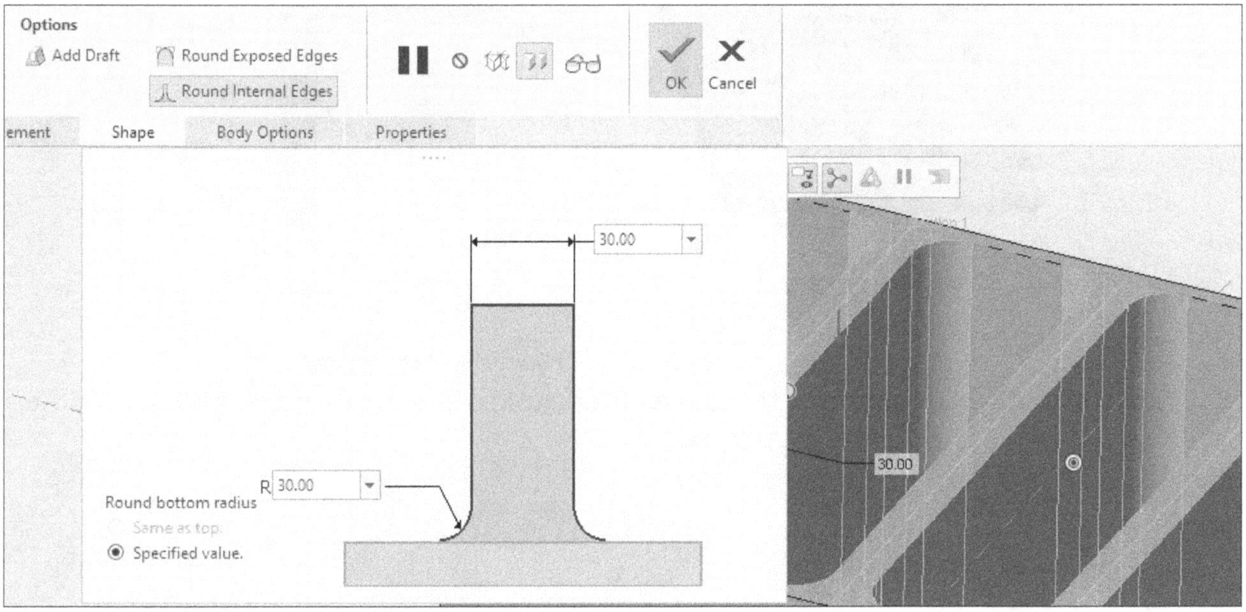

Figure-63. Preview of rib feature with rounds on internal edges

- Specify desired values for the **Round Internal Edges** option in the edit boxes displayed in the **Shape** tab.
- Specify desired width for rib feature in the edit box from the **Width** area in the **Ribbon**.
- Click on the **Flip Direction** button from the **Depth** area of the **Ribbon** to change the depth direction of rib feature.
- Click on the **OK** button from the **Trajectory Rib** contextual tab to create the rib feature.

Profile Rib

- Click on the **Profile Rib** tool from the **Rib** drop-down in the **Engineering** panel of the **Ribbon**. The **Profile Rib** contextual tab will be displayed; refer to Figure-64.

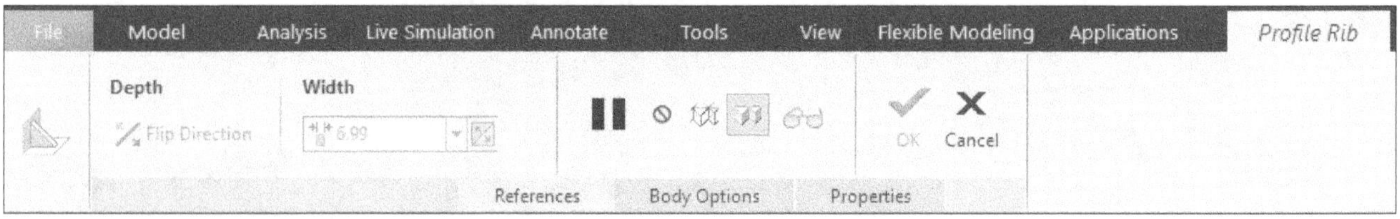

Figure-64. Profile Rib contextual tab

- Click on the **References** tab and click on the **Define** button from the tab; the **Sketch** dialog box will be displayed.
- Select the plane to create the profile; refer to Figure-65.
- Create the sketch of the profile at the plane as shown in Figure-66. Note that the end points of the spline created in the figure are coincident to the vertices of the model.

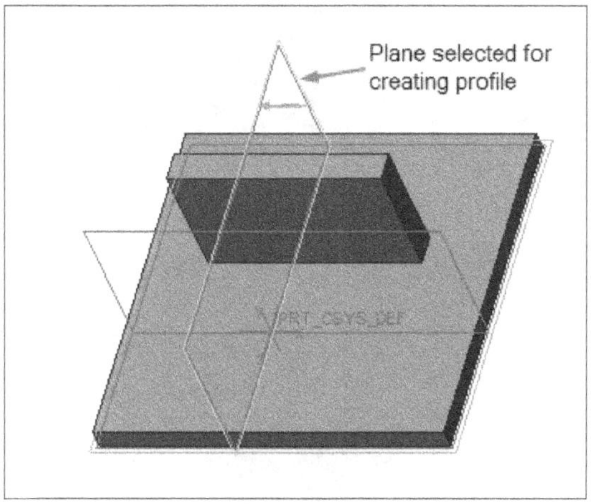

Figure-65. Plane for creating profile

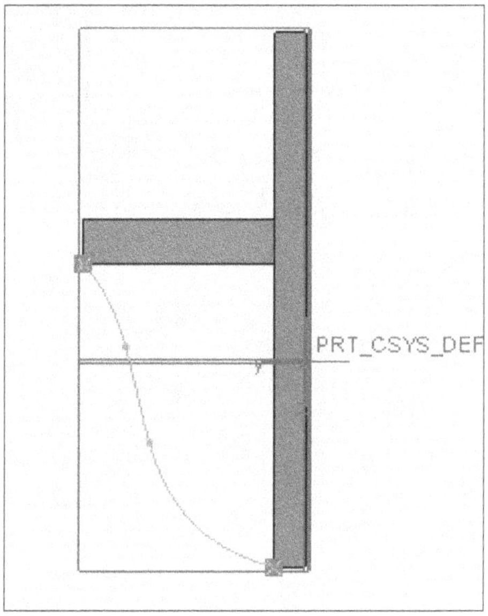

Figure-66. Profile created

- Click on the **OK** button from the **Sketch** contextual tab. Preview of the profile rib will be displayed; refer to Figure-67.

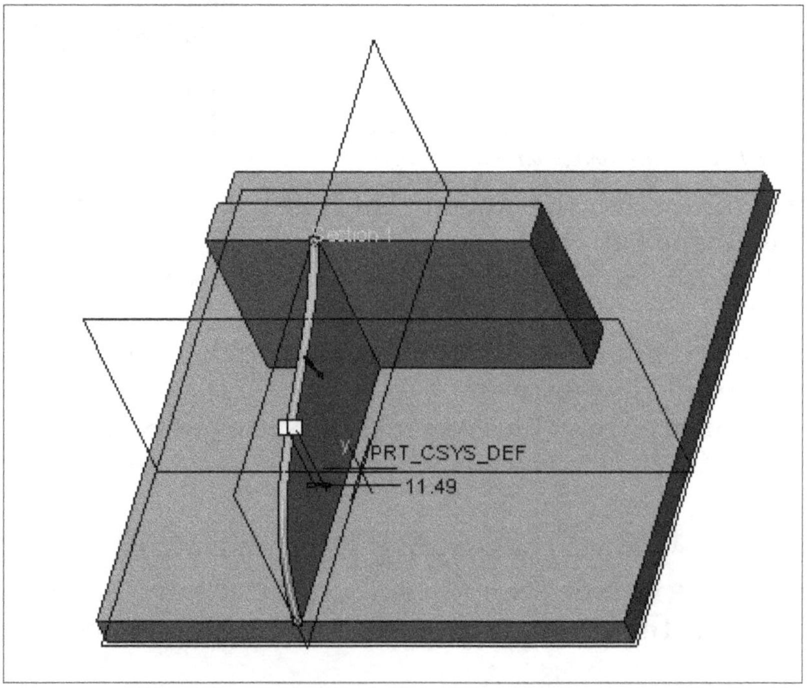

Figure-67. Preview of profile rib

- Specify desired thickness value and click on the **OK** button from the **Profile Rib** contextual tab.

Toroidal Bend

The **Toroidal Bend** tool is used to bend solids, surfaces, and datum curves to form toroidal shapes like forming tire from flat solid. The procedure to use this tool is given next.

- Click on the **Toroidal Bend** tool from the expanded **Engineering** panel in the **Ribbon**. The **Toroidal Bend** contextual tab will be displayed; refer to Figure-68.

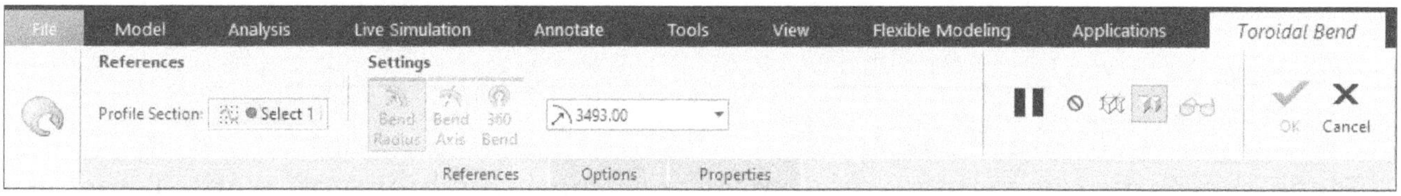

Figure-68. Toroidal Bend contextual tab

- Click on the **References** tab in the **Ribbon** and then click on the **Define** button. You will be asked to select a sketching plane.
- Select the flat face of the model which is to be kept fixed during bending; refer to Figure-69. The orientation references will be selected automatically. You can change the orientation as discussed in earlier chapters.

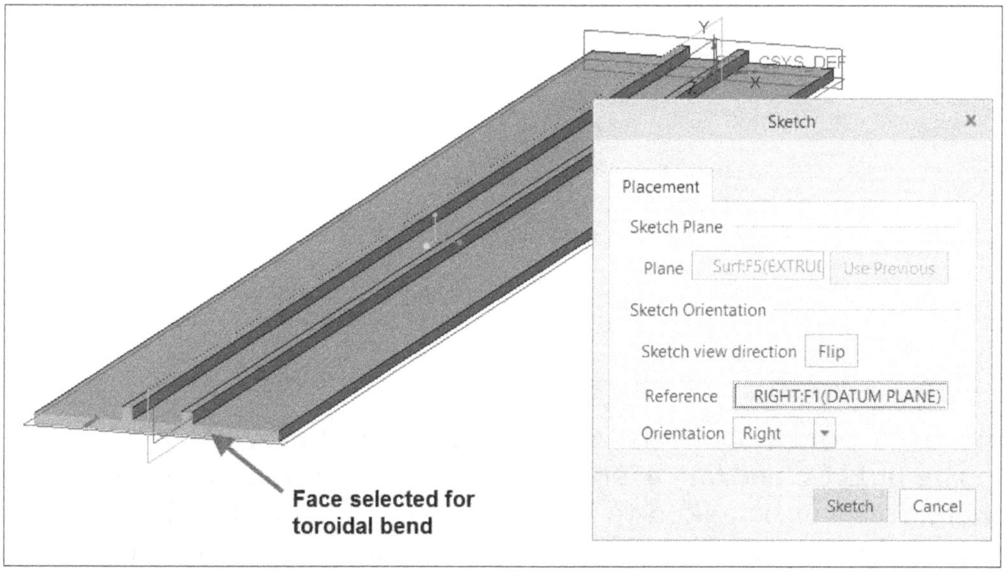

Figure-69. Face selected for toroidal bend

- Click on the **Sketch** button from the dialog box and create the sketch of profile in which you want to bend the work piece; refer to Figure-70.

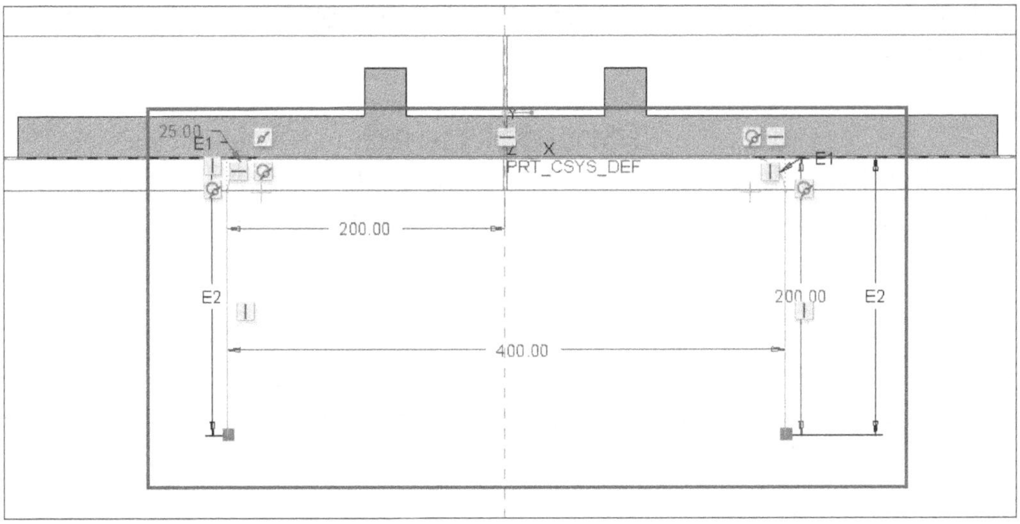

Figure-70. Sketch created for bend

- Place the datum coordinate system at the location which you want to make as neutral plane. Most of the time the coordinate system is placed on/near the sketch profile; refer to Figure-71.

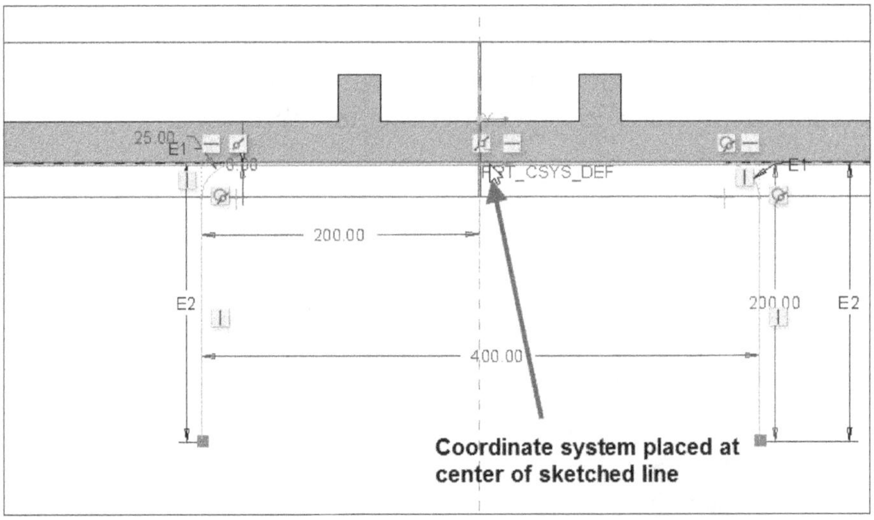

Figure-71. Placing coordinate system

- Click on the **OK** button from the **Sketch** contextual tab.
- Click on the **Quilts and/or a solid body** selection box in the **References** tab of the **Ribbon**. You will be asked to select the surfaces or a solid body.
- Select the surfaces or a solid body from the modeling area. Preview of bend feature will be displayed; refer to Figure-72.
- By default, the **Bend Radius** option is selected in the **Settings** area of the **Ribbon**. Specify desired radius of bend in the **Bend Radius** edit box. If you want to bend the part about an axis then select the **Bend Axis** option from the **Settings** area and select desired axis.
- To create a full 360 degrees bend, select the **360 Bend** option from the **Settings** area. You will be asked to select two faces that define the total length of solid; refer to Figure-73.

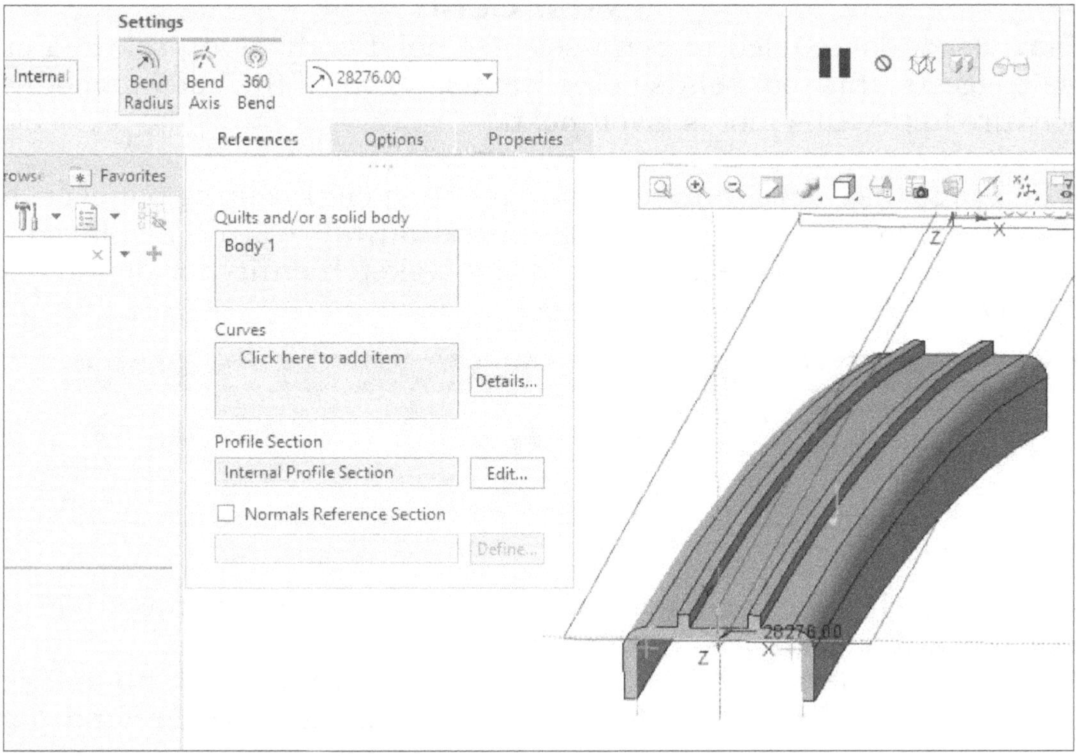

Figure-72. Preview of toroidal bend

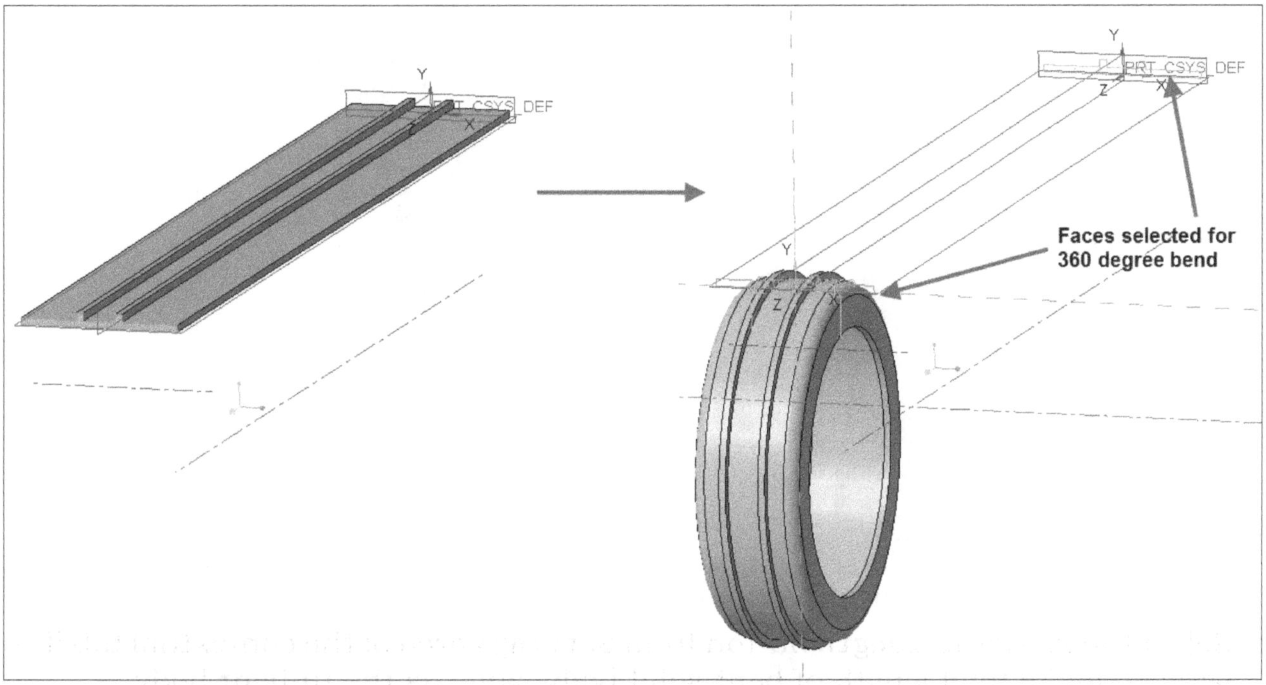

Figure-73. Preview of 360 degree toroidal bend

- If you want to bend a curve using the toroidal bend then after activating the tool, click on the **Curves** selection box in the **References** tab of the **Ribbon**. You will be asked to select the curves. Rest of the procedure is same.
- Click on the **OK** button from the **Ribbon** to create the bend.

Spinal Bend

The **Spinal Bend** tool is used to bend selected solid body along selected curve. As the name suggests, this tool bends spine (center curve) of the body to modify shape. The procedure to use this tool is given next.

- Click on the **Spinal Bend** tool from the expanded **Engineering** panel in the **Model** tab of the **Ribbon**. The **Spinal Bend** contextual tab will be displayed; refer to Figure-74. Also, you will be asked to select a sketch entity for defining shape of solid body.

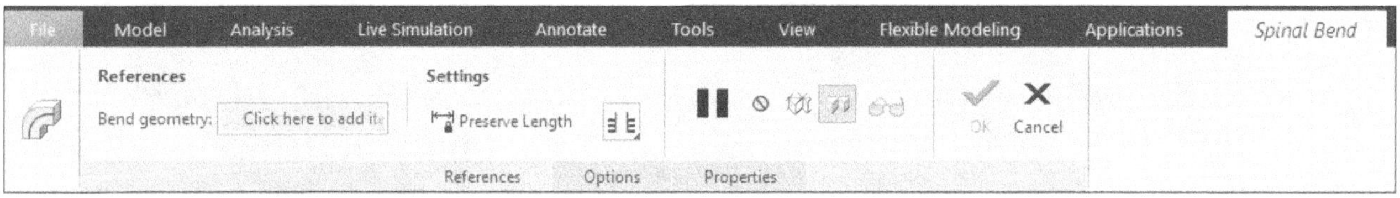

Figure-74. Spinal Bend contextual tab

- Select the sketch entity as shown in Figure-75. To change the origin of curve, click on the arrow displayed on the curve.
- Click in the **Bend Geometry** selection box from the contextual tab and select the solid geometry to be bent. Preview of the bend will be displayed; refer to Figure-76.

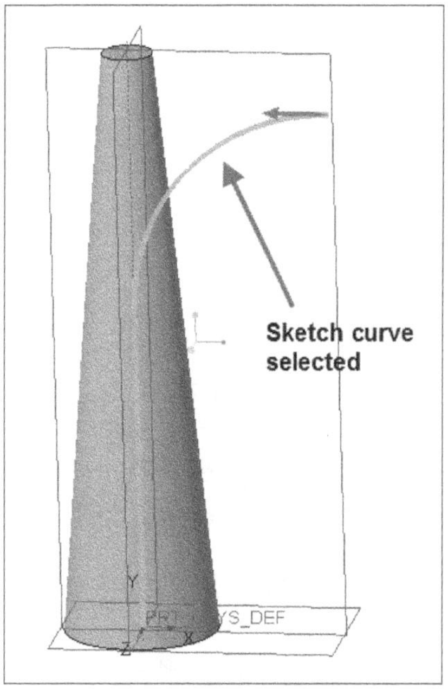

Figure-75. Sketch curve selected for spinal bend

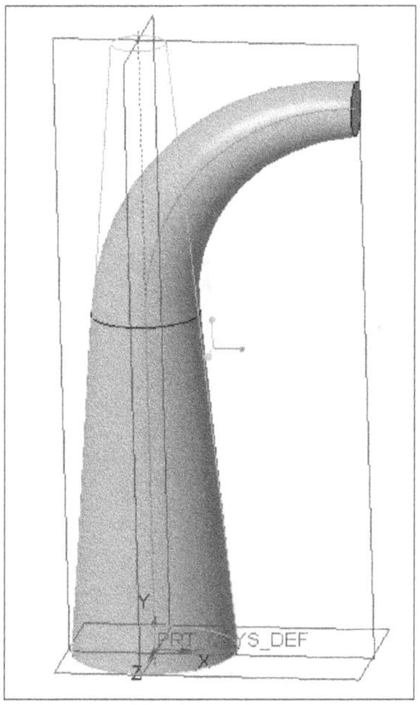

Figure-76. Preview of spinal bend

- Select the **Preserve Length** button from **Settings** area of the contextual tab if you want to make total length of bent solid body same as the unbent body.
- If you want to change the extent up to which you want to bend the solid body then select desired option from **Bend Extent** drop-down in the **Ribbon**; refer to Figure-77.

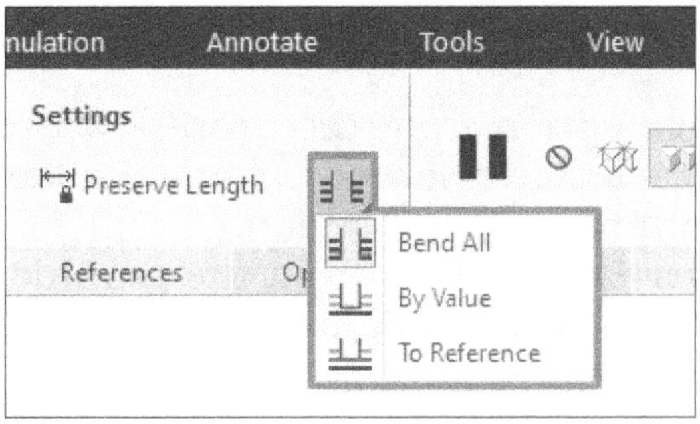

Figure-77. Bend Extents drop-down

- Select the **Bend All** option from the drop-down to bend the entire selected geometry from the spine start. The preview of bend will be displayed as shown in Figure-78.

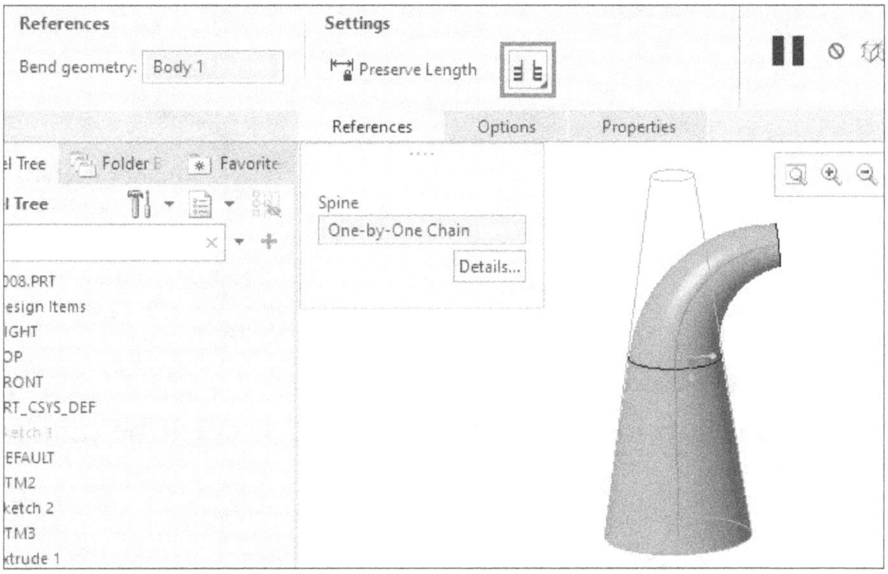

Figure-78. Bend All option

- Select the **By Value** option from the drop-down to bend the geometry between the spine start and the specified offset. The preview of bend will be displayed as shown in Figure-79.

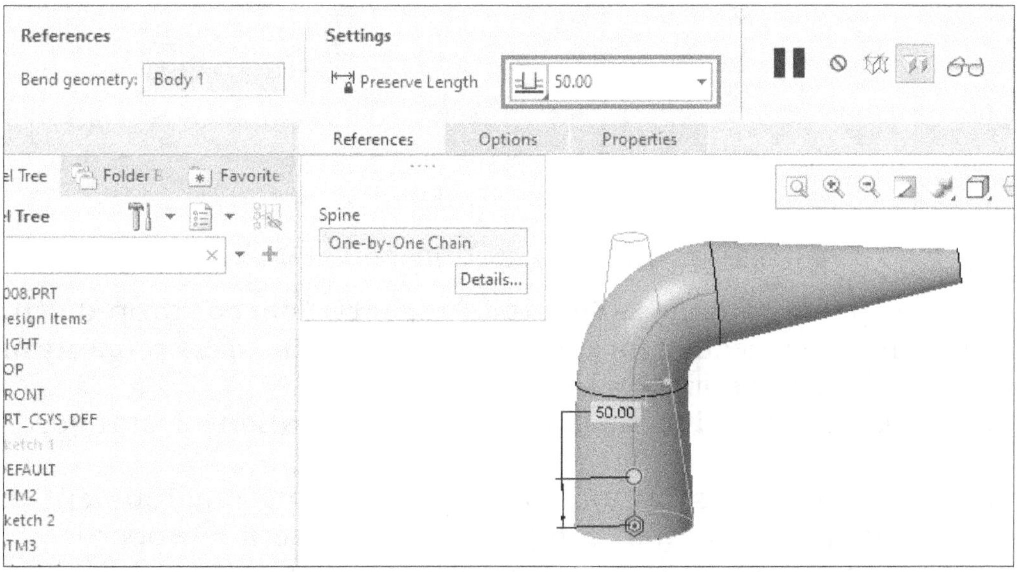

Figure-79. By Value option

- Specify desired value for depth of the bend region in the edit box displayed next to the drop-down.
- Select the **To Reference** option from the drop-down to bend geometry between the spine start and the selected reference. You are asked to select a point, vertex, or plane to specify depth of the bend region.
- Select desired point, vertex, or plane from the graphics window. The preview of bend will be displayed as shown in Figure-80.

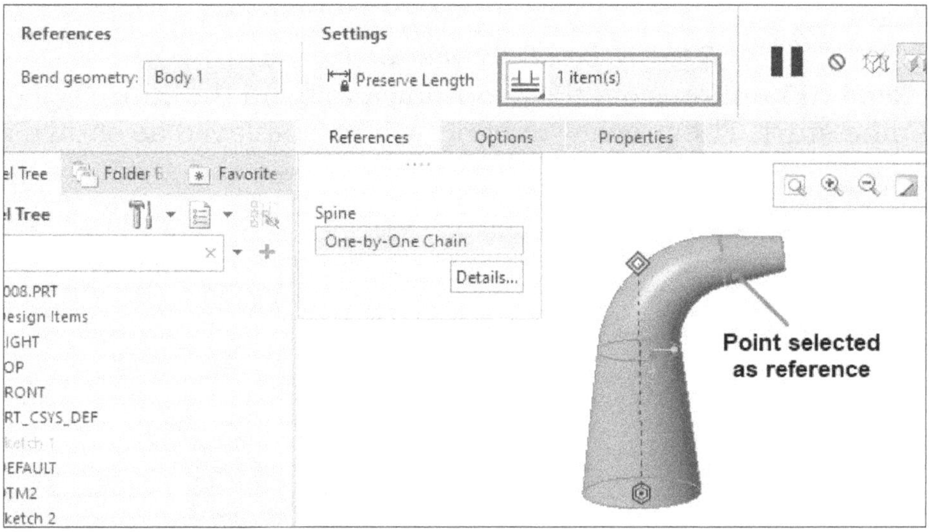

Figure-80. To Reference option

- Click on the **Options** tab in the **Ribbon**. The options will be displayed as shown in Figure-81.

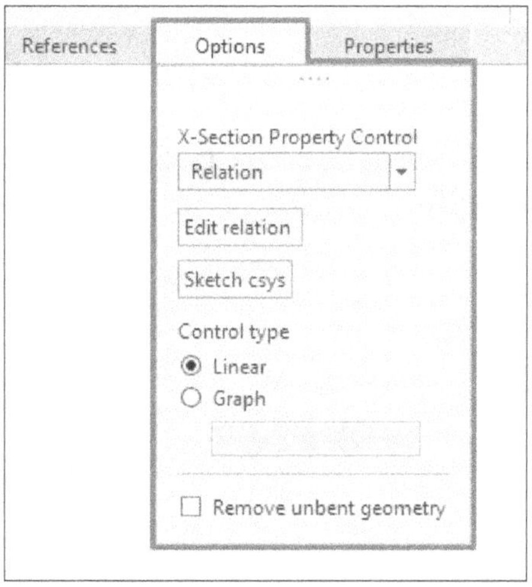

Figure-81. Options tab of Spinal Bend contextual tab

- Select desired option from the **X-Section Property Control** drop-down to control properties of the cross-section for the distribution of the mass property of a varying cross-section along the spine.
- Click on the **Edit relation** button to enter a relation of standard x-section properties.
- Click on the **Sketch csys** button to enter sketching environment and create coordinate system to be used in computation of x-section properties.
- Select the **Linear** radio button from the **Control type** area of the tab to place the x-sections such that the property varies linearly. Select the **Graph** radio button to place the x-sections such that the property varies according to the selected graph feature.

- Select the **Remove unbent geometry** check box to remove the geometry outside of the bend region.
- After specifying desired parameters, click on the **OK** button from the **Ribbon** to create the spinal bend feature.

Cosmetic Sketch

The **Cosmetic Sketch** tool is used to create a sketch that is used for representation only. You can not use a cosmetic sketch as base feature for other modeling tools. The tool is available in the expanded **Engineering** panel of the **Ribbon**. The tool works in the same way as **Sketch** tool works.

Cosmetic Thread

The **Cosmetic Thread** tool is used to create a simple representation of threads. The procedure to use this tool is given next.

- Click on the **Cosmetic Thread** tool from the expanded **Engineering** panel in the **Model** tab of the **Ribbon**. The **Thread** contextual tab will be displayed in the **Ribbon**; refer to Figure-82. Also, you will be asked to select the surface on which thread representation is to be applied.

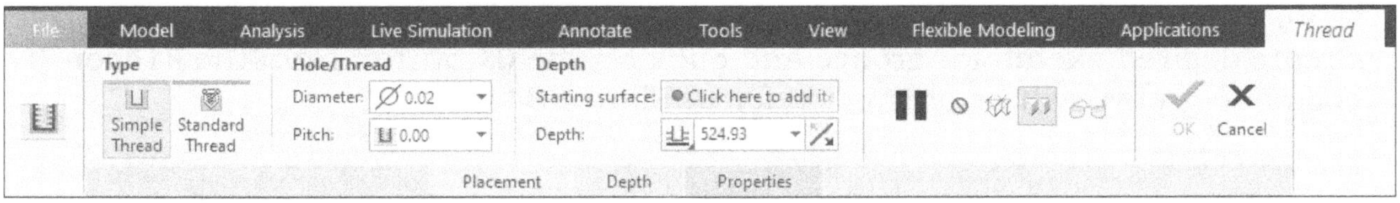

Figure-82. Thread contextual tab

- Select the round face of the hole/boss feature. You will be asked to select the starting face for the thread.
- Select the flat face of part from where the thread starts.
- Specify desired pitch value in the **Pitch** edit box from the **Hole/Thread** area of the **Ribbon**.
- Set desired depth of threading in the **Depth** edit box from **Depth** area of the **Ribbon**. Preview of thread feature will be displayed; refer to Figure-83.

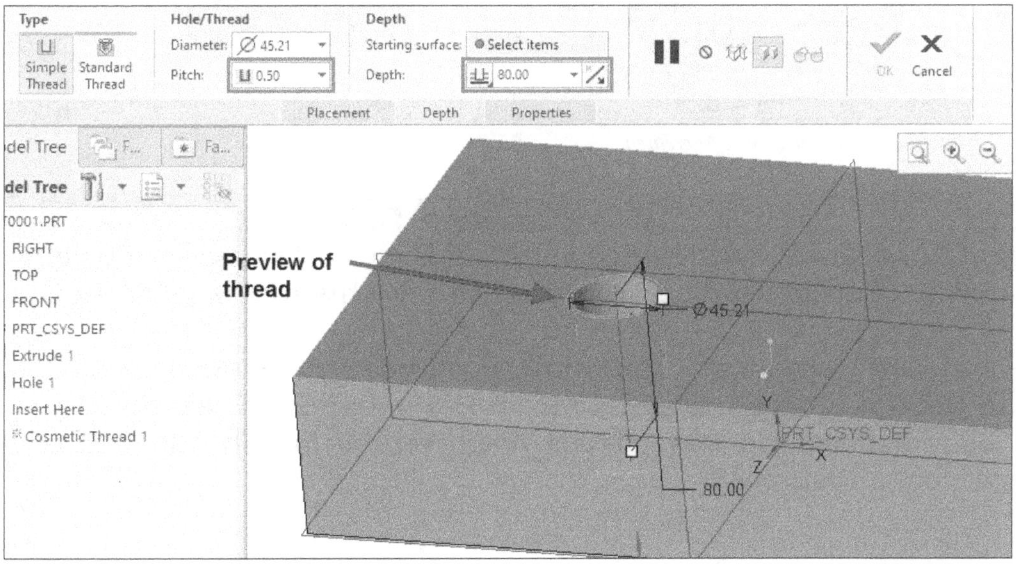

Figure-83. Preview of Thread

- By default, simple threads are created by this tool. If you want to create standard threads then click on the **Standard Thread** button from **Type** area of the **Ribbon**. Now, select desired standard from the **Thread Type** drop-down and then select desired thread size from the **Thread Size** drop-down.
- Click on the **OK** button to create the feature.

Cosmetic Groove

The **Cosmetic Groove** tool is used to create impression of groove sketch on surface based on which groove cut can be created using Creo Manufacturing tools. The procedure to use this tool is given next.

- Click on the **Cosmetic Groove** tool from the expanded **Engineering** panel of the **Ribbon**. The **FEATURE REFS Menu Manager** will be displayed asking you to select the surface/face on which cosmetic groove is to be created.
- Select desired surface/face and press the **Middle Mouse Button** twice. You will be asked to select a sketching plane.
- Select desired plane (Note that plane should be parallel to selected surface so that sketch can be projected on the surface). You will be asked to specify the sketch direction.
- Click on the **Okay** or **Flip** button as required from the **Menu Manager**. Set the required orientation of the sketch by using desired button from the **Menu Manager**.
- Create desired sketch for groove and click on the **OK** button from the **Ribbon**. The cosmetic groove will be created; refer to Figure-84.

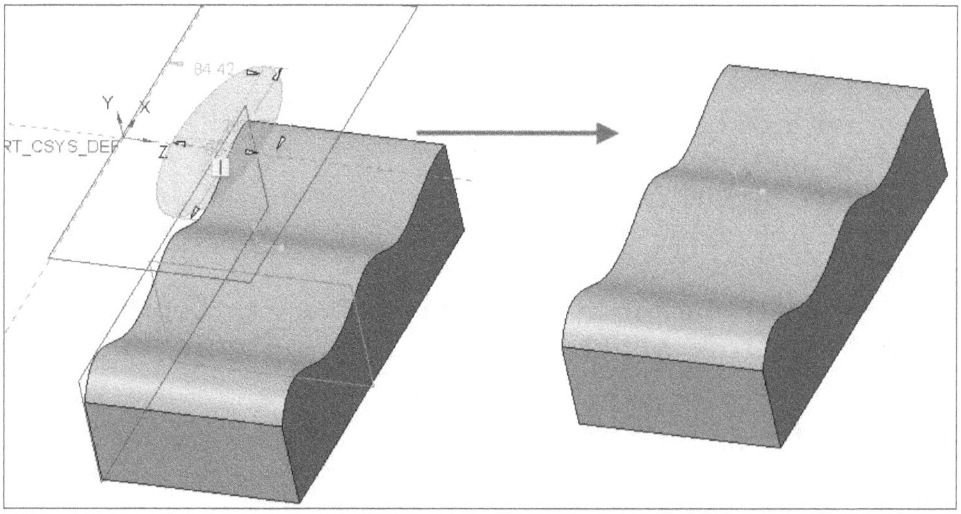

Figure-84. Cosmetic Groove created

Designated Area

The **Designated Area** tool in expanded **Engineering** panel is used to designate selected area for specific operations. The procedure to use this tool is given next.

- Create a closed loop sketch on the area you want to be designated.
- Click on the **Designated Area** tool from the expanded **Engineering** panel of the **Model** tab in **Ribbon**. The **Designated Area** contextual tab will be displayed in the **Ribbon**; refer to Figure-85.

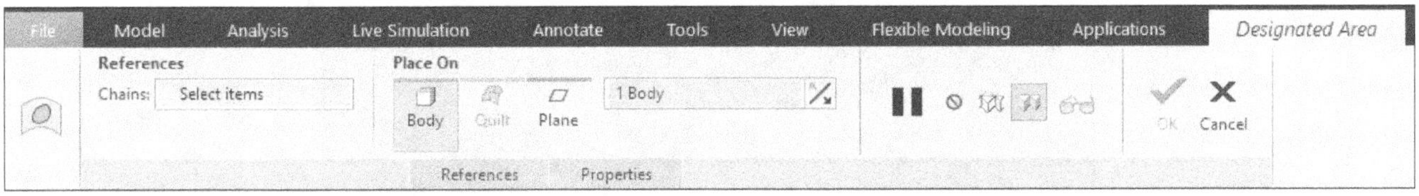

Figure-85. Designated Area contextual tab

- Select the closed loop sketch from model. Preview of designated area will be displayed; refer to Figure-86. You can also select the edges of model forming a closed loop for defining designated area.

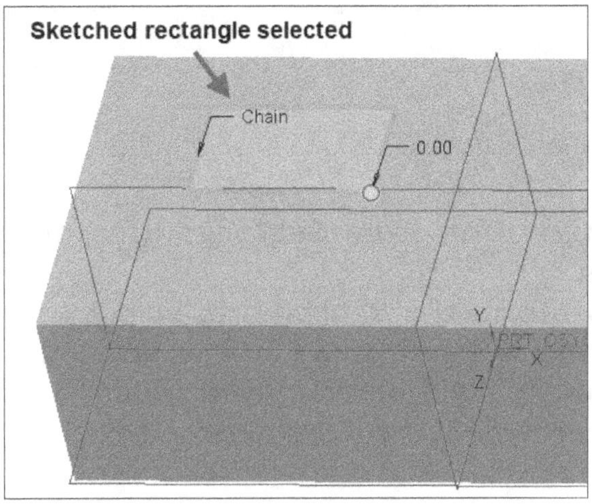

Figure-86. Preview of designated area

- Click on the **OK** button from the **Ribbon** to create the feature.

ECAD Area

The **ECAD Area** tool is used to assign selected area on the model to electronic circuits. The procedure to use this tool is given next.

- Click on the **ECAD Area** tool from the expanded **Engineering** panel of the **Ribbon**. The **ECAD Area** contextual tab will be displayed; refer to Figure-87.

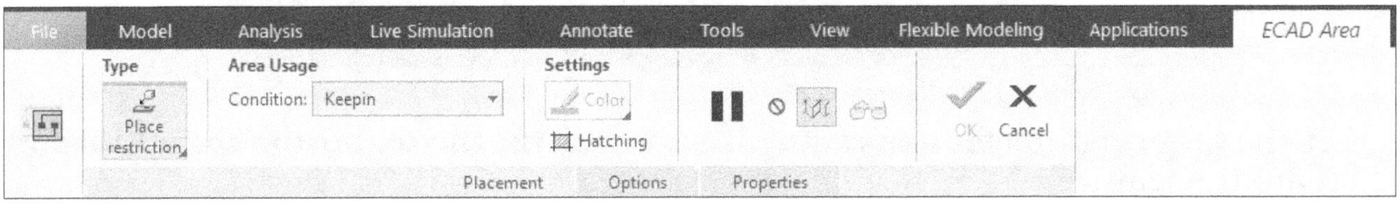

Figure-87. ECAD Area contextual tab

- Click on the face of model on which you want to create ECAD area. The sketching environment will become active automatically.
- Create the boundary of electronic circuit in the form of a closed loop; refer to Figure-88. After creating sketch, click on the **OK** button from **Ribbon** to exit sketching environment.

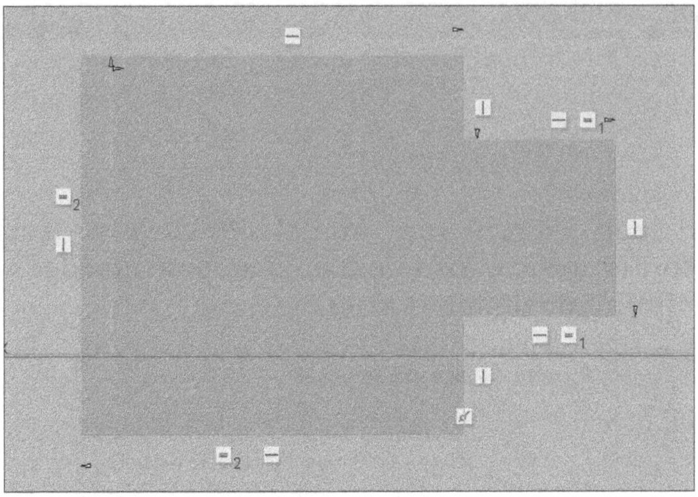

Figure-88. Sketch created for ECAD area

- Click on the **Hatching** button from **Settings** area of the **Ribbon** to display the ecad area in hatching.
- Click on the **Options** tab in the **Ribbon** and select the **3D Volume** check box to create extruded volume of ecad area. Define desired depth options and depth value. Preview of ecad area will be displayed; refer to Figure-89.

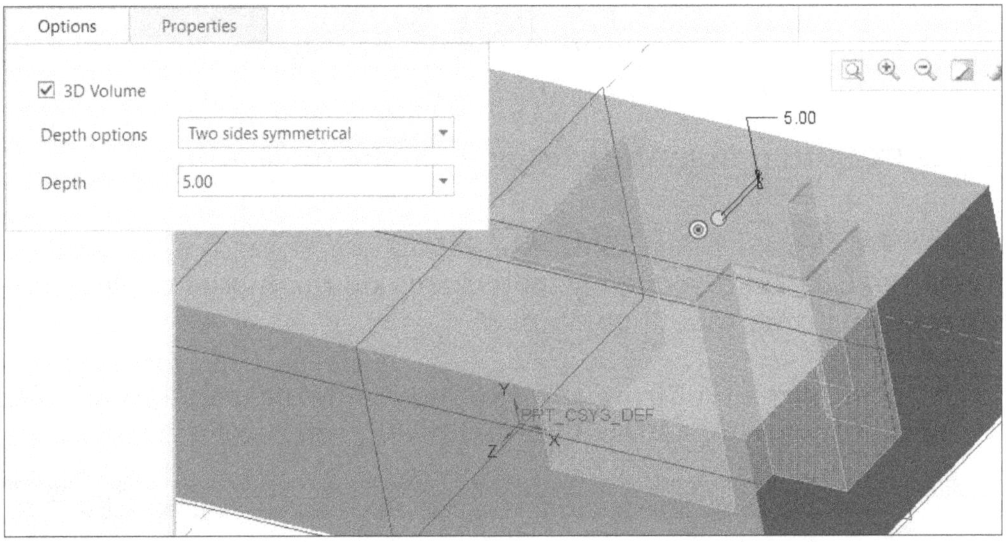

Figure-89. Preview of ECAD area

- Set the other parameters as required and click on the **OK** button from **Ribbon** to create the feature.

You will learn about **Lattice** tool later in this book. Till this point, we have learned about the most commonly used tools in the **Engineering** panel. Now, we will discuss tools used for editing.

COMPOSITES

A composite is combination of layers of difference substances (materials) joined by resins like carbon fiber, kevlar, glass fiber, solar panels, and so on. The **Composite** tool is used to create a composite feature by defining laminate objects on a surface of given boundaries. The procedure to use this tool is discussed next.

- Click on the **Composite** tool from expanded **Engineering** panel of **Model** tab in the **Ribbon**. The **Composite** tab will be added in the **Ribbon**; refer to Figure-90.

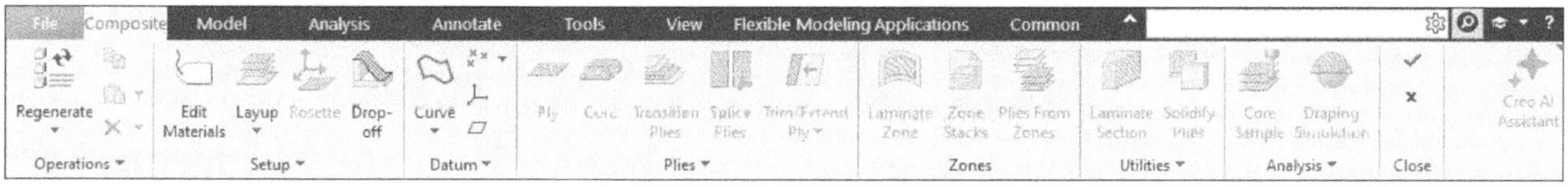

Figure-90. Composite tab

Edit Materials

The **Edit Materials** tool is used to edit materials of the model. The procedure to use this tool has been discussed earlier.

Layup Surface

The **Layup Surface** tool is used to define the surface to use for creating the geometry of the plies. This surface acts as base reference for the composite. The origin of the Rosette and the curves defining the boundaries of the plies must lie on the layup surface. The procedure to use this tool is discussed next.

- Click on the **Layup Surface** tool from **Layup** drop-down in the **Setup** panel of **Composite** tab in the **Ribbon**. The **Layup Surface** dialog box will be displayed; refer to Figure-91.
- Click on the **Model references** selection box from **Reference** tab and select desired reference surface(s) that define the layup surface.
- Click on the **Details** button, the **Surface Sets** dialog box will be displayed; refer to Figure-92.

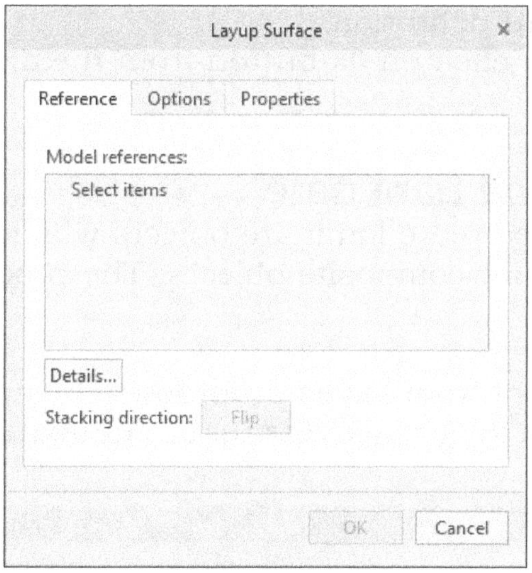

Figure-91. Layup Surface dialog box

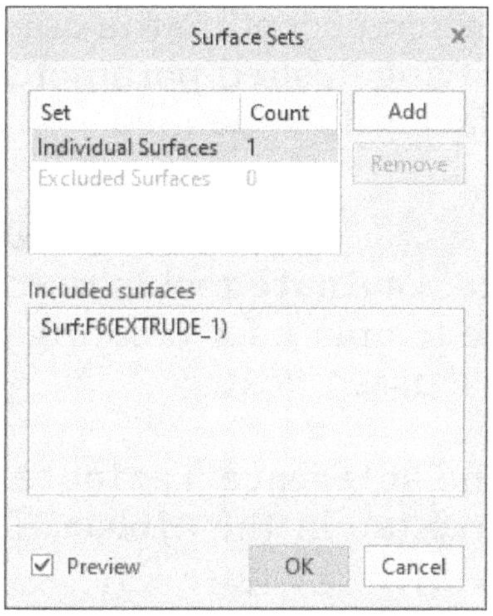

Figure-92. Surface Sets dialog box

- Select desired item from **Set** column to view or change its definition.
- Click on **Add** button to insert a rule-based surface set and click on **Remove** button to remove the selected surface set.
- Click on the **Included surfaces** selection box and select desired number of surfaces to include.
- After specifying desired parameters, click on the **OK** button to create surface sets.
- Click on the **Flip** button from **Stacking direction** area to flip the direction in which plies stack up.

- Click on the **Options** tab of **Layup Surface** dialog box, the options will be displayed as shown in Figure-93.

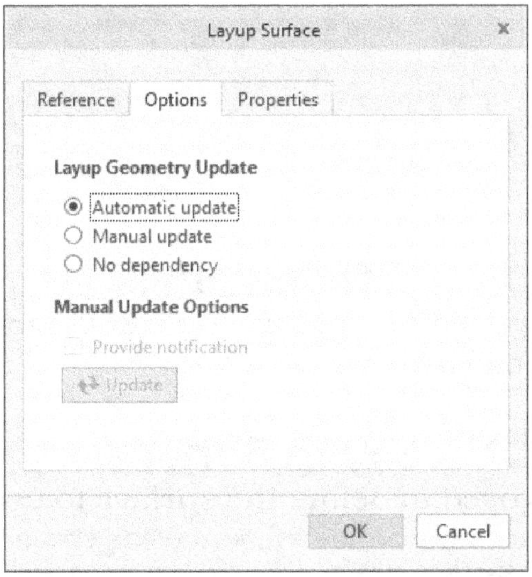

Figure-93. Options tab of Layup Surface dialog box

- Select the **Automatic update** radio button from the **Layup Geometry Update** area to update the feature automatically when the source model is modified and in session. Select the **Manual update** radio button to update the feature at any time manually when the source geometry is available. On selecting the **No dependency** radio button, there is no dependency between the feature and the source geometry. The feature will not be updated.
- Select the **Provide notification** check box from the **Manual Update Options** area to get a notification when the feature is outdated.
- Click on the **Update** button to update feature geometry relative to the reference geometry when accepting the current definition.
- After specifying desired parameters, click on **OK** button from the dialog box. The layup surface will be defined.

Reference Laminate

The **Reference Laminate** tool is used to create laminate objects which can be used as a reference template for creating other composite objects. The procedure to use this tool is discussed next.

- Click on the **Reference Laminate** tool from **Layup** drop-down in the **Setup** panel of **Composite** tab in the **Ribbon**. The **Reference Laminate** contextual tab will be displayed; refer to Figure-94.

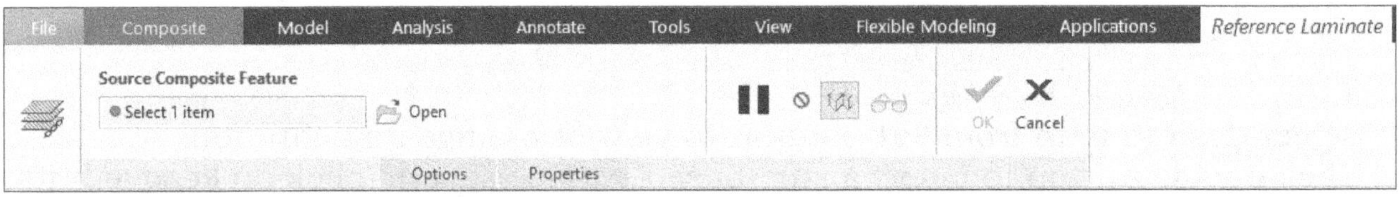

Figure-94. Reference Laminate contextual tab

- Click on **Open** button from the **Ribbon**, the **Open** dialog box will be displayed to open a reference model. Select desired composite feature from the dialog box and click on the **OK** button; refer to Figure-95.

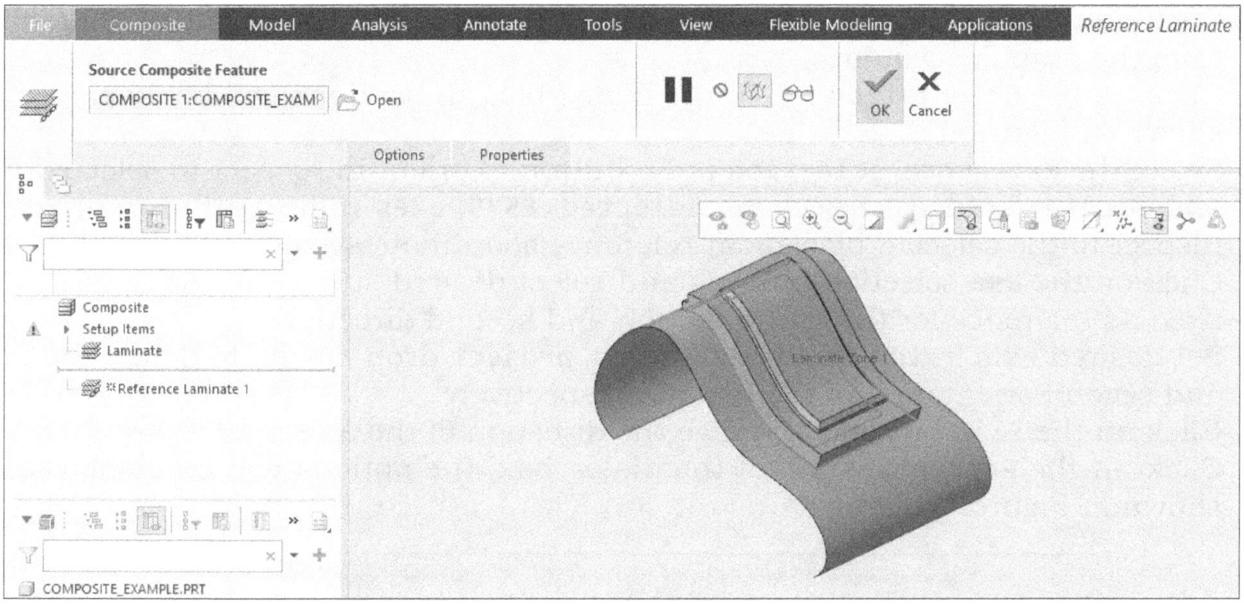

Figure-95. Composite feature selected

- On selecting the **Automatic update** option from **Options** tab of the **Ribbon**, the feature will be automatically updated when the source model is modified. Select **Manual** update option to update the feature manually on modifying the source model. On selecting the **No dependency** option, there will be no link between the feature and the source model and the feature will not be updated.
- After specifying desired parameters, click on **OK** button from the **Ribbon**. The laminate object will be created.

Rosette

The **Rosette** tool is used to define the default coordinate system for the composite design. The zero position of plies and cores will be defined based on this coordinate system. The procedure to use this tool is discussed next.

- Click on the **Rosette** tool from the **Setup** panel in the **Composite** tab of the **Ribbon**. The **Rosette Coordinate System** dialog box will be displayed; refer to Figure-96.

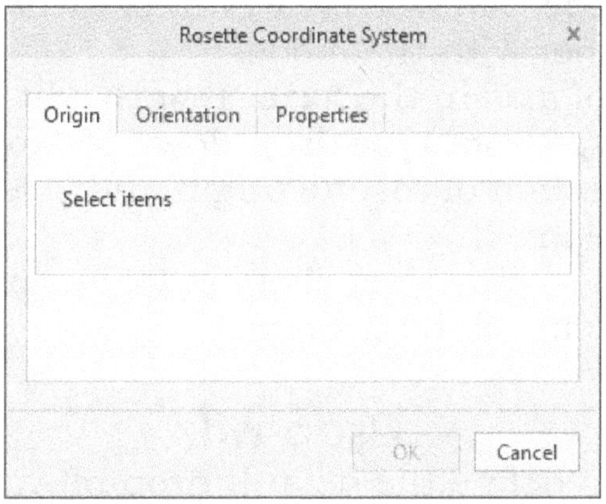

Figure-96. Rosette Coordinate System dialog box

- Click on the **Placement Reference** selection box from **Origin** tab and select a reference surface/plane that defines the placement of the rosette.
- Select **Linear** option from **Type** drop-down to place coordinate system by using two linear dimensions. Select **Radial** or **Diameter** option from the drop-down to place coordinate system by using a linear dimension and an angular dimension.

- Click on the **Offset references** selection box and select desired offset references from the graphics window.
- Click on the **Orientation** tab of the dialog box, the options will be displayed as shown in Figure-97.
- Select the **Reference selection** radio button to orient in respect to selected two additional references. Select the **Selected CSYS axes** radio button to orient in respect to the selected placement reference coordinate system.
- Click on the **Use** selection buttons and select desired surface of the model to be used as reference for the first direction and second direction.
- Set desired axis in **to determine** and **to project** drop-downs to define the first and second orientation of the rosette, respectively.
- Click on the **Flip** button to change the direction of the axis.
- Click on the **Properties** tab of the dialog box, the options will be displayed as shown in Figure-98.

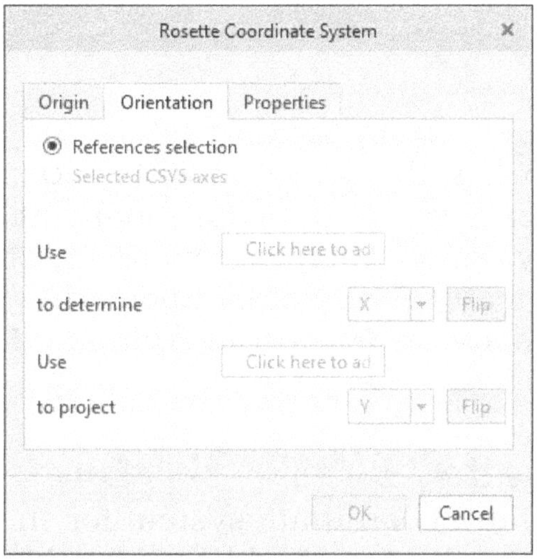

Figure-97. Orientation tab

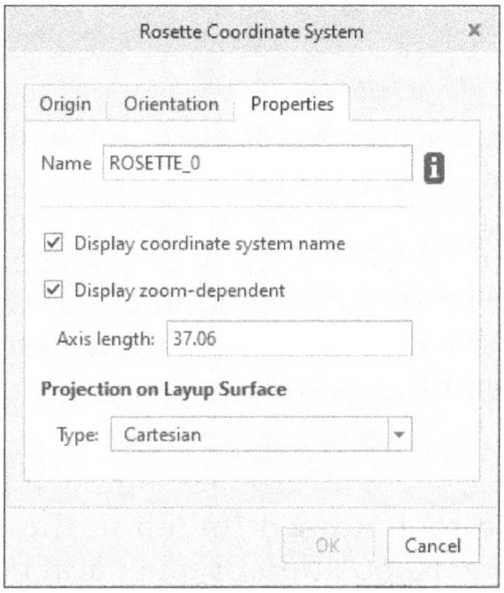

Figure-98. Properties tab

- Specify desired name of the feature in the **Name** edit box.
- Select **Display coordinate system name** check box to set whether or not to show coordinate system name.
- Select **Display zoom-dependent** check box to set whether or not the coordinate system is zoomed together with the model.
- Specify desired length of axis in the **Axis length** edit box.
- Select desired rosette type from **Type** drop-down of **Projection on Layup Surface** area to specify the projection of rosette origin and direction on the layup surface for the draping simulation.
- After specifying desired parameters, click on **OK** button from the dialog box. The Rosette coordinate system will be defined.

Drop-off

The **Drop-off** tool is used to define the default drop-off value for new plies. Drop-off is the distance at the end of ply where high amount of resin is applied as compared to rest of ply for bonding. The procedure to use this tool is discussed next.

- Click on the **Drop-off** tool from the **Setup** panel in the **Composite** tab of the **Ribbon**. The **Drop-off** dialog box will be displayed; refer to Figure-99.

- Specify desired distance between the sidewall of the bottom ply and the dropped ply in the edit box and click on the **OK** button. The drop-off value will be defined.

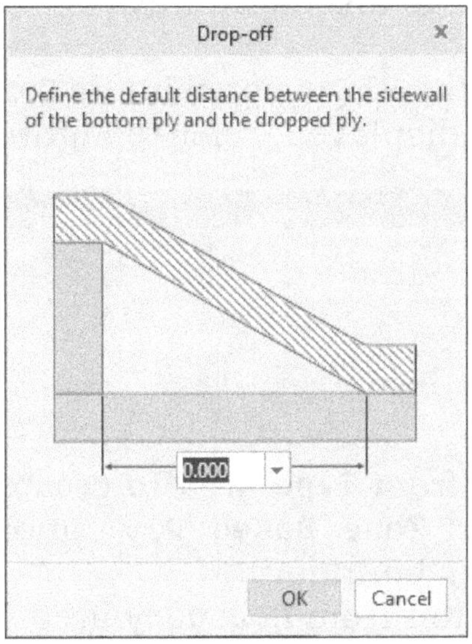

Figure-99. Drop-off dialog box

Color Mapping

The **Color Mapping** tool is used to manage the color of plies that share the same material and orientation. This tool becomes active when one or more plies have been created in the design. The procedure to use this tool is discussed next.

- Click on the **Color Mapping** tool from the expanded **Setup** panel in the **Composite** tab of the **Ribbon**. The **Color Mapping** dialog box will be displayed; refer to Figure-100.

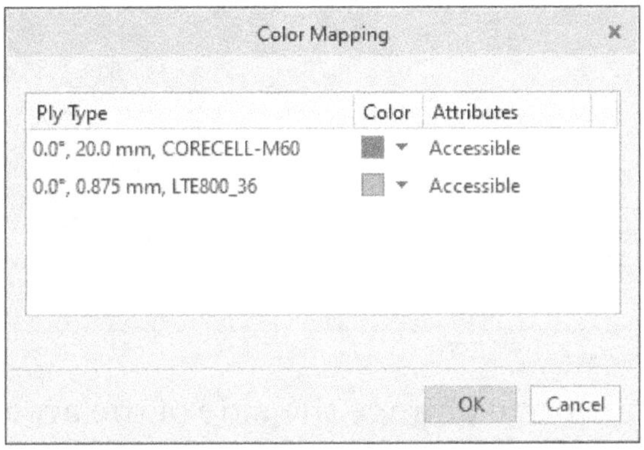

Figure-100. Color Mapping dialog box

- Specify desired color of the plies by clicking on the **Color** drop-down and click on **OK** button from the dialog box. The appearance of the plies will be changed.

Mass Properties Computation

Select desired mass properties computation method from **Mass Properties Computation** cascading menu. On selecting the **Based on layup surface** radio button from the cascading menu, the mass properties of plies and cores are calculated based on their geometry on the layup surface. On selecting the **Based on underlying plies** radio button from the cascading menu, the mass properties of plies and cores are calculated considering the underlying plies in the laminate stack. This calculation method takes longer than layup surface based calculation.

Ply

The **Ply** tool is used to create a single ply by defining its boundary and properties. The procedure to use this tool is discussed next.

- Click on the **Ply** tool from the **Plies** panel in the **Composite** tab of the **Ribbon**. The **Ply** contextual tab will be displayed; refer to Figure-101.

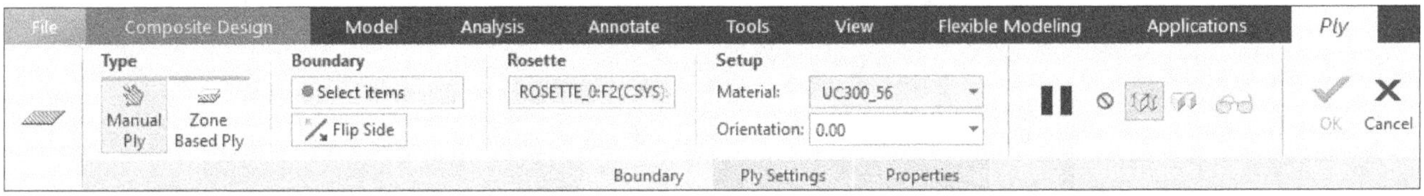

Figure-101. Ply Contextual tab

- Select **Manual Ply** option from **Type** area to create a ply by selecting chains to define its boundary. Select **Zone Based Ply** option to create a ply by selecting laminate zones to define its boundary.
- Click on the selection button from **Boundary** area to collect chains to define the boundary; refer to Figure-102.

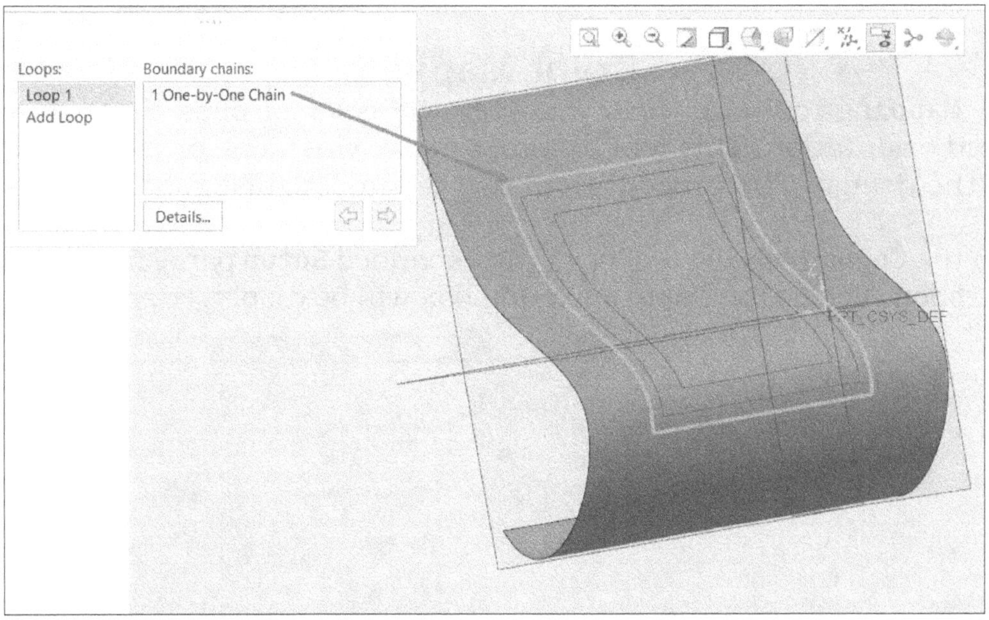

Figure-102. Chains selected

- Toggle the **Flip Side** button to change the side of the area created by the boundary references.
- Click on the selection button from **Rosette** area and select a rosette coordinate system to define the orientation of the ply.
- Select desired material of the ply from **Material** drop-down in the **Setup** area. Enter desired value in the **Orientation** edit box to specify the orientation of the ply relative to the X axis of the rosette.
- Specify desired value for the ply drop-off offset from the sidewall in the **Drop-off** edit box from **Ply Settings** tab of the **Ribbon**.
- After specifying desired parameters, click on **OK** button from the contextual tab. The ply will be created.

Core

The **Core** tool is used to create a core ply. Core ply is a thick ply made from stronger materials that bind well with other plies and it acts as base for other plies. The procedure to use this tool is discussed next.

- Click on the **Core** tool from **Plies** panel in the **Composite** tab of the **Ribbon**. The **Core** contextual tab will be displayed; refer to Figure-103.

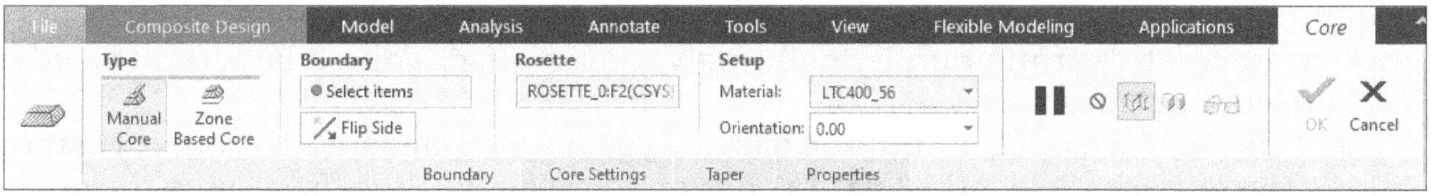

Figure-103. Core contextual tab

- After selecting chains to define the boundary as discussed earlier, click on the **Taper** tab in the **Ribbon**. The options will be displayed as shown in Figure-104.
- Click on the **Taper chains** selection box and select desired chains to define the taper; refer to Figure-105.

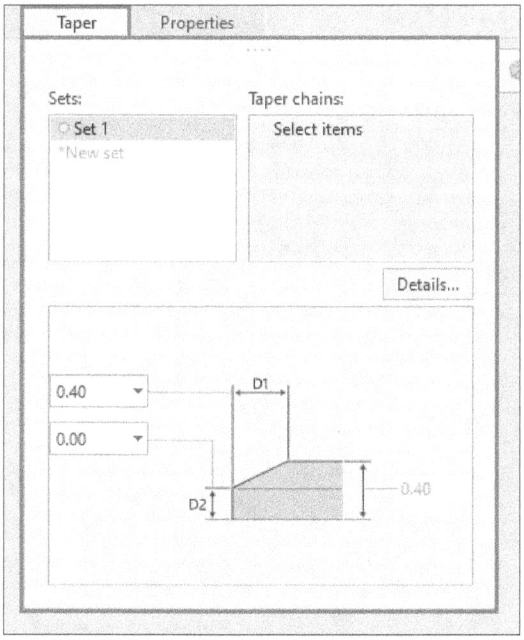

Figure-104. Taper tab options

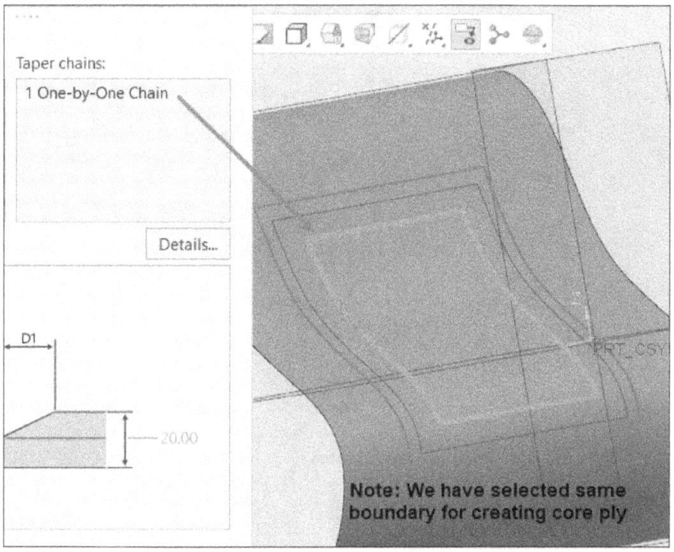

Figure-105. Selecting chains to define the taper

- Enter desired horizontal and vertical taper dimensions in their respective edit boxes.
- Other parameters in the **Ribbon** have been discussed earlier. After specifying desired parameters, click on the **OK** button from the **Ribbon**. The core ply will be created.

Transition Plies

The **Transition Plies** tool is used to shorten and extend plies created using the same boundary to create a transition effect. The procedure to use this tool is discussed next.

- Click on the **Transition Plies** tool from **Plies** panel in the **Composite** tab of the **Ribbon**. The **Transition Plies** contextual tab will be displayed; refer to Figure-106.

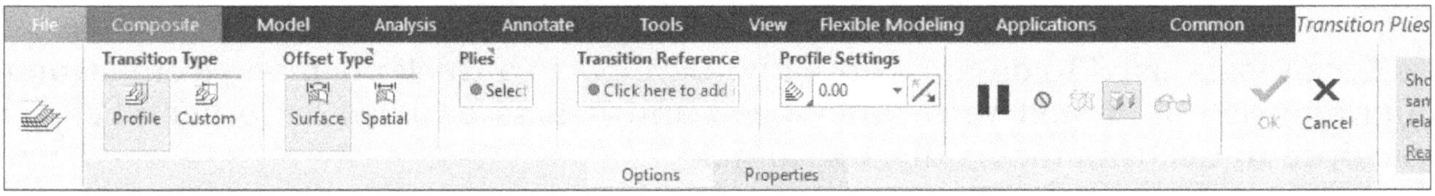

Figure-106. Transition Plies contextual tab

- Select the **Profile** option from **Transition Type** area to create a transition by defining a constant offset between the edges of consequent plies. Select **Custom** option to create a transition by defining variable offset values between the edges of consequent plies.
- Select the **Surface** option from the **Offset Type** area to measure the offset distance along the surface. Select the **Spatial** option to measure the offset using the spatial distance.
- Click on the selection button of **Plies** area and select plies of which boundary will be shorten or extended; refer to Figure-107.

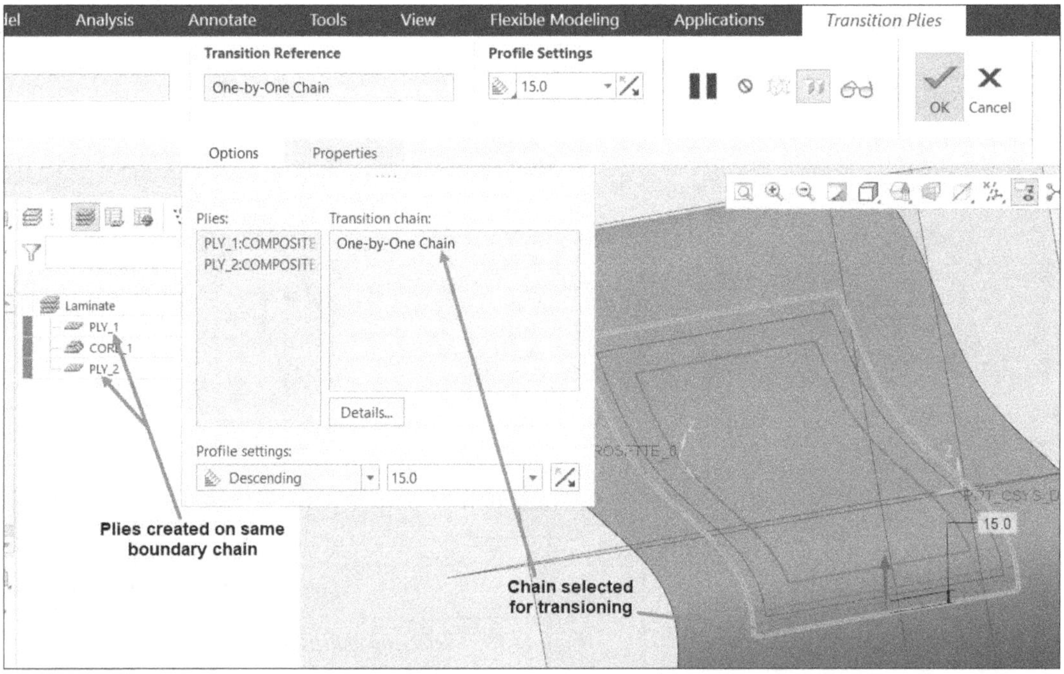

Figure-107. Selecting ply and transition chain

- Click on the selection button of **Transition Reference** area and select a chain of edges to define the reference for transition offsets. You can only select the edges that are common to all the selected plies; refer to Figure-107.
- Select **Descending** or **Ascending** option from drop-down in the **Profile Settings** area to create a descending or ascending transition, respectively. Enter desired value in the edit box to specify spacing between edges of consequent plies after transition. Toggle the direction of profile by clicking on the button.
- After specifying desired parameters, click on **OK** button from the **Ribbon**. The transition will be created in plies.

Splice Plies

The **Splice Plies** tool is used to splice or cut selected plies by selecting a splicing curve, a connection type, and optionally a stagger. The procedure to use this tool is discussed next.

- Click on the **Splice Plies** tool from **Plies** panel in the **Composite** tab of the **Ribbon**. The **Splice Plies** contextual tab will be displayed; refer to Figure-108.

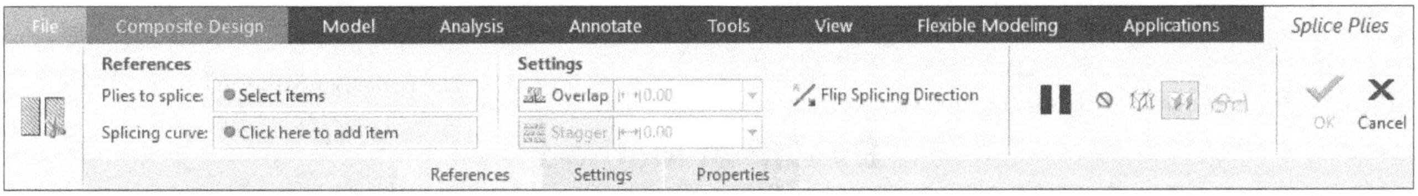

Figure-108. Splice Plies Contextual tab

- Click on the **Plies to splice** selection box and select plies and cores to be spliced or darted.
- Click on the **Splicing curve** selection box and select a curve that defines the splicing or darting trajectory; refer to Figure-109.

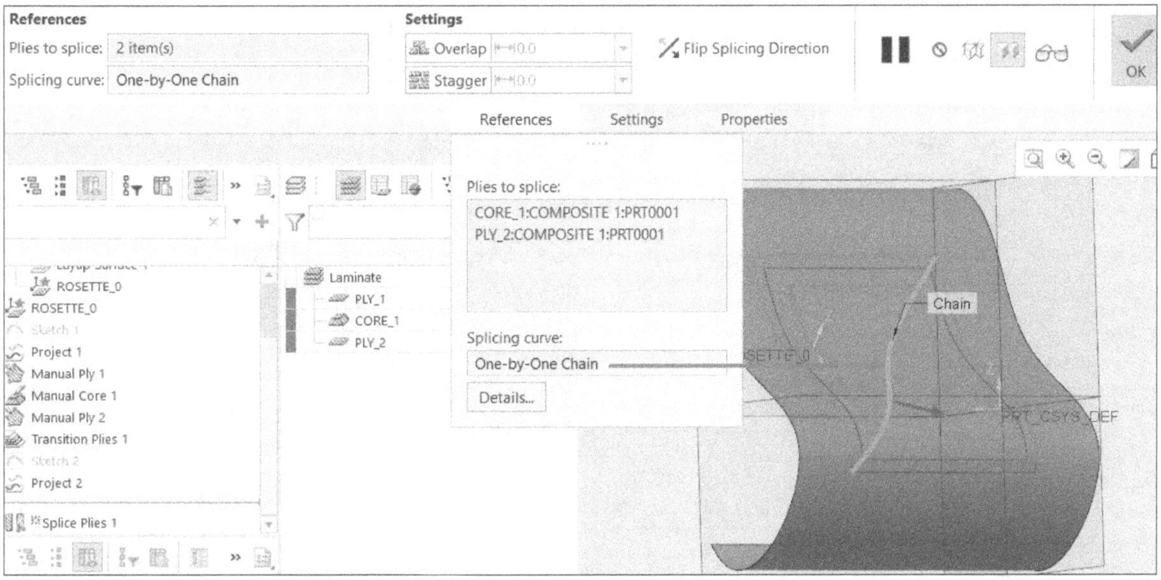

Figure-109. Selecting ply and splicing curve

- Click on the **Overlap** button from the **Settings** area and enter desired overlapping offset value in the respective edit box to specify whether plies created as a result of splicing the original ply overlap each other. Click on the **Stagger** button and enter desired stagger offset value in the respective edit box to specify whether plies created as a result of splicing the original ply are staggered. Click on the **Flip Splicing Direction** button to toggle the direction of overlap and stagger offsets.
- After specifying desired parameters, click on **OK** button from the **Ribbon**. The ply will be spliced.

Trim/Extend Ply

The **Trim/Extend Ply** tool is used to trim or extend the ply boundary by specifying distance, by selecting reference, or by joining it with another closed loop contour. The procedure to use this tool is discussed next.

- Click on the **Trim/Extend Ply** tool from **Plies** panel in the **Composite** tab of the **Ribbon**. The **Trim/Extend Ply** contextual tab will be displayed with the **Extend** option selected in the **Operation** area; refer to Figure-110.

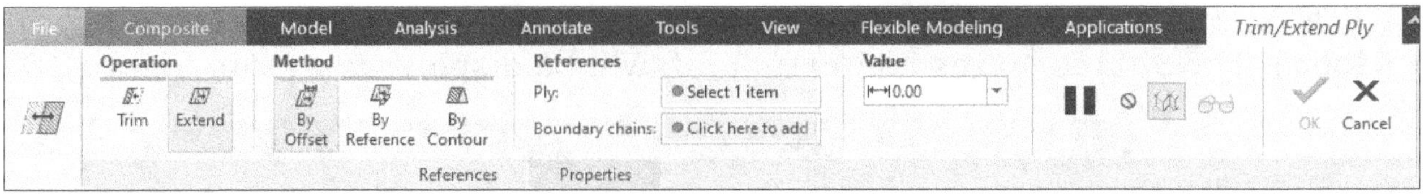

Figure-110. Trim Extend Ply contextual tab

By Offset Method

- Select **By Offset** option from **Method** area of the contextual tab, the options will be displayed as shown in Figure-110.
- Click on the **Ply** selection button from **References** area and select a ply or a core to extend. Click on the **Boundary chains** selection button and select chains to define the extended boundary; refer to Figure-111.

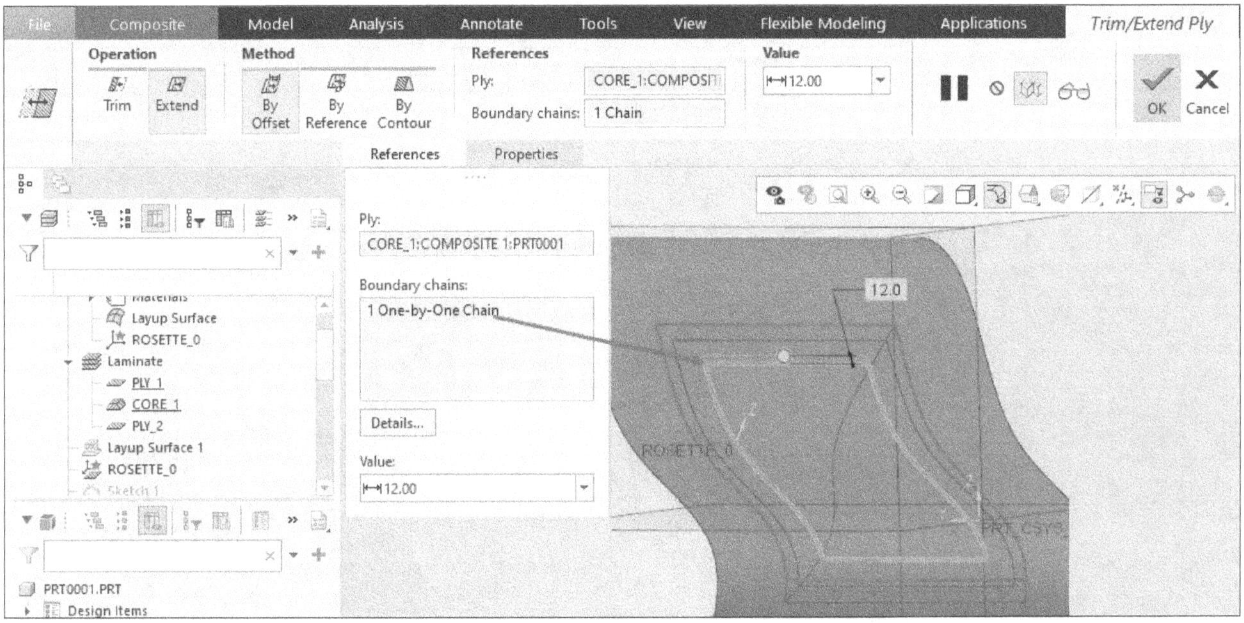

Figure-111. Ply and edge selected

- Enter desired distance value to extend ply in the edit box of **Value** area.
- After specifying desired parameters, click on **OK** button from the **Ribbon**. The ply boundary will be extended.

By Reference Method

- Select **By Reference** option from **Method** area of the contextual tab, the options will be displayed as shown in Figure-112.

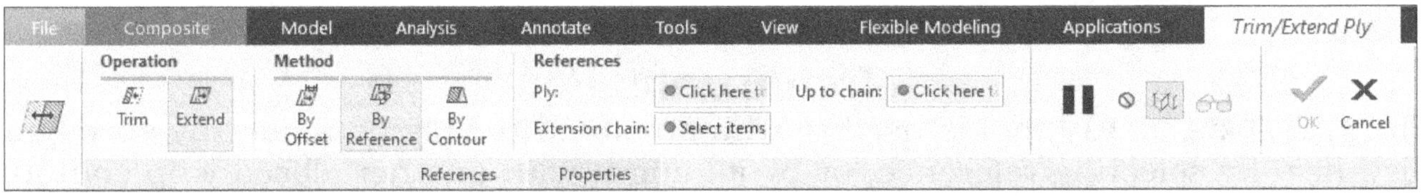

Figure-112. By Reference Method options

- Click on the **Ply** selection button from **References** area and select a ply to extend. Click on the **Extension chains** selection button and select a chain to define the boundary of the ply to be extended. Click on the **Up to chains** selection button and select a chain up to which the boundary of the ply is extended; refer to Figure-113.

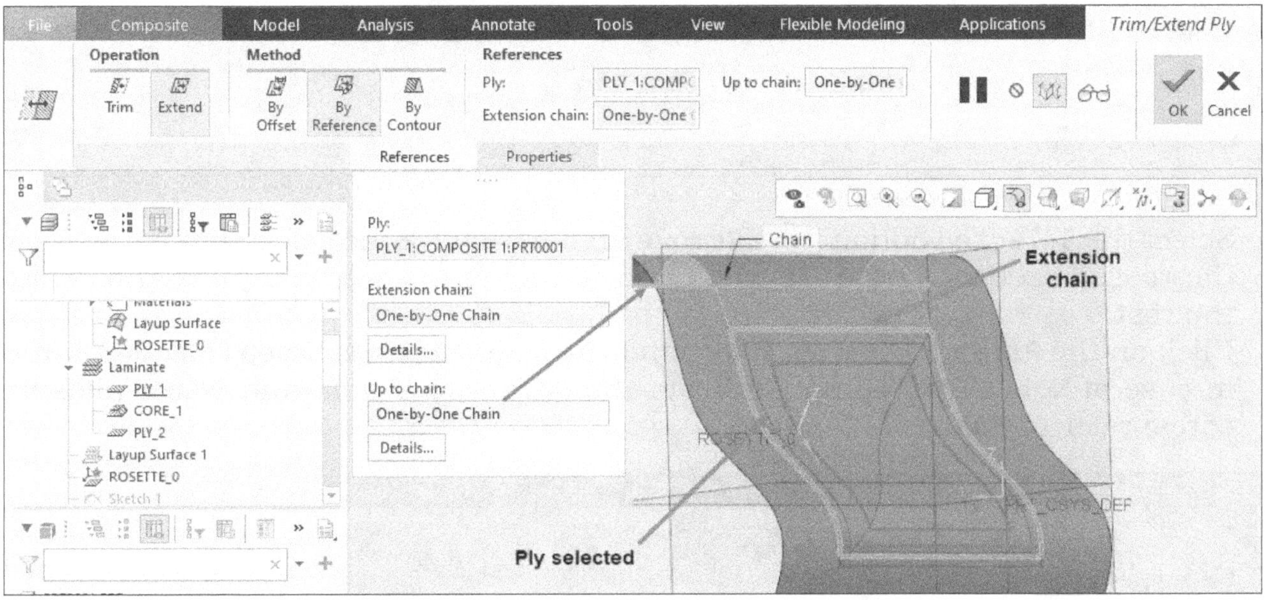

Figure-113. Ply and edge selected

- After specifying desired parameters, click on **OK** button from the **Ribbon**. The ply boundary will be extended.

By Contour Method

- Select **By Contour** option from **Method** area of the contextual tab, the options will be displayed; refer to Figure-114.

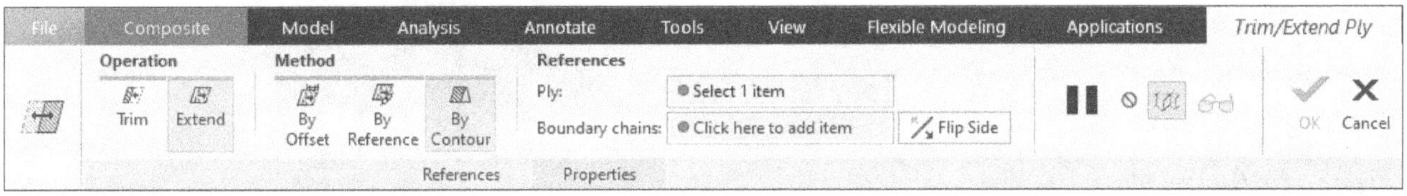

Figure-114. By Contour Method options

- Click on the **Ply** selection button from **References** area and select a ply to be extended. Click on the **Boundary chains** selection button and select chains to define the boundary. Click on the **Flip Side** button to change the side of the area created by the boundary references.
- After specifying desired parameters, click on **OK** button from the **Ribbon**. The ply boundary will be extended.

Similarly, you can use **Trim** option from **Operation** area of the **Trim/Extend Ply** contextual tab.

Remove Ply

The **Remove Ply** tool is used to create a feature to consume a ply. The ply cannot be used further, and its geometry is removed. The procedure to use this tool is discussed next.

- Click on the **Remove Ply** tool from the expanded **Plies** panel of **Composite** tab in the **Ribbon**. The **Remove Ply** contextual tab will be displayed; refer to Figure-115.

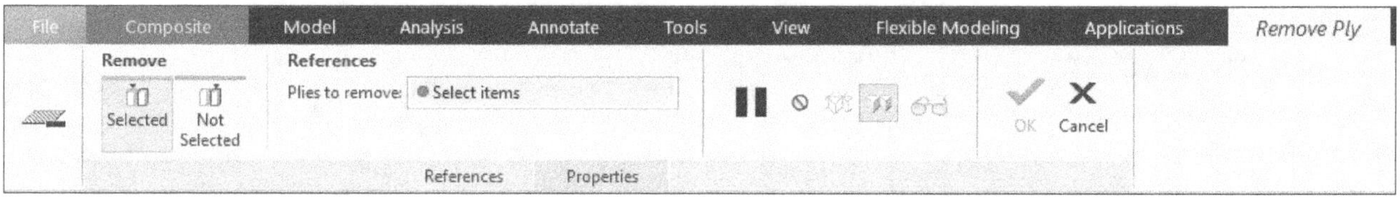

Figure-115. Remove Ply contextual tab

- Select the **Selected** option from **Remove** area to remove the selected plies and keep the rest. Select the **Not Selected** option to keep the selected plies and remove the rest.
- Click on the **Plies to remove** selection button or (**Plies to keep** selection button in case of **Not Selected** option) from the **References** area and select plies and cores; refer to Figure-116.

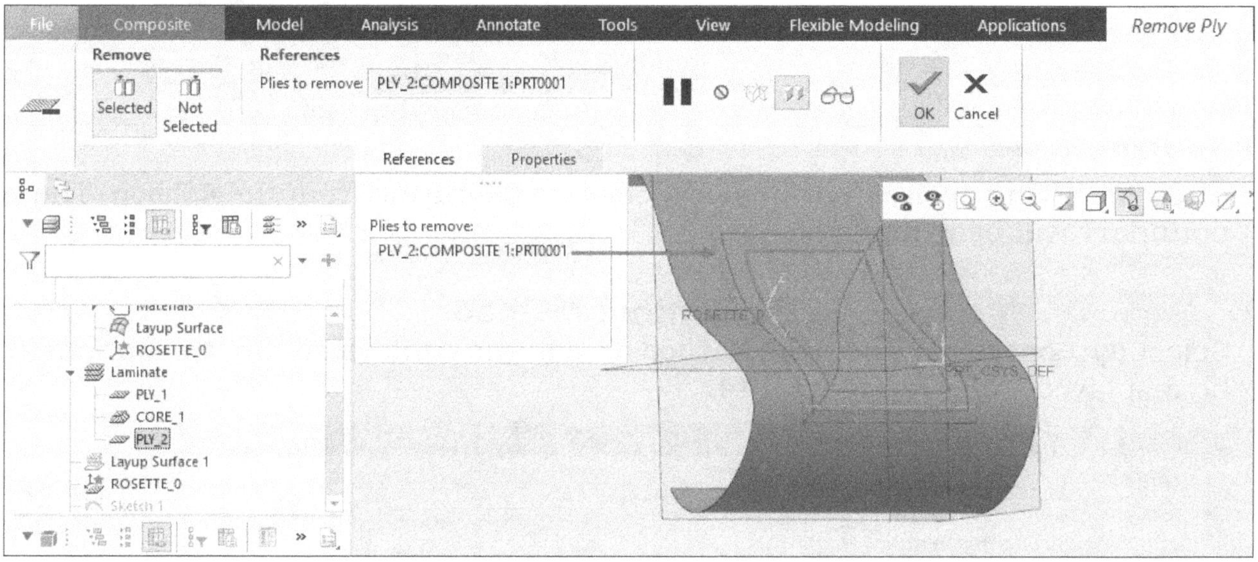

Figure-116. Remove plies

- After specifying desired parameters, click on **OK** button from the **Ribbon**. The plies will be removed.

Laminate Zone

The **Laminate Zone** tool is used to create a laminate zone by defining its boundary. This zone can be used to group plies and cores based on specific categorization. The procedure to use this tool is discussed next.

- Click on the **Laminate Zone** tool from **Zones** panel in the **Composite** tab of the **Ribbon**. The **Laminate Zone** contextual tab will be displayed; refer to Figure-117.

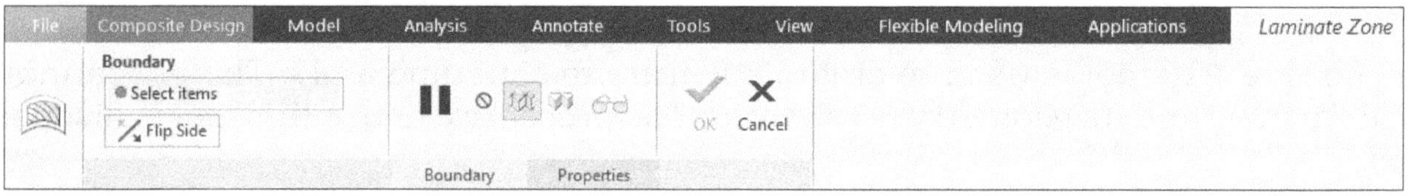

Figure-117. Laminate Zone contextual tab

- Click on the selection button from **Boundary** area and select chains to define the boundary; refer to Figure-118.

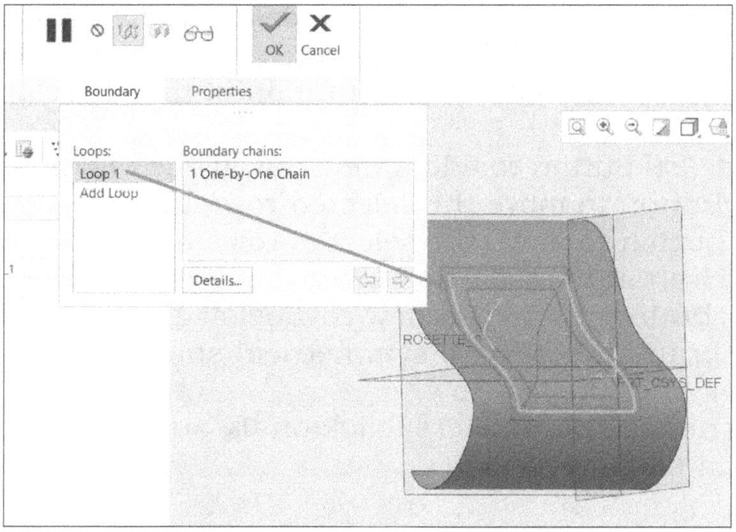

Figure-118. Laminate zone selected boundary

- Click on the **Flip Side** button to change the side of the area created by the boundary references.
- After specifying desired parameters, click on **OK** button from the **Ribbon**. The laminate zone will be created.

Zone Stacks

The **Zone Stacks** tool is used to create and modify stacks that you can use for creating plies from zones. The procedure to use this tool is discussed next.

- Click on the **Zone Stacks** tool from the **Zones** panel in the **Composite** tab of the **Ribbon**. The **Zone Stacks** dialog box will be displayed; refer to Figure-119.

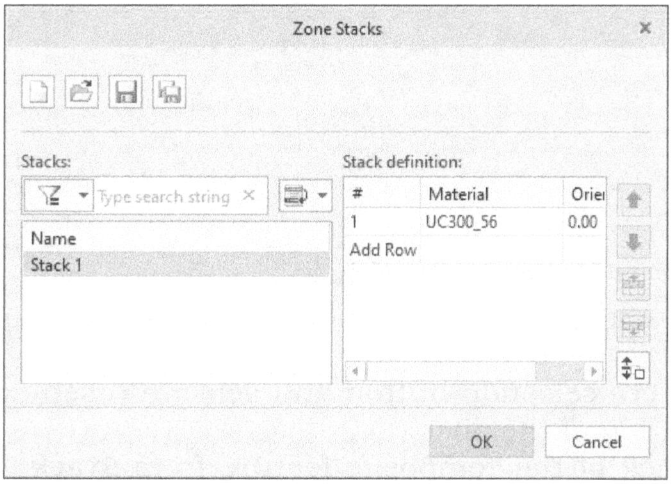

Figure-119. Zone Stacks dialog box

- Click on the button to create a new stack and add it to the list.
- Click on the button, the **Open** dialog box will be displayed to open an existing stack and edit it to the list.
- Click on the button to save the selected stack to a location defined by the composite stacks dir configuration option.
- Click on the button to save the selected stack with a new name to selected location.

- Click on the **Material** column from **Stack definition** area and select material of the ply from the list of materials assigned to the composite feature. Click on the **Orientation** column to specify the orientation of the ply relative to the X axis of the Rosette.
- Click on the **Add Row** button to add a new row at the end of the table.
- Click on the button to move the selected rows up.
- Click on the button to move the selected rows down.
- Click on the button to insert a new row above the selected row.
- Click on the button to insert a new row below the selected row.
- Click on the button to create a symmetrical stack by adding mirror copies of the existing rows after the last row.
- After specifying desired parameters, click on **OK** button from the dialog box. The stack will be created.

Plies From Zones

The **Plies From Zones** tool is used to create a stack of zone based plies using earlier created zone, rosette, and zone stack. The procedure to use this tool is discussed next.

- Click on the **Plies From Zones** tool from the **Zones** panel in the **Composite** tab of the **Ribbon**. The **Plies from Zones** dialog box will be displayed; refer to Figure-120.

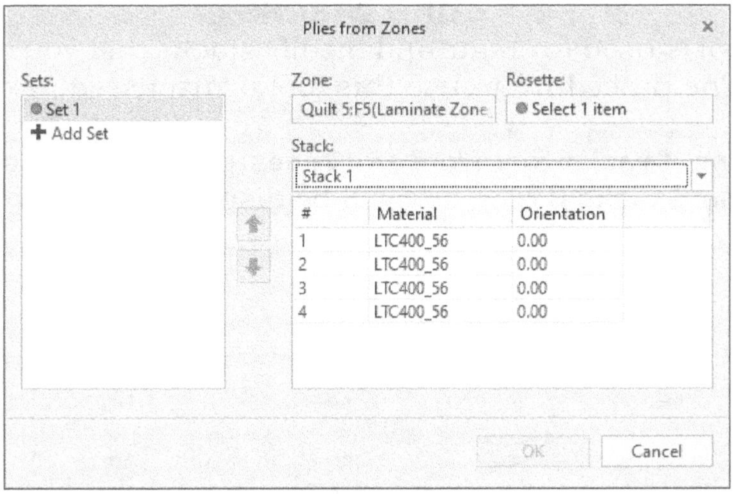

Figure-120. Plies from Zones dialog box

- Click on the **Zone** selection button and select zone feature to define the boundary of the plies.
- Click on the **Rosette** selection button and select a rosette coordinate system to define the orientation of the plies.
- Select desired stack of the composite feature from **Stack** drop-down to use for the set.
- Select desired material of the ply from **Material** column and specify desired orientation of the ply in the **Orientation** column.
- After specifying desired parameters, click on **OK** button from the dialog box. The stack of zone-based plies will be created.

Laminate Section

The **Laminate Section** tool is used to create a cross section of the laminate by using selected plane as cutting reference. The procedure to use this tool is discussed next.

- Click on the **Laminate Section** tool from **Utilities** panel in the **Composite** tab of the **Ribbon**. The **Section** contextual tab will be displayed; refer to Figure-121.

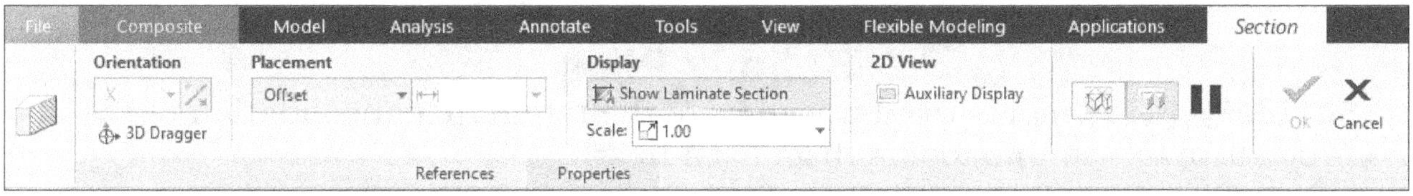

Figure-121. Section contextual tab

- Select the plane using which you want to create section of the laminate. Preview of the section will be displayed; refer to Figure-122.

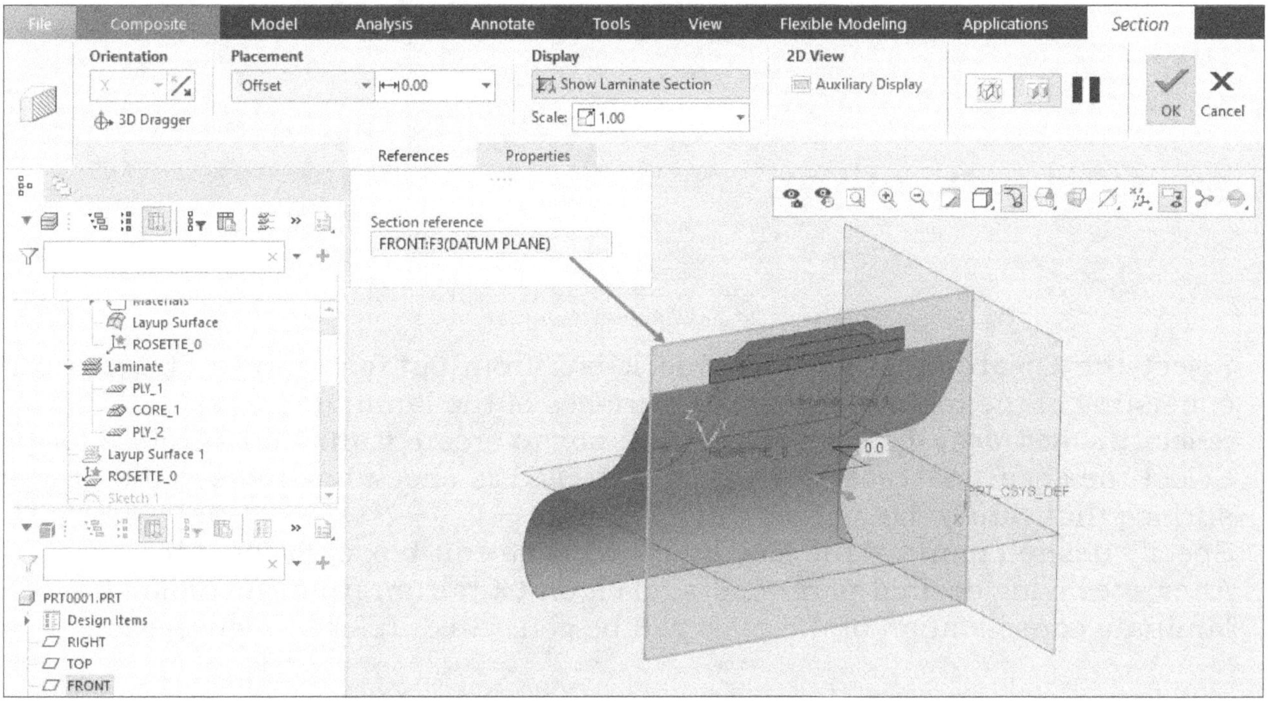

Figure-122. Coordinate system selected

- Select desired direction of the referenced coordinate system from the drop-down of **Orientation** area to create the cross-section. Click on the button to flip the clipping direction of the cross section.
- Click on the **3D Dragger** button to enable free positioning of the clipping plane.
- Select the **Offset** option from **Placement** drop-down and enter desired value in the edit box to set distance of the cross section from the reference. Select the Through option from the drop-down if you want to create cross-section at selected plane.
- Select the **Show Laminate Section** button from **Display** area to display preview section of the laminate at the specified scale. Enter desired value in the **Scale** edit box to scale the laminate section display.
- Select the **Auxiliary Display** button from **2D View** area to display a 2D view of the cross section in a separate window. The **2D Section Viewer** will be displayed; refer to Figure-123.

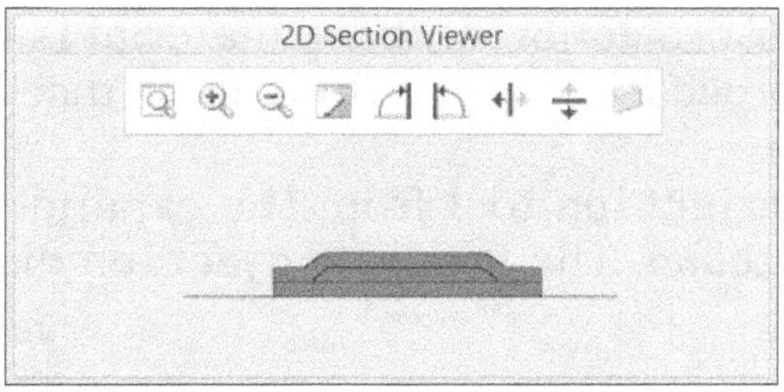

Figure-123. 2D Section Viewer

- After specifying desired parameters, click on **OK** button from the **Ribbon**. The cross section of the laminate will be created.

Solidify Plies

The **Solidify Plies** tool is used to generate the laminate consolidation of the plies. The procedure to use this tool is discussed next.

- Click on the **Solidify Plies** tool from **Utilities** panel in the **Composite** tab of the **Ribbon**. The **Solidify Plies** dialog box will be displayed; refer to Figure-124.

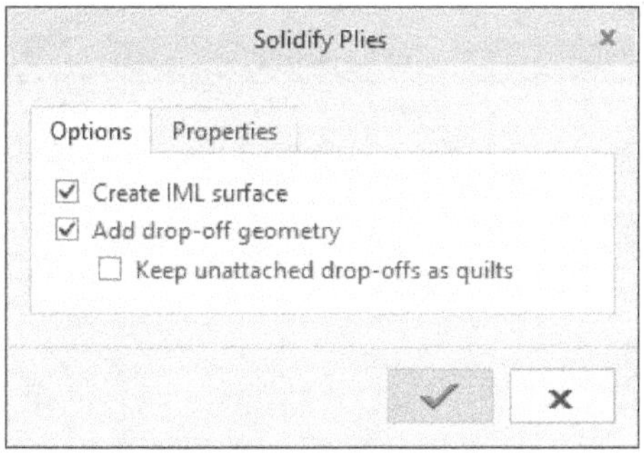

Figure-124. Solidify Plies dialog box

- Select the **Create IML surface** check box from **Options** tab to create a quilt consisting of the top most and side surfaces of the laminate.
- Select the **Add drop-off geometry** check box to create transition surfaces for ply.
- Select the **Keep unattached drop-offs as quilts** check box to keep the drop-off surface that cannot be merged.
- Specify desired name of the feature in the **Name** edit box of **Properties** tab.
- After specifying desired parameters, click on **OK** button from the dialog box. The laminate consolidation of the plies will be generated; refer to Figure-125.

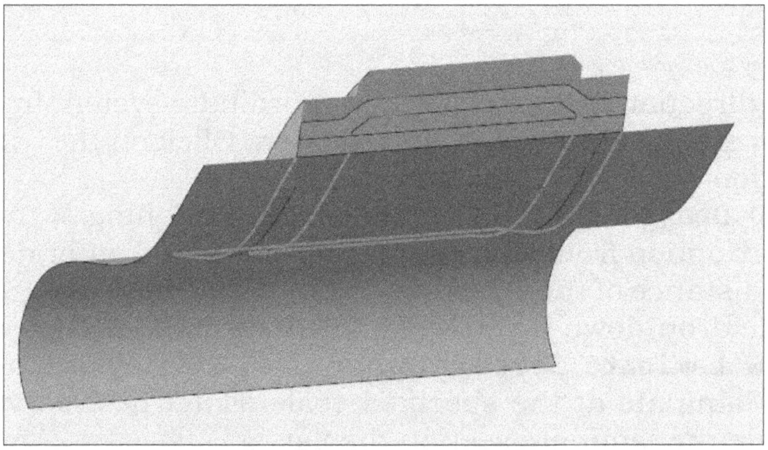

Figure-125. Solidified plies

Laser Projection

The **Laser Projection** tool is used to create projection data and calibration files for laser projectors. This laser projection on base material is later used as reference for sizing of laminates. The procedure to use this tool is discussed next.

- Click on the **Laser Projection** tool from the expanded **Utilities** panel in the **Composite** tab of the **Ribbon**. The **Laser Projection** dialog box will be displayed; refer to Figure-126.

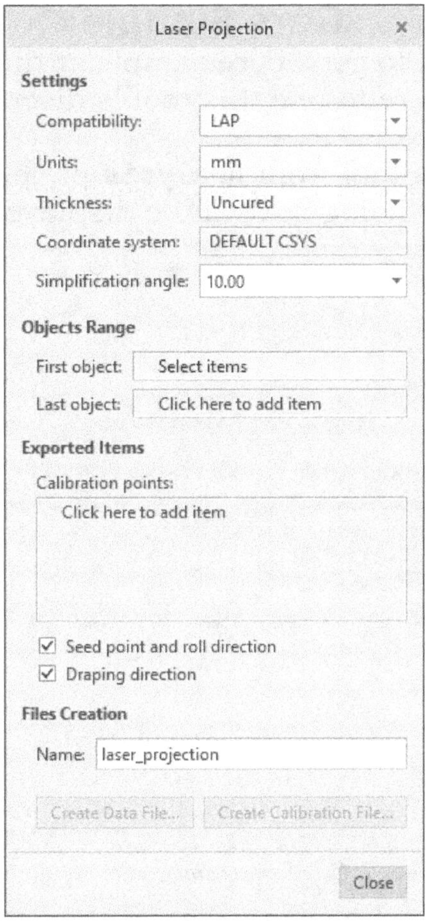

Figure-126. Laser Projection dialog box

- Select desired laser projection system from **Compatibility** drop-down of **Settings** area to create files in a compatible format for this system. Select desired unit from **Units** drop-down to use for creating the exported data. Select desired thickness option for laser projection from **Thickness** drop-down. Click on the **Coordinate system** selection box and select a coordinate system for calculating the coordinates of the projected geometry and the calibration points. Specify desired angle between polyline segments below which the segments may be merged in the **Simplification angle** edit box.
- Click on the **First object** selection box from **Objects Range** area and select a ply or a core object to define the first object in the range. Click on the **Last object** selection box and select a ply or a core object to define the last object in the range.
- Click on the **Calibration points** selection box from **Exported Items** area and select datum points to define the calibration points of the laser projection system. Select **Seed point and roll direction** check box to add a seed point and roll direction marker for each ply to the laser projection data file. Select **Draping direction** check box to add a draping direction indication for each ply to the laser projection data file.
- Specify desired name of the file in the **Name** edit box from **Files Creation** area. Click on the **Create Data File** button, the **Save a Copy** dialog box will be displayed to create a data file in a format compatible with the selected laser projection system. Click on the **Create Calibration File** button, the **Save a Copy** dialog box will be displayed to create a calibration file in a format compatible with the selected laser projection system.
- After specifying desired parameters, click on **Close** button to exit the dialog box.

Core Sample

The **Core Sample** tool is used to get a core sample at the selected location to analyze its composition. The procedure to use this tool is discussed next.

- Click on the **Core Sample** tool from **Analysis** panel in the **Composite** tab of the **Ribbon**. The **Core Sample** dialog box will be displayed; refer to Figure-127.

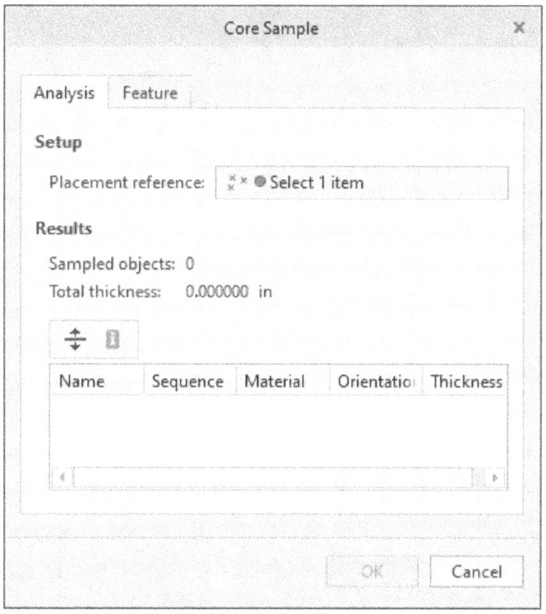

Figure-127. Core Sample dialog box

- Click on the **Placement reference** selection box from **Setup** area and select a datum point at the location where it intersects with laminate zone. Preview of core sample at selected point will be displayed; refer to Figure-128.

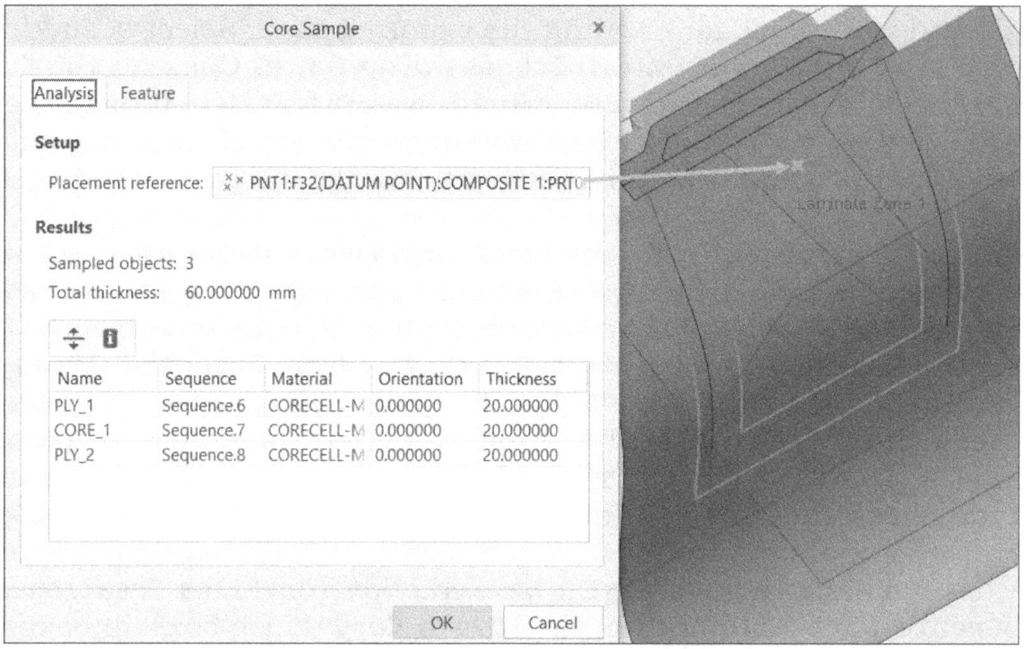

Figure-128. Preview of core sample

- The **Sampled objects** area of **Results** section displays the list of laminate objects included in the selected sample. The **Total thickness** area displays the total material thickness of intersected objects at the sampled location.

- Click on the button to toggle the order of the listed plies.
- Click on **Feature** tab of the dialog box, the options will be displayed as shown in Figure-129.

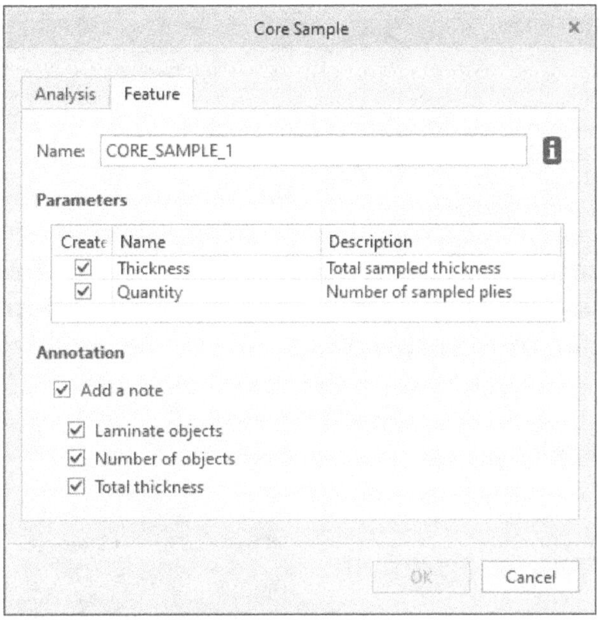

Figure-129. Feature tab options

- Specify desired name of the feature in the **Name** edit box.
- Select the **Add a note** check box from **Annotation** area is used to create a core sample note to display the results form the results table. Select the **Laminate objects** check box to include the list of the sampled laminate objects in the note. Select the **Number of objects** check box to include the number of the sampled laminate objects in the note. Select the **Total thickness** check box to include the total material thicknesses of the sampled laminate objects in the note.
- After specifying desired parameters, click on **OK** button from the dialog box. The core sample feature will be created and annotation will be displayed on the model; refer to Figure-130.

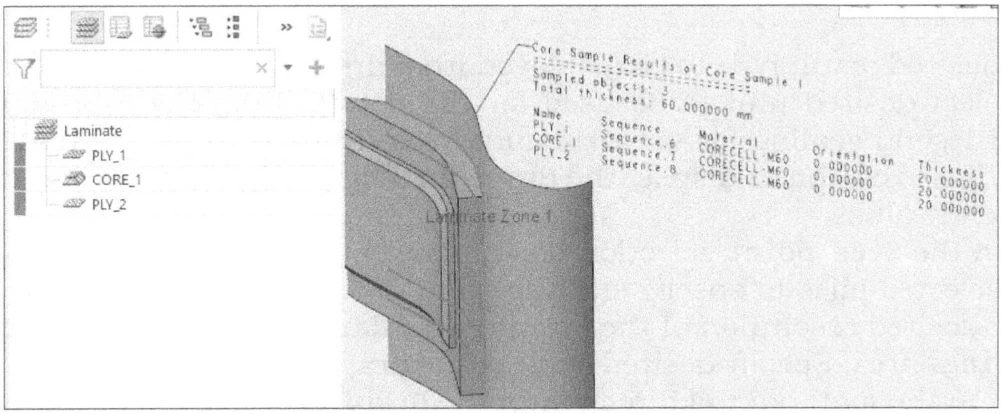

Figure-130. Core sample annotation

Draping Simulation

The **Draping Simulation** tool is used to run draping simulations to analyze ply production-ability and calculate ply flat patterns. The procedure to use this tool is discussed next.

- Click on the **Draping Simulation** tool from **Analysis** panel in the **Composite** tab of the **Ribbon**. The **Draping Simulation** contextual tab will be displayed; refer to Figure-131.

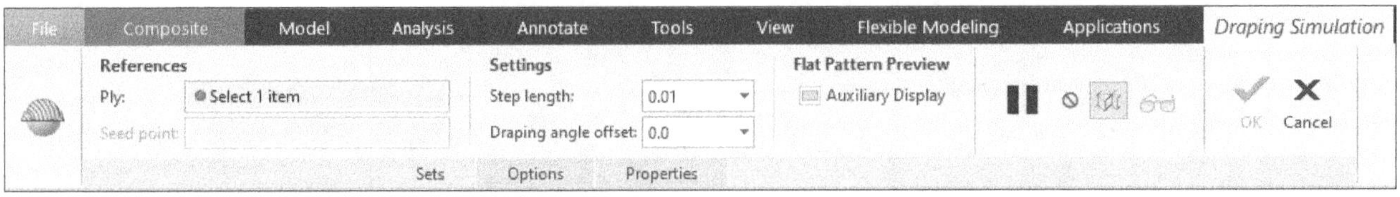

Figure-131. Draping Simulation contextual tab

- Click on the **Ply** selection box from **References** area and select a ply from draping manager or graphics area to perform draping simulation. The **Results Summary** will be displayed; refer to Figure-132.

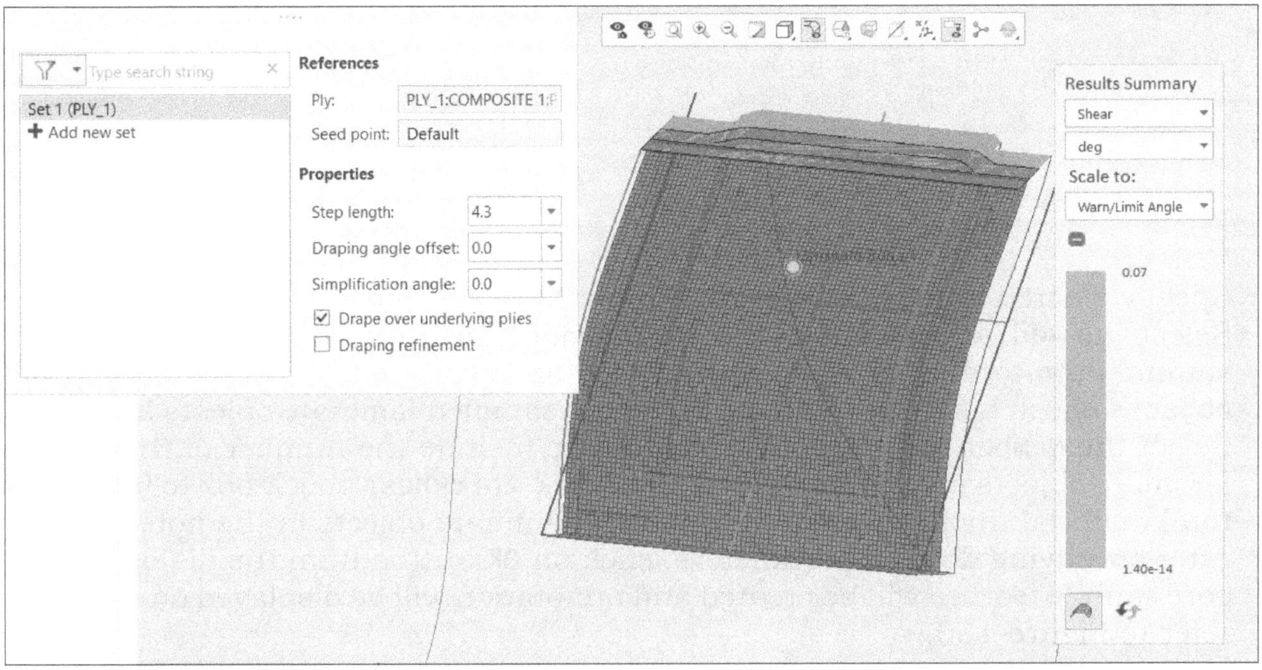

Figure-132. Results Summary

- Select desired result type to be displayed from drop-down in the **Results Summary** box. Select desired unit to be used for the results from the drop-down. Select desired legend scaling for shear results from drop-down in the **Scale to** area. Select the button to display the drape fishnet. Click on the button to reset the legend values.
- Click on the **Seed point** selection box and select a location inside the boundary of the selected plies to specify starting point of the draping simulation.
- Specify desired resolution of the draping simulation in the **Step length** edit box of **Settings** area. Specify desired angle of the draping simulation progression with respect to the material roll direction in the **Draping angle** offset edit box.
- Click on the **Sets** tab in the **Ribbon** and specify desired angle between polyline segments below which the segments may be merged in the **Simplification angle** edit box. Select the **Drape over underlying plies** check box to consider the ply's height in the laminate stack when performing draping analysis. Select the **Draping refinement** check box to increase the refinement of the drape, particularly for smaller plies.

- Select the **Auxiliary Display** button from **Flat Pattern Preview** area to display a preview of the flat pattern in a separate window; refer to Figure-133.

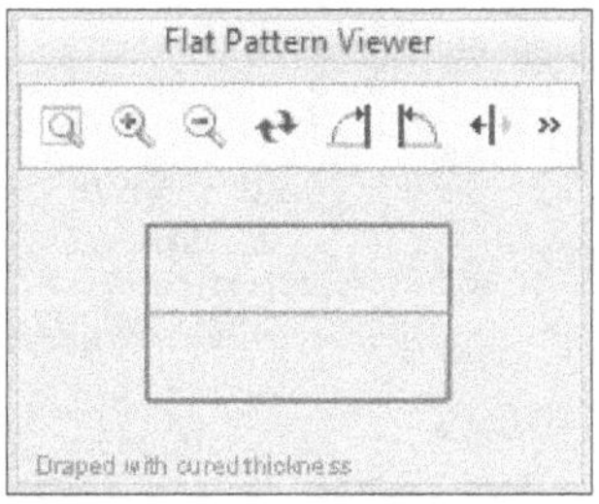

Figure-133. Flat pattern preview

- After specifying desired parameters, click on **OK** button from the contextual tab. The draping simulation feature will be added in the **Composite Tree**.

Export Draping Summary

The **Export Draping Summary** tool is used to export a summary report of draping results. The procedure to use this tool is discussed next.

- This tool is inactive if draping simulation has not been performed. You can also perform draping simulation using **Laminate Tree**. Click on the **Laminate Tree** option from the **Navigation Trees** toolbar; refer to Figure-134. The **Laminate Tree** will be displayed; refer to Figure-135.

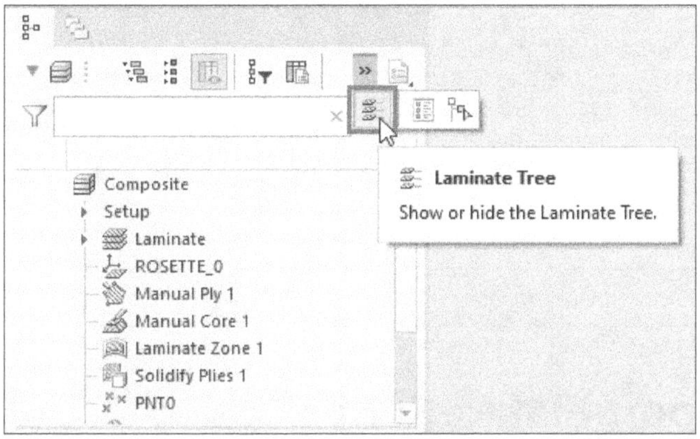

Figure-134. Laminate Tree option

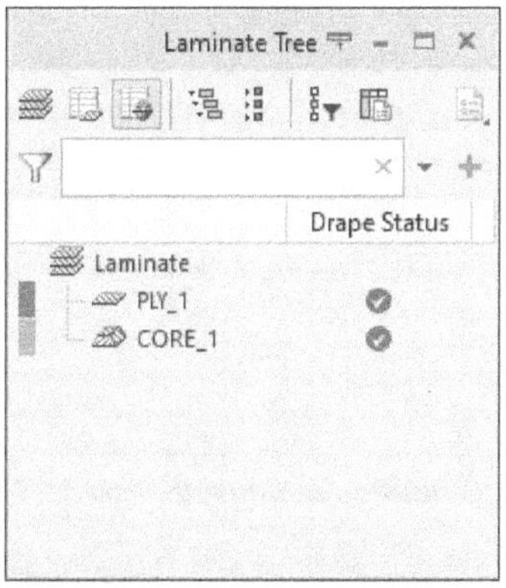

Figure-135. Laminate Tree

- Click **RMB** on the ply feature created and click on the **Draping Simulation** option; refer to Figure-136. The **Draping Simulation** contextual tab will be displayed.
- Specify desired parameters in the contextual tab which have been discussed earlier and click on the **OK** button. The **Export Draping Summary** tool will be activated.
- Click on the **Export Draping Summary** tool from the expanded **Analysis** panel in the **Composite** tab of the **Ribbon**. The **Draping Summary Report** will be displayed; refer to Figure-137.

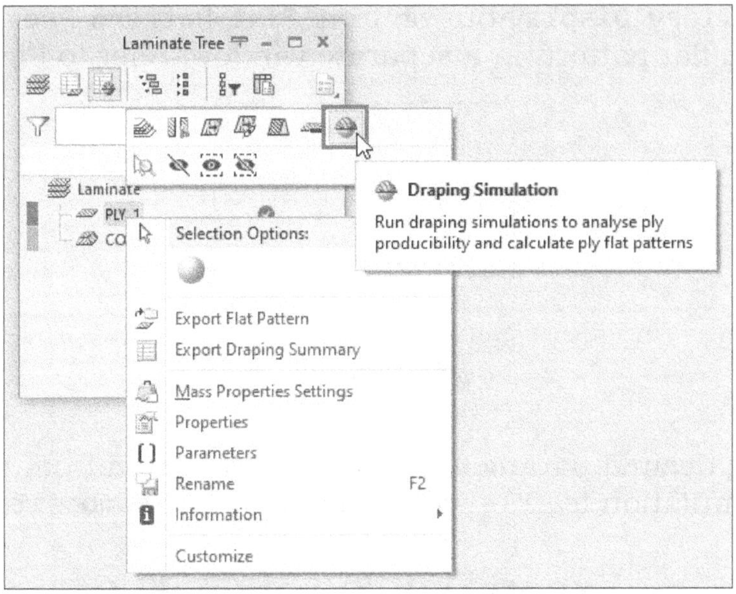

Figure-136. Draping Simulation option

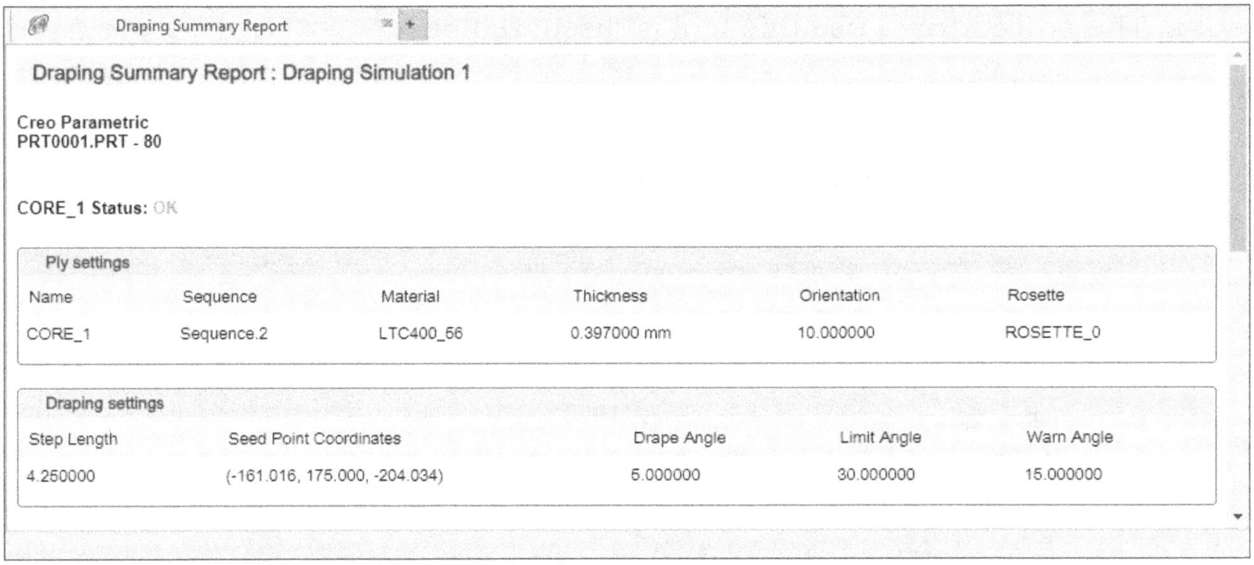

Figure-137. Draping Summary Report

Export Flat Pattern

The **Export Flat Pattern** tool is used to set up export properties, preview the results, and output plies to another format. The procedure to use this tool is discussed next.

- Click on the **Export Flat Pattern** tool from the expanded **Analysis** panel in the **Composite** tab of the **Ribbon**. The **Export Setup** dialog box will be displayed; refer to Figure-138.
- Select **DXF** or **DWG** radio button from **Format** area as the publish deliverable. Click on the **Settings** button, the **Export Environment** dialog box will be displayed to edit the settings for the selected format; refer to Figure-139.
- Select desired version of file from **Version** drop-down.
- Select **As Points** or **As Shapes** radio button from **Points** area of **Entities** tab to export point as points or as shapes, respectively.
- Select **Export multi-line note as MTEXT** check box from **Notes** area of **Annotations** tab to export multi-line note as MTEXT entity. Select **UNICODE encoding** check box to write non-ASCII characters in UNICODE encoding.

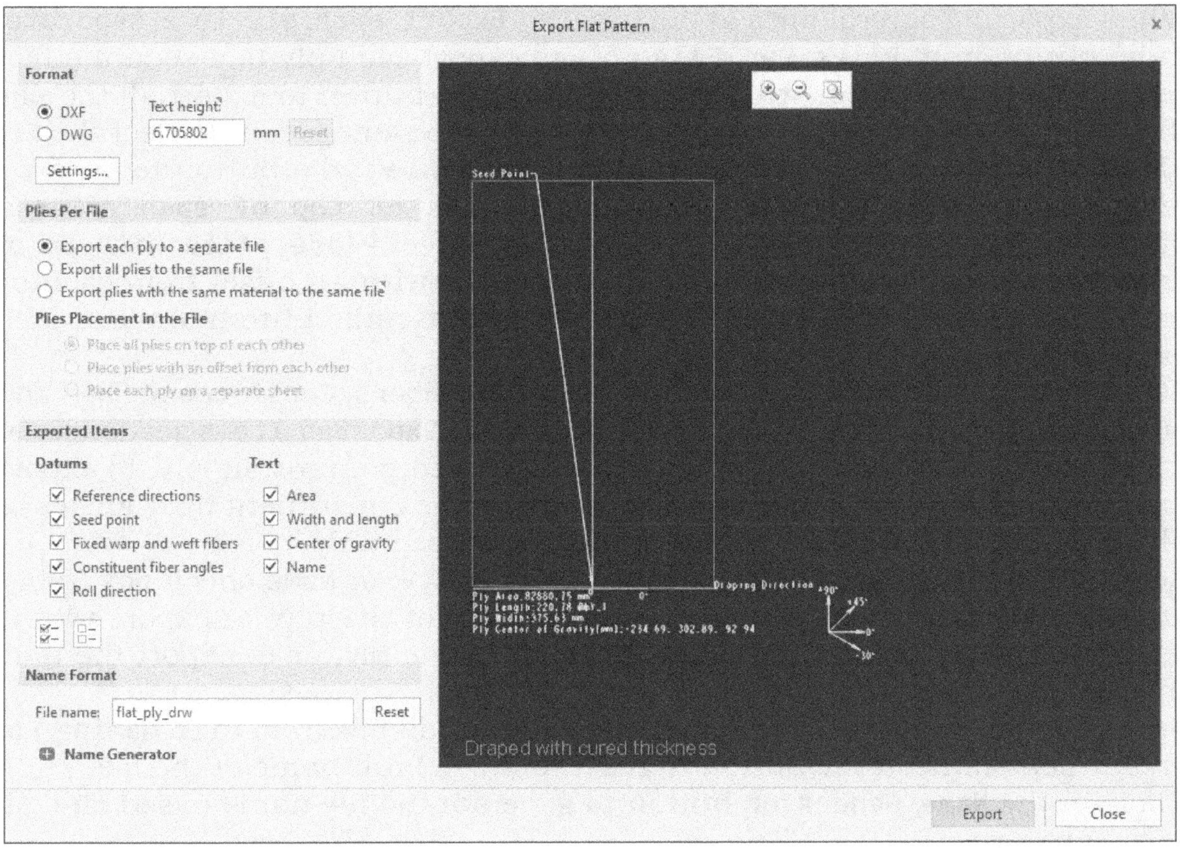

Figure-138. Export Setup dialog box

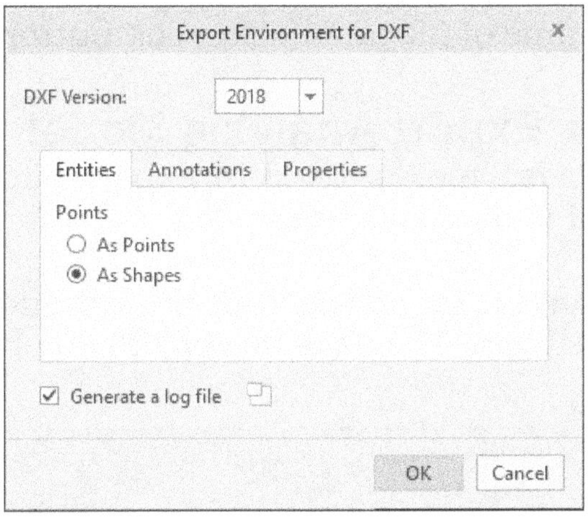

Figure-139. Export Environment dialog box

- Select the **As Is** option from the **Text Alignment** drop-down to export notes with their original alignment values. Select the **Fit** option from the drop-down to export notes with FIT alignment.
- Select the **Generate a log file** check box to generate a log file after you export the drawing.
- Select the button to open the log file in a new window.
- Click on the **Properties** tab of the dialog box to specify parameters related to line fonts, text fonts, colors, and layers.
- After specifying desired parameters, click on the **OK** button.
- Click in the **Text height** edit box and specify desired value to define the height of text character.
- Click on the **Reset** button to restore the default text height specified in the detail options file.

- When exporting several plies at once, select **Export each ply to a separate file** radio button from **Plies Per File** area to export each ply to a separate file and select **Export all plies to the same file** radio button to export all the plies to the same file. When exporting several plies to the same file and select the **Export plies with the same material to the same file** radio button to export plies with same material file, select **Place all plies on top of each other** radio button to place all plies on top of each other, select **Place plies with an offset from each other** radio button to place all plies with an offset from each other, and select **Place each ply on a separate sheet** radio button to place each ply on an individual sheet.
- Select **Rosette**, **Seed point**, **Fixed warp and weft fibers**, **Constituent fiber angles**, or **Roll direction** check box from **Datums** area of **Exported Items** section to export the reference rosette of the ply, to export the seed point of the ply, to export the fixed warp and weft fibers of the ply, to export the constituent fiber angles of the ply, or to export the roll direction of the ply, respectively.
- Select **Area**, **Width and length**, **Center of gravity**, or **Name** check box from **Text** area of **Exported Items** section to export area of the ply, to export width and length of the ply, to export center of gravity of the ply, or to export the name of the ply, respectively.
- Specify desired name of the file in the **File name** edit box from **File Naming Format** area. Click on the **Reset** button to reset to the default name of the file.
- Click on the **Name Generator** button to generate the file name based on callouts of ply properties.
- Click on the **Export** button, the **Save a Copy** dialog box will be displayed. Specify desired location and name of file and click on **OK** button. The file will be exported.

Export Analysis Model

The **Export Analysis Model** tool is used to export plies to analysis model. The procedure to use this tool is discussed next.

- Click on the **Export Analysis Model** from the expanded **Analysis** panel in the **Composite** tab of the **Ribbon**. The **Save a Copy** dialog box will be displayed; refer to Figure-140.

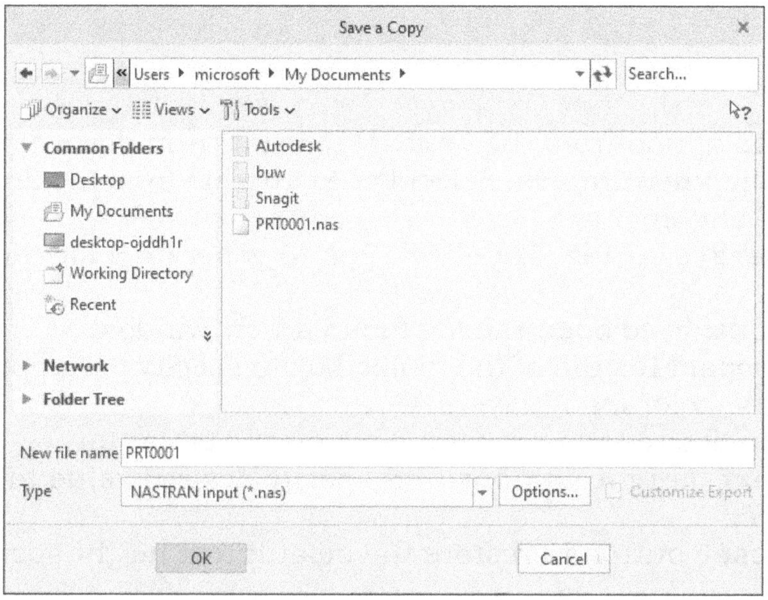

Figure-140. Export analysis model

- Specify desired name and location of the file and click on the **OK** button. The plies will be exported.
- After specifying desired parameters, click on the **OK** button from the **Close** panel in the Ribbon.

Conformal Cooling

The **Conformal Cooling** tool is used to create cooling channels that follow profile of the selected surface to create cooling channels in the mold. You can use this tool to create inner cavity in a model as an alternate use. To use this tool, you must have a sketch profile of cooling channel and a body representing mold core/cavity; refer to Figure-141. The procedure to use this tool is discussed next.

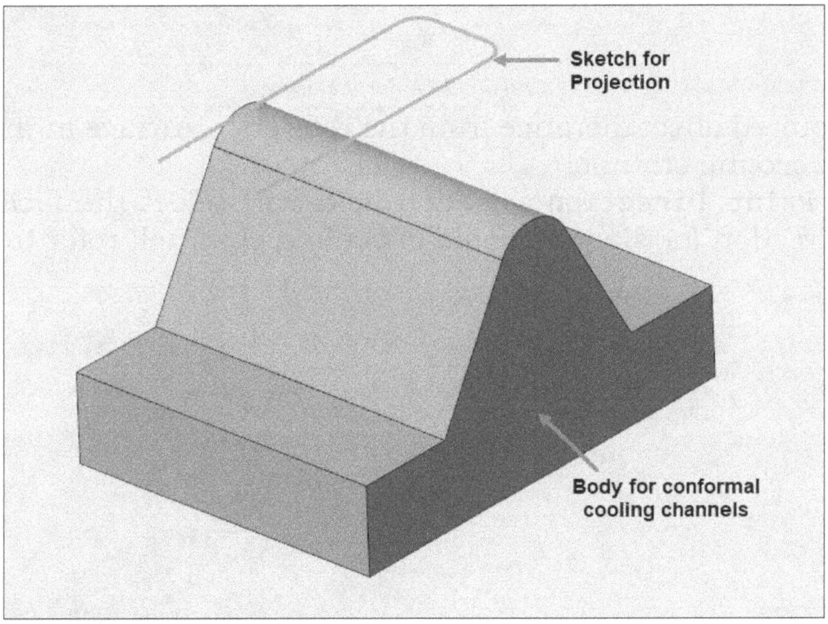

Figure-141. Model for conformal cooling

- Click on the **Conformal Cooling** tool from **Engineering** panel in the **Model** tab of the **Ribbon**. The **Conformal Cooling** contextual tab will be displayed; refer to Figure-142.

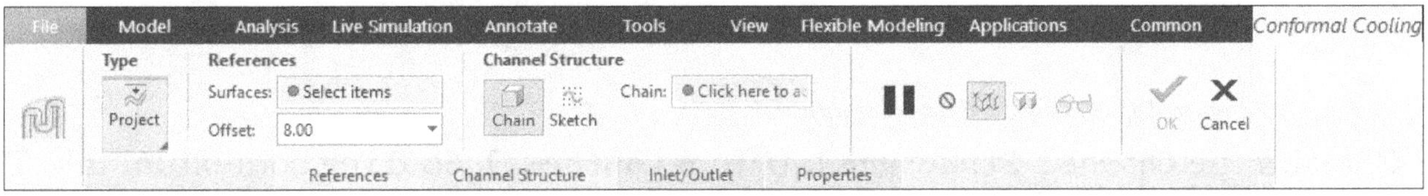

Figure-142. Conformal Cooling contextual tab

- Select **Project** option from the **Type** drop-down to create a projected cooling channel (Selected in our case). Select **Spiral** option to create a spiral cooling channel, generally for cylindrical models.
- Click on the **References** tab from **Conformal Cooling** contextual tab. The options in the tab will be displayed as shown in Figure-143.
- Select desired surface of the model for creating the cooling channel; refer to Figure-144.
- Click on the **Details** button to review and modify the surface property. The **Surface Sets** dialog box will be displayed. The options of the dialog box have been discussed earlier.

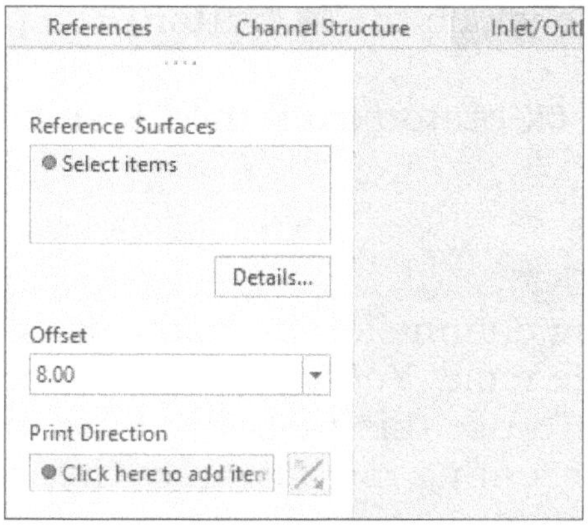

Figure-143. References tab

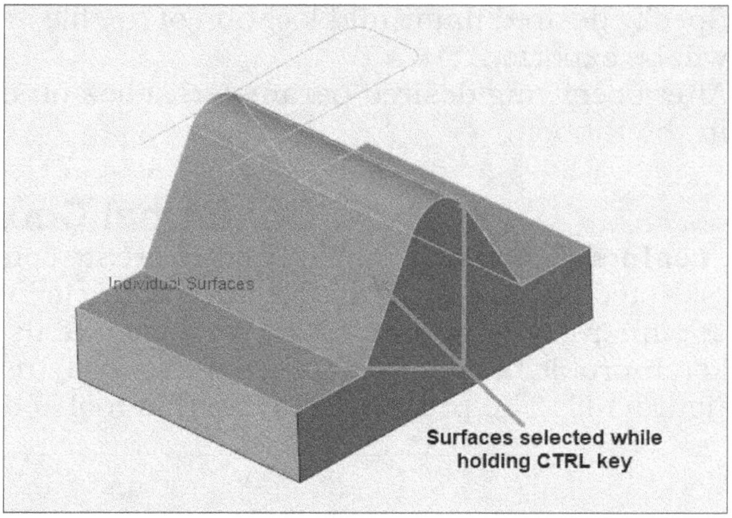

Figure-144. Surfaces selected

- Enter the required offset distance from the reference surface in the **Offset** edit box to create the cooling channel.
- Click in the **Print Direction** selection field and select the face/edge to define projection direction for sketch profile of cooling channel; refer to Figure-145.

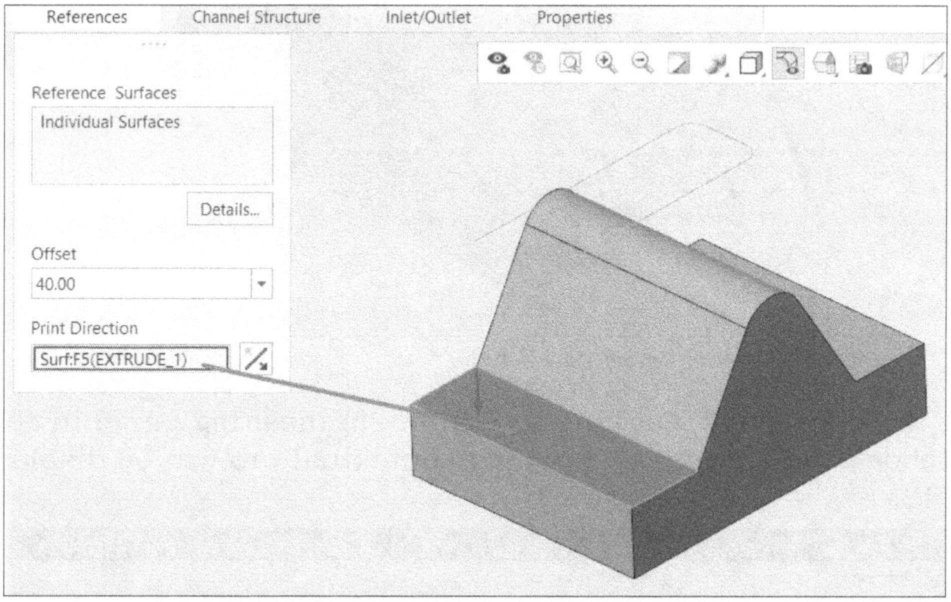

Figure-145. Face selected for print direction

- Click on the **Channel Structure** tab from **Conformal Cooling** contextual tab. The options in the tab will be displayed as shown in Figure-146.
- Set desired option in the **Section Profile** drop-down to define the profile used for creating channel.
- Click in the **Diameter** edit box and specify desired value to define size of the section for the cooling channel.
- Click in the **Turn Radius** edit box define the channel turning radius.
- Select the **Chain** radio button from the **Project** area to use already created sketch profile (Selected in our case). Select the **Sketch** radio button to create a new sketch profile of cooling channel.

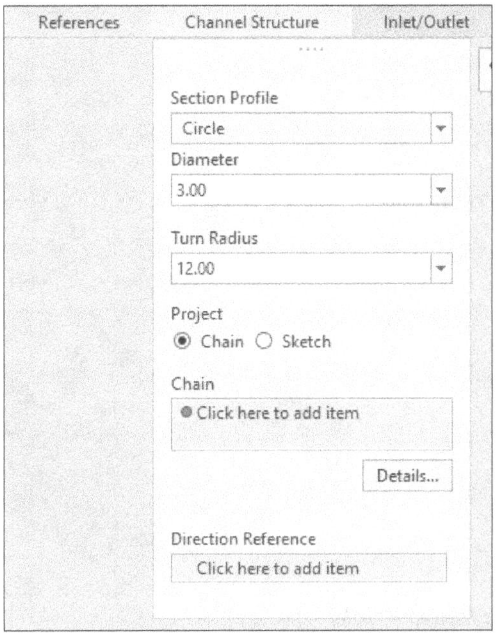

Figure-146. Channel Structure tab

- Click in the **Chain** selection field and select the reference sketch to be projected. Preview of the conformal cooling channel will be displayed; refer to Figure-147. Click on the purple arrow shown on sketch profile to toggle inlet point of cooling channel.

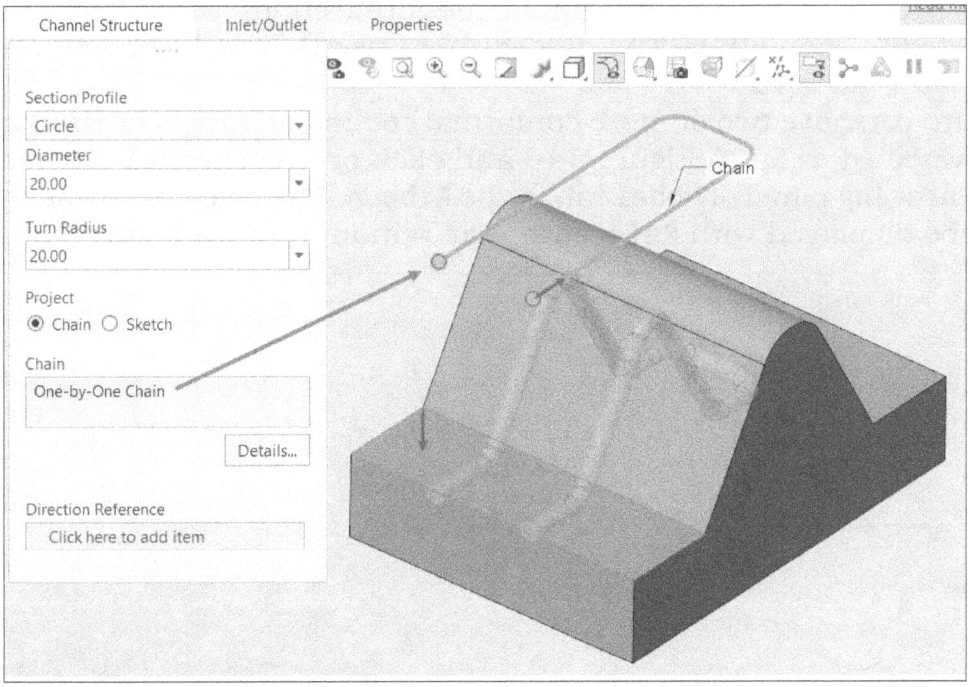

Figure-147. Selecting the sketch of conformal cooling

- Click on the **Inlet/Outlet** tab to define references for inlet and outlet. Click in the **Inlet Reference** selection field and select face of model to extent the channel upto selected face for defining inlet position; refer to Figure-148. Similarly, you can use other options in this tab to define outlet reference.
- Select the **Create Counterbore** check box to change profile of pipe into a counterbore hole. Set the parameters as discussed earlier.

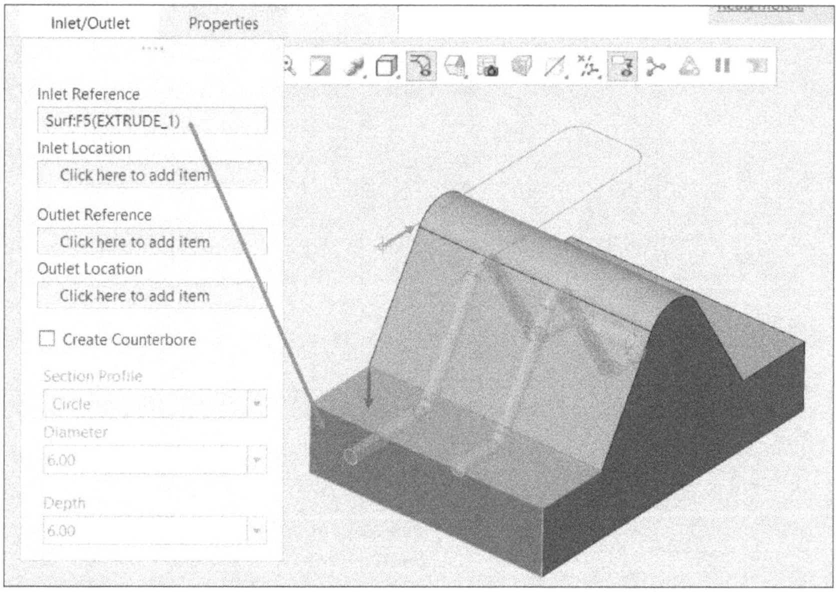

Figure-148. Face selected as inlet reference

- After setting parameters, click on the **OK** button from **Ribbon** to create conformal cooling channel.

Channel Connect

The **Channel Connect** tool is used to join two or more conformal cooling channels. Generally, multiple cooling channels are created in the mold and they are interconnected to each other. The procedure to use this tool is given next.

- Make sure you have two or more conformal cooling channels created in the model to be connected; refer to Figure-149 and click on the **Channel Connect** tool from the **Engineering** panel of **Model** tab in the **Ribbon**. The **Channel Connect** contextual tab will be displayed with **References** tab option; refer to Figure-150.

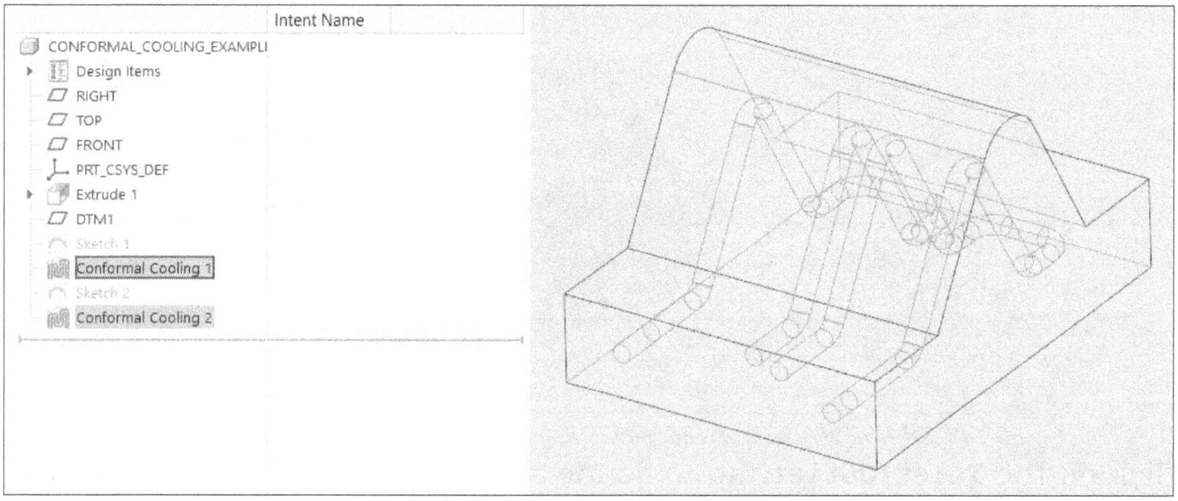

Figure-149. Cooling channels created

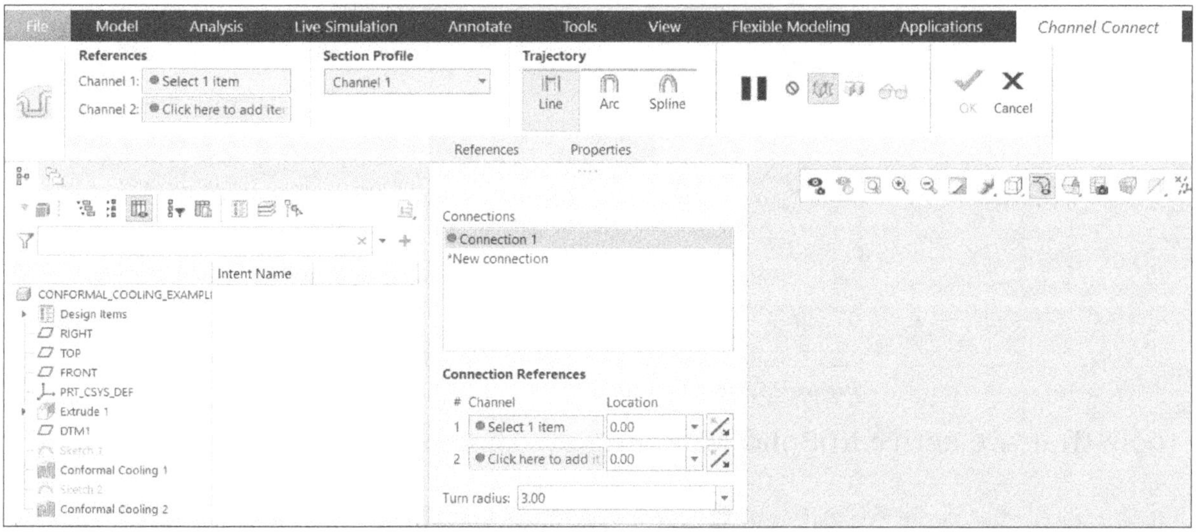

Figure-150. Channel Connect contextual tab

- Select the two channels to be connected and use **Flip** buttons in **References** tab to make sure connection points are near each other. Preview of connection will be displayed; refer to Figure-151.

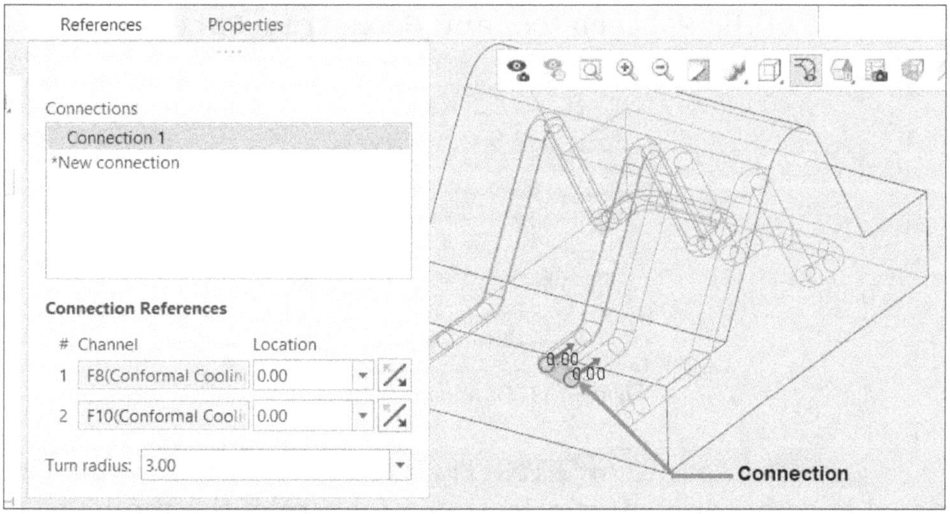

Figure-151. Preview of connection

- Select the **Arc** or **Spline** button from **Trajectory** area of contextual tab to modify shape of connecting line.
- Set the other parameters as discussed earlier and click on the **OK** button from **Ribbon** to create the feature.

EDITING TOOLS

The editing tools are available in the **Editing** panel of the **Ribbon**; refer to Figure-152. Note that very few tools are active in the **Editing** panel and rest of the tools cannot be used at present. Some of the tools like **Mirror**, **Pattern**, and so on are active after selecting a feature. Some of the tools will not be used in the solid modeling and hence will not be active.

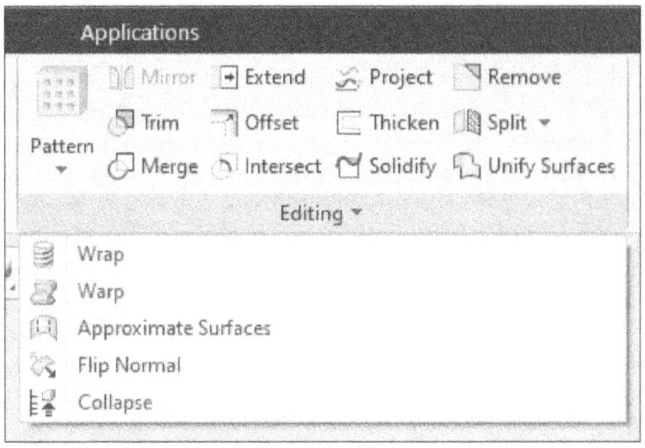

Figure-152. Editing panel

The tools that are active in Solid Modeling are discussed next.

Pattern Tools

There are three tools in the **Pattern** drop-down: **Pattern**, **Geometric Pattern**, and **Pattern Table**; refer to Figure-153. The **Pattern** tool is used to create multiple copies of the selected feature. The **Geometric Pattern** tool is used to create pattern of geometry. The **Pattern Table** tool is used to create a table of patterns. We will now learn about use of the **Pattern** tool and **Geometric Pattern** tool.

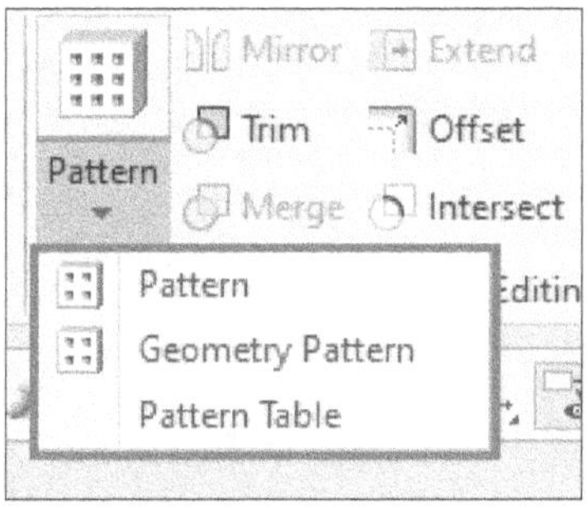

Figure-153. Pattern drop-down

Pattern Tool

The **Pattern** tool is active only after selecting a feature of the model to be patterned. The procedure to use this tool is given next.

- Select the feature from the model that you want to pattern; refer to Figure-154.

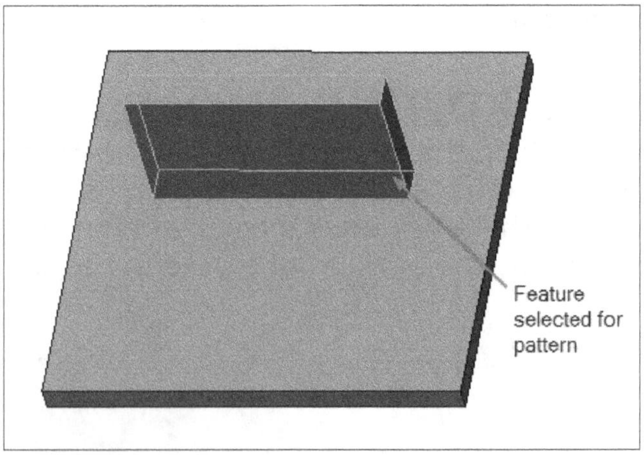

Figure-154. Feature selected to pattern

- Click on the **Pattern** tool from the **Pattern Tools** drop-down. The **Pattern** contextual tab will be displayed; refer to Figure-155.

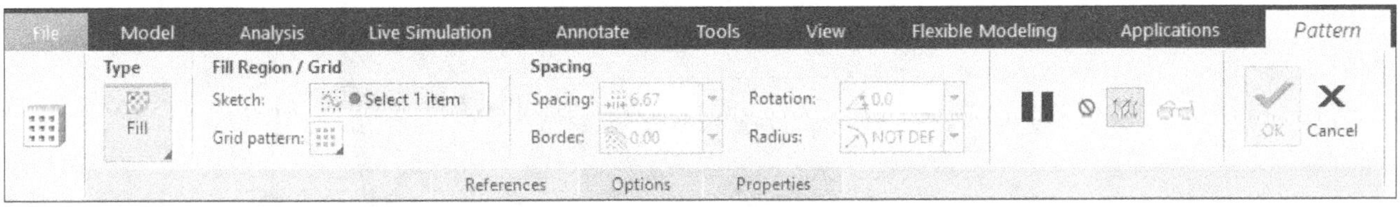

Figure-155. Pattern contextual tab

Now, we have different pattern types to select from the drop-down in the **Type** area of the contextual tab; refer to Figure-156.

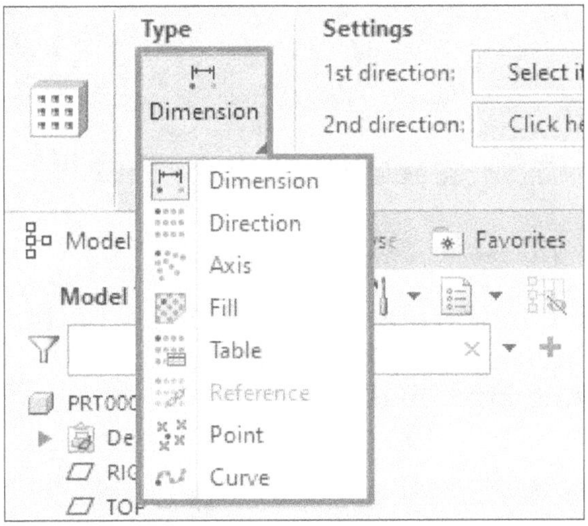

Figure-156. Pattern type drop-down

We will discuss about creating a pattern by each of the option.

Creating pattern using Dimension option

- Select the **Dimension** option from the drop-down in the **Type** area of the contextual tab if not selected by default. The dimensions of the selected feature will be displayed; refer to Figure-157.

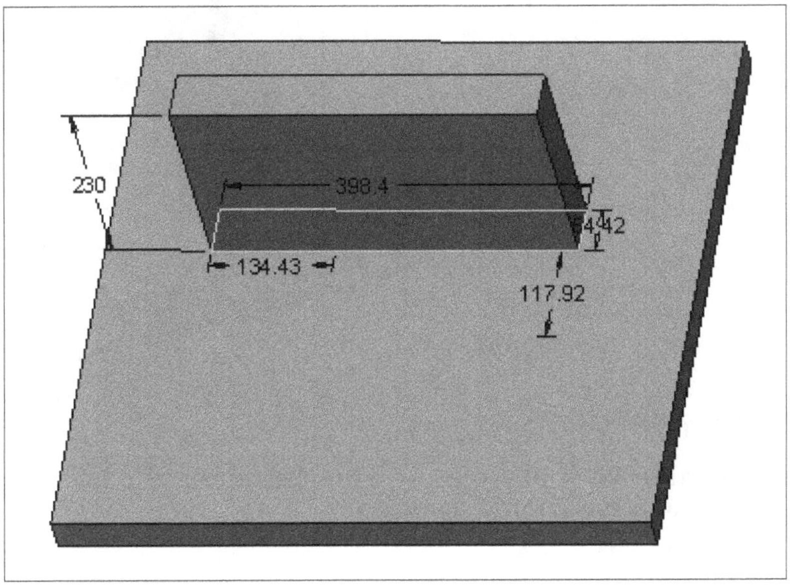

Figure-157. Dimensions displayed on model

- Select a dimension as reference along which you want to create the pattern; refer to Figure-158.

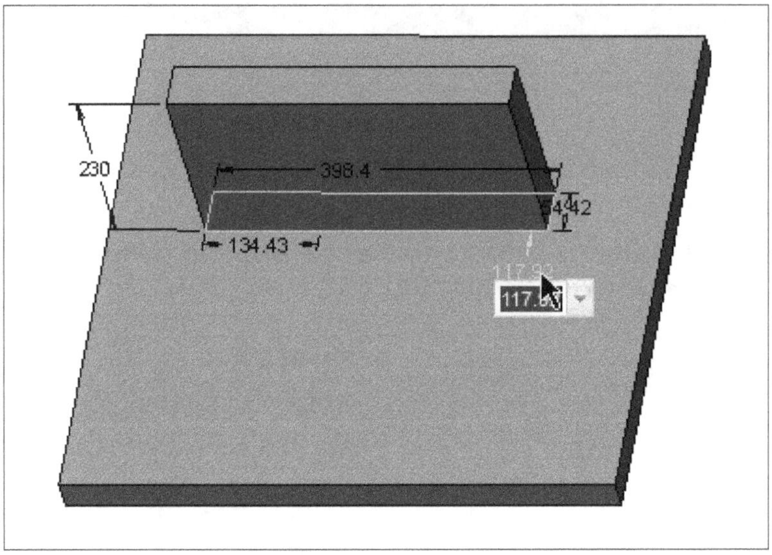

Figure-158. Dimension selected for first direction

- Specify desired distance in the active box. Preview of the pattern will be displayed; refer to Figure-159. Click on the **Dimensions** tab in the contextual tab to change the value of the distance specified.

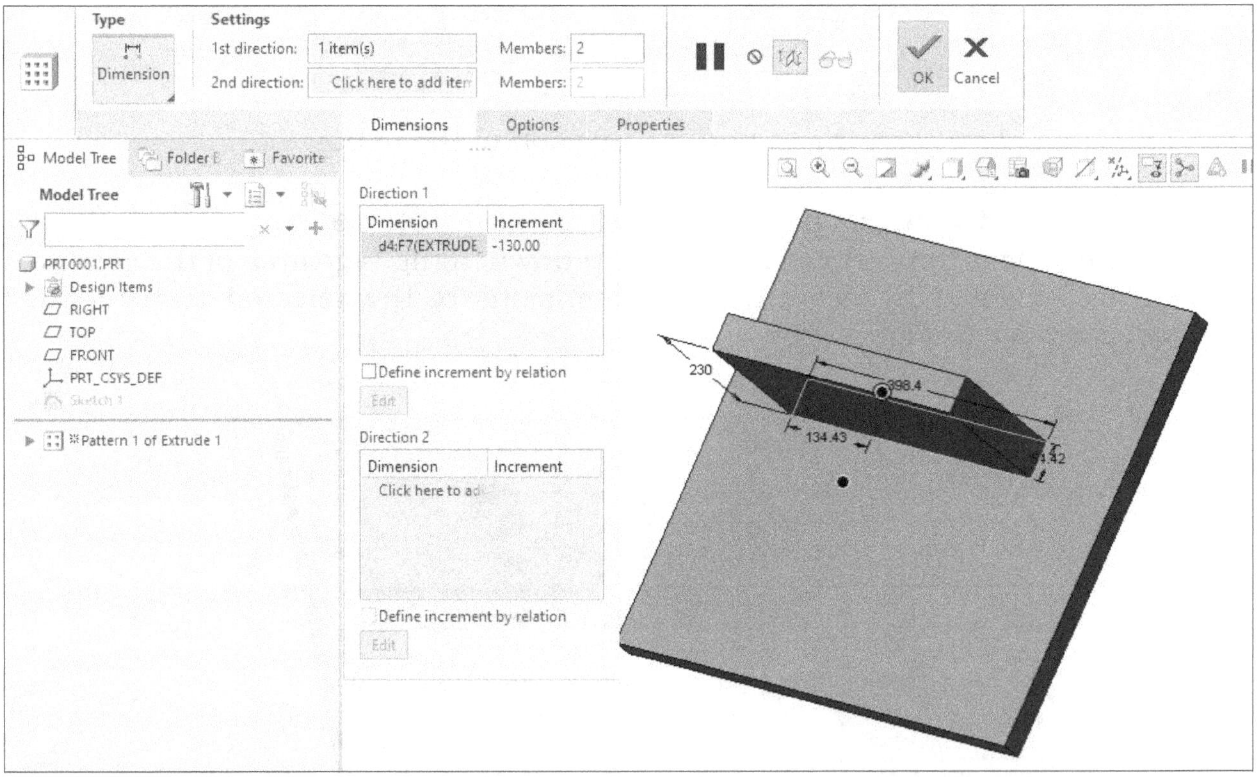

Figure-159. Preview of dimension pattern

- Specify desired number of instances in the **Members** edit box from **Settings** area of the contextual tab; refer to Figure-160.

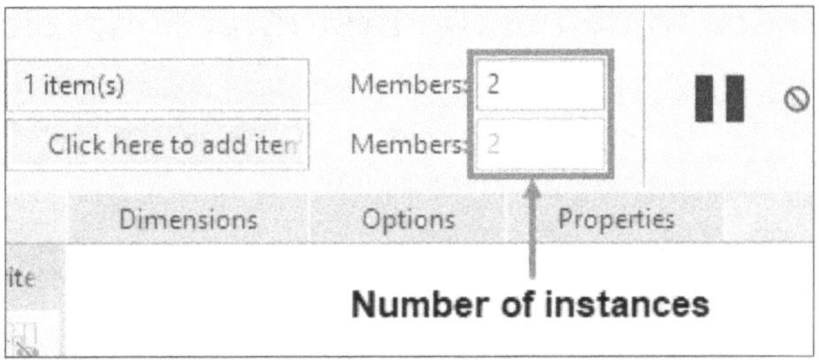

Figure-160. Number of instances for pattern

- Click in the **2nd direction** collector from **Settings** area of the contextual tab and select the second dimension to create a rectangular pattern; refer to Figure-161.

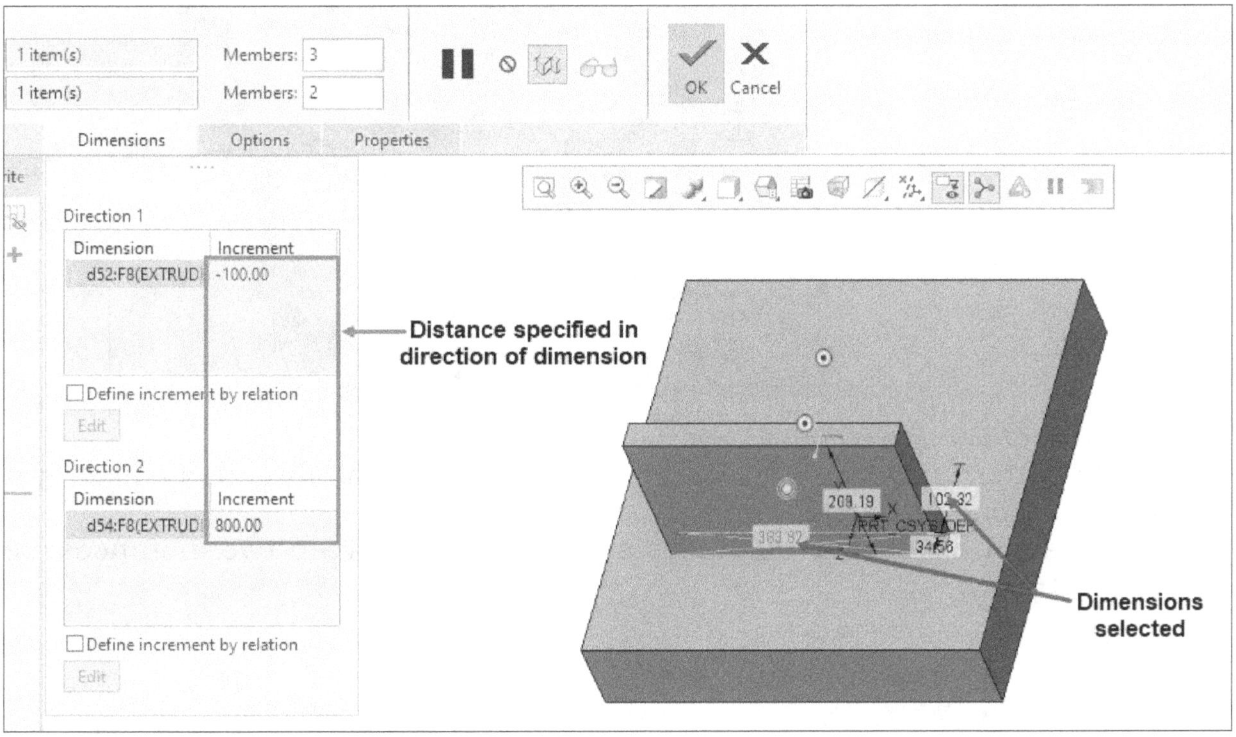

Figure-161. Dimension selection for second direction

- Click on the **OK** button from the contextual tab to create the pattern.

Creating pattern using Direction option

- Select the **Direction** option from the drop-down in the **Type** area of the contextual tab. The **Pattern** contextual tab will be displayed as shown in Figure-162.

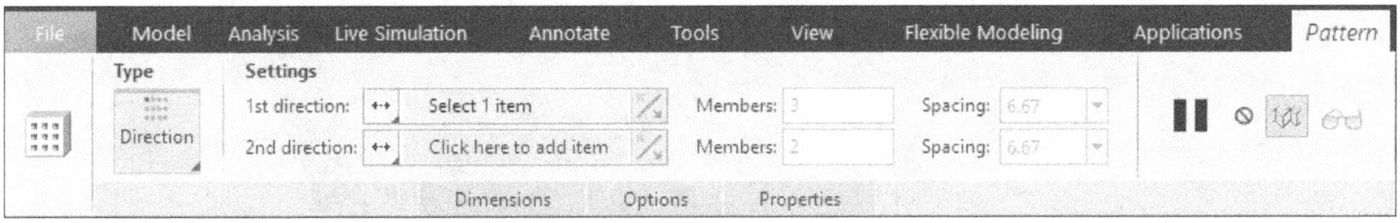

Figure-162. Pattern contextual tab for direction option

- Select a plane/face/edge to define the first direction; refer to Figure-163.

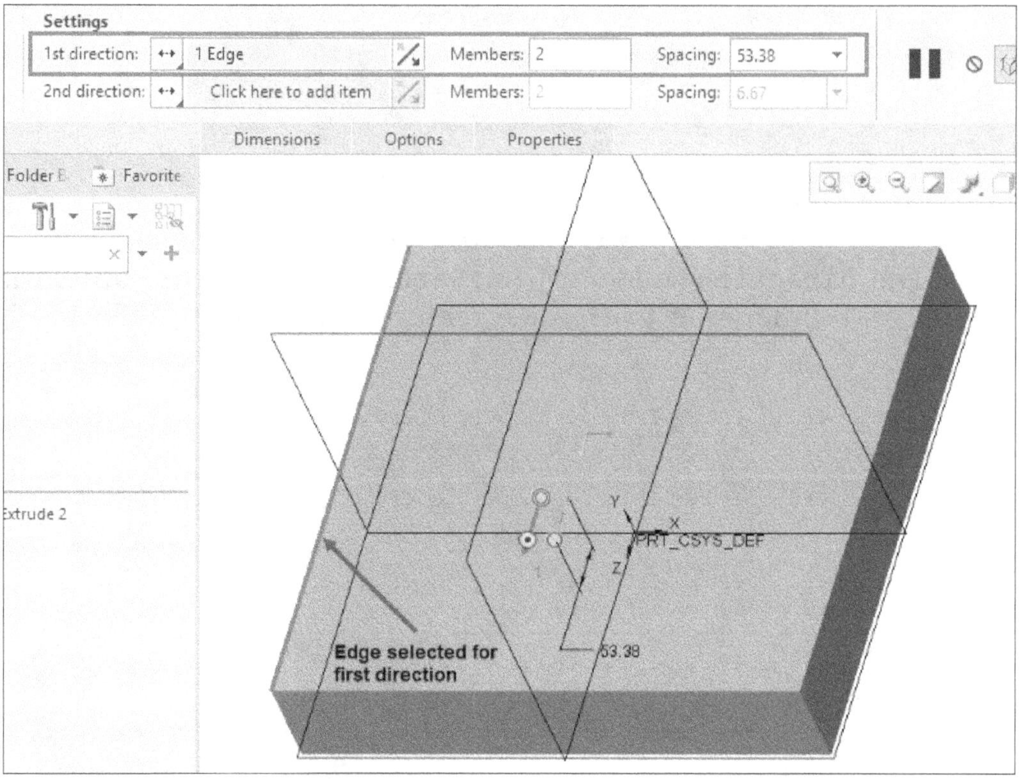

Figure-163. Edge selected for first direction

- To create pattern in second direction, click in the second direction collector and select the second reference.
- Specify desired number of instances and distance between two instances; refer to Figure-164.

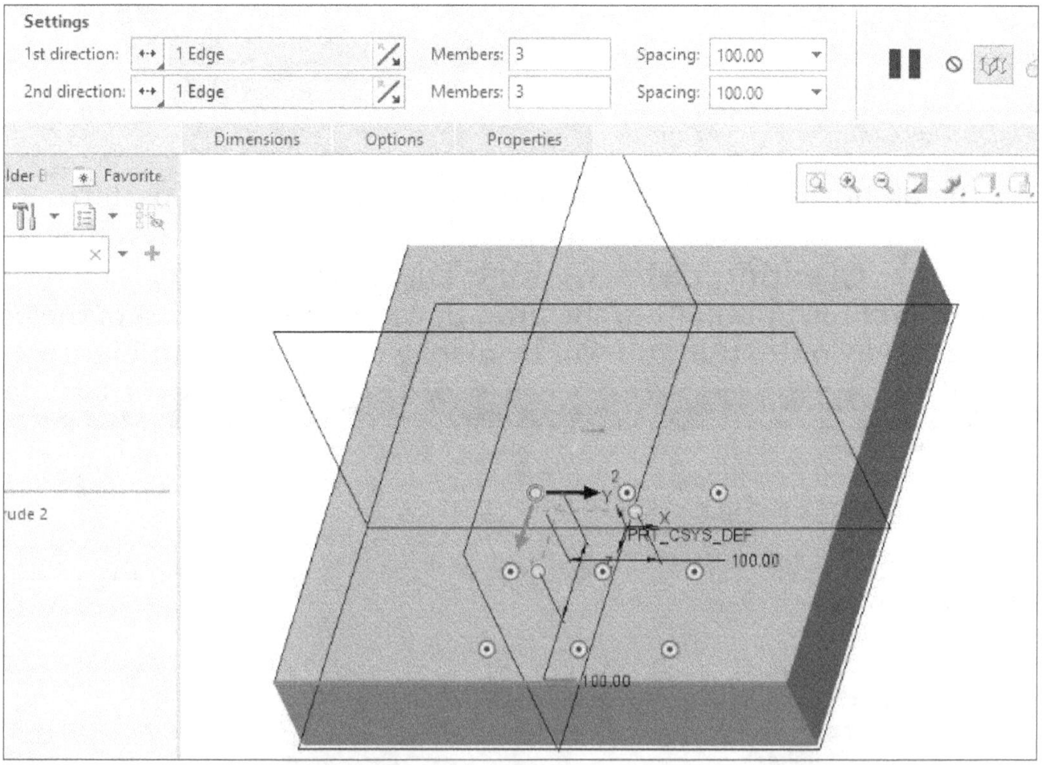

Figure-164. Edge selected for second direction

- Click on the **OK** button from the contextual tab to create the pattern.

Creating pattern using Axis option

- Select the **Axis** option from the drop-down in the **Type** area of the contextual tab. The **Pattern** contextual tab will be displayed as shown in Figure-165. Also, you are asked to select a reference.

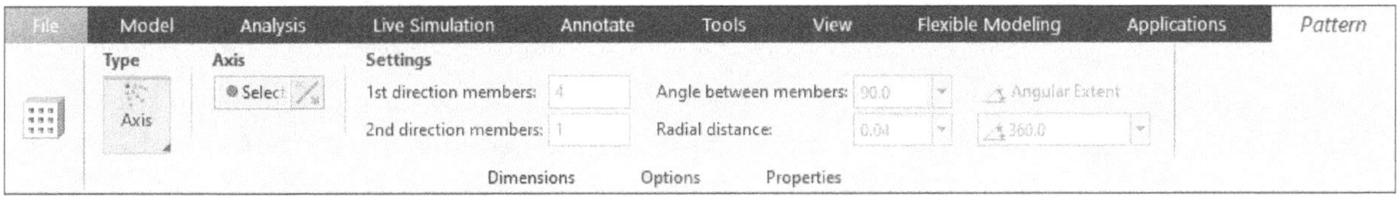

Figure-165. Pattern contextual tab for axis option

- Select the axis of coordinate system or geometric centerline created. Preview of the pattern will be displayed; refer to Figure-166.

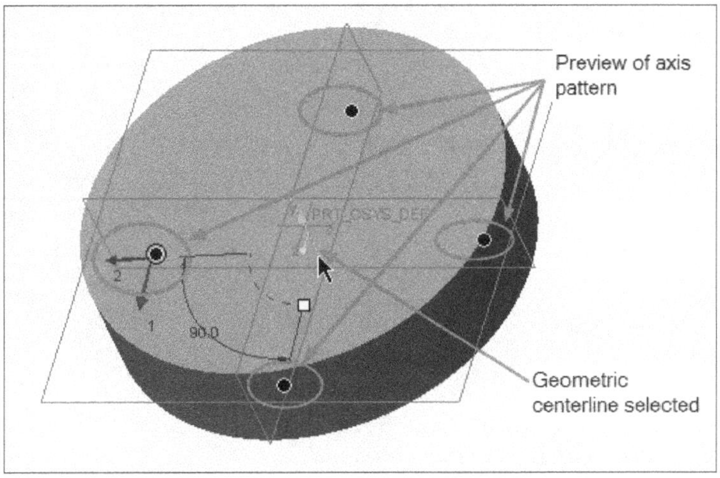

Figure-166. Preview of axis pattern

- Specify the number of instances for the first direction in the respective edit box in the contextual tab.
- Next, specify the angular distance between the two instances of the pattern or you can specify the total angular span; refer to Figure-167.

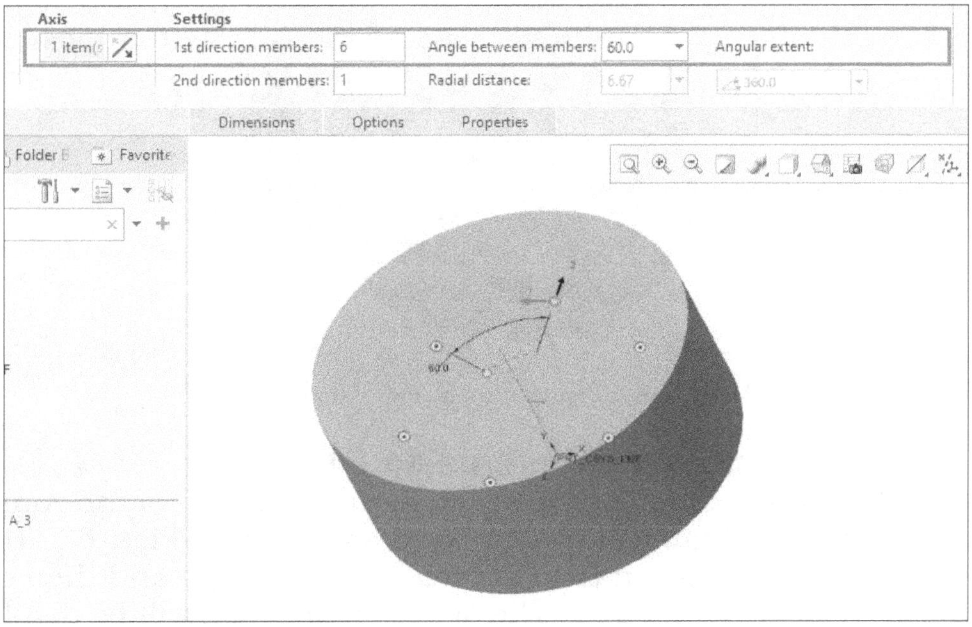

Figure-167. Options to create angular pattern

- Similarly, you can create angular pattern along the second direction by specifying the value in the second direction; refer to Figure-168.

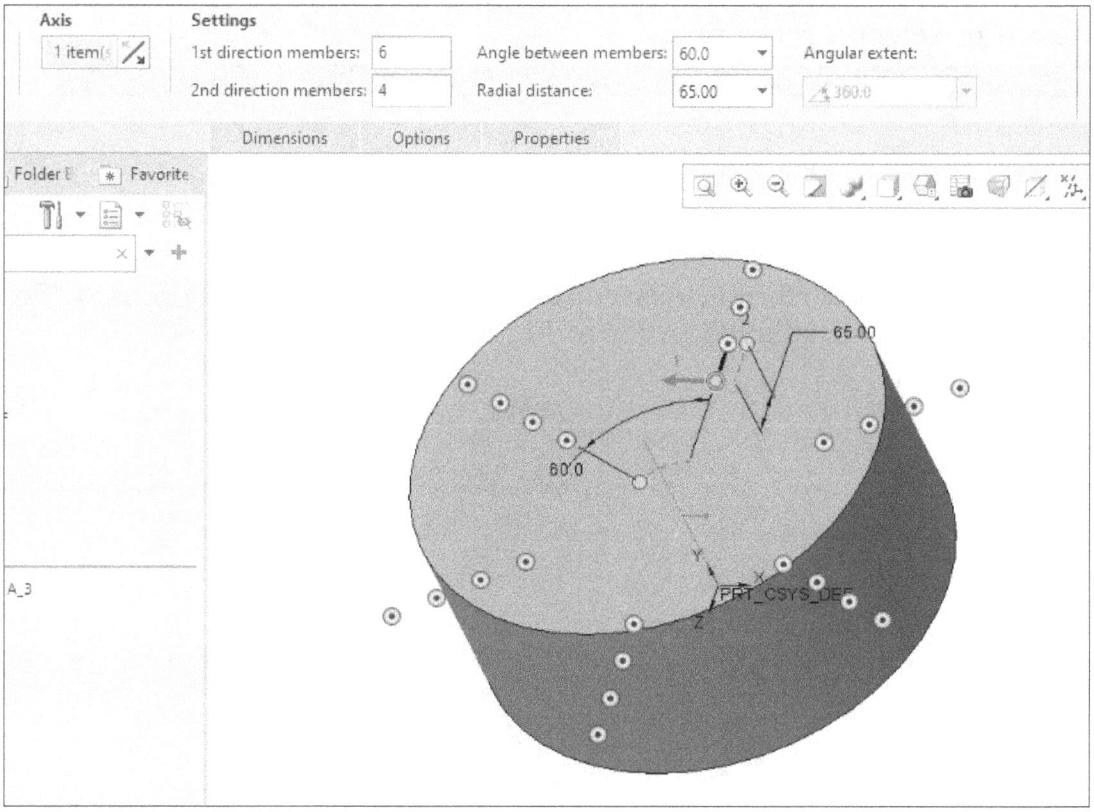

Figure-168. Angular pattern with second direction selected

- Click on the **OK** button from the contextual tab to create the pattern; refer to Figure-169.

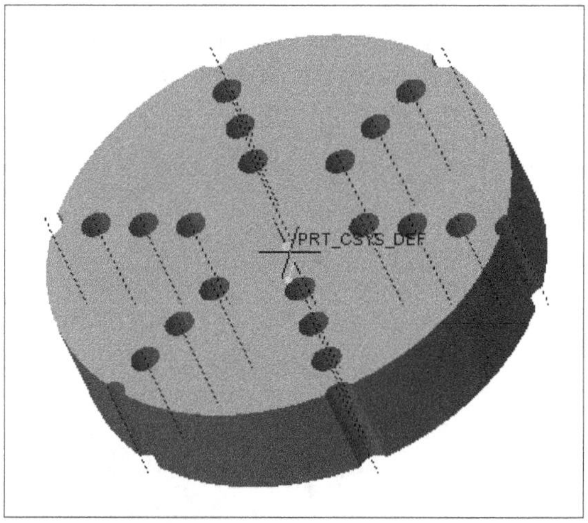

Figure-169. Angular pattern created

Creating pattern using Fill option

- Select the **Fill** option from the drop-down in the **Type** area of the contextual tab. The **Pattern** contextual tab will be displayed as shown in Figure-170.
- Click on the **References** tab in the **Pattern** contextual tab and then click on the **Define** button; refer to Figure-171. The **Sketch** dialog box will be displayed.
- Create a closed sketch on the face of the model which you want to fill by using the instances of the selected feature to be patterned; refer to Figure-172.

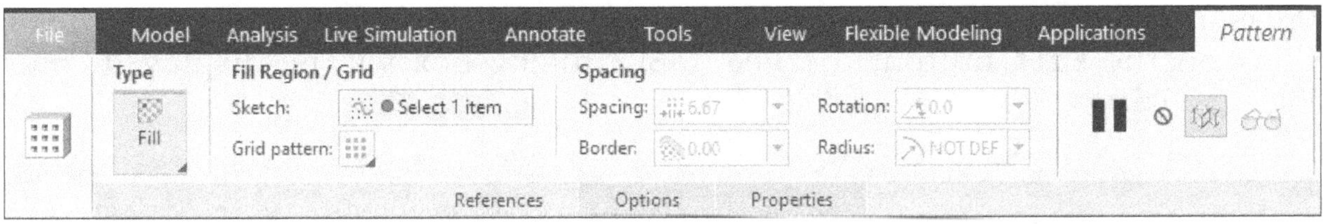

Figure-170. Pattern contextual tab for fill option

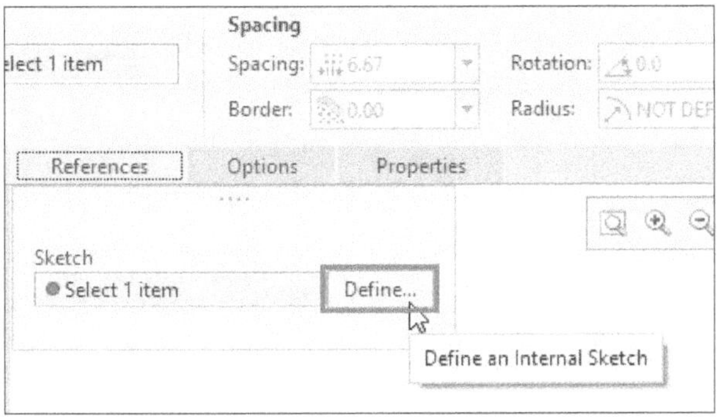

Figure-171. Define button to be selected

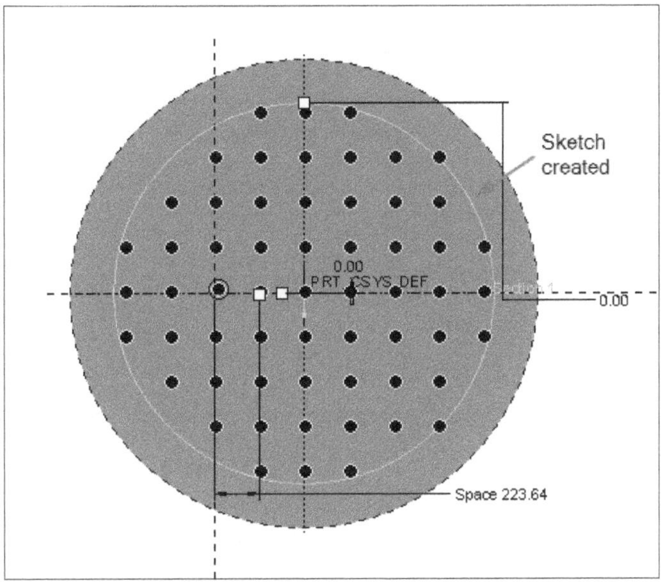

Figure-172. Sketch created for pattern

- Specify the distance between two instances of the pattern.
- Using options of the **Grid pattern** drop-down, you can change the grid pattern; refer to Figure-173.

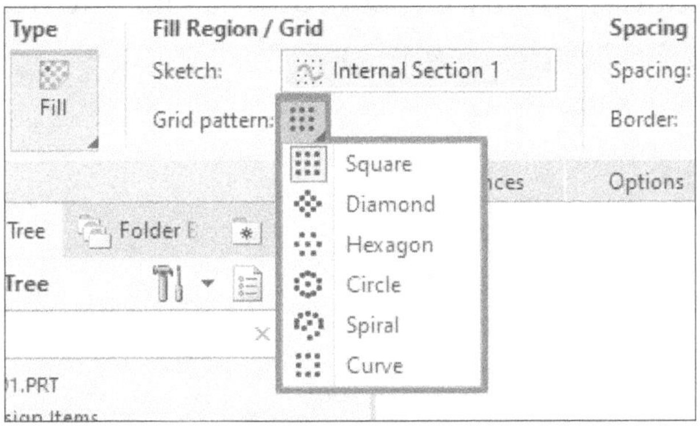

Figure-173. Grid type for fill pattern

- After specifying desired options, click on the **OK** button from the **Pattern** contextual tab.

Creating pattern using Table option

- Select the **Table** option from the drop-down in the **Type** area of the contextual tab. The **Pattern** contextual tab will be displayed as shown in Figure-174.

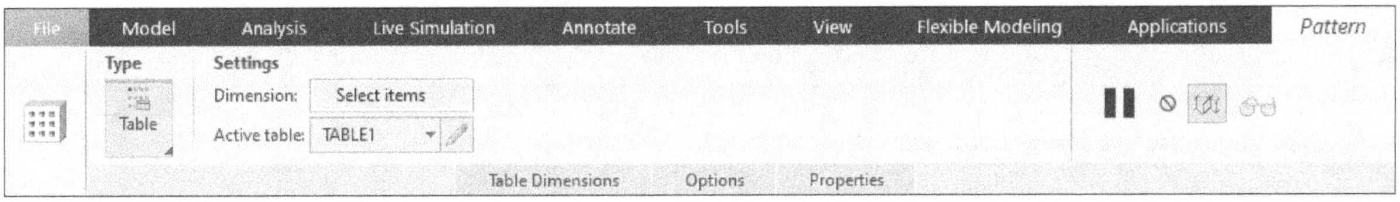

Figure-174. Pattern contextual tab for table option

- Press the **CTRL** key and select dimensions as per which you want to create the table.
- Click on the **Edit** button, the **Pro/TABLE** dialog box will be displayed; refer to Figure-175.

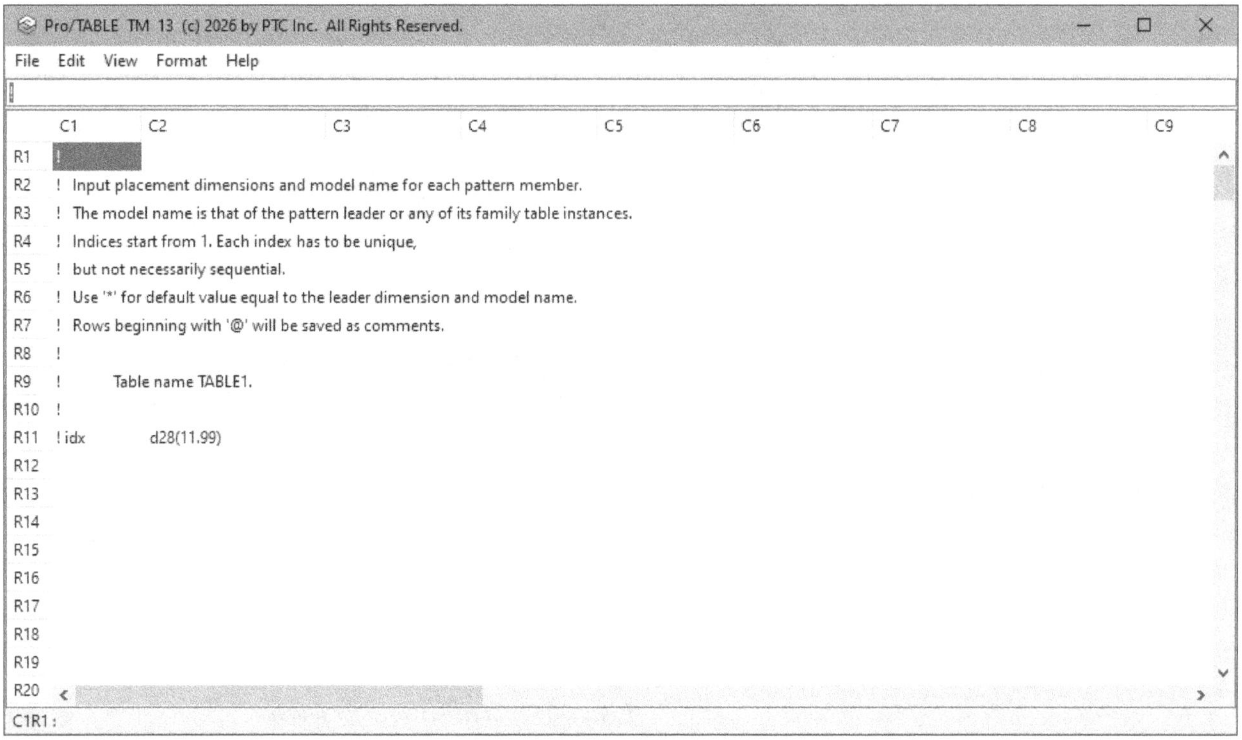

Figure-175. Pro-Table dialog box

- Under the **idx** column, specify the index number for pattern instance.
- Under the other columns, specify the coordinates for the holes; refer to Figure-176.

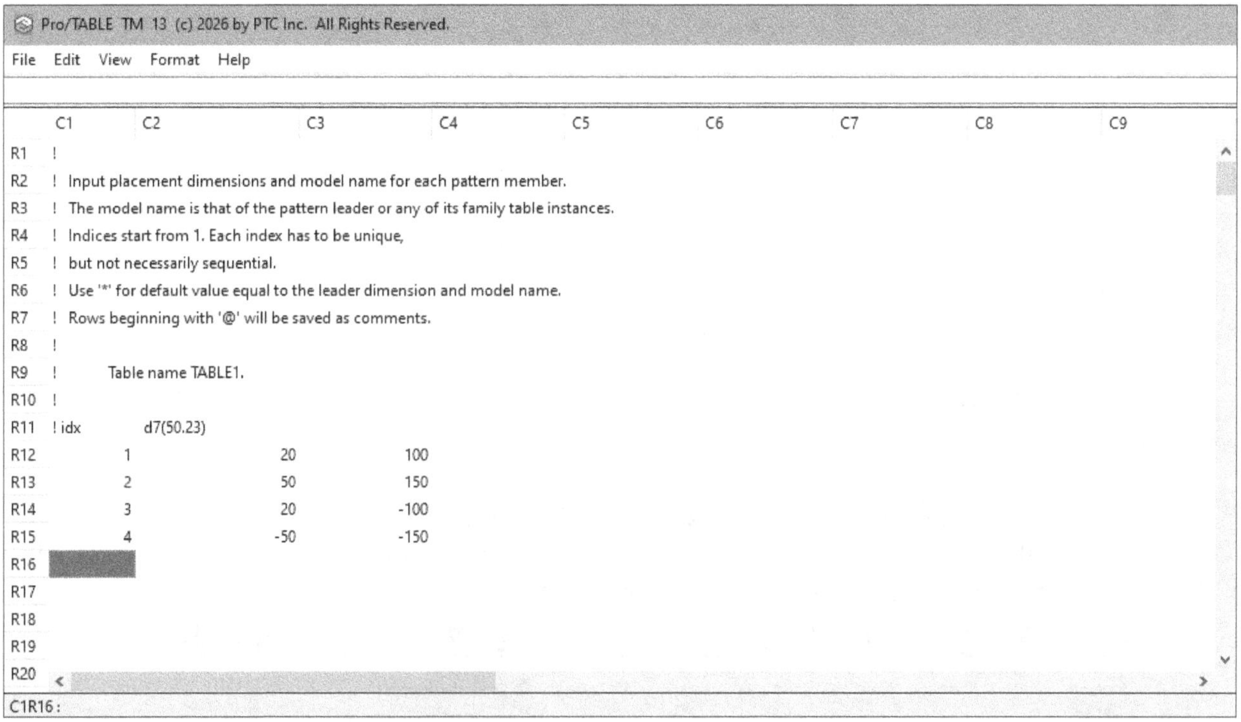

Figure-176. Table after specifying coordinates

- After specifying the coordinates, click on the **Exit** option from the **File** menu in the dialog box. Preview of the pattern will be displayed.
- Click on the **OK** button from the **Pattern** contextual tab.

Creating pattern using Curve option

- Select the **Curve** option from the drop-down in the **Type** area of the contextual tab. The **Pattern** contextual tab will be displayed as shown in Figure-177.

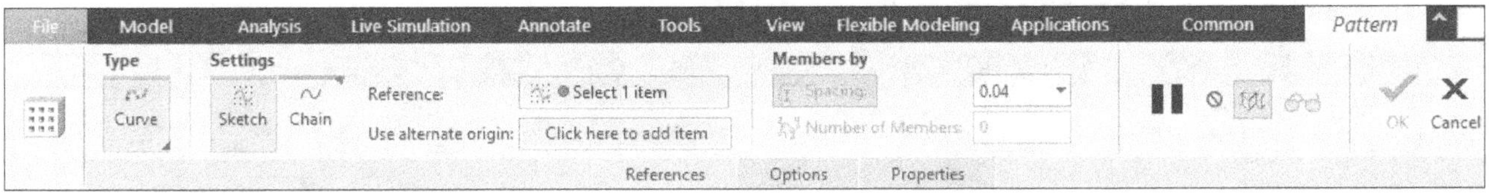

Figure-177. Pattern contextual tab for curve option

- Click on the **References** tab and click on the **Define** button from it; refer to Figure-178. The **Sketch** dialog box will be displayed.

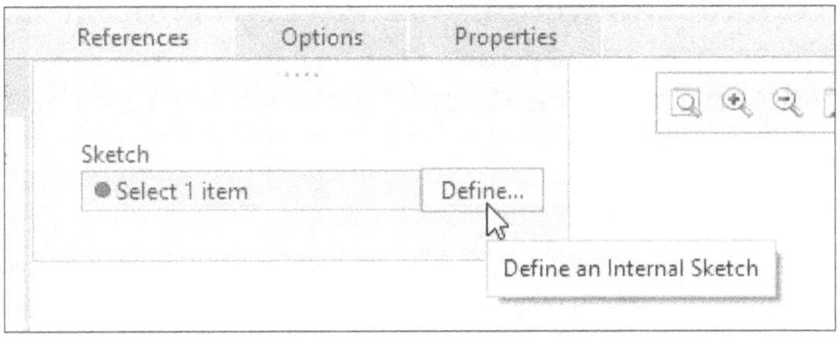

Figure-178. Reference tab

- Create a curve along which you want to create the pattern; refer to Figure-179. Click on the **OK** button from the **Sketch** contextual tab. Preview of the pattern will be displayed.

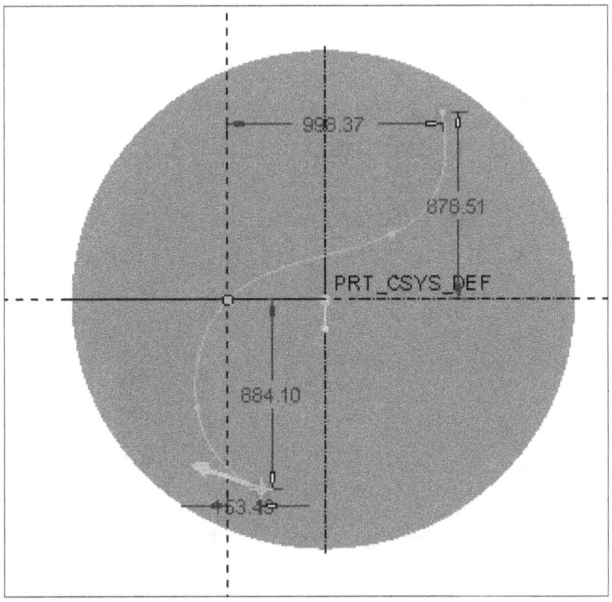

Figure-179. Curve for pattern

- Click on the **OK** button from the **Pattern** contextual tab.

You can use the **Point** option of the pattern in the same way as the **Curve** option do. Note that when you click in the empty area of model when **Pattern** tool is active then options to switch between various pattern types will be displayed in a mini toolbar.

Geometry Pattern

The **Geometry Pattern** tool works in the same way as the **Pattern** tool do but you can use the **Geometry Pattern** tool to also pattern the geometric entities like centerline, curves, and so on. The procedure to use this tool is given next.

- Select the entity that you want to pattern and click on the **Geometry Pattern** tool from the **Pattern** drop-down in the **Ribbon**. The **Geometry Pattern** contextual tab will be displayed as shown in Figure-180.

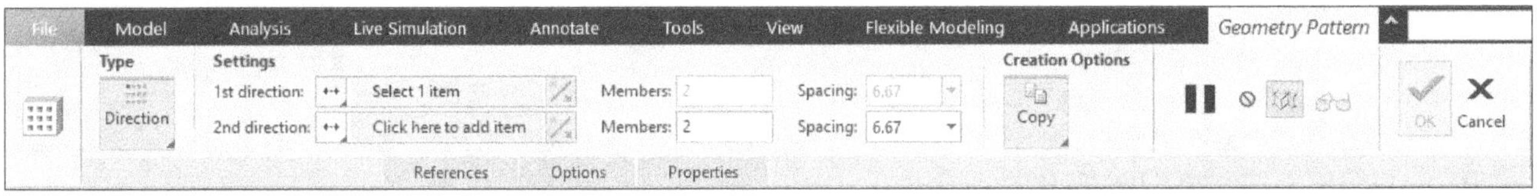

Figure-180. Geometry Pattern contextual tab

- The options in the drop-down of **Type** area in the **Geometry Pattern** contextual tab has the same options as were in the **Pattern** contextual tab. So, we are not going to discuss these options again.
- Click on the drop-down from **Creation Options** area of the contextual tab; refer to Figure-181.

Figure-181. Options for changing pattern topology

- The options in the drop-down are discussed next.

Attach button : Using this option, you can create geometric pattern trimmed automatically to adjust with the base surface; refer to Figure-182.

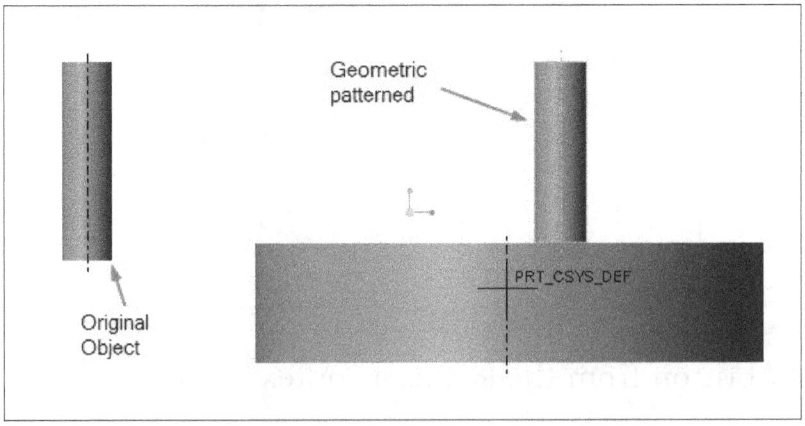

Figure-182. Geometric pattern with Flexible modeling attach

Copy button : Using this option, you can create only geometries and the attached solid/surface is not copied; refer to Figure-183.

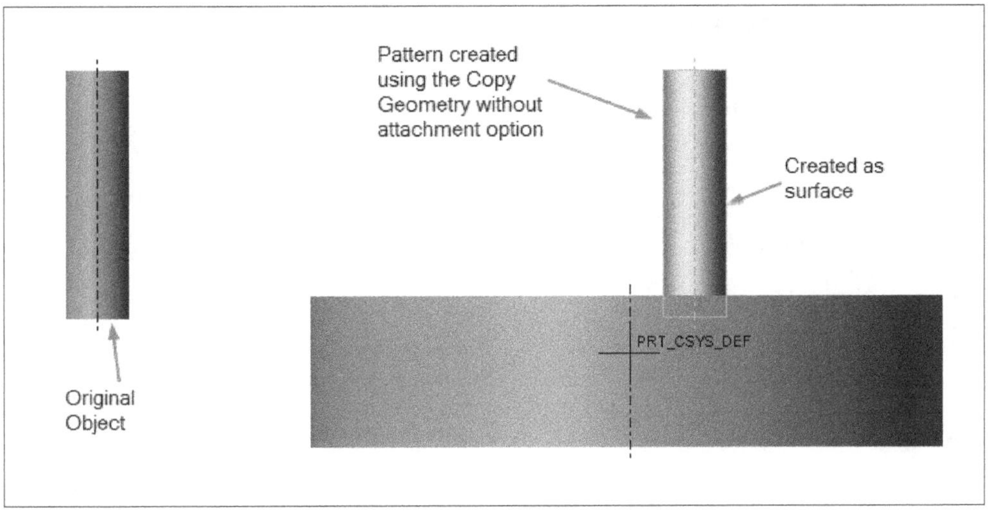

Figure-183. Geometric pattern using copy geometry without attachment

Fill with Solid button : Using this option, you can create solid models delimited by contacting surfaces.

Similarly, you can use the other options in the drop-down.

Pattern Table

The **Pattern Table** tool is used to manage various tables of pattern used in part or assembly. The procedure to use this tool is given next.

- Click on the **Pattern Table** tool from the **Pattern** drop-down in the **Editing** panel of the **Ribbon**. The **TABLES** dialog box will be displayed; refer to Figure-184. Note that in this example, we have already created two patterns using the **Table** option.

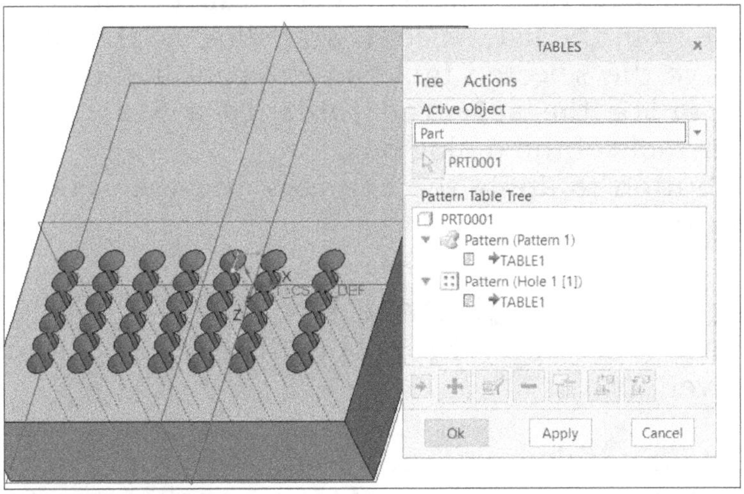

Figure-184. TABLES dialog box

- Double-click on the table that you want to edit from the dialog box. The **Pro/TABLE** dialog box for selected table will be displayed; refer to Figure-185.

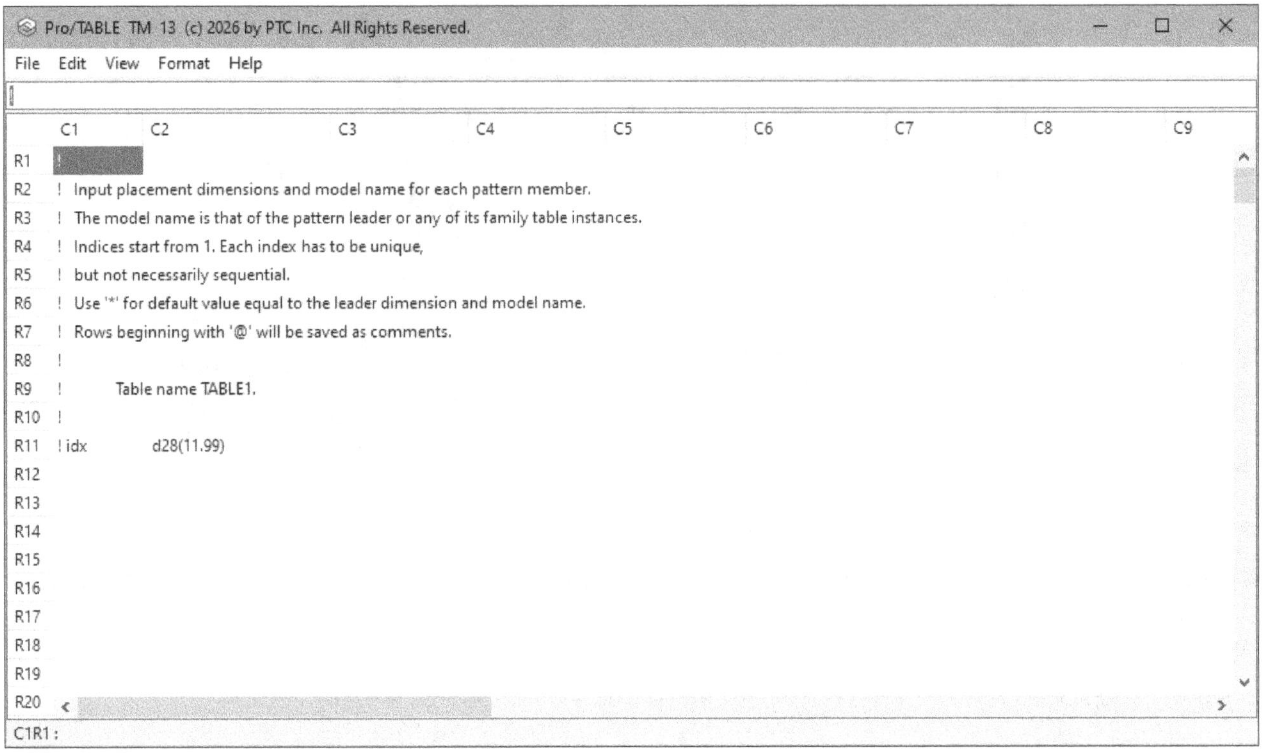

Figure-185. ProTable dialog box

- Edit the table and close the dialog box.
- To add a new table, click on the button at the bottom in the dialog box. You will be prompted to specify name of the table. Enter desired name of table. The **Pro/TABLE** dialog box will be displayed as discussed earlier. Specify desired parameters and close the dialog box.
- If you want to activate the newly created table then select the table from the dialog box and click on the **Activate the selected table** button.
- To remove a table from the list, select it and click on the **Remove** button.
- If you want to save the selected table as external file in the Working Directory then click on the **Write the selected table to a file** button. Similarly, you can use the other tools of the dialog box.
- Click on the **OK** button to apply the changes and then click on the **Regenerate** button to refresh the model.

Mirror Tool

The **Mirror** tool is used to create a mirror copy of the selected entities. The procedure to use this tool is given next.

- Select the entity/entities that you want to be mirrored.
- Click on the **Mirror** tool from the **Editing** panel in the **Ribbon**. The **Mirror** contextual tab will be displayed; refer to Figure-186.

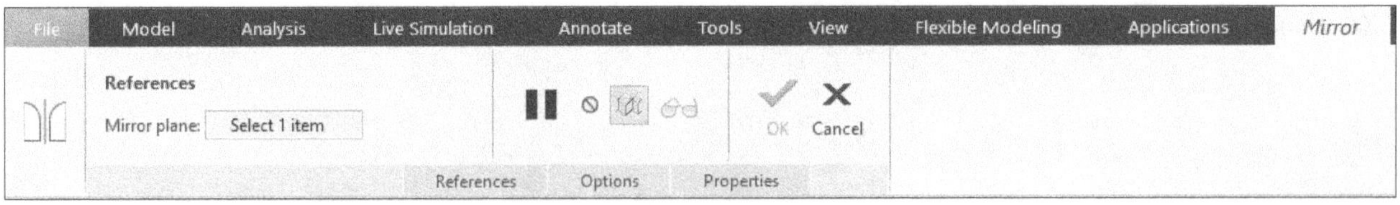

Figure-186. Mirror contextual tab

- Select the plane about which you want to create the mirror copy; refer to Figure-187.
- Click on the **Options** tab and clear the **Dependent copy** check box if you want to create copy of the feature as independent entity.
- Select the **Dependent copy** check box if you want to mirror feature to be dependent on parent feature. Select the **Partially dependent** radio button from **Options** tab to make the dimensions of mirror copy dependent on parent body. Select the **Fully dependent with options to vary** radio button from **Options** tab to make the mirrored body fully dependent on parent body.
- Click on the **OK** button from the **Ribbon**. The mirror copy of the entity will be created; refer to Figure-188.

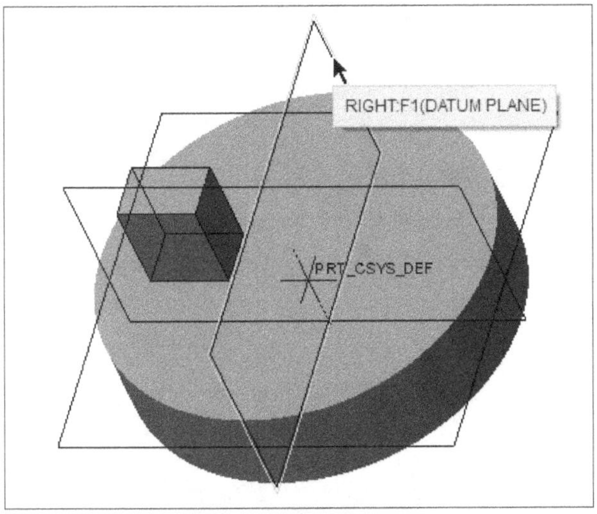

Figure-187. Plane selected for mirroring

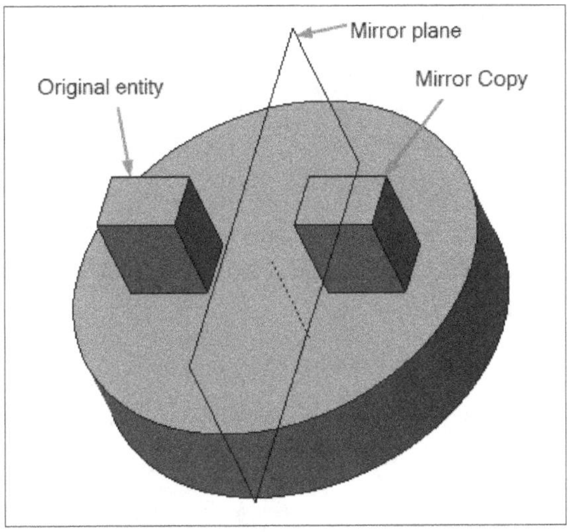

Figure-188. Mirror copy created

Extending Geometry

The **Extend** tool is used to extend a curve, edge, or surface to a selected boundary or distance. The procedure to use this tool is given next.

- Select the **Extend** tool from the **Editing** panel in the **Ribbon**. The **Extend** contextual tab will be displayed; refer to Figure-189.

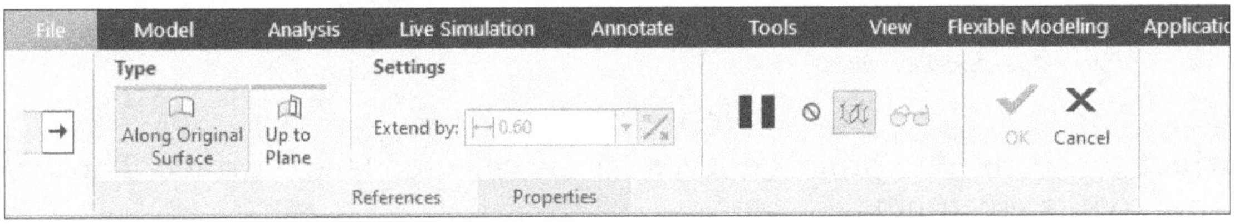

Figure-189. Extend contextual tab

- Select the **Along Original Surface** option from the **Type** area to extend the surface by a value along the original surface. Click in the **Extend by** edit box and specify desired value to define the distance to extend geometry.
- Select the **Up to Plane** option to extend the surface to the reference plane. Select desired plane which you want to extend the edge chain.
- Select the edge which you want to extend the selected boundary; refer to Figure-190. The Preview of the extend will be displayed; refer to Figure-191.

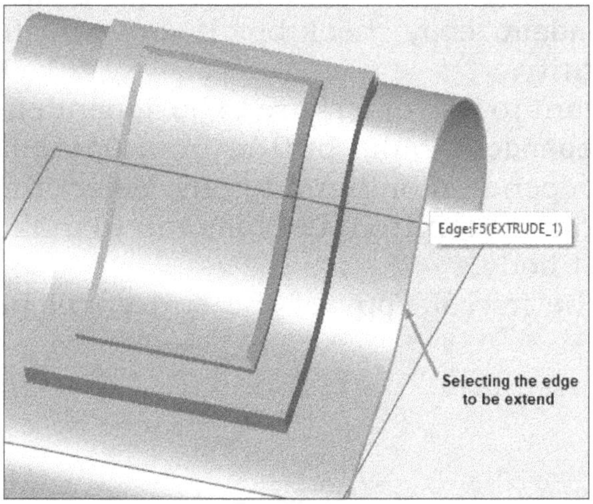

Figure-190. Selecting the edge of faces

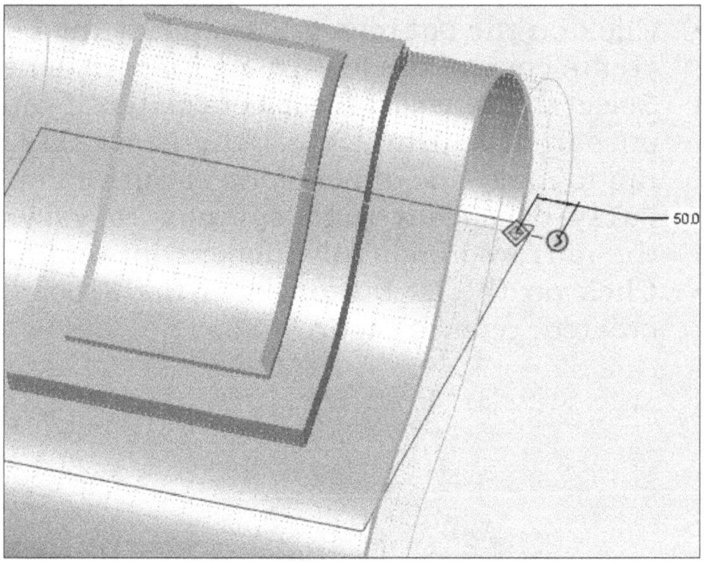

Figure-191. Preview of extend

- Click on the **OK** button from the **Ribbon**. The extend will be displayed; refer to Figure-192.

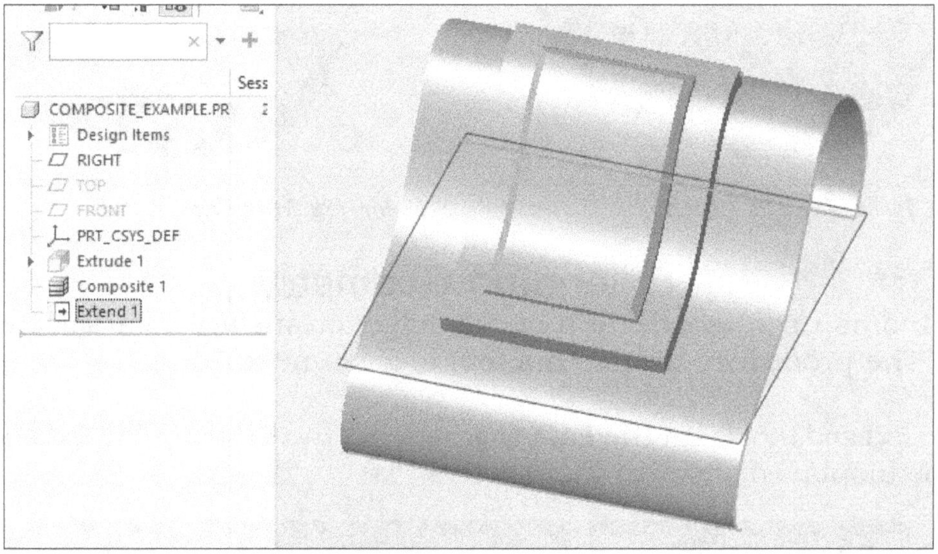

Figure-192. Extend created

Project Tool

The **Project** tool is used to project curves on the selected face/surface. The procedure to use this tool is given next.

- Select the **Project** tool from the **Editing** panel in the **Ribbon**. The **Project** contextual tab will be displayed; refer to Figure-193.

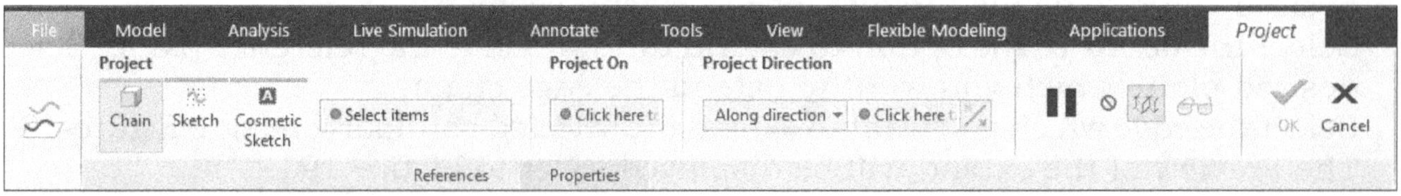

Figure-193. Project contextual tab

- Click on the **References** tab in the **Ribbon**. The expanded **References** tab will be displayed; refer to Figure-194.

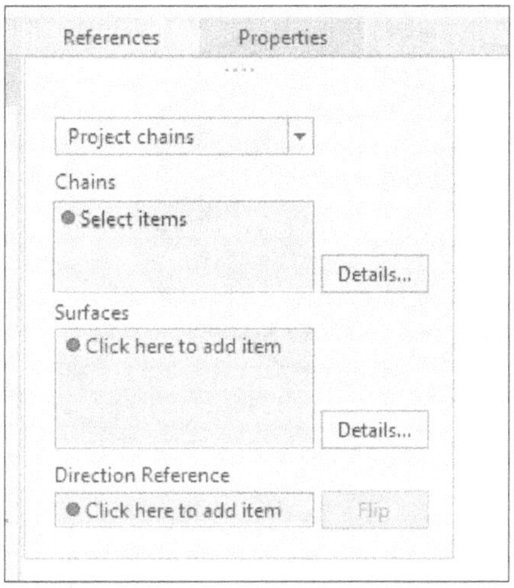

Figure-194. References tab for Project tool

- Click in the **Chains** collector in the **References** tab and select the curves which you want to project.
- Click in the **Surfaces** collector and select the surface/surfaces/face/faces on which you want to project the curves.
- Click in the **Direction Reference** collector and select a plane/edge for referencing direction of projection.
- Preview of the projected curves will be displayed; refer to Figure-195.

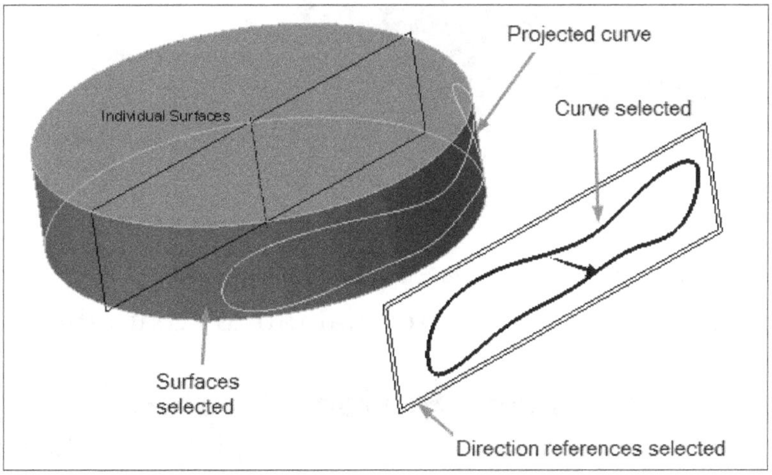

Figure-195. Curve projected

- Click in the drop-down from **Project Direction** area of the **Projected Curve** contextual tab and select desired option from the drop-down; refer to Figure-196.

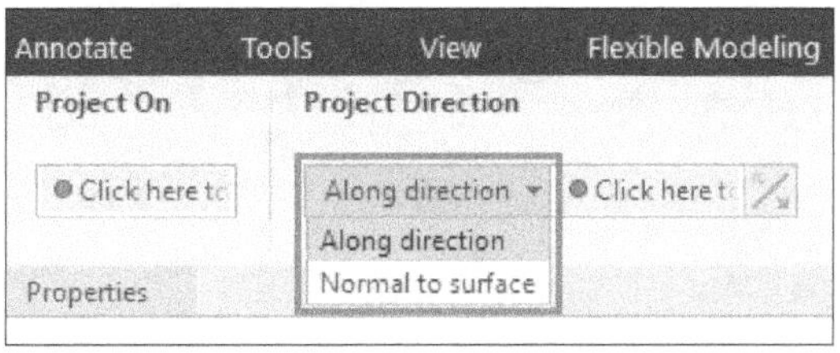

Figure-196. Direction drop-down

- Selecting the **Along direction** option generates a projected curve in the specified direction; refer to Figure-197.

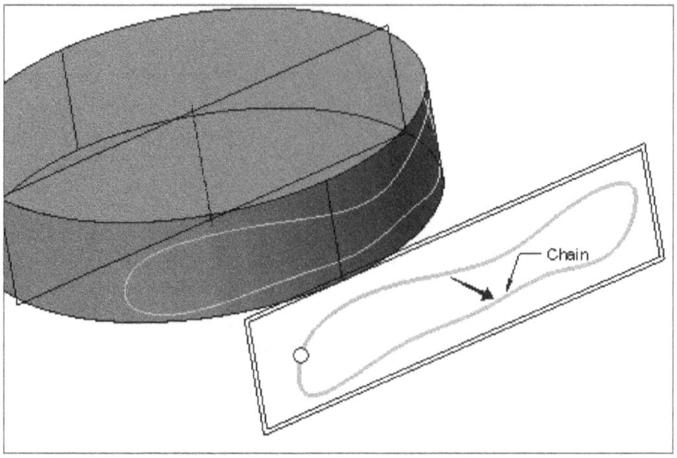

Figure-197. Curve projected using along direction option

- Selecting the **Normal to surface** option generates a projected curve normal to the selected surface/surfaces; refer to Figure-198.

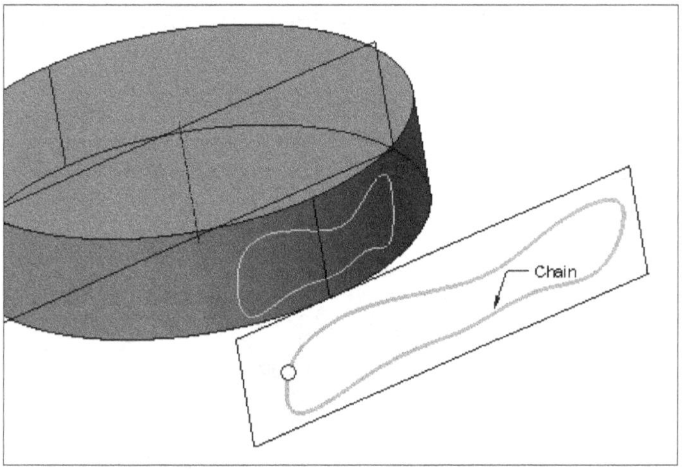

Figure-198. Curve projected using normal to surface option

- Click on the **OK** button from the contextual tab to create the projected curve.

Separate Surface Region

The **Separate Surface Region** tool is used to separate surface regions from the original surface to a new surface. The procedure to use this tool is discussed next.

- Click on the **Separate Surface Region** tool from **Split** drop-down in the **Editing** panel of the **Ribbon**. The **Separate Surface Region** contextual tab will be displayed; refer to Figure-199.

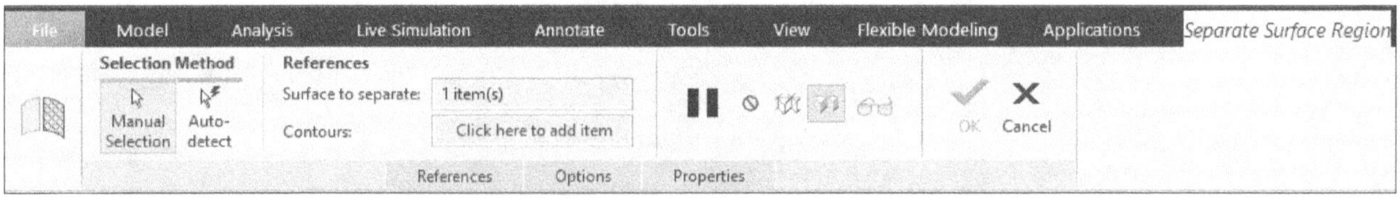

Figure-199. Separate Surface Region contextual tab

- Select desired option from **Selection Method** area of the contextual tab. Select **Manual Selection** option to select the surface(s) manually. Select the **Auto-detect** option to automatically detect the surfaces to be separated.
- Click on the **Surface to separate** collector from **References** area of the **Ribbon** and select the surface region you want to separate.

- Click on the **Contours** collector from **References** area of the **Ribbon** and select the surface region you want to separate to form a new surface; refer to Figure-200.

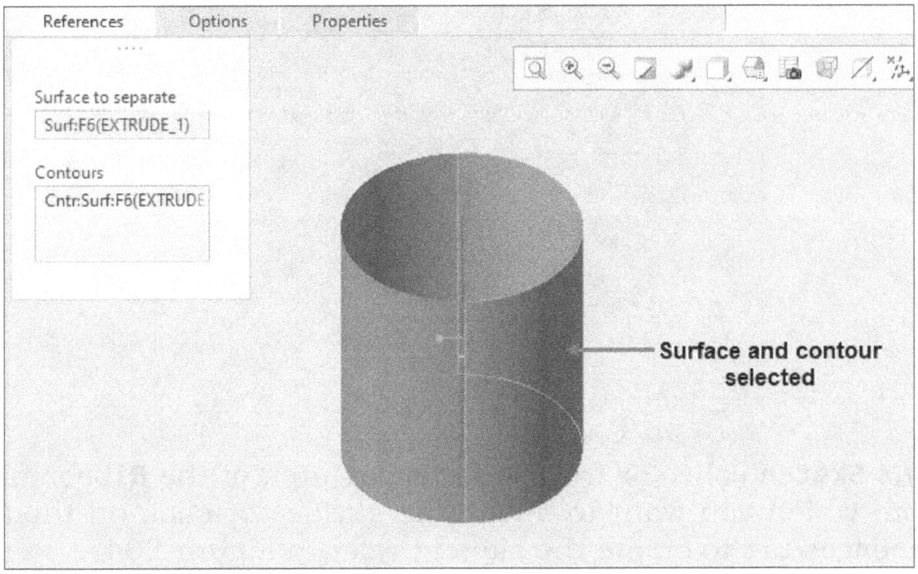

Figure-200. Surface and contour selected

- Select desired option from **Options** tab of the **Ribbon** to create the new surface.
- After specifying desired parameters click on the **OK** button from the contextual tab. A new separate surface will be created; refer to Figure-201.

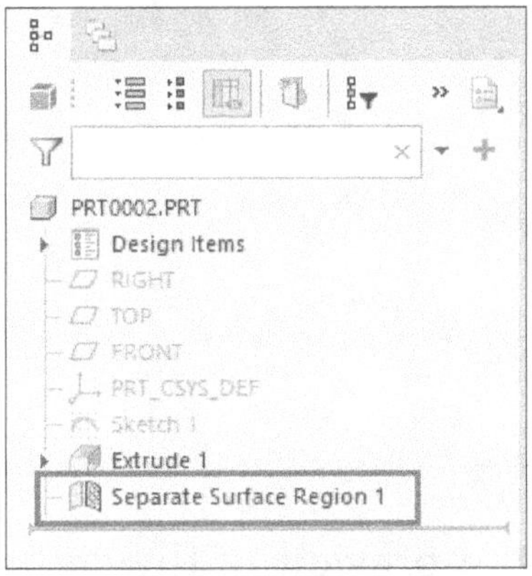

Figure-201. Separate surface created

Divide Surface Tool

The **Divide Surface** tool is used to split a surface to allow you to apply loads, constraints, measures or idealizations on a particular portion of a surface. The procedure to use this tool is discussed next.

- Click on the **Divide Surface** tool from **Split** drop-down in the **Editing** panel of the **Ribbon**. The **Divide Surface** contextual tab will be displayed; refer to Figure-202.

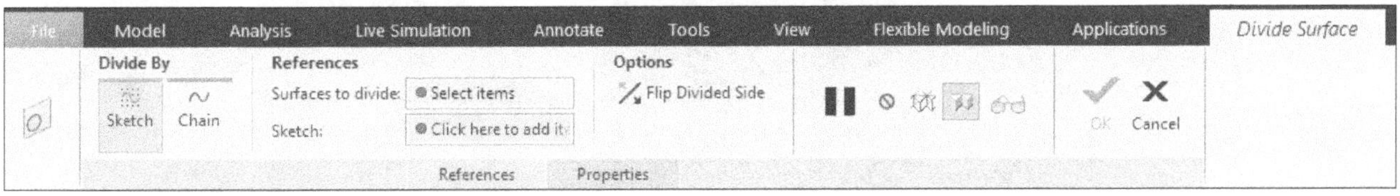

Figure-202. Divide Surface contextual tab

- Click in the **Surfaces to divide** collector from **References** area of the **Ribbon** and select the surface you want to divide; refer to Figure-203.

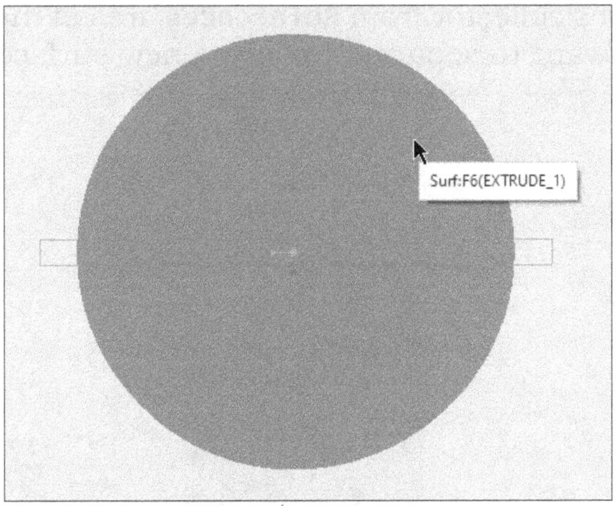

Figure-203. Selecting the surface to split

- Click in the **Sketch** collector from **References** area of the **Ribbon** and select the sketch from which you want to divide the surface or click on the **Define** button from **References** tab to create the sketch; refer to Figure-204.

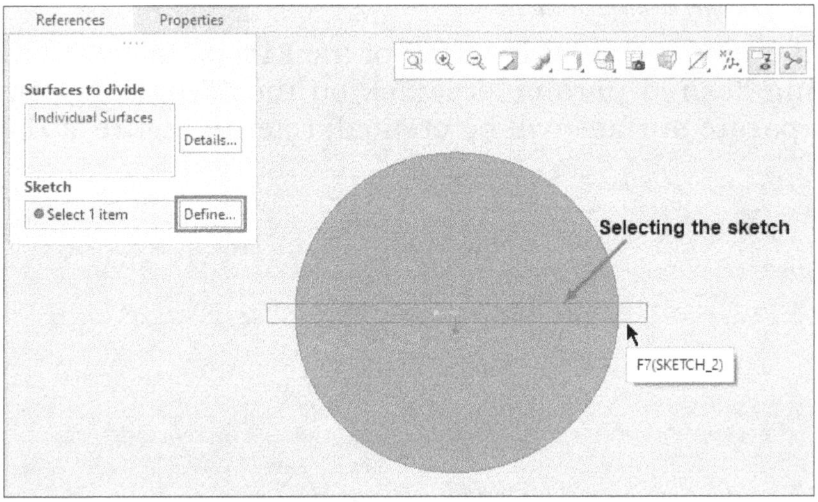

Figure-204. Selecting the sketch

- After selecting the sketch, the preview of divided surface will be displayed; refer to Figure-205.

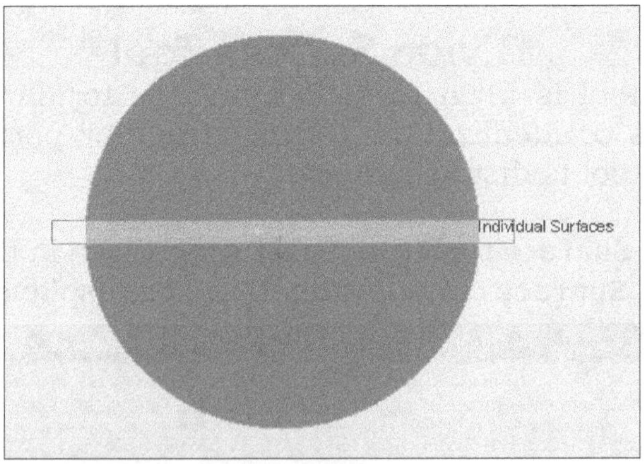

Figure-205. Preview of divided surface

- Click on the **Flip Divided Side** button from **Options** area of the **Ribbon** to flip the side that will become the new surface.

- After specifying desired parameters, click on the **OK** button from the contextual tab. The surface will be divided.

Unify Surfaces Tool

The **Unify Surfaces** tool is used to unify consecutive geometry surfaces into a single surface. The procedure to use this tool is discussed next.

- Click on the **Unify Surfaces** tool from **Editing** panel in the **Ribbon**. The **Unify Surfaces** contextual tab will be displayed; refer to Figure-206.

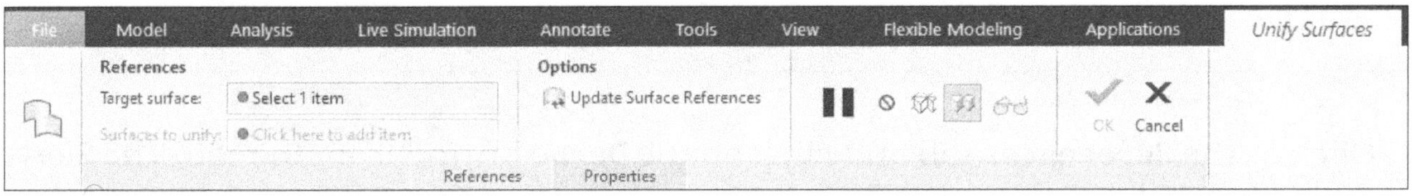

Figure-206. Unify Surfaces contextual tab

- Click in the **Target surface** collector from **References** area of the **Ribbon** and select the surface which you want to retain in the resulting geometry; refer to Figure-207.
- Click in the **Surfaces** to unify collector from **References** area and select the surface you want to merge into the target surface; refer to Figure-208.

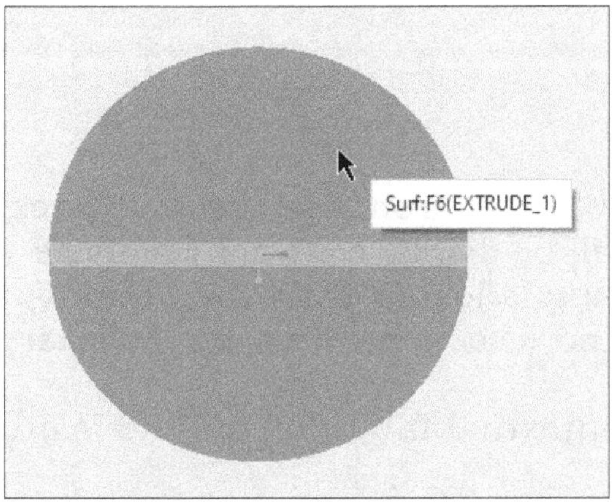

Figure-207. Selecting the surface

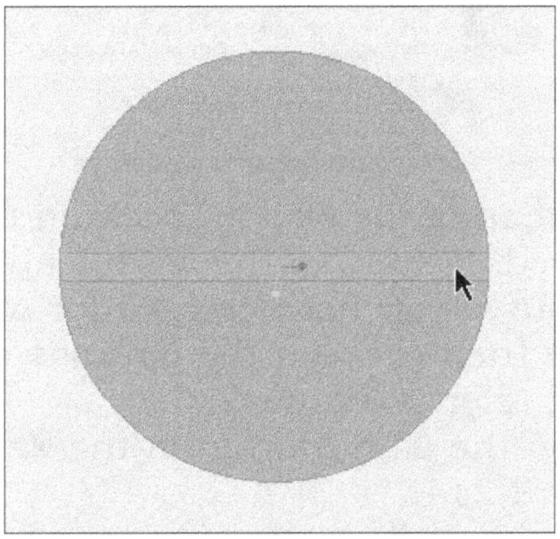

Figure-208. Selecting the other surface to be merged

- After specifying desired parameters, click on the **OK** button from the contextual tab. The surfaces will be merged; refer to Figure-209.

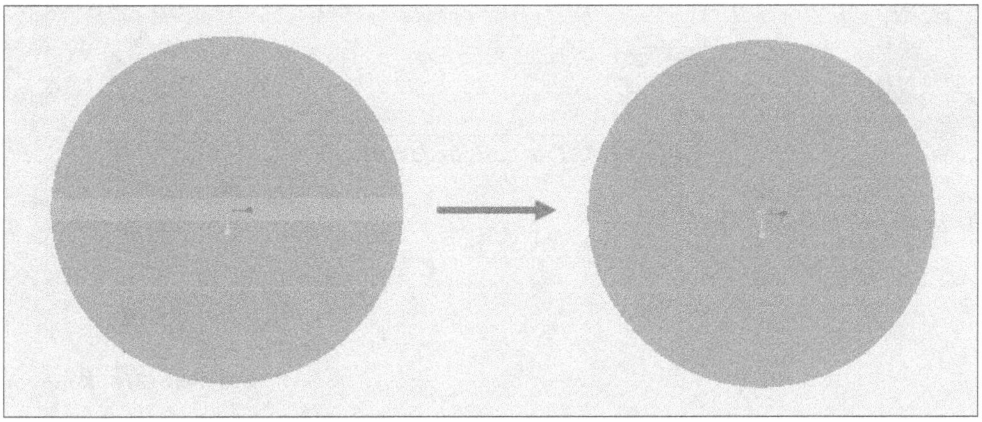

Figure-209. Surfaces merged

Wrap Tool

The **Wrap** tool, as the name suggests, is used to wrap a curve around the selected cylindrical surface. The procedure to use this tool is given next.

- Click on the **Wrap** tool from the expanded **Editing** panel in the **Ribbon**. The **Wrap** contextual tab will be displayed; refer to Figure-210.

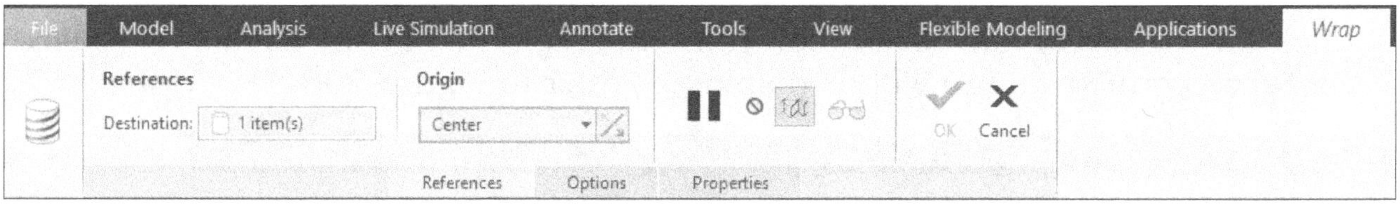

Figure-210. Wrap contextual tab

- Click in the **References** tab and click on the **Define** button from the tab. The **Sketch** dialog box will be displayed.
- Create a sketched curve with coordinate system; refer to Figure-211. Note that the sketch curve will be wrapped around the cylinder.

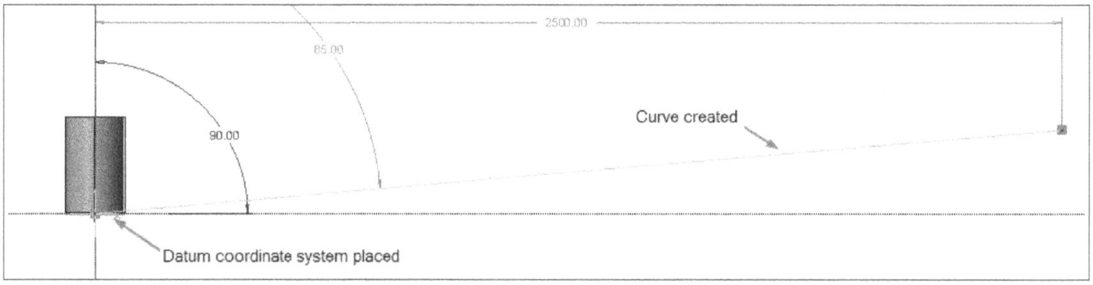

Figure-211. Sketch created for wrap feature

- After creating the sketch, click on the **OK** button from the **Sketch** contextual tab displayed. Preview of the wrap feature will be displayed; refer to Figure-212.
- If the curve you have created for wrapping is longer than the limits of selected surface then click on the **Options** tab and select the **Trim at boundary** option from it; refer to Figure-213.
- Click on the **OK** button from the **Wrap** contextual tab to create the feature; refer to Figure-214.

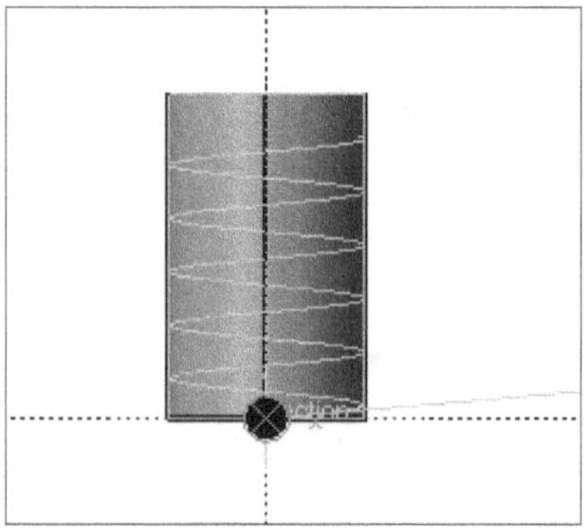

Figure-212. Preview of wrap feature

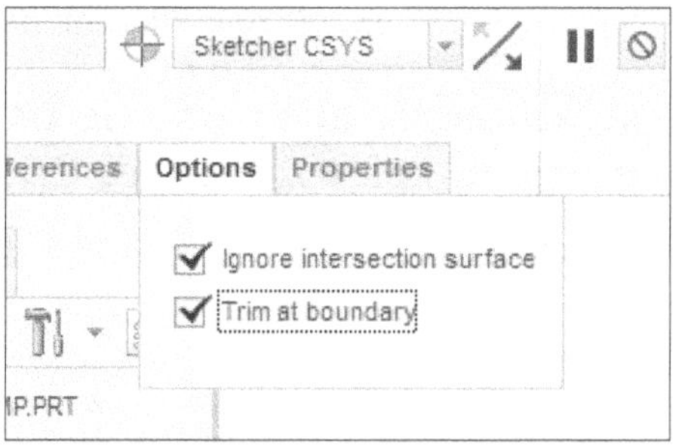

Figure-213. Trim at boundary option

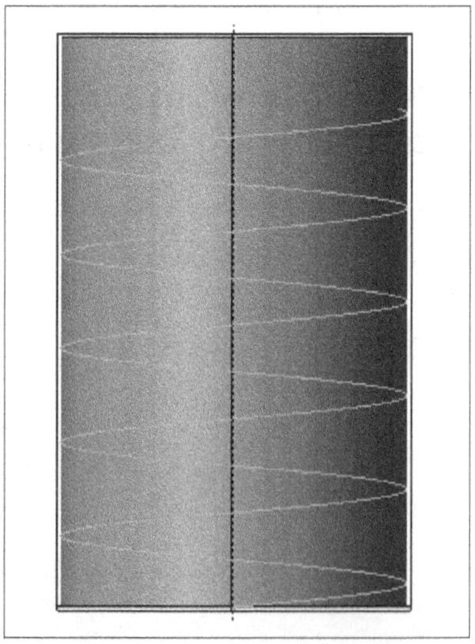

Figure-214. Wrap feature created

Warp Tool

The **Warp** tool is used to modify the shape of selected solid model. The procedure to use this tool is given next.

- Click on the **Warp** tool from the expanded **Editing** panel in the **Ribbon**. The **Warp** contextual tab will be displayed; refer to Figure-215.

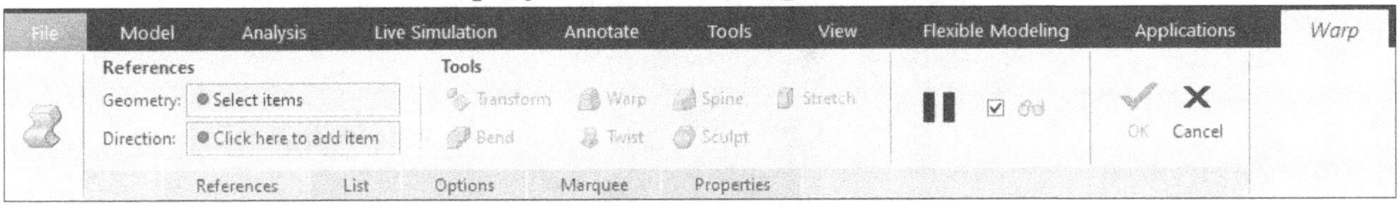

Figure-215. Warp contextual tab

- Select the solid model that you want to deform. The options in the **Warp** contextual tab will become active; refer to Figure-216.

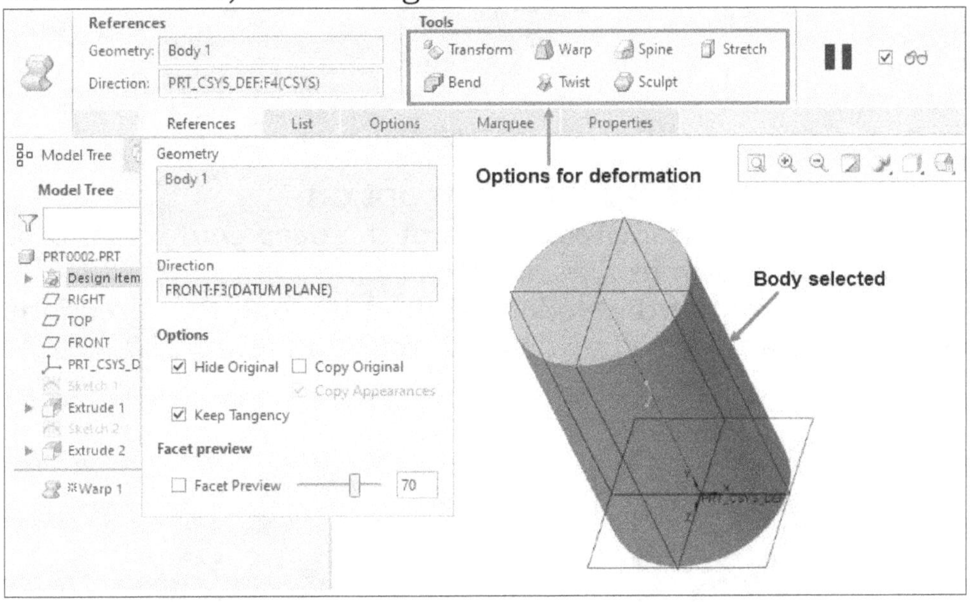

Figure-216. Warp contextual tab with active options

The use of each deformation option is given next.

Using the Transform option

- Click on the **Transform** option from **Tools** area of the **Warp** contextual tab. The model will be displayed as shown in Figure-217.

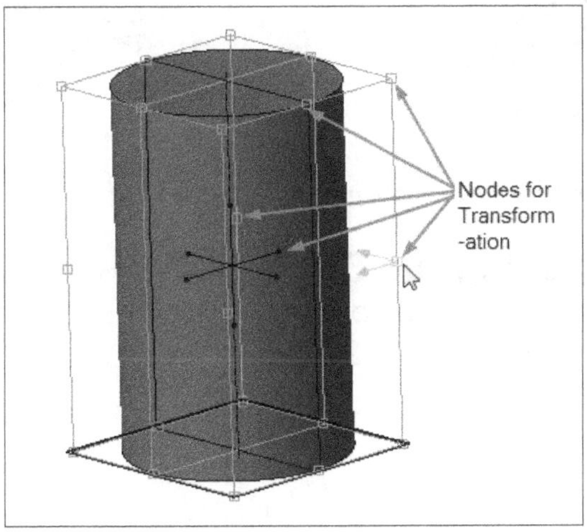

Figure-217. Model after selecting Transform option

- Move the cursor on any of the node and drag it along the directions displayed. The model will be transformed as desired; refer to Figure-218.

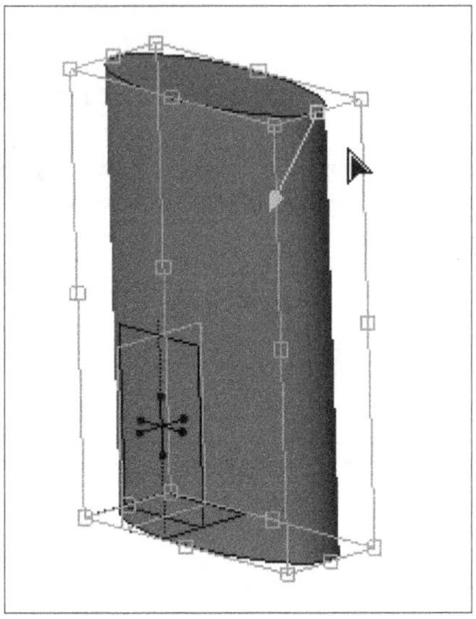

Figure-218. After transformation

Using the Warp option

- Click on the **Warp** option from **Tools** area of the **Warp** contextual tab. The model will be displayed as shown in Figure-219.
- Move the cursor on any of the node and drag it along the directions displayed. The model will be transformed as desired; refer to Figure-220.

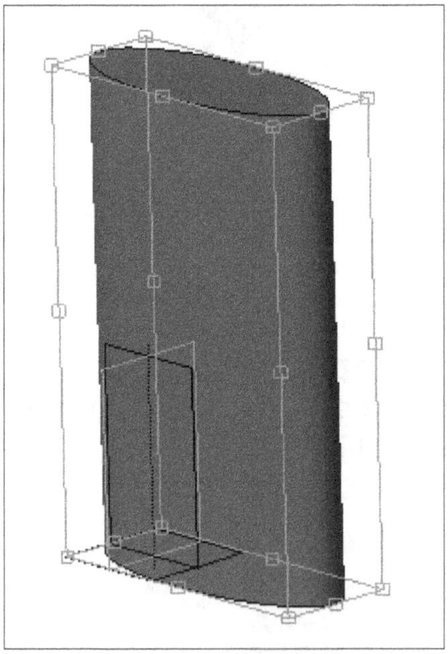

Figure-219. Model after selecting Warp option

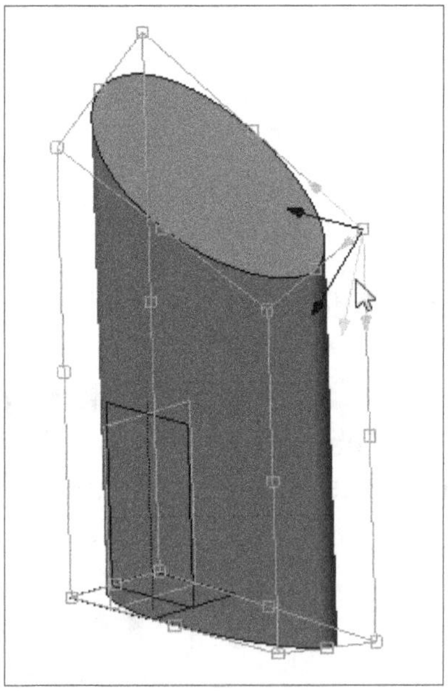

Figure-220. Model after applying warp option

Using the Spine option

- For using the **Spine** option of **Warp** tool, we must have a spline already created in the modeling area; refer to Figure-221.

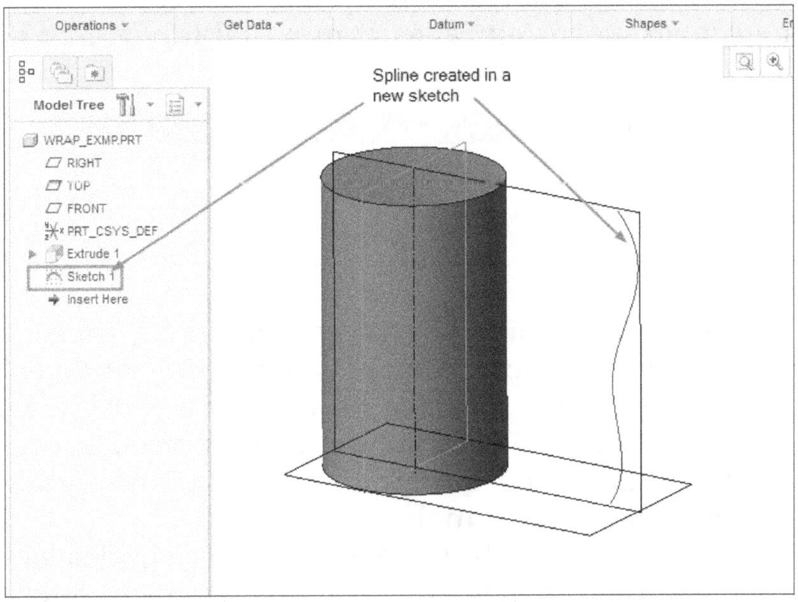

Figure-221. Spline sketched

- Now, start the **Warp** tool, select the model and click on the **Spine** option from **Tools** area of the **Warp** contextual tab. You are asked to select the spline. Select the spline sketched. The model will be displayed as shown in Figure-222.
- Move the cursor on any of the node and drag it along the directions displayed. The model will be transformed as desired; refer to Figure-223.

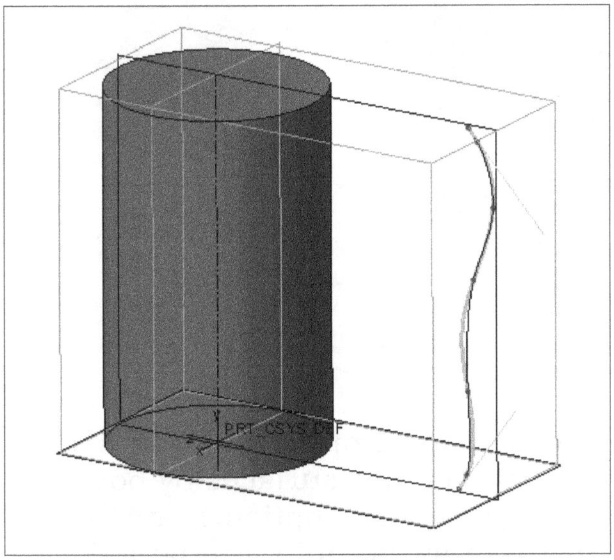

Figure-222. Model after selecting Spline option

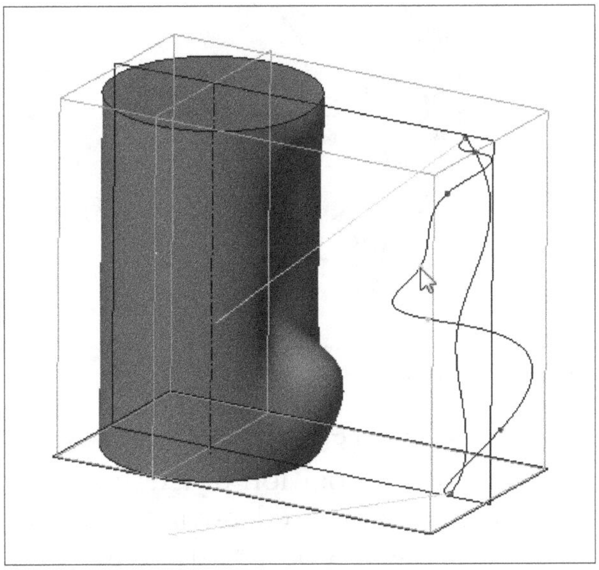

Figure-223. Model after using Spline option

- Similarly, you can use the other options.

Note that for engineering point of view, the **Warp** tool does not find much significance but if you want to display deformed objects then you can use this tool.

Approximate Surfaces

The **Approximate Surfaces** tool is used to create a new surface based on the selected surfaces, either to replace them or to make a copy. The procedure to use this tool is discussed next.

- Click on the **Approximate Surfaces** tool from the expanded **Editing** panel in the **Ribbon**. The **Approximate Surfaces** contextual tab will be displayed; refer to Figure-224.

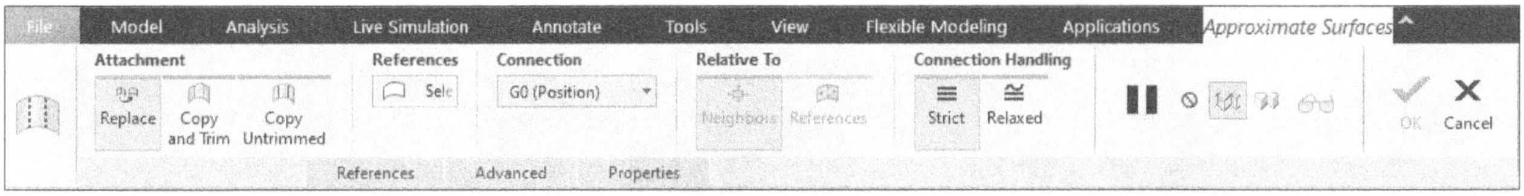

Figure-224. Approximate Surfaces contextual tab

- On selecting the **Replace** option from **Attachment** area, the referenced surfaces will be replaced by the new approximated surface. Select **Copy and Trim** option to create a new approximated surface as a separate quilt, while keeping the original surfaces unchanged. Select the **Copy Untrimmed** option to create a new approximated surface as a separate quilt without trimming its boundaries and the original surfaces will remain unchanged.
- Click on the **Select items** button from **References** area and select desired surfaces from a single body to create a new approximated surface; refer to Figure-225.

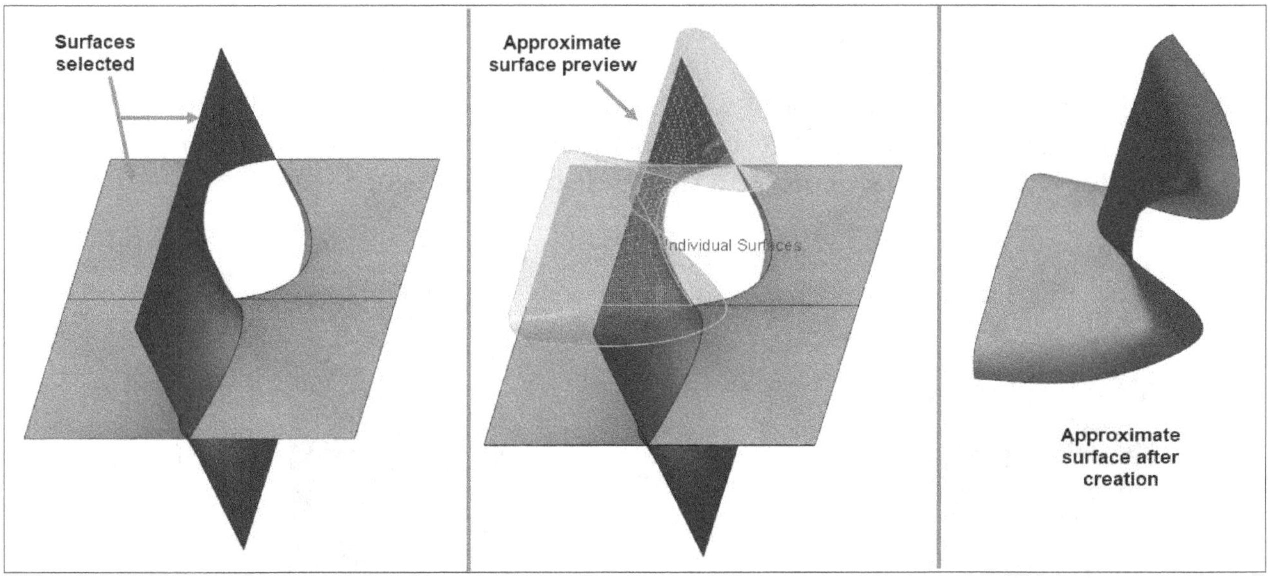

Figure-225. Approximate surface created

- Select the **G0 (Position)** option from the **Connection** drop-down in the **Ribbon** to maintain the position of the boundaries of the reference surfaces by boundaries of the approximated surface. Select the **G1 (Tangency)** option from the drop-down to maintain the tangency of the reference surfaces by the boundaries of the approximated surface.
- Select the **Neighbors** option from the **Relative To** area to maintain tangency of the neighboring surfaces by boundaries of the approximated surface. Select the **References** option to tangent the approximated surface to the reference surfaces.
- Select the **Strict** option from the **Connection Handling** area to met all the boundary conditions. Select the **Relaxed** option to allow tolerance for the boundary conditions.
- Click on the **Advanced** tab of the **Ribbon**. The options will be displayed; refer to Figure-226.

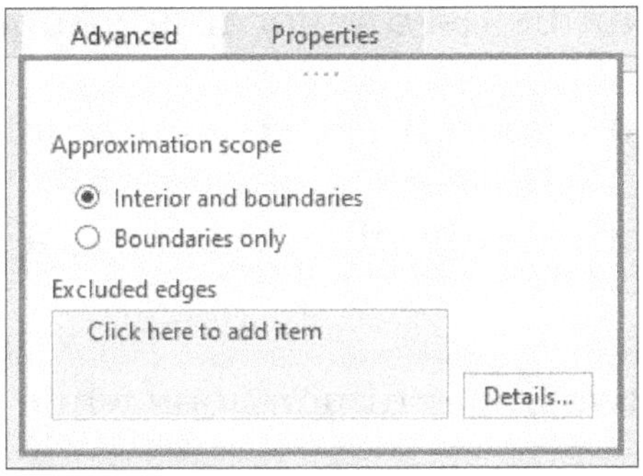

Figure-226. Advanced tab

- Select **Interior and boundaries** radio button from the **Approximation scope** area to create the approximated surface using the boundary edges and the surface area. Select **Boundaries only** radio button to create the approximated surface using only on the boundary edges.
- Click on the **Excluded edges** selection button and select desired edges to be excluded to create approximated surface.
- After specifying desired parameters, click on **OK** button from the **Ribbon**. The approximated surface will be created; refer to Figure-207.

In the next chapter, we will work on some practical and then we will practice on some complex models.

SELF ASSESSMENT

1. The **Hole** tool is available in .... panel of the **Ribbon**.

(a) Shapes (b) Engineering
(c) Datum (d) Editing

2. Which of the following tools is used to create rounds and fillet at the sharp edges.

(a) Draft (b) Shell
(c) Round (d) Chamfer

3. Which of the following tool is used to modify shape of selected solid body using drag points?

(a) Wrap (b) Warp
(c) Toroidal Bend (d) Spinal Bend

4. The .... tool is used to create round at the all sharp edges of the model at once.

5. The .... tool is used to create chamfer at the corner created by intersection of edges.

6. The .... tool is used to project curves on the selected face/surface.

7. The **Shell** tool is used to apply taper to the faces. (T/F)

8. The **Toroidal Bend** tool can be used to form tire from flat solid. (T/F)

9. The cosmetic sketch as an important base feature for other modeling tools. (T/F)

10. The **Pattern** tool is active only after selecting a feature of the model to be patterned. (T/F)

11. If you want to reference two linear dimensions while placing a hole, which option should you select?

a) Radial
b) Coaxial
c) Linear
d) Sketched

12. What is the use of the Sketched button in the Hole tool?

a) Create counterbore holes
b) Add predefined standard holes
c) Use custom profile sketches for holes
d) Create draft angles

13. What does the Standard button in the Hole tool allow you to do?

a) Apply lighting effects
b) Define custom shapes
c) Create holes with standard dimensions and thread types
d) Paint the hole surface

14. What does the Round tool primarily help with?

a) Coloring surfaces
b) Modeling with NURBS
c) Reducing stress at sharp edges
d) Meshing geometry

15. Which option in the Round tool is used to modify the round shape where three edges meet?

a) Draft
b) Transition
c) Sketch
d) Hole

16. What is the Auto Round tool used for?

a) Automatically apply fillets to sketches
b) Add texture to surfaces
c) Round all sharp edges of a model at once
d) Apply chamfer with constant radius

17. Which Dimension Scheme allows specifying two distances independently in the Edge Chamfer tool?

a) D x Angle
b) D1 x D2
c) Diameter x Radius
d) Chamfer Edge

18. How is a Corner Chamfer different from Edge Chamfer?

a) It applies chamfer to curved faces only
b) It uses user-defined profiles
c) It is applied at intersecting vertex of edges
d) It blends with round surfaces

19. What is the purpose of the Draft tool?

a) Hollow out a model
b) Apply tapered angle to faces
c) Add threads to a hole
d) Convert surfaces into solids

20. Which button is used in the Draft tool to include nearby tangent faces automatically?

a) Include Threads
b) Propagate Draft Surfaces
c) Add Profile
d) Include Sketched Hole

21. What happens if "Preserve Inlying Rounds" is selected in the Draft tool?

a) It removes chamfers
b) It removes sharp edges
c) It retains the rounds at transition faces
d) It reverses the draft direction

22. Which Draft Split option pivots the whole surface about the draft hinge?

a) Split by draft hinge
b) No split
c) Split by sketch
d) Independent split

23. What is the Shell tool used for?

a) Adding edges
b) Creating fillets
c) Hollowing out a model
d) Applying textures

24. In Shell tool, which option lets you give different thickness to specific faces?

a) Propagate
b) Draft angle
c) Non-default thickness
d) Exclude Surface

25. Which Shell option prevents shelling from cutting through solid at concave corners?

a) Extend Excluded Surfaces
b) Convex corners
c) Concave corners
d) Hollow corners

26. What must be selected first when using the Toroidal Bend tool?

a) Reference axis
b) Sketch entity
c) Flat face to fix during bending
d) Coordinate system

27. What option allows you to create a full 360-degree bend using Toroidal Bend?

a) Full Loop
b) Complete Bend
c) Full Rotation
d) 360 Bend

28. What is the primary function of the Spinal Bend tool?

a) To create thread profiles
b) To mirror solid bodies
c) To bend solid along a curve
d) To flatten a toroidal part

29. Which drop-down in Spinal Bend controls how far the body is bent?

a) Control Axis
b) Bend Extent
c) Bend Settings
d) Radius Extent

30. What does the Cosmetic Sketch tool allow you to do?

a) Create editable base geometry
b) Create visual-only sketches
c) Trim model edges
d) Define sweep paths

31. What is required for the groove sketch to be projected correctly?

a) Sketch on curved surface
b) Sketch on perpendicular plane
c) Plane must be parallel to surface
d) Surface must be hidden

32. What does the Designated Area tool define?

a) Cosmetic finish
b) Assembly connections
c) Functional region on the model
d) Threaded area

33. Which of the following is required before using Designated Area tool?

a) 3D curve
b) Datum axis
c) Closed loop sketch
d) Shell geometry

34. What is the ECAD Area tool used for?

a) Thermal analysis
b) Sketch optimization
c) Assigning circuit layout area
d) Adding structural ribs

35. What feature allows volume creation for ECAD areas?

a) Shape generator
b) Volume Mesh
c) 3D Volume checkbox
d) Thread Length

36. What does the Composite tool create?

a) Swept blend
b) Cosmetic thread
c) Laminate-based feature
d) Pattern

37. What is the purpose of the Layup Surface tool?

a) Define axis of symmetry
b) Define geometry of plies
c) Analyze draft angle
d) Create loft surface

38. What must the origin of Rosette and boundaries lie on in a Layup Surface?

a) Any surface
b) Coordinate system
c) Sketch plane
d) Layup surface

39. What is the main purpose of the Rosette tool in composite design?

a) To generate a mesh for simulation
b) To define material properties
c) To define the default coordinate system
d) To analyze stress distribution

40. What is the use of the Drop-off tool in ply creation?

a) To change ply thickness
b) To calculate weight
c) To define distance at ply ends for bonding
d) To connect two plies

41. When does the Color Mapping tool become active?

a) When you select a material
b) When a core is defined
c) When plies are created
d) After simulation is completed

42. Which mass computation method considers underlying plies in the laminate stack?

a) Based on mesh
b) Based on simulation
c) Based on layup surface
d) Based on underlying plies

43. Which type of ply requires selecting laminate zones?

a) Core Ply
b) Manual Ply
c) Zone Based Ply
d) Rosette Ply

44. Which option in the Solidify Plies dialog box is used to create a quilt consisting of the topmost and side surfaces of the laminate?

a) Add drop-off geometry
b) Keep unattached drop-offs as quilts
c) Create IML surface
d) Properties tab

45. What is the function of the Core tool?

a) To trim ply boundaries
b) To assign orientation
c) To create a thick base ply
d) To define stacking order

46. What does the Transition Plies tool help you create?

a) 3D laminate view
b) Material properties
c) Constant/variable offset between plies
d) Axis definitions for rosettes

47. What defines the splicing or darting trajectory in the Splice Plies tool?

a) Rosette system
b) Color map
c) Splicing curve
d) Drop-off offset

48. Which method in the Trim/Extend Ply tool allows you to extend up to a selected chain?

a) By Offset
b) By Contour
c) By Reference
d) By Chain

49. What can you do with the Laminate Zone tool?

a) Measure resin drop-off
b) Create a ply boundary
c) Group plies and cores by boundary
d) Simulate ply stress

50. Which function allows movement of rows up/down in the Zone Stacks dialog box?

a) Drop-down
b) Orientation column
c) Arrow buttons
d) Rosette selection

51. What is needed to create plies from zones using Plies From Zones tool?

a) Only material and orientation
b) Only rosette
c) Zone, rosette, and zone stack
d) Only a boundary chain

52. In the Laminate Section tool, which option enables free positioning of the clipping plane?

a) Orientation drop-down
b) 3D Dragger
c) Offset edit box
d) Auxiliary Display

53. What does the Auxiliary Display button do in Laminate Section tool?

a) Generates 3D mesh
b) Creates a new ply
c) Opens a 2D view of the section
d) Displays laminate stack table

54. What is the primary purpose of the Solidify Plies tool?

a) To simulate draping of plies
b) To create a laminate consolidation of the plies
c) To export plies as DXF files
d) To generate calibration files

55. In the Solidify Plies tool, what does the 'Create IML surface' option do?

a) It creates a pattern of plies
b) It displays ply boundaries
c) It creates a quilt of top and side surfaces
d) It resets all input parameters

56. Which tool is used to generate projection data and calibration files for laser projectors?

a) Draping Simulation
b) Solidify Plies
c) Export Flat Pattern
d) Laser Projection

57. What is the function of the Core Sample tool?

a) Project laser paths
b) Analyze ply geometry
c) Analyze laminate composition at a point
d) Export ply reports

58. Which section displays the total thickness in the Core Sample tool?

a) Results Summary
b) Setup area
c) Results section
d) Feature tab

59. What does the Draping Simulation tool calculate?

a) Ply thermal conductivity
b) Ply flat patterns and production-ability
c) Ply mechanical strength
d) Calibration data

60. What happens if you haven't performed draping simulation and try to use Export Draping Summary?

a) Tool exports default data
b) It prompts for material properties
c) The tool remains inactive
d) It opens draping settings automatically

61. Which tab allows you to export notes with FIT alignment?

a) Annotations tab
b) Properties tab
c) File Naming Format tab
d) Datums tab

62. What does selecting 'Export each ply to a separate file' do?

a) Exports plies as single object
b) Saves time
c) Creates individual files for each ply
d) Merges ply annotations

63. In Dimension type pattern, what is needed to define pattern direction?

a) Angle
b) Reference dimension
c) Axis
d) Sketch

64. Which pattern type requires defining angular distance?

a) Fill
b) Direction
c) Axis
d) Curve

65. What is the purpose of the Fill option in pattern types?

a) Create circular pattern
b) Create a filled sketch with instances
c) Export patterns
d) Add material thickness

66. In Table pattern option, what is specified in idx column?

a) File name
b) Distance between instances
c) Index number for instances
d) Sketch constraints

67. What is the main difference between the Pattern tool and the Geometry Pattern tool?

a) Geometry Pattern can only pattern solids
b) Geometry Pattern can pattern geometric entities like curves and centerlines
c) Pattern tool is used for 2D shapes only
d) Pattern tool is not available in Creo

68. What is the purpose of the Pattern Table tool?

a) It creates mirror features
b) It manages various pattern tables used in part/assembly
c) It joins multiple patterns
d) It wraps geometry around surfaces

69. What action allows you to save a pattern table as a file in the Working Directory?

a) Activate selected table
b) Remove
c) Write the selected table to a file
d) OK

70. Which option in the Mirror tool makes the mirrored feature fully dependent but allows dimension variation?

a) Dependent copy
b) Partially dependent
c) Fully dependent with options to vary
d) Independent copy

71. Which tool separates a portion of a surface into a new surface?

a) Divide Surface
b) Separate Surface Region
c) Project
d) Unify Surfaces

72. What does the Divide Surface tool allow you to do?

a) Unify two surfaces
b) Apply loads and constraints on part of a surface
c) Mirror the body
d) Create patterns

73. What is the purpose of the Unify Surfaces tool?

a) To separate surfaces
b) To create mirrored bodies
c) To combine consecutive surfaces into one
d) To split sketches

74. Which collector allows selection of the surface to keep during surface unification?

a) References
b) Target surface
c) Merge
d) Main panel

75. What is the Wrap tool used for?

a) Copying solids
b) Projecting edges
c) Wrapping a curve around a cylindrical surface
d) Editing sketches

76. What option should be selected in the Wrap tool if the curve exceeds the surface boundary?

a) Wrap beyond
b) Trim at boundary
c) Clip excess
d) Boundary limit

77. What does the Warp tool do in Creo?

a) Projects curves
b) Unifies surfaces
c) Deforms solid models
d) Mirrors geometry

78. What is required to use the Spine option in the Warp tool?

a) A predefined mirror
b) A sketched spline
c) A solid pattern
d) A wrapped surface

FOR STUDENT NOTES

Answers to Self Assessment Questions

1. (b) **2.** (c) **3.** (b) **4.** Auto Round **5.** Corner Chamfer **6.** Project **7.** F **8.** T **9.** F **10.** T

Chapter 7

3D Modeling Advanced Practical and Practice

Topics Covered

The major topics covered in this chapter are:

- ***Practical 1***
- ***Practical 2***
- ***Practice 1 to Practice 6***

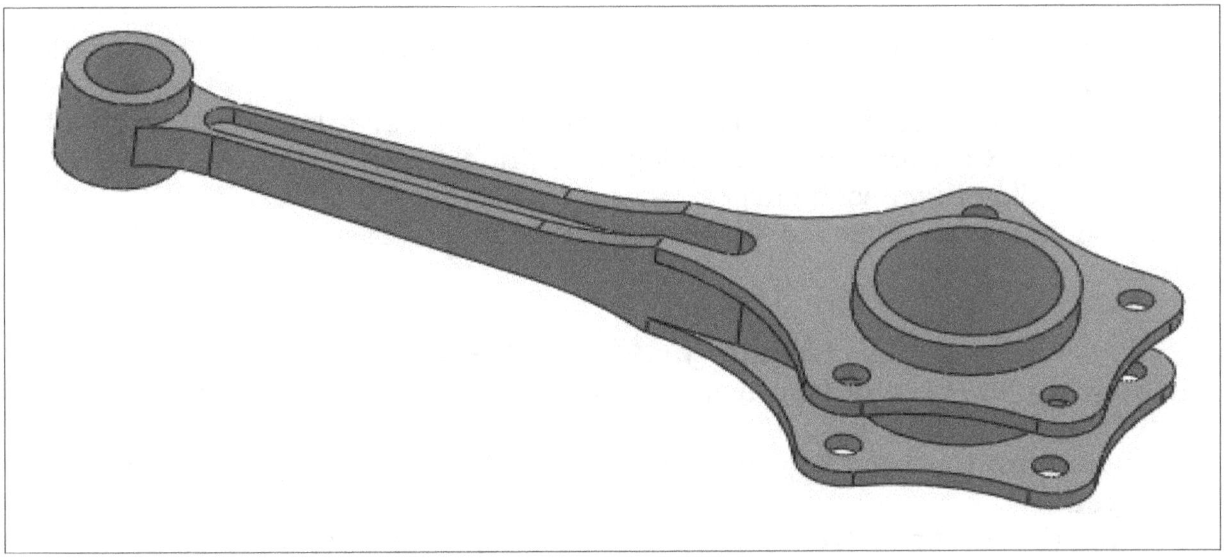

PRACTICAL 1

In this practical, we will create the model of a lever as shown in Figure-1.

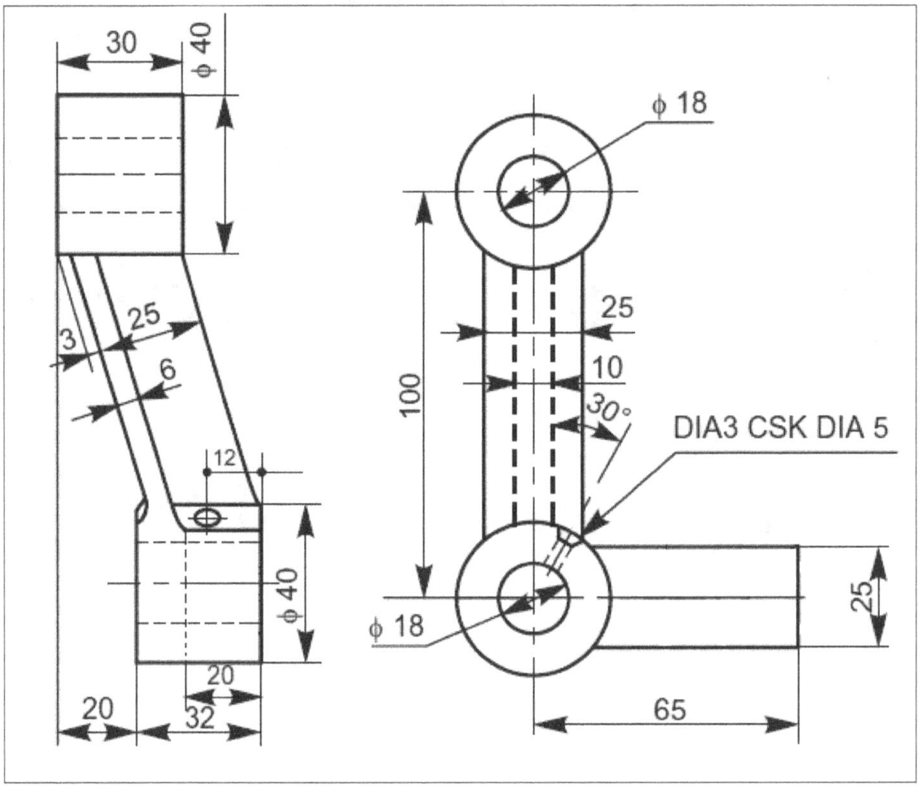

Figure-1. Practical 1

Starting Part Modeling

- Double-click on the Creo Parametric icon from the desktop to start Creo Parametric if not started already.
- Click on the **New** button from the **Data** panel in the **Ribbon**. The **New** dialog box will be displayed.
- Specify desired name for the file and clear the **Use default template** check box.
- Click on the **OK** button from the dialog box. The **New File Options** dialog box will be displayed as discussed earlier.
- Select the **mmns part solid abs** option from the dialog box and click on the **OK** button.

Creating Revolve feature

- Click on the **Revolve** button from the **Shapes** panel in the **Ribbon**. The **Revolve** contextual tab will be displayed.
- Select the **RIGHT** plane from the **Model Tree**. The sketching environment will be displayed.
- Click on the **Sketch View** button from the **In-Graphics** toolbar to make the sketching plane parallel to the screen if not gets by default.
- Create the sketch with geometric centerline as shown in Figure-2.
- Click on the **OK** button from the **Sketch** contextual tab. Preview of the revolve feature will be displayed.
- Click on the **OK** button from the **Revolve** contextual tab. The feature will be displayed; refer to Figure-3.

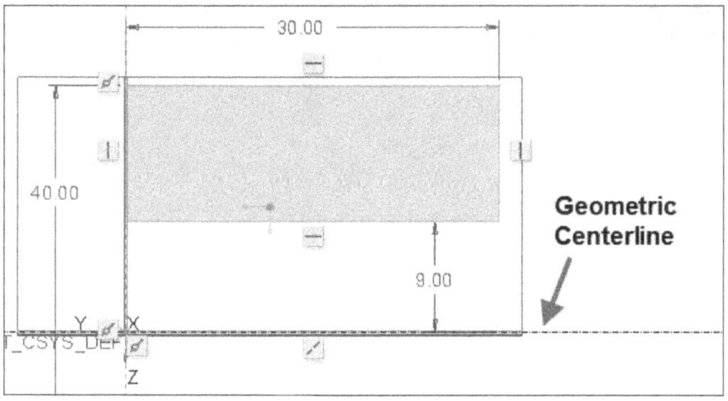

Figure-2. Sketch for revolve

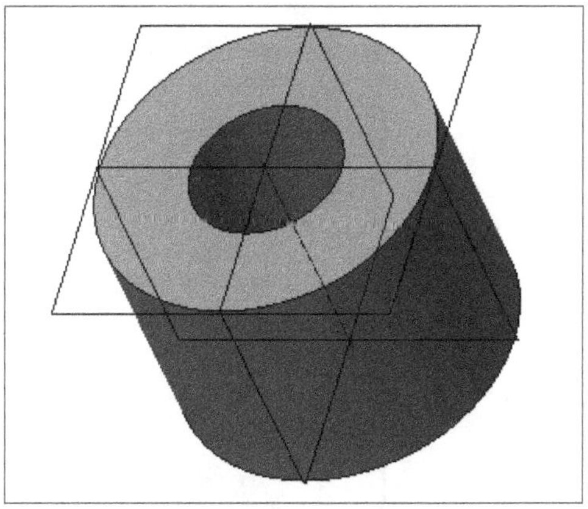

Figure-3. Revolve feature created

Creating another revolve feature

- Click on the **Revolve** tool from the **Shapes** panel in the **Ribbon**. The **Revolve** contextual tab will be displayed.
- Select the **RIGHT** plane and create the sketch as shown in Figure-4.
- Click on the **OK** button from the **Sketch** contextual tab and then from the **Revolve** contextual tab. The model will be displayed as shown in Figure-5.

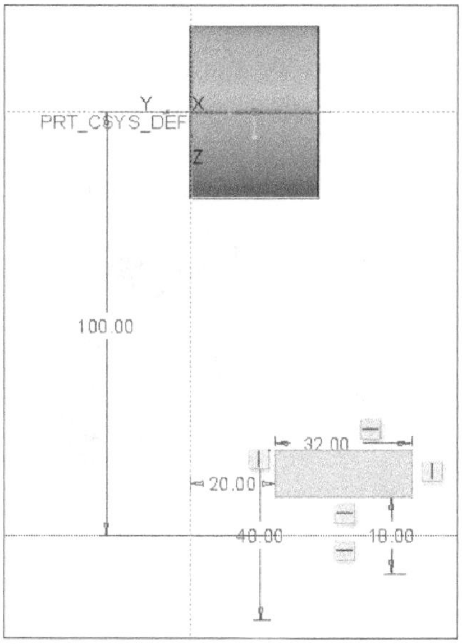

Figure-4. Sketch for other revolve feature

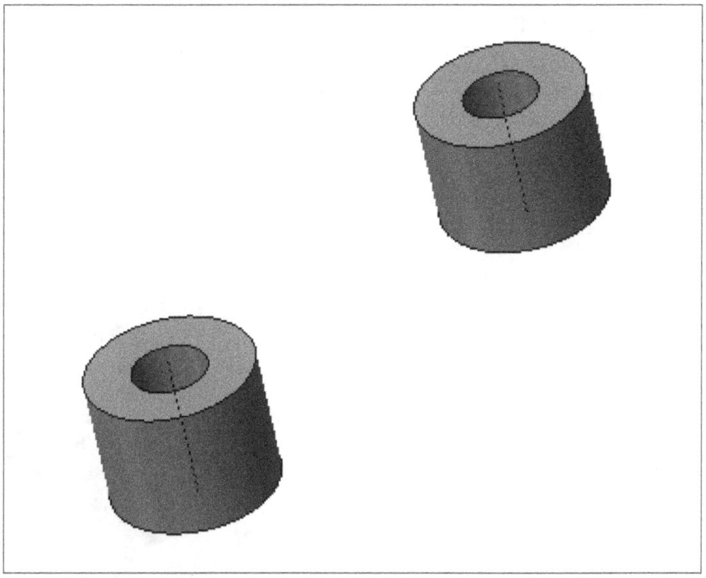

Figure-5. Model with revolved features

Creating the Extrude feature

- Click on the **Extrude** tool from the **Shapes** panel in the **Ribbon**. The **Extrude** contextual tab will be displayed.
- Select the **RIGHT** plane from the **Model Tree**. The sketching environment will be displayed.
- Click on the **Sketch View** button from the **In-Graphics** toolbar.
- Create a line coincident to the two vertex of the revolve features; refer to Figure-6.
- Click on the **Offset** tool from the **Sketching** panel in the **Ribbon** and create a line at offset distance of **3** mm; refer to Figure-7.
- Again, create a line at an offset distance of **6** mm from the recently offsetted line; refer to Figure-8.

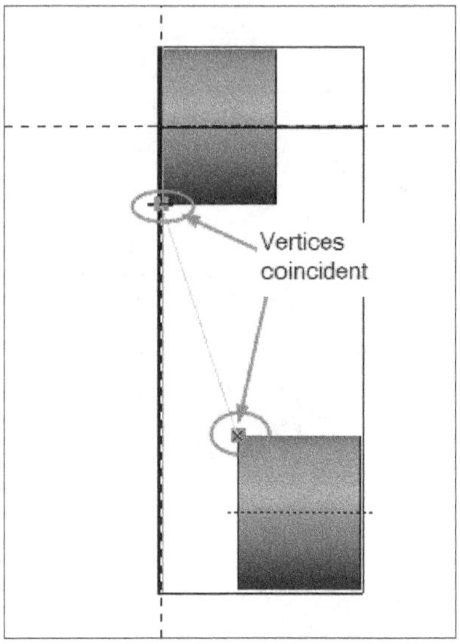

Figure-6. Line coincident to vertices

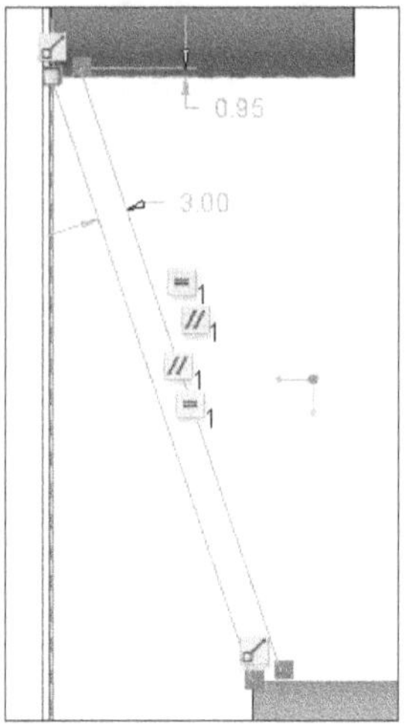

Figure-7. Line offsetted

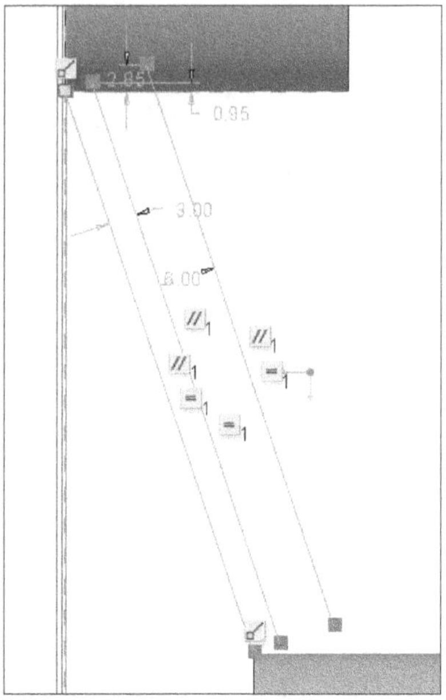

Figure-8. Second line offsetted

- Delete the first line created earlier and make the end points of the two offsetted lines closed by a line after extending them; refer to Figure-9. Note that you need to extend the lines by using the **Line** tool in such a way that it does not cross the revolve features.
- Click on the **OK** button from the **Sketch** contextual tab. Preview of the extrude feature will be displayed; refer to Figure-10.

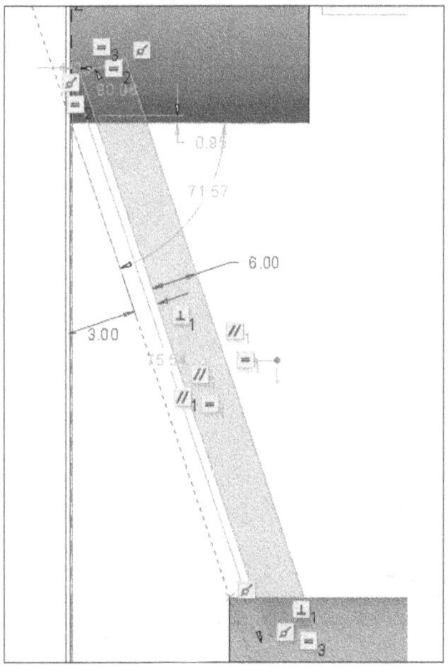

Figure-9. Lines closed after extending

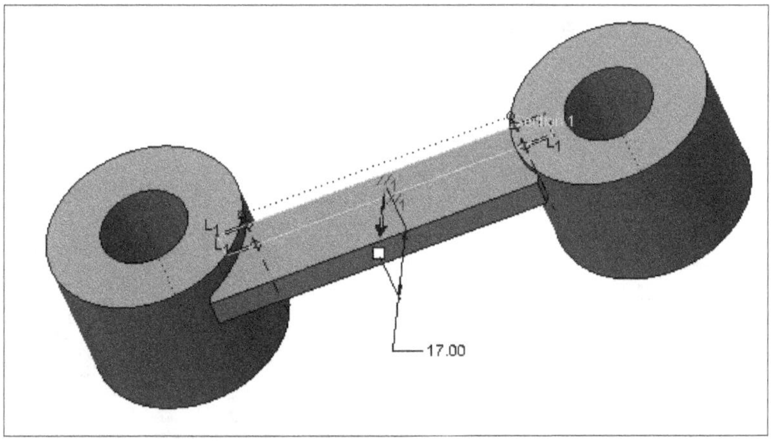

Figure-10. Preview of the extrude feature

- Click on the **Symmetric** option from the drop-down in the **Depth** area of the contextual tab; refer to Figure-11.
- Click in the edit box and specify the value as **25**. Click on the **OK** button from the **Extrude** contextual tab. The model will be displayed as shown in Figure-12.

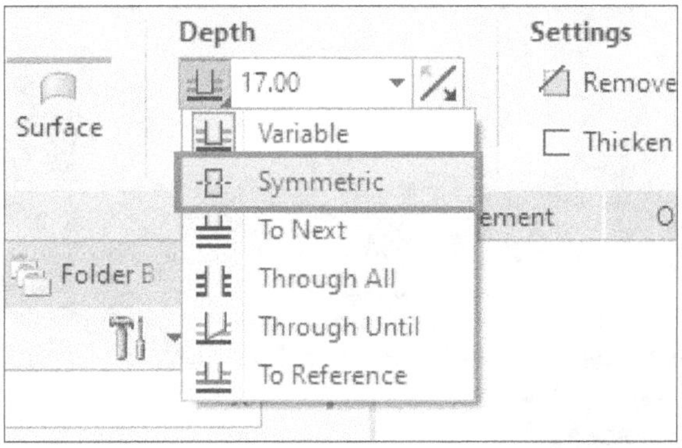

Figure-11. Both side extrude

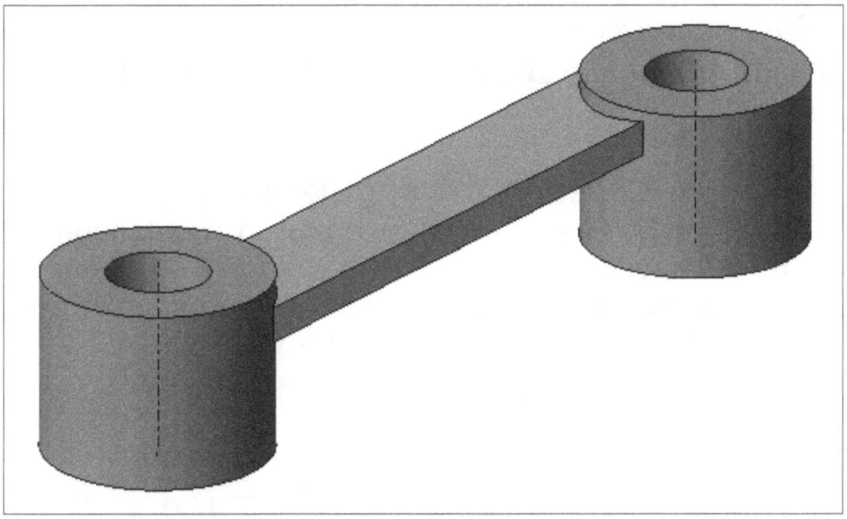

Figure-12. Model after creating extrude feature

Creating the Rib feature

- Click on the **Profile Rib** tool from the **Rib** drop-down in the **Engineering** panel of the **Ribbon**. The **Profile Rib** contextual tab will be displayed in the **Ribbon**.
- Click on the **RIGHT** plane from the **Model Tree**. The sketching environment will be displayed. Click on the **Sketch View** button from the **In-Graphics** toolbar.
- Click on the **Line Chain** tool from the **Line** drop-down in the **Sketching** panel of the **Ribbon**. Create a line coincident with the vertices of revolve features created earlier; refer to Figure-13.

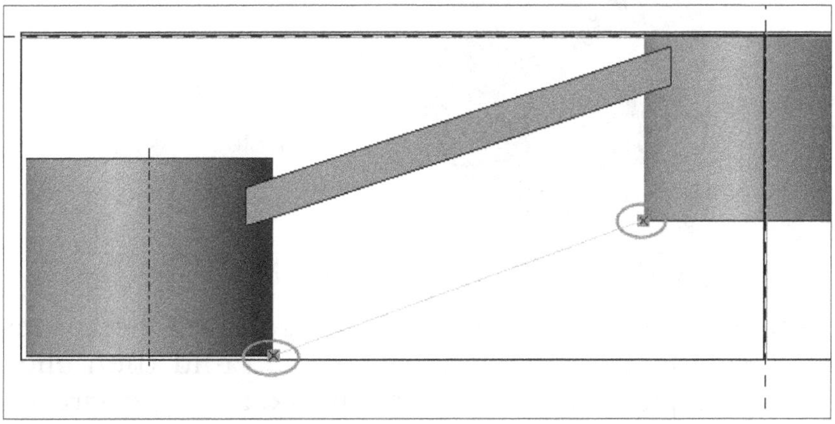

Figure-13. Line created coincident with vertices

- Click on the **OK** button from the **Sketch** contextual tab. Preview of the rib feature will be displayed; refer to Figure-14.

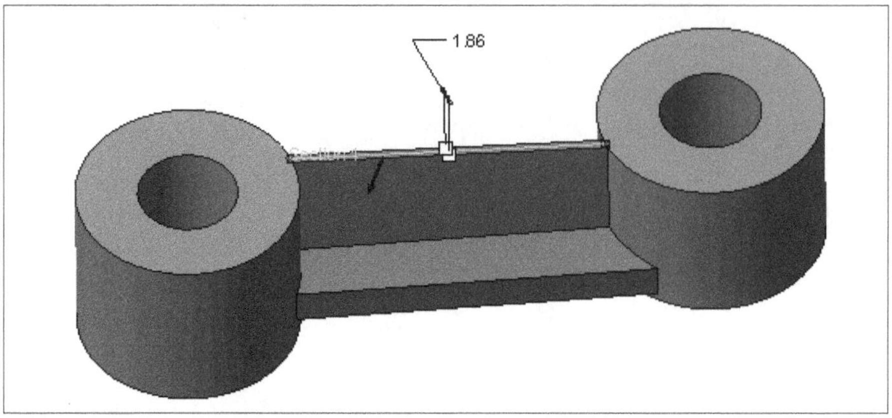

Figure-14. Preview of Rib feature

- Change the thickness value to **10** and then click on the **OK** button from the **Profile Rib** contextual tab.

Creating the angular hole

- Click on the **Plane** button from the **Datum** panel in the **Ribbon**. The **Datum Plane** dialog box will be displayed.
- Select the top face of the revolve feature at the higher level; refer to Figure-15. Preview of the offset datum plane will be displayed.

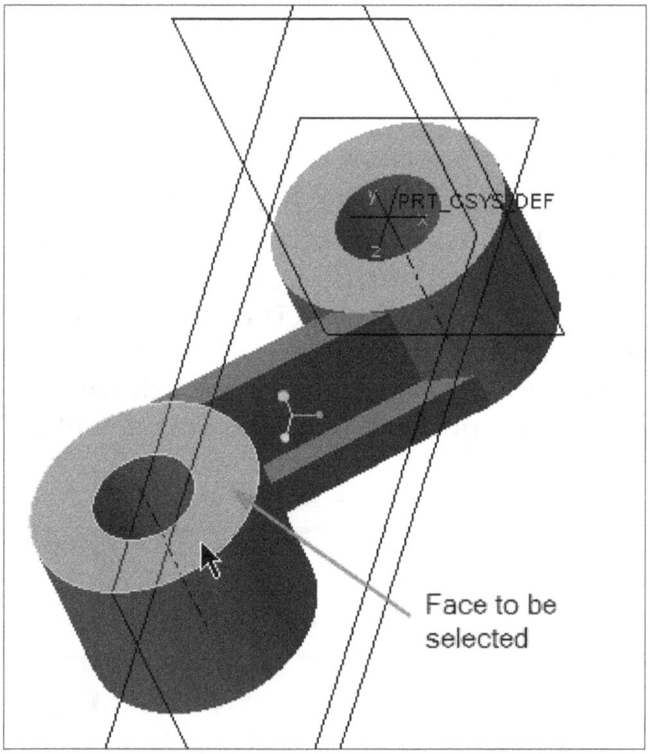

Figure-15. Face to be selected for creating plane

- Create the plane at a distance of **20** below the selected face; refer to Figure-16.
- Make sure the recently created plane is selected and then click on the **Sketch** button from the **Datum** panel in the **Ribbon**. The sketching environment will become active.
- Create a datum centerline by using the **Centerline** tool from the **Datum** panel in the **Ribbon**; refer to Figure-17.

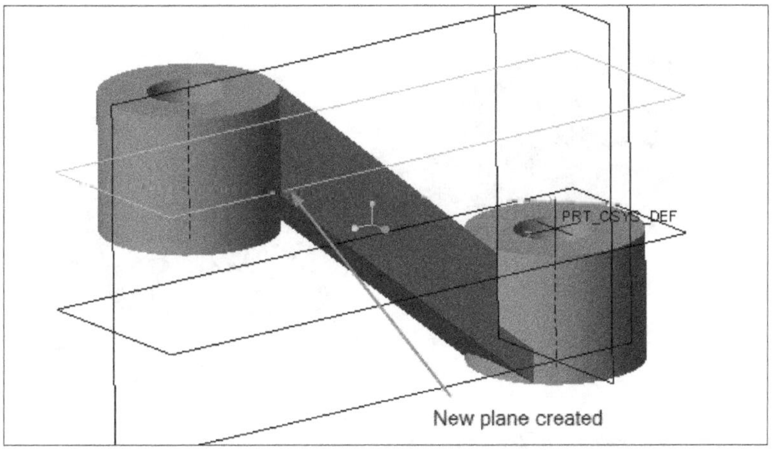

Figure-16. Plane to be created

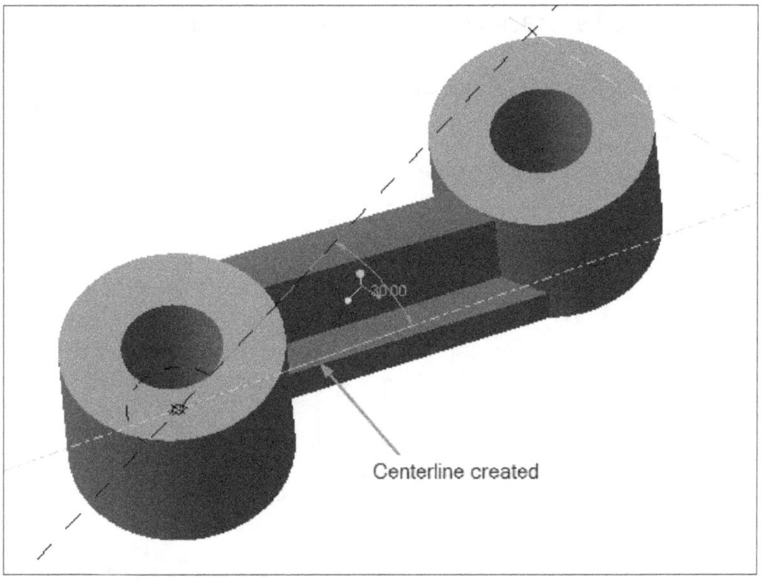

Figure-17. Centerline created for hole

- Click on the **OK** button from the **Close** panel in the **Sketch** contextual tab.
- Click on the **Hole** tool from the **Engineering** panel in the **Ribbon**. The **Hole** contextual tab will be displayed.
- Select the centerline recently created and select the round face of the respective revolve feature; refer to Figure-18. Preview of the hole will be displayed; refer to Figure-19.

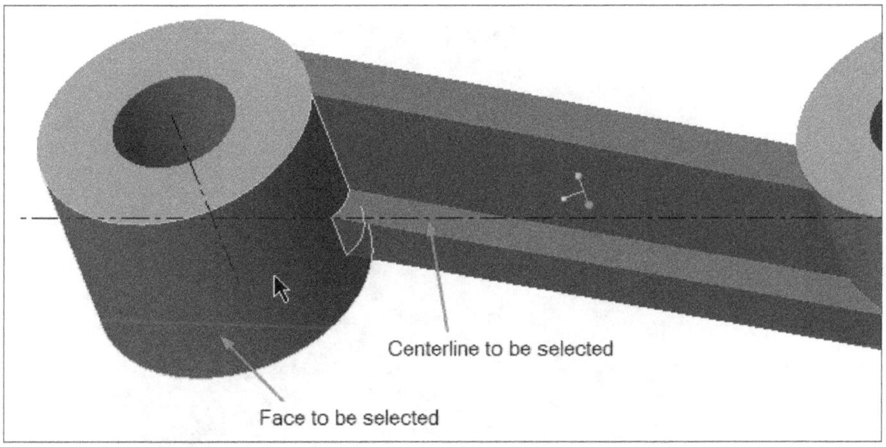

Figure-18. Entities to be selected for creating hole

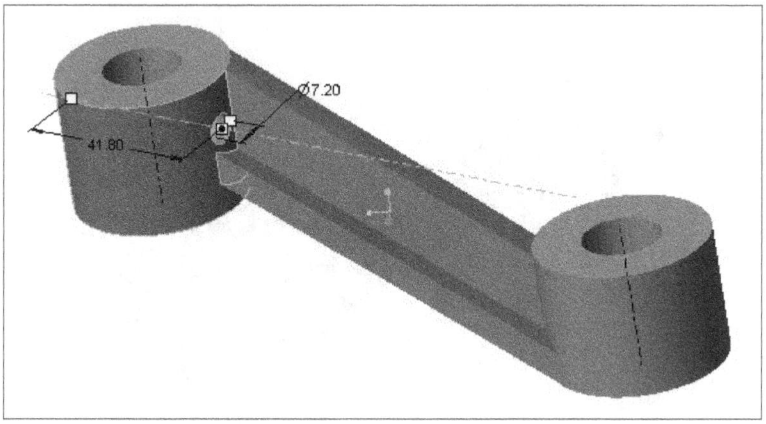

Figure-19. Preview of the hole feature

- Click on the **Standard** button from **Type** area of the **Hole** contextual tab and then click on the **Straight**, **Clearance**, and **Countersink** buttons from **Profile** area of the contextual tab.
- Click on the **Shape** tab and specify the values as shown in Figure-20.

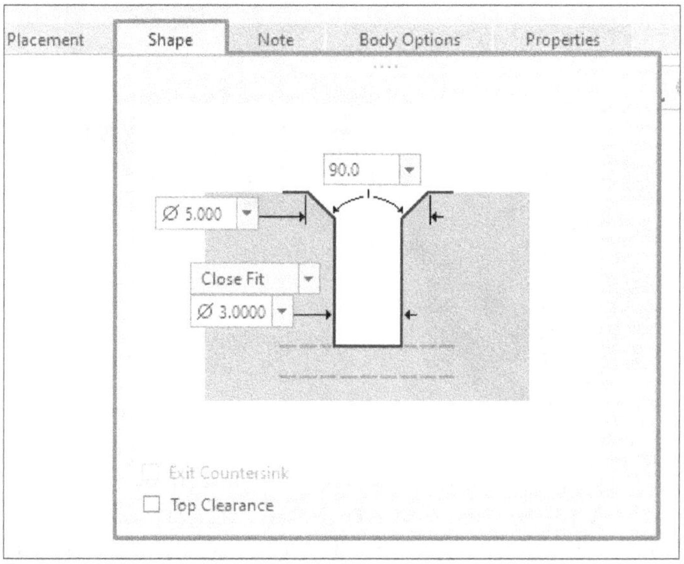

Figure-20. Values in Shape tab

- Click on the **OK** button from the contextual tab to create the hole. The hole will be created as shown in Figure-21.

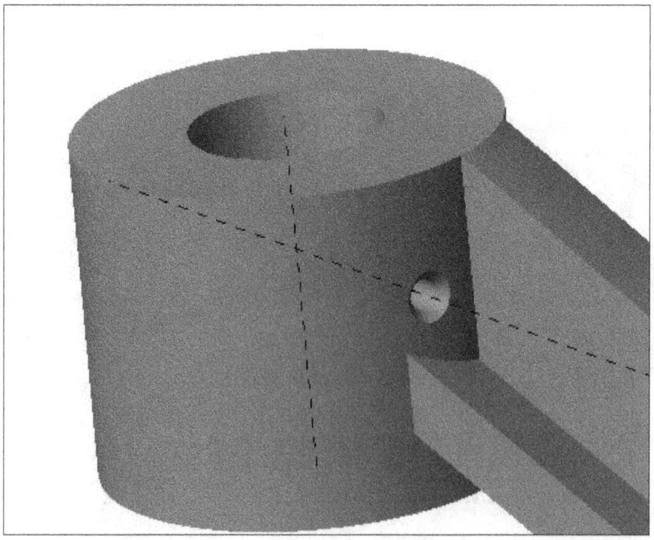

Figure-21. Hole created

Creating handle of lever

- Click on the **Extrude** tool from the **Shapes** panel in the **Ribbon**. The **Extrude** contextual tab will be displayed.
- Select the face as shown in Figure-22. The sketching environment will be displayed.
- Create the sketch as shown in Figure-23.

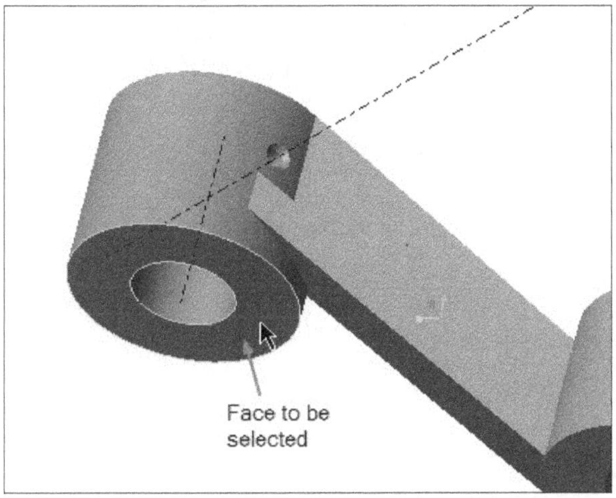

Figure-22. Face to be selected for creating extrude feature

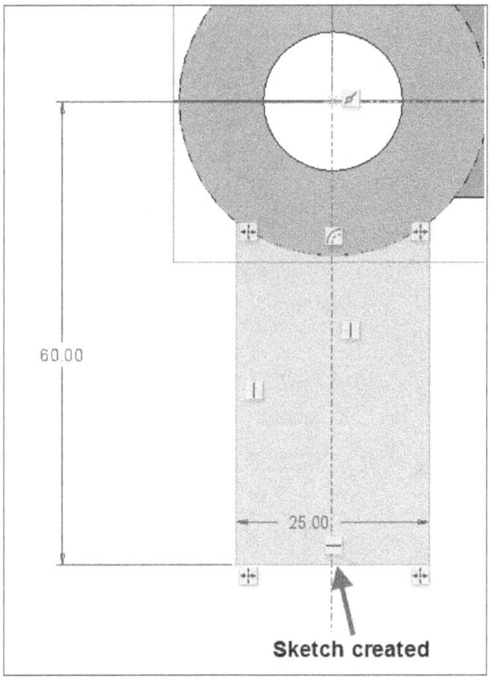

Figure-23. Sketch for extrude

- Click on the **OK** button from the **Sketch** contextual tab and specify the depth of extrusion as **12**.
- Click on the **OK** button from the **Extrude** contextual tab to create the feature.

PRACTICAL 2

Create the model as shown in Figure-24. The dimensions are given in Figure-25.

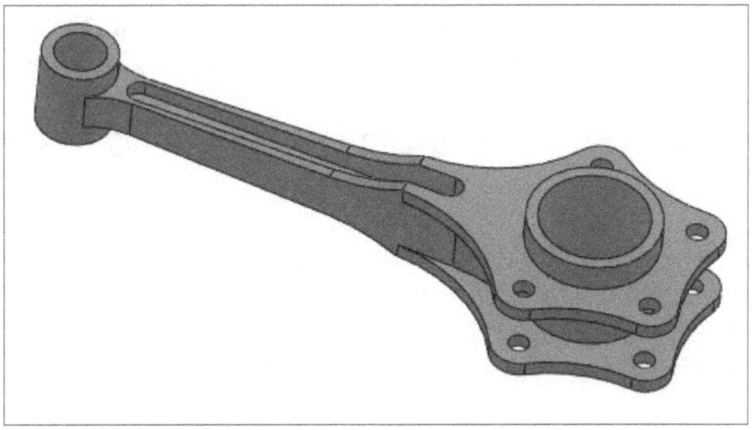

Figure-24. Practical 2

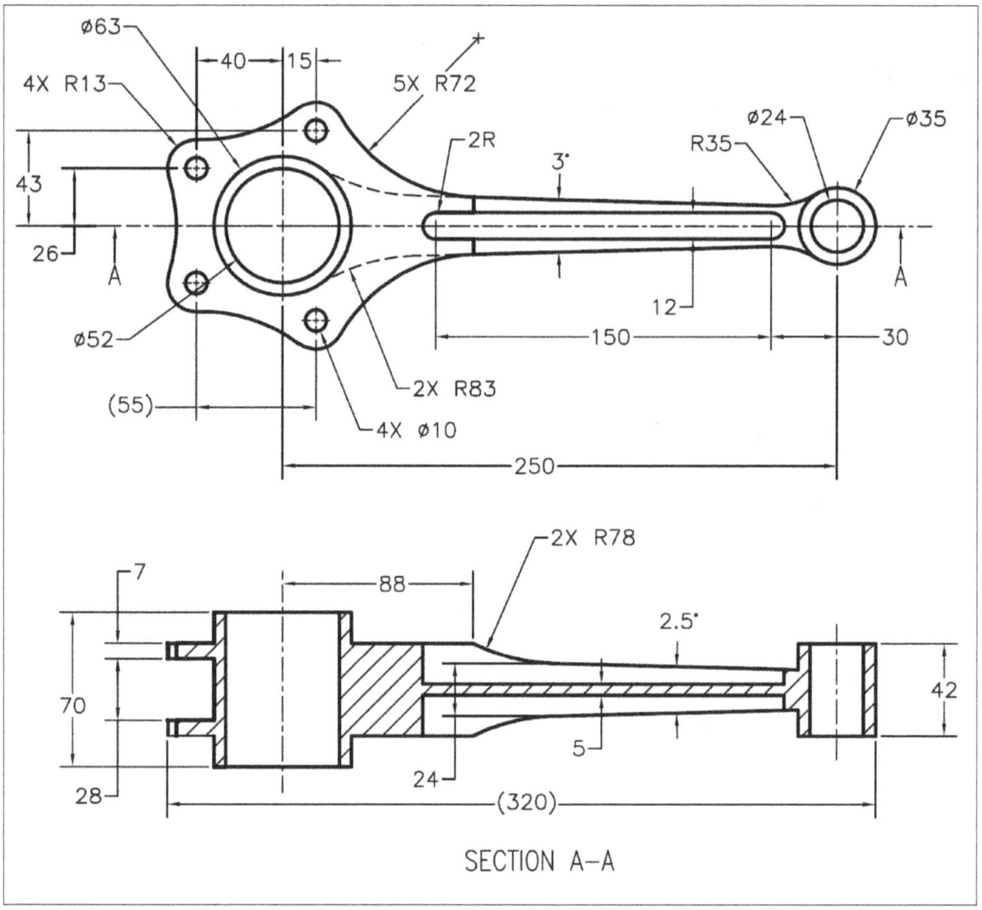

Figure-25. Practical 2 drawing

Starting Part Modeling

- Double-click on the Creo Parametric icon from the desktop to start Creo Parametric if not started already.
- Click on the **New** button from the **Data** panel in the **Ribbon**. The **New** dialog box will be displayed.
- Specify desired name for the file and clear the **Use default template** check box.
- Click on the **OK** button from the dialog box. The **New File Options** dialog box will be displayed as discussed earlier.
- Select the **mmns part solid abs** option from the dialog box and click on the **OK** button.

Creating the base feature

- Click on the **Extrude** button from the **Shapes** panel in the **Ribbon**. The **Extrude** contextual tab will be displayed.
- Select the **TOP** plane from the **Model Tree**. The sketching environment will be displayed.
- Create the sketch as shown in Figure-26.

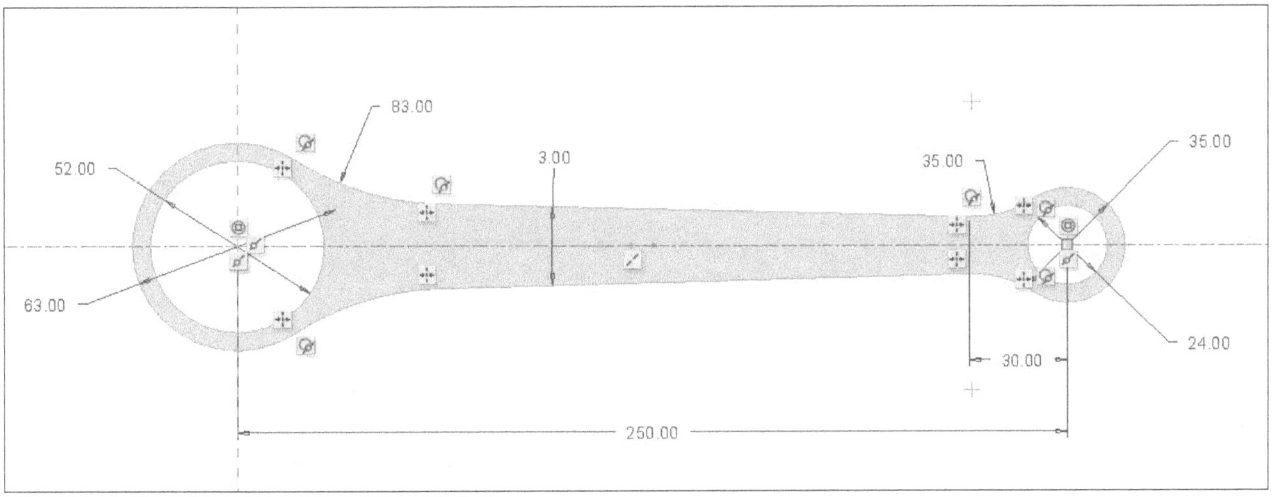

Figure-26. Sketch for base feature

- Click on the **OK** button from the **Sketch** contextual tab. Preview of the extrude feature will be displayed.
- Specify the depth value as **42** and select the both side extrude option from **Depth** area of the contextual tab; refer to Figure-27.

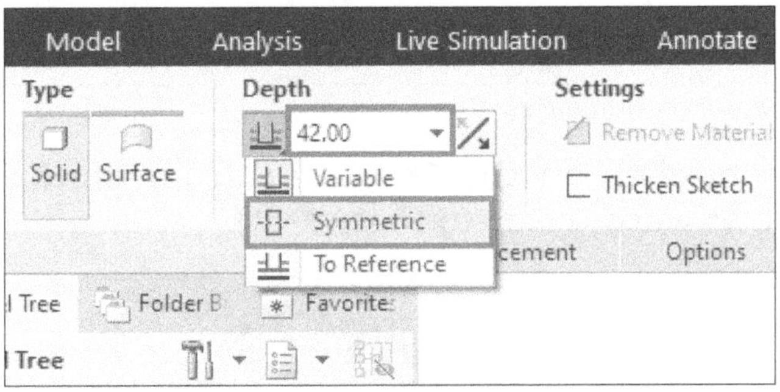

Figure-27. Depth value for extrusion

- Click on the **OK** button from the **Extrude** contextual tab.

Creating the second extrude feature

- Click on the **Extrude** button from the **Shapes** panel. The **Extrude** contextual tab will display.
- Click on the top face of the base feature; refer to Figure-28. The sketching environment will get activated.

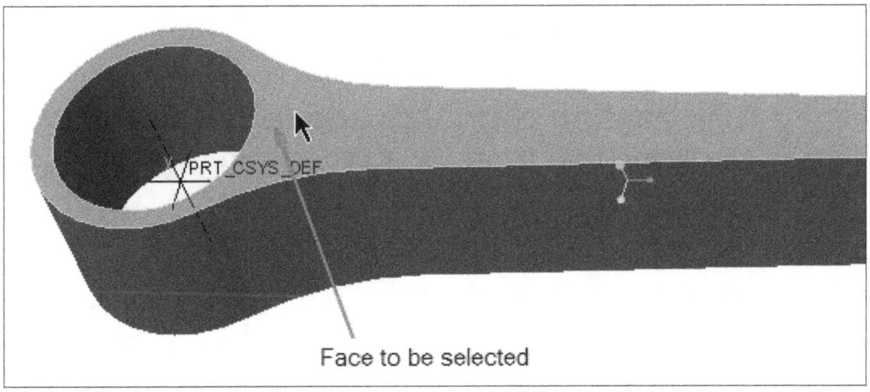

Figure-28. Top face to be selected

- Create the sketch as shown in Figure-29.

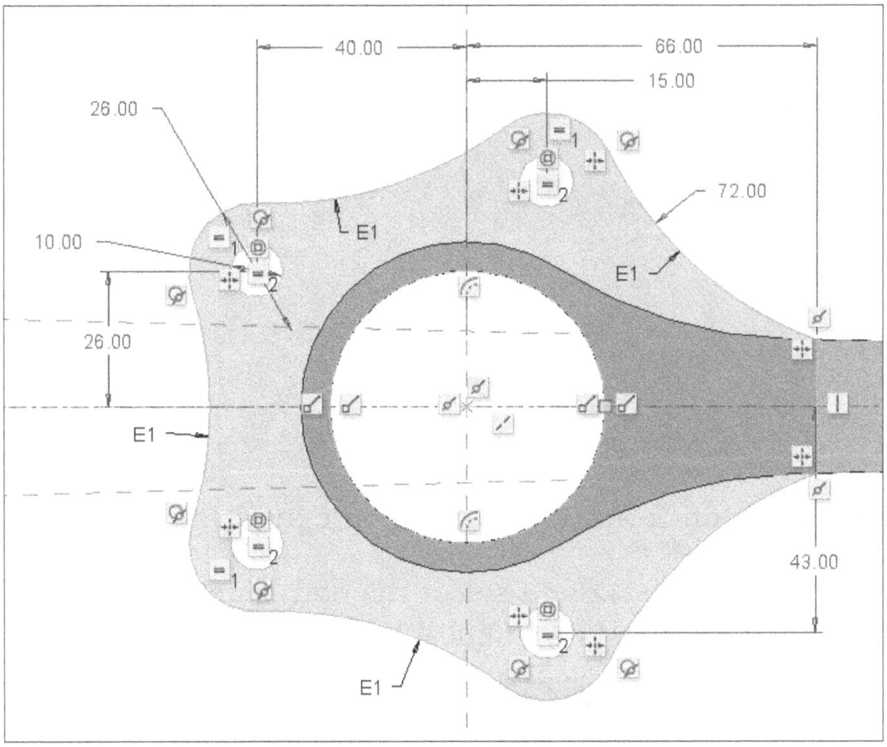

Figure-29. Sketch to be created

- After creating sketch, click on the **OK** button from the **Ribbon** and extrude the feature by **7** mm downward; refer to Figure-30.

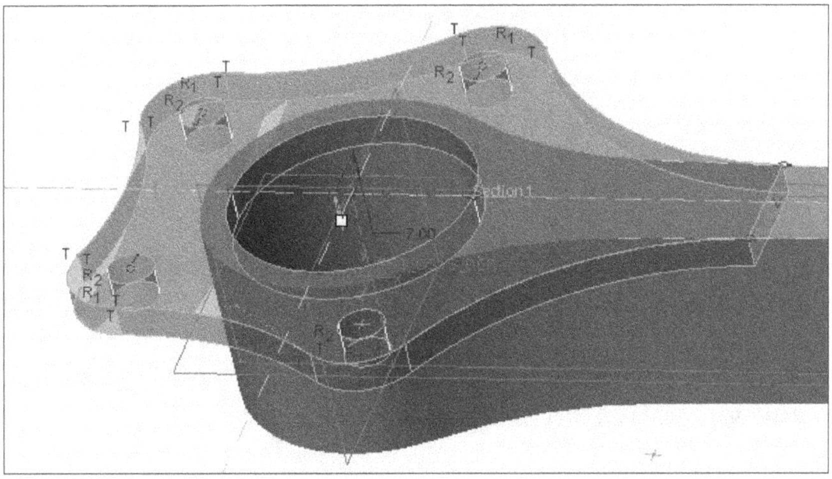

Figure-30. Extruding second feature

Creating third extrude feature

- Again, click on the **Extrude** tool from the **Ribbon** and create the sketch as shown in Figure-31.

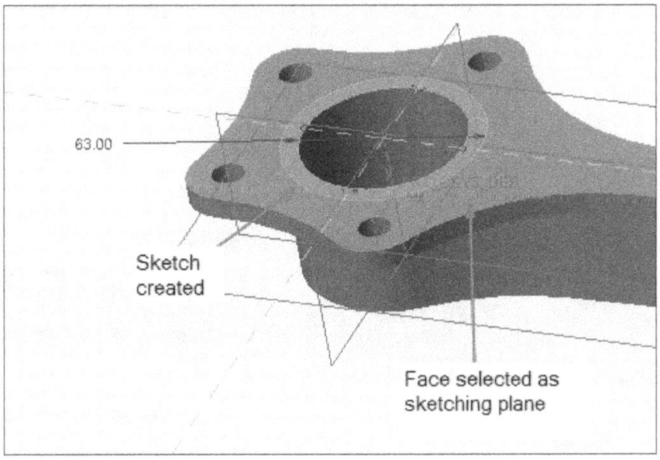

Figure-31. Sketch for third extrusion

- Extrude the sketch to a height of **14**; refer to Figure-32.

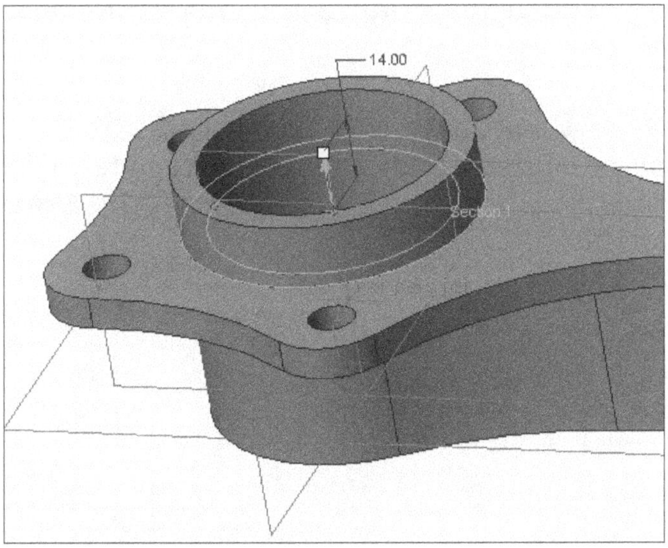

Figure-32. Preview of third extrusion

Creating Mirror feature

- Select the second and third extruded feature and then click on the **Mirror** tool from the **Editing** panel in the **Ribbon**. The **Mirror** contextual tab will be displayed and you are asked to select a plane.
- Select the top plane as mirror reference; refer to Figure-33.

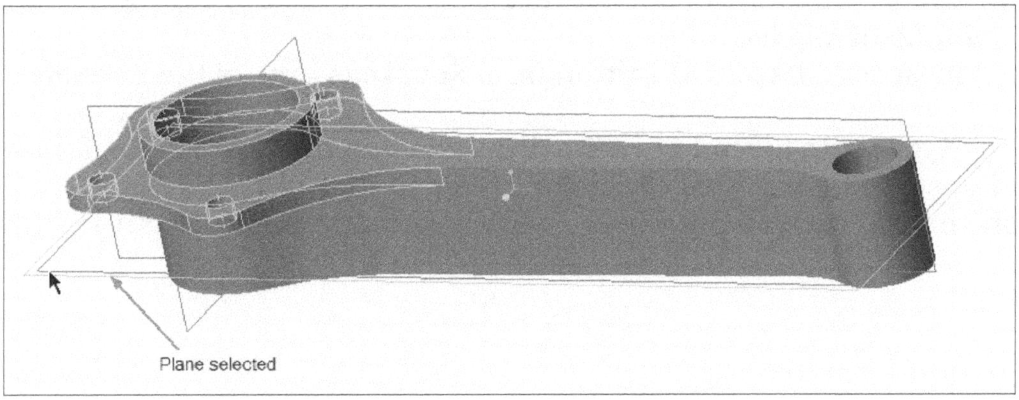

Figure-33. Plane selected for mirror reference

- Click on the **OK** button from the contextual tab. The mirror feature will be created; refer to Figure-34.

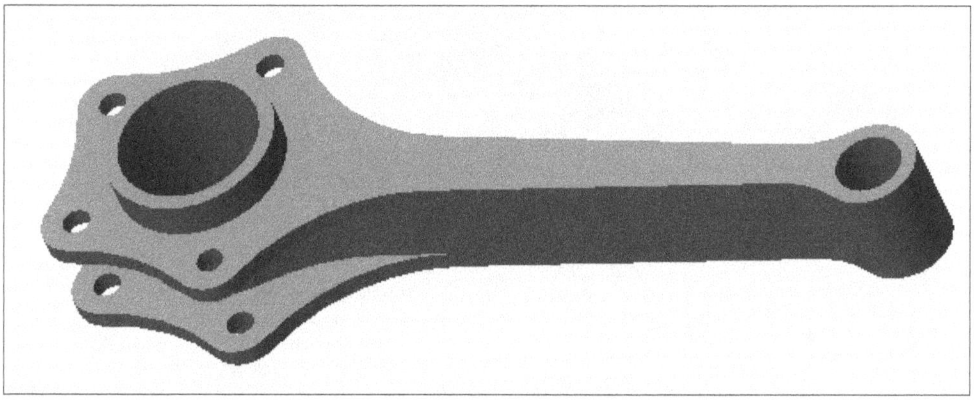

Figure-34. Mirror feature created

Till this point, we have added material in the model. Rest of the features are for removing the material.

Creating First Extruded cut

- Select the **Front** plane and then click on the **Extrude** tool from the **Ribbon**. The sketching environment will be activated. Click on the **Sketch View** button from the **In-Graphics** toolbar.
- Create the sketch as shown in Figure-35.

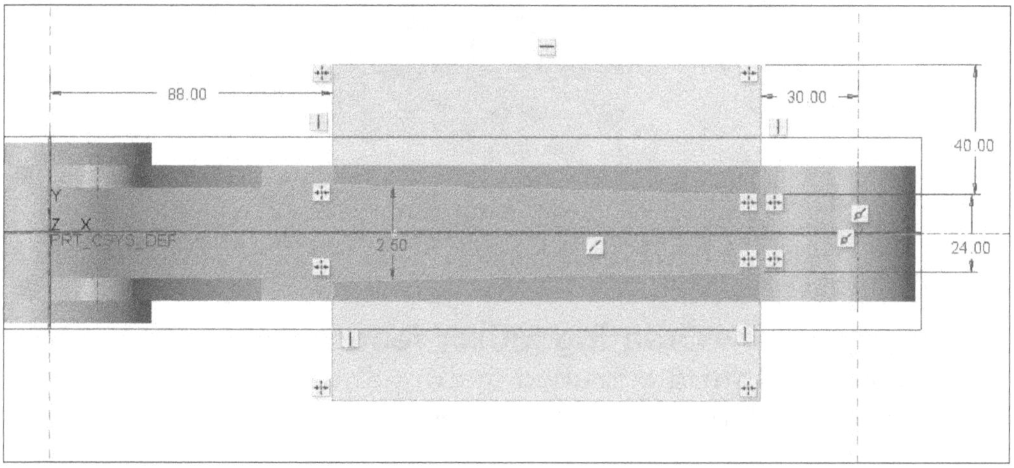

Figure-35. Sketch for first cut feature

- Click on the **OK** button from the **Sketch** contextual tab. Preview of the extrude feature will be displayed.
- Click on the **Remove Material** button from **Settings** area of the **Extrude** contextual tab.
- Select the **Symmetric** button from the drop-down in the **Depth** area of the contextual tab and specify the value of extrusion; refer to Figure-36.
- Click on the **OK** button from the contextual tab to create the cut feature.

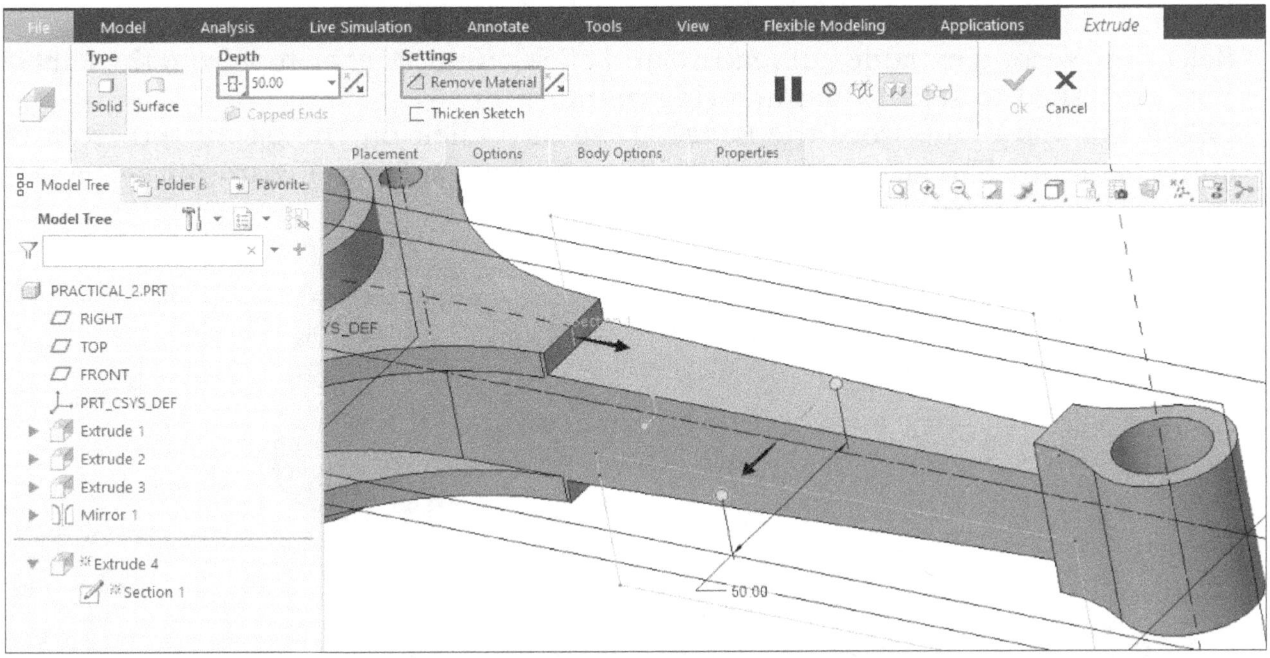

Figure-36. Options specified for extrude cut

Creating Second Extruded cut

- Select the top face of the model as shown in Figure-37 and then click on the **Extrude** tool from the **Ribbon**. The sketching environment will be activated. Click on the **Sketch View** button from the **In-Graphics** toolbar.

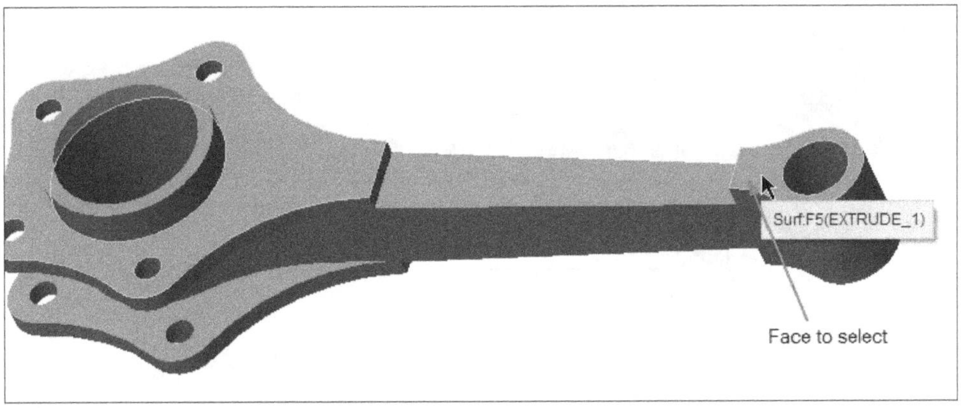

Figure-37. Face selected for second cut feature

- Create the sketch as shown in Figure-38 by using the **Project** tool.
- Click on the **OK** button and create the extrude cut up to the surface of first cut feature; refer to Figure-39.

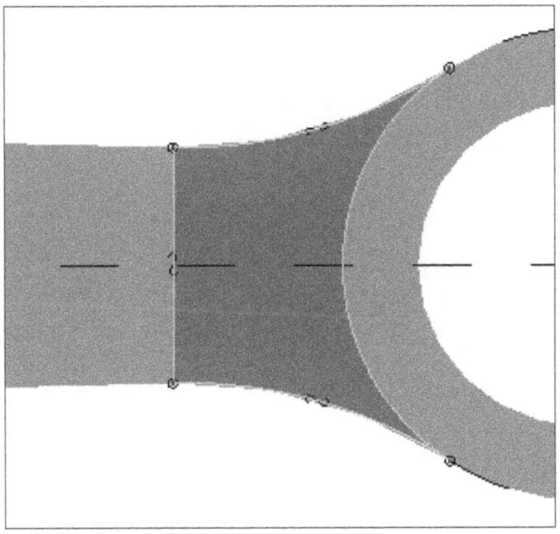

Figure-38. Sketch for second cut

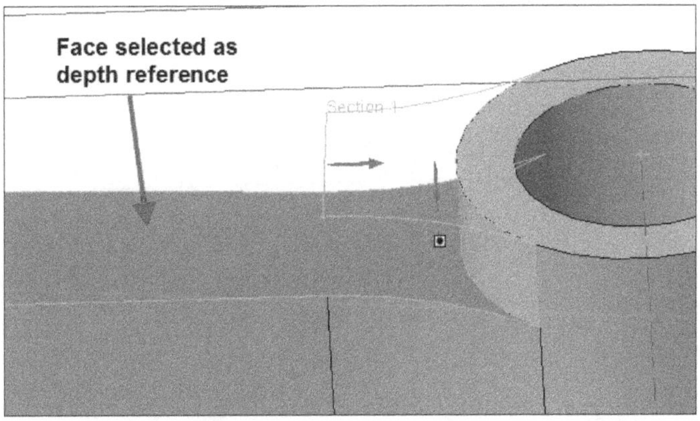

Figure-39. Depth of extrude cut

Mirroring the cut feature

- Select the second extrude cut feature and click on the **Mirror** tool from the **Ribbon**. You are asked to select the mirroring plane.
- Select the **Top** plane from the **Model Tree** and click on the **OK** button from the contextual tab. The mirror feature will be created; refer to Figure-40.

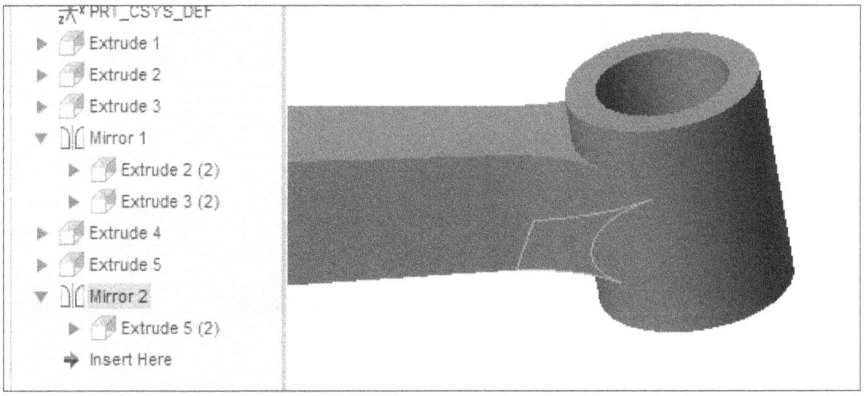

Figure-40. Mirror feature of extruded cut

Creating Third Extruded Cut

- Click on the **Plane** tool from the **Datum** panel in the **Ribbon** and select the **Top** plane.
- Create a plane at an offset distance of **2.5** from the **Top** plane; refer to Figure-41.

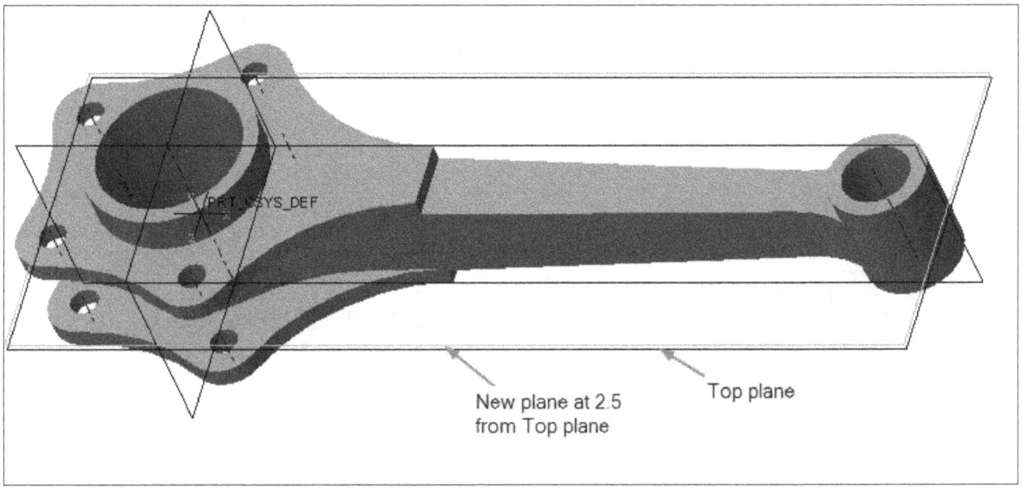

Figure-41. New plane created

- Select the newly created plane and click on the **Extrude** tool from the **Ribbon**. The sketching environment will be displayed.
- Create the sketch as shown in Figure-42.

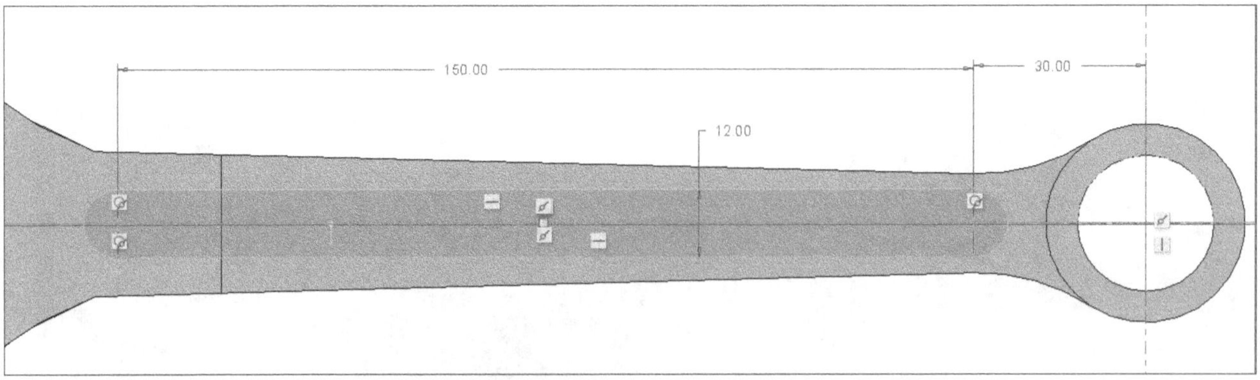

Figure-42. Sketch for third cut feature

- Click on the **OK** button from the **Sketch** contextual tab and click on the **Remove Material** button from **Settings** area of the **Extrude** contextual tab. Preview of the extruded cut will be displayed.
- Click on the **Through All** button from drop-down in the **Depth** area of the **Extrude** contextual tab; refer to Figure-43 and then click on the **OK** button from the **Extrude** contextual tab to create the feature. Make surc that the direction of extrusion is upward.

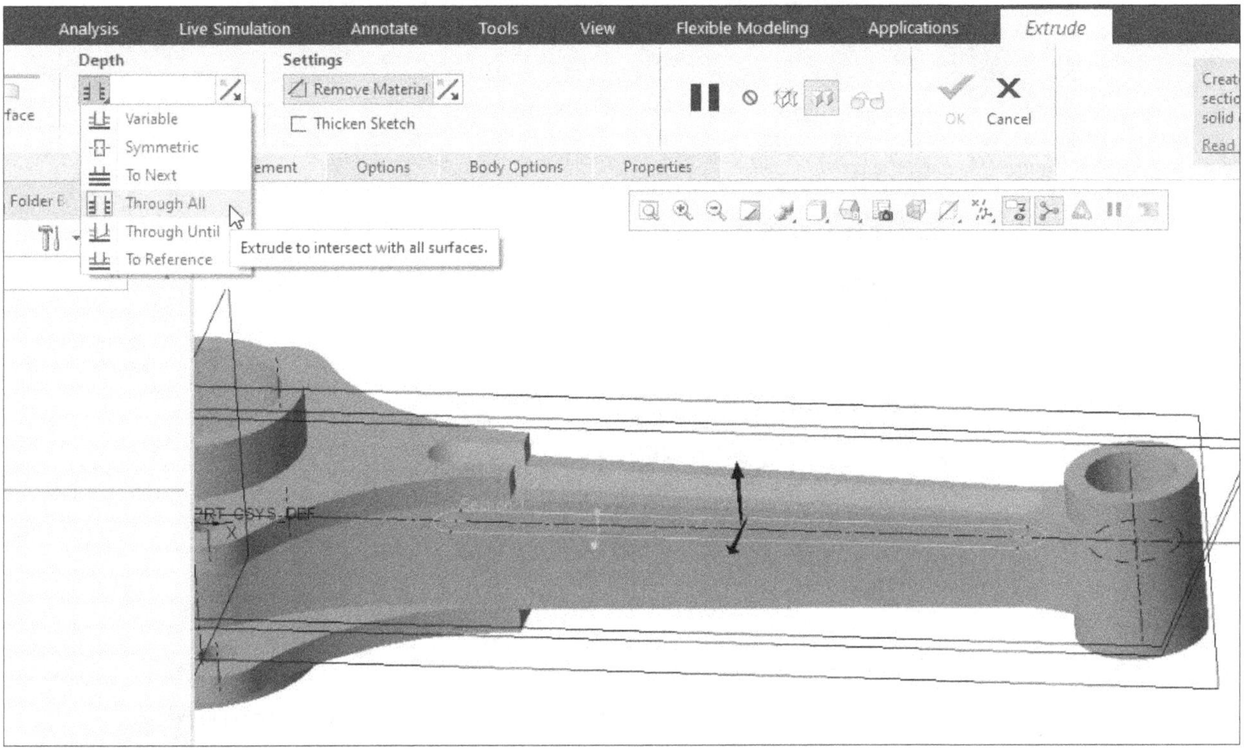

Figure-43. Through All button

- Create mirror feature of this extruded cut with respect to the **Top** plane; refer to Figure-44.

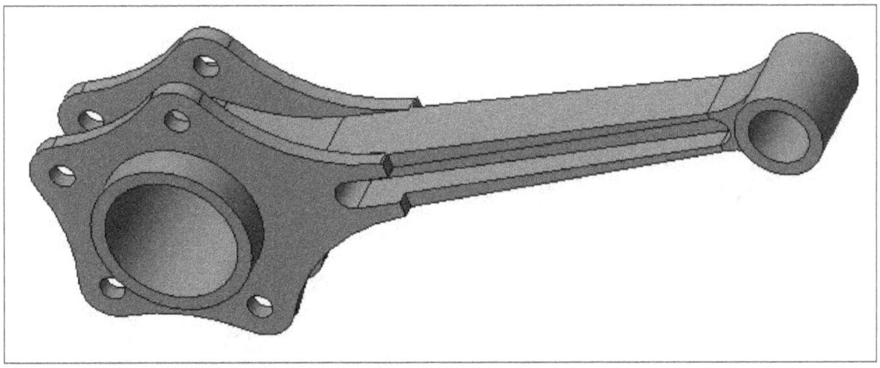

Figure-44. Mirror feature of third extruded cut

Creating Fillet

- Click on the **Round** tool from the **Engineering** panel in the **Ribbon**. The **Round** contextual tab will be displayed.
- Specify the value of fillet radius as **78** in the edit box available in the contextual tab.
- One by one, select the four edges as shown in Figure-45. Preview of the fillet will be displayed; refer to Figure-46.

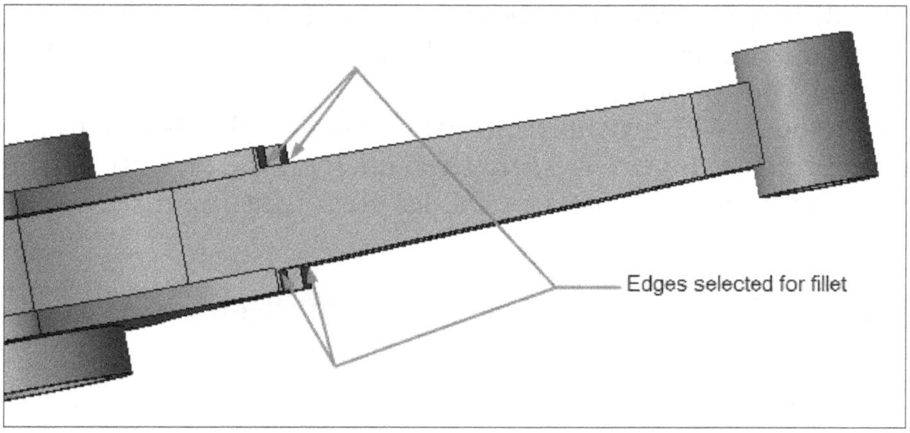

Figure-45. Edges selected for fillet

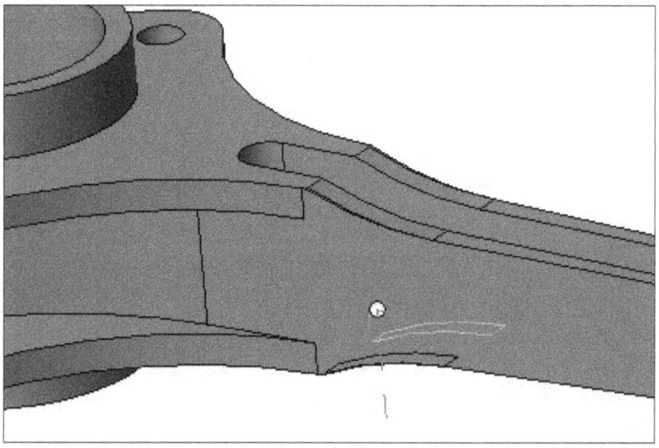

Figure-46. Preview of fillet

- Click on the **OK** button from the contextual tab to create the feature.

PRACTICE 1

Create the model(isometric view) as shown in Figure-47. The dimensions of the model are given in Figure-48.

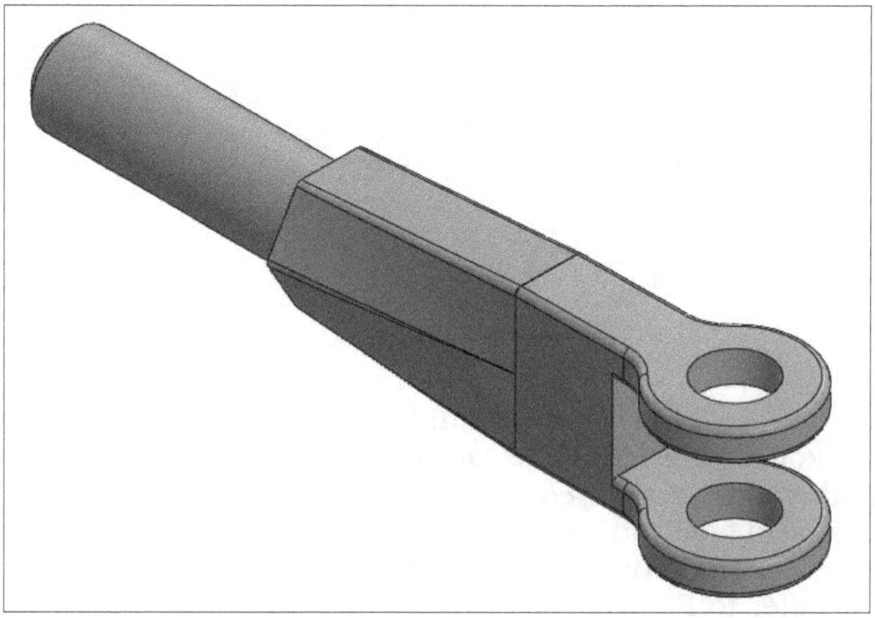

Figure-47. Model for Practice 1

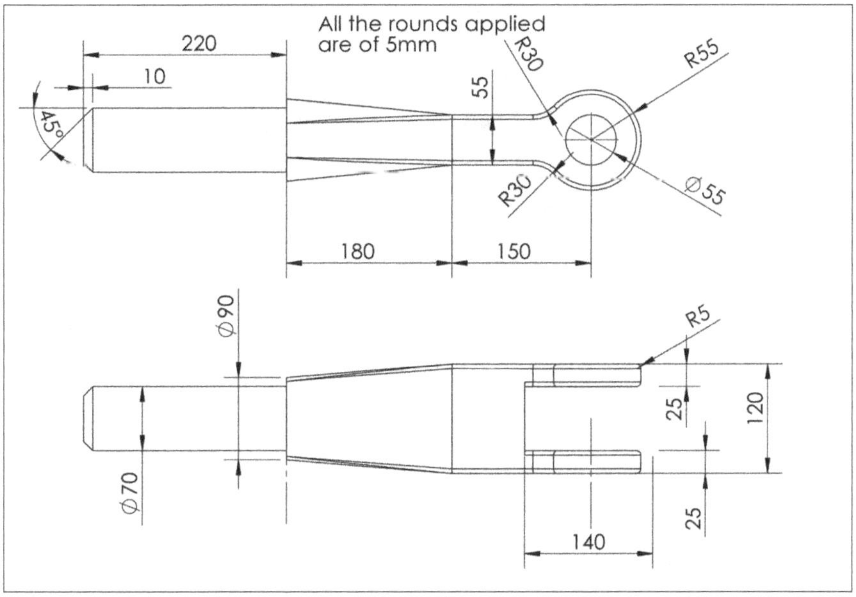

Figure-48. Practice 1 drawing views

PRACTICE 2

Create the model using the drawings shown in Figure-49.

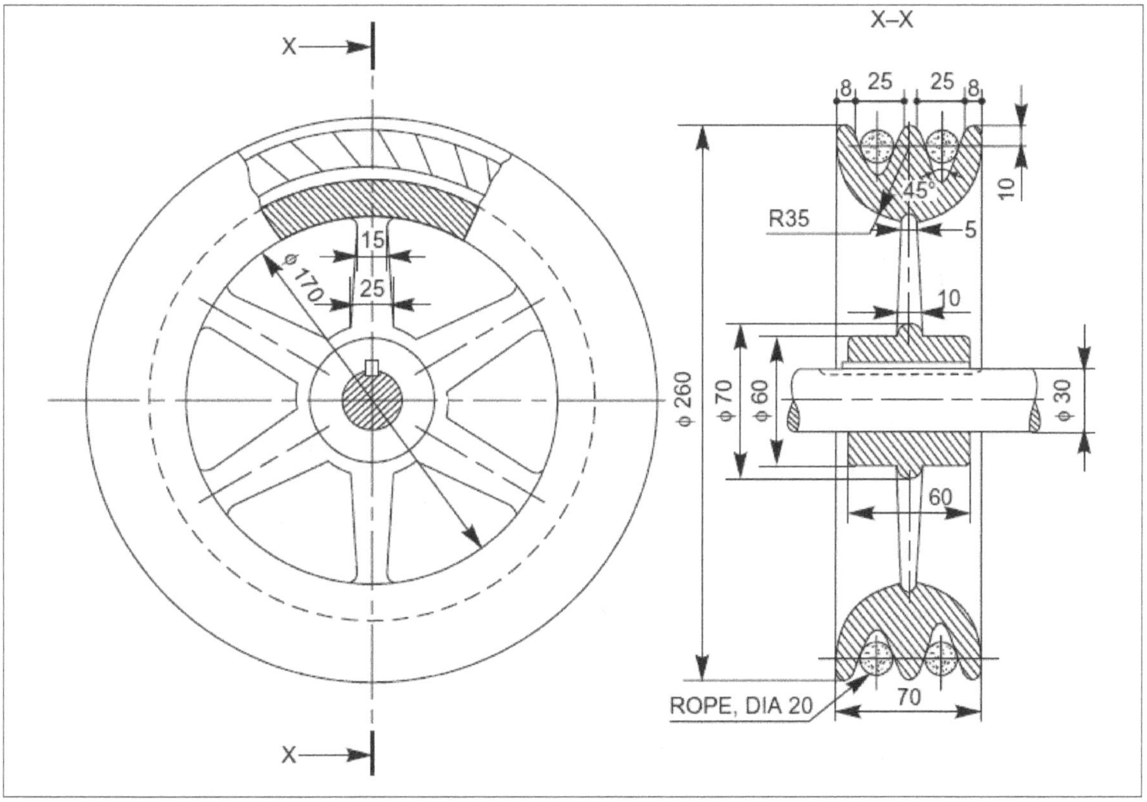

Figure-49. Rope Pulley

PRACTICE 3

Create the model as shown in Figure-50. Dimensions are given in Figure-51. Assume the missing dimensions.

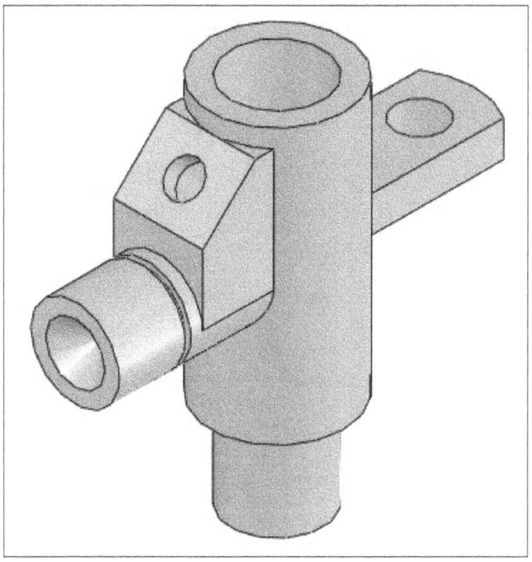

Figure-50. Practice3 model

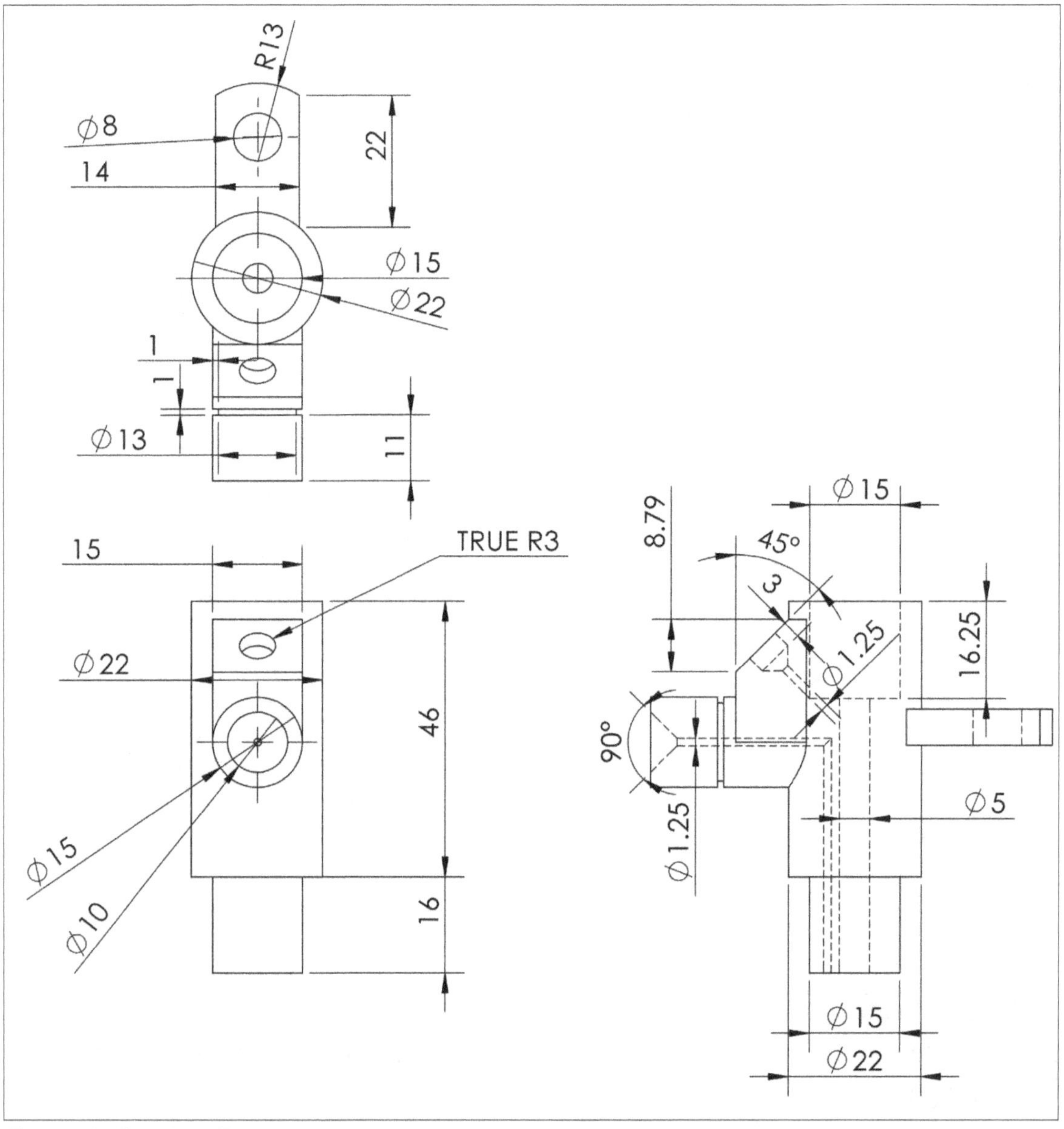

Figure-51. Practice 3 Drawing

PRACTICE 4

Create the model by using the dimensions given in Figure-52.

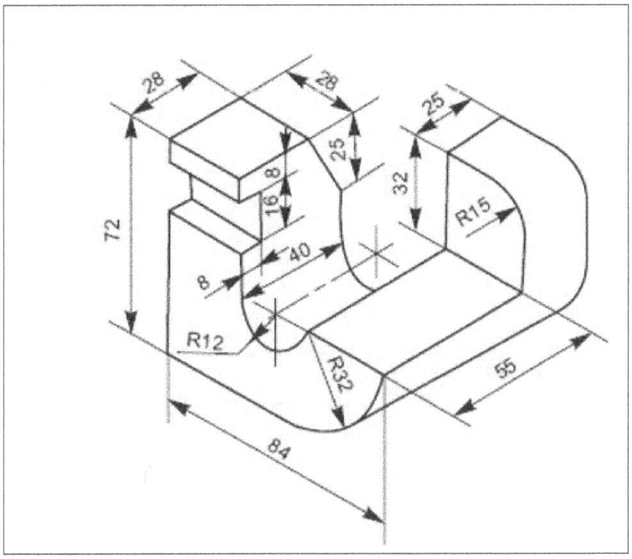

Figure-52. Practice 4

PRACTICE 5

Create the model by using the dimensions given in Figure-53.

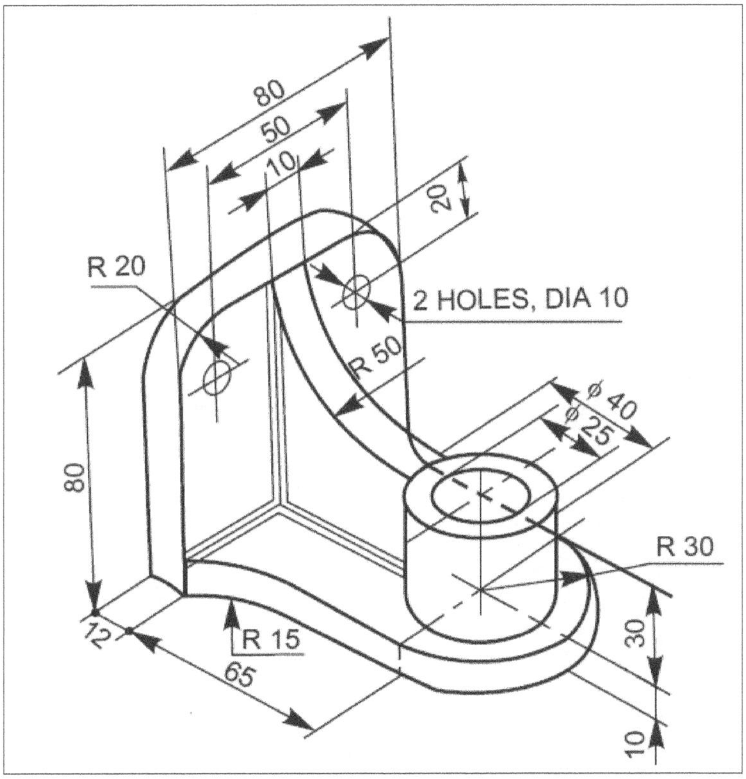

Figure-53. Practice 5

PRACTICE 6

Create the model by using the dimensions given in Figure-54.

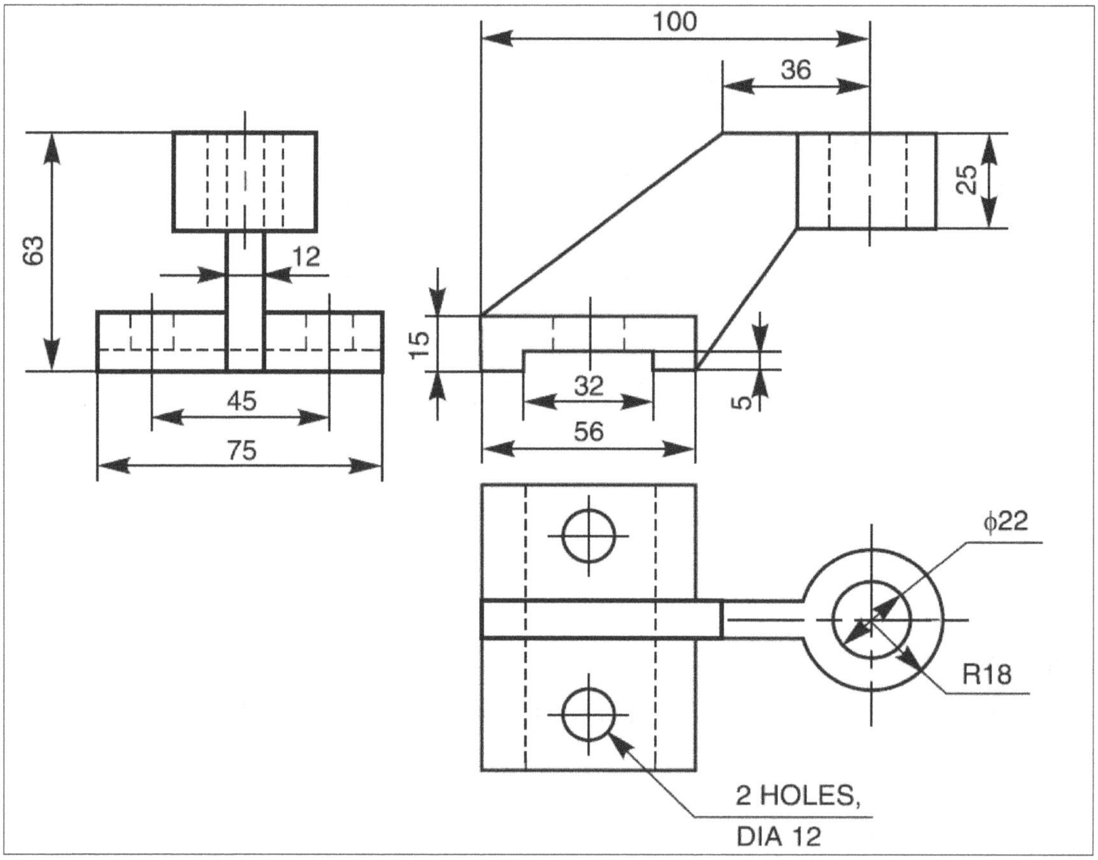

Figure-54. Practice 6

Chapter 8

3D Modeling Advanced-II

Topics Covered

The major topics covered in this chapter are:

- ***Datum Reference***
- ***Datum Graph***
- ***User-Defined Feature (UDF)***
- ***Scaling Model***
- ***Setting Features Read-Only***
- ***Family Table***
- ***Importing Part/Assembly***
- ***Merge/Inheritance***
- ***Collapse feature***
- ***Rendering***

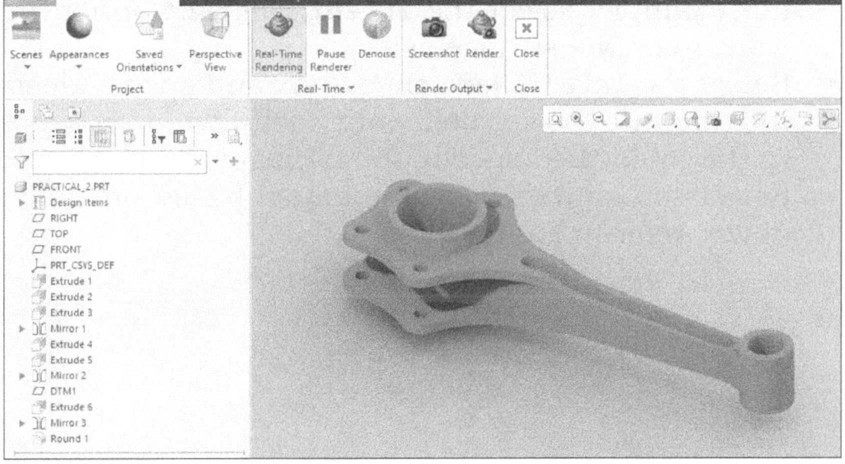

INTRODUCTION

In previous chapters, you have learned about 3D modeling tools and you have created many parts. The tools that are discussed till now are sufficient for common work in industries. But, you can also customize the software as per your company needs so that you can be more productive in lesser time. Along with customizing, there are some other part modeling tools which are discussed in this chapter.

DATUM REFERENCE

Datum reference features are user-defined surface sets, edge chains, datum planes, datum axes, datum points, or datum coordinate systems. Each datum reference feature can create an intent object, which you can use to show your design intent in a model. The **Datum Reference** tool is used to create Datum reference feature. The procedure to use this tool is given next.

- Click on the **Reference** tool from the expanded **Datum** panel in the **Model** tab of the **Ribbon**. The **Datum Reference** dialog box will be displayed; refer to Figure-1.

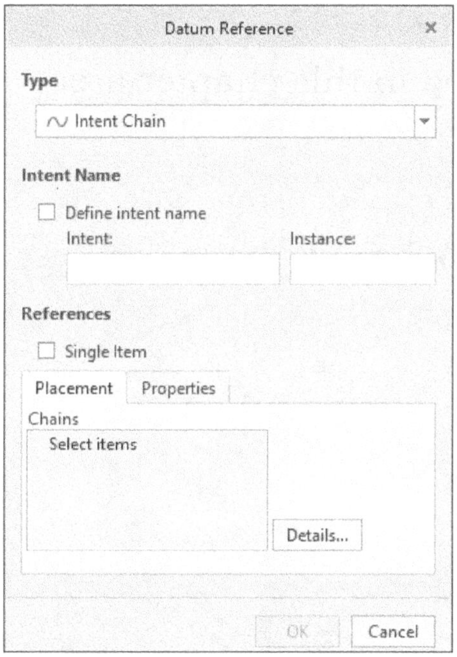

Figure-1. Datum Reference dialog box

- Select the type of datum reference from the **Type** drop-down in the dialog box. For example, select the **Intent Surface** option from the **Type** drop-down if you want to create surface set.
- Select the **Intent Name** check box and specify desired name in the edit box below it to identify the selected entity set. Like, surfaces selected belong to boss feature in the mold then specify the name of the feature BOSS Feature.
- Select the entities from the model based on the type selected in the **Type** drop-down; refer to Figure-2.

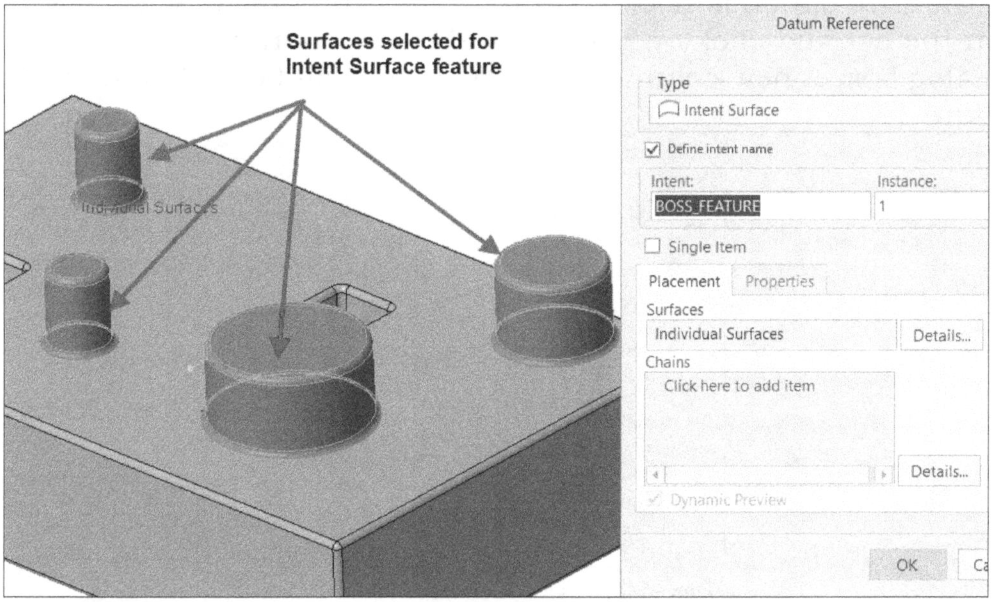

Figure-2. Surfaces selected for Intent Surface feature

- Click on the **OK** button from the dialog box to create the feature.

Note that by default, the names of intent objects are not displayed in the **Model Tree**. To display the name of intent objects, click on the **Tree Columns** option in the **Model Tree**; refer to Figure-3. The **Model Tree Columns** dialog box will be displayed; refer to Figure-4.

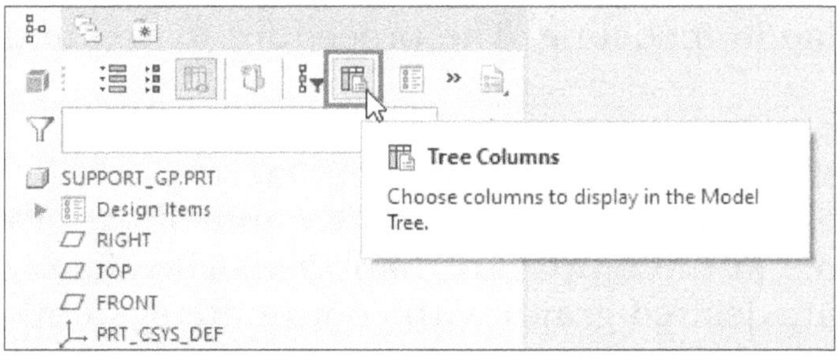

Figure-3. Tree Columns option

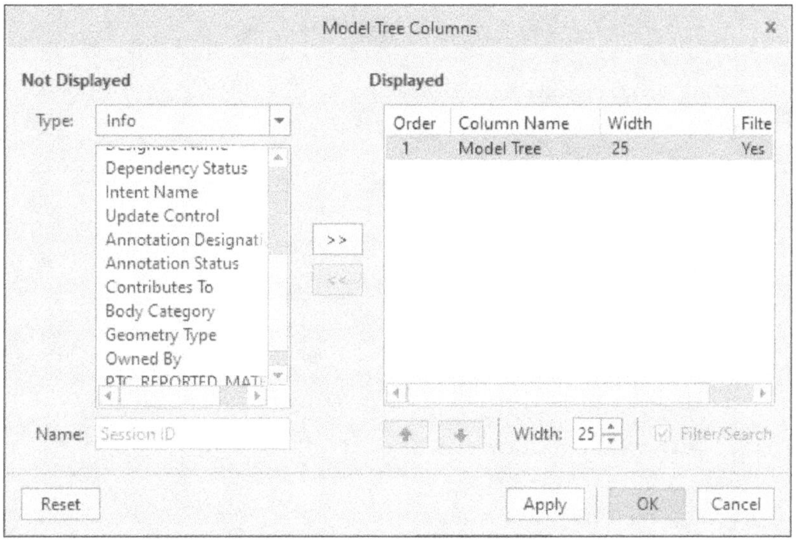

Figure-4. Model Tree Columns dialog box

Make sure the **Info** option is selected in the **Type** drop-down. Select the **Intent Name** option from the list and click on the **Add Column** button. Click on the **OK** button from the dialog box. A new column of intent name will be added to the **Model Tree**; refer to Figure-7.

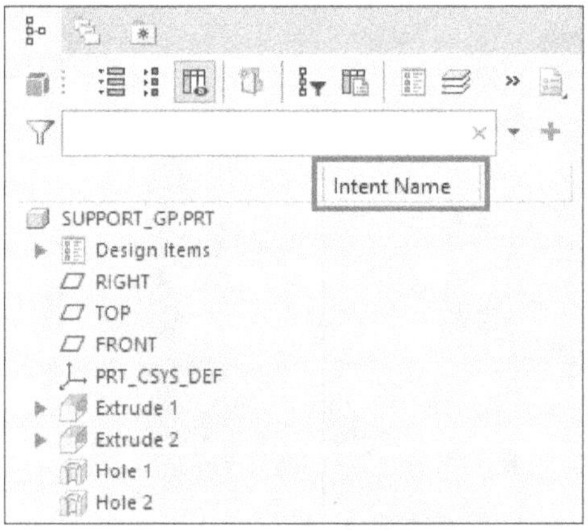

Figure-5. Intent Name column in Model Tree

Now, you will ask what is the benefit of using this feature. Once you have created a datum reference feature, you can annotate your design intent, search for intent objects with the **Search** tool, define saved queries, and automatically place user-defined features (UDFs). You will learn about all these options later in this book.

DATUM GRAPH

The datum graph is used to create a sketch graph which can be used in various relations and formulae in modeling. The procedure to create datum graph is given next.

- Click on the **Graph** tool from the expanded **Datum** panel in the **Model** tab of the **Ribbon**. You will be prompted to specify the name of the graph.
- Enter desired name in the input box displayed. The sketching environment will be activated. Create desired graph with coordinate system; refer to Figure-6.

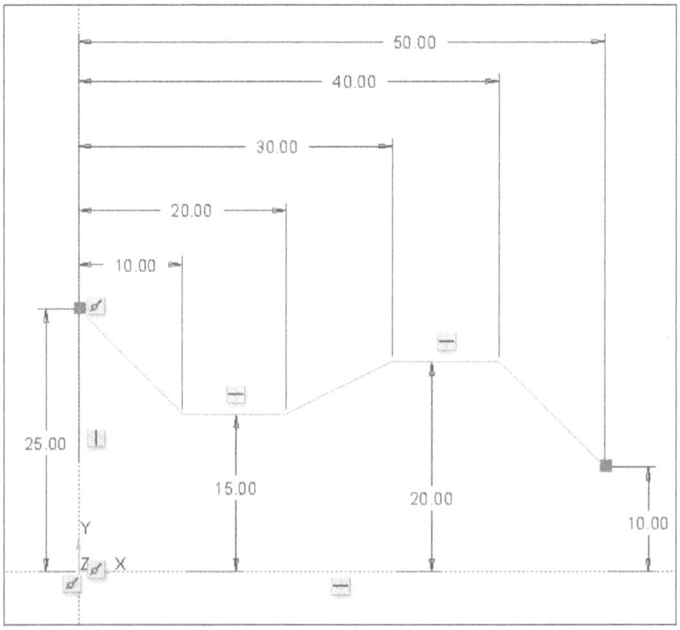

Figure-6. Graph created

- After creating graph, click on the **OK** button from the **Ribbon**. The graph will be added in the **Model Tree**; refer to Figure-7.

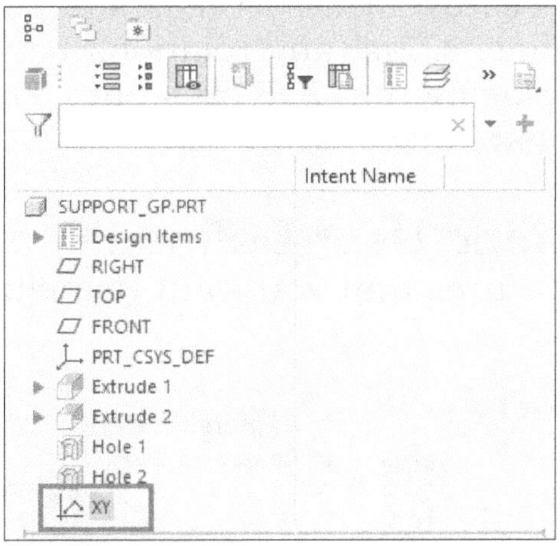

Figure-7. Graph added in Model Tree

The main use of graph is in making relations in the model. Like, you can make the length of a block change automatically based on specified value of width using graph; refer to Figure-8.

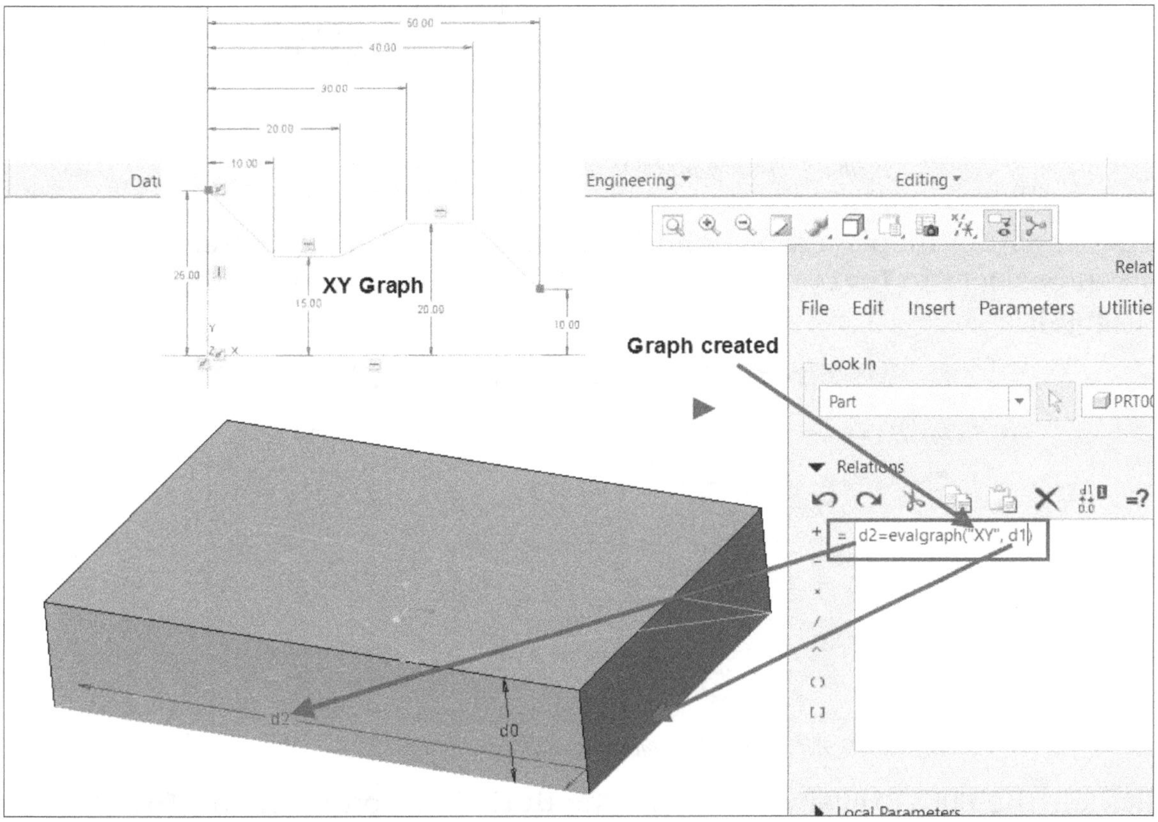

Figure-8. Relation applied using graph

In the above example, if you change the value of **d1** then using the graph, value of **d2** will change automatically. Like, if **d1** is **10** then **d2** will be **15** and if **d1** is **30** then **d2** will be **20**.

USER-DEFINED FEATURE

A User-Defined Feature is a combination of features that can be applied to part at one place. A User-Defined Feature (UDF) consists of selected features (holes/cuts etc.), all their associated dimensions, any relations between the selected features, and a list of references for placing the UDF on a part. The procedures to create and apply User-defined features are discussed next.

Creating User-Defined Feature

- Create the model with features that you want to include in User Defined Feature (UDF); refer to Figure-9.

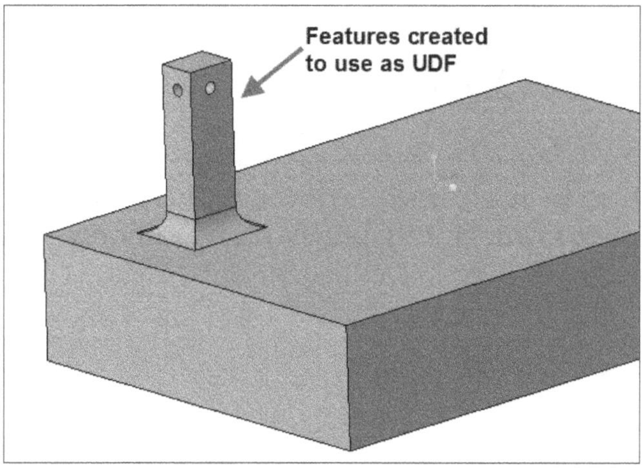

Figure-9. Features for UDF

If **Tools** tab is not displayed by default in the **Ribbon** then right-click on any tab of **Ribbon** and select the **Tools** check box in **Tabs** cascading menu of the shortcut menu; refer to Figure-10.

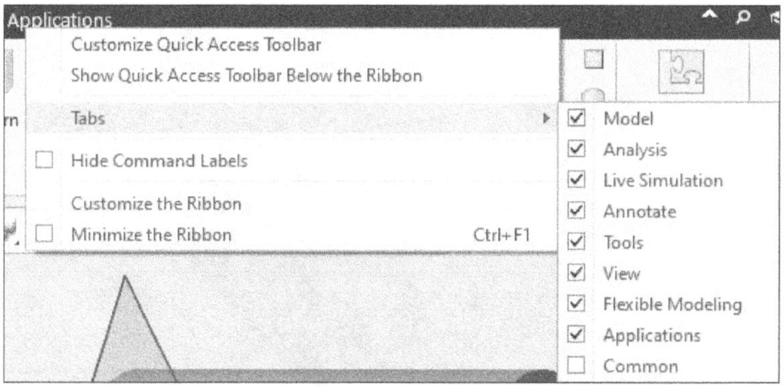

Figure-10. Activating Tools tab in Ribbon

- Click on the **UDF Library** tool from the **Utilities** panel of the **Tools** tab in the **Ribbon**. The **UDF Menu Manager** will be displayed; refer to Figure-11.
- Click on the **Create** option from the **Menu Manager**. You will be prompted to specify the name of the UDF.
- Enter desired name like we have specified the name as "Support" and press **Enter**. **UDF OPTIONS** sub-menu will be displayed asking you to select **Stand Alone** or **Subordinate** option from the menu; refer to Figure-12. A standalone UDF copies all the original model information into the UDF file. Because of this, a standalone UDF requires more storage space than a subordinate UDF. If you make any changes to the reference model, they are not reflected in the UDF. A subordinate UDF

gets its values directly from the original model at run time, so the original model must be present for the subordinate UDF to function. If you make any changes to the dimension values in the original model, they are automatically reflected in the UDF. We will discuss the use of **Stand Alone** option. You can apply the same method for Subordinate UDF.

Figure-11. UDF Menu Manager

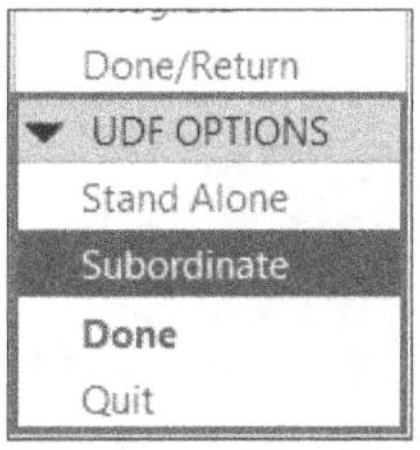

Figure-12. UDF OPTIONS sub-menu

- Select the **Stand Alone** option from sub-menu and click on the **Done** button. You will be asked whether to include the reference part or not. Click **Yes** if you want to display a preview of UDF while inserting in the Part. Click **No** if you do not want to display the preview of the UDF. (We have selected **Yes** button). You will be asked to select the features to be included in UDF.
- Select the features from **Model Tree** while holding the **CTRL** key and then press Middle Mouse Button(**MMB**) thrice. You will be prompted to specify names of various references used for making these features.
- Enter desired names of references (highlighted in the model) in the input box. After specifying all the reference names, press **MMB**.
- You can click on the **OK** button and create the UDF but the dimensional variation will not be available while inserting the feature. If you want to change the shape and size of the UDF while inserting in the part, select the **Var Dims** option from the **UDF** dialog box and click on the **Define** button; refer to Figure-13. You will be prompted to select the dimensions that you want to be changed; refer to Figure-14.

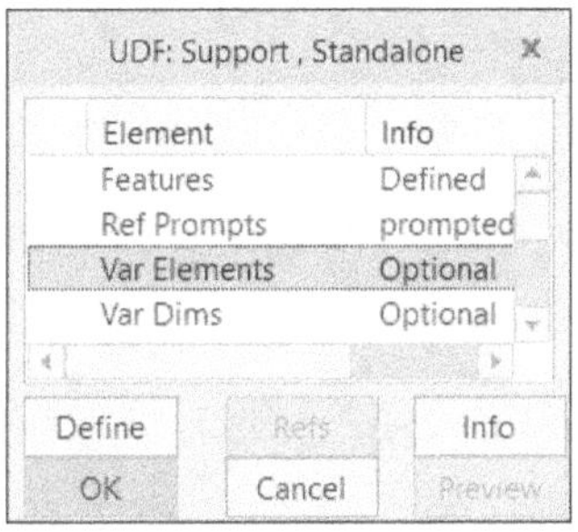

Figure-13. UDF dialog box

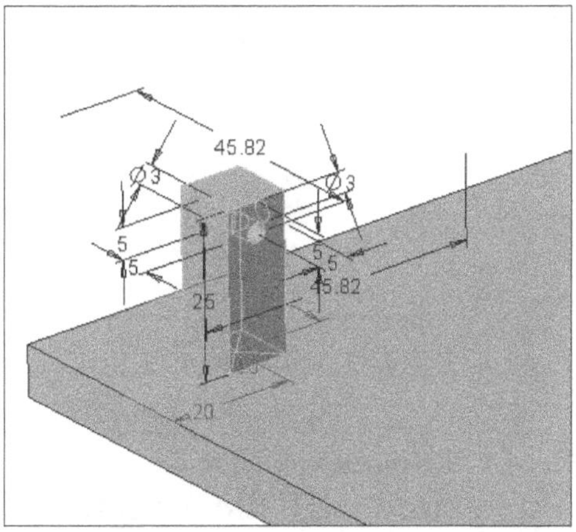

Figure-14. Dimensions displayed for UDF

- Select the dimensions that you want to be variable while holding the **CTRL** key. The selected dimensions will be highlighted in green color.
- Press the **MMB** thrice. You will be asked to specify names of various dimension variables.
- Enter desired names like hole diameters; refer to Figure-15.

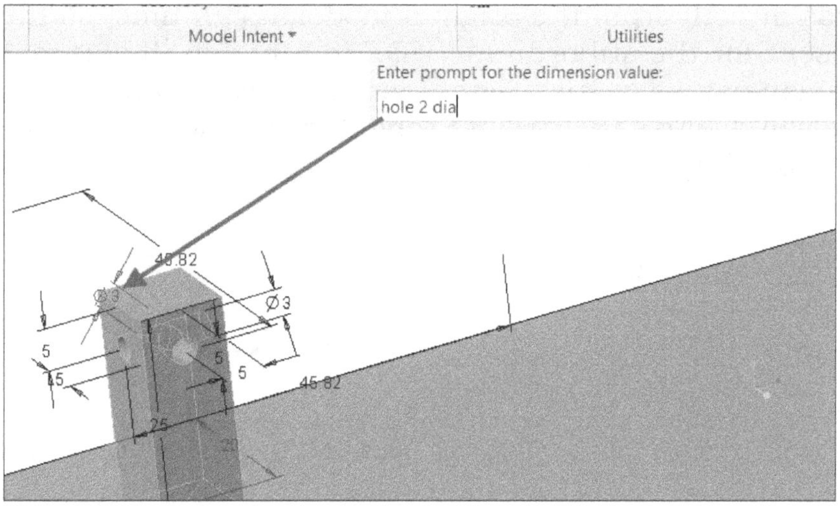

Figure-15. Specifying names for dimensional variables

- After specifying all the dimensions, click on the **OK** button from the dialog box. The **UDF Menu Manager** will be activated again.
- Click on the **Done/Return** option from the **Menu Manager**. The UDF will be saved in the current working directory.

Inserting User-Defined Feature

- Click on the **User-Defined Feature** tool from the **Get Data** panel in the **Model** tab of the **Ribbon**. The **Open** dialog box will be displayed with UDF files in working directory; refer to Figure-16.

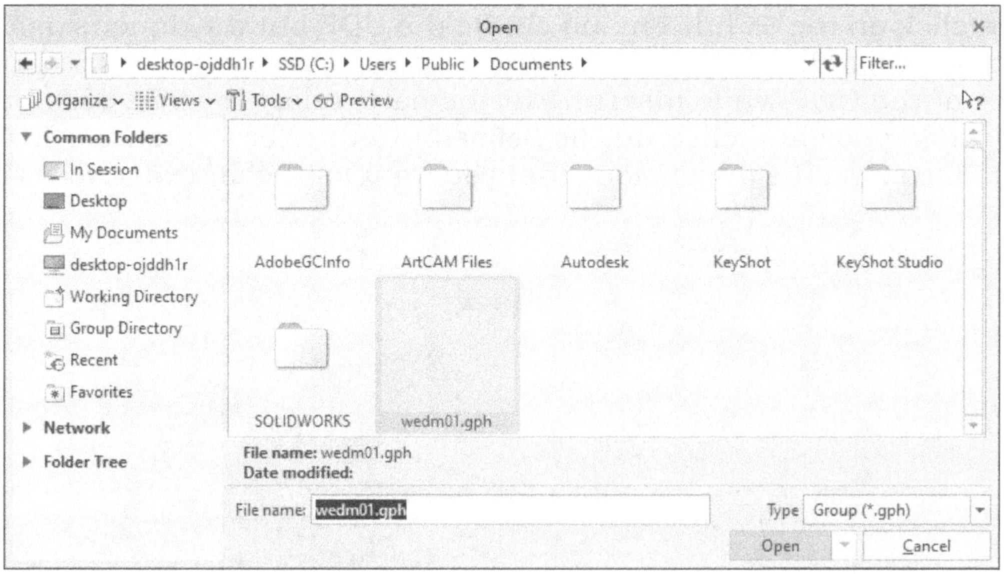

Figure-16. Open dialog box with UDF file

- Double-click on desired UDF file from the dialog box. Note that the file extension for UDF file is ".gph". The **Insert User-Defined Feature** dialog box will be displayed; refer to Figure-17.

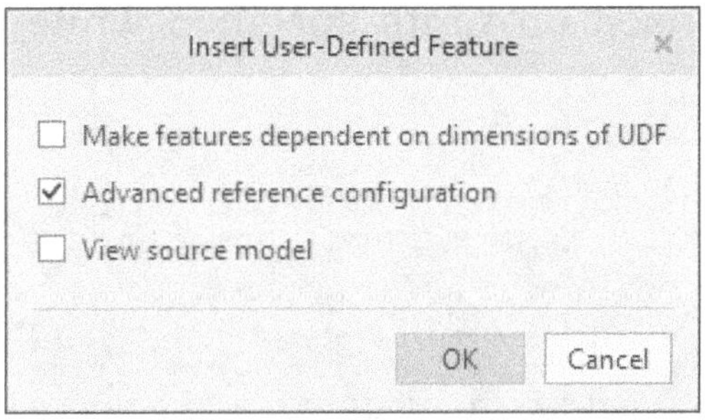

Figure-17. Insert User-Defined Feature dialog box

- Select the **Advanced reference configuration** check box if you want to map the UDF references to the selected references. (This option is required for placing UDF properly otherwise you might need to redefine the whole feature again in the model.) Select the **View source model** check box if you want to view the source model while inserting UDF. Select the **Make features dependent on dimensions of UDF** check box to make all the features of UDF dependent on the dimensions specified for UDF. Select desired check box and click on the **OK** button (We have selected the **Advanced reference configuration** check box and the **View source model** check box). The **User-Defined Feature Placement** dialog box will be displayed with preview of source model; refer to Figure-18. Also, you will be asked to select the references for UDF one by one.

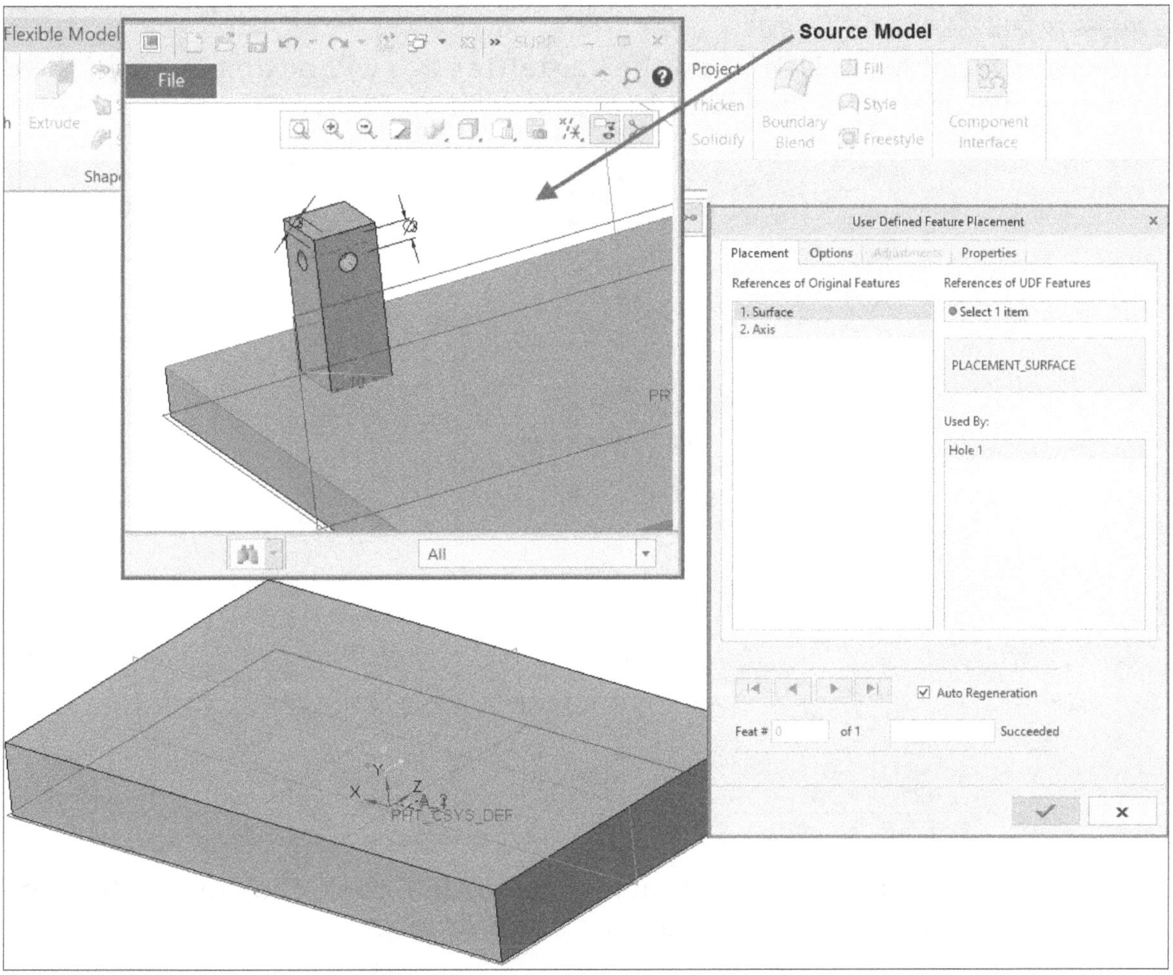

Figure-18. User Defined Feature Placement dialog box with source model preview

- Select the references based on hints specified while creating the UDF; refer to Figure-19.

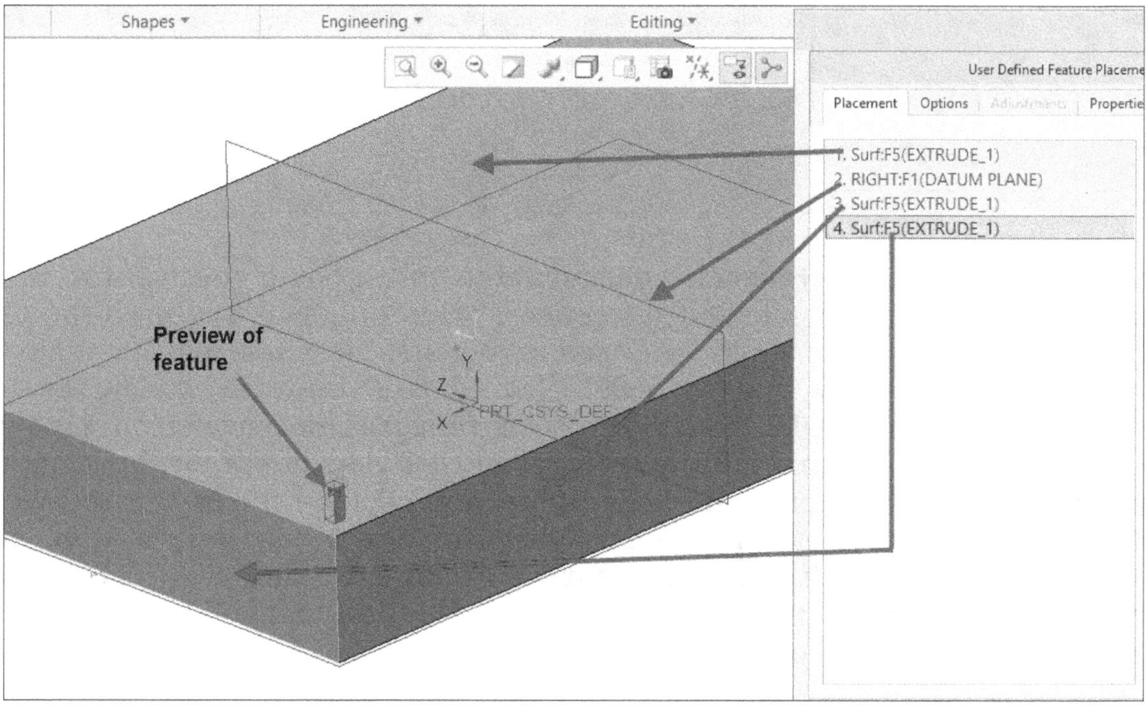

Figure-19. Reference selection for UDF

- If there are variables in UDF then the **Variables** tab will be displayed in the dialog box where you can specify desired values; refer to Figure-20.

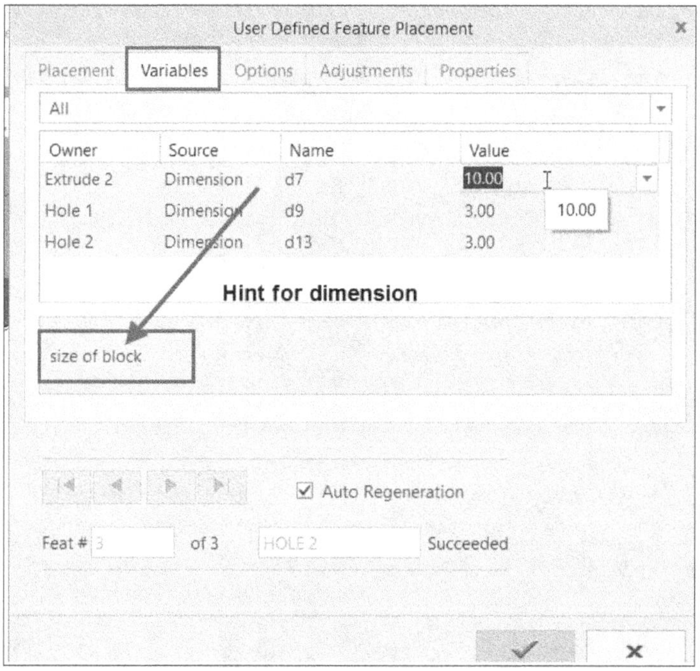

Figure-20. Variables tab in User Defined Feature Placement dialog box

- If you want to modify any individual feature of UDF then click on the **Options** tab. The dialog box will be displayed as shown in Figure-21.

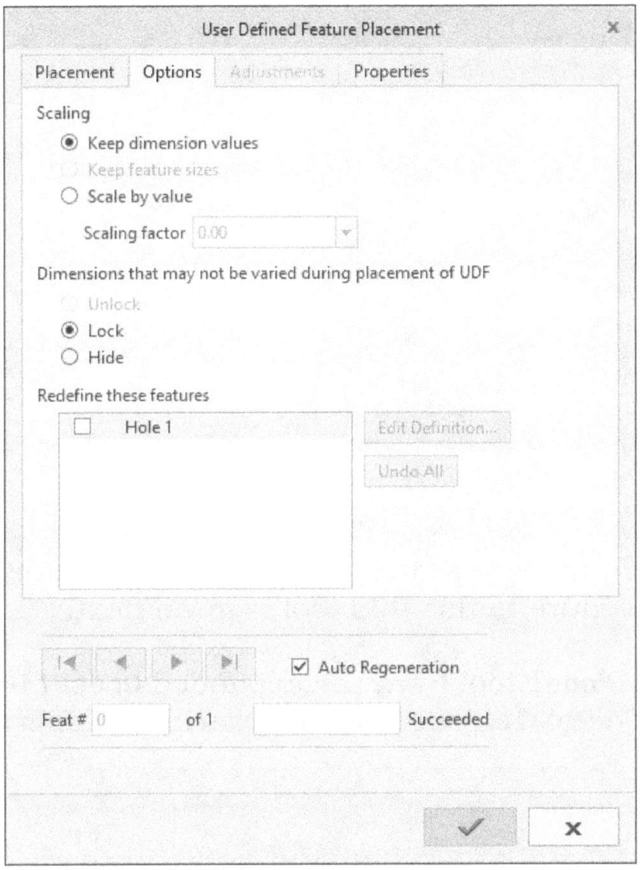

Figure-21. Options tab in User Defined Feature Placement dialog box

- If you want to scale up/down the dimensions of UDF which are not variable then click on the **Scale by value** radio button and specify desired scale value.
- Select desired radio button for dimensions that can not be varied while placing UDF. If you select the **Unlock** radio button then these dimensions can be edited manually after placing UDF. If you select the **Lock** radio button then the dimensions will be locked. If you select the **Hide** radio button then the dimensions will be hidden.
- If you want to redefine any feature like, you want to change the depth of extrude feature in UDF or you want to change a sketch then select the check box(es) for feature(s) which you want to redefine from the **Redefine these features** area of the dialog box and click on the **Edit Definition** button. The related contextual tabs will be displayed providing the options to redefine feature(s). Modify the features as required.
- If you want to exclude the last features of UDF then clear the **Auto Regeneration** check box and set desired number of features upto which you want to create the UDF; refer to Figure-22.
- If you have features that can be flipped in orientation then click on the **Adjustments** tab and click on the **Flip** button.
- Click on the **OK** button from the dialog box to create the feature and exit the dialog box.

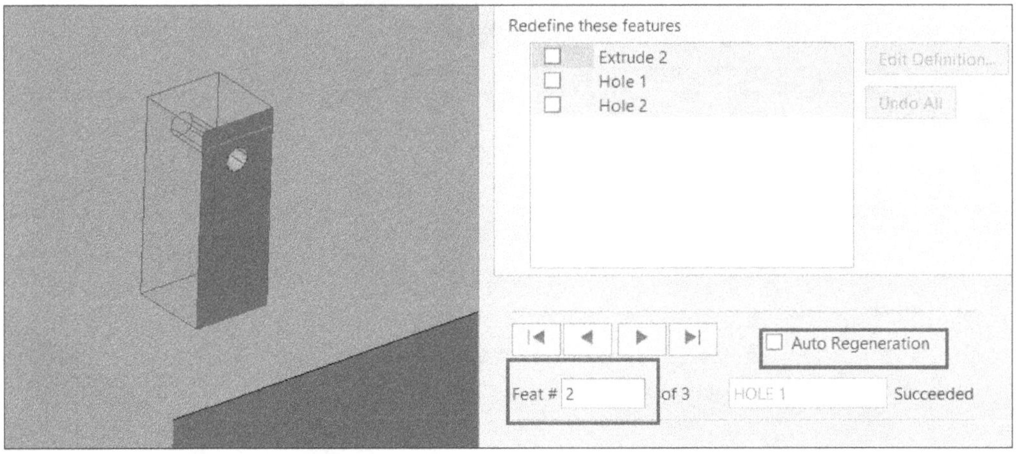

Figure-22. Modifying number of features

SCALING MODEL

The **Scale Model** tool in the **Operations** panel is used to scale-up or scale-down the whole model. The procedure to use this tool is given next.

- Click on the **Scale Model** tool from the expanded **Operations** panel in the **Model** tab of the **Ribbon**. The **Scale Model** dialog box will be displayed; refer to Figure-23.

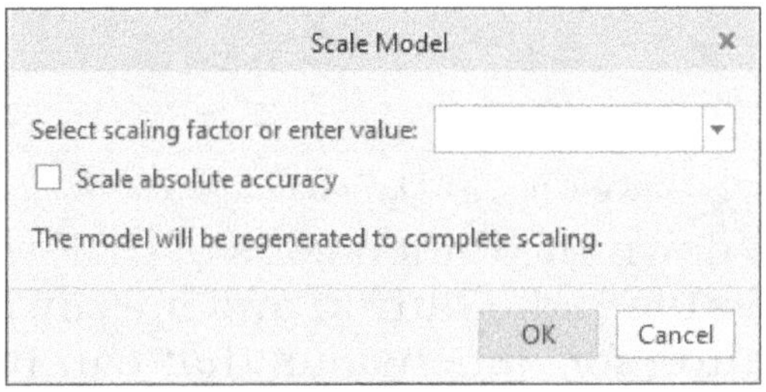

Figure-23. Scale Model dialog box

- Specify desired value of scale in the edit box. You can specify the scale value in the range of 0.00001 to 10000. If you want to scale down the model then specify the value less than 1.
- If you want to change the absolute accuracy of model according to the scale value then select the **Scale absolute accuracy** check box. Here, accuracy means the lowest size that can be displayed properly in Creo Parametric. Accuracy plays important role in meshing the model and performing analysis.
- After specifying the value, click on the **OK** button. The model will be scaled accordingly.

SETTING FEATURES READ-ONLY

Sometimes features get changed unintentionally while working on the model. To safeguard from such incidents, you can make the features read-only after creating them. The procedure to do so is given next.

- Select the feature up to which you want to make all the features read only. Click on the **Set as last read only** option from the **Read Only** cascading menu in the expanded **Operations** panel of the **Model** tab in the **Ribbon**. The features up to the selected feature will become read only; refer to Figure-24.

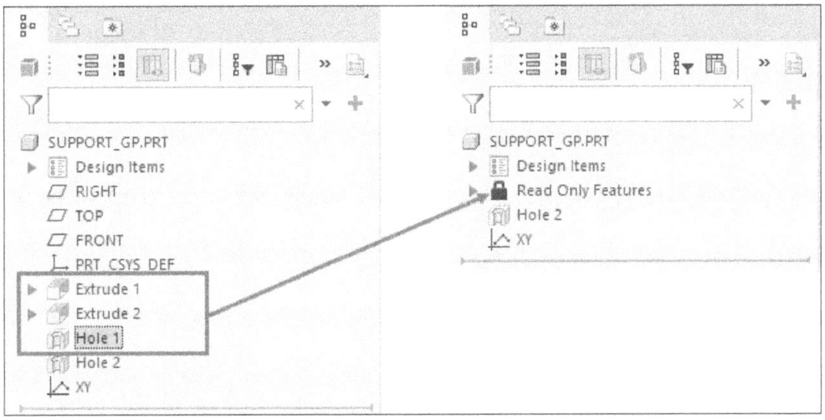

Figure-24. Making features read only

- If you want to make all the features of model read-only, then click on the **Set all as read only** option from the **Read Only** cascading menu in the expanded **Operations** panel of the **Ribbon**.
- To clear read-only from feature, right-click on **Read Only Features** in the **Model Tree** and select the **Clear All Read Only** option; refer to Figure-25.

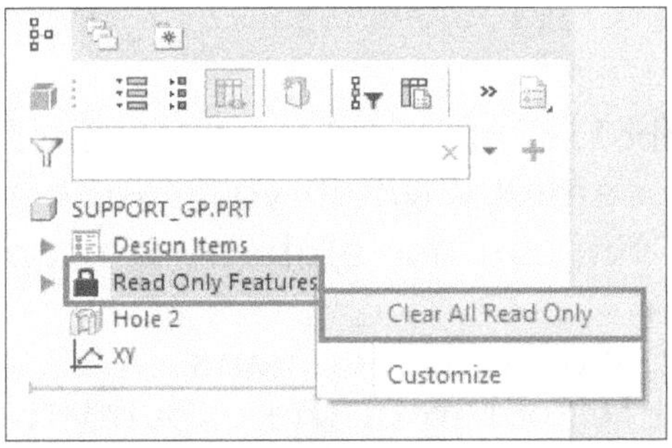

Figure-25. Clear All Read Only option

FAMILY TABLE

The **Family Table** tool is used to create multiple instances of same part with some dimensional or feature variation. The procedure to create a family table is given next.

- Create a model of part for which you want to create family table; refer to Figure-26.
- Double-click on any flat face of the part to activate dynamic edit box. The dynamic editing mode will become active; refer to Figure-27. Or, you can right-click on the feature from **Model Tree** and select the **Edit dimension** button; refer to Figure-28. The dynamic editing mode will become active.

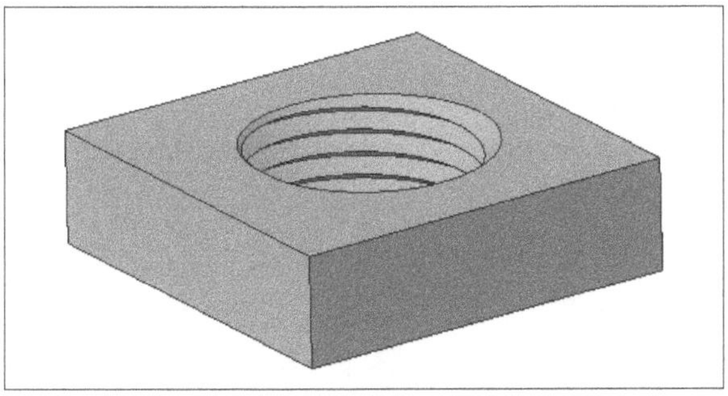

Figure-26. Square nut for family table

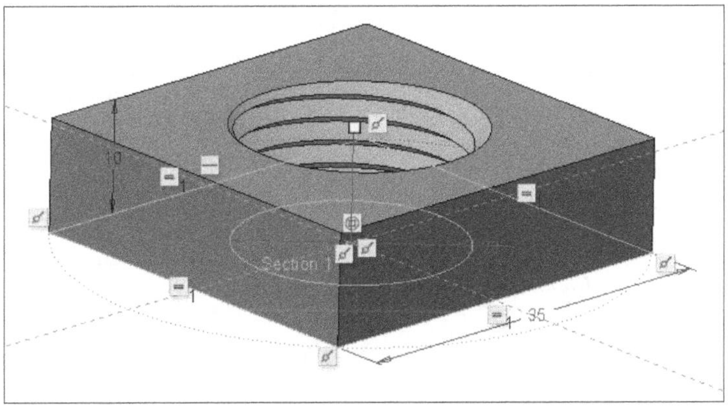

Figure-27. Dynamic editing mode of part

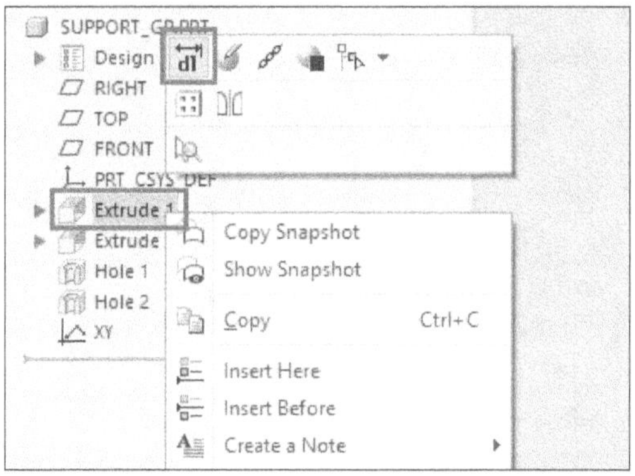

Figure-28. Edit Dimension button

- Select a dimension of the model that you want to include in the family table. The **Dimension** contextual tab will be displayed in the **Ribbon**; refer to Figure-29.

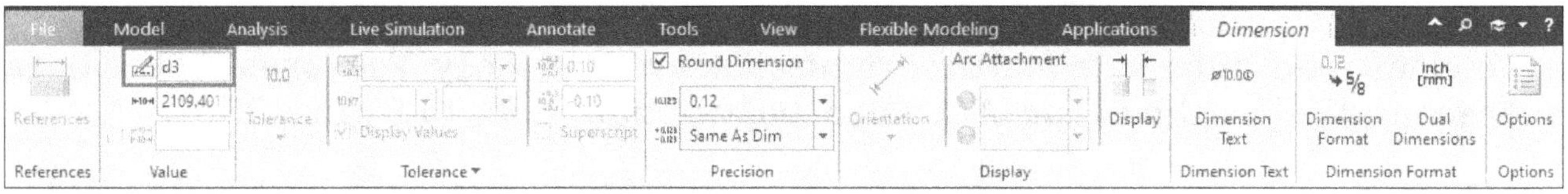

Figure-29. Dimension contextual tab

- Click in the **Modify symbolic name of the dimensions** edit box highlighted in Figure-29 and enter the name by which you can identify the dimension in table like **Nut size**. Note that you can use alphabets, numerics, and _ (Underscore) in specifying name.
- Similarly, set the names of other dimensions.
- Click on the **Family Table** tool from the expanded **Model Intent** panel in the **Model** tab of the **Ribbon**. The **Family Table** dialog box will be displayed; refer to Figure-30.

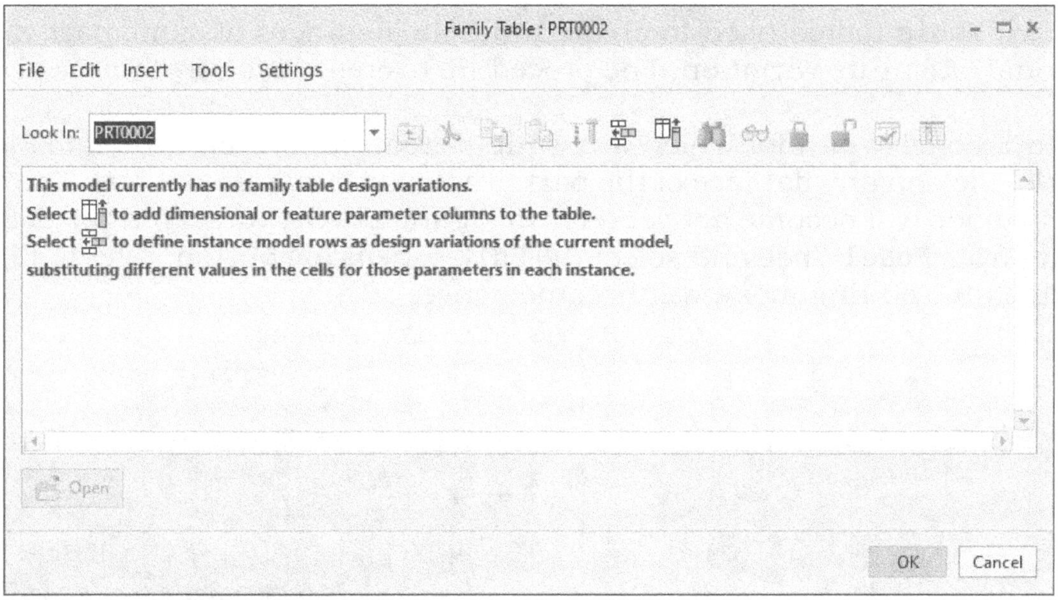

Figure-30. Family Table dialog box

- Click on the **Add/delete the table columns** button from the toolbar in the dialog box. The **Family Items** dialog box will be displayed; refer to Figure-31. By default, the **Dimension** radio button is selected, so you are asked to select dimensions to be included in the table.
- Click on the feature of model whose dimensions are to be included in family table. The dimensions of feature will be displayed; refer to Figure-32.

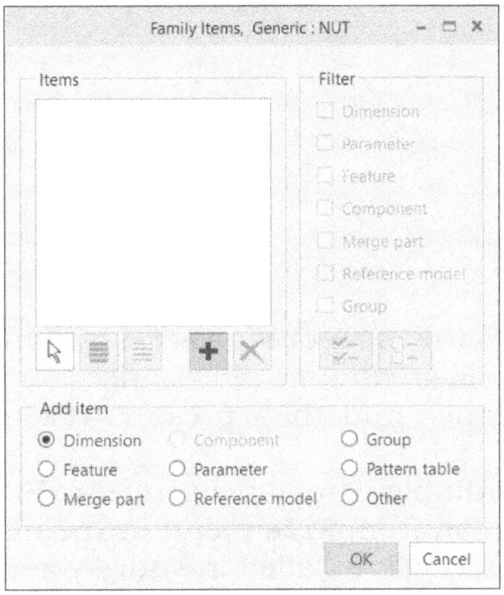

Figure-31. Family Items dialog box

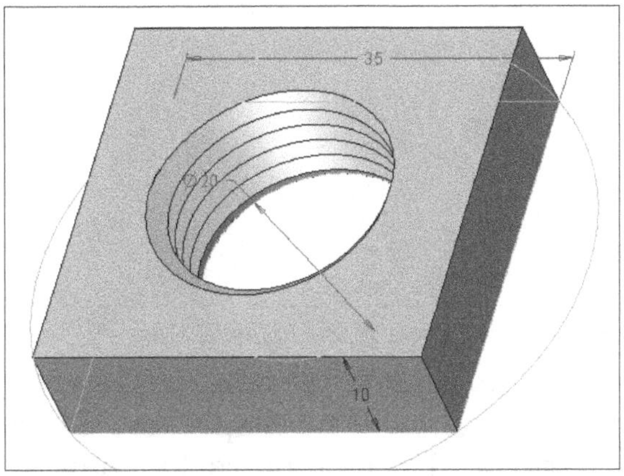

Figure-32. Dimension of extrude feature displayed

- Click one by one on the dimensions to be included in table; refer to Figure-33.

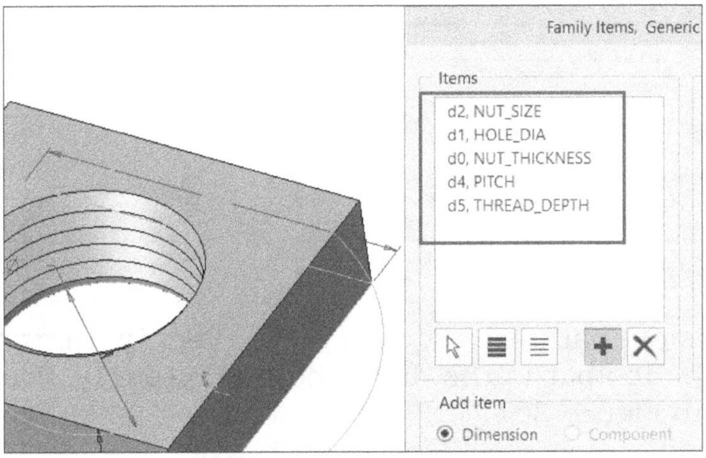

Figure-33. DImensions added in the table

- If you want to add/remove a feature from the part using Yes/No option in the table then select the **Feature** radio button from the dialog box and select the features from the model. Similarly, you can include other items in the family table.
- Click on the **OK** button from the dialog box. The parameters of part will be displayed in the table; reefer to Figure-34.

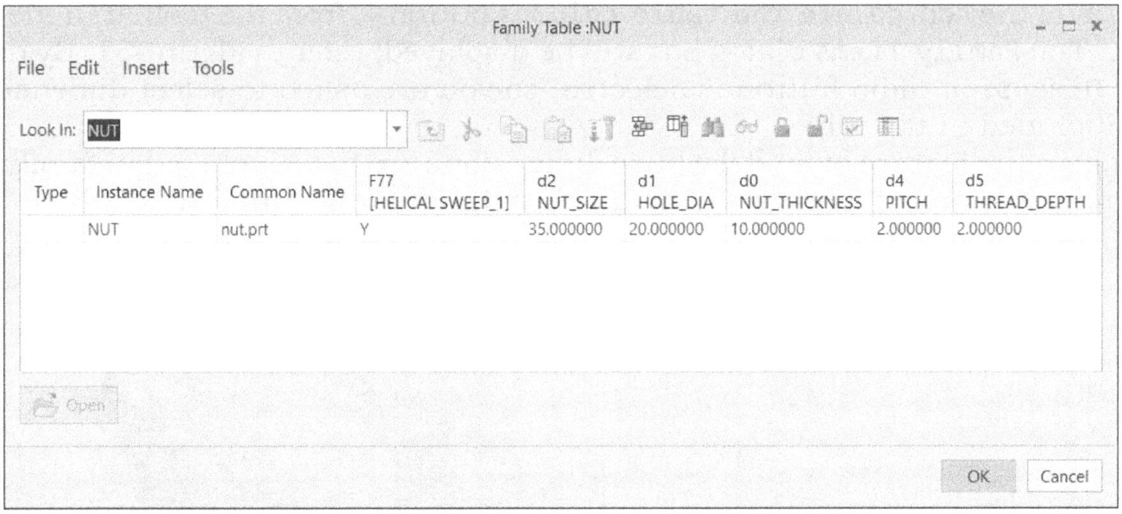

Figure-34. Parameters of part in family table

- Click on the **Insert a new instance at the selected row** button. A new instance of part will be displayed. Specify desired name of instance.
- Specify desired parameters for new instance and then press **ENTER** to create another instance.
- Repeat the process until you get required number of instances; refer to Figure-35. You can click on the **Edit with Excel** option from **File** menu in the dialog box to edit table in Microsoft Excel if Microsoft Excel installed in your system.

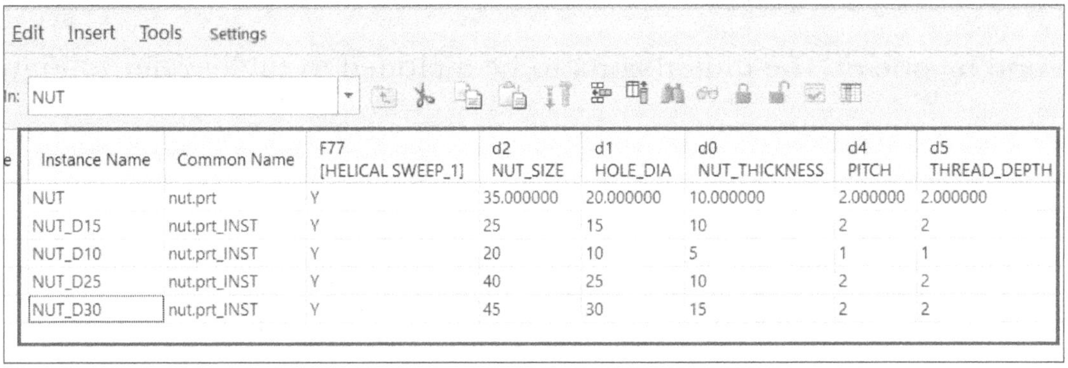

Figure-35. Parameters specified for nut

- After entering desired parameters, click on the **Verify instances of the family** button from the toolbar in the dialog box. The **Family Tree** dialog box will be displayed; refer to Figure-36.

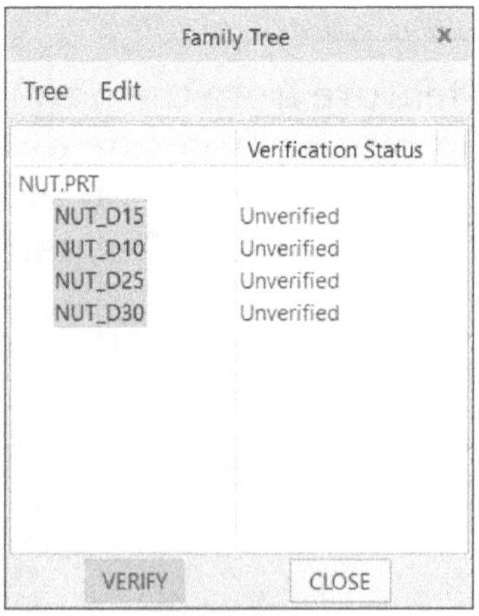

Figure-36. Family Tree dialog box

- Click on the **Verify** button from the dialog box. If verification status for all the instances are **Success** then close the dialog box and click on the **OK** button from the **Family Table** dialog box. If verification status for any of the instances is **Failure** then close the dialog box, change the parameters for instance, and then again click on the **Verify** button from the **Family Table** dialog box. Once all the instances are successful, click on the **OK** button to create the table.
- Save the file using **Save** button from the **Quick Access Toolbar**. Close the file.

Opening a Family Table Part

- Click on the **Open** button from the **Quick Access Toolbar**. The **File Open** dialog box will be displayed.
- Select the part for which family table was created earlier and click on the **Open** button. The **Select Instance** dialog box will be displayed; refer to Figure-37.

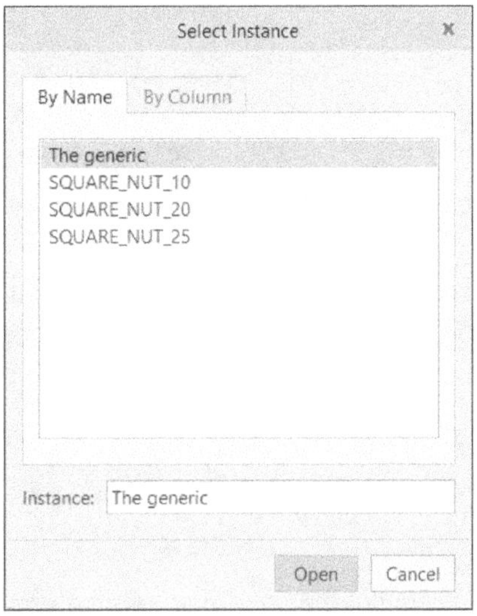

Figure-37. Select Instance dialog box

- Select desired instance and click on the **Open** button. The selected instance of part will open.

IMPORTING PART/ASSEMBLY

You can import parts/assemblies of third party CAD software by using the Import tool. The procedure to use **Import** tool is given next.

- Click on the **Import** tool from the expanded **Get Data** panel in the **Model** tab of the **Ribbon**. The **Open** dialog box will be displayed.
- Double-click on the third party CAD part/assembly file. The **File** dialog box will be displayed as shown in Figure-38.
- Select desired radio button from **Import type** area of the dialog box. Like, select the **Geometry** radio button to import part as geometry or **Facet** radio button to import part as surfaces. If you are not sure what type of object is there in imported part then select the **Automatic** radio button.
- To modify the profile of importing part, click on the **Details** button from the dialog box. The **Import Profile** dialog box will be displayed as shown in Figure-39.

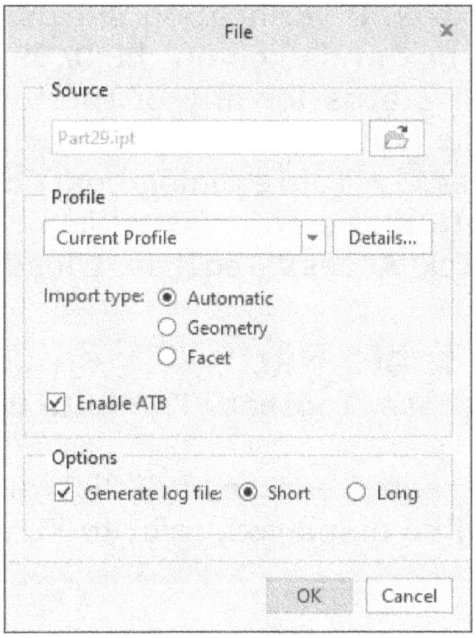

Figure-38. File dialog box

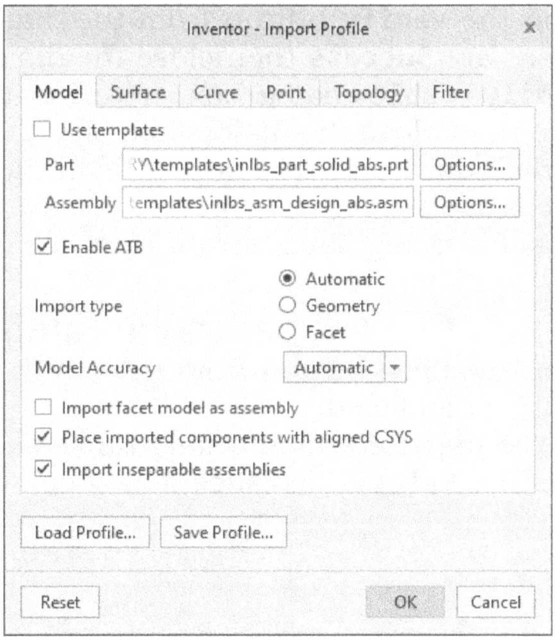

Figure-39. Import Profile dialog box

- Select the **Use templates** check box if you want to use Creo Parametric template while importing the part.
- Click on the **Surface** tab in the dialog box to modify parameters of the surface. The dialog box will be displayed as shown in Figure-40.

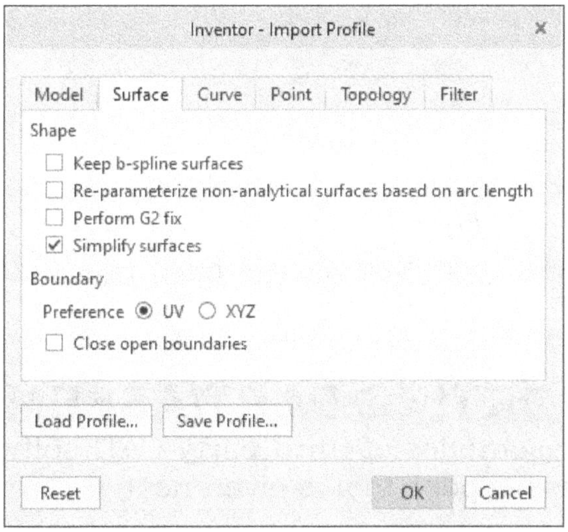

Figure-40. Surface tab in the Import Profile dialog box

- Select desired parameters like select the **Keep b-spline surfaces** check box to keep b-spline surfaces in the imported model. In the same way, you can modify the other parameters of the profile.
- Click on the **OK** button from the **Import Profile** dialog box to apply changes.
- Click on the **OK** button from the **File** dialog box. Preview of the imported part will be displayed; refer to Figure-41.
- Click on the **Add Bodies** button from **Import As** area of the contextual tab if you want to add the solid part in the existing model. Click on the **Add Geometry** button to combine merged model with present model. Click on the **Remove Geometry** button to subtract merged model from present model. Click on the **Add Surfaces** button if you want to import the part as surface.
- Click on the **OK** button from the contextual tab.

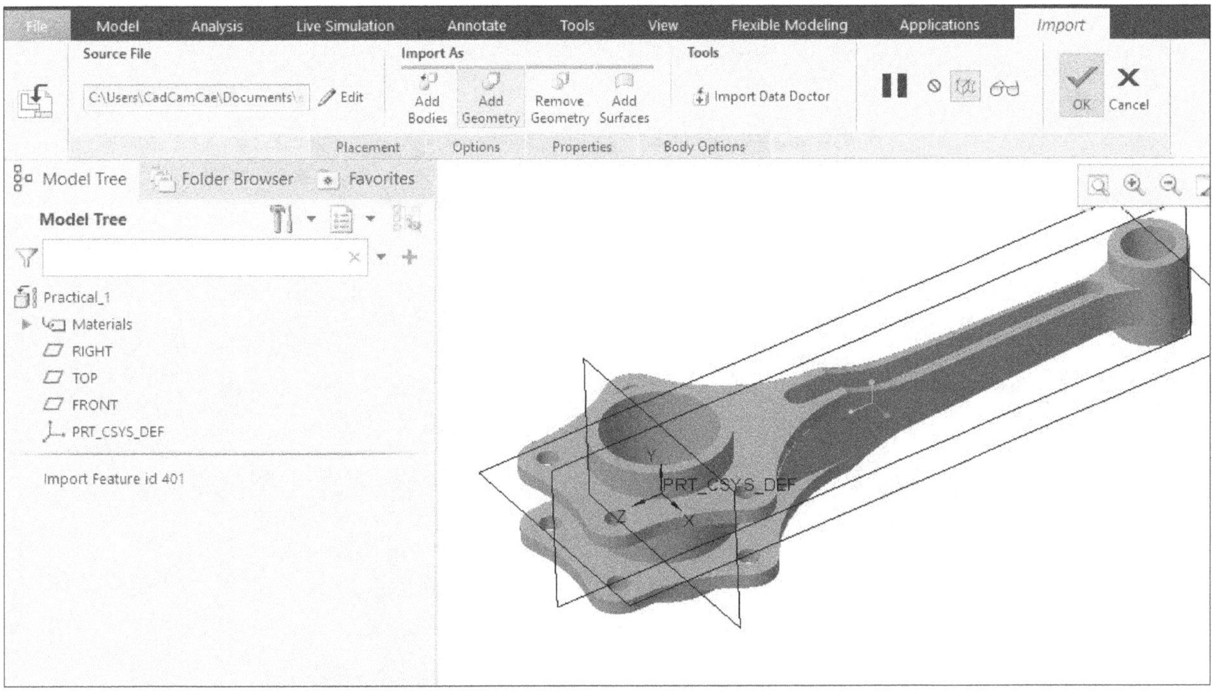

Figure-41. Preview of imported part

MERGE/INHERITANCE

The **Merge/Inheritance** tool is used to perform boolean operation of part with another part using the assembly constraints. The procedure is given next.

- Click on the **Merge/Inheritance** tool from the expanded **Get Data** panel in the **Model** tab of the **Ribbon**. The **Merge/Inheritance** contextual tab will be displayed; refer to Figure-42.

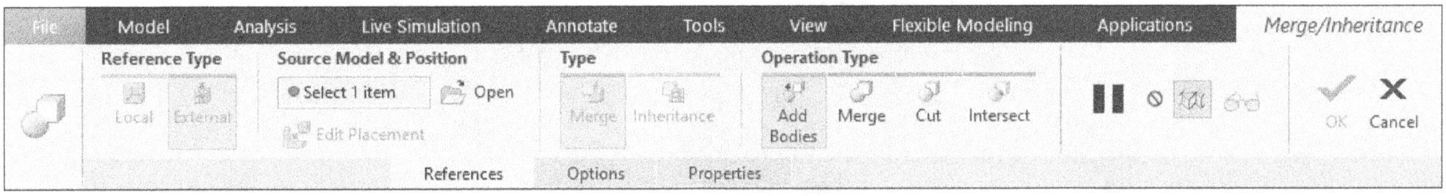

Figure-42. Merge Inheritance contextual tab

- Click on the **Open** button from the contextual tab. The **Open** dialog box will be displayed.
- Double-click on the part file that you want to merge with the model in drawing area. Preview of the part will be displayed with **Component Placement** dialog box; refer to Figure-43.
- Select the faces of model in drawing area and part to be merged as required using the constraints. Note that the use of various constraints is discussed in Chapter 9 of this book. So, you can check the chapter and come back for practicing this tool.
- Apply desired constraints (We have used **Default** constraint which places the inserted part at default coordinate system) and click on the **OK** button from the dialog box. The buttons in contextual tab will become active and if you click on the **Preview** button then you can check the preview of merge feature; refer to Figure-44. Click on the **Preview** button again to return.

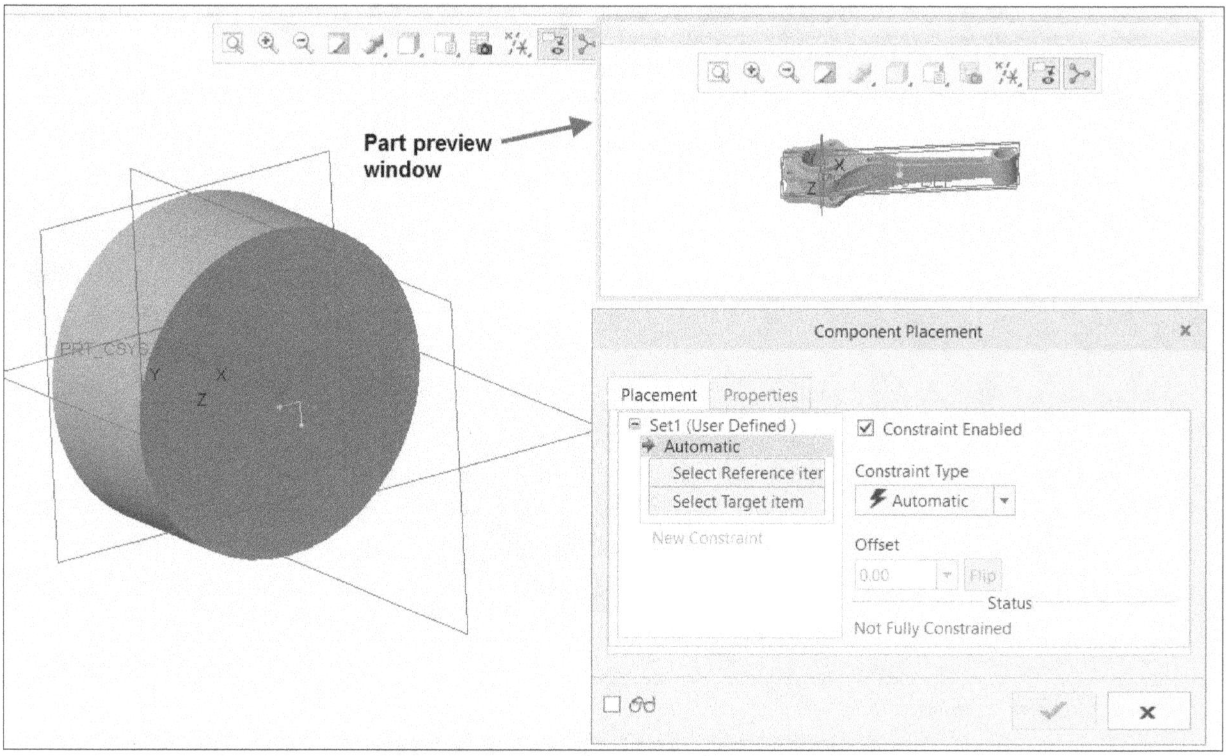

Figure-43. Part preview with Component Placement dialog box

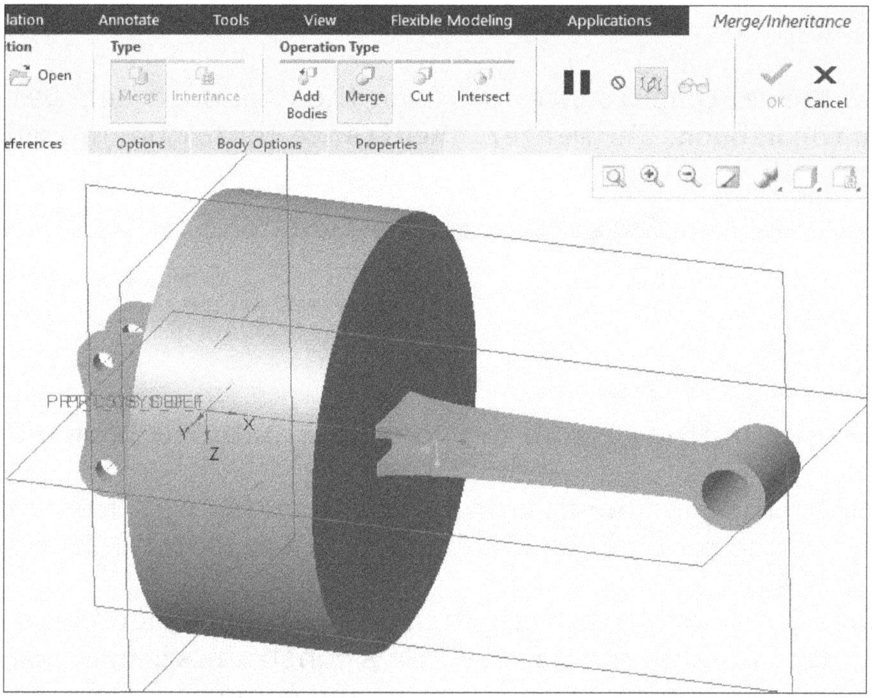

Figure-44. Preview of merge feature

- Click on the **Merge/Inheritance** button from **Type** area of the contextual tab if you want to inherit all the parameters and features of the model to be merged. On doing so, you can later modify the features of inherited model using the **Model Tree**; refer to Figure-45.

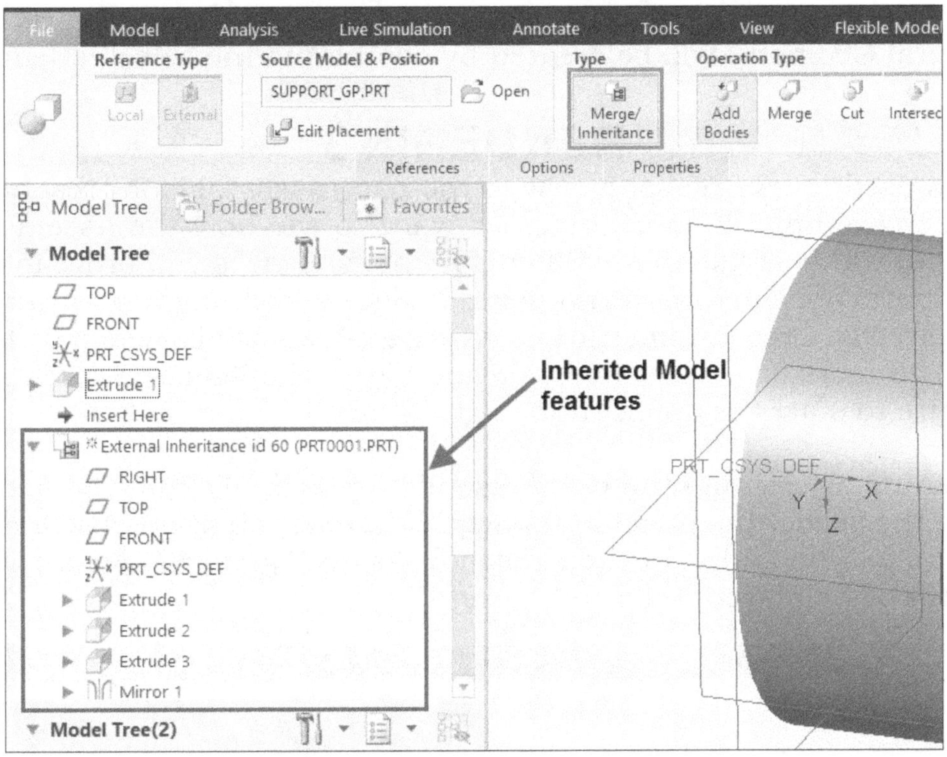

Figure-45. Inherited model features

- To perform boolean operation, click on desired button from the **Ribbon**. Click on the **Add Bodies** button from **Operation Type** area of the **Ribbon** if you want to add the solid part in the existing model. Click on the **Merge** button to combine merged model with present model. Click on the **Cut** button to subtract merged model from present model. Click on the **Intersect** button to create intersection part of the merging models.
- Click on the **OK** button from the contextual tab to create the feature.

COLLAPSE

The **Collapse** tool is used to merge various features of the model to form one feature. In this way, you can hide the details of modeling features. The procedure to use this tool is given next.

- Select the features you want to combine from the **Model Tree** and then click on the **Collapse** tool from the expanded **Editing** panel in the **Ribbon**. The **Collapse** dialog box will be displayed; refer to Figure-46.

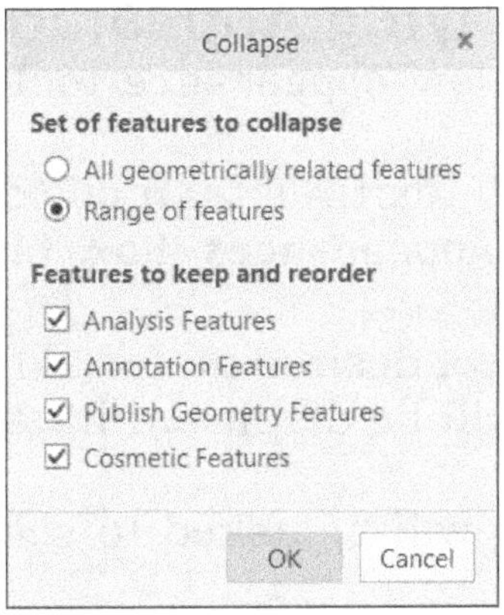

Figure-46. Collapse dialog box

- Select desired options from the dialog box and click on the **OK** button. An Incremental Geometry will be created by combining the selected features.

RENDERING

Rendering is used to give realistic view to the part/assembly for presentation to the customer. For example, if your customer want to see how the assembly of watch created by you will look like in real life before he/she gives you order for production then it is better to present him the rendered image of product rather than starting the production directly. Creo Parametric has a very sophisticated system of photo realistic rendering. The tools for rendering are available in the **Render Studio** Application. The procedure to start the application is given next.

- After opening or creating the part/assembly model, click on the **Render Studio** tool from the **Rendering** panel in the **Applications** tab of the **Ribbon**. The **Render Studio** tab will be added in the **Ribbon**; refer to Figure-47. Also, the preview of render will be displayed; refer to Figure-47.

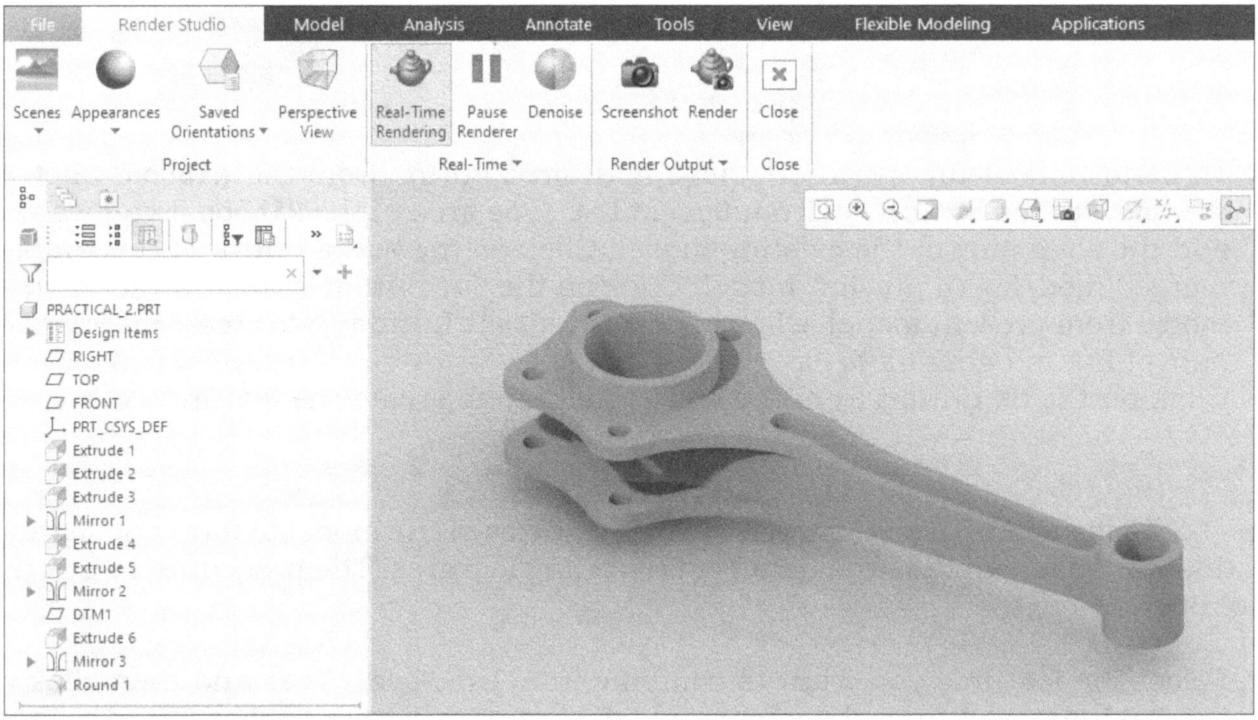

Figure-47. Render Studio tab

Applying Appearances

- Click on the down arrow below **Appearance** tool and select desired appearance from the list.
- If you want to apply material textures then click on the down arrow in the right side of **Library** node in the **Appearances box**. List of material categories will be displayed; refer to Figure-48.
- Expand the category and select desired material type from the Material categories box. The related materials will be displayed in the **Library** node of **Appearances box**.
- Select desired material. You will be asked to select the object to apply material texture.

- Select the **Part** filter from the **Selection Filter** drop-down at the bottom-right corner of the application window and select the part/face of the model.
- Press the Middle Mouse Button (MMB) to apply texture.

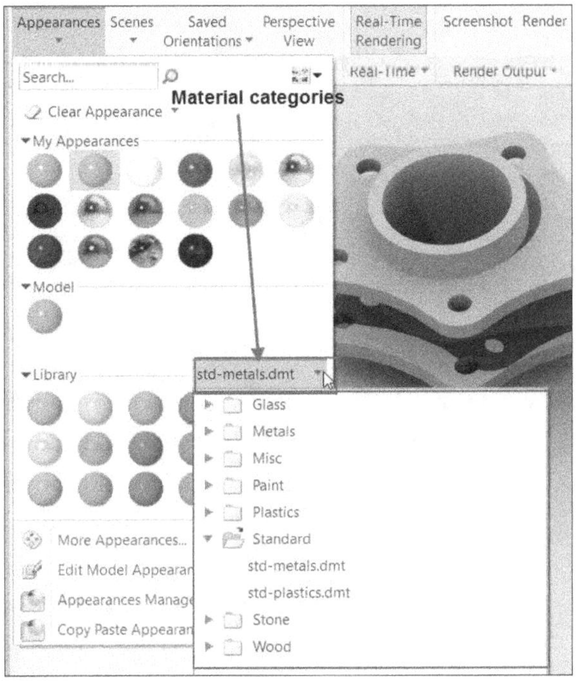

Figure-48. Material categories

User Defined Textures

If you want to use a texture downloaded from internet or saved in your computer then follow the steps given next.

- Click on the down arrow below **Appearances** button in the **Project** panel of the **Render Studio** tab in the **Ribbon** and then select the **More Appearances** button from the **Appearances box**. The **Appearance Editor** dialog box will be displayed; refer to Figure-49.
- Specify desired name for texture in the **Name** edit box.
- Set desired class and sub-class for material using the drop-downs in the **Properties** tab of the dialog box and specify the other related parameters.
- Click on the **Texture** tab to edit the options related to texture of material. Select the **Image** option from the drop-down in the tab. The **Browse** button next to drop-down will become active.
- Click on the **Browse** button and select the texture of material downloaded from internet or saved in your computer in image format.
- Similarly, you can add bump and decal to the material texture using the related tab options in the dialog box.
- Click on the **Close** button. The texture will be activated and you will be asked to select the object to apply texture. Select the object and press **MMB** to apply texture.
- Note that you can later find this texture in the class and sub-class that you have selected while creating the material texture.

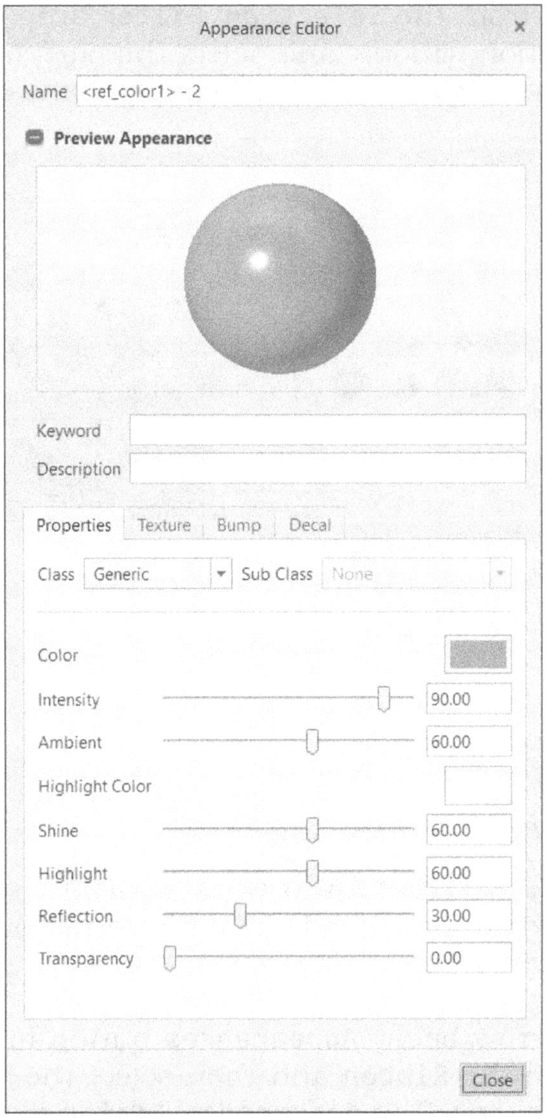

Figure-49. Appearance Editor dialog box

Applying Scenes

- Click on the down arrow below **Scenes** button in the **Project** panel of the **Render Studio** tab in the **Ribbon** and select desired scene for rendering.

Similarly, select desired orientation of part/assembly from the **Saved Orientations** drop-down in the **Ribbon**.

Real-Time Rendering

Real-Time Rendering tool allows to check the rendering of model while applying textures to the model. To activate real-time rendering, click on the **Real-Time Rendering** toggle button from the **Real-Time** panel in the **Render Studio** tab of the **Ribbon** to set it as On. The rendering will be displayed. To edit the parameters of rendering, follow the steps given next.

- Click on the **Real-Time Settings** tool from the expanded **Real-Time** panel of the **Render Studio** tab in the **Ribbon**. The **Real-Time Rendering Settings** dialog box will be displayed; refer to Figure-50.

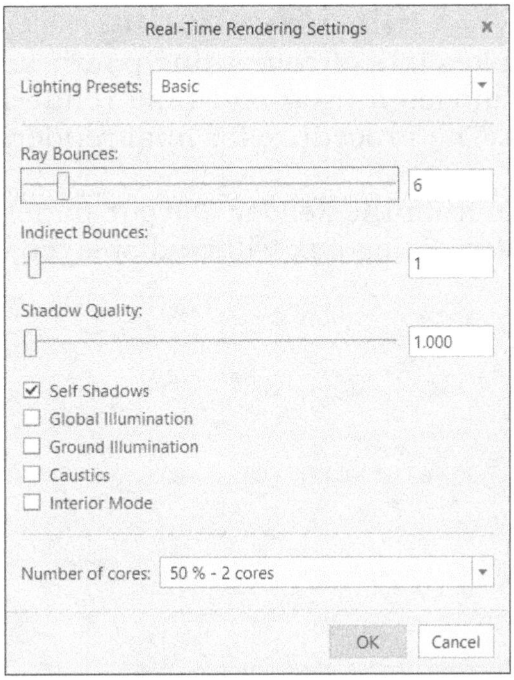

Figure-50. Real-Time Rendering Settings dialog box

- Set desired parameters in the dialog box or select desired preset from the **Lighting Presets** drop-down to system defined settings.
- Click on the **OK** button from the dialog box to apply changes.

Denoise

The **Denoise** tool is used to reduce the noise while rendering the model.

Taking Screenshot

- Click on the **Screenshot** tool from the **Render Output** panel in the **Render Studio** tab of the **Ribbon** to save the current rendering state of model as image file. The **Save screenshot** dialog box will be displayed; refer to Figure-51.

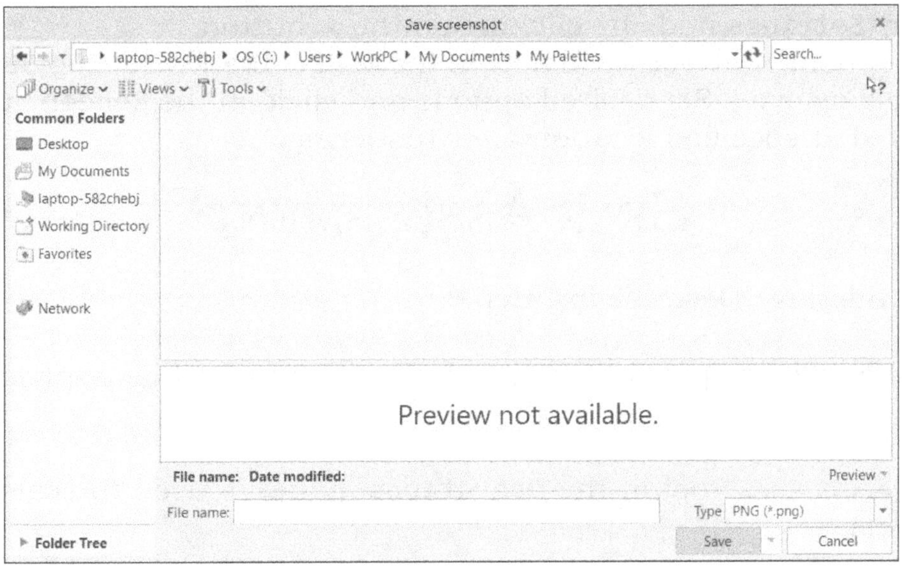

Figure-51. Save screenshot dialog box

- Specify a name for the file and click on the **Save** button to save the screenshot.

Final Rendering

A good quality of render takes lots of computing power and time to render. So, it is advisable to first make changes during real-time rendering then move on to final render to save reattempts. The procedure for final rendering is given next.

- Click on the **Render** tool from the **Render Output** panel in the **Render Studio** tab of the **Ribbon**. The **Render** dialog box will be displayed; refer to Figure-52.

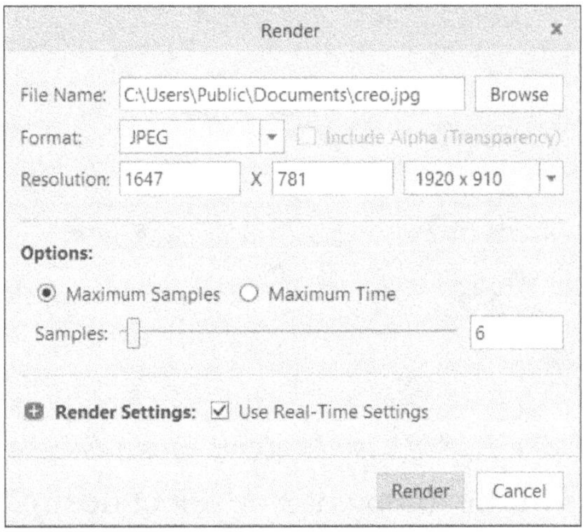

Figure-52. Render dialog box

- Specify the name and location of render file in the **File Name** edit box of the dialog box.
- Set desired format for output file from the **Format** drop-down. For TIF and PNG format, you can also include transparency by selecting the **Include Alpha (Transparency)** check box next to drop-down.
- Set desired resolution for output image file in the **Resolution** edit boxes.
- Set the termination condition of render from the **Options** area of the dialog box. You can specify maximum time or maximum samples for render termination.
- If you want to use the same settings as used for real-time rendering then select the **Use Real-Time Settings** check box otherwise clear the check box and expand the **Render Settings** node by clicking on the **+** button.
- The same options that were available in the **Real-Time Rendering Settings** dialog box will be displayed. Set desired options and click on the **Render** button. The file will be saved at specified location after rendering.

Self Assessment

1. What is Rendering? Describe in brief.

2. Which tool is used to preview the rendering of model while applying textures to the model?

3. The .... tool in the **Operations** panel is used to scale-up or scale-down the model.

4. The .... tool is used to create multiple instances of same part with some dimensional or feature variation.

5.The .... tool is used to perform boolean operation of part with another part using the assembly constraints.

6. The .... tool is used to merge various features of the model to form one feature.

7. The datum graph is used to create a sketch graph which can be used in various relations and formulae in modeling. (T/F)

8. A User-Defined Feature is a combination of features that can be applied to part at one place. (T/F)

9. What is the primary purpose of the Datum Reference tool in Creo Parametric?

a) To create solid models
b) To annotate drawing sheets
c) To create datum reference features showing design intent
d) To edit dimension values

10. What is the main use of a datum graph?

a) To print design reports
b) To build rendering scenes
c) To create solid extrusions
d) To drive model relations and formulas

11. Which file extension is associated with User-Defined Feature (UDF) files?

a) .prt
b) .asm
c) .gph
d) .drw

12. What is the difference between Stand Alone and Subordinate UDFs?

a) Subordinate UDFs are more detailed
b) Stand Alone UDFs require less memory
c) Subordinate UDFs fetch data from the reference model
d) Stand Alone UDFs update automatically with model changes

13. What happens if you clear the Auto Regeneration checkbox while inserting a UDF?

a) The model won't regenerate
b) Only selected features of UDF will be included
c) It regenerates all UDFs twice
d) It hides dimensions

14. What is the valid scale range when using the Scale Model tool?

a) 0.1 to 100
b) 0.00001 to 10000
c) 1 to 1000
d) 0.01 to 10

15. What does selecting the "Scale absolute accuracy" checkbox do in the Scale Model tool?

a) Locks the scale value permanently
b) Changes the model accuracy with scale
c) Reduces the file size
d) Converts model to 2D

16. What is the purpose of setting features as read-only in Creo Parametric?

a) To delete unnecessary features
b) To lock the dimensions permanently
c) To prevent accidental changes to features
d) To hide features from the Model Tree

17. Which option makes all features in the model read-only?

a) Set as last read only
b) Clear All Read Only
c) Set all as read only
d) Set model as read only

18. How can you clear the read-only status from features?

a) Use the Clear option in Operations panel
b) Click on Set as editable
c) Right-click on Read Only Features and select Clear All Read Only
d) Reopen the model without saving

19. What is the Family Table used for?

a) Analyzing assemblies
b) Creating multiple versions of a part with variations
c) Exporting models
d) Locking model dimensions

20. Which file format is required to edit Family Table using Excel?

a) TXT
b) CSV
c) XLSX
d) DOCX

21. What happens if an instance verification status is "Failure"?

a) It gets deleted
b) The table is locked
c) You need to change parameters and verify again
d) It gets automatically corrected

22. What does the Import tool allow in Creo Parametric?

a) Print documents
b) Merge multiple workspaces
c) Bring in parts/assemblies from other CAD software
d) Backup your workspace

23. What is the function of the Merge/Inheritance tool?

a) Create screenshots of model
b) Perform boolean operation using assembly constraints
c) Edit material appearance
d) Hide features from Model Tree

24. Which boolean operation subtracts the merged part from the existing model?

a) Add Bodies
b) Merge
c) Cut
d) Intersect

25. What is the purpose of the Collapse tool?

a) Flatten the model
b) Merge features into one to hide detail
c) Export the model
d) Verify model dimensions

26. What does the Real-Time Rendering toggle button do?

a) Saves screenshot
b) Enables live preview of rendering
c) Applies shadows
d) Merges textures

27. What is required to apply user-defined textures in Render Studio?

a) Save file in .txt format
b) Enter texture manually
c) Browse and select texture image from computer
d) Only use default appearances

28. How can you save a rendered image?

a) By clicking Screenshot tool in Render Output panel
b) Using Export option in File tab
c) From Save As in View tab
d) By taking a manual printscreen

29. What must be set to include transparency in final rendering output?

a) Use default format
b) Select the Include Alpha checkbox
c) Choose BMP format
d) Enable snapshot mode

Answers to Self Assessment Questions :

2. Real-Time Rendering **3.** Scale Model **4.** Family Table **5.** Merge/Inheritance **6.** Collapse **7.** T **8.** T

Chapter 9

Assembly and Practical

Topics Covered

The major topics covered in this chapter are:

- ***Introduction***
- ***Inserting Components in Assembly***
- ***Assembly constraints and relationships***
- ***Exploded View***
- ***Copying components in assembly with constraint***
- ***Practice***

INTRODUCTION

Most of the things you find around you in real-world are assembly of various components; the computer you are working on is an assembly, the automotive you may be driving or sitting in for traveling is an assembly, there are lots of examples. Till this point, we have learned to create solid parts. But most of the time, we need to assemble the parts to get some use of them. In this chapter, we will work on the Assembly environment of Creo Parametric in which we will be assembling two or more components using assembly constraints.

STARTING ASSEMBLY ENVIRONMENT

The procedure to start assembly environment is given next.

- Click on the **New** button from the **Quick Access Toolbar** or **Ribbon**. The **New** dialog box will be displayed.
- Select the **Assembly** radio button from the **Type** area in the dialog box and **Design** radio button from the **Sub-type** area of the dialog box.
- Clear the **Use default template** check box and click on the **OK** button from the dialog box. The **New File Options** dialog box will be displayed.
- Select the **mmns asm design** option from the list box to make assembly in Millimeter Newton Second unit system; refer to Figure-1 and click on the **OK** button from the dialog box. The assembly environment will be displayed; refer to Figure-2.

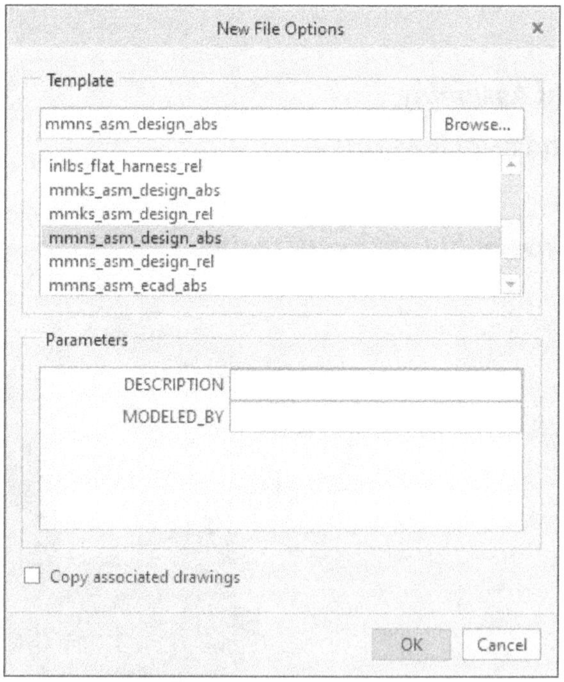

Figure-1. New File Options dialog box

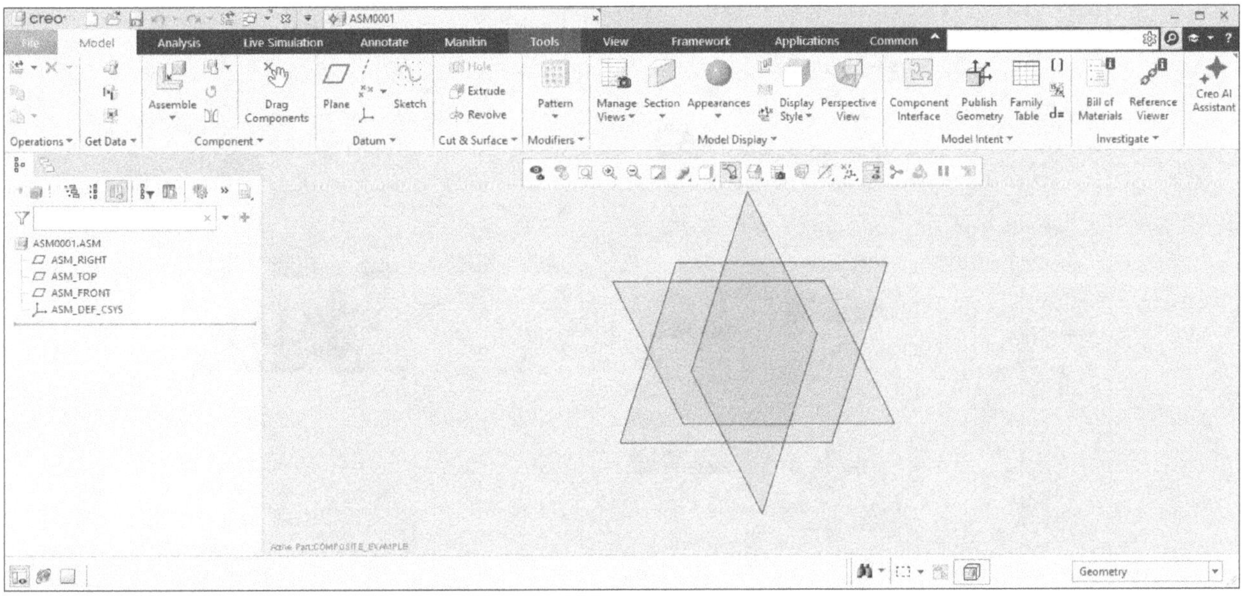

Figure-2. Assembly environment of Creo

Note that you can change the units of assembly in the same way as discussed in Chapter 1. Changing the unit system will also affect the size of parts in the model.

INSERTING BASE COMPONENT IN ASSEMBLY

In an assembly created in any CAD software, the first component is assumed to be the base component and it is generally fixed to its location. Afterwards, all the components are assembled with respect to the base component. The procedure of inserting components in assembly is given next.

- Click on the **Assemble** button from the **Assemble** drop-down in the **Component** panel of the **Ribbon**; refer to Figure-3.

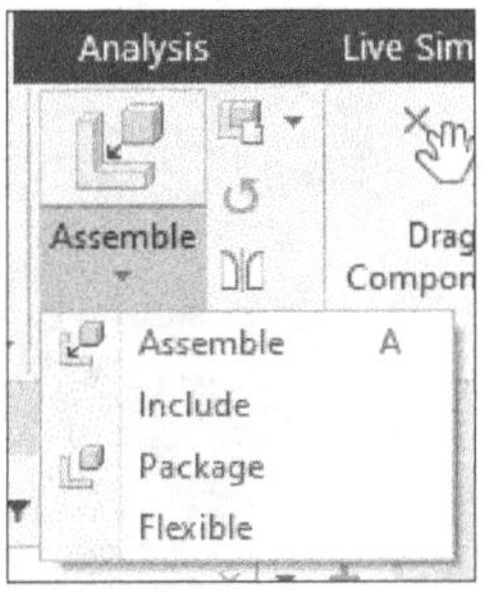

Figure-3. Assemble button

- On doing so, the **Open** dialog box will be displayed; refer to Figure-4.

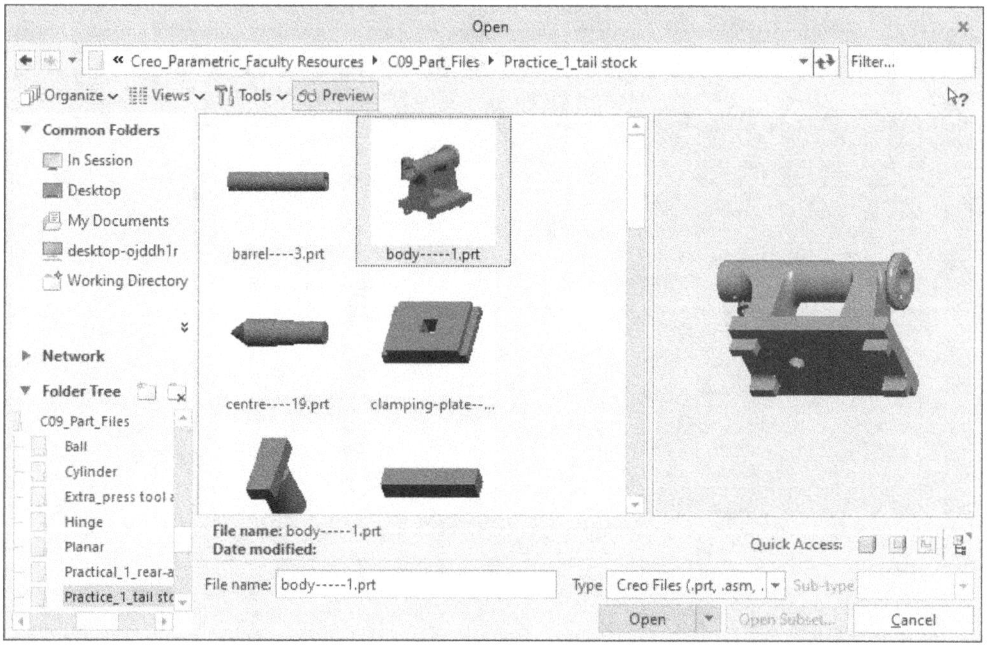

Figure-4. Open dialog box

- Select the base component from the dialog box and click on the **Open** button. The model will be displayed with a transformation triad and **Component Placement** contextual tab will be displayed; refer to Figure-5.

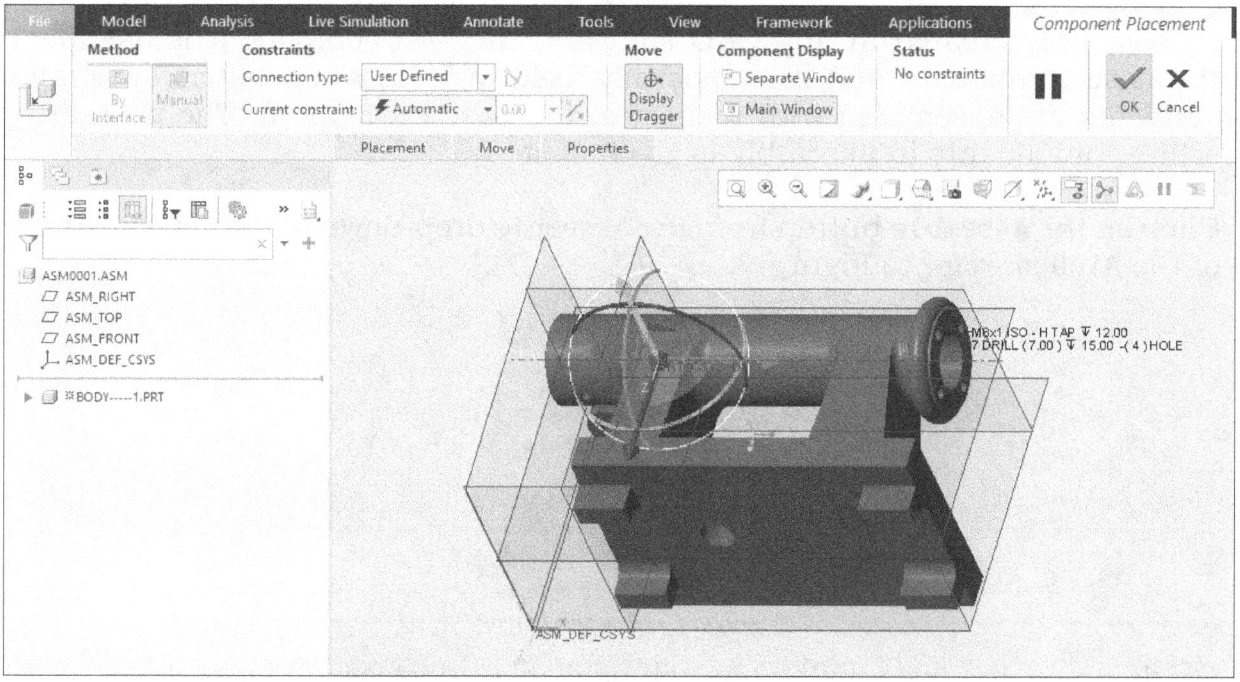

Figure-5. Component Placement contextual tab

- Sometimes, we may create the model in a different orientation than the required one in assembly. In such cases, hover the cursor on desired arrow or ring of the triad and drag it in desired direction; refer to Figure-6. Click on the **Display Dragger** button  from the contextual tab to show/hide the triad.

- After rotating the part, click on the **Current constraint** drop-down from the contextual tab; refer to Figure-7. The list of constraints will be displayed.

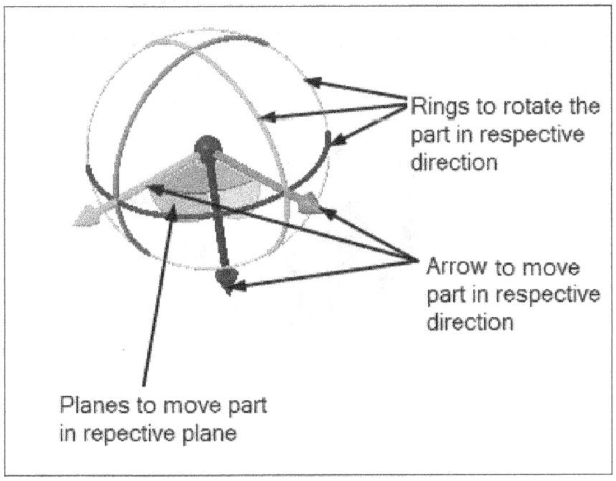

Figure-6. Transformation triad

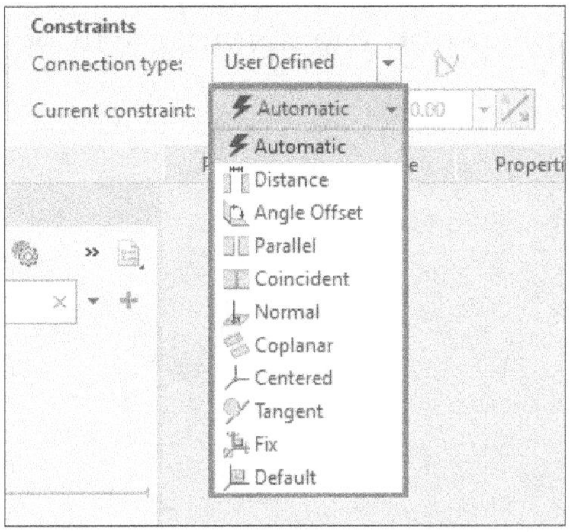

Figure-7. List of relationship constraints

- Generally, either **Default** or **Fix** option is selected from the **Current constraint** drop-down to place the base component. Select desired constraint and click on the **OK** button from the contextual tab. During the chapter, you will get to know about each option in the contextual tab. Details of various constraints in **Current constraint** drop-down is given next.

CONSTRAINTS IN CURRENT CONSTRAINT DROP-DOWN

There are 11 options available in the **Current constraint** drop-down to place components in the assembly. These options are discussed next.

Distance

As the name suggests, this constraint is used to place the component at a specified distance from the selected reference. The procedure to use this option is given next.

- Click on the **Distance** option from the **Current constraint** drop-down in the contextual tab or from the **Constraint Type** drop-down in the **Placement** tab; refer to Figure-8. You are asked to select one reference from component and one reference from assembly.

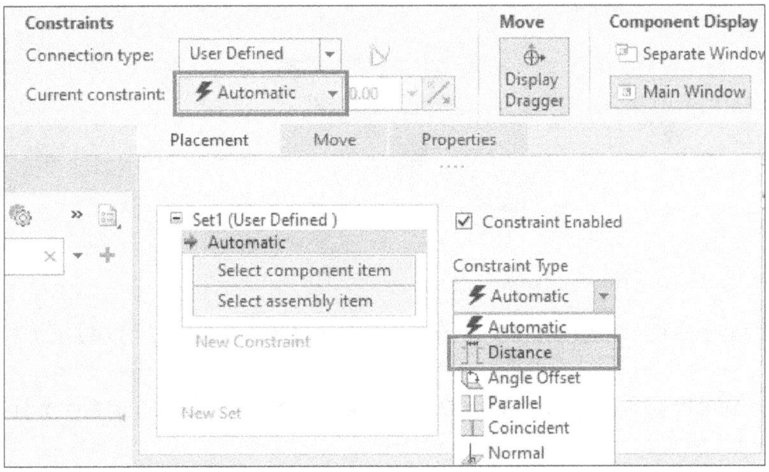

Figure-8. Distance constraint

- Select a face/plane/edge/axis/point from the component. You are asked to select a reference from assembly. Also a cosmetic line gets attached to the cursor.
- Select a face/plane/edge/axis/point of assembly. The distance constraint will be applied and the distance will be displayed as a dimension; refer to Figure-9.

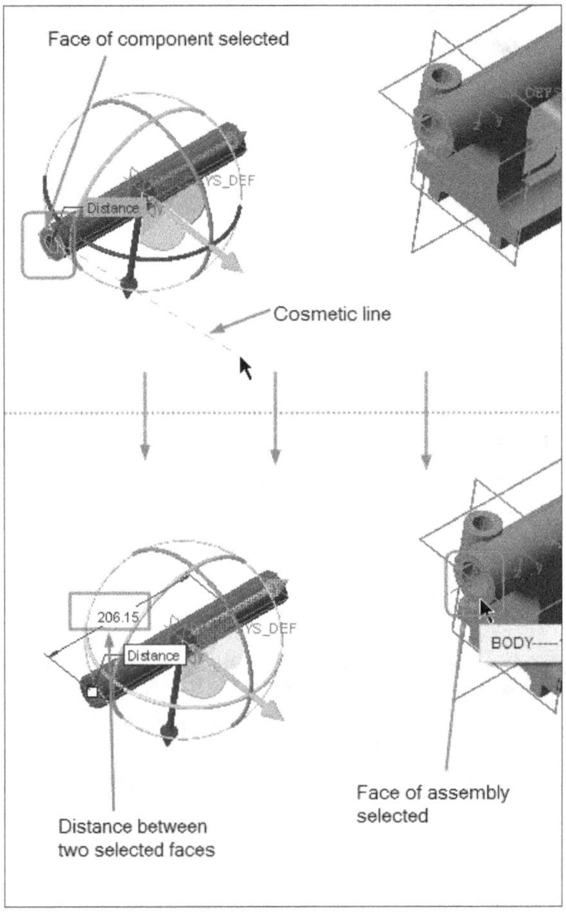

Figure-9. Selecting faces for distance constraint

- Double-click on the dimension value or specify desired distance value in the **Offset** edit box; refer to Figure-10.

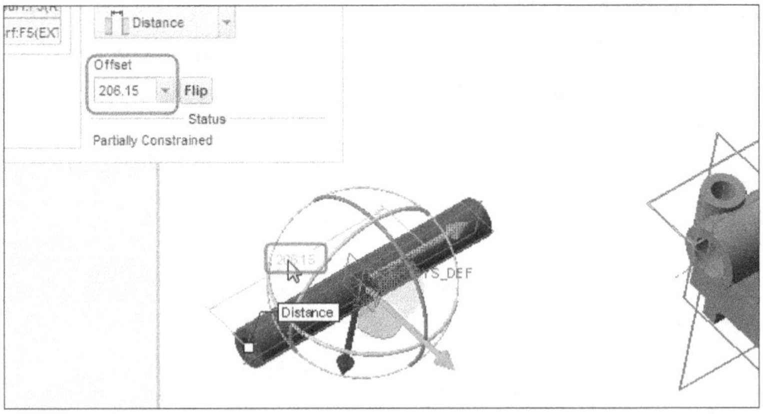

Figure-10. Distance value

- Click on the **Flip** button next to the **Offset** edit box to flip the component in offset direction.
- To apply next constraint, click on the **New Constraint** option from the **Placement** tab; refer to Figure-11.

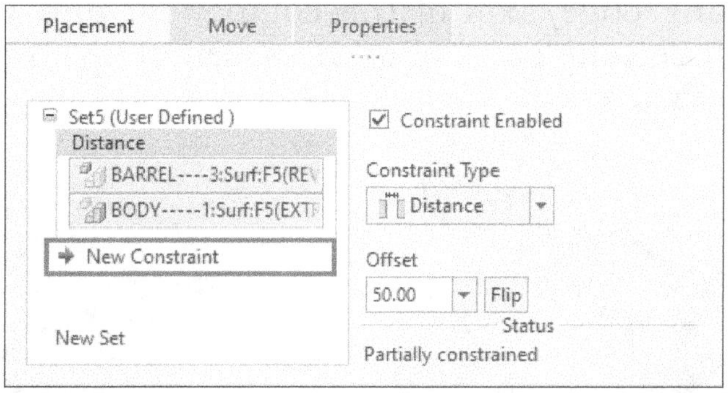

Figure-11. New Constraint option

Angle Offset

As the name suggests, this constraint is used to set an angle between the selected planes/faces/edges of component and assembly. The procedure to use this constraint is given next.

- Click on the **Angle Offset** option from the **Current constraint** drop-down in the contextual tab or from the **Constraint Type** drop-down in the **Placement** tab. You are asked to select one reference from component and one reference from assembly.
- Select the face/plane/edge/axis of the component and then of the assembly. The angle offset constraint will be applied; refer to Figure-12.
- Specify desired angle value. To apply the next constraint, click on the **New Constraint** option from the **Placement** tab.

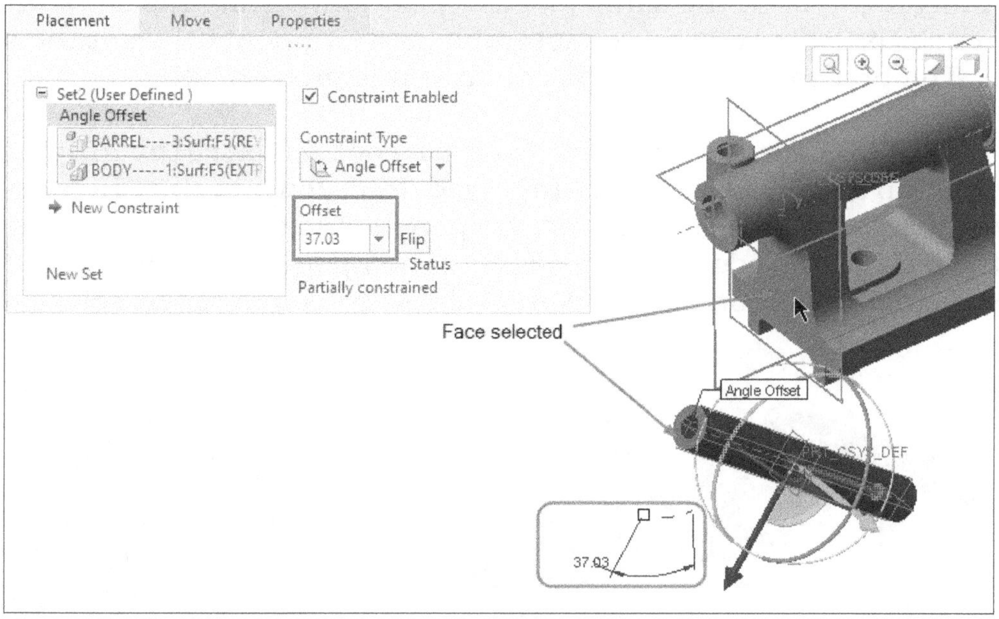

Figure-12. Angle offset constraint applied

Parallel

As the name suggests, this constraint is used to set the component and assembly parallel for selected faces/planes/edges/axes. The procedure to use this constraint is given next.

- Click on the **Parallel** option from the **Current constraint** drop-down in the contextual tab or from the **Constraint Type** drop-down in the **Placement** tab. You are asked to select one reference from component and one reference from assembly.

- Select the face/plane/edge/axis of the component and then of the assembly. The component will become parallel to the assembly with respect to the selected references; refer to Figure-13.

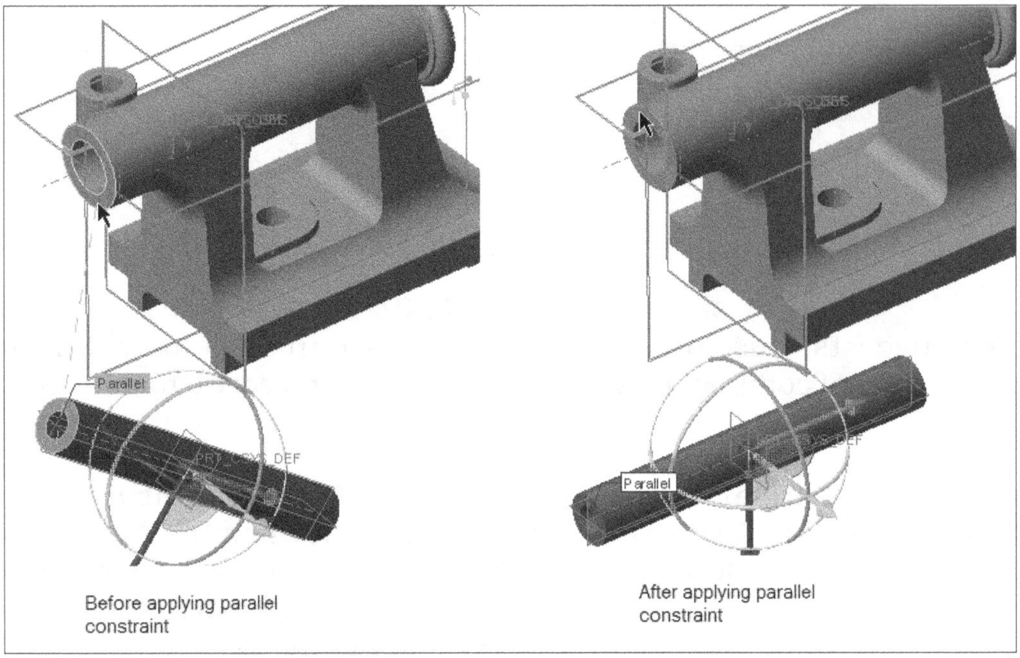

Figure-13. Applying parallel constraint

Coincident

Coincident means, to be at the same place or position. Using this constraint, we can make references (selected entities of assembly and component) lie at the same place or position. The procedure to use this constraint is given next.

- Click on the **Coincident** option from the **Current constraint** drop-down in the contextual tab or from the **Constraint Type** drop-down in the **Placement** tab. You are asked to select one reference from component and one reference from assembly.
- Select the face/plane/edge/axis/point of the component and then of the assembly. The component will become coincident at the selected reference; refer to Figure-14.

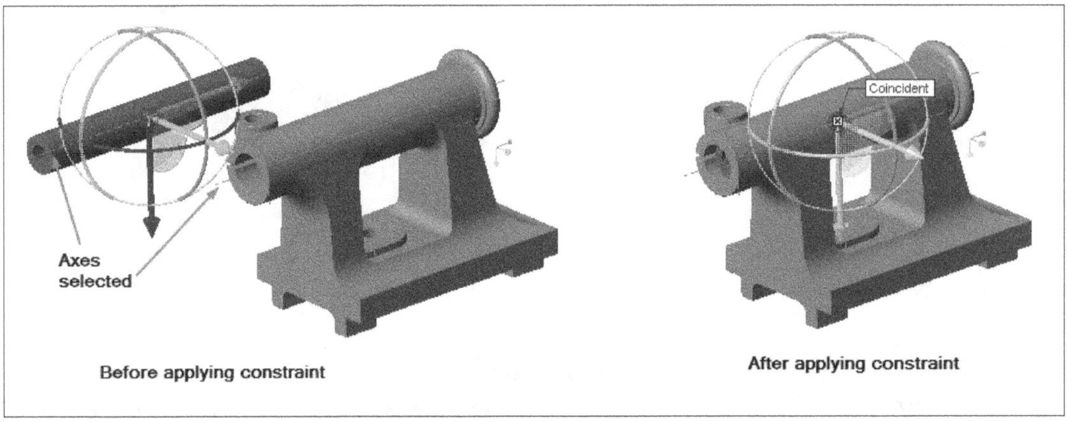

Figure-14. Applying coincident constraint

Normal

Normal constraint is used to make references (selected entities of assembly and component) perpendicular to each other. The procedure to use this constraint is given next.

- Click on the **Normal** option from the **Current constraint** drop-down in the contextual tab or from the **Constraint Type** drop-down in the **Placement** tab. You are asked to select one reference from component and one reference from assembly.
- Select the face/plane/edge/axis of the component and then of the assembly. The component will become perpendicular to assembly at the selected reference; refer to Figure-15.

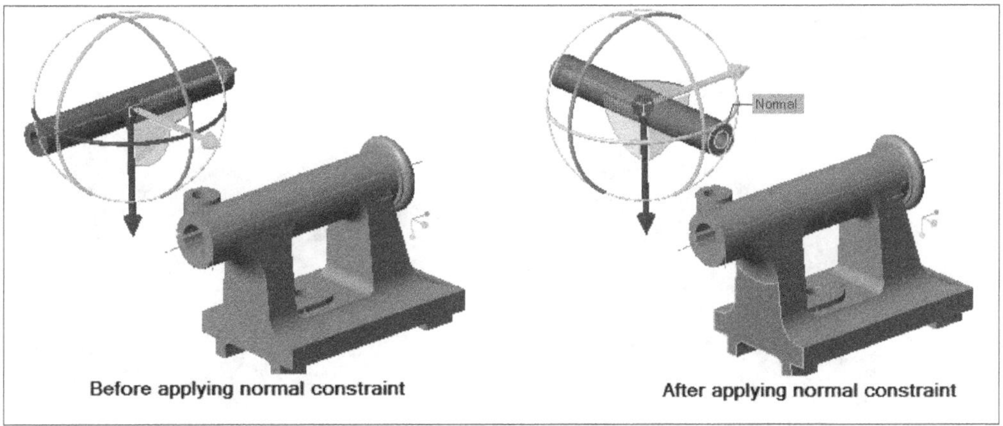

Figure-15. Applying Normal constraint

Coplanar

Coplanar constraint is used to make references (selected entities of assembly and component) share the same plane. The procedure to use this constraint is given next.

- Click on the **Coplanar** option from the **Current constraint** drop-down in the contextual tab or from the **Constraint Type** drop-down in the **Placement** tab. You are asked to select one reference from component and one reference from assembly.
- Select the axis of the component and then of the assembly. The component will become coplanar to assembly at the selected reference; refer to Figure-16.

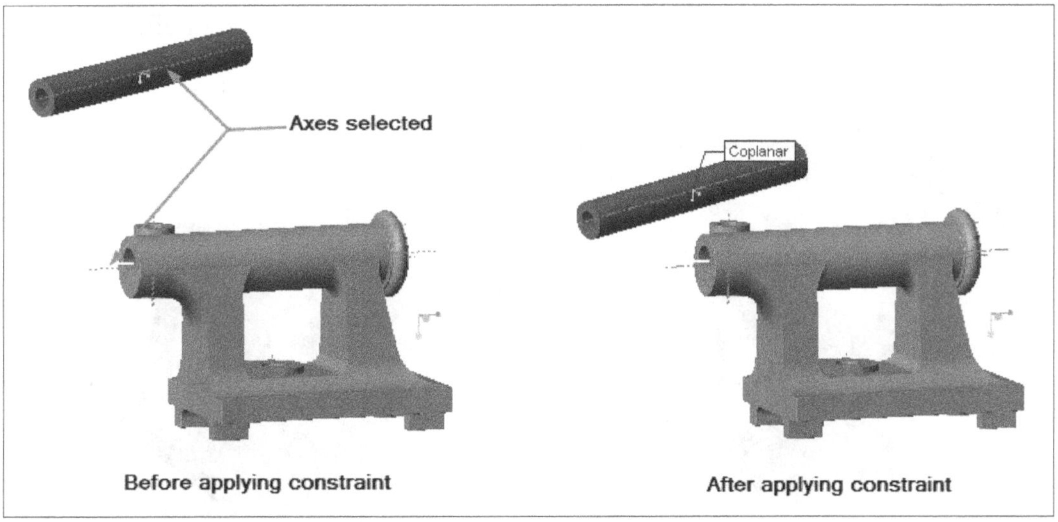

Figure-16. Applying Coplanar constraint

Centered

Centered constraint is used to make component centered to the assembly with respect to the selected round face. The procedure to use this constraint is given next.

- Click on the **Centered** option from the **Current constraint** drop-down in the contextual tab or from the **Constraint Type** drop-down in the **Placement** tab. You are asked to select one reference from component and one reference from assembly.
- Select a round face of the component and then of the assembly. The component will become centered to assembly at the selected reference; refer to Figure-17.

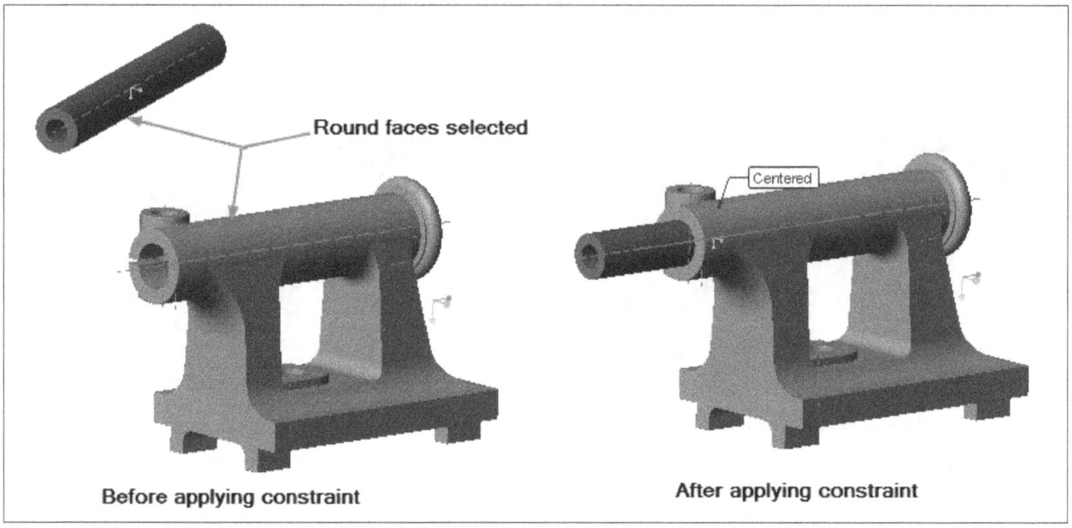

Figure-17. Applying centered constraint

Tangent

Tangent constraint is used to make component tangent to the assembly with respect to the selected round face. The procedure to use this constraint is given next.

- Click on the **Tangent** option from the **Relationship Type** drop-down in the contextual tab or from the **Constraint Type** drop-down in the **Placement** tab. You are asked to select one reference from component and one reference from assembly.
- Select a round face of the component and then of the assembly. The component will become centered to assembly at the selected reference; refer to Figure-18.

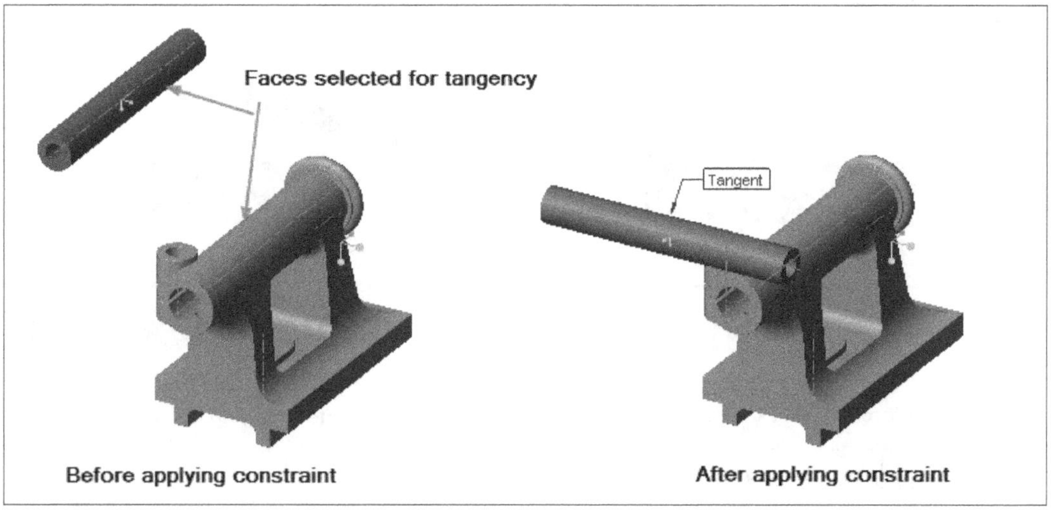

Figure-18. Applying tangent constraint

Fix

As the name suggests, Fix constraint is used to fix the component at its present location. This constraint is generally used to place the base component of the assembly. The procedure to use this constraint is given next.

- Click on the **Fix** option from the **Current constraint** drop-down in the contextual tab or from the **Constraint Type** drop-down in the **Placement** tab. The component will be fixed at its current location. Note that when the component is fully defined, its color changes from violet to dark orange. It shows that the component cannot move from its location due to any motion-simulation relation; refer to Figure-19.

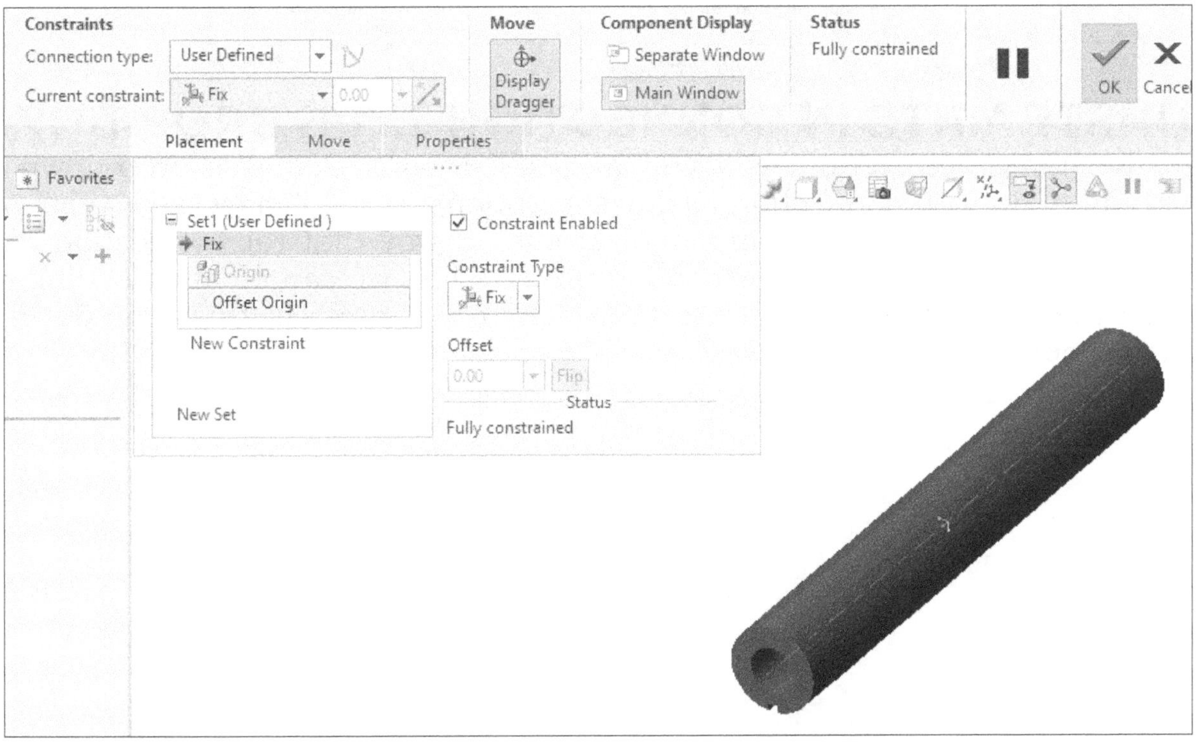

Figure-19. Component fixed at its location

Default

As the name suggests, Default constraint is used to place the component at its default position in assembly. It means- Front plane of component will be coincident with Front plane of assembly, Right plane of component will be coincident with the Right plane of assembly and similarly, the Top plane of component will be coincident with the Top plane of assembly. Primarily, this constraint is used to place the base component in the assembly. The procedure to use this constraint is given next.

- Click on the **Default** option from the **Current constraint** drop-down in the contextual tab or from the **Constraint Type** drop-down in the **Placement** tab. The component will be placed according to the default planes of assembly; refer to Figure-20.

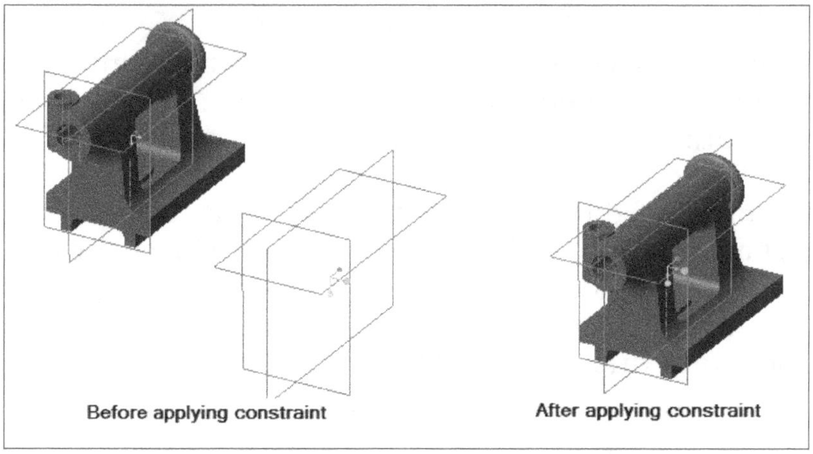

Figure-20. Applying default constraint

CONSTRAINTS IN CONNECTION TYPE DROP-DOWN

From the name Connection, you can have a fair idea that this drop-down has something to do with connection. Using the options in the **Connection type** drop-down, we can constrain the component in such a way that the connection reacts as real-machine mechanism; refer to Figure-21. Like, we can create a sliding joint between the two components in assembly. The constraints in this drop-down are discussed next.

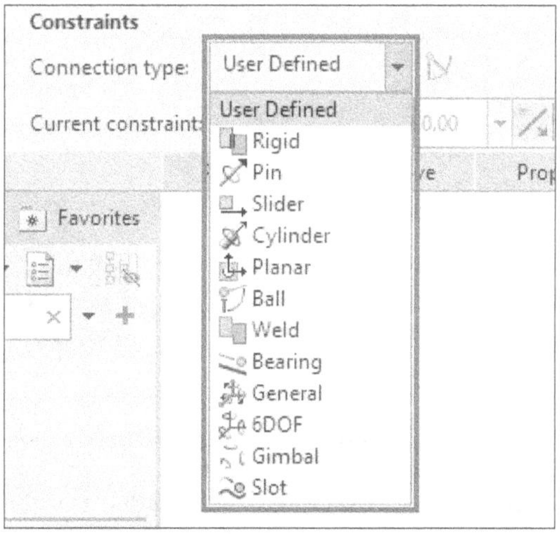

Figure-21. Connection type drop-down

Rigid

As the name suggests, **Rigid** option is used to apply rigid connection between two components of an assembly. Select this option and you are allowed to use all the constraints that are available in the **Current constraint** drop-down.

Pin

Pin constraint is used to assemble the component in such a way that they act like hinged at the selected reference. The procedure to use this constraint is given next.

- After inserting component, click on the **Pin** option from the **Connection type** drop-down; refer to Figure-22.

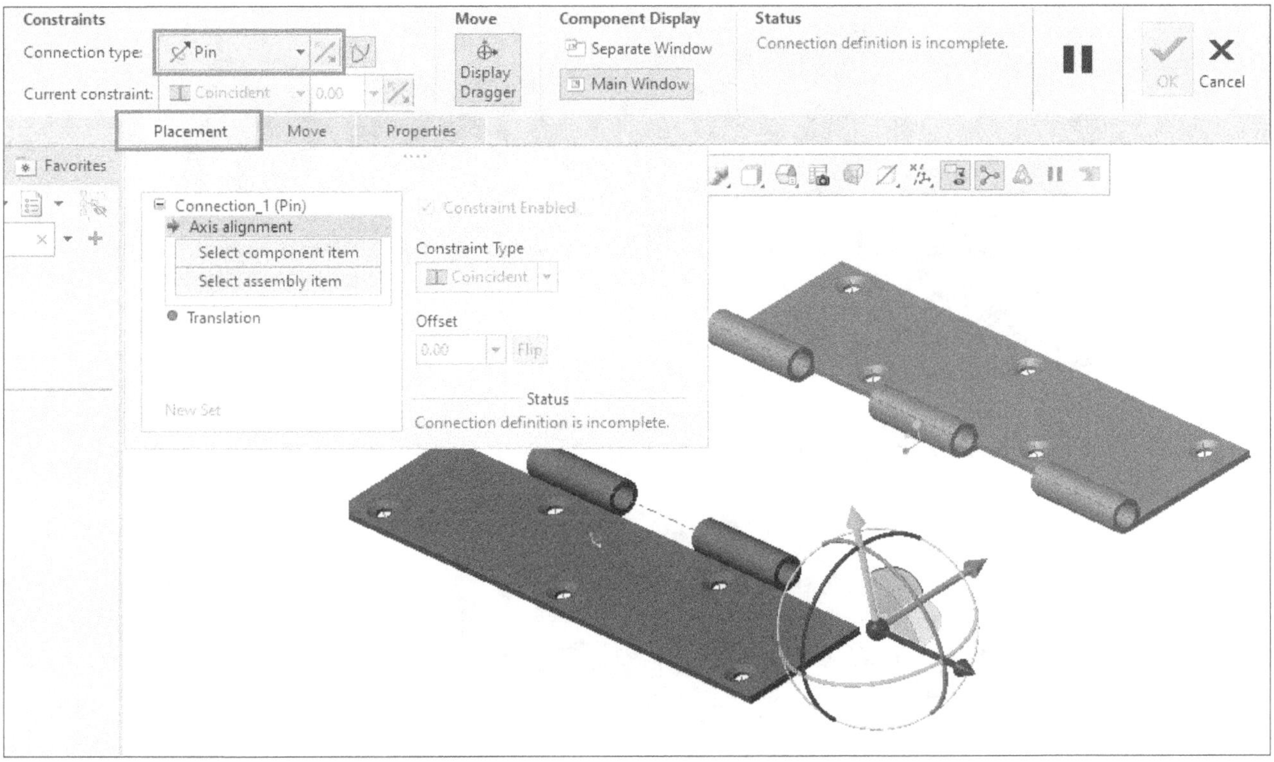

Figure-22. Pin constraint

- Click on the **Placement** tab and check the requirements under **Connections** tab. The first requirement of constraint is axis alignment.
- Select an axis of component and then of the assembly. The axes will be aligned; refer to Figure-23. You are asked to select references for restricting the translation of component.

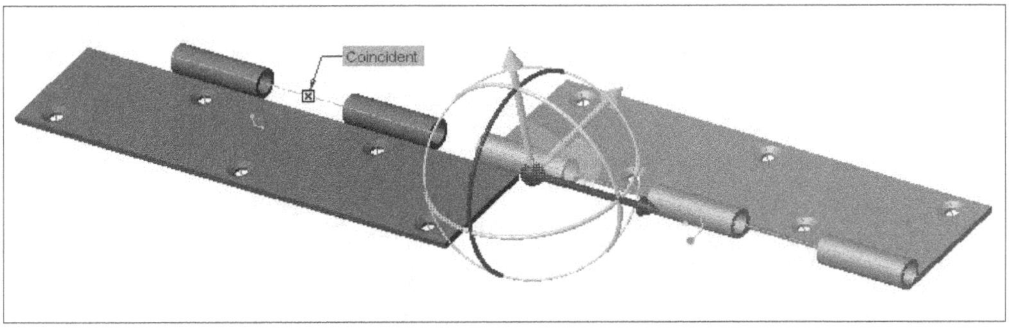

Figure-23. Axes alignment

- Select a face/plane/vertex of component and then of the assembly. The coincident relation will be applied to restrict the translation; refer to Figure-24 and Figure-25.

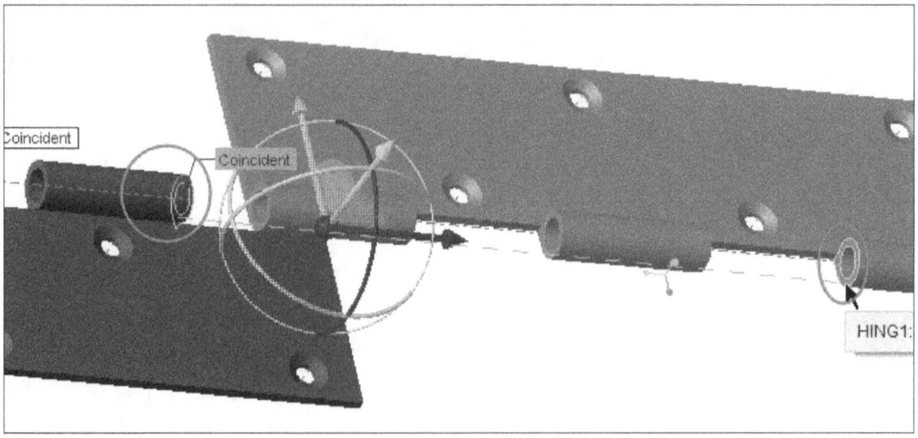

Figure-24. Restricting translation of component

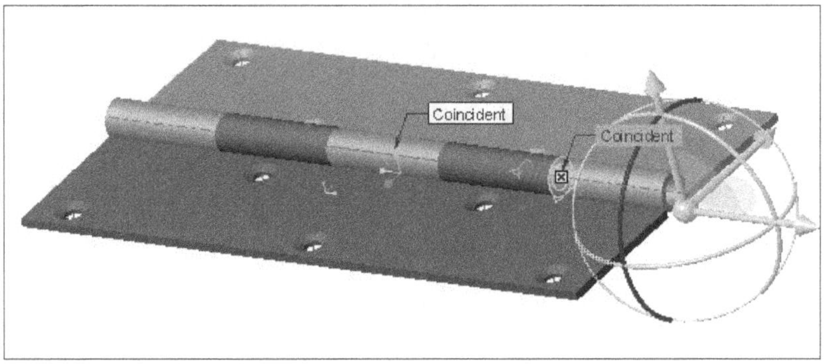

Figure-25. Applying pin constraint

- Using the Blue ring in 3D dragger (so called triad), you can rotate the hinged plate.
- Click on the **Rotation Axis** option from the **Placement** tab and select one face of each component and assembly; refer to Figure-26.

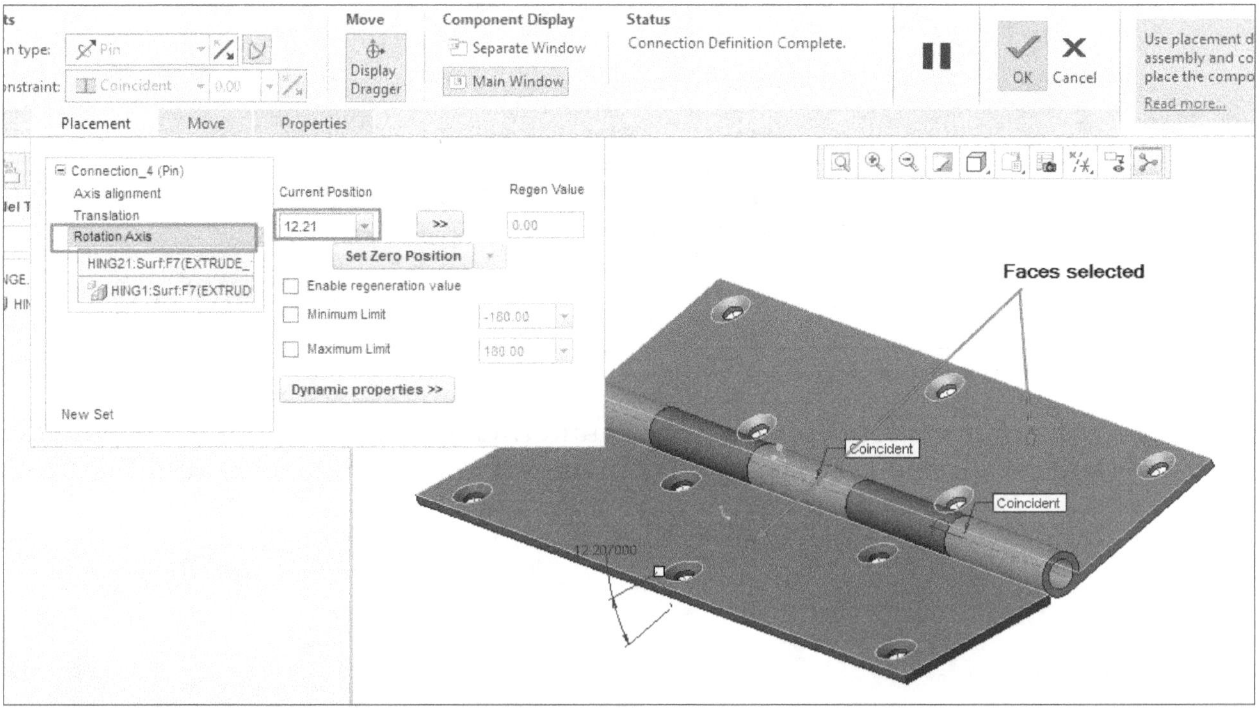

Figure-26. Rotation limit for pin

- Click in the **Current Position** edit box and specify the value as **0**. Select the **Minimum Limit** and **Maximum Limit** check boxes and specify the rotation limits.
- Click on the **OK** button from the contextual tab to apply the constraint.

Slider

Slider constraint is used to assemble the component in such a way that it acts like hinged at the selected reference. The procedure to use this constraint is given next.

- After inserting component, click on the **Slider** option from the **Connection type** drop-down; refer to Figure-27.

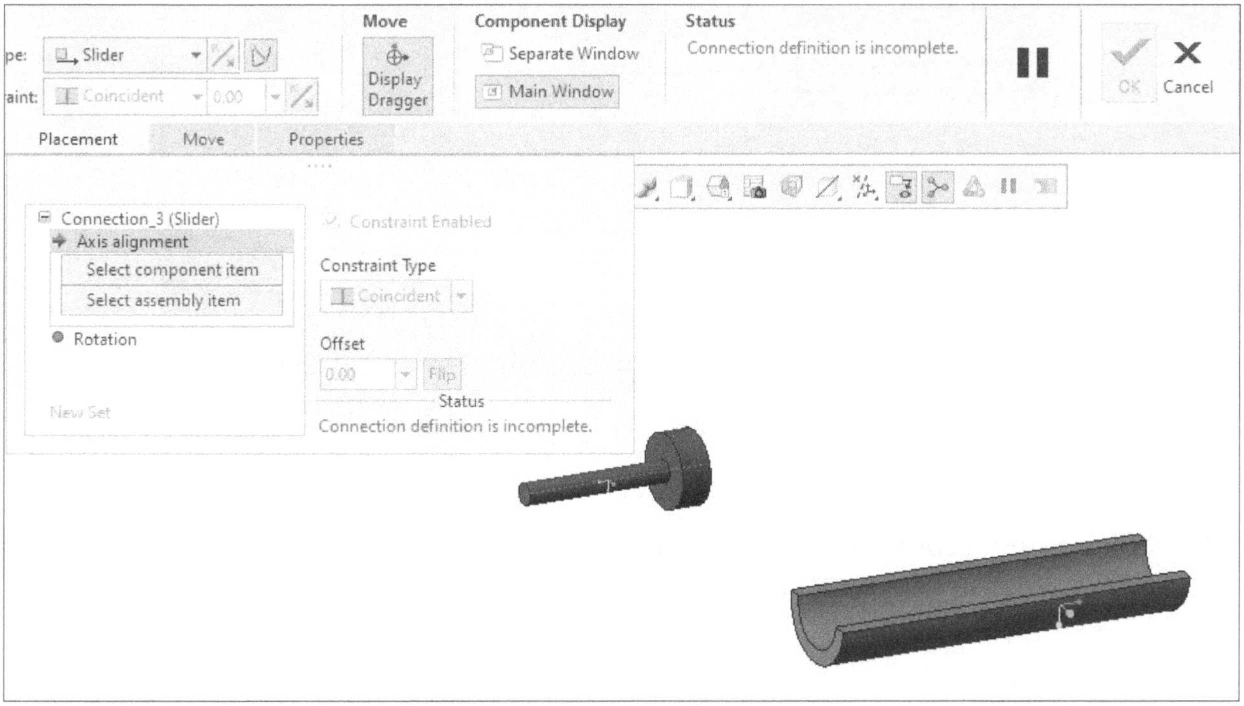

Figure-27. Slider constraint

- Click on the **Placement** tab and check the requirements under **Connections** tab. The first requirement of constraint is axis alignment.
- Select an axis of component and then of the assembly. The axes will be aligned; refer to Figure-28. You are asked to select references for restricting the rotation of component.

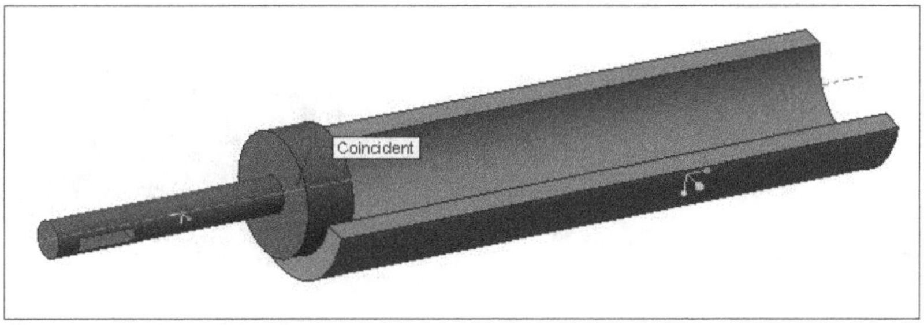

Figure-28. Axes aligning

- Select face/plane of component and then of assembly; refer to Figure-29.

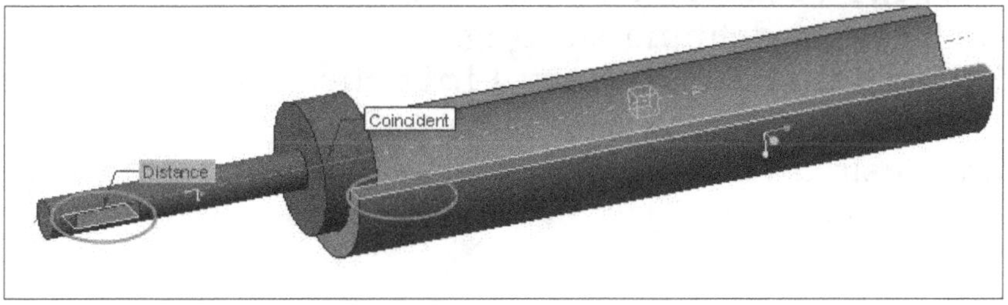

Figure-29. Restricting rotation of part

- Click on the **Translation Axis** option from the **Placement** tab. You are asked to select reference for translation limits; refer to Figure-30.

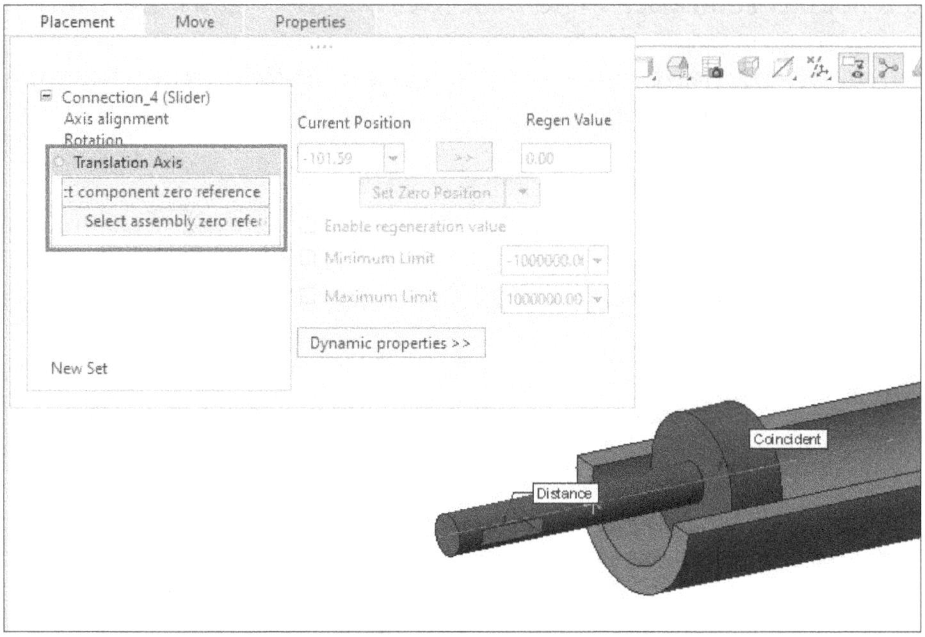

Figure-30. Translation Axis option

- Select face of component and then of the assembly; refer to Figure-31.

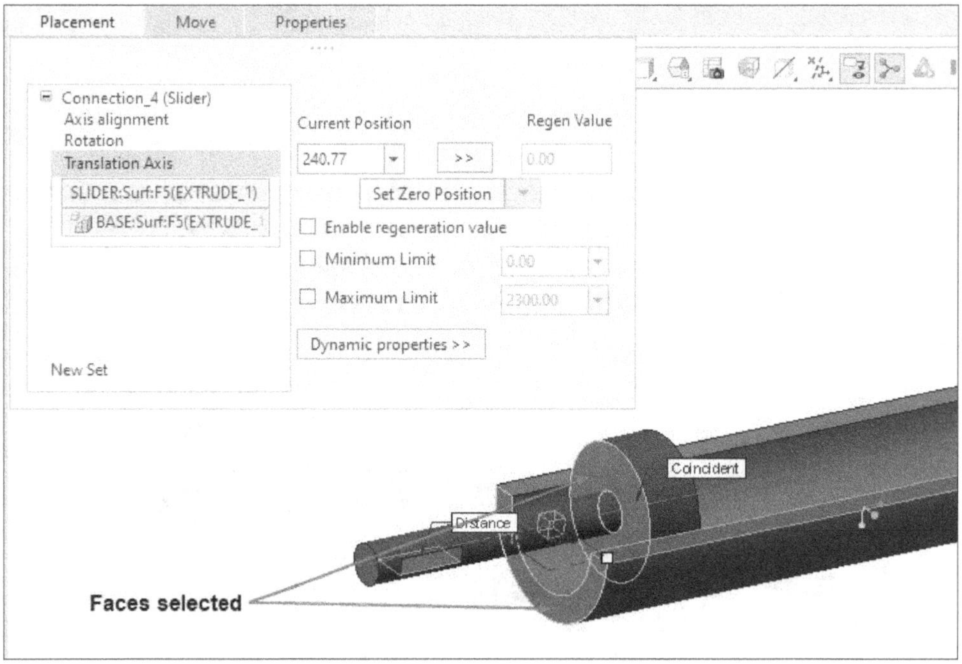

Figure-31. Faces selected for translation

- Click in the **Current Position** edit box and specify the value as **0** if you want to match the two faces for defining starting.
- Select the **Minimum Limit** and **Maximum Limit** check boxes and specify the values, respectively.
- After specifying desired values, click on the **OK** button from the contextual tab to create the connection.

Confirm Motion of Components

Once you have applied a connection then you can check it by using the **Drag Components** button. The procedure for checking motion of slider in previous example is given next.

- Click on the **Drag Components** button from the **Ribbon**.  You are asked to select a component.
- Click on the slider(Component) and move the cursor. The component will be able to slide on the base only.

Cylinder

Cylinder constraint is used to assemble the component in such a way that the component is free to move along the selected axis and free to rotate about the same selected axis. But, you can specify the limits for rotation as well as translation. The procedure to use this constraint is given next.

- After inserting component, click on the **Cylinder** option from the **Connection type** drop-down.
- Click on the **Placement** tab from the contextual tab. You are asked to select axis for alignment.
- Select an axis of component and then of the assembly.
- Specify desired limitations for translation and rotation. Refer to Figure-32.

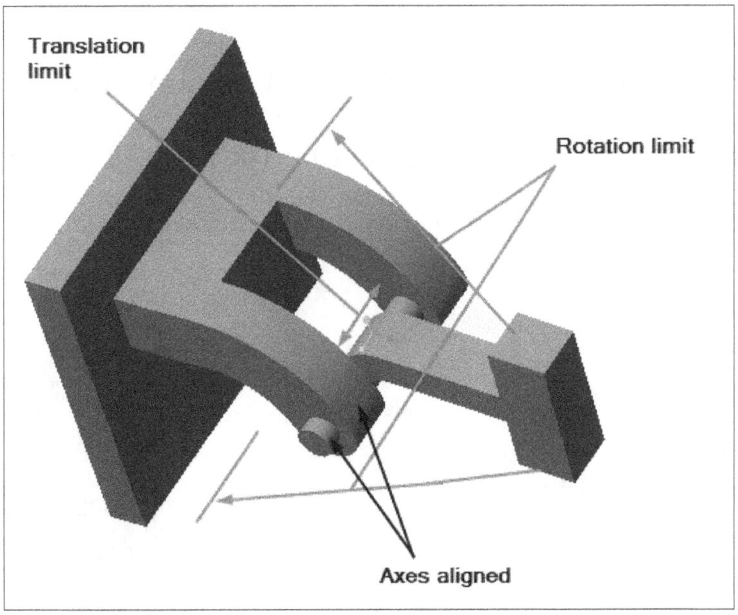

Figure-32. Cylinder constraint

Planar

Planar constraint is used to assemble the component in such a way that the component can move along the selected plane in defined boundary. You need to specify the limits for rotation and translation. The procedure to use this constraint is given next.

- After inserting component, click on the **Planar** option from the **Connection type** drop-down.

- Click on the **Placement** tab from the contextual tab. You are asked to select a face/plane for applying coincident relation.
- Select a face of component and then of the assembly.
- Specify desired limitations for translation and rotation. Figure-33 shows an application of Planar constraint.

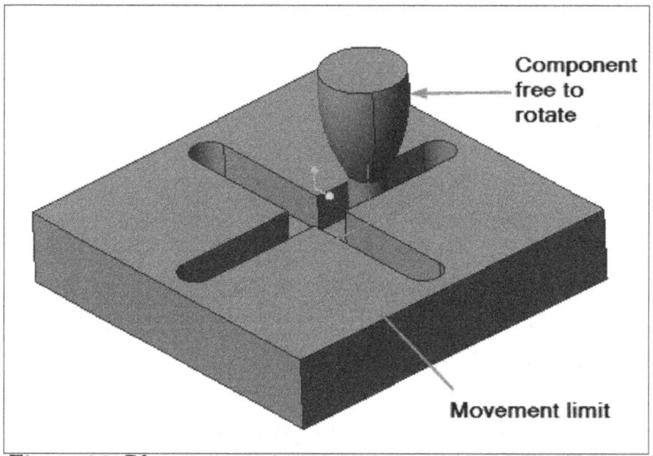

Figure-33. Planar constraint

Ball

Ball constraint is used to assemble the component in such a way that the component is free to move 360 degree in 3D space pivoted to a point. This kind of connection is required when there is a ball joint in the assembly. The procedure to use this constraint is given next.

- After inserting component, click on the **Ball** option from the **Connection type** drop-down.
- Click on the **Placement** tab from the contextual tab. You are asked to select a point/vertex for applying coincident relation.
- Select a point of component and then of the assembly; refer to Figure-34.

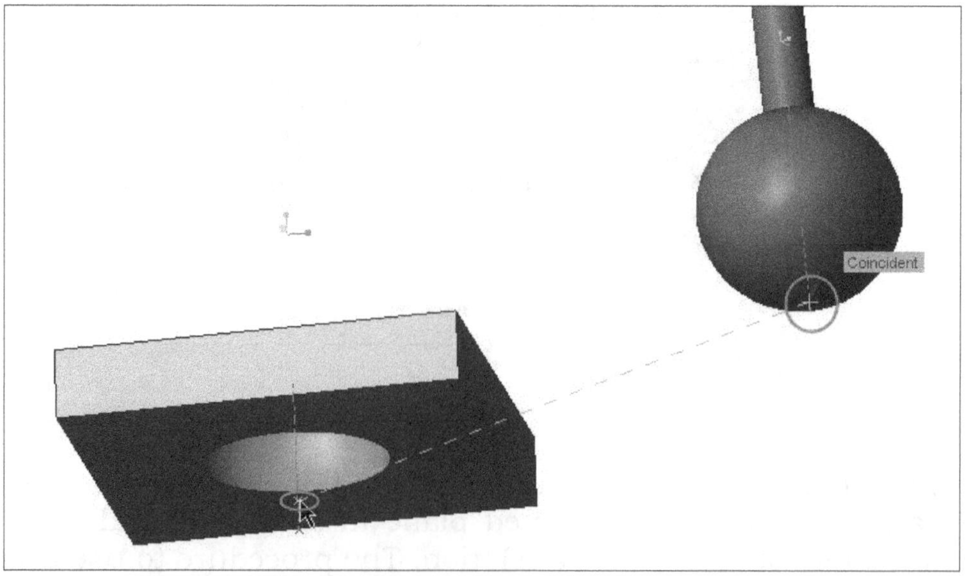

Figure-34. Point selection for ball joint

- Click on the **Cone Axis** option to specify limitations to rotation of ball joint. You are asked to select axis of the component.
- Select the center axis of the ball. You are asked to select a reference point on the assembly.

- Select a point of the assembly. Preview of cone will be displayed; refer to Figure-35.

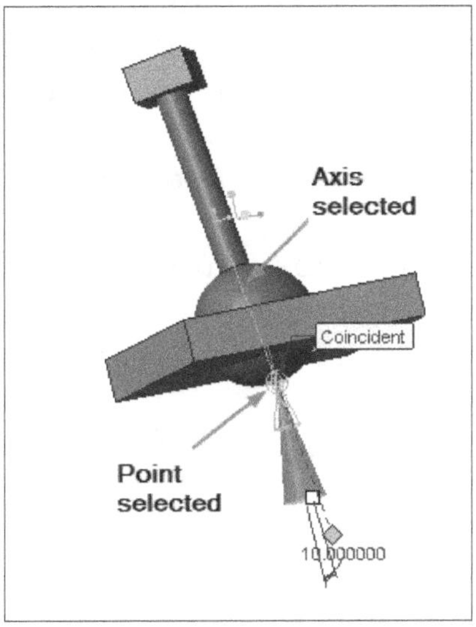

Figure-35. Preview of rotation limiting cone

- Specify the opening angle of the cone as shown in above figure. Note that you may need to select the **Flip** button from the **Placement** tab to get such a cone.
- Click on the **OK** button from the contextual tab to create the joint.
- Use the **Drag Components** button to check motion of the ball joint.

Weld

Weld constraint is used to permanently join component to the assembly. This constraint is same like fixing a component at a place. But in this case, the component will move along with the assembly. The procedure to use this constraint is given next.

- After inserting component, click on the **Weld** option from the **Connection type** drop-down.
- Click on the **Placement** tab from the contextual tab. You are asked to select a coordinate systems.
- Select the coordinate system of component and then of the assembly. The color component will change to orange showing that the component is fully placed.

Bearing

Bearing constraint is used to apply the same motion to the component which is applied on a ball in the ball bearing. After applying Bearing constraint, the component can rotate in any direction but can move only along the selected direction. This constraint is a combination of slider and ball constraints discussed earlier. The procedure to use this constraint is given next.

- After inserting component, click on the **Bearing** option from the **Connection type** drop-down.
- Click on the **Placement** tab from the contextual tab. You are asked to select a point/vertex of the component.
- Select the point component. You are asked to select an edge/axis of the assembly.
- Select an edge or axis of the assembly.
- Specify the translation and rotation limits as discussed earlier in this chapter.
- Click on the **OK** button from the contextual tab to apply the constraint.

General

General constraint is a kind of master tool for constraining the components. Using the **General** constraint, you can apply any of the joint/connection we have discussed earlier. The procedure to use this constraint is given next.

- After inserting component, click on the **General** option from the **Connection type** drop-down.
- Click on the **Placement** tab from the contextual tab. We have three constraints to apply, primarily; refer to Figure-36.

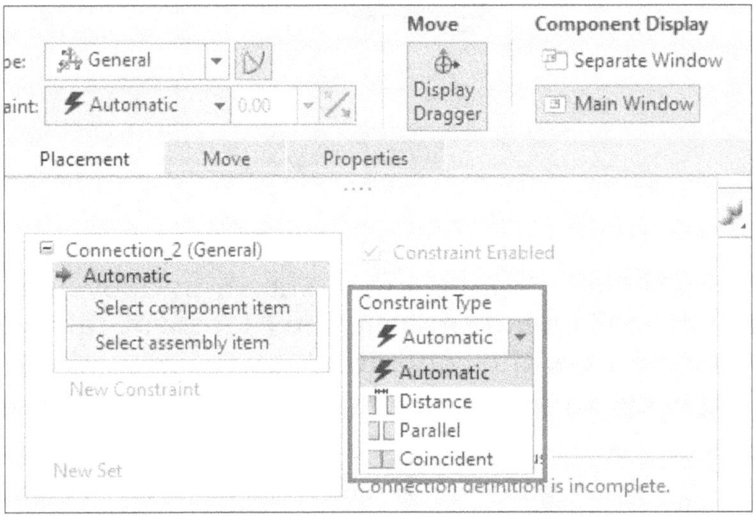

Figure-36. General constraint

- Select one reference from component and one reference from assembly, and then apply desired relation from the available three constraints. You are asked to either specify more constraints or you can specify translational/rotational limits; refer to Figure-37.

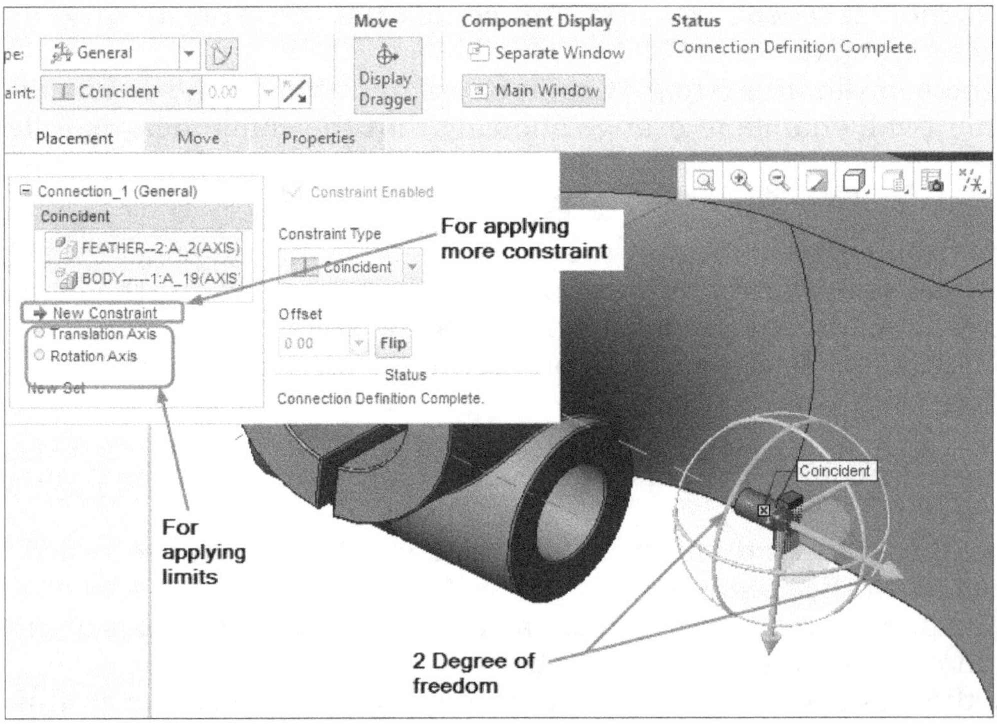

Figure-37. Applying General constraint

- Set desired option and click on the **OK** button from the contextual tab to apply the constraint.

6DOF

6DOF (6 Degree of Freedom) constraint is used to specify the limits of movement of component in each direction. Using this constraint, you can not restrict the component rotation. Procedure to apply this constraint is similar to **Weld** constraint but in this case, component is free to move.

Gimbal

Gimbal constraint is used to make the component centered to the assembly with respect to the selected coordinate system. Procedure to apply this constraint is similar to **Weld** constraint but in this case, component is free to rotate.

Slot

Slot constraint is used to make the component follow path created on the assembly component. The procedure to use this constraint is given next.

- After inserting component, click on the **Slot** option from the **Connection type** drop-down.
- Click on the **Placement** tab from the contextual tab. You are asked to select a vertex or point of the component.
- Select the vertex of the component; refer to Figure-38. You are asked to select an edge/axis/curve along which the follower will move.

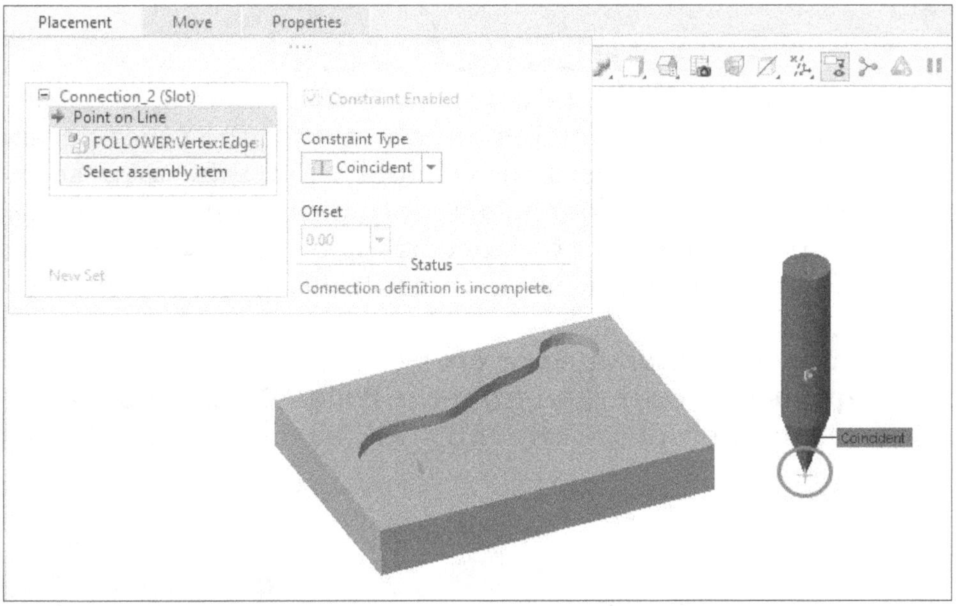

Figure-38. Vertex selected

- Select the sketched curve/edge/axis along which you want to make the follower move; refer to Figure-39.

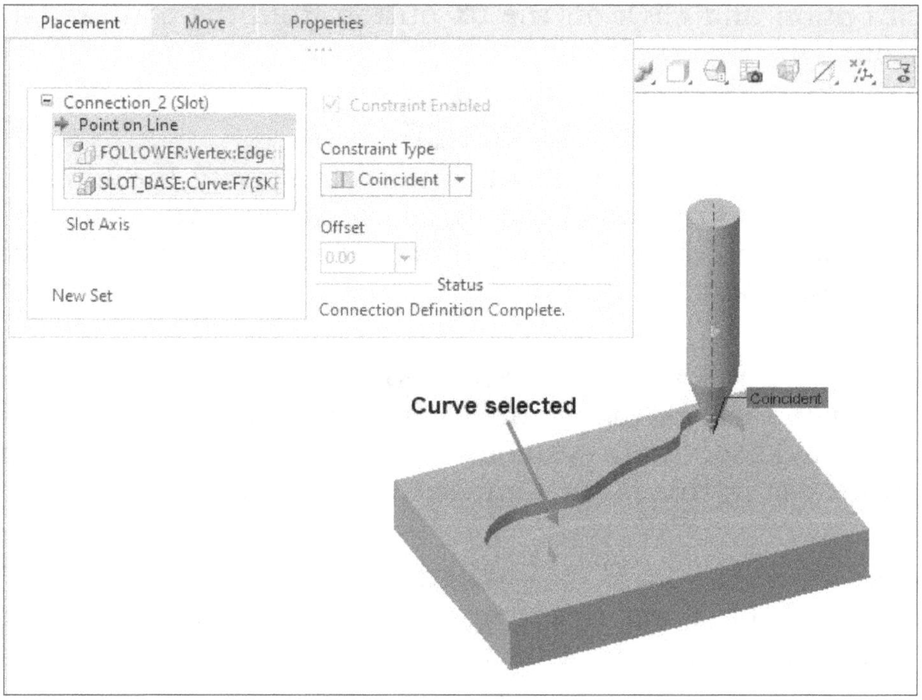

Figure-39. Curve selected for path

- Click on the **OK** button from the contextual tab to apply the constraint. Using the **Drag Components** tool you can check the motion of the component.
- You can apply more constraints to the follower so that it remain perpendicular to the face of the assembly base. Like, you can use the **General** constraint after selecting **New Set** option in the **Placement** tab and use the Parallel relationship.

EXPLODED VIEW

We have learned about assembling the component till now. But, on paper, we need to display the components of assembly in such a way that the other person can easily find out the location of a component in assembly. For this purpose, we create an exploded view of assembly. In exploded view, the components are disassembled and placed at some distance from each other according to their sequence of assembling. The procedure to create exploded view of an assembly is given next.

- Open any assembly earlier created or create an assembly.
- Click on the **Exploded View** button from the **Model Display** panel of the **Ribbon**. The default exploded view of the assembly will be displayed; refer to Figure-40.

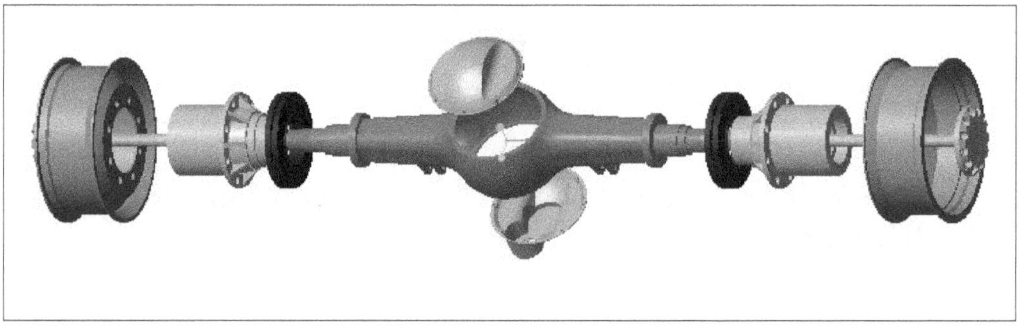

Figure-40. Default exploded view

- The exploded view displayed in the above figure is created by placing each component at default specified distance from other. Also, the components are displaced as per their assembly sequence. We suggest you to maintain the same assembly sequence although you can change the distance between them for a clear view.
- To change the distance between components, click on the **Edit position** button from the **Model Display** panel in the **Ribbon**. The **Explode Tool** contextual tab will be displayed.
- Click on the component that you want to move. A triad will be displayed with the component allowing you to displace the component; refer to Figure-41.
- Click on an arrow and drag the component to desired location. Similarly, you can displace the other components of the assembly.
- You can also apply cosmetic lines to show the connection of components to each other in the assembly. To do so, click on the **Cosmetic Lines** button from the contextual tab. The **Cosmetic Offset Line** dialog box will be displayed; refer to Figure-42 and you are asked to select two references.

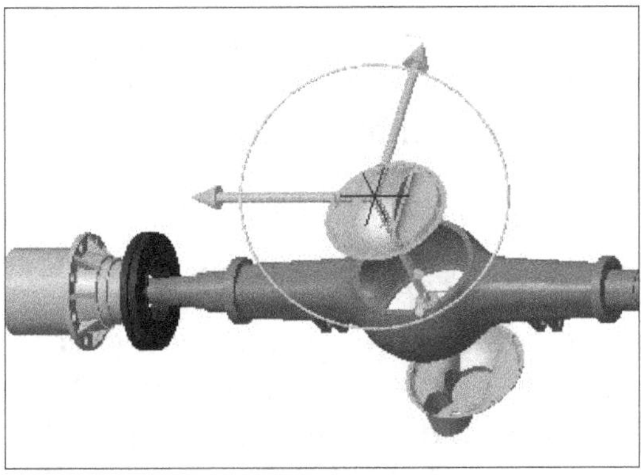

Figure-41. Component to be moved

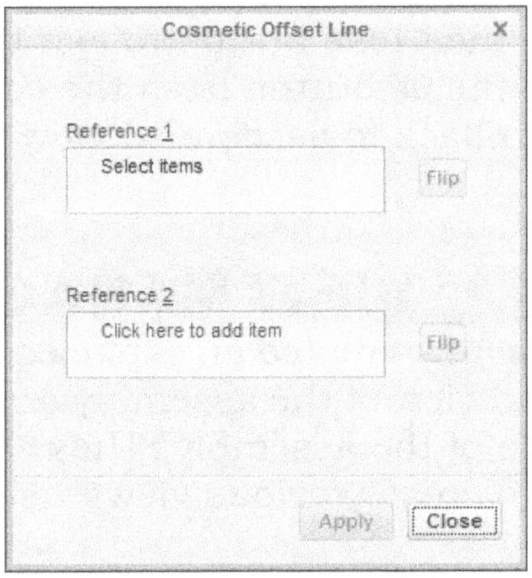

Figure-42. Cosmetic Offset Line dialog box

- Click any two references of the components between which you want to create the cosmetic line; refer to Figure-43.

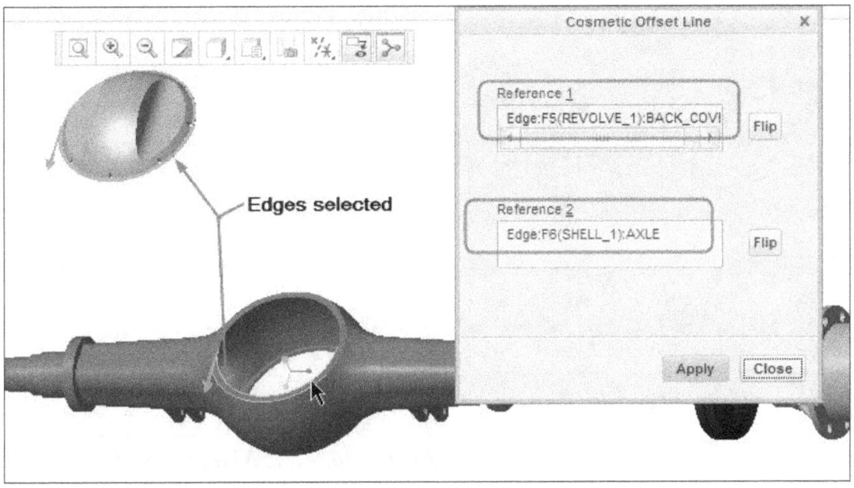

Figure-43. References selected cosmetic line

- Click on the **Apply** button to create the cosmetic line; refer to Figure-44.

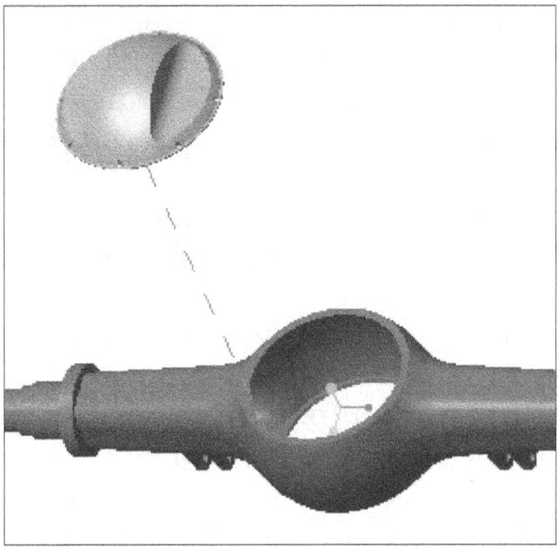

Figure-44. Cosmetic line created

- Continue the process till you have desired cosmetic lines to show the connections between components.
- Click on the **Close** button to exit the **Cosmetic Offset Line** dialog box.
- Click on the **OK** button from the contextual tab to apply the exploded view.
- To return back to assembled view of assembly, click again on the **Exploded View** button.

VIEW MANAGER AND ITS ROLE

Recently, we have created an exploded view of the assembly. You can create more than one exploded view of the assembly and you can also create sections of the assembly to see inside of the assembly. These all options are available in **View Manager**. The procedure to create various views using the **View Manager** is given next.

- Click on the **View Manager** button from the **Manage Views** drop-down in the **Model Display** panel of the **Ribbon**; refer to Figure-45. The **View Manager** dialog box will be displayed; refer to Figure-46.

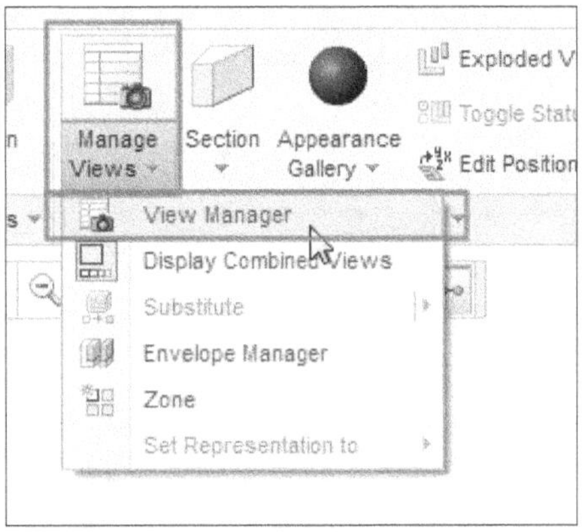

Figure-45. View Manager button

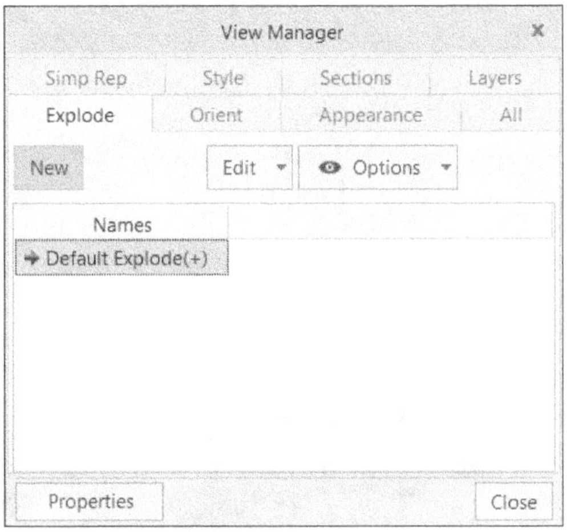

Figure-46. View Manager dialog box

- Click on the **Explode** tab in the dialog box if not selected by default.
- Click on the **New** button from the dialog box to create a new exploded view.
- Specify the name of the view as desired and press the Middle Mouse Button. Using the **Edit Position** button from the **Ribbon**, change the position of components.
- Right-click on the newly created exploded view; refer to Figure-47.

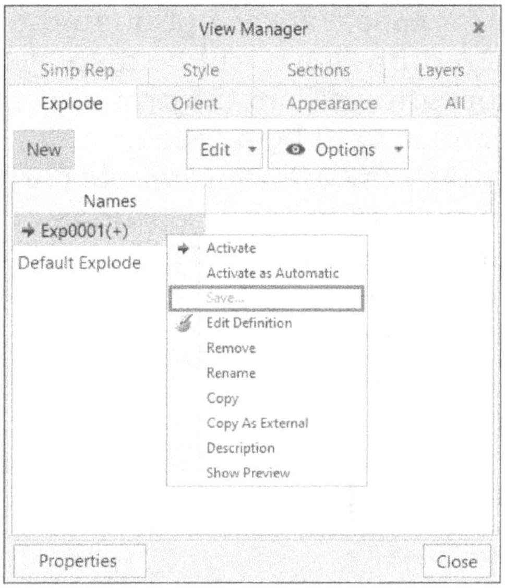

Figure-47. View Manager with newly created exploded view

- Click on the **Save** button from the shortcut menu and then click on the **OK** button from the **Save Display Elements** dialog box displayed.
- To switch between various exploded views, right-click on desired view in the **View Manager** dialog box and select the **Activate** option.

APPEARANCE

For most of the parts, appearance is automatically applied when a material is assigned to them. But if you want to change the appearance of a part in assembly then the options are available in the **Appearances** drop-down; refer to Figure-48. The procedure to apply appearances is given next.

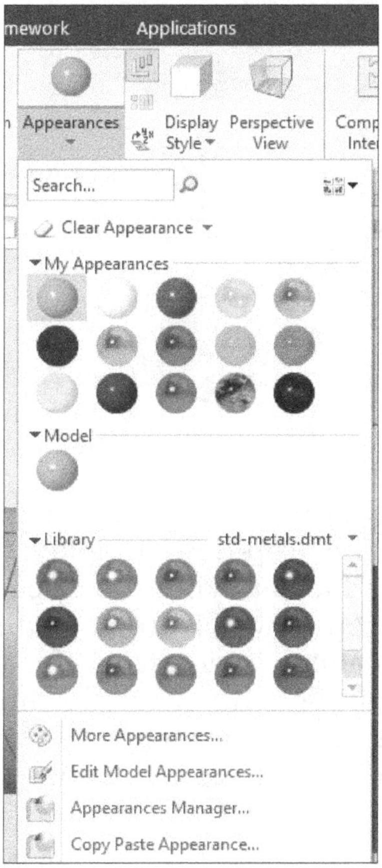

Figure-48. Appearances drop-down

- Click on the down arrow for **Appearances** option in the **Model Display** panel of the **Model** tab in the **Ribbon**. A drop-down will be displayed as shown in Figure-48.
- Click on desired color/appearance from the drop-down. You will be asked to select the item to which appearance is to be applied.
- Click on the part to apply the appearance to whole part. Hold the **CTRL** key to select multiple parts. If you want to select some portions of part in place of whole part then select **Surface** from the **Selection Filter** drop-down at the bottom-right corner of the application window and then select multiple portions of part while holding the **CTRL** key; refer to Figure-49.

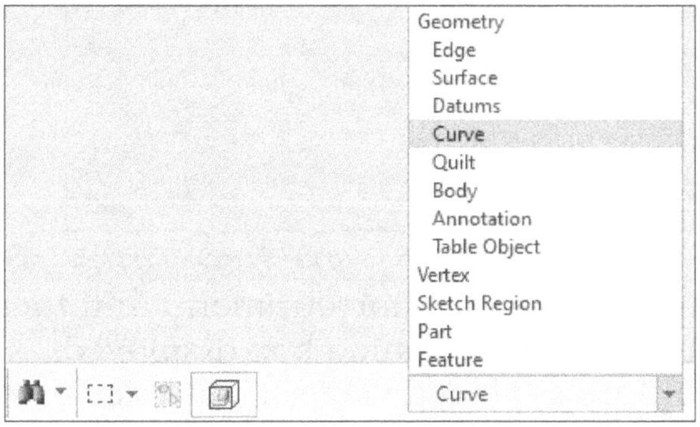

Figure-49. Selection Filter drop-down

- After selection, press the Middle Mouse Button. The selected portion will be colored accordingly; refer to Figure-50.

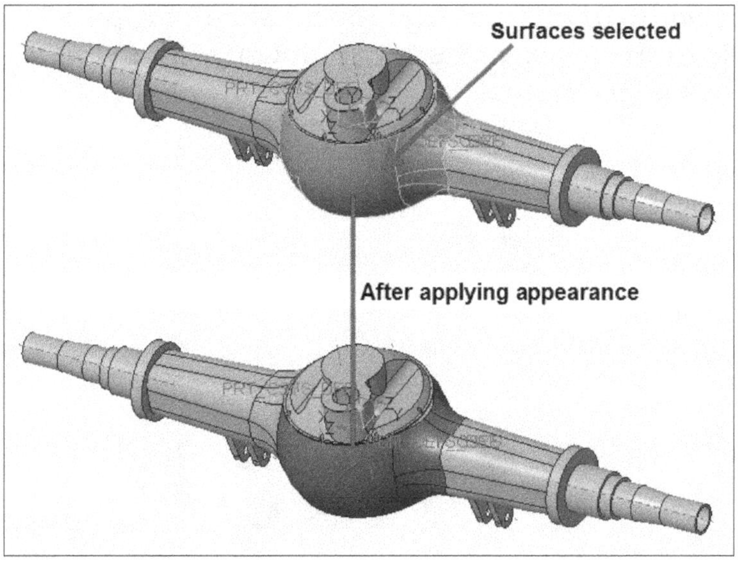

Figure-50. Applying appearances

To remove appearances, click on the down arrow next to **Clear Appearance** option and select desired option from the drop-down displayed; refer to Figure-51. To remove desired appearance, select the faces having the appearance and click on the **Clear Appearance** option from the drop-down. To remove all assembly appearances, click on the **Clear Assembly Appearances** option from the drop-down. Note that on using this option, the appearances applied in Part environment will not be removed. Click on the **Clear All Appearances** option to remove all the appearances. More advanced options of appearance are out of scope of this book.

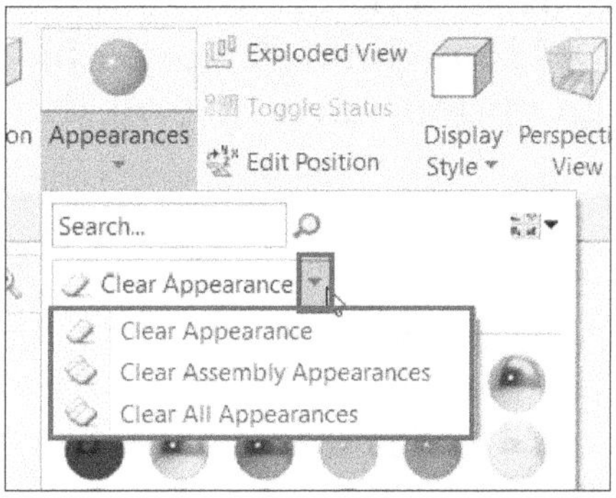

Figure-51. Clear Appearance drop-down

PRACTICAL 1

Create the real axle assembly as shown in Figure-52. The exploded view of assembly is given in Figure-53.

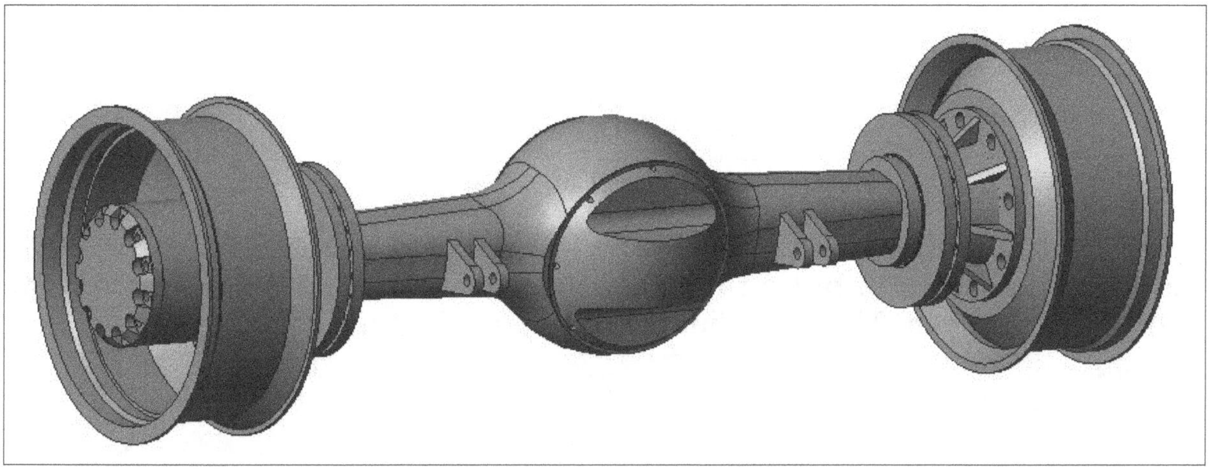

Figure-52. Rear axle assembly

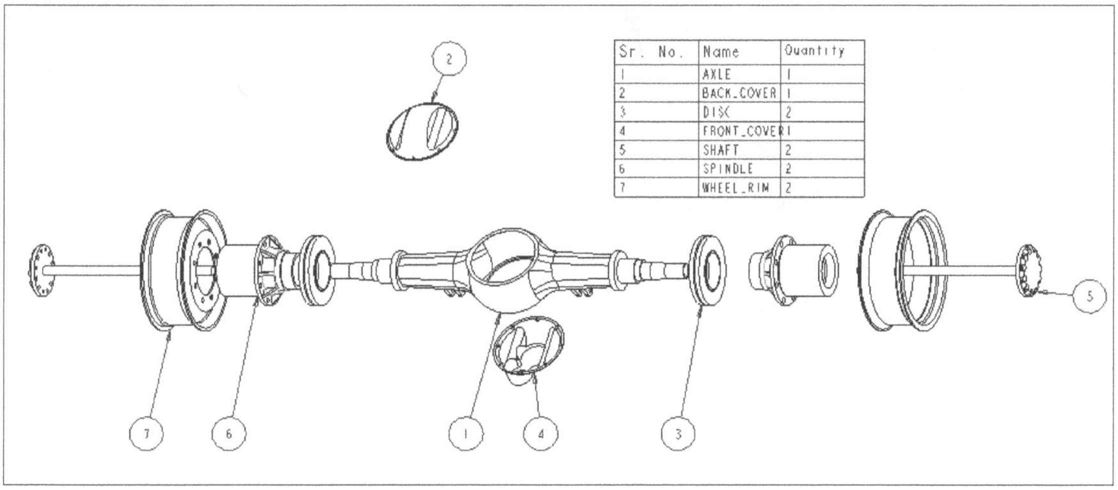

Figure-53. Exploded view of the assembly

Starting assembly file

- Start Creo Parametric and click on the **New** button from the **Quick Access toolbar**. The **New** dialog box will be displayed.
- Click on the **Assembly** radio button from the **Type** area and **Design** option from the **Sub-type** area.
- Specify desired name of the file.

- Clear the **Use default template** check box and click on the **OK** button from the dialog box. The **New File Options** dialog box will be displayed; refer to Figure-54.
- Select the **mmns asm design** option and click on the **OK** button.

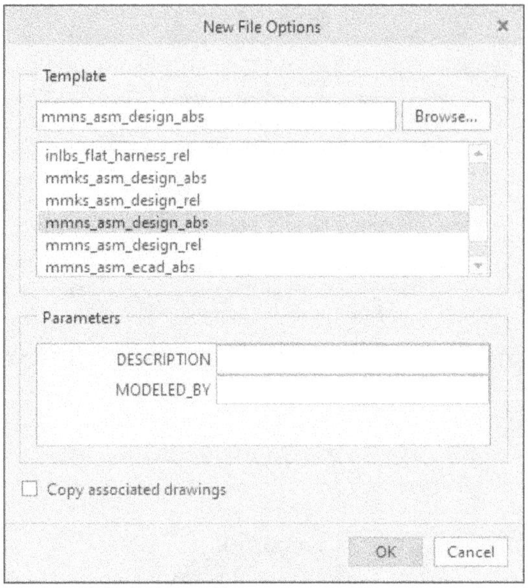

Figure-54. New File Options dialog box

Inserting the Base Component (Axle)

- Click on the **Assemble** button from the **Assemble** drop-down in the **Components** panel of the **Ribbon**. The **Open** dialog box will be displayed; refer to Figure-55.

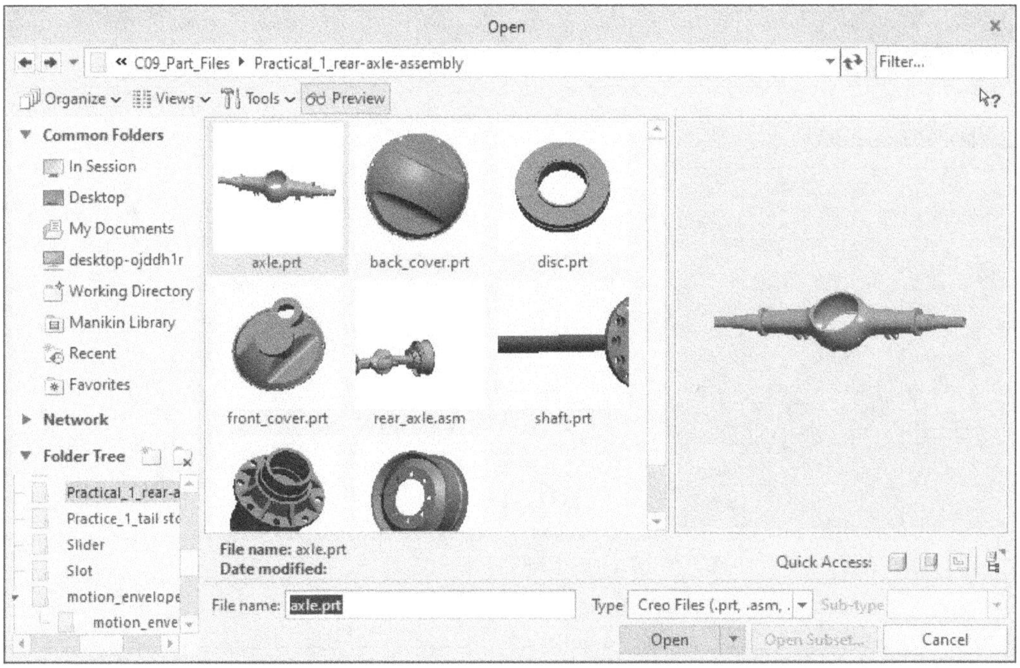

Figure-55. Open dialog box

Note that if preview of component is not displaying in your case then click on the **Preview** button at right corner of the dialog box. The preview window will be displayed. Move the cursor in the preview window and scroll up/down to check the preview. Press the middle button of mouse and drag to rotate the component.

- Select the part file of axle from dialog box and click on the **Open** button. The axle will be displayed in the assembly window; refer to Figure-56.

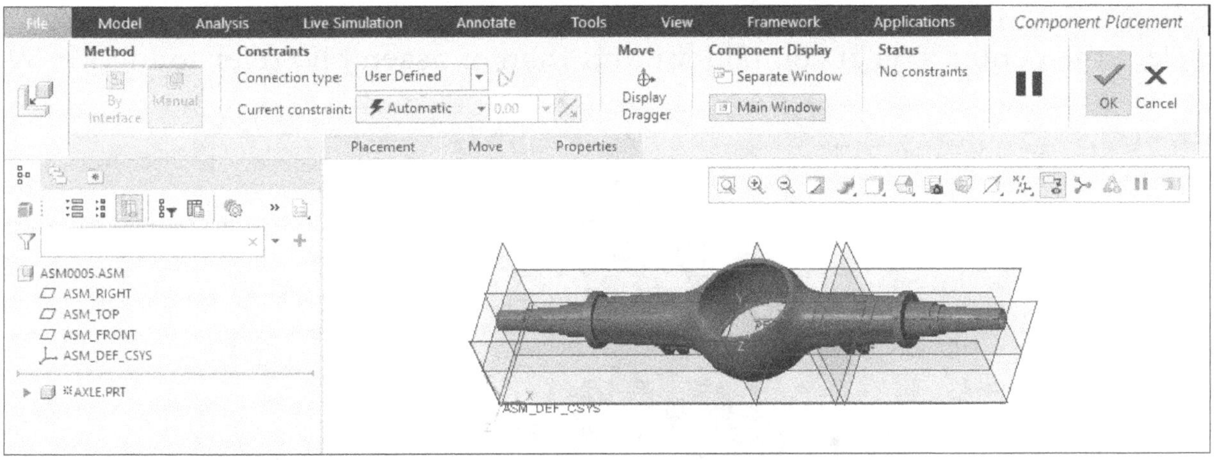

Figure-56. Preview of axle

- Select the **Default** option from the **Current constraint** drop-down in the **Component Placement** contextual tab; refer to Figure-57.

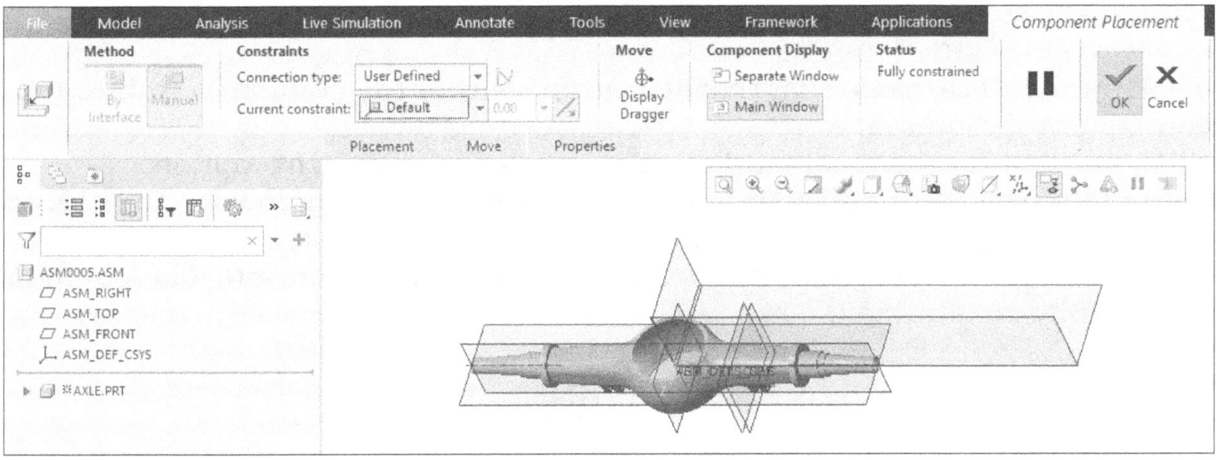

Figure-57. Placing axle

- Click on the **OK** button from the contextual tab to place the axle.

Inserting the Front Cover

- Click on the **Assemble** button from the **Assemble** drop-down in the **Component** panel of the **Ribbon**. The **Open** dialog box will be displayed.
- Select the part file of **Front Cover** and click on the **Open** button from the dialog box.
- Hide the display of planes using the **Datum Display Filters** drop-down in the **In-Graphics** toolbar; refer to Figure-58.

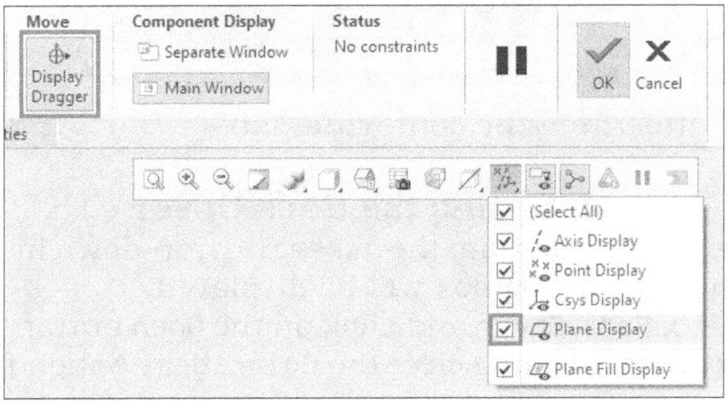

Figure-58. Hiding planes and 3D Dragger

- Select the **Coincident** relation from the **Current constraint** drop-down.
- Select the center axis of component and then of assembly; refer to Figure-59.

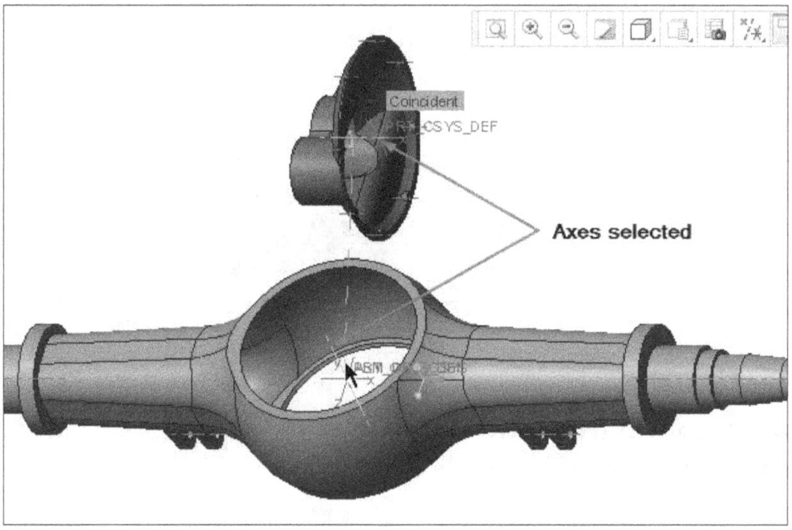

Figure-59. Axes selected

- Click on the **Flip axis constraint** button from the contextual tab to flip the component if required.
- Click on the **Placement** tab and click on the **New Constraint** option.
- Select the **Coincident** option from the **Constraint Type** drop-down in the **Placement** tab.
- Select the flat face of Front cover and Axle; refer to Figure-60. The component will be fully constrained.

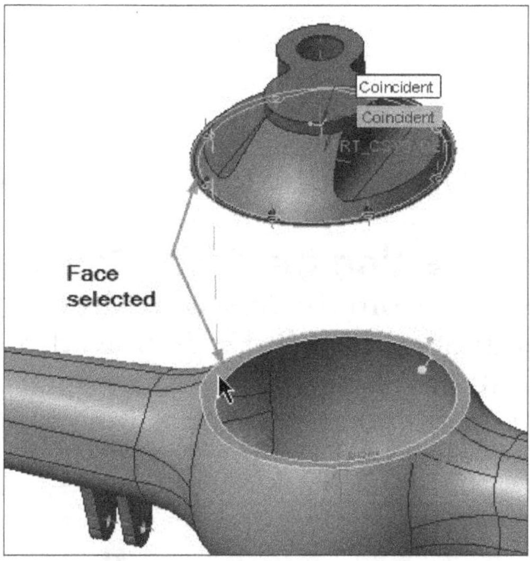

Figure-60. Faces selected for coincident constraint

- Click on the **OK** button from the contextual tab.

Inserting the Back Cover

- Click on the **Assemble** button from the **Assemble** drop-down in the **Component** panel of the **Ribbon**. The **Open** dialog box will be displayed.
- Select the part file of **Back Cover** and click on the **Open** button from the dialog box.
- Click on the **Placement** tab and select the **Coincident** option from the **Constraint Type** drop-down.
- Select the flat face of component and then of assembly; refer to Figure-61.

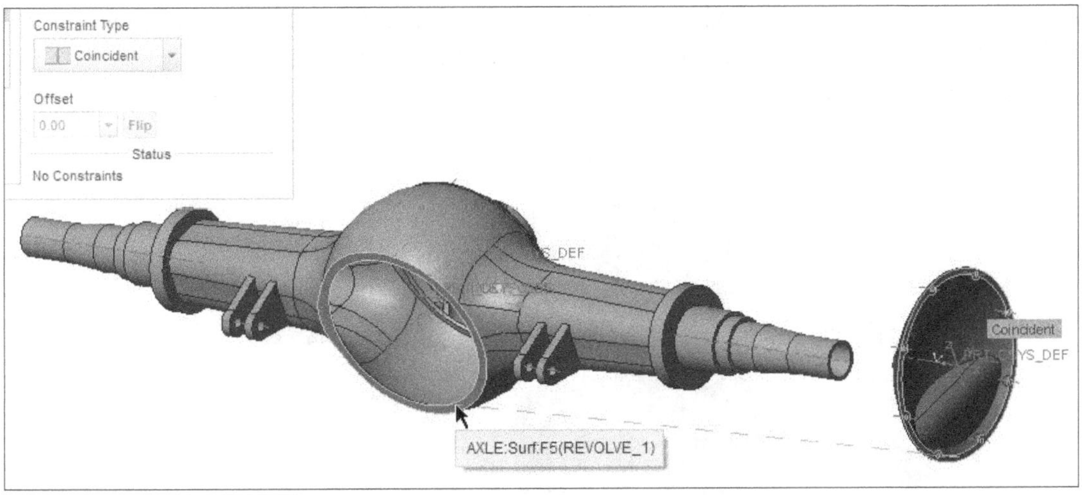

Figure-61. Select flat faces

- Click on the **New Constraint** option from the **Placement** tab and select the **Coincident** option from the **Constraint Type** drop-down.
- One by one select the axis of Back plate and Axle; refer to Figure-62.
- Click on the **OK** button from the contextual tab to apply the constraint.

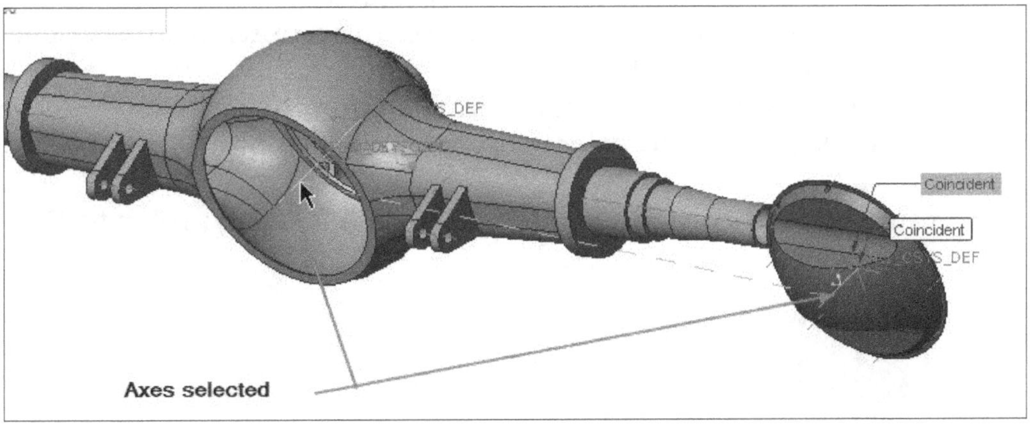

Figure-62. Axes selected for coincident constraint

Inserting the Disc

- Click on the **Assemble** button from the **Assemble** drop-down in the **Component** panel of the **Ribbon**. The **Open** dialog box will be displayed.
- Select the part file of **Disc** and click on the **Open** button from the dialog box.
- Click on the **Placement** tab and select the **Coincident** option from the **Constraint Type** drop-down.
- Select the flat face of component and then of assembly; refer to Figure-63.

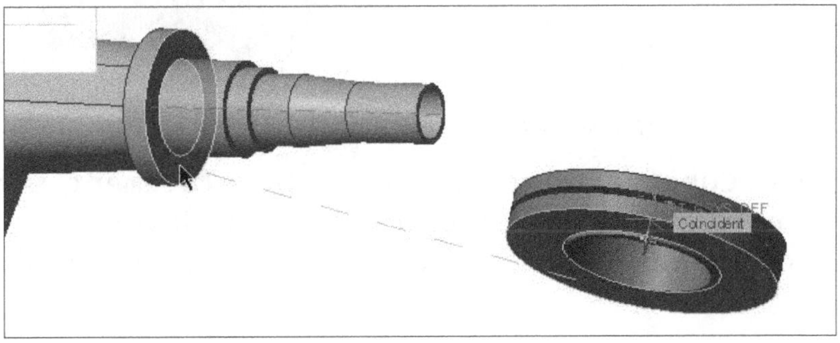

Figure-63. Selecting flat faces of disc and axle

- Click on the **New Constraint** option from the **Placement** tab and select the **Coincident** option from the **Constraint Type** drop-down.
- One by one select the axis of Disc and Axle; refer to Figure-64.

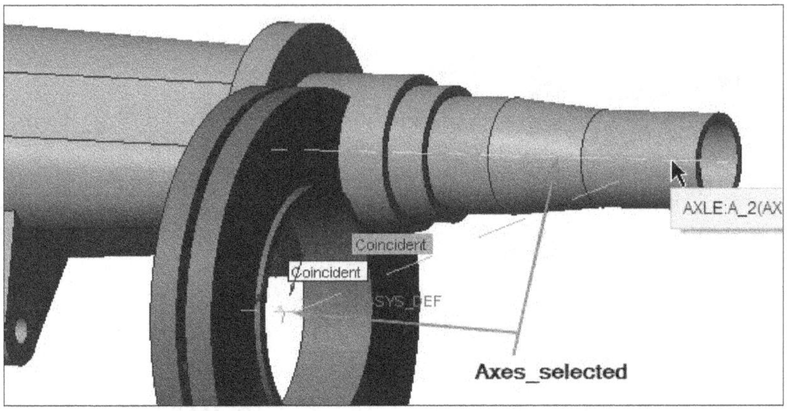

Figure-64. Selecting axes

- Click on the **OK** button from the contextual tab to apply the constraints.

Inserting the Spindle

- Click on the **Assemble** button from the **Assemble** drop-down in the **Component** panel of the **Ribbon**. The **Open** dialog box will be displayed.
- Select the part file of **Spindle** and click on the **Open** button from the dialog box.
- Click on the **Placement** tab and select the **Coincident** option from the **Constraint Type** drop-down.
- Select the center axis of component and then of assembly; refer to Figure-65.

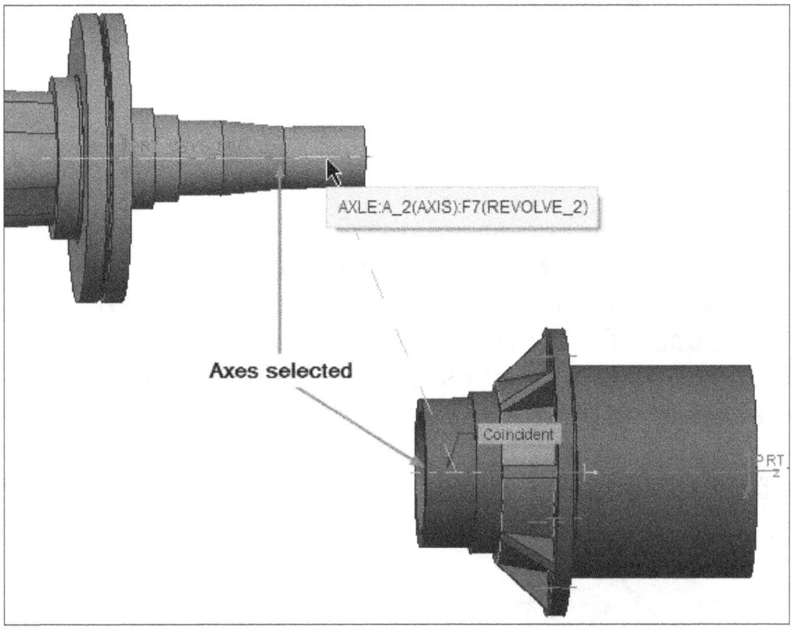

Figure-65. Axes of spindle and axle

- Click on the **New Constraint** option from the **Placement** tab and select the **Coincident** option from the **Constraint Type** drop-down.
- One by one select the faces of Disc and Axle; refer to Figure-66.

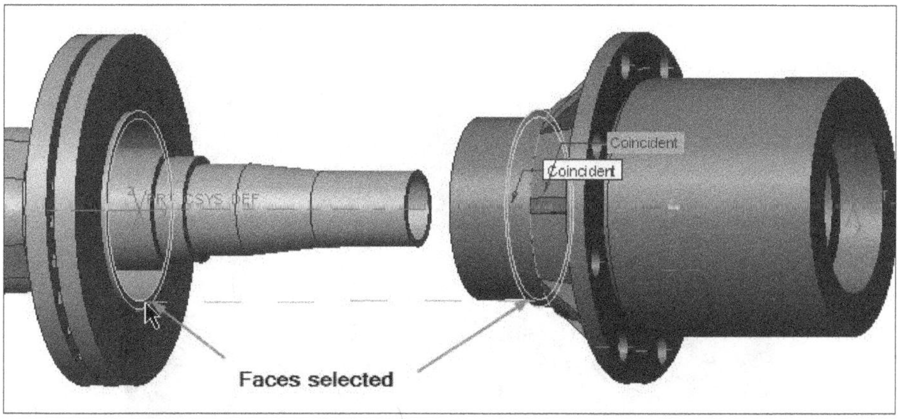

Figure-66. Faces of spindle and axle selected

- Click on the **OK** button from the contextual tab to apply the constraint.

Inserting the Wheel Rim

- Click on the **Assemble** button from the **Assemble** drop-down in the **Component** panel of the **Ribbon**. The **Open** dialog box will be displayed.
- Select the part file of **Wheel rim** and click on the **Open** button from the dialog box.
- Click on the **Placement** tab and select the **Coincident** option from the **Constraint Type** drop-down.
- Select the center axis of component and then of assembly; refer to Figure-67.

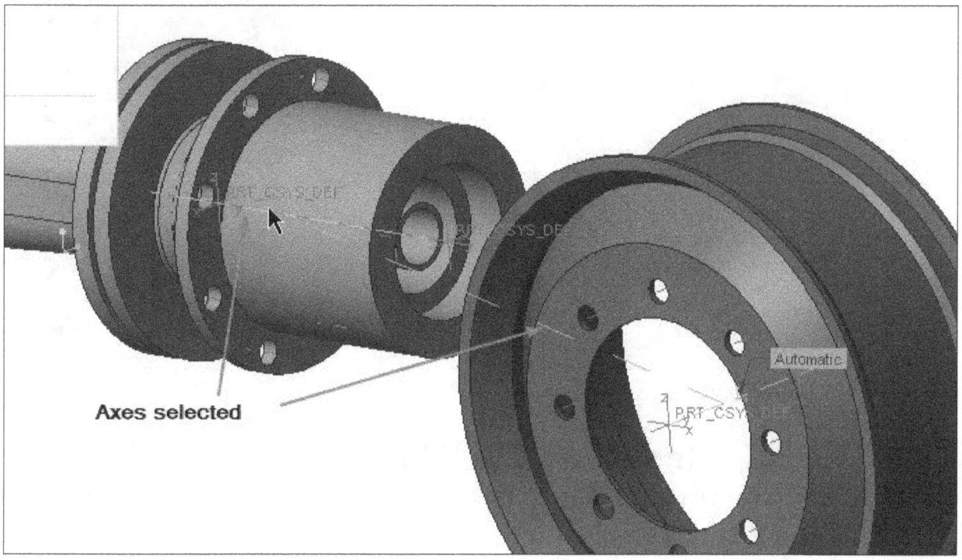

Figure-67. Axes alignment of wheel rim

- Click on the **New Constraint** option from the **Placement** tab and select the **Coincident** option from the **Constraint Type** drop-down.
- Select the hole axis of Spindle and then of the Wheel Rim; refer to Figure-68.

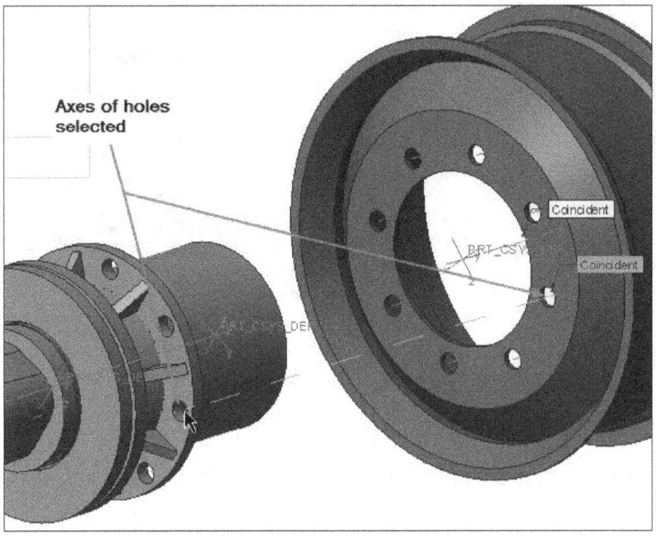

Figure-68. Axes of holes aligned

- Again, click on the **New Constraint** option from the **Placement** tab and select the **Coincident** option from the **Constraint Type** drop-down.
- Select the flat faces of Spindle and Wheel Rim; refer to Figure-69.

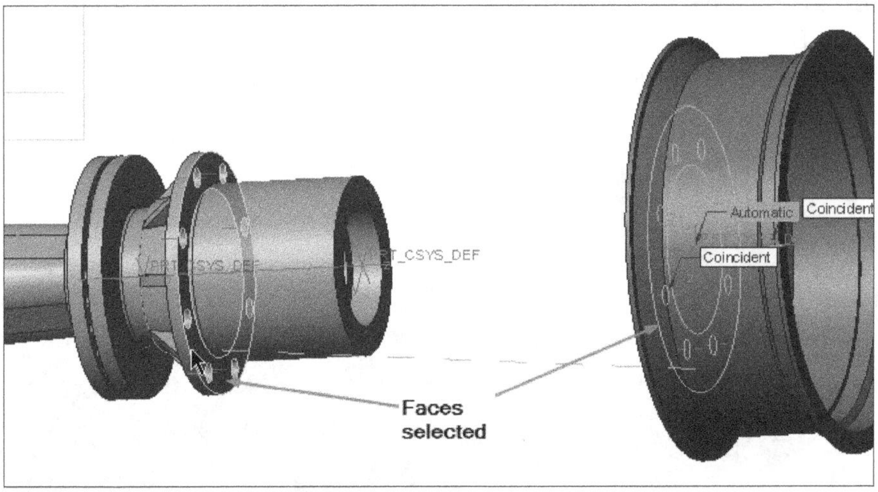

Figure-69. Flat faces selected

Inserting the Wheel Rim

- Click on the **Assemble** button from the **Assemble** drop-down in the **Components** panel of the **Ribbon**. The **Open** dialog box will be displayed.
- Select the part file of **Shaft** and click on the **Open** button from the dialog box.
- Click on the **Placement** tab and select the **Coincident** option from the **Constraint Type** drop-down.
- Select the center axis of component and then of assembly; refer to Figure-70.

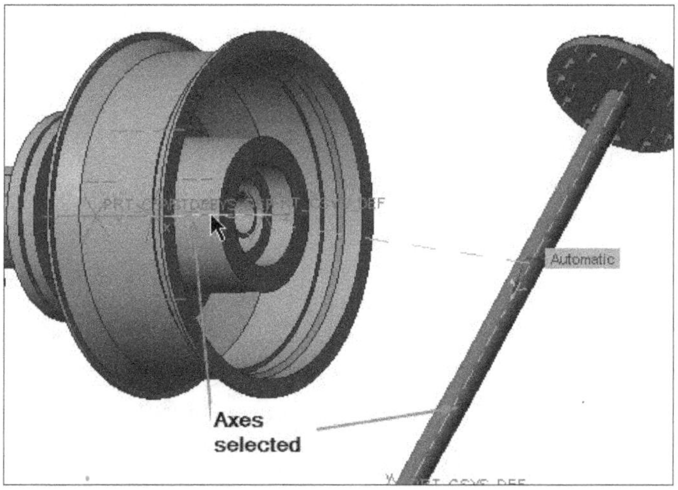

Figure-70. Aligning axis of shaft

- Click on the **New Constraint** option from the **Placement** tab and select the **Coincident** option from the **Constraint Type** drop-down.
- Select the flat faces of Shaft and Wheel Rim; refer to Figure-71.

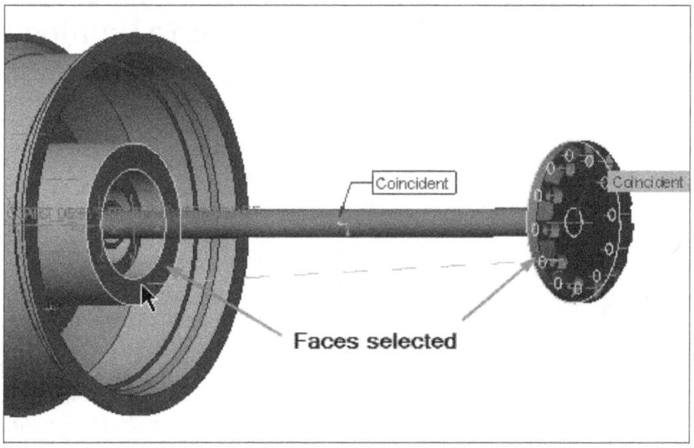

Figure-71. Faces of wheel rim and shaft selected

We have done the assembly on one side. Now, we will learn how to create copy of components in assembly with assembly constraints.

Copying Components in Assembly

- Select Disc, Spindle, Wheel Rim, and Shaft from the **Model Tree** while holding the **CTRL** key; refer to Figure-72.
- Hold the **RMB**. A shortcut menu will be displayed.
- Select the **Copy** option from the shortcut menu; refer to Figure-73.

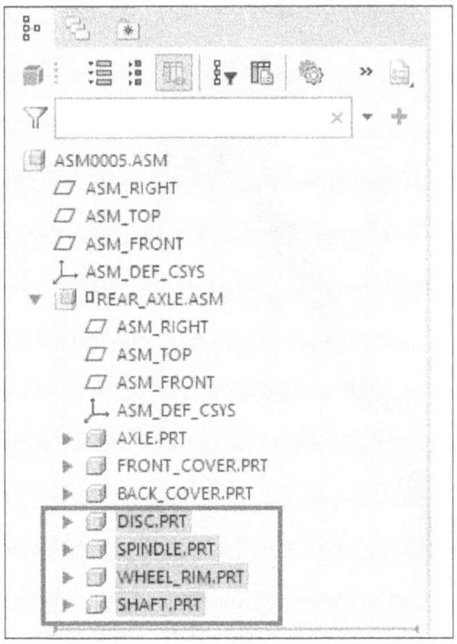

Figure-72. Components selected from Model Tree

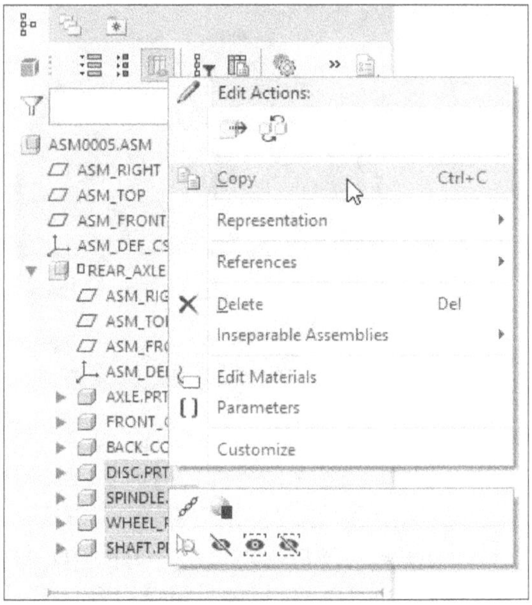

Figure-73. Copy option

- Right-click anywhere in the screen and select the **Paste option with dependency configuration**; refer to Figure-74. The **Paste Special** dialog box will be displayed; refer to Figure-75.

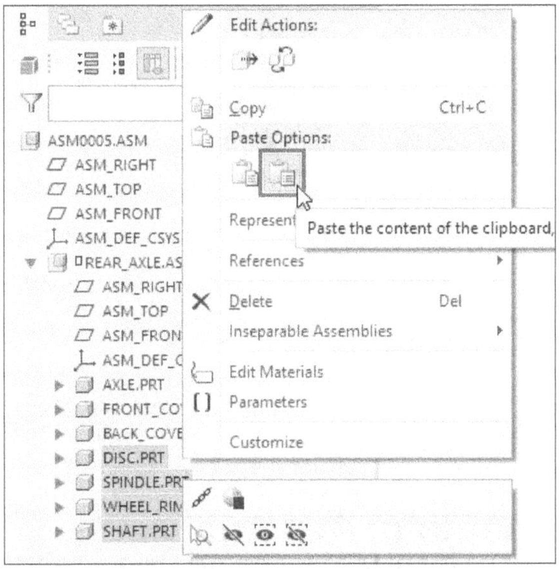

Figure-74. Paste option with dependency configurations

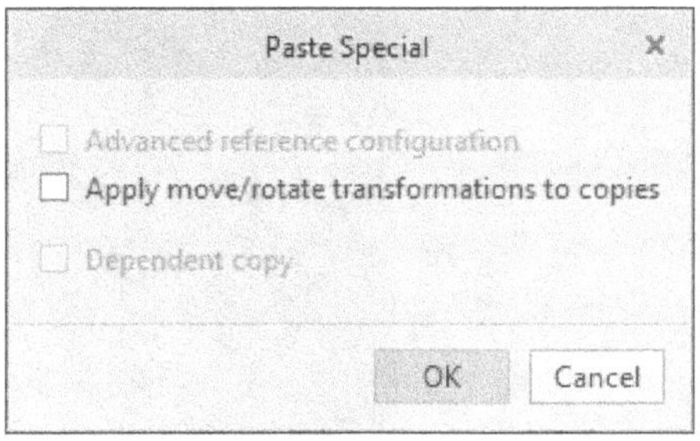

Figure-75. Paste Special dialog box

- Select the **Advanced reference configuration** check box from the dialog box and then click on the **OK** button from the dialog box. The **Advanced Reference Configuration** dialog box will be displayed; refer to Figure-76.
- Through this dialog box, you are asked to specify the replacement references for the reference entities displayed in the left list box. By default, the Surf:F7(REVOLVE 2):AXLE reference surface is selected in the left box.
- Select the same face on the other side of the axle; refer to Figure-77. You are asked to select the replacement of axis.
- Select the same axis on the other side of the axle; refer to Figure-78.
- Click on the **OK** button from the dialog box. The copy will be created with the same constraints on other side; refer to Figure-79.

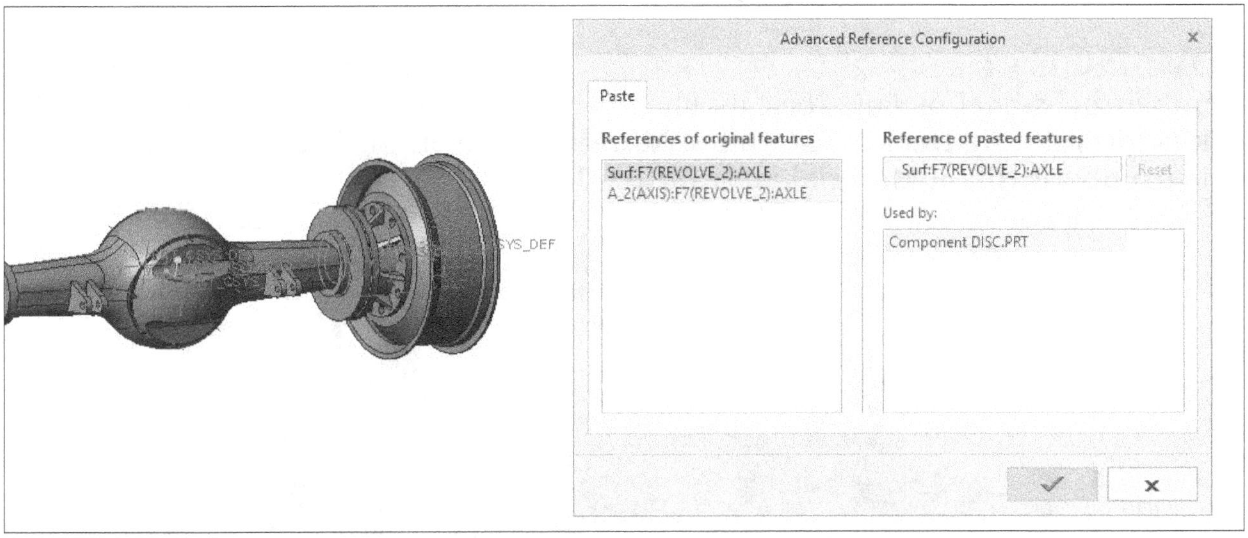

Figure-76. Advanced Reference Configuration dialog box

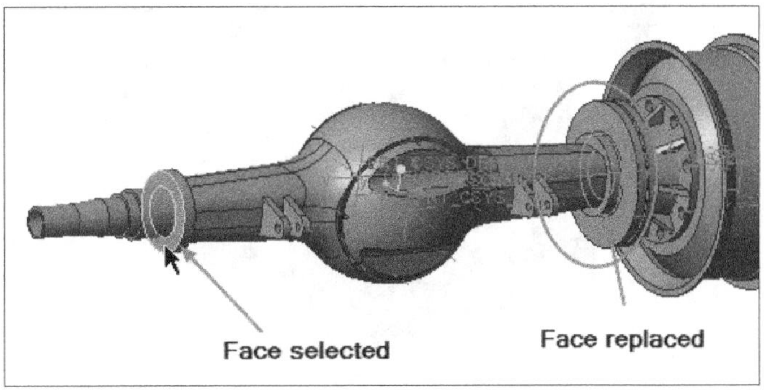

Figure-77. Face replaced

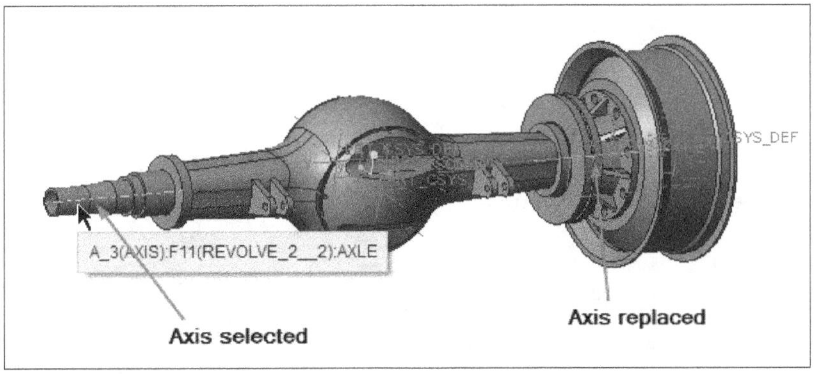

Figure-78. Axis replaced

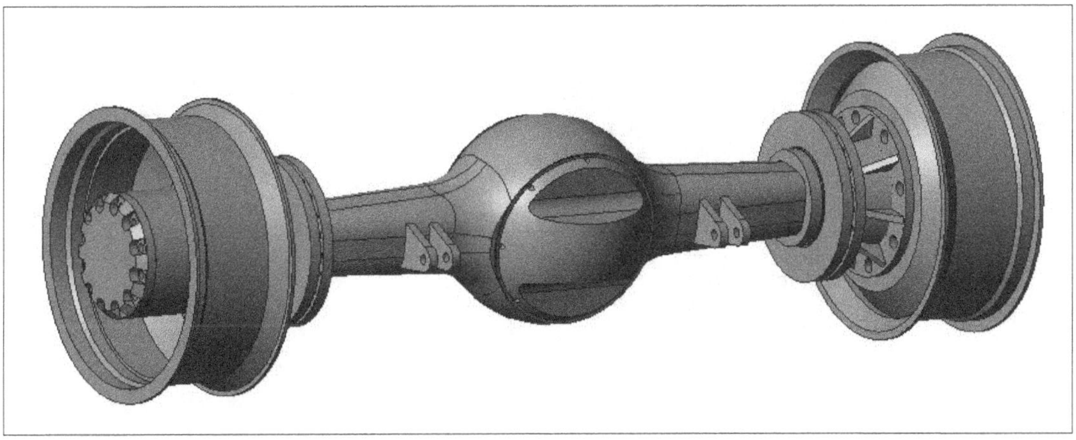

Figure-79. Assembly after copy

PRACTICE 1

Assemble the model of tail stock as shown in Figure-80. The exploded view of tail stock is given in Figure-81. The Bill of Material is given in Figure-82. Note that you will learn about Bill of Material later in this book.

Figure-80. Practice 1

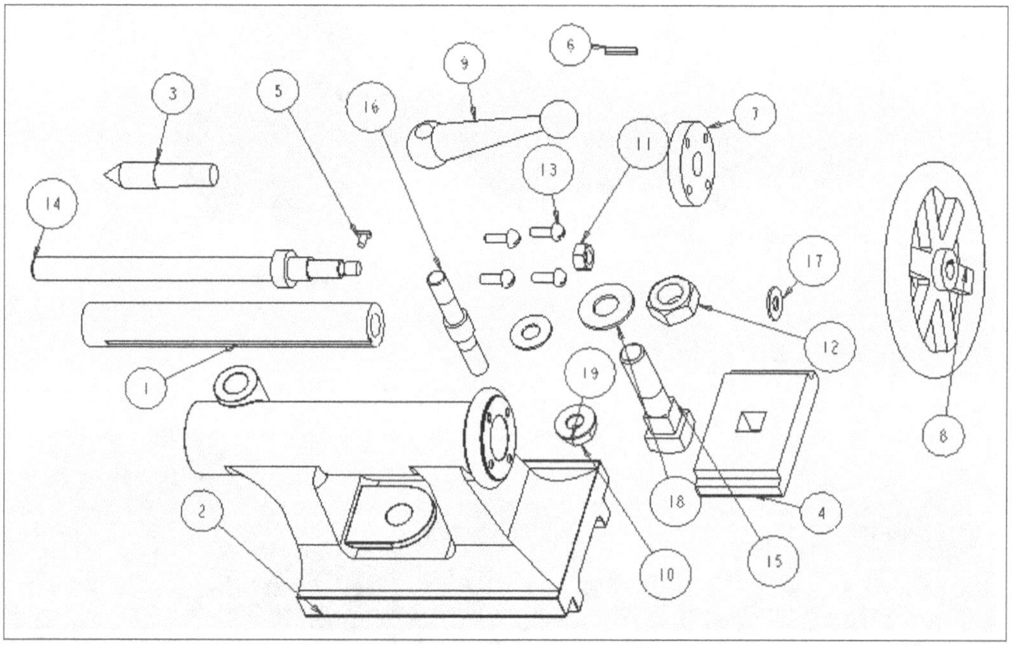

Figure-81. Exploded view of tail stock

Sr. No.	Component Name	Qty.
1	BARREL----3	1
2	BODY-----1	1
3	CENTRE----19	1
4	CLAMPING-PLATE----15	1
5	FEATHER--2	1
6	FEATHER-KEY--7	1
7	FLANGE---5	1
8	HAND-WHEEL-------8	1
9	HANDLE---13	1
10	HEXAGONAL---NUT--M16--------14	1
11	HEXAGONAL---NUT-M12------10	1
12	HEXAGONAL-NUT-M22--------18	1
13	SCREW---6	4
14	SCREW--SPINDILE---4	1
15	SQ-HEADED-BOLT--16	1
16	STUD---11	1
17	WASHER----M12------9	1
18	WASHER----M22-STD----------17	1
19	WASHER-M16----------12	2

Figure-82. Bill of Material

SELF ASSESSMENT

1. Which of the following constraints is used to permanently join component to the assembly?

(a) Weld (b) Fix
(c) Pin (d) Coplanar

2. Which of the following constraints is used to make the component follow path created on the assembly component?

(a) Pin (b) Slot
(c) Coplanar (d) Gimbal

3. The .... constraint is used to set the component and assembly parallel for selected faces/planes/edges/axes.

4. .... constraint is used to make references(selected entities of assembly and component) share the same plane.

5. .... constrain is used to fix the component at its present location.

6. .... constraint is used to assemble the component in such a way that they act like hinged at the selected reference.

7. .... constraint is used to assemble the component in such a way that the component is free to move 360 degree in 3D space pivoted to a point.

8. What is the primary purpose of using the Assembly environment in Creo Parametric?

a) To simulate motion of parts
b) To modify individual part designs
c) To combine two or more components using constraints
d) To create 2D sketches

9. Which option must be selected in the 'New' dialog box to create an assembly in Millimeter Newton Second unit system?

a) mmkg sec design
b) mmns asm design
c) inch lbm sec design
d) mmns part design

10. In Creo, what is typically the status of the first component inserted in an assembly?

a) Movable
b) Deleted
c) Base and fixed
d) Hidden

11. What does the "Display Dragger" button control?

a) Shows/hides the default planes
b) Flips component orientation
c) Enables 3D dragger (triad) visibility
d) Hides unused constraints

12. What happens when you apply the "Fix" constraint to a component?

a) It floats freely
b) It becomes the base
c) It is constrained at a specified angle
d) It becomes unmovable from its location

13. Which constraint aligns planes of the component and assembly in the same direction?

a) Tangent
b) Parallel
c) Coincident
d) Normal

14. Which constraint places component and assembly references at the same location?

a) Coincident
b) Coplanar
c) Parallel
d) Angle Offset

15. What does the "Centered" constraint do?

a) Centers components at origin
b) Aligns flat faces
c) Aligns circular faces concentrically
d) Sets parts tangent

16. Which constraint should you use to create a sliding joint between components?

a) Ball
b) Pin
c) Slider
d) Fix

17. Which constraint provides both rotational and translational freedom along an axis?

a) Cylinder
b) Planar
c) Weld
d) Angle Offset

18. What is the purpose of the "Drag Components" button?

a) Drag toolbar items
b) Rotate sketch entities
c) Test motion of constrained components
d) Add animation effects

19. Which constraint allows 360-degree movement around a pivot point?

a) Slider
b) Planar
c) Ball
d) Cylinder

20. What does the Weld constraint signify?

a) Rotational constraint
b) Temporary placement
c) Permanent joining of component
d) No constraint

21. What type of motion does the Bearing constraint allow for a component?

a) Only rotational motion in one direction
b) Only translational motion along one axis
c) Rotation in any direction and translation only in one direction
d) Fixed in all directions

22. What is the General constraint primarily used for?

a) Creating motion limits
b) Applying material properties
c) Applying any type of constraint discussed
d) Animating components

23. How many primary constraints can be applied using the General constraint option?

a) One
b) Two
c) Three
d) Four

24. What does the 6DOF constraint allow?

a) Unlimited rotation
b) Restriction of component rotation
c) No movement at all
d) Free movement in all directions with rotational limits

25. How is the 6DOF constraint similar to Weld?

a) It does not allow any motion
b) It restricts motion in all directions
c) The procedure of application is similar
d) It is used to apply materials

26. What is the main feature of the Gimbal constraint?

a) Fixes the part completely
b) Aligns component center with coordinate system
c) Allows slot-like motion
d) Restricts translation but not rotation

27. The Slot constraint makes a component follow:

a) A fixed point
b) A circular path
c) A sketched curve or edge
d) A flat surface

28. What is the main purpose of an Exploded View?

a) Animate the model
b) Disassemble model for manufacturing
c) Display component positions clearly
d) Apply constraints

29. How can the distance between components be changed in an exploded view?

a) Using Appearance tab
b) Using Edit Position button
c) Using Connection drop-down
d) Using Assembly Constraints

30. What tool is used to visually show connections between components in exploded view?

a) Distance Tool
b) Gimbal Axis
c) Cosmetic Lines
d) Appearance Filter

31. Which tab helps to return back to the assembled view from exploded view?

a) Placement tab
b) Explode tab
c) Model Display panel
d) Cosmetic Lines dialog box

32. What is the use of View Manager in Creo?

a) Apply animations
b) Manage material properties
c) Create, manage and switch between exploded views
d) Insert new components

33. Which command in View Manager helps in modifying the exploded positions of components?

a) Cosmetic Lines
b) Appearance Settings
c) Edit Position
d) Activate

34. What happens when you use Clear Assembly Appearances?

a) All appearances including part environment ones are removed
b) Only appearances from part environment are removed
c) Only appearance in assembly is removed
d) Nothing happens

35. How do you apply a color to only a portion of a part?

a) Select Face from the Appearance Filter
b) Use General constraint
c) Use Cosmetic Lines
d) Apply via View Manager

FOR STUDENT NOTES

Answers to Self Assessment Questions :

1. (a) **2.** (b) **3.** Parallel **4.** Coplanar **5.** Fix **6.** Pin **7.** Ball

Chapter 10

Advanced Assembly and Introduction to Mechanism

Topics Covered

The major topics covered in this chapter are:

- ***Introduction***
- ***Bottom-Up Assembly Approach***
- ***Modifying Part in Assembly***
- ***Mechanism Design***

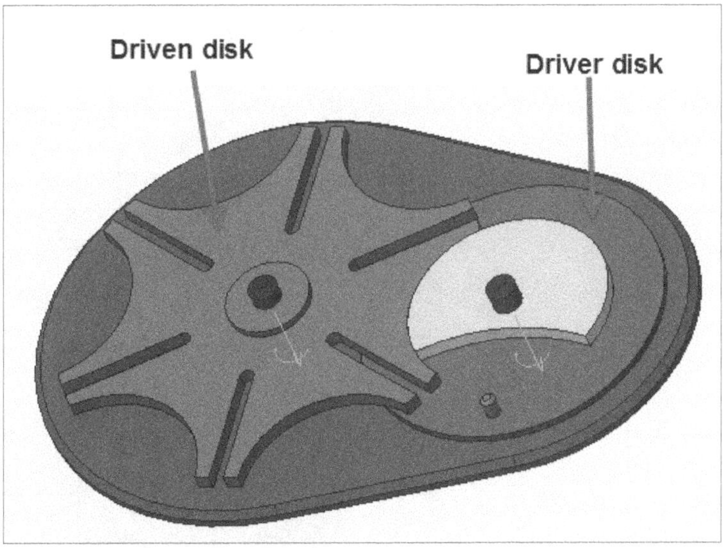

INTRODUCTION

In previous chapter, you have learned about inserting components in assembly and performing simple assembly operations. In this chapter, you will learn about creating parts in the assembly (also called Bottom-Up Assembly approach), performing mechanism simulations, and many other advanced operations. We will start the chapter with Bottom-Up Assembly approach.

BOTTOM-UP ASSEMBLY APPROACH

In the previous chapter, we inserted the components in assembly file which were already created. Now, we will create components as per the requirement of assembly. For this, we have opened an already created assembly in Creo Parametric as shown in Figure-1. In this assembly, we will create a lever that can join the boss features of two sliders as shown in Figure-2. Before that we will change the shuttle part shown in the figure because it is overlapping with the base part. The procedure is discussed next.

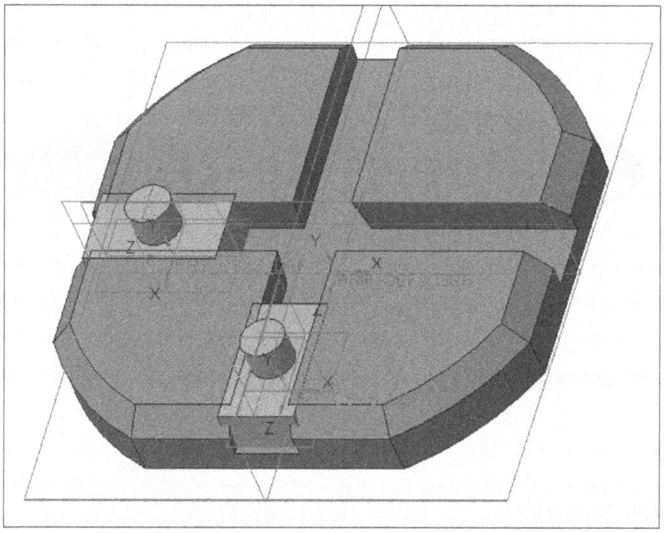

Figure-1. Assembly for Bottom Up Approach

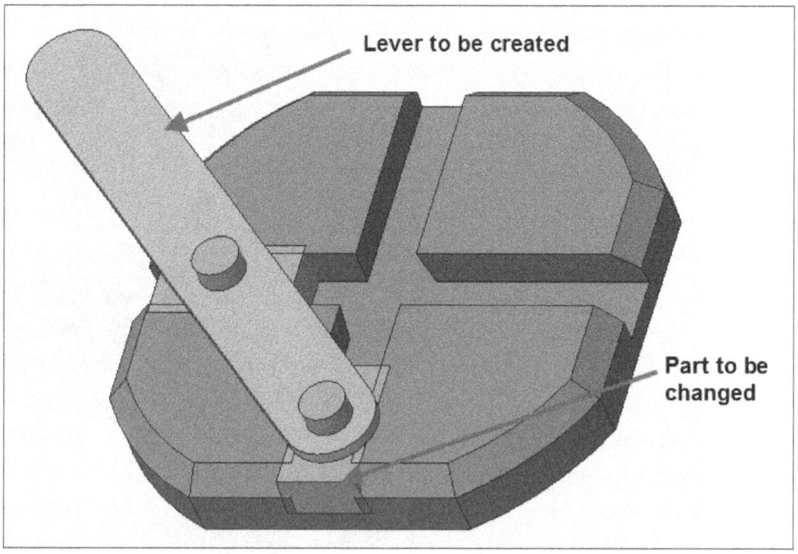

Figure-2. Lever to be created

Modifying Part in Assembly

- Open the assembly with the name **Bottom-Up Approach.asm** from the resources available for this book in Chapter 10. The assembly will be displayed as shown in Figure-1.
- Right-click on any of the **Shuttle.prt** from **Model Tree** and click on the **Activate** button; refer to Figure-3. The part will be activated in drawing area; refer to Figure-4.

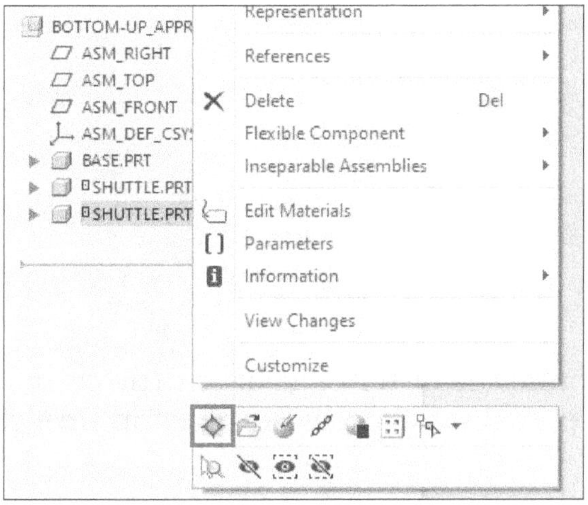

Figure-3. Activate button

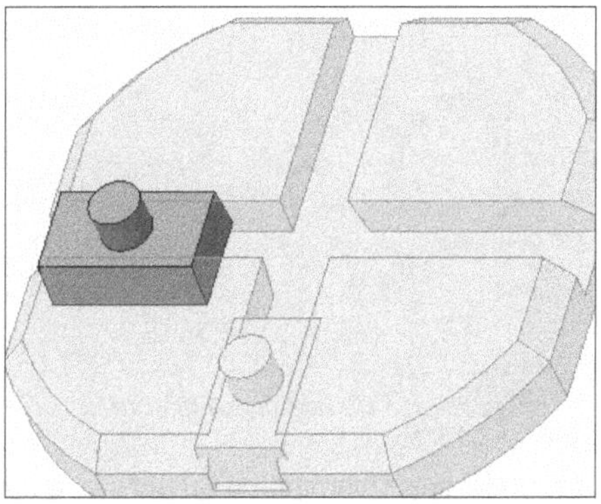

Figure-4. Shuttle part activated in assembly

- Click on the right face of the shuttle part. Mini Toolbar will be displayed; refer to Figure-5.

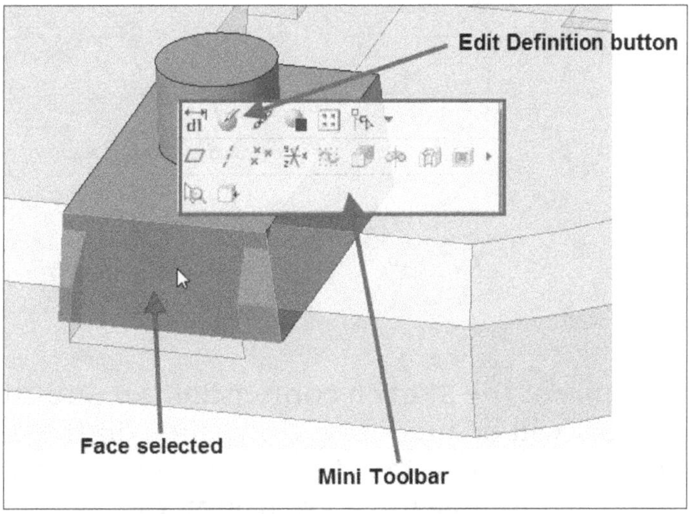

Figure-5. Mini toolbar on selecting face of part

- Click on the **Edit Definition** button from the Mini toolbar. The **Extrude** contextual tab will be displayed and part will change to editing mode.
- Click on the **Placement** tab and then click on the **Edit** button. The sketch editing mode will become active; refer to Figure-6.

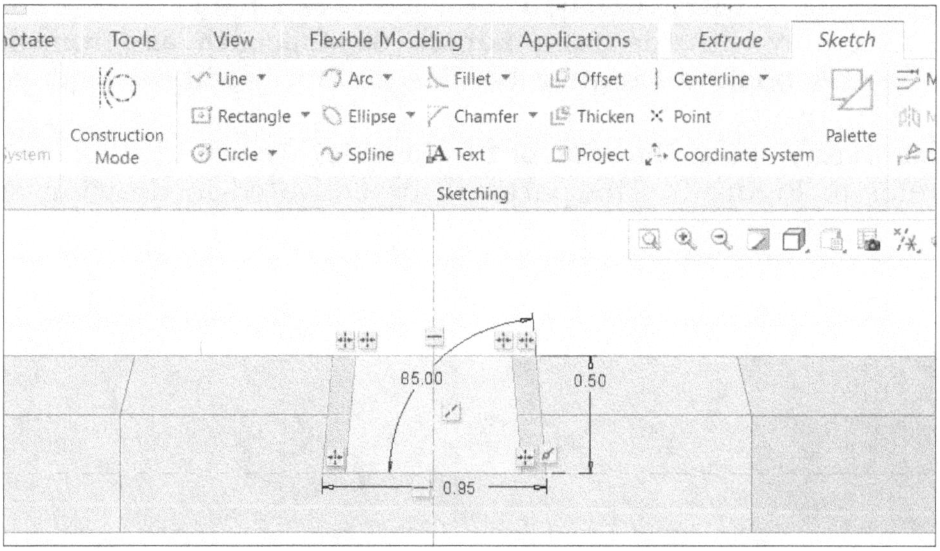

Figure-6. Editing sketch of shuttle

- Delete the dimensions of sketch and make the outer edge of shuttle coincident with edge of groove in base; refer to Figure-7. Similarly, make the top line coincident with upper edge; refer to Figure-8.

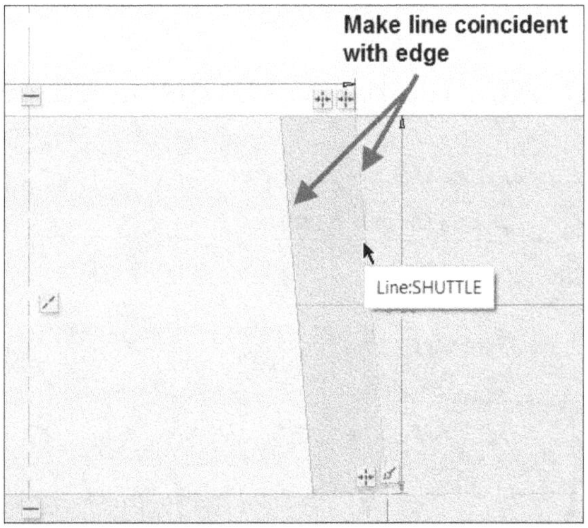

Figure-7. Making line coincident

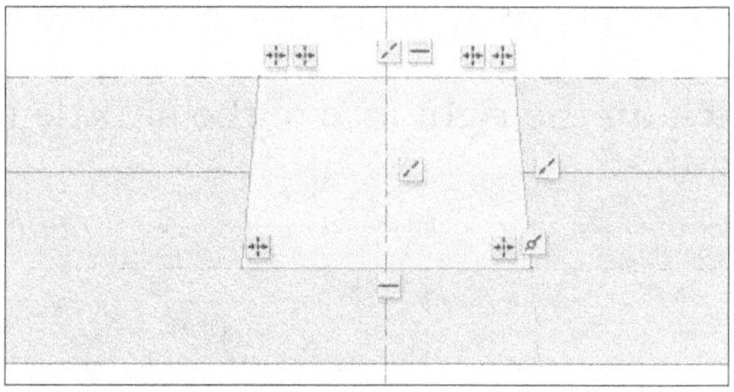

Figure-8. Sketch after making coincident

- Click on the **OK** button from the **Sketch** contextual tab and then from the **Extrude** contextual tab. The part will be modified. Now, click on the assembly file name in the **Model Tree** and click on the **Activate** button from the Mini toolbar displayed; refer to Figure-9 to return to assembly environment.

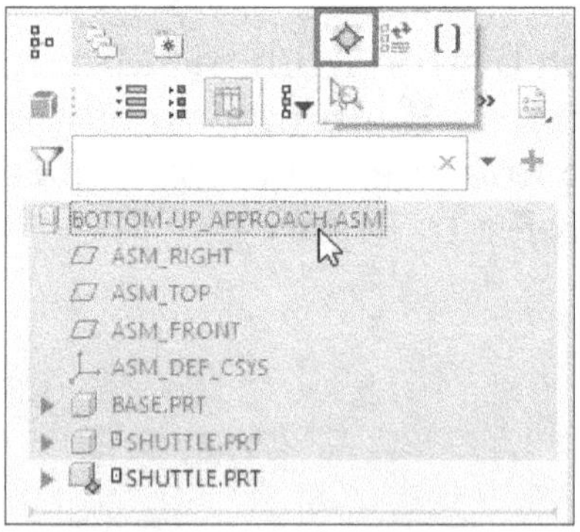

Figure-9. Activate button for assembly

Creating Part in Assembly

- Click on the **Create** button from the **Component** panel of the **Model** tab in the **Ribbon**. The **Create Component** dialog box will be displayed; refer to Figure-10.
- Make sure the **Part** radio button is selected in the **Type** area and **Solid** radio button is selected in the **Sub-Type** area of the dialog box. Type the name as **Lever** in the **Name** edit box.
- Click on the **OK** button from the dialog box. The **Creation Options** dialog box will be displayed; refer to Figure-11.

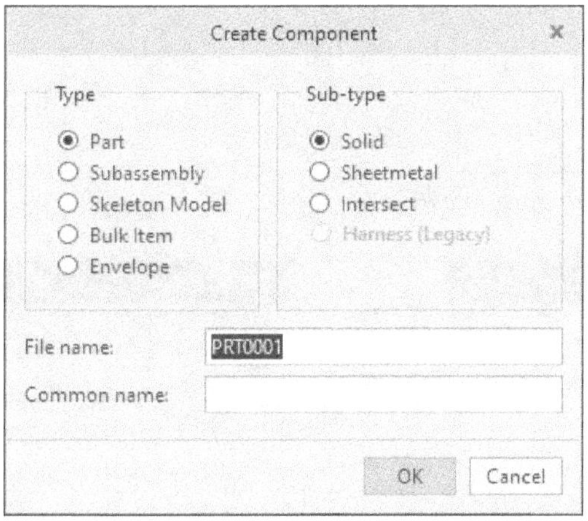

Figure-10. Create Component dialog box

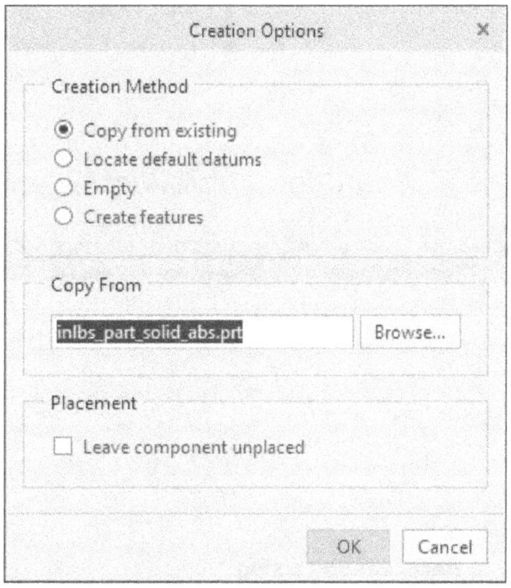

Figure-11. Creation Options dialog box

Using Copy From Existing option

- If you want to use any already created file as template then select the **Copy from existing** radio button from the **Creation Method** area of the dialog box and click on the **Browse** button to select desired file. The **Choose template** dialog box will be displayed.
- Select desired template and click on the **OK** button. The selected file will get selected as template.
- Click on the **OK** button from the dialog box. The **Component Placement** contextual tab will be displayed and you will be asked to place the template part using assembly constraints.
- Place the part using desired constraints and click on the **OK** button from the contextual tab. Now, you can modify the part as discussed earlier.

Using Locate Default Datums option

- Select the **Locate Default Datums** option from the **Creation Options** dialog box and select desired method of locating datums from the **Locate Datums Method** area of the dialog box; refer to Figure-12.
- Click on the **OK** button from the dialog box. You will be asked to select the reference according to radio button selected in the **Locate Datums Method** area of the dialog box.
- Select the datums and then create the model using the part modeling tools; refer to Figure-13.

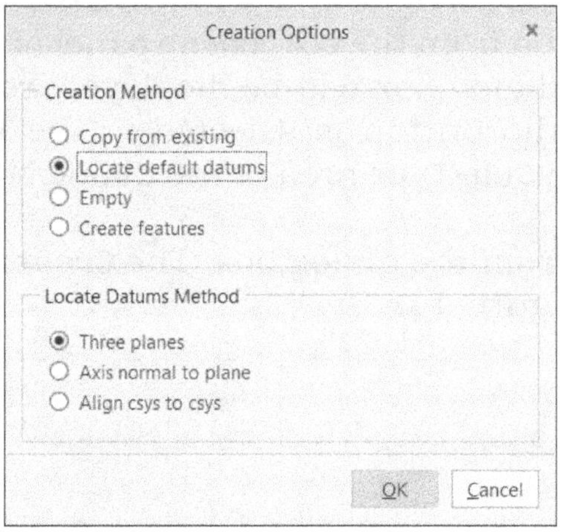

Figure-12. Locate default datums option

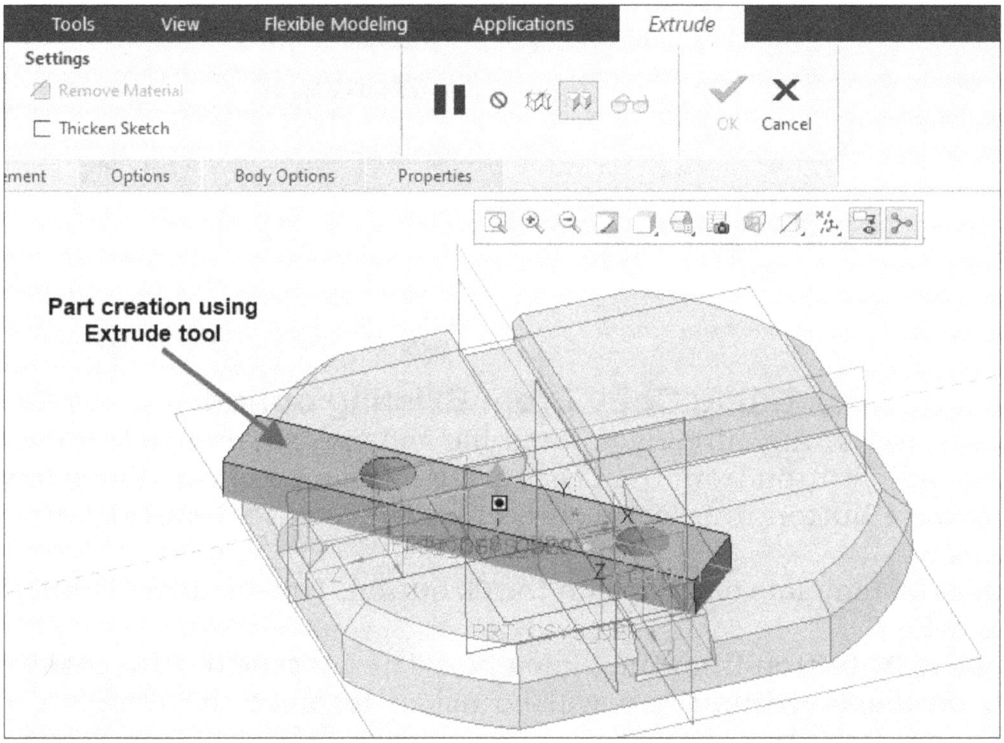

Figure-13. Creating part in assembly

- Activate the assembly file from **Model Tree** as discussed earlier after creating part. Now, you can redefine the assembly constraints of the created part.

Using Empty option

- Select the **Empty** radio button from the **Creation Options** dialog box and click on the **OK** button. A new empty part will be created. Modify the newly added part using the method discussed earlier. Note that on using this option, you will not be able to define assembly constraints for the component. So, you should not create part using this option if you are concerned about assembly constraints.

Create Features option

- Select the **Create Features** radio button from the **Creation Options** dialog box and click on the **OK** button. A new part file will be created and the part modeling environment will be displayed; refer to Figure-14.

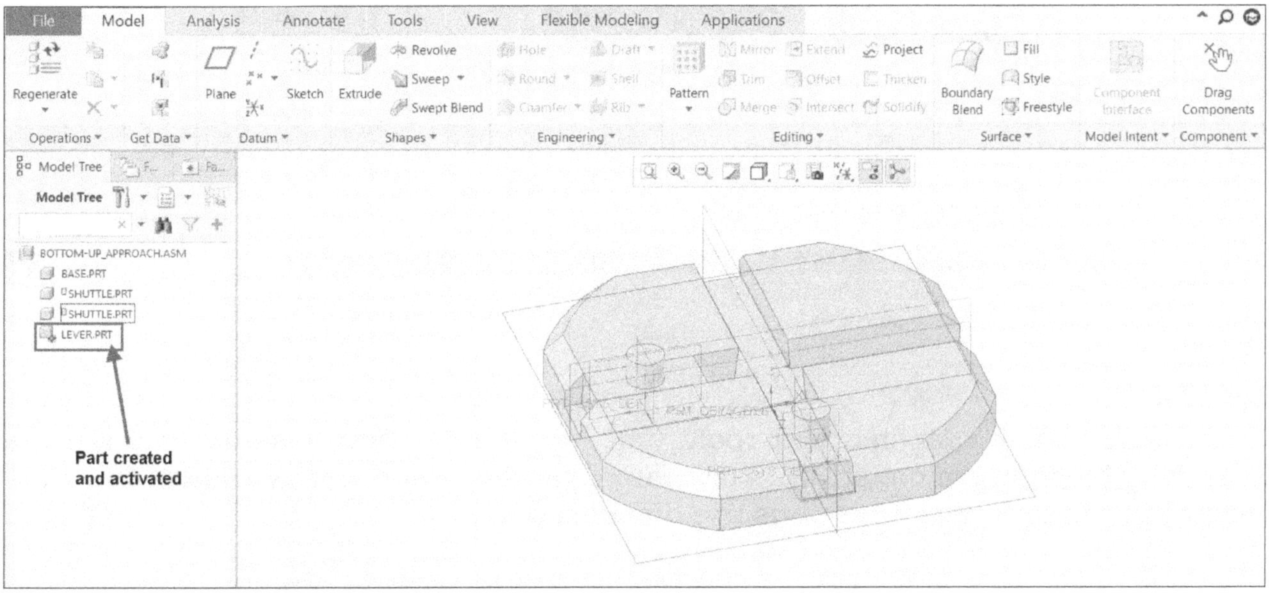

Figure-14. Part modeling environment

- Create the part using the modeling tools. Note that you can use the assembly geometry as reference while creating the part. For example, you can project the edges of shuttle part while creating sketch for feature or you can use the top face of shuttle as extrude depth reference; refer to Figure-15.

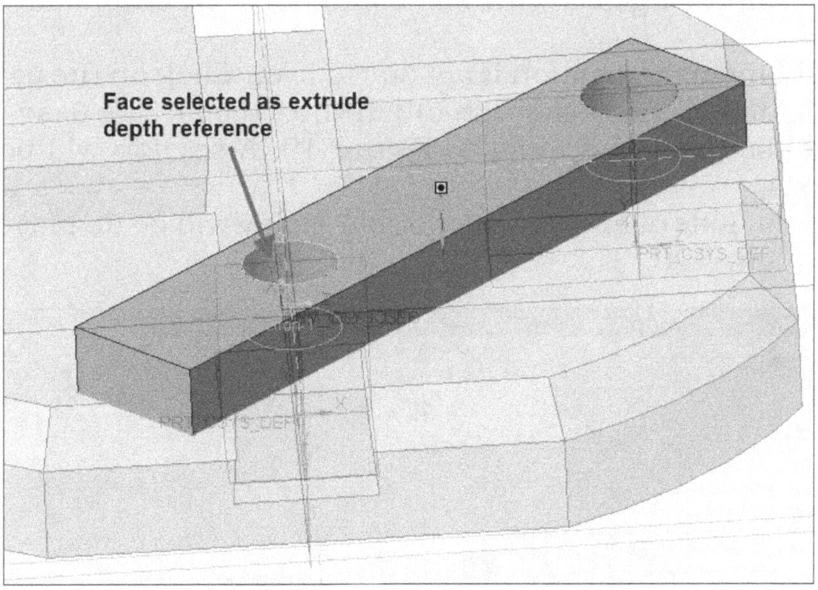

Figure-15. Face of assembly part selected as reference

Note that on using this option, you will not be able to define assembly constraints for the component. So, you should not create part using this option if you are concerned about assembly constraints.

MECHANISM DESIGN

The tools for designing mechanism are available in the Mechanism application of Creo Parametric. The procedure to start Mechanism application is given next.

- Click on the **Mechanism** tool from the **Motion** panel of the **Applications** tab in the **Ribbon** while in Assembly environment; refer to Figure-16. The **Mechanism** tab will be added to the **Ribbon**; refer to Figure-17.

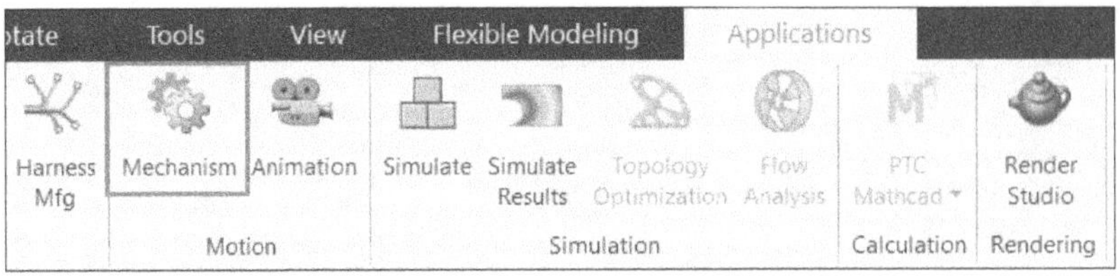

Figure-16. Mechanism button

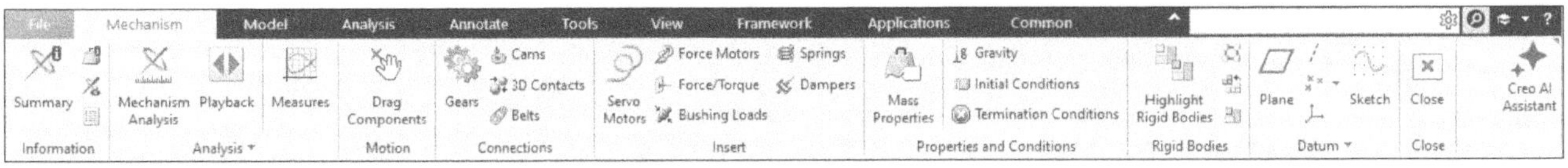

Figure-17. Mechanism tab in Ribbon

Note that for using Mechanism tools, you must have the assembly constraints defined by Mechanism constraints like Pin, Cylinder, Rigid, etc. Various tools in the **Mechanism** tab and their functions are discussed next.

APPLYING GEAR RELATIONS

Gears are the backbone of modern locomotives. You can create real dynamics of a gear mechanism in the **Mechanism** environment of **Creo Parametric**. The procedure to do so is given next.

- Create an assembly of gears with **Pin** connection type applied to them; refer to Figure-18.
- Start the Mechanism application if not started yet. Click on the **Gears** tool from the **Connections** panel of the **Mechanism** tab in the **Ribbon**. The **Gear Pair Definition** dialog box will be displayed; refer to Figure-19. Also, you will be asked to select the motion axis.
- Select the motion axis of first gear. A double-arrow will be displayed on the motion axis; refer to Figure-20.

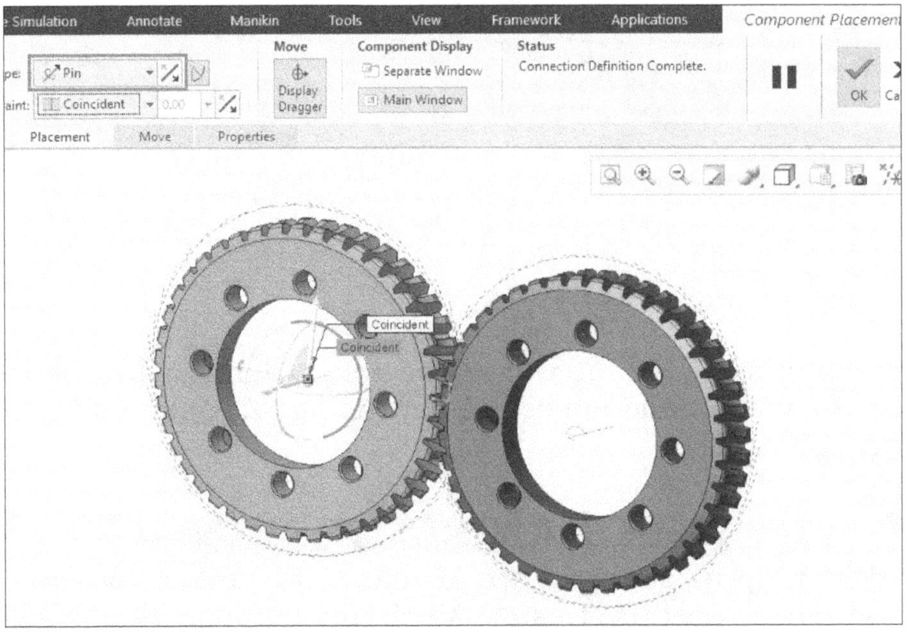

Figure-18. Assembly of gears

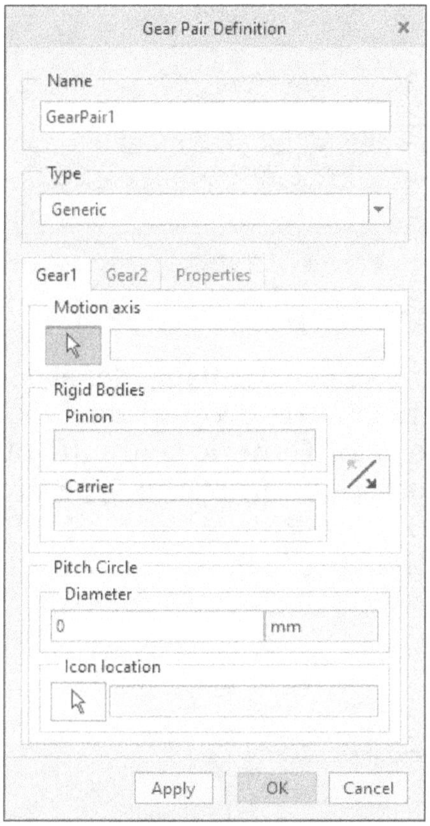

Figure-19. Gear Pair Definition dialog box

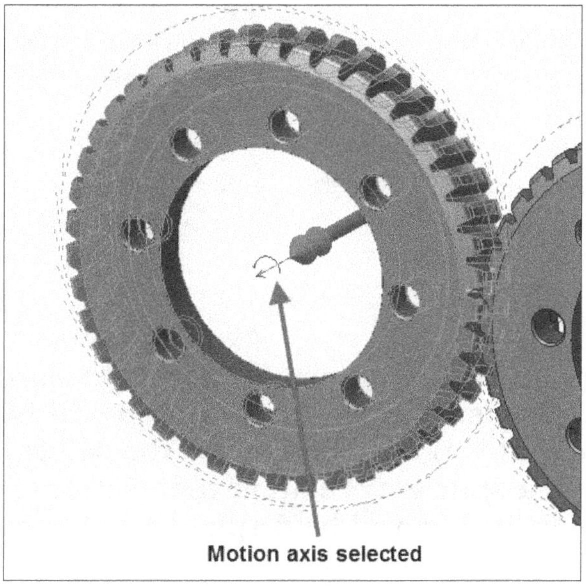

Figure-20. Selecting motion axis

- Specify desired value of pitch circle diameter in the **Diameter** edit box of the **Pitch Circle** area of the dialog box; refer to Figure-21. Note that the gear ratio will be calculated based on the Pitch Circle Diameter specified here.

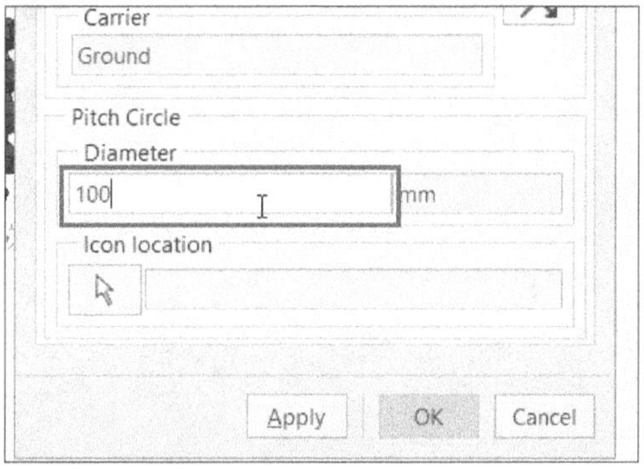

Figure-21. Diameter edit box

- Click on the **Gear 2** tab in the dialog box. You will be asked to select the motion axis of second gear. If you are not prompted to select the axis then click on the selection button from the **Motion axis** area of the dialog box.
- Select the motion axis of the second gear. The motion arrow will be displayed on the motion axis. Note that this time, the direction is opposite because mating gears rotate in opposite direction. If you want to reverse the direction of gear motion then click on the **Flip** button in **Motion axis** area of the dialog box.
- Specify the Pitch Circle Diameter for **Gear 2** in the **Diameter** edit box.
- Click on the **Properties** tab to change the properties of the gear mechanism relation. The options in the dialog box will be displayed as shown in Figure-22.

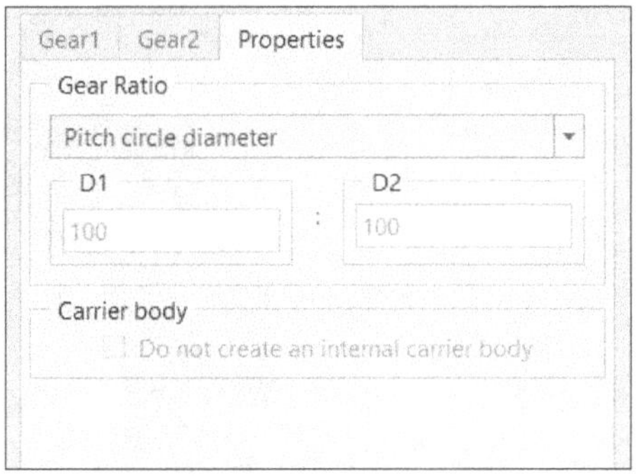

Figure-22. Properties options

- Click in the drop-down of **Gear Ratio** area and select the **User defined** option to manually specify the gear ratio in edit boxes below the drop-down.
- Note that you have performed the whole process for Generic gears. If you want to create a spur gear relation then select the **Spur** option from the **Type** drop-down. The dialog box will be displayed as shown in Figure-23.

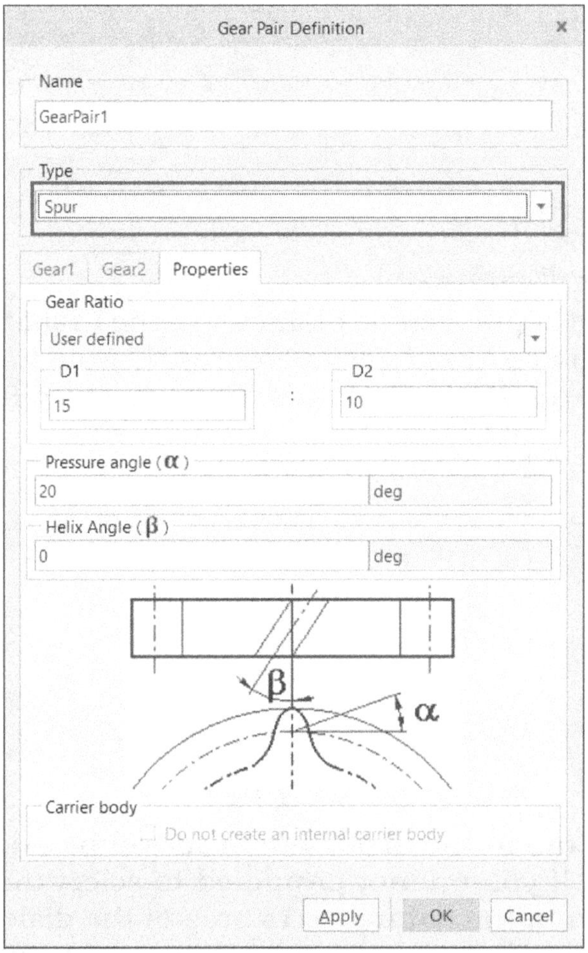

Figure-23. Gear Pair Definition dialog box for spur gear

- Specify the parameters related to spur gear like pressure angle and helix angle in respective edit boxes of **Properties** tab.
- In the same way, you can make Bevel gear, Worm gear, or Rack and Pinion mechanism relation by selecting the respective option from the **Type** drop-down.
- Click on the **OK** button to create the mechanism relation.
- Click on the **Drag Components** button and drag one of the gear to rotate it. The other gear will rotate accordingly. Save the file at desired location.

APPLYING CAM-FOLLOWER RELATION

The most common example of cam-follower relation for a mechanical engineer is cam valve system in an engine. In Creo Parametric, we can create this relation by using the **Cams** tool. The procedure to create Cam-follower relation is given next.

- Create/open a cam-follower assembly; refer to Figure-24.
- Start Mechanism application if not started yet.
- Click on the **Cams** tool from the **Connections** panel of the **Mechanism** tab in the **Ribbon**. The **Cam-Follower Connection Definition** dialog box will be displayed; refer to Figure-25 and you will be asked to select the surface/curve of cam.

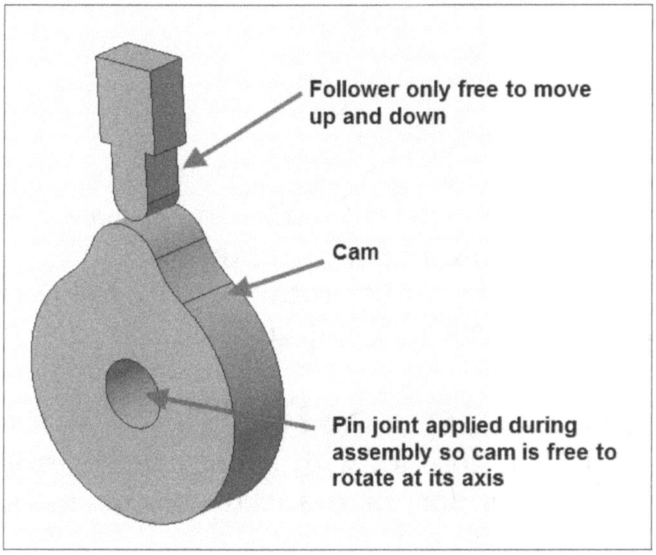

Figure-24. Cam follower assembly

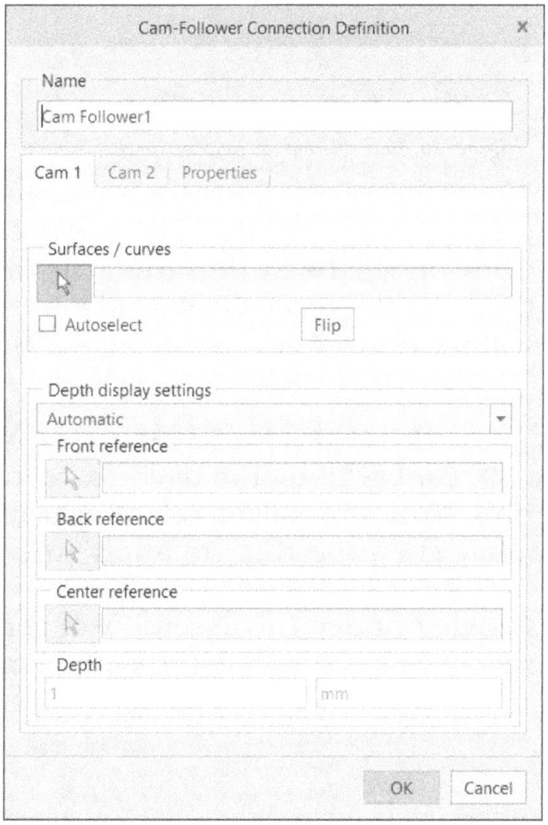

Figure-25. Cam-Follower Connection Definition dialog box

- Select the surfaces/curves of Cam profile while holding the **CTRL** key or select the **Autoselect** check box in **Surfaces/Curves** area of the dialog box and then select one of the cam profile surface/curve, all the adjoining surfaces/curves will be selected automatically. After selecting the faces, press the **MMB**.
- Click on the **Cam 2** tab from the dialog box. You will be asked to select the face of follower.
- Select the face of follower as shown in Figure-26 and press **MMB**.
- Click on the **Properties** tab of the dialog box and specify the parameters like liftoff and friction coefficient in respective fields if required; refer to Figure-27.
- Select **Smoothen the cam curves** check box from **Smoothen** area of the tab to use smooth splines instead the original references.

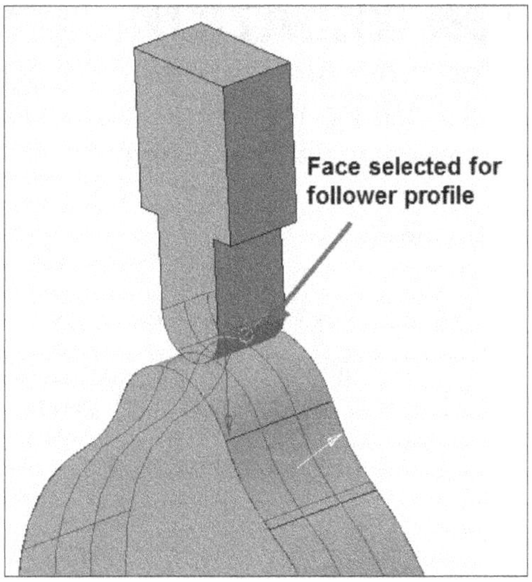

Figure-26. Face selected for follower profile

Figure-27. Properties tab of Cam-Follower Connection dialog box

- Click on the **OK** button from the dialog box to create the connection.
- Click on the **Drag Components** button and drag the cam to rotate it. The follower will move up-down accordingly. Save the file at desired location.

APPLYING 3D CONTACT RELATION

The **3D Contacts** tool is used to keep two bodies in contact with each other during motion. You can select references like sphere, cylinder, or plane to establish 3D contact. The procedure to apply this relation is given next.

- Create or open the assembly of geneva mechanism (You can find the assembly in resources of this book; refer to Figure-28.

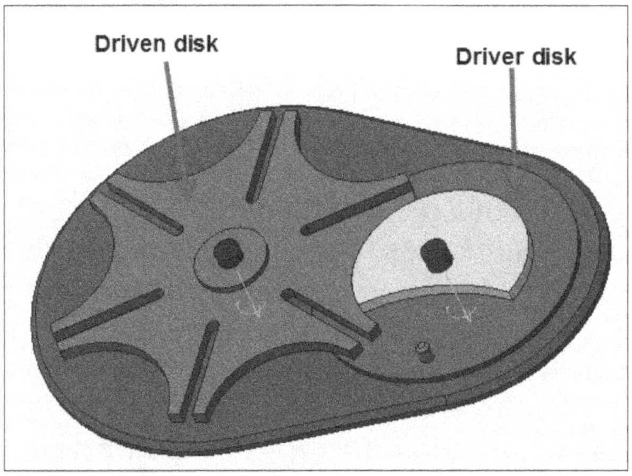

Figure-28. Geneva mechanism

- Start the Mechanism application if not started yet. Now, using the **Drag Components** tool in the **Motion** panel, try to rotate the driver disk. You will find that pin does not rotate the driven disk but it passes through it. This is not desired in geneva mechanism, so we will apply 3D contact here to make software understand our purpose.
- Click on the **3D Contacts** tool from the **Connections** panel in the **Mechanism** tab of the **Ribbon**. The **3D Contact** contextual tab will be displayed in the Ribbon; refer to Figure-29 and you will be asked to select the contact references.

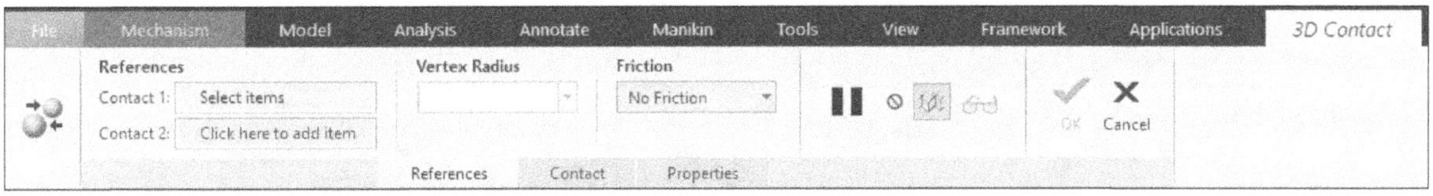

Figure-29. 3D Contact contextual tab

- Click on the **References** tab and select the round face of pin; refer to Figure-30. You will be asked to select face of second reference.

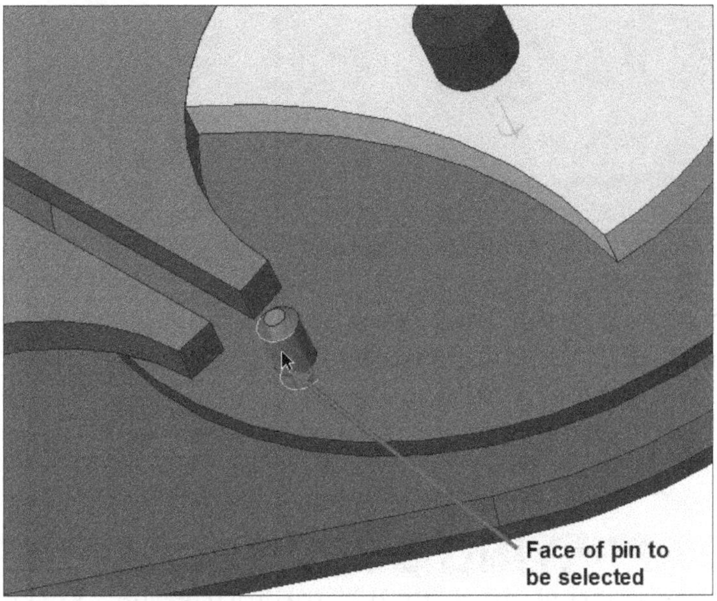

Figure-30. Face of pin selected

- Select the faces of driven disk as shown in Figure-31.

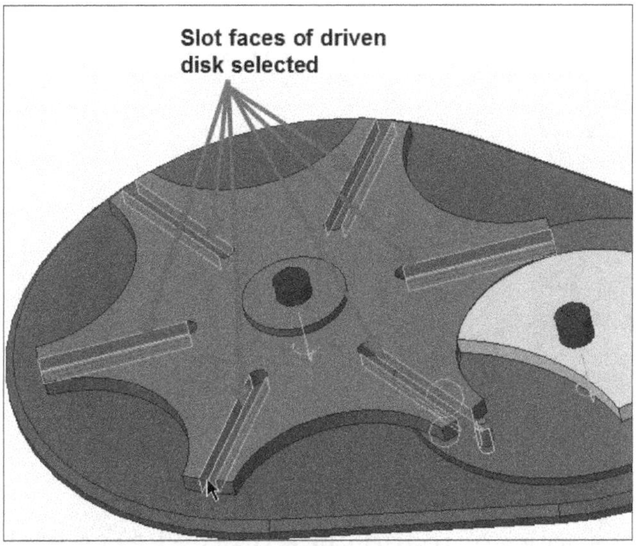

Figure-31. Faces of driven disk selected

- Click on the **Contact** tab and specify the material properties for both sides of contact; refer to Figure-32.
- If you want to select a material in place of explicitly specifying properties then select the **Select material** option from the drop-down in the **Contact** tab; refer to Figure-33 and click in the **More** field next to it. The **Materials** dialog box will be displayed as discussed in earlier chapters. Select desired material from the dialog box and click on the **OK** button.

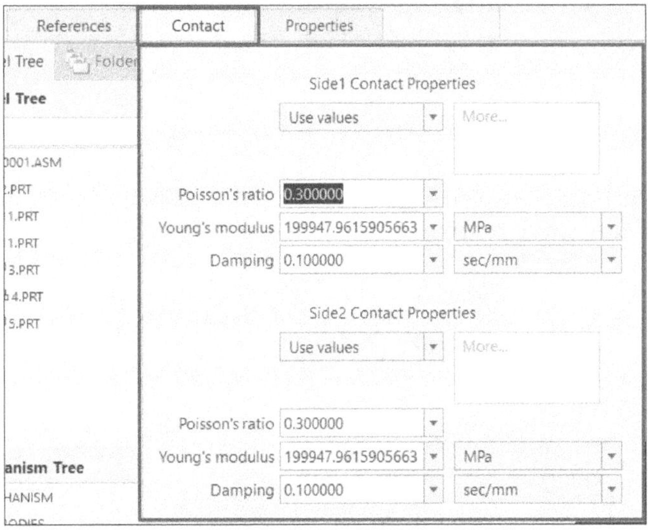

Figure-32. Contact tab

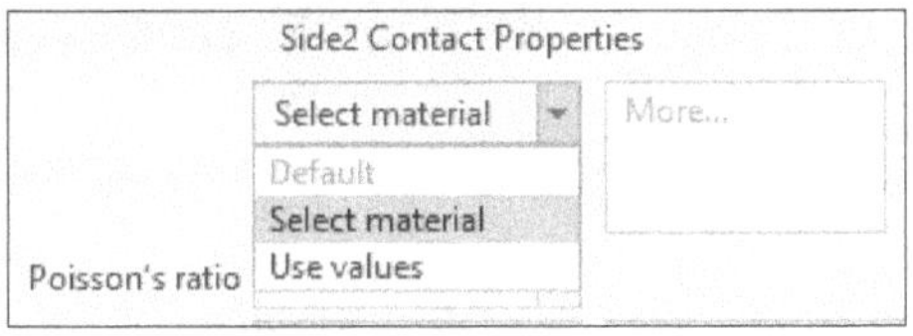

Figure-33. Select material option

- If you want to specify friction between the two contact references then select the **With Friction** option from the **Friction** drop-down of contextual tab in **Ribbon** and specify desired friction coefficients.
- Click on the **OK** button to create the relation. Save the file at desired location, we will run this mechanism later.

APPLYING BELT RELATION

Belt mechanism has many uses in daily life and industries. You can find a belt in the car which runs the engine and alternator. You can also find belts in wheat crushing machines. The procedure to apply the belt relation is given next.

- Create or open the assembly in which you want to apply the belt relation; refer to Figure-34.

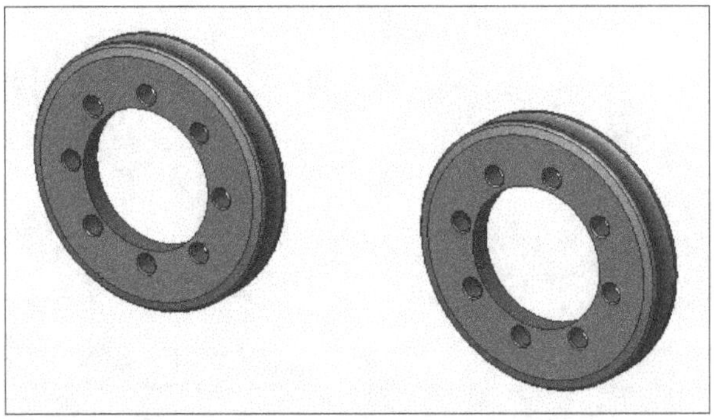

Figure-34. Assembly for applying belt mechanism

- Start the **Mechanism** application and click on the **Belts** tool from the **Connections** panel of the **Mechanism** tab in the **Ribbon**. The **Belt** contextual tab will be displayed; refer to Figure-35. Also, you will be asked to select the faces/edges of both pulleys.

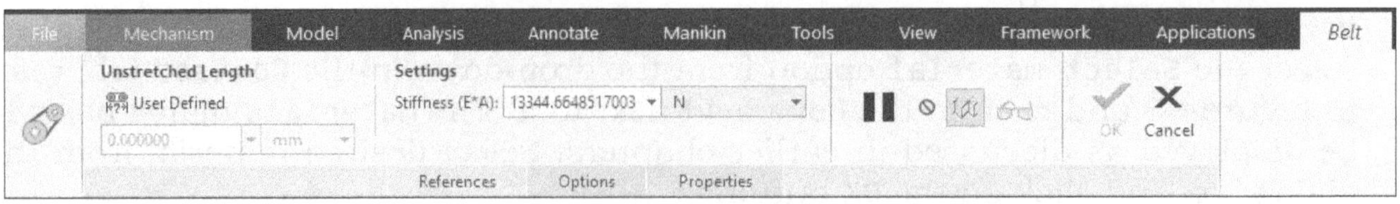

Figure-35. Belt contextual tab

- Select round face/edge of first pulley and then of second pulley while holding the **CTRL** key; refer to Figure-36. Preview of belt relation will be displayed; refer to Figure-37.

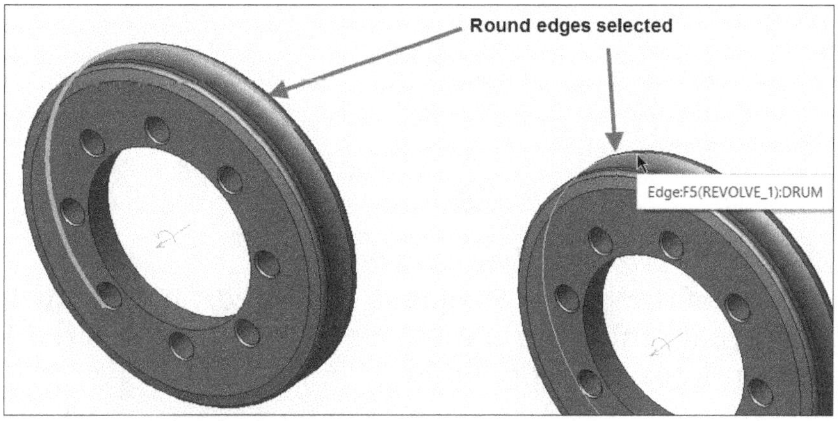

Figure-36. Selecting edges of pulleys

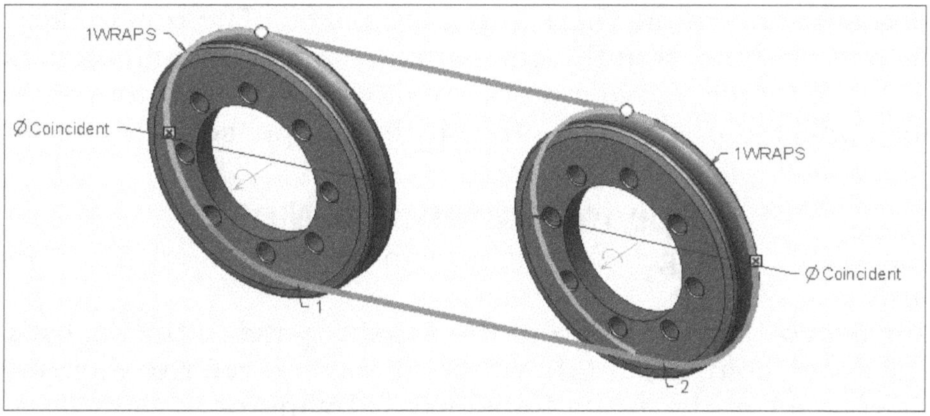

Figure-37. Preview of belt relation

- Click in the **Belt plane** selection box of **References** tab in the **Belt** contextual tab and select desired plane for belt placement; refer to Figure-38.

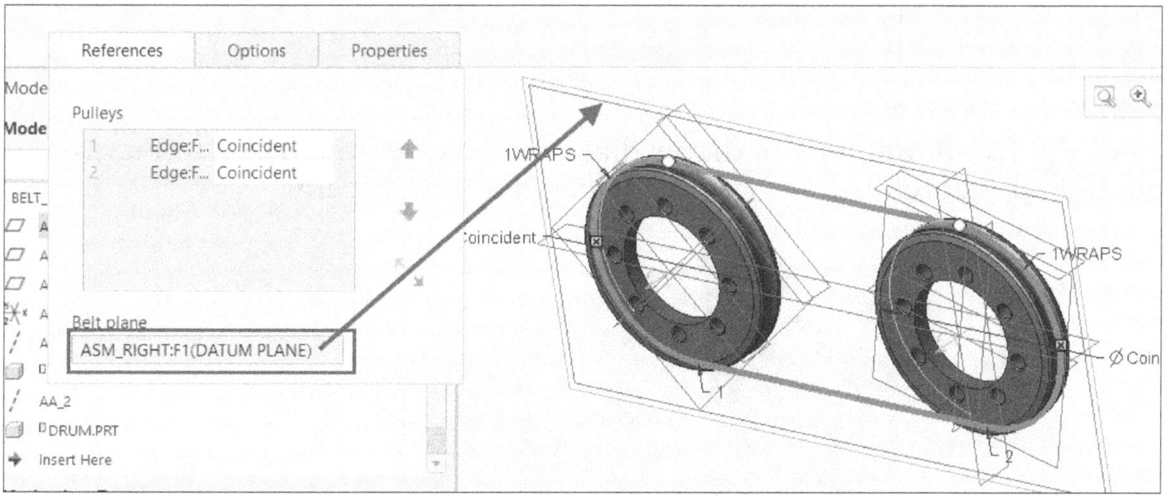

Figure-38. Belt plane selection

- Click on the **Options** tab and specify desired number of wraps of belt on each pulley; refer to Figure-39.

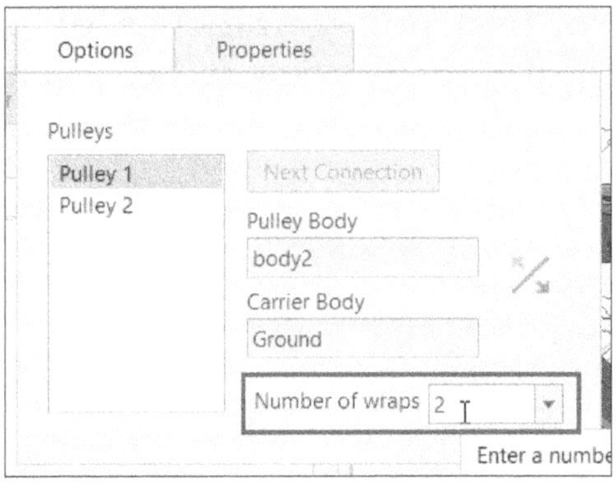

Figure-39. Number of wraps option

- Specify the tension of the belt in **Stiffness (E*A)** edit box of the **Ribbon**. Click on the **OK** button to create the belt relation. Save the file at desired location, we will analyze the motion later in this chapter.

SERVO MOTORS

In Creo Mechanism application, there is always a need of motion maker that rotates/ translates one or more objects in the mechanism. One of the motion making object in Mechanism is servo motor. Servo motors are like electrical motors which give rotary motion to the connected object. The procedure to apply servo motor is given next.

Applying Rotational Motor

- Open the assembly file of geneva mechanism earlier created. Start the Mechanism application.
- Click on the **Servo Motors** tool from the **Insert** panel in the **Mechanism** tab of the **Ribbon**. The **Motor** contextual tab will be displayed; refer to Figure-40. Also, you will be asked to select the entity to be driven by motor.

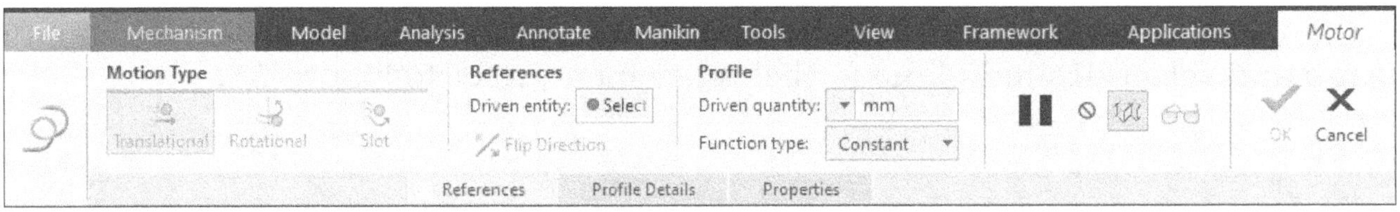

Figure-40. Motor contextual tab

- Select the rotational axis of driver disk in the assembly; refer to Figure-41. The **Rotational motion** button will get selected automatically.

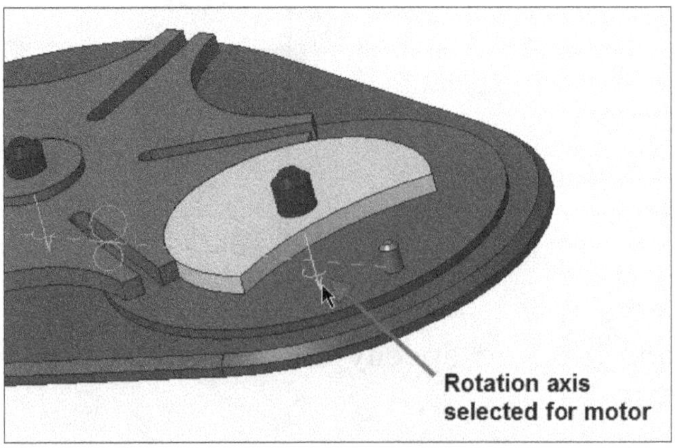

Figure-41. Rotation axis selected for motor

- Click on the **Profile Details** tab in the **Ribbon**. The options to modify motor profile will be displayed; refer to Figure-42.

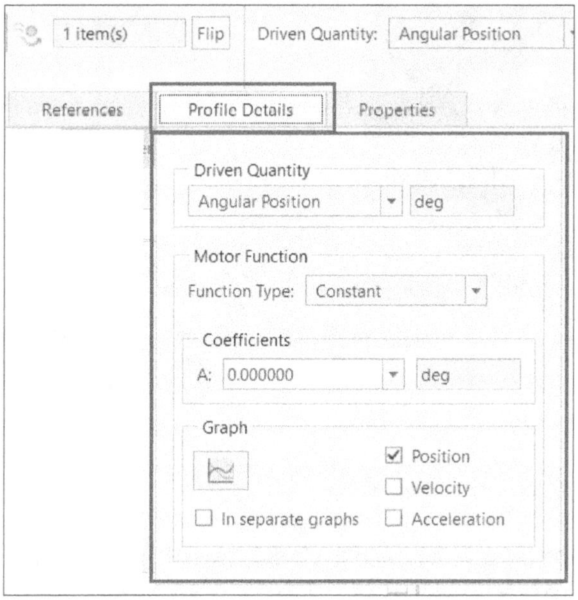

Figure-42. Profile Details tab

- Click in the **Driven Quantity** drop-down and select desired parameter (like Velocity) to be used for applying motion. Specify desired value of parameter in the **Coeficients** edit box.
- If you want to set a function for parameter value then click in the **Function Type** drop-down and select desired function; refer to Figure-43. Specify desired parameters for the function.

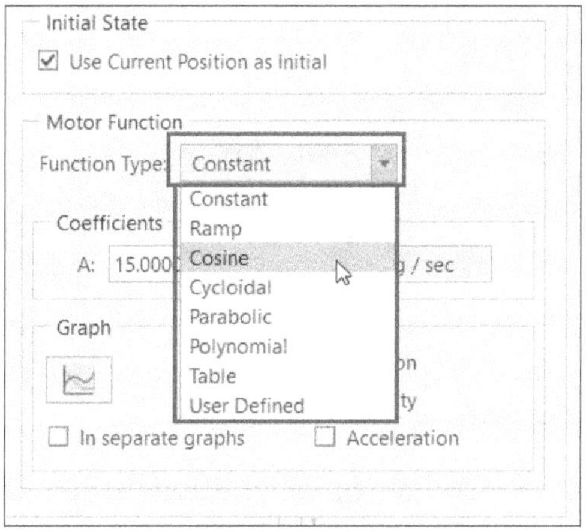

Figure-43. Function Type drop-down

- Click on the **OK** button from the **Ribbon** to apply motor. Save the file.

Applying Translational Motor

Translational motor is useful when we need to check the effect of translational motion of a component in assembly. For example, in Rack and Pinion assembly; refer to Figure-44.

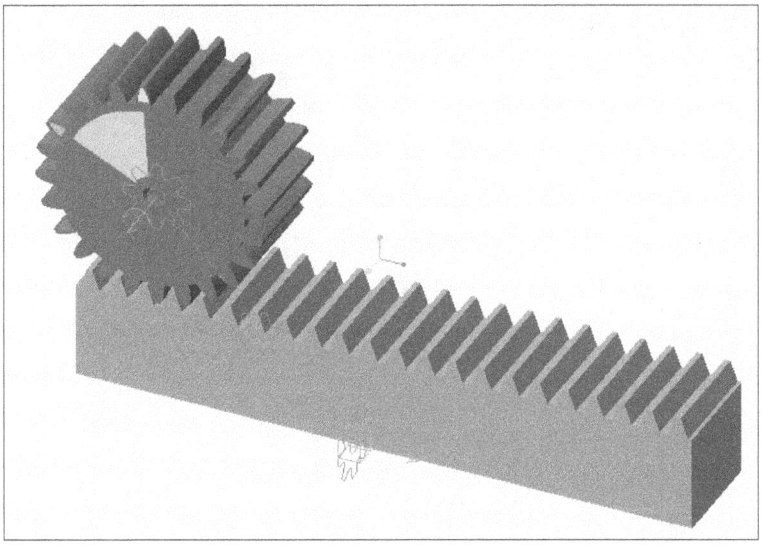

Figure-44. Rack pinion assembly

- Click on the **Servo Motors** tool from the **Insert** panel in the **Mechanism** tab of the **Ribbon**. The **Motor** contextual tab will be displayed as discussed earlier.
- Select the translational motion axis of model created by slider joints; refer to Figure-45.

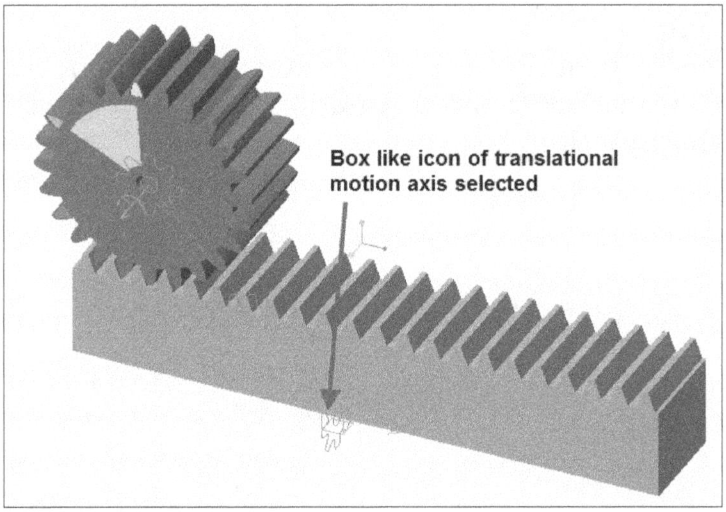

Figure-45. Translational motion axis selected

- Now, specify the position, velocity, or acceleration as discussed in previous topic.

Note that the part files with mechanism applied to them are available in the resources of this book.

APPLY FORCE MOTORS

Force motors are used to represent the force/torque applied to a component in assembly. The procedure to apply force motor is given next.

- Click on the **Force Motors** tool from the **Insert** panel in the **Mechanism** tab of the **Ribbon**. The **Motor** contextual tab will be displayed in the **Ribbon**. Also, you will be asked to select the joint axis or component on which force motor is to be applied.

- Select the linear joint axis of assembly; refer to Figure-46. Click on the **Flip** button from the **Ribbon** to change the direction of force if required.

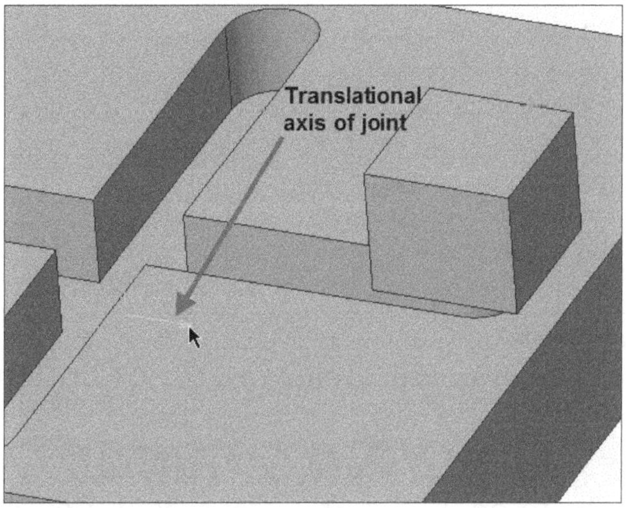

Figure-46. Axis of joint to be selected

- Click in the **Profile Details** tab of the **Ribbon** and specify the value of force in respective edit box.
- Set the other parameters as required and then click on the **OK** button.
- Save the file as we will later perform analysis on these mechanism.

In the same way, you can use the **Force/Torque** tool.

APPLYING BUSHING LOAD

The **Bushing Load** tool is used to simulate movement between two bodies, specify the spring stiffness, and the damping coefficient. The procedure to use this tool is discussed next.

- Click on the **Bushing Loads** tool from the **Insert** panel in the **Mechanism** tab of the **Ribbon**. The **Bushing Load** contextual tab will be displayed; refer to Figure-47.

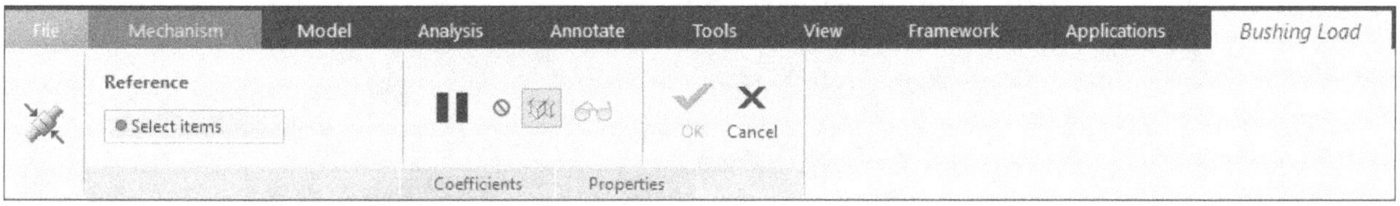

Figure-47. Bushing Load contextual tab

- Select desired weld or 6DOF connection as the reference from the drawing area.
- Click on the **Coefficients** tab in the **Ribbon**. The options to specify **Spring Stiffnesses** and **Damping Coefficients** will be displayed; refer to Figure-48.

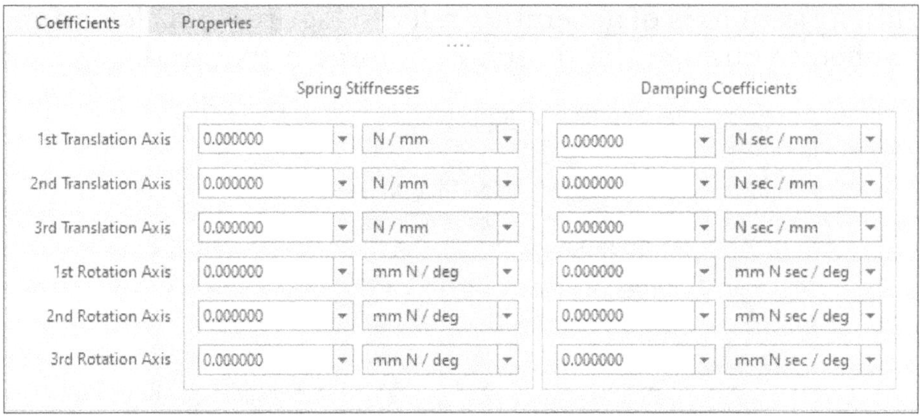

Figure-48. Coefficients tab

- After specifying desired parameters, click on the **OK** button to exit the tool.

APPLYING SPRINGS

The **Springs** tool is used to apply dynamic representation of spring in the model. The procedure to apply spring is given next.

- Click on the **Springs** tool from the **Insert** panel in the **Mechanism** tab of the **Ribbon**. The **Spring** contextual tab will be displayed; refer to Figure-49.

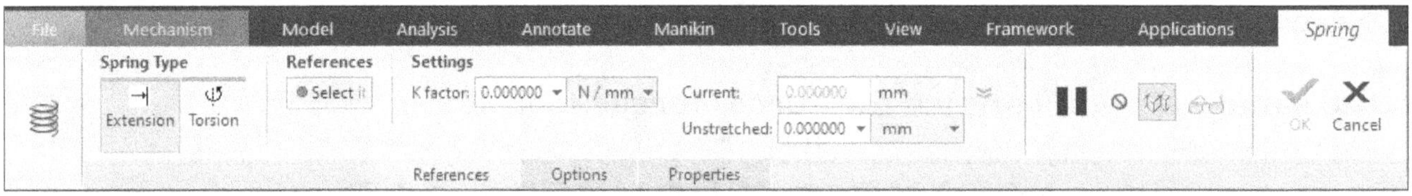

Figure-49. Spring contextual tab

- Select desired button from the contextual tab to specify type of spring. Click on the **Extension and compression springs** button to create an extension/compression spring or click on the **Torsion springs** button to create a torsion spring.
- Select two vertices of assembly if you are creating extension/compression spring; refer to Figure-50. Select the rotational joint axis of the assembly if you want to create torsion spring; refer to Figure-51.

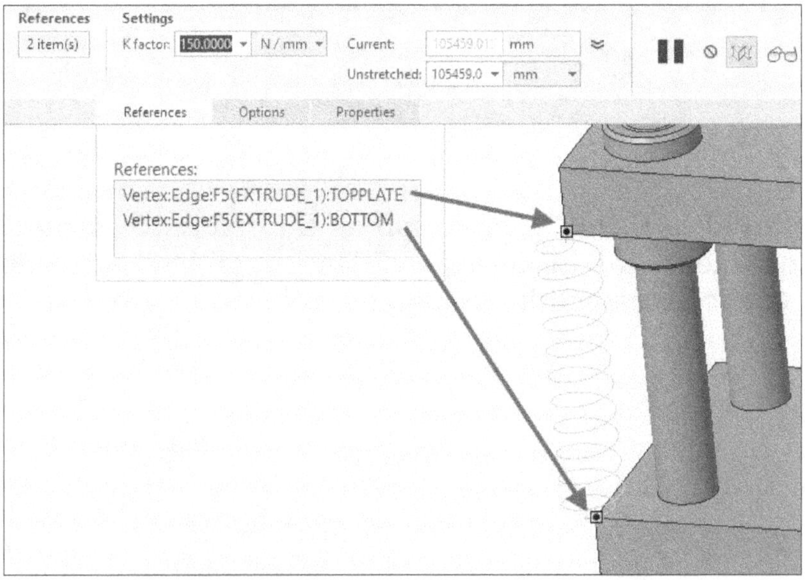

Figure-50. Vertices selected for extension spring

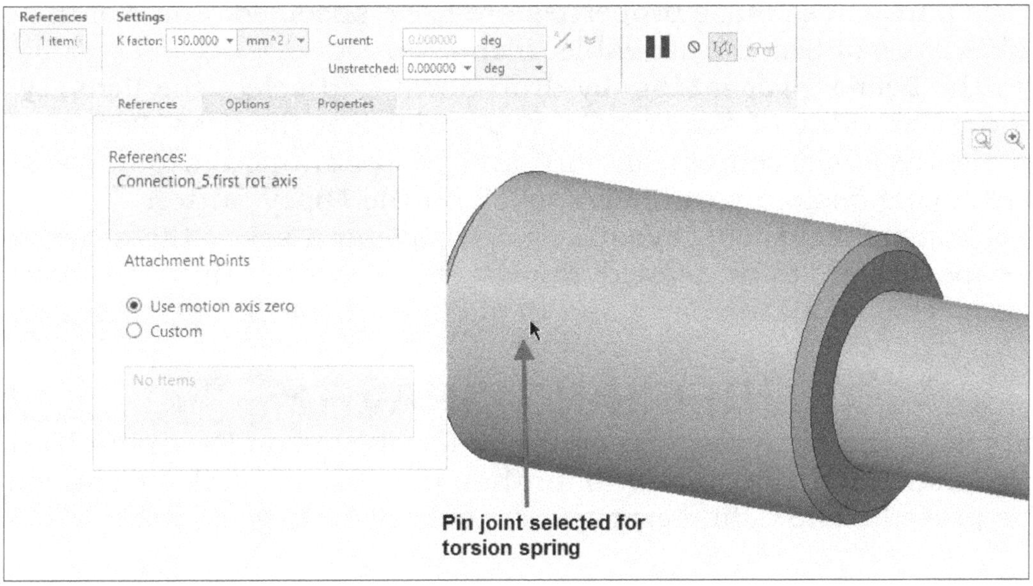

Figure-51. Torsion spring

- Specify desired value of spring stiffness in the **Stiffness coefficient** edit box of the **Ribbon**. Select desired unit of stiffness from the drop-down next to edit box.
- Set desired equilibrium distance and click on the **OK** button.

The Dampers are applied in the same way as springs.

SPECIFYING MASS PROPERTIES

Mass properties of a component define the behavior of that component due to its mass like it defines moment of inertia, effect of gravity on component, and so on. The procedure to specify mass properties of assembly components is given next.

- Click on the **Mass Properties** tool from the **Properties and Conditions** panel of the **Mechanism** tab in the **Ribbon**. The **Mass Properties** dialog box will be displayed; refer to Figure-52.

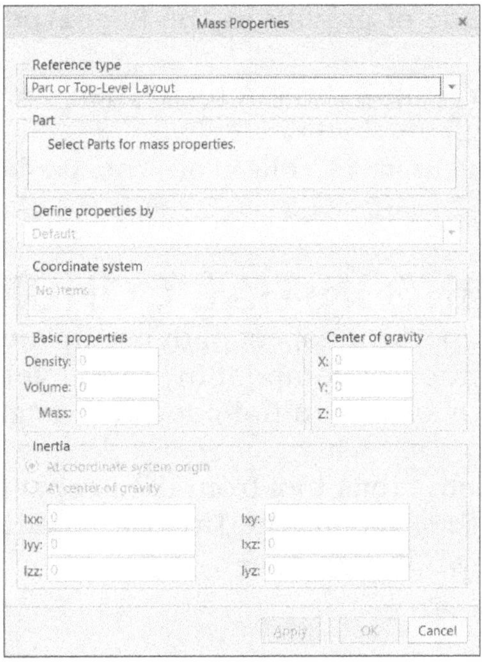

Figure-52. Mass Properties dialog box

- Select the part whose mass properties are to be specified. Some of the options in the dialog box will become available to choose.
- Click in the **Define properties by** drop-down and select the **Density** option to specify desired value of density. Or, you can select the **Mass Properties** option and specify the mass, center of gravity, and other parameters for the selected part.
- After specifying desired parameters, click on the **Apply** button.
- Now, click in the **Part or Layout** selection box and select the other part whose mass properties are to be defined. Repeat the procedure until you have specified mass properties of all the parts and then click on the **OK** button to exit.

DEFINING GRAVITY

Although most of the analyses are performed for objects on Earth but if you want to test your mechanism on Moon or Jupiter then it is also possible by changing gravity value!! The procedure to define gravity for mechanism is given next.

- Click on the **Gravity** tool from the **Properties and Conditions** panel of the **Mechanism** tab in the **Ribbon**. The **Gravity** dialog box will be displayed; refer to Figure-53.

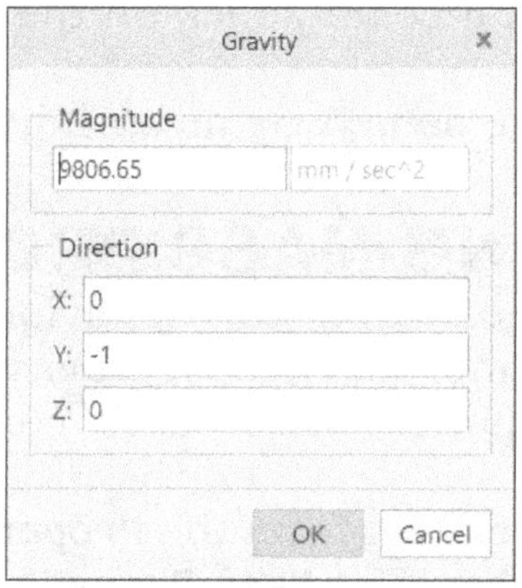

Figure-53. Gravity dialog box

- Specify desired magnitude of gravity in the **Magnitude** edit box. For Earth, it is **9806.65**.
- Set desired ratio for X, Y, and Z directions in their respective edit boxes to define direction of gravity force.
- After specifying the parameters, click on the **OK** button to apply gravity on mechanism.

DEFINING INITIAL CONDITIONS

Initial condition is a very important aspect of dynamic analysis. In initial conditions, we specify the starting position of component, initial velocity, motion axis velocity, and so on. The procedure to specify initial condition is given next.

- Click on the **Initial Conditions** tool from the **Properties and Conditions** panel of the **Mechanism** tab in the **Ribbon**. The **Initial Condition Definition** dialog box will be displayed as shown in Figure-54.

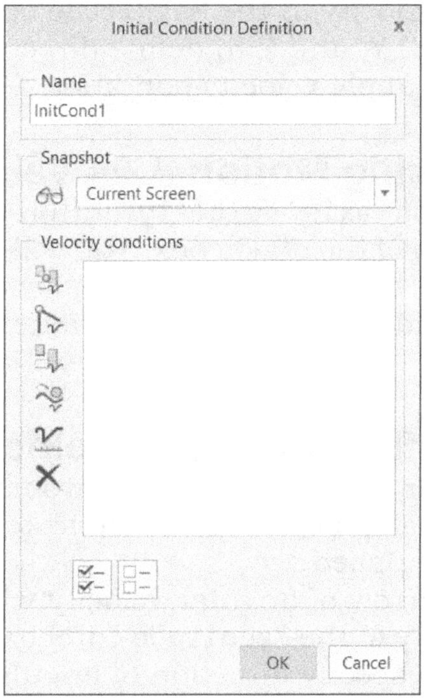

Figure-54. Initial Condition Definition dialog box

- If you now click on the **OK** button then the current state of model will be saved as initial condition for mechanism which can later be used as initial state of assembly for analysis.
- If your model has some initial velocity then select desired button from the left panel in the **Velocity conditions** area of the dialog box. The procedures to use each button in this area are discussed in next topic.
- After specifying velocity conditions, click on the **OK** button from the dialog box.

Defining Initial Velocity of a Point

- Click on the **Define velocity of a point** button from the left panel in the **Velocity conditions** area of the dialog box. You will be asked to select the vertex whose velocity is to be defined.
- Click on desired vertex of the model. The options in the dialog box will be displayed as shown in Figure-55.

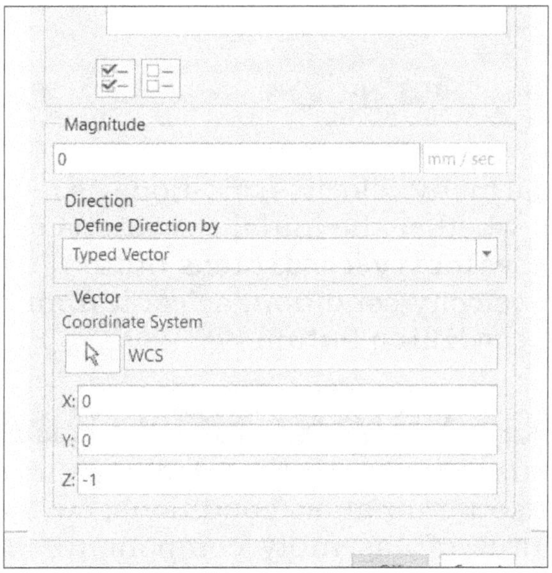

Figure-55. Options for velocity

- Specify desired value of velocity in the **Magnitude** edit box.
- Set the required ratio of X, Y, and Z to define direction of velocity.
- Click on the **OK** button to apply velocity condition.

Defining Motion Axis Velocity

- Click on the **Define motion axis velocity** button from the left panel in the **Velocity conditions** area of the dialog box. You will be asked to select the motion axis.
- Select the motion axis and enter the velocity value in the **Magnitude** edit box of the dialog box.

Defining Angular Velocity

- Click on the **Define angular velocity** button from the left panel in the **Velocity conditions** area of the dialog box. You will be asked to select the part to which angular velocity is being applied.
- Select the part. Preview arrow of angular velocity will be displayed.
- Specify the angular velocity in the **Magnitude** edit box in dialog box and also define the ratio of X, Y, and Z to specify direction of angular velocity.

Defining Tangential Slot Velocity

- Click on the **Define tangential slot velocity** button from the left panel in the **Velocity conditions** area of the dialog box. You will be asked to select the slot-follower connection to which velocity is being applied.
- Click on the slot-follower connection and enter the velocity value in **Magnitude** edit box of the dialog box; refer to Figure-56.

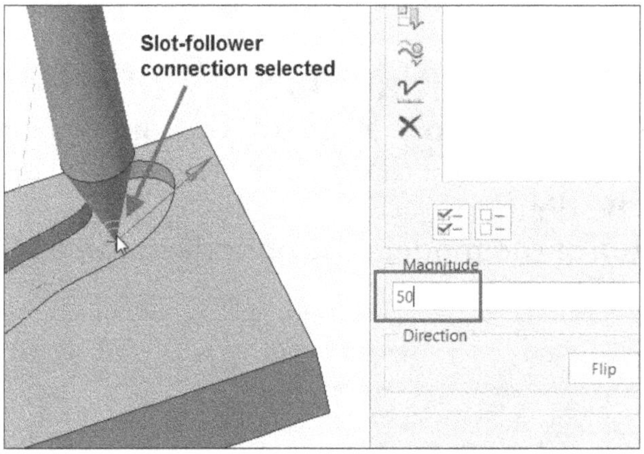

Figure-56. Slot follower connection selected

Note that you can define as many velocity conditions as required but they must form a valid relation. To check whether the initial conditions specified are valid, click on the **Evaluate model with velocity conditions** button from the left panel in the dialog box. To delete any velocity condition, select it from the list and then click on the **Delete highlighted condition** button.

DEFINING TERMINATION CONDITIONS

Termination condition is used to specify the conditions where the dynamic analysis should be stopped. To use termination conditions, we need some variables that represent dynamic features of assembly components. The procedure to create variables and apply termination conditions are discussed next.

Creating Variables for Mechanism

- Click on the **Measures** tool from the **Analysis** panel in the **Mechanism** tab of the **Ribbon**. The **Measure Results** dialog box will be displayed; refer to Figure-57.
- Click on the **Create new measure** button from the **Measures** area of the dialog box. The **Measure Definition** dialog box will be displayed; refer to Figure-58, and you will be prompted to select a point or motion axis.

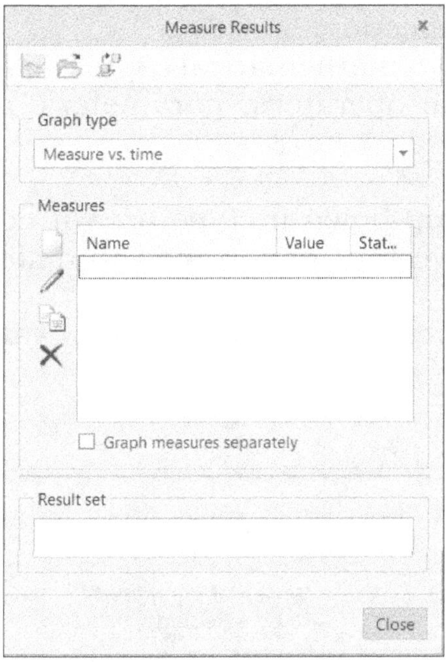

Figure-57. Measure Results dialog box

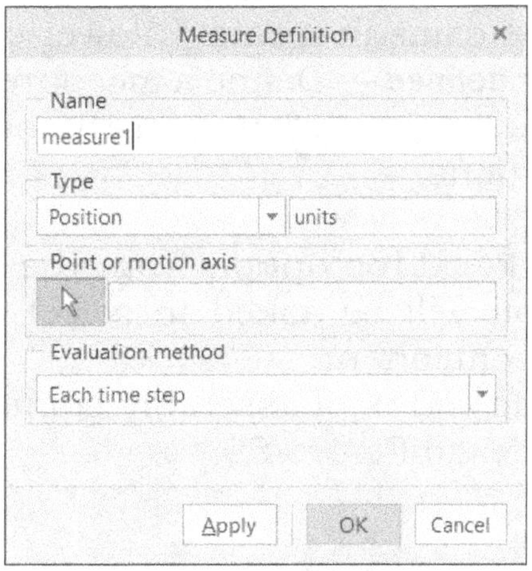

Figure-58. Measure Definition dialog box

- Click in the **Name** edit box of the dialog box and specify desired name. (Like, we have specified "**Max Travel**".)
- Click in the drop-down of **Type** area and select desired type of measurement variable. Short description of each measure type is given next. We will use **Position** type for this topic. You can use the other variable types accordingly.

  - **Position** — Measure the location of a point, vertex, or motion axis during the analysis.
  - **Velocity** — Measure the velocity of a point, vertex, or motion axis during the analysis.
  - **Acceleration** — Measure the acceleration of a point, vertex, or motion axis during the analysis.
  - **Connection reaction** — Measure the reaction forces and moments at joint, gear-pair, cam-follower, or slot-follower connections.
  - **Net load** — Measure the magnitude of a force load on a spring, damper, servo motor, force, torque, or motion axis. You can also confirm the force load on a force motor.
  - **Loadcell reaction** — Measure the load on a load cell lock during a force balance analysis.
  - **Impact** — Determine whether impact occurred during an analysis at a joint limit, slot end, or between two cams.
  - **Impulse** — Measure the change in momentum resulting from an impact event. You can measure impulses for joints with limits, for cam-follower connections with liftoff, or for slot-follower connections.

- **System** — Measure several quantities that describe the behavior of the entire system.
- **Rigid body** — Measure several quantities that describe the behavior of a selected body.
- **Separation** — Measure the separation distance, separation speed, and change in separation speed between two selected points.
- **Cam** — Measure the curvature, pressure angle, and slip velocity for either of the cams in a cam-follower connection.
- **User defined** — Define a measure as a mathematical expression that includes measures, constants, arithmetical operators, parameters, and algebraic functions.

- Select the **Position** option from the drop-down in **Type** area if not selected by default. You will be asked to select a vertex/motion axis to define position of assembly component.
- Click on the vertex of assembly component to whom a position variable is to be applied; refer to Figure-59.

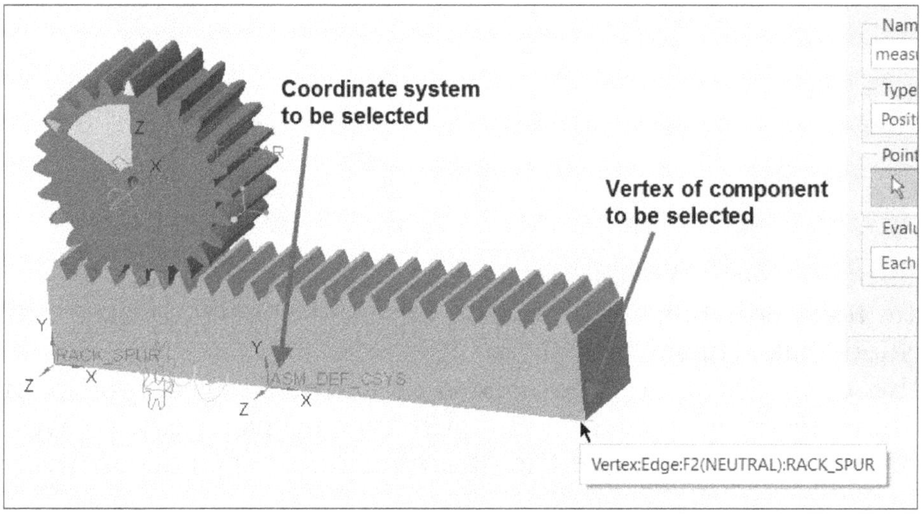

Figure-59. Vertex and coordinate system selected for position variable

- Click on the selection button in the **Coordinate system** area of the dialog box and select desired coordinate system; refer to Figure-59.
- Click in the drop-down of **Component** area in the dialog box and select desired directional component of position to be measures. We have selected the **X-component** option as we want to measure horizontal distance covered by rack gear.
- From the **Evaluation Method** drop-down, select desired option to specify evaluation method for measuring the selected component of position. Like, we are concerned about the Maximum distance covered by rack so we have selected **Maximum** option.
- Click on the **OK** button from the dialog box to create the variable. The variable will be created and you will return to **Measure Results** dialog box.
- Create more variables if required by using the same method. Click on the **Close** button from the **Measure Results** dialog box to exit.

Specifying Termination Conditions

- Click on the **Termination Conditions** tool from the **Properties and Conditions** panel in the **Mechanism** tab of the **Ribbon**. The **Termination Condition Definition** dialog box will be displayed; refer to Figure-60.

- Specify desired name for termination condition in the **Name** edit box.
- Click on the **Insert variable from list** button from the **Termination condition** area of the dialog box to use variables earlier saved. The **Variables** dialog box will be displayed; refer to Figure-61.
- Double-click on the variable in the dialog box to insert it in the expression and create the equation for termination condition; refer to Figure-62.

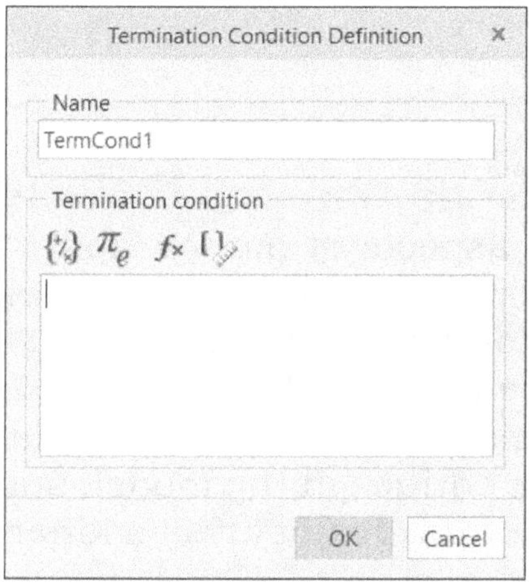

Figure-60. Termination Condition Definition dialog box

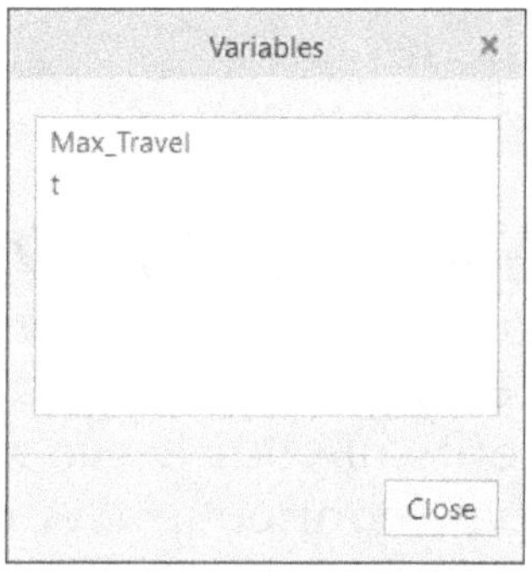

Figure-61. Variables dialog box

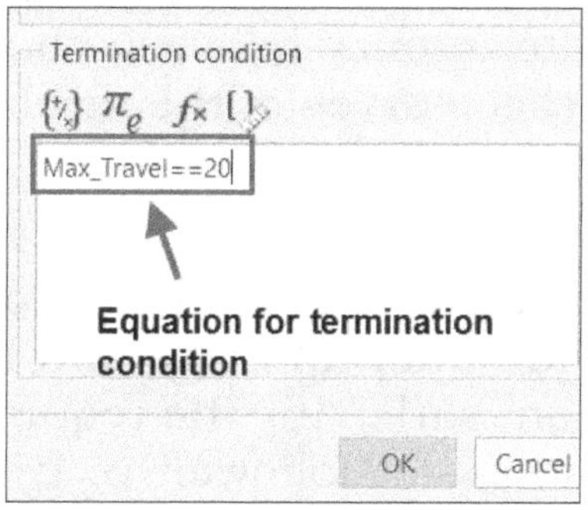

Figure-62. Equation for termination condition

- Click on the **OK** button after creating the equation to exit the dialog box.

Now, we are ready to perform analysis on the mechanism as we have applied motors/ force, initial conditions, termination conditions, and other parameters of mechanism analysis. The procedure to perform analysis is given next.

PERFORMING MECHANISM ANALYSIS

Before we move on to perform mechanism analysis, it is important to understand that in Creo Parametric Mechanism Analysis, we can perform five type of analyses: Position Analysis, Kinematic Analysis, Dynamic Analysis, Static Analysis, and Force balance analysis. The description of each analysis is given next.

Position Analysis

A position analysis is a series of assembly analyses driven by servo motors. Only motion axes or geometric servo motors can be included in position analyses. Force motors do not appear in the list of possible motor selections when adding a motor for a position analysis.

- Position analyses were called kinematic or repeated assembly analysis in previous releases of Mechanism Design.
- If you edit an analysis that you created as a kinematic or repeated assembly analysis in a previous release of Mechanism Design, it will be regenerated as a position analysis.

A position analysis simulates the mechanism's motion, satisfying the requirements of your servo motor profiles and any joint, cam-follower, slot-follower, or gear-pair connections, and records position data for the mechanism's various components. It does not take force and mass into account when performing the analysis. Therefore, you do not have to specify mass properties for your mechanism. Dynamic entities in the model, such as springs, dampers, gravity, forces/torques, and force motors, do not affect a position analysis.

Use a position analysis to study:

- Positions of components over time
- Interference between components
- Trace curves of the mechanism's motion

Kinematic Analysis

Kinematics is a branch of dynamics that deals with aspects of motion apart from consideration of mass and force. A kinematic analysis simulates the mechanism's motion, satisfying the requirements of your servo motor profiles and any joint, cam-follower, slot-follower, or gear-pair connection. A kinematic analysis does not take forces into account. Therefore, you cannot use force motors, and you do not have to specify mass properties for your mechanism. Dynamic entities in the model, such as springs, dampers, gravity, forces/torques, and force motors, do not affect a kinematic analysis.

If your servo motor has a noncontinuous profile, an attempt is made to make the profile continuous before running a kinematic analysis. If the profile is such that the software cannot make it continuous, the motor is not used for the analysis.

Use a kinematic analysis to obtain information on:

- Position, velocity, and acceleration of geometric entities and connections.
- Interference between components.
- Trace curves of the mechanism's motion.
- Motion envelopes that capture the mechanism's motion as a part.

Dynamic Analysis

Dynamic analysis is a branch of mechanics that deals with forces and their relation primarily to the motion, but sometimes also to the equilibrium, of bodies. You can use a dynamic analysis to study the relationship between the forces acting on a body, the mass of the body, and the motion of the body.

Keep the following key points in mind when running a dynamic analysis:

- Motion axis-based servo motors are active for the duration of a dynamic analysis. For this reason, the From and To times derived from the time domain for the analysis appear as the uneditable Start and End values.
- You can add both servo and force motors.
- If your servo or force motor has a noncontinuous profile, an attempt is made to make the profile continuous before running a dynamic analysis. If the profile cannot be made continuous, the motor is not used for the analysis.
- You can add forces or torques using the **External loads** tab.
- You can turn gravity and friction on or off.

You can evaluate the positions, velocities, accelerations, and reaction forces at the beginning of your dynamic analysis by specifying a zero time duration and running as usual. A suitable time interval for the calculations is determined automatically. If you graph measures from the analysis, the graph will contain only a single line.

Static Analysis

Statics is the branch of mechanics that deals with forces acting on a body when it is at equilibrium. Use a static analysis to determine the state of a mechanism when it is subject to known forces. The application searches for a configuration in which all the loads and forces in your mechanism balance and the potential energy is zero. A static analysis can identify a static configuration faster than a dynamic analysis because it does not consider velocity in the calculation.

Keep the following key points in mind when running a static analysis:

- If you do not specify an initial configuration, the static analysis starts from the currently displayed position of the model when you click **Run**.
- When you run a static analysis, a graph of acceleration versus iteration number appears, showing the maximum acceleration of the mechanism's entities. As the analysis calculation proceeds, both the graph display and the model display change to reflect the intermediate positions reached during the calculation. When the maximum acceleration for the mechanism reaches 0, your mechanism has reached a static configuration.
- You can adjust the maximum step size between each iteration of the static analysis by changing the **Maximum step factor** on the **Preferences** tab of the **Analysis Definition** dialog box. Reducing this value reduces the positional change between each iteration and can be useful when analyzing mechanisms incorporating large accelerations.
- If a static configuration for your mechanism cannot be found, the analysis ends and the mechanism remains in the last configuration reached during the analysis.
- Any measures computed will be for the final times and positions, not a time history for the settling process.

Force Balance Analysis

A force balance analysis is an inverse static analysis. In a force balance analysis, you derive the resulting reaction forces from a specific static configuration, whereas, in a static analysis, you apply forces to a mechanism to derive the resulting static configuration. Use a force balance analysis to determine the forces required to keep a mechanism fixed in a particular configuration.

Before you can run a force balance analysis, you must reduce the number of degrees of freedom in the mechanism to zero. Use connection locks, body locks between two bodies, a load cell lock at a point, or apply active servo motors to motion axes. Use the items in the Analysis Definition dialog box to evaluate the DOFs on your mechanism and apply constraints to it until you achieve zero DOF.

The procedure of performing all these analysis is similar. Here, we will discuss the procedure of performing dynamic analysis. You can apply the procedure to other analyses in the same way.

Performing Dynamic Analysis

- Click on the **Mechanism Analysis** button from the **Analysis** panel in the **Mechanism** tab of the **Ribbon**. The **Analysis Definition** dialog box will be displayed; refer to Figure-63.

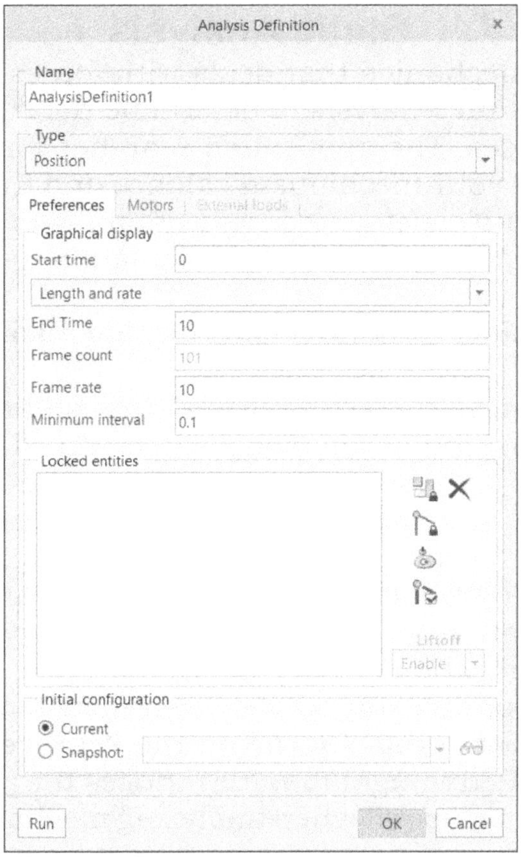

Figure-63. Analysis Definition dialog box

- Specify desired name of analysis in the **Name** edit box.
- Click in the **Type** drop-down and select the **Dynamic** option.
- Specify the parameters in **Preferences** tab like duration of analysis, frame rate for analysis, minimum interval in their respective edit box. If you want to evaluate the positions, velocities, accelerations, and reaction forces of the entities in your mechanism at the beginning of your dynamic analysis, enter 0 for Duration. You can use this method as a quick check before running a longer dynamic analysis. Note that **Frame Rate = 1/Interval & Frame Count = Frame Rate * Length + 1**.
- If you want to lock any connection then click on the **Create connection lock** button from the **Locked entities** area of the dialog box. You will be asked to select the connection. Select a connection and press the **MMB**. The locked connection will be listed in the **Locked entities** area of the dialog box. Clear the check box for connection from the list if you want to deactivate the lock. In the same way, you can use other buttons of the area.
- Click on the **I.C.State** radio button from the **Initial configuration** area of the dialog box and select desired initial condition from the drop-down. Similarly, select desired termination condition from the **Termination condition** area of the dialog box.
- Click on the **Motors** tab and select desired motors to be used for analysis.
- Click on the **External Loads** tab and select the forces/torques to be applied in mechanism.

- If you want to check the effect of friction and gravity in your analysis then make sure the **Enable gravity** and **Enable all friction** check boxes are selected in the **External Loads** tab of the dialog box.
- Click on the **Run** button from the dialog box to run the analysis. If the parameters specified are correct then the analysis will run as expected otherwise you need to recheck all thc paramctcrs.
- Click on the **OK** button from the dialog box. The analysis will be saved in the **Mechanism Tree**.

Using the **Playback** tool in **Analysis** panel in **Ribbon**, you can play the mechanism animation again. Now, you can run mechanism on all the examples of assemblies that we have discussed earlier. Part files for all the examples are available in resources.

SELF ASSESSMENT

1. Write down the difference between Top-Down assembly approach and Bottom-Up assembly approach.

2. Discuss the procedure of performing a kinematic analysis using a suitable example in Creo Mechanism.

3. Which of the following relations should be applied in mechanism design to keep two bodies in contact with each other during motion?

(a) Gear Relation
(b) Belt Relation
(c) 3D-Contact Relation
(d) None of the Above

4. Which of the following initial conditions is used in mechanism design?

(a) Motion Axis Velocity
(b) Tangential Slot Velocity
(c) Both a and b
(d) None of the Above

5. In Creo Mechanism application, ... is one of the motion making object that rotates/translates one or more objects in the mechanism.

6. Termination condition is used to specify the conditions where the dynamic analysis should be stopped. To use termination conditions, we need some .... that represent dynamic features of assembly components.

7. .... analysis is used to study the relationship between the forces acting on a body, the mass of the body, and the motion of the body.

8. In Creo Mechanism application, translational motor is used to check the force/ torque applied to a component in the assembly. (T/F)

9. In Creo Mechanism Analysis, a position analysis is used to study the interference between components. (T/F)

10. In force balance analysis, use the items in **Analysis Definition** dialog box to evaluate the DOFs on the mechanism. (T/F)

11. Which method allows you to use an existing part as a template when creating a new component in an assembly?

a) Create Features
b) Locate Default Datums
c) Copy From Existing
d) Empty

12. What happens if you use the "Empty" option while creating a part in the assembly?

a) You can define assembly constraints easily
b) A template is automatically selected
c) Assembly constraints cannot be defined
d) The part is imported from another assembly

13. When using the "Create Features" option, what can be used as a reference while creating a new part?

a) Only standard templates
b) Geometry of other software
c) Geometry of the assembly
d) External files

14. What must be true before using Mechanism tools in Creo Parametric?

a) Assembly should be saved in a template format
b) Assembly constraints must be defined using Mechanism types
c) Only parts should be active
d) All components must be hidden

15. What does the Gear Ratio depend on when creating gear relations?

a) Number of parts
b) Volume of gears
c) Pitch Circle Diameter
d) Shaft length

16. What is the primary purpose of 3D Contact relation in Mechanism design?

a) Create part modeling
b) Analyze material stress
c) Keep two bodies in contact during motion
d) Define datum constraints

17. In a belt relation, what can be adjusted to change the tightness of the belt?

a) Plane selection
b) Number of belt wraps
c) Material density
d) Stiffness (E*A)

18. Which tool is used in Creo Mechanism to rotate a component using a motor?

a) Force Motors
b) Servo Motors
c) Springs
d) Bushing Load

19. While applying a rotational motor, which parameter must be selected to specify motion?

a) Acceleration
b) Position
c) Velocity
d) Gravity

20. What type of motor is used to simulate translational motion in a mechanism?

a) Rotational Motor
b) Force Motor
c) Translational Motor
d) Gravity Motor

21. What is the purpose of the Force Motors tool?

a) To rotate components
b) To apply gravity
c) To apply force/torque
d) To apply bushing loads

22. Which tool allows specifying spring stiffness and damping coefficients?

a) Spring Tool
b) Servo Motors
c) Force Motors
d) Bushing Loads

23. What must be selected when applying a torsion spring?

a) Two vertices
b) Part file
c) Translational joint
d) Rotational joint axis

24. In the Mass Properties tool, which option can be used to define part properties manually?

a) Profile
b) Density
c) Velocity
d) Rotation

25. What is the default gravity value used in Creo for Earth?

a) 9.80665
b) 980.665
c) 98.0665
d) 9806.65

26. Which tool is used to define the starting velocity of a point in a mechanism?

a) Mass Properties
b) Define angular velocity
c) Define velocity of a point
d) Initial Conditions

27. Which type of analysis considers mass and forces?

a) Static Analysis
b) Position Analysis
c) Dynamic Analysis
d) Kinematic Analysis

28. Which tool allows measuring motion aspects like position or velocity in Creo?

a) Motor
b) Playback
c) Measures
d) Conditions

29. What must be achieved before performing a Force Balance Analysis?

a) Gravity must be disabled
b) Zero Degrees of Freedom
c) Rotational motion
d) High spring stiffness

30. Which analysis type simulates motion without considering force or mass?

a) Dynamic
b) Static
c) Force Balance
d) Kinematic

31. Which tool is used to stop the analysis based on certain conditions?

a) Initial Conditions
b) Gravity
c) Termination Conditions
d) External Loads

32. Which measure type is used to determine if a cam-follower loses contact?

a) Acceleration
b) Reaction
c) Impact
d) User defined

33. What does a static analysis aim to achieve?

a) Trace curves
b) Zero potential energy
c) Tangential motion
d) Maximum spring tension

34. In the Mechanism Analysis dialog box, what does Frame Rate equal to?

a) Frame Count * Interval
b) Interval * Duration
c) 1/Interval
d) Interval / Frame Count

35. Which measure type calculates the magnitude of spring or motor force?

a) System
b) Net load
c) Connection reaction
d) Impulse

36. Which tool is used to animate the results after a mechanism analysis?

a) Force Motors
b) Mass Properties
c) Playback Tool
d) Velocity Conditions

FOR STUDENT NOTES

Answers to Self Assessment Questions :

3. (c) **4.** (c) **5.** Servo Motors **6.** Variables **7.** Dynamic **8.** F **9.** T **10.** T

Chapter 11

Sheetmetal Design

Topics Covered

The major topics covered in this chapter are:

- ***Introduction***
- ***Starting Sheetmetal***
- ***Modeling tools in Sheetmetal environment***
- ***Walls***
- ***Bend, Unbend, Bend Back, and Flat Pattern***
- ***Part to Sheetmetal***
- ***Rip tools***
- ***Forming Tools***
- ***Flexible Modeling for Sheetmetal***

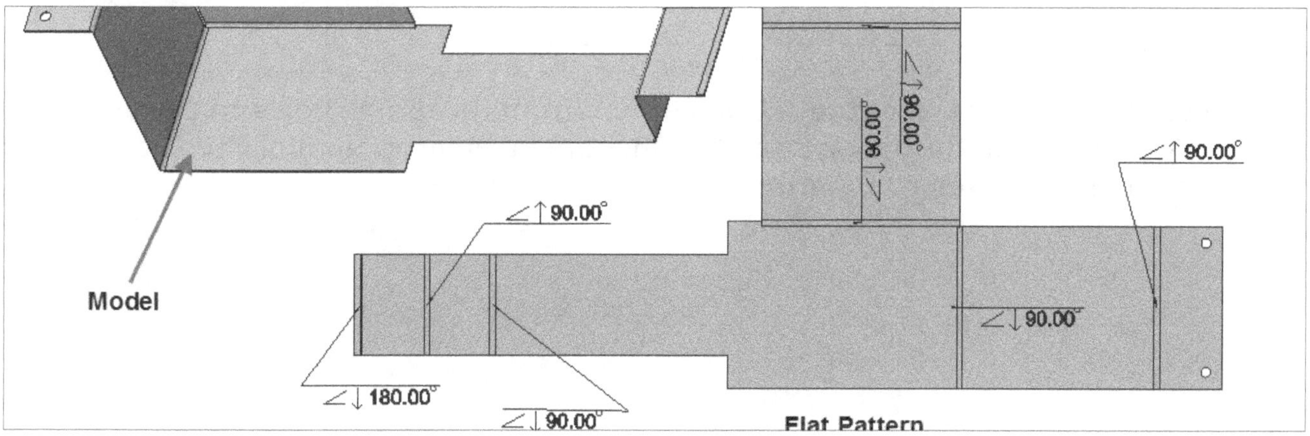

INTRODUCTION

Sheet metal work is an important aspect of Mechanical engineering. Many parts around us are manufactured via sheetmetal processes. For example, car body, vents in houses, Air-conditioner ducts, spoon, metal bowls, and so on. The sheetmetal parts generally have thickness ranging from fraction of millimeter to 12.5 millimeters i.e. up to half inch. Like welding and machining, sheetmetal also has its own processes like, bending, punching, stamping, spinning, rolling, and so on. In this chapter, we will discuss about the tools available in Creo Parametric related to sheetmetal designing.

STARTING SHEETMETAL DESIGN

- Start Creo Parametric and click on the **New** button from the **Quick Access Toolbar**. The **New** dialog box will be displayed.
- Click on the **Part** radio button in the **Type** area and **Sheetmetal** radio button from the **Sub-type** area of the dialog box.
- Clear the **Use default template** check box and then click on the **OK** button from the dialog box. The **New File Options** dialog box will be displayed; refer to Figure-1.

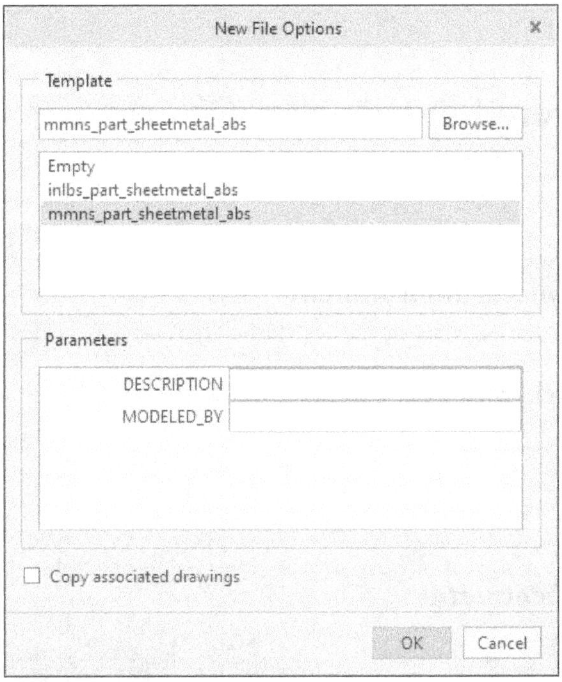

Figure-1. New File Options dialog box

- Select the **mmns part sheetmetal abs** option from the dialog box and then click on the **OK** button from the dialog box. The Sheetmetal environment of Creo Parametric will be displayed; refer to Figure-2.

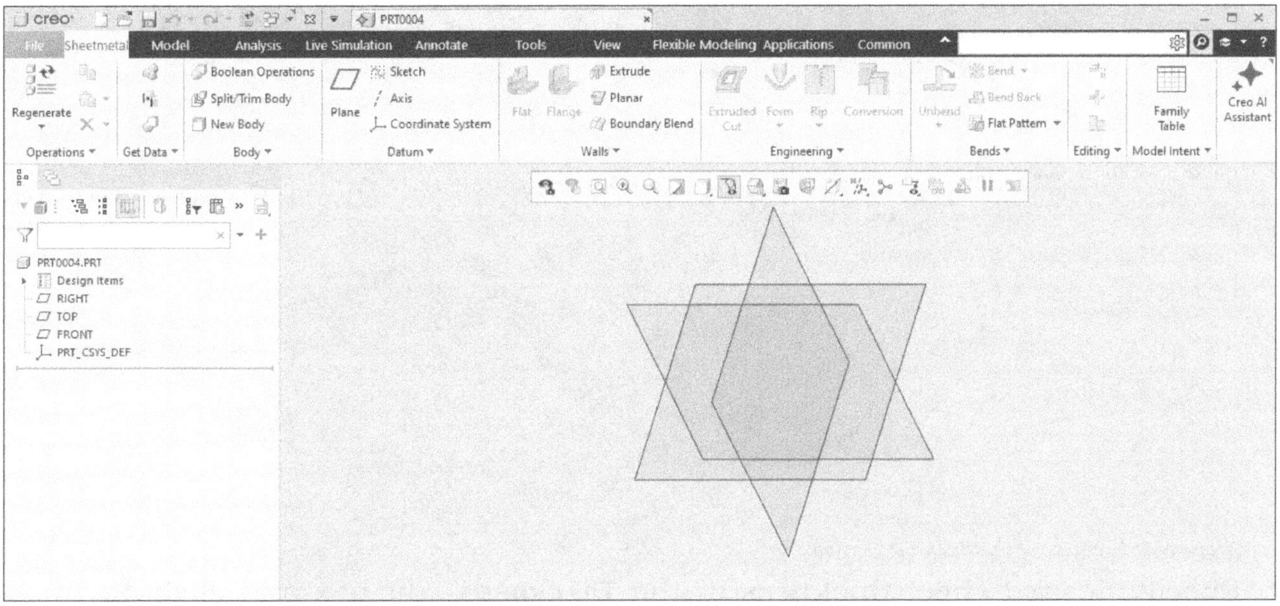

Figure-2. Sheetmetal environment

There is a long list of tools used for creating sheetmetal parts in various panels of Creo Parametric. You will also find some familiar tools like Extrude, Revolve, and so on in these panels. In this chapter, we will be discussing sheetmetal application of all these familiar tools. We will also be discussing the tools that are specifically meant for sheetmetal. These tools are discussed next.

EXTRUDE FOR SHEETMETAL

The **Extrude** tool in sheetmetal environment works similar to the one in Part environment but, in sheetmetal environment, you need to specify the thickness of sheet while extruding the sketch. The procedure is given next.

- Click on the **Extrude** tool from the **Walls** panel in the **Sheetmetal** tab of the **Ribbon**. The **Extrude** contextual tab will be displayed; refer to Figure-3. You are asked to select a sketch or sketching plane.

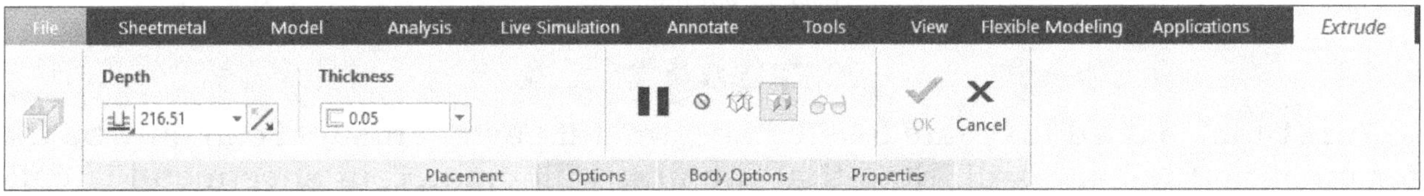

Figure-3. Extrude contextual tab

- Select a sketch if you have already created, otherwise click on the **Define** button from **Placement** tab of the **Ribbon**. You are asked to select a sketching plane.
- On selecting the sketching plane, sketching environment will be displayed. Create a sketch and click on the **OK** button from the **Ribbon**. Note that you can create close or open both type of sketches but the sketch must not be self-intersecting.
- On doing so, the preview of sheetmetal extrusion will be displayed; refer to Figure-4.

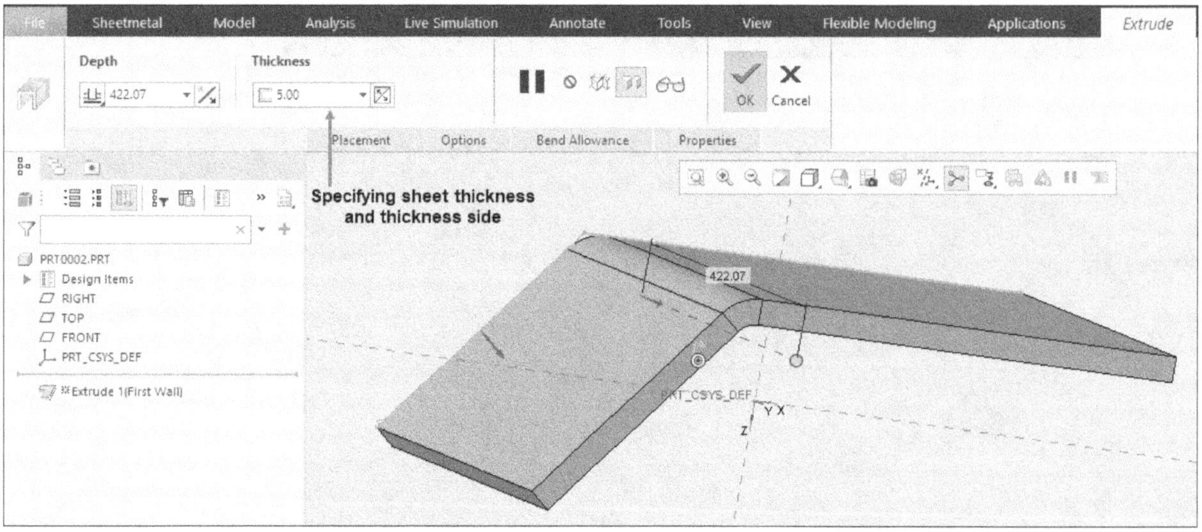

Figure-4. Preview of sheetmetal extrusion

- Specify desired sheet thickness in the **Thickness** edit box and click on the **OK** button to create the sheetmetal extrusion.

In the same way, you can use the other tools that have been discussed in chapter for Part Modeling; refer to Figure-5.

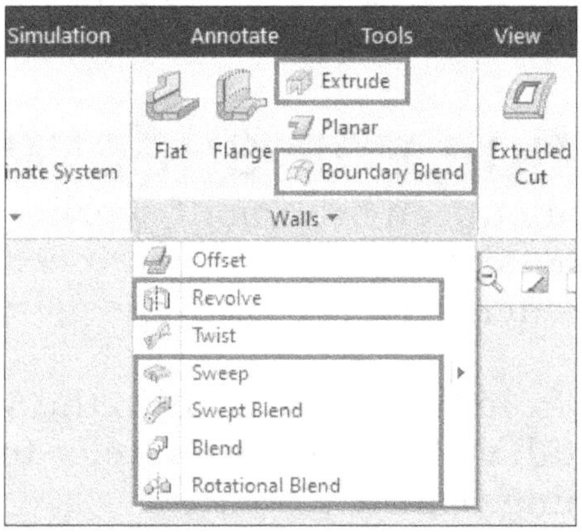

Figure-5. Tools already discussed

TWIST

The **Twist** tool is used to create twisted sheetmetal parts. This tool can only be used after creating the base wall. Note that the first wall created in sheetmetal is called base wall. The base wall can be created by any of the part modeling creation tools. The procedure to use **Twist** tool is given next.

- Click on the **Twist** tool from the expanded **Walls** panel in the **Ribbon**. The **Twist** contextual tab will be displayed; refer to Figure-6 and you will be asked to select an edge to which twisted wall would be attached.

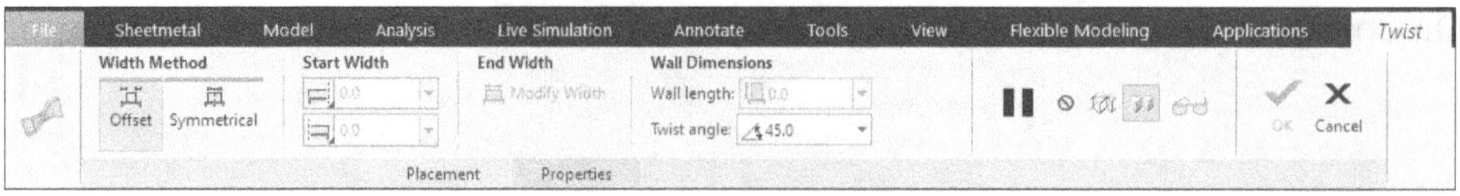

Figure-6. Twist contextual tab

- Select an edge of the base wall; refer to Figure-7. Note that this edge will become base sketch for twist feature.

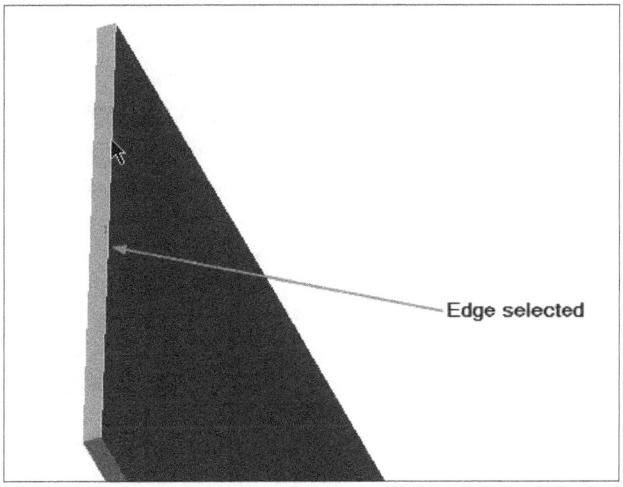

Figure-7. Edge selected for twisting

- On selecting the edge, preview of the twisted wall will be displayed; refer to Figure-8.

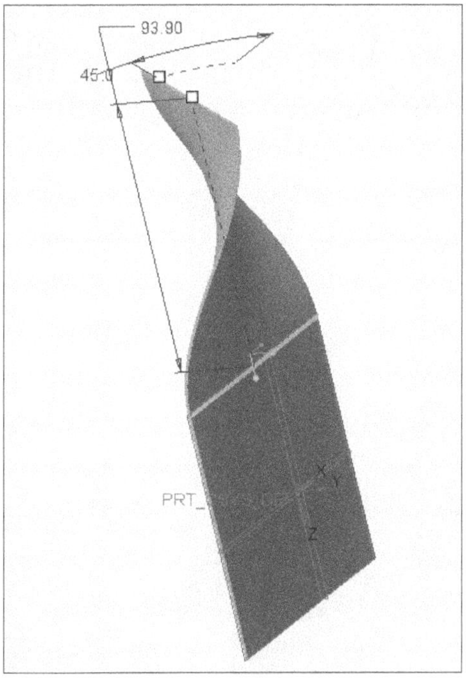

Figure-8. Preview of twisted wall

- Set desired length and angle of twisted wall by double-clicking on the respective dimensions in the model area or you can specify the value in edit boxes in the contextual tab.
- By default, the wall width of twisted wall is calculated using offset dimension of selected edge. So, you can specify desired offset distances from end points of selected edge in **Start Width** edit boxes. If you want to define wall width by specifying desired value then click on the **Symmetrical** button and specify desired value in the next edit box; refer to Figure-9. The width of twisted wall will be symmetric with respect to end points of selected edge.

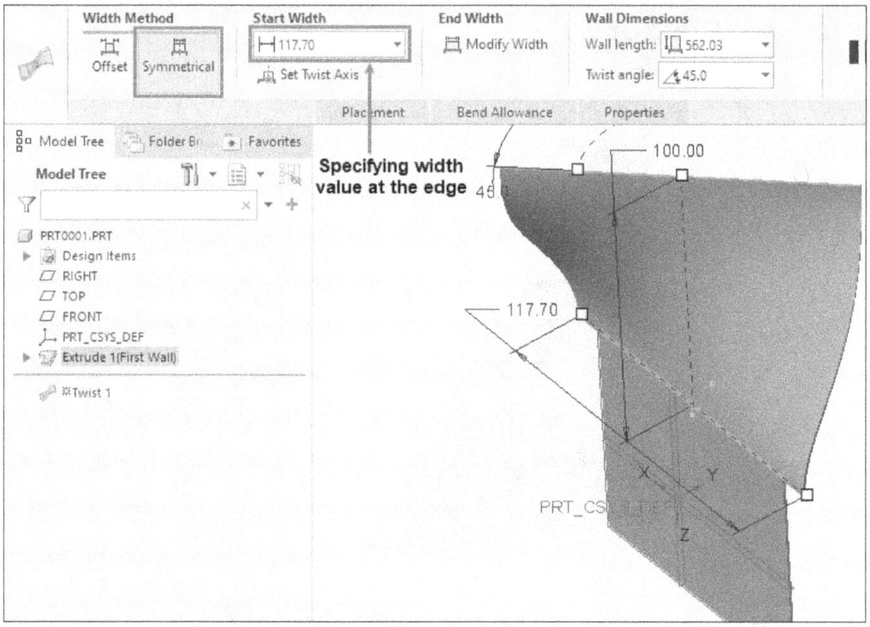

Figure-9. Specifying width of twist feature at edge

- By default, the twist axis is at the center of the selected edge. If you want to specify the location of twist axis explicitly then click on the **Set Twist Axis** button and select the datum point through which the twist axis should pass; refer to Figure-10.

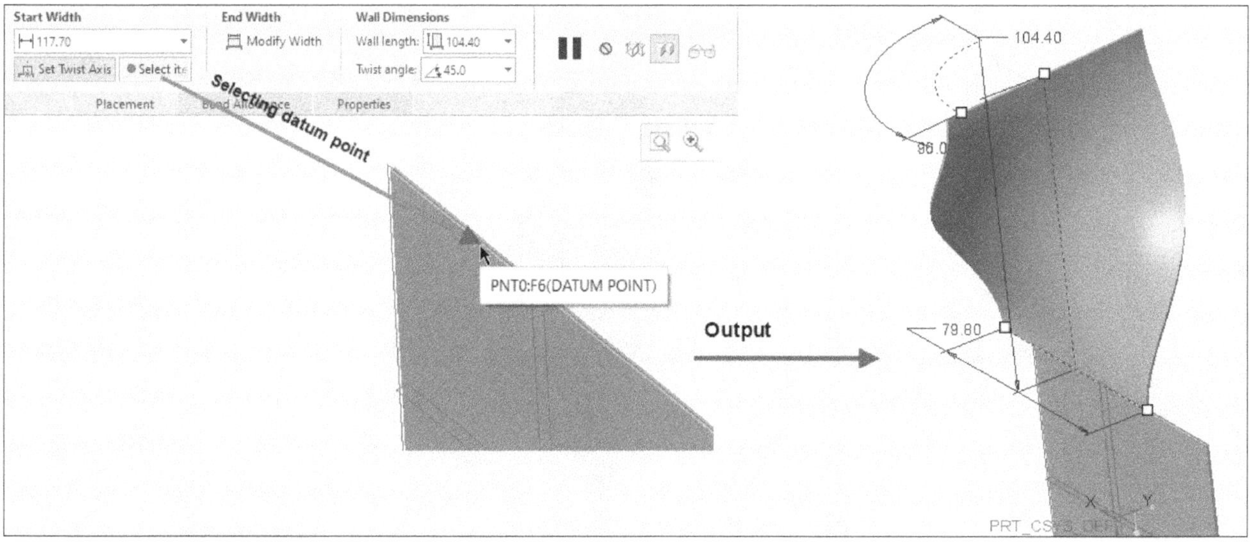

Figure-10. Selecting datum point for axis

- If you want to modify the width of twisted wall at the end then click on the **Modify Width** button from the contextual tab and specify desired value of width in next edit box.
- Click on the **Bend Allowance** tab in the **Ribbon** and specify desired value of unbent wall length in the **Wall length in an unbent state** edit box.
- Click on the **OK** button from the contextual tab to create the twisted wall.

FLAT TOOL

The **Flat** tool is used to create flat walls of sheetmetal. In manufacturing, these walls are created by bending or drawing processes. The procedure to use this tool is given next.

- Click on the **Flat** tool from the **Walls** panel in the **Ribbon**. The **Flat** contextual tab will be displayed; refer to Figure-11 and you will be asked to select an edge.

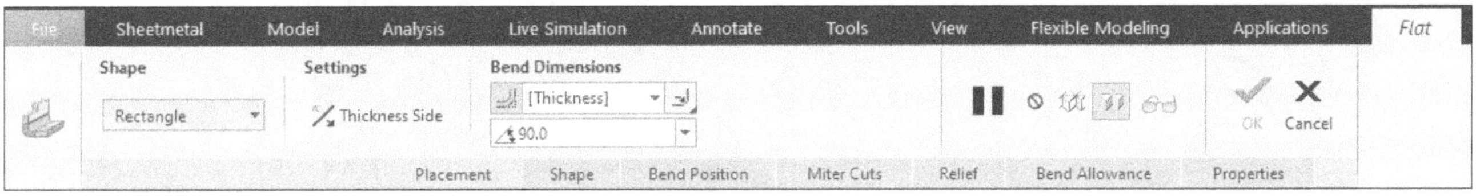

Figure-11. Flat contextual tab

- Select an edge. Preview of the flat wall will be displayed; refer to Figure-12.

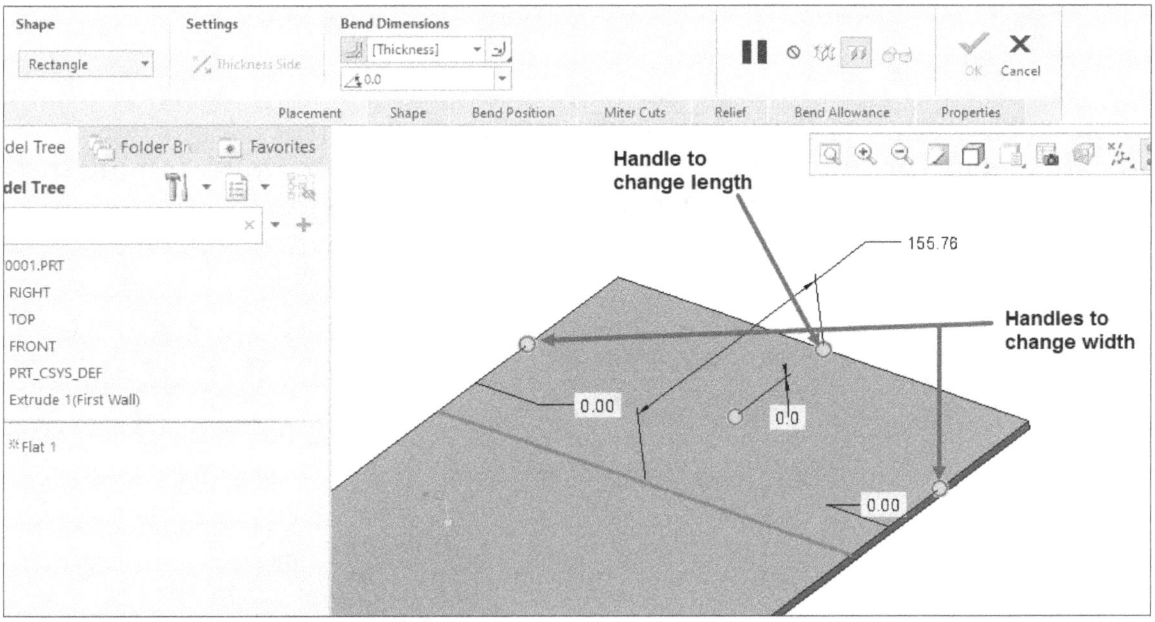

Figure-12. Preview of flat wall

- Using the handles displayed in preview, you can change the width, length, and angle of the flat wall.
- Select desired shape of wall from the **Shapes** drop-down in the **Ribbon**; refer to Figure-13. Preview of the wall will change accordingly; refer to Figure-14.

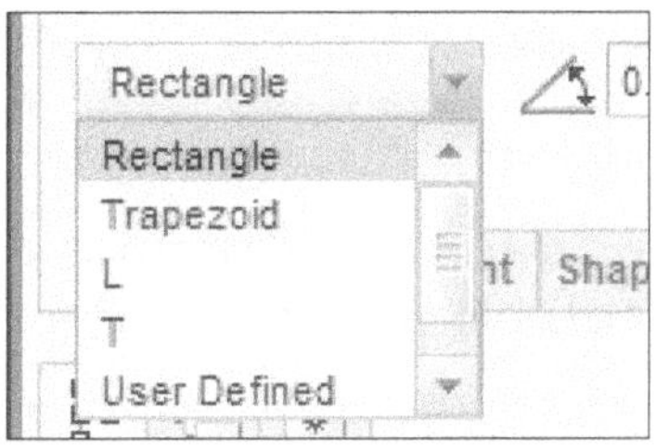

Figure-13. Shapes drop-down

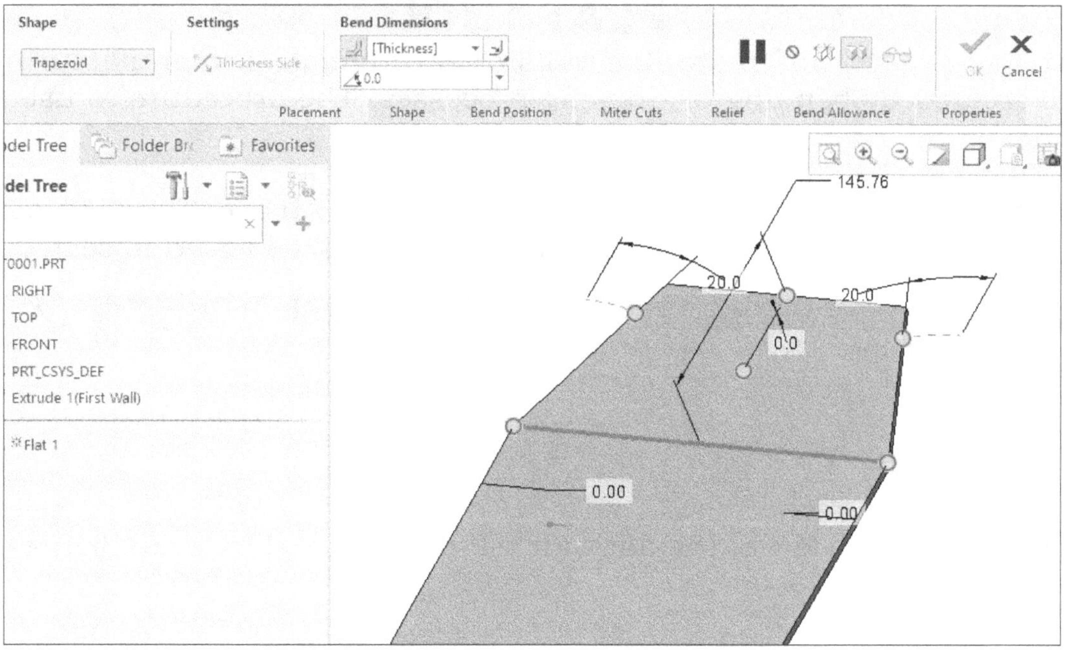

Figure-14. Flat wall preview

- Double-click on any of the value in preview to change it.
- You can specify the angle of wall with respect to the base wall by using the **Angle** edit box in the contextual tab (**Ribbon**); refer to Figure-15.

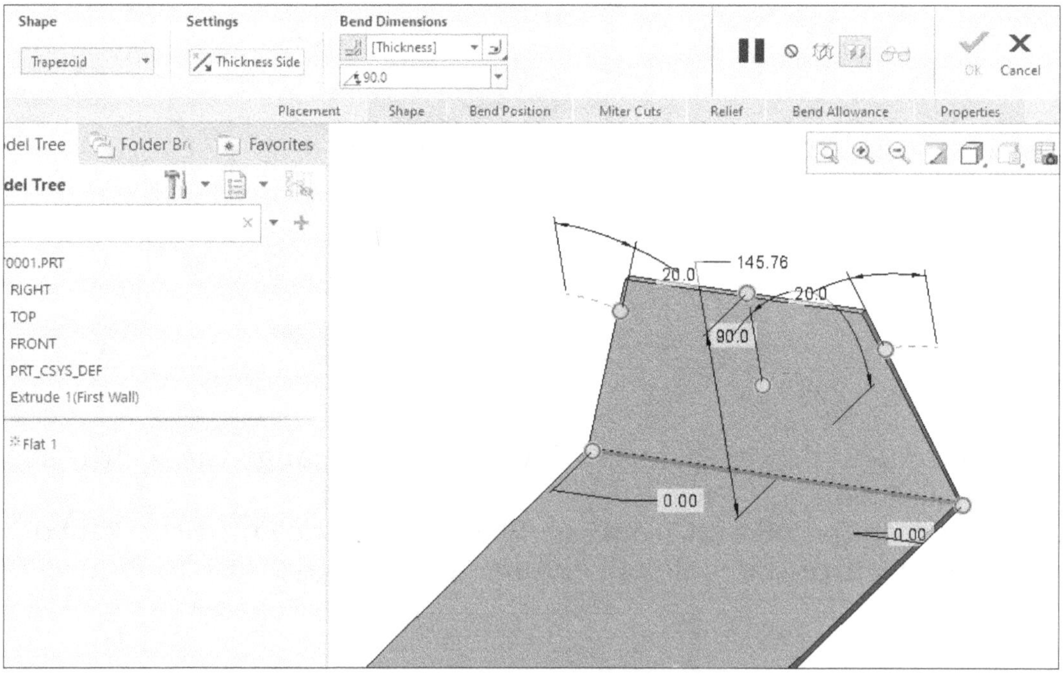

Figure-15. Angle of wall specified

- If you want to specify the bend radius at turning edge then click on the **Add bends** button from the contextual tab and specify the bend radius; refer to Figure-16.

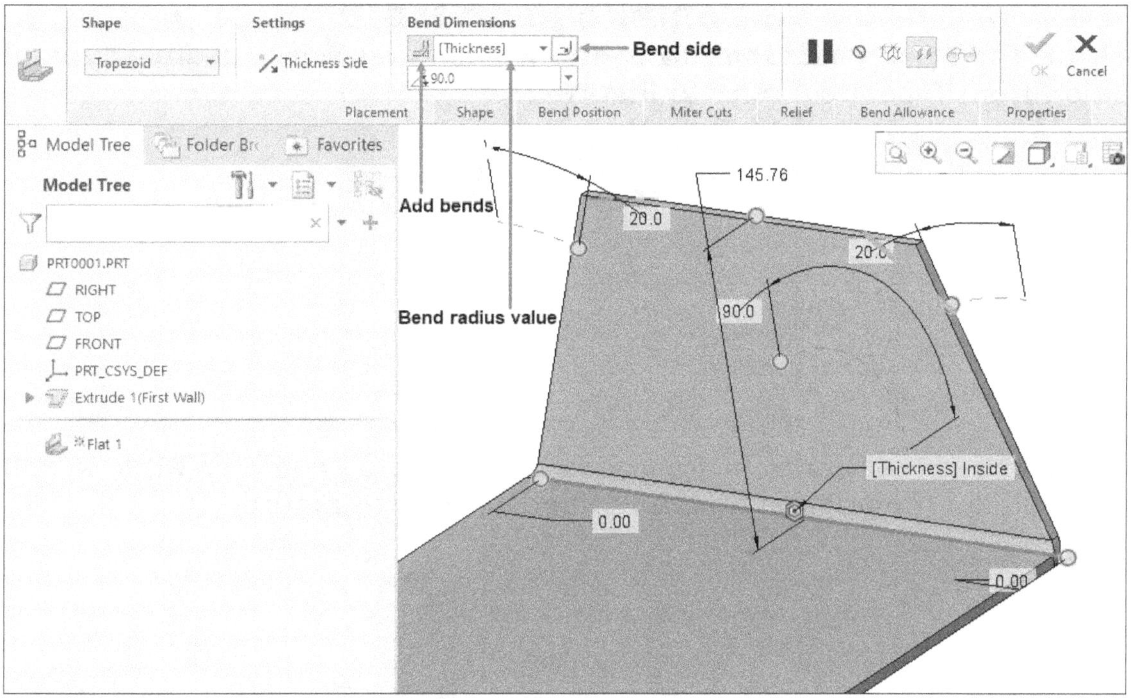

Figure-16. Bend radius

Shape tab

- Using the options in the **Shape** tab of the contextual tab, you can create or modify desired shape of flat wall with the help of creating/created sketch; refer to Figure-17. Click on the **Sketch** button to activate sketching environment to create a shape or edit the wall dimensions. Note that you need to create a closed loop sketch with one of its side attached to edge earlier selected. Click on the **Open** button to open the shape for wall from the local drive. Click on the **Save as** button to save the profile you created in the local drive.

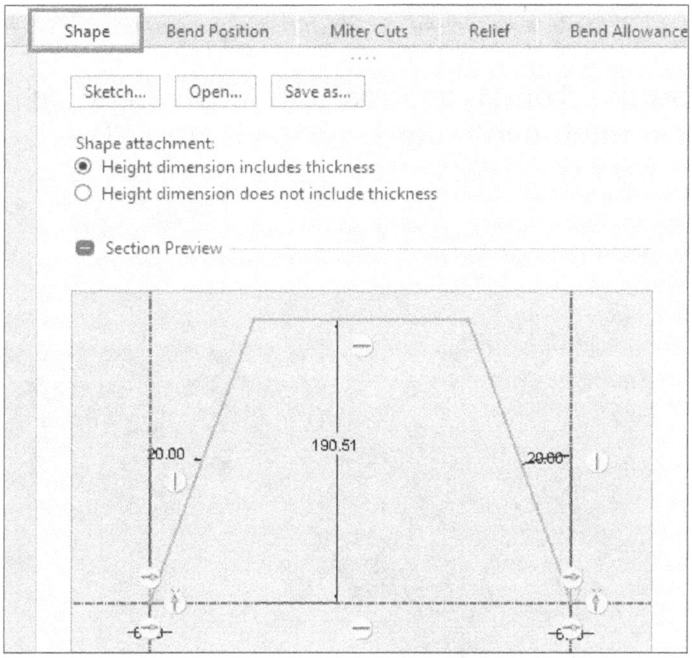

Figure-17. Shape tab

Bend Position tab

- Click on the **Bend Position** tab in the **Ribbon** and select desired type of bend position from **Type** area; refer to Figure-18.

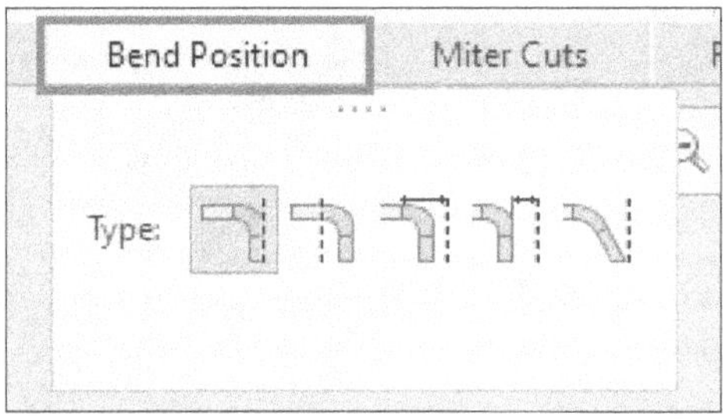

Figure-18. Bend Position tab of Flat tool

- Click on the button from **Type** area to add bend geometry while keeping the wall profile on the original attachment edge; refer to Figure-19.

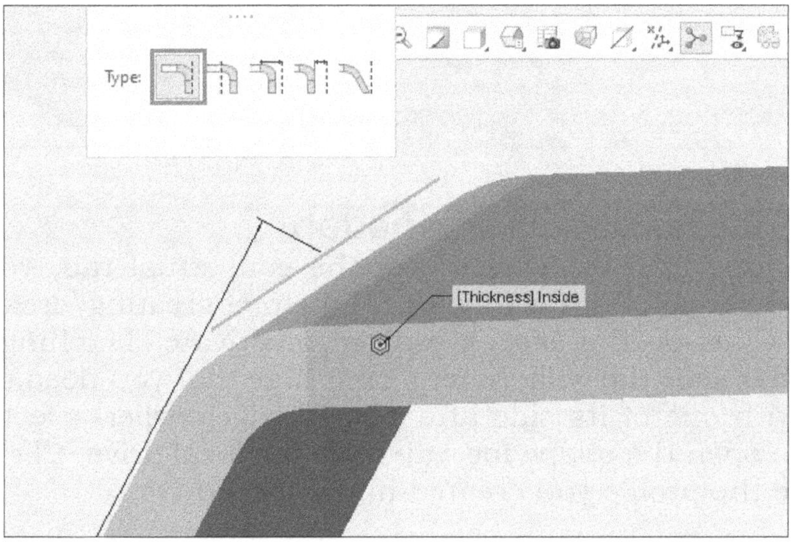

Figure-19. When keeping the wall profile on the original attachment edge

- Click on the button from **Type** area to add the bend geometry with the bend line tangent to the attachment edge; refer to Figure-20.

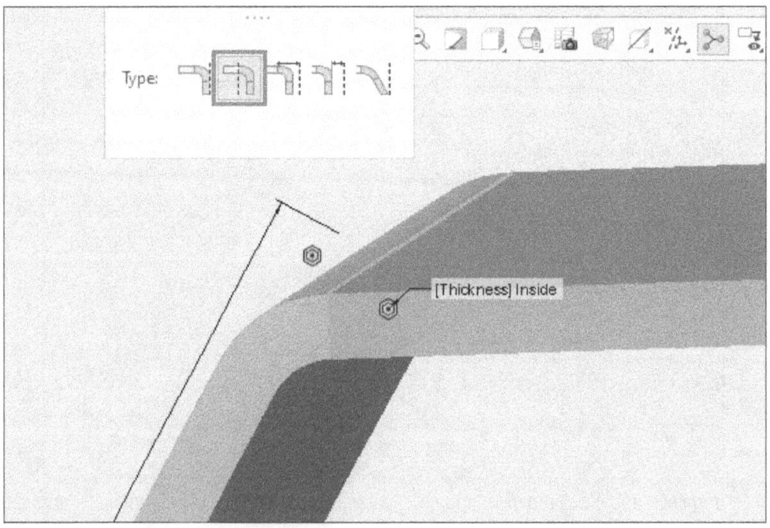

Figure-20. When bend line tangent to the attachment edge

- Click on the button from **Type** area to measure the offset from the attachment edge to the Bend Start; refer to Figure-21. Specify desired value for the offset in the **Value** edit box.

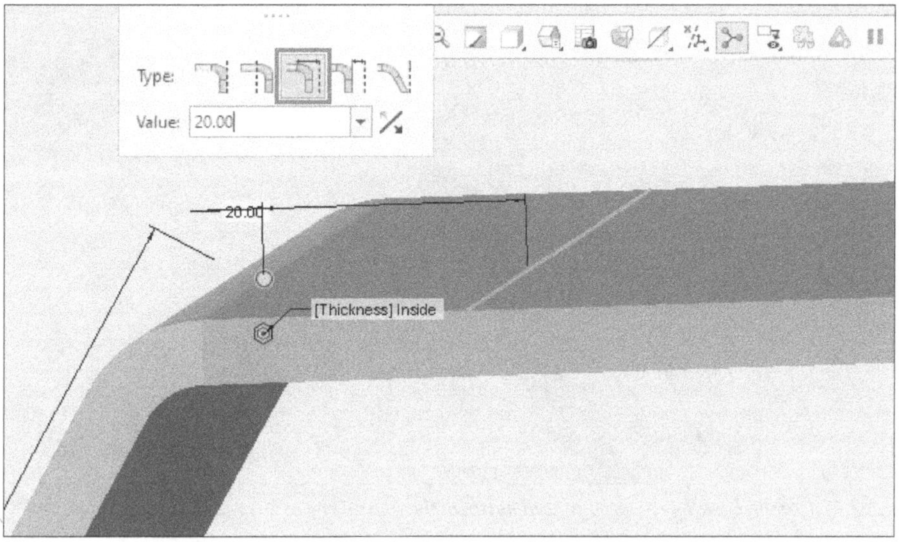

Figure-21. Specifying offset from the attachment edge to the Bend Start

- Click on the button from **Type** area to measure the offset from the attachment edge to the Bend Apex; refer to Figure-22. Specify desired value for the offset in the **Value** edit box.

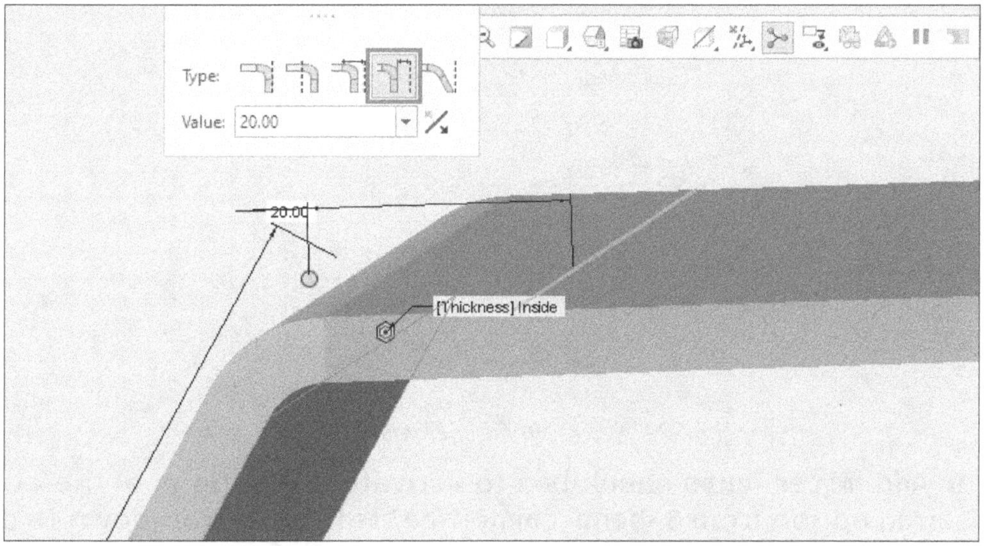

Figure-22. Specifying offset from the attachment edge to the Bend Apex

- Click on the button from **Type** area to place the attached wall geometry within the boundary of the attachment edge; refer to Figure-23.

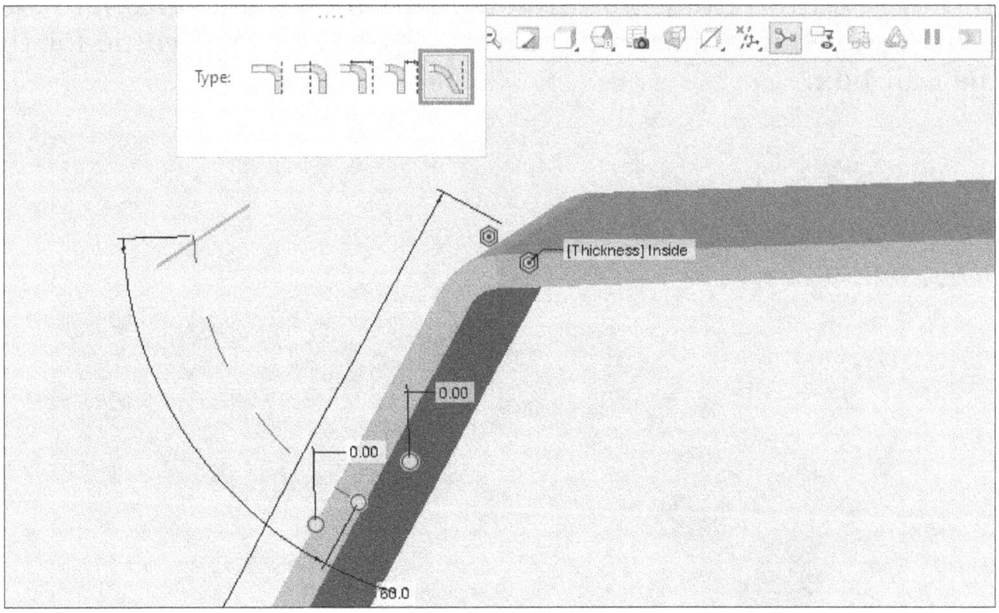

Figure-23. Attached wall geometry placed within the boundary of attachment edge

Miter Cuts tab

- Click on the **Miter Cuts** tab in the **Ribbon** to define the way the segments intersect. The options will be displayed; refer to Figure-24.

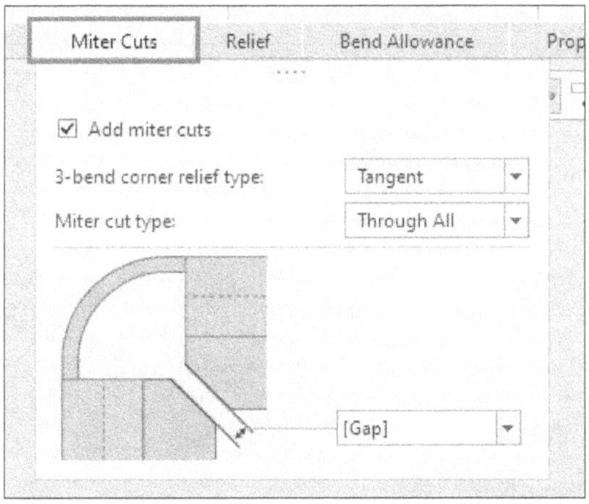

Figure-24. Miter Cuts tab of Flat tool

- Select the **Add miter cuts** check box to activate the options of the tab.
- Select desired option from **3-bend corner relief type** drop-down to define relief at corner. Select **Tangent** option to create the relief cuts tangent to the middle bend edges. Select **Open** option to create linear relief cuts to the side bend vertices. Select **Closed** option to create a corner patch that will be flattened as a deformation area. Select **Rip** option to create rips for the relief.
- Select desired option from **Miter cut type** drop-down. Select **Obround** option to create an obround shape groove. Select **Through All** option to create the groove through to the corner relief. Select **No Gap** option to create the groove with zero width.

Relief tab

- Click on the **Relief** tab in the **Ribbon**. The **Bend Relief** category is selected by default. The options related to **Bend Relief** category is displayed; refer to Figure-25.

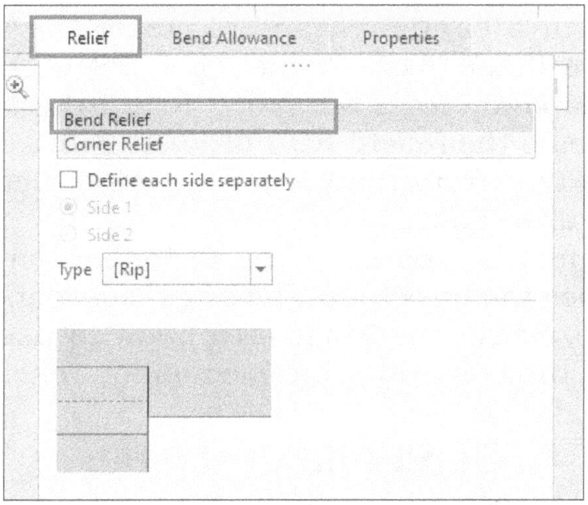

Figure-25. Bend Relief options in the Relief tab

- Select **Define each side separately** check box to define different relief at each bend side.
- Select desired type of bend relief from **Type** drop-down. Select **No relief** option to make the geometry without relief. Select **Rip** option to tear the material normal to attachment edge. Select **Stretch** option to use material stretching to provide relief. Select **Rectangular** option to use rectangle shape to provide relief. Select **Obround** option to use obround shape to provide relief.
- Select **Corner Relief** category from the **Relief** tab. The options related to **Corner Relief** category is displayed; refer to Figure-26.

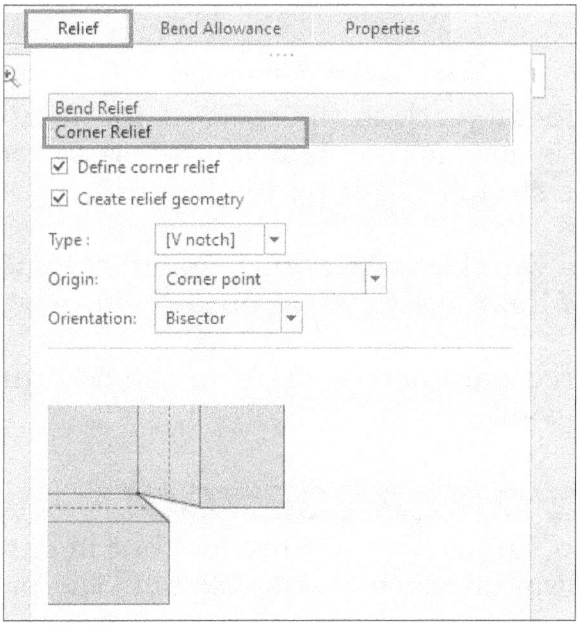

Figure-26. Corner Relief options in the Relief tab

- Select **Define corner relief** check box to display the options related to **Corner Relief** category.
- Select **Create relief geometry** check box if you want to define the corner but create the geometry using Unbend or Flat Pattern features.

- Select desired type of corner relief from the **Type** drop-down. Select the **No Relief** option to attach the wall without relief. Select the **V-notch** option to retain the default V-notch characteristic of the corner. Select the **Normal** option to cut from the corner up to and normal to the bend end to create the relief. Select the **Circular** option to cut a circular shape to create the relief. Select the **Square** option to cut a square shape to create the relief. Select the **Rectangular** option to cut a rectangular shape to create the relief. Select the **Obround** option to cut an obround shape to create the relief.
- Select desired origin type from the **Corner point** or **Bend lines intersection** option in the **Origin** drop-down.
- Select desired orientation type from the **Orientation** drop-down. Select the **Bisector** option to use the bisector of the angle between the bend edges as relief orientation reference. Select the **Diagonal** option to use the line that connects the corner point and the bend lines intersection as relief orientation reference.

Bend Allowance tab

- Click on the **Bend Allowance** tab to specify bending allowance for sheet; refer to . Figure-27. You can specify K factor or Y factor, or you can use the bend table to specify bending allowance.

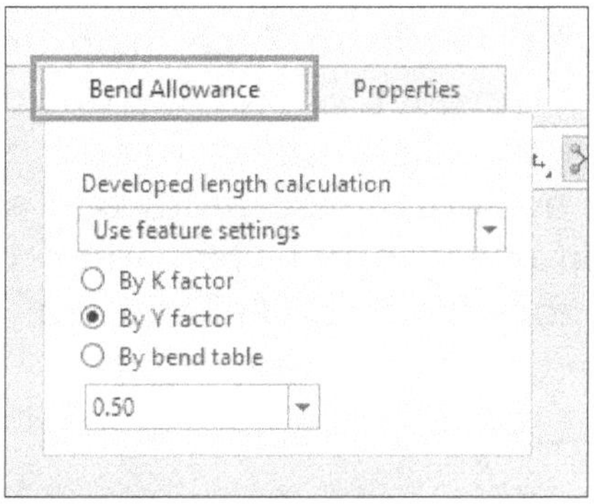

Figure-27. Bend Allowance tab

The K-Factor in sheet metal work is the ratio of the neutral axis to the material thickness. The K-Factor is used to calculate flat patterns because it is directly related to how much material is stretched during the bend.

The Y-Factor is simply a variable based on the more commonly used K-Factor. It is derived by taking half of the K-Factor multiplied by PI.

- After specifying desired parameters, click on the **OK** button from the contextual tab to create the flat wall.

FLANGE TOOL

The **Flange** tool works in similar way to **Flat** tool but in case of **Flange** tool, we can modify cross-section of wall in place of base sketch. The procedure to use this tool is given next.

- Click on the **Flange** tool from the **Walls** panel in the **Ribbon**. The **Flange** contextual tab will be displayed; refer to Figure-28.

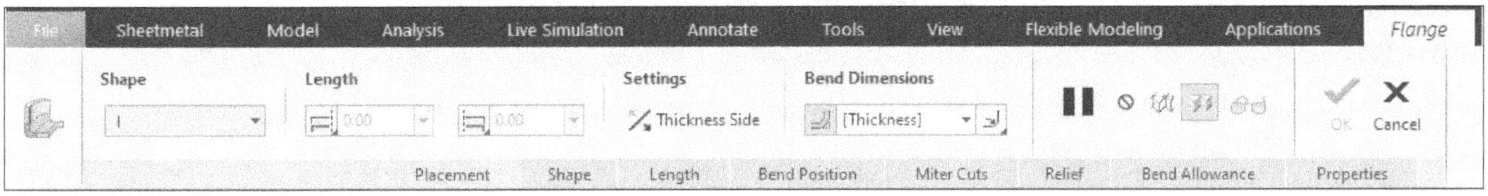

Figure-28. Flange contextual tab

- Select an edge to create a flange wall attached to it. Preview of the flange wall will be displayed; refer to Figure-29.

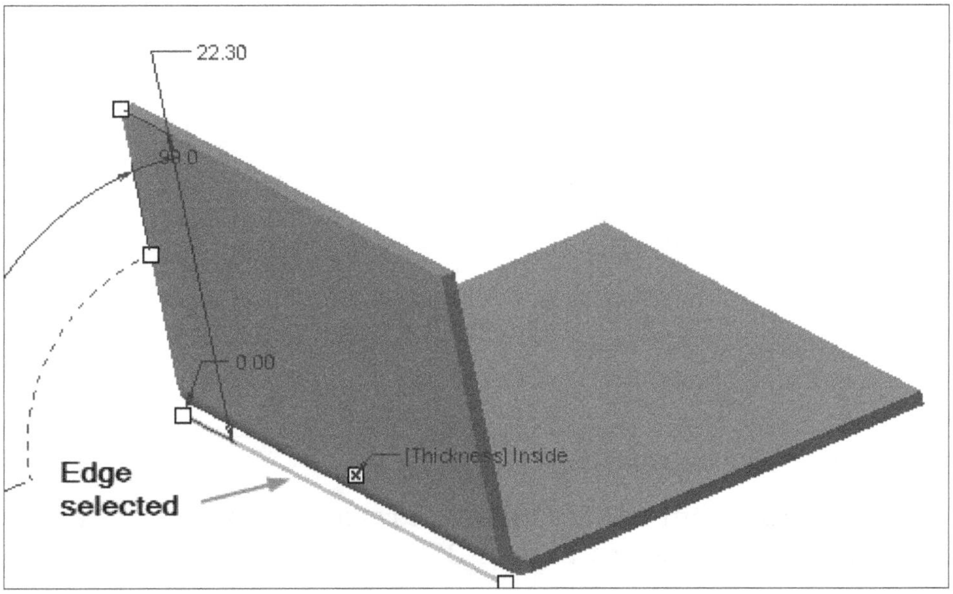

Figure-29. Edge selected for flange wall

- To make multiple selections at a time, click on the **Placement** tab and then click on the **Details** button; refer to Figure-30. The **Chain** dialog box will be displayed; refer to Figure-31.

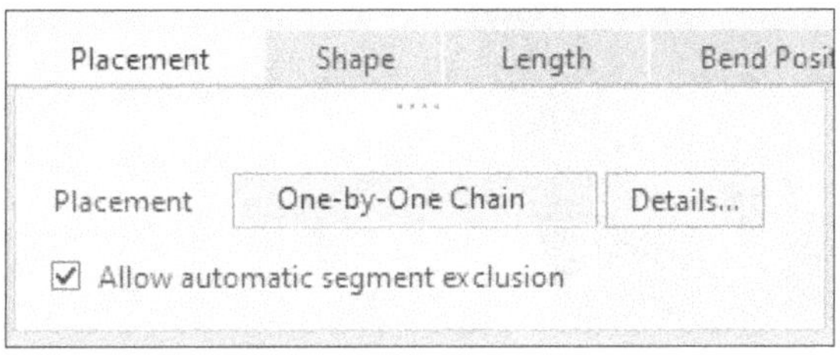

Figure-30. Details button

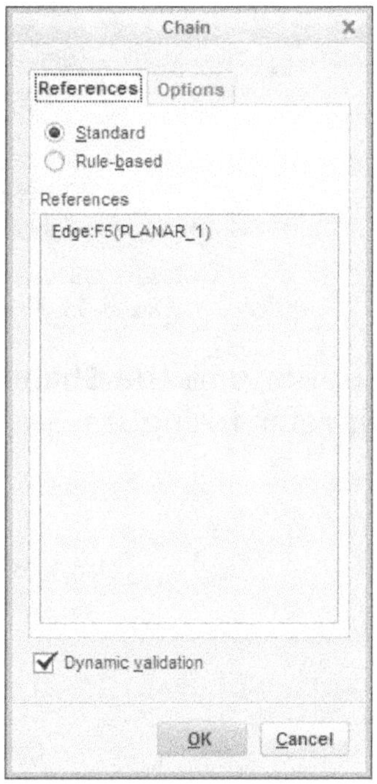

Figure-31. Chain dialog box

- Hold the **CTRL** key from Keyboard and select the edges one by one; refer to Figure-32.

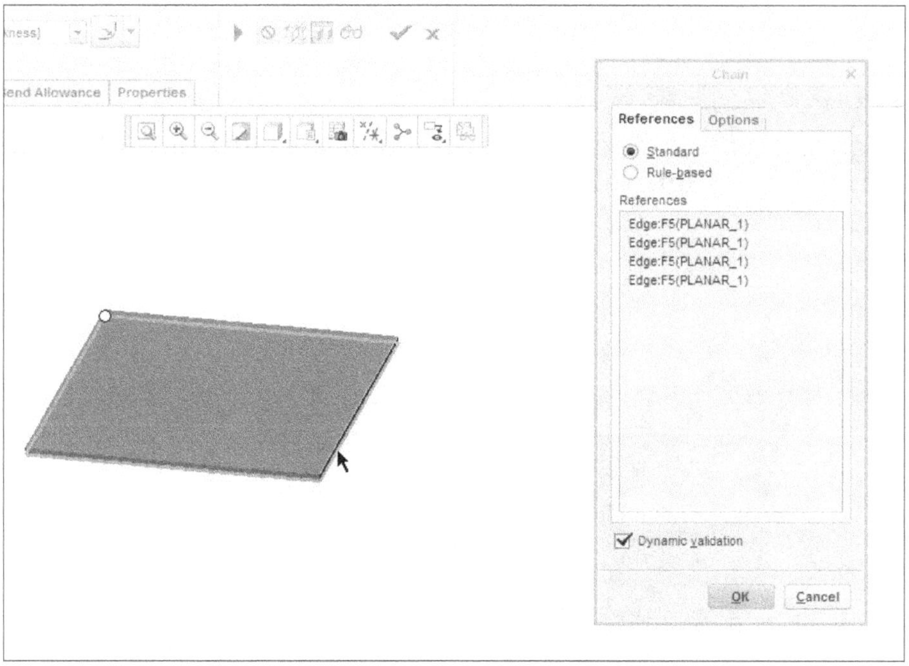

Figure-32. Multiple edges selected

- Click on the **OK** button from the dialog box. Preview of the flange wall with multiple edges will be displayed; refer to Figure-33.

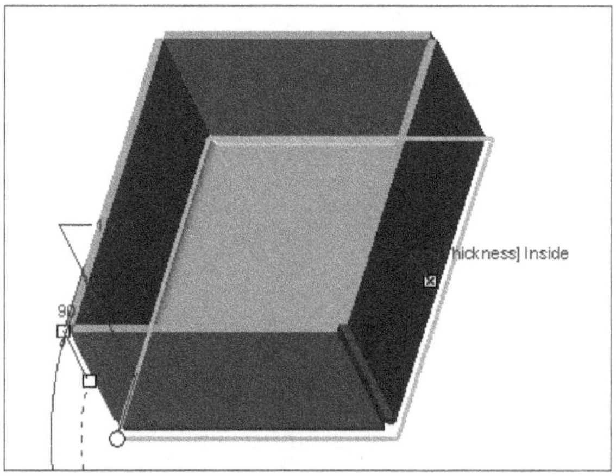

Figure-33. Preview of flange wall

- Using the options in the **Shape** tab, you can create desired cross-section for the flange wall; refer to Figure-34.

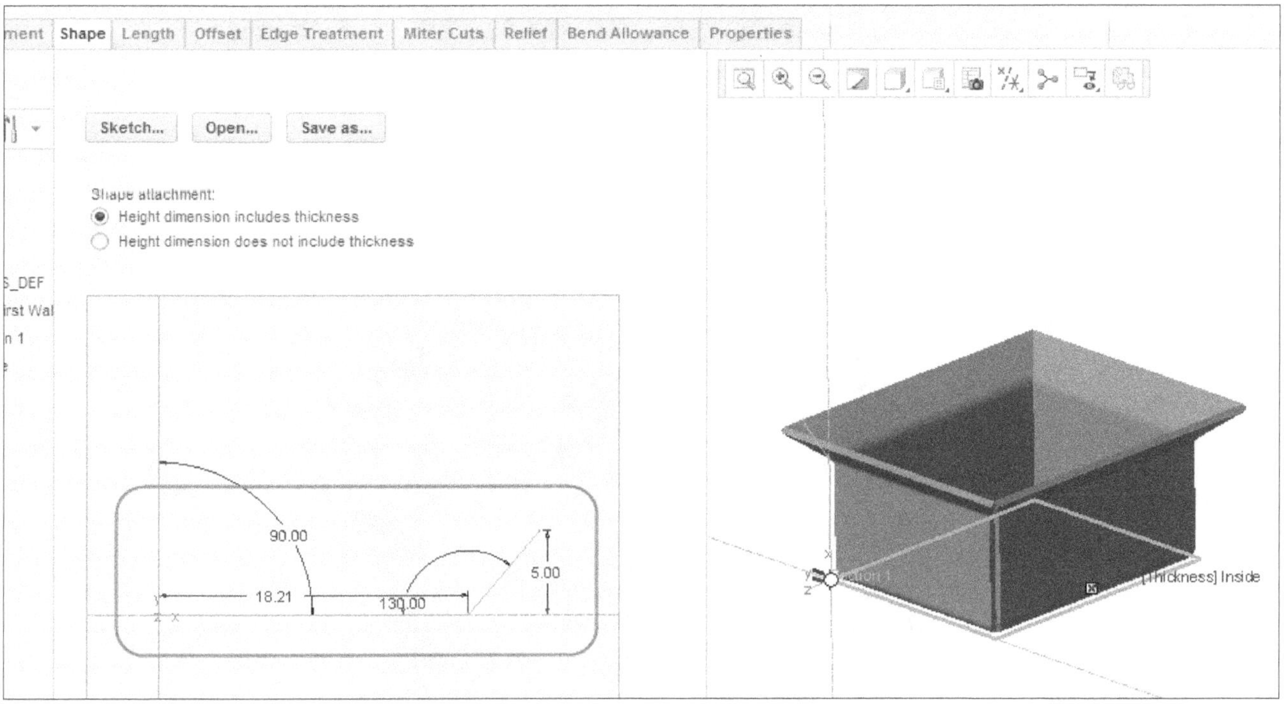

Figure-34. Sketched cross-section of flange wall

- Using the options in **Length** tab, you can specify the starting and end limit of the flange wall; refer to Figure-35.

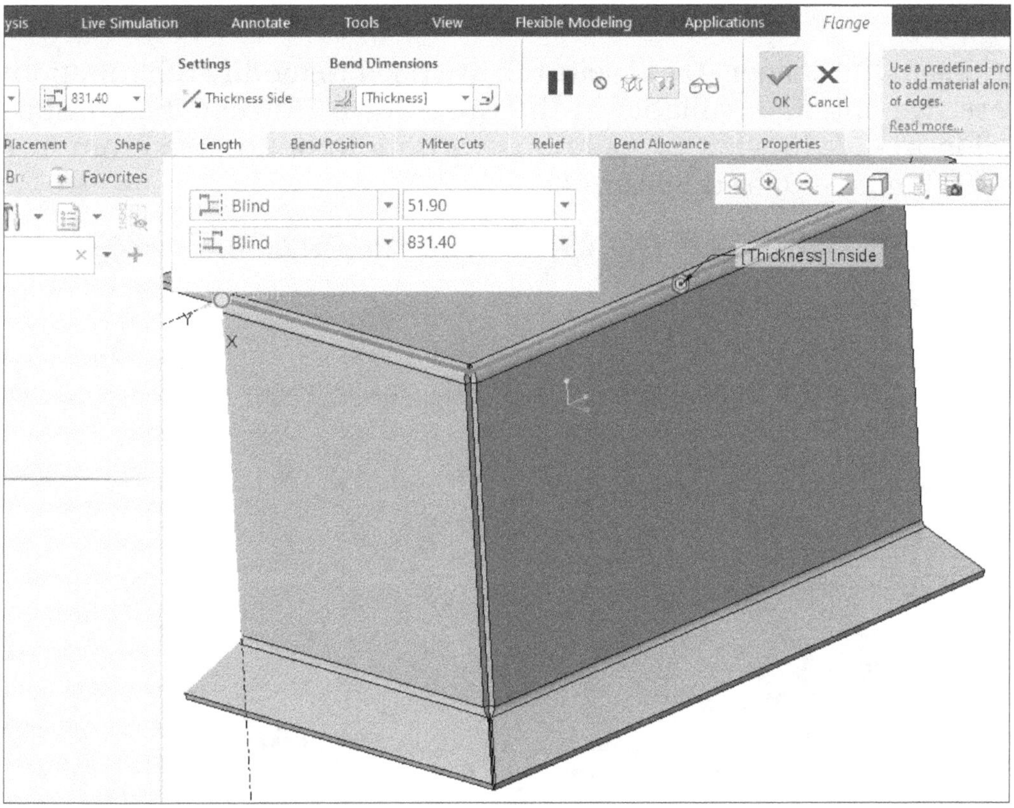

Figure-35. Flange wall after specifying desired length

- Select desired option from the **Bend Position** tab to define location of bend; refer to Figure-36.

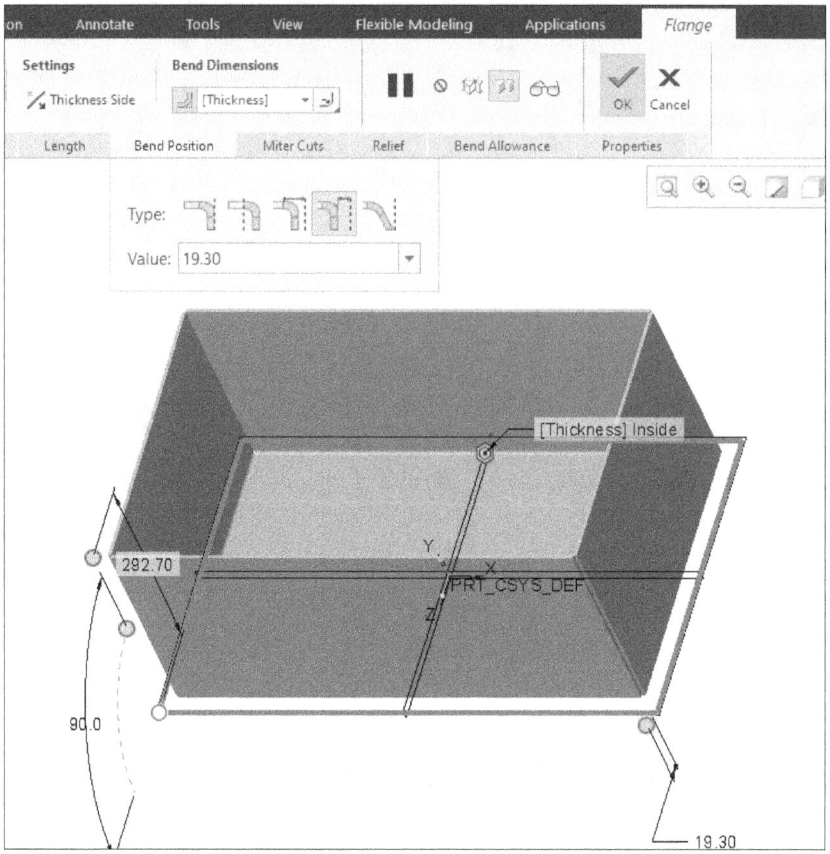

Figure-36. Defining Bend position

- The options in the **Corner Treatment** tab are used to modify the junctions of edges. There are five options available in the drop-down to treat the corner junctions; refer to Figure-37. Preview of junctions with main options is given in Figure-38, Figure-39, Figure-40, and Figure-41.

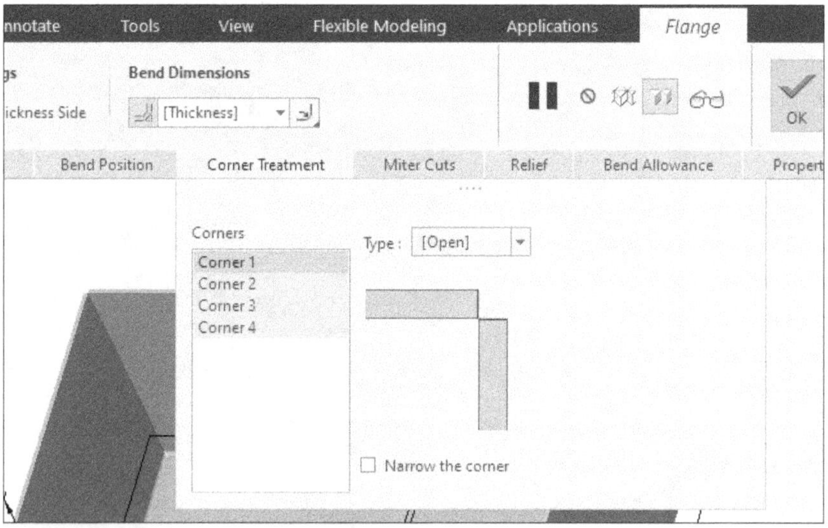

Figure-37. Edge Treatment options

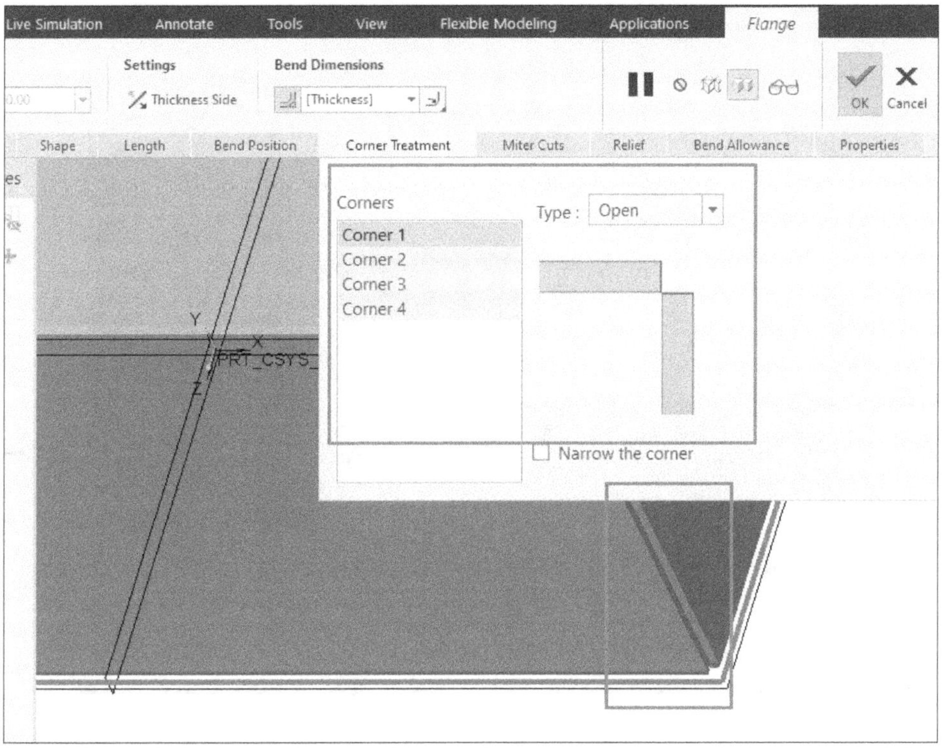

Figure-38. Open edge treatment

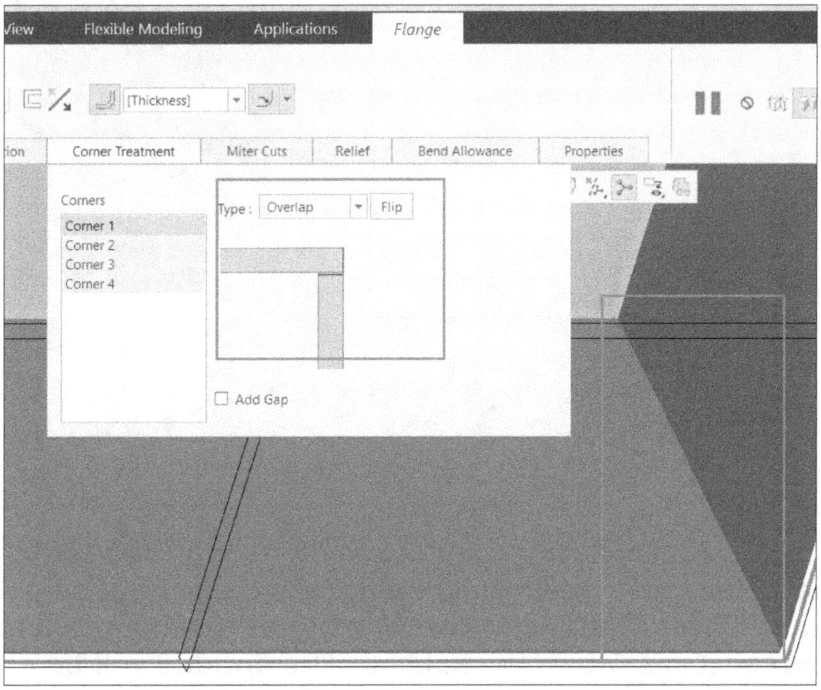

Figure-39. Overlap corner treatment

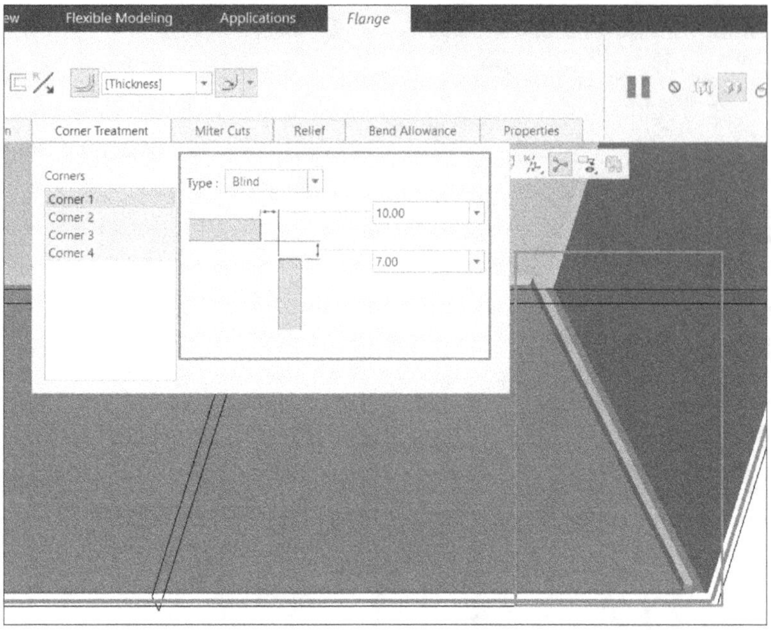

Figure-40. Blind corner treatment

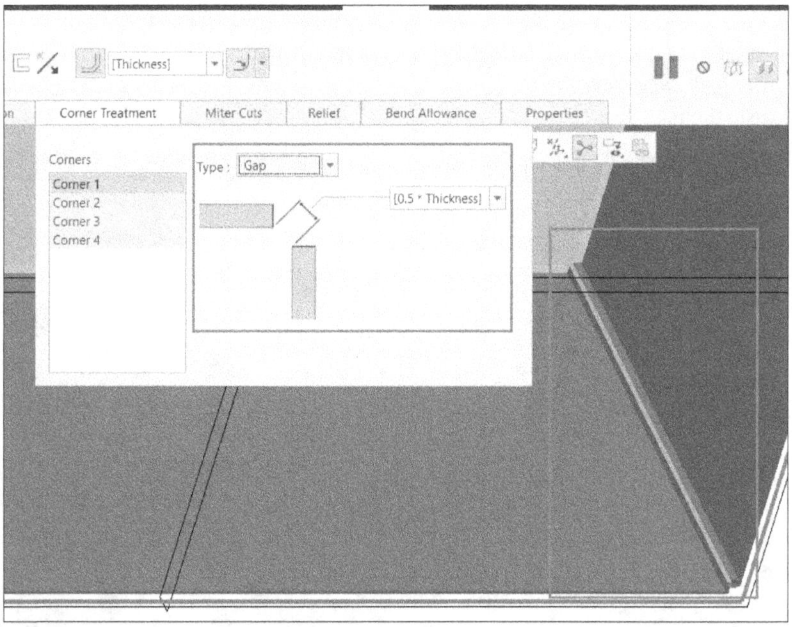

Figure-41. Gap corner treatment

- The options in the **Miter Cuts** tab make their use in **Flat** pattern of sheetmetal part. Note that after creating the sheetmetal part, our final step is to create a flat pattern so that a sheet of that size can be cut and transformed into desired part.
- Click on the **Miter Cuts** tab in the **Ribbon**. The options will be displayed; refer to Figure-42.

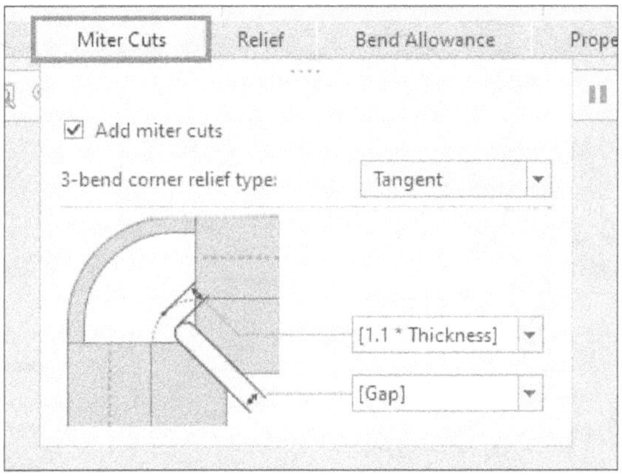

Figure-42. Miter Cuts tab of Flange tool

- Select **Add miter cuts** check box to activate the options of the **Miter Cuts** tab.
- Select desired option from **3-bend corner relief type** drop-down. Select **Tangent** option to create relief cuts tangent to the middle bend edges. Select **Closed** option to create a corner patch that will be flattened as a deformation area.
- After specifying desired parameters, the miter cuts feature will be created; refer to Figure-43.

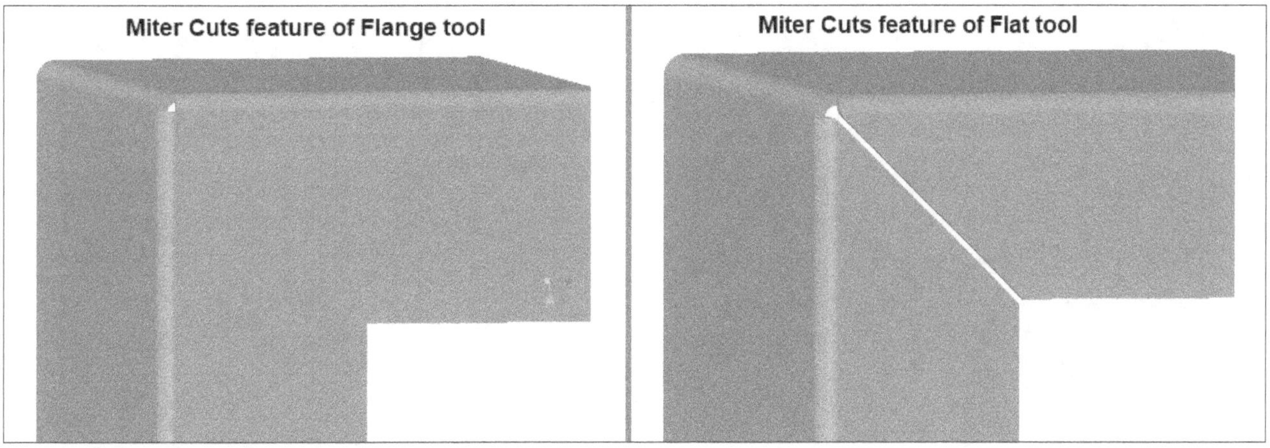

Figure-43. Miter Cuts feature of Flange and Flat tool

- Click on the **Relief** tab to provide relied in sheetmetal part so that the part can be bent or unbent on the machine without material overlapping and loss. There are two categories by which we can apply relief; **Bend Relief** and **Corner Relief**; refer to Figure-44. The Bend relief is applied to set the shape of relief at the bends whereas Corner relief change the shape of relief at corners formed by walls; refer to Figure-45 and Figure-46.

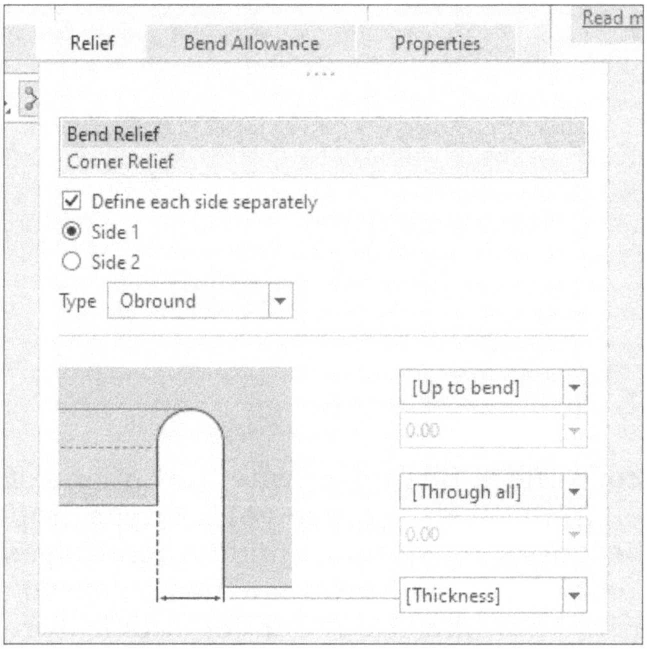

Figure-44. Relief categories

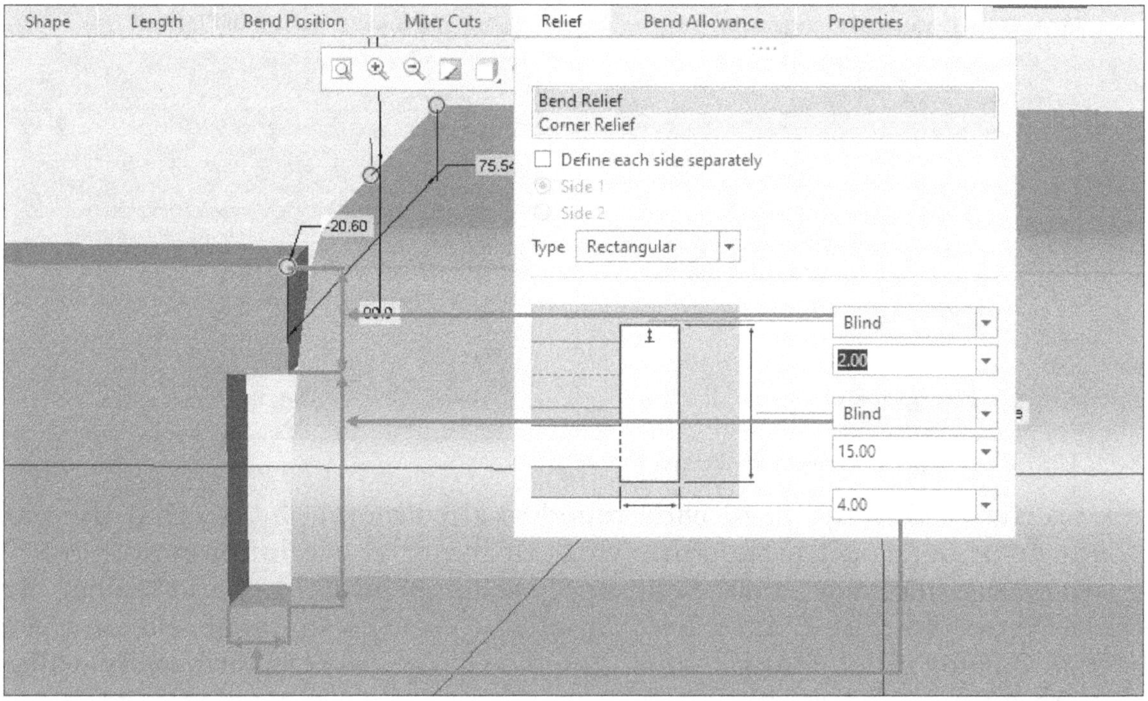

Figure-45. Bend relief preview

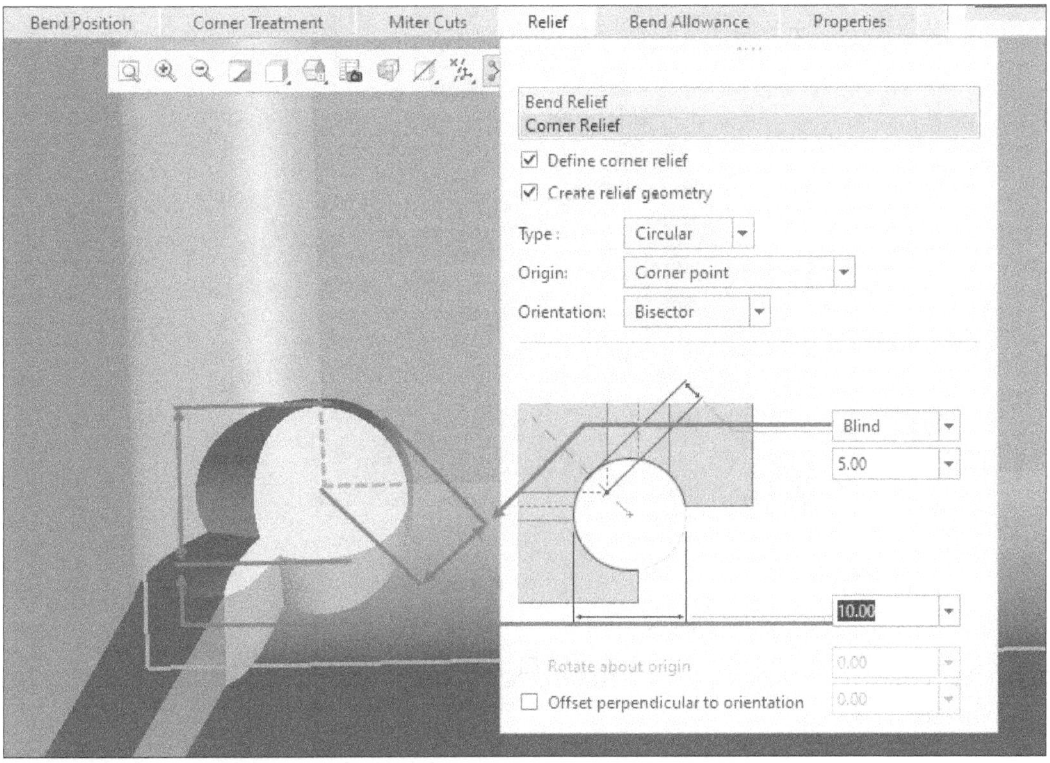

Figure-46. Corner relief

- Select desired options and specify related values to create desired relief in part. Note that you can specify Bend relief only when you bend the sheetmetal at some distance from edge ends. If the sheet is bent for the full edge then effect of Bend relief will not be displayed.
- Other options in the contextual tab are same as discussed for Flat wall earlier. After specifying desired parameters, click on the **OK** button from the contextual tab to create the flange walls.

PLANAR TOOL

The **Planar** tool is used to create base wall like extrude and other part modeling software. Using this tool, you can create base wall on the basis of a selected/created closed sketch. This tool works as patch in surface design. The procedure to use this tool is given next.

- Click on the **Planar** tool from the **Walls** panel in the **Ribbon**. The **Planar** contextual tab will be displayed; refer to Figure-47 and you will be asked to select or create a sketch.

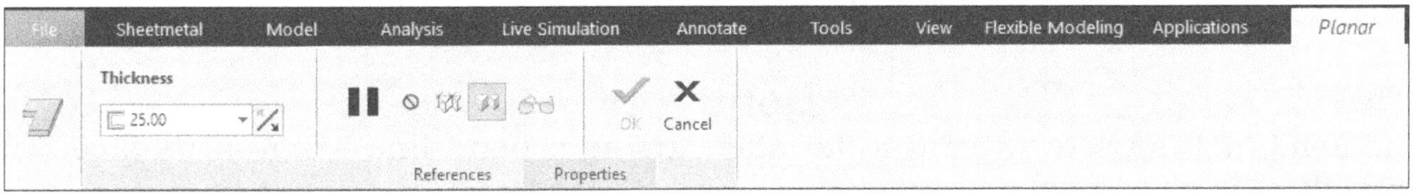

Figure-47. Planar contextual tab

- If you already have a closed sketch in the modeling area then select it otherwise, click on the **References** tab and click on the **Define** button to create a sketch.
- Create a closed sketch at desired plane and then click on the **OK** button to exit the sketching environment. Preview of the wall will be displayed; refer to Figure-48.

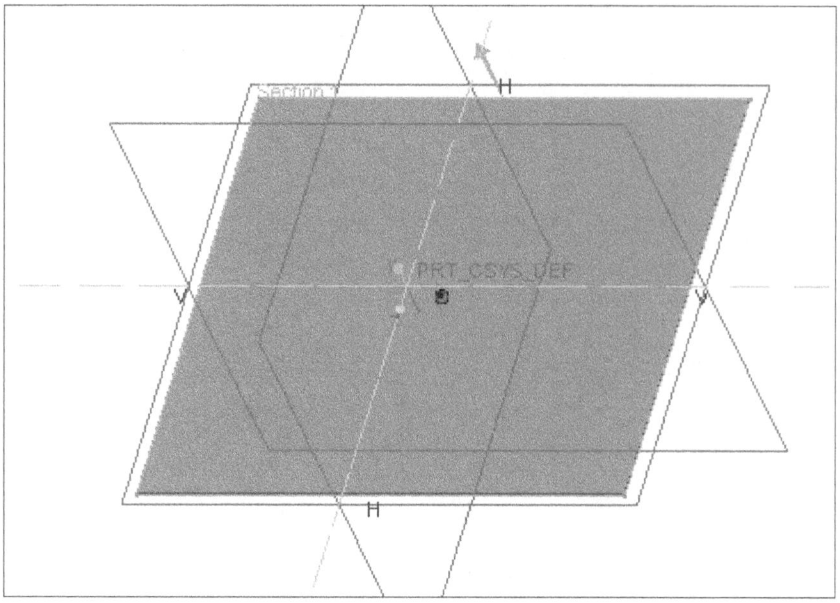

Figure-48. Preview of planar wall

- Click in the **Thickness** edit box and specify desired thickness for the planar wall; refer to Figure-49.

Figure-49. Thickness edit box

- Click on the **OK** button to create the wall.

BENDING TOOLS

The Bending tools, as the name suggests, are used to bend the sheet along the specified bend line. There are three tools in Creo Parametric to perform bending; Bend, Edge Bend, and Planar Bend; refer to Figure-50. These tools are discussed next.

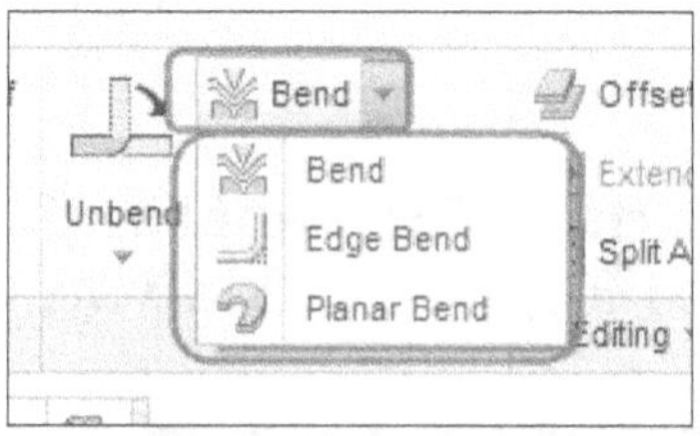

Figure-50. Bending tools

Bend tool

The **Bend** tool is used to bend a flat sheet using a bend line lying on its face. The procedure is given next.

- Click on the **Bend** tool from the **Bend** drop-down in the **Bends** panel of the **Ribbon**. The **Bend** contextual tab will be displayed; refer to Figure-51.

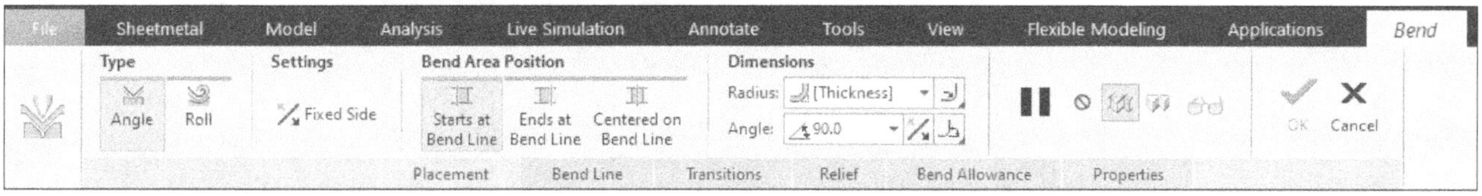

Figure-51. Bend contextual tab

- Click on the **Placement** tab. You will be asked to select a surface for defining bend line; refer to Figure-52.

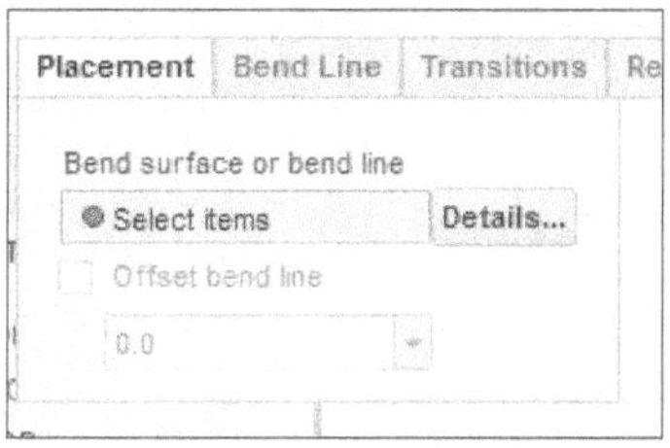

Figure-52. Placement tab of Bend contextual tab

- Select a face of wall that you want to bend; refer to Figure-53. Preview of the bend line will be displayed.

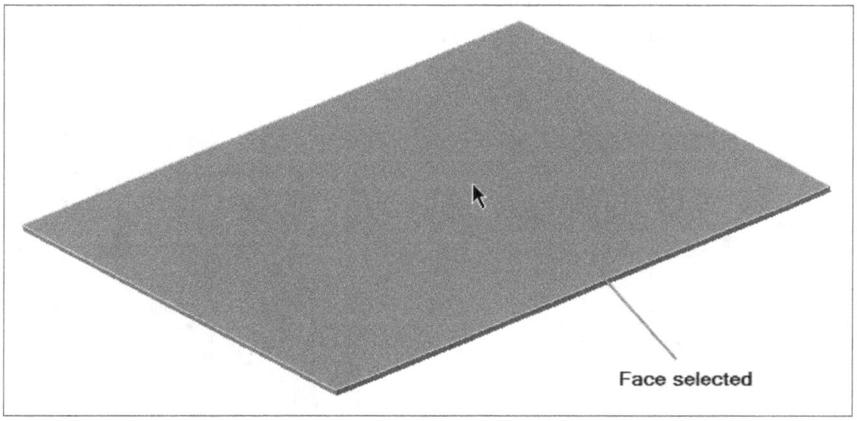

Figure-53. Face selected

- One by one, drag the green handles of bend line to the references edges; refer to Figure-54.

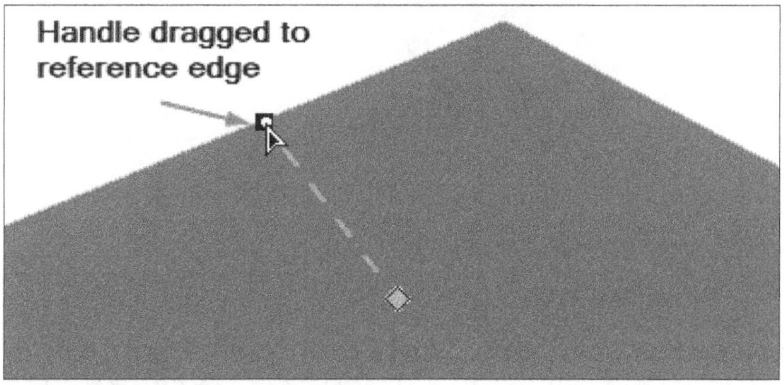

Figure-54. Dragging reference handle

- If you face problem in dragging the handle then you can define the references in the **Bend Line** tab of contextual tab; refer to Figure-55.

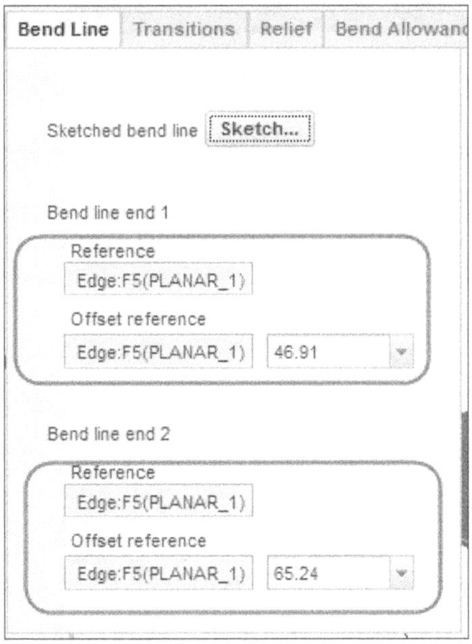

Figure-55. Bend line references

- You can also use the **Sketch** button to sketch the bend line in place of selecting references. **Note that while sketching the bend line, you are allowed to create only one line**; refer to Figure-56.

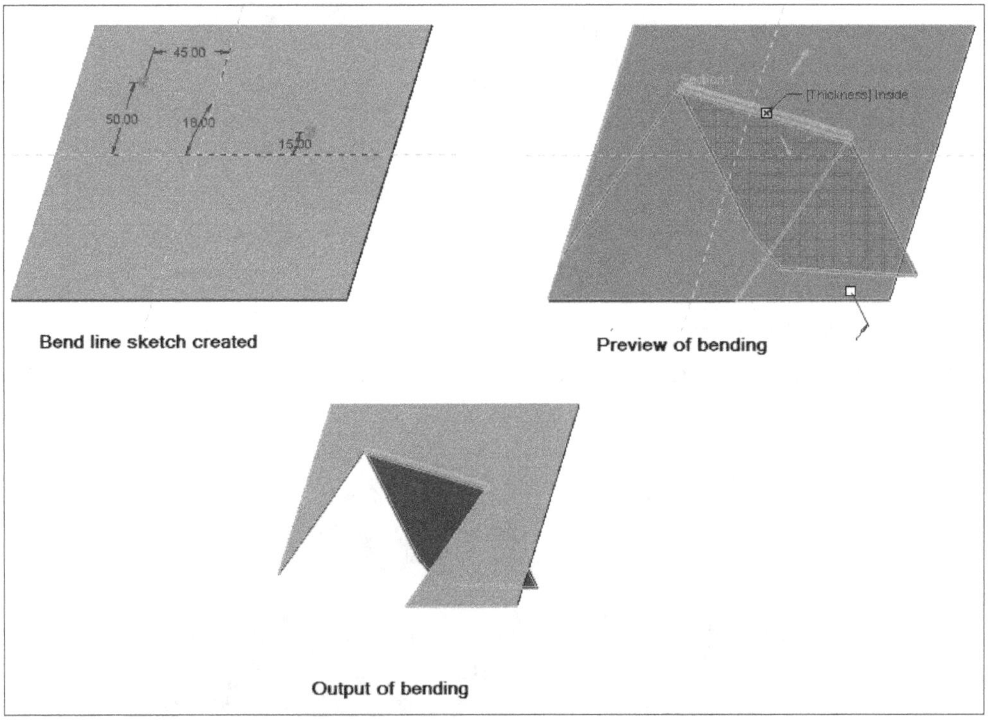

Figure-56. Bending by sketched line

- The three options in the **Bend Area Position** area of the contextual tab are used to decide the bending side of material with respect to the bending line; refer to Figure-57. The effects of selecting an option out of the three is given in Figure-58, Figure-59, and Figure-60.

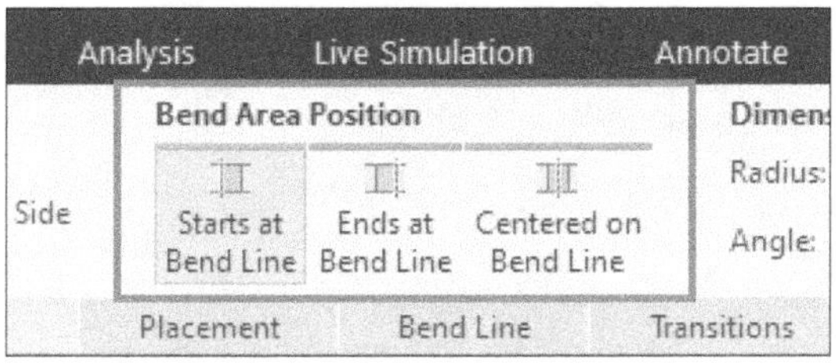

Figure-57. Bend Area Position options

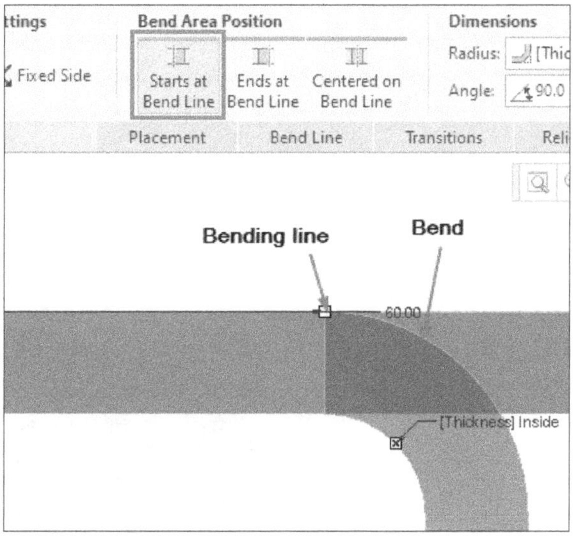

Figure-58. Starts at Bend Line option

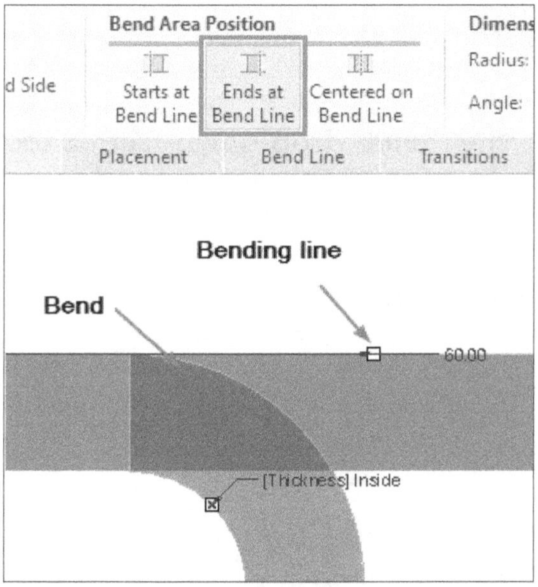

Figure-59. Ends at Bend Line option

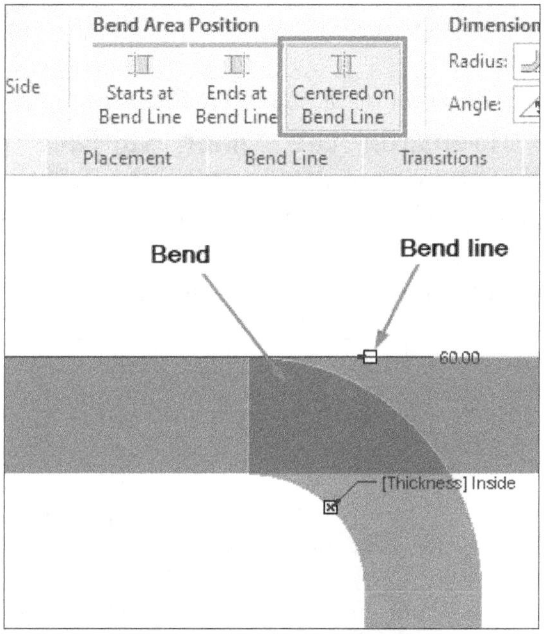

Figure-60. Centered on Bend Line option

- You can change the fixed side of bend by using the **Fixed Side** button in the **Settings** area of the contextual tab.
- Till this point, we have used **Angle** button from **Type** area. Which practically means, the sheet is bent on a punch press. But, we can also bend the sheet on a roller. To do so, click on the **Roll** button from **Type** area. The **Angle** edit box in the **Dimension** area of the **Ribbon** will be deactivated and you are asked to specify radius of bend.
- Specify desired bend radius. Preview of the bend will be displayed; refer to Figure-61. Note that the preview will be displayed only when you have specified a possible radius in the edit box.

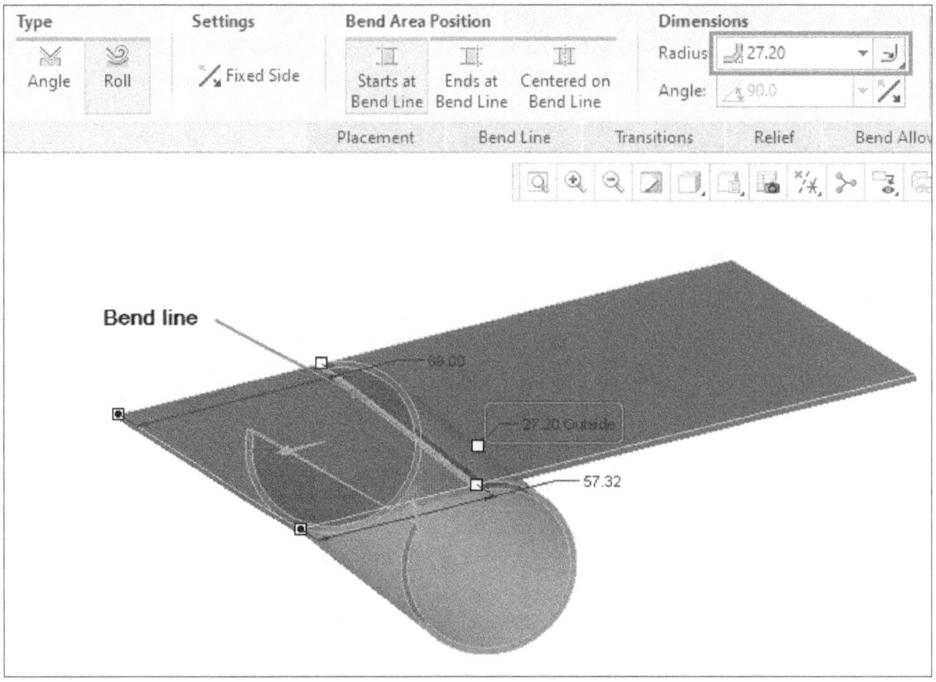

Figure-61. Bend using Roll button

- Use **Dimension the inner surface of the bend** drop-down from **Dimensions** area of the contextual tab to change the radius from inner to outer and vice-versa.
- To apply the transition, click on the **Transitions** tab and click on the **Add Transition** button. The **Sketch** button will become active. Click on it and draw two lines defining limits of transition; refer to Figure-62.

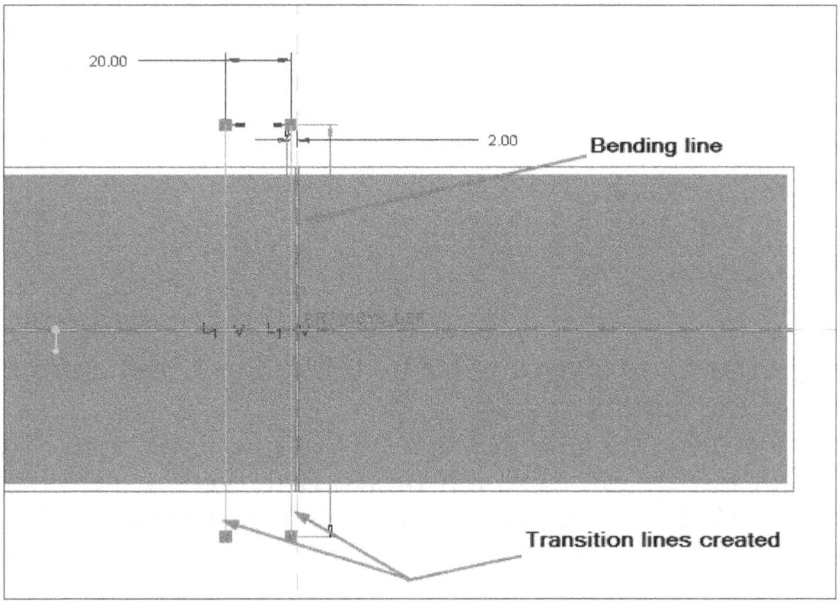

Figure-62. Sketch of transition lines

- Click on the **OK** button from the sketching environment. Preview of the bend with transition will be displayed; refer to Figure-63.

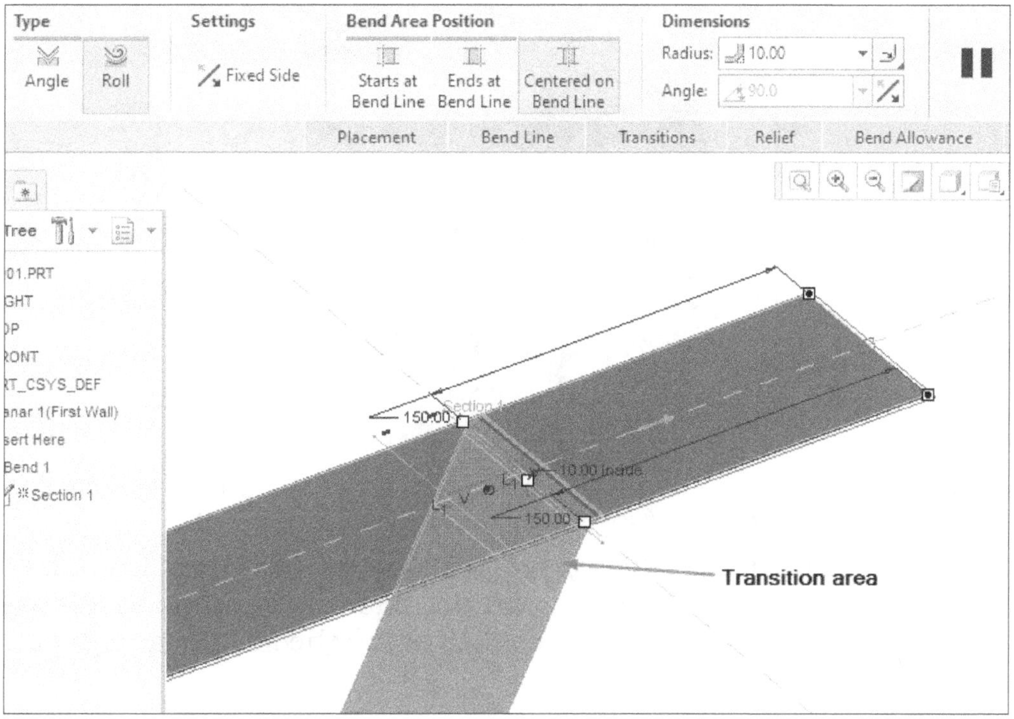

Figure-63. Transition area of bend

- After specifying desired parameters, click on the **OK** button from the contextual tab to create the bend.

Edge Bend

The **Edge Bend** tool is used to apply bend at the sharp edges of the sheetmetal part. This tool is generally used when you convert solid part to sheetmetal in Creo Parametric. The procedure is given next.

- Click on the **Edge Bend** tool from the **Bend** drop-down in the **Bends** panel of the **Ribbon**. The **Edge Bend** contextual tab will be displayed; refer to Figure-64.

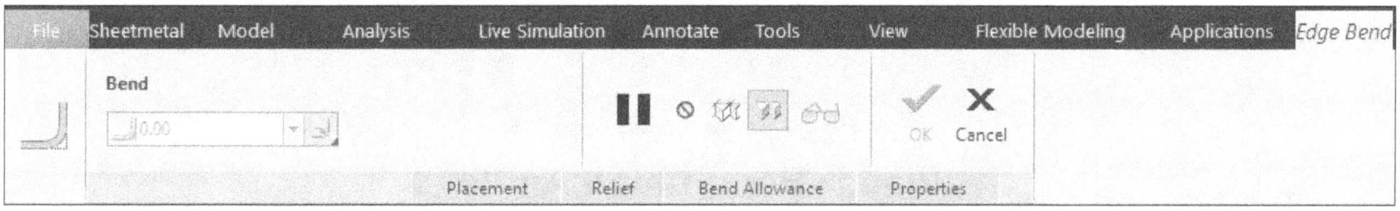

Figure-64. Edge Bend contextual tab

- Select the sharp edges of the model. Preview of the bend will be displayed; refer to Figure-65.

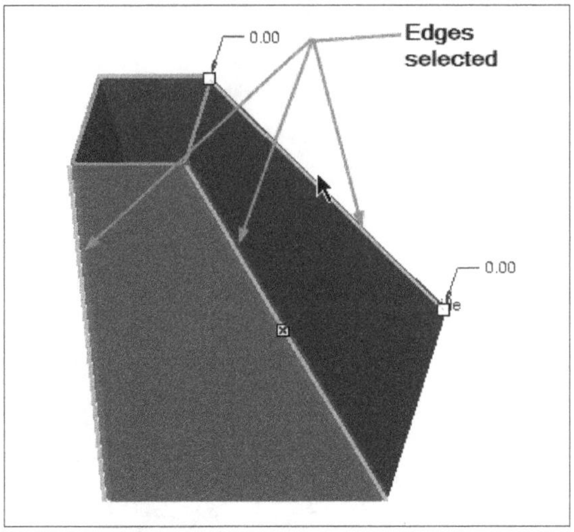

Figure-65. Edges selected

- Specify desired radius in the edit box and click on the **OK** button from the contextual tab to apply the bend. Note that you can provide relief and bend allowance to the bends in the same way as discussed earlier using the **Relief** and **Bend Allowance** tabs in the contextual tab.

Planar Bend

The **Planar Bend** tool is used to bend the sheet by specified radius or angle in its own plane. The procedure is given next.

- Click on the **Planar Bend** tool from the **Bend** drop-down in the **Bends** panel of the **Ribbon**. The **Menu Manager** with two options will be displayed; refer to Figure-66.

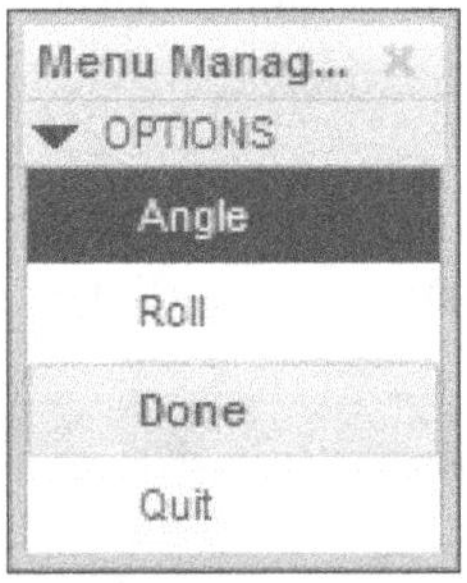

Figure-66. Menu Manager

Planar Bend using Angle

- Select the **Angle** option from the **Menu Manager** and click on the **Done** button (or press MMB). The **Bend Options** dialog box will be displayed with angle options and **USE TABLE** options will be displayed in the **Menu Manager**; refer to Figure-67 and Figure-68.

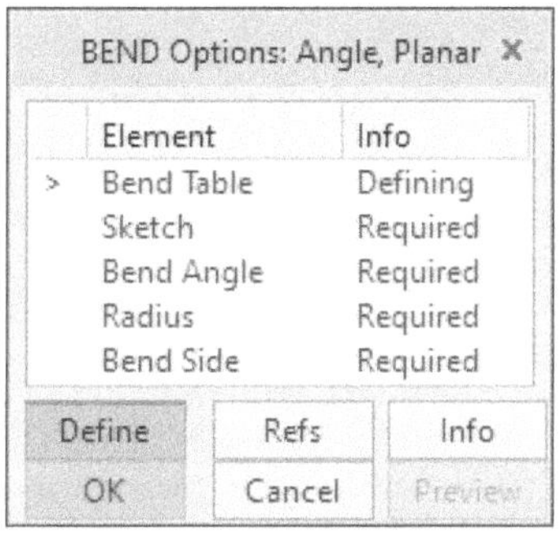

Figure-67. Bend Options dialog box

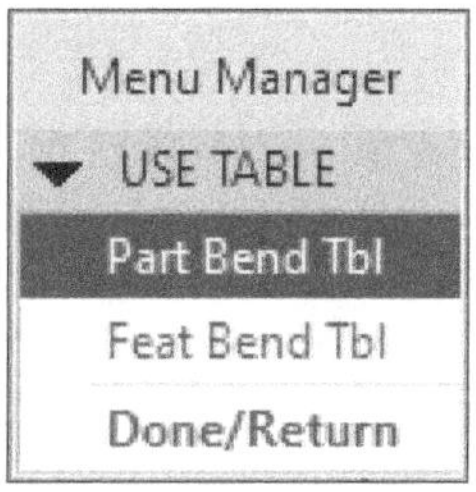

Figure-68. USE TABLE options in Menu Manager

- Select the **Part Bend Tbl** option from the **Menu Manager** and press the Middle button of Mouse (MMB). You are asked to select a sketching plane for specifying bending line.
- Select a plane. You are asked to specify sketching direction. Press the MMB and specify references as we do for sketching.
- Create a sketch line for specifying bend line; refer to Figure-69.

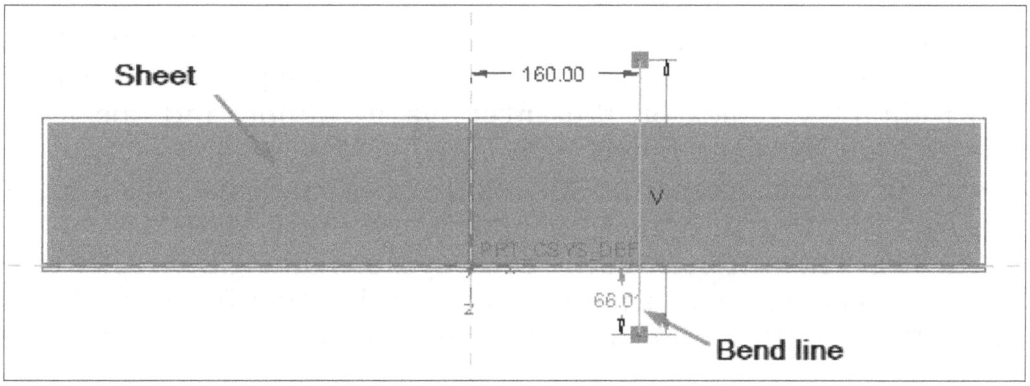

Figure-69. Bending line

- Click on the **OK** button from **Ribbon** to exit sketching environment.
- Select the **Flip** button from the **Menu Manager** displayed if you want to flip the bending side.
- Click **Okay** from the **Menu Manager**. You are asked to specify the direction of **Angle**.
- Click on the **Okay** button after specifying desired direction. You are asked to specify the angle; refer to Figure-70.

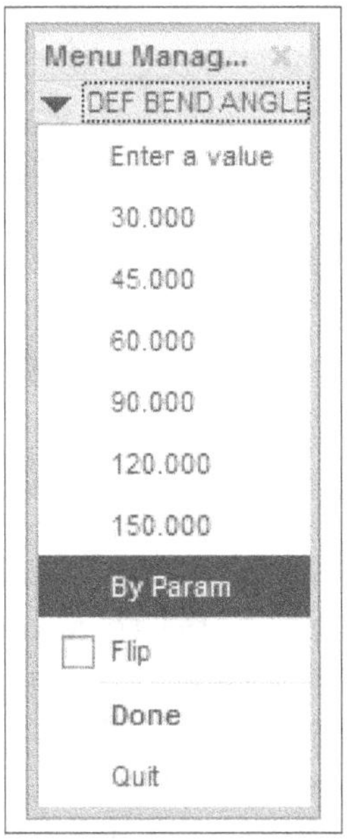

Figure-70. Menu Manager with angle values

- Specify desired angle and click on the **Done** button from the **Menu Manager**. The **SEL RADIUS** option will be displayed in the **Menu Manager**. If you want to specify a custom radius then click on the **Enter Value** option and specify the radius otherwise, default parameters will be applied.
- After specifying radius, press the MMB. You are asked to specify direction of bend.
- Select desired side by using the **Flip** option and press MMB.
- Click on the **Preview** button from the **Bend Options** dialog box; refer to Figure-71. If you want to make changes then select desired option from the dialog box and click on the **Define** button otherwise, click on the **OK** button to create the bend.

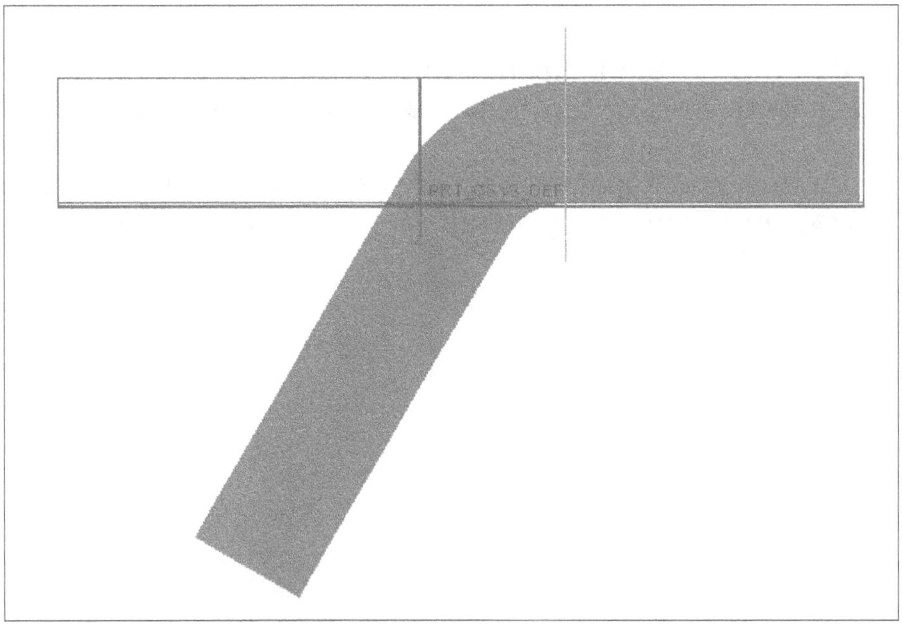

Figure-71. Preview of planar bend

Planar Bend using Roll

- Select the **Roll** option after clicking on the **Planar Bend** tool and then click on the **Done** option from the **Menu Manager**.

- Select the **Part Bend Tbl** option and press the Middle button of Mouse **(MMB)**. You are asked to select a sketching plane for specifying bending line.
- Select a plane. You are asked to specify sketching direction. Press the **MMB** and specify references as we do for sketching.
- Create a sketch line for specifying bend line.
- Click on the **OK** button from **Ribbon** to exit sketching environment.
- Select the **Flip** button from the **Menu Manager** displayed if you want to flip the bending side.
- Click **Okay** from the **Menu Manager**. The **SEL RADIUS** option will be displayed in the **Menu Manager**. Click on the **Enter Value** option and specify the radius otherwise, default parameters will be applied.
- After specifying radius, press the MMB. You are asked to specify direction of bend.
- Select desired side by using the **Flip** option and press **MMB**.
- Click on the **Preview** button from the dialog box. Preview of the roll planar bend will be displayed; refer to Figure-72. If you want to make changes then select desired option from the dialog box and click on the **Define** button otherwise, click on the **OK** button to create the bend.

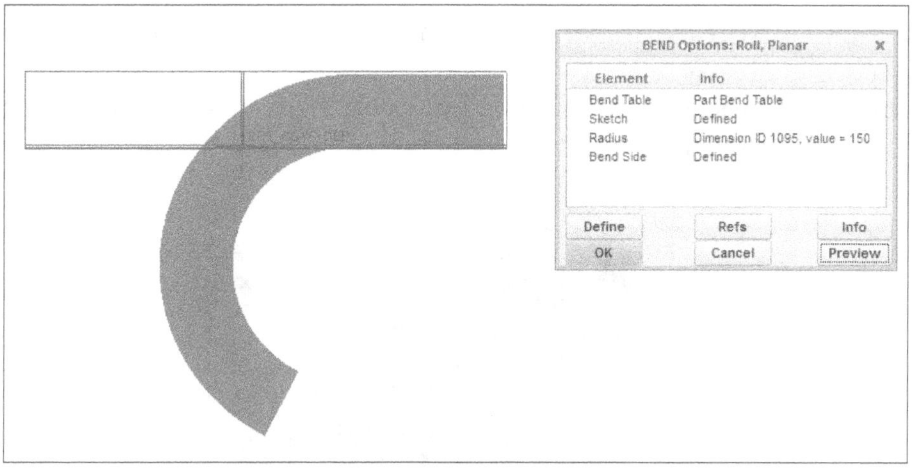

Figure-72. Preview of planar roll bend

UNBEND

The **Unbend** tools are used to perform the reversal of **Bend** tools. There are three tools to perform unbend operation. The most commonly used of the three is **Unbend** tool which is discussed next.

Unbend tool

- Click on the **Unbend** tool from the **Unbend** drop-down in the **Bends** panel of the **Ribbon**; refer to Figure-73. The **Unbend** contextual tab will be displayed with the preview of unbending in modeling area; refer to Figure-74.

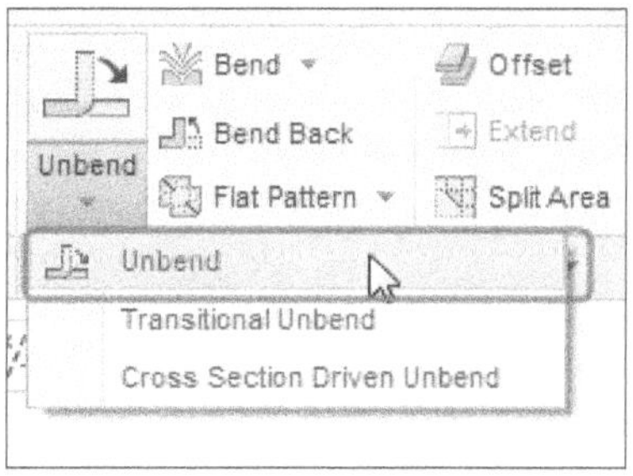

Figure-73. Unbend drop-down

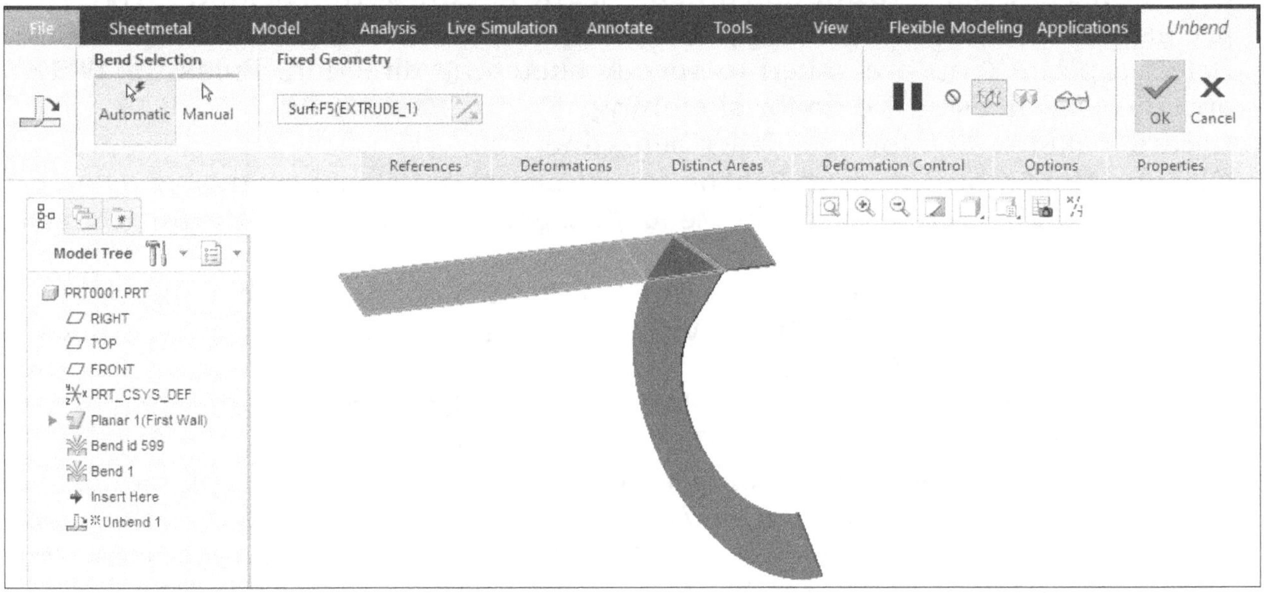

Figure-74. Unbend contextual tab with unbending preview

- Click on the **OK** button from the contextual tab to perform unbending.

Most of the time the Unbending process is simple but what to do if we have a closed sheetmetal part as shown in Figure-75.

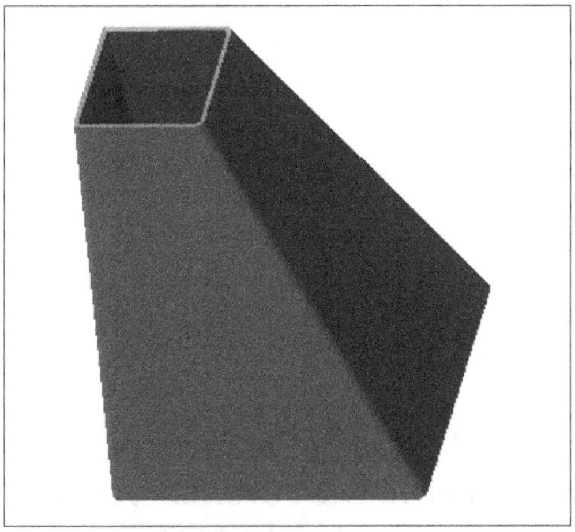

Figure-75. Closed sheetmetal part

In such cases, we can use the **Deformation** options in the **Unbend** contextual tab. The steps are given next.

- After selecting the **Unbend** tool, click on the **Deformations** tab; refer to Figure-76.

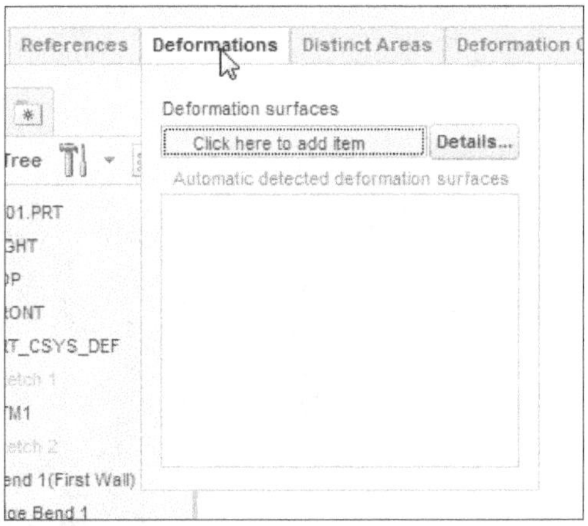

Figure-76. Deformations tab

- Click in the **Deformation Surfaces** collector in the tab and select a face on which you want to apply the deformations so that our part can unbend; refer to Figure-77. Preview of deformation will be displayed; refer to Figure-78.

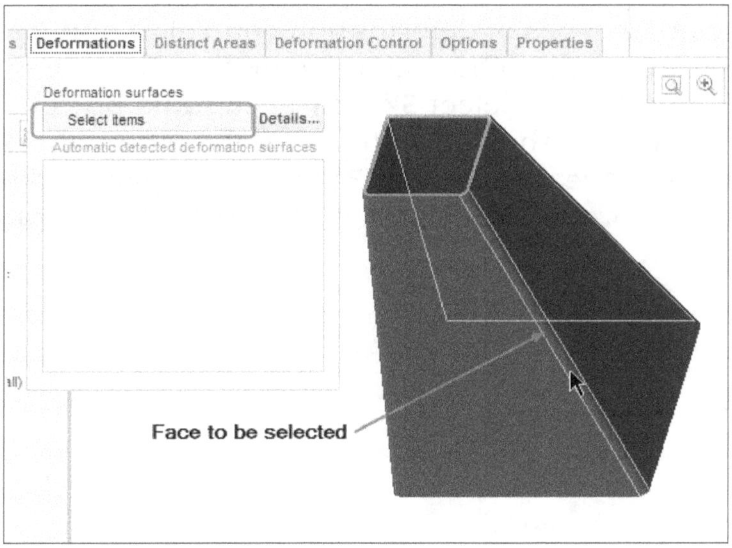

Figure-77. Deformation surfaces collector

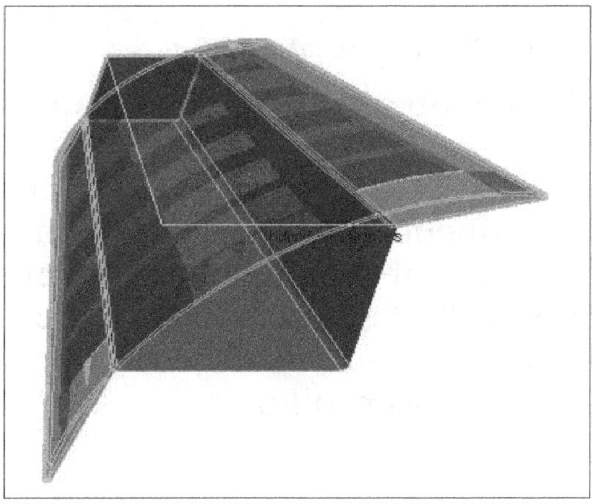

Figure-78. Preview of deformation

- But still, we can not unbend the part. So, click on the **Deformation Control** tab and select the **Rip area** radio button. Preview of unbent sheet will be displayed; refer to Figure-79.

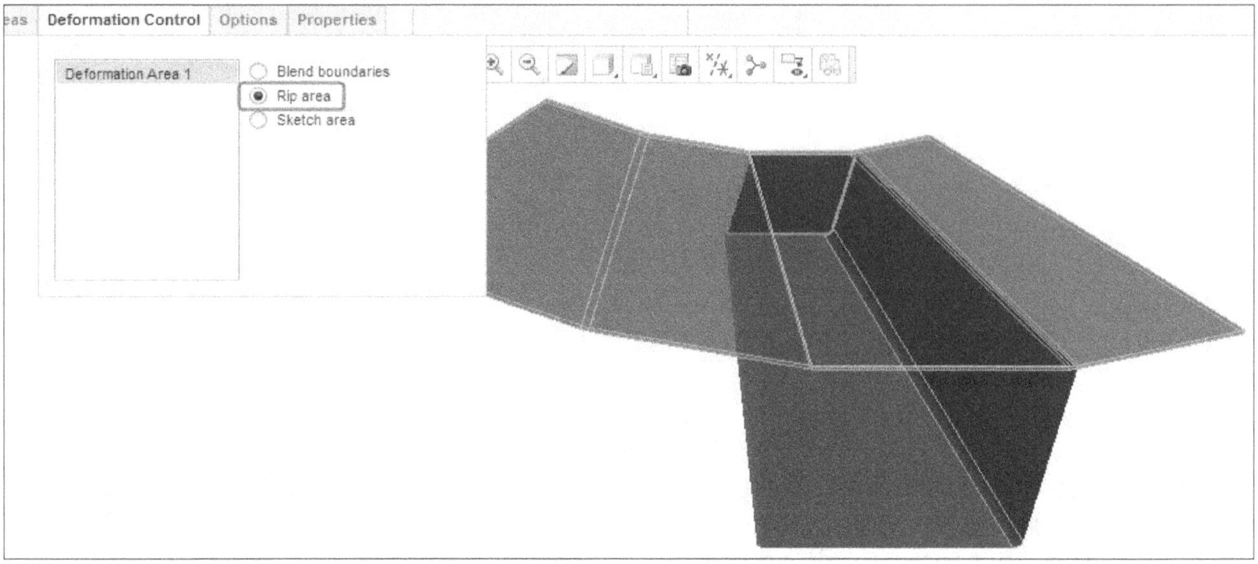

Figure-79. Preview of unbent sheet

- You can also use other types of deformation control to apply to the selected area. Select **Blend boundaries** radio button to create the shape of the deformation area by blending the boundaries. Select **Sketch area** radio button to define the shape of the deformation area in the flat state using Sketcher window.
- Click on the **Distinct Areas** tab in the **Ribbon** to display and set a fixed geometry reference for one or more distinct areas in the part. The options will be displayed; refer to Figure-80.

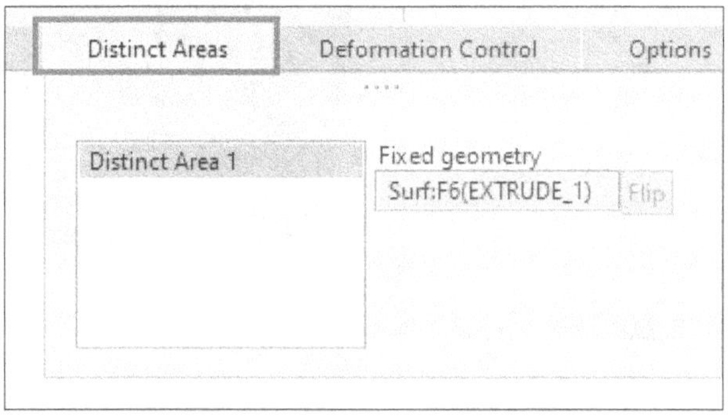

Figure-80. Distinct Areas tab of Unbend tool

- The **Distinct Area** list in the tab displays all automatically detected distinct area references.
- The **Fixed geometry** selection button displays the surface or edge reference that remains fixed during the unbend operation. Click on the **Flip** button to flip the side of the non-tangent edge that remains fixed during the unbend operation.
- Click on the **Options** tab in the **Ribbon** to create the relief geometry during the Unbend operation and to define if side surfaces in the same location are removed. The options will be displayed; refer to Figure-81.

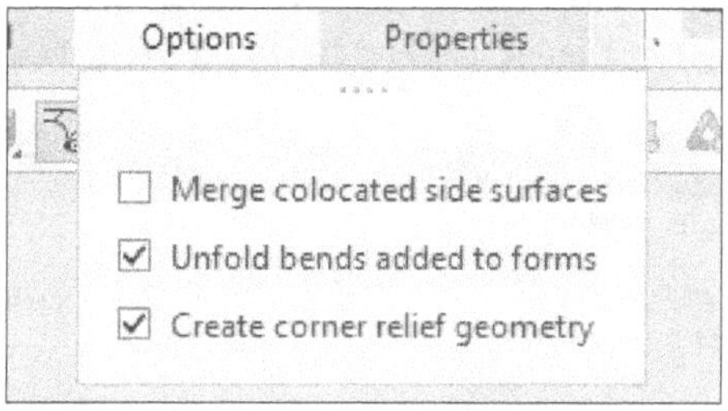

Figure-81. Options tab of Unbend tool

- Select the **Merge colocated side surfaces** check box to remove side surfaces that have common location.
- Select the **Unfold bends added to forms** check box to unbend the geometry that was added to a form and is not part of the original form. When forms are also flattened, geometry is first unbent.
- Select the **Create corner relief geometry** check box to create corner relief geometry as set in the **Relief** area of the **Sheetmetal Preferences** dialog box.
- After specifying desired parameters, click on the **OK** button to apply unbending.

BEND BACK

The **Bend Back** tool is used to reverse the operation done by **Unbend** tool but it does not reverse the deformation done in the part during unbending. The procedure is given next.

- Click on the **Bend Back** tool from the **Bends** panel of the **Ribbon**. Preview of the bending back will be displayed with the **Bend Back** contextual tab; refer to Figure-82.

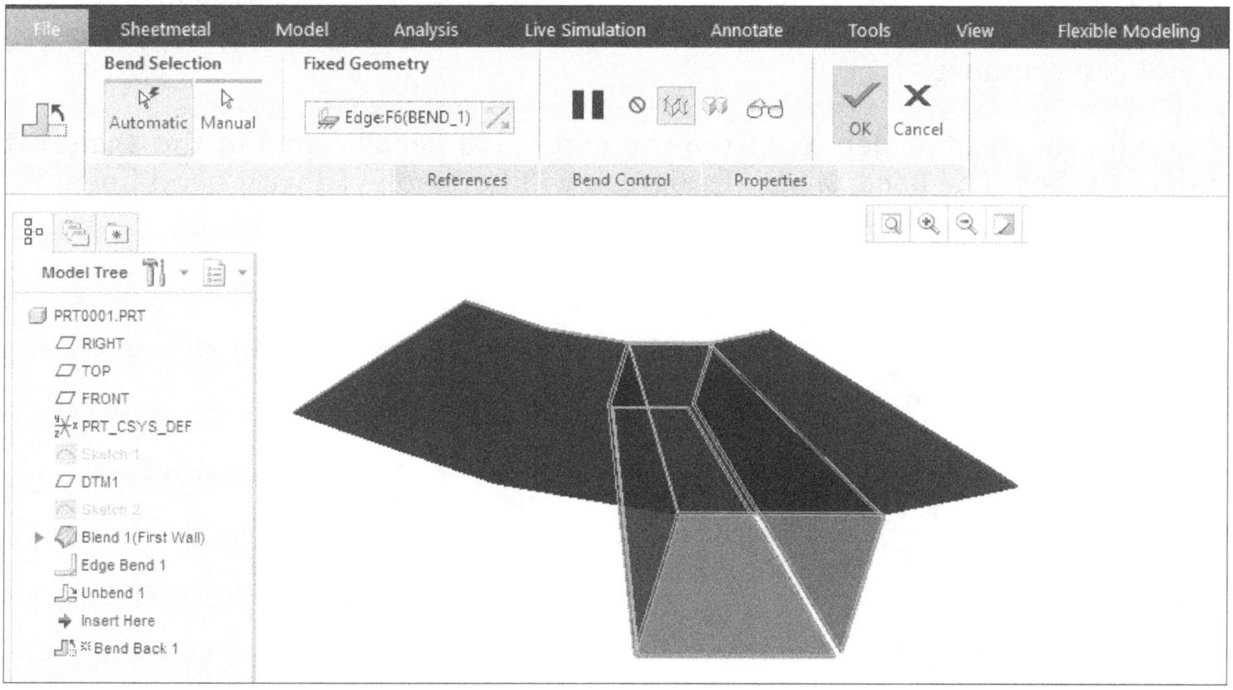

Figure-82. Bend Back contextual tab

- Select desired face to make it reference and click on the **OK** button from the contextual tab to create the feature.

- You can use the **Manual** button from **Bend Selection** area of the contextual tab and select each face to bent back manually; refer to Figure-83.

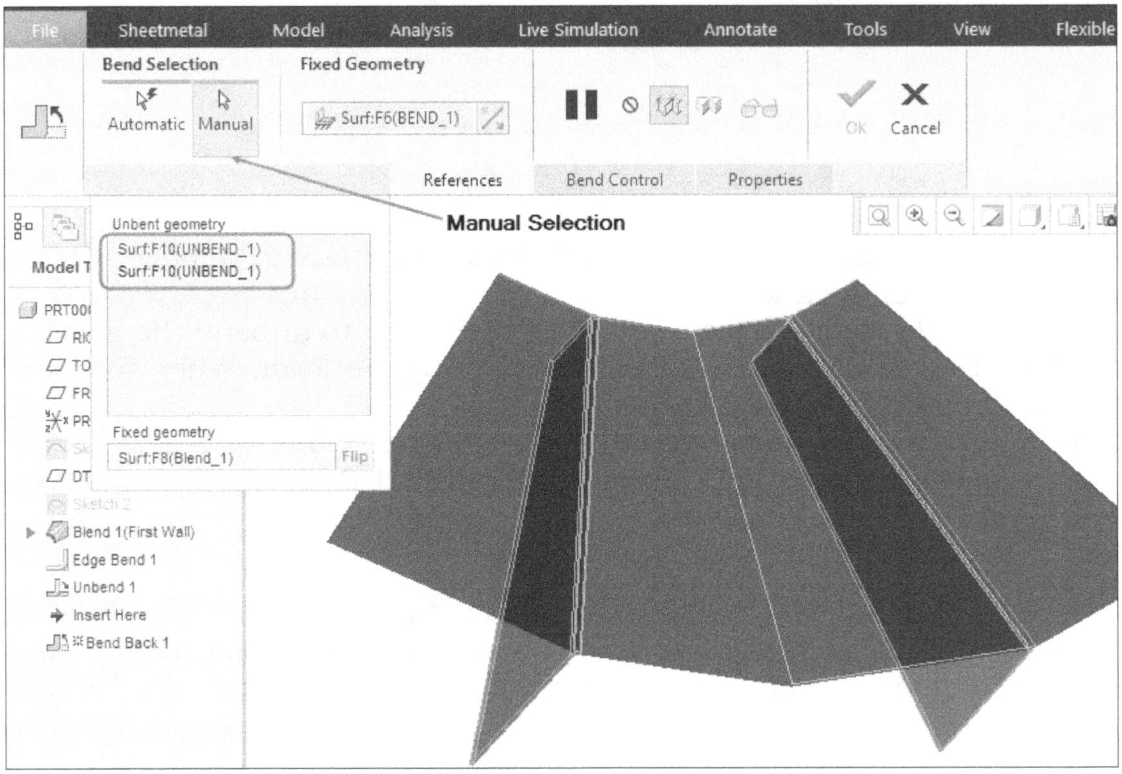

Figure-83. Bend back preview for manual face selection

BEND ORDER

The **Bend Order** tool is available in the expanded **Bends** panel of **Ribbon**. This tool is used to mark the order in which sheet metal need to be bent. The procedure to use this tool is given next.

- Click on the **Bend Order** tool from the expanded **Bends** panel in the **Sheetmetal** tab of **Ribbon**. The **Bend Order** dialog box will be displayed with bend lines in the model; refer to Figure-84.

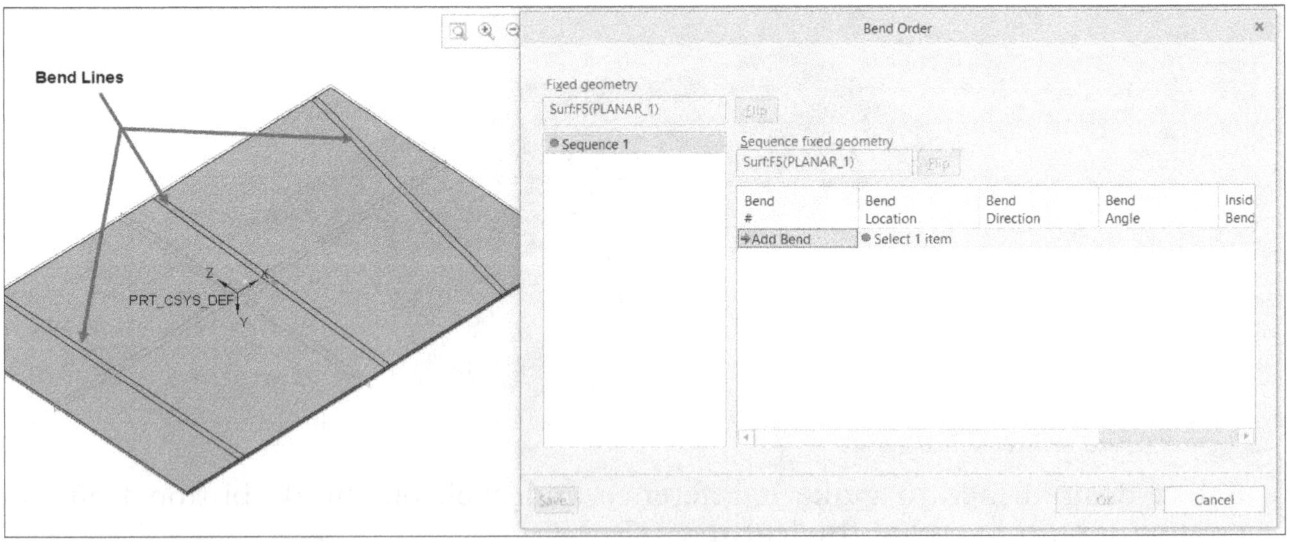

Figure-84. Bend Order dialog box

- Select the bend lines from the model in order by which you want to number bends in the flat pattern; refer to Figure-85.

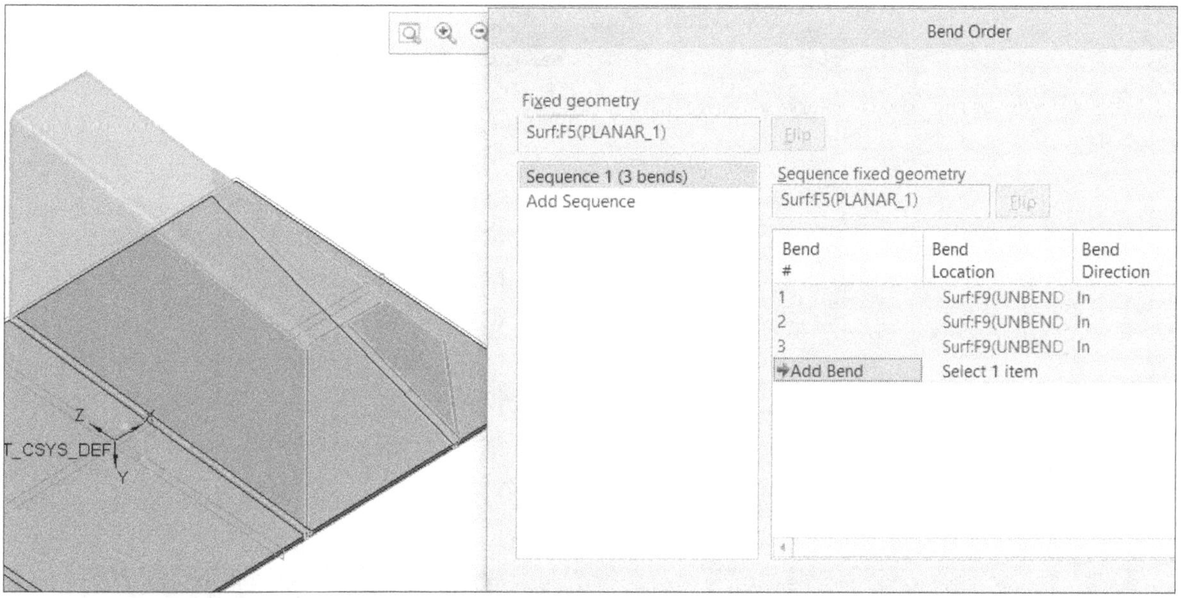

Figure-85. Selecting bend lines

- Click on the **OK** button from the dialog box to apply the changes.

SOLID TO SHEETMETAL CONVERSION

Although there is so much flexibility in working with Sheetmetal environment to create sheetmetal part but still there are some situations where we need to create the part in Part Modeling environment. We can bring the part from Part Modeling to Sheetmetal environment and convert it to sheetmetal part by using the **Convert to Sheet Metal** tool in Part Modeling environment and **Conversion** tool in Sheetmetal environment.

The procedure and workflow of converting a solid part into a sheetmetal part is given next.

- Open or create the solid model of part; refer to Figure-86.

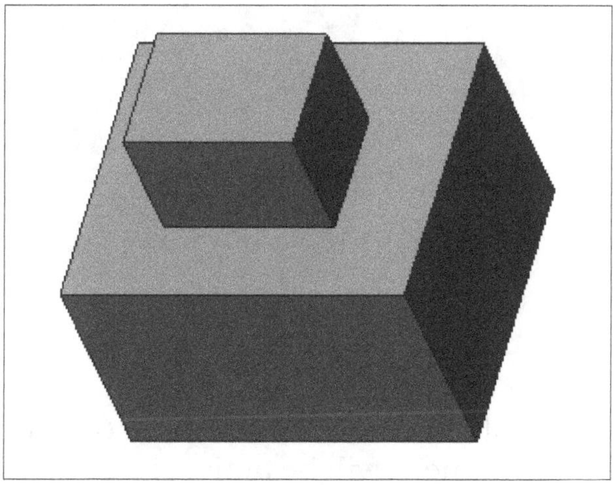

Figure-86. Solid model of part

- Expand the **Operations** panel in the **Model** tab of Part environment and click on the **Convert to Sheet Metal** tool; refer to Figure-87. The **Convert** contextual tab will be displayed; refer to Figure-88.

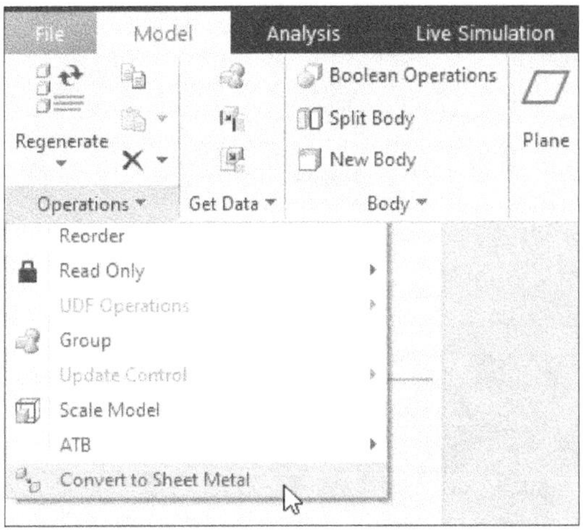

Figure-87. Convert to Sheet Metal tool

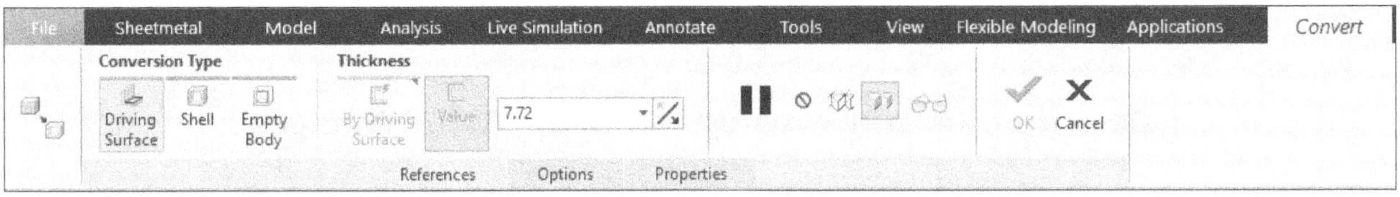

Figure-88. Convert contextual tab

- Select the **Shell** option from the **Conversion Type** area in the **Convert** contextual tab; refer to Figure-89.

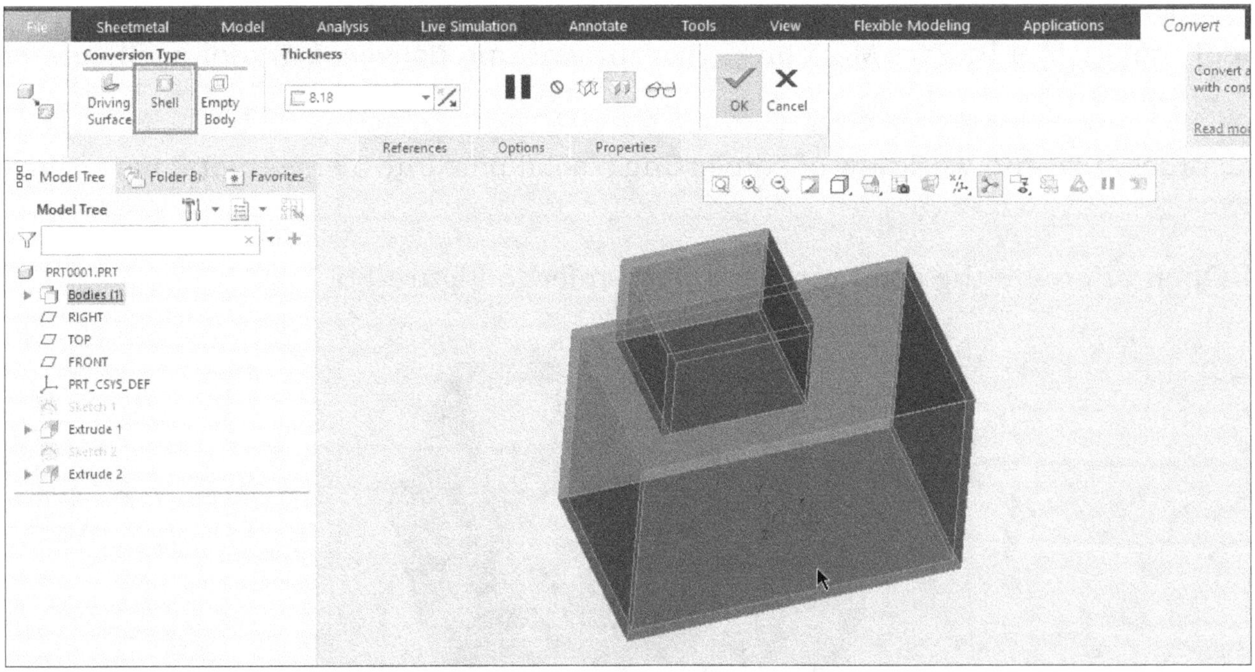

Figure-89. Conversion method selection

- Specify desired thickness of sheet and click on the **OK** button from the contextual tab. The Sheet Metal environment will be active; refer to Figure-90. (We have done half-way but remember the ultimate goal is Flat Pattern)

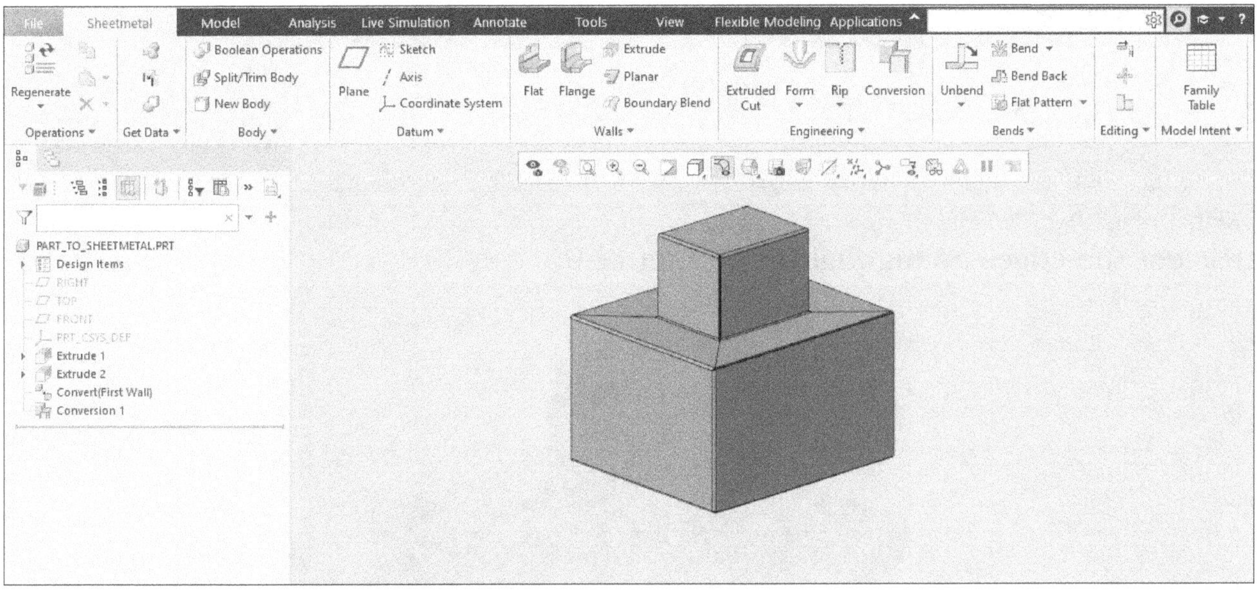

Figure-90. Part to Sheetmetal environment

- Click on the **Conversion** tool from the **Engineering** panel of the **Ribbon**. The **Conversion** contextual tab will be displayed; refer to Figure-91. (There are four tools in the tab to cut down the edges and faces so that we can unwrap the model for flat pattern.)

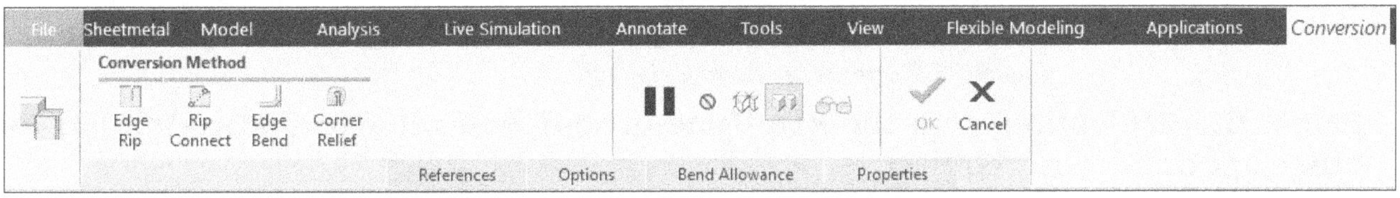

Figure-91. Conversion contextual tab

- Click on the **Options** tab in the contextual tab and make sure the **Inside** option for radius is selected in the drop-down; refer to Figure-92. If **Outside** option is selected then bends as shown in Figure-93 will not be created during conversion.

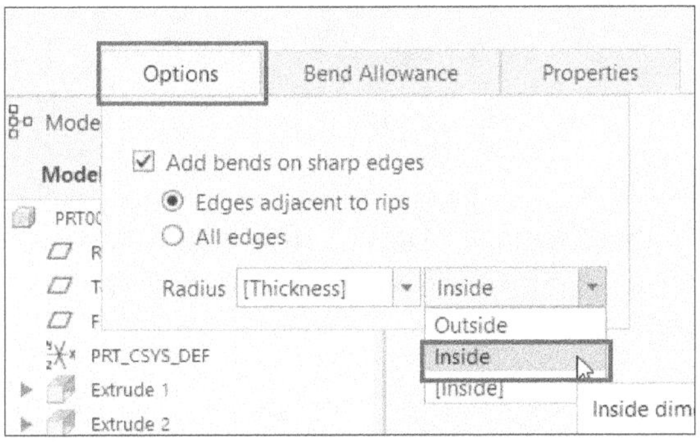

Figure-92. Inside option for bend

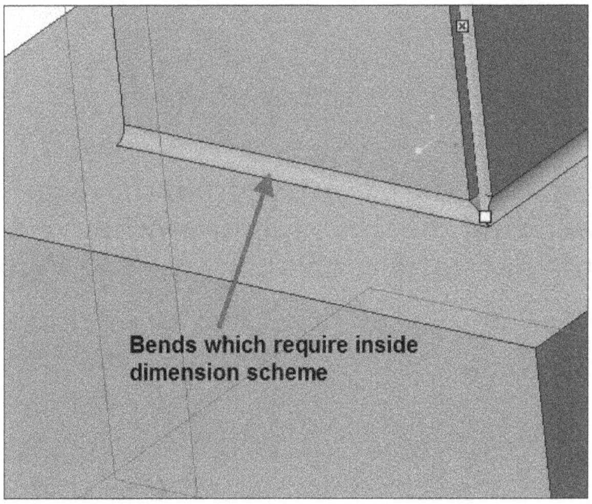

Figure-93. Bends that require inside dimensioning

- Click on the **Edge Rip** button from **Conversion Method** area of the contextual tab. The **Edge Rip** contextual tab will be displayed; refer to Figure-94.

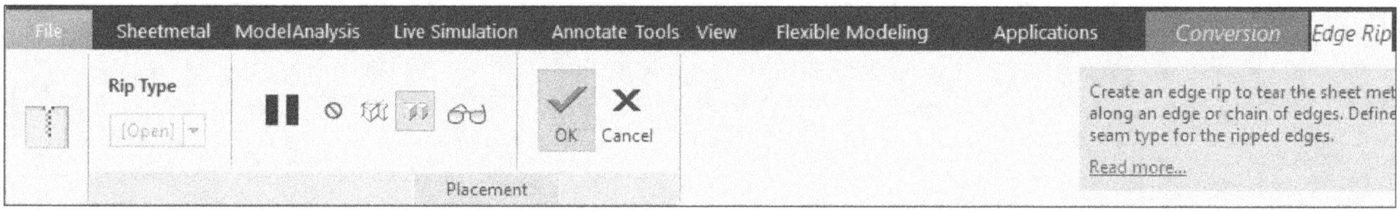

Figure-94. Edge Rip contextual tab

- Select the edges as highlighted in Figure-95.

Figure-95. Edges selected for edge ripping

- Select the **Gap** option from the **Rip Type** drop-down; refer to Figure-96. (Or any other option as you require).

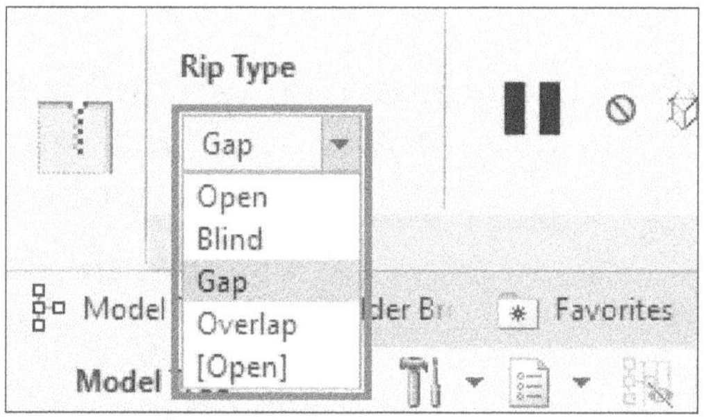

Figure-96. Rip Type drop-down

- Click on the **OK** button from the **Edge Rip** contextual tab. The edges will be ripped allowing the unwrapping of walls; refer to Figure-97. (Now, we got a face stopping the flat pattern creation; refer to Figure-98.)

Figure-97. Ripped edges

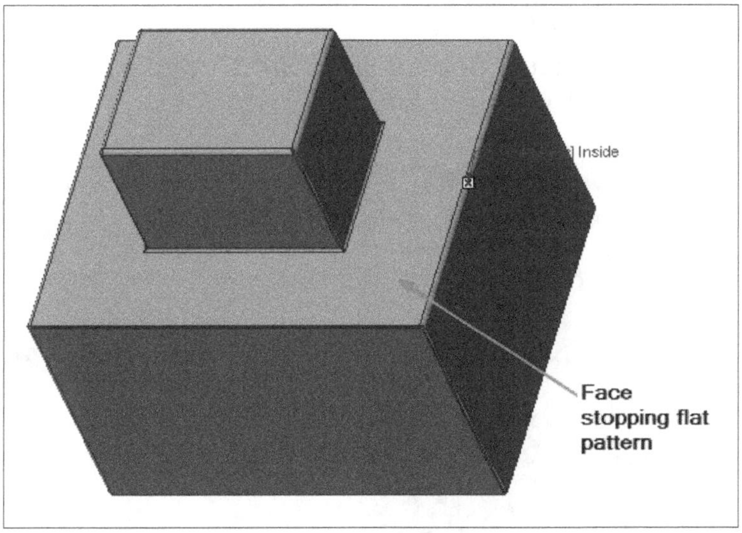

Figure-98. Face causing problem

- Click on the **Rip Connect** button from **Conversion Method** area of the **Conversion** contextual tab (displayed again). The **Rip Connect** contextual tab will be displayed with preview of edge rip; refer to Figure-99.

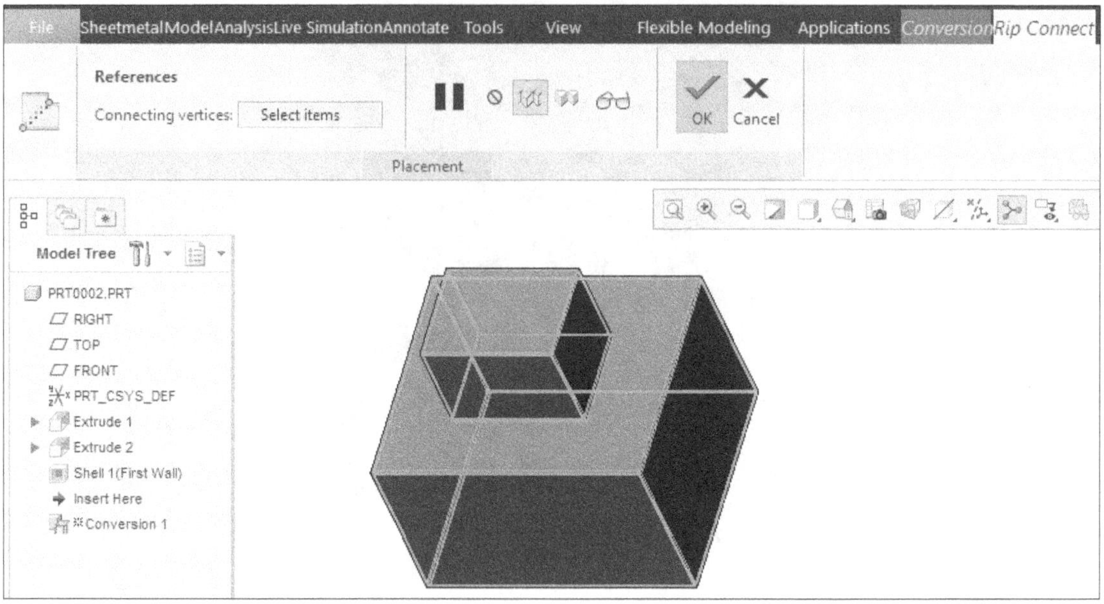

Figure-99. Rip Connect contextual tab

- Select two consecutive vertex points of ripped edges as shown in Figure-100. Preview of rip connect will be displayed; refer to Figure-101.

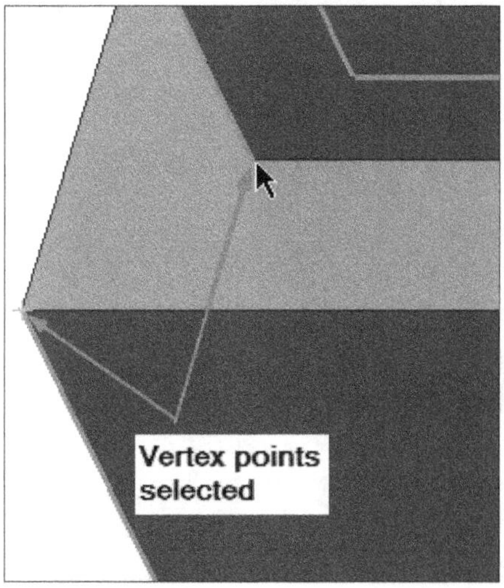

Figure-100. Vertex selected

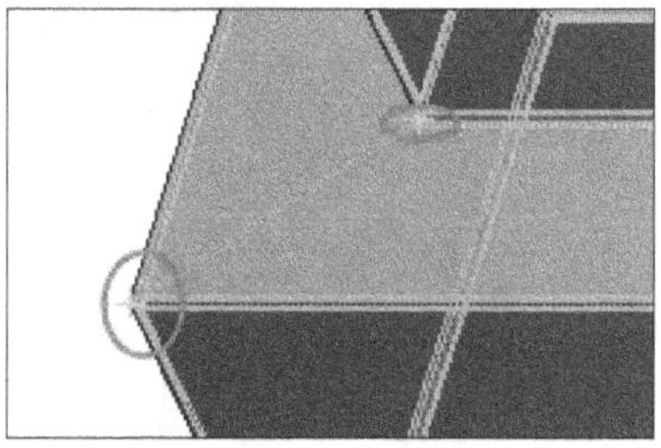

Figure-101. Preview of rip connect

- Click on the **Placement** tab from the contextual tab and click on the **New Set** option; refer to Figure-102.

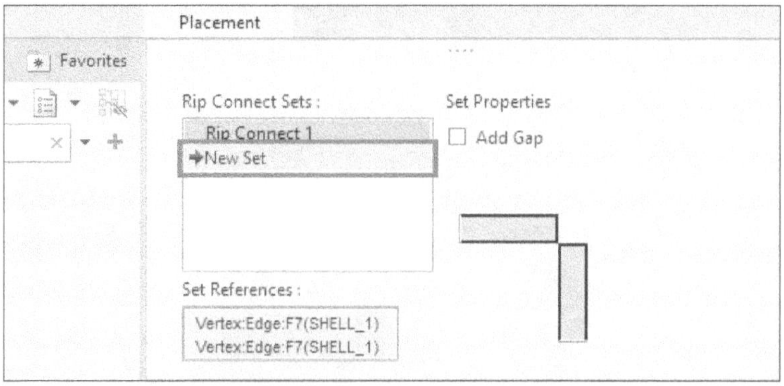

Figure-102. New Set option

- Select the other two consecutive vertices; refer to Figure-103.

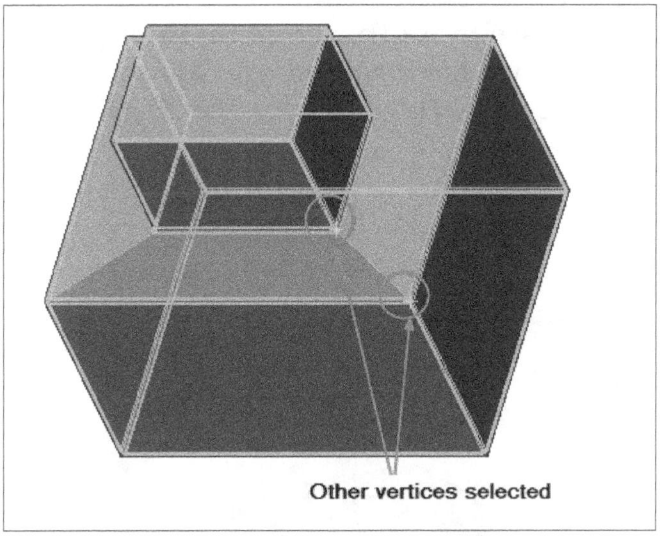

Figure-103. Other vertices selected

- Repeat the procedure for other edge rips. The model will be displayed as shown in Figure-104.

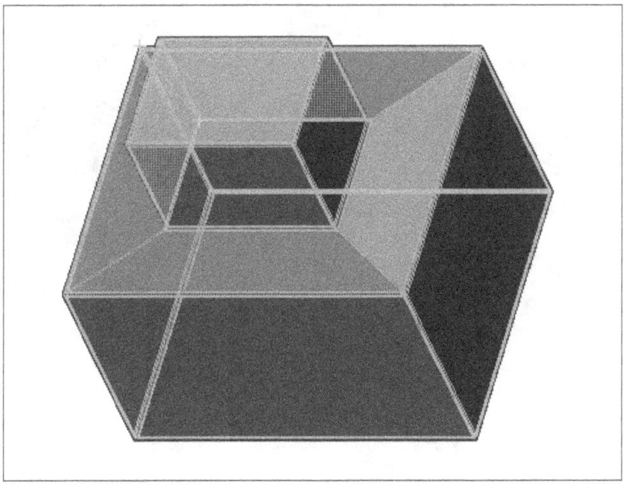

Figure-104. Model after rip connect

- Click on the **OK** button from the **Rip Connect** contextual tab and then from the **Conversion** contextual tab.
- Click on the **Flat Pattern** button from the **Bends** panel in the **Ribbon**. Preview of pattern will be displayed; refer to Figure-105.

Figure-105. Preview of flat pattern

Note that you should always check the number of distinct pieces at the bottom bar; refer to Figure-106. If there are more than one distinct pieces then flat pattern will not be created. For example, we have ripped one more edge of the model discussed recently as shown in Figure-107. Now, if you use the **Flat Pattern** tool, an error message will be displayed.

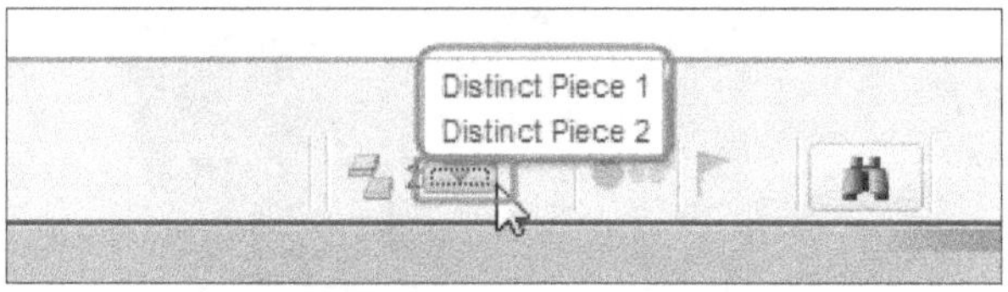

Figure-106. Distinct pieces

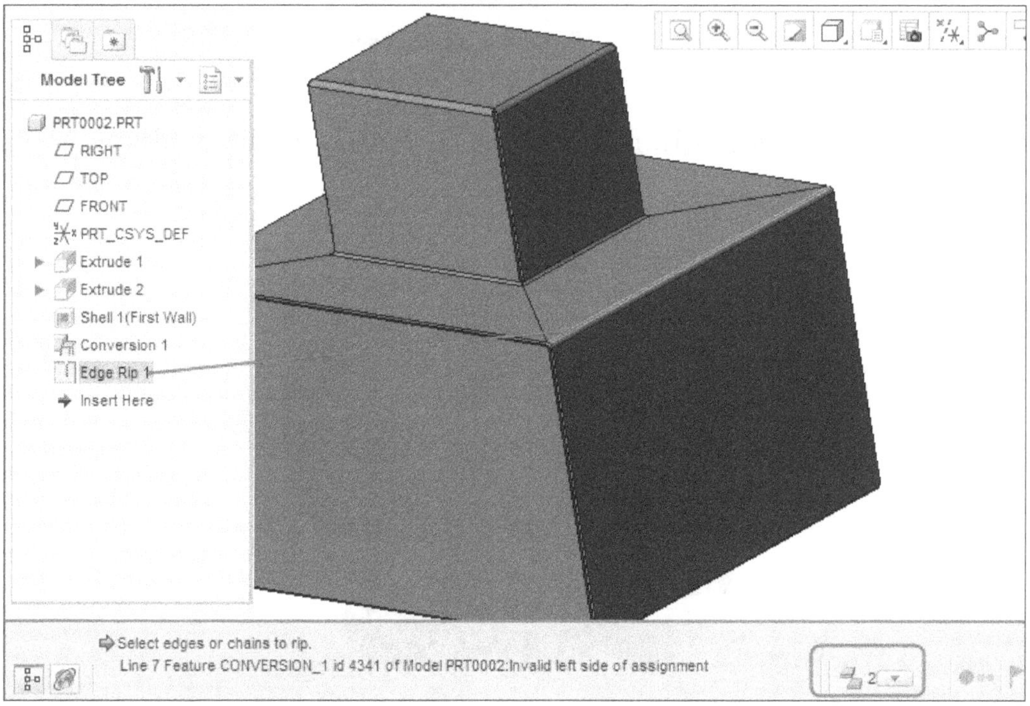

Figure-107. One more edge ripped

RIP TOOLS

Rip tool is used to make a straight cut in the sheet metal. We use rip when we want to divide a sheet metal piece along an edge or line. There are four tool in **Rip** drop-down of **Engineering** panel in the **Ribbon** to perform this operation; refer to Figure-108. You have used the **Edge Rip** and **Rip Connect** tools in previous topics. Now, we will discuss the use of **Surface Rip** and **Sketched Rip** tools.

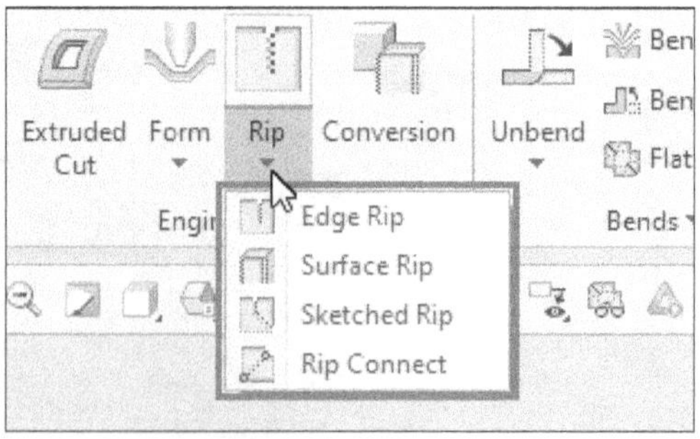

Figure-108. Rip drop-down

Surface Rip

The **Surface Rip** tool is used to rip selected surfaces. The procedure to use this tool is given next.

- Click on the **Surface Rip** tool from the **Rip** drop-down in the **Engineering** panel of the **Ribbon**. The **Surface Rip** contextual tab will be displayed; refer to Figure-109. Also, you will be asked to select the surface to be ripped.

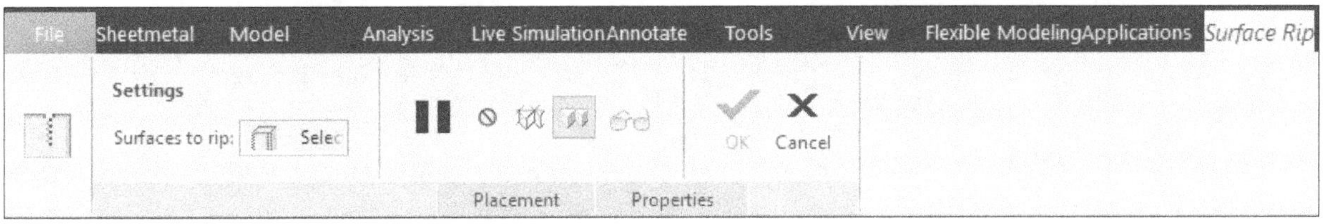

Figure-109. Surface Rip contextual tab

- Select the surfaces of sheetmetal part that you want to be removed. Preview of the surface rip feature will be displayed; refer to Figure-110.

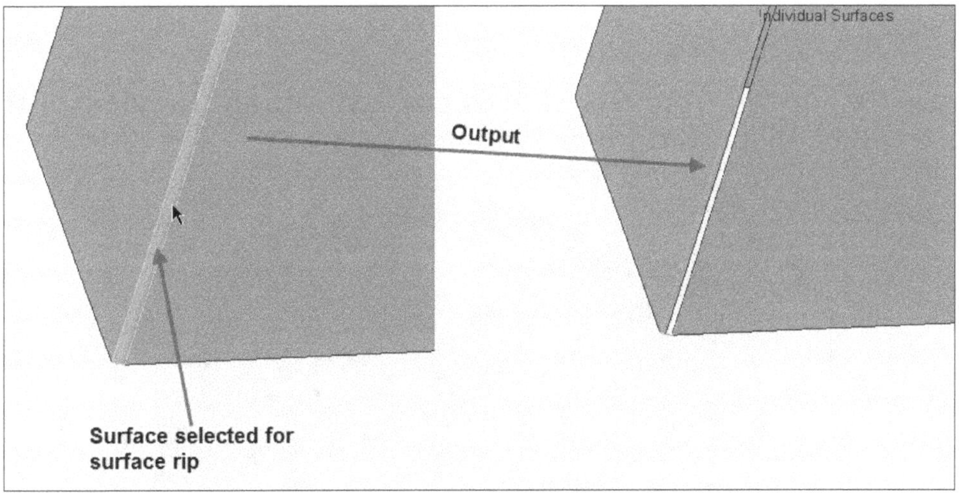

Figure-110. Surface rip

- Click on the **OK** button from the **Ribbon** to create the feature.

Sketched Rip

The **Sketched Rip** tool is used to create rip based on the sketch created. The procedure to use this tool is given next.

- Click on the **Sketched Rip** tool from the **Rip** drop-down in the **Engineering** panel of the **Ribbon**. The **Sketched Rip** contextual tab will be displayed in the **Ribbon**; refer to Figure-111. Also, you will be asked to select a face on which the rip feature is to be created.

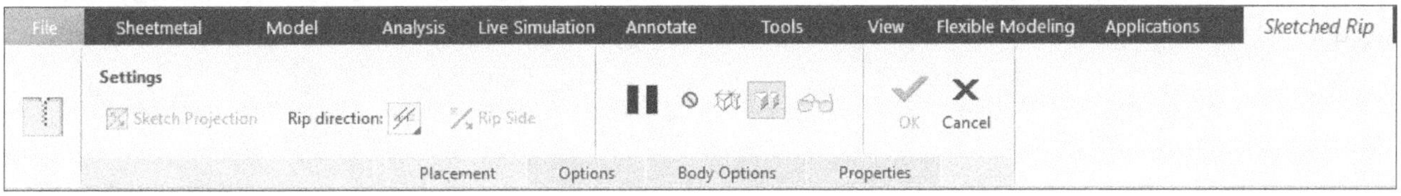

Figure-111. Sketched Rip contextual tab

- Select the face of sheetmetal part on which you want to create the sketched rip feature. The sketching environment will be displayed.
- Create the sketch for rip feature; refer to Figure-112.

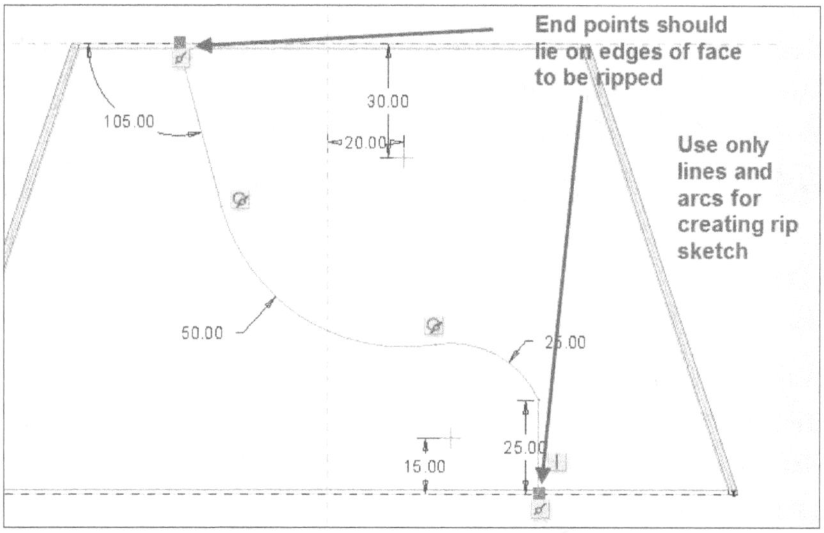

Figure-112. Sketch for sketched rip feature

- Click on the **OK** button from the **Sketch** contextual tab. Preview of the sketched rip feature will be displayed; refer to Figure-113.

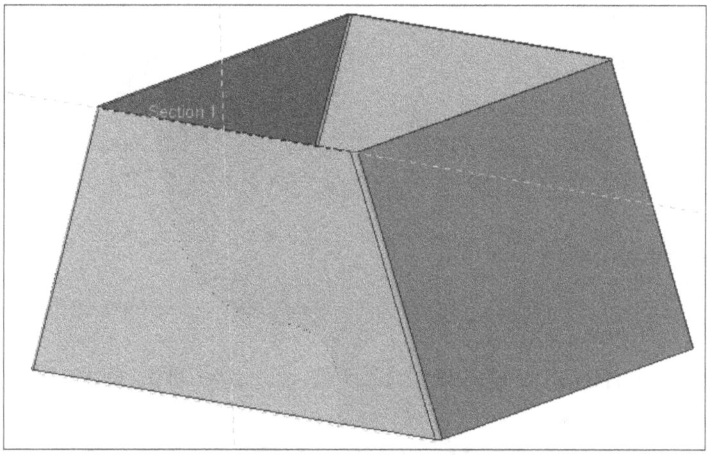

Figure-113. Preview of sketched rip feature

- Set desired rip side using the flip buttons in the **Ribbon**.
- Click on the **OK** button from the **Ribbon** to create the rip feature.

CORNER RELIEF

The **Corner Relief** tool is used to apply relief at the corner formed by three joining edges of sheetmetal part. Note that this tool is applicable for place where corner relief has not been defined earlier like at corner created by two flat walls; refer to Figure-114. The procedure to use this tool is given next.

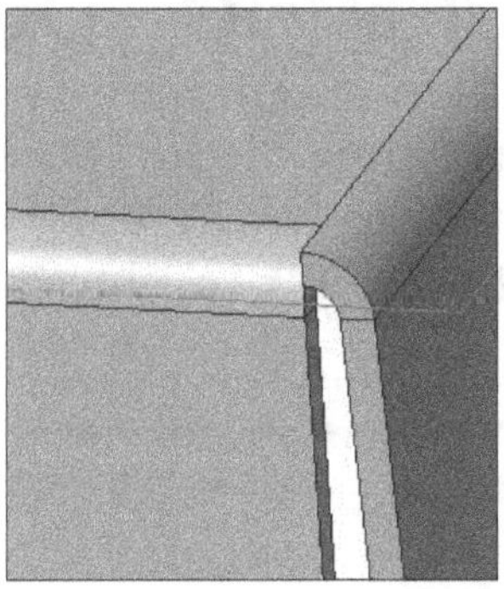

Figure-114. Corner created by flat walls

- Click on the **Corner Relief** tool from the expanded **Engineering** panel in the **Ribbon**. The **Corner Relief** contextual tab will be displayed; refer to Figure-115.

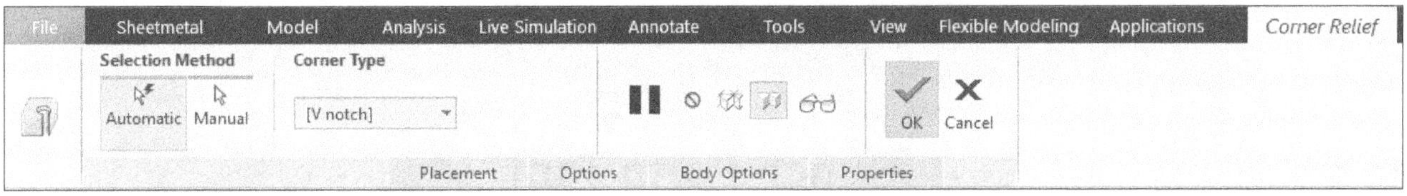

Figure-115. Corner Relief contextual tab

- By default, all the corners of sheet metal part are selected. If you want to specify corner relief for a specific corner then click on the manual selection button from the **Ribbon**.
- After selecting the corners, select desired type of corner relief from the drop-down in the **Corner Type** area of the **Ribbon**.
- Click on the **Placement** tab and set the parameters for the corner relief in the tab; refer to Figure-116.

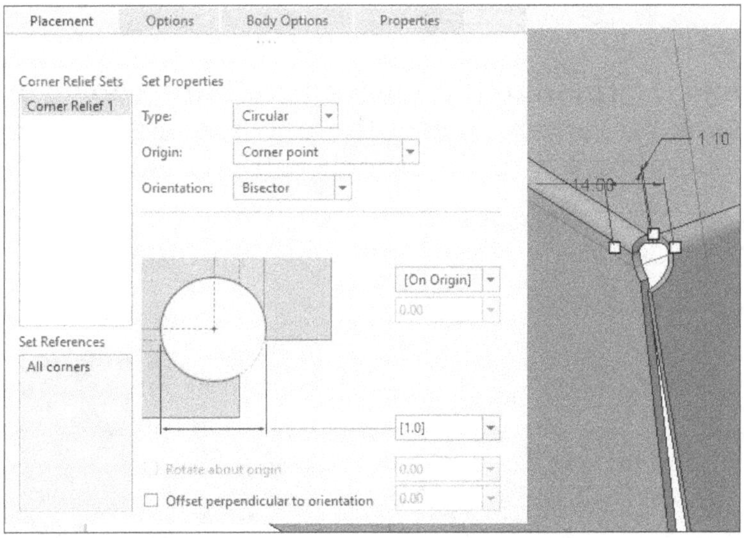

Figure-116. Specifying parameters for corner relief

- The options in the **Placement** tab have been discussed earlier in this chapter.
- Click on the **Options** tab in the **Ribbon** and select **Create relief geometry** check box to create the relief geometry in the feature. Clear the check box, if you want to create the relief only during the unbend and flat pattern operations.
- Click on the **OK** button from the **Ribbon** to create the feature.

FORMING TOOL

Forming is a process of sheetmetal in which a die/punch is applied to the sheetmetal with mechanical force and impression of die/punch is made on the part. All the sheetmetal forming tools are available in the **Form** drop-down of **Engineering** panel in the **Sheetmetal** tab of the **Ribbon**; refer to Figure-117. The procedure to use each forming tool is given next.

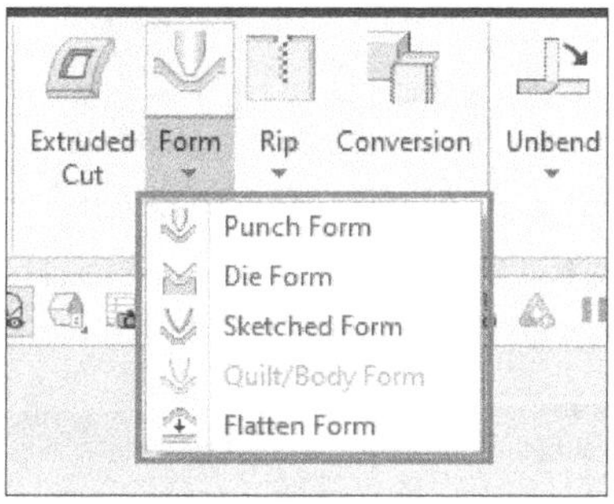

Figure-117. Form drop-down

Punch Form Tool

The **Punch Form** tool is used to form punch mark on sheet metal part. The procedure to use this tool is given next.

- Click on the **Punch Form** tool from the **Form** drop-down in the **Engineering** panel of the **Ribbon**. The **Punch Form** contextual tab will be displayed; refer to Figure-118.

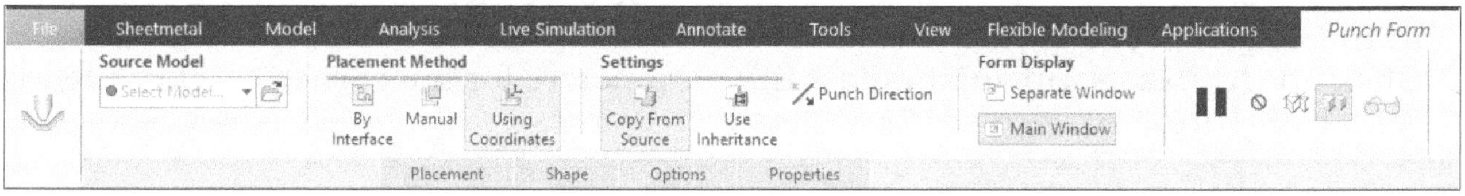

Figure-118. Punch Form contextual tab

- Select desired punch form from the **Source Model** drop-down in the contextual tab or click on the **Open** button and select the part file of punch you want to form on the sheetmetal part. Preview of the punch will be displayed; refer to Figure-119.

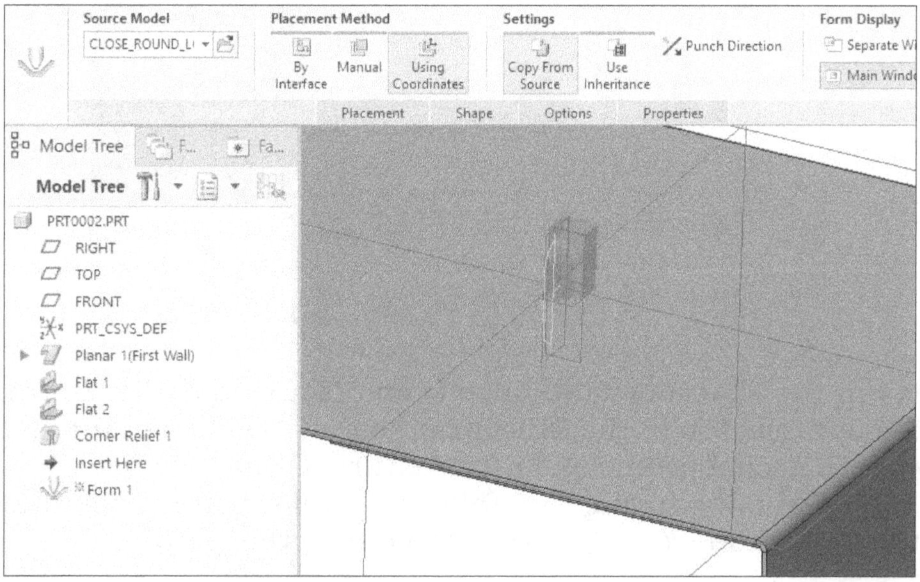

Figure-119. Preview of punch

- If you have selected a punch from the drop-down in the **Ribbon** then select the face of sheet metal part on which you want to apply punch. You will be asked to specify distance references. Drag the green handles to edges of face for defining distance; refer to Figure-120.

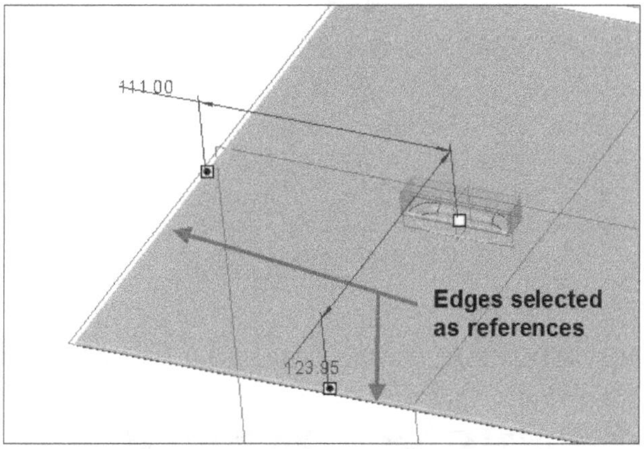

Figure-120. Placing punch

- If you are using a part file as punch using the **Open** button in the **Ribbon** then place the punch at desired location using the assembly constraints; refer to Figure-121.

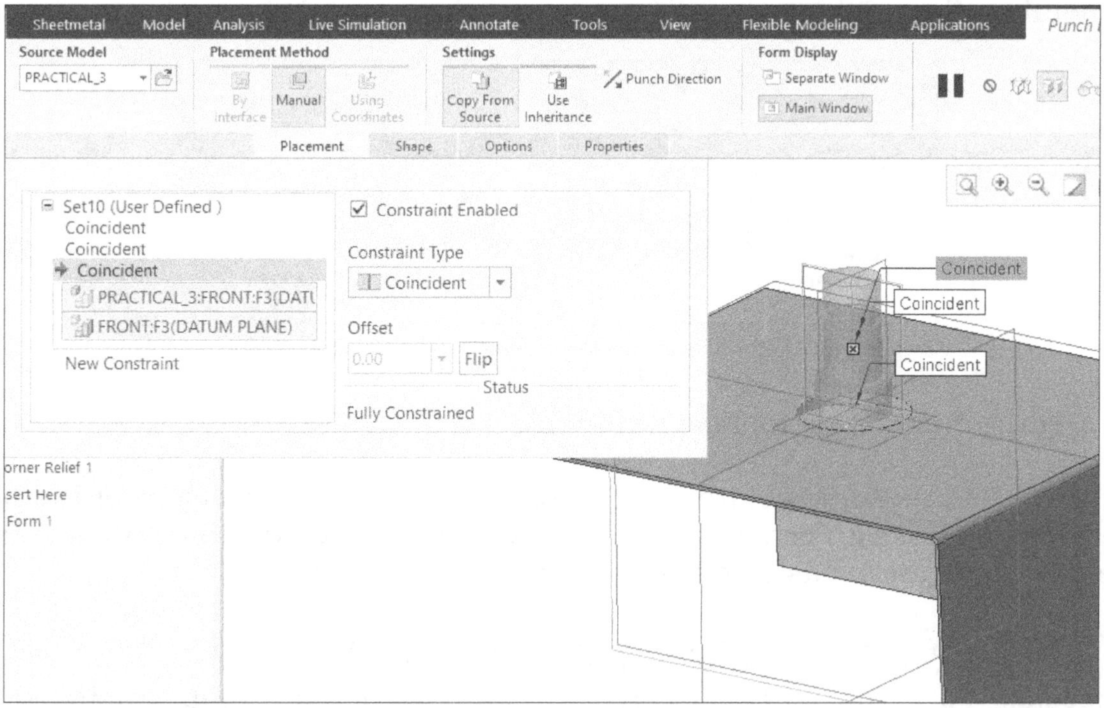

Figure-121. Punch placed using assembly constraints

- If you want to rotate the punch (template punch selected from drop-down in **Ribbon**) then select the **Add rotation about the first axis** check box in the **Placement** tab and specify desired angle of rotation.
- If round is not applied at the punch mark then select the **Placement edges** check box from the **Options** tab and specify desired radius for round (fillet).
- If you want to remove a portion of sheet metal after punching then click in the **Exclude punch model surfaces** selection box and select the respective face; refer to Figure-122.

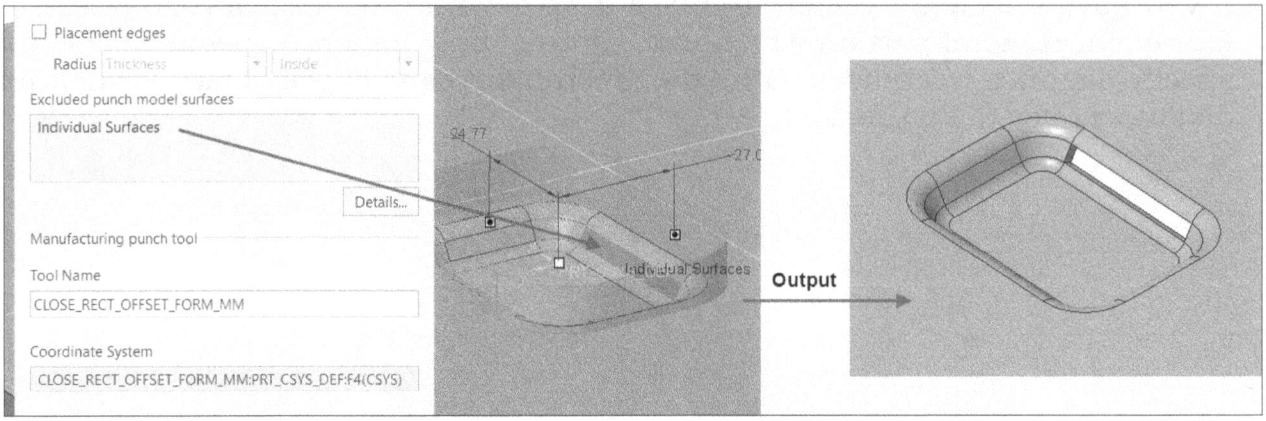

Figure-122. Excluding punch model surface

- Click on the **OK** button from the contextual tab to create the punch mark.

DIE FORM TOOL

Die creates an opposite impression of punch. In practical, when we apply force on punch then punch presses sheet metal and creates an indent. Opposite to it, in die forming- sheet metal is placed on die and a flat hammer strikes on sheet metal to push sheet metal in die which creates die indent on sheet metal part; refer to Figure-123.

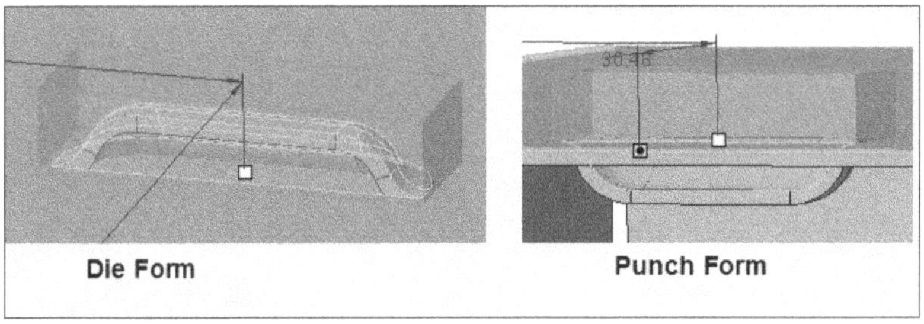

Figure-123. Die forming and punch forming

The procedure to use this tool is given next.

- Click on the **Die Form** tool from the **Form** drop-down in the **Engineering** panel of the **Ribbon**. The **Die Form** contextual tab will be displayed. Now, the procedure to use this tool is same as discussed for **Punch Form** tool.

Sketched Form Tool

The **Sketched Form** tool is used to create a die or punch form mark using sketched shape. The procedure to use this tool is given next.

- Click on the **Sketched Form** tool from the **Form** drop-down in the **Engineering** panel of the **Sheetmetal** tab in the **Ribbon**. The **Sketched Form** contextual tab will be displayed; refer to Figure-124. Also, you will be asked to select a face to create form tool sketch.

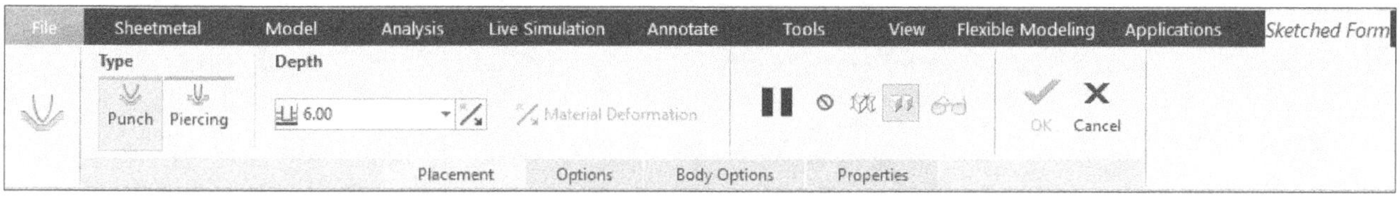

Figure-124. Sketched Form contextual tab

- Select the face on which you want to apply the form tool. The Sketching environment will be displayed.
- Create a closed loop sketch to define shape of form tool; refer to Figure-125.

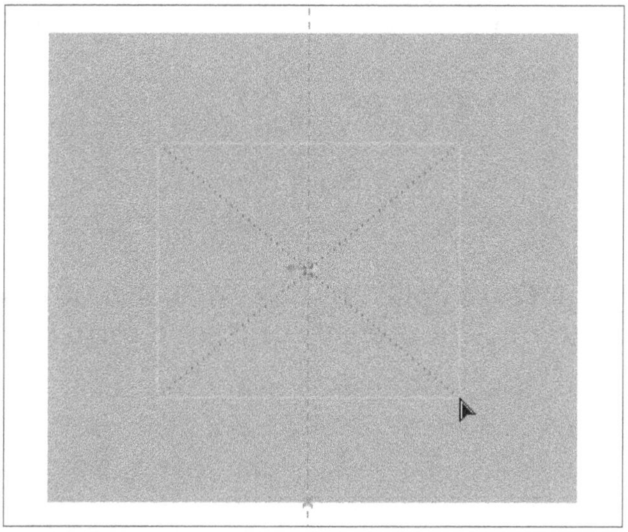

Figure-125. Sketch created for form tool

- After creating sketch, click on the **OK** button from the **Sketch** contextual tab. Preview of sketched forming will be displayed; refer to Figure-126.

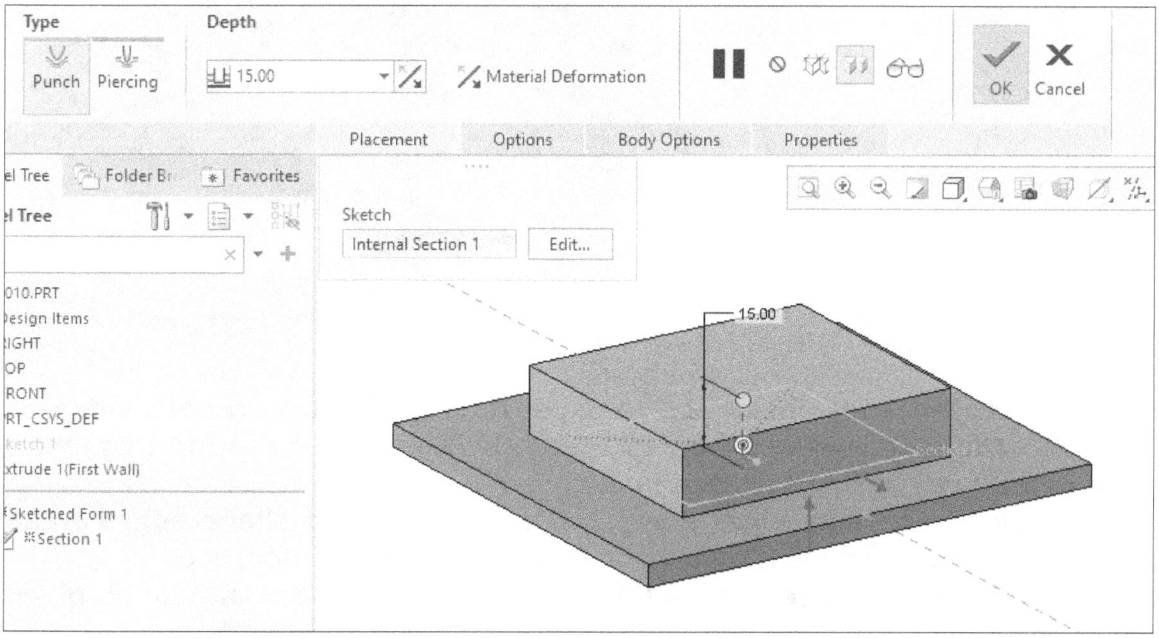

Figure-126. Preview of sketched forming

- Click on the **Options** tab in the **Ribbon**. The options will be displayed; refer to Figure-127.

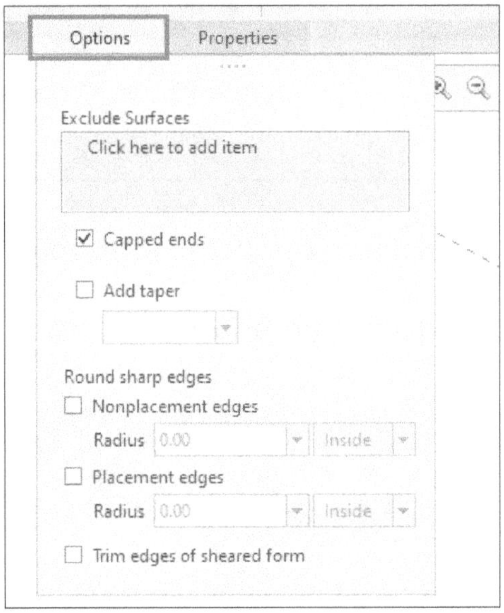

Figure-127. Options tab of Sketched Form tool

- Click on the **Exclude Surfaces** collector box and collect the surfaces to be excluded during the form operation. The preview of punch form will be displayed; refer to Figure-128.

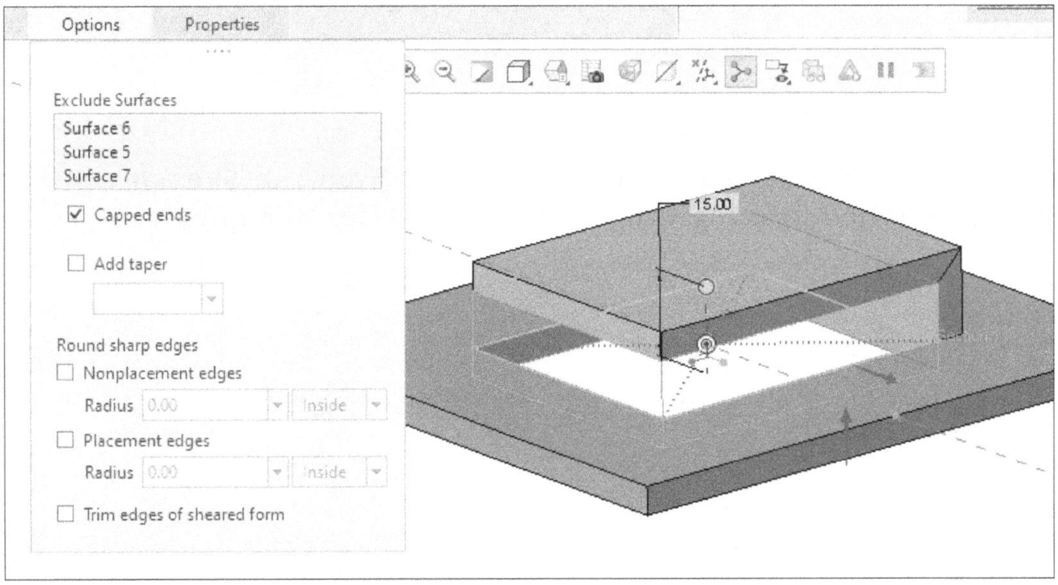

Figure-128. Preview of punch after excluding surfaces

- Select the **Capped ends** check box to caps the form feature in both sides.
- Select the **Add taper** check box to taper the sides of the punch by specifying desired value in the edit box displayed.
- Select the **Nonplacement edges** check box from the **Round sharp edges** area of the tab to round sharp edges that do not lie on placement reference.
- Select the **Placement edges** check box to round sharp edges that lie on placement reference.
- Select the **Trim edges of sheared form** check box to finish the formed part along its new open boundary by removing excess material from its sloping side surfaces in order to align them with the original boundary edges.
- Specify desired depth value of the punch or piercing in the edit box of the **Depth** area in the **Ribbon**.

- Click on the button in the **Depth** area to flip the direction of the punch or piercing.
- Click on the **Material Deformation** button in the **Ribbon** to flip the material thickness direction of a punch.
- After specifying desired parameters, click on the **OK** button to create the feature.

Quilt/Body Form Tool

The **Quilt/Body Form** tool is active in the **Form** drop-down when a quilt/surface is available in the modeling area; refer to Figure-129 (You will learn about creating surfaces later in this book).

The procedure to use this tool is given next.

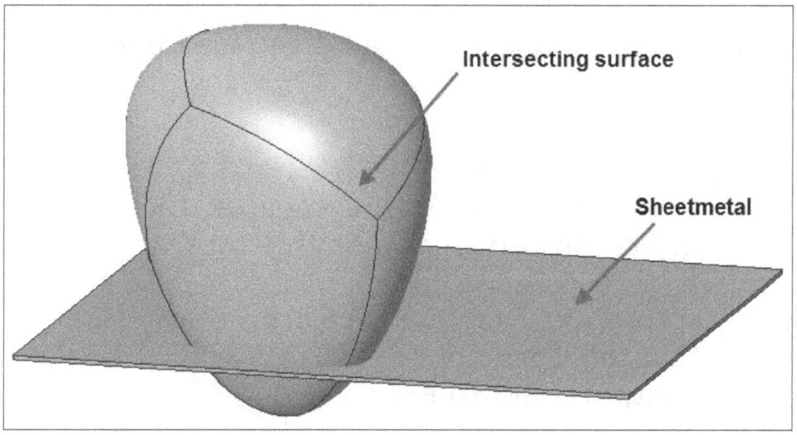

Figure-129. Surface for forming

- Click on the **Quilt/Body Form** tool from the **Form** drop-down in the **Engineering** panel of the **Ribbon**. The **Quilt/Body Form** contextual tab will be displayed; refer to Figure-130.

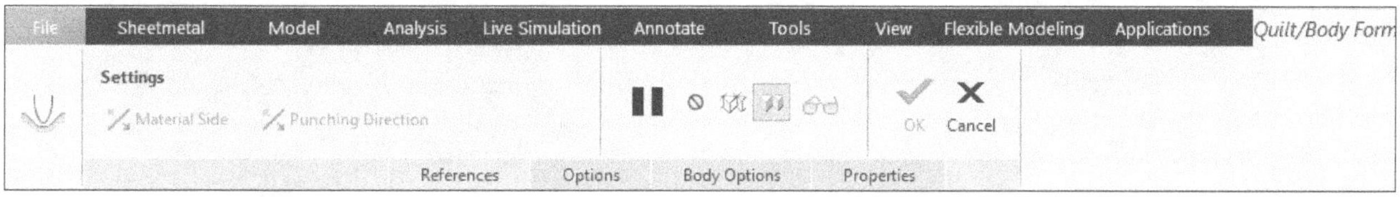

Figure-130. Quilt Body Form contextual tab

- Select the surface/quilt to specify the forming tool and set the direction of forming using the arrows in modeling area; refer to Figure-131.

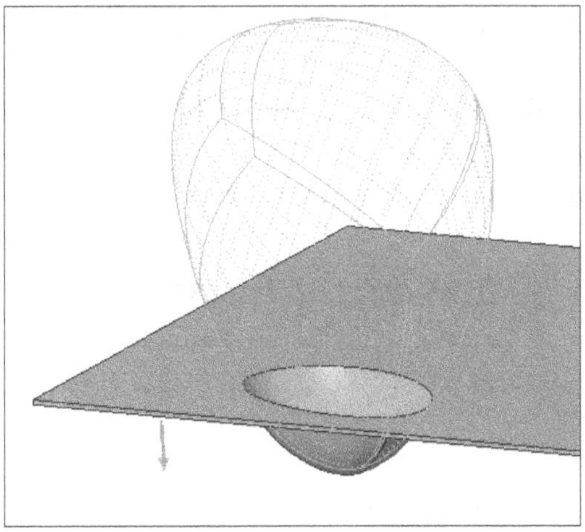

Figure-131. Sheetmetal forming using Quilt Form tool

- Set desired options in the **Options** tab as discussed earlier and click on the **OK** button.

Flatten Form Tool

The **Flatten Form** tool is used to flatten the sheet at the locations where forming tools have been applied. The procedure to use this tool is given next.

- Click on the **Flatten Form** tool from the **Form** drop-down in the **Engineering** panel of the **Ribbon**. The **Flatten Form** contextual tab will be displayed and preview of flattening will be displayed; refer to Figure-132.

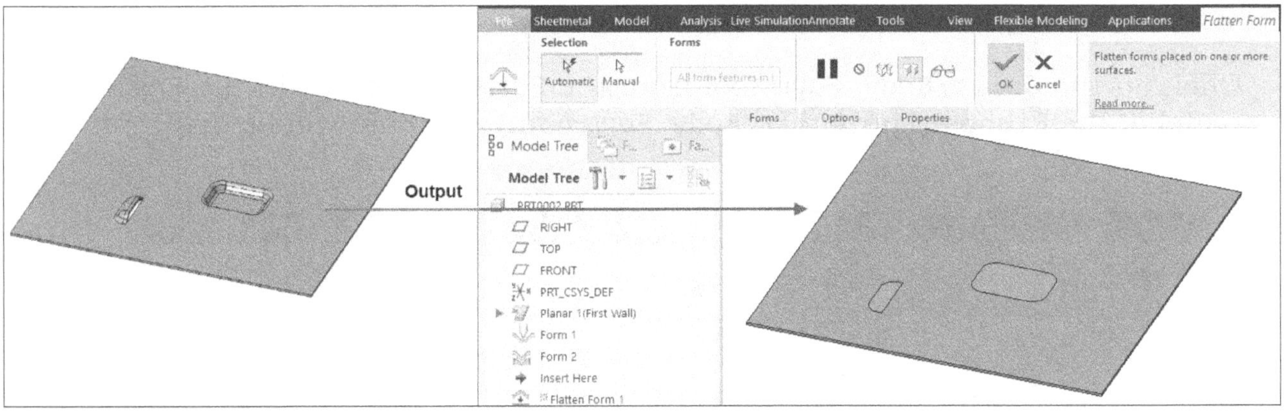

Figure-132. Flatten Form contextual tab with preview

- By default, all the form marks are flattened by this tool but if you want to flatten a specific form mark then click on the **Manual** button from **Selection** area of the contextual tab in the **Ribbon**. You will be asked to select the form marks to be flattened.
- Select the form marks, preview of flattening will be displayed. If you also want to display projected cuts/holes in flattened sheetmetal then select the **Project cuts and holes** check box from the **Options** tab in the **Flatten Form** contextual tab in the **Ribbon**.
- Click on the **OK** button from the **Ribbon** to create the feature.

EXTRUDED CUT

The **Extruded Cut** tool is used to create sheet metal cuts that remove solid material from the sheet metal wall, normal to the driven or to the offset surface, or normal to both sufaces. It is also used to create solid cuts that remove solid material from the sheet metal wall, normal to the sketch plane. The procedure to use this tool is discussed next.

- Click on the **Extruded Cut** tool from **Engineering** panel in the **Sheetmetal** tab of the **Ribbon**. The **Extruded Cut** contextual tab will be displayed; refer to Figure-133, and you are asked to select an existing sketch or select a plane or a surface as a sketching plane to create the sketch.

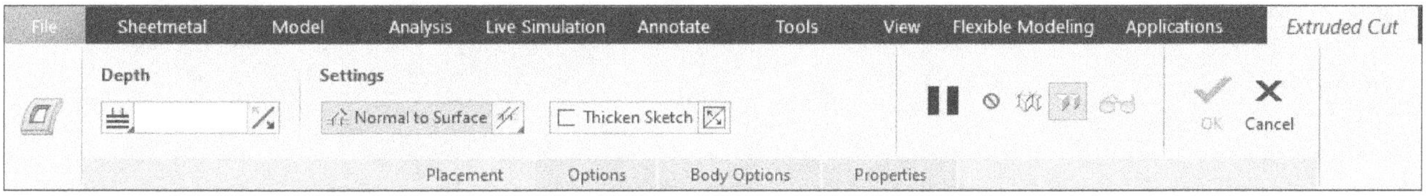

Figure-133. Extruded Cut contextual tab

- Select desired face of the plane as a sketching plane and create the sketch; refer to Figure-134.

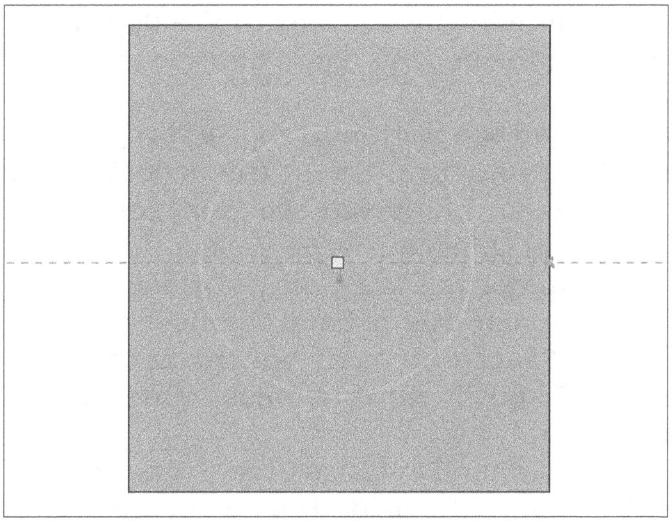

Figure-134. Sketch created for extruded cut feature

- Click on the **OK** button from **Sketch** contextual tab. The preview of extruded cut feature will be displayed; refer to Figure-135.

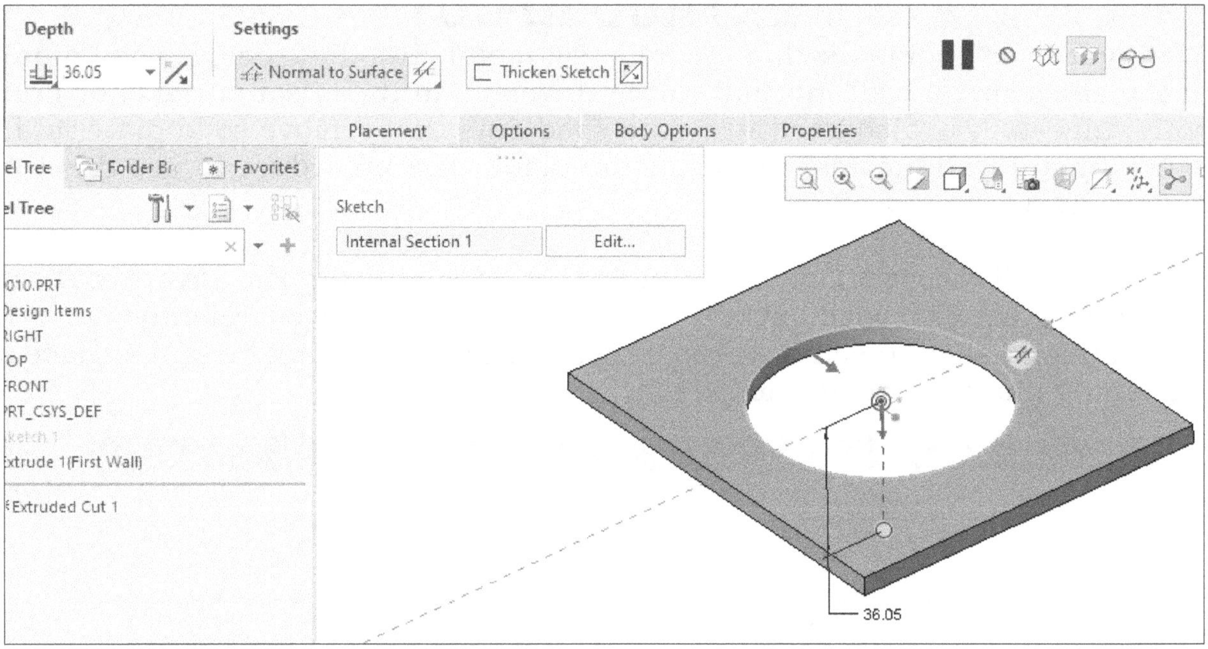

Figure-135. Preview of extruded cut feature

- Select desired depth option from the drop-down in the **Depth** area of the **Ribbon**. The options in this drop-down have been discussed earlier in this book.
- Specify desired depth value in the edit box of the **Depth** area.
- Click on the button in the **Depth** area to change the depth direction of extrude to other side of sketch.
- Click on the **Normal to Surface** button in the **Settings** area to toggle between the sheet metal and solid cuts feature. Select the **Normal to Both Surfaces** option from the drop-down next to the **Normal to Surface** button to remove material normal to both Driving and Offset surfaces. Select the **Normal to Driving Surface** option to remove material normal to Driving surface. Select the **Normal to Offset Surface** option to remove material normal to offset surface.
- Click on the **Thickness Sketch** button from the **Settings** area to add thickness to the sketch curves by specifying thickness value in the edit box next to the **Thickness Sketch** button.
- Click on the button from the **Settings** area to change the direction of extruded cut between one side, other side, or both sides of sketch.
- Click on the **Options** tab in the **Ribbon**. The options will be displayed; refer to Figure-136.

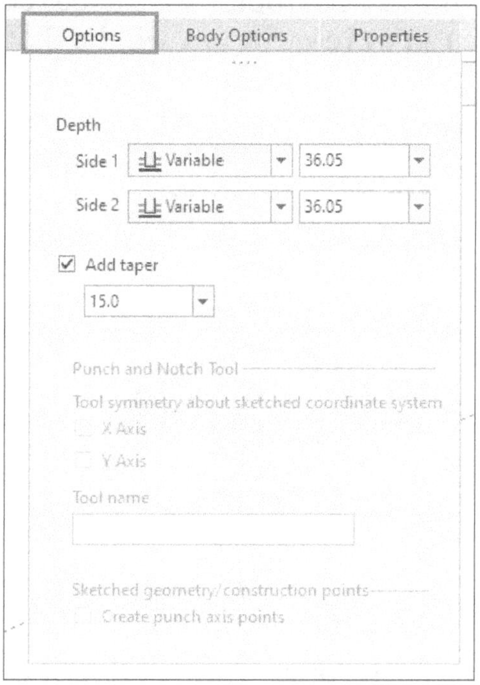

Figure-136. Options tab of Extruded Cut tool

- Select desired depth option from the **Side 1** and **Side 2** drop-down in the **Depth** area of the **Options** tab and specify desired depth value in their respective edit boxes.
- Select the **Add taper** check box to taper the geometry by specifying desired value in the edit box displayed.
- Click on the **Body Options** tab in the **Ribbon**. The options will be displayed; refer to Figure-137.

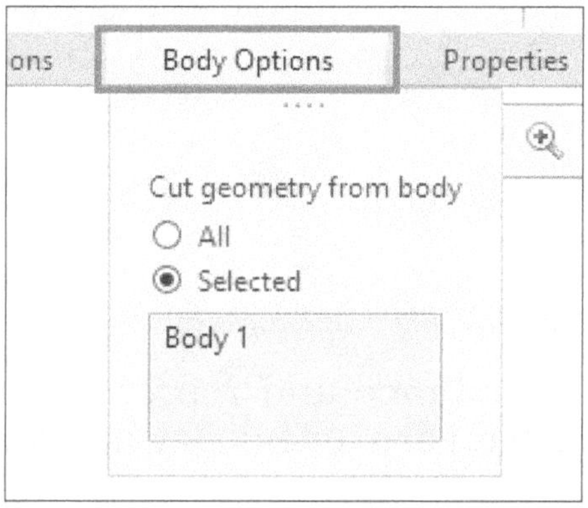

Figure-137. Body Options tab of Extruded Cut tool

- Select the **All** radio button from the **Cut geometry from body** area of the tab to cut all the geometries from the body.
- Select the **Selected** radio button to cut the selected geometry from the body.
- After specifying desired parameters, click on the **OK** button from the contextual tab to create the feature.

FLAT PATTERN PREVIEW

The **Flat Pattern Preview** tool in **Quick Access Toolbar** is used to check the preview of flat pattern while working on sheet metal part. The procedure to use this tool is given next.

- Click on the **Flat Pattern Preview** tool from the **Quick Access Toolbar** below the **Ribbon**. The **Flat Pattern Preview** window will be displayed with related options; refer to Figure-138.

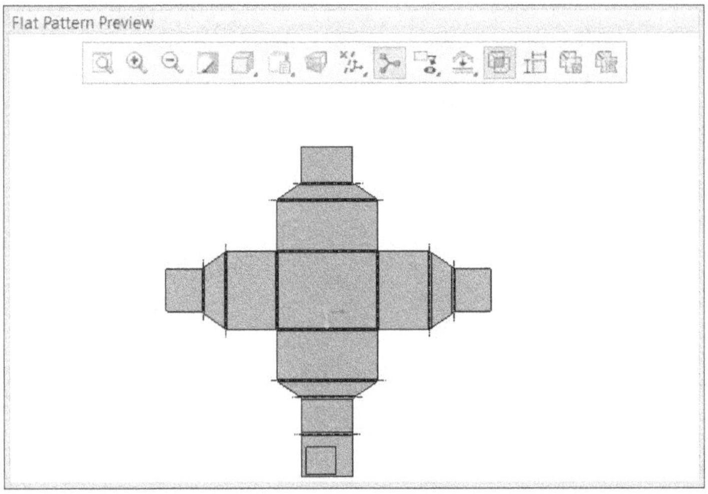

Figure-138. Flat Pattern Preview window

- Select desired check boxes from **Form geometry** flyout in the toolbar of **Flat Pattern Preview** window to display respective entities in the preview.
- Select the **Bounding Box** button from the toolbar to get dimensions of required blank; refer to Figure-139.

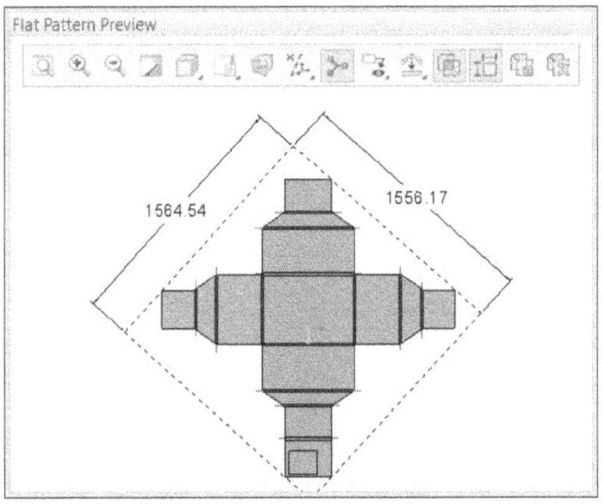

Figure-139. Blank size displayed

- You can create the family instance and representation by using the respective buttons in toolbar of **Flat Pattern Preview** window.

Click again on the **Flat Pattern Preview** tool from the **Quick Access Toolbar** to exit the **Flat Pattern Preview** window.

FLAT PATTERN

The **Flat Pattern** tool is used to create flat pattern of the sheetmetal part which is our ultimate goal for using the software. The procedure to use this tool is same as discussed for **Unbend** tool and options for the tool are also same; refer to Figure-140.

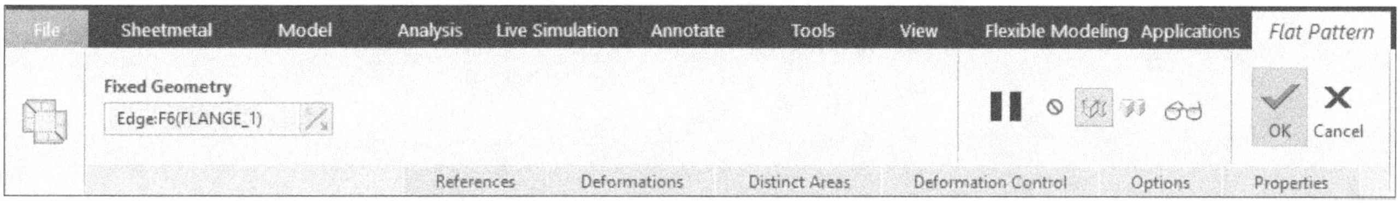

Figure-140. Flat Pattern contextual tab

FLEXIBLE MODELING FOR SHEETMETAL

Flexible modeling is new concept relative to conventional CAD modeling. The tools to perform flexible modeling operations are available in the **Flexible Modeling** tab of the **Ribbon** in Sheetmetal environment; refer to Figure-141. The tools of sheetmetal flexible modeling are discussed next.

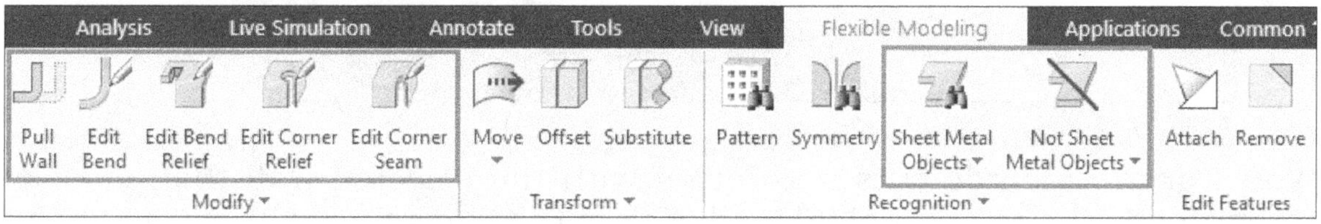

Figure-141. Flexible Modeling tab for sheetmetal

Pull Wall Tool

The **Pull Wall** tool is used to stretch a flange or flat wall by specified value. The procedure is given next.

- Click on the **Pull Wall** tool from the **Modify** panel in the **Flexible Modeling** tab of the **Ribbon**. The **Pull Wall** contextual tab will be displayed in the **Ribbon**; refer to Figure-142 and you will be asked to select a wall.

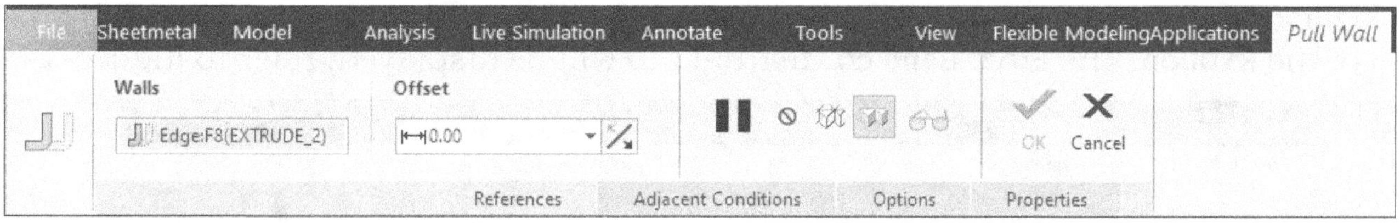

Figure-142. Pull Wall contextual tab

- Select the wall to be pulled and specify desired distance value in the **Offset** edit box of contextual tab. Preview of the feature will be displayed; refer to Figure-143.

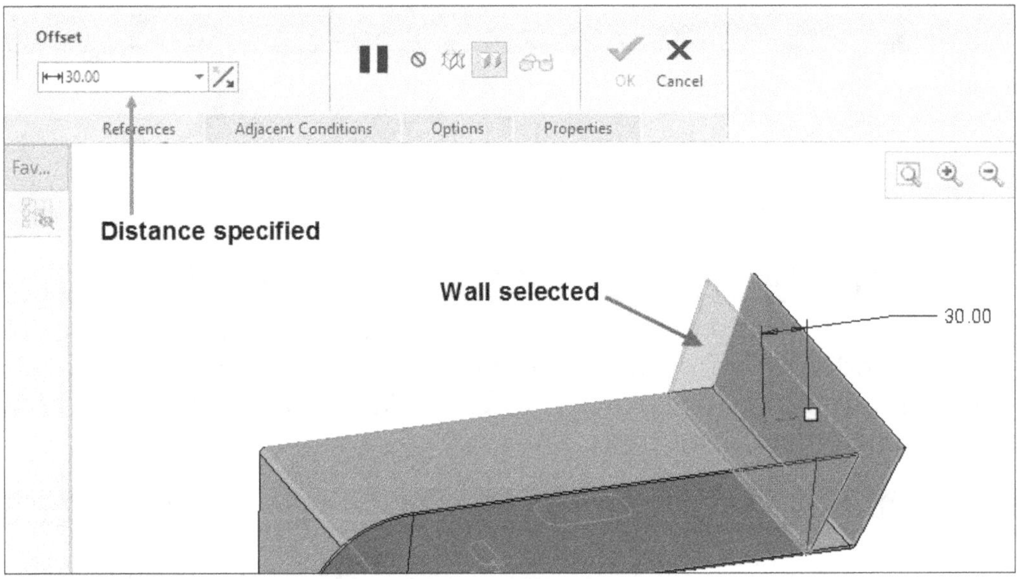

Figure-143. Preview of pull wall feature

- If you want to include cuts and forms with the selected wall then click on the **Options** tab in the contextual tab and click in the selection box. Now, you can select the cuts and form features that you want to include with the wall to be pulled.
- Using the options in the **Adjacent Conditions** tab, you specify the conditions for features that are adjacent to select wall. Click on the **OK** button to create the feature.

Edit Bend Tool

The **Edit Bend** tool is used for editing bend dynamically. The procedure to use this tool is given next.

- Click on the **Edit Bend** tool from the **Modify** panel in the **Flexible Modeling** tab of the **Ribbon**. The **Edit Bend** contextual tab will be displayed; refer to Figure-144.

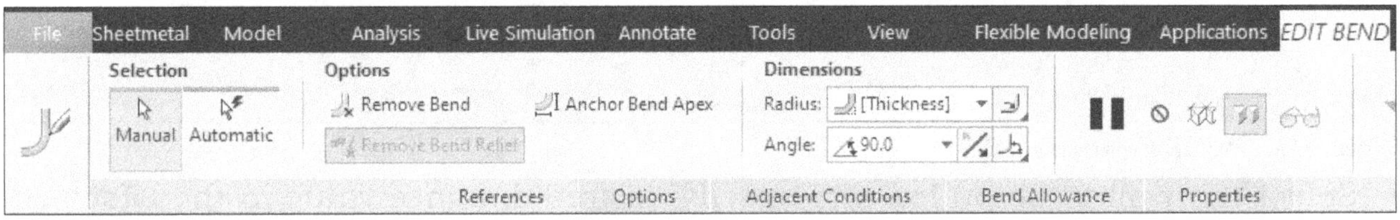

Figure-144. Edit Bend contextual tab

- Select the bend that you want to modify. Tools in the contextual tab will become active.
- You can change the angle and bend radius by using the handles displayed in modeling area; refer to Figure-145. Change the other parameters as required using the options in the contextual tab.

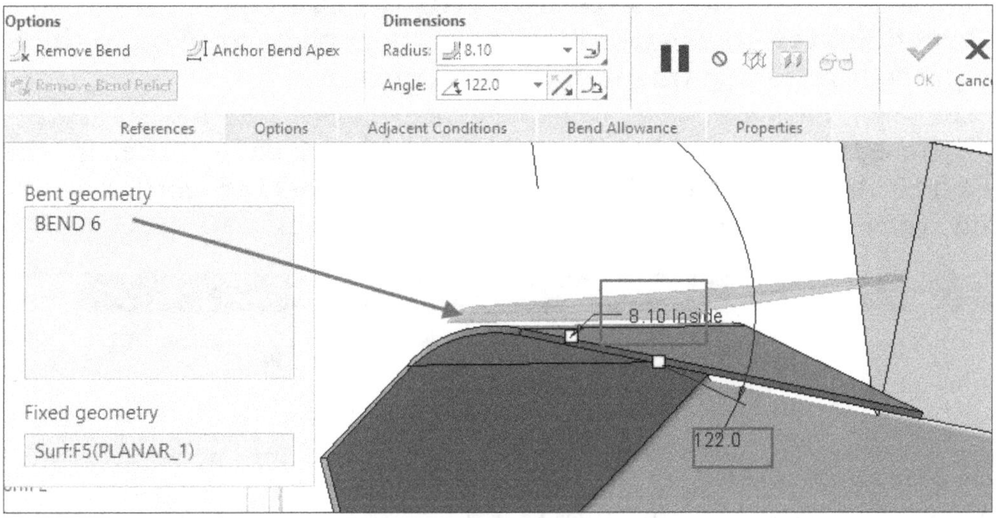

Figure-145. Editing bend

- Click on the **OK** button to apply modifications.

Edit Bend Relief Tool

The **Edit Bend Relief** tool is used to edit relief provided for the bend of flanges and other walls. The procedure to use this tool is given next.

- Click on the **Edit Bend Relief** tool from the **Modify** panel in the **Flexible Modeling** tab of the **Ribbon**. The **Edit Bend Relief** contextual tab will be displayed; refer to Figure-146.

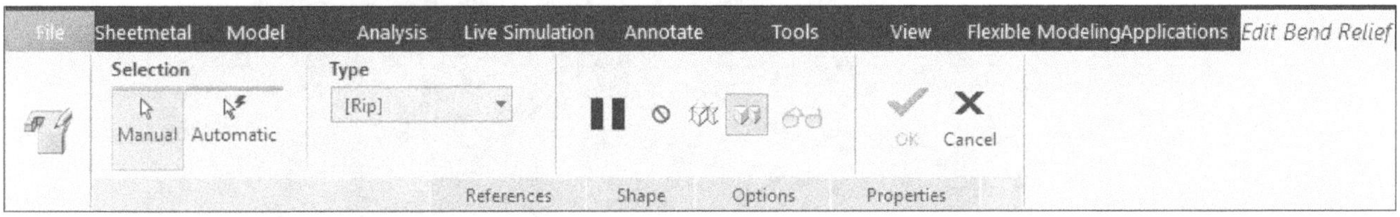

Figure-146. Edit Bend Relief contextual tab

- Select the bend whose relief is to be modified and then select desired option from the drop-down in the contextual tab. Preview of the bend relief will be displayed; refer to Figure-147.

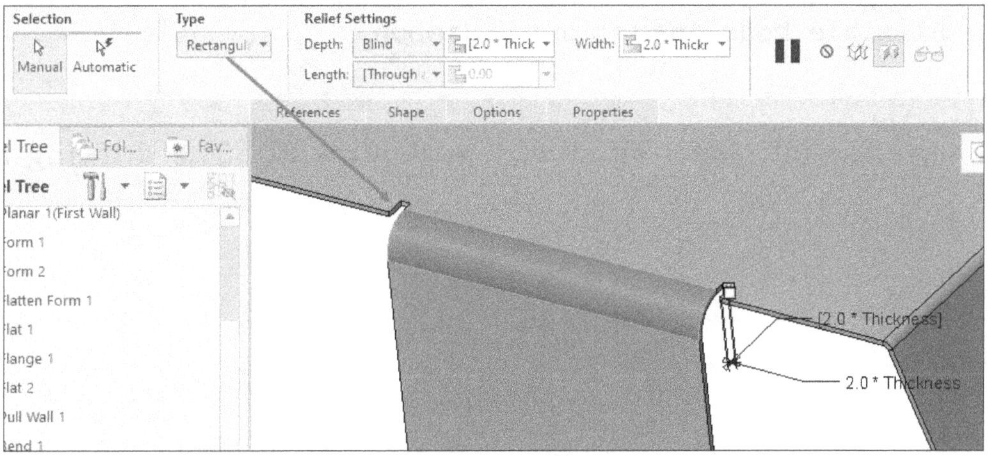

Figure-147. Preview of editing bend relief

- Click on the **OK** button to apply modifications.

Edit Corner Relief Tool

The **Edit Corner Relief** tool is used to edit corner reliefs applied to the sheet metal model. The procedure to use this tool is given next.

- Click on the **Edit Corner Relief** tool from the **Modify** panel in the **Flexible Modeling** tab of the **Ribbon**. The **Edit Corner Relief** contextual tab will be displayed; refer to Figure-148.

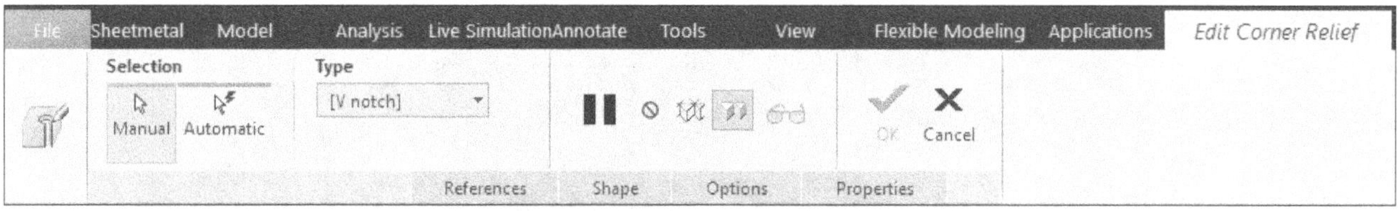

Figure-148. Edit Corner Relief contextual tab

- Select the corners to be modified. Select desired corner relief shape from the drop-down in contextual tab and specify the related parameters. Preview of the corner relief will be displayed; refer to Figure-149.

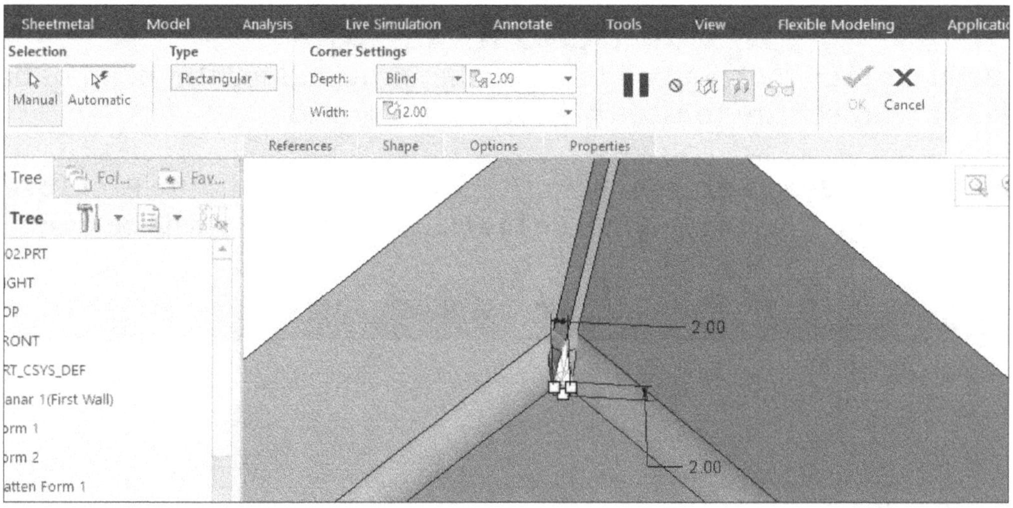

Figure-149. Preview of editing corner relief

- Click on the **OK** button to apply the modifications.

In the same way, you can use the **Edit Corner Seam** tool available in the **Modify** panel of the **Flexible Modeling** tab of the **Ribbon**.

PRACTICAL 1

Create the sheet metal model as shown in Figure-150. The drawing is given in Figure-151.

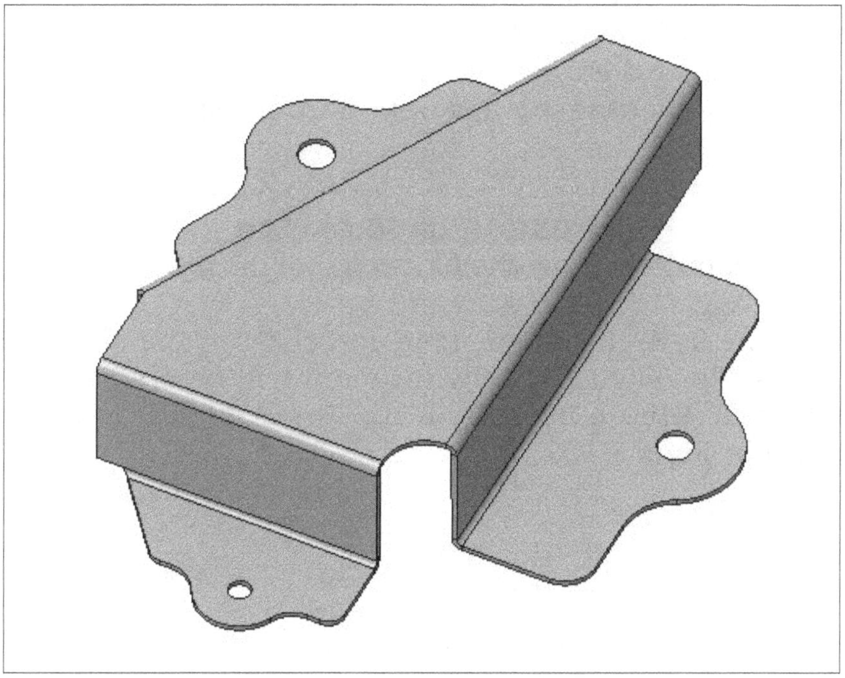

Figure-150. Model for Practical 1

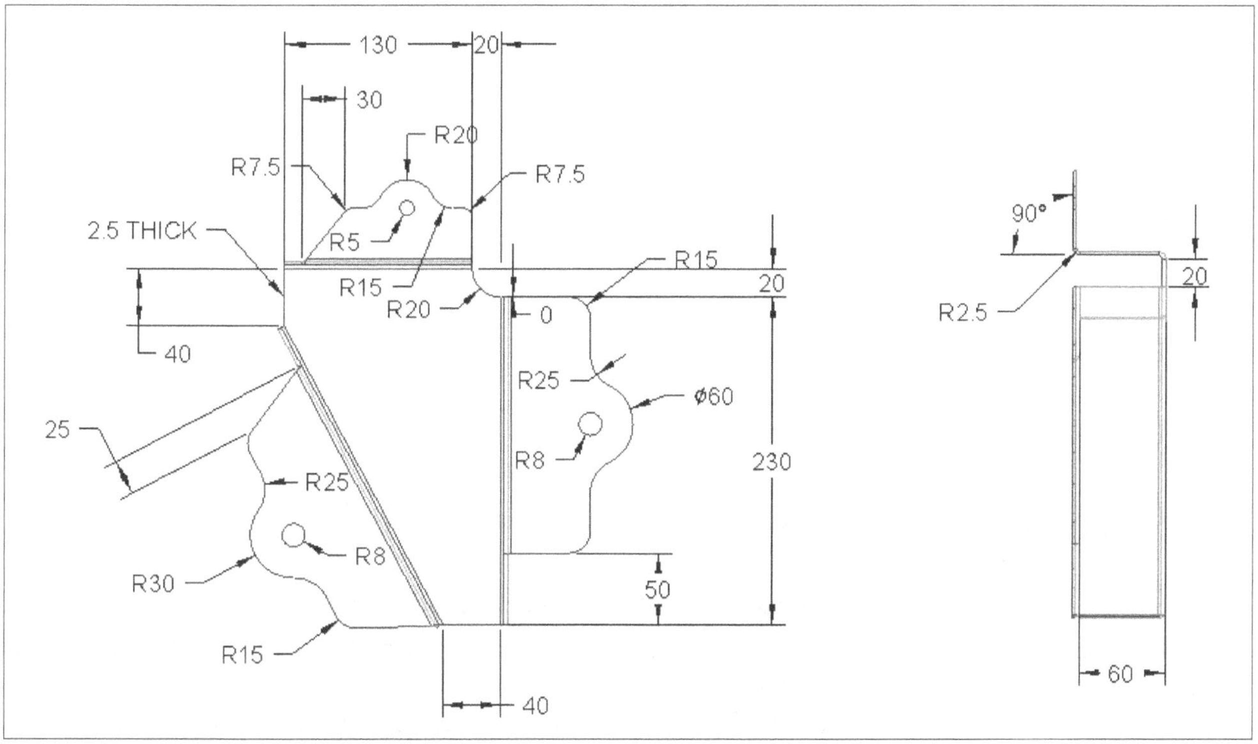

Figure-151. Drawing for Practical 1

Starting New Sheet Metal Part

- Double-click on the Creo Parametric icon from the desktop to start Creo Parametric if not started already.
- Click on the **New** button from the **Data** panel in the **Ribbon**. The **New** dialog box will be displayed.
- Select **Part** radio button from **Type** area and select **Sheetmetal** radio button from **Sub-type** area.

- Specify desired name for the file and clear the **Use default template** check box.
- Click on the **OK** button from the dialog box. The **New File Options** dialog box will be displayed as discussed earlier.
- Select the **mmns part sheetmetal abs** option from the dialog box and click on the **OK** button.

Creating base sketch

- Click on the **Sketch** button from the **Datum** panel in the **Ribbon**. The **Sketch** dialog box will be displayed.
- Select the **TOP** plane from the **Model Tree** and click on the **Sketch** button from the **Sketch** dialog box. The sketching environment will be displayed.
- Click on the **Sketch View** button from the **In-Graphics** toolbar and create the sketch as shown in Figure-152.

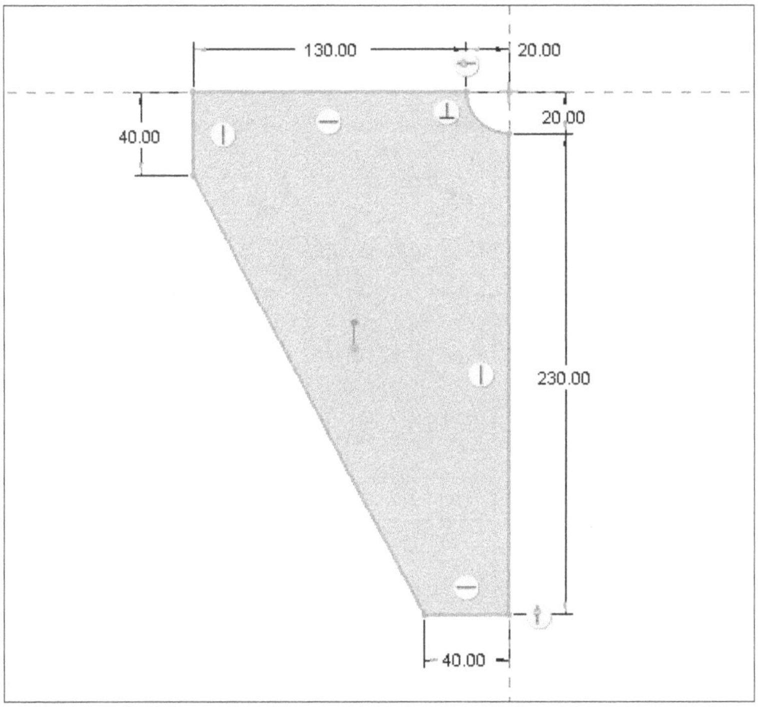

Figure-152. Base sketch for the model

- Click on the **OK** button from the **Sketch** contextual tab.

Creating Planar feature

- Click on the **Planar** tool from the **Walls** panel in the **Sheetmetal** tab of the **Ribbon**. The **Planar** contextual tab will be displayed.
- Select the sketch earlier created. Preview of the planar feature will be displayed; refer to Figure-153.

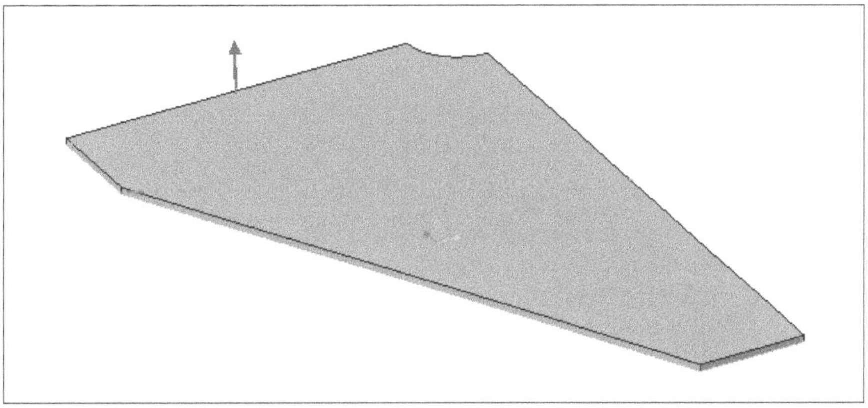

Figure-153. Preview of planar feature

- Specify the thickness value for planar feature as **2.50** in the **Thickness** edit box.
- Click on the **OK** button from **Planar** contextual tab to create the feature.

Creating Flat Walls

As per the model and drawing displayed in Figure-150 and Figure-151, there are three flat walls created on the edges of the base with depth of **60** mm. The steps to create flat walls are given next.

- Click on the **Flat** tool from the **Walls** panel in the **Sheetmetal** tab of the **Ribbon**. The **Flat** contextual tab will be displayed and you will be asked to select edges.
- Select the lower edges of the side faces as shown in Figure-154. The preview of the flat walls will be displayed.

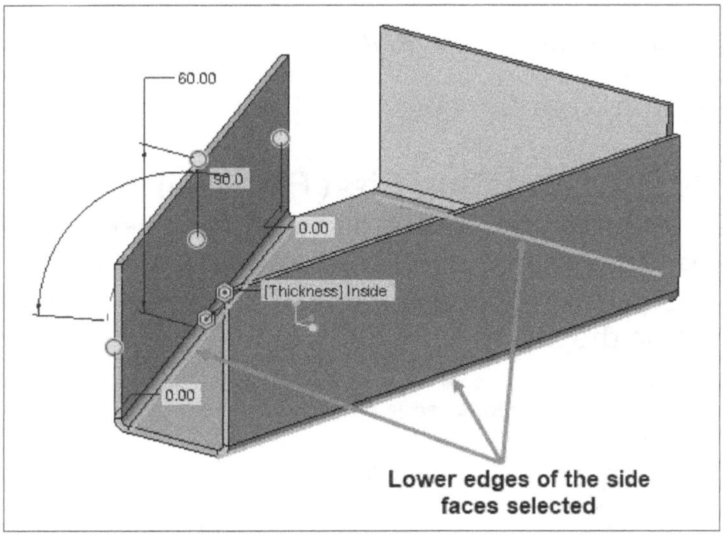

Figure-154. Preview of the flat wall feature

- Specify the depth of wall as **60** from **Section Preview** area in the **Shape** tab of the **Ribbon**; refer to Figure-155. Make sure the other parameters is same as given in Figure-156.

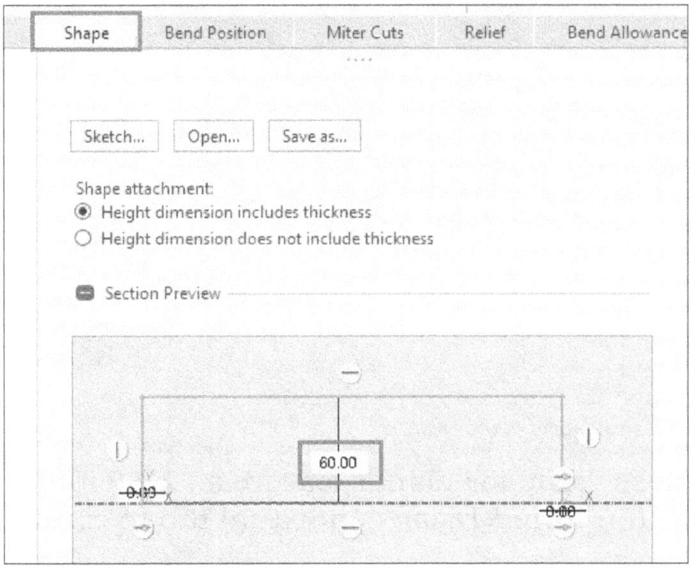

Figure-155. Specifying depth of wall

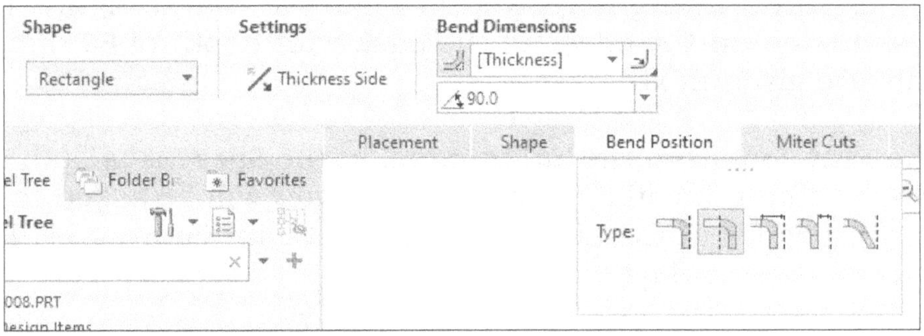

Figure-156. Specifying the parameters for flat wall

- Click on the **OK** button from the contextual tab. The flat wall will be created.

Creating First Flat Wall

- Click on the **Flat** tool from the **Walls** panel in the **Sheetmetal** tab of the **Ribbon**. The **Flat** contextual tab will be displayed and you will be asked to select edges.
- Select the inner edge of the newly created wall as shown in Figure-157. The preview of the flat wall will be displayed.

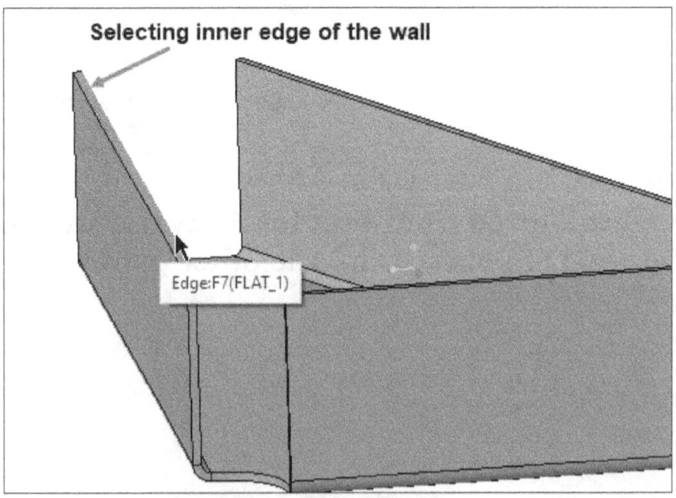

Figure-157. Selecting inner edge of the wall

- Specify the parameters for the wall as shown in Figure-158.

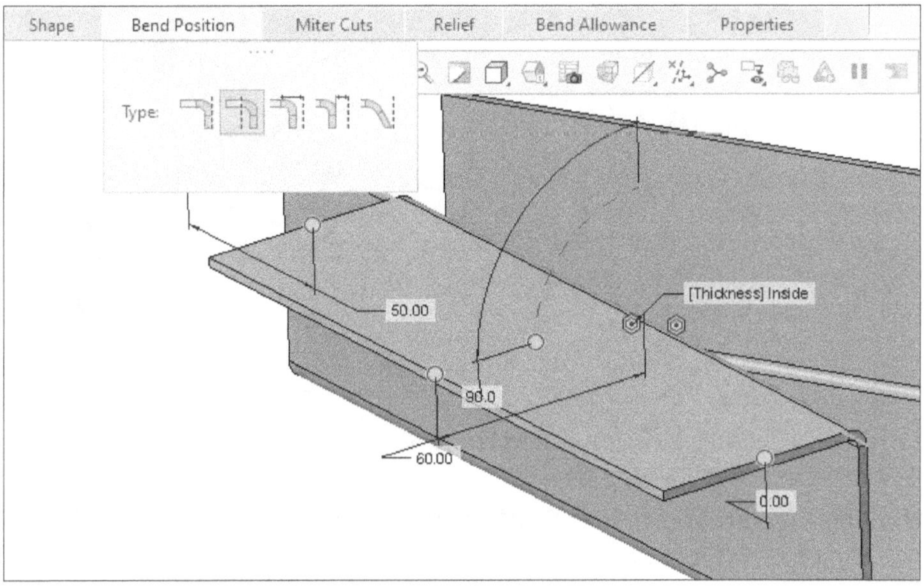

Figure-158. Specifying parameters for first wall

- Click on the **Sketch** button from **Shape** tab in the **Ribbon** to activate sketching environment and modify the sketch as shown in Figure-159.

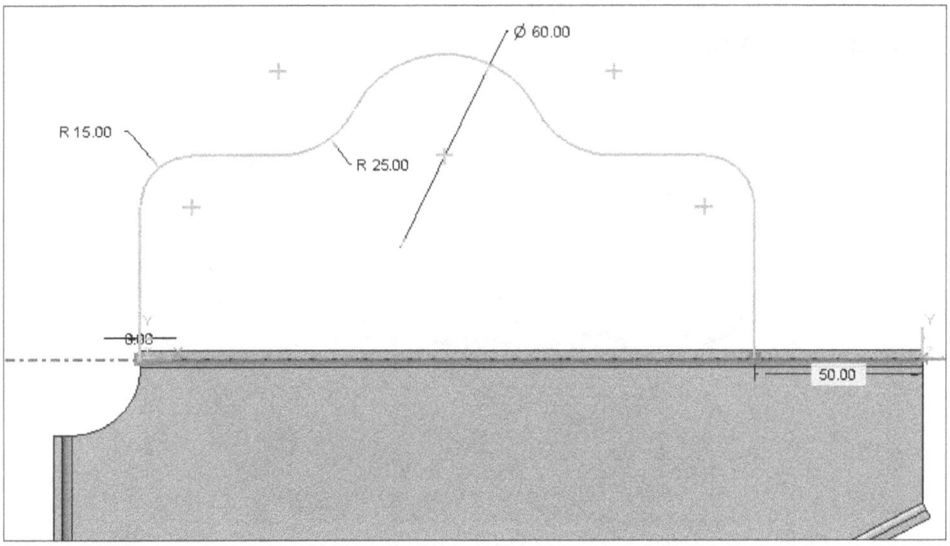

Figure-159. Modifying the sketch

- Click on the **OK** button from **Sketch** contextual tab. The preview of modified flat wall will be displayed; refer to Figure-160.

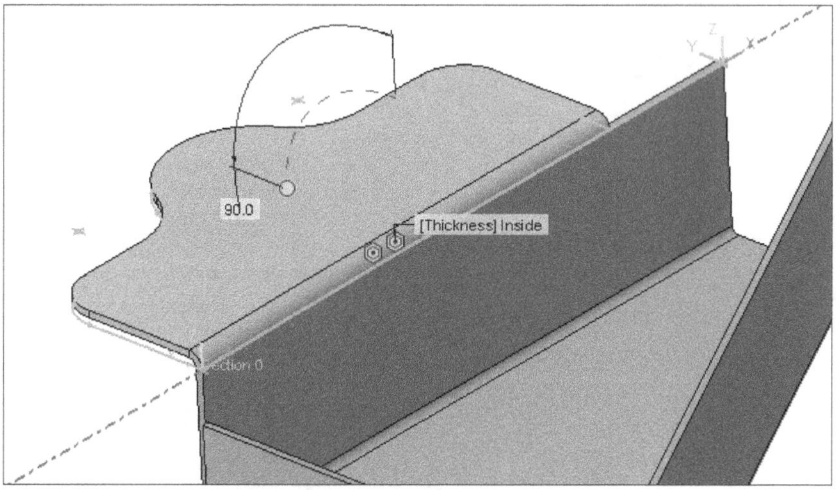

Figure-160. Preview of modified flat wall

- Click on the **OK** button from the **Flat** contextual tab to create the feature.

Creating First Extruded Cut

- Click on the **Extruded Cut** tool from **Engineering** panel in the **Sheetmetal** tab of the **Ribbon**. The **Extruded Cut** contextual tab will be displayed and you are asked to create or select the sketch.
- Select face of the newly created flat wall as shown in Figure-161. The sketching environment will be displayed.

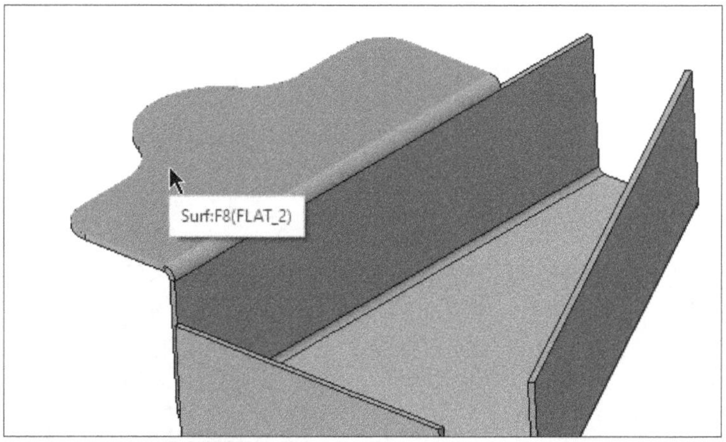

Figure-161. Selecting face of wall

- Click on the **Sketch View** button from the **In-Graphics** toolbar and create the sketch as shown in Figure-162.

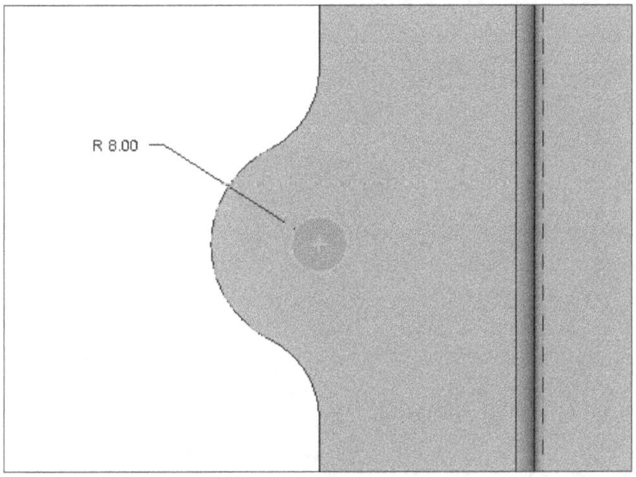

Figure-162. Creating the sketch for extruded cut

- Click on the **OK** button from **Sketch** contextual tab. The preview of extruded cut feature will be displayed; refer to Figure-163.

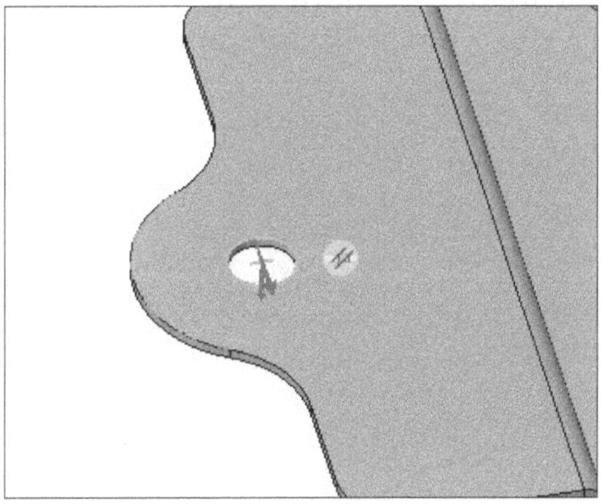

Figure-163. Preview of extruded cut feature

- Click on the **OK** button from **Extruded Cut** contextual tab to create the feature.

Creating Second Flat Wall

- Click on the **Flat** tool from the **Walls** panel in the **Sheetmetal** tab of the **Ribbon**. The **Flat** contextual tab will be displayed and you will be asked to select edges.
- Select the inner edge of the second wall as shown in Figure-164. The preview of the second flat wall will be displayed.

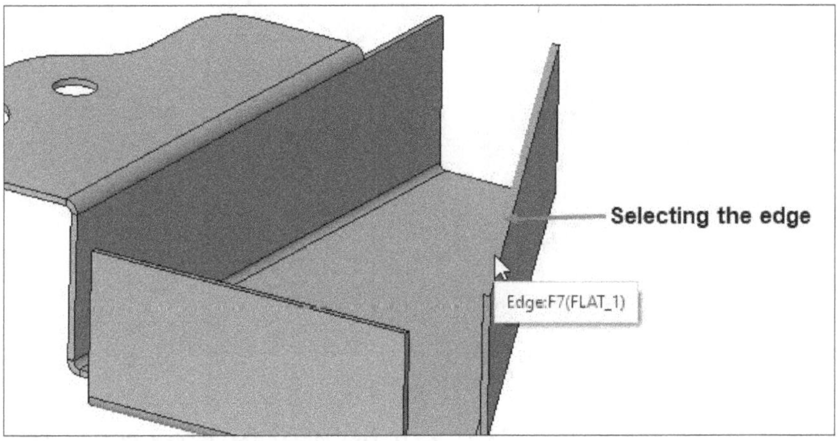

Figure-164. Selecting inner edge of the second wall

- Specify the parameters for the second wall as shown in Figure-165.

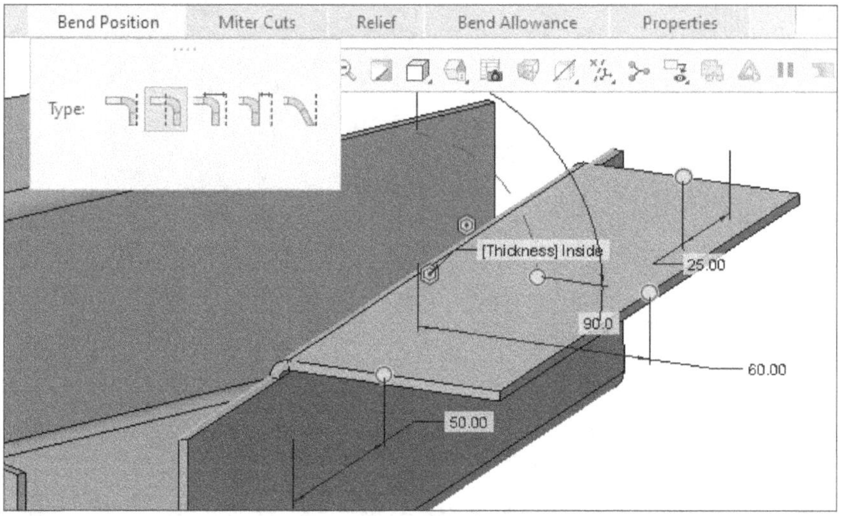

Figure-165. Specifying parameters for second wall

- Click on the **Sketch** button from **Shape** tab in the **Ribbon** to activate sketching environment and modify the sketch as shown in Figure-166.

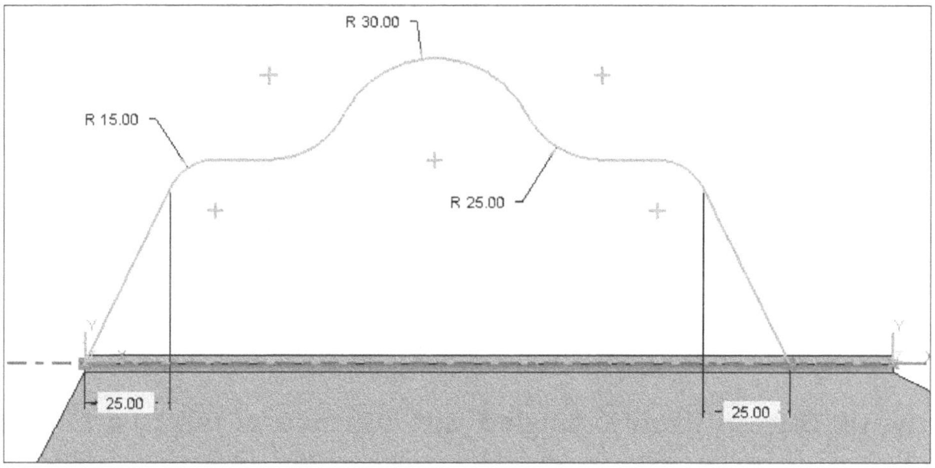

Figure-166. Modifying the sketch for second wall

- Click on the **OK** button from **Sketch** contextual tab. The preview of modified second flat wall will be displayed; refer to Figure-167.

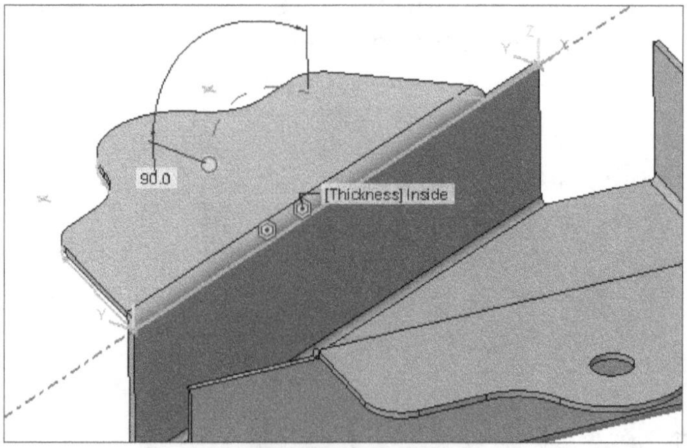

Figure-167. Preview of modified second flat wall

- Click on the **OK** button from the **Flat** contextual tab to create the feature.

Creating Second Extruded Cut

- Click on the **Extruded Cut** tool from **Engineering** panel in the **Sheetmetal** tab of the **Ribbon**. The **Extruded Cut** contextual tab will be displayed and you are asked to create or select the sketch.
- Select face of the newly created second flat wall as shown in Figure-168. The sketching environment will be displayed.

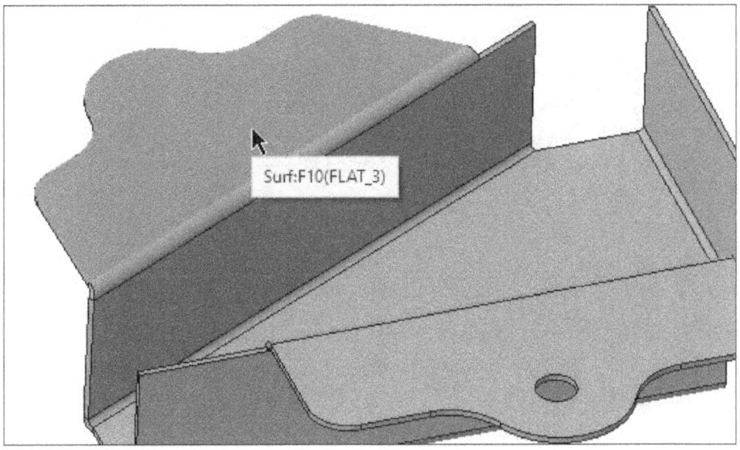

Figure-168. Selecting face of second wall

- Click on the **Sketch View** button from the **In-Graphics** toolbar and create the sketch as shown in Figure-169.

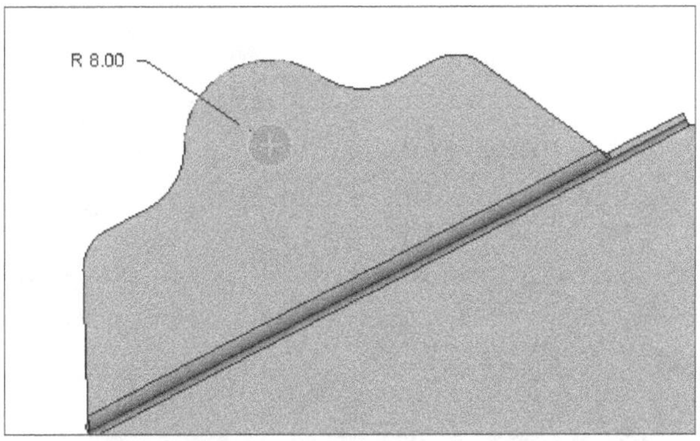

Figure-169. Creating the sketch for second extruded cut

- Click on the **OK** button from **Sketch** contextual tab. The preview of second extruded cut feature will be displayed; refer to Figure-170.

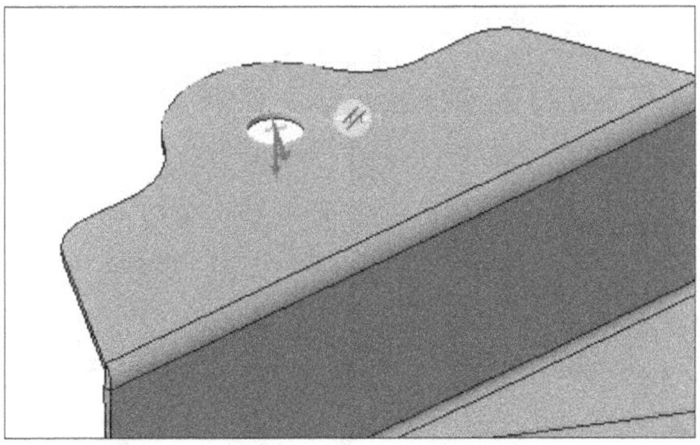

Figure-170. Preview of second extruded cut

- Click on the **OK** button from **Extruded Cut** contextual tab to create the feature.

Creating Third Flat Wall

- Click on the **Flat** tool from the **Walls** panel in the **Sheetmetal** tab of the **Ribbon**. The **Flat** contextual tab will be displayed and you will be asked to select edges.
- Select the inner edge of the third wall as shown in Figure-171. The preview of the third flat wall will be displayed.

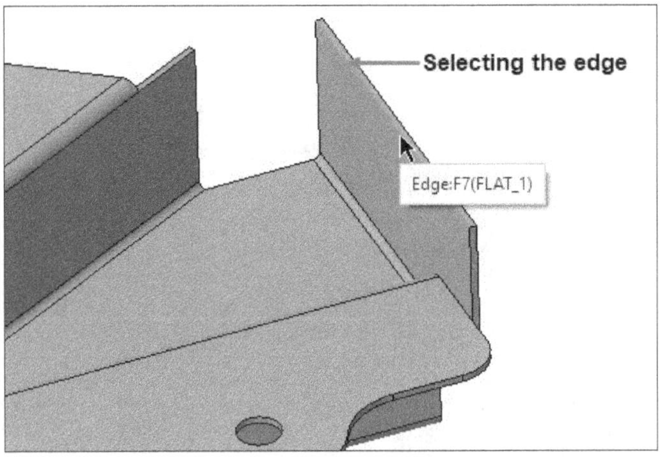

Figure-171. Selecting inner edge of the third wall

- Specify the parameters for the third wall as shown in Figure-172.

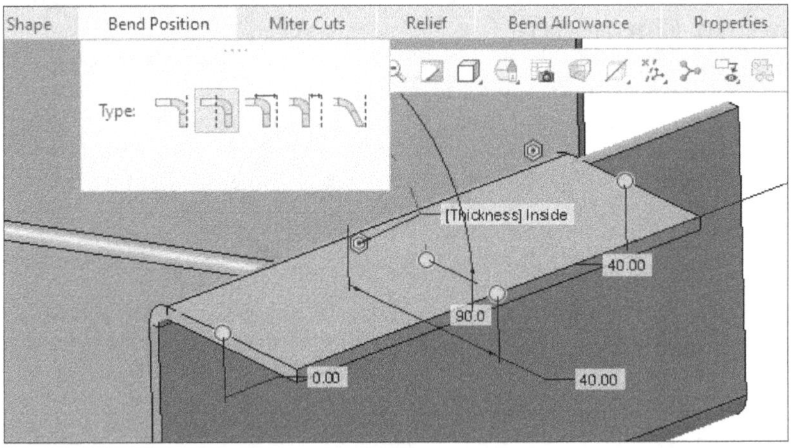

Figure-172. Specifying parameters for third wall

- Click on the **Sketch** button from **Shape** tab in the **Ribbon** to activate sketching environment and modify the sketch as shown in Figure-173.

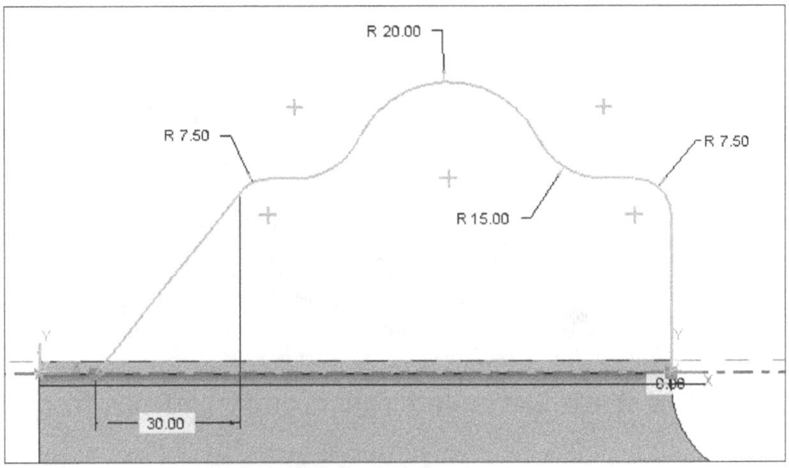

Figure-173. Modifying the sketch for third wall

- Click on the **OK** button from **Sketch** contextual tab. The preview of modified third flat wall will be displayed; refer to Figure-174.

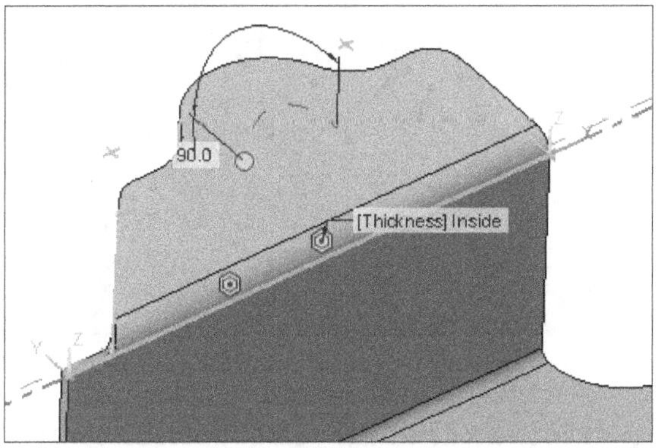

Figure-174. Preview of modified third flat wall

- Click on the **OK** button from the **Flat** contextual tab to create the feature.

Creating Third Extruded Cut

- Click on the **Extruded Cut** tool from **Engineering** panel in the **Sheetmetal** tab of the **Ribbon**. The **Extruded Cut** contextual tab will be displayed and you are asked to create or select the sketch.
- Select face of the newly created third flat wall as shown in Figure-175. The sketching environment will be displayed.

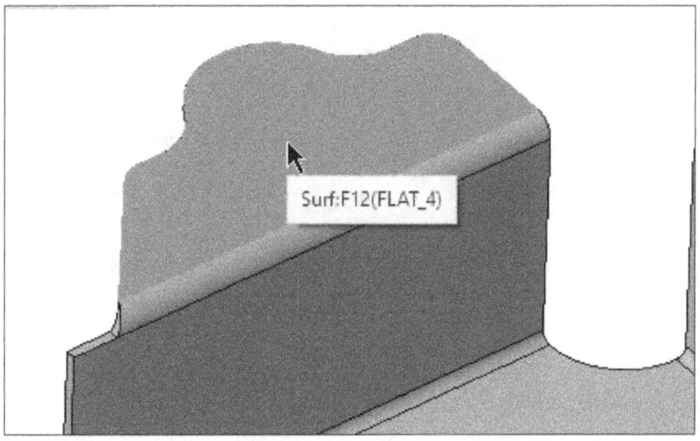

Figure-175. Selecting the face of third wall

- Click on the **Sketch View** button from the **In-Graphics** toolbar and create the sketch as shown in Figure-176.

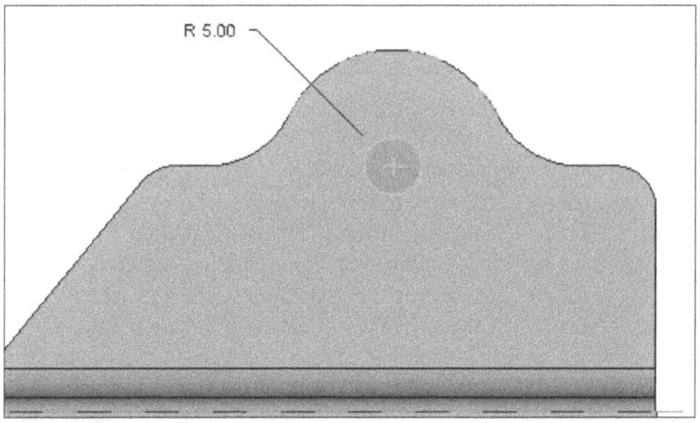

Figure-176. Creating the sketch for third extruded cut

- Click on the **OK** button from **Sketch** contextual tab. The preview of third extruded cut feature will be displayed; refer to Figure-177.

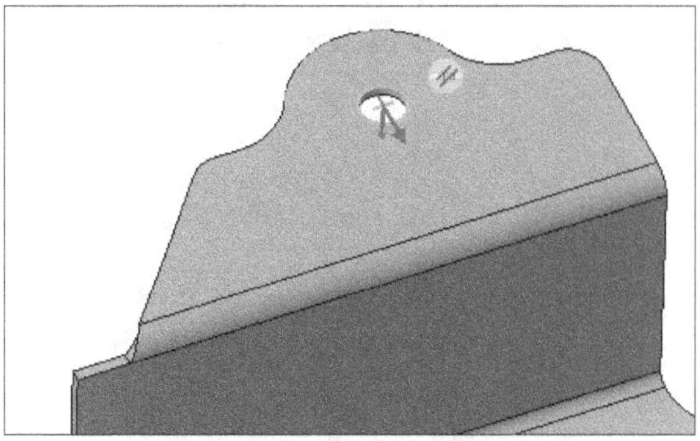

Figure-177. Preview of third extruded cut feature

- Click on the **OK** button from **Extruded Cut** contextual tab to create the feature. The final sheetmetal model will be created; refer to Figure-178.

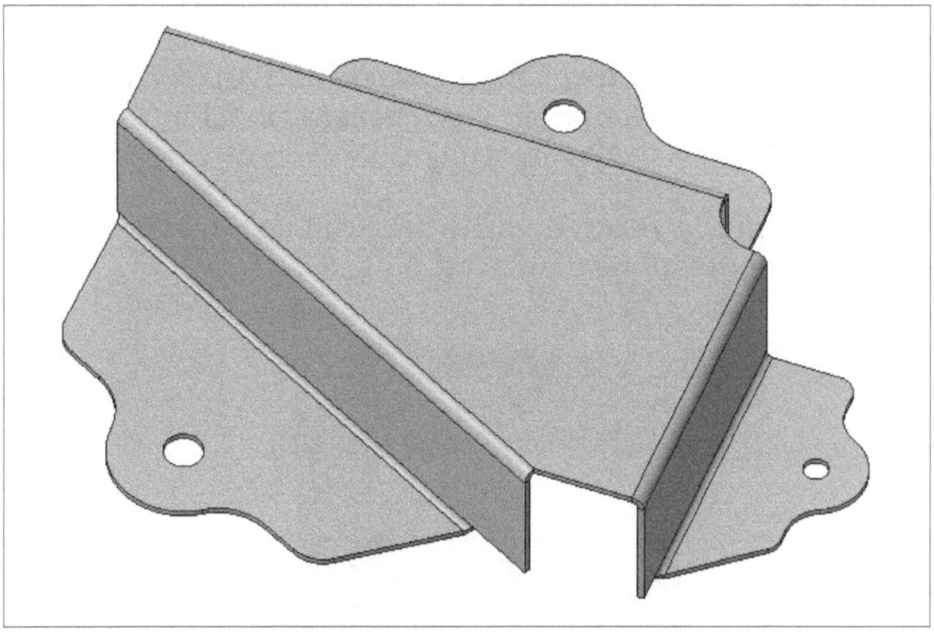

Figure-178. Final sheetmetal model created

PRACTICE 1

Create the sheet metal model as shown in Figure-179. Dimensions are given in Figure-180.

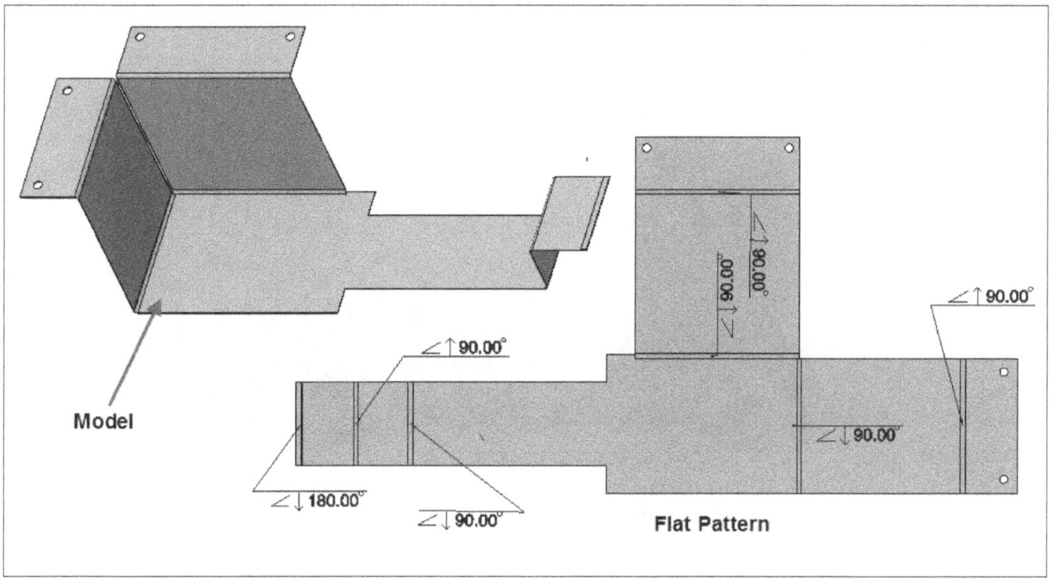

Figure-179. Sheet metal model

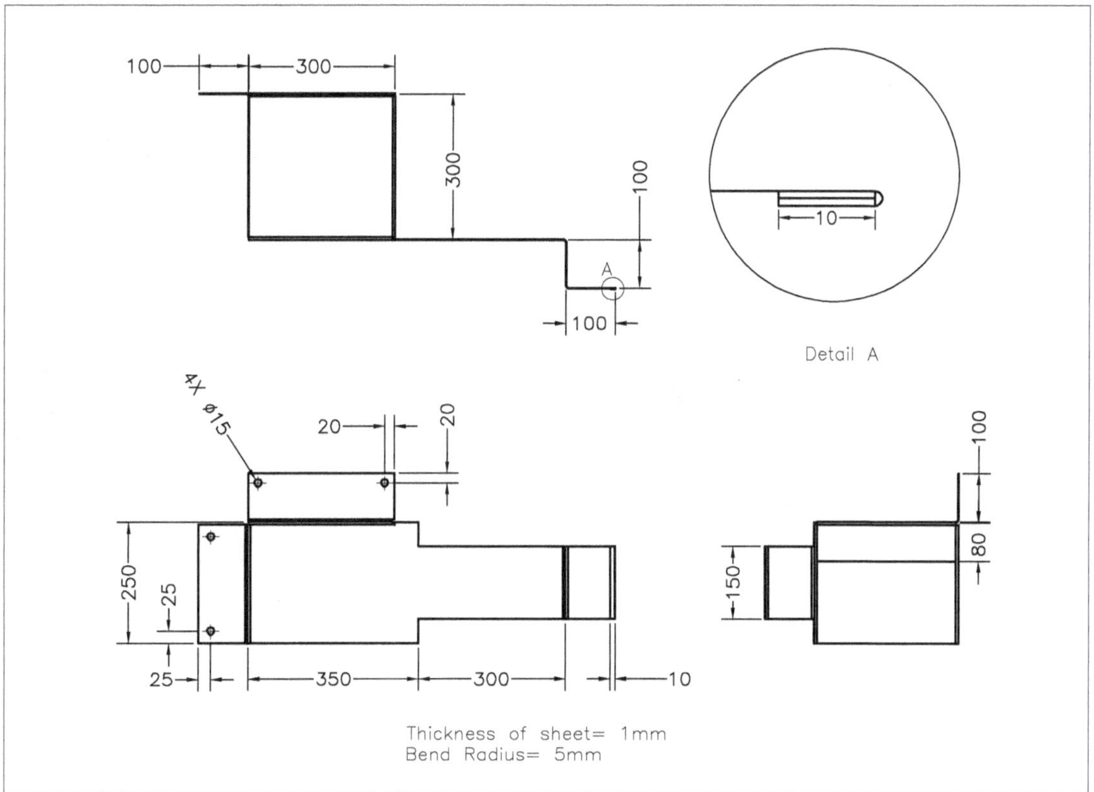

Figure-180. *Drawing views*

PRACTICE 2

Create the sheet metal model as shown in Figure-181. Dimensions are given in Figure-182.

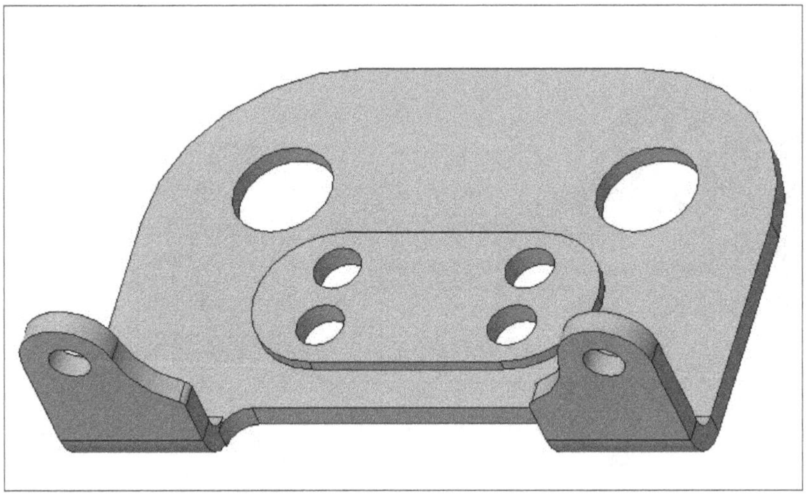

Figure-181. Practice 2 Model

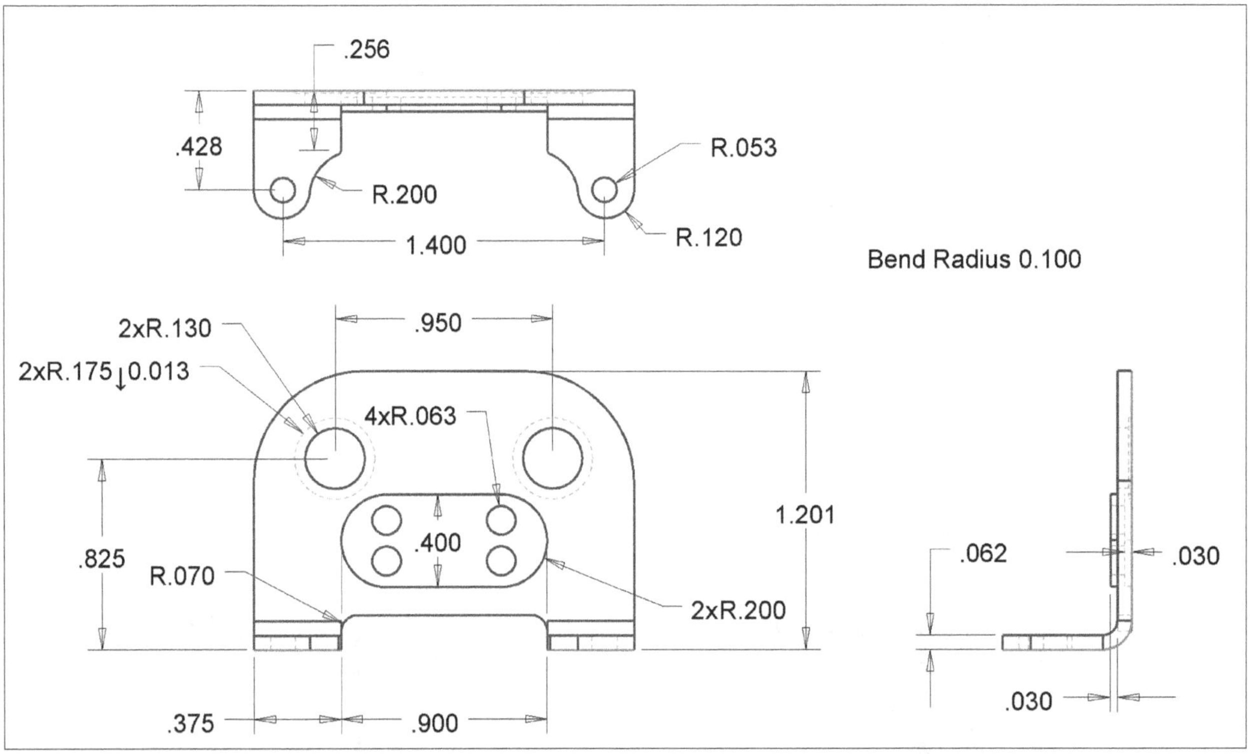

Figure-182. Practice 2 Drawing Views

SELF ASSESSMENT

1. Which parts are called sheet metal parts?

2. What is K-factor in case of sheet metal design?

3. Write down the difference between punch forming and die forming process.

4. Which of the following buttons in the **Bend Position** tab of **Flat** tool is used to add the bend geometry with the bend line tangent to the attachment edge?

a)  b)  c)  d) 

5. Which of the following tools in **Sheetmetal** design works as **Patch** tool in **Surface** design?

a) Extrude
b) Flat
c) Flange
d) Planar

6. The .... tool is used to create twisted sheetmetal parts.

7. The .... tool is used to reverse the operation done by **Unbend** tool.

8. The .... tool is used to create sheet metal cuts that remove solid material from the sheet metal wall, normal to the driven or to the offset surface, or normal to both sufaces.

9. While sketching the bend line, you are allowed to create only one line. (T/F)

10. **Forming** is a process of sheetmetal in which a die/punch is applied to the sheetmetal with mechanical force and impression of die/punch is made on the part. (T/F)

11. The **Quilt/Body Form** tool is used to flatten the sheet at the locations where forming tools have been applied. (T/F)

12. What is the typical thickness range of sheetmetal parts?

a) 0.1 mm to 5 mm
b) 1 mm to 25 mm
c) Fraction of mm to 12.5 mm
d) 5 mm to 50 mm

13. In the sheetmetal environment, what is additionally required while using the Extrude tool compared to part modeling?

a) Material type
b) Sketch dimension
c) Sheet thickness
d) Layer setting

14. What is the term for the first wall created in sheetmetal design?

a) Master wall
b) Main wall
c) Base wall
d) Starter wall

15. What is the purpose of the “Bend Position” tab in wall creation?

a) Set color and texture
b) Define wall thickness
c) Select bend origin
d) Specify location of bend geometry

16. Which relief option cuts a circular shape at the corner?

a) Rip
b) V-notch
c) Circular
d) Obround

17. What does the K-Factor in sheetmetal represent?

a) Ratio of inner radius to outer radius
b) Thickness divided by width
c) Ratio of neutral axis to material thickness
d) A measure of bend angle

18. What is the derived factor based on K-Factor and π?

a) Twist Factor
b) Y-Factor
c) Z-Factor
d) Radius Factor

19. Which tool is similar to Flat tool but allows section shape modification instead of base sketch?

a) Planar
b) Flange
c) Twist
d) Relief

20. How can you attach a flange to multiple edges at once?

a) Use Modify Width
b) Use Shape tab
c) Use Chain dialog box
d) Use Sketch tab

21. Which tool is primarily used to create a base wall using a closed sketch?

a) Extrude
b) Bend
c) Planar
d) Flange

22. What tool would you use to bend a sheet along a sketch line drawn on its face?

a) Edge Bend
b) Planar Bend
c) Flange
d) Bend

23. In Planar Bend, what are the two types of bends that can be performed?

a) Angle and Radius
b) Radius and Curve
c) Angle and Roll
d) Roll and Flat

24. What is the main function of the Unbend tool in sheetmetal modeling?

a) To merge separate parts
b) To create a flat pattern
c) To reverse the bend operation
d) To cut sheet metal into parts

25. What is NOT reversed by the Bend Back tool?

a) Face selection
b) Sketch
c) Deformation
d) Bend order

26. What does the Rip Connect tool require for operation?

a) Two parallel edges
b) Selection of bend lines
c) Selection of two vertex points
d) A flat surface

27. What condition causes the Flat Pattern tool to show an error?

a) More than one distinct piece
b) No bends applied
c) Shell not selected
d) Thickness too small

28. What does the Surface Rip tool do?

a) Cuts using a sketch
b) Rips based on surface selection
c) Adds material
d) Merges two parts

29. What must you create before using the Sketched Rip tool?

a) A deformation
b) A flat pattern
c) A closed loop sketch
d) A forming tool

30. Which of the following does the Corner Relief tool modify?

a) Forming die
b) Flat walls only
c) Joining corners of three edges
d) Sketch planes

31. What is the purpose of the Punch Form tool?

a) Cuts metal into a pattern
b) Applies mechanical deformation using punch
c) Defines a bend order
d) Sketches surface cuts

32. What's the primary difference between Punch and Die Form tools?

a) Punch cuts while Die joins
b) Punch removes material, Die adds
c) Punch creates indent using force, Die forms using hammer
d) Punch creates round edges only

33. What feature allows forming using a user-created shape sketch?

a) Punch Form
b) Die Form
c) Sketched Form
d) Flatten Form

34. The Extruded Cut tool removes material from the wall using what method?

a) Dragging from feature list
b) Applying force
c) Extruding sketch normal to surface
d) Directly flattening part

35. The Pull Wall tool is used to:

a) Bend the sheet
b) Flatten formed area
c) Stretch a wall by value
d) Create a cut

36. The Edit Bend tool allows you to change:

a) Material type
b) Forming direction
c) Bend angle and radius
d) Thickness only

37. Which tool is used to edit the relief at a bent corner?

a) Pull Wall
b) Edit Corner Relief
c) Punch Form
d) Sketched Rip

FOR STUDENT NOTES

Answer to Self Assessment Questions:

1. Those parts which are created by bending, punching, or forming piece of metal sheets **2.** The K-Factor in sheet metal work is the ratio of the neutral axis to the material thickness. The K-Factor is used to calculate flat patterns because it is directly related to how much material is stretched during the bend. **3.** Die creates an opposite impression of punch. In practical, when we apply force on punch then punch presses sheetmetal and creates an indent. Opposite to it, in die forming- sheetmetal is placed on die and a flat hammer strikes on sheetmetal to push sheetmetal in die which creates die indent on sheetmetal part. **4.** (a) **5.** (d) **6.** Twist **7.** Bend Back **8.** Extruded Cut **9.** T **10.** T **11.** F

Chapter 12

Surface Design

Topics Covered

The major topics covered in this chapter are:

- ***Introduction***
- ***Starting with Surface Design***
- ***Solid Modeling tools for surfacing***
- ***Boundary Blend and Fill surfaces***
- ***Trimming, Merging, and Offsetting surfaces***
- ***Thickening, Solidifying, and Editing surfaces***

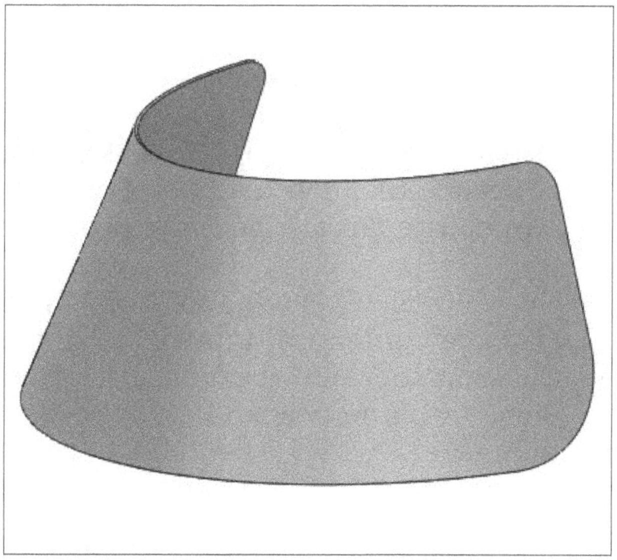

INTRODUCTION

Surface Designing or Surfacing is a technique used to create complex shapes. The most general application of Surfacing can be seen in the objects that are made with good aerodynamics like car body, aeroplanes, ships, and so on. Sometimes, surfacing is also used to add attractiveness in the models. The models created by surfacing are called surface models and they do not exist in real world. Since, surface models do not have mass properties. So, in the end of surface designing, we are required to convert the surface model into a solid part for manufacturing.

In Creo Parametric, there is no separate environment for creating surface designs. We have all the surfacing tools available in the **Part** Modeling environment; refer to Figure-1. Note that we have also enclosed the tools of **Shapes** panel for surfacing tool. We have used these tools earlier in Solid modeling and now we will use them in surface designing.

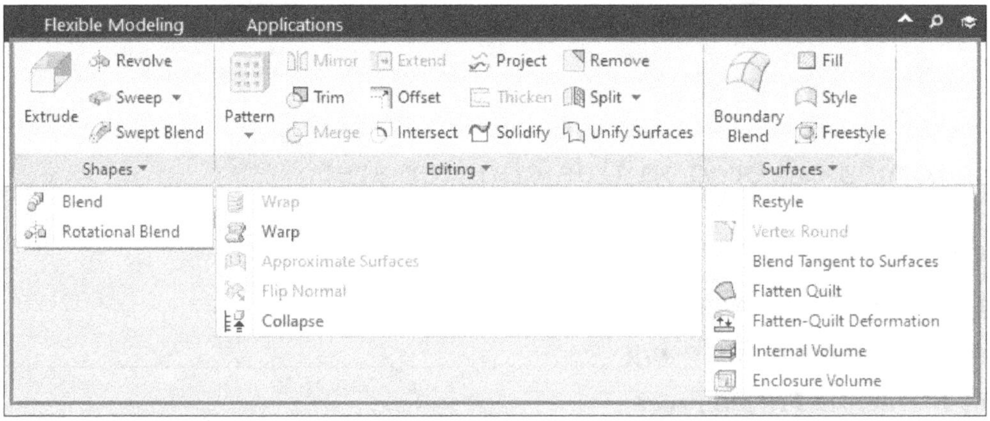

Figure-1. Surfacing tools

EXTRUDED SURFACE

The **Extrude** tool can also be used to create the extruded surfaces. Using this tool, we can create flat surface; the procedure is given next.

- Click on the **Extrude** tool from the **Shapes** panel in the **Model** tab of **Ribbon**. The **Extrude** contextual tab will be displayed as discussed earlier in the book.
- Click on the **Surface** button from **Type** area of the contextual tab.
- Select a plane perpendicular to which you want the surface to be created; refer to Figure-2.

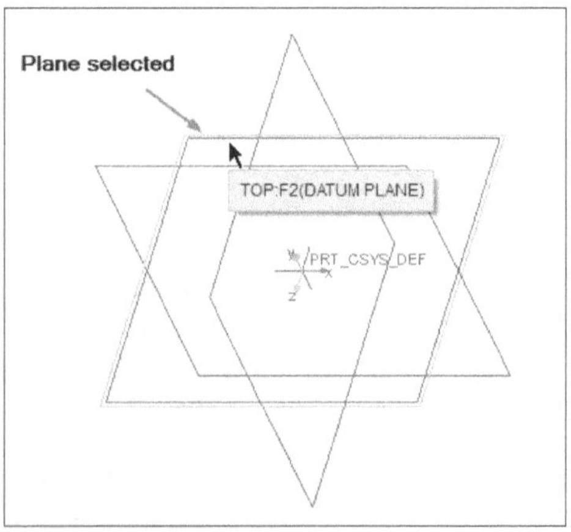

Figure-2. Plane selected

- Create the sketch and click on the **OK** button from the **Sketch** contextual tab. Note that the sketch can be open as well as closed. There is no restriction of closed sketch like in Part modeling.
- On exiting the sketching environment, preview of the extruded surface will be displayed; refer to Figure-3.

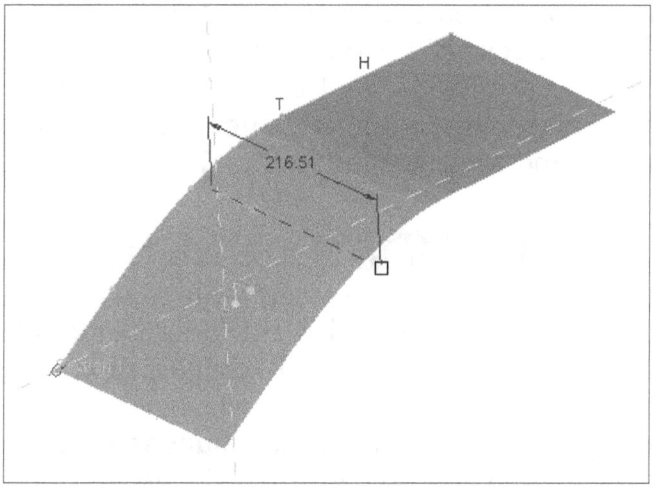

Figure-3. Preview of extruded surface

- If you have created a closed sketch then you can click on the **Capped Ends** button from **Depth** area or you can select **Capped ends** check box from the **Options** tab in the **Extrude** contextual tab to close the open ends of surface; refer to Figure-4.

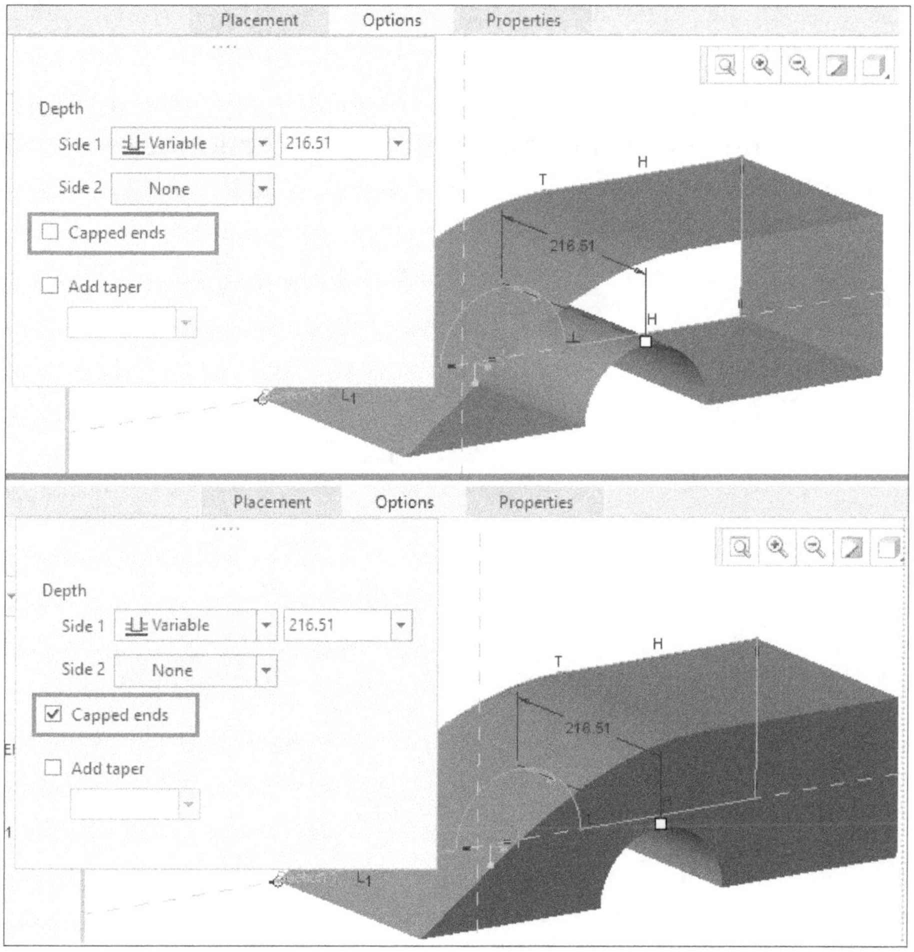

Figure-4. Capped ends option

- You can also make the surface taper by using the **Add taper** check box as done earlier for solid extrusion.
- Click on the **OK** button from the contextual tab to create the surface.

OTHER SOLID MODELING TOOLS FOR SURFACING

The other tools in **Shapes** panel can also be used in the same way as discussed in **Chapter 4:3D Modeling Basics** of the book. The only difference while creating the features will be selecting surface modeling button in place of solid modeling button. You can now create surfaces by using **Revolve**, **Sweep**, **Helical Sweep**, **Blend**, **Swept Blend**, and **Rotational Blend** tools by following the procedures discussed earlier.

BOUNDARY BLEND

The **Boundary Blend** tool is one of the most used tools in Creo Parametric for surfacing. Using this tool, you can create surface with the help of sketched curves or edges of other entities. The procedure to use this tool is given next.

- Click on the **Boundary Blend** tool from the **Surfaces** panel in the **Model** tab of **Ribbon**. The **Boundary Blend** contextual tab will be displayed; refer to Figure-5.

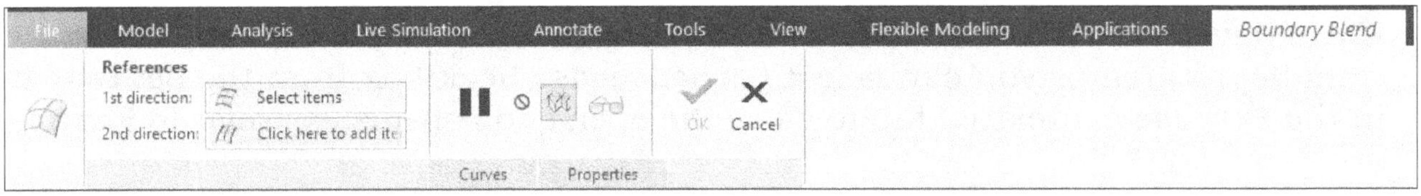

Figure-5. Boundary Blend contextual tab

- There are two curve collectors in the contextual tab; refer to Figure-5. Click in the first collector and select the curves in first direction. Preview of surface will be displayed; refer to Figure-6.

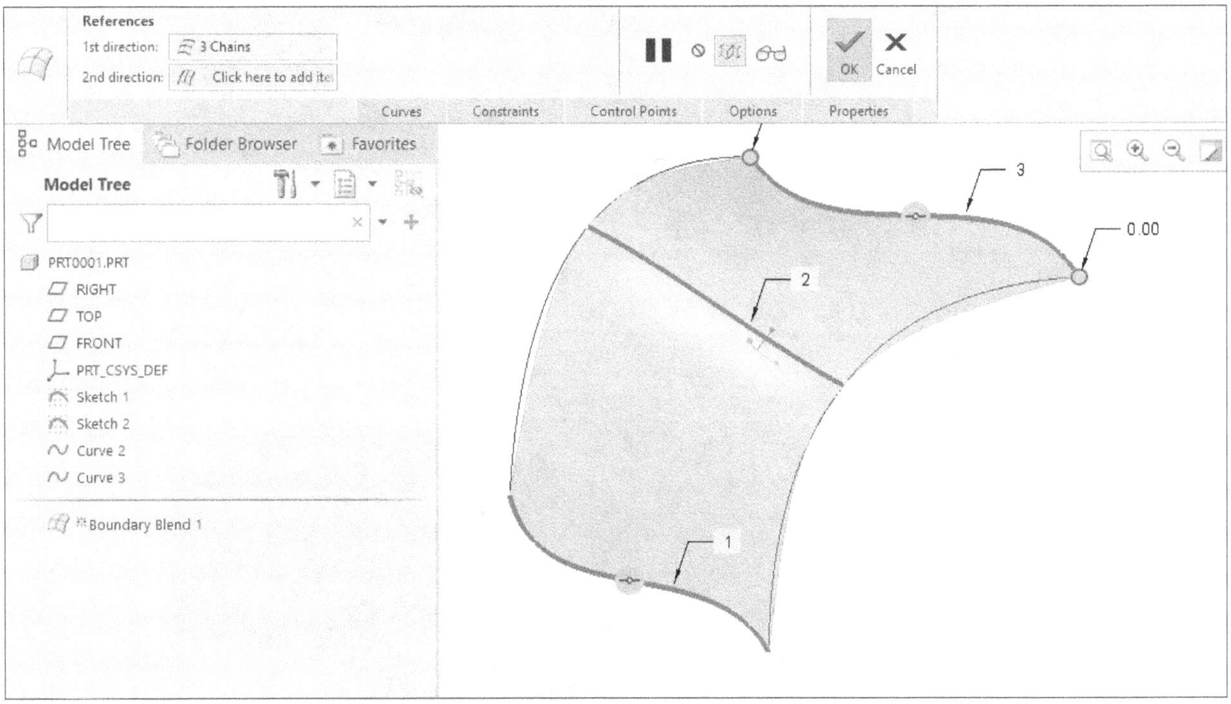

Figure-6. Preview of boundary blend with 1direction curves

- To add curves of 2nd direction, click in the **2nd Direction** collector and select the curves. Preview of boundary blend will be displayed; refer to Figure-7.

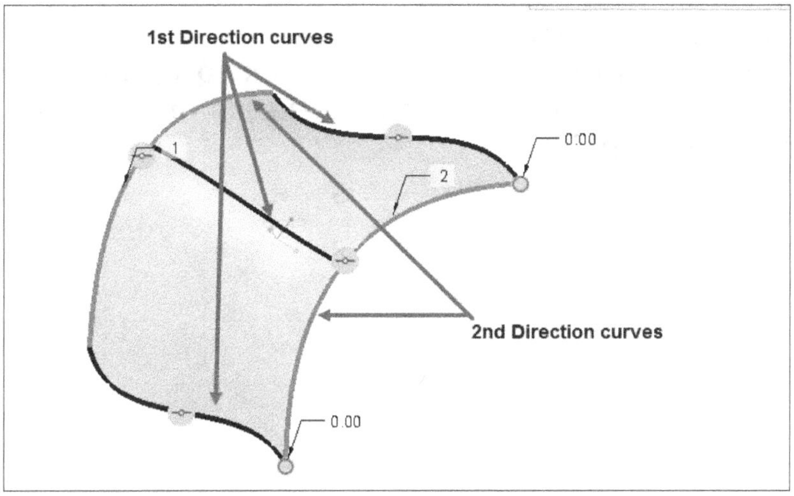

Figure-7. Boundary blend with curves in both direction

Curves tab

- Click on the **Curves** tab in the **Ribbon**. The options will be displayed; refer to Figure-8.

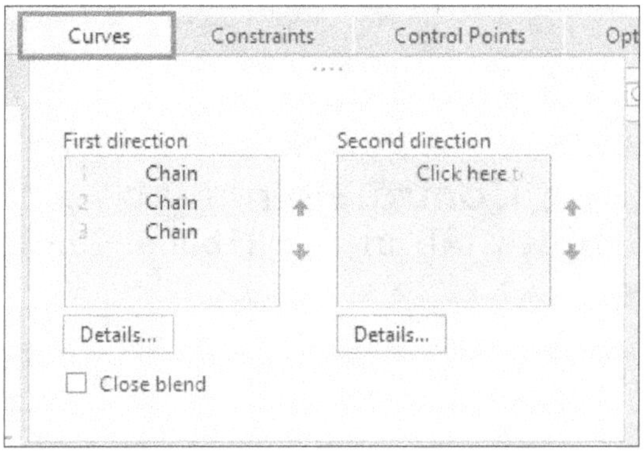

Figure-8. Curves tab of Boundary Blend tool

- The **First direction** and **Second direction** collector box displays curve or edge chain references that create a blended surface in the first and second direction, respectively.
- Select the **Close blend** check box to close the blend by connecting the last chain with the first chain.

Constraint tab

- Click on the **Constraints** tab in the **Ribbon**. The options will be displayed; refer to Figure-9.
- The **Boundary** area in the box of the tab displays the chains in the boundary blend.
- The **Condition** area in the box controls the boundary conditions including tangency conditions for edge alignment. Possible conditions for each chain are **Free**, **Tangent**, **Curvature**, and **Normal**.
- Specify desired stretch coefficient value in the **Stretch value** edit box.
- Select the **Show stretch handles** check box to display the drag handles for adjusting the stretch coefficients.

- Select the **Add side curve influence** check box to use influence of side curve to control the shape of the surface.
- Select the **Add inner edge tangency** check box to use inner edge tangency to control the shape of the surface.
- Select the **Optimize surface shape** check box to optimize the surface shape in situations where four single entity boundaries are selected with tangent or curvature connections applied.

Figure-9. Constraints tab of Boundary Blend tool

Control Points tab

- Click on the **Control Points** tab in the **Ribbon**. The options will be displayed; refer to Figure-10.

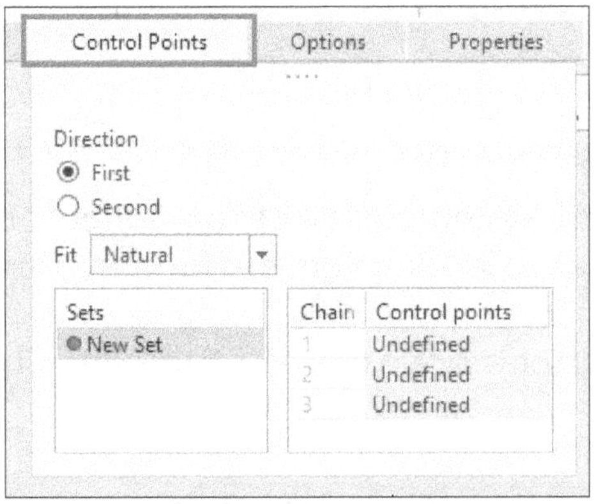

Figure-10. Control Points tab of Boundary Blend tool

- Select the **First** radio button from **Direction** area of the tab to add or remove control points in the first direction. Select the **Second** radio button to add or remove control points in the second direction.
- Select desired predefined control options from the **Fit** drop-down in the tab. Select the **Natural** option to create a uniform connection between points. Select the **Arclength** option to maintain the same arc along the length of curve connecting points. Select the **Piece to piece** option to create uniform piece by piece connection. Select the **Point to Point** option to create blend by connecting Point 1 in the first curve to the Point 2 in the second curve and so forth. Select the **Developable** option if two tangent curves in one direction are selected.

- The **Sets** box in the tab display the set of control points.
- The **Control Points** box shapes the surface by mapping control points locations on input curves.

Options tab

- You can also use an influcncing curve to change the shape of boundary blend. To do so, click on the **Options** tab in the **Boundary Blend** contextual tab. The options will be displayed as shown in Figure-11.

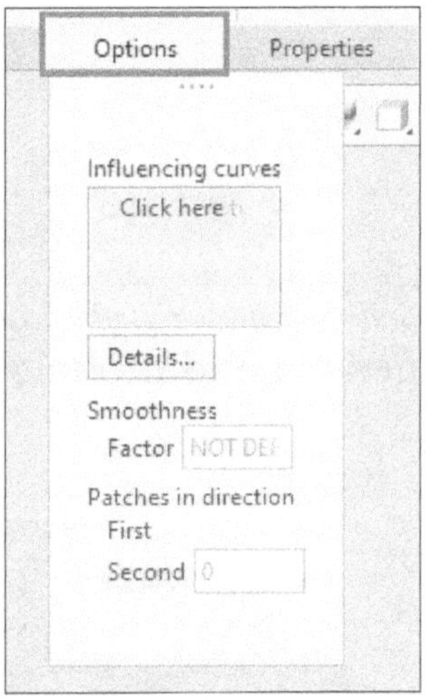

Figure-11. Options tab of Boundary Blend tool

- Click in the **Influencing curves** collector and select the sketched curve that you want to use for influencing the surface; refer to Figure-12. Preview of the boundary blend will be displayed; refer to Figure-13.

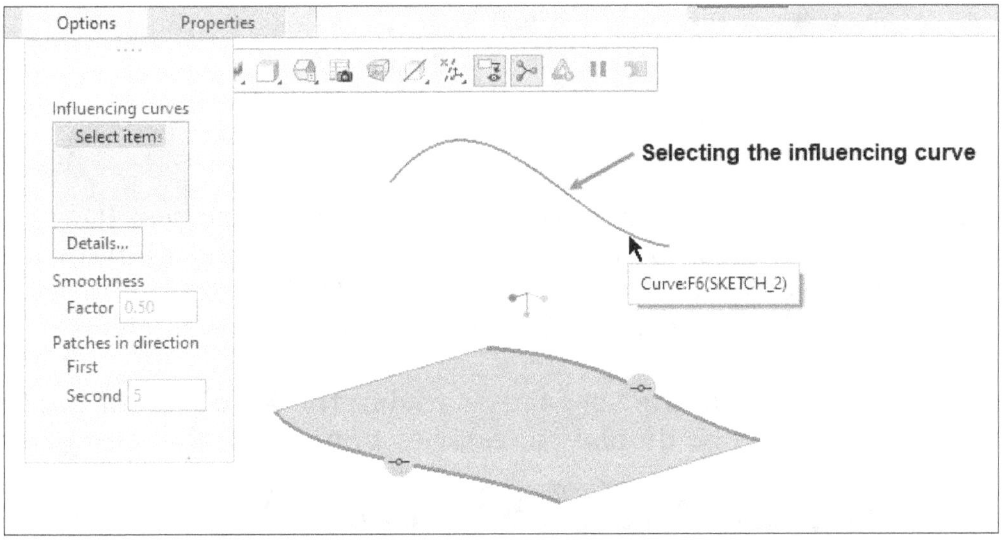

Figure-12. Selecting the influencing curve

- Specify desired smoothness factor value in the **Factor** edit box from **Smoothness** area of the tab to control the surface roughness, irregularities, or projections.
- Specify desired number of patches between 1 and 29 for the first and second directions in the **First** and **Second** edit boxes, respectively, from **Patches in direction** area of the tab to form the resultant surface.
- After specifying desired parameters, click on the **OK** button from the contextual tab to create the surface.

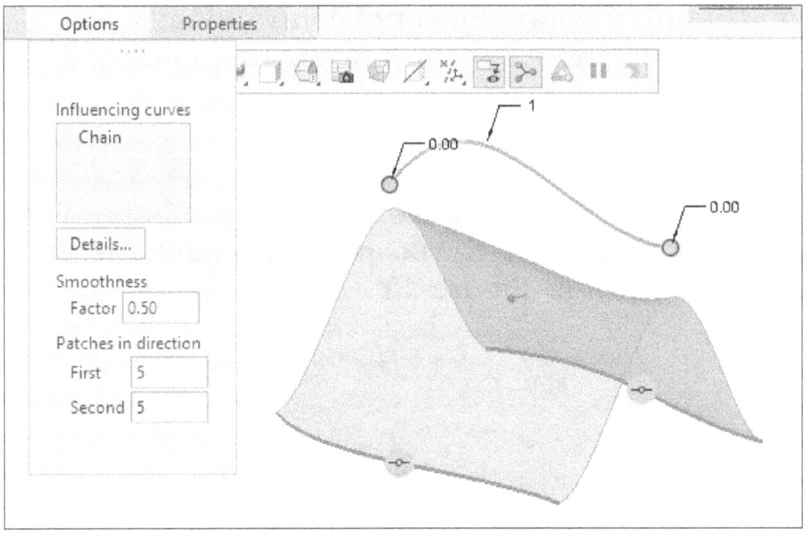

Figure-13. Preview of boundary blend with influencing curve

Note that you can also use the edges of solid models to create boundary blends; refer to Figure-14.

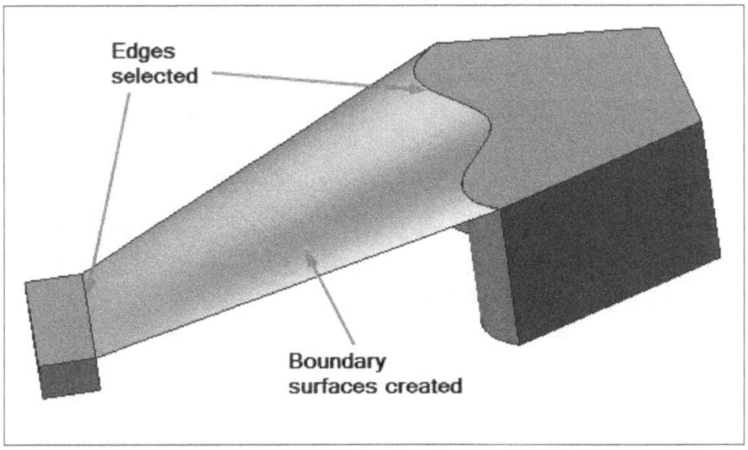

Figure-14. Boundary blend using edges of solids

FILL

The **Fill** tool is used to fill the void areas of solids and surfaces. It works with the help of closed sketches. Most of the time, we use it to create planar surfaces with irregular shapes but we can also use it along with **Project** tool to fill gaps between other solids/surfaces. The procedure for both the conditions is given next.

- Click on the **Fill** tool from the **Surfaces** panel in the **Model** tab of the **Ribbon**. The **Fill** contextual tab will be displayed; refer to Figure-15.

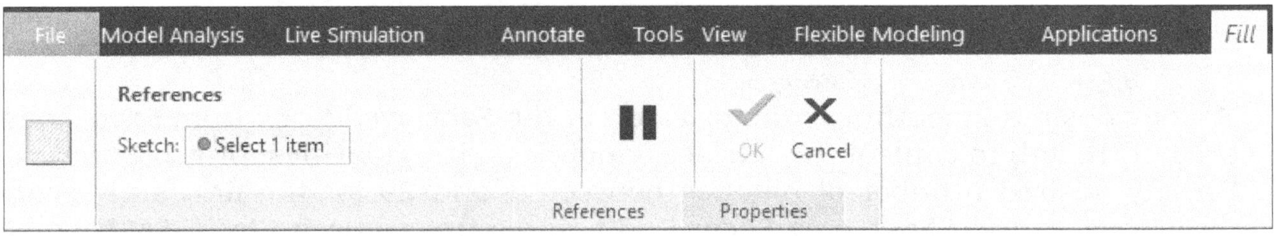

Figure-15. Fill contextual tab

- Click on the **References** tab and then click on the **Define** button from it.
- Select desired plane and create the sketch for planar surface. Note that the sketch must be closed one loop.

- After creating the sketch, click on the **OK** button from the **Sketch** contextual tab. The preview of the surface will be displayed; refer to Figure-16.

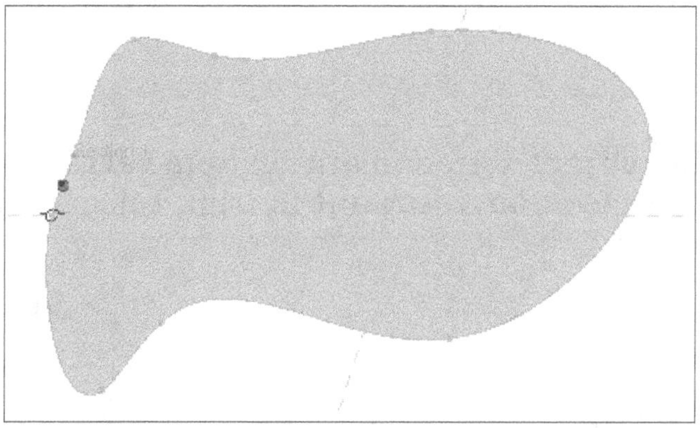

Figure-16. Preview of fill surface

- If you want to fill the gap on a planar surface then project the edges of the gap using the **Project** tool from the **Sketching** panel to form a closed loop; refer to Figure-17.

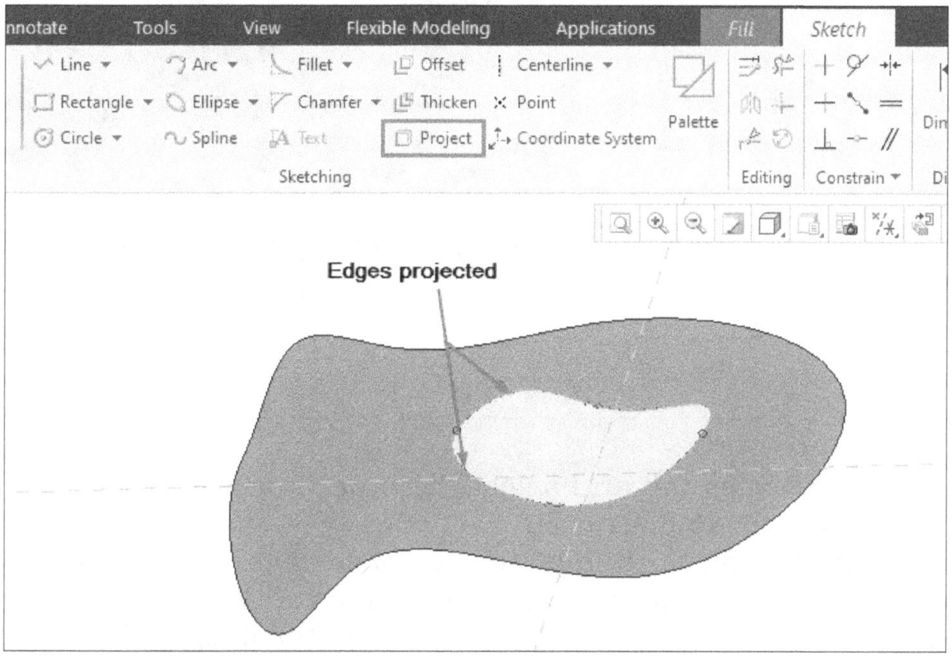

Figure-17. Edges projected to fill gap

- Click on the **OK** button from the **Fill** contextual tab to create the surface.

TRIMMING SURFACES

Trimming is an important step while creating surface models. As we trim sketched entities while sketching, in the same way we can trim the surfaces intersecting with other surfaces. The procedure for trimming surfaces is given next.

- Click on the **Trim** tool from **Editing** panel in the **Model** tab of the **Ribbon**. The **Trim** contextual tab will be displayed and you are asked to select the surface that you want to trim; refer to Figure-18.

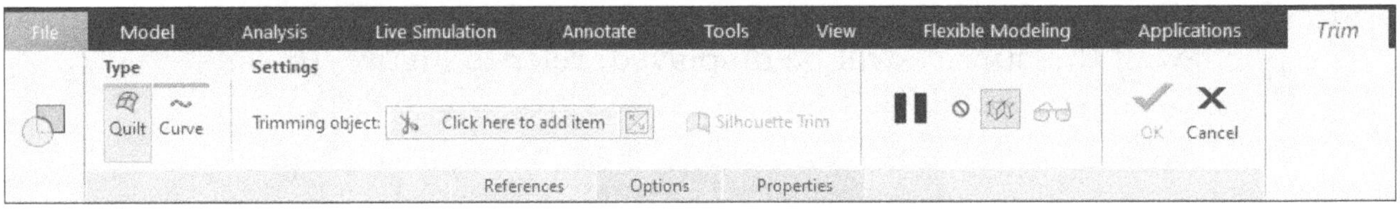

Figure-18. Trim contextual tab

- Click on the **Trimming object** selection button from **Settings** area of the contextual tab and select the surface that you want to trim; refer to Figure-19.

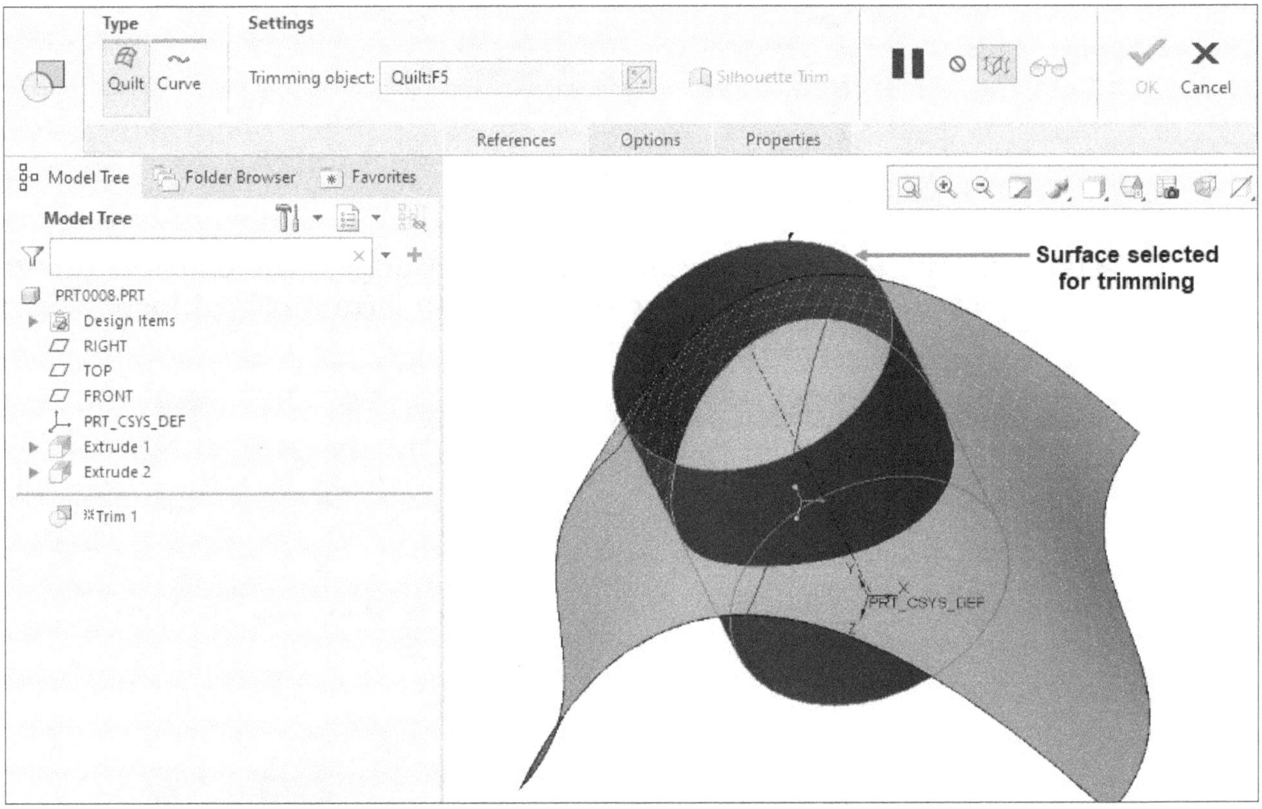

Figure-19. Surface selected for trimming

- Click on the **References** tab and select the other surface which you want to use as trimming tool; refer to Figure-20.
- Click on the **Flip** button to change the side of surface which you want to remain. Note that the portion of surface which is displayed with orange dotted net will remain and other portion will be trimmed. Clear the **Keep trimming quilt** check box from the **Options** tab of **Trim** contextual tab if you want to remove the trimming tool.
- Click on the **OK** button from the contextual tab. The other side of surface will be trimmed; refer to Figure-21.

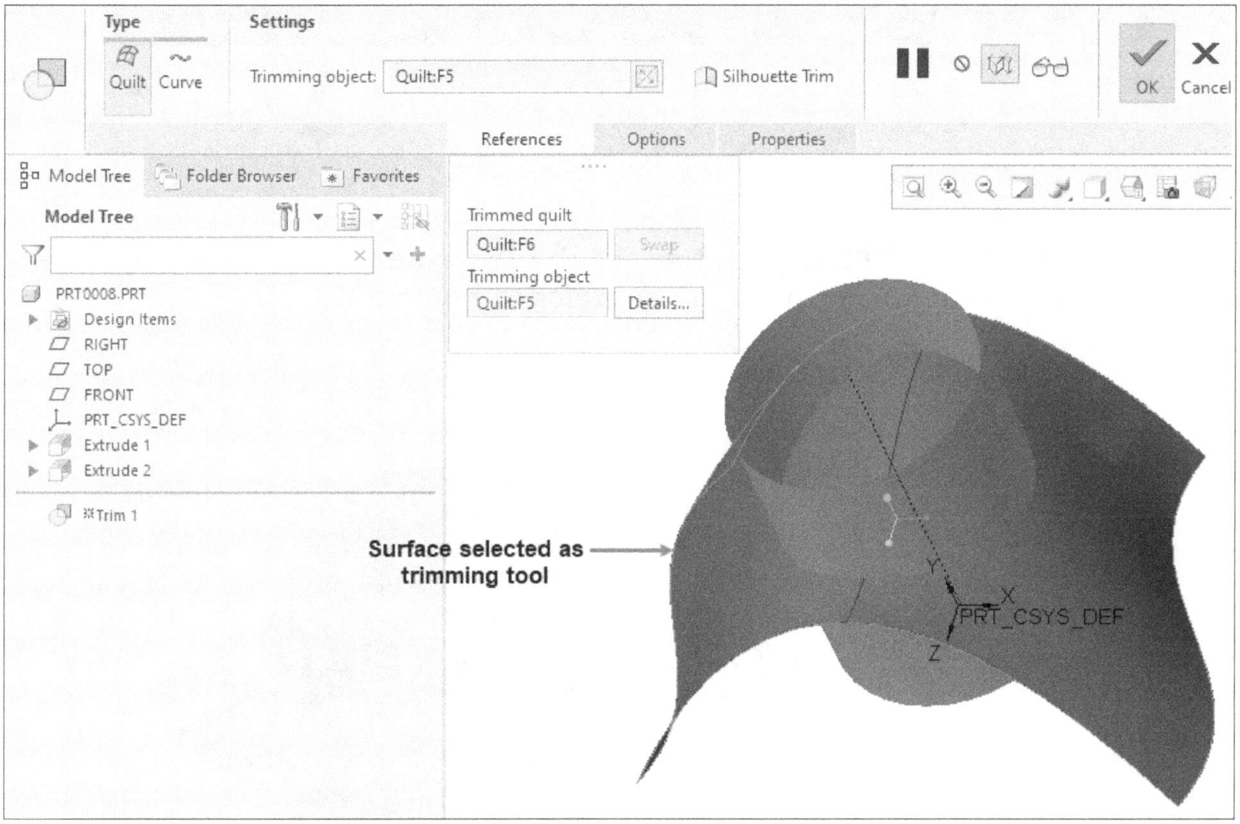

Figure-20. Selecting trimming surface

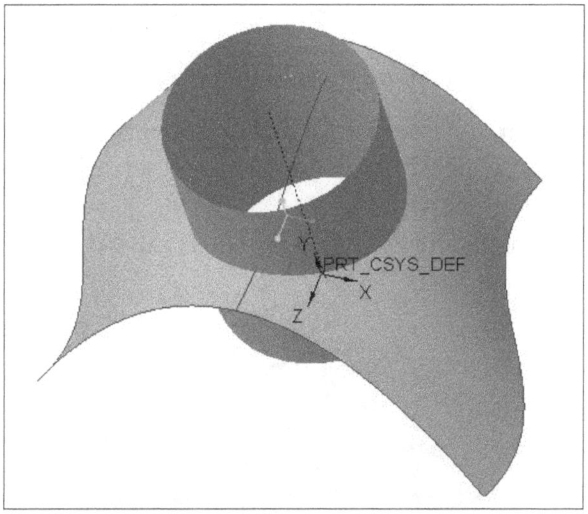

Figure-21. Surface after trimming

MERGING SURFACES

There can be various purposes of merging two or more surfaces; like applying same thickness to all the surfaces later, creating a closed surface to form solid, and so on. We will learn to form solid using surfaces later in this chapter. The procedure to merge surfaces is given next.

- Click on the **Merge** tool from **Editing** panel in the **Model** tab of the **Ribbon**. The **Merge** contextual tab will be displayed and you are asked to select the two intersecting surfaces; refer to Figure-22.

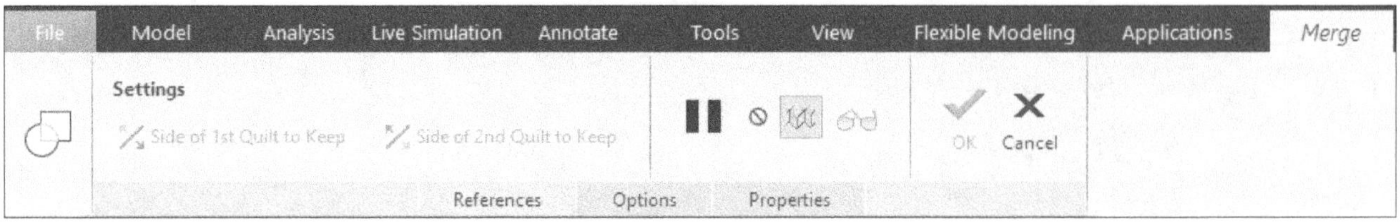

Figure-22. Merge contextual tab

- Press and hold the **CTRL** key and select the two intersecting surfaces from the modeling area that you want to merge; refer to Figure-23.

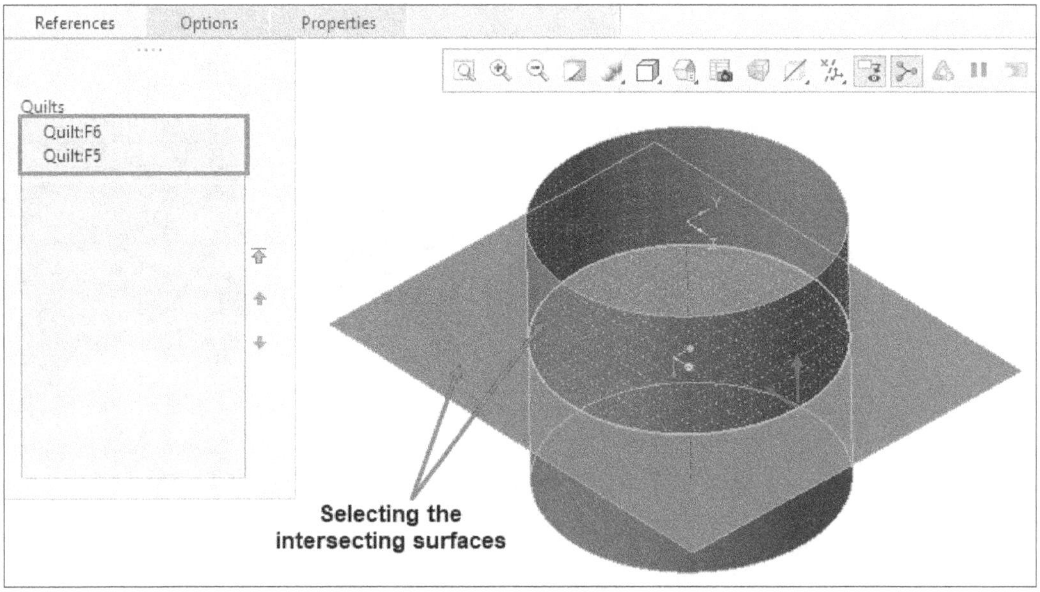

Figure-23. Selecting the intersecting surfaces

- Using the two **Flip** buttons from **Settings** area of the contextual tab, you can change the sides of surfaces. The direction in which the Pink arrows point will remain and others will be trimmed.
- Click on the **OK** button from the **Merge** contextual tab to merge the surfaces; refer to Figure-24.

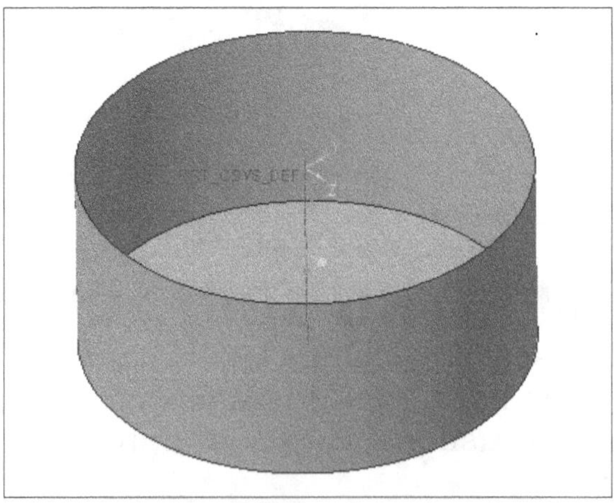

Figure-24. Merged surfaces

OFFSETTING SURFACES

The **Offset** tool in surfacing works in the same way as it does in sketching for sketched entities. The **Offset** tool is used to create copy of the selected entity at a specified distance. The procedure to offset surfaces is given next.

Surface Offset Type

- Click on the **Offset** tool from **Editing** panel in the **Model** tab of the **Ribbon**. The **Offset** contextual tab will be displayed with **Surface** offset type selected in the **Type** area of the contextual tab and you are asked to select the surface that you want to offset; refer to Figure-25.

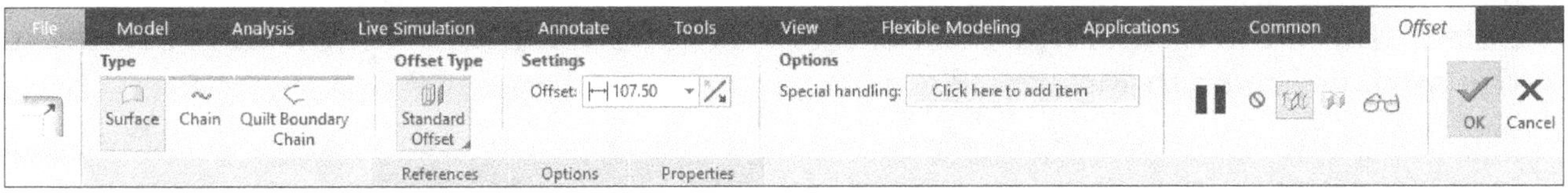

Figure-25. Offset contextual tab

- Select the surface that you want to offset, preview of the offsetted surface will be displayed; refer to Figure-26.

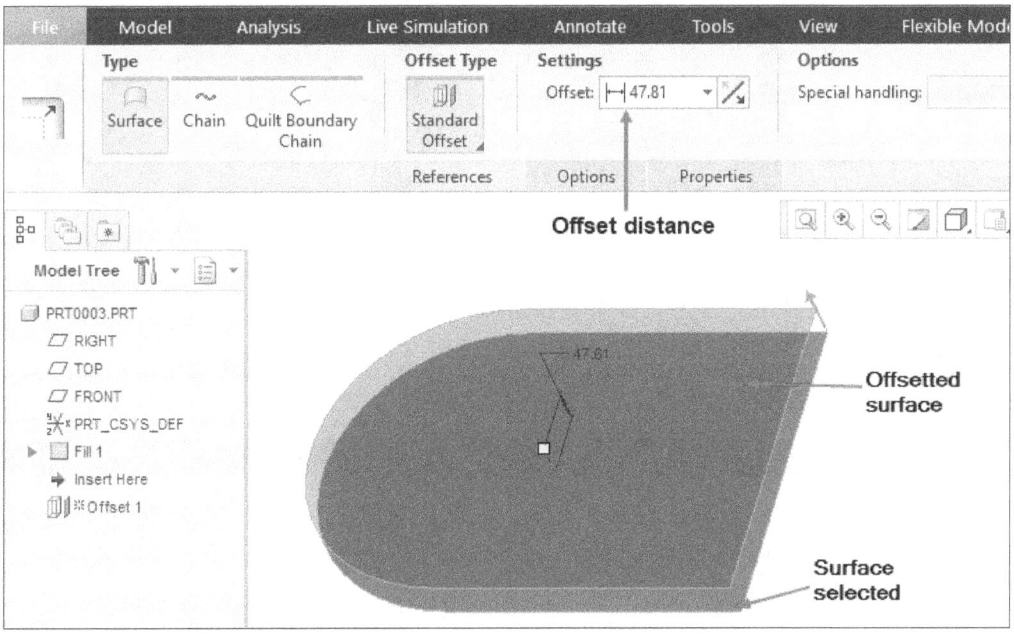

Figure-26. Preview of Offset

- The offset preview displayed in above figure is the most common use of **Offset** tool. But, there are three more options in which we can apply the **Offset** tool in surfacing; **Offset With Draft**, **Offset With Expand**, and **Offset With Replace Surface**. These options are available in the **Offset Type** drop-down in the contextual tab; refer to Figure-27.

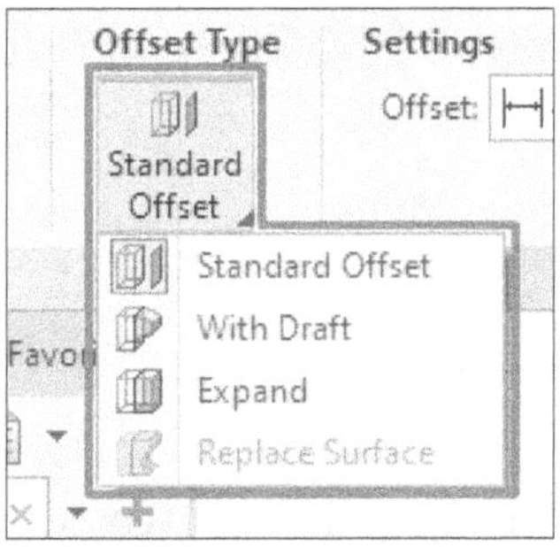

Figure-27. Offset Type drop-down

With Draft Feature

- Click on the **With Draft** option from the **Offset Type** drop-down. You will be asked to select or create a sketch.
- Select the closed sketch if you have in modeling area otherwise click on the **References** tab and select the **Define** button. You will be asked to select the sketching plane.
- Select the plane and create a closed sketch in such a way that it intersects with the surface; refer to Figure-28.

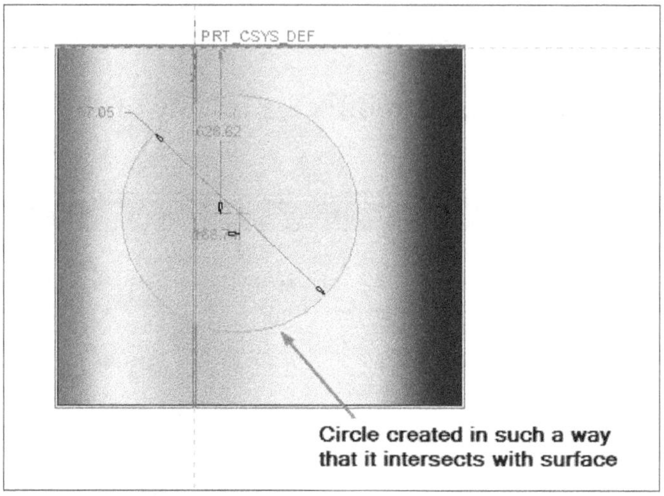

Figure-28. Sketch created

- After creating sketch, click on the **OK** button from the **Sketch** contextual tab. The preview will be displayed; refer to Figure-29.

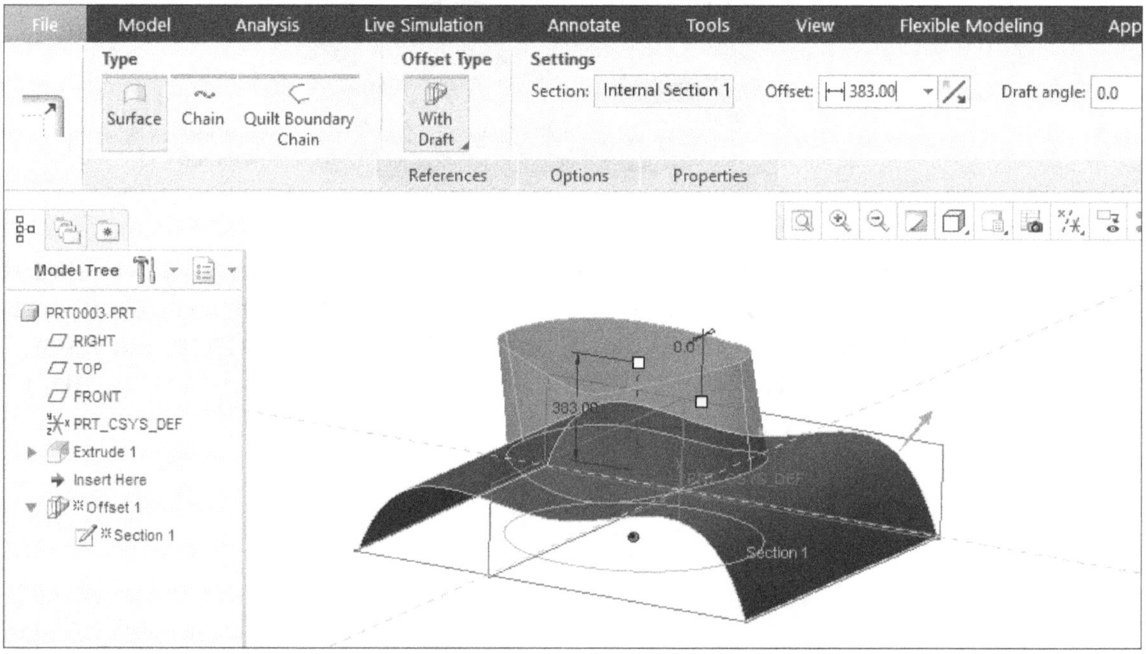

Figure-29. Preview of Offset with draft feature

- Specify desired height and draft angle in the edit boxes available in the contextual tab and click on the **OK** button from the contextual tab. The surface will be created with offsetted region coming out from the base surface; refer to Figure-30.

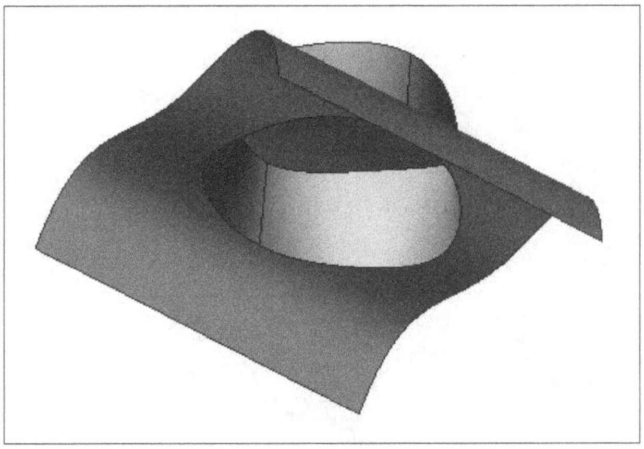

Figure-30. Offsetted surface viewed from bottom

Expand Feature

You can offset the surface in same way as done using **With Draft** option but without applying draft, by using the **Expand** option. The procedure is same as for **With Draft** option.

Replace Surface Feature

The **Replace Surface** option is used to replace the face of a solid model with an intersecting surface. In other words, the selected face takes the shape of surface selected as replacement. The procedure to use this option is given next.

- Click on the **Offset** tool from the **Editing** panel of the **Ribbon**. The **Offset** contextual tab will be displayed. You are asked to select the surface to be offset.
- Select the surface of the solid model to be offset; refer to Figure-31.

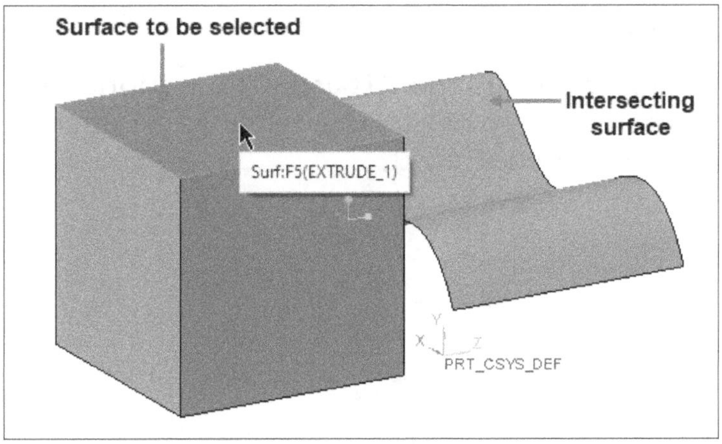

Figure-31. Face of solid model selected for replacement

- Select the **Replace Surface** option from the **Offset Type** drop-down in the contextual tab. You are asked to select the replacement surface.
- Select the replacement surface which is intersecting with the model parallel to replacement face. Preview of replaced surface will be displayed; refer to Figure-32.

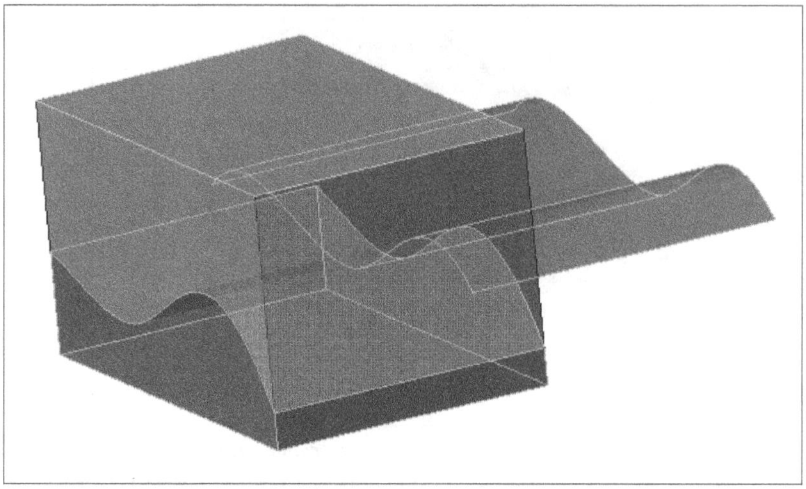

Figure-32. Preview of replaced surface

- Select the **Keep replace quilt** check box from **Options** tab in the **Offset** contextual tab to prevent the replace quilt from being absorbed by the offset feature.
- Click on the **OK** button from the contextual tab to create the replacement.

Chain Offset Type

- Select the **Chain** option from the **Type** area of the **Offset** contextual tab. The updated **Offset** contextual tab will be displayed; refer to Figure-33.

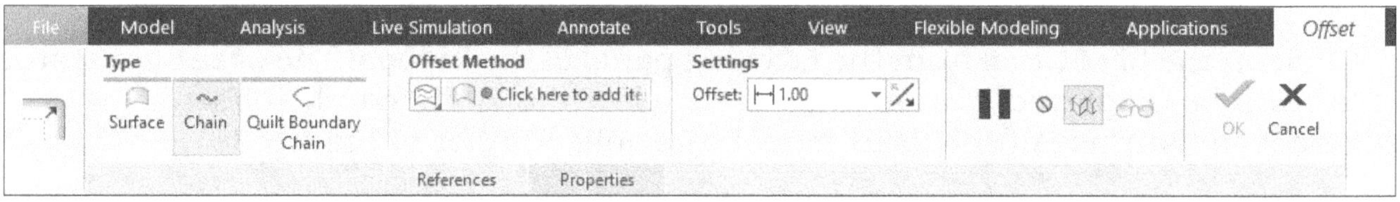

Figure-33. Offset contextual tab with Chain offset type options

- Click on the **References** tab in the **Ribbon**. The options will be displayed; refer to Figure-34. You are asked to select the curve to be offset and select the quilt, plane, or surface as a reference quilt.

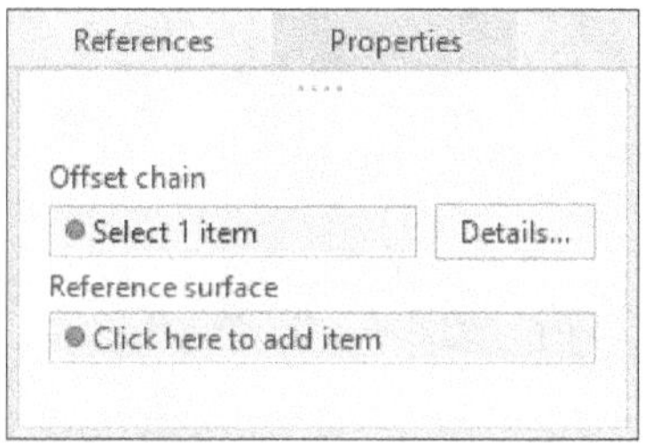

Figure-34. References tab of Chain offset type

- Click in the **Offset chain** collector box and select the curve to be offset. The **Reference quilt** collector box displays the reference quilt, plane, or surface selected; refer to Figure-35.

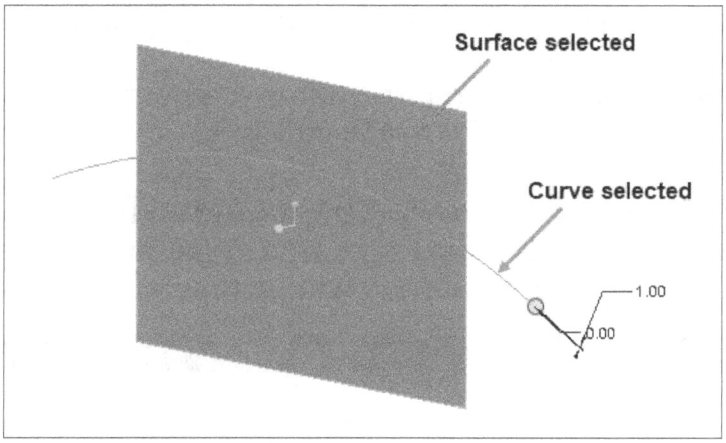

Figure-35. Curve and surface selected

- Select desired offset method from the drop-down in the **Offset Method** area of the contextual tab; refer to Figure-36. Select the **Along Surface** option to offset the curve along the reference surface. Select the **Normal to Surface** option to offset the curve normal to the reference surface.
- On selecting the **Along Surface** option from the drop-down, the **Measurements** tab will be displayed in the **Ribbon**; refer to Figure-37.

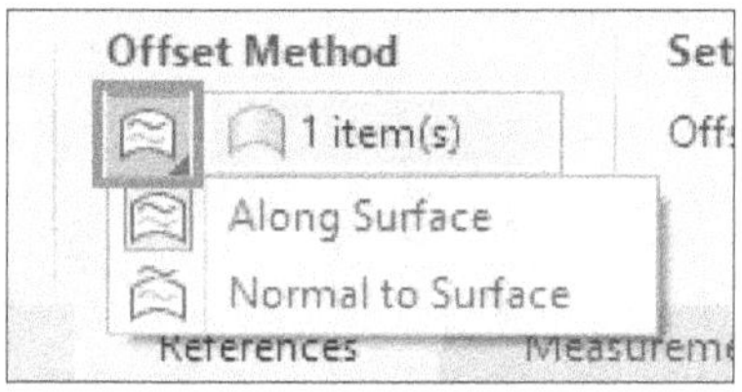

Figure-36. Offset Method drop down

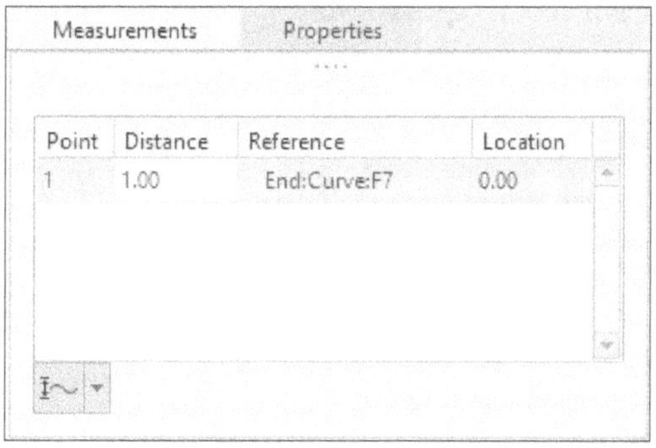

Figure-37. Measurements tab of the Chain offset type

- The **Point** area of the tab lists the points used in the offset. Right-click on the number and click on the **Add** or **Delete** button to add or delete a point, respectively.
- The **Distance** area specifies the offset distance. You can either drag the handle in the graphics window or click on the **Distance** cell to enter a new value.
- The **Reference** area activates the reference collector for this point.
- The **Location** area specifies the length ratio of the point.
- Select the button to measure the offset distance in the direction normal to the curve.
- Select the button to measure the offset distance in the direction parallel to the selected datum plane.
- On selecting the **Normal to Surface** option from the **Offset Method** area of the contextual tab. The **Options** tab will be displayed in the **Ribbon**; refer to Figure-38.

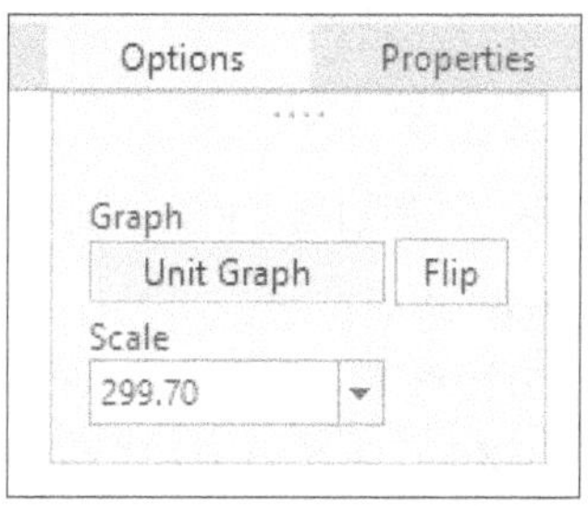

Figure-38. Options tab of Curve offset type

- Click on the **Unit Graph** button from **Graph** area of the tab to collect the graph used as the offset reference.
- Click on the **Flip** button to reverse the offset direction.
- Specify desired offset value in the **Scale** edit box.

Quilt Boundary Chain Offset Type

- Select **Quilt Boundary Chain** offset type from **Type** area of the **Offset** contextual tab. The updated **Offset** contextual tab will be displayed; refer to Figure-39.

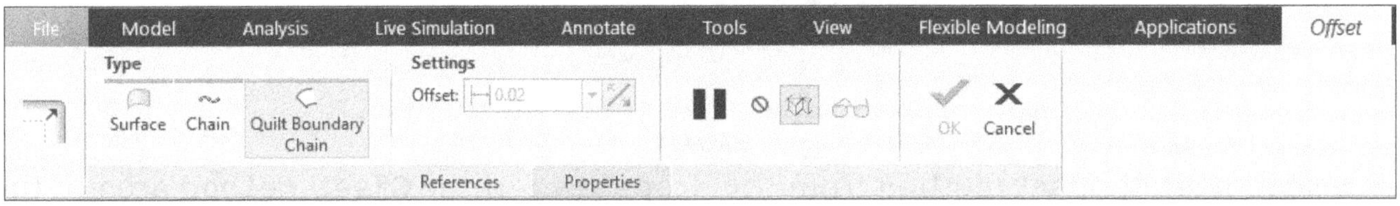

Figure-39. Offset contextual tab with Quilt Boundary Chain offset type options

- Click on the **References** tab in the **Ribbon**. The options will be displayed; refer to Figure-40. You are asked to select the boundary edges to be offset.
- Select the chain of boundary edges of a surface you want to offset; refer to Figure-41. On selecting the edges, the **Measurements** tab will be displayed in the **Ribbon**; refer to Figure-42.

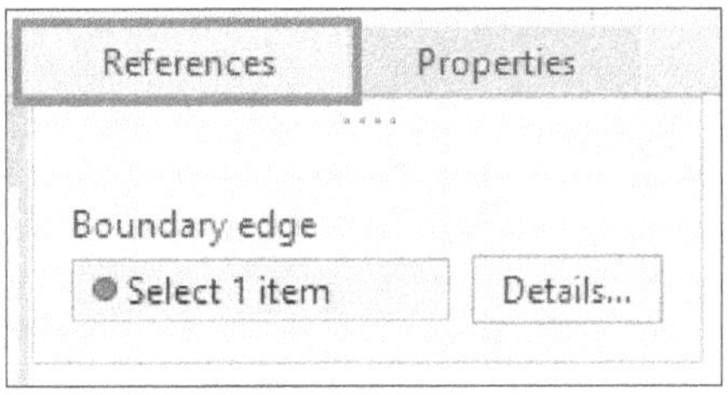

Figure-40. References tab of Quilt Boundary Chain offset type

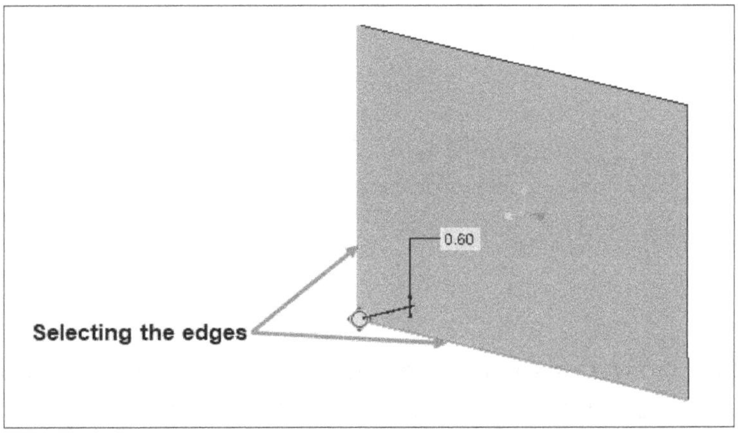

Figure-41. Selecting the boundary edges to be offset

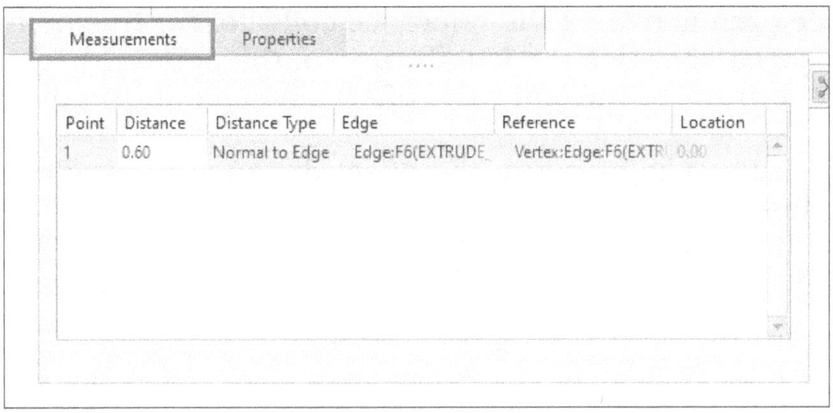

Figure-42. Measurements tab of the Quilts Boundary Chain offset type

- Select desired option from the drop-down in the **Distance Type** area of the tab. Select **Normal to Edge** option to measure the offset distance normal to the boundary edge. Select **Along Edge** option to measure the offset distance along the measurement edge. Select the **To Vertex** option to start offset curve at the vertex and parallel to the boundary edge. Note that the only **Normal to Edge** option will be displayed on selecting the multiple edges of surface boundary. The other options will be displayed on selecting the single edge only.

- The **Edge** area displays the boundary edge for this point.
- Rest of the options have been discussed earlier in this tool.
- Specify desired offset distancc in the **Offset** edit box from **Settings** area of the contextual tab.
- Click on the button from **Settings** area to change the direction of offset to the other side.
- After specifying desired parameters, click on the **OK** button from the contextual tab to create the feature.

THICKEN

The **Thicken** tool is used to add desired thickness to a surface. This tool used once you have performed all the surfacing operations. The procedure to use this tool is given next.

- Click on the **Thicken** tool from **Editing** panel in the **Model** tab of the **Ribbon**. The **Thicken** contextual tab will be displayed; refer to Figure-43. You are asked to select the surface to be thicken.

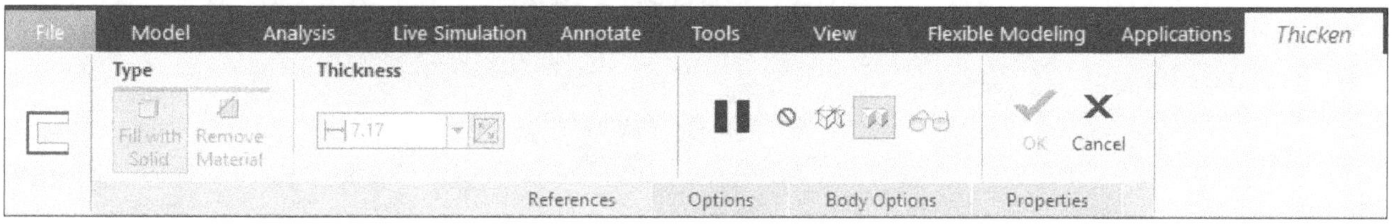

Figure-43. Thicken contextual tab

- Select the surface to which you want to apply thickness. Preview of thickened surface will be displayed; refer to Figure-44.

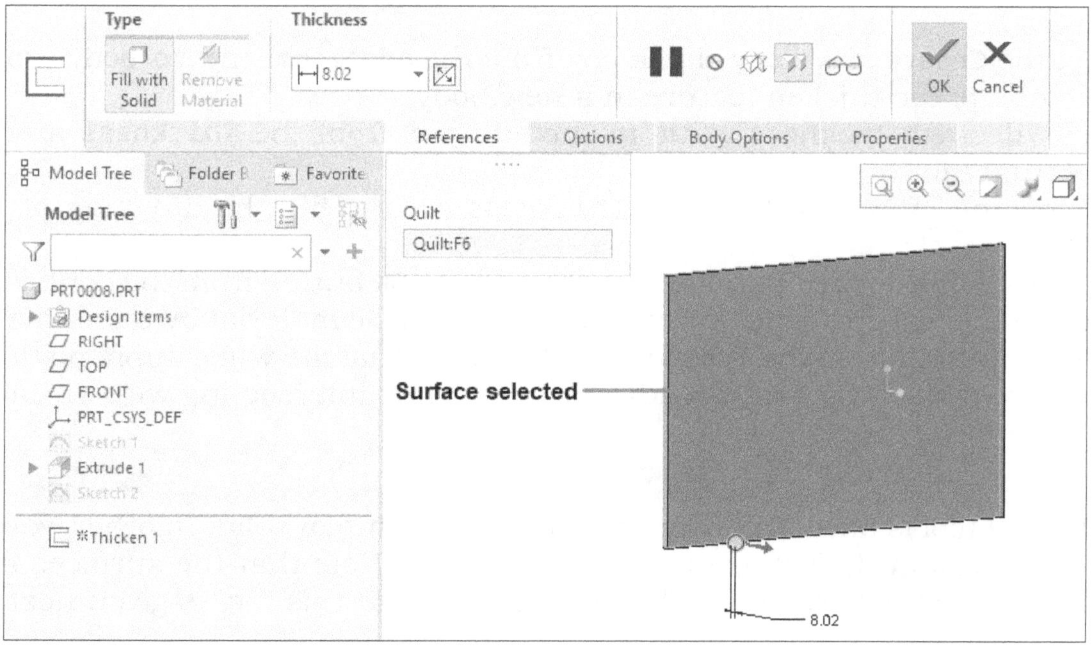

Figure-44. Preview of Thickened surface

Options tab

- Click on the **Options** tab in the **Ribbon**. The options will be displayed; refer to Figure-45.

Figure-45. Options tab of Thicken tool

- Select the **Normal to surface** option from the drop-down in the tab to offset the thickened surface normal to the original surface. Select the **Automatic fit** option from the drop-down to scale and translate the thickened surface in relation to an automatically determined coordinate system. Select the **Controlled fit** option from the drop-down to scale the original surface about a selected coordinate system, and then translate it along a specified axis.

Body Options tab

- Click on the **Body Options** tab in the **Ribbon**. The options will be displayed; refer to Figure-46.

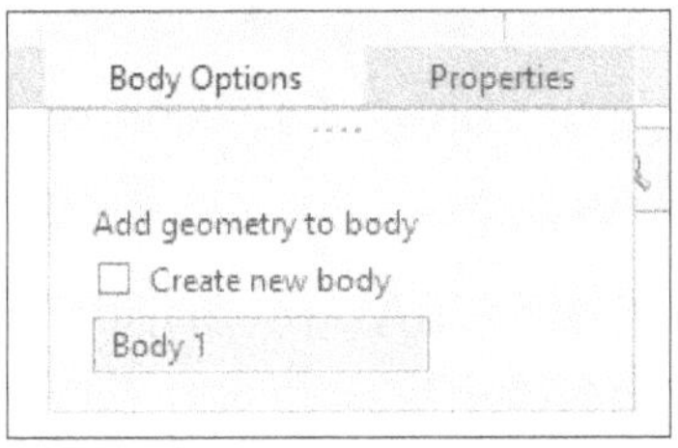

Figure-46. Body Options tab of Thicken tool

- Select the **Create new body** check box from the **Add geometry to body** area of the tab to create the thicken feature in a new body.
- Specify desired thickness value in the edit box from the **Thickness** area of the contextual tab.
- Click on the button from the **Thickness** area to flip the direction of thicken feature.
- After specifying desired parameters, click on the **OK** button from the contextual tab to create the feature. Note that you can also remove material by using the **Remove Material** button from the **Type** area of the contextual tab while applying thickness to surface if a solid model already exists which is intersecting with surface.

SOLIDIFY

The **Solidify** tool is used to convert closed surfaces into a solid. In other words, this tool fills material in the volume closed by surfaces. Note that the surfaces must be merged by using the **Merge** tool. The procedure to use this tool is given next.

- Click on the **Solidify** tool from **Editing** panel in the **Model** tab of the **Ribbon**. The **Solidify** contextual tab will be displayed; refer to Figure-47. You are asked to select the surface to be solidify.

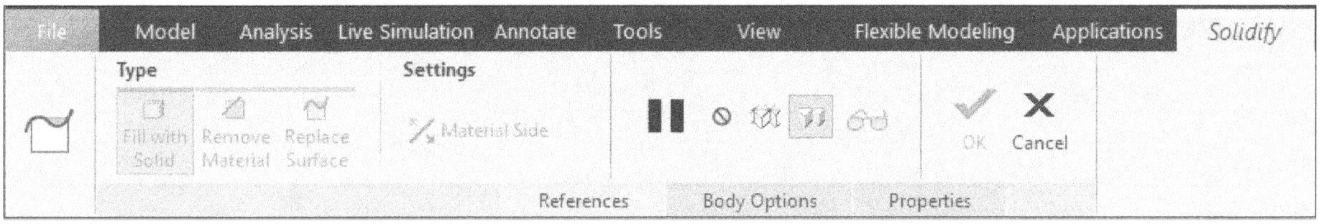

Figure-47. Solidify contextual tab

- Select the merged surfaces forming closed volume that you want to solidify; refer to Figure-48.

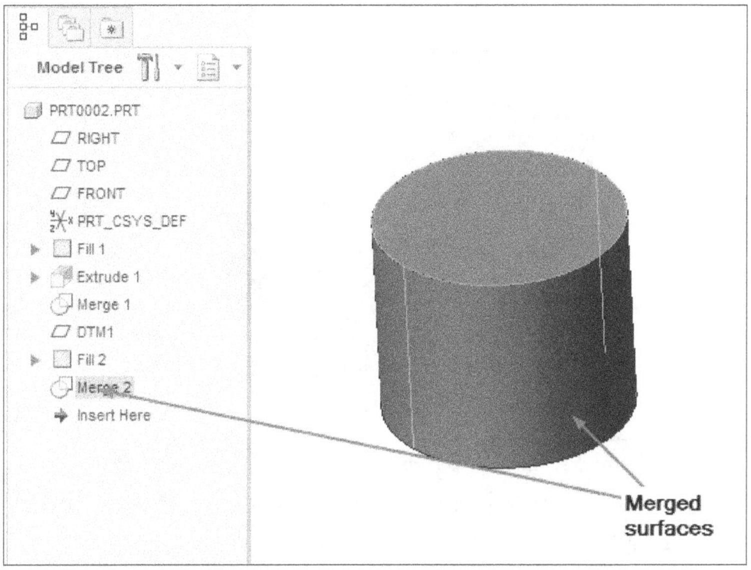

Figure-48. Merged surfaces selected

- Click on the **Material Side** button from **Settings** area in the **Ribbon**.
- The other options in the contextual tab is same as discussed in previous tool.
- Click on the **OK** button from the contextual tab. Solid will be created using the surface boundaries.

EDITING SURFACES USING CONTROL POINTS

We can modify the shape of a surface/face by using the control points. **This operation is generally done after creating solid from surface.** The tools to do so are available in the **Style** contextual tab. The procedure to modify surface/face using control points is given next.

- Click on the **Style** tool from the **Surfaces** tab in the **Model** tab of **Ribbon**. The **Style** contextual tab will be displayed; refer to Figure-49.

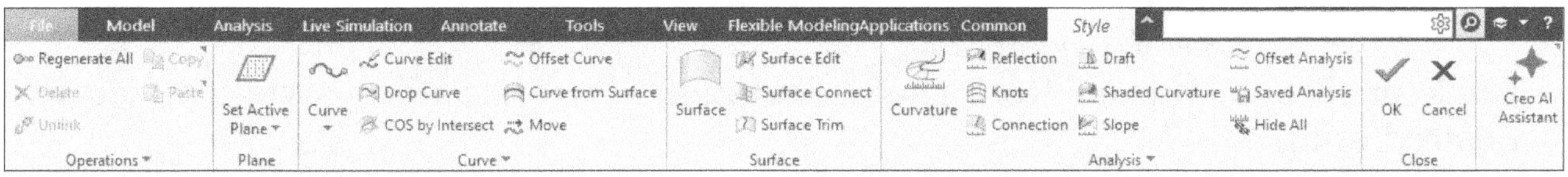

Figure-49. Style contextual tab

- Click on the **Surface Edit** tool from the **Surface** panel in the contextual tab. The **Style: Surface Edit** contextual tab will be displayed; refer to Figure-50.

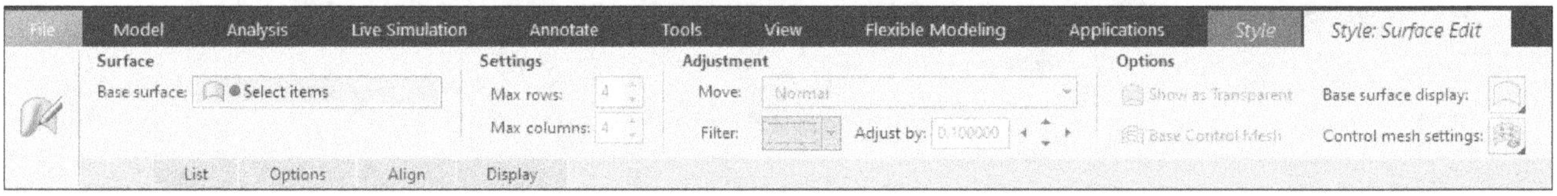

Figure-50. Style Surface Edit contextual tab

- Select the surface/face of model that you want to modify. Control points will be displayed on the surface/face; refer to Figure-51.

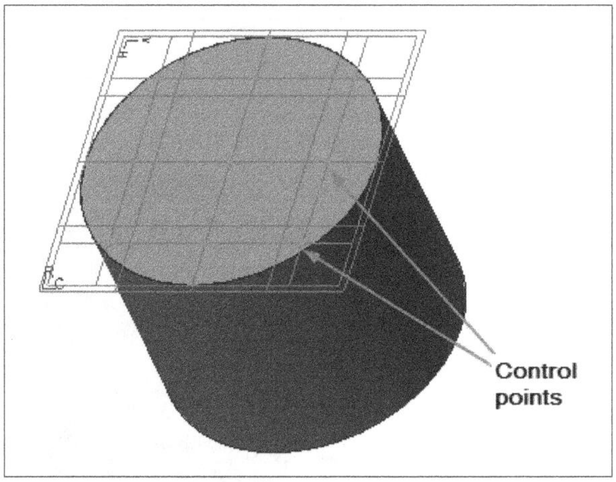

Figure-51. Face with control points

- Increase the number of control points by using the **Max rows** and **Max columns** spinners from **Settings** area of the contextual tab.
- Drag the control points from the modeling area to modify the shape of surface; refer to Figure-52.

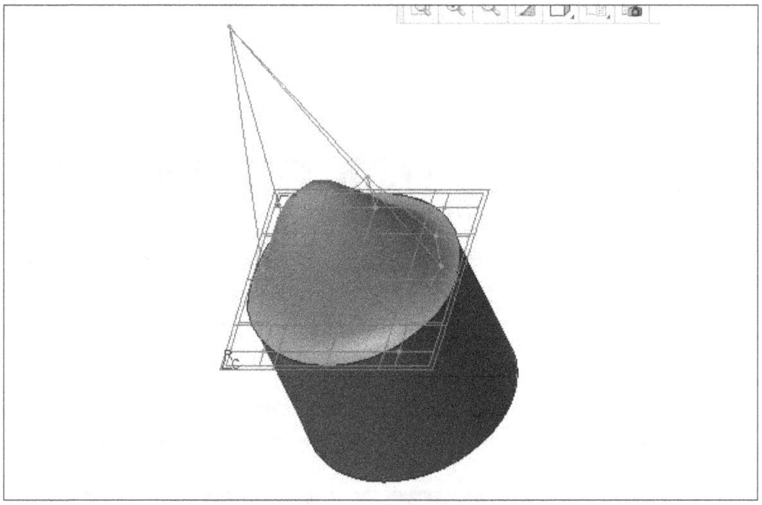

Figure-52. Surface editted

- Click on the **OK** button from the contextual tab to create a style surface with desired shape.
- Click on the **OK** button from the **Style** contextual tab to create the feature. You will notice that it has become a separate surface; refer to Figure-53. If you want this surface to be applied on solid model, use the **Replace Surface** option in the **Offset** tool. The model after replacing the face with style surface will be displayed as shown in Figure-54.

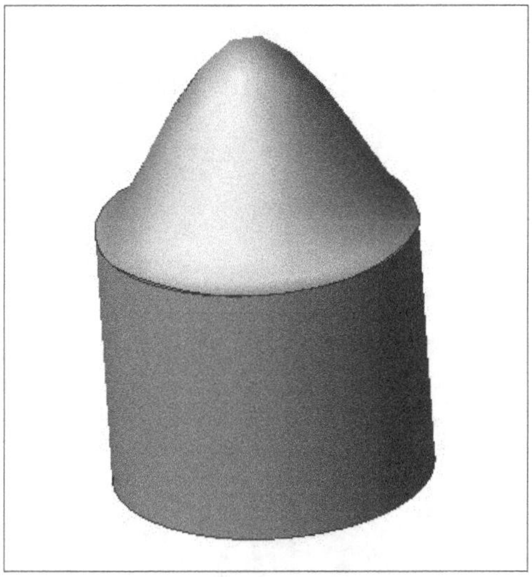

Figure-53. Style surface created

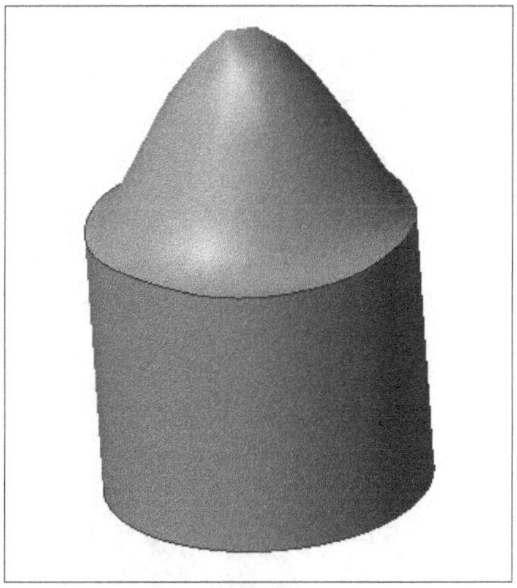

Figure-54. Model after replacing the face

VERTEX ROUND

The **Vertex Round** tool is used to apply round at the sharp vertex of a surface. The procedure to use this tool is given next.

- Click on the **Vertex Round** tool from the expanded **Surfaces** panel of the **Model** tab in the **Ribbon**. The **Vertex Round** contextual tab will be displayed and you will be asked to select vertices to be rounded.
- Select the vertices. Preview of the round will be displayed; refer to Figure-55.

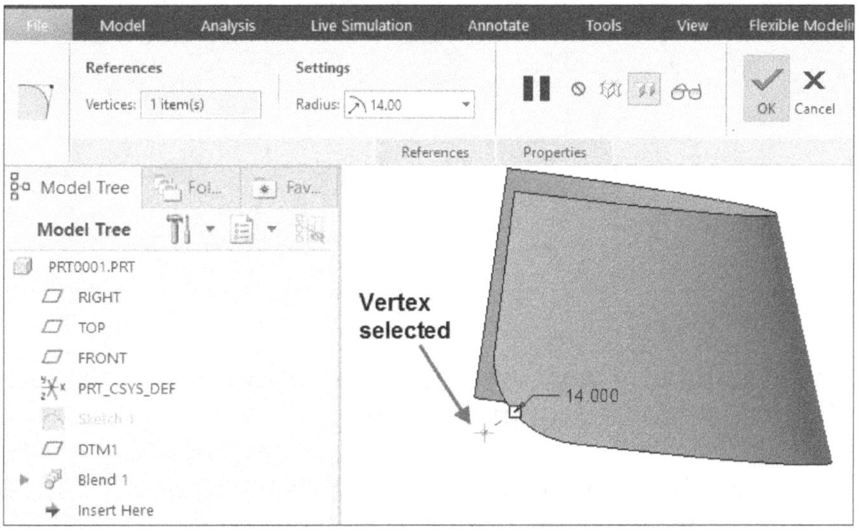

Figure-55. Preview of vertex round

- Specify desired value of radius in the **Settings** area of the contextual tab and click on the **OK** button from the **Ribbon** to create the feature.

PRACTICAL 1

Create the model of helmet glass as shown in Figure-56. The dimensions of the model are given in Figure-57.

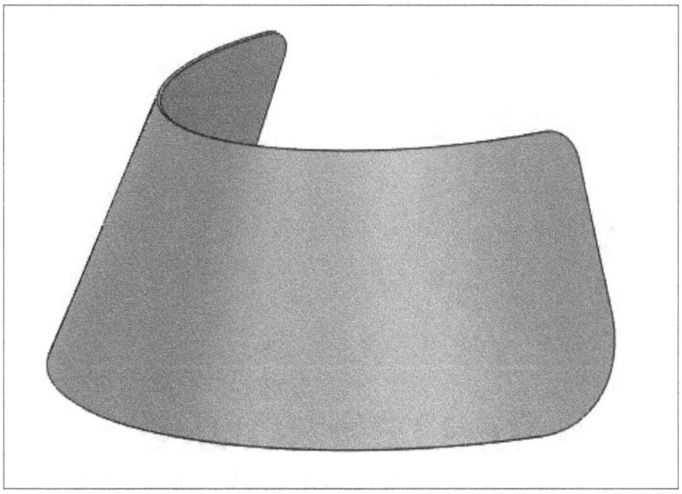

Figure-56. Practical1 model

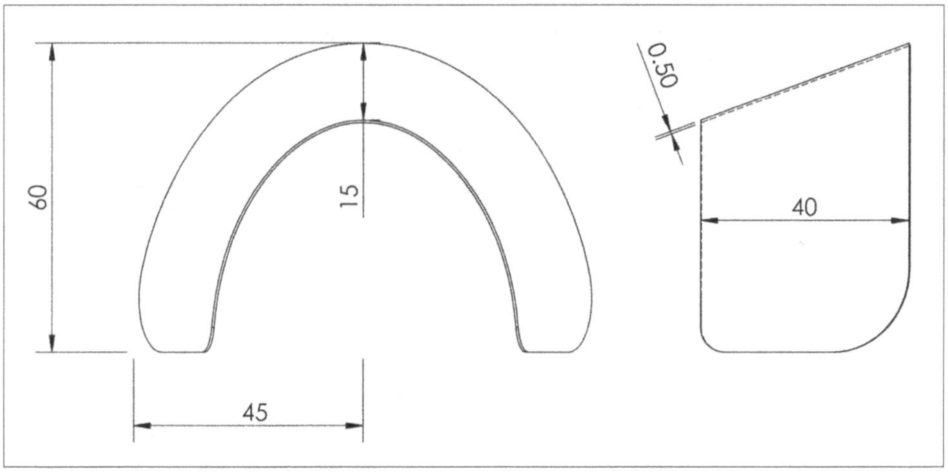

Figure-57. Practical 1 drawing

The model displayed is having very low thickness and its having complex 3D shape. So, its a good idea to use surfacing in this case.

We can create this model by **Blend** tool easily. For that, we need to have two sketches. Start the Part Modeling environment of Creo Parametric.

Creating first sketch

- Click on the **Sketch** tool from the **Datum** panel in the **Model** tab of the **Ribbon**. The **Sketch** dialog box will be displayed and you will be prompted to select a sketching plane.
- Select the **Top** plane and click on the **Sketch** button. The sketching environment will display.
- Click on the **Center and Axis Ellipse** tool from the **Ellipse** drop-down in the **Sketching** panel of the **Ribbon** and draw an ellipse as shown in Figure-58.

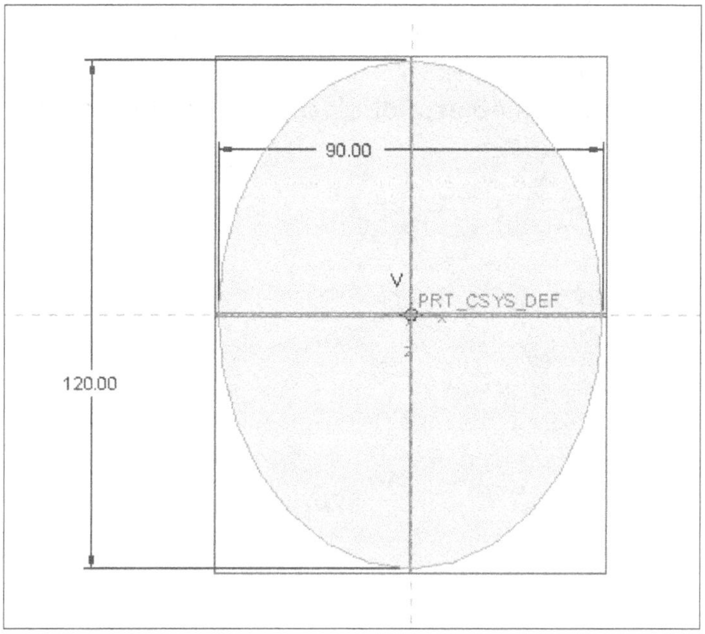

Figure-58. Ellipse to be drawn

- Trim the ellipse by using the **Delete Segment** tool in such a way that upper half of ellipse is left; refer to Figure-59.

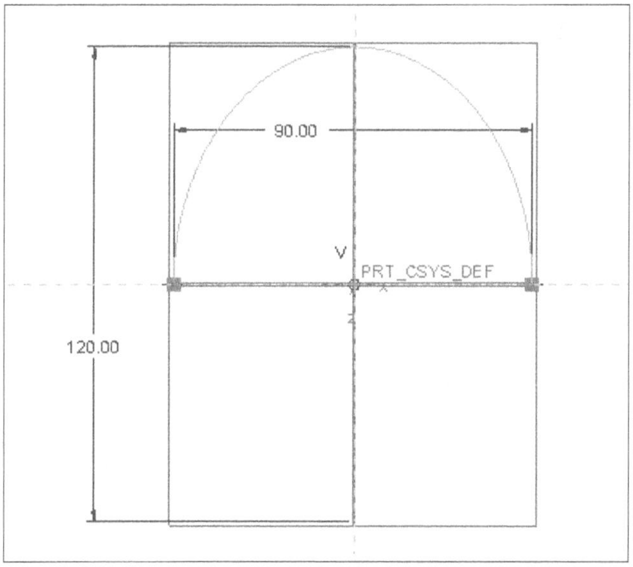

Figure-59. Trimmed ellipse

- Click on the **OK** button from **Sketch** contextual tab to exit the sketch.

Creating blended surface

- Click on the **Blend** tool from expanded **Shapes** panel in **Model** tab of the **Ribbon**. The **Blend** contextual tab will be displayed; refer to Figure-60.

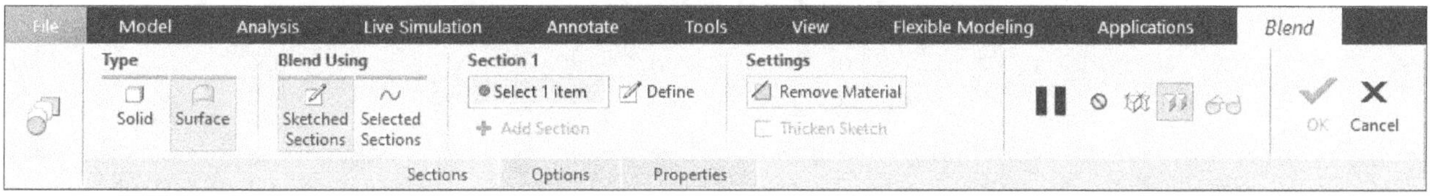

Figure-60. Blend contextual tab

- Select the **Surface** button from **Type** area of the contextual tab.
- Click on the **Sections** tab and select the sketch created. You are asked to specify offset distance for second sketch.
- Specify the offset distance as **40** and click on the **Sketch** button; refer to Figure-61.

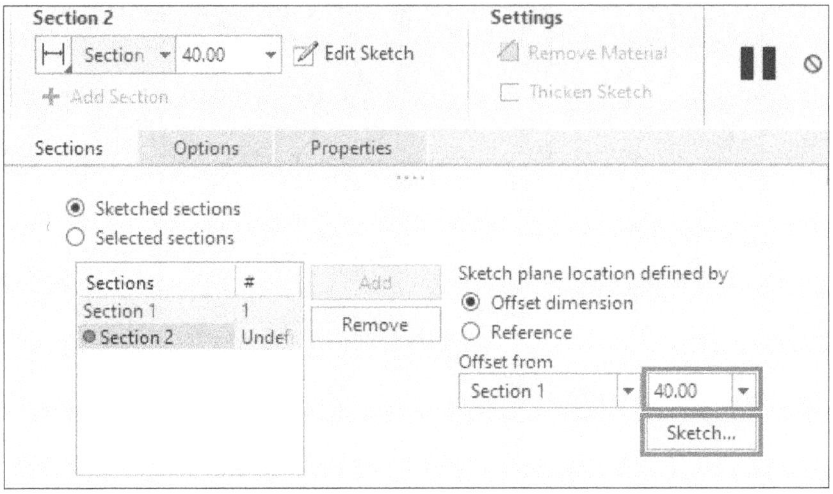

Figure-61. Offset distance specified

- Click on the **Offset** tool from the **Sketching** panel in the **Ribbon** and select the earlier created sketch.
- Specify the value of offset as **-15** if offset direction is **outward** and **15** if offset direction is **inward** in the input box displayed; refer to Figure-62.

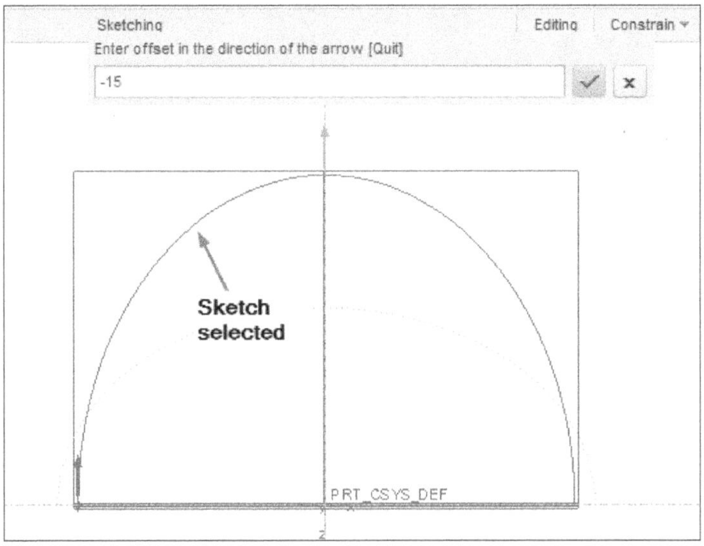

Figure-62. Sketch offsetted

- Click on the **OK** button from the Input box and **Close** button from the **Type** Menu Manager displayed to create the offset curve; refer to Figure-63. Note that the starting points of curves should be properly aligned. After aligning the starting points, the sketch should display like Figure-64.

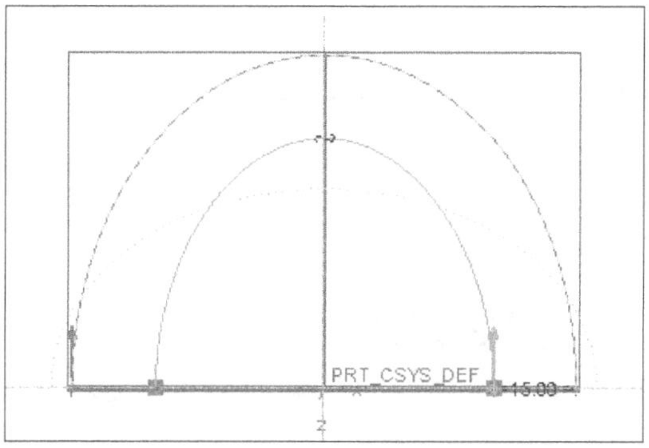

Figure-63. Offset sketch created

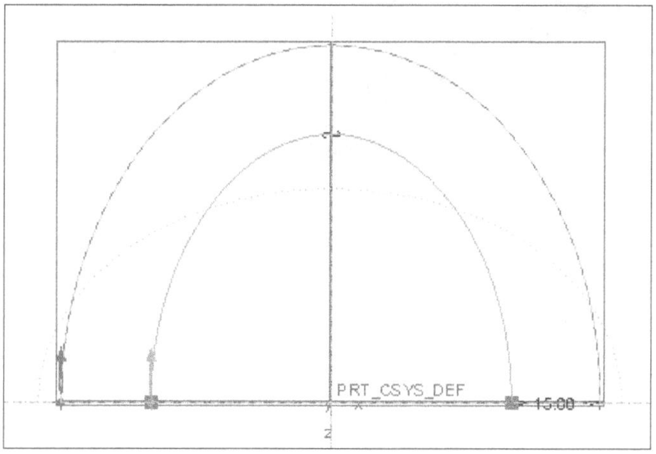

Figure-64. Sketch after aligning starting points

- Exit the sketching environment by pressing **OK** button. Preview of blended surface will be displayed; refer to Figure-65.

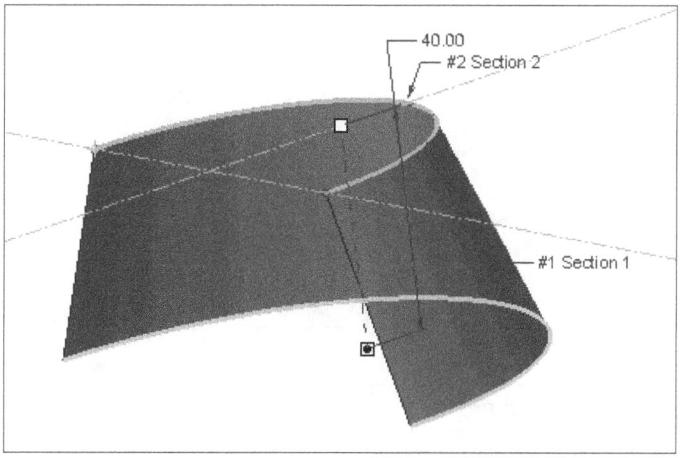

Figure-65. Blended surface

- Click on the **OK** button from the **Blend** contextual tab to create the surface.

Thickening surface and applying fillet

- Click on the **Thicken** tool from the **Ribbon** and select the surface. Preview of thickened surface will display.
- Enter the thickness value as **0.5**.
- Click **OK** to create the solid.
- Click on the **Fillet** tool and apply suitable fillets at the small edges on the corners.

PRACTICE 1

Create the surface model of tank as shown in Figure-66. The dimensions of the model are given in Figure-67.

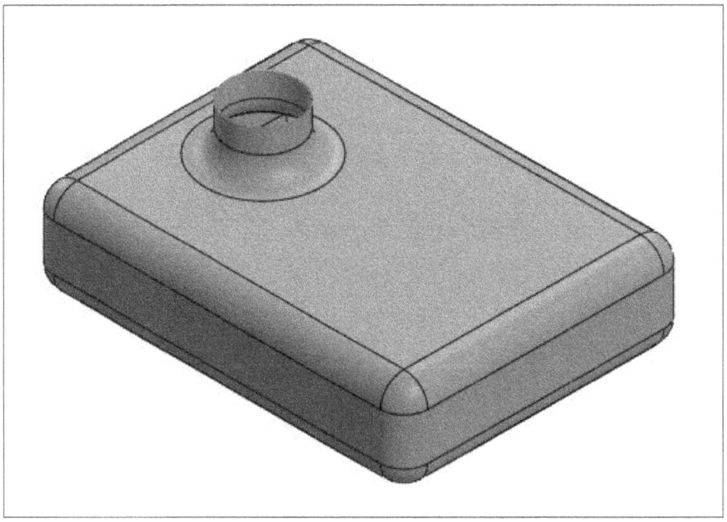

Figure-66. Practice1 model

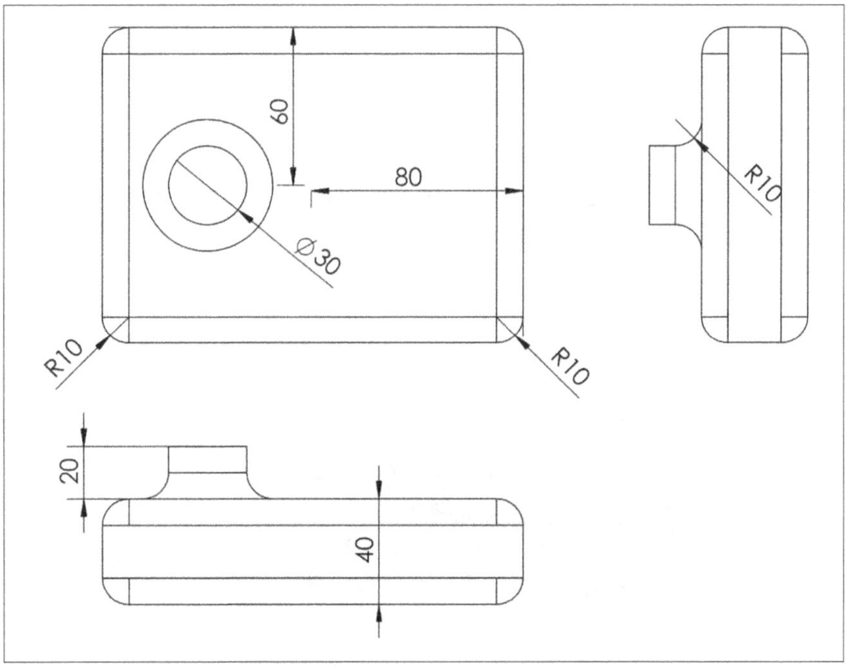

Figure-67. Practice1 drawing

PRACTICE 2

Create the surface model of car bumper as shown in Figure-68. The dimensions of the model are given in Figure-69. **Assume the missing dimensions. (Hint:** You will need the **Style** tools to modify the surface after using **Swept Blend** tool.**)**

Figure-68. Practice 2 model

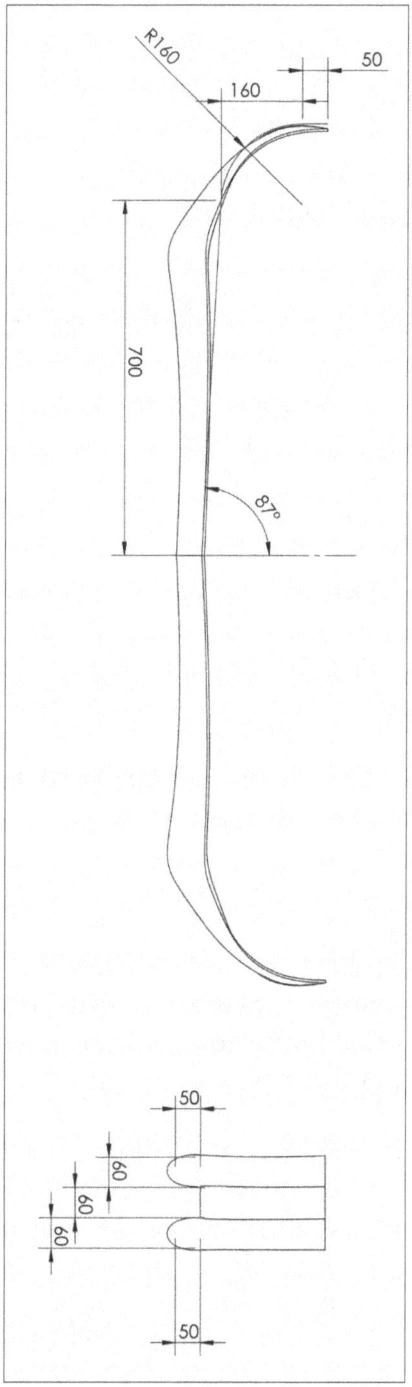

Figure-69. Car bumper

SELF ASSESSMENT

1. The tools to create surface are available in :

(a) Part Modeling Environment
(b) Drawing Environment
(c) Assembly Environment
(d) Manufacturing Environment

2. Which of the following option should be used in **Extrude** tool to close the open ends of surface?

(a) Thicken Sketch
(b) Add taper
(c) Capped ends
(c) Create new body

3. The .... tool is used to create surface using sketched curves or edges of other entities as boundaries.

4. The tools to modify the shape of a surface/face by using the control points are available in the .... contextual tab.

5. The .... tool is used to convert closed surfaces into a solid.

6. The .... tool is used to apply round at the sharp corner of a surface.

7. The **Enclosure Volume** tool is used to fill the void areas of solids and surfaces. It works with the help of closed sketches. (T/F)

8. The **Replace Surface** tool is used to replace the face of a solid model with an intersecting surface. (T/F)

9. What is the major difference between solid and surface models in Creo Parametric?

a) Surface models have mass properties
b) Solid models cannot be manufactured
c) Surface models lack mass properties
d) Solid models cannot be visualized

10. What is the use of the Capped Ends option during extrusion?

a) To create curves automatically
b) To sketch on 3D surfaces
c) To close open ends of a surface
d) To open closed ends of a surface

11. Which tool is commonly used for creating surfaces with sketched curves or edges of other entities?

a) Fill tool
b) Trim tool
c) Boundary Blend tool
d) Merge tool

12. What happens when you select the 'Close blend' checkbox in Boundary Blend?

a) It opens the blend curves
b) It makes the surface transparent
c) It joins the last and first chain
d) It merges surfaces

13. What is the use of the Smoothness Factor in the Options tab of Boundary Blend?

a) Controls file size
b) Controls mass properties
c) Controls surface roughness
d) Controls extrusion depth

14. What is required to use the Fill tool to create planar surfaces?

a) An open sketch
b) A projected curve
c) A closed sketch
d) No sketch at all

15. Which tool is used to remove unwanted intersecting areas of surfaces?

a) Extrude
b) Trim
c) Merge
d) Sweep

16. What indicates which side of the surface will remain during trimming?

a) Red arrow
b) Blue line
c) Orange dotted net
d) Green highlight

17. What is the purpose of merging surfaces in Creo Parametric?

a) To delete surfaces
b) To change colors of surfaces
c) To combine surfaces for further operations like thickening
d) To generate exploded views

18. How do you select multiple surfaces for merging?

a) Use the ALT key
b) Use the Shift key
c) Use the CTRL key
d) Use the ESC key

19. What does the Offset tool do in surfacing?

a) Creates a new surface from scratch
b) Copies a surface at a specified distance
c) Merges two surfaces
d) Adds material to a surface

20. Which option allows you to offset a surface while adding a draft?

a) Offset with Replace
b) Offset with Expand
c) Offset with Draft
d) Chain Offset

21. What does the Replace Surface option do?

a) Deletes the existing surface
b) Adds new surface to a body
c) Replaces a face of solid with another surface
d) Offsets a surface with curve

22. What should you select to prevent the replace quilt from being absorbed by the offset feature?

a) Flip button
b) Keep replace quilt checkbox
c) Remove material button
d) Normal to surface option

23. What does Chain Offset allow you to do?

a) Offset multiple models
b) Offset surface with volume
c) Offset a curve based on a reference surface
d) Replace surfaces in sequence

24. The Quilt Boundary Chain Offset tool requires selection of:

a) Solid model
b) Reference surface
c) Boundary edges of a surface
d) Control points

25. What does the Thicken tool do?

a) Adds draft to surfaces
b) Solidifies closed quilts
c) Adds thickness to a surface
d) Replaces a surface

26. What does the Automatic Fit option do in the Thicken tool?

a) Applies draft
b) Uses a graph to modify shape
c) Adjusts scale and position automatically
d) Adds chain offset

27. Which tool converts merged closed surfaces into a solid?

a) Thicken
b) Offset
c) Solidify
d) Expand

28. What are control points used for in surface editing?

a) Applying offset
b) Merging surfaces
c) Modifying surface shape
d) Creating solids

29. What must be increased to get more control points while editing a surface?

a) Curve depth
b) Sketch constraints
c) Max rows and Max columns
d) Offset thickness

30. How can a styled surface be applied to a solid model?

a) Using Thicken
b) Using Draft
c) Using Replace Surface
d) Using Expand

31. What does the Vertex Round tool do?

a) Adds fillet to edges
b) Adds radius to sharp surface corners
c) Merges vertex into one
d) Replaces sharp surface

FOR STUDENT NOTES

Answers to Self Assessment Questions:

1. (a) **2.** (c) **3.** Boundary Blend **4.** Style **5.** Solidify **6.** Vertex Round **7.** F **8.** T

Chapter 13

Drawing

Topics Covered

The major topics covered in this chapter are:

- ***Introduction***
- ***Starting Drawing***
- ***Inserting new sheets***
- ***Placing base view***
- ***Creating Projection view, Detail view, Section View, Broken Views, and so on***
- ***Applying dimensions to views***
- ***Creating Geometric tolerance, surface finish, and datum symbols***
- ***Creating Tables, Bill of Materials, and Balloons***

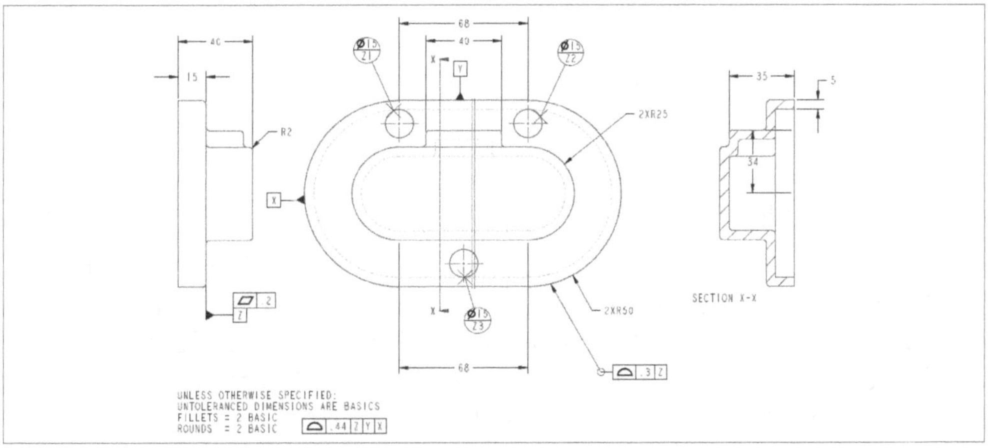

INTRODUCTION

We create models and assemblies in Creo Parametric for manufacturing. These models are not useful for manufacturer until we give complete **Product Manufacturing Information** (PMI) to them. The manufacturer will not be able to find the dimension of product by barely looking at the model that does not display any dimension or geometric tolerances in a computer system/gadget. So, we need to represent the models and assemblies in such a way that all the dimensions and geometric tolerances are available for easy interpretation. You can also use **Model Based Definition** tools to put Product Manufacturing Information directly on model or assembly and then you can use it at shop floor for manufacturing (You will learn about MBD later). But, still most of the industries use drawings printed on papers for their manufacturing. To represent real objects on paper, we use engineering drawings at the workshops. In this chapter, we will be discuss about the tools available in Creo Parametric related to drawing creation.

STARTING DRAWING

- Start Creo Parametric and click on the **New** button from the **Quick Access Toolbar**. The **New** dialog box will be displayed; refer to Figure-1.

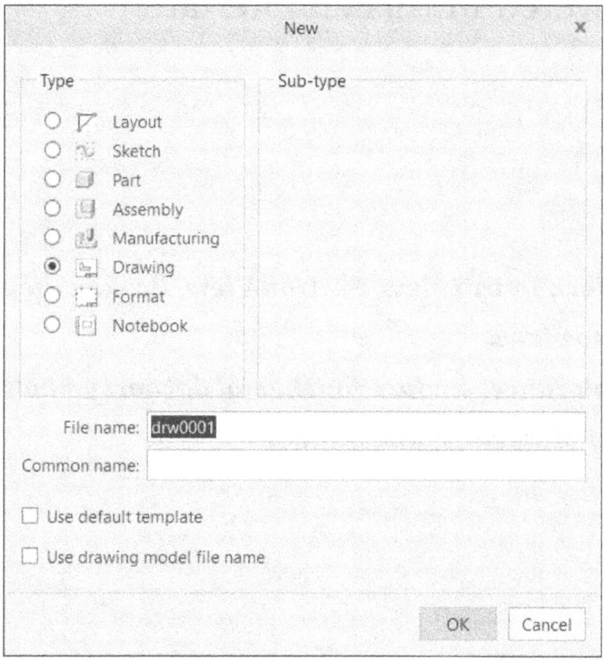

Figure-1. New dialog box

- Select the **Drawing** radio button from the **Type** area of the dialog box. Clear the **Use default template** check box to manually select the template. Select the **Use drawing model file name** check box to use the name of model imported in drawing as drawing file name and click on the **OK** button from the dialog box. The **New Drawing** dialog box will be displayed; refer to Figure-2.

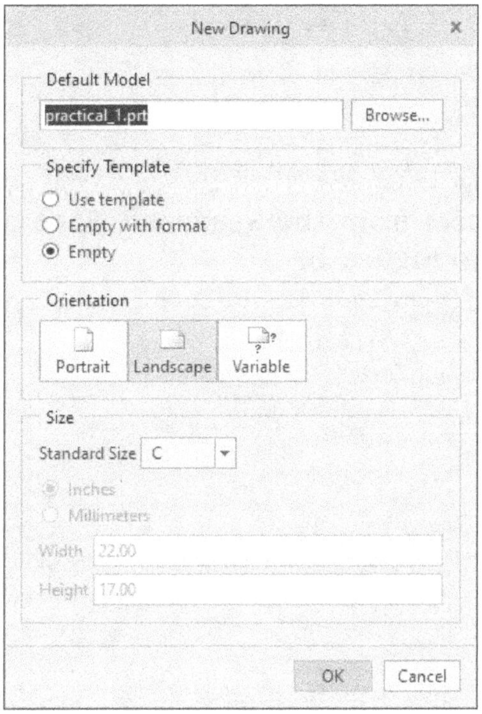

Figure-2. New Drawing dialog box

- Click on the **Browse** button from the **Default Model** area of the dialog box. The **Open** dialog box will be displayed; refer to Figure-3.

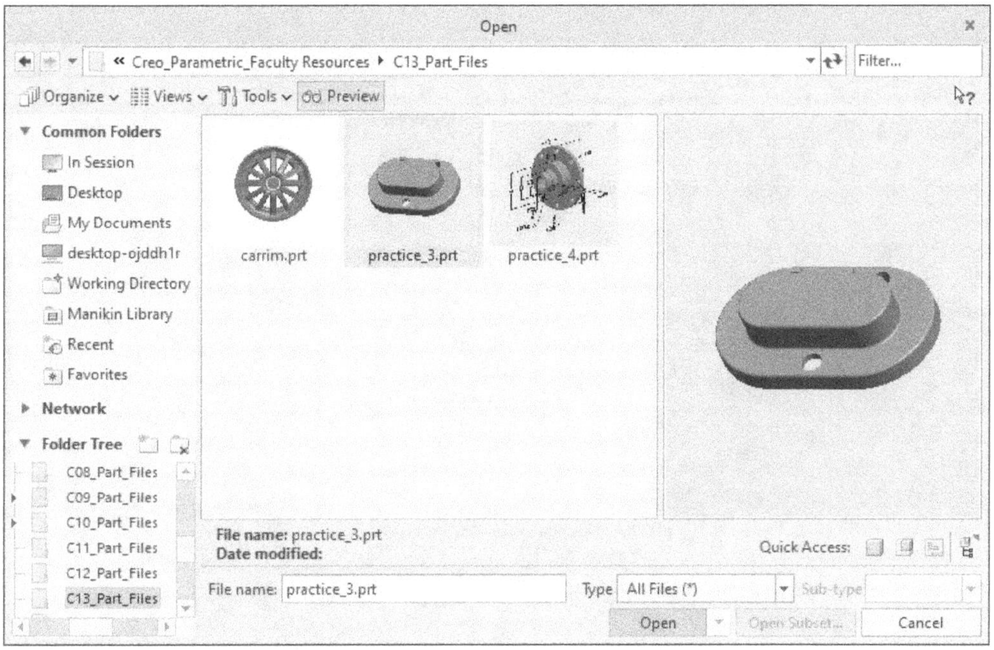

Figure-3. Open dialog box

- Select the part/assembly model for which you want to create the drawing and click on the **Open** button from the dialog box.
- Select desired orientation of page from the **Orientation** area of the dialog box; refer to Figure-4.

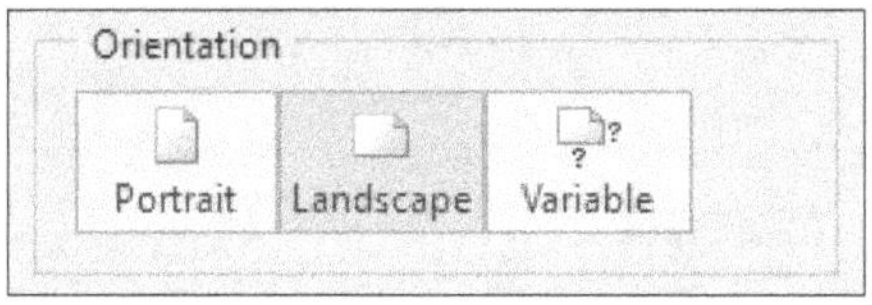

Figure-4. Orientation area of dialog box

- Select desired size of sheet from the **Standard Size** drop-down in the **Size** area of the dialog box; refer to Figure-5.

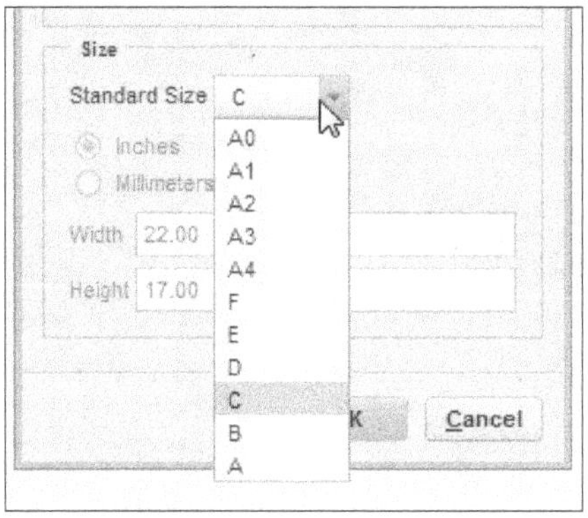

Figure-5. Sheet size drop-down

- Click on the **Variable** button from the **Orientation** area of the dialog box to specify custom size of the sheet.
- After specifying desired parameters, click on the **OK** button from the dialog box. The Drawing environment of Creo Parametric will be displayed; refer to Figure-6.

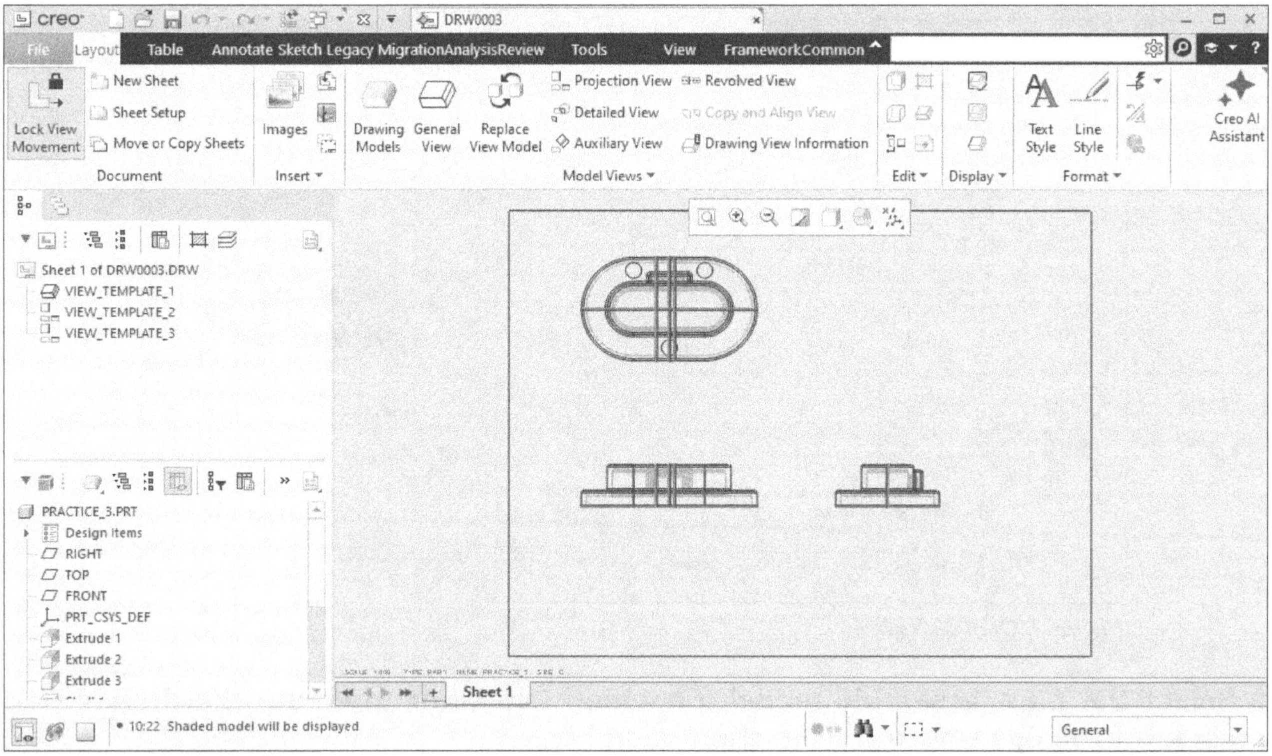

Figure-6. Drawing environment

Drawing environment of Creo Parametric

There is a lot we do using Drawing environment of Creo Parametric so that a person on manufacturing facilities can manufacture the part without any doubt. Following are the general things that we do using the Drawing environment:

- We insert various views of model in the drawing sheet.
- We dimension the views both geometrically and dimensionally.
- We create Tables in the drawing.
- We create Bill of Materials and Balloons.
- We insert images and other data for presentation purpose.

We will start with inserting various type of views in the drawing sheet. But, before that we will learn to create more drawing sheets.

INSERTING DRAWING SHEETS

Drawing sheet is the base for various drawing views. Without drawing sheet, we cannot create drawings in Creo. The drawing sheets are displayed in **Drawing Sheet** tabs at the bottom of the drawing area; refer to Figure-7. Here, Sheet 1 is the name of the sheet. Double click on it to change the name. The procedure to insert new drawing sheets is given next.

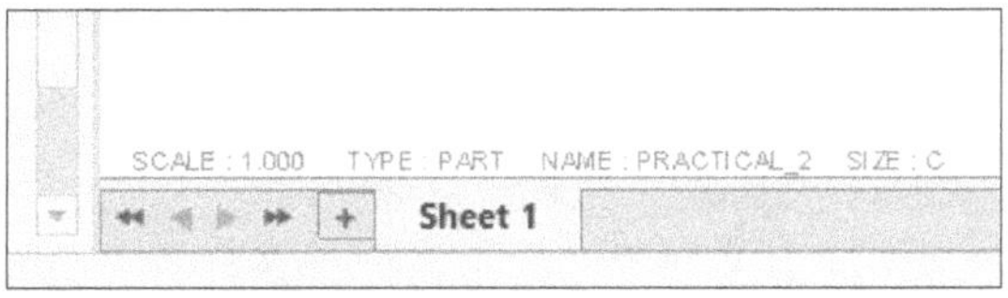

Figure-7. Drawing Sheet tab

- Click on the **Layout** tab of the **Ribbon** if not selected by default. The options related to sheet will be displayed in the **Document** panel of the **Ribbon**; refer to Figure-8.

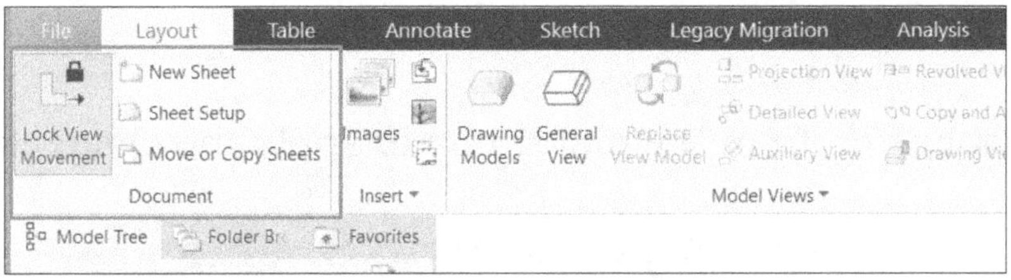

Figure-8. Document panel in Layout tab

- Click on the **New Sheet** tool from the **Document** panel. A new sheet will be added in the **Sheet** tabs at the bottom with the name **Sheet 2**.
- By default, the new sheet has the same parameters as we have set while starting the drawing environment. To change the parameters of the sheet, click on the **Sheet Setup** button from the **Document** panel of the **Layout** tab in **Ribbon**. The **Sheet Setup** dialog box will be displayed; refer to Figure-9.

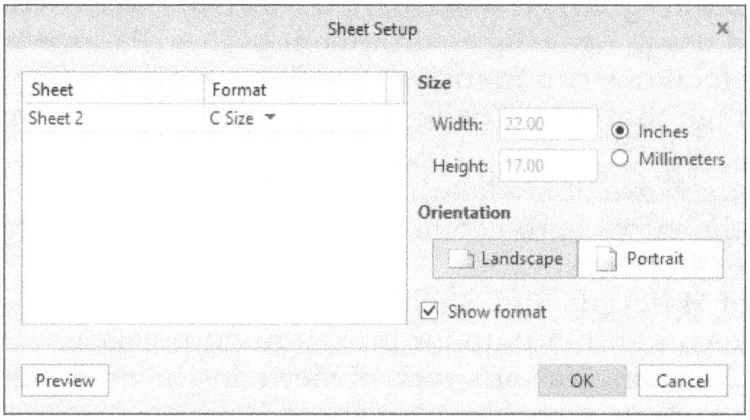

Figure-9. Sheet Setup dialog box

- Click in the cell under **Format** column of the dialog box. It will change to a drop-down. Select desired size for the sheet; refer to Figure-10. You can select the **Custom Size** option and specify the sheet size as required in the edit boxes of **Size** area in the dialog box.

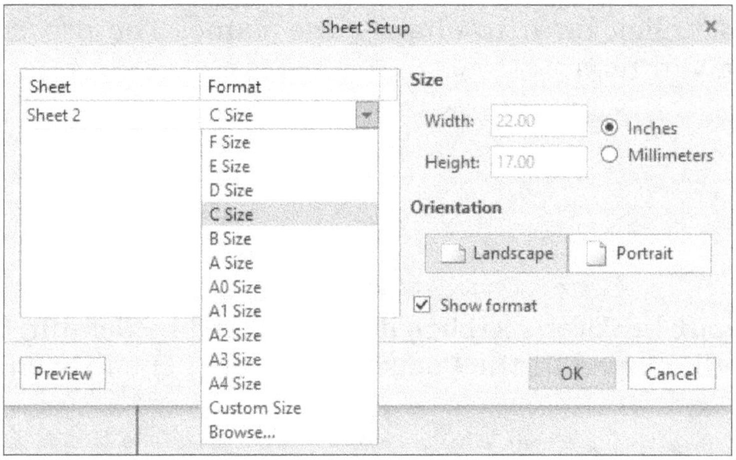

Figure-10. Format drop-down

- Click on the **OK** button from the dialog box to apply the changes.

Moving or Coping Sheets

The **Move or Copy Sheets** tool is used to move or copy selected sheets between drawings or within the same drawing. The procedure to use this tool is discussed next.

- Click on the **Move or Copy Sheets** button from the **Document** panel of the **Layout** tab in **Ribbon**. The **Move or Copy Sheet** dialog box will be displayed; refer to Figure-11.

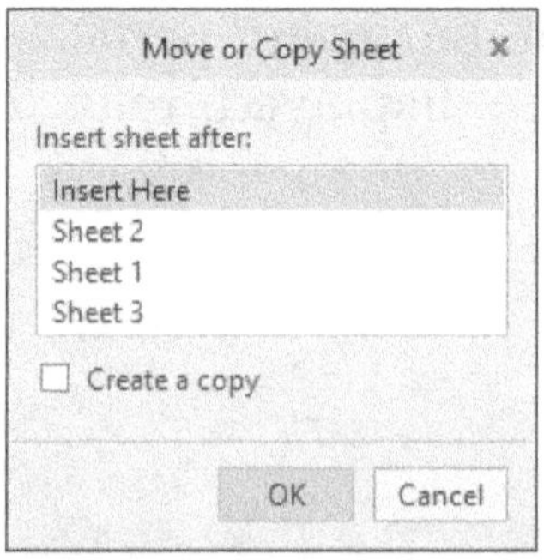

Figure-11. Move or Copy Sheet dialog box

- Select desired sheets from the **Insert sheet after** area to place the moved or copied sheet.
- Select the **Create a copy** check box to create a duplicate copy of the selected sheet.
- After specifying desired parameters, click on the **OK** button from the dialog box. The copy sheet will be created.

ADDING MODEL TO THE DRAWING

It might be possible that you have selected a wrong model and have started the drawing or you have not selected any model but are in the drawing environment. So, the steps to add or replace the model for drawing are given next.

- Click on the **Drawing Models** tool from the **Model Views** panel of the **Ribbon**. The **DWG MODELS** Menu Manager will be displayed; refer to Figure-12.

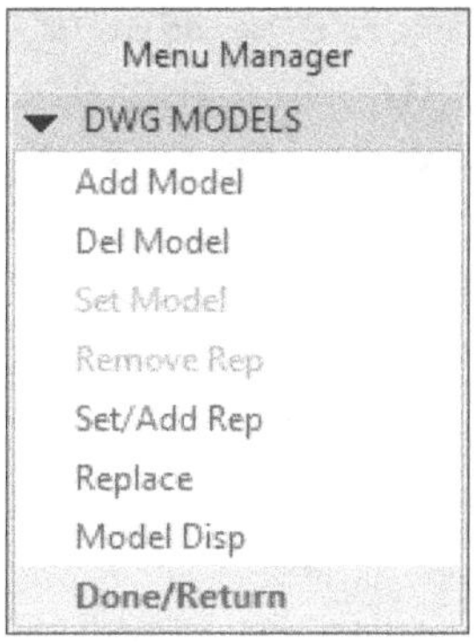

Figure-12. DWG MODELS Menu Manager

- Click on the **Add Model** option if you have not selected any model while starting the drawing environment. The **Open** dialog box will be displayed as discussed earlier.
- Select the part/assembly file for which you want to create the drawing views and click on the **OK** button from the dialog box. The model will be fetched in the drawing memory.
- If you want to change the model, then click on the **Del Model** option from the **Menu Manager**. A confirmation message box will be displayed; refer to Figure-13.

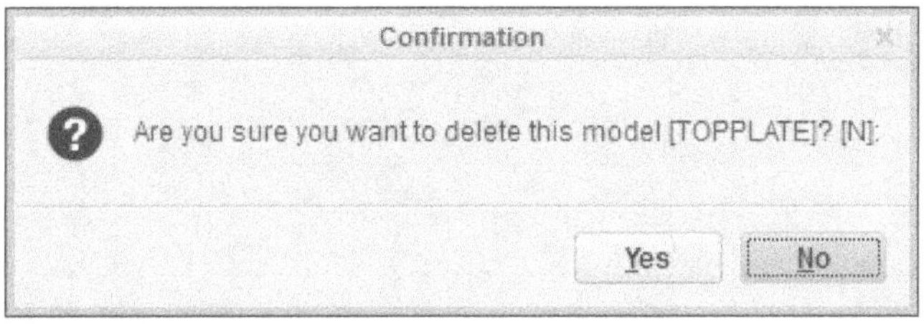

Figure-13. Confirmation box

- Click on the **Yes** button to accept the deletion.
- Click on the **Drawing Models** tool again from the **Model Views** panel and then click on the **Add Model** option. Rest of the procedure has already been discussed.
- After adding the model, click on the **Done/Return** option from the Menu Manager.

PLACING THE FIRST VIEW (BASE VIEW)

First View or **Base View** is an independent view and all other views are placed with reference to this view either directly or indirectly. The Base view is placed by using the **General View** tool. The procedure to place base view is given next.

- Click on the **General View** tool from the **Model Views** panel of the **Ribbon**. The **Select Combined State** dialog box will be displayed; refer to Figure-14.

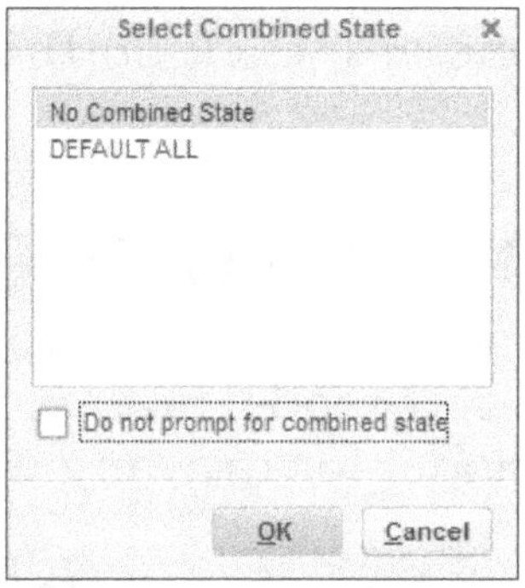

Figure-14. Select Combined State dialog box

- Select the **No Combined State** option from the dialog box and select the **Do not prompt for combined state** check box. Using the **No Combined State** option, you specify that no user defined states are required in the drawing mode.
- Click on the **OK** button from the dialog box. You are asked to specify the center location for the base view.
- Click in the drawing area at desired location to place the base view. As soon as you click in the drawing area, the default view of model and **Drawing View** dialog box are displayed; refer to Figure-15.

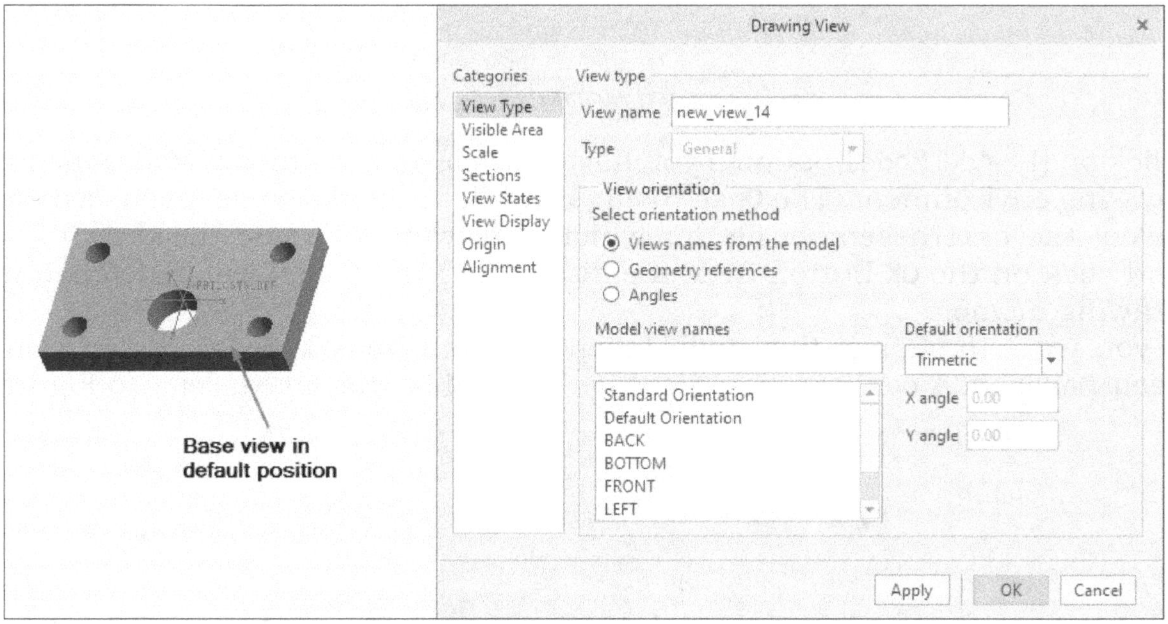

Figure-15. Base view with Drawing View dialog box

View Type options

- Click in the **View name** edit box in the dialog box and specify desired name for the view, like Front view or Top view.
- Select desired model view from the **Model view names** list box. Like, FRONT or TOP. You can select the **Default Orientation** option and specify it as **Trimetric**, **Isometric**, or **User Defined** by using the option in the **Default orientation** drop-down in the dialog box.
- After selecting desired view, click on the **Apply** button from the dialog box.

Visible Area options

- To clip the view or, display half or partial view; click on the **Visible Area** option from the **Categories** list box in the dialog box. The dialog box will be displayed as shown in Figure-16.

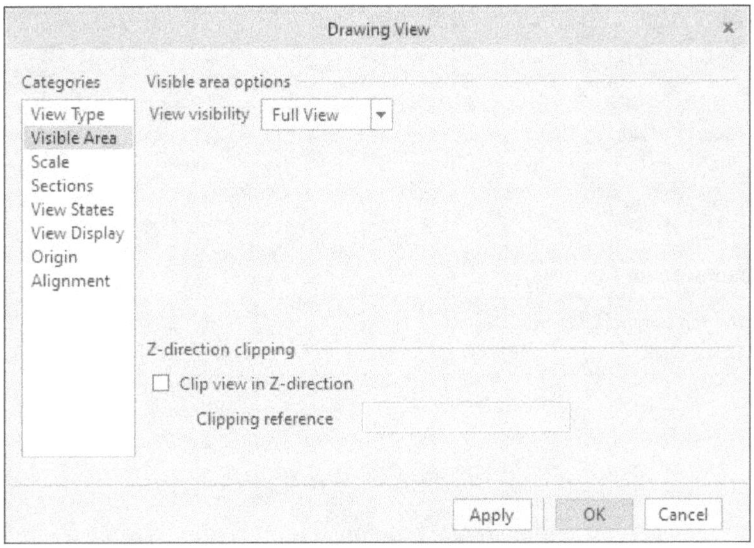

Figure-16. Drawing View dialog box with Visible Area options

Half-View

- Click in the **View visibility** drop-down and select desired option. If you select the **Half view** option then you need to select a plane normal to the selected view. Select the side that you want to keep by using the **Flip** button and then click on the **Apply** button to see the half-view; refer to Figure-17.

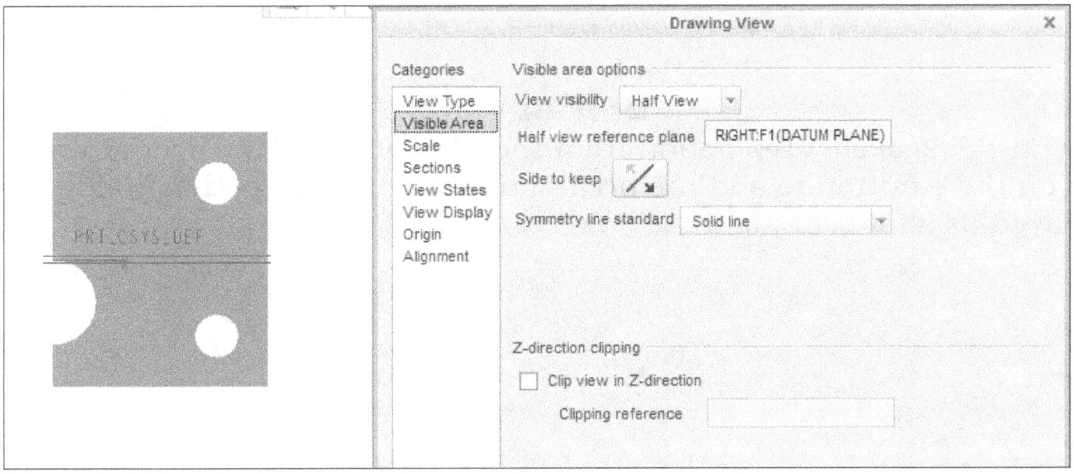

Figure-17. Half-view of model

Partial View

- To create the partial view, click on the **Partial View** option from the **View visibility** drop-down. You are asked to select a reference point. Select a point and then create a spline around it; refer to Figure-18. Click on the **Apply** button from the dialog box to check the partial view; refer to Figure-19.

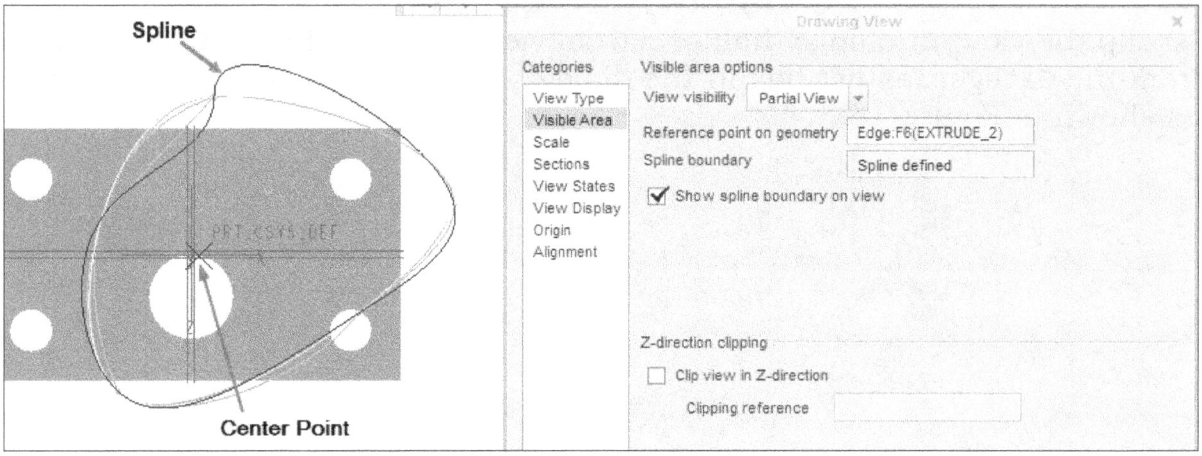

Figure-18. Spline created for partial view

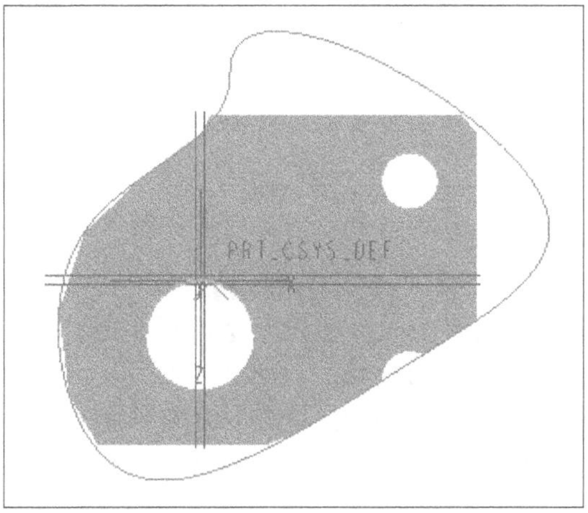

Figure-19. Partial view

Broken View

- Click on the **Broken View** option from the **View visibility** drop-down and then click on the **+** button to add the break lines. The **Drawing View** dialog box will be displayed as shown in Figure-20.

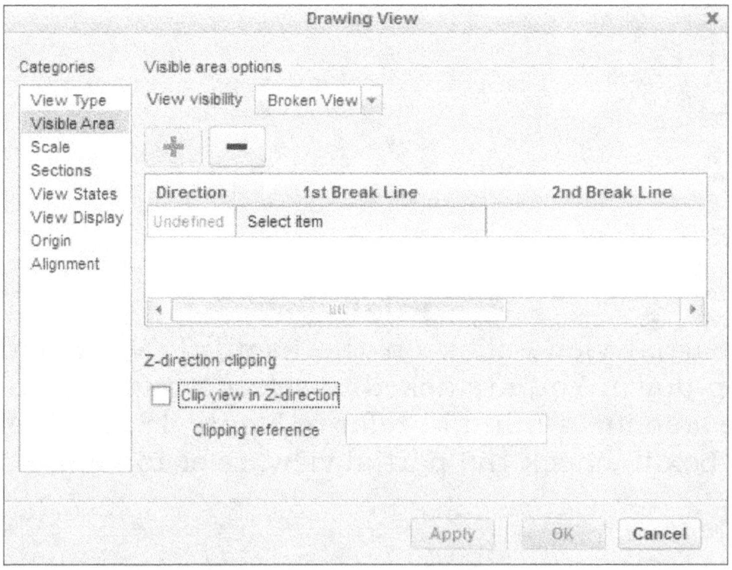

Figure-20. Drawing View dialog box for broken view

- Click on the straight edge of the model to define the starting point of break line; refer to Figure-21.

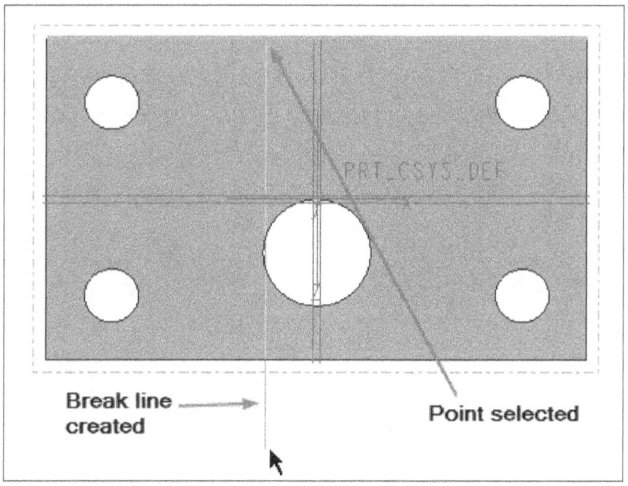

Figure-21. Break line creation

- Click to specify the end point of the break line. You are asked to specify the starting point for the second break line.
- Click to specify starting point of second break line. The break line will be created; refer to Figure-22.

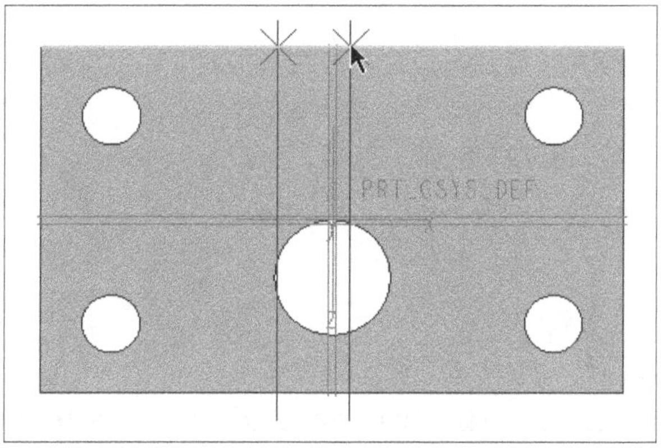

Figure-22. Second break line

- Move the slider in the dialog box to right and select desired **Break Line Style** from the drop-down; refer to Figure-23.

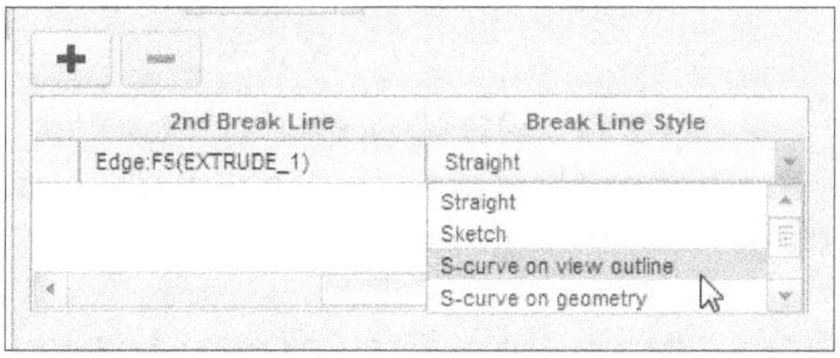

Figure-23. Break line style options

- After selecting desired style, click on the **Apply** button from the dialog box to create the broken view; refer to Figure-24.

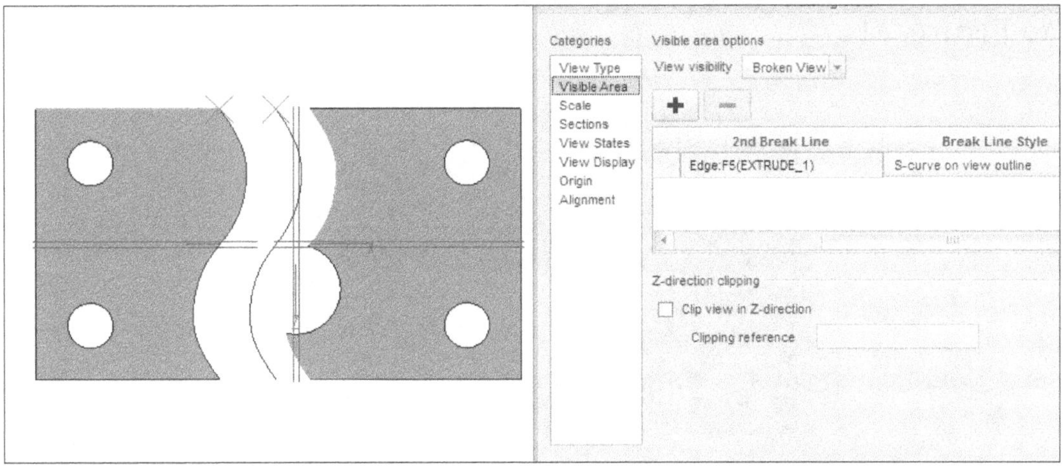

Figure-24. Broken view created

Scale Options

- Click on the **Scale** option from the **Categories** list box to display the options related to scaling; refer to Figure-25.

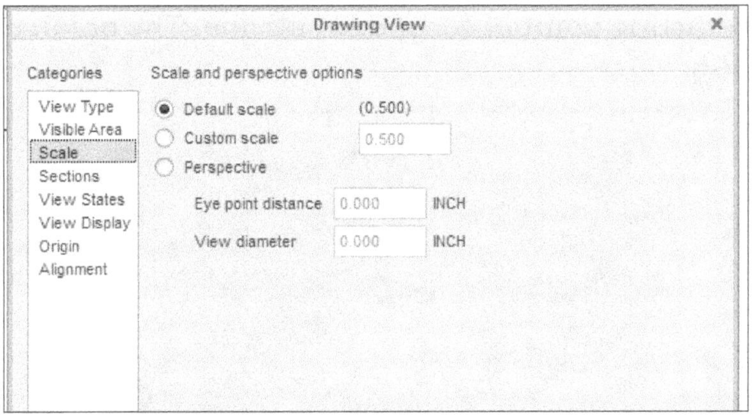

Figure-25. Scale options

- Select on the **Custom scale** radio button and specify desired value for scaling the view in the adjacent edit box.
- Click on the **Apply** button to apply the scaling.

The options for **Sections** will be discussed later in the chapter. Now, we will continue to **View States** options.

View States options

The **View States** options are generally used for assembly models, so you should have assembly model selected as Drawing Model.

- Click on the **View States** option from the **Categories** list box. The options in the dialog box will be displayed as shown in Figure-26.

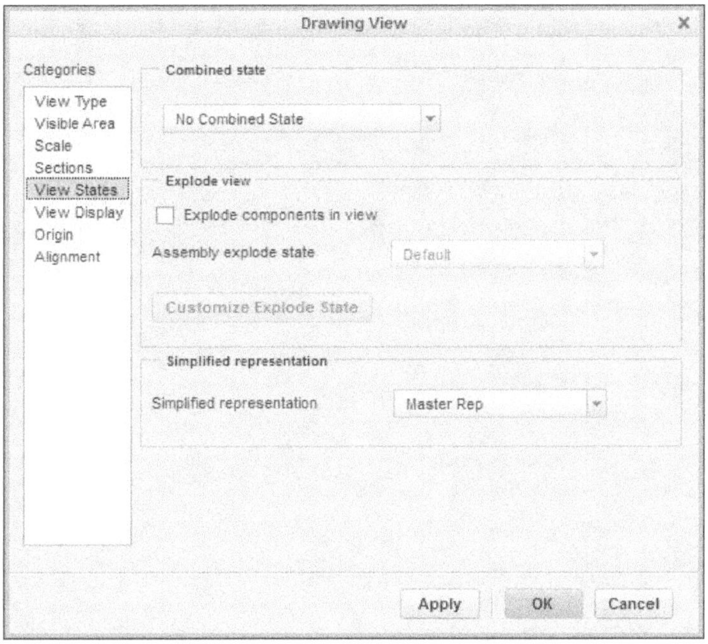

Figure-26. Drawing View dialog box with View States options

- Select the **Explode components in view** check box to enable the options related to exploded view of assembly model.
- Select desired exploded state of the model from the **Assembly explode state** drop-down and click on the **Apply** button to display the exploded view; refer to Figure-27.

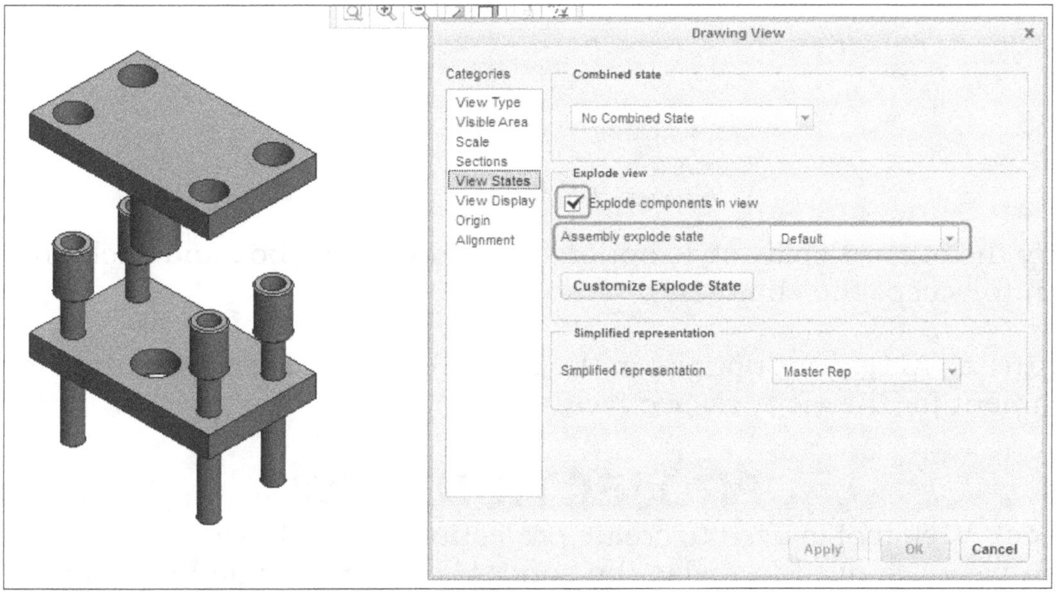

Figure-27. Exploded view of assembly

- Select desired representation from the **Simplified representation** drop-down. By default, **Master Rep** is selected in the drop-down.

View Display options

- Click on the **View Display** option from the **Categories** list box. The options in the dialog box will be displayed as shown in Figure-28.

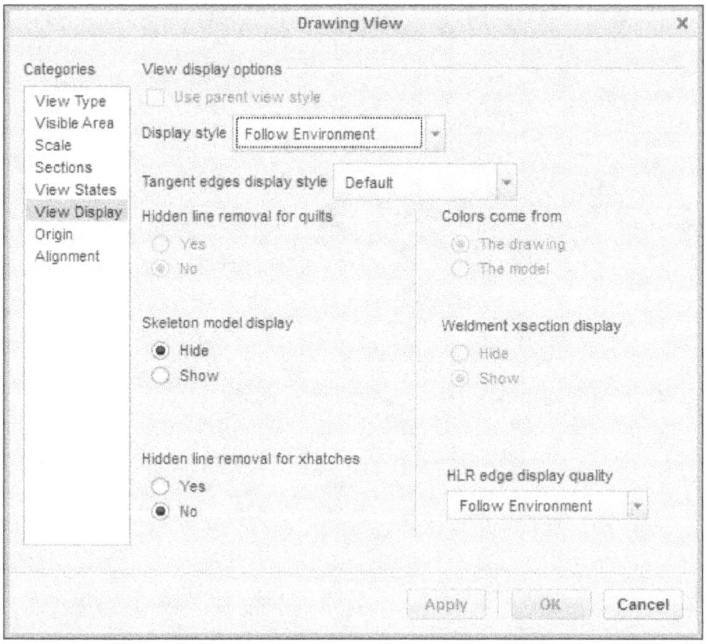

Figure-28. Drawing View dialog box with View Display options

- Click on the **Display style** drop-down and select desired option from the drop-down to specify the display style; refer to Figure-29.

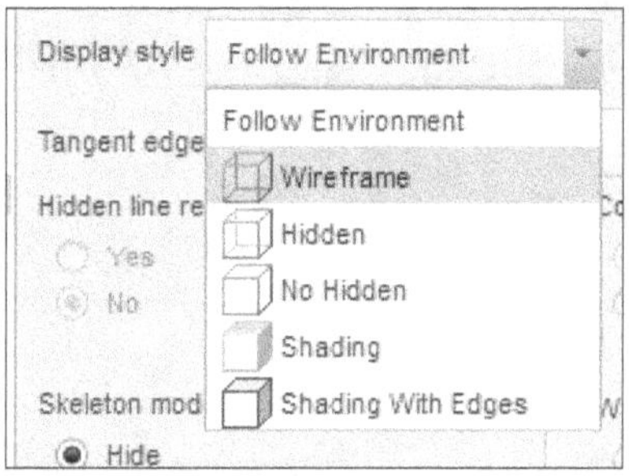

Figure-29. Display style drop-down

- Specify the other display style options from the dialog box and click on the **Apply** button to accept the changes.

The **Origin** and **Alignment** options in the dialog box are used to specify origin of view and alignment for the view, respectively.

PROJECTION VIEW

The **Project View** tool is used to create projections of the base view. Before we go for projection view, we need to revise the concepts of First Angle Projection and Third Angle Projection. Figure-30 shows an object with different view directions say, a, b, c, d, e, and f.

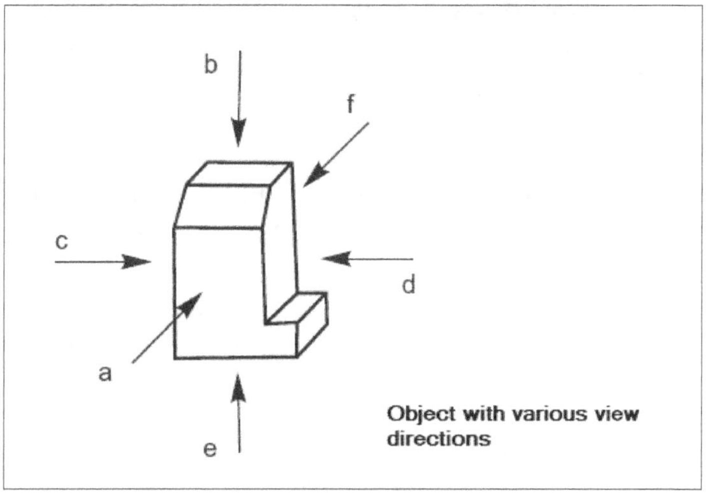

Figure-30. Object with view directions

Here,

1. View in the direction a = view from the front
2. View in the direction b = view from top
3. View in the direction c = view from the left
4. View in the direction d = view from the right
5. View in the direction e = view from bottom
6. View in the direction f = view from the back

In First Angle projection, these views are arranged as shown in Figure-31. In Third Angle projection, these views are arranged as shown in Figure-32.

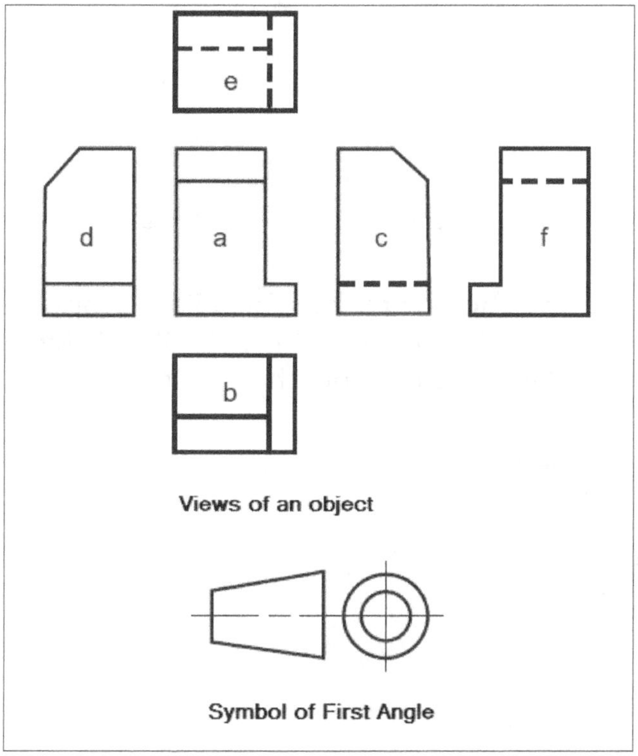

Figure-31. Views in First Angle projection

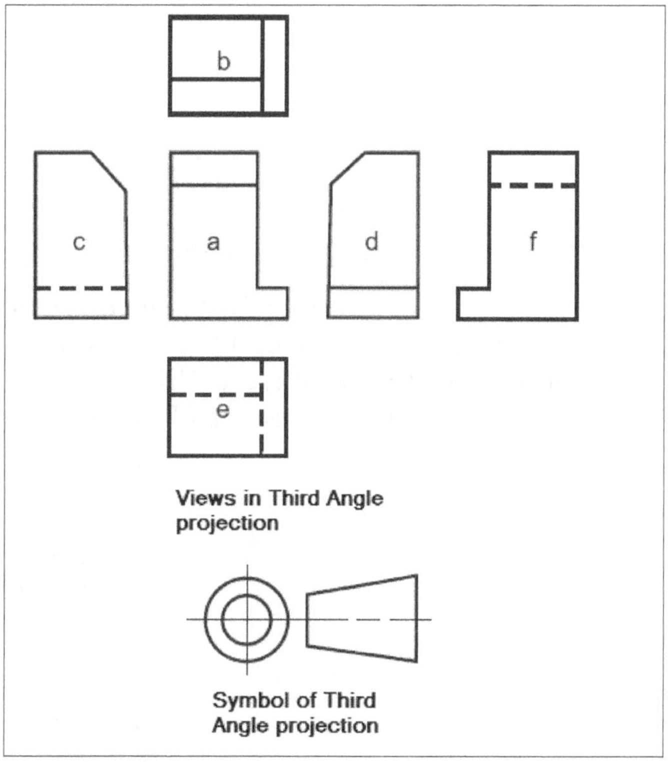

Figure-32. Views in Third Angle projection

Setting Projection Type

In Creo Parametric, we can set the project type between First Angle and Third Angle by using the **Drawing Properties** option in the **File** menu. The procedure is given next.

- Expand the **File** menu and select **Drawing Properties** option from the **Prepare** cascading menu; refer to Figure-33. The **Drawing Properties** dialog box will be displayed; refer to Figure-34.

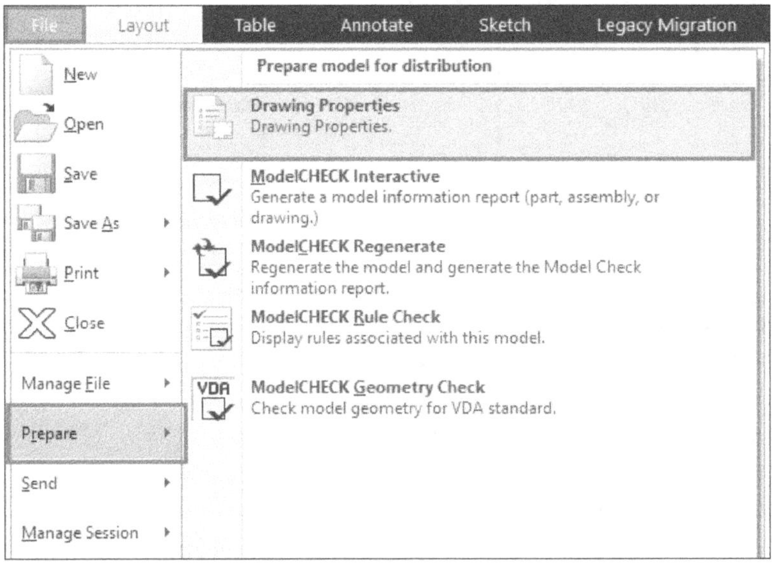

Figure-33. Drawing Properties option

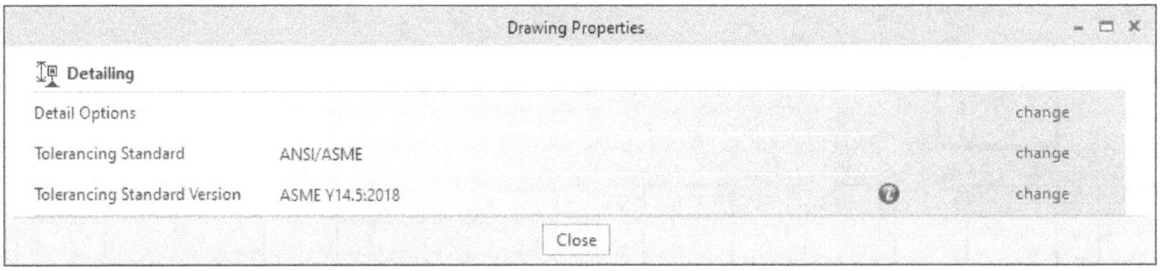

Figure-34. Drawing Properties dialog box

- If you want to change the tolerance standard then click on the **change** option in the end of **Tolerancing Standard** row in the dialog box. The **TOL SETUP Menu Manager** will be displayed. Click on the **Standard** option and then select desired tolerance standard; refer to Figure-35.

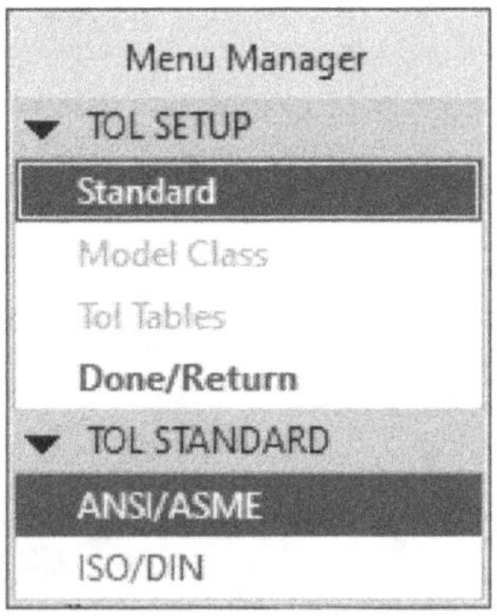

Figure-35. TOL SETUP Menu Manager

- Click on the **change** option next to **Detail Options** in the dialog box. The **Options** dialog box will be displayed as shown in Figure-36.

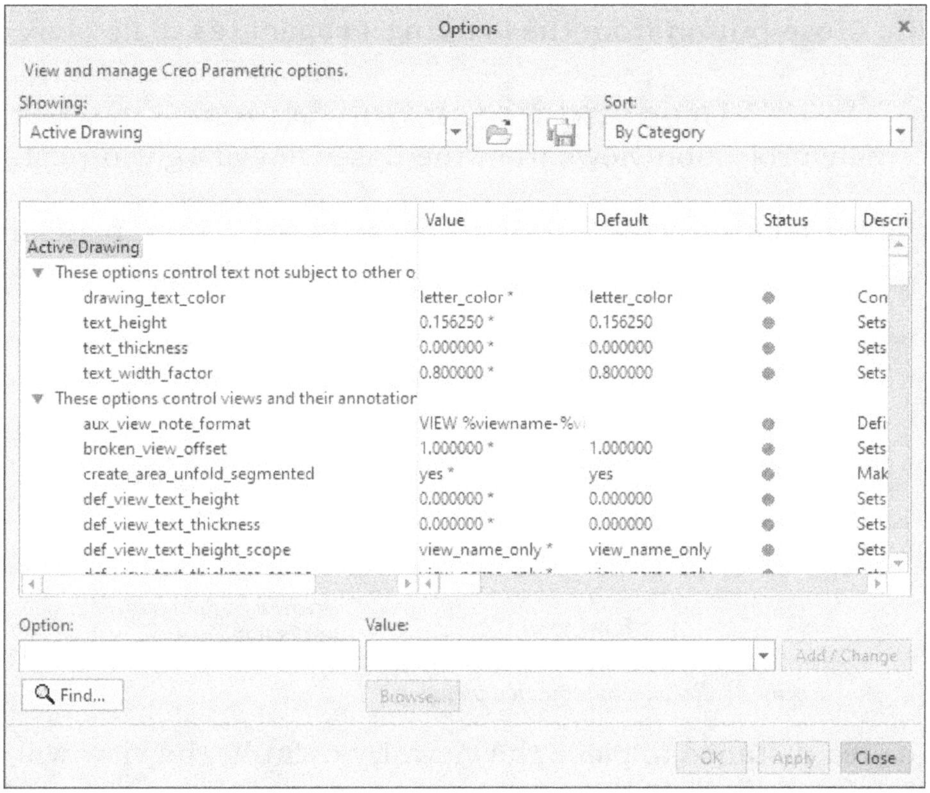

Figure-36. Options dialog box

- Type **projection type** in the **Option** edit box at the bottom of the dialog box. Two options will be displayed under the **Value** drop-down; refer to Figure-37.

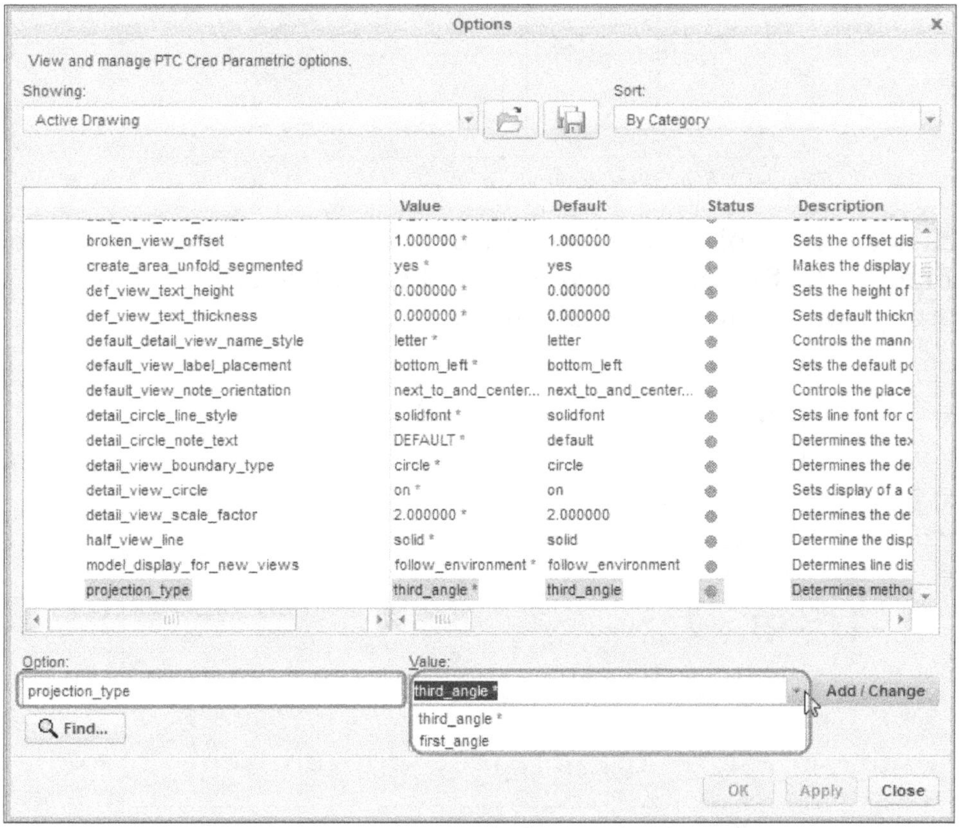

Figure-37. Projection type options

- Select desired projection type from the drop-down. Click on the **Add/Change** option and then click on the **OK** button to change the projection type in the drawing. (We will continue with the default one i.e. third angle in this book.)
- Click on the **Close** button from the **Drawing Properties** dialog box to exit.

Creating Projection Views

The steps to create projection views from the base view are given next.

- Click on the **Projection View** button from the **Model Views** panel in the **Ribbon**. Projection of the base view will get attached to the cursor; refer to Figure-38.

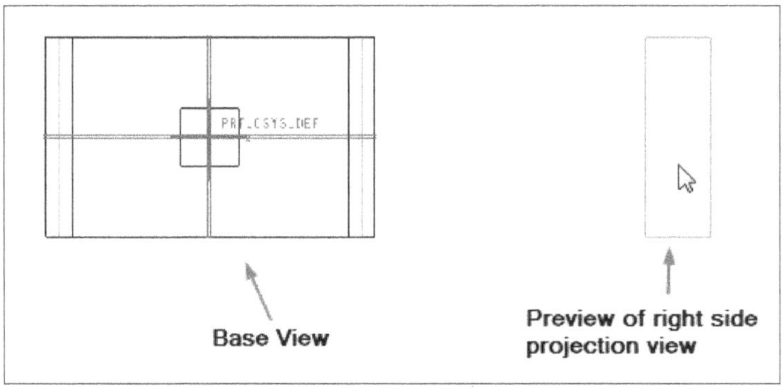

Figure-38. Preview of projection view

- Click at desired distance to place the view. By default, the view will be displayed as shaded; refer to Figure-39.

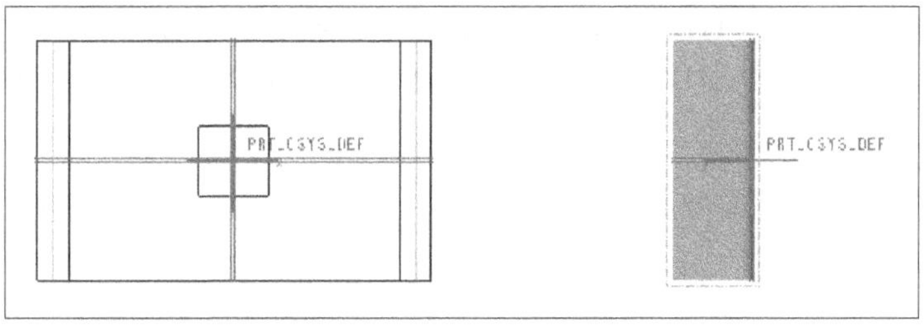

Figure-39. Shaded projection view

- Double-click on the projection view. The **Drawing View** dialog box will be displayed; refer to Figure-40. Select the **Add projection arrows** check box if you want to display projection arrows in the drawing.

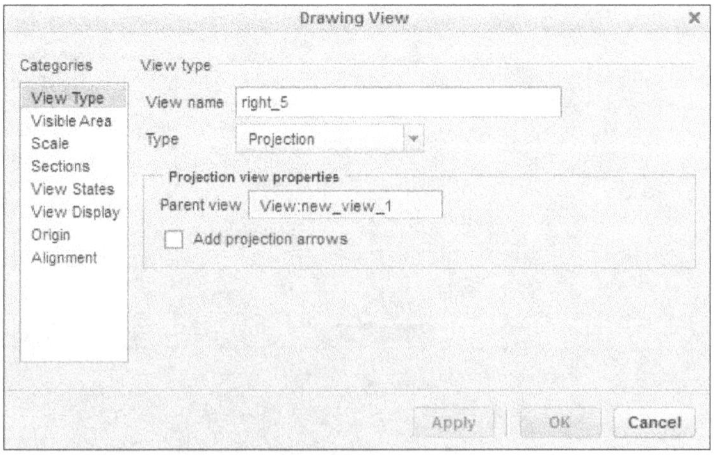

Figure-40. Drawing View dialog box

- Using the options in the **View Display** category, you can change the display of view to **Hidden**, **No Hidden**, or **Wireframe** for presentation purpose.
- Click on the **OK** button from dialog box.
- Click again on the **Projection View** button and select the base view as parent view for projection. Repeat the same procedure to place other views; refer to Figure-41.

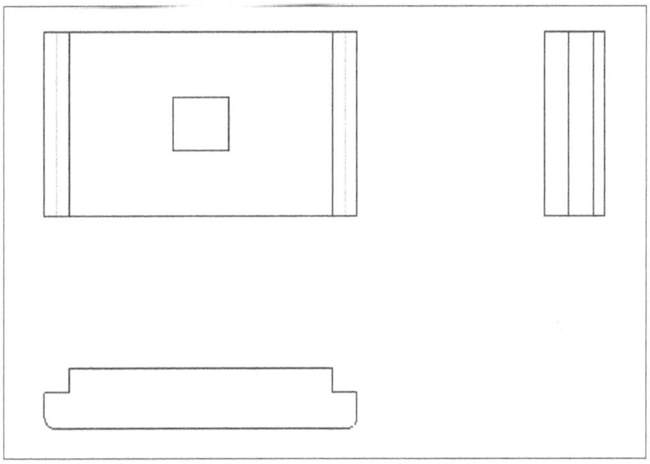

Figure-41. Views placed in drawing

Detailed View

The detailed views are used to highlight a small section of drawing which has minute details that are to be considered while manufacturing. The procedure to create detailed views is given next.

- Click on the **Detailed View** tool from the **Model Views** panel in the **Ribbon**. You are asked to specify the center point for the view.
- Click at the location on model which is center for your detailed view; refer to Figure-42. You are asked to draw a non-self-intersecting spline.

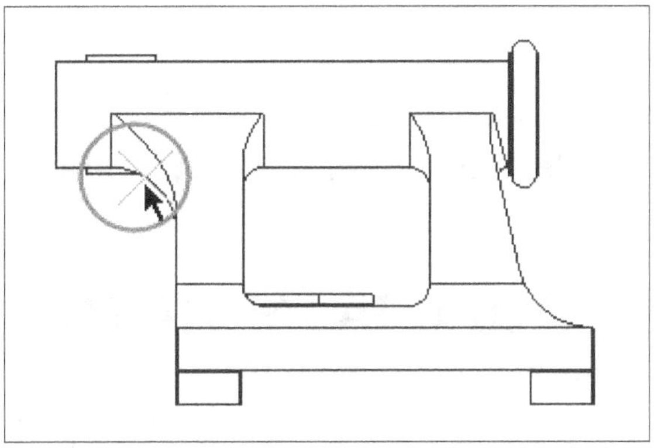

Figure-42. Center point selection

- Create a closed spline around the center point which is covering all the entities that you want to include in the detailed view; refer to Figure-43 and press the **MMB**. A circle will be drawn around the center point and you are asked to specify placement point for detailed view.

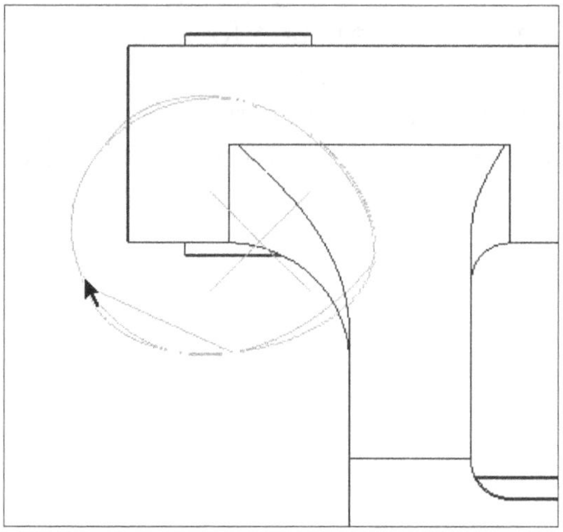

Figure-43. Spline created for detailed view

- Click at desired location in the drawing sheet to place the detailed view; refer to Figure-44.

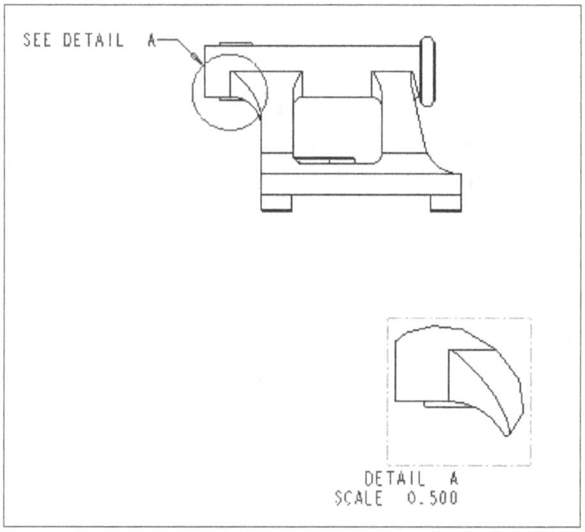

Figure-44. Detailed view

- Double-click on the detailed view to change the details like display style, scale, and so on.

AUXILIARY VIEW

Auxiliary views are orthographic views taken from a direction of sight other than top, front, right side, left side, bottom, or rear. Auxiliary views are often used to show inclined and oblique surface's true size. Inclined and oblique surfaces do not show true size in the standard views. The procedure to create auxiliary view is given next.

- Click on the **Auxiliary View** tool from the **Model Views** panel in the **Ribbon**. You are asked to select an edge, axis, datum plane, or surface.
- Select the entity through which you want to create the auxiliary view. The view will get attached to the cursor; refer to Figure-45.

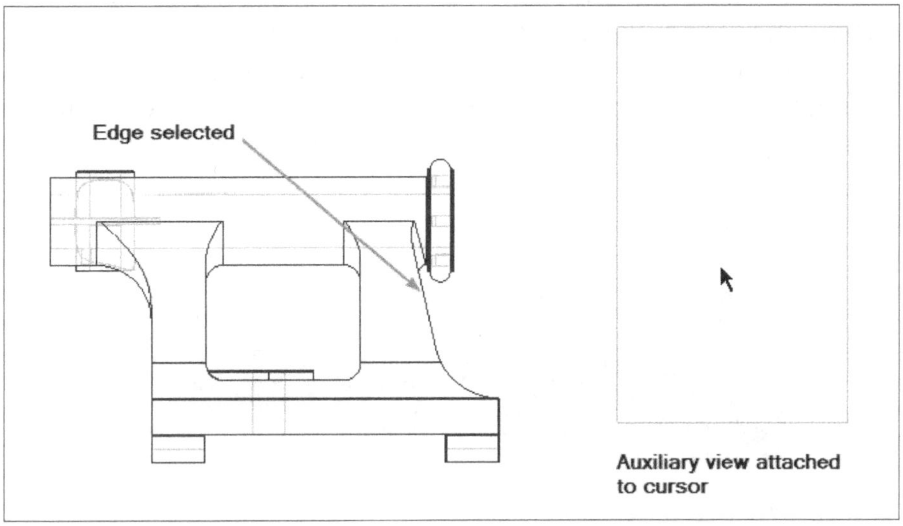

Figure-45. Auxiliary view attached to cursor

- Click at desired location to place the view; refer to Figure-46.

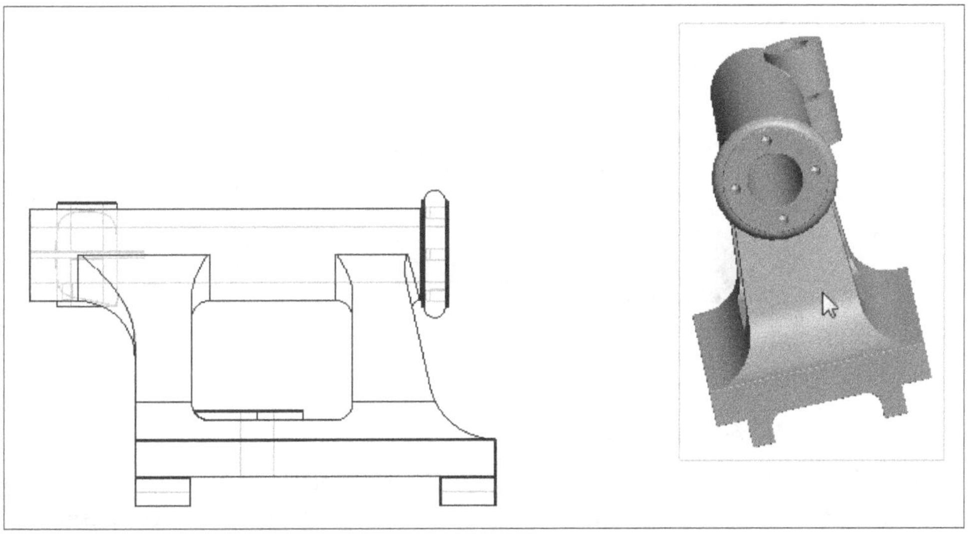

Figure-46. Auxiliary view placed

REVOLVED VIEW

The Revolved view is created to show detail of a part after revolving and sectioning a specific area of part. This type of view is used to show hidden details of part. The procedure is given next.

- Click on the **Revolved View** tool from the **Model Views** panel in the **Ribbon**. You are asked to select parent view.
- Select the view for which you want to create the revolved view. You are asked to specify center point for revolved view.
- Click at desired location to place the view. The **XSEC CREATE Menu Manager** will be displayed along with the **Drawing View** dialog box.
- Select the **Planar** and **Single** option from the **Menu Manager** and click on the **Done** button from the **Menu Manager**. You are asked to specify name for the section. (You will learn about other options later in this chapter).
- Enter desired name in the input box displayed. The **SETUP PLANE Menu Manager** will be displayed.

- Click on the **Make Datum** option and select desired option from the **DATUM PLANE** area in the **Menu Manager**. Note that we are going to create a datum plane which will act as cutting plane for creating the cross-section.
- After selecting desired option (which is Through in our case), select the respective reference (which is an edge in our case; refer to Figure-47.)

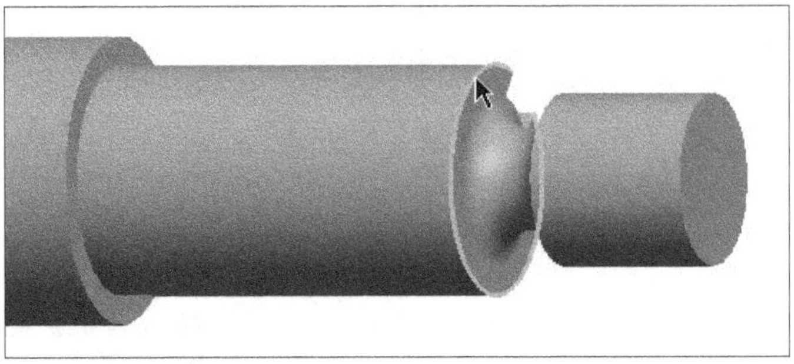

Figure-47. Edge selected

- Click on the **Done** option from the **Menu Manager**. Preview of the revolve view will be displayed. Note that it can be overlapping with the parent view; refer to Figure-48.

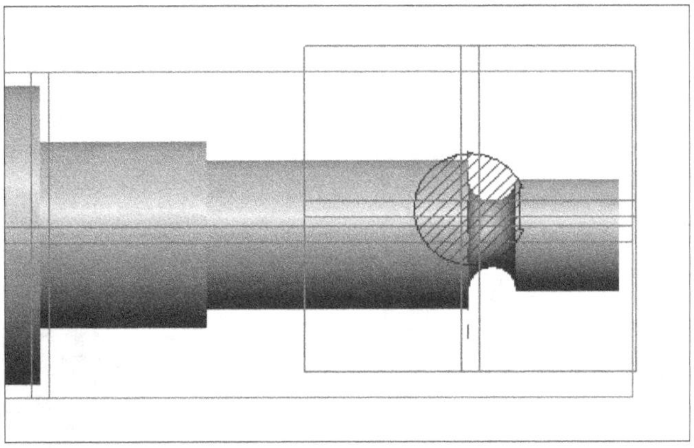

Figure-48. Preview of revolved view

- Click on the **OK** button from the **Drawing View** dialog box to create the view.
- Release the **Lock View Movement** toggle button from the **Document** panel in the **Ribbon** and drag the view to desired distance from the base view; refer to Figure-49.

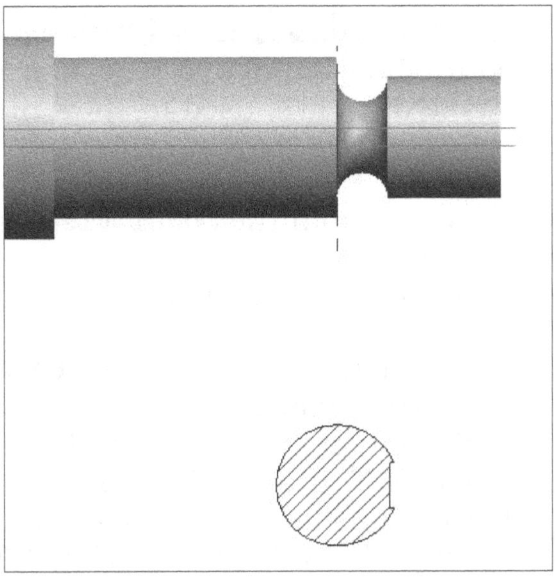

Figure-49. Revolved view

CREATING SECTION VIEWS

Section views are used to display hidden details of an object by cutting it from selected reference. To create a section view in Creo, you must have a view already present in the drawing that can be sectioned. The procedure to create section views is given next.

- Create the view that you want to be sectioned; refer to Figure-50.

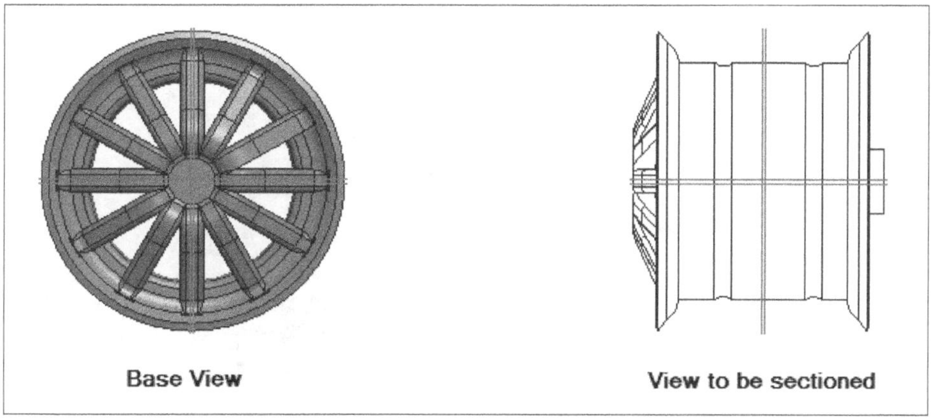

Figure-50. View created for sectioning

- Double-click on the view to be sectioned. The **Drawing View** dialog box will be displayed.
- Click on the **Sections** option from the **Categories** list box. The dialog box will be displayed as shown in Figure-51.

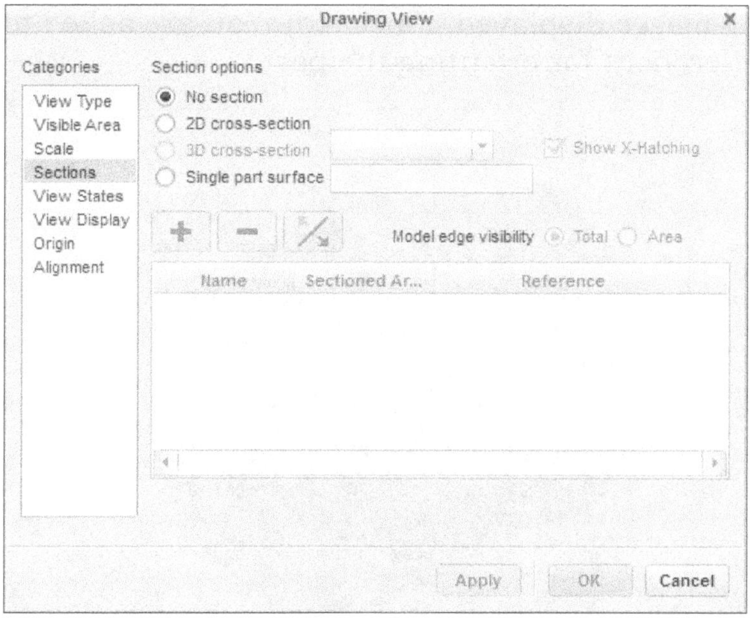

Figure-51. Drawing View dialog box with Section options

2D Cross-sectioning

Here, we will section the part in 2 Dimensional plane.

- Select the **2D cross-section** radio button and click on the **+** button from the dialog box. The **XSEC CREATE Menu Manager** will be displayed as discussed earlier. We have discussed planar section options earlier. Now, we will start with Offset section.
- Select the **Offset**, **Both Sides**, and **Single** option from the **XSEC CREATE Menu Manager** and then click on the **Done** button. You are asked to specify the name for section.

- Specify desired name in the Input box displayed on screen and click on the **OK** button from the Input box. A separate window with sketching options will be displayed; refer to Figure-52.

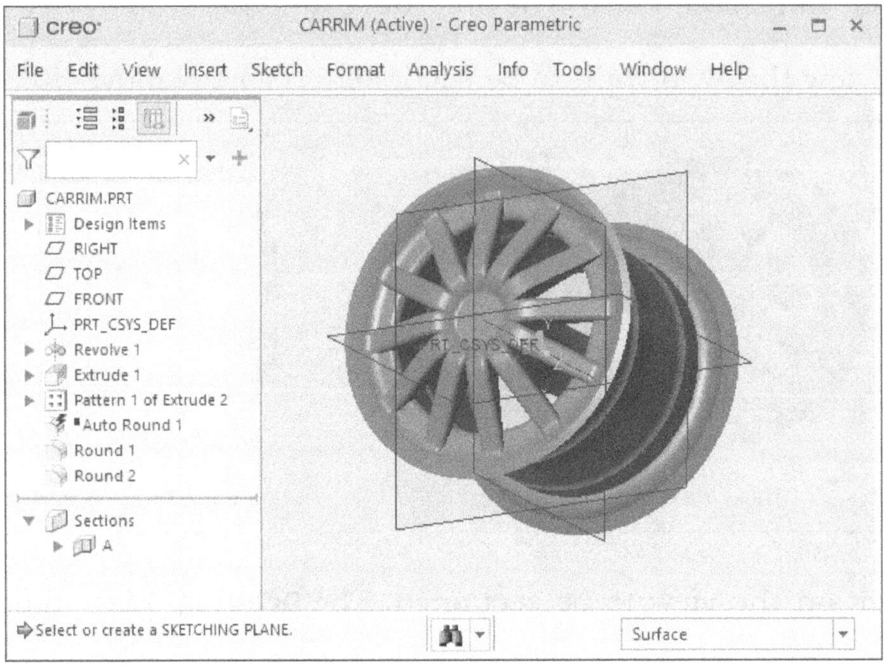

Figure-52. Window for sketching cross-section boundary

- Select the sketching plane; refer to Figure-53. (You can create a datum plane by using the **Menu Manager** displayed, if needed). You are asked to specify sketching direction and references for orienting the part.

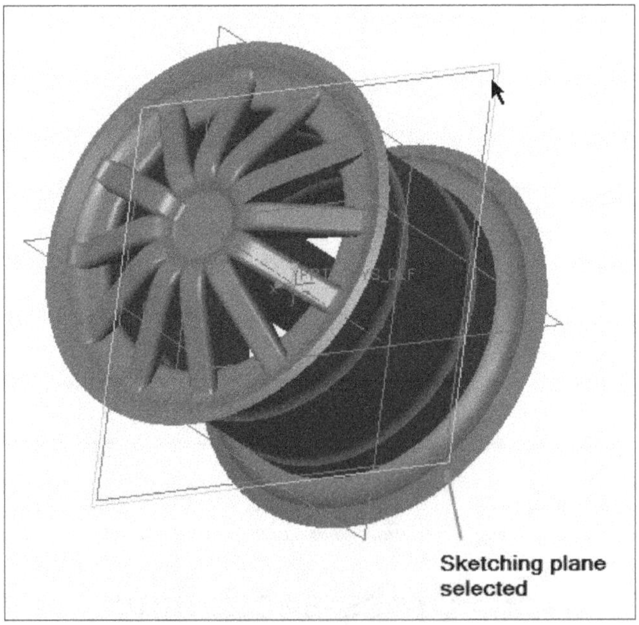

Figure-53. Sketching plane selected

- Select the default options or as required. Now, we need to orient the part parallel to screen for sketching, if not oriented by default.
- Click on the **View Manager** tool from the **Manage Views** drop-down in the **View** menu; refer to Figure-54. The **View Manager** dialog box will be displayed.

- Click on the **Orient** tab. Various predefined orientations will be displayed; refer to Figure-55.

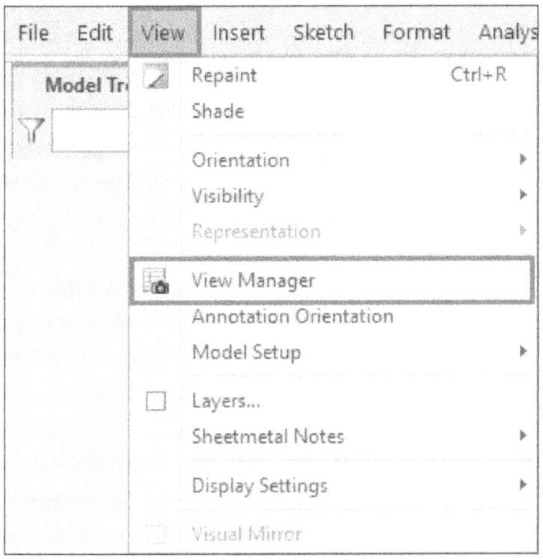

Figure-54. View Manager

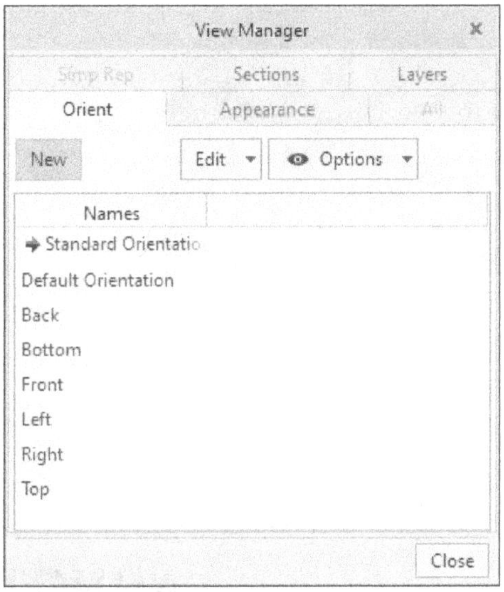

Figure-55. View Manager with Orient tab

- Double-click on the orientation which makes the sketching plane parallel to screen.
- Click on the **Close** button from the **View Manager** dialog box to exit.
- Select the **Line** tool from the **Sketch** menu and create a line sketch for making cross-section boundary; refer to Figure-56.

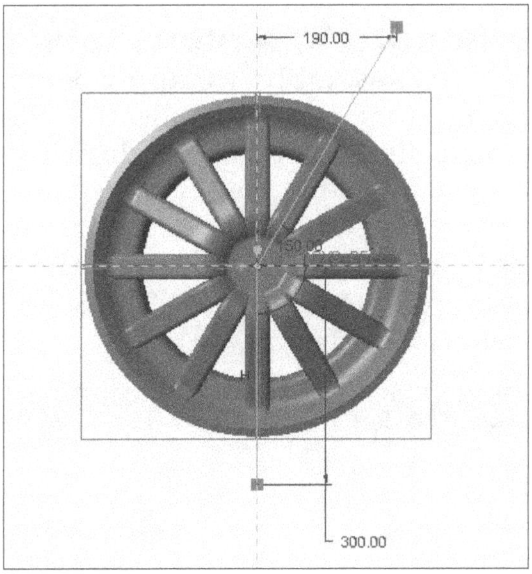

Figure-56. Sketch drawn

- After drawing sketch, click on the **Done** button from the **Sketch** menu. The section name will appear with a green tick mark in the **Section** options area of the **Drawing View** dialog box. The Green tick mark denotes that selected section is applicable on selected view. If a red cross mark is displayed in place of the green tick mark, then either the view you have selected for sectioning is not correct or the section sketch you have created is not intersecting the view.
- Click on the **Apply** button to create the section; refer to Figure-57.

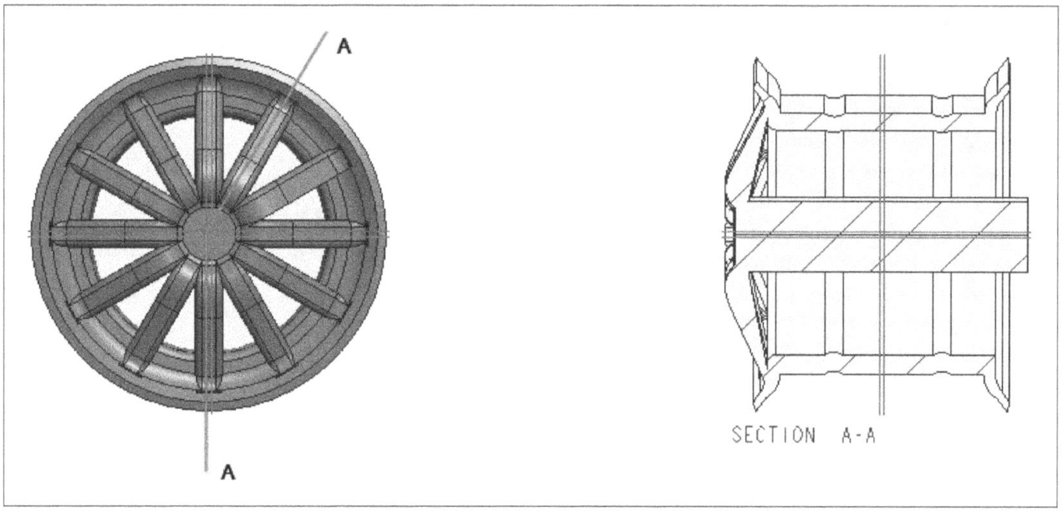

Figure-57. Model with section view

ANNOTATIONS

Annotations are used to display geometric and dimensional tolerances of the parts. In Creo Parametric, you can apply the dimensions manually or you can import the dimensions from Part or assembly environment. First, we will discuss the method to import dimensions from Part/Assembly environment and then we will discuss the method to manually apply dimensions.

Importing dimensions

When we create model of a part/assembly, we apply some dimensions to it in Part/ Assembly environment. These dimensions decide the shape and size of the part/ assembly. We can import these dimensions in the drawing environment by following the steps given next.

- Click on the **Show Model Annotations** tool from the **Annotations** panel in the **Annotate** tab of the **Ribbon**; refer to Figure-58. The **Show Model Annotations** dialog box will be displayed; refer to Figure-59.

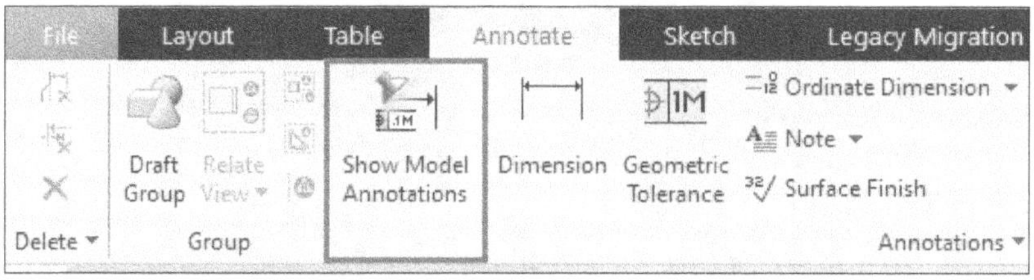

Figure-58. Show Model Annotations button

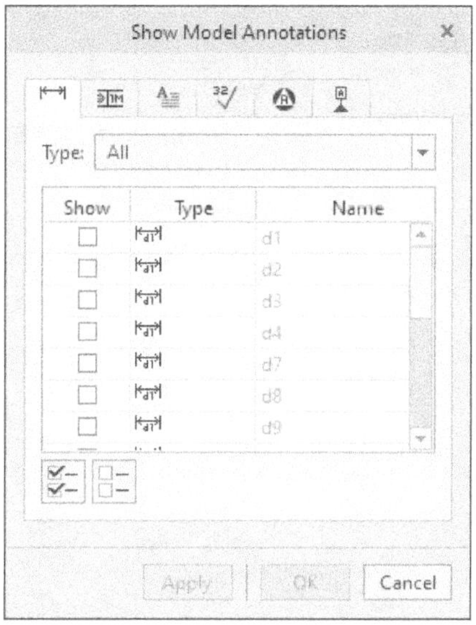

Figure-59. Show Model Annotations dialog box

- Select the view to which you want to apply the annotations. Dimensions will be displayed on the view; refer to Figure-60. Note that you can select multiple views by holding the **CTRL** key while selecting.

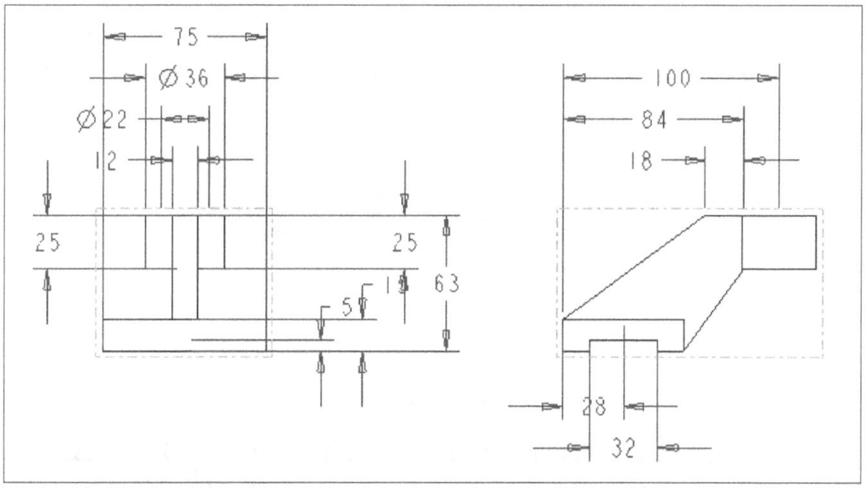

Figure-60. Dimensions displayed with the views

- One by one, click on the dimensions in the drawing that you want to keep or click on the **Select All** button to display all the dimensions.
- Click on the **Apply** button to display the selected dimension in the view.
- In the same way, you can import other data by using other tabs in the **Show Model Annotations** dialog box. The purpose of various tabs is shown in Figure-61.

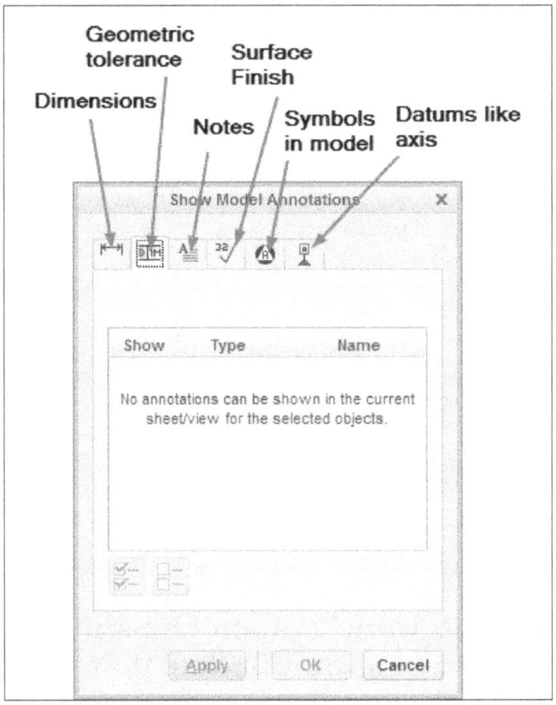

Figure-61. Detail of tabs

To change any of the dimension, double-click on it and specify desired value. On selecting the **Regenerate** button from **Quick Access Toolbar** (refer to Figure-62), the modifications are applied to the model.

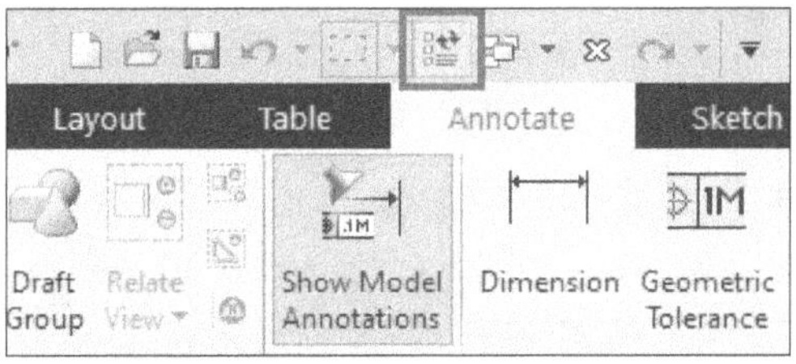

Figure-62. Regenerate button

Manual Dimensioning (Dimension Tool)

Like Part environment, we also have manual dimensioning tool in Drawing environment. The only drawback of using manual dimensioning in Drawing environment is that, the model do not update as per the dimensions. For example, if you have changed manual dimension of a line then it will display as changed but the line will remain the same. The procedure to apply manual dimensions is given next.

- Click on the **Dimension** tool from the **Annotations** panel in the **Ribbon**. The **Select Reference** dialog box will be displayed; refer to Figure-63.

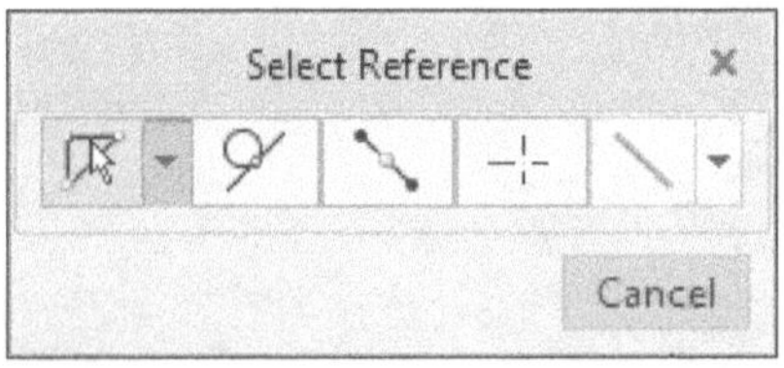

Figure-63. Select Reference dialog box

- Select the entities like we have done in the chapter for sketching and place the dimensions by pressing **MMB**.
- Select the **Tangent** button from the **Select Reference** dialog box and you will be able to dimension circles and arcs at their tangency points; refer to Figure-64.

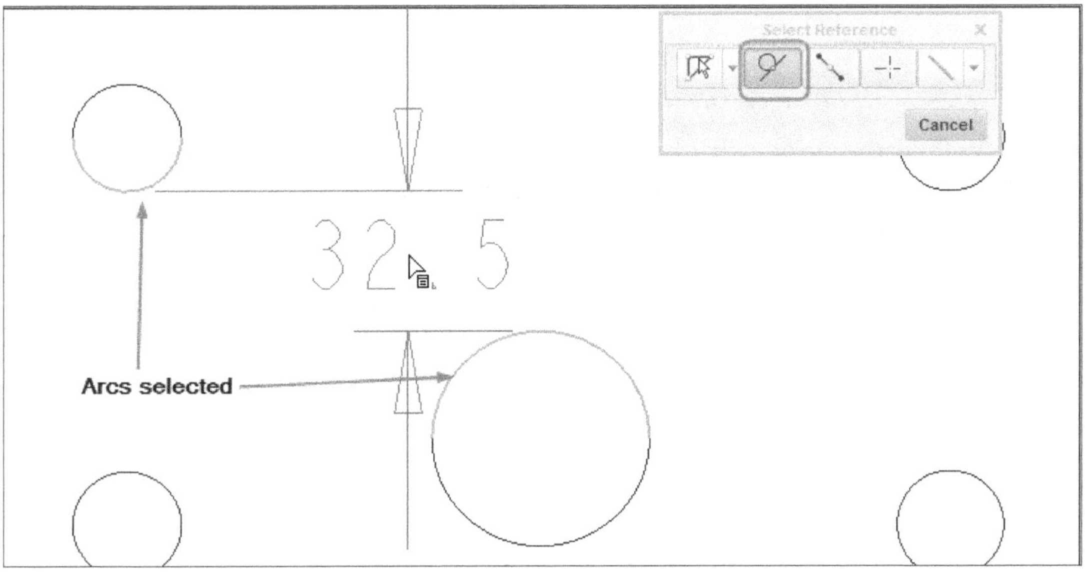

Figure-64. Dimensioning arc at tangency

- Using the **Midpoint** button, you can dimension the entities with reference to their mid points; refer to Figure-65. Note that you can select multiple entities by holding the **CTRL** key while selecting entities.

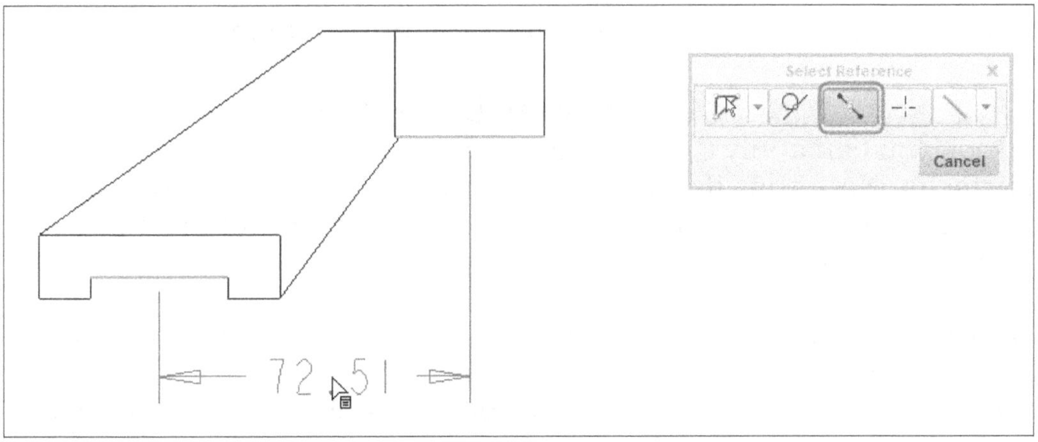

Figure-65. Dimensioning with reference to mid points

- Similarly, you can use the other options in **Select Reference** dialog box.

Ordinate Dimension

The **Ordinate Dimension** tool works in the same way as it does in Part environment. The procedure is given next.

- Click on the **Ordinate Dimension** tool from the **Ordinate Dimension** drop-down in the **Annotations** panel of the **Ribbon**; refer to Figure-66. The **Select Reference** dialog box will be displayed.

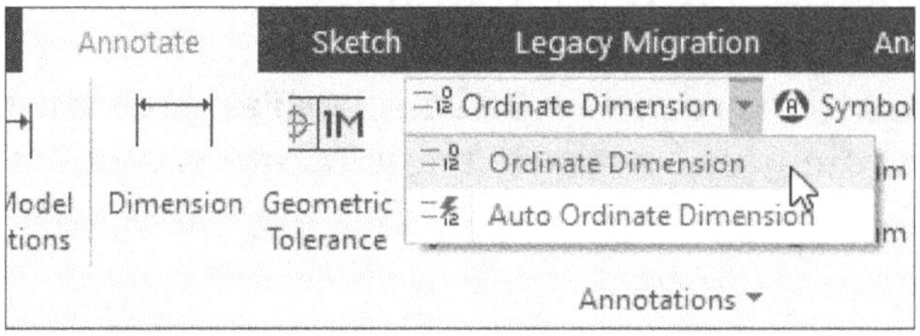

Figure-66. Ordinate Dimension tool

- Select the reference edge which will be set a zero reference and then select all the entities to which you want to apply the dimensions while holding the **CTRL** key. Preview of ordinate dimensions will be displayed; refer to Figure-67.

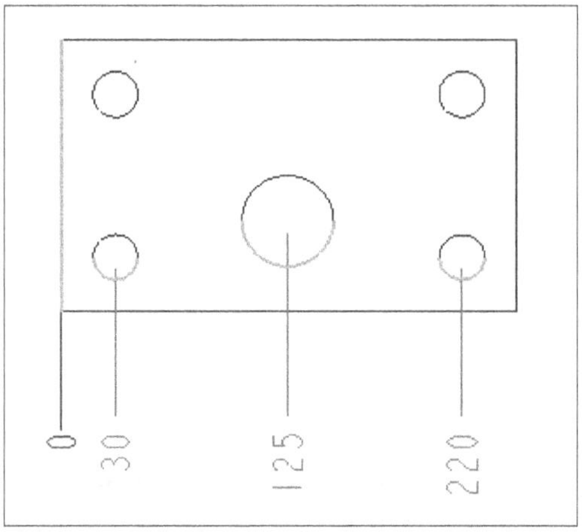

Figure-67. Preview of ordinate dimensions

- Press the **MMB** at desired location to place the dimensions.

Auto Ordinate Dimension

Using this tool, you can apply the ordinate dimension to all the entities on the selected surface/surfaces. Note that if you want to apply ordinate dimension to more than one surfaces then the surfaces must be parallel to each other. The procedure to use **Auto Ordinate Dimension** tool is given next.

- Click on the **Auto Ordinate Dimension** tool from the **Ordinate Dimension** drop-down. You are asked to select one or more surfaces.
- Select the surface whose entities are to be dimensioned; refer to Figure-68.

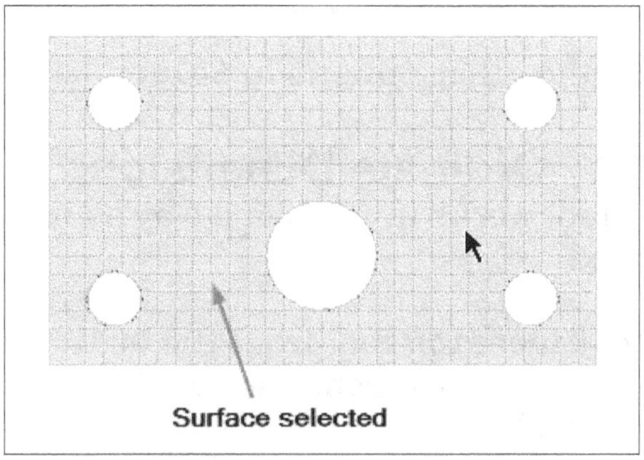

Figure-68. Surface selected

- Press the **MMB**. You are asked to select a base line entity.

- Select an edge, curve, or datum plane. Preview of ordinate dimensions will be displayed; refer to Figure-69.

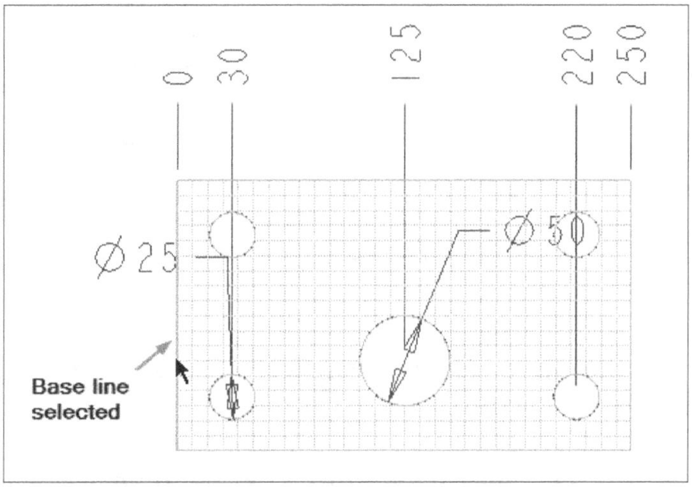

Figure-69. Ordinate dimension created

- Click on the **Select Base Line** option from the **Menu Manager** displayed to select base line for other direction; refer to Figure-70.
- Press the Middle Mouse Button to apply the dimensions.

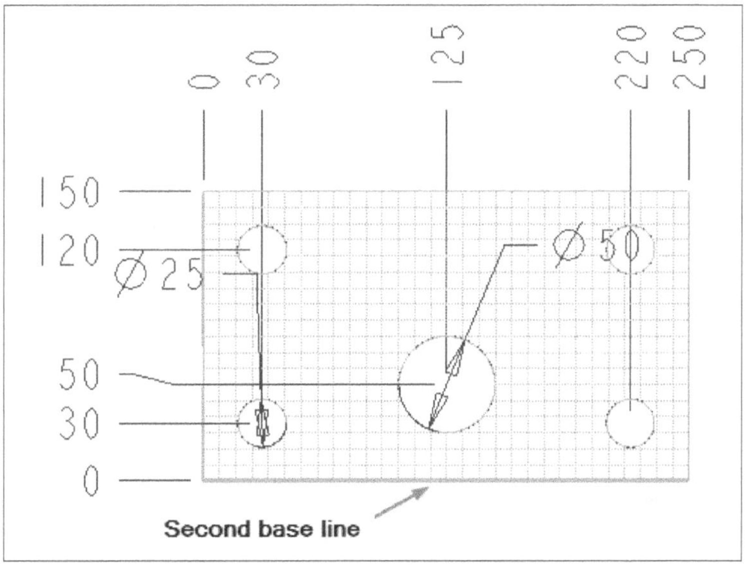

Figure-70. Ordinate dimension with two base lines

GEOMETRIC TOLERANCE

Geometrical tolerance is defined as the maximum permissible overall variation of form or position of a feature.

Geometrical tolerances are used,
(i) to specify the required accuracy in controlling the form of a feature.
(ii) to ensure correct functional positioning of the feature.

Figure-71 shows a geometric symbol with meaning of each box.

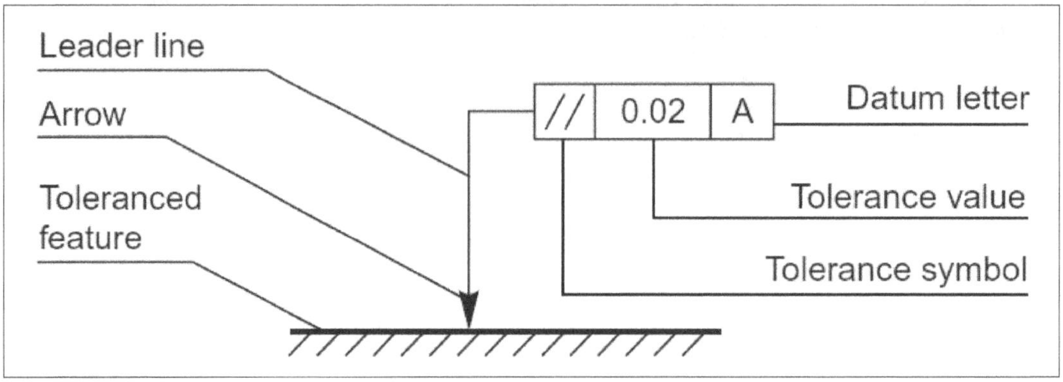

Figure-71. Geometric Tolerance symbol

Before we start using the tools in Creo Parametric, it is important to understand the meaning of each Tolerance Symbol.

Meaning of various geometric tolerance symbols are given in Figure-72.

Characteristics to be toleranced		*Symbols*
Form of single features	Straightness	⏤
	Flatness	⏥
	Circularity (roundness)	○
	Cylindricity	⌭
	Profile of any line	⌒
	Profile of any surface	⌓
Orientation of related features	Parallelism	//
	Perpendicularity (squareness)	⊥
	Angularity	∠
Position of related features	Position	⌖
	Concentricity and coaxiality	◎
	Symmetry	⌯
	Run-out	↗

Figure-72. Meaning of geometric Tolerance symbol

Figure-73 and Figure-74 shows the use of geometric tolerances in real-world.

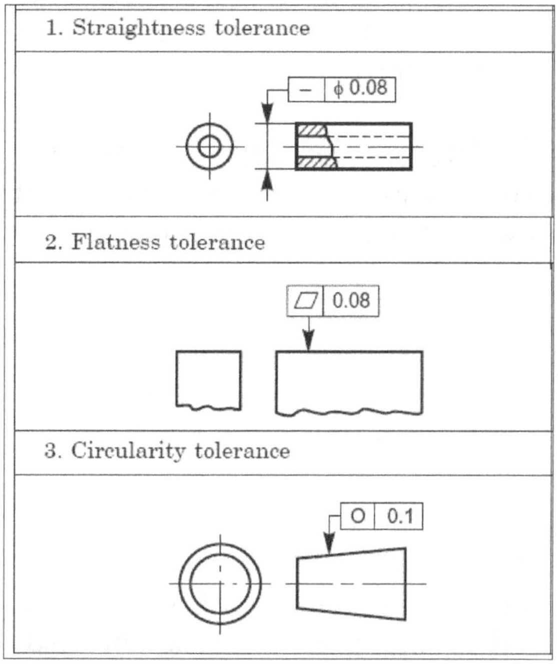

Figure-73. Use of geometric tolerance 1

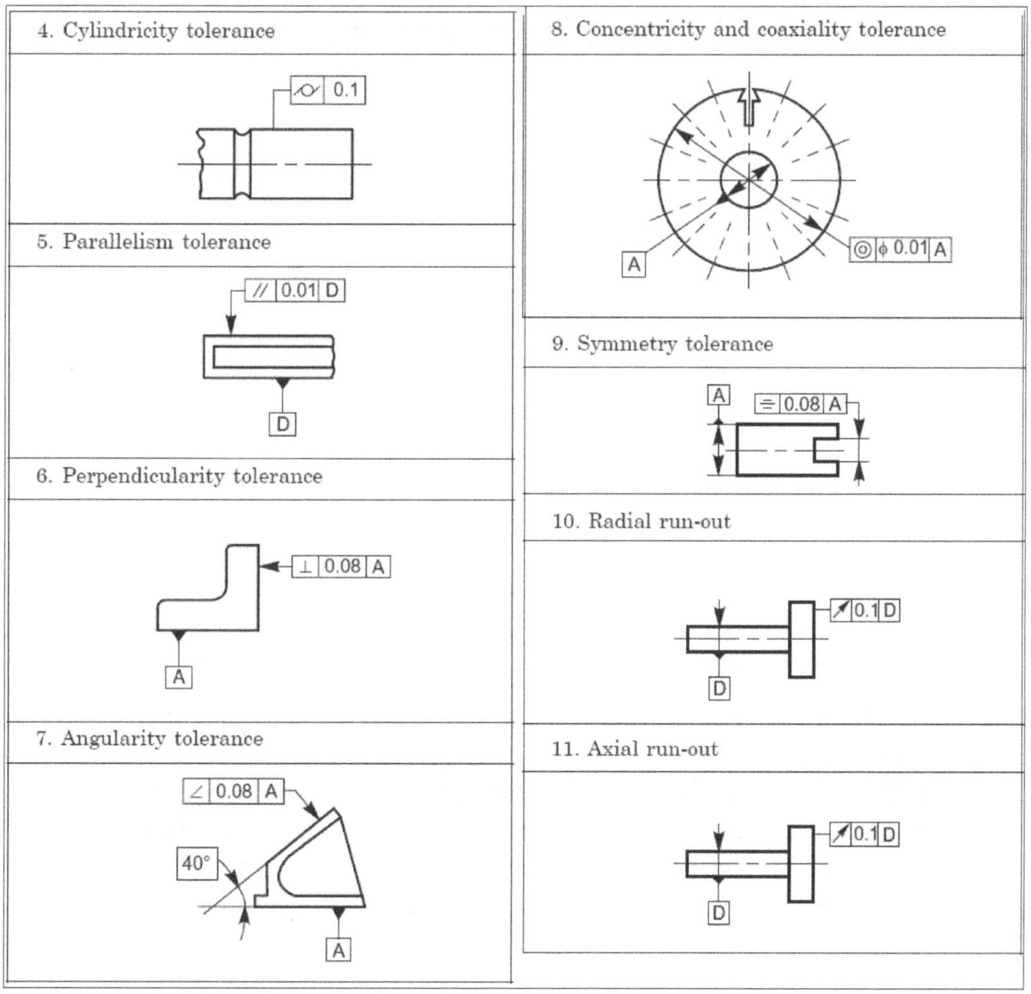

Figure-74. Use of geometric tolerance 2

Note that in applying most of the Geometrical tolerances, you need to define a datum plane like in Perpendicularity, Parallelism, and so on. So, before we place geometric tolerance symbol, we need to understand how to place the datum plane symbol.

Placing Datum symbol

- Click on the **Datum Feature Symbol** tool from the **Annotations** panel in the **Ribbon**; refer to Figure-75. You will be asked to select entity to which datum symbol is to be applied.

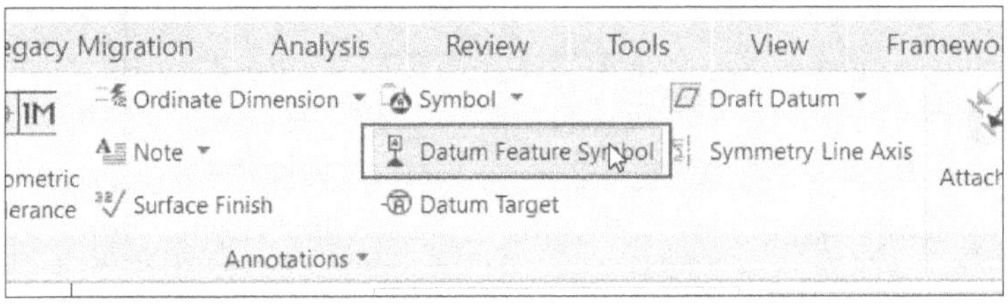

Figure-75. Datum Feature Symbol tool

- Click on the edge of model, plane, axis, or dimension in drawing view. The datum symbol will get attached to the cursor. Press the **MMB** at desired location. The symbol will be placed and **Datum Feature** contextual tab will be displayed in the **Ribbon**; refer to Figure-76.

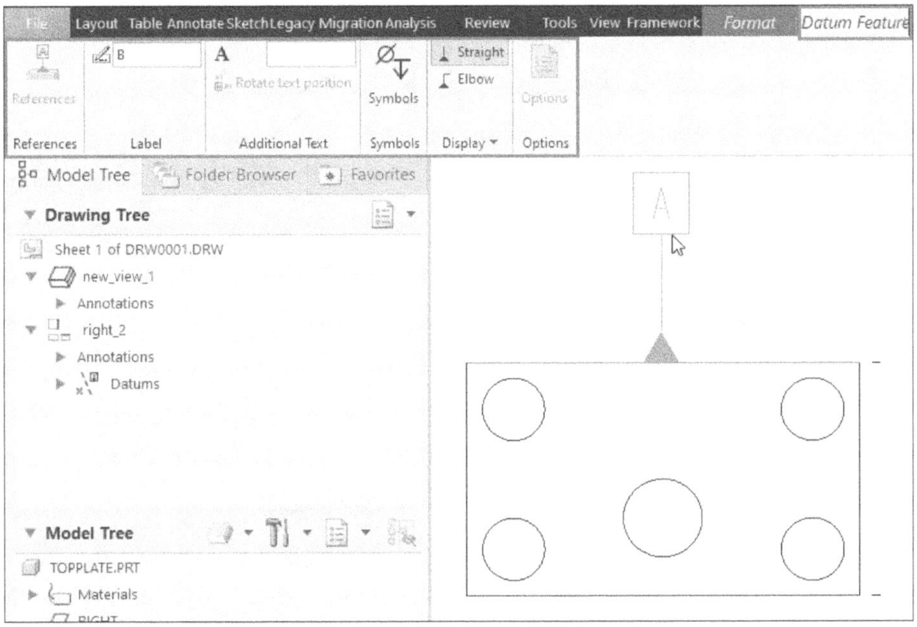

Figure-76. Datum Feature contextual tab

- Specify desired label (A,B,C, etc.) for datum feature in the **Label** edit box.
- If you want to specify additional text with datum feature then click in the **A** edit box next to **Label** edit box in the **Ribbon** and enter desired text.
- Click on the **Symbols** button from **Symbols** panel of the contextual tab. The **Symbols** dialog box will be displayed; refer to Figure-77. Select desired symbol from the dialog box to add it to the current annotation.

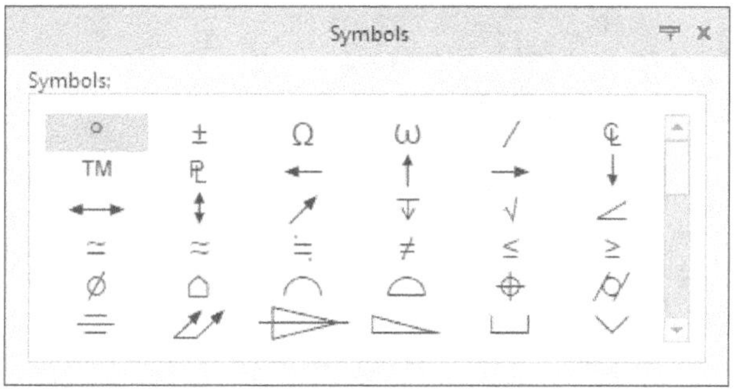

Figure-77. Symbols dialog box

- If you want to modify the symbol from straight to elbow type then select the **Elbow** button. If you want to display the symbol as per **ASME Y14.5m-1982** standard then select the **Display per ASME Y14.5m-1982** check box from the expanded **Display** panel of the **Ribbon**.
- Drag the datum symbol at desired location and click in the blank area of the drawing to exit the contextual tab.

Inserting Geometric Tolerance

- Click on the **Geometric Tolerance** button from the **Annotations** panel in the **Ribbon**; refer to Figure-78. The symbol will get attached to the cursor.

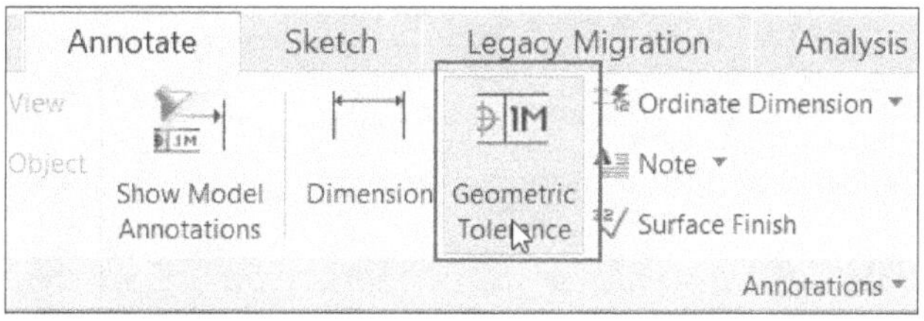

Figure-78. Geometric Tolerance button

- Click on the edge/face/curve/dimension to which you want to apply geometric tolerance and press the **MMB** to specify location. The **Geometric Tolerance** contextual tab will be displayed in the **Ribbon**; refer to Figure-79.

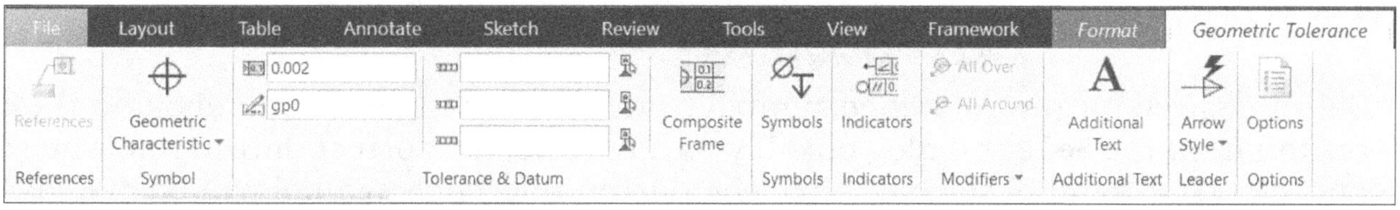

Figure-79. Geometric Tolerance contextual tab

- Click on the **Geometric Characteristic** button from the **Symbol** panel in the contextual tab and select desired GTOL (Geometric Tolerance) symbol; refer to Figure-80.

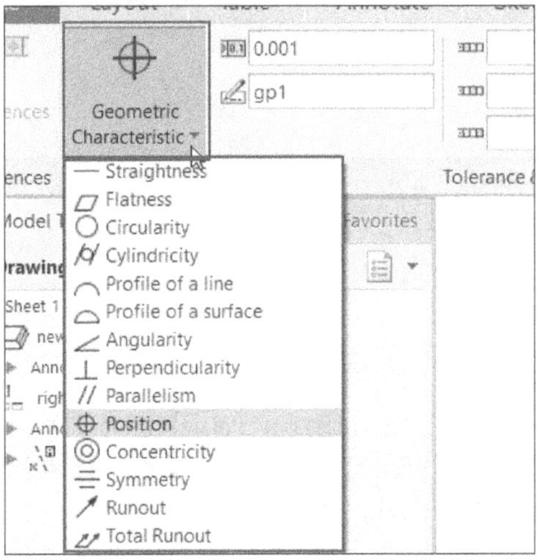

Figure-80. Geometric Characteristic drop-down

- Specify desired value of geometric tolerance in the **Tolerance value** edit box in the contextual tab.
- Click on the **Select datum reference** button next to **Primary datum reference** edit box. The **Select** dialog box will be displayed and you will be asked to select a datum reference; refer to Figure-81.

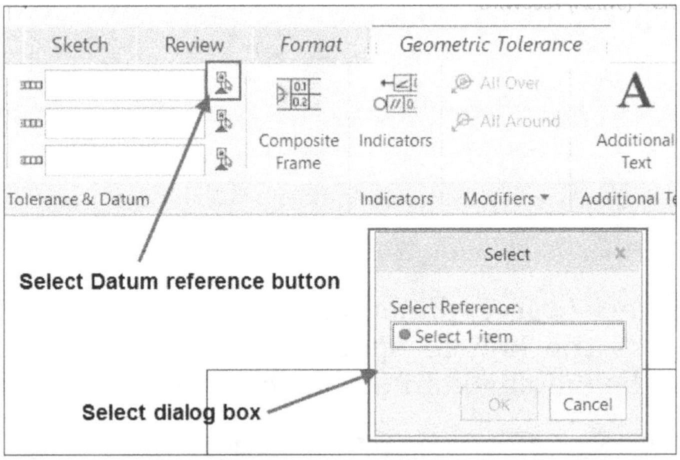

Figure-81. Select dialog box

- Select desired datum reference symbol from the drawing area and click on the **OK** button from the **Select** dialog box. If you have selected correct datum reference as per the GTOL symbol selected then the datum reference symbol will be displayed in green color in the **Primary datum reference** edit box; refer to Figure-82. If the symbol selected is not as per the datum reference then a red line will be displayed below the symbol name in the **Primary datum reference** edit box; refer to Figure-82.

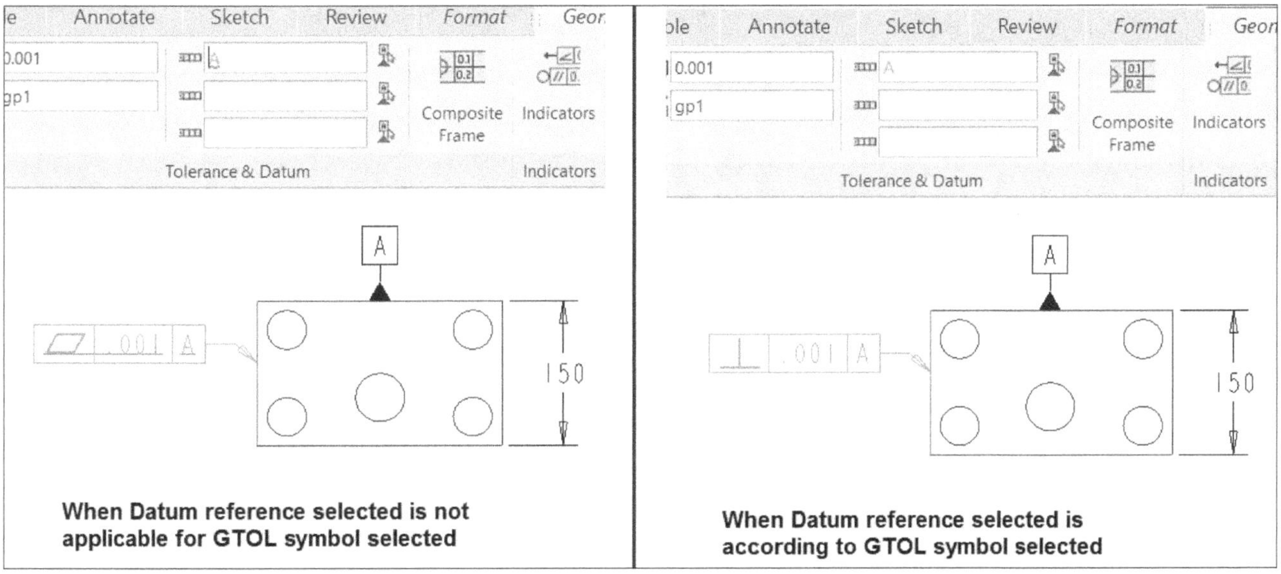

Figure-82. GTOL symbol and datum reference selection

- Similarly, you can specify Secondary and Tertiary datum references using the respective options in the **Tolerance & Datum** panel of the **Geometric Tolerance** contextual tab.

Composite Frame

- If you want to create a composite tolerance frame then click on the **Composite Frame** button from the **Tolerances & Datum** panel of the contextual tab. The box to define parameters of **composite tolerance frame** will be displayed; refer to Figure-83.

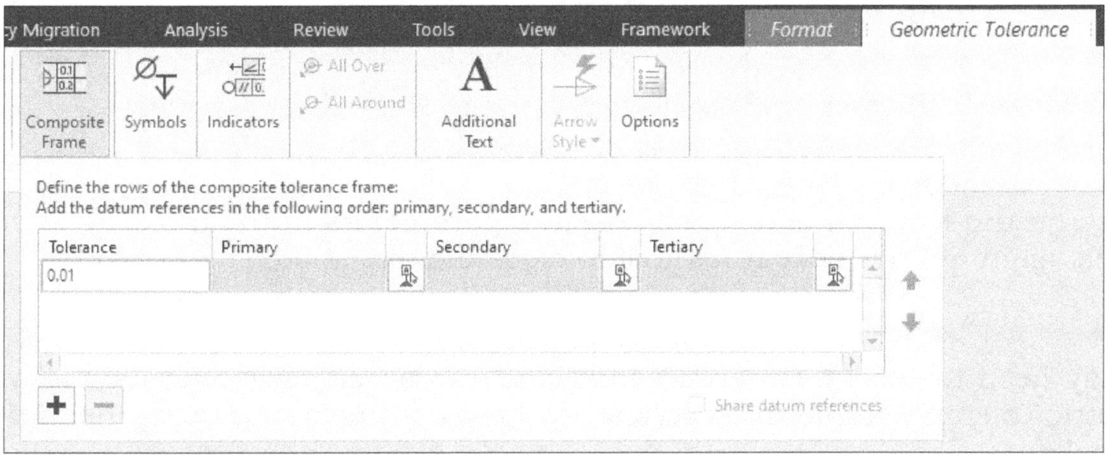

Figure-83. Composite tolerance frame box

- Click on the **+** button at the bottom in the box. A new row will be added to the Geometric Tolerance frame.
- Specify desired tolerance value and select the related datum reference; refer to Figure-84. Click on the **Composite Frame** tool again to close the box.

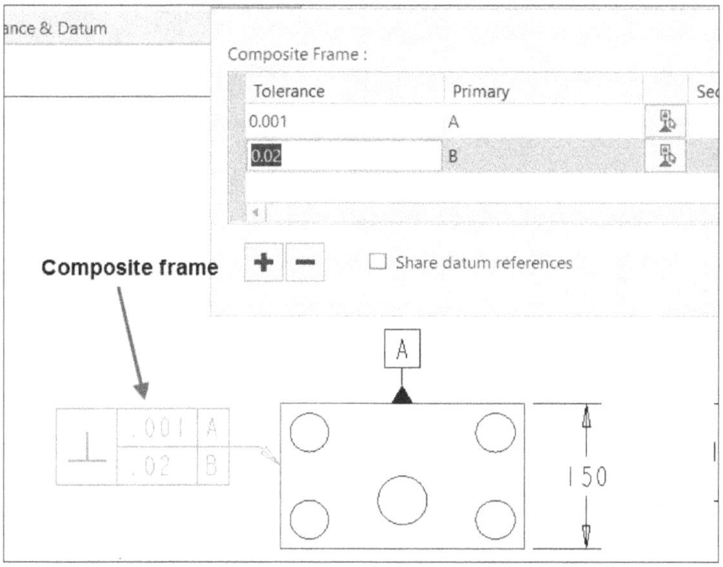

Figure-84. Composite frame created

Indicators Frame

- Click on the **Indicators** tool from the **Indicators** panel in the **Geometric Tolerance** contextual tab of the **Ribbon**. The **Indicators Frame** dialog box will be displayed to define indicators; refer to Figure-85.

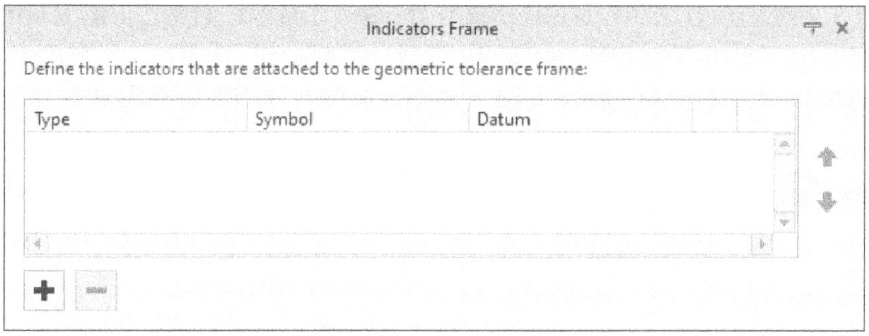

Figure-85. Indicators Frame dialog box

- Click on the **+** button and specify desired parameters in the table.
- Click again on the **Indicators** tool to close the dialog box.

Additional Text

You may need to specify material conditions and other parameters along with the Geometric Tolerance frame. You can specify these parameters by using the **Additional Text** tool.

- Click on the **Additional Text** tool from the **Additional Text** panel in the **Geometric Tolerance** contextual tab. The input box will be displayed; refer to Figure-86.

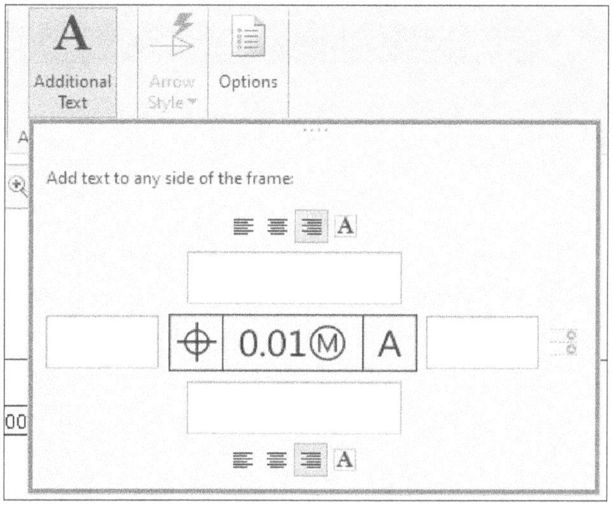

Figure-86. Additional Text box

- Click in the box around the frame in which you want to specify additional text and enter desired text in it.
- Click on the **Additional Text** tool again to close the box.

Click in the blank area of drawing to exit the contextual tab. If you want to modify a tolerance frame then click on it, the **Geometric Tolerance** contextual tab will display again.

SURFACE FINISH SYMBOL

As the name suggests, this symbol is used to define the surface finish of face of a part. The procedure to add surface finish symbol is given next.

- Click on the **Surface Finish** tool from the **Annotations** panel of the **Ribbon**. The **Surface Finish** contextual tab will be displayed; refer to Figure-87.

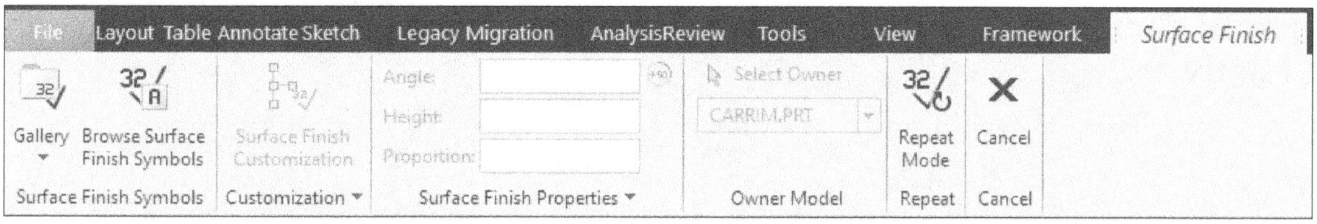

Figure-87. Surface Finish contextual tab

- Click on the **Gallery** drop-down button from **Surface Finish Symbols** panel. All the symbols to define the surface finish will be displayed; refer to Figure-88.

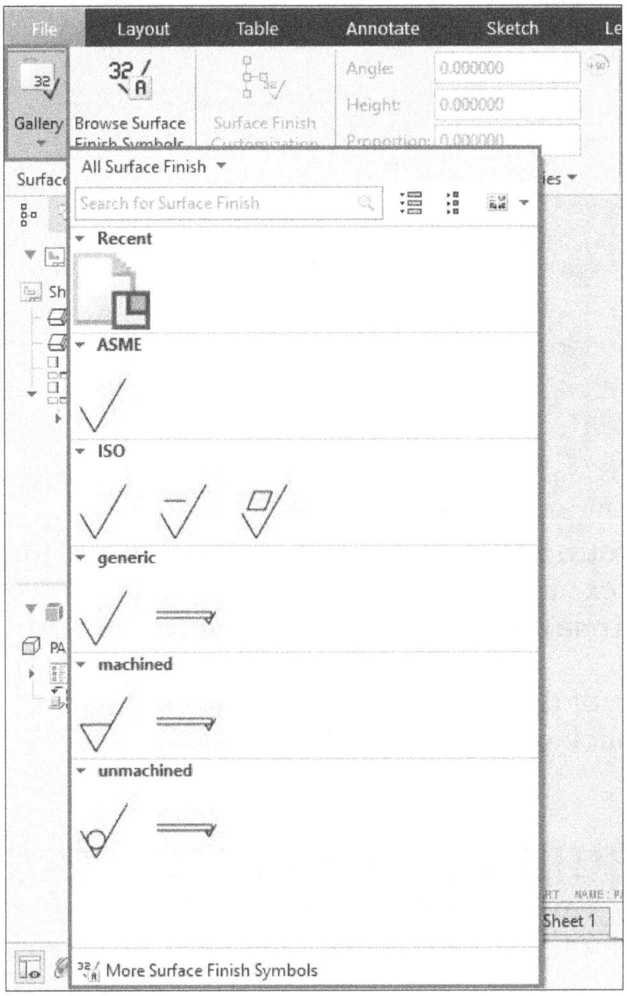

Figure-88. Symbols to define surface finish

- Or, click on the **Browse Surface Finish Symbols** tool from **Surface Finish Symbols** panel in the contextual tab. The **Open** dialog box will be displayed; refer to Figure-89.

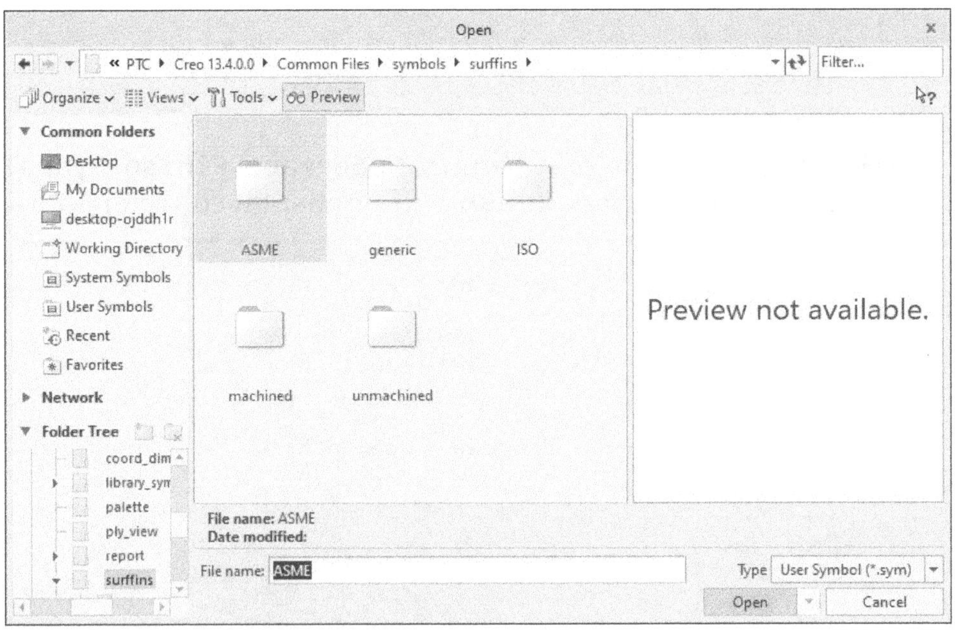

Figure-89. Open dialog box with surface finish symbol

- There are five categories available: ASME, ISO, generic, machined, unmachined. Double-click on desired folder and select the standard symbol in the folder.
- Click on the **Open** button from the dialog box. The symbol will get attached to the cursor; refer to Figure-90.

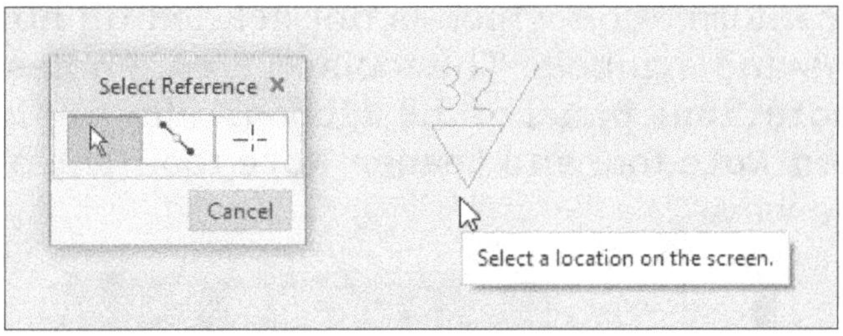

Figure-90. Symbol attached to cursor along with Select Reference dialog box

- Place the symbol by selecting the entity corresponding to option selected in **Select Reference** dialog box; refer to Figure-91.

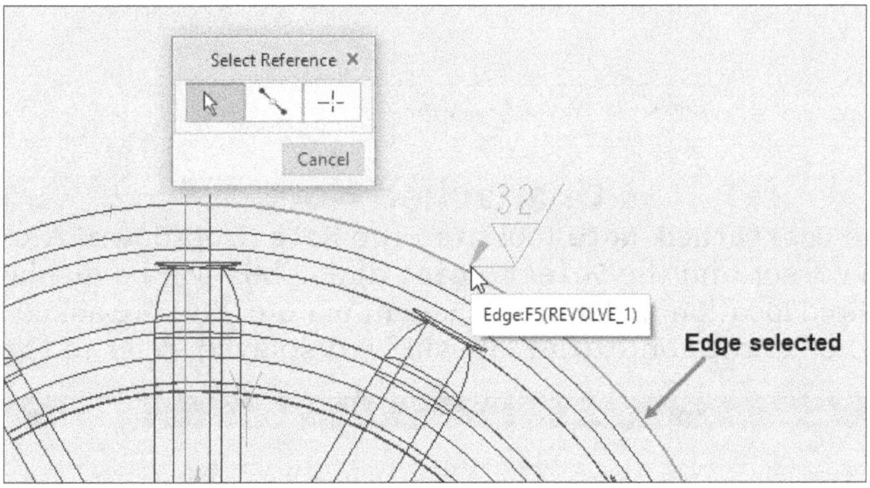

Figure-91. Reference selected for placing surface finish symbol

- Set desired height and angle for the symbol by using options in the **Surface Finish Properties** panel of the contextual tab.
- Click on the **Surface Finish Customization** button from **Customization** panel. The **Surface Finish Customization** dialog box will be displayed; refer to Figure-92.

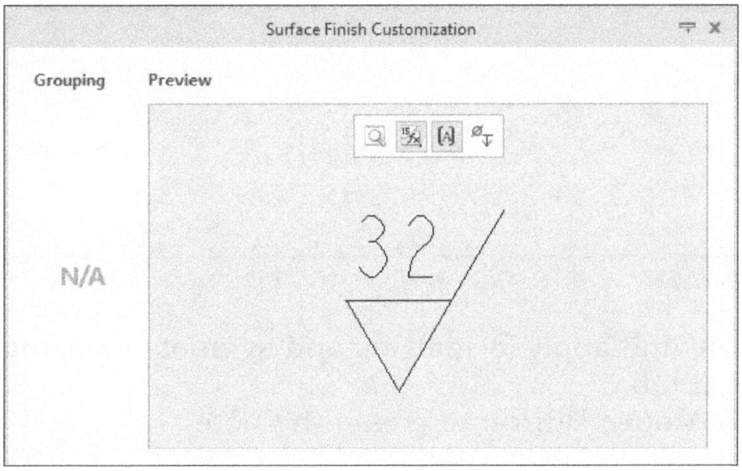

Figure-92. Surface Finish Customization dialog box

- After specifying desired parameters, press the Middle Mouse Button to place the surface finish symbol.

NOTES

Notes are used to give information which is not defined till now in the drawing with the help of dimensions and symbols. The tools to create notes are given in the **Note** drop-down in the **Annotations** panel of the **Ribbon**; refer to Figure-93. Here, we will discuss the **Unattached Note** tool and **Leader Note** tool. The other tools for creating note work in the same way.

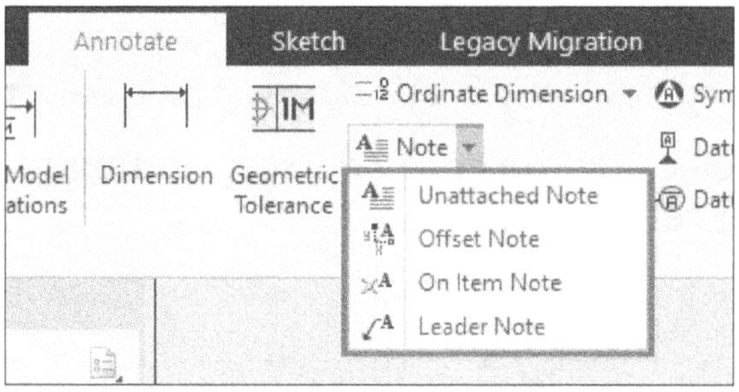

Figure-93. Note drop-down

Unattached Note

- Click on the **Unattached Note** tool from the **Note** drop-down. A text box will get attached to cursor and the **Select Point** dialog box will be displayed.
- Click at desired location to define placement of note. You are asked to type desired text. Also, the **Format** contextual tab will be displayed; refer to Figure-94.

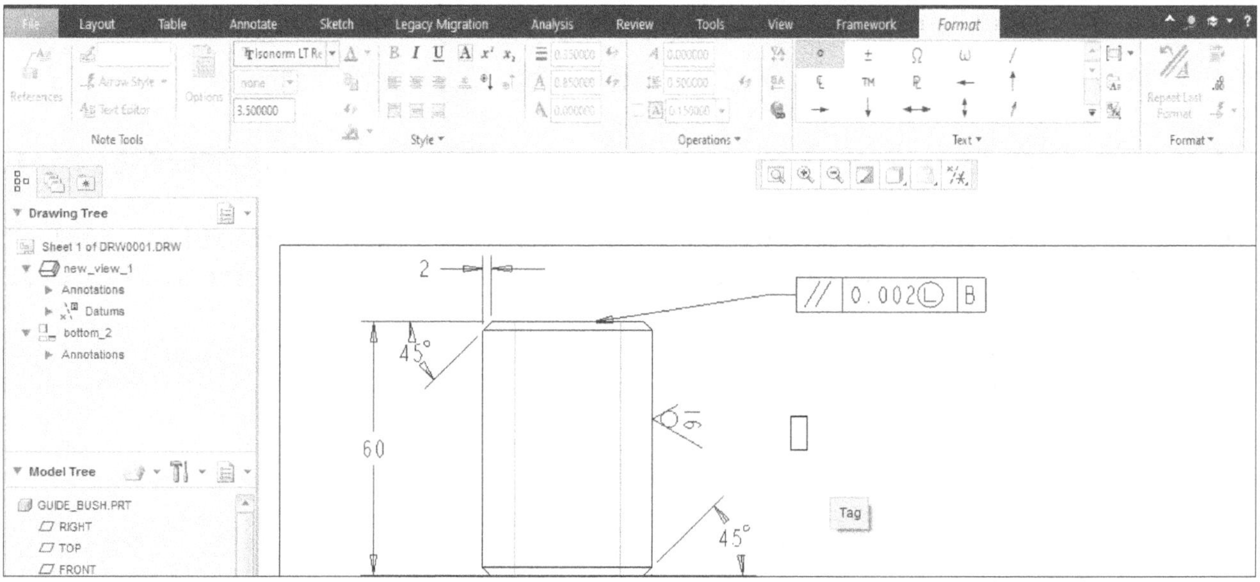

Figure-94. Format contextual tab

- Write desired note and apply formatting and symbols by using the options in the **Format** contextual tab.
- Press the Middle Mouse Button to create the note.

Leader Note

- Click on the **Leader Note** tool from the **Note** drop-down. A text box with leader will get attached to cursor and the **Select Reference** dialog box will be displayed.
- Click at desired location to specify the starting point of the leader. You are asked to specify the end point of the leader.
- Press the middle mouse button (MMB) to specify the end point of leader. Rest of the procedure is same as discussed for **Unattached Note** tool.

MODIFYING DIMENSION STYLE

- Select the **Annotation** option from the **Selection Filter** drop-down at the bottom right corner of the interface and then select all the dimensions for changing their dimension style; refer to Figure-95. The **Dimension** contextual tab will be displayed in the **Ribbon**.

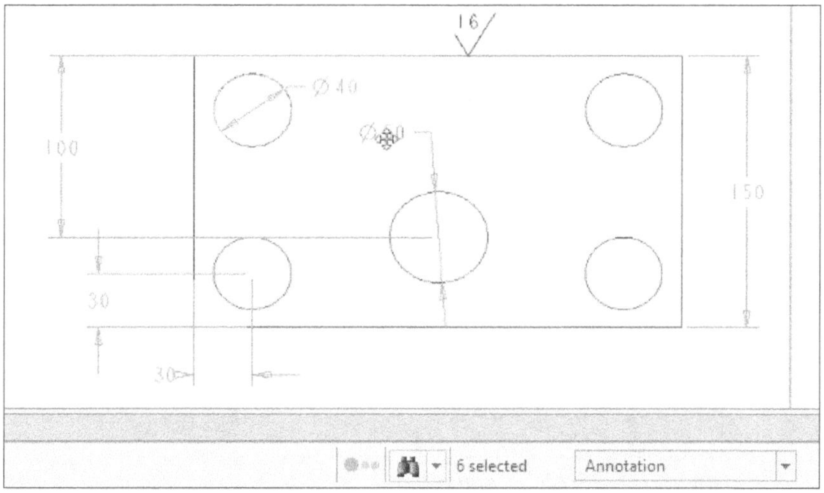

Figure-95. Dimensions selected

- Click on the **Display** tool from the contextual tab. The options will be displayed as shown in Figure-96.

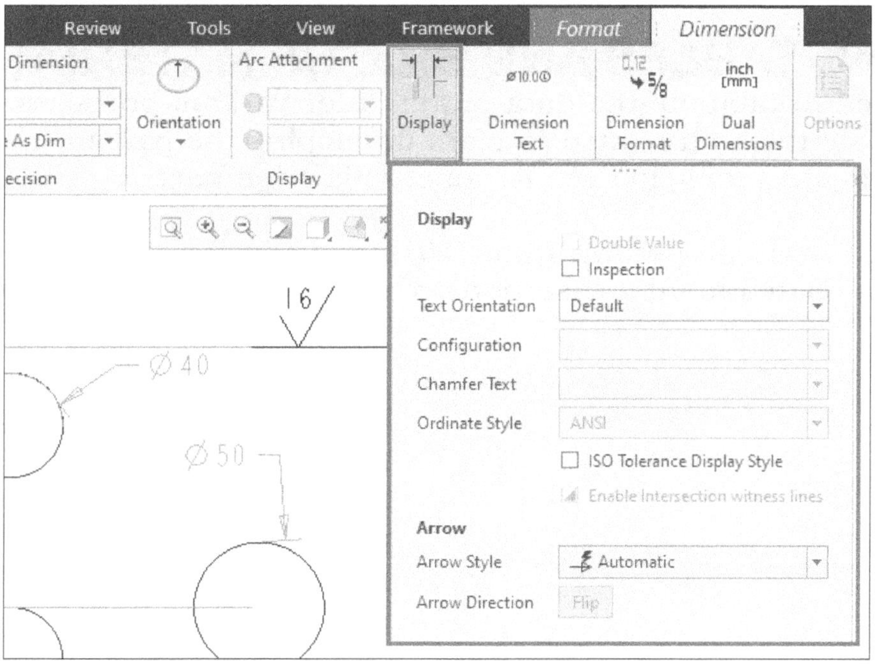

Figure-96. Display options

- Set desired parameters like change the arrow style using the **Arrow Style** drop-down or change the orientation of text using the **Text Orientation** drop-down. You can set the selected dimensions as inspection dimension using the **Inspection** check box in the box.
- If you want to change the text font or other text styles then select all dimensions and click on the **Text Style** tool from the **Annotate** tab of the **Ribbon**. The **Text Style** dialog box will be displayed; refer to Figure-97.

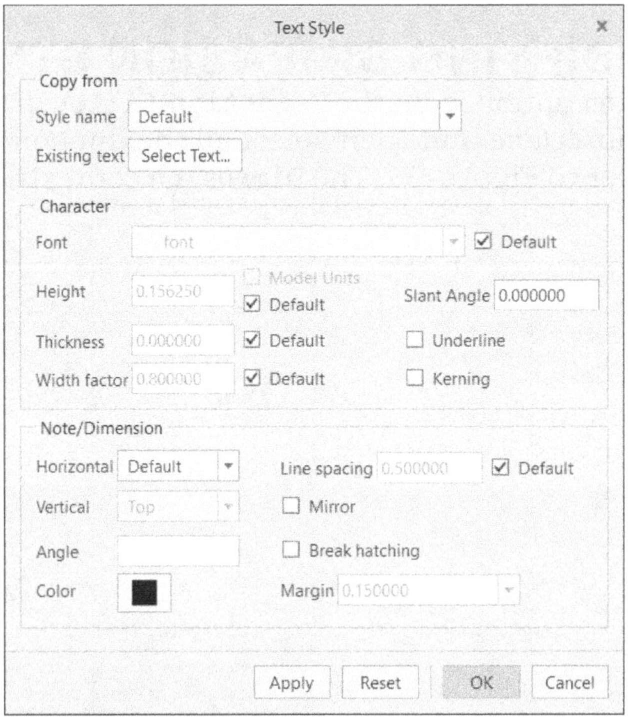

Figure-97. Text Style dialog box

- Clear the **Default** check box and select desired font from the **Font** drop-down.
- Specify the other parameters related to text using the options in the dialog box and click on the **OK** button to apply the changes.

CREATING TABLES AND BILL OF MATERIALS (BOM)

Tables are used to tabulate the data required for various purposes. For example, you can tabulate the data related to team developing the part in the drawing. The procedure to create a table in Creo Parametric is given next.

- Click on the **Table** drop-down from **Table** panel in the **Table** tab of the **Ribbon**. The options related to table insertion are displayed; refer to Figure-98.

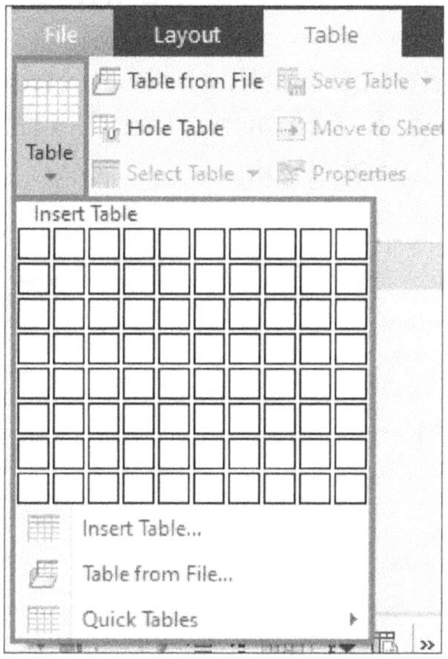

Figure-98. Table drop-down

Inserting Table dynamically

- Hover the cursor over the boxes to define the number of rows and columns of table. Click on the boxes when you get desired number of rows and columns. Preview of table attached to cursor will be displayed; refer to Figure-99.

Figure-99. Preview of table attached

- Click to place the table; refer to Figure-100.

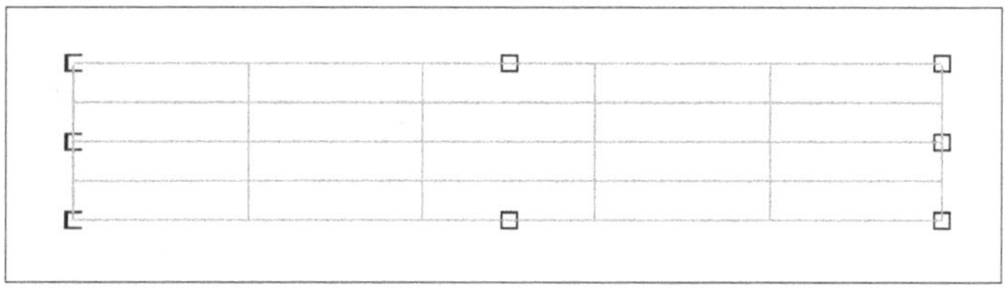

Figure-100. Table placed

- To enter data in any field, double click on it. (Make sure you have **General** option selected in the **Selection Filter** drop-down at the bottom-right corner of the interface.)
- You can perform the operations like merging cells, unmerging cells, and so on by using the tools in the **Rows & Columns** panel in the **Ribbon**; refer to Figure-101.

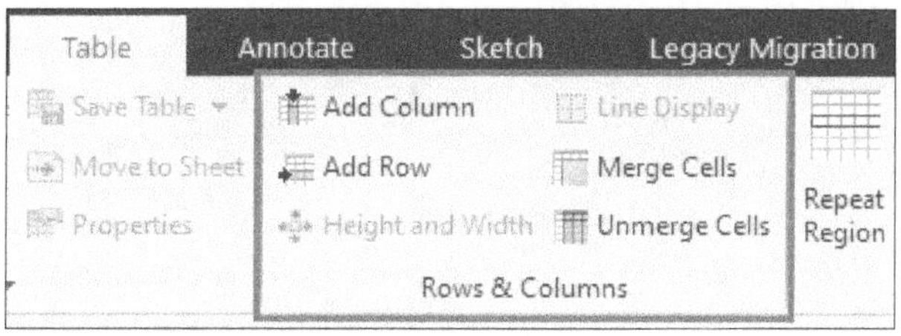

Figure-101. Rows and Columns panel

- To merge the cells, select two or more cells while holding the **CTRL** key and click on the **Merge Cells** tool.
- To adjust the height and width of a cell, click on the cell and then select the **Height and Width** tool from the **Rows & Columns** panel. The **Height and Width** dialog box will be displayed; refer to Figure-102.

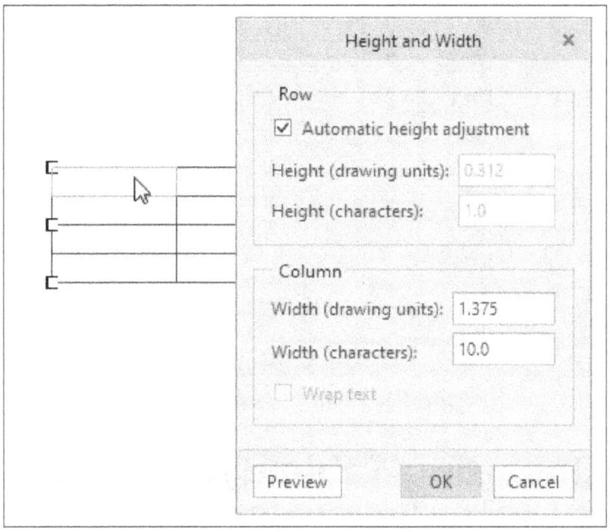

Figure-102. Height and Width dialog box

- By default, the **Automatic height adjustment** check box is selected. So, the height of column is automatically adjusted according to the data entered in the cell. To define a specific height, clear the check box and specify the value in the **Height (drawing units)** or **Height (characters)**edit box. Similarly, you can change the width of the cell.

Inserting Table by dialog box

- Click on the **Insert Table** tool from the **Table** drop-down in the **Table** panel of **Table** tab in the **Ribbon**. The **Insert Table** dialog box will be displayed; refer to Figure-103.

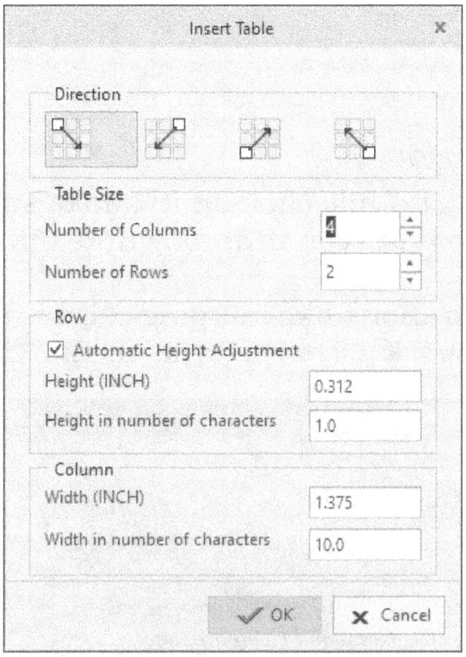

Figure-103. Insert Table dialog box

- Specify the number of columns and rows of the table by using the spinners in the **Table Size** area of the dialog box.
- Specify height and width of cells by using the related edit boxes and click on the **OK** button from the dialog box. The **Select Point** dialog box will be displayed and you will be prompted to specify the insertion point for the table.
- Click in the drawing to place the table. Rest of the procedure is same as discussed earlier.

Quick Tables

There are various predefined templates of tables available in the **Quick Tables** cascading menu in the **Table** drop-down; refer to Figure-104. If your desired table matches with the templates then click on desired template and place it at desired location. Rest of the procedure is same as discussed earlier.

Figure-104. Quick Tables

Bill of Materials (BOM)

Bill of Material is used to tabulate the specifications of components used in the current assembly drawing. In Creo Parametric, we have a standard method to insert BOM. We do not need to enter each component description manually in Creo. The procedure to create Bill of Materials is given next.

- Insert a table with desired number of columns and three rows. (Generally in BOMs, we have three columns: one for serial number, second for name of component, and third for quantity. Also in First Row, we type name of table i.e. Bill of Materials; in second row, we type description of columns i.e. Sr. No., Name of component, etc. Note that you need to merge the cells in first row to write description of table; refer to Figure-105.)

Bill of Material		
Sr. No.	Name of Component	Quantity

Figure-105. Bill of material table template

- Click on the **Repeat Region** tool from the **Data** panel in the **Ribbon**; refer to Figure-106. The **TBL REGIONS Menu Manager** will be displayed; refer to Figure-107.

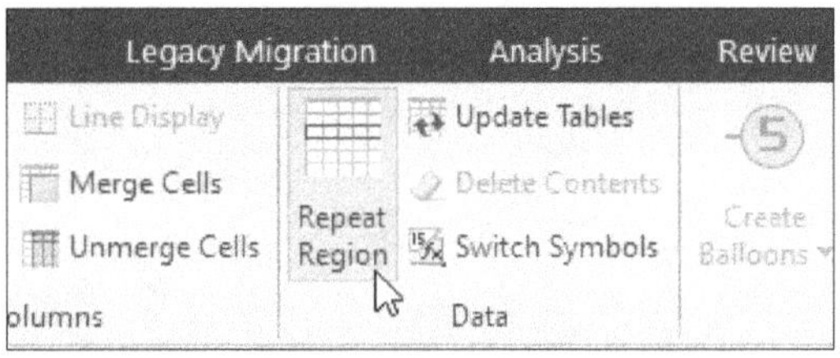

Figure-106. Repeat Region tool

Figure-107. TBL REGIONS Menu Manager

- Click on the **Add** option from the **Menu Manager** and select first and last cell of the third row in the table; refer to Figure-108.

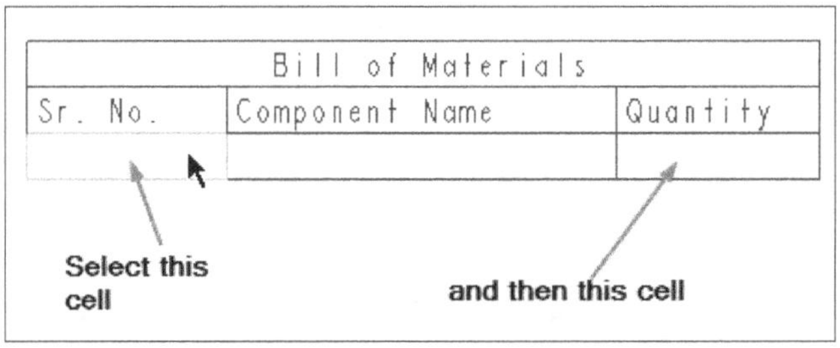

Figure-108. Cells selected for repeat regions

- Press the **Middle Mouse Button** (**MMB**) once.
- Click on the **Attributes** option from the **TBL REGIONS Menu Manager** and select a cell we have added in the regions. The attribute options will be displayed in the **Menu Manager**; refer to Figure-109. (If you find that you have selected only one cell and all the three cells in same row get selected! Don't worry they have become part of a region now).

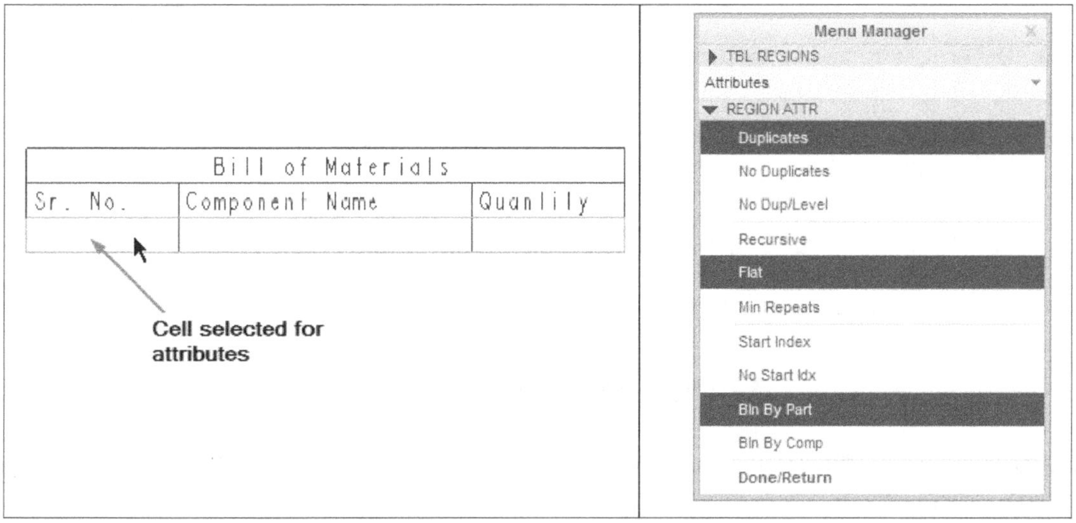

Figure-109. Region with Attribute options

- Select the **No Duplicates** option from the **Menu Manager** and press the **MMB** thrice to exit the **Menu Manager**.

Filling Repeat Region Parameters in Table

- Double-click on the first cell of the region created (i.e. under Sr. No. column). The **Report Symbol** dialog box will be displayed; refer to Figure-110. In this dialog box, you can see various categories in their short form like, asm stands for assembly, dgm stands for diagram, and so on. Details of each category and its symbols is given later in this chapter. Now, we will continue with the most basic BOM.

Figure-110. Report Symbol dialog box

- Select the **rpt** option and then **index** option from the **Report Symbol** dialog box.
- Double-click on the middle cell in the third row and select **asm** then **mbr** and then **name** from the **Report Symbol** dialog box displayed.
- Double-click on the last cell of third row in table and select **rpt** and then **qty** from the **Report Symbol** dialog box displayed.
- Click on the **Update Tables** tool from the **Data** panel in the **Table** tab of the **Ribbon** to update the Bill of Materials table. Refer to Figure-111 for generated Bill of Materials.

Bill of Materials		
Sr. No.	Component Name	Quantity
1	BOTTOM	1
2	GUIDE_BUSH	4
3	GUIDE_PILLAR	4
4	TOPPLATE	1

Figure-111. Bill of materials generated

Categories in Report Symbol

asm stand for assembly, so you can find all the parameters related to assembly components in it.

dgm stand for diagram, so you can find all the parameters related to electrical diagrams in it.

fam stand for family, so you can find all the parameters related to family components in it.

harn stand for harness, so you can find all the parameters related to pipe/wire harness components in it.

lay stand for layout, so you can find all the parameters related to assembly components in it.

material stand for material, so you can find all the parameters related to material in it like tensile strength.

mbr stand for member, so you can find all the parameters related to members of current wiring/piping/cabling diagram in it.

mdl stand for model, so you can find all the parameters related to model in it.

mfg stand for manufacturing, so you can find all the parameters related to manufacturing components in it.

prs stand for process step, so you can find all the parameters related to process planning in it.

rpt stand for report, so you can find all the parameters related to quantity in it like quantity of a component in assembly.

weldasm stand for welding assembly, so you can find all the parameters related to welding assembly components in it.

But, we do not use all the categories in our general use. Here are some commonly used report symbols:

Parameter Name	Definition
asm.mbr.cparams.name	Lists the names of all user-defined parameters in an assembly component. This parameter is defined for the parts making up the connector outside of the cabling environment.
asm.mbr.cparams.value	Lists the values of all user-defined parameters in an assembly component. This parameter is defined for the parts making up the connector outside of the cabling environment.
asm.mbr.cparam.User Defined	Lists the specified user-defined parameters used in an assembly component. These parameters are defined for the parts making up the Connector outside of the cabling environment.
asm.mbr.name	Displays the name of an assembly member.
asm.mbr.param.name	Lists the names of all user-defined parameters in an assembly member
mdl.param.name	Lists the names of all user-defined parameters in a model.
rpt.index	Displays the number assigned to each record in a repeat region
rpt.level	Shows the recursive depth of an item.
rpt.qty	Displays the quantity of an item.

GENERATING BALLOONS

Balloons are used to identify the components by their index numbers. Balloons are generally used in combination with Bill of Materials. The procedure to generate balloons is given next.

- Click on the **Create Balloons** drop-down from the **Balloons** panel in the **Ribbon**. The tools related to balloons will be displayed; refer to Figure-112.

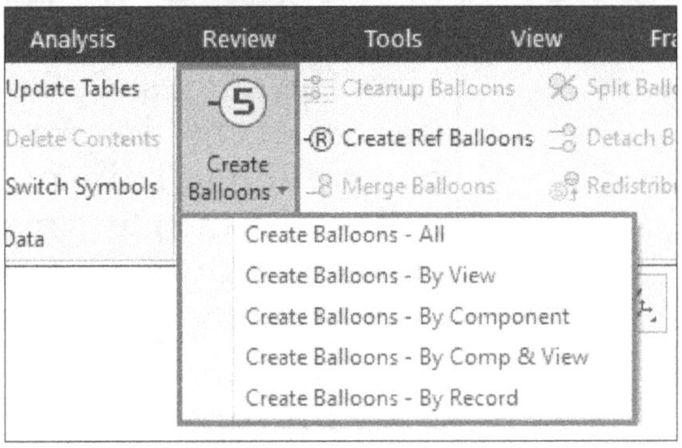

Figure-112. Create Balloons drop-down

- Click on the **Create Balloons-All** tool from the drop-down. The balloons will be created attached to the respective component; refer to Figure-113.

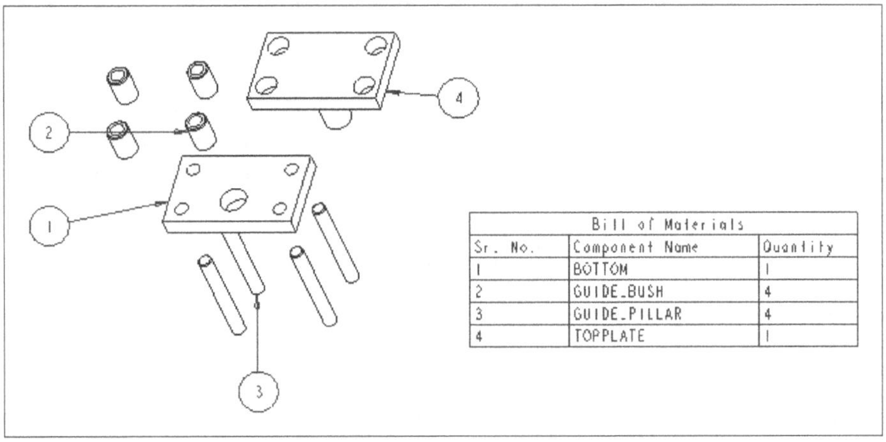

Figure-113. Balloons created

- Click on the balloon and drag it to desired location if it is out of sheet boundary.

PRACTICE 1

Generate the drawing views of all the solid models we have created in Practices and Practicals in the previous chapters.

PRACTICE 2

Generate the exploded views, bill of materials, and balloons from all the assembly models we have worked on till this chapter.

PRACTICE 3

Create the model and drawing given in Figure-114.

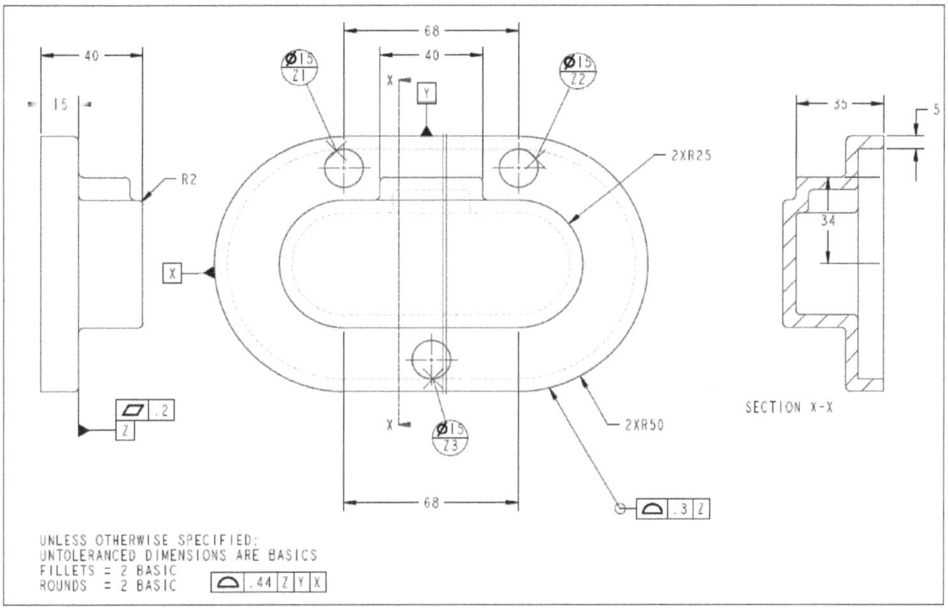

Figure-114. Practice 3

PRACTICE 4

Create the model and drawing given in Figure-115.

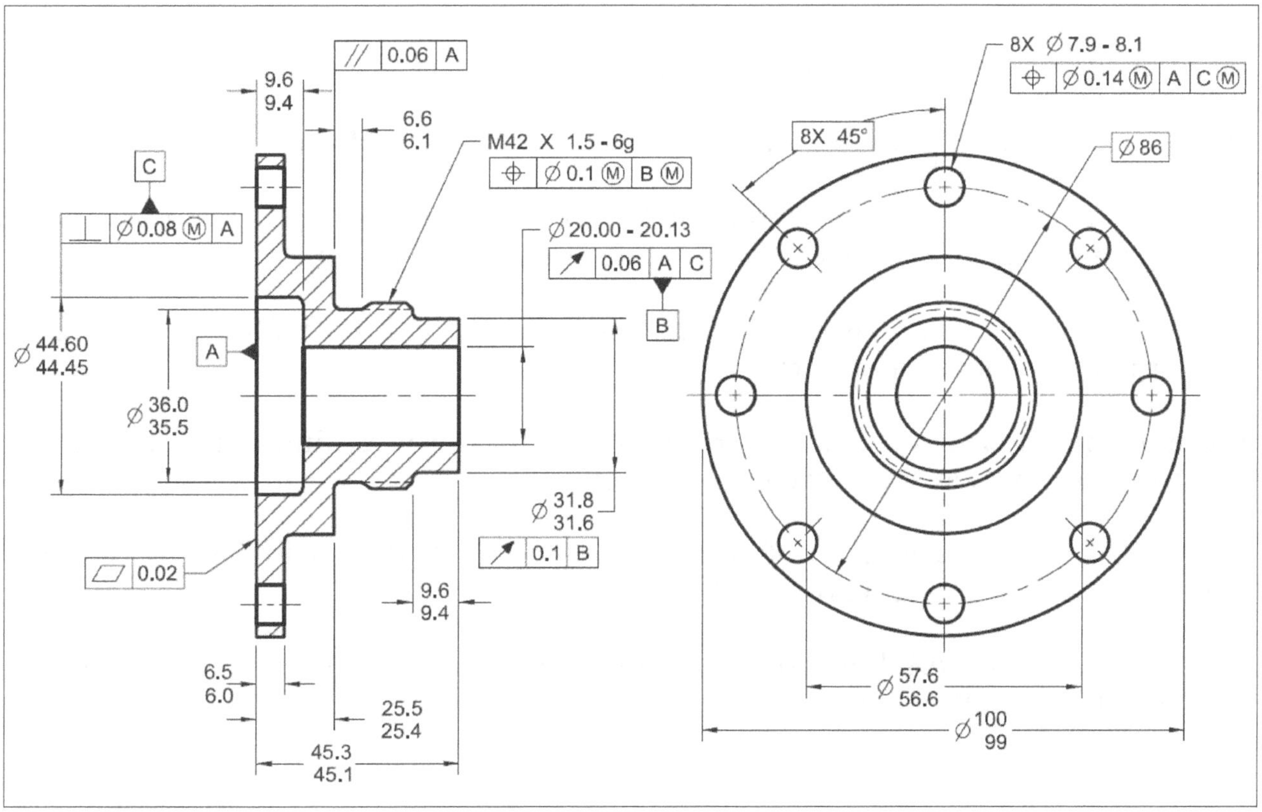

Figure-115. Practice 4

Note that the drawing given in this book are for practice purpose only.

SELF ASSESSMENT

1. What is the full form of PMI in case of Manufacturing Technology?

2. Explain First Angle and Third Angle projections with example.

3. Which of the following symbols is for cylindricity in Geometric Tolerance box?

(a) ⌓ (b) ⌒

(c) ⌭ (d) ○

4. Which of the following symbols is for roundness in Geometric Tolerance box?

(a) ⌓ (b) ⌒

(c) ⌭ (d) ○

5. In which category of report symbols can we find the numbers of components in assembly while generating bill of material?

(a) **`asm`** (b) **`fam`**

(c) **`rpt`** (d) **`mdl`**

6. In Drawing environment, base view is placed by using the .... tool.

7. The .... tool is used to create projections of the base view.

8. The .... are used to highlight a small section of drawing which has minute details that are to be considered while manufacturing.

9. The .... is created to show detail of a part after revolving and sectioning a specific area of part.

10. Using this .... tool, you can apply the ordinate dimension to all the entities on the selected surface/surfaces.

11. **`Geometrical tolerance`** is defined as the maximum permissible overall variation of form or position of a feature. (T/F)

12. **`mbr`** stand for material, so you can find all the parameters related to material in it like tensile strength. (T/F)

13. Why is Product Manufacturing Information (PMI) important in Creo Parametric models?

a) To make models look attractive
b) To save storage space in CAD files
c) To help manufacturers interpret dimensions and tolerances
d) To enable 3D animation features

14. Which tool allows placing Product Manufacturing Information directly on the model or assembly?

a) Drawing View
b) Layout Tab
c) Model Based Definition
d) Projection View

15. What is the purpose of the General View tool?

a) To insert an exploded view
b) To create a base view
c) To edit sheet size
d) To add a table

16. Which option is used to create a Half View in Creo Parametric?

a) View Display
b) View Visibility
c) Model View
d) Layout Setup

17. What needs to be done to create a Partial View in a drawing?

a) Select a view and add a break
b) Select a point and draw a spline
c) Select the default orientation
d) Use the Drawing Properties option

18. What does the Broken View option allow you to do?

a) Create a duplicate model
b) Add tables to your drawing
c) Break a model view with lines
d) Align all views automatically

19. What must be done before creating Projection Views?

a) Add projection arrows
b) Review Display styles
c) Understand First and Third Angle projection
d) Set sheet format

20. Which type of view is used to highlight a small section with minute details?

a) Projection View
b) Auxiliary View
c) Detailed View
d) Section View

21. What is the use of Auxiliary Views?

a) To enlarge views automatically
b) To show inclined surfaces' true size
c) To show exploded views
d) To hide dimensions

22. What is the purpose of a Revolved View in Creo?

a) To rotate the part completely
b) To show exploded view of the model
c) To show hidden details by revolving a sectioned area
d) To create an animation of the part

23. Which option must be selected in the Menu Manager to create a Revolved View?

a) Radial and Double
b) Linear and Multiple
c) Planar and Single
d) Offset and Both Sides

24. What is the purpose of creating a datum plane during the Revolved View process?

a) To mirror the part
b) To define the center of gravity
c) To act as the cutting plane
d) To add color shading

25. When creating a 2D cross-section, what happens if the sketch does not intersect the view properly?

a) Section will still be created
b) View will automatically adjust
c) A red cross mark will be shown
d) Green tick mark will be displayed

26. Which tool is used to import dimensions from the part/assembly into the drawing?

a) Dimension Tool
b) Manual Annotations
c) Show Model Annotations
d) Model Dimension Importer

27. What does the green tick mark indicate in the Drawing View dialog box after sectioning?

a) Section not applicable
b) Sketch has errors
c) Section is successfully applied
d) View is hidden

28. What is the limitation of applying manual dimensioning in the Drawing environment?

a) Dimensions can't be seen
b) Dimensions change the model
c) Model does not update with changes
d) Only circles can be dimensioned

29. What does the Tangent button help you to do in the Dimension tool?

a) Create straight lines
b) Dimension circular arcs at tangency points
c) Add datums
d) Apply geometric tolerances

30. What must be true to use Auto Ordinate Dimension on multiple surfaces?

a) They must have same color
b) They must be perpendicular
c) They must be parallel
d) They must belong to the same body

31. What do geometric tolerances control?

a) Part color and texture
b) File size
c) Form and position accuracy
d) Exploded view placement

32. What symbol status shows if an incorrect datum is selected for the tolerance frame?

a) Green tick
b) Red background
c) Red underline
d) Blue asterisk

33. What is the purpose of the Composite Frame tool in tolerance annotation?

a) To rotate the drawing
b) To add multiple tolerance rows
c) To apply color schemes
d) To convert drawing into 3D

34. How can you add material conditions or extra notes to the tolerance frame?

a) Use the Regenerate tool
b) Use Additional Text tool
c) Use Sketch tool
d) Use Auto Ordinate tool

35. What happens when you click on the balloon attached to a tolerance frame?

a) Deletes the tolerance
b) Resets dimensions
c) Allows repositioning
d) Opens main menu

36. What is the purpose of the Surface Finish symbol in Creo Parametric?

a) To define the tolerance value
b) To create dimensions automatically
c) To define the surface finish of a face
d) To set the material property

37. How can you access different standard symbols in the Surface Finish tool?

a) Using Format tab
b) By clicking on the Open Model tool
c) From the Gallery drop-down or Browse Surface Finish Symbols
d) From the Dimension Style drop-down

38. Which tool is used to create a text note not attached to any reference?

a) Leader Note
b) Balloon Note
c) Table Note
d) Unattached Note

39. Which tool is used to change the font of dimension text?

a) Dimension Style
b) Font Manager
c) Text Style tool
d) Arrow Options

40. What happens when you hover over boxes while inserting a table dynamically?

a) It selects existing tables
b) It allows you to define rows and columns
c) It opens the Table Dialog box
d) It changes the height of cells

41. What must you do to merge cells in a table?

a) Select one cell and right-click
b) Press Shift and click
c) Select multiple cells and click Merge Cells
d) Click Insert Table

42. What tool is used to insert a table using dialog box method?

a) Add Row
b) Insert Table
c) Merge Cells
d) New Layout

43. What should be done in the first row of BOM table?

a) Leave it empty
b) Add the serial numbers
c) Merge the cells and add table title
d) Add part descriptions

44. What is the purpose of the Repeat Region tool in BOM creation?

a) To sort the table
b) To merge table cells
c) To automate row entries for components
d) To adjust column widths

45. Which category in Report Symbol represents assembly-related parameters?

a) mdl
b) asm
c) mfg
d) lay

46. Which Report Symbol is used to show the quantity of items?

a) asm.mbr.name
b) rpt.level
c) rpt.qty
d) asm.param

47. What does rpt.index represent in a BOM table?

a) Name of a part
b) Drawing name
c) Serial number/index
d) File path

48. Which symbol represents model-related parameters in a report?

a) mfg
b) mdl
c) prs
d) dgm

49. What are Balloons used for in an engineering drawing?

a) To show text formatting
b) To display material types
c) To identify components by index numbers
d) To highlight drawing errors

50. What is the tool to generate all balloons at once in a BOM?

a) Auto Label
b) Create Balloons-All
c) Label Manager
d) Generate Tags

Answers to Self Assessment Questions :

1. Product Manufacturing Information **3.** (c) **4.** (d) **5.** (c) **6.** General View **7.** Project View **8.** Detailed views **9.** Revolved view **10.** Auto Ordinate Dimension **11.** T **12.** F

Chapter 14

Model Based Definition (MBD) and 3D Printing

Topics Covered

The major topics covered in this chapter are:

- ***Introduction***
- ***Annotation Planes***
- ***Displaying Annotations***
- ***Combined Views Bar***
- ***GD&T Advisor***
- ***Model Based Definition***
- ***3D PDF Creation***
- ***3D Printing Processes***
- ***Part Preparation***
- ***Lattice Creation***
- ***Adding 3D Printer***
- ***3D Printing in Creo Parametric***

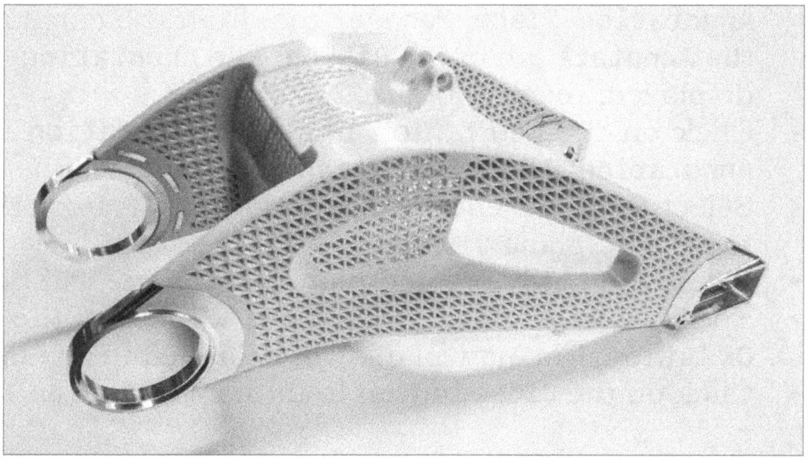

INTRODUCTION

In this chapter, you will learn about the latest trend of CAD - Model Based Definition and 3D Printing. Model Based Definition is a new way of putting Product Manufacturing Information (PMI) in CAD. Earlier, all the dimensions and tolerances were in 2D drawing but now you will learn to insert PMI directly in model. The tools to apply MBD are available in the **Annotate** tab of the **Ribbon** in Part/Assembly environment; refer to Figure-1. Various tools in this tab are discussed next.

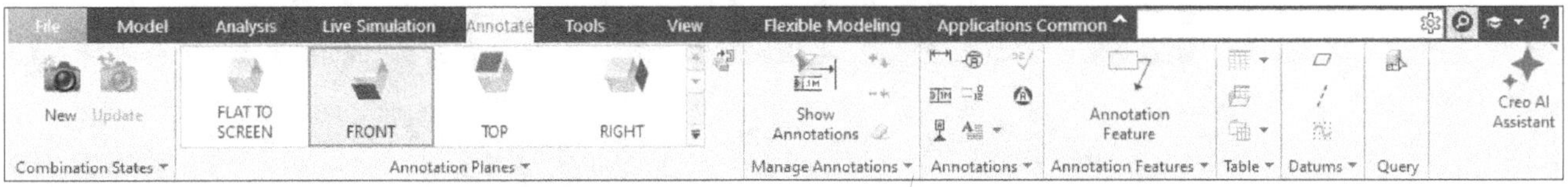

Figure-1. Annotate tab

ANNOTATION PLANES

Annotation planes are used as foundation for various annotations in Part/Assembly environment. The procedure to select an annotation plane is given next.

- Hover the cursor on a button in the **Annotation Planes Names** selection box of the **Annotation Planes** panel in the **Annotate** tab of the **Ribbon**. The plane will be displayed in the form of grid. Click on the button if you want to create annotations on this plane.
- Click on the **Active Annotation Plane** tool from the **Annotation Planes** panel in the **Ribbon**. The selected plane will become parallel to the screen.

Annotation Plane Manager

Note that by default, **FLAT TO SCREEN**, **FRONT**, **TOP**, **RIGHT**, **BACK**, **BOTTOM**, and **LEFT** buttons are available in the **Annotation Planes Names** selection box. If you want to add more planes in the selection box then follow the steps given next.

- Create a plane which you want to use as annotation plane and then click on the **Annotation Plane Manager** tool from the expanded **Annotation Planes** panel of the **Annotate** tab in the **Ribbon**. The **Annotation Plane Manager** dialog box will be displayed; refer to Figure-2.
- Click on the **New** button from the **Annotation Plane Manager** dialog box. The **Annotation Plane Definition** dialog box will be displayed; refer to Figure-3.
- Select the **Reference Plane** radio button from the dialog box. You will be asked to select a plane.
- Select the newly created plane. The plane will be displayed with grid lines.
- Specify desired name in the **Name** edit box of the dialog box and then click on the **OK** button. The new plane will be added in the list.
- Click on the **Close** button from the **Annotation Plane Manager** dialog box to exit.

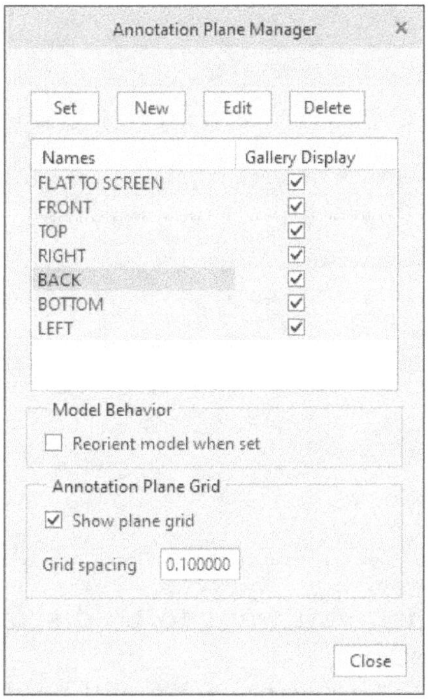

Figure-2. Annotation Plane Manager dialog box

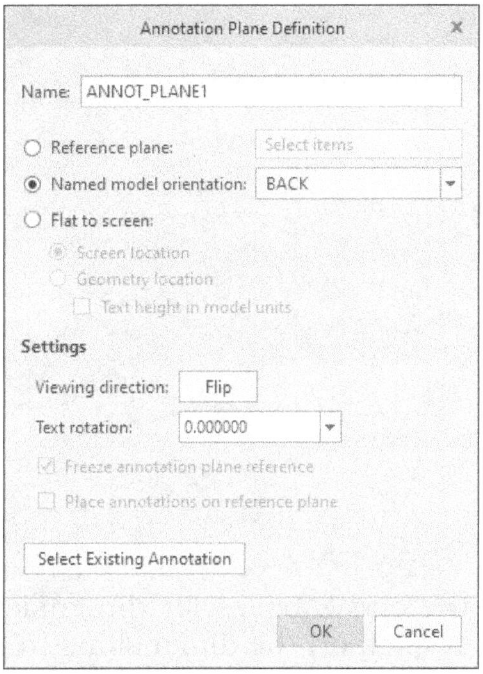

Figure-3. Annotation Plane Definition dialog box

Active Annotation Plane

The **Active Annotation Plane** tool is used to show the active annotation orientation that is used for new annotations; refer to Figure-4.

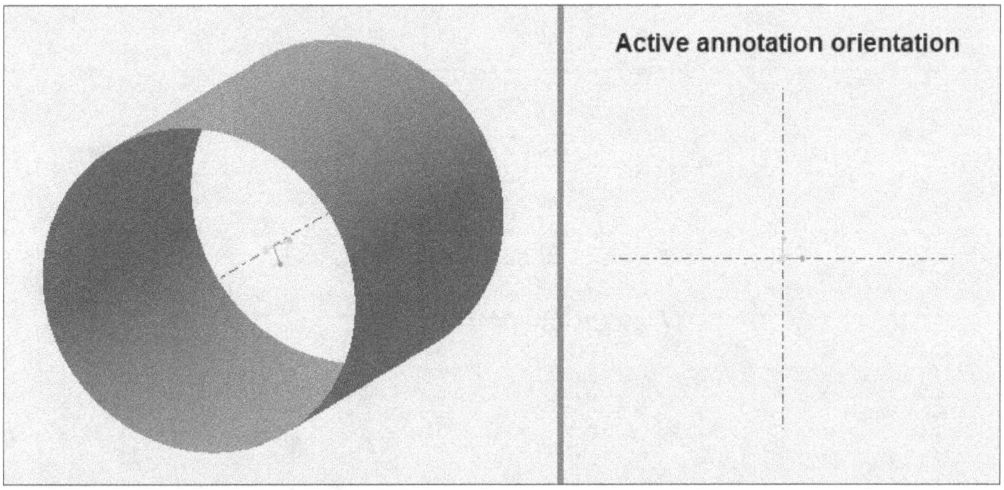

Figure-4. Active annotation orientation

SHOW ANNOTATIONS

The **Show Annotations** tool is used to display annotations assigned to the model while creating it. The procedure to use this tool is given next.

- Click on the **Show Annotations** tool from the **Manage Annotations** panel in the **Annotate** tab of the **Ribbon**. The **Show Annotations** dialog box will be displayed as discussed in previous chapter.
- Select the features of model to display their dimensions while holding the **CTRL** key. Respective dimension will be displayed; refer to Figure-5.

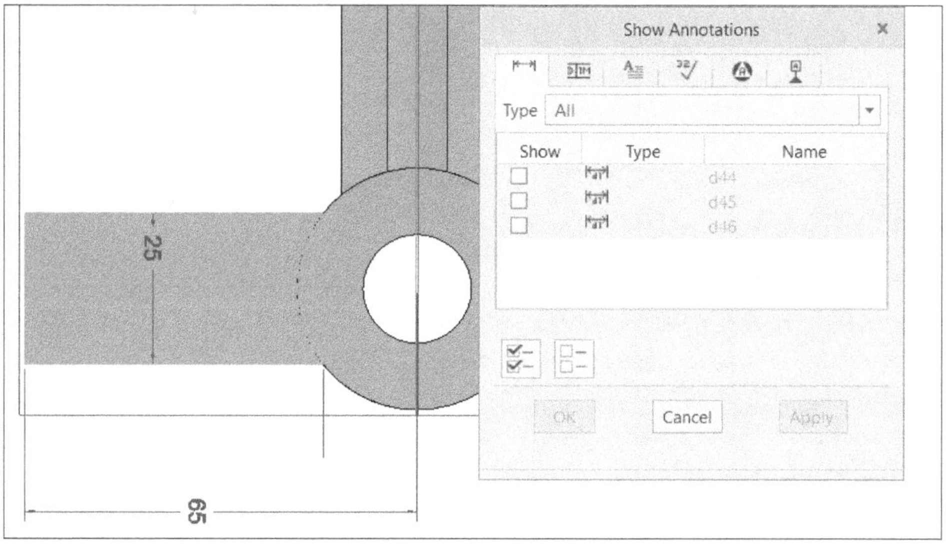

Figure-5. Preview of annotations

- Select the check boxes for dimensions which you want to be displayed on the model or click on the dimensions in the model.
- Click on the **OK** button from the dialog box. The annotations will be displayed on the model. Drag the annotations to place them at desired location.
- If you want to remove any annotation then select the annotation. The **Dimension** contextual tab will be displayed along with the mini toolbar.
- Click on the **Erase** button from the mini toolbar displayed; refer to Figure-6. The annotation will be removed. Figure-7 shows a model after applying annotations (MBD).

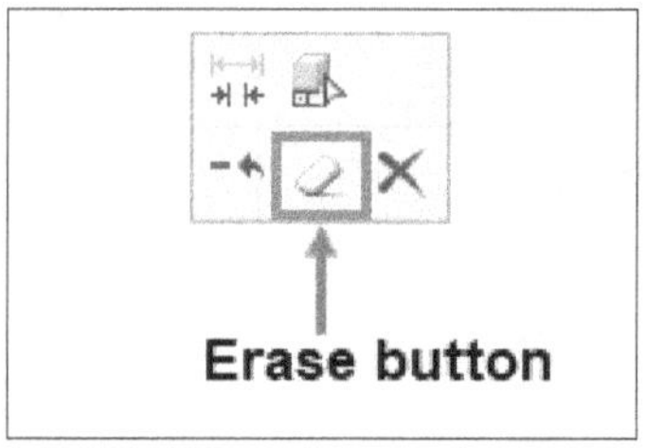

Figure-6. Erase button

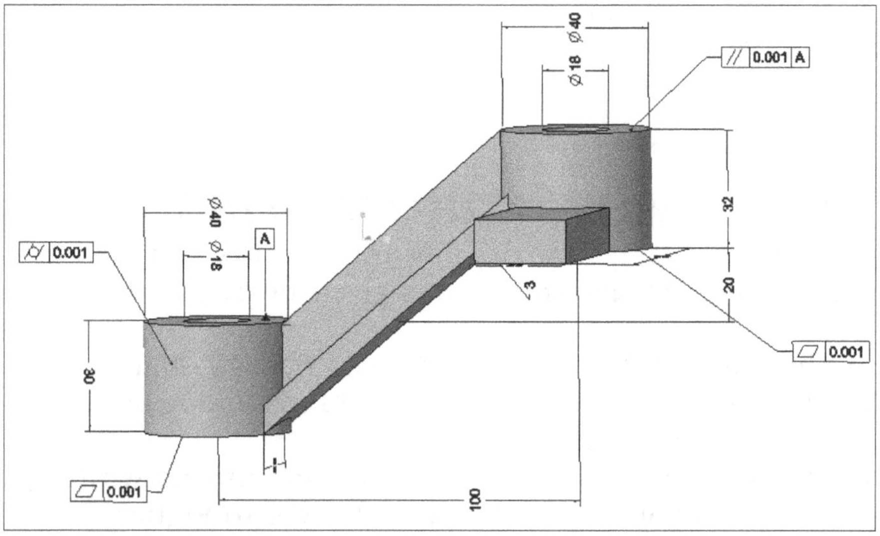

Figure-7. Model Based Definition example

Similarly, you can use the other tools in the **Annotate** tab of the **Ribbon** which work in the same way as discussed in previous chapter on drawings.

DATUM TARGET

The **Datum Target** tool is used to create datum target symbol. The procedure to use this tool is discussed next.

- Click on the **Datum Target** tool from **Annotations** panel of the **Ribbon**. The **Select Reference** dialog box will be displayed along with the datum target symbol attached to the cursor; refer to Figure-8. You will be asked to select geometry, point, or an axis.

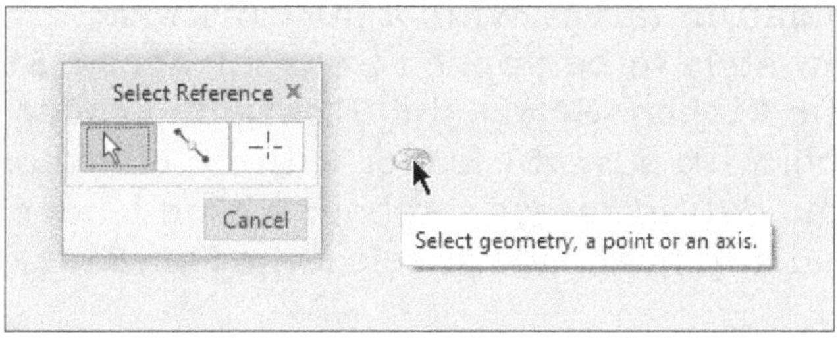

Figure-8. Select Reference dialog box along with datum target symbol

- Select desired geometry, point, or an axis on which you want to create datum target symbol. The datum target symbol will be applied; refer to Figure-9 and the **Datum Target** contextual tab will be displayed; refer to Figure-10.

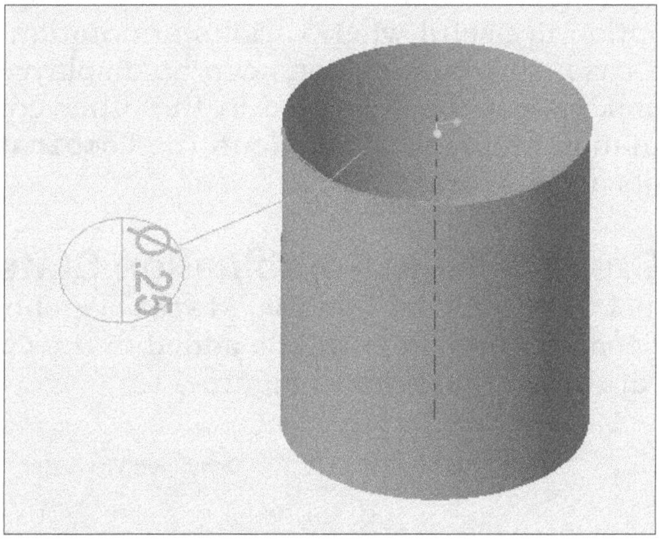

Figure-9. Datum target symbol applied

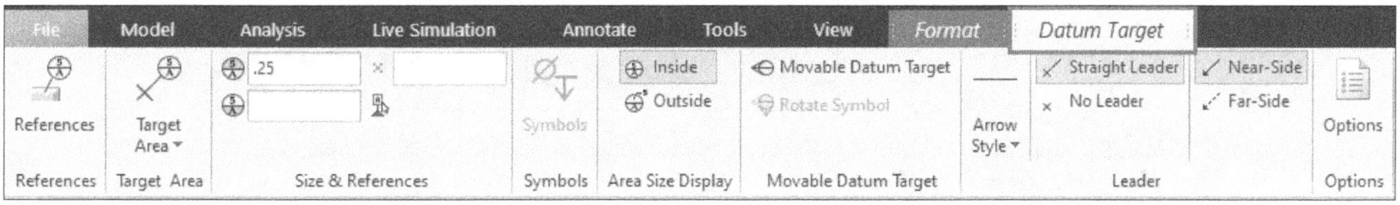

Figure-10. Datum Target contextual tab

- Click on the **References** button from **References** panel of the **Ribbon** to select additional references for the datum target symbol.

- Select desired target area from the **Target Area** drop-down in the **Target Area** panel of the **Ribbon**.
- Specify desired value of width, height, and datum reference in the respective edit boxes of the **Size & References** panel. Select the button to select the datum reference from the model.
- Select the **Symbols** option from the **Symbols** area to select the symbol to add it to the current annotation.
- Select the **Inside** option from the **Area Size Display** panel to place the target area size within the datum target symbol or select the **Outside** option to place the target area size outside the datum target symbol with a separate leader.
- Select the **Movable Datum Target** option from the **Movable Datum Target** panel to set the datum target symbol to be movable and set the **Rotate Symbol** option to rotate the movable datum target symbol 90^{0} clockwise.
- Select desired arrow style to be applied from the **Arrow Style** drop-down in the **Leader** panel of the **Ribbon**. Select the **Straight Leader** option to display the datum target symbol with straight leader with no elbow or select the **No Leader** option to display the datum target symbol with no leader. Select the **Near-Side** option to set the leader to near-side or select the **Far-Side** option to set the leader to far-side.
- Click on the **Options** button from the **Options** panel of the **Ribbon** and select desired check boxes to place the datum target symbol.

COMBINATION STATES

The Combination State is used to define the state of model with various annotation combinations. This option is useful when various annotations are to be displayed on the model. In that case, some dimensions can be displayed in one combination state and other dimensions can be displayed in the other combination state. The tools to create combination state are available in the **Combination States** panel of the **Ribbon**. These tools are discussed next.

Creating New Combination State

- Click on the **New** tool from the **Combination States** panel of the **Annotate** tab in the **Ribbon**. A new combination state will be added in the **Combined Views Bar** at the bottom in the drawing area; refer to Figure-11.

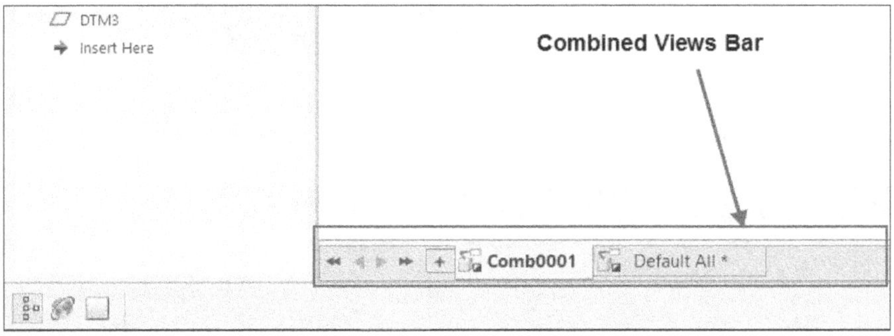

Figure-11. Combined Views Bar

- Apply annotations to the model and click on the **Update** button from the **Combination States** panel of the **Annotate** tab in the **Ribbon**.

GD&T ADVISOR

The **GD&T Advisor** is an application from Sigmetrix used for applying and analyzing the model for geometric dimensioning and tolerances. The procedure to start this application is given next.

- Click on the **GD&T Advisor** tool from the **GD&T** panel in the **Applications** tab of the **Ribbon** in Part environment. The **GD&T Advisor** tab will be added in the **Ribbon**; refer to Figure-12.

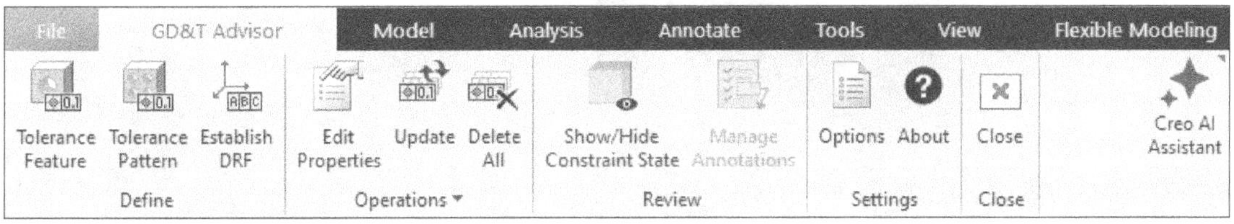

Figure-12. GD&T Advisor tab

The tools in this tab are discussed next.

Tolerance Feature

The **Tolerance Feature** tool is used to apply tolerance features and dimensions to the part in GD&T environment. The procedure to use this tool is given next.

- Click on the **Tolerance Feature** tool from the **Define** panel in the **GD&T Advisor** tab of the **Ribbon**. You will be asked to select one or more surfaces to apply dimensioning and tolerances.
- Select the surface(s). The **Add Feature** dialog box will be displayed with selected surfaces in the surface list; refer to Figure-13. If you select surface of a hole then other surface of hole will get automatically selected and will be identified by the software. If you select a pattern surface then **Add entire pattern** check box will be selected automatically in the dialog box and the current tolerance feature will be applied to whole pattern; refer to Figure-14.

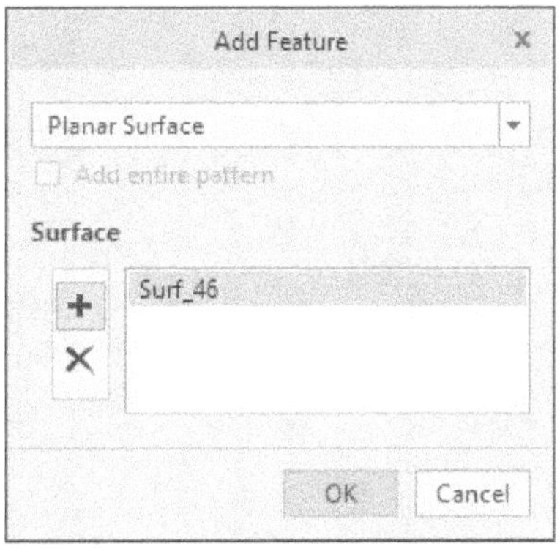

Figure-13. Add Feature dialog box

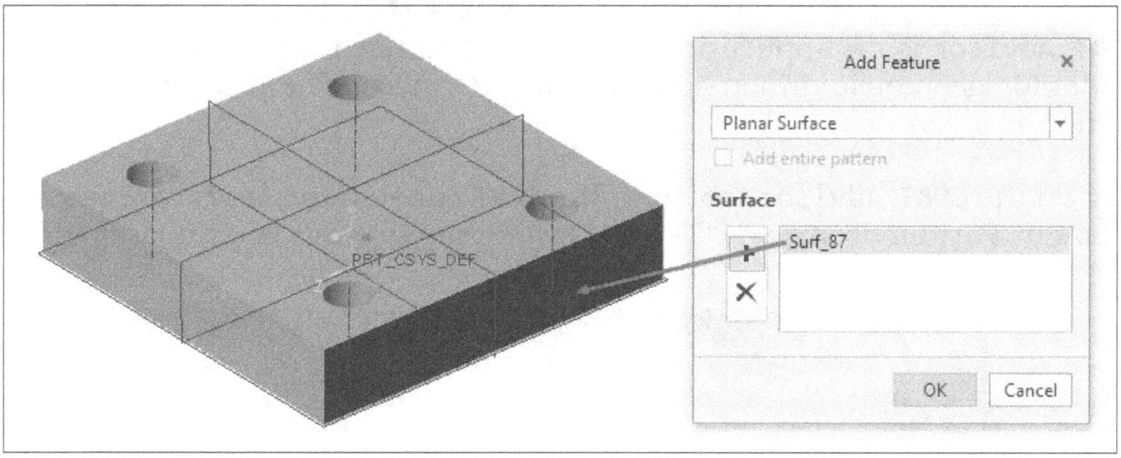

Figure-14. Add Feature dialog box for pattern

- Click on the **OK** button from the dialog box. The **Tolerance Feature** contextual tab will be displayed in the **Ribbon** according to the object selected in the dialog box; refer to Figure-15 (**Tolerance Feature** contextual tab on selecting planar surface). If you have selected the pattern then **Tolerance Pattern** contextual tab will be displayed which will be discussed later.

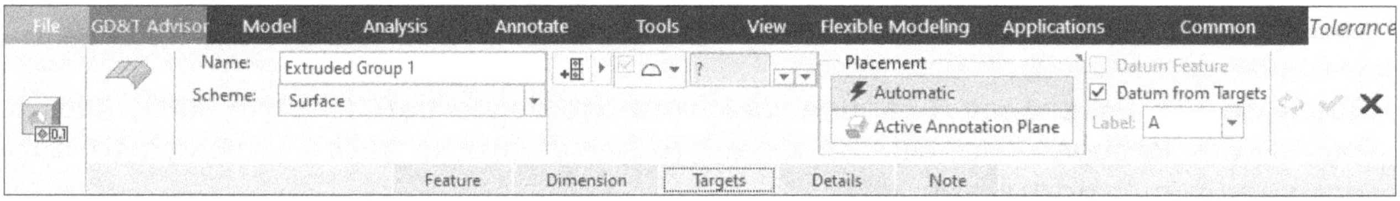

Figure-15. Tolerance Feature contextual tab

- Select desired tolerance symbol from the **Geometric Characteristic Symbol Selector** drop-down and specify related tolerance value in the adjacent field; refer to Figure-16.

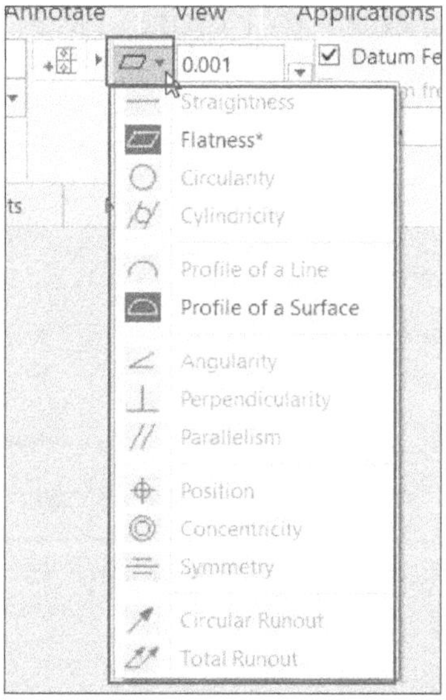

Figure-16. Geometric Characteristic Symbol Selector drop-down

- If you want to add a datum feature symbol to the selected face then select the **Datum Feature** check box and enter desired label for datum feature in the **Label** edit box of the contextual tab; refer to Figure-17.

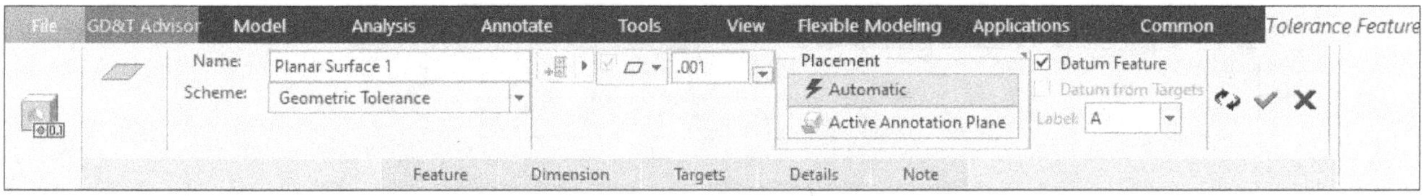

Figure-17. Specifying parameters in the contextual tab

- Click on the **OK** button from the contextual tab to assign the GTOL; refer to Figure-18.

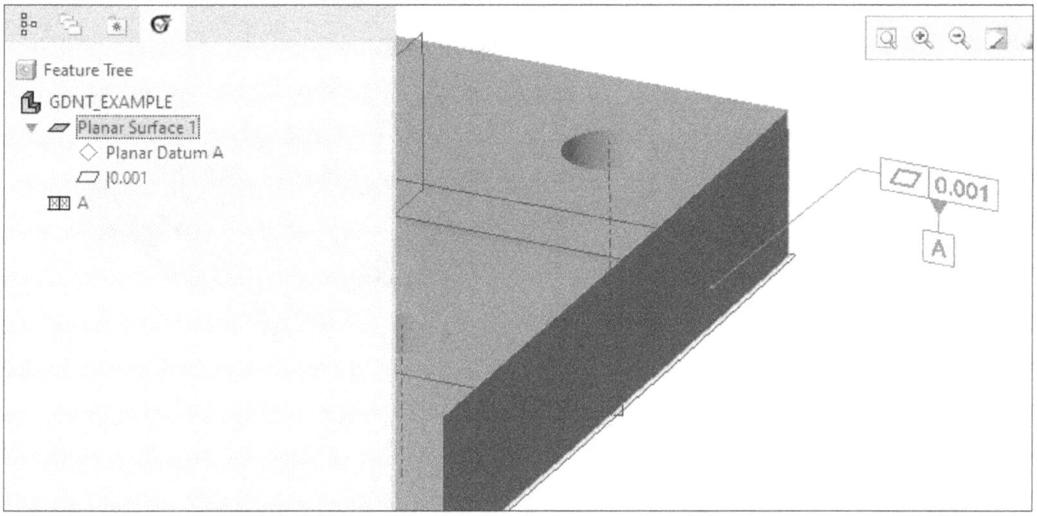

Figure-18. Datum feature assigned

- Note that if there is parallel face to the selected face at some distance then you can select the **Slab** option from the **Add Feature** dialog box; refer to Figure-19. In this way, you can also get the distance dimension between the two faces; refer to Figure-20. Click on the **Add independent segment** button from **Tolerance Feature** contextual tab to add more boxes in GTOL for creating composite GTOL box; refer to Figure-20. If you want to remove a segment from the GTOL then expand the **Segment Control Selector** flyout and select the **Remove segment** button to remove last GTOL box; refer to Figure-21.

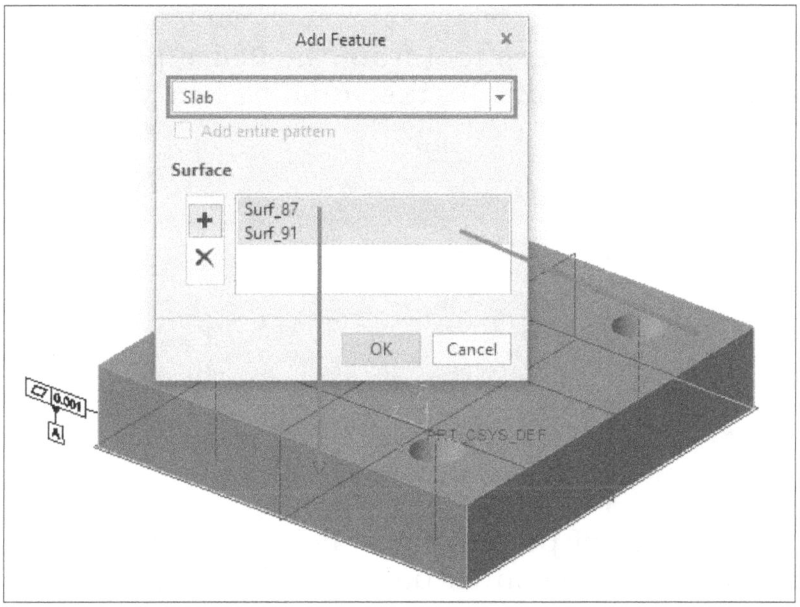

Figure-19. Slab option in Add Feature dialog box

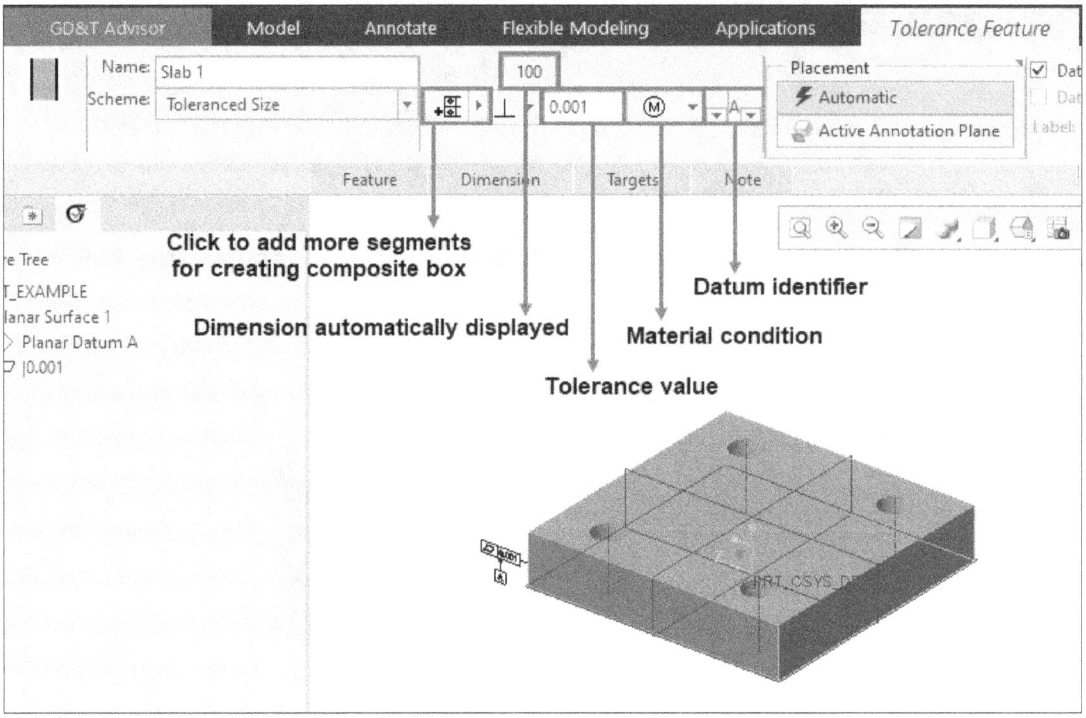

Figure-20. Slab GTOL

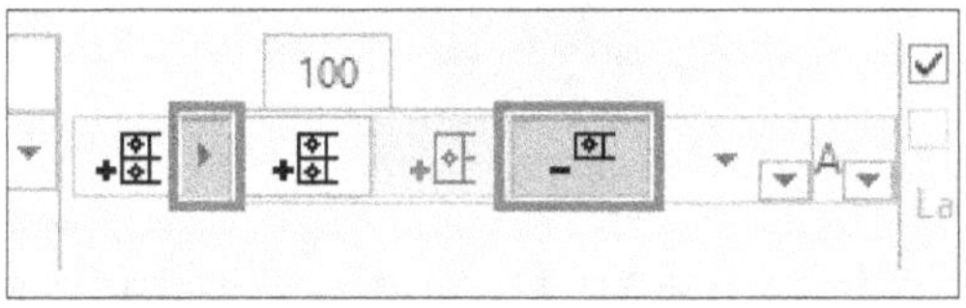

Figure-21. Remove segment button

Similarly, you can apply GTOL to other faces of the model.

Tolerance Pattern

The **Tolerance Pattern** tool is used to apply geometric tolerance and dimensioning to the whole pattern, like you can apply tolerance to the pattern of holes at single place. The procedure to use this tool is given next.

- Click on the **Tolerance Pattern** tool from the **Define** panel in the **GD&T Advisor** tab of the **Ribbon**. The **Add/Edit Pattern** dialog box will be displayed; refer to Figure-22.

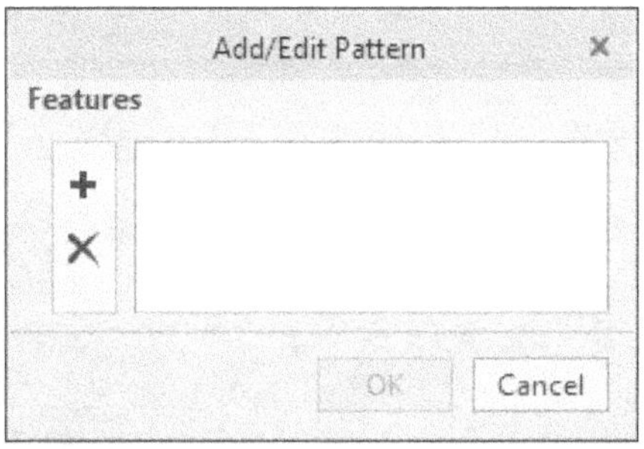

Figure-22. Add/Edit Pattern dialog box

- Select one of the feature of pattern and click on the **OK** button from the dialog box. The **Tolerance Pattern** contextual tab will be displayed; refer to Figure-23.

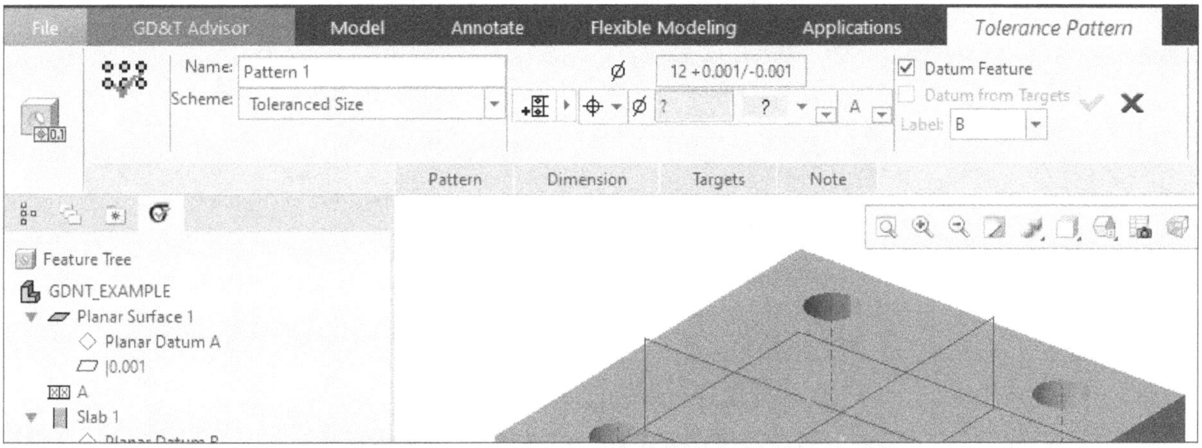

Figure-23. Tolerance Pattern contextual tab

- Specify desired parameters in the tab as discussed earlier and click on the **OK** button to create the feature.

Establish DRF

The **Establish DRF** tool is used to link geometric tolerance specified in model using the **Annotation** panel tools with the datum reference specified in the GD&T Advisor environment. The procedure to use this tool is discussed next.

- Click on the **Establish DRF** tool from **Define** panel in the **GD&T Advisor** tab of the **Ribbon**. The **Add DRF** dialog box will be displayed; refer to Figure-24.

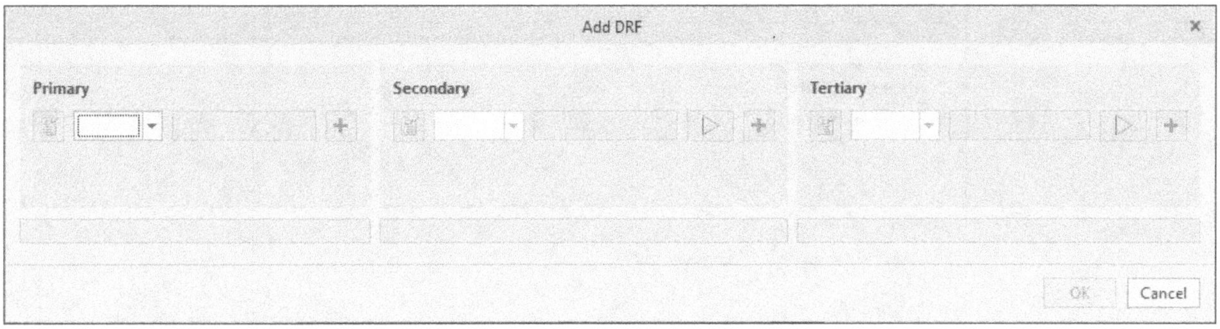

Figure-24. Add DRF dialog box

- Select desired datum feature from **Datum Feature Selector** drop-down in the **Primary** section of the dialog box.
- Similarly, you can select desired datum feature from **Secondary** and **Tertiary** section of the dialog box.
- After specifying desired parameters, click on the **OK** button from the dialog box. The DRF will be specified; refer to Figure-25.

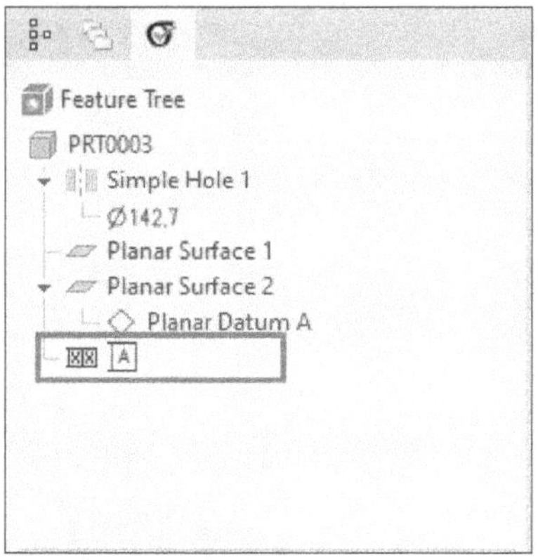

Figure-25. DRF specified

Editing Properties for GD&T

The **Edit Properties** tool is used to set the standard and other parameters for applying GD&T using GD&T Advisor. The procedure to use this tool is given next.

- Click on the **Edit Properties** tool from the **Operations** panel in the **GD&T Advisor** tab of the **Ribbon**. The **Edit Model Properties** dialog box will be displayed; refer to Figure-26.

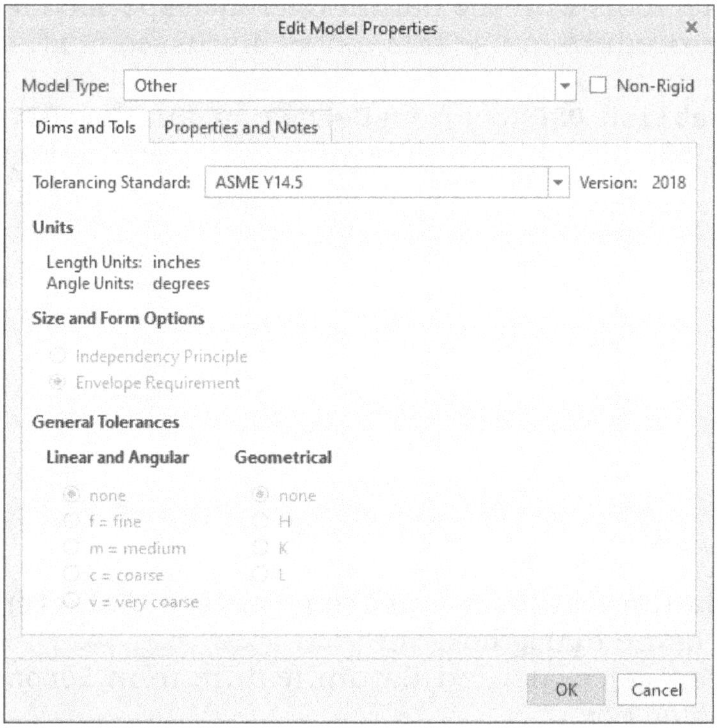

Figure-26. Edit Model Properties dialog box

- Select the type of part for which you want to apply GD&T from the **Part Type** drop-down. Select the **Non-Rigid** check box if the part is not rigid.
- In the next options, set the desired standard for tolerancing and other parameters, and then click on the **Accept** button from the dialog box.

The **Update** tool in **Operations** panel of the **GD&T Advisor** tab is used to update the recent changes made in GD&T of part using the tools in the **GD&T Advisor** tab of the **Ribbon**.
The **Delete All** tool in the **Operations** panel is used to delete all the GD&T data specified by using the tools in the **GD&T Advisor** tab of the **Ribbon**.

The **Show/Hide Constraint State** tool in the **Review** panel of the **GD&T Advisor** tab is used to display the constrained and unconstrained areas of the part; refer to Figure-27.

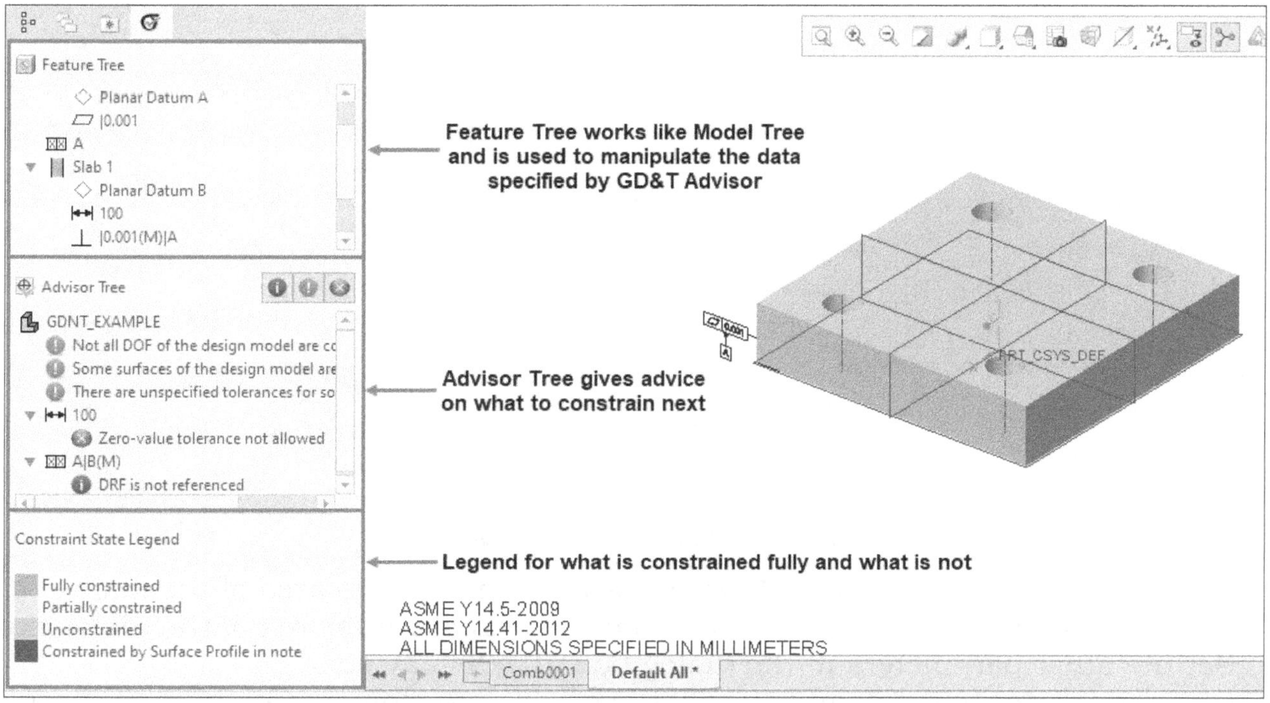

Figure-27. Displaying constrained state of part

Click on the **Close** button from the **GD&T Advisor** tab to exit the application. Now, you can manipulate all the GTOLs applied by **GD&T Advisor** in the same way as you have edited them earlier using the tools in **Annotate** tab of the **Ribbon**.

3D PDF CREATION

Although, iges and other CAD portability formats are useful data for engineers and designers but they are not useful data for marketing. For market executives, there is requirement of a format by which they can display important features of model with some dimensions. 3D PDF is one of the important format for this purpose. The procedure to create 3D PDF is given next.

- Click on the **Save a Copy** tool from the **Save As** cascading menu in the **File** menu. The **Save a Copy** dialog box will be displayed as discussed earlier.
- Select the **PDF U3D (*.pdf)** format from the **Type** drop-down in the dialog box and specify desired name for the file. Click on the **OK** button from the dialog box. The **PDF U3D Export Settings** dialog box will be displayed; refer to Figure-28.

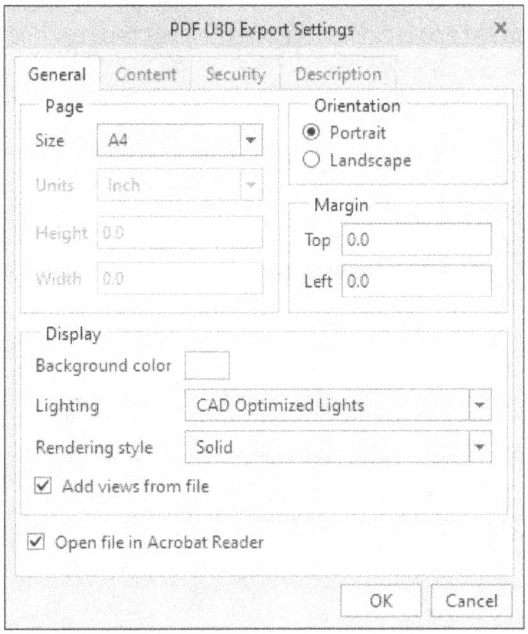

Figure-28. PDF U3D Export Settings dialog box

- Select the paper size from the **Size** drop-down in the **Page** area of the dialog box.
- Set the desired orientation of paper from the **Orientation** area of the dialog box.
- Set the other parameters in the dialog box like display style.
- Click on the **Content** tab and specify the other non-geometry features that are to be included in the 3D PDF.
- Similarly, set the other parameters and then click on the **OK** button from the dialog box. The 3D PDF will be created and opened in the PDF reader.

3D PRINTING

3D Printing also known as Additive Manufacturing is not a new concept as it was developed in 1981 but since then 3D Printing technology is continuously evolving. In early stages, the 3D printers were able to create only prototypes of objects using the polymers. But now a days, 3D printers are able to produce final products using metals, plastics, and biological materials. 3D printers are being used for making artificial organs, architectural art pieces, complex design objects, etc. Although, 3D Printing technique was created for manufacturing industry but now, it has found more applications in medical field.

In Creo Parametric, there is a very simple and robust mechanism for 3D printing. The procedure of 3D Printing itself is not difficult but it is important to prepare your part well for 3D printing. We will first discuss the part preparation for 3D Printing and then we will use Creo Parametric tools for performing 3D print.

PART PREPARATION FOR 3D PRINTING

Part preparation is very important step for 3D Printing. If your part is not stable in semi molten state then it is less suitable for 3D printing. Stability of model is directly dependent on the material you are using for 3D Printing. We will know more about part preparation but before that it is important to understand different type of processes available in 3D Printing.

3D Printing Processes

Not all 3D printers use the same technology. There are several ways to print and all those available are additive, differing mainly in the way layers are build to create the final object.

Some methods use melting or softening material to produce the layers. Selective laser sintering (SLS) and fused deposition modeling (FDM) are the most common technologies using this way of 3D printing. Another method is when we talk about curing a photo-reactive resin with a UV laser or another similar power source one layer at a time. The most common technology using this method is called stereolithography (SLA).

In 2010, the American Society for Testing and Materials (ASTM) group "ASTM F42 – Additive Manufacturing", developed a set of standards that classify the Additive Manufacturing processes into 7 categories according to Standard Terminology for Additive Manufacturing Technologies. These seven processes are:

1. Vat Photopolymerisation
2. Material Jetting
3. Binder Jetting
4. Material Extrusion
5. Powder Bed Fusion
6. Sheet Lamination
7. Directed Energy Deposition

Brief introduction to these processes is given next.

Vat Photopolymerisation

A 3D printer based on the Vat Photopolymerisation method has a container filled with photopolymer resin which is then hardened with a UV light source; refer to Figure-29.

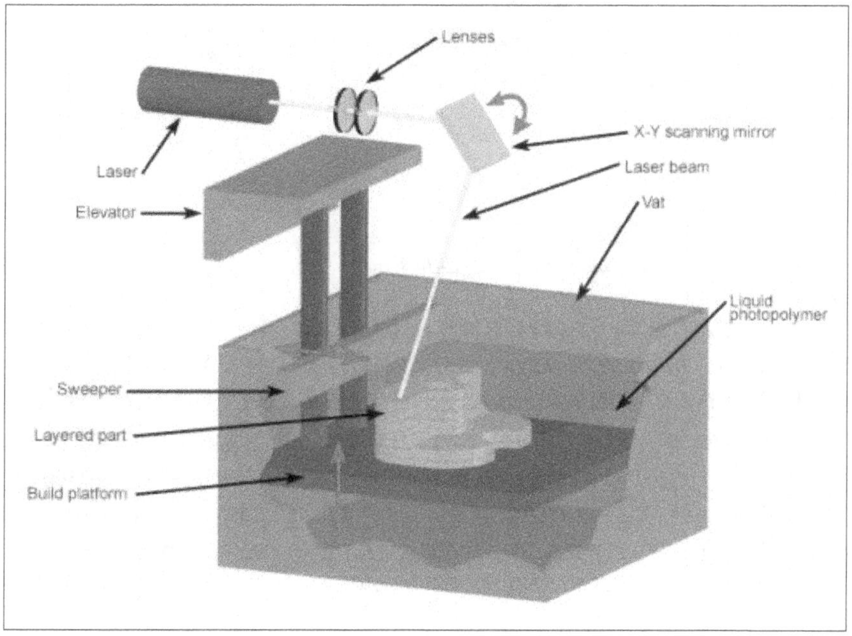

Figure-29. 3D Printing via vat-photopolymerisation

The most commonly used technology in this processes is Stereolithography (SLA). This technology employs a vat of liquid ultraviolet curable photopolymer resin and an ultraviolet laser to build the object's layers one at a time. For each layer, the laser beam traces a cross-section of the part pattern on the surface of the liquid resin. Exposure to the ultraviolet laser light cures and solidifies the pattern traced on the resin and joins it to the layer below.

After the pattern has been traced, the SLA's elevator platform descends by a distance equal to the thickness of a single layer, typically 0.05 mm to 0.15 mm (0.002″ to 0.006″). Then, a resin-filled blade sweeps across the cross section of the part, re-coating it with fresh material. On this new liquid surface, the subsequent layer pattern is traced, joining the previous layer. The complete three dimensional object is formed by this project. Stereolithography requires the use of supporting structures which serve to attach the part to the elevator platform and to hold the object because it floats in the basin filled with liquid resin. These are removed manually after the object is finished.

Material Jetting

In this process, material is applied in droplets through a small diameter nozzle, similar to the way a common inkjet paper printer works, but it is applied layer-by-layer to a build platform making a 3D object and then hardened by UV light; refer to Figure-30.

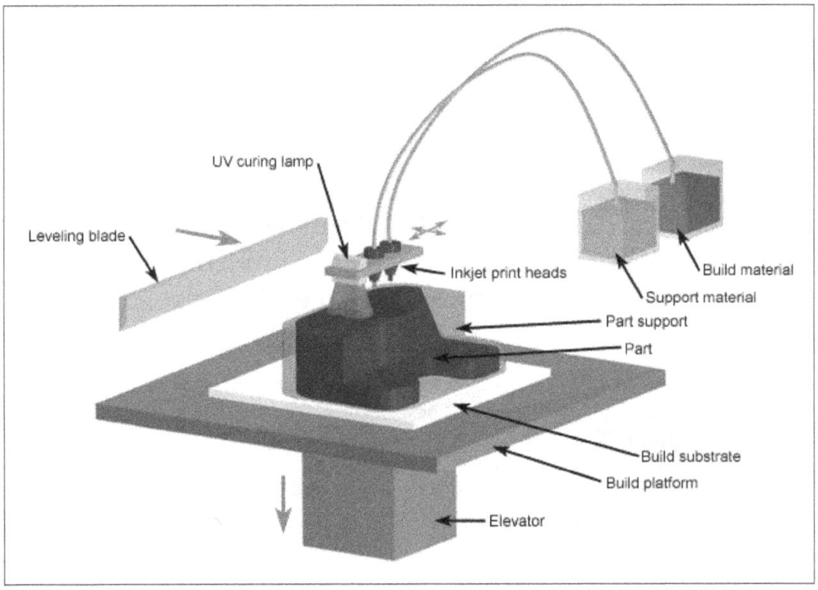

Figure-30. 3D Printing via Material-Jetting

Binder Jetting

With binder jetting, two materials are used: powder base material and a liquid binder. In the build chamber, powder is spread in equal layers and binder is applied through jet nozzles that "glue" the powder particles in the shape of a programmed 3D object; refer to Figure-31. The finished object is "glued together" by binder remains in the container with the powder base material. After the print is finished, the remaining powder is cleaned off and used for 3D printing the next object.

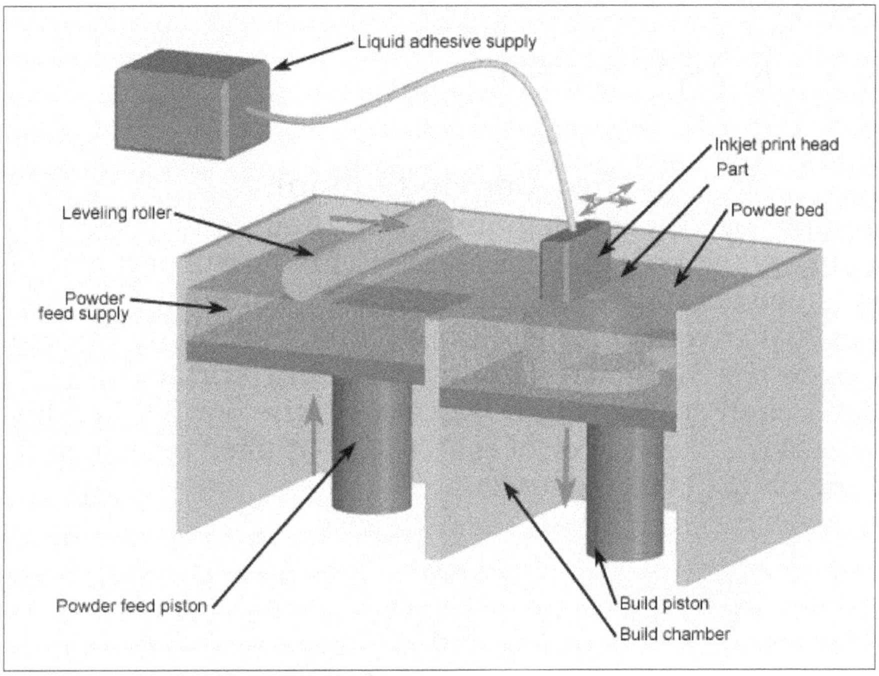

Figure-31. 3D Printing via binder-jetting

Material Extrusion

The most commonly used technology in this process is Fused deposition modeling (FDM). The FDM technology works using a plastic filament or metal wire which is unwound from a coil and supplying material to an extrusion nozzle which can turn the flow on and off. The nozzle is heated to melt the material and can be moved in both horizontal and vertical directions by a numerically controlled mechanism, directly controlled by a computer-aided manufacturing (CAM) software package; refer to Figure-32. The object is produced by extruding melted material to form layers as the material hardens immediately after extrusion from the nozzle. This technology is most widely used with two plastic filament material types: ABS (Acrylonitrile Butadiene Styrene) and PLA (Polylactic acid) but many other materials are available ranging in properties from wood filed, conductive, flexible, etc.

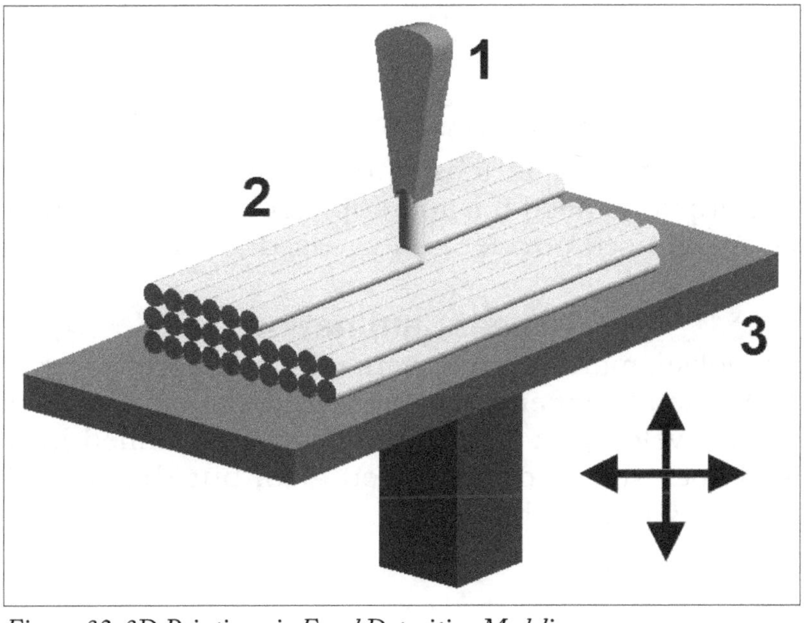

Figure-32. 3D Printing via Fused Deposition Modeling

In the above figure:
1 – nozzle ejecting molten material (plastic),
2 – deposited material (modelled part),
3 – controlled movable table.

Powder Bed Fusion

The most commonly used technology in this processes is Selective laser sintering (SLS). This technology uses a high power laser to fuse small particles of plastic, metal, ceramic, or glass powders into a mass that has desired three dimensional shape. The laser selectively fuses the powdered material by scanning the cross-sections (or layers) generated by the 3D modeling program on the surface of a powder bed; refer to Figure-33. After each cross-section is scanned, the powder bed is lowered by one layer thickness. Then, a new layer of material is applied on top and the process is repeated until the object is completed.

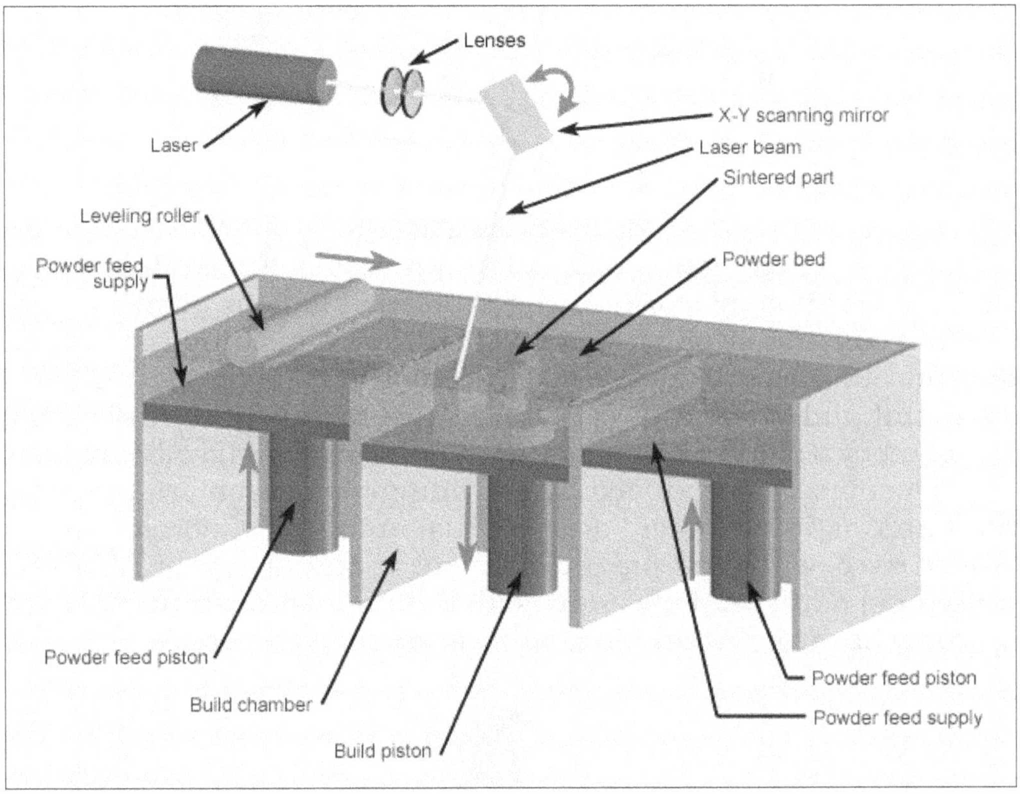

Figure-33. 3D Printing via Selective Laser Sintering

All untouched powder remains as it is and becomes a support structure for the object. Therefore, there is no need for any support structure which is an advantage over SLS and SLA. All unused powder can be used for the next print.

Sheet Lamination

Sheet lamination involves material in sheets which is bound together with external force. Sheets can be metal, paper, or a form of polymer. Metal sheets are welded together by ultrasonic welding in layers and then CNC milled into a proper shape; refer to Figure-34. Paper sheets can be used also, but they are glued by adhesive glue and cut in shape by precise blades.

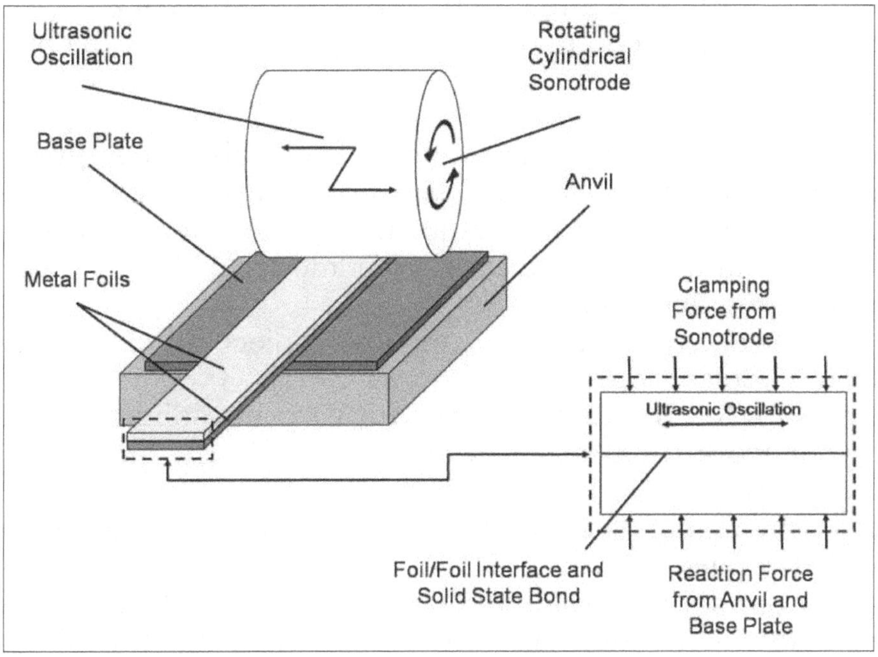

Figure-34. 3D Printing via Ultrasonic Sheet Lamination

Directed Energy Deposition

This process is mostly used in the high-tech metal industry and in rapid manufacturing applications. The 3D printing apparatus is usually attached to a multi-axis robotic arm and consists of a nozzle that deposits metal powder or wire on a surface and an energy source (laser, electron beam, or plasma arc) that melts it, forming a solid object; refer to Figure-35.

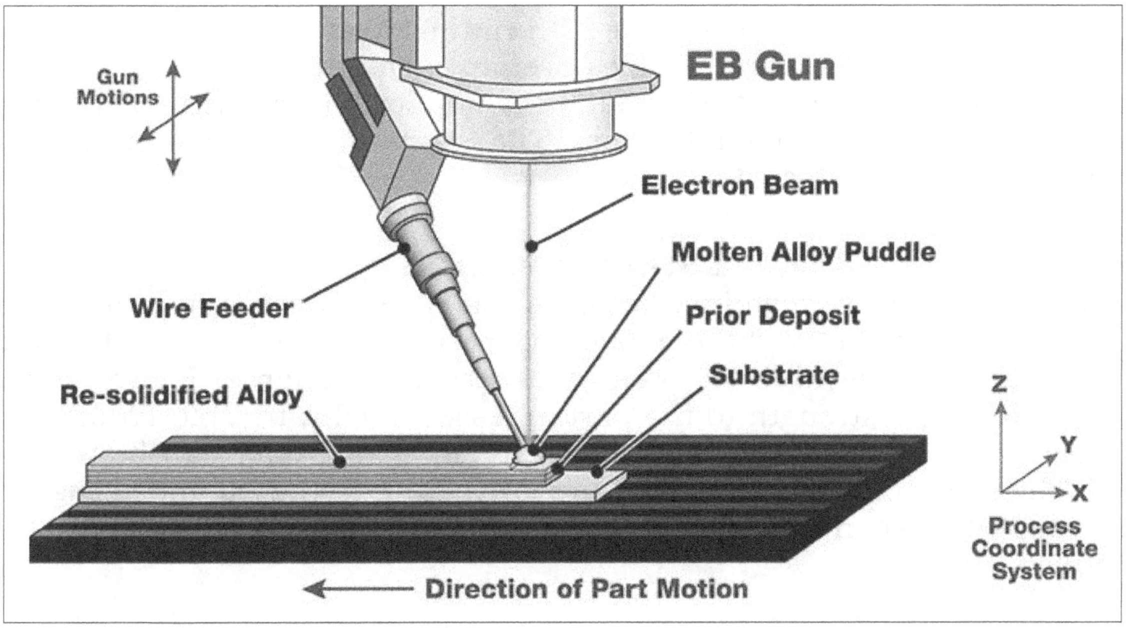

Figure-35. 3D Printing via Direct Energy Deposition

Now, you know about different 3D Printing techniques so it is clear from different processes that the main work of 3D printer is to solidify material at your will, through different techniques. Now, we will learn about the points to be taken care of while preparing model for 3D printing.

Part Preparation for 3D Printing

Various important points to remember while preparing part for 3D printing are given next.

- You should avoid holes in the areas where model is not supported. Holes can cause material to flow out in various 3D printing processes.
- Use the Solid models. It does not mean that you cannot use surface modeling tools but you should avoid surfaces in your model. Thicken your surfaces after performing modeling operations.
- Make sure that you have not left any unwanted piece inside the model enclosure after performing boolean operations.
- Shell your model after creating it. You can 3D print solid model but if a hollow box can do your work then why to waste material on solid cube. Less material means cost efficient.
- If you want to write text on your model then check the specification of your printer for possible font range.
- The textures you apply on model in Creo Parametric will not be exported for 3D printing so do not waste your time on them. Although, the color will be applied to the 3D Printed model if it is available for the printer.
- 3D printing is closer to mesh modeling than solid modeling. So, check your mesh model by exporting solid model in .stl file.
- If your file has quite a bit of text and multiple emboss/engrave features, try exporting the file as a vector. Vector files are more appropriate for extremely complex files. Try .iges or .step.
- Orientation is particularly important when it comes to 3D printing in order to determine the interior and exterior of an object. Orient your part the same way as you want it in 3D Printing.
- Don't make a multi-body model for 3D printing. Your printer may die thinking what to do when two separate bodies overlap each other!!
- A bidirectional exchange of information is supported between Creo Parametric and Stratasys & 3D Systems Printers. The Stratasys Connex Family of 3D and other models are supported.

Lattice Creation

Lattice structures involve repetitive patterns of a particular cell shape or type. There are libraries of cell types, and the density of these cells in a design is based on the application and loading that the design experiences; refer to Figure-36. Lattice structures give more strength to the part in lesser weight. In Creo Parametric, you can convert your part to lattice structure directly which later can be used for 3D Printing. The tool to create lattice structure is available in the expanded **Engineering** panel of the **Model** tab in **Ribbon** of Part environment. The procedure to use this tool is given next.

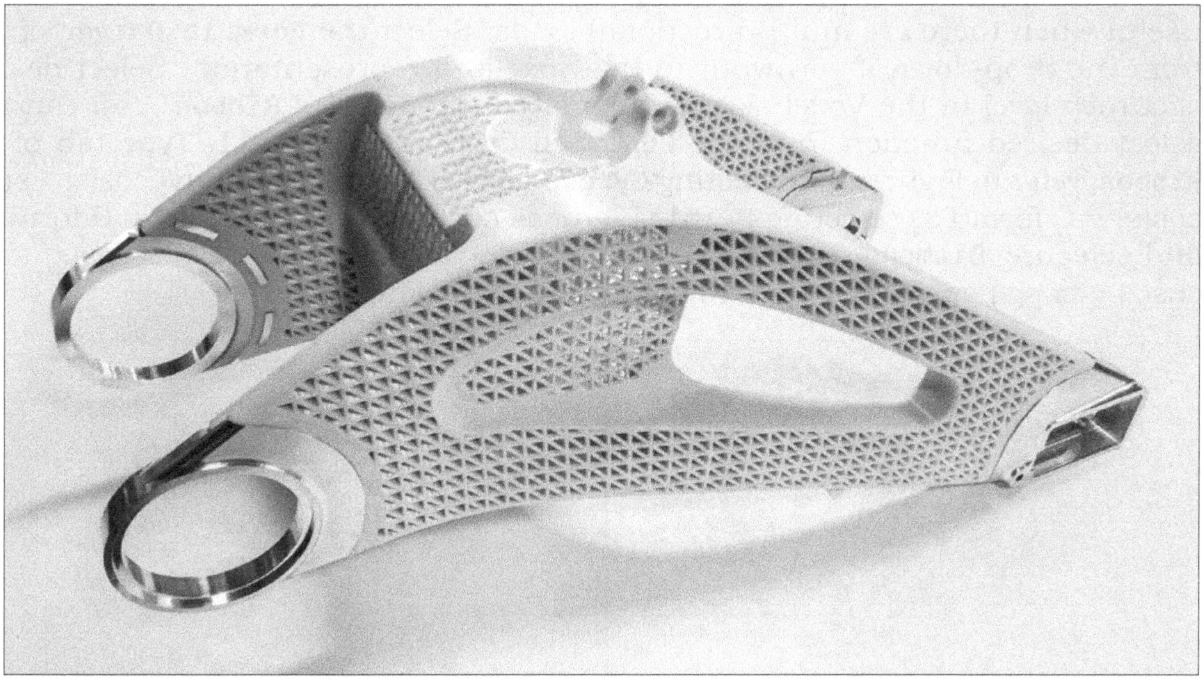

Figure-36. Lattice structure

Click on the **Lattice** tool from the expanded **Engineering** panel of the **Model** tab in the **Ribbon** of Part environment; refer to Figure-37. The **Lattice** contextual tab will be displayed; refer to Figure-38.

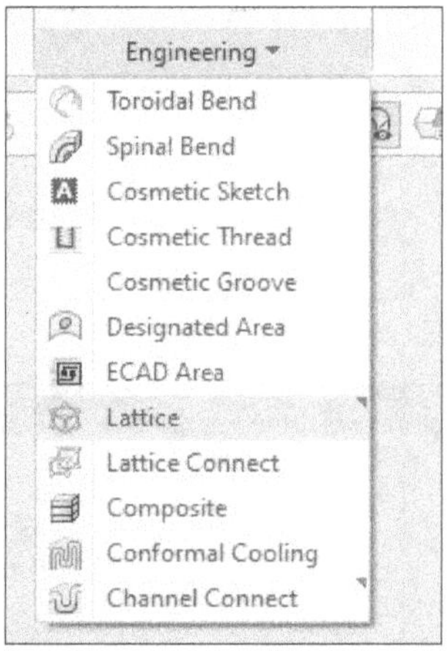

Figure-37. Lattice tool

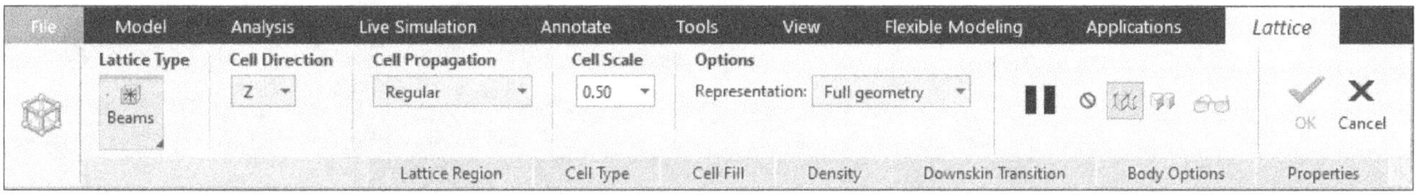

Figure-38. Lattice contextual tab

- Select the lattice type from the drop-down in the **Lattice Type** area of the **Ribbon**. There are four options for lattice type; **Beams**, **2.5D**, **Formula Driven**, and **Custom**. Select the **2.5D** option if you need not control the structure of lattice but need to define the element shape. Select the **Beams** option if you want to control shape as well as structure of lattice. Figure-39 shows a component made by 2.5D lattice and Beam lattice. Note that 2.5D lattice are created faster on 3D printer and give enough strength for axial load. The Beam lattice takes time on 3D printer but is useful when there are multi-directional loads. Select the **Formula Driven** option from the drop-down if you want to use voxelized representation. Select desired accuracy level in the Voxel size and density drop-down of **Ribbon**. You can also select desired function from the **Function** drop-down in **Cell Type** tab of the **Ribbon**; refer to Figure-40. Selecting **Gyroid** uses sin(x) cos(y) + sin(y) cos(z) + sin(z) cos(x) = 0 formula, selecting **Primitive** uses cos(x) + cos(y) + cos(z) = 0 formula, and selecting **Diamond** uses sin(x) sin(y) sin(z) + sin(x) cos(y) cos(z) + cos(x) sin(y) cos(z) + cos(x) cos(y) sin(z) = 0 to define shape of element.

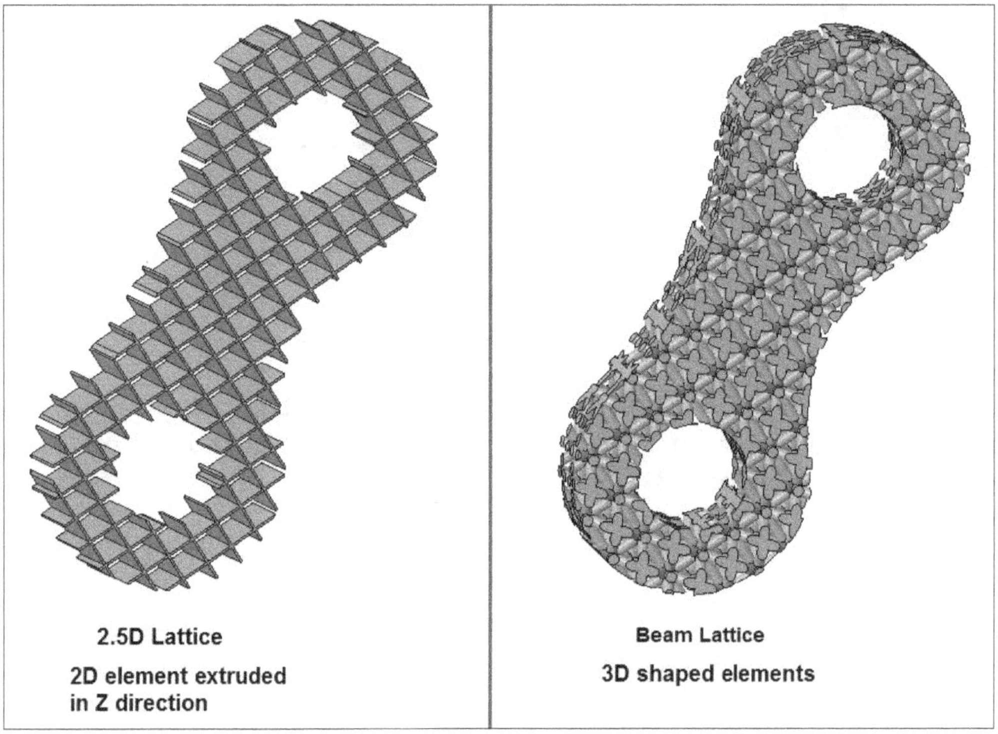

Figure-39. Difference between 2.5D and 3D lattice

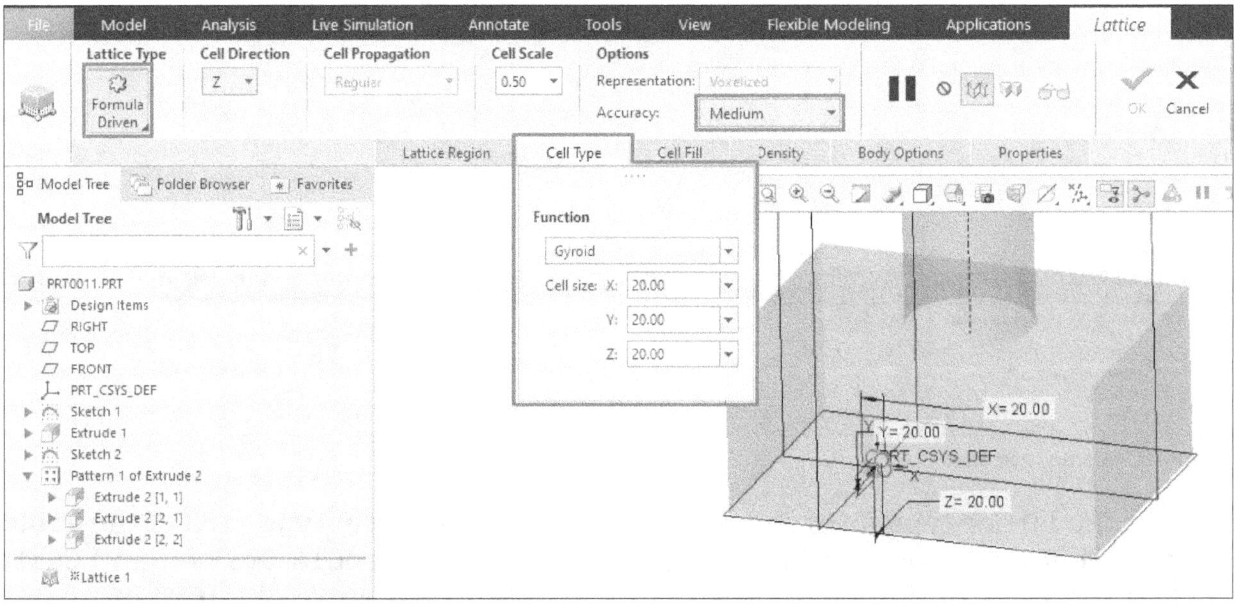

Figure-40. Formula Driven lattice type

- Select the **Custom** option from the drop-down in the **Lattice Type** area of the **Ribbon** if you want to use a part model earlier created in Creo Parametric as element for lattice. The options in **Lattice** contextual tab will be as shown in Figure-41. Click on the **Open Cell** button from **Lattice Type** area in the **Ribbon** and open desired model to be used as element for lattice.

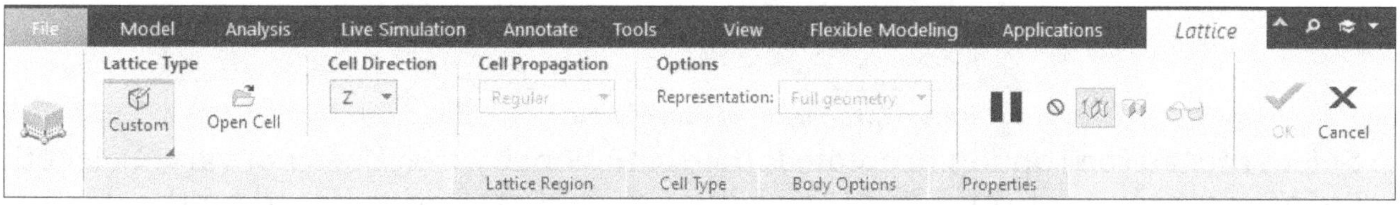

Figure-41. Lattice contextual tab with Custom lattice type options

- Select the **Z** direction for lattice element from the drop-down in the **Cell Direction** area of the **Ribbon**.
- Using the dimensions displayed on the element preview, change the size of lattice element as required; refer to Figure-42.
- Select the multiplication method for lattice cells from the drop-down in the **Cell Propagation** area of the **Ribbon**. Note that the selected method can highly affect the strength of 3D printed part.
- Similarly, select desired representation and specify desired scale value in the **Ribbon**.
- Select the **Replace body with lattice** check box from the **Lattice Region** tab of the **Ribbon** to fill the part with lattice while printing.
- If you want to create a shell of part along with lattice then select the **Create Shell** check box from the **Lattice Region** tab in the **Ribbon** and specify desired thickness of shell in the next edit box; refer to Figure-43.

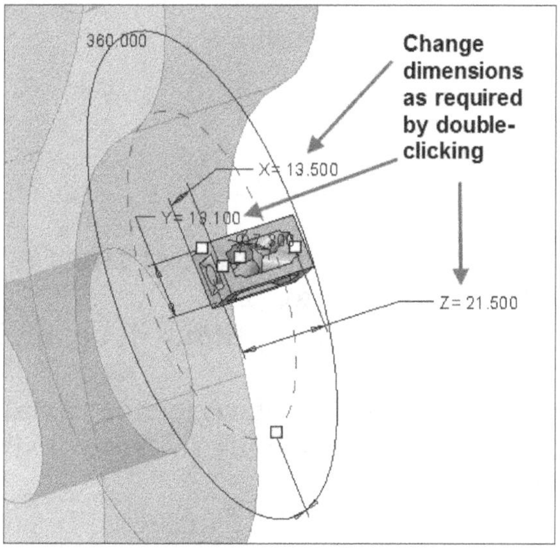

Figure-42. Lattice element preview

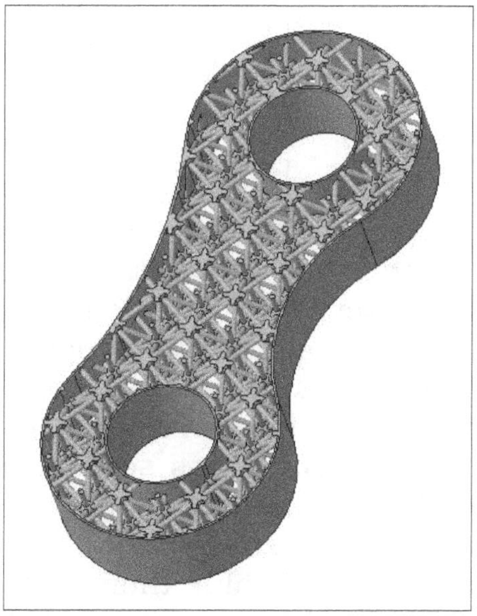

Figure-43. Lattice with shell of solid

- To change the parameters of cells and beams of element, click on the respective tab in the **Lattice** contextual tab and set desired parameters. Note that you can change the cell size and beam size only for 3D type lattices.
- If you want to create a variable density lattice then click on the **Density** tab in the contextual tab. The options will be displayed as shown in Figure-44.

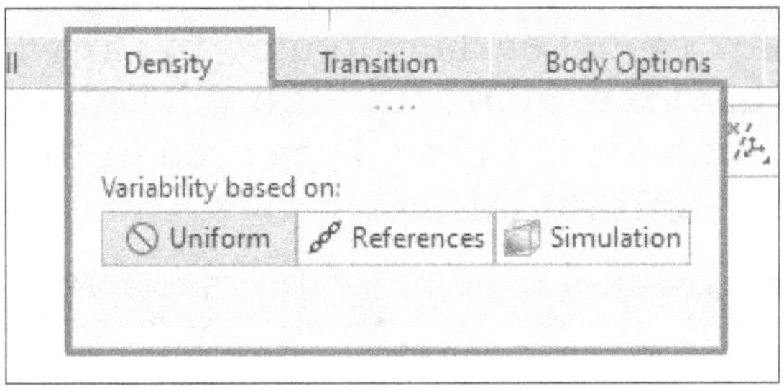

Figure-44. Variability options of density

- Select the **Uniform** option to create lattice with density that does not vary. Select the **References** option to create lattice with density that varies based on the distance from references. Select the **Simulation** option to create lattice with density that varies based on simulation results (density and stress maps).
- On selecting the **References** option, the options will be displayed as shown in Figure-45.

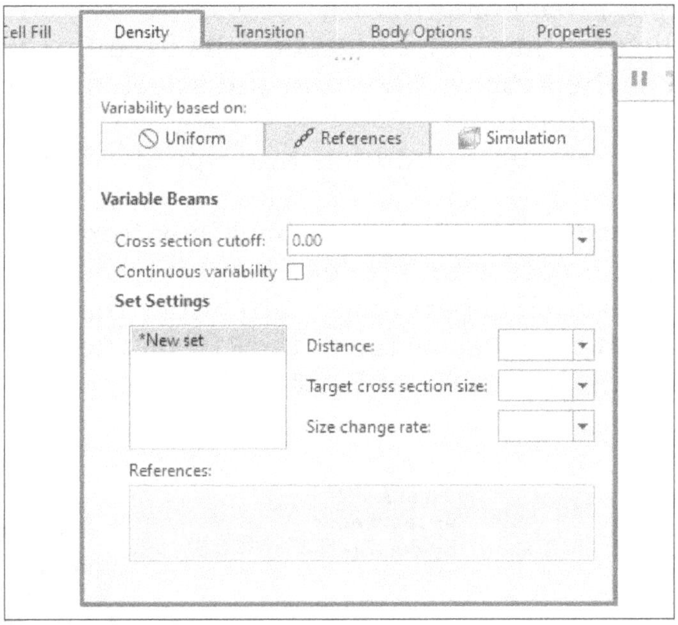

Figure-45. References options in Density tab

- Click on the ***New set** option from the list box in the **Set Settings** area of the tab. A new set of variable density will be added as **Set 1**.
- Specify the distance up to which the variable density option will be applicable to lattice in the **Distance** edit box.
- Set desired size of beam cross-section at the selected reference for variable lattice form in the **Target cross section Size** edit box and specify the rate of size change in the **Size change rate** edit box of the tab.
- Specify desired size of section up to which lattice will be created. If section size is below specified value then lattice will not be created.
- Select the **Continuous variability** check box from **Variable Beams** area if you want to create lattice with continuous variability.
- Click in the **References** selection box in the tab and select the faces/surfaces, edges, points, etc. as starting reference for variable density lattice.
- Set desired parameters in the **Cell Fill** tab of contextual tab in the **Ribbon**.
- Click on the **OK** button from the **Lattice** contextual tab after specifying desired parameters to create the lattice. Save the part file in STL, OBJ, or VRML format to give it to your 3D Print Provider.

Beams Lattice Type

- Select the **Beams** option from the drop-down in the **Lattice Type** area of the **Lattice** contextual tab in the **Ribbon** if you want to control shape as well as structure of lattice. The options in the **Lattice** contextual tab will be as shown in Figure-46.

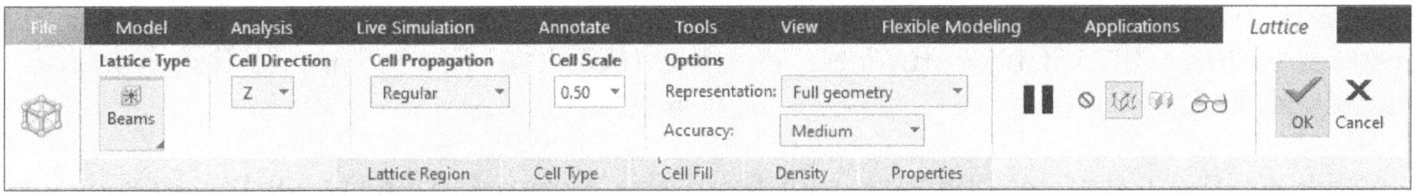

Figure-46. Lattice contextual tab with Beams lattice type options

- Select the **Z** direction for lattice element from the drop-down in the **Cell Direction** area of the **Ribbon**.
- Using the dimensions displayed on the element preview, change the size of lattice element as required; refer to Figure-47.
- Click on the **Cell Type** tab of the **Ribbon**, the options will be displayed as shown in Figure-48.

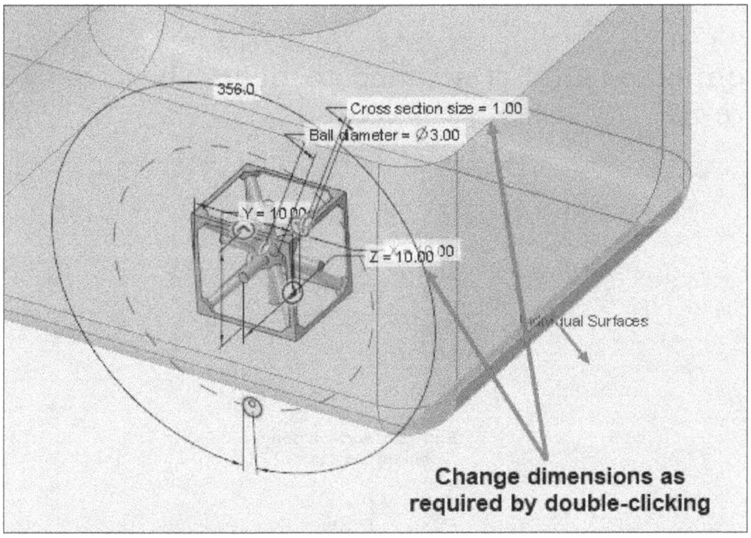

Figure-47. Lattice element preview

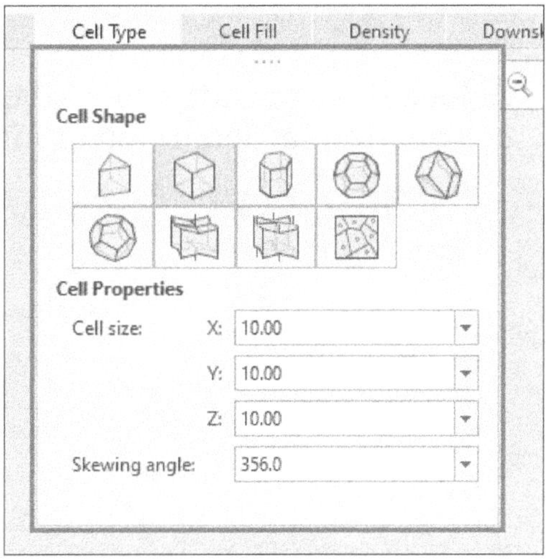

Figure-48. Cell Type tab options

- Select desired cell shape of the beam from the **Cell Shape** area and specify desired properties of the cell in the **Cell Properties** area of the **Cell Type** tab.
- Click on the **Downskin Transition** tab of the **Ribbon**, the options will be displayed as shown in Figure-49.

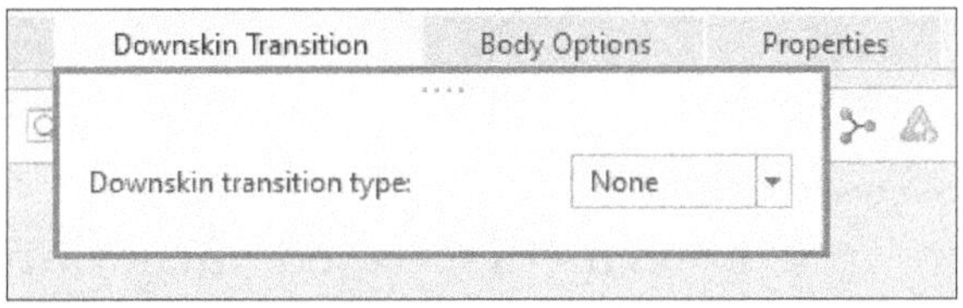

Figure-49. Downskin Transition tab options

- Select the **None** option from the **Downskin transition type** drop-down to not create any transition beams. Select the **Vertical** option from the drop-down to create transition beams with an elbow so that they stand vertically where they connect to the wall in the model. Select the **Slanted** option from the drop-down to create transition beams that are slanted from an elbow where they connect to the model wall.
- Other parameters in the dialog box is same as discussed earlier.

Similarly, you can create lattice using **2.5D** and **Formula Driven** lattice type.

Lattice Connect

The **Lattice Connect** tool is used to create continuous lattice structure by connecting two or more existing lattices. Note that lattices created with **Full geometry** representation will not be connected by this tool. The procedure to use this tool is discussed next.

- Click on the **Lattice Connect** tool from the expanded **Engineering** panel of the **Model** tab in the **Ribbon**. The **Lattice Connect** contextual tab will be displayed; refer to Figure-50.

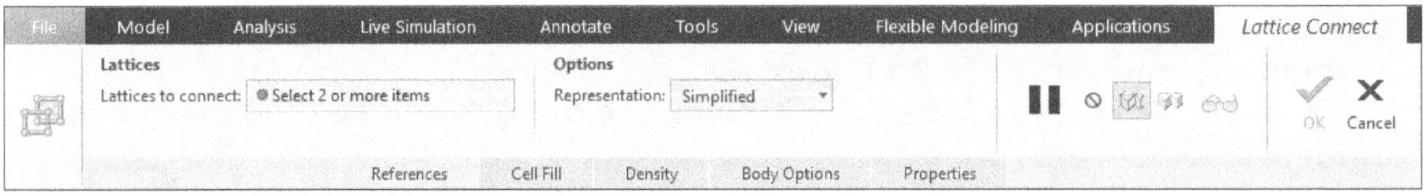

Figure-50. Lattice Connect contextual tab

- Select desired lattices to be connected and a surface to define boundary of connecting lattice; refer to Figure-51.

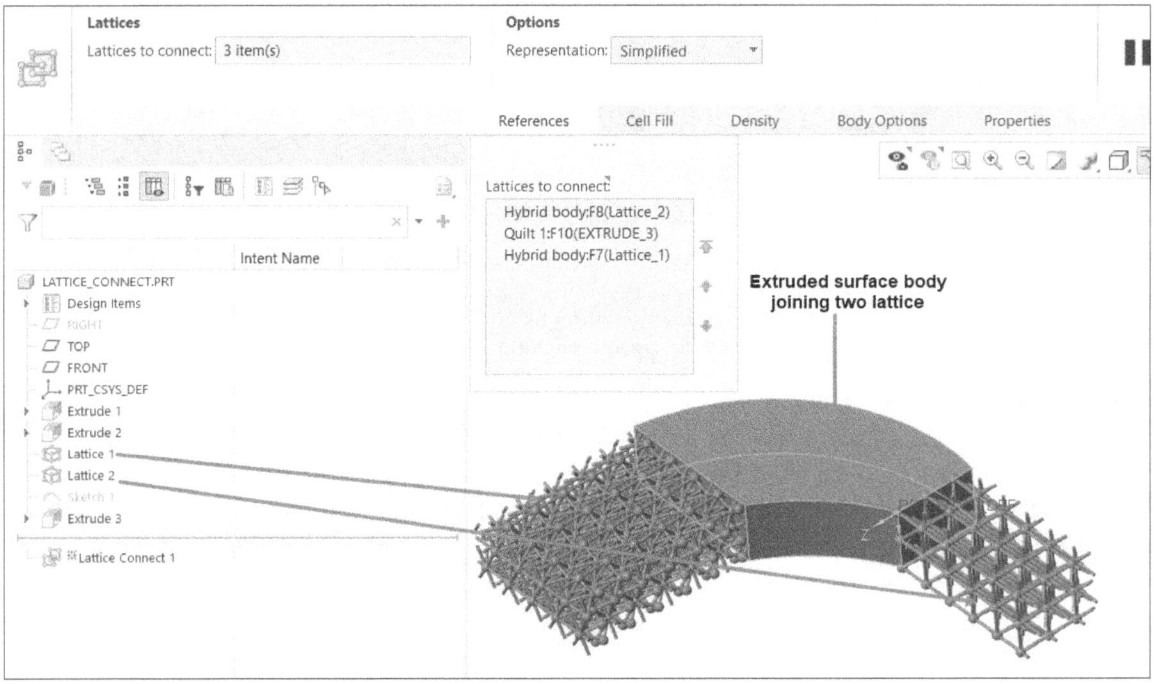

Figure-51. Selection for lattice connect

- Specify the parameters in **Ribbon** as discussed earlier and click on the **OK** button from the **Ribbon**. A new lattice structure will be created; refer to Figure-52.

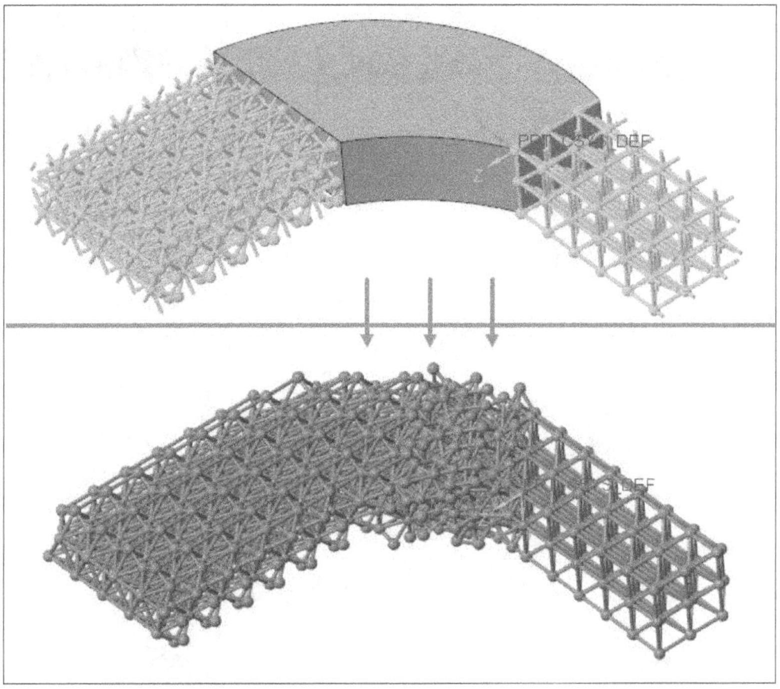

Figure-52. Lattice connect feature

3D Printing in Creo Parametric

- Click on the **Prepare for 3D Printing** tool from the **Print** cascading menu in the **File** menu; refer to Figure-53. The **Tray** tab will open in a new Creo Parametric window with tray assembly of current part; refer to Figure-54.

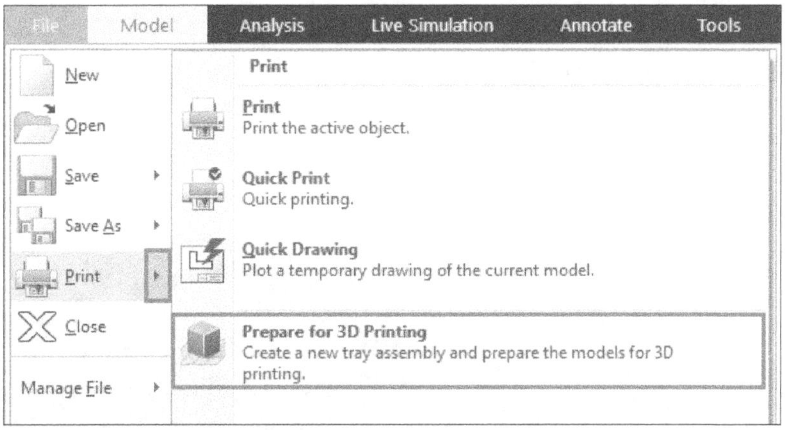

Figure-53. Prepare for 3D Printing tool

- Note that the grid line is the total area of 3D Printer available for printing.
- Click on the **Assemble** button from **Preparation** panel in the **Ribbon** and insert more parts if required. Note that you need to assemble the inserted parts with tray in such a way that the bottom face of part is directly on the tray; refer to Figure-55.

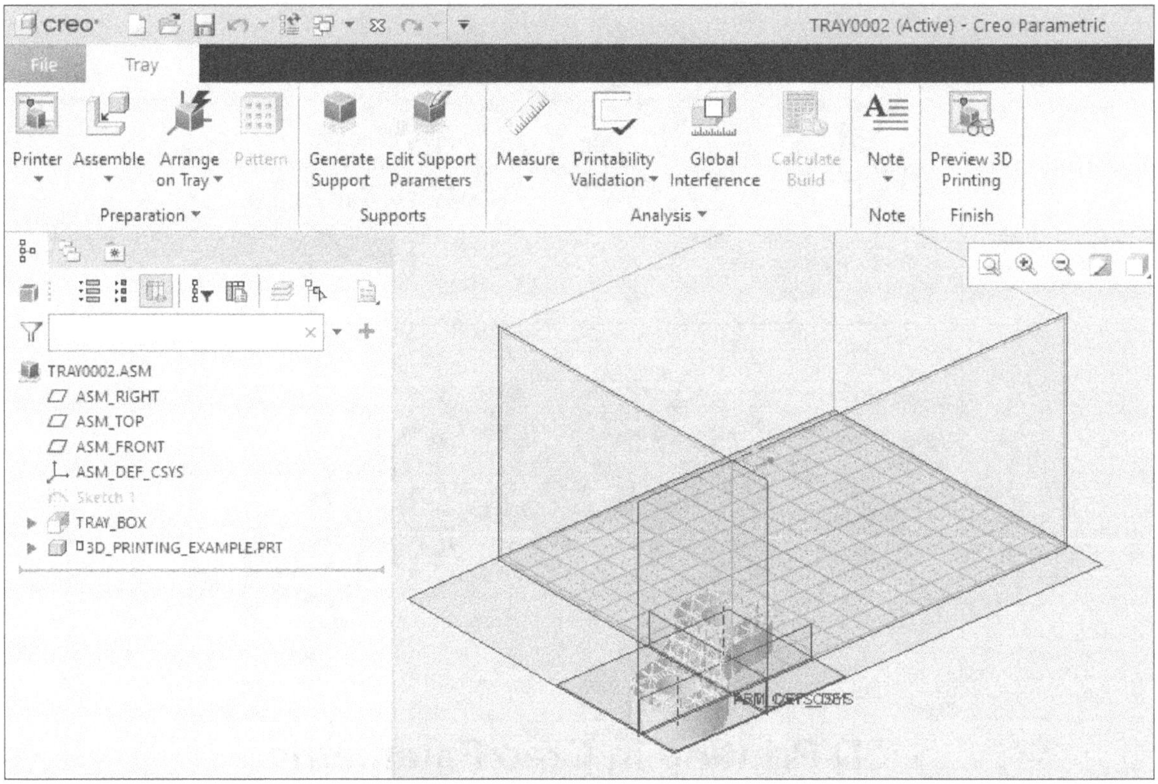

Figure-54. Tray assembly of part

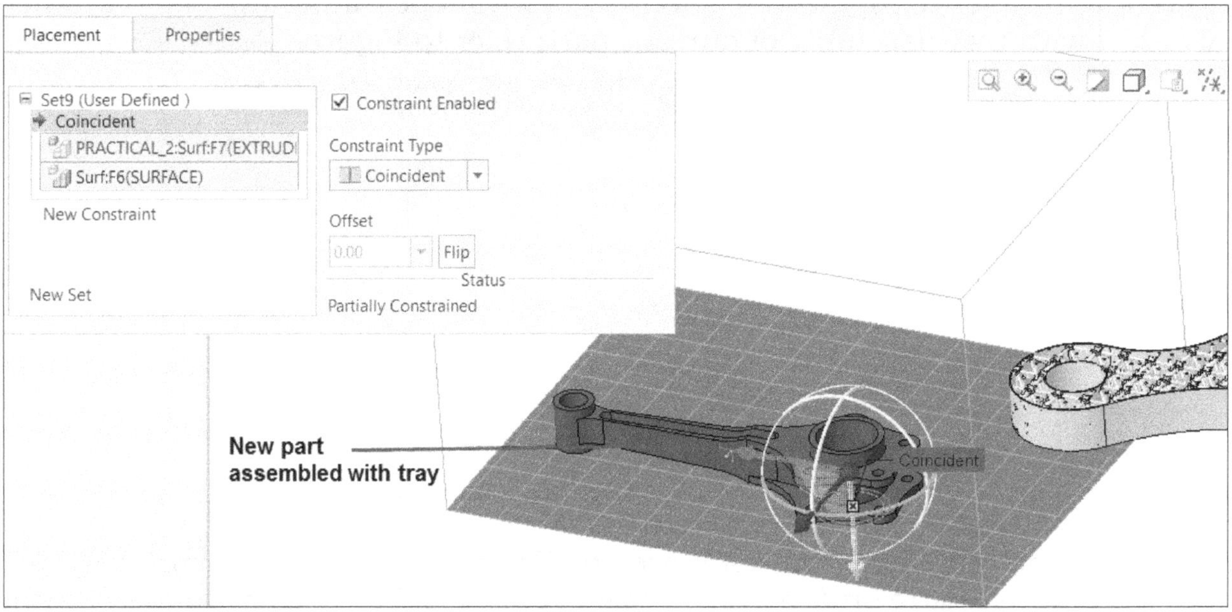

Figure-55. Assembling part with tray

- After inserting the parts, click on the **Arrange on Tray** button from **Preparation** panel in the **Ribbon**. The parts will be placed automatically at suitable location on the table.
- Select the part and create pattern of part using the **Pattern** tool from the **Ribbon** as discussed in previous chapters; refer to Figure-56.
- Click on the **Arrange on Tray** tool from the **Preparation** panel or **Nesting** tool from the expanded **Preparation** panel of the **Ribbon** to place the parts on tray automatically.

- Check the minimum thickness and gap your 3D Printer can produce from the product manual of printer. Click on the **Validate Thin Walls** tool from the **Printability Validation** drop-down in the **Analysis** panel of the **Ribbon**. The **Measure: Verify Thin Walls** dialog box will be displayed; refer to Figure-57.

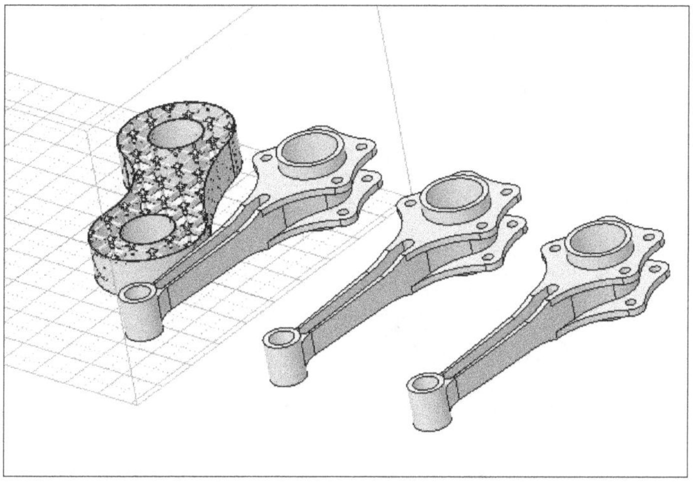

Figure-56. Pattern of part on tray

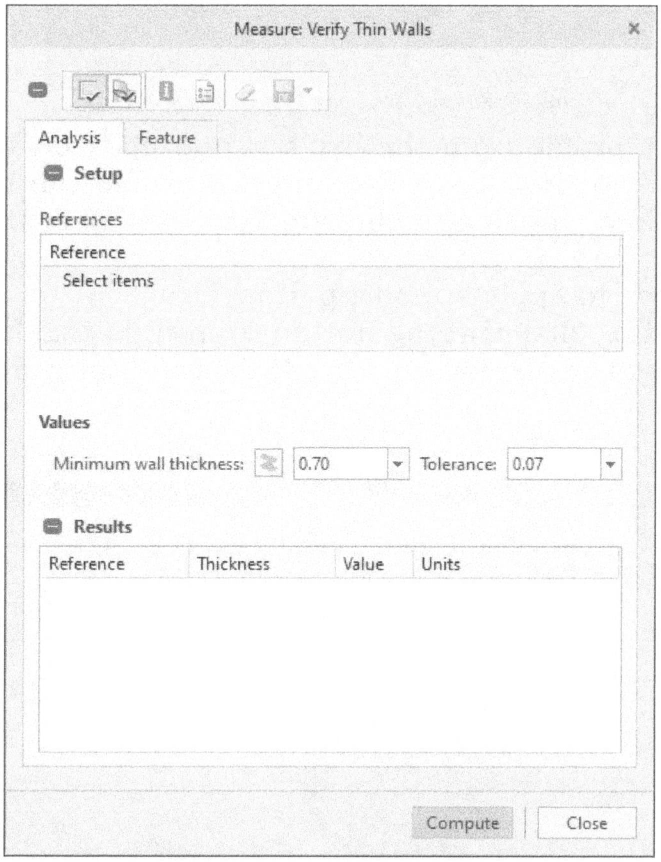

Figure-57. Measure Verify Thin Walls dialog box

- Select the part and specify the minimum thickness to be checked in the part. Click on the **Compute** button at the bottom in the dialog box. Increase the thickness of part by using the **Flexible modeling** tools if required.
- In the same way, you can perform the **Validate Narrow Gaps** analysis.
- Click on the **Generate Support** tool from the **Supports** panel in the **Ribbon** to generate support automatically.

- Click on the **Edit Support Parameters** tool from the **Supports** panel in the **Ribbon**. The **Support Structure Profiles** dialog box will be displayed; refer to Figure-58.

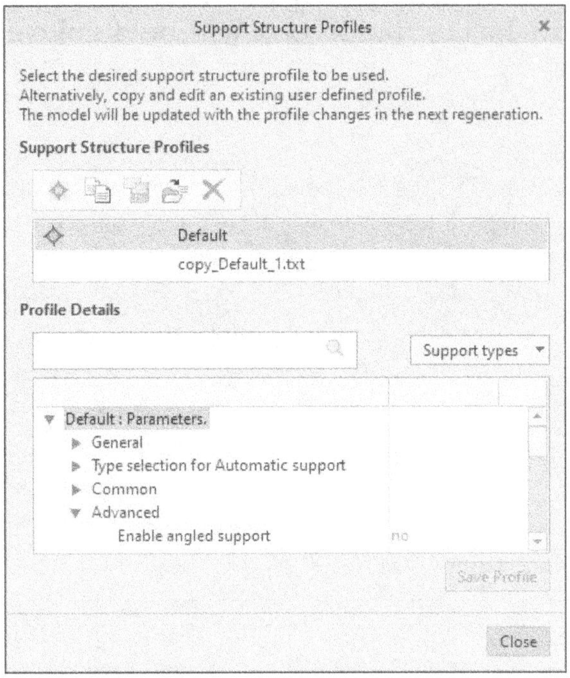

Figure-58. Support Structure Profiles dialog box

- Select the **Default** profile from the list box and click on the **Copy the profile** button from the dialog box. Duplicate copy of profile will be created which can be edited. Set desired values and click on **Set the current profile** button from the dialog box.
- Close the dialog box to apply support parameters.
- Click on the **Preview 3D Printing** button from the **Finish** panel in the **Ribbon**. The **3D Print** tab will be displayed in the **Ribbon** with preview of 3D printed parts; refer to Figure-59.

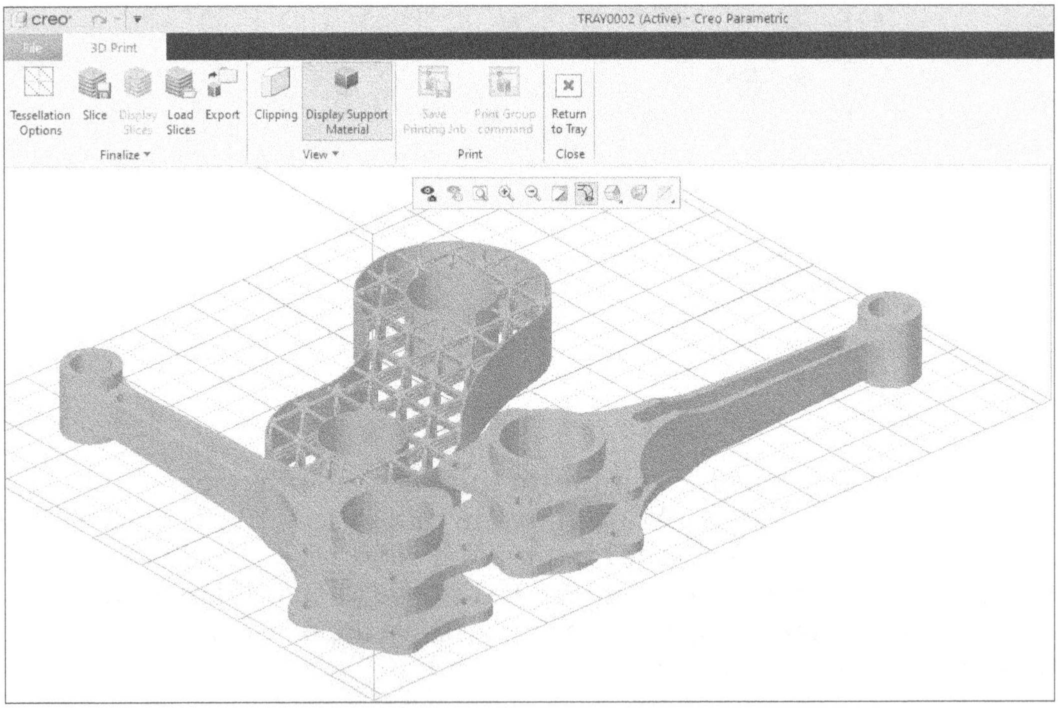

Figure-59. 3D Print tab in Ribbon with preview

- If you have a 3D Printer connected to your system then **Print** tool will be available in the **Print** panel of the **3D Print** tab in the **Ribbon**. Click on the tool to directly 3D print the parts.

Till this point, we have worked for generic printers but in Creo Parametric there is a direct cost calculation and printing option if you select the **i.materialise** option from the **Printer** drop-down in the **Preparation** panel of the **Tray** tab in the **Ribbon**; refer to Figure-60.

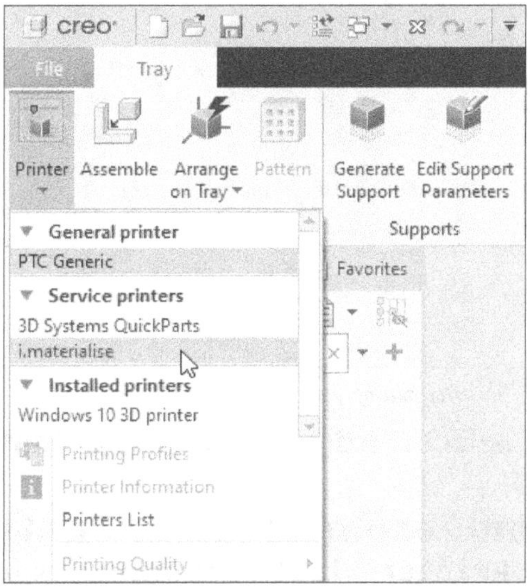

Figure-60. Printer drop-down

Adding 3D Printer to Creo Parametric

- Click on the **Printers List** tool from the **Printer** drop-down in the **Preparation** panel of the **Tray** tab in the **Ribbon**. The **3D Printers** dialog box will be displayed; refer to Figure-61.

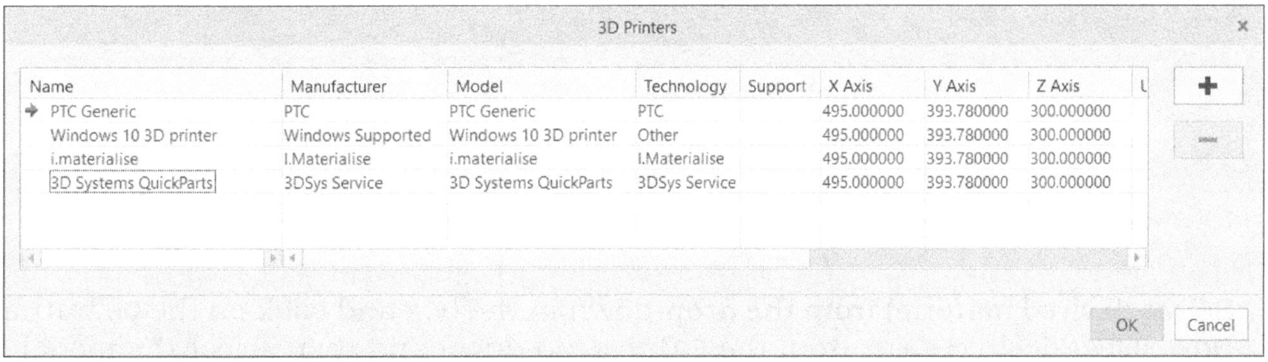

Figure-61. 3D Printers dialog box

- Click on the + button from the dialog box. The **Add Printer** dialog box will be displayed; refer to Figure-62. If you have Stratasys printer or 3DSystems printer then there are direct buttons available in the dialog box to connect them with Creo Parametric.
- Select desired option and click on the **Next** button. Follow the information given in the dialog box and create a new printer by clicking on the **Finish** button at the end in the dialog box.

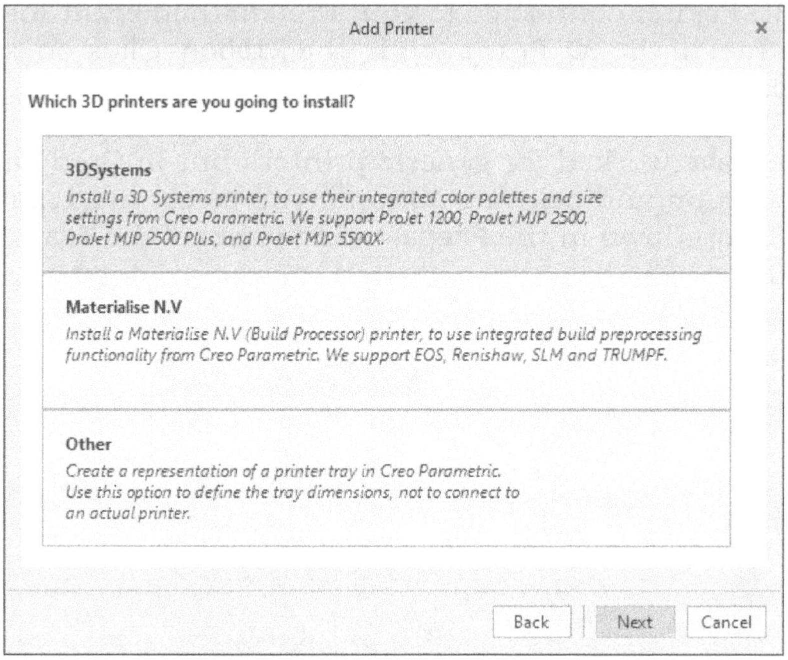

Figure-62. Add Printer dialog box

- After adding the printer, select it from the **Printers list** in the **Printer** drop-down.

Applying Texture to the 3D Printed Part

- Select a printer from the **Printers list** that supports textures like **i.materialise**.
- Click on the **Manage Appearances** button from the expanded **Preparation** panel in the **Tray** tab of the **Ribbon**. The **Appearance** contextual tab will be added in the **Ribbon.**
- Select the **Palette Selection** button from the **Colors** drop-down in the **Appearance** contextual tab. The **Material Selection** box will be displayed; refer to Figure-63.

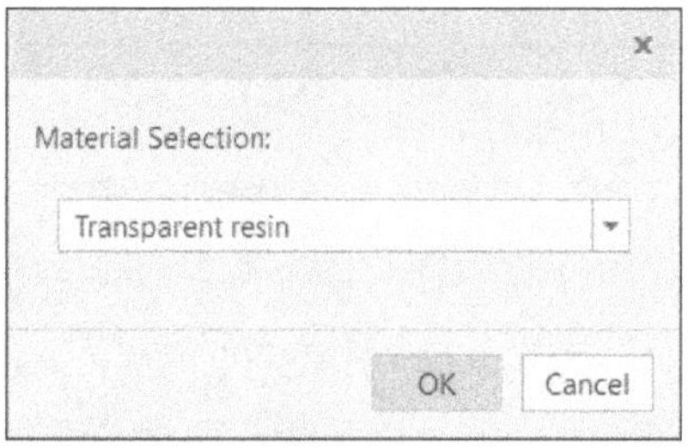

Figure-63. Material Selection box

- Select desired material from the drop-down in the box and click on the **OK** button.
- Now select desired color from the **Color** drop-down and then select the model to apply the color/texture. Click in the empty area to exit the tool.

SELF ASSESSMENT

1. Explain the Vat Photopolymeriation process of 3D printing.

2. Explain the binder jetting process of 3D Printing.

3. Which of the following planes is not available in the **Annotation Planes Names** selection box?

(a) FLAT TO SCREEN
(b) FRONT
(c) FLAT TO FACE
(d) TOP

4. In which of the following 3D Printing processes, the material is applied in droplets through a small diameter nozzle?

(a) Binder Jetting
(b) Material Jetting
(c) Sheet Lamination
(d) None of the Above

5. In which of the following 3D Printing processes, the Selective laser sintering (SLS) technology is used?

(a) Power Bed Fusion
(b) Directed Energy Deposition
(c) Vat Photopolymerisation
(d) None of the Above

6. The Fused deposition modeling (FDM) technology is used in .... process of 3D Printing.

7. The .... tool is used to display annotations assigned to the model while creating it.

8. The .... tool is used to set the standard and other parameters for applying GD&T using GD&T Advisor.

9. The **GD&T Advisor** is an application from Sigmetrix used for applying and analyzing the model for geometric dimensioning and tolerances. (T/F)

10. The **Tolerance Feature** tool is used to apply geometric tolerance and dimensioning to the whole pattern, like you can apply tolerance to the pattern of holes at single place. (T/F)

11. Select the **2.5D** lattice type if you do not want to control the structure of lattice but want to define the element shape. (T/F)

12. What is the primary benefit of using Model Based Definition (MBD) in CAD?

a) It replaces 3D models with 2D drawings
b) It allows PMI to be added directly to 3D models
c) It reduces the size of CAD files
d) It converts models to PDF files automatically

13. Which of the following is NOT a default annotation plane in Creo Parametric?

a) FRONT
b) RIGHT
c) ISO
d) BOTTOM

14. What does the Show Annotations tool do?

a) Displays PMI in 2D drawing only
b) Removes all annotations
c) Displays dimensions assigned during model creation
d) Changes annotation text size

15. Which action will remove an annotation from the model?

a) Clicking on Update button
b) Using the Erase option in the mini toolbar
c) Using the Tolerance Pattern tool
d) Selecting Inside option in Symbol panel

16. What does the Combination State help manage?

a) File conversion formats
b) Different dimension combinations in model views
c) Printing speed of 3D printers
d) Editing part materials

17. What is the use of the GD&T Advisor?

a) To measure total volume of model
b) To apply and analyze geometric tolerances
c) To convert model to PDF
d) To color 3D annotations

18. What is the use of Establish DRF tool?

a) Export model to IGES format
b) Rotate datum targets
c) Link GD&T annotations with datum references
d) Measure wall thickness

19. What does the Edit Properties tool in GD&T Advisor allow?

a) Delete features
b) Export geometry
c) Set tolerancing standards and part types
d) Save drawing as DWG

20. What is the function of the Show/Hide Constraint State tool?

a) Highlight visible annotations only
b) Show constrained and unconstrained areas of part
c) Hide datum targets
d) Create new datum features

21. What is the main benefit of 3D PDF over IGES for marketing use?

a) It includes only technical data
b) It reduces file size drastically
c) It can be used to show important features and dimensions visually
d) It exports tool paths directly

22. What is 3D Printing also commonly known as?

a) Virtual Modeling
b) Additive Manufacturing
c) Parametric Rendering
d) Selective Drawing

23. What is the primary goal of part preparation in 3D printing?

a) To decorate the model before printing
b) To ensure stability of the part in semi molten state
c) To color the part for aesthetics
d) To improve the printer speed

24. Which of the following processes is classified under Vat Photopolymerisation?

a) FDM
b) SLA
c) SLS
d) DED

25. In SLA, what is used to cure the resin?

a) Heated nozzle
b) Infrared rays
c) UV laser
d) Magnetic beam

26. What is a key benefit of Powder Bed Fusion like SLS?

a) No requirement for mesh model
b) It needs external support structures
c) It doesn't waste any powder
d) All unused powder can be reused

27. Which material types are most commonly used in FDM technology?

a) Resin and glue
b) ABS and PLA
c) Ceramic and glass
d) Ink and toner

28. What does Material Jetting use to apply material?

a) Blade
b) UV lamp
c) Nozzle
d) Extruder

29. Which process involves a robotic arm and melting metal powder?

a) SLA
b) FDM
c) DED
d) Binder Jetting

30. Why should you shell your 3D model before printing?

a) To improve its color
b) To make it hollow and save material
c) To enhance mesh quality
d) To add extra layers

31. What should you avoid when modeling for 3D printing?

a) Using solid models
b) Exporting files in .iges
c) Creating multi-body models
d) Using surface modeling

32. What are lattice structures mainly used for?

a) Coloring the model
b) Increasing weight
c) Strength with less material
d) Supporting surface modeling

33. Which lattice type is created fastest and suitable for axial loads?

a) Beam lattice
b) 2.5D lattice
c) Formula Driven
d) Custom

34. What does the "Gyroid" function use as its formula?

a) $\sin(x) + \sin(y) + \sin(z) = 0$
b) $\sin(x)\cos(y) + \sin(y)\cos(z) + \sin(z)\cos(x) = 0$
c) $\cos(x) + \cos(y) + \cos(z) = 0$
d) $x + y + z = 0$

35. What is required for the Custom lattice option in Creo Parametric?

a) Texture settings
b) Importing .jpg image
c) Using a pre-created part as element
d) Coloring the lattice

36. What does selecting “Replace body with lattice” do?

a) Applies new texture
b) Replaces part with surface
c) Fills part with lattice structure
d) Converts model into sheet metal

37. What does the “References” option do in variable density lattice?

a) Keeps density same
b) Changes lattice density based on distance
c) Applies uniform thickness
d) Removes cell patterns

38. What does the Validate Thin Walls tool help you check?

a) Color accuracy
b) Mesh complexity
c) Wall thickness
d) Print speed

39. What does the Generate Support tool in Creo Parametric do?

a) Adds color
b) Automatically creates supports
c) Applies glue
d) Adds textures

40. Which function allows setting variable beam sizes in lattice structure?

a) Shell
b) Validate
c) Density tab
d) Prepare

FOR STUDENT NOTES

Answer to Self Assessment Questions:

3. (c) **4.** (b) **5.** (a) **6.** Material Extrusion **7.** Show Annotations **8.** Edit Properties **9.** T **10.** F **11.** T

Chapter 15

Introduction to Sheetmetal Manufacturing

Topics Covered

The major topics covered in this chapter are:

- ***Introduction***
- ***Parts setting***
- ***Work cell Settings***
- ***Operation Setting***
- ***NC Sequencing***
- ***Program Output Generation***

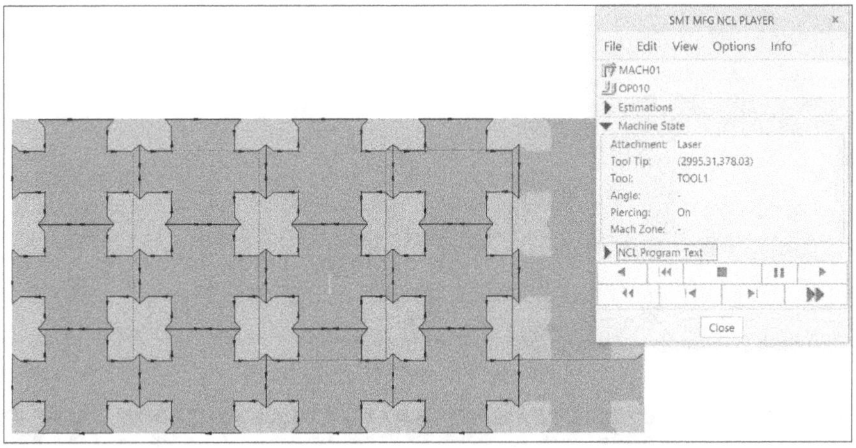

INTRODUCTION

You have learned about creating flat pattern of various sheet metal parts in the previous chapters. You have also learned to create drawings for them. Now, you will learn about creating NC programs for automated sheet metal cutting and forming machines. In this chapter, you will learn about arranging flat patterns of various parts on a sheet so that you can maximize the usage of sheet to produce more sheet metal parts. The tools to manufacture sheet metal parts are available in the Sheet Metal Manufacturing environment. The procedure to start the manufacturing environment is given next.

- Click on the **New** tool from the **Ribbon** or **Quick Access Toolbar**. The **New** dialog box will be displayed.
- Select the **Manufacturing** radio button from the **Type** area and **Sheetmetal** radio button from the **Sub-type** area of the dialog box.
- Specify desired name in the **File name** edit box and click on the **OK** button from the dialog box. The sheet metal manufacturing environment will be displayed along with the **SMT MFG MACHINING** dialog box as shown in Figure-1.

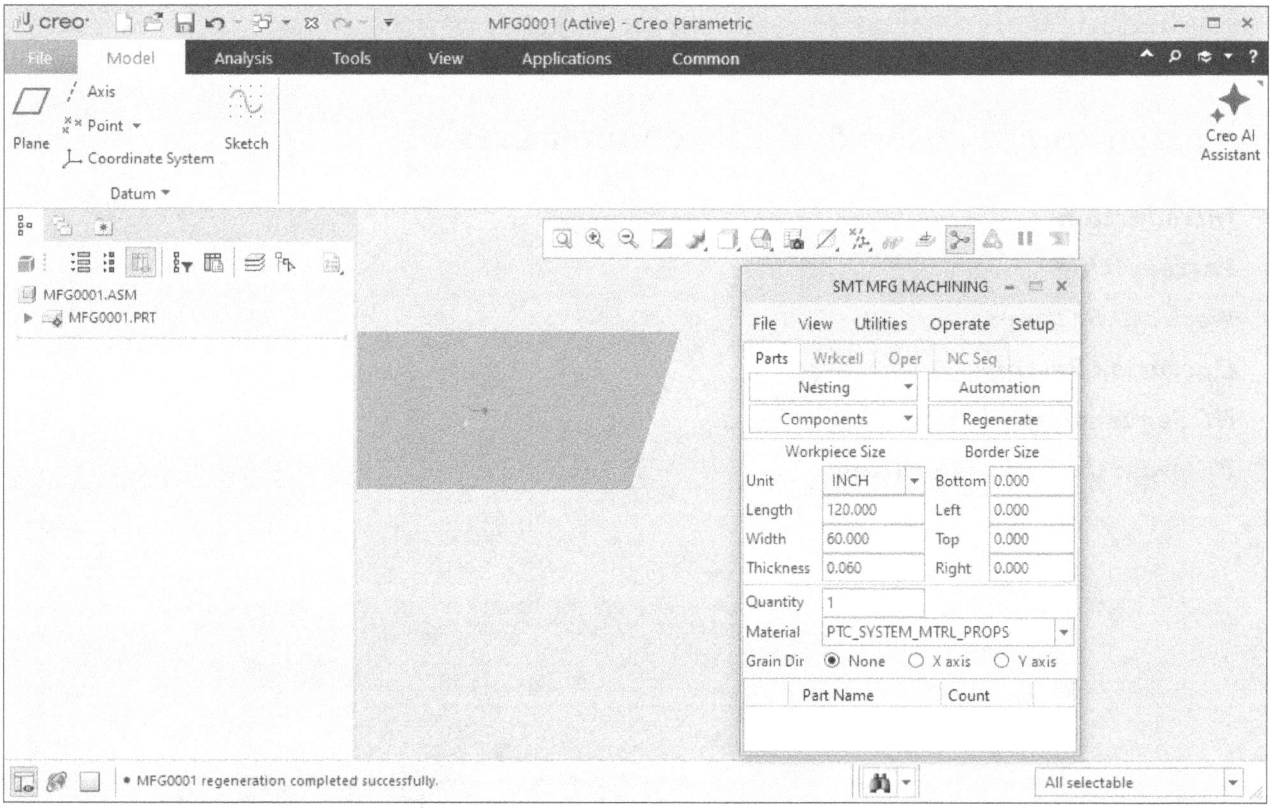

Figure-1. Sheetmetal Manufacturing environment

SETTING WORKPIECE AND MACHINE

The options to set workpiece size are available in **Parts** tab of **SMT MFG MACHINING** dialog box. The procedure to set workpiece is given next.

Setting Workpiece

- Select desired option from the **Unit** drop-down in the **Parts** tab of the dialog box.
- Specify desired parameters in the **Length**, **Width**, and **Thickness** edit boxes to define size of metal sheet.

- Set desired offset values in the edit boxes of **Border Size** area of the dialog box.
- Select desired material from the **Material** drop-down and set desired **Grain Dir** radio button.

Setting Machine

- Select the **Wrkcell** tab from the dialog box. The options of dialog box will be displayed as shown in Figure-2.

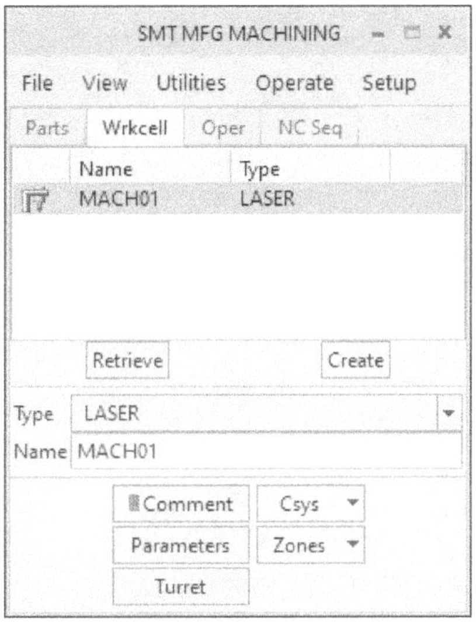

Figure-2. Wrkcell tab

- Select desired machine type from the **Type** drop-down and specify desired name in the **Name** edit box. Select the **LASER** option from the drop-down if you want to cut flat pattern from the metal sheet. Select the **PUNCH** option from the drop-down if you want to create punch deformation in sheet metal. Select the **LASER-PUNCH** option from the drop-down if you want to perform cutting and punching both on the sheet metal. Select the **FLAME** option from the drop-down to select a flame cutting machine. Select the **FLAME-PUNCH** option from the drop-down to select flame punching machine.
- Select the **Select** option from the **Csys** drop-down at the bottom in the **Wrkcell** tab of the dialog box and select the coordinate system to be used for machine. If you want to create a new coordinate system then click on the **Create** option from the **Csys** drop-down. The **Coordinate System** dialog box will be displayed; refer to Figure-3.

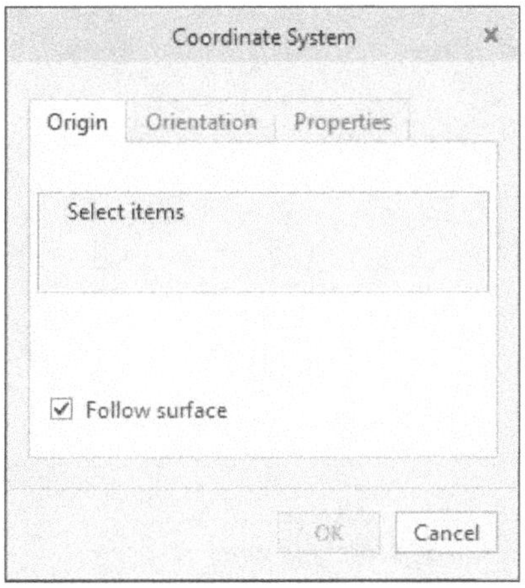

Figure-3. Coordinate System dialog box

- Create the coordinate system as discussed earlier and click on the **OK** button.
- Click on the **Parameters** option from the **Wrkcell** tab of the dialog box to modify parameters of machine. The **SMM PARAMETERS** dialog box will be displayed; refer to Figure-4.

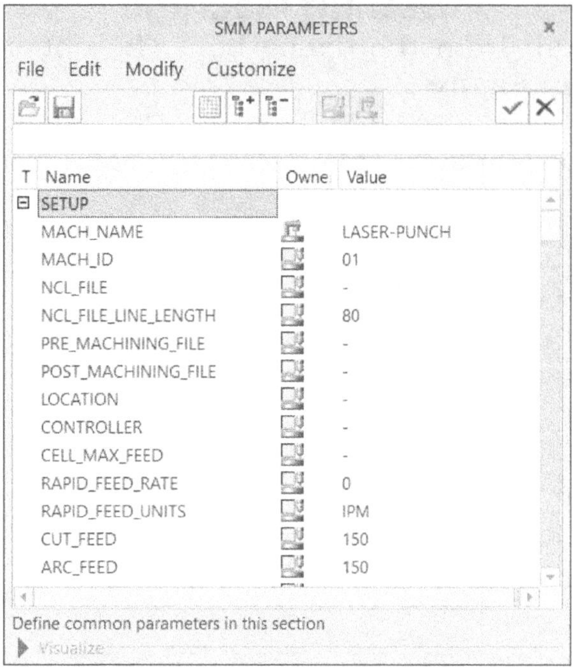

Figure-4. SMM PARAMETERS dialog box

- Set desired parameters in the dialog box and click on the **OK** button.
- If you want to define a machining zone then click on the **Create** option from the **Zones** drop-down. The **Machine Zone** dialog box will be displayed with preview of machine zone; refer to Figure-5.

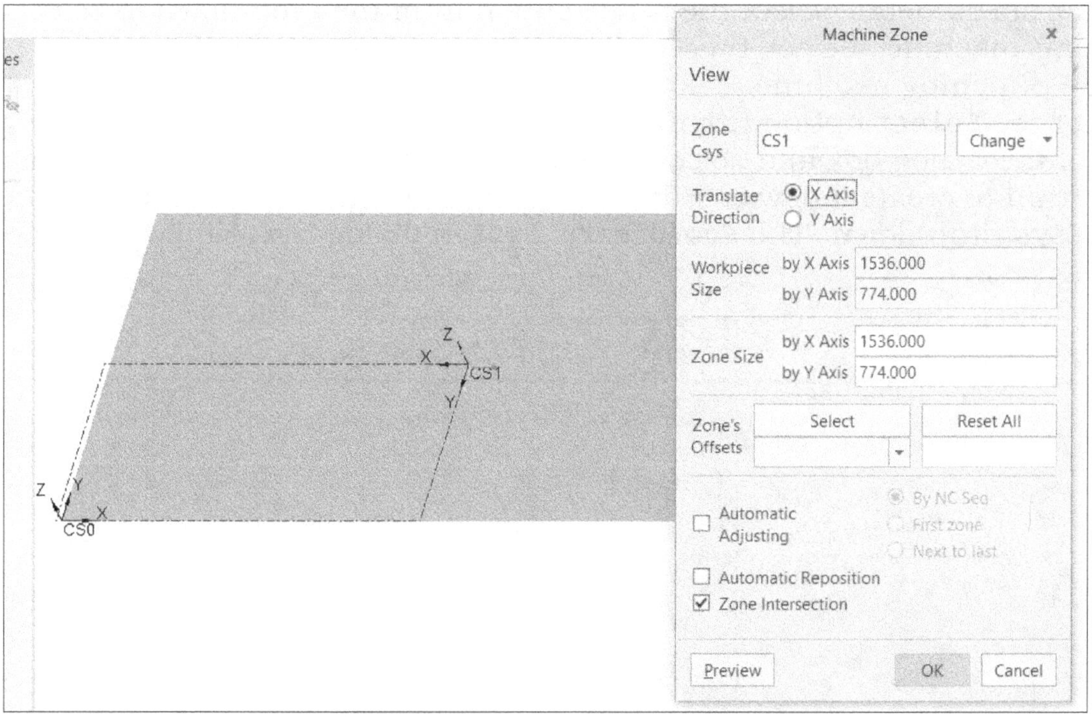

Figure-5. Machine Zone dialog box with preview of zone

- Set desired parameters in the dialog box and click on the **OK** button.

Tool Settings

- If you are using turret machine and want to create multiple tools for turret then click on the **Turret** button from **SMT MFG MACHINING** dialog box. The **TURRET MANAGER** dialog box will be displayed; refer to Figure-6.

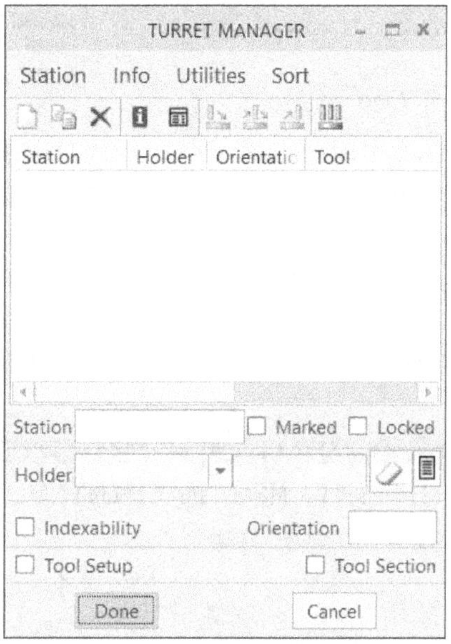

Figure-6. TURRET MANAGER dialog box

- Click on **Create New** button from the dialog box to create 1st index of tool turret. Double-click on the station to setup tool. The **TOOL SETUP** dialog box will be displayed; refer to Figure-7.

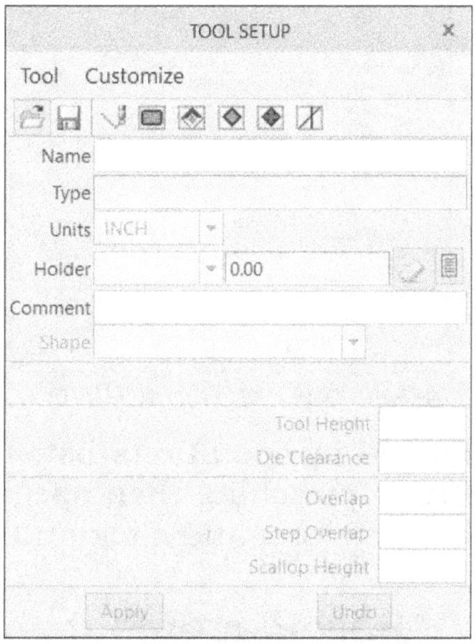

Figure-7. TOOL SETUP dialog box

- Click on desired button from the dialog box. There are 6 tool options available in this dialog box viz. New contouring tool, New standard punch tool, New form tool, New UDF punch tool, New solid punch tool, and New shear tool; refer to Figure-8.

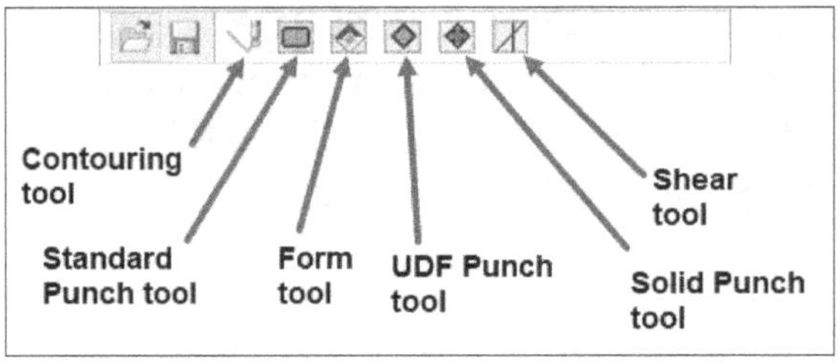

Figure-8. Tools

- The options for selected tool will be displayed in the **TOOL SETUP** dialog box. Specify desired name of tool in the **Name** edit box. Set the other parameters as desired and click on the **Apply** button.
- Click on the **Tools/Stations Switch** tool from the toolbar in the dialog box to check tools used in machine.
- Click on the **Done** button from the dialog box to apply changes.

Creating Operations

- Click on the **Oper** tab of the **SMT MFG MACHINING** dialog box to display options related to NC operation; refer to Figure-9.

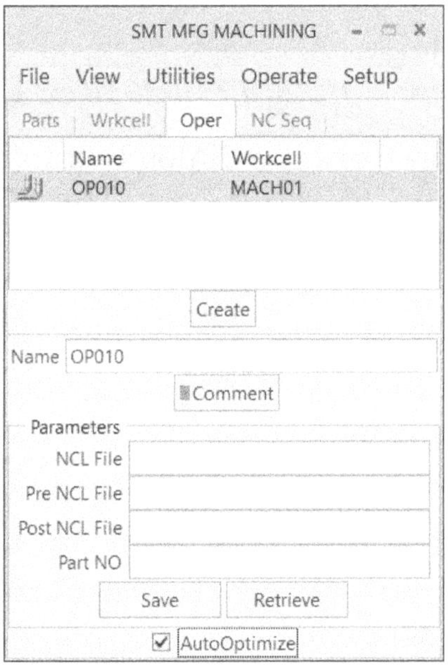

Figure-9. Oper tab of SMT MFG MACHINING dialog box

- By default, OP010 is available in operations list. If you want to create a new operation like sheet cutting or punching then specify desired name in the **Name** edit box, set the NCL file parameters, and click on the **Create** button.

Part Placement

There are three options in **Parts** tab of **SMT MFG MACHINING** dialog box; Nesting, Automation, and Components. Select the **Automation** option if you want to multiple instances of same component. Select the **Components** option if you want to assemble a component with the workpiece. The procedures to perform part placement are discussed next.

Part Placement with Nesting

Select the **Nesting** option if you want to create multiple different types of components. The procedure to use this option is given next.

- Click on the **Nesting** option from the top in the **Parts** tab of the dialog box. A drop-down will be displayed; refer to Figure-10.

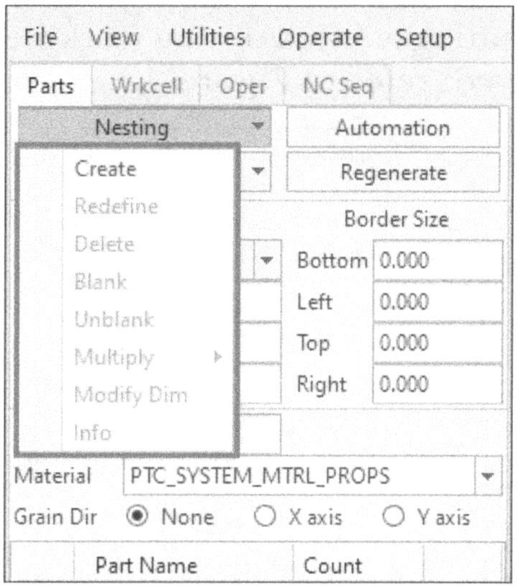

Figure-10. Nesting drop-down

- Click on the **Create** option from the **Nesting** drop-down. The **NEST CELL Menu Manager** will be displayed.
- Click on the **Add Part** option from the **Menu Manager**. The **Open** dialog box will be displayed; refer to Figure-11.

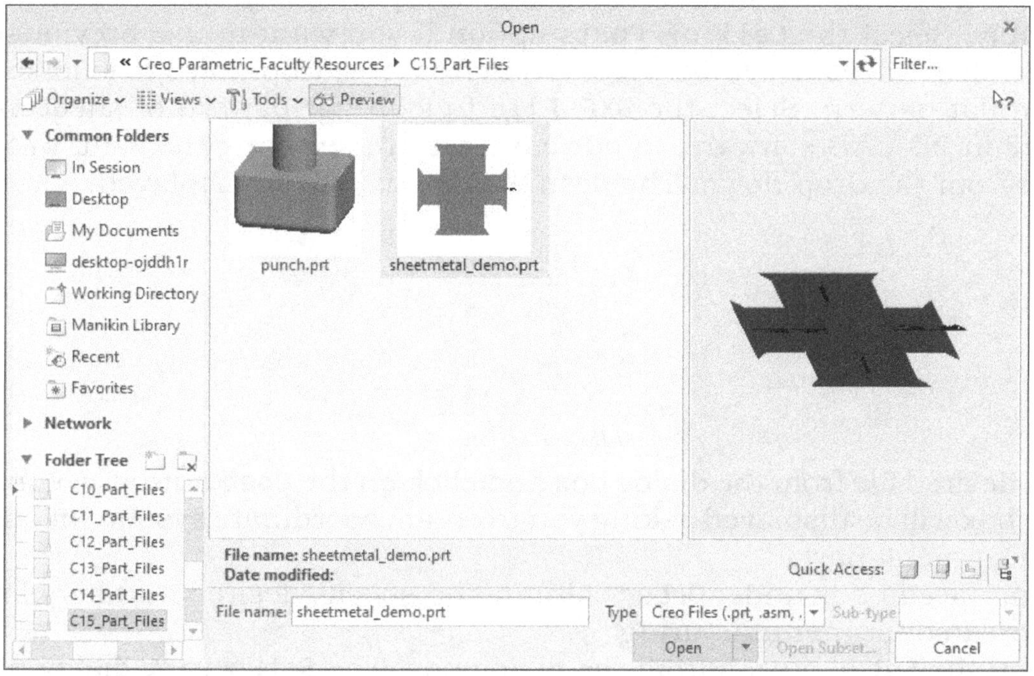

Figure-11. Open dialog box

- Select desired sheet metal part with flat pattern and click on the **Open** button. The **PART PLACE** menu will be displayed in **Menu Manager**. Select the **DragOrigin** check box from the **Menu Manager** to place the flat pattern by dragging and click on the **Done** button. You will be asked to select the coordinate system.

- Select desired coordinate system and place the component at desired location.
- Click on the **Done** button from the **Menu Manager**.
- Select desired option from the **Nesting** drop-down and modify the part placement as desired.

Part Placement with Automation

- Click on the **Automation** button from the dialog box to create multiple instances of a sheet metal part automatically fitted on the workpiece. The **SMT MFG AUTOMATION** dialog box will be displayed; refer to Figure-12.

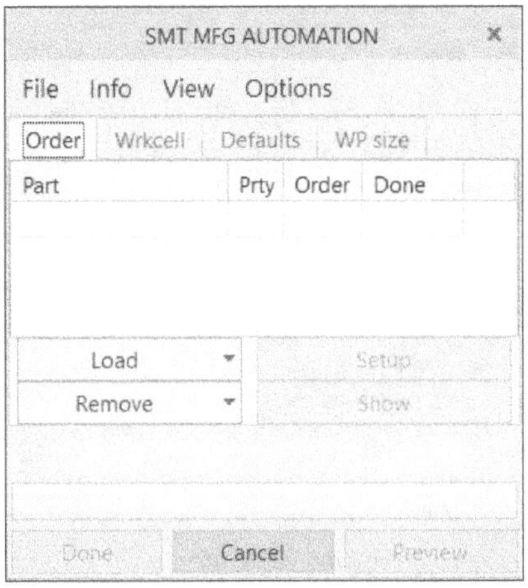

Figure-12. SMT MFG AUTOMATION dialog box

- Click on the **Load** option from the dialog box. The drop-down will be displayed as shown in Figure-13. There are 4 options in this drop-down; **Parts from Mfg**, **Cell of Parts**, **Part w/o NC Seqs**, and **DXF File**. Select the **Parts from Mfg** option if you want to import sheet metal part from previously created manufacturing assembly. Select the **Cell of Parts** option if you want to use previously nested parts. Select the **Part w/o NC Seqs** option from the drop-down to load sheet metal part in flat pattern. Select the **DXF File** to load flat pattern of sheet metal part created in 2D CAD software. In our case, we are selecting the **Part w/o NC Seqs** option from the drop-down. The **Open** dialog box will be displayed.

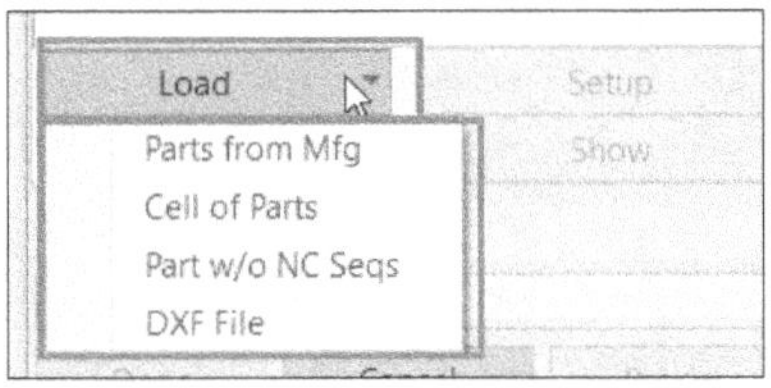

Figure-13. Load options

- Select desired file from the dialog box and click on the **Open** button. A confirmation dialog box will be displayed asking you to create coordinate system for assembling the sheet metal part.
- Click in the edit box under **Order** column and specify desired number of instances to be created for manufacturing.
- Click on the **Setup** button from the dialog box. The **Setup Part** dialog box will be displayed; refer to Figure-14.

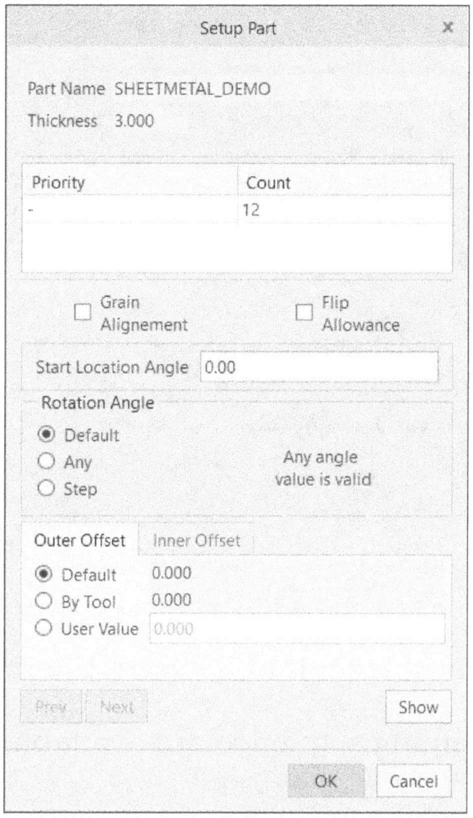

Figure-14. Setup Part dialog box

- Select the **User Value** radio button and specify desired offset value. This offset will be the material left while cutting the sheet metal parts.
- Click on the **OK** button from the dialog box. The **SMT MFG AUTOMATION** dialog box will be displayed again with number of instances specified and number of instances that could be created on specified workpiece; refer to Figure-15.

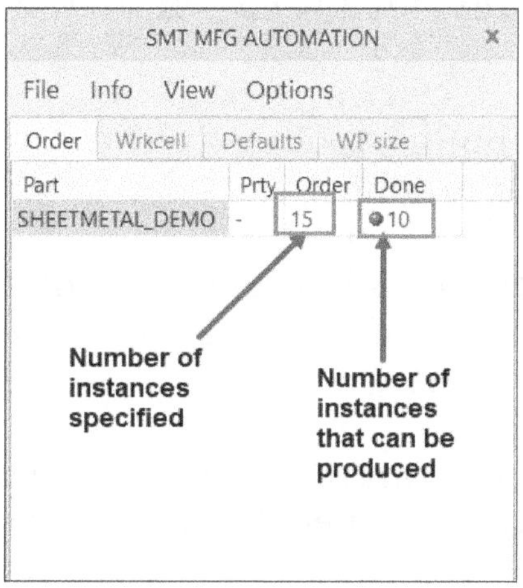

Figure-15. Instances for sheetmetal manufacturing

- Similarly, you can load other sheetmetal parts on same sheet if there is material left and parts can fit in there.
- Click on the **Done** button from the dialog box after specifying the parameters.

Creating NC Sequence

The tools in the **NC Seq** tab of the **SMT MFG MACHINING** dialog box are used to define toolpaths and parameters for create sheet metal part on machine; refer to Figure-16.

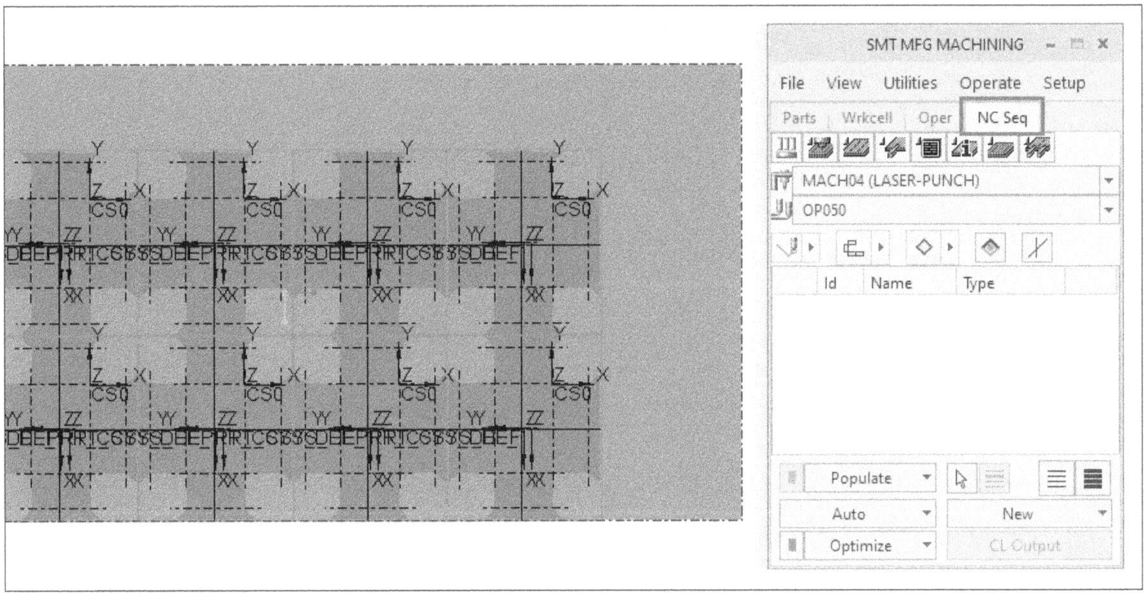

Figure-16. NC Seq tab

- Select desired machine and operation file from the respective drop-downs at the top in the dialog box.
- The tools to create machining sequence are available below the **Operation** drop-down. These tools are:

Contouring : The contouring tool is used to cut sheet metal based on selected part boundaries.

Slitting : The slitting tool is used to split the remaining sheet metal after punching and finish cutting.

Approach Punching : The approach punching tool is used to punch the primary impression on sheet metal.

Edge Nibbling : The edge nibbling tool is used to cut contour on sheet metal by successive overlapping slits or notches.

Similarly, you can use the other tools in the dialog box to create respective toolpaths. Here, we will discuss the process of creating toolpath for contouring. You can use the same procedure for other tools.

- Click on the **Contouring** tool from the dialog box. The **TURRET MANAGER** dialog box will be displayed if you have not specified tool earlier. Create desired contouring tool as discussed earlier.
- After selecting the tool, the options will be displayed as shown in Figure-17.

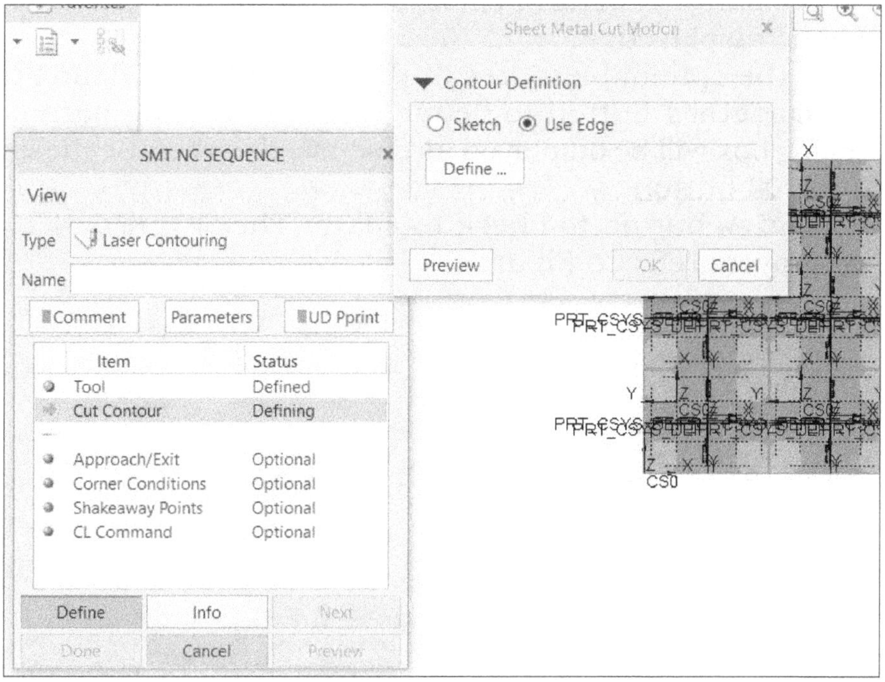

Figure-17. Laser contouring options

- Select the **Use Edge** radio button and click on the **Define** button from the dialog box.
- Select the edges of flat pattern part to be cut from sheet metal by contour tool; refer to Figure-18. Click on the **OK** button from the **Select Edges** dialog box. The **Sheet Metal Cut Motion** dialog box will be displayed; refer to Figure-19.

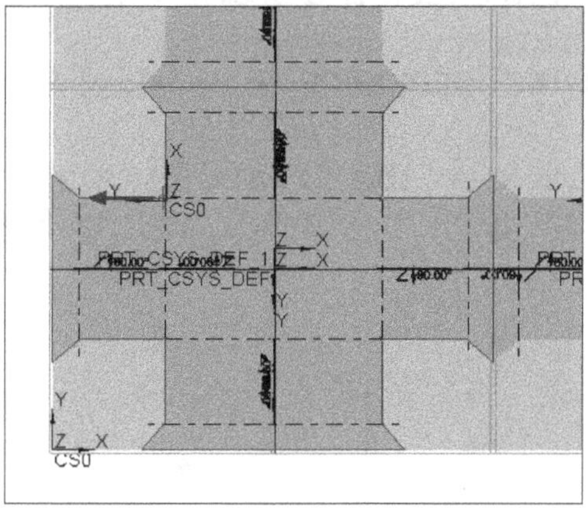

Figure-18. Edges of flat pattern selected for contouring

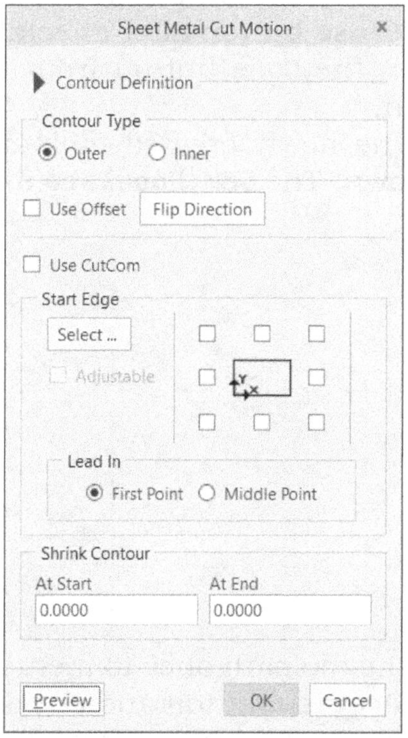

Figure-19. Sheet Metal Cut Motion dialog box

- Click on the **Select** button in **Start Edge** area of the dialog box and select desired edge from where you want cutting operation to begin.
- Select the **Use CutCom** check box if you want to specify the cutter compensation. Set desired parameters after selecting the check box.

- Specify the other parameters and click on the **OK** button. The **SMT NC SEQUENCE** dialog box will be displayed.
- Double-click on the optional features in this dialog box to define them.
- Click on the **Parameters** button to define machine cutting parameters. The **SMM PARAMETERS** dialog box will be displayed as discussed earlier. Set desired parameters and click on the **OK** button.
- Click on the **Preview** button to check toolpath. The **SMT MFG NCL PLAYER** dialog box will be displayed; refer to Figure-20.

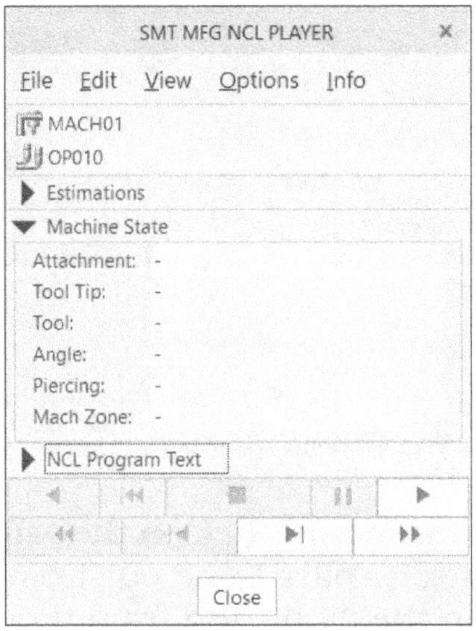

Figure-20. SMT MFG NCL PLAYER dialog box

- Click on the **Play** button in this dialog box to check the preview of toolpath. Click on the **Close** button after checking the preview.
- Click on the **Done** button from the **SMT NC SEQUENCE** dialog box to create the toolpath.
- Select the newly created toolpath and click on the **Create** button of **Populate** drop-down. The **SMM Populate** dialog box will be displayed; refer to Figure-21.

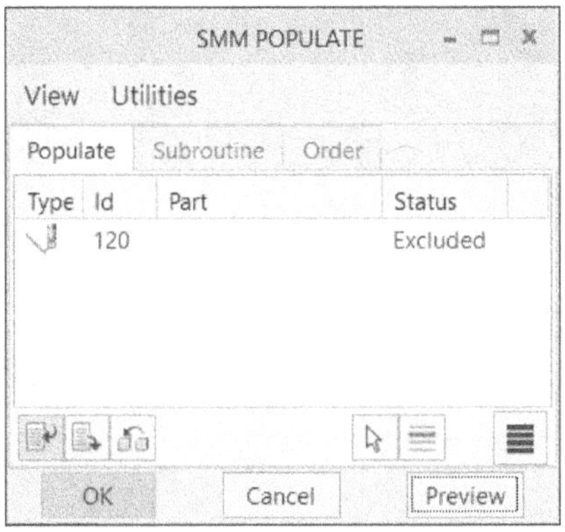

Figure-21. SMM POPULATE dialog box

- Select the toolpath once to include it. The status will be shown as included. Click on the **Preview** button and check if all instances of the part have been included.
- Click on the **OK** button from the **SMM POPULATE** dialog box to create toolpath including all instances.
- Click on the **Create** button from the **Optimize** drop-down at the bottom in the dialog box to automatically optimize toolpaths based on selected tool and machines. The **SMM Optimize** dialog box will be displayed; refer to Figure-22.

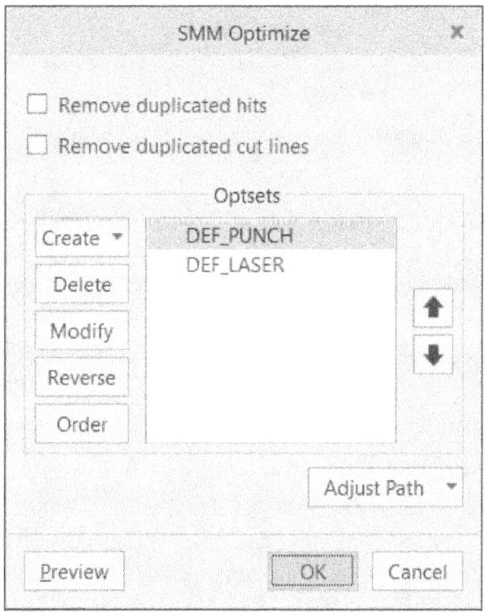

Figure-22. SMM Optimize dialog box

- Select desired optimization definition like select **DEF LASER** option from the list box to optimize toolpaths for laser cutting and click on the **OK** button from the dialog box.

Generating CL Output

- Select desired NC sequence from the **SMT MFG MACHINING** dialog box and click on the **CL Output** button. The **SMT MFG NCL PLAYER** dialog box will be displayed as discussed earlier. Check the toolpath by clicking on the play button; refer to Figure-23.

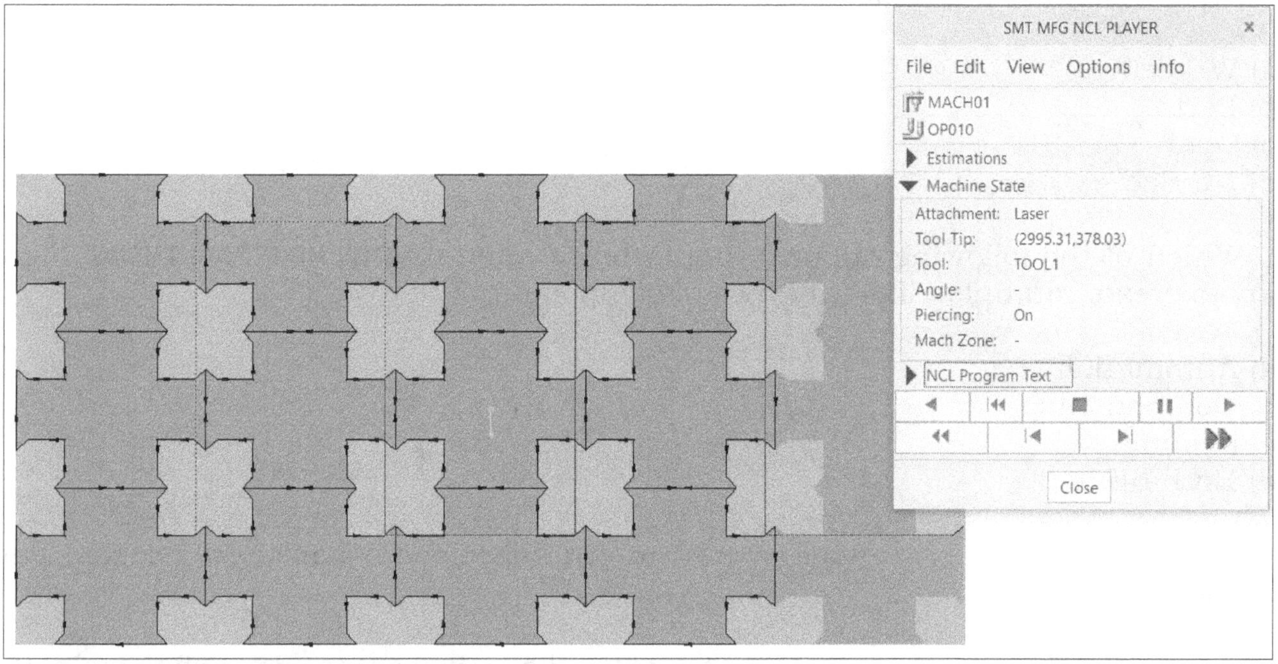

Figure-23. Toolpath for sheetmetal contouring

- Click on the **Save As** option from the **File** menu. The **Save a Copy** dialog box will be displayed; refer to Figure-24.

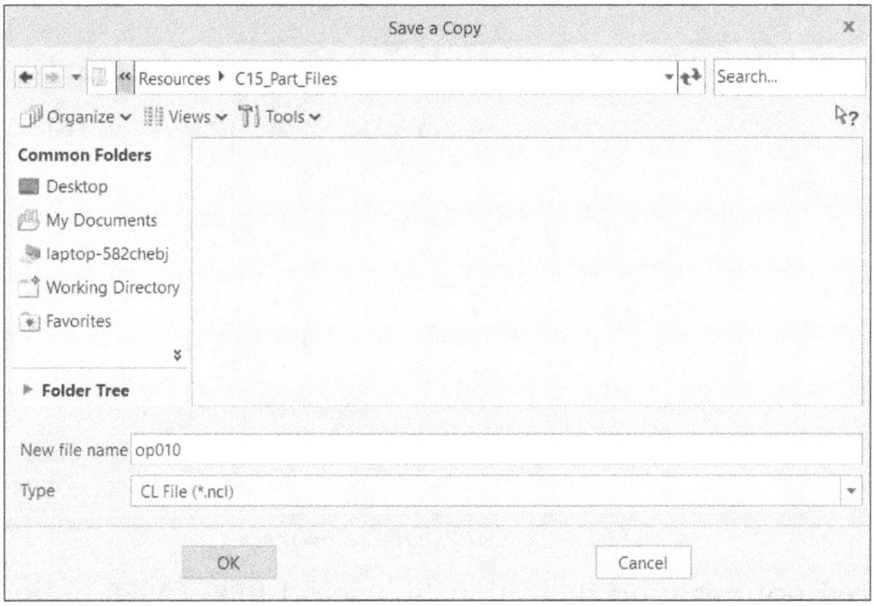

Figure-24. Save a Copy dialog box

- Specify desired name and location for the file and click on the **OK** button. The output file will be created.
- Save the manufacturing file at desired location to reuse later.

SELF ASSESSMENT

1. In which of the following tabs of **SMT MFG MACHINING** dialog box, the options to set workpiece size are available?

a) Wrkcell
b) Parts
c) Oper
d) NC Seq

2. Which of the following options should be selected in **SMT MFG MACHINING** dialog box to create multiple different types of components?

a) Automation
b) Components
c) Nesting
d) Both b & c

3. The .... tool is used to cut sheet metal based on selected part boundaries.

4. The tools in the .... tab of the dialog box are used to define toolpaths and parameters for create sheet metal part on machine.

5. The **Slitting** tool is used to punch the primary impression on sheet metal. (T/F)

6. The **Edge Nibbling** tool is used to cut contour on sheet metal by successive overlapping slits or notches. (T/F)

7. Which option should you select from the Wrkcell tab to define the type of machine used for sheet metal cutting or punching?

a) Coordinate System
b) Parameters
c) Type
d) Tool Settings

8. What does the LASER option in the Wrkcell tab signify?

a) Punching the metal sheet
b) Cutting the metal sheet
c) Flame heating the metal sheet
d) Deforming the metal sheet

9. Which dialog box is used to set the dimensions and material of the sheet metal workpiece?

a) Oper tab
b) SMT MFG AUTOMATION
c) Parts tab of SMT MFG MACHINING
d) Tool Setup

10. Which button is used to create multiple tools in a turret machine setup?

a) Create New in Tool Setup
b) Setup in SMT MFG AUTOMATION
c) Turret in SMT MFG MACHINING
d) Parameters in Wrkcell tab

11. What is the purpose of the Contouring tool in the NC Seq tab?

a) To split the leftover metal
b) To punch holes in the sheet
c) To cut the sheet based on part boundaries
d) To smoothen the edges of a part

12. What should you do if you want to load a flat pattern created in a 2D CAD software?

a) Select the Parts from Mfg option
b) Select the Cell of Parts option
c) Select the Part w/o NC Seqs option
d) Select the DXF File option

13. What is the function of the Populate tool in NC Sequence creation?

a) Save NC files to a directory
b) Preview toolpath before generating CL data
c) Include toolpath for all instances of part
d) Create tools for turret

14. What is the final step to generate the NC output after verifying toolpath?

a) Click on Create in Optimize
b) Click on CL Output and save using Save As
c) Select the Automation option
d) Click on Setup button

15. What option should you use in the Parts tab to arrange multiple different parts on a single sheet?

a) Automation
b) Components
c) Nesting
d) Oper

Answers to Self Assessment Questions :

1. (b) **2.** (c) **3.** Contouring **4.** NC Seq **5.** F **6.** T

Chapter 16

Simulation Studies in Creo Parametric

Topics Covered

The major topics covered in this chapter are:

- ***Introduction***
- ***Structure Simulation Study***
- ***Thermal Simulation Study***
- ***Modal Simulation Study***
- ***Fluid Simulation Study***

INTRODUCTION

Simulation is the study of effects caused on an object due to real-world loading conditions. Computer Simulation is a type of simulation which uses CAD models to represent real objects and it applies various load conditions on the model to study the real-world effects. Creo Parametric is a CAD-CAM-CAE software package. In Creo Parametric Simulation, we apply loads on a constrained model under predefined environmental conditions and check the result (visually and/or in the form of tabular data). The types of simulation studies that can be performed in Creo Parametric are given next.

Creo Live Simulation is a tool in Creo CAD software that lets engineers perform simulation in real time on a parametric model. So, every time you make a change in your model, you'll see the consequences instantaneously in the modeling environment. Creo Live Simulation is an integration of ANSYS engineering simulation software, embedded within the 3D Creo Parametric modeling environment that provides real-time analysis for static structural, thermal, and modal (vibration) simulation.

STARTING SIMULATION IN CREO PARAMETRIC

In Creo Parametric, every workspace is available in a seamless manner. To start simulation in Creo Parametric 13.0, open the model on which you want to do the simulation and click on **Live Simulation** tab from the **Ribbon**. The Simulation workspace will become active; refer to Figure-1.

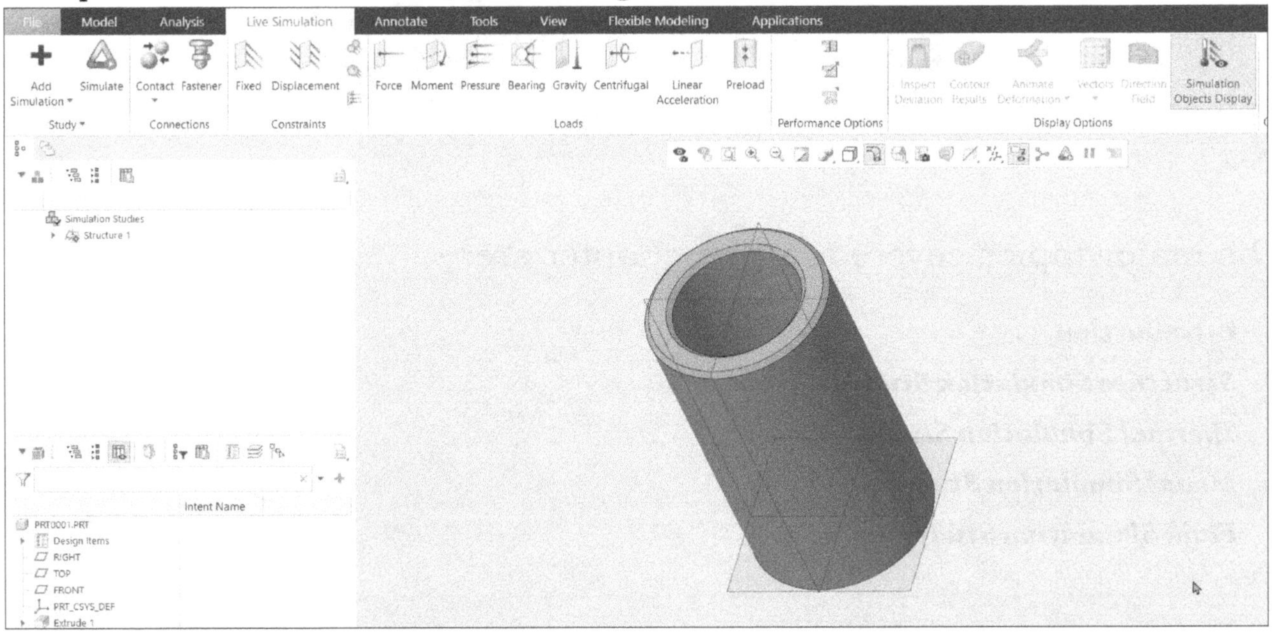

Figure-1. Simulation workspace

STARTING STRUCTURE SIMULATION STUDY

The **Structure Simulation Study** is used to evaluate stress and deformation of a solid model. This study determines the structural integrity of components subjected to real-world constraints and loads. It also examines stress and deflection results.

- Click on the **Structure Simulation Study** option from the **Add Simulation** drop-down in the **Study** panel of the **Ribbon**. The tools related to **Structure Simulation Study** will be displayed in the toolbar; refer to Figure-2.

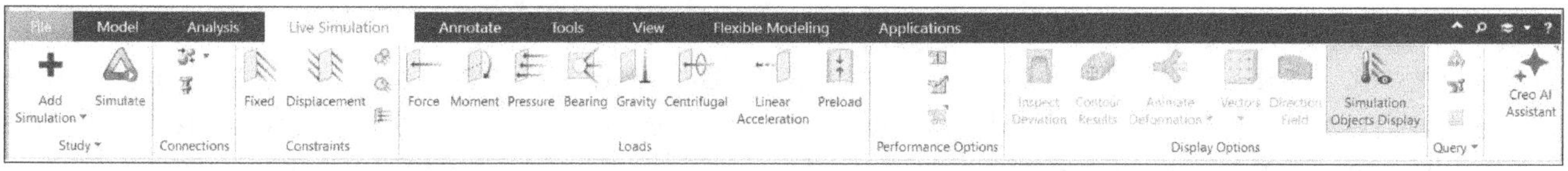

Figure-2. Structure Simulation Study tools

Scope

The **Scope** tool is used to specify which components of the assembly are to be included in the simulation live study. The procedure to use this tool is discussed next.

- Click on the **Scope** tool from **Setup** panel of the **Ribbon**. The **Simulation Scope** dialog box will be displayed; refer to Figure-3.

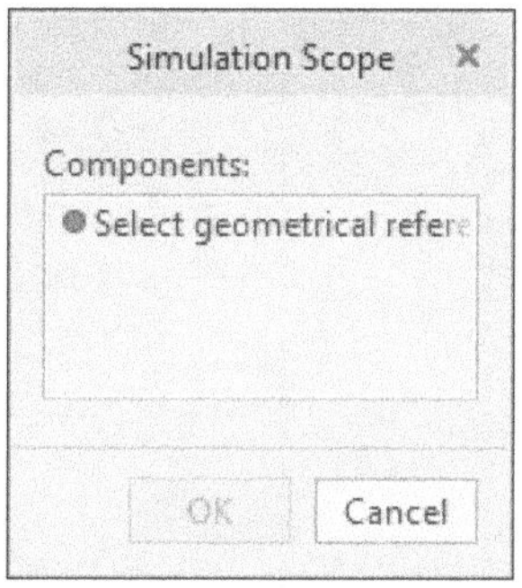

Figure-3. Simulation Scope dialog box

- Select desired components of the assembly as references; refer to Figure-4 and click on the **OK** button. The scope will be added to the **Model tree**; refer to Figure-5.

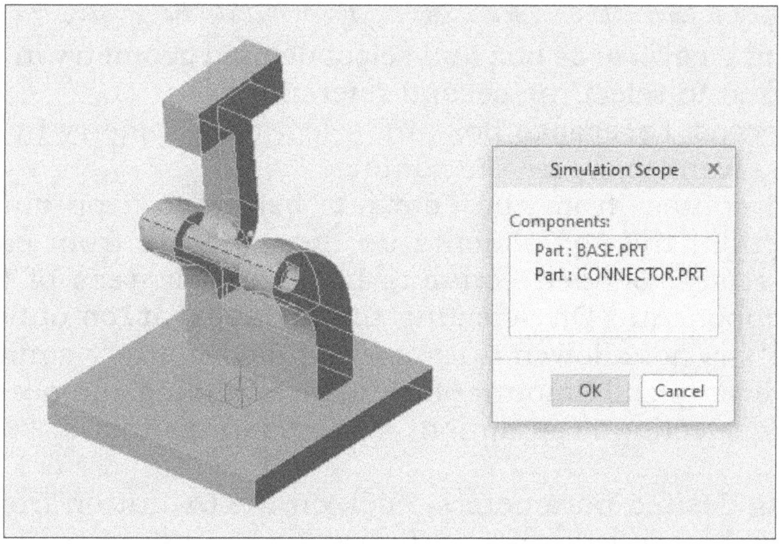

Figure-4. Components selected

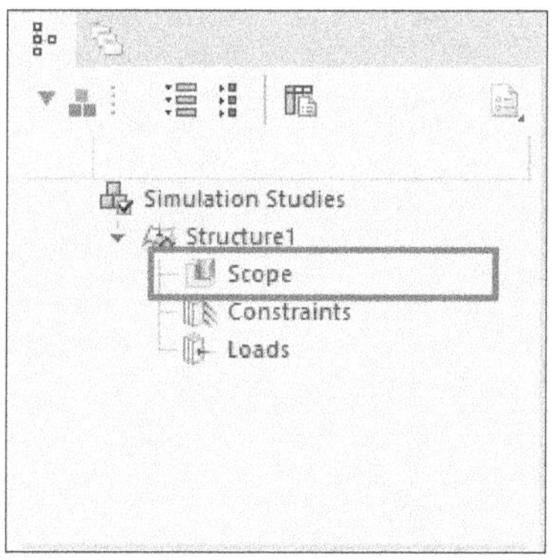

Figure-5. Scope added

Applying contact

The **Contact** tool is used to create contacts between references within your model either manually or automatically. You can create contacts between surfaces, edges, and vertices. The procedure to use this tool is discussed next.

- Click on the **Contact** tool from **Contact** drop-down in the **Connections** panel of the **Ribbon**. The **Contact Definition** dialog box will be displayed; refer to Figure-6. You will be asked to select the first reference.
- Specify desired name of the contact in the **Name** edit box of the dialog box.
- Click on the **Change the color** button next to the **Name** edit box and select desired color of the contact from the **Color Editor** dialog box; refer to Figure-7.

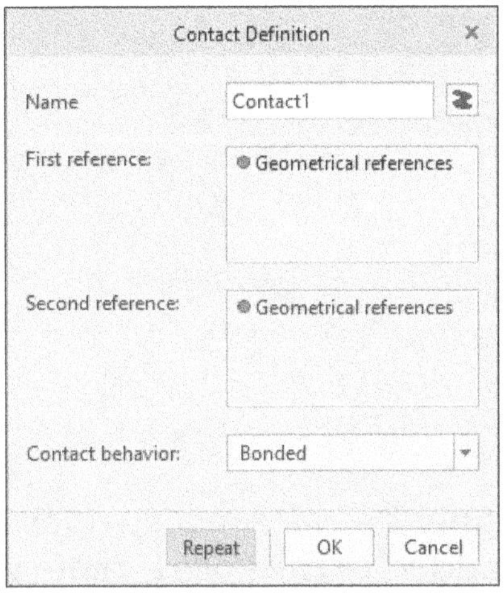

Figure-6. Contact Definition dialog box

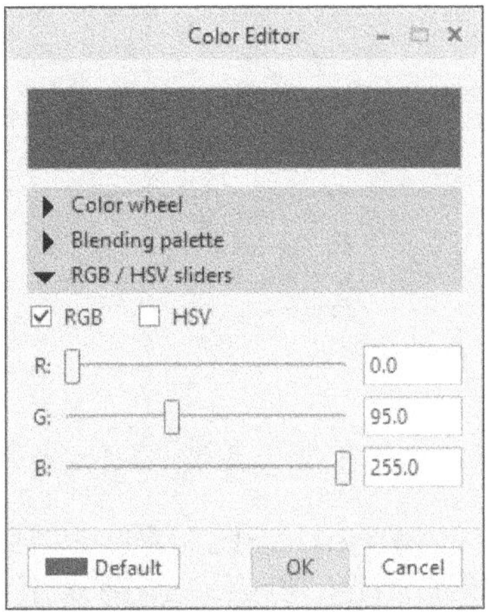

Figure-7. Color Editor dialog box

- Click in the **First reference** box and select desired geometry in the drawing area. You will be asked to select the second reference.
- Click in the **Second reference** box and select the geometry in the drawing area with which you want to create the contact.
- Select desired contact from the **Contact behavior** drop-down. On selecting the **Bonded** option, the components do not separate from each other during a simulation study. Bonded contacts have zero degrees of freedom between interfacing components. On selecting the **No separation** option, separation of the components is not allowed during a simulation study similar to the bonded contacts. However, small amount of frictionless sliding can occur along surfaces in contact. On selecting **Free** option, surfaces in contact have no effect on one another.
- After specifying desired parameters, click on the **OK** button from the dialog box. The contact will be applied; refer to Figure-8.

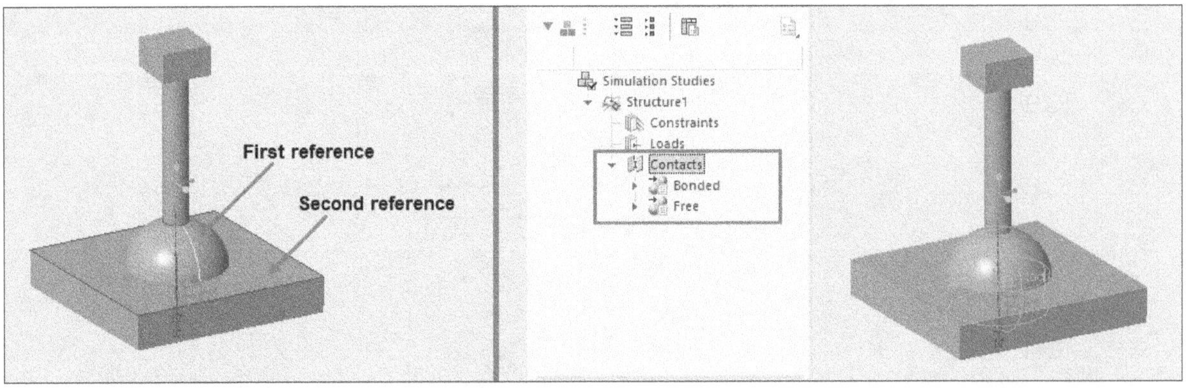

Figure-8. Contact applied

Detecting Contacts

The **Detect Contacts** tool is used to detect contacts between two or more selected solid bodies or components that are within a specified distance from each other for the active simulation study. The procedure to use this tool is discussed next.

- Click on the **Detect Contacts** tool from **Contact** drop-down in the **Connections** panel of the **Ribbon**. The **Detect Contacts** dialog box will be displayed; refer to Figure-9. You will be asked to select the geometrical references.

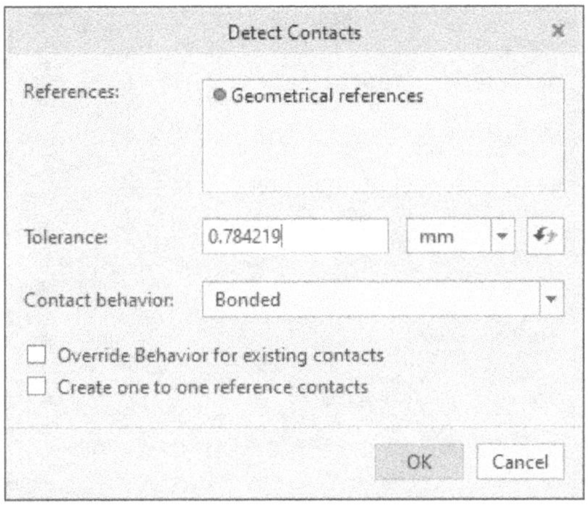

Figure-9. Detect Contacts dialog box

- Click in the **References** box and select desired references in the drawing area.
- Specify desired tolerance value in the **Tolerance** edit box to define the limit of contact detection gap and select desired unit from the drop-down next to the **Tolerance** edit box.
- Select desired contact from **Contact behavior** drop-down.
- Select **Override Behavior for existing contacts** check box to apply specified behavior to all contacts, overriding the current behavior.
- Select **Create one to one reference contacts** check box to create contacts for model containing shell pairs.
- After specifying desired parameters, click on the **OK** button from the dialog box. The contacts will be detected; refer to Figure-10.

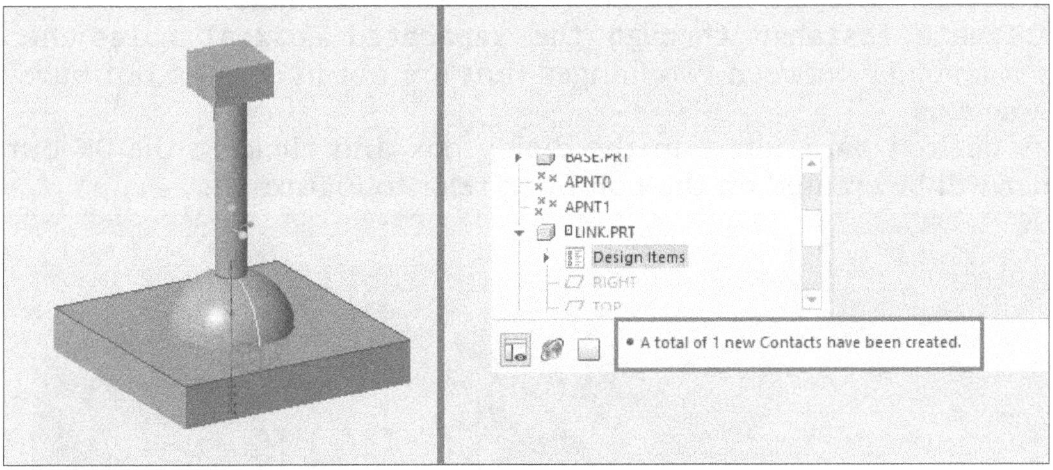

Figure-10. Contacts detected

Fastener

The **Fastener** tool is used to create fasteners that are simplified versions of bolted joints. These fasteners help analyze how loads are transferred between parts and calculate the resulting stress and deformation in the model. The procedure to use this tool is discussed next.

- Click on the **Fastener** tool from **Connections** panel in the **Live Simulation** tab of the **Ribbon**. The **Fastener Definition** dialog box will be displayed; refer to Figure-11.

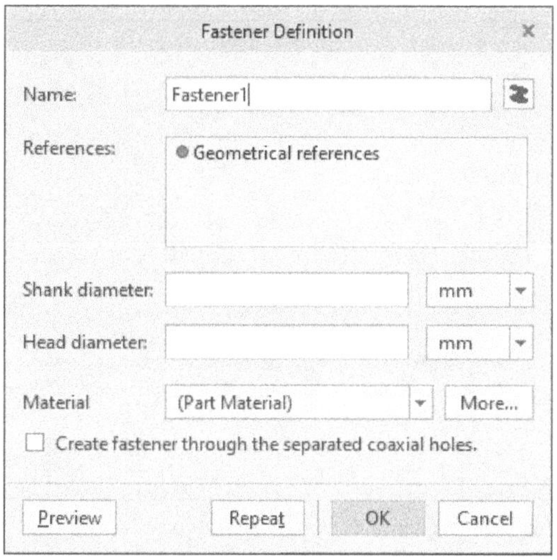

Figure-11. Fastener Definition dialog box

- Specify desired name of the fastener in the **Name** edit box. Click on **Change the color** button to change the color of fastener to be created.
- Click on the **References** selection box and select inner surface of desired hole as a geometrical reference through which the fastener is to be created. The dimension of the fastener to be created will be automatically calculated and displayed in the **Shank diameter** and **Head diameter** edit boxes. Make sure that the shank diameter is less than the bolt hole diameter and the head diameter is more than the bolt hole diameter.
- Specify desired material for the fastener from **Material** drop-down.
- Click on the **More** button, the **Material** dialog box will be displayed as discussed earlier in this book to define desired material for the fastener.
- Select **Create fastener through the separated coaxial holes** check box to create a fastener between two flanges that are not in contact but have holes on the same axis.
- Specify desired parameters in the dialog box and click on the **OK** button. The fastener will be created on the bolt hole; refer to Figure-12.

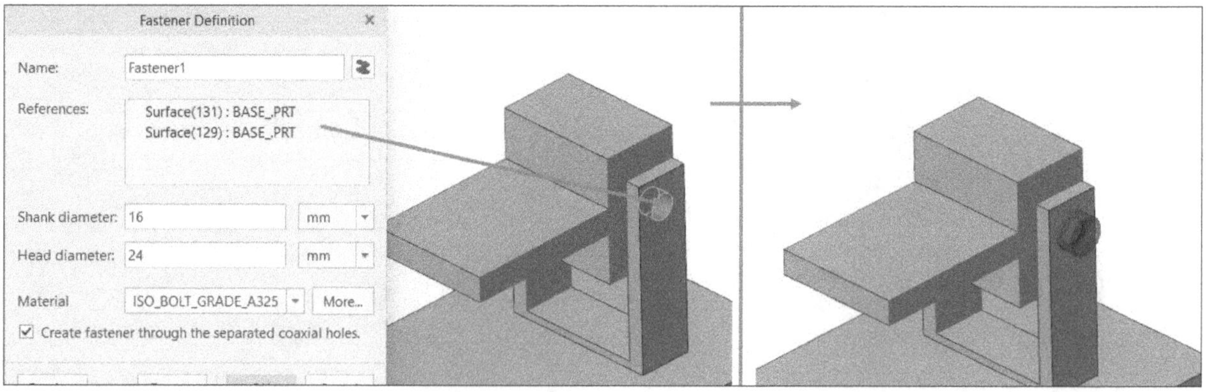

Figure-12. Fastener created

APPLYING CONSTRAINTS

Constraints are used to restrict motion of part when load is applied to form equilibrium. The tools to apply constraints are available in **Constraints** panel of **Live Simulation** tab in the **Ribbon**; refer to Figure-13.

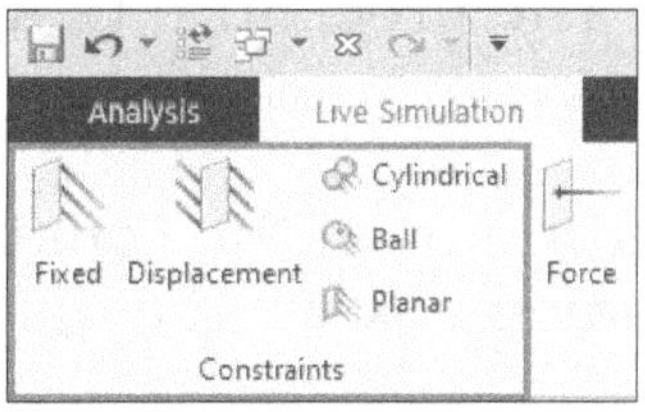

Figure-13. Constraints panel

The procedure to apply different type of constraints are discussed next.

Applying Fixed Constraint

A fixed constraint prevents selected surface from moving or deforming, that is it removes all degrees of freedom from the surface. The procedure to apply fixed constraint is given next.

- Click on the **Fixed** button from the **Constraints** panel of the **Ribbon**. The **Fixed Constraint** dialog box will be displayed; refer to Figure-14.

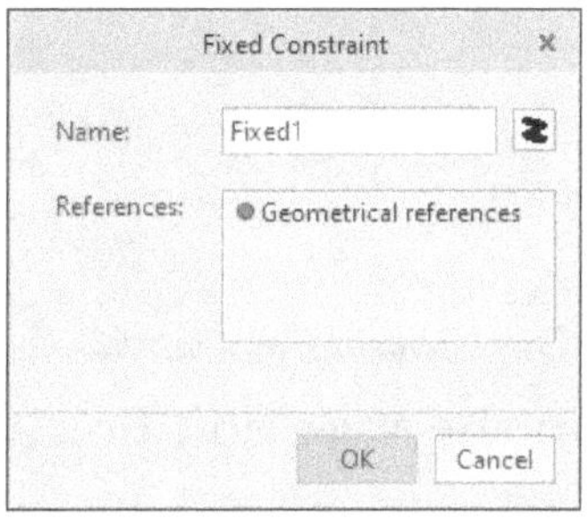

Figure-14. Fixed Constraint dialog box

- Specify the constraint name in the **Name** edit box as desired.
- Click on **Change the color** button next to the **Name** edit box if you want to change the color of icon, distribution, or text of the constraint.
- Select one or more surfaces of the solid model that you want to be fixed; refer to Figure-15.

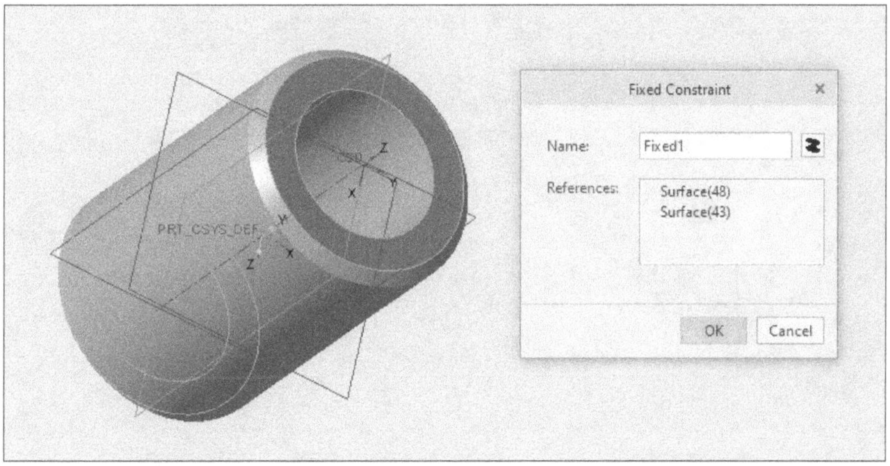

Figure-15. Surfaces selected for fixed constraint

- Click on the **OK** button from the dialog box to fix the selected geometries.

Applying Displacement Constraint

A displacement constraint creates an enforced translation displacement in a specified direction for a selected surface. The procedure to apply displacement constraint is given next.

- Click on the **Displacement** button from the **Constraints** panel of the **Ribbon**. The **Displacement Constraint** dialog box will be displayed; refer to Figure-16.

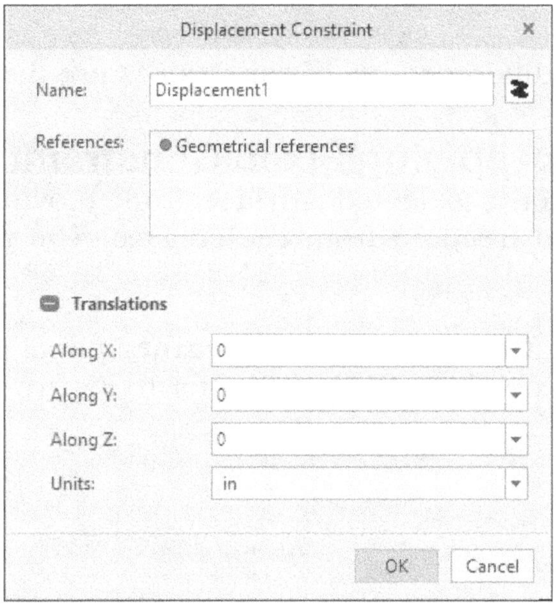

Figure-16. Displacement Constraint dialog box

- Specify the constraint name in the **Name** edit box as you want or accept the default name.
- Click on **Change the color** button next to the **Name** edit box if you want to change the color of the constraint.
- Select the surfaces of the model which you want to be displaced; refer to Figure-17.

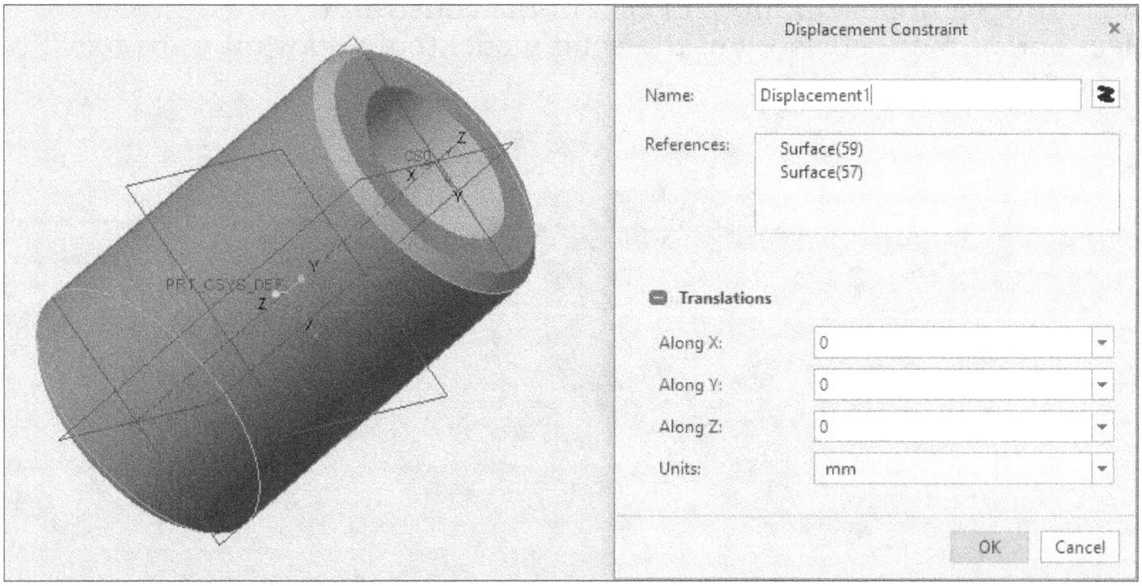

Figure-17. Surface selected for displacement constraint

- Specify desired value in the **X**, **Y**, or **Z** edit boxes from the **Translations** area of the dialog box to define translation limit in respective directions. Specifying **0** in edit box will restrict movement in that direction.
- Select desired unit for displacement from the **Units** drop-down.
- Click on the **OK** button from the dialog box to create the constraint.

Applying Cylindrical Constraint

A cylindrical constraint controls the axial movement of a cylindrical surface, while allowing angular movement, and keeping radial movement fixed. It is particularly useful when a surface must move in one or more directions, but must be fixed in the remaining directions. The procedure to apply cylindrical constraint is given next.

- Click on the **Cylindrical** button from **Constraints** panel of the **Ribbon**. The **Cylindrical Constraint** dialog box will be displayed; refer to Figure-18.

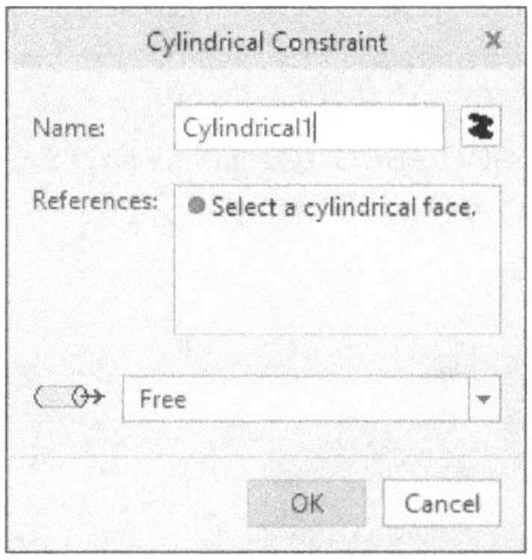

Figure-18. Cylindrical Constraint dialog box

- Specify the parameters as discussed for previous constraints. Select surface of the model which you want to be constrained cylindrical; refer to Figure-19.

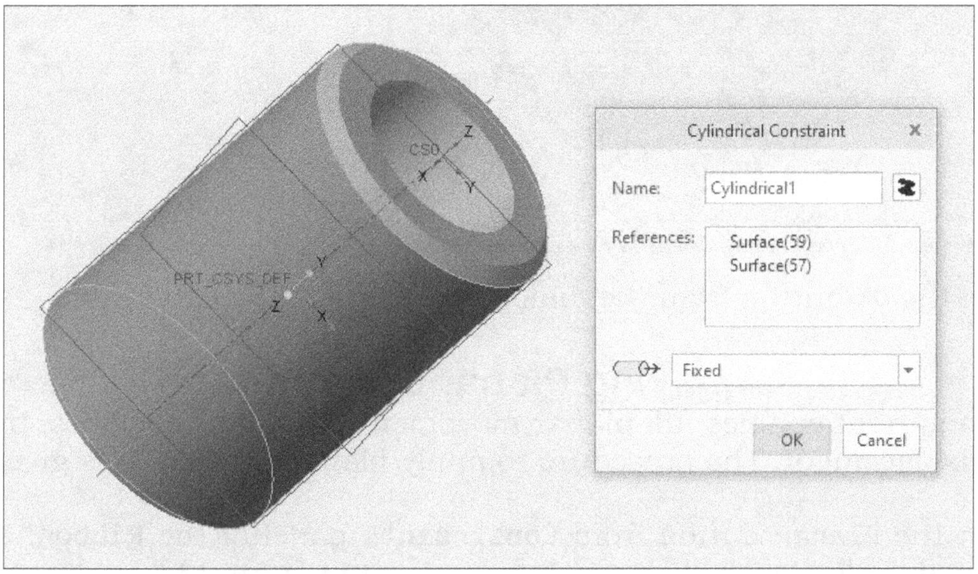

Figure-19. Surface selected for cylindrical constraint

- Select desired option from the **Axial displacement** drop-down. Select **Free** option to allow the axial displacement and select **Fixed** option to constrain the axial displacement.
- Click on the **OK** button from the dialog box to apply the constraint.

Applying Ball Constraint

A ball constraint is a surface constraint that represents a ball joint where the translation is fixed and the rotation is free. The procedure to apply ball constraint is given next.

- Click on the **Ball** button from the **Constraints** panel of the **Ribbon**. The **Ball Constraint** dialog box will be displayed; refer to Figure-20.

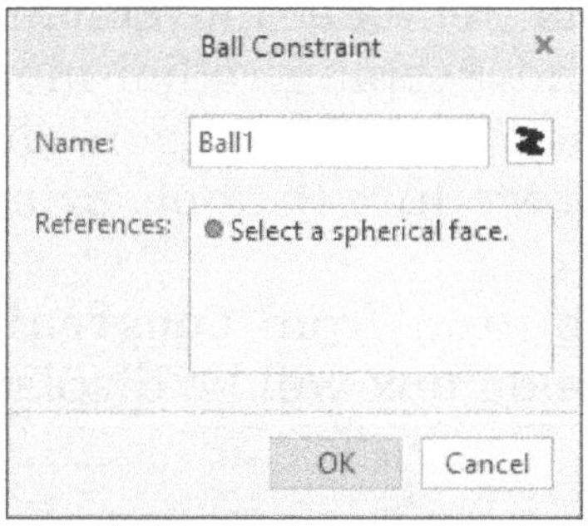

Figure-20. Ball Constraint dialog box

- Specify the parameters as discussed for previous constraints. Select the spherical surfaces of the model as shown in Figure-21.

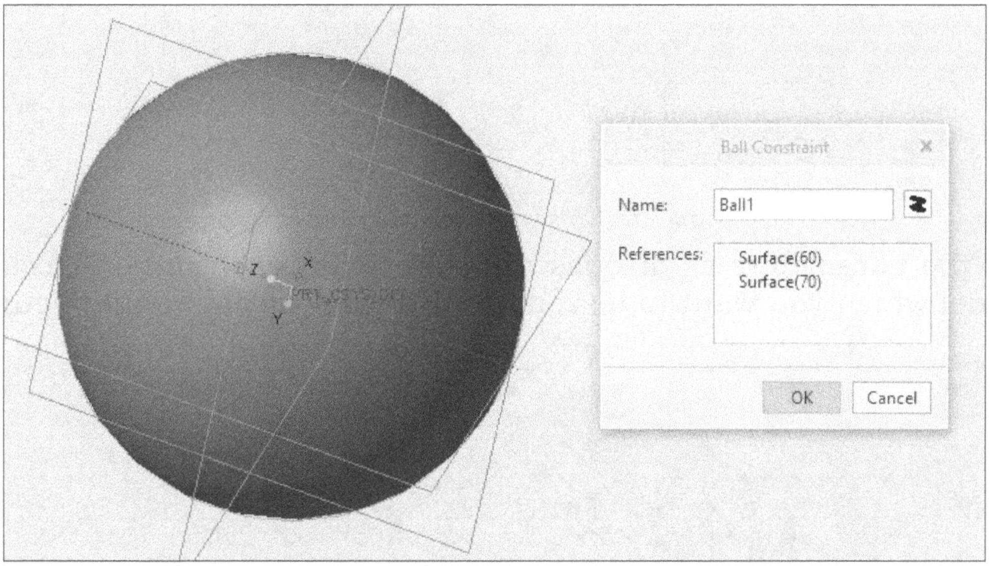

Figure-21. Spherical surface selected for ball constraint

- Click on the **OK** button from the dialog box to apply the constraint.

Applying Planar Constraint

A planar constraint enables full planar movement for planar surfaces, but restricts off-plane displacement. The procedure to apply planar constraint is given next.

- Click on the **Planar** button from **Constraints** panel of the **Ribbon**. The **Planar Constraint** dialog box will be displayed; refer to Figure-22.

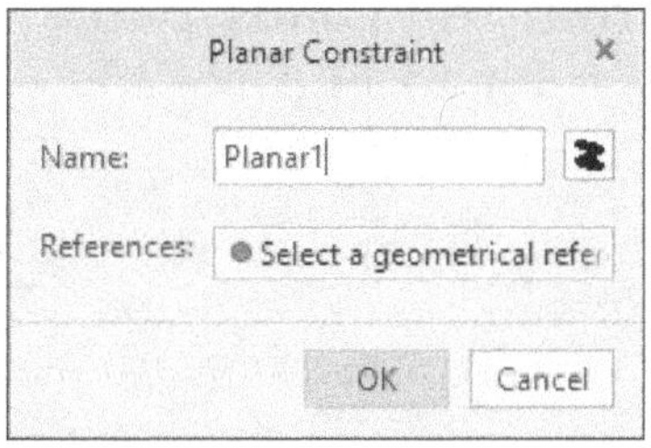

Figure-22. Planar Constraint dialog box

- Specify the parameters as discussed for previous constraints. Select planar face of the model to constrain; refer to Figure-23. You can also select the geometry before opening the dialog box.

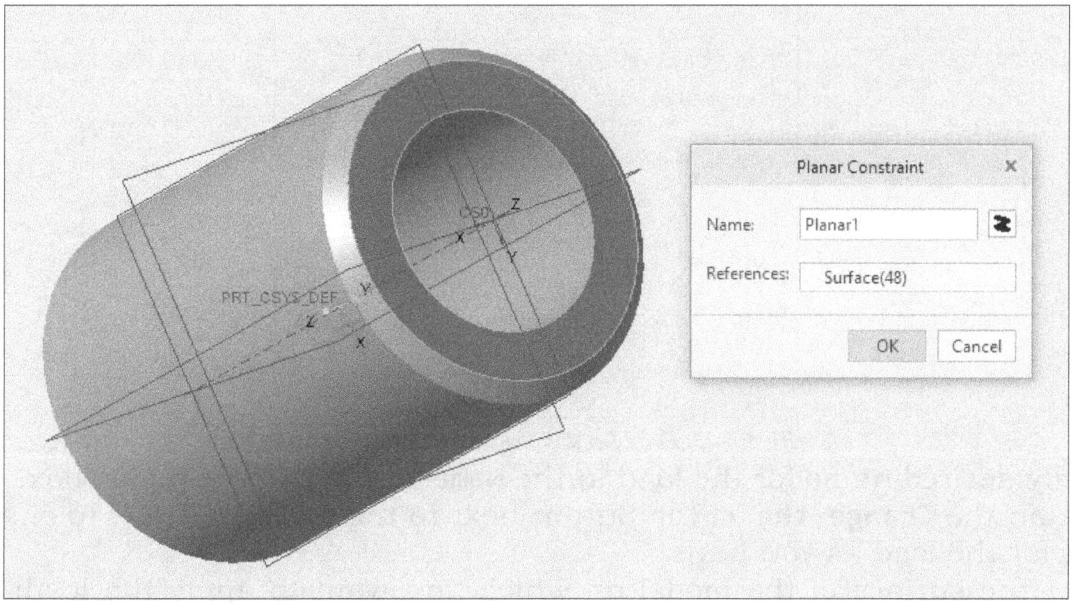

Figure-23. Plane surface selected for planar constraint

- Click on the **OK** button from the dialog box to create the constraint.

APPLYING LOADS

Loads in Creo Parametric are the representation of forces and loads applied on the part in real application. The tools to apply loads are available in the **Loads** panel in the **Toolbar**; refer to Figure-24.

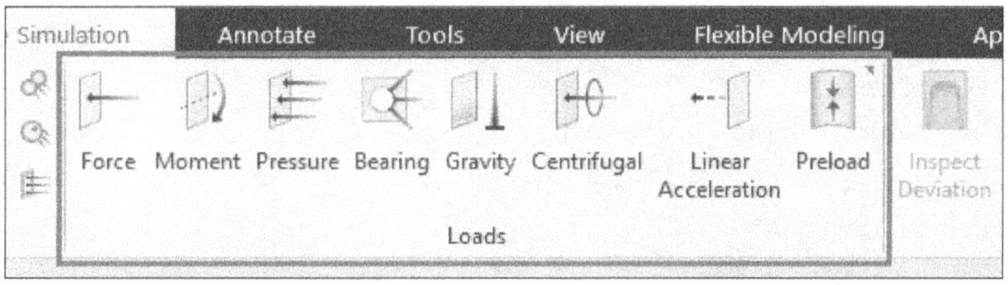

Figure-24. Loads panel

The procedures to apply different type of loads are discussed next.

Applying Force Load

You can apply force load on the faces of your model. The procedure to apply force load is given next.

- Click on the **Force** button from the **Loads** panel in the **Ribbon**. The **Force Load** dialog box will be displayed; refer to Figure-25.

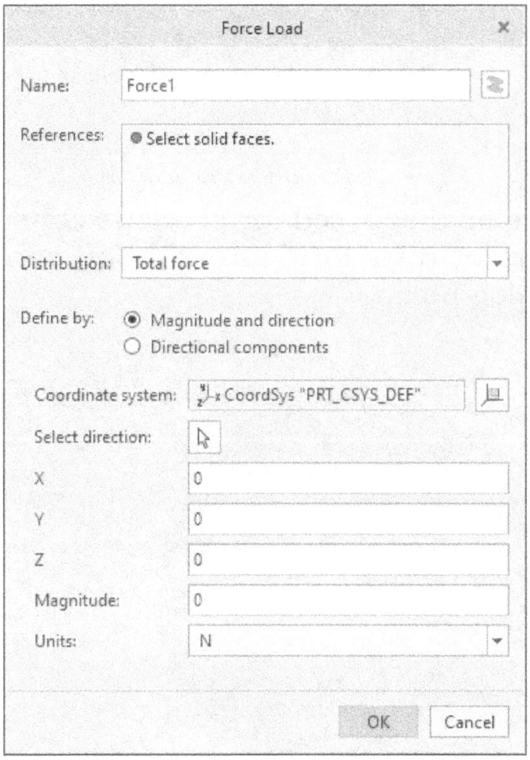

Figure-25. Force Load dialog box

- Specify desired name for the load in the **Name** edit box of the dialog box.
- Click on the **Change the color** button next to the name edit box to change the color for the load as you want.
- Select the surface of the model on which you want to apply the load; refer to Figure-26.

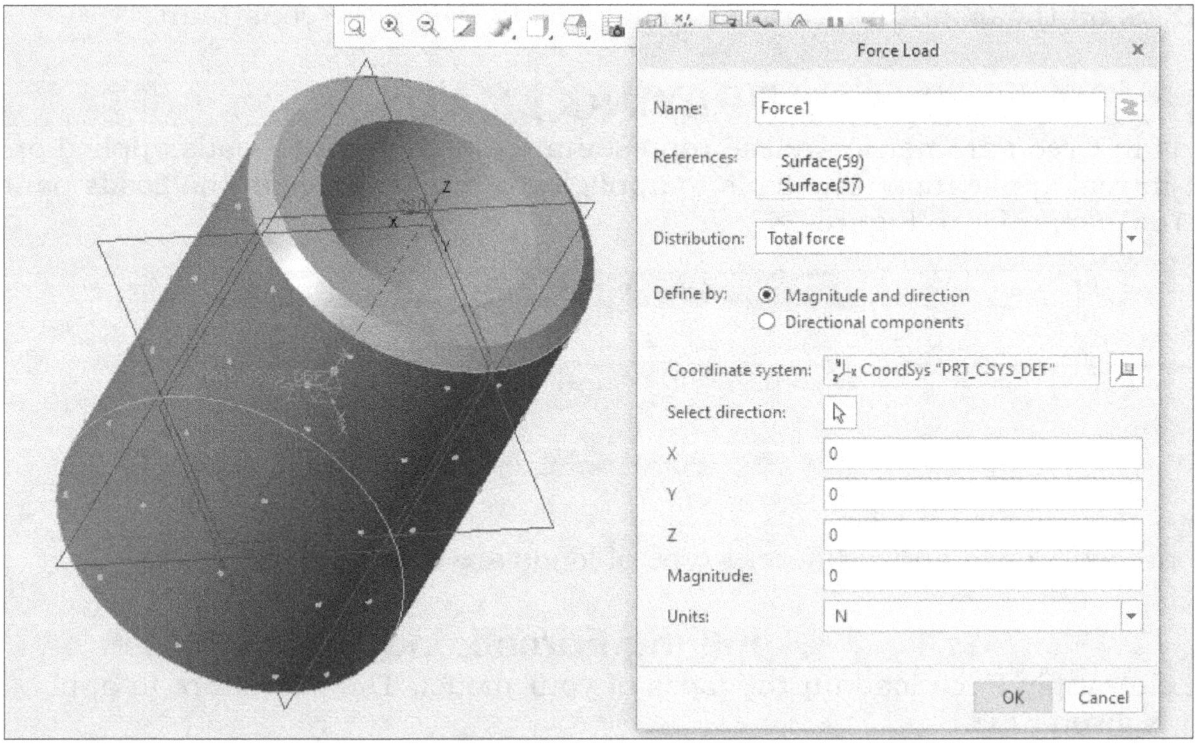

Figure-26. Surface selected to apply the force load

- Select the **Total force** option from the **Distribution** drop-down to define the total force for the selected surface.
- Select the **Total load at point** option from the **Distribution** drop-down to define a distributed load that is statically equivalent to a load applied to a single point.
- Select the **Magnitude and direction** option from the **Define by** area of the dialog box to specify the direction for the load in the **X**, **Y**, or **Z** edit box. Alternatively, click on the **Select direction** button and select a linear edge or planar surface to specify the direction of the load. Specify the magnitude of the load in the **Magnitude** edit box.
- Select the **Directional components** option from the **Define by** area to specify the components of the load for each coordinate direction **X**, **Y**, or **Z** and specify the value of the unit vectors for the direction in the **X**, **Y**, or **Z** edit boxes.
- Select desired units for the load from the **Units** drop-down.
- Click on the **OK** button from the dialog box to apply the load on the model.

Applying Moment Load

The **Moment** tool in **Loads** panel is used to apply bending load on selected faces of model. The procedure to apply the moment load is discussed next.

- Click on the **Moment** button from the **Loads** panel in the **Ribbon**. The **Moment Load** dialog box will be displayed; refer to Figure-27.

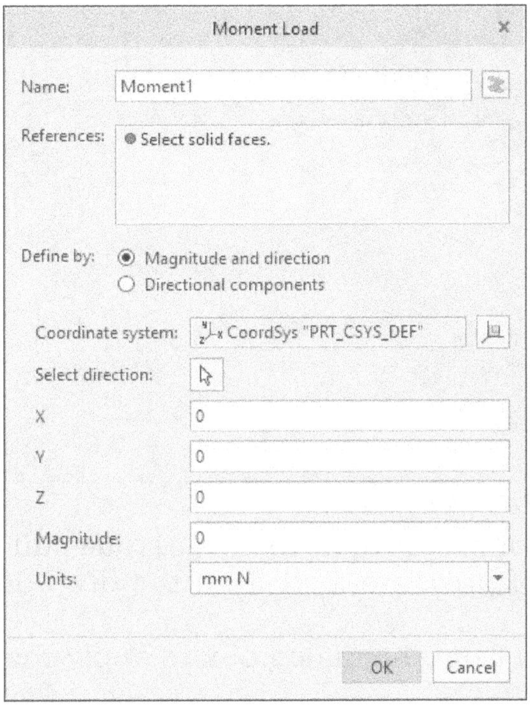

Figure-27. Moment Load dialog box

- Specify the parameters as discussed for the force load and click on the **OK** button from the dialog box to apply the moment load.

Applying Pressure Load

Pressure loads are applied on model faces. A positive pressure load always acts opposite to the normal direction of the surface at every location, even if the surface is curved. The procedure to apply the pressure load is given next.

- Click on the **Pressure** button from the **Loads** panel in the **Ribbon**. The **Pressure Load** dialog box will be displayed; refer to Figure-28.

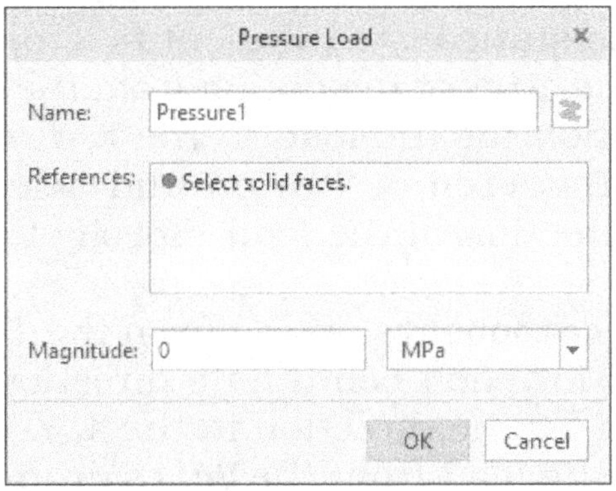

Figure-28. Pressure Load dialog box

- Specify desired name for the load in the **Name** edit box.
- Click on **Change the color** button next to the name edit box to specify desired color for the load.
- Select the faces on which you want to apply the pressure load; refer to Figure-29.

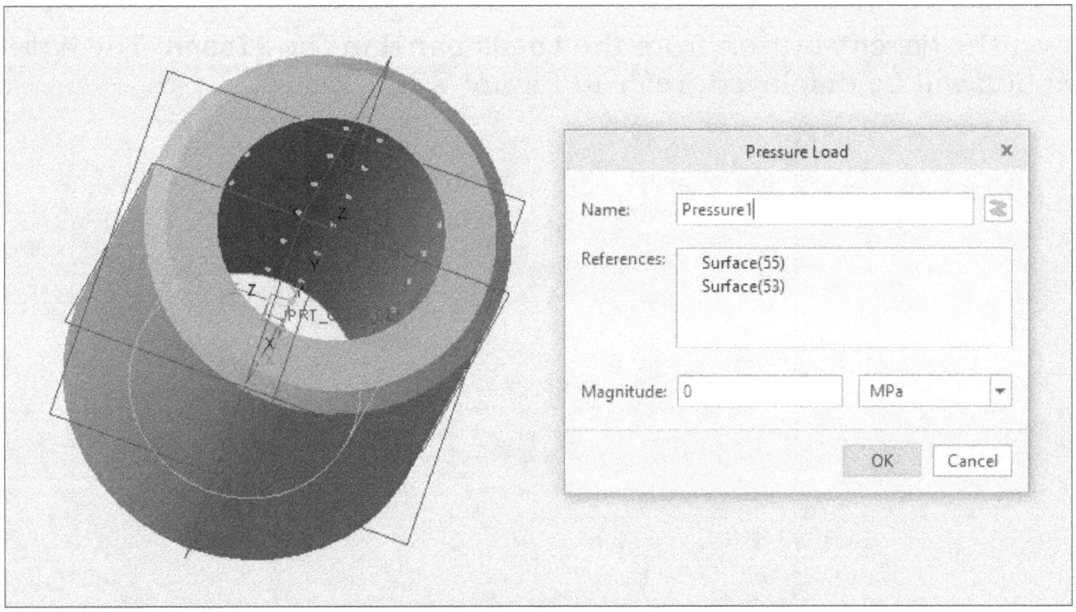

Figure-29. Surface selected to apply the pressure load

- Specify desired value of pressure in the **Magnitude** edit box.
- Specify desired unit of pressure load from the drop-down available next to the magnitude edit box.
- Click on the **OK** button from the dialog box to apply the load.

Applying Gravity Load

Gravity loads are body loads that simulate the force of gravity as it affects your model. When you define a gravity load, you specify the components of gravitational acceleration along one of the coordinate directions. You can also specify a negative value in the edit box for opposite direction load. The procedure to apply the gravity load is discussed next.

- Click on the **Gravity** button from the **Loads** panel in the **Ribbon**. The **Gravity Load** dialog box will be displayed; refer to Figure-30.

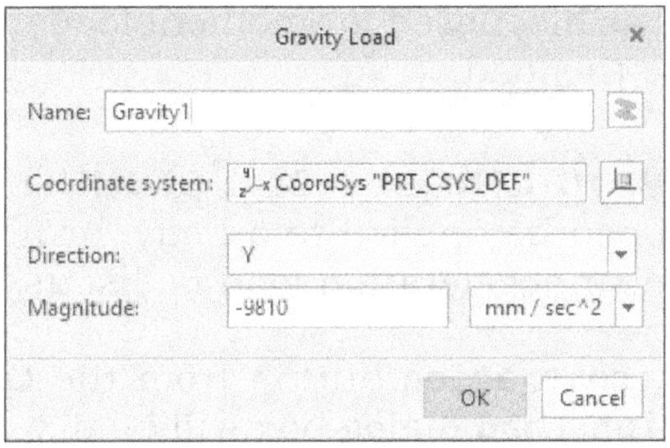

Figure-30. Gravity Load dialog box

- Specify desired name for the load in the **Name** edit box and specify desired color for the load by clicking on **Change the color** button available next to the name edit box.
- The default coordinate system of the model is the reference coordinate system and is displayed in the **Coordinate system** box. You can select difference reference coordinate system from the **Model Tree**.
- Select the direction of gravitational acceleration for the X, Y, or Z directions from the **Directions** drop-down.
- Specify desired value of gravity load in the **Magnitude** edit box and specify desired units for the gravitational acceleration from the drop-down available next to the magnitude edit box.
- Click on the **OK** button from the dialog box to create the load.

Applying Centrifugal Load

Centrifugal loads are body loads that simulate rigid body rotation for your model. When you define a centrifugal load, you specify either the vector components of angular velocity, or the direction vector and magnitude. The resulting body load acts in the direction opposite to the direction of centripetal and tangential velocity. The procedure to create centrifugal load is given next.

- Click on the **Centrifugal** button from the **Loads** panel in the **Ribbon**. The **Centrifugal Load** dialog box will be displayed; refer to Figure-31.

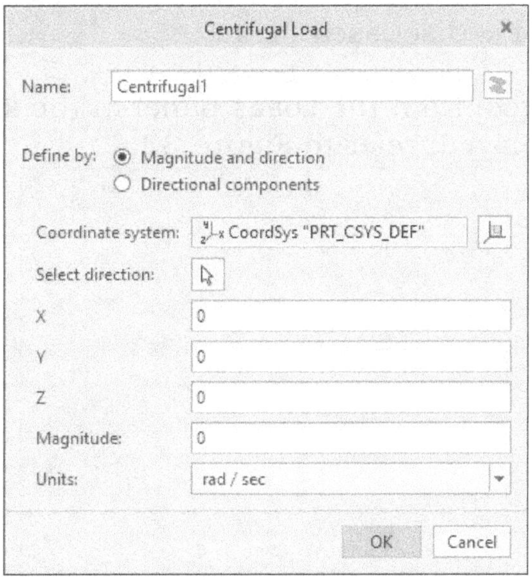

Figure-31. Centrifugal Load dialog box

- Specify the parameters as discussed for moment load and click on **OK** button from the dialog box to create the load.

Applying Linear Acceleration Load

A linear acceleration load can be applied to a body, or multiple bodies in a model. The procedure to apply linear acceleration load is discussed next.

- Click on the **Linear Acceleration** button from the **Loads** panel in the **Ribbon**. The **Linear Acceleration Load** dialog box will be displayed; refer to Figure-32.

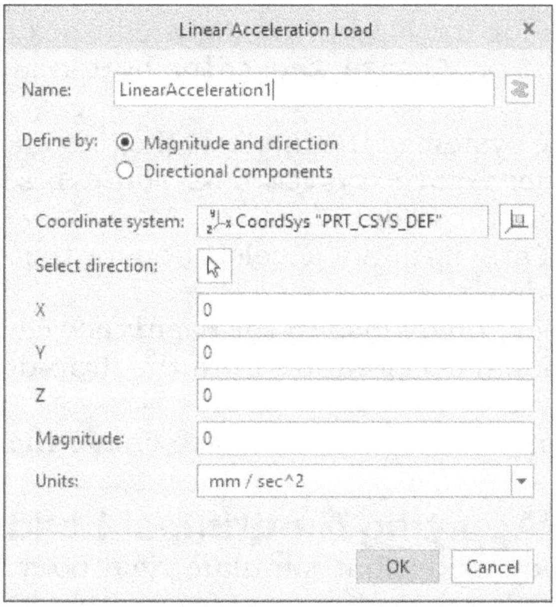

Figure-32. Linear Acceleration Load dialog box

- Specify the parameters as discussed for moment load and click on **OK** button from the dialog box to create the load.

Applying Preload

The **Preload** tool is used to simulate the condition where a fastener is tightened using torque to the bolt head or nut, even though no external load is applied. The procedure to use this tool is discussed next.

- Click on the **Preload** tool from the **Loads** panel in the **Ribbon**. The **Preload Load** dialog box will be displayed; refer to Figure-33.

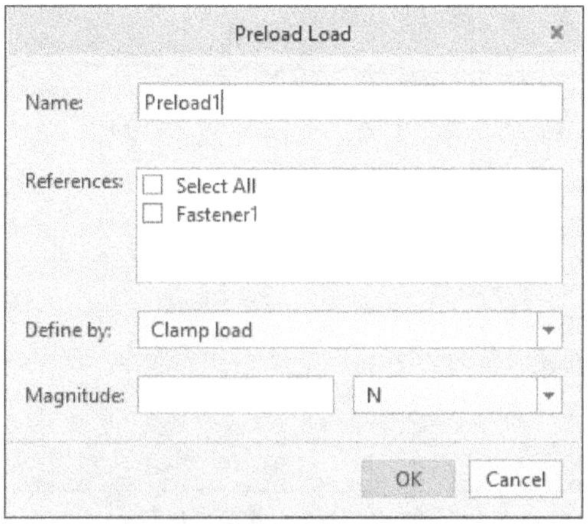

Figure-33. Preload Load dialog box

- Select the **Clamp load** option from the **Define by** drop-down and enter desired preload value applied to the bolt shank using appropriate force units. Select **Grip length adjustment** option from the drop-down and specify how much the flanges are compressed due to the preload using the appropriate length units. Select **Torque** option from the drop-down and enter desired value of torque needed to tighten the bolt to its required preload.
- Other parameters in the dialog box is same as discussed earlier.
- After specifying desired parameters, click on the **OK** button from the dialog box. The preload will be applied.

SETTING PERFORMANCE OPTIONS

The tools in the **Performance Options** panel are used to define balance between accuracy and performance; refer to . When you perform any FEA on computer, it is always a compromise between accuracy and speed at which results are achieved. If you try to get more accurate result then number of equations and their complexity increases hence increasing overall solution time.

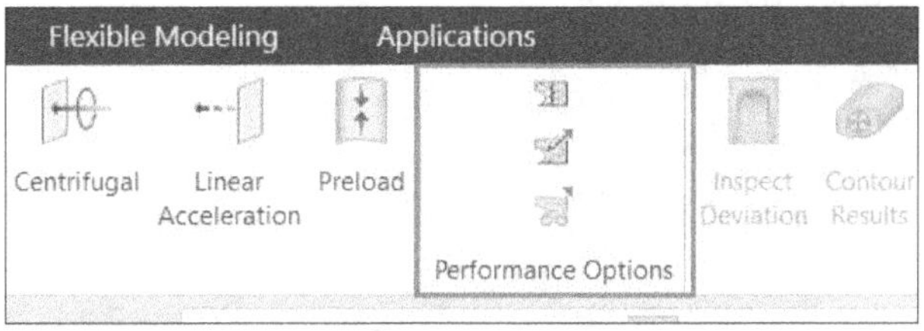

Figure-34. Performance Options panel

Defining Global Fidelity

The **Global Fidelity** tool is used to define accuracy level to be achieved in simulation result. At deeper understanding level, it defines the size of individual mesh elements. A lower size means more number of mesh elements in same body and better accuracy in results. On clicking this tool, the **Global Fidelity** dialog box is displayed; refer to Figure-35. Set the slider towards Accuracy to get more accurate results with longer processing time.

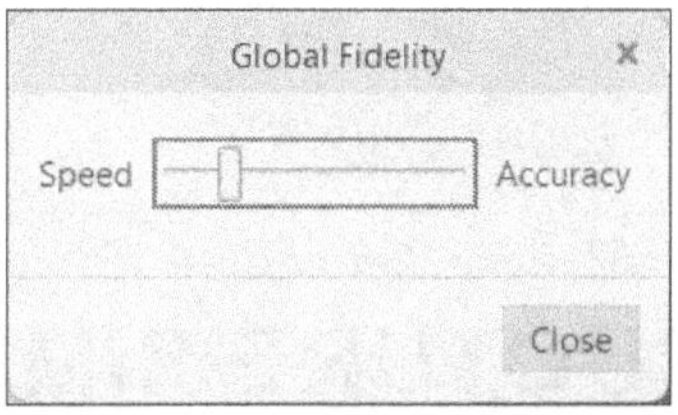

Figure-35. Global Fidelity dialog box

Local Refinement

The local refinement is used to set special size of mesh for selected body from the model. The local refinement is performed to increase accuracy in the area of interest where you expect the part to fail. The procedure to perform local refinement is given next.

- Click on the **Local Refinement** tool from the **Performance Options** panel in the **Live Simulation** tab of the **Ribbon**. The **Local Refinement** dialog box will be displayed; refer to Figure-36 and you will be asked to select body(s) for defining mesh size.
- Select the body to which you want to apply local mesh size refinement and set desired size of mesh elements in the **Size** edit box.
- Click on the **OK** button from the dialog box. The refinement will be applied.

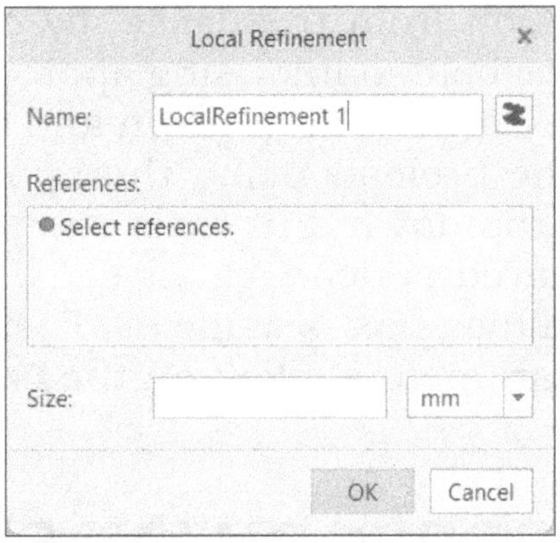

Figure-36. Local Refinement dialog box

Checking Element Size

The **Display Element Size** tool of **Performance Options** panel is used to show size of element on which you are hovering cursor in the model after running the analysis. Click on this tool after selecting **Simulate** tool from **Ribbon** and hover the cursor to check element size; refer to Figure-37.

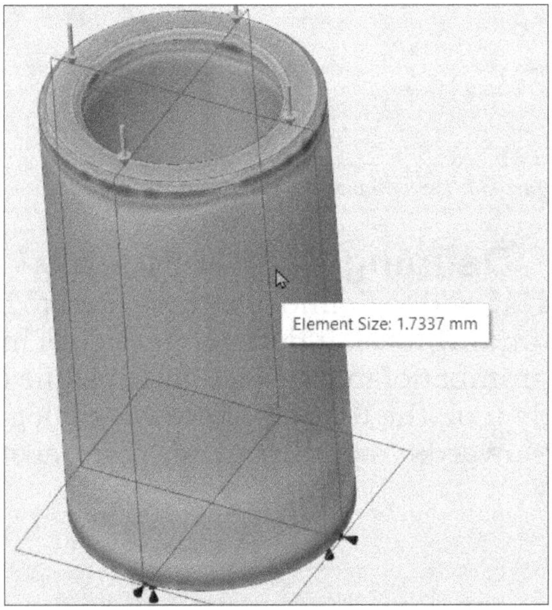

Figure-37. Showing element size

RUNNING A STRUCTURE SIMULATION STUDY

Simulation lets you examine how your model will behave in the real world, reducing the need for costly prototype iterations. The Simulation helps you evaluate your model's structural characteristics, thermal profile, and provide powerful tools for examining mechanism performance. Simulation help to learn about creating a simulation model that reflects the loads, materials, and boundary conditions you expect your model to undergo. Simulation helps in running a wide range of analyses and design studies, review results, and optimize the model to fulfil the specific design benchmarks. The procedure to perform the structure simulation study is discussed next.

- Click on the **Simulate** button from **Study** panel of the **Ribbon**. A fringe plot of the results is displayed in the graphics window; refer to Figure-38.

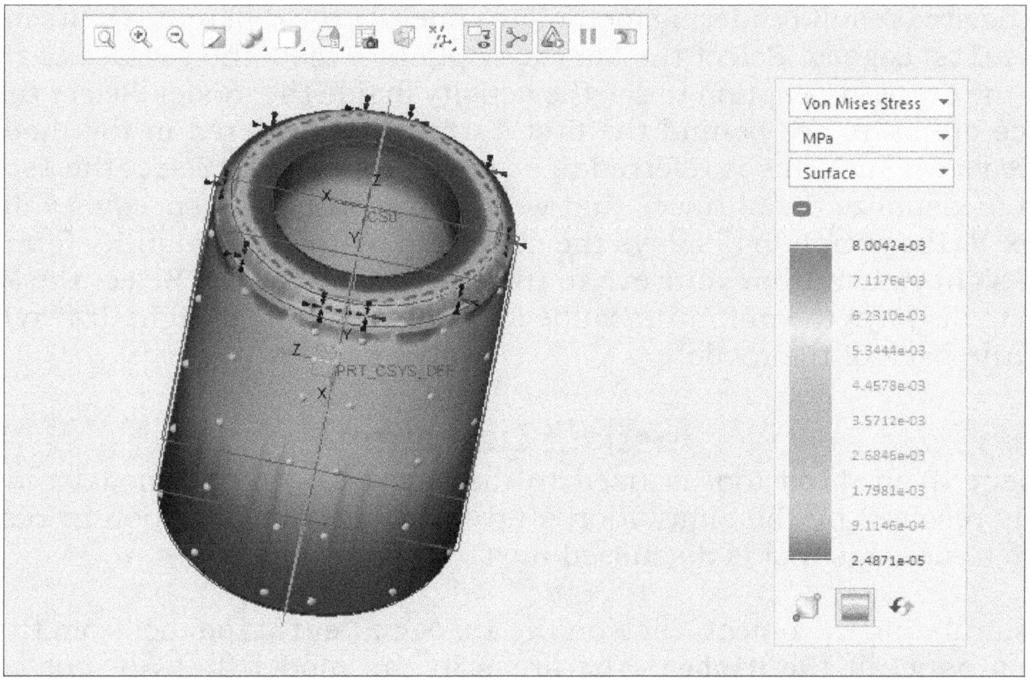

Figure-38. Simulation results

- Select the type of result quantity from the **Results Legend** that appears for a simulation study. When you change the selected result type, the results that appear in the graphics window change instantly. The result types available depend on the active simulation study.

The following result types are available in the **Results Legend**; refer to Figure-39.

Result Type	Description
Von Mises Stress	A combination of all stress components.
Deformation	Deformation.
X Normal Stress	Normal stress along the X-axis.
Y Normal Stress	Normal stress along the Y-axis.
Z Normal Stress	Normal stress along the Z- axis.
XY Shear Stress	Shear stress acting in the Y- direction on the plane whose outward normal is parallel to the X- axis.
YZ Shear Stress	Shear stress acting in the Z- direction on the plane whose outward normal is parallel to the Y axis.
XZ Shear Stress	Shear stress acting in the Z- direction on the plane whose outward normal is parallel to the X axis.
Maximum Principal Stress	Maximum principal stress.
Middle Principal Stress	The principal stress that has a numerical value between maximum principal and minimum principal.
Minimum Principal Stress	Minimum principal stress.
Local Reaction Force	Force acting in the direction opposite to the applied force.
Reaction Resultant	The sum of all the different forces acting on the model.

Figure-39. Result types in Results Legend

- Select desired result rendering method to generate the different results image from the **Results Legend**. Select the **Surface** option to view the surface of the model. Select the **Composite** option to see the activity inside the model. Select the **Inverse Surface** option to see behind the first surface encountered in the model from a specific viewpoint. This is referred to as surface skipping. Select the **Iso-Surface** option to visualize the surfaces that would form when you specify a value. Select the **Max Value** option to displays the maximum value of a quantity found along a line of sight drawn from your eye to the back of the model. Select the **Min Value** option to displays the minimum value found along a line of sight drawn from your eye to the back of the model.

Inspect Deviation

The **Inspect Deviation** tool is used to display areas in the model that are not completely resolved by the simulation study and show degradation in results. The procedure to use this tool is discussed next.

- After simulating the object, click on the **Inspect Deviation** tool from the **Display Options** panel in the **Ribbon**. The areas in the model that are not completely resolved after simulation will be displayed; refer to Figure-40.

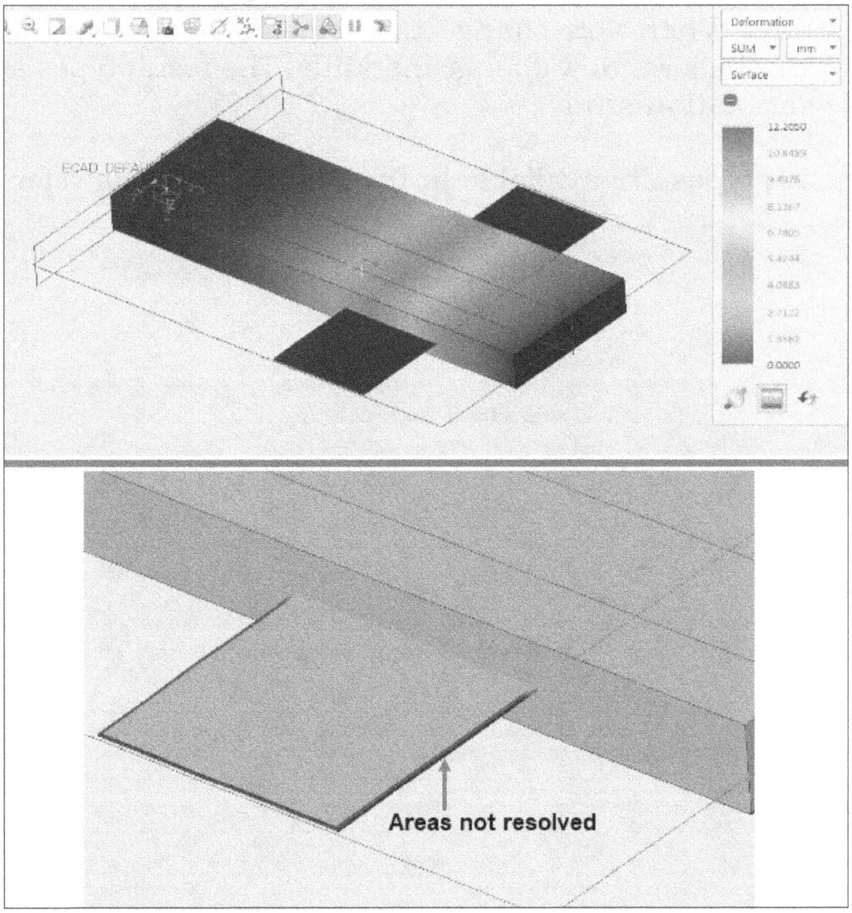

Figure-40. Areas not resolved

STARTING THERMAL SIMULATION STUDY

The **Thermal Simulation Study** is used to calculate the thermal response to heat loads, depending on the prescribed temperatures, applied convection conditions, or both.

- Click on the **Thermal Simulation Study** option from the **Add Simulation** drop-down in the **Study** panel of the **Ribbon**. The tools related to **Thermal Simulation Study** will be displayed in the toolbar; refer to Figure-41.

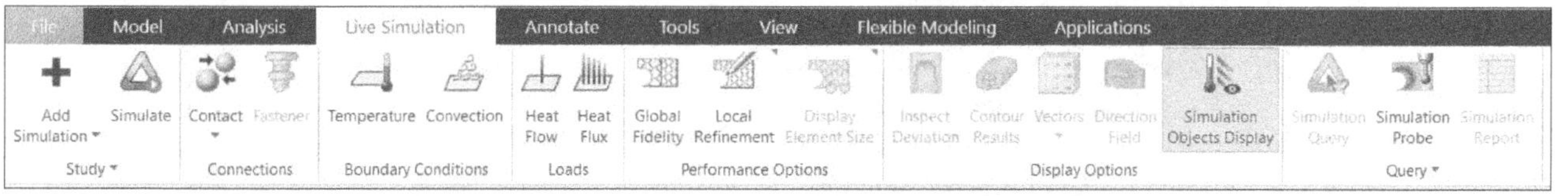

Figure-41. Thermal Simulation Study tools

APPLYING BOUNDARY CONDITIONS

In an analysis model, the loads are the mechanical forces and thermal loading which act on the object or part. The boundary conditions are the environmental factors influencing the behavior of the object or part under normal use. The tools to apply boundary conditions are available in the **Boundary Conditions** panel of the **Live Simulation** tab in the **Ribbon**; refer to Figure-42.

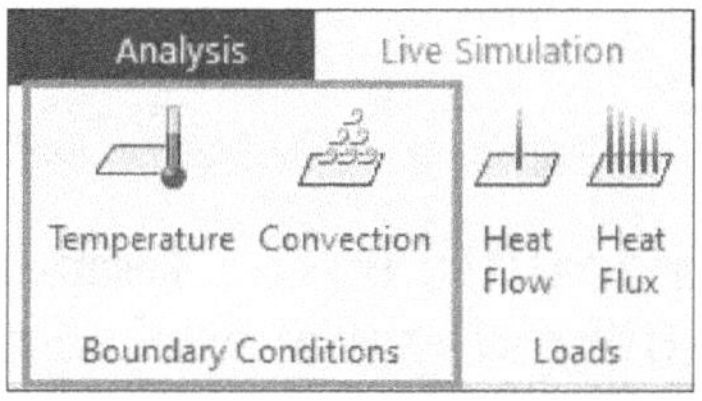

Figure-42. Boundary Conditions panel

The procedure to apply different type of boundary conditions are discussed next.

Temperature Boundary Condition

A prescribed temperature is a thermal boundary condition that limits the temperature of your model. Use this boundary condition to set the temperature of selected faces. The temperature is applied uniformly to the surface. The procedure to apply temperature boundary condition is discussed next.

- Click on the **Temperature** button from the **Boundary Conditions** panel of the **Ribbon**. The **Prescribed Temperature** dialog box will be displayed; refer to Figure-43.

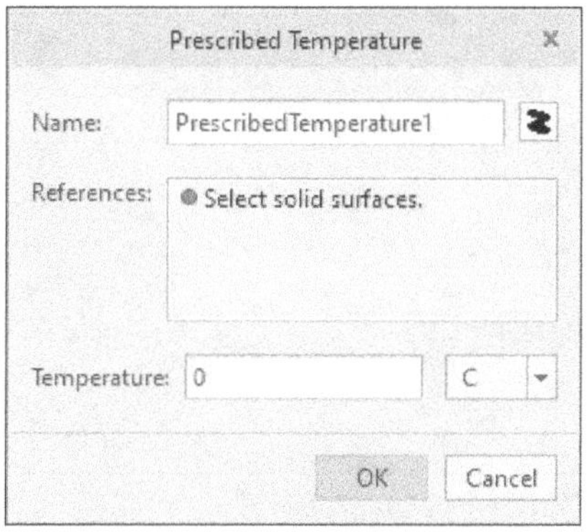

Figure-43. Prescribed Temperature dialog box

- Specify desired name for the boundary condition in the **Name** edit box and click on **Change the color** button next to the name edit box to specify desired color for temperature boundary condition.
- Select one or more faces of the model on which you want to apply the temperature boundary condition; refer to Figure-44.

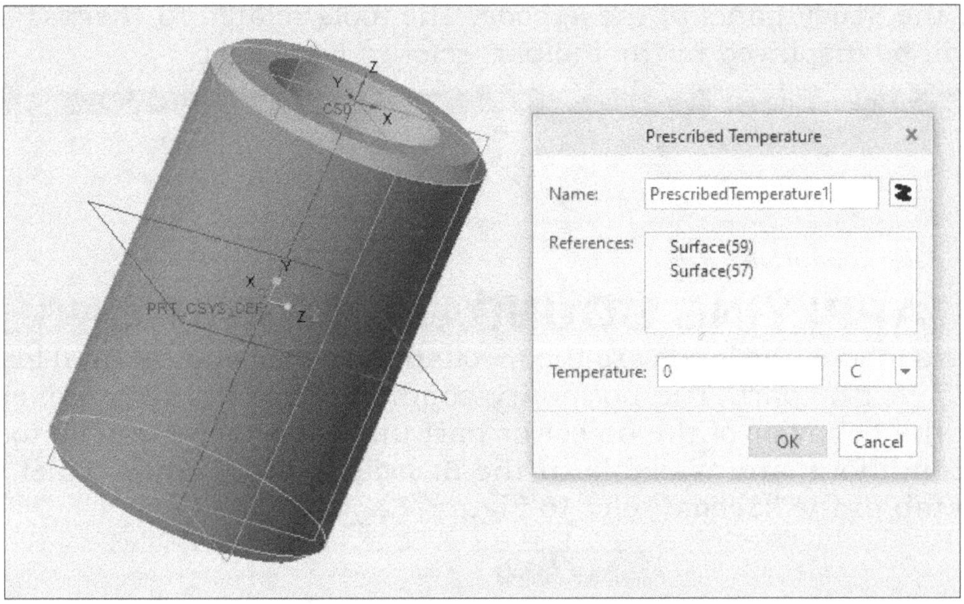

Figure-44. Surfaces selected to apply temperature boundary condition

- Specify desired value of temperature in the **Temperature** edit box and specify the unit of temperature from the drop-down available next to the temperature edit box.
- Click on the **OK** button from the dialog box to apply the temperature boundary condition.

Convection Boundary Condition

A convection boundary condition simulates convection heating or cooling at a selected surface. It overrides the default ambient temperature in the solution. The procedure to apply convection boundary condition is discussed next.

- Click on the **Convection** button from **Boundary Conditions** panel of the **Ribbon**. The **Convection** dialog box will be displayed; refer to Figure-45.

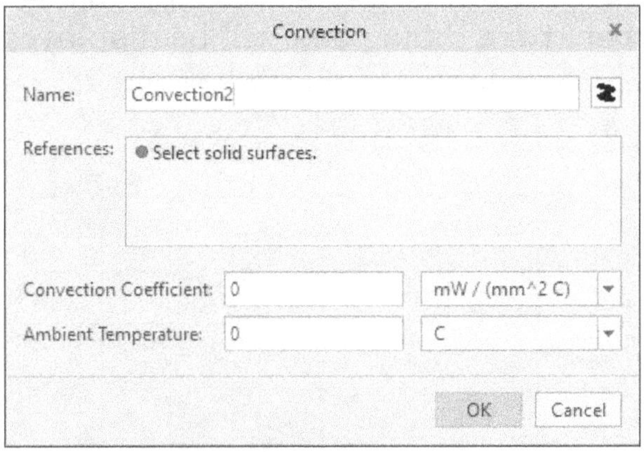

Figure-45. Convection dialog box

- Specify the parameters as discussed earlier.
- Select a surface on which you want to apply the convection boundary condition; refer to Figure-46.

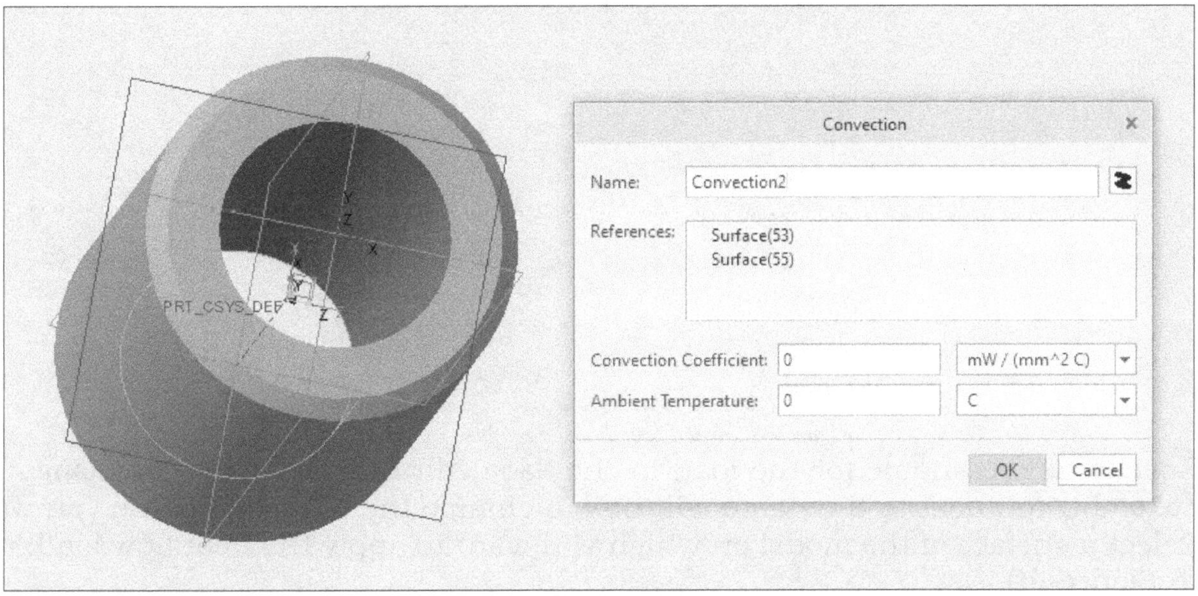

Figure-46. Surface selected to apply convection boundary condition

- Specify the positive constant value in the **Convection Coefficient** edit box.
- In the **Ambient Temperature** edit box, specify the temperature of the surrounding fluid.
- Specify desired unit for ambient temperature from the drop-down available next to the convection coefficient edit box.
- Click on the **OK** button from the dialog box to apply the convection boundary condition.

APPLYING LOADS

Creo Simulate allows you to simulate thermal conditions. A steady state thermal analysis calculates effects of constant thermal loads on a model and is used to determine temperatures, heat flow rates, and the heat fluxes in a part. The tools to apply loads are available in the **Loads** panel in the **Toolbar**; refer to Figure-47.

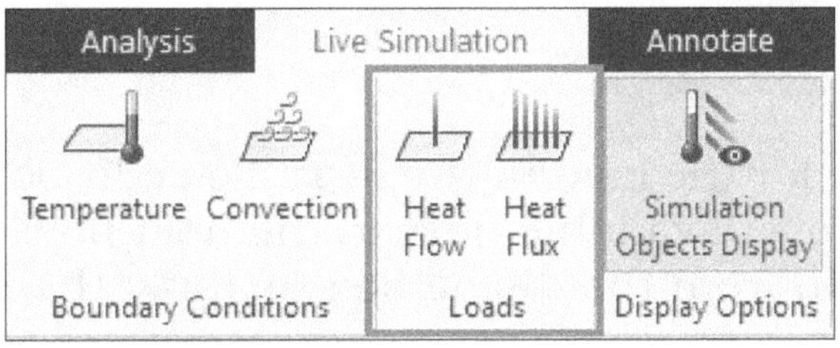

Figure-47. Loads panel

The procedures to apply different type of loads are discussed next.

Applying Heat Flow Load

Heat flow loads simulate local heat sources and sinks for your model. A heat flow load sets the rate of heat energy transfer of selected surfaces. You can apply heat flow loads to both internal and external surfaces of your model. The procedure to apply heat flow load is discussed next.

- Click on the **Heat Flow** button from **Loads** panel in the **Ribbon**. The **Heat Flow** dialog box will be displayed; refer to Figure-48.

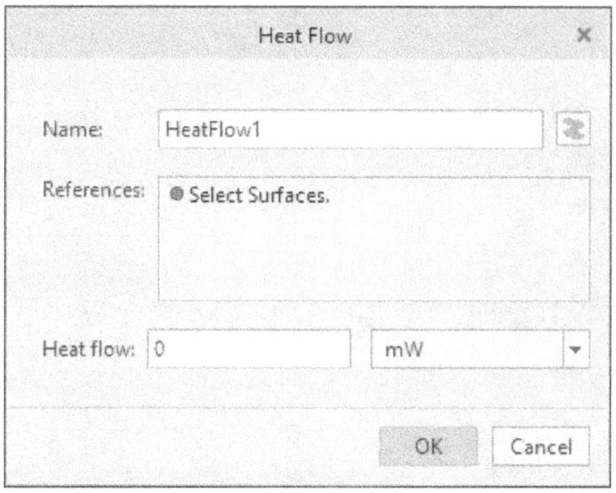

Figure-48. Heat Flow dialog box

- Specify desired name for the load in the **Name** edit box and click on **Change the color** button next to the name edit box to change the color of load as you want.
- Select a surface of the model on which you want to apply the heat flow load; refer to Figure-49.

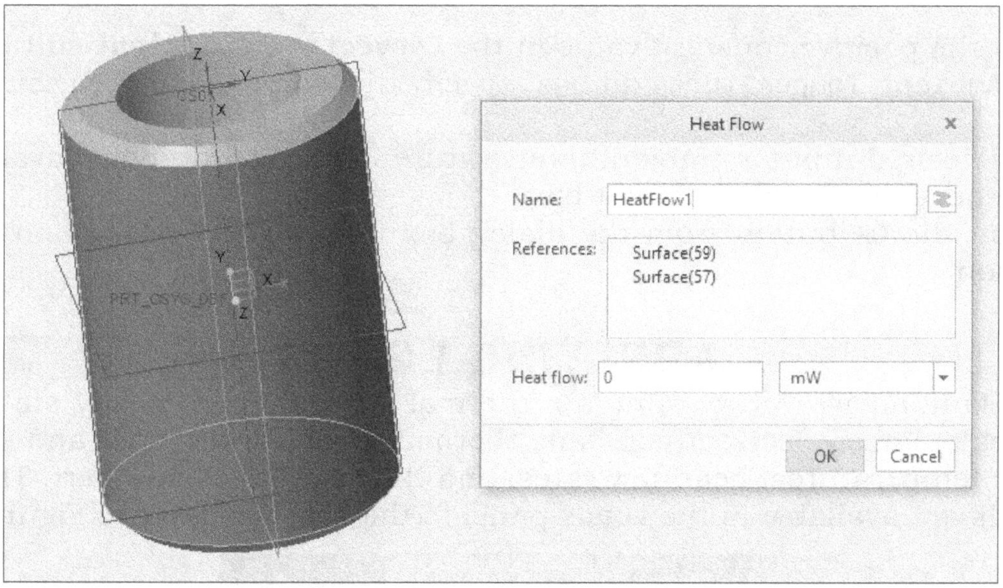

Figure-49. Surface selected to apply the heat flow load

- Specfiy desired value for the load in the **Heat flow** edit box and and select desired unit from the drop-down available next to the heat flow edit box.
- Click on the **OK** button from the dialog box to apply the heat flow load.

Applying Heat Flux Load

Heat flux loads set the rate of heat energy transfer per unit area of selected surface. You can apply heat flux loads to model for internal heat generation or flux. The procedure to apply heat flux load is discussed next.

- Click on the **Heat Flux** button from the **Loads** panel in the **Ribbon**. The **Heat Flux** dialog box will be displayed; refer to Figure-50.

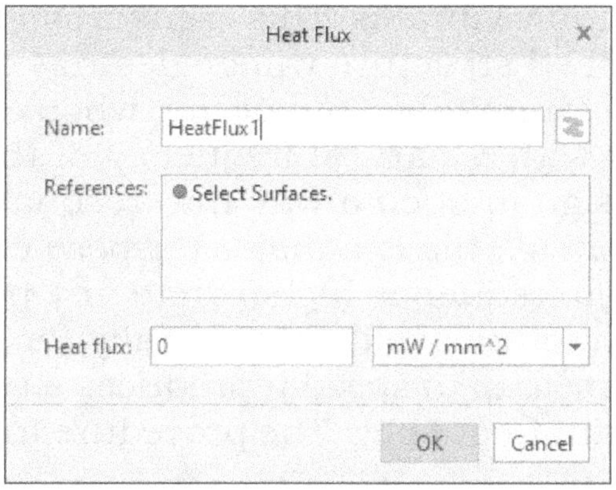

Figure-50. Heat Flux dialog box

- Specify desired name for the load in the **Name** edit box and click on **Change the color** button to change the color of the load as you want.
- Select a surface of the model on which you want to apply the load; refer to Figure-51.

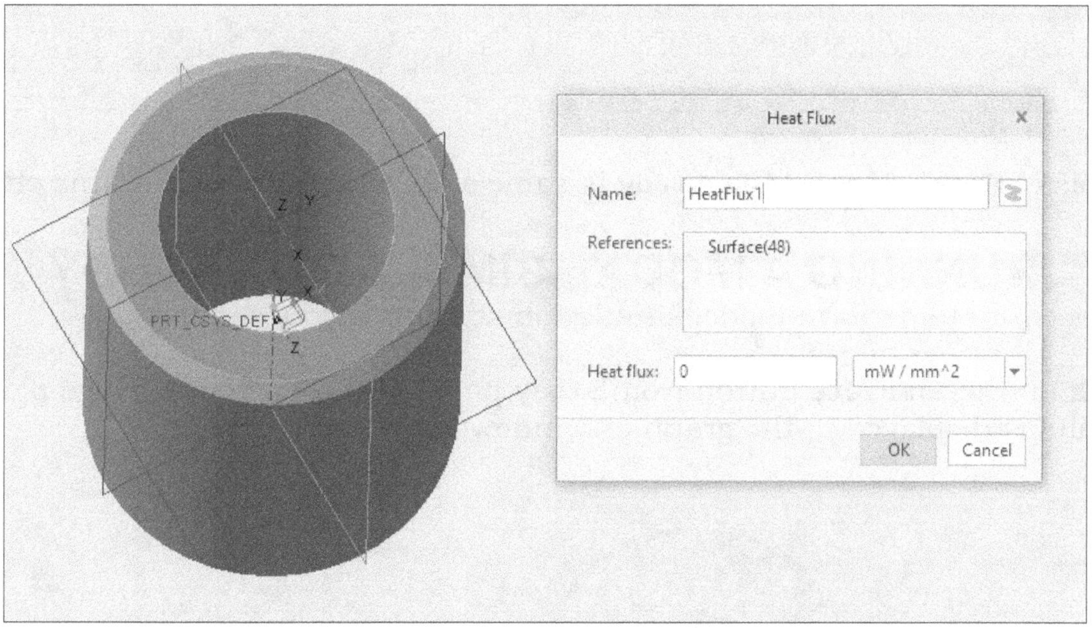

Figure-51. Surface selected to apply the Heat Flux Load

- Specify desired value for the load in the **Heat flux** edit box and select desired unit from the drop-down available next to the heat flux edit box.
- Click on the **OK** button from the dialog box to apply the heat flux load.

The procedure to perform a thermal simulation study is same as discussed earlier in this chapter.

STARTING MODAL SIMULATION STUDY

Harmonics and overtones occur because individual sections of the string can vibrate independently within the larger vibration forming different shapes. These various shapes are called "modes". The base frequency is said to vibrate in the first mode, and so on up the ladder. Each mode shape will have an associated frequency. Higher mode shapes have higher frequencies. The most disastrous kinds of consequences occur when a power-driven device such as a motor, produces a frequency at which an attached structure naturally vibrates. This event is called "resonance." If sufficient power is applied, the attached structure will be destroyed. Note that armies, which normally marched "in step," were taken out of step when crossing bridges. If the beat of the marching feet align with a natural frequency of the bridge then it could fall down. Engineers must design in such a way that resonance does not occur during regular operation of machines. This is a major purpose of Modal Simulation Study. Ideally, the first mode has a frequency higher than any potential driving frequency. Frequently, resonance cannot be avoided, especially for short periods of time. For example, when a motor comes up to speed it produces a variety of frequencies. So, it may pass through a resonant frequency. The procedure to create a modal simulation study is discussed next.

- Click on the **Modal Simulation Study** option from **Add Simulation** drop-down in the **Study** panel of the **Ribbon**. The tools related to **Modal Simulation Study** will be displayed; refer to Figure-52.

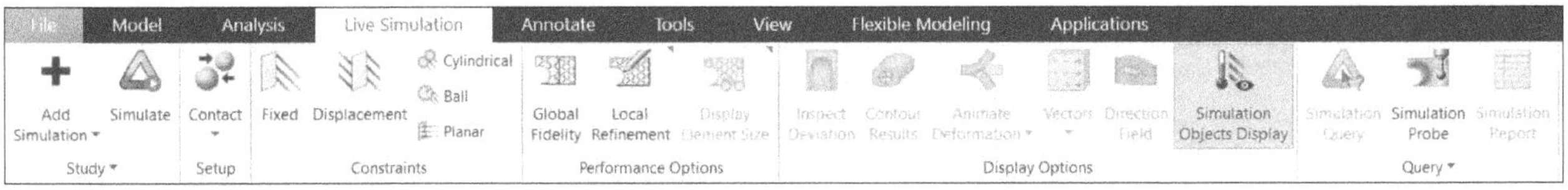

Figure-52. Modal Simulation Study tools

The tools of **Modal Simulation Study** is same as discussed earlier in this chapter.

RUNNING A MODAL SIMULATION STUDY

The procedure to perform model simulation study is discussed next.

- Click on the **Simulate** button from **Study** panel of the **Ribbon**. A fringe plot of the results is displayed in the graphics window; refer to Figure-53.

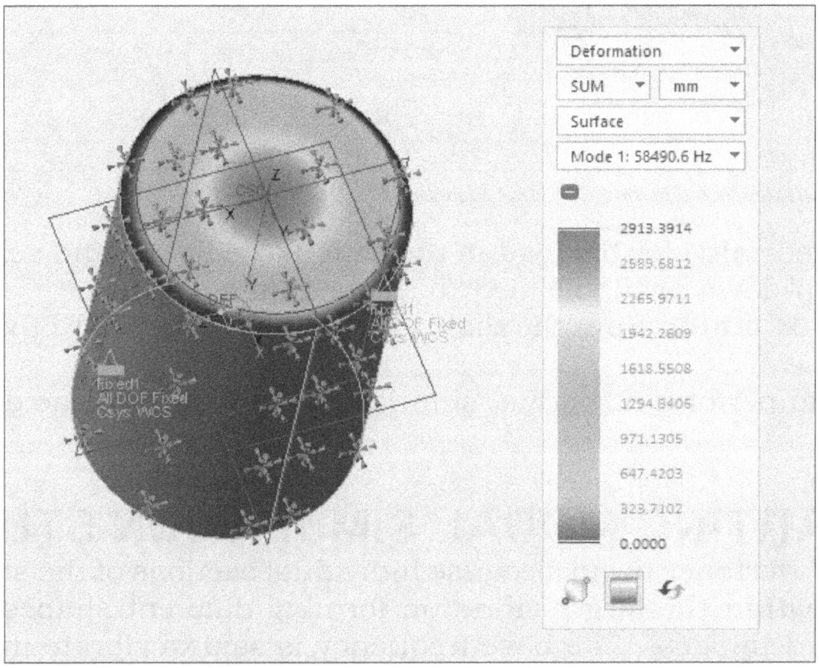

Figure-53. Simulation results

The different type of results in the **Results Legend** have been discussed earlier in this chapter. Here, we will discuss only about **Mode** result type in the **Results Legend**.

- Select desired option from the **Mode** drop-down in the **Results Legend** to specify the number of modes you want **Creo Simulate** to calculate above a specified minimum frequency.

STARTING FLUID SIMULATION STUDY

Fluid Simulation Study helps predict the performance of a system or product involving internal or external fluid flow and heat transfer. It also helps easier fluid volume extraction and automated meshing. The procedure to create a fluid simulation study is discussed next.

- Click on the **Fluid Simulation Study** option from **Add Simulation** drop-down in the **Study** panel of the **Ribbon**. The tools related to **Fluid Simulation Study** will be displayed; refer to Figure-54.

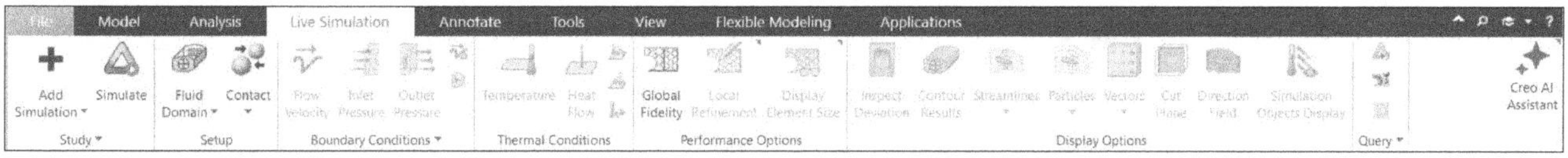

Figure-54. Fluid Simulation Study tools

FLUID SETUP

The tools in the **Fluid Setup** group are used to define the volume to be used for performing CFD analysis. Various tools in this group are discussed next.

Creating Internal Volume

The **Internal Volume** tool is used to create fluid volume for performing CFD analysis. The procedure to use this tool is given next.

- Click on the **Internal Volume** tool from the **Fluid Domain** drop-down in the **Fluid Setup** panel of **Live Simulation** tab in the **Ribbon**. The **Internal Volume** contextual tab will be displayed in the **Ribbon**.
- Select two bounding faces (holding **CTRL** key) of the model forming fluid volume. Preview of the internal volume will be displayed; refer to Figure-55.

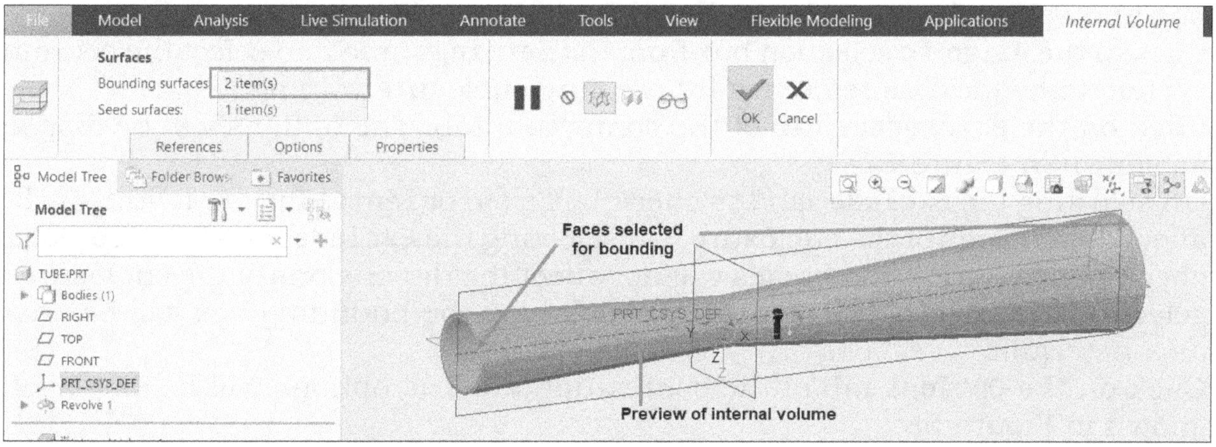

Figure-55. Preview of internal volume

- If you want to close the holes in the internal volume then click on the **Options** tab and click in the **Fill holes** selection box. You will be asked to select the surfaces/ faces to be used for filling holes.
- Select desired faces/surfaces.
- Click on the **OK** button from the **Ribbon** to create the volume.

Creating Enclosure Volume

The **Enclosure Volume** tool is used to create an external fluid volume for CFD analysis around desired solid objects. This tool is specially useful when performing aerodynamic analysis on objects. The procedure to use this tool is given next.

- Click on the **Enclosure Volume** tool from the **Fluid Domain** drop-down in the **Fluid Setup** panel of the **Live Simulation** tab in the **Ribbon**. The **Enclosure Volume** contextual tab will be displayed in the **Ribbon** with the preview of rectangular enclosure volume; refer to Figure-56.

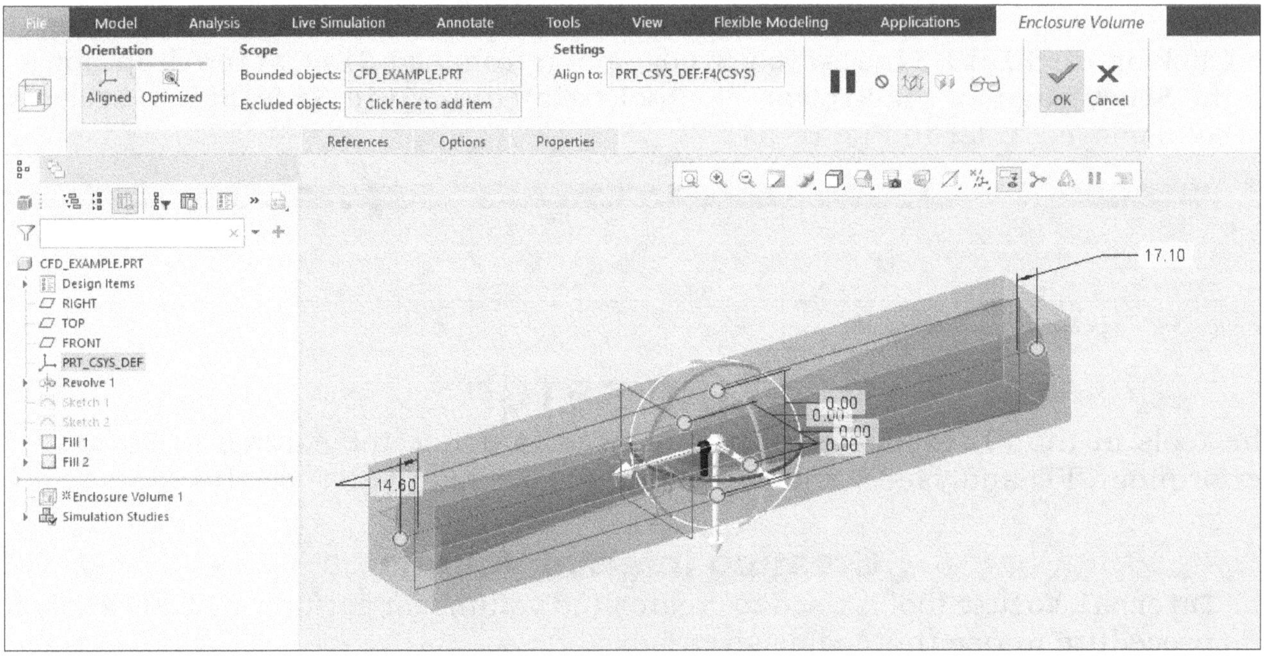

Figure-56. Enclosure Volume contextual tab with preview of enclosure volume

- Select the **Aligned** option from the **Orientation** area to orient the bounding box according to selected coordinate system. Select the **Optimized** option to create bounding box of minimal volume.
- Click in the **Bounded objects** selection box from the **Scope** area and select objects to be enclosed inside the box. Similarly, click in the **Excluded objects** selection box and select objects to be excluded from the enclosure.
- Click in the **Align to** selection box from the **Settings** area and select the coordinate system to be used as reference for creating enclosure volume.
- Click on the **References** tab of the contextual tab. The options will be displayed as shown in Figure-57.
- On selecting the **Exclude quilts** check box from **Orientation** area, quilts will not affect dimensions of the enclosure. On selecting the **Exclude construction bodies** check box, construction bodies will not affect the dimensions of the enclosure. On selecting the **Create box geometry** check box, the bounding box will be created as a new quilt.
- Click on the **Options** tab of the contextual tab. The options will be displayed as shown in Figure-58.
- Select the **Uniform** radio button from the **Linear Offsets** area and specify desired offset value in the edit box to offset the box uniformly in all directions. Select the **Non-uniform** radio button and specify desired values in the edit boxes to offset each side, individually.

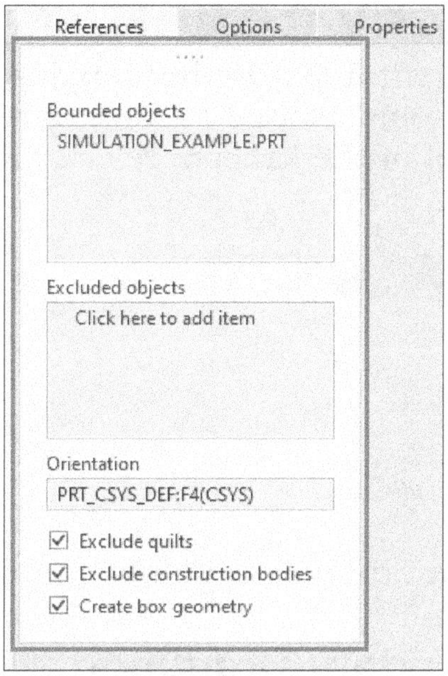

Figure-57. References tab options

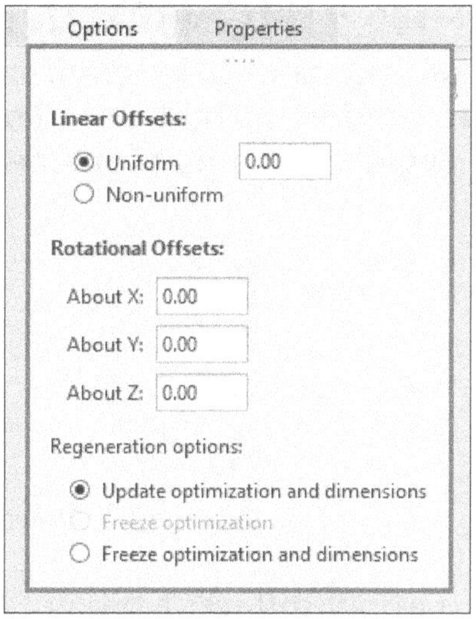

Figure-58. Options tab options

- Specify desired value in the **About X**, **About Y**, and **About Z** edit boxes from the **Rotational Offsets** area to rotate the components about X, Y, and Z axes, respectively.
- Select the **Update optimization and dimensions** radio button from the **Regeneration options** area to recalculate box optimization and dimensions. Select the **Freeze optimization** radio button to recalculate box dimensions but keep orientation unchanged.
- Drag the key points of the enclosure volume to modify its volume.
- After specifying desired parameters, click on the **OK** button from the **Ribbon** to create the volume.

Selecting Fluid Domain

The **Fluid Domain** tool is used to select quilts to be used as fluid domain. The procedure to use this tool is given next.

- Click on the **Fluid Domain** tool from the **Fluid Domain** drop-down in the **Fluid Setup** panel of the **Live Simulation** tab in the **Ribbon**. The **Fluid Domain Definition** dialog box will be displayed; refer to Figure-59.

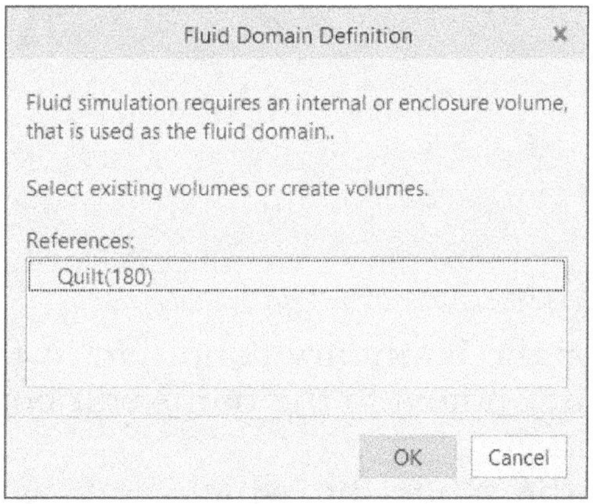

Figure-59. Fluid Domain Definition dialog box

- Select desired internal or enclosure volume to be used for fluid domain and click on the **OK** button.

APPLYING BOUNDARY CONDITIONS

The boundary conditions are the environmental factors influencing the behavior of the object or part under normal use. The tools related to boundary conditions are available in the **Boundary Conditions** panel of the **Ribbon**; refer to Figure-60.

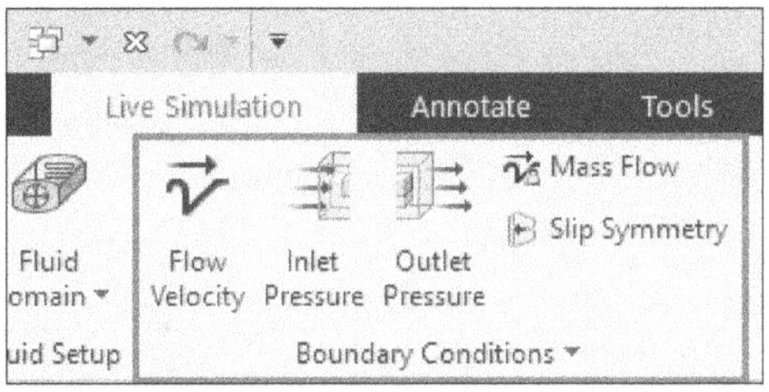

Figure-60. Boundary Conditions panel

The procedure to apply different type of boundary conditions are discussed next.

Flow Velocity Boundary Condition

When defining a fluid simulation study, the flow velocity at the inlet is one of the required boundary conditions. The **Flow Velocity** command is available in the **Boundary Conditions** group when a fluid simulation study is active. The procedure to apply flow velocity boundary condition is discussed next.

- Click on the **Flow Velocity** button from **Boundary Conditions** panel of the **Ribbon**. The **Fluid Flow Velocity** dialog box will be displayed; refer to Figure-61.

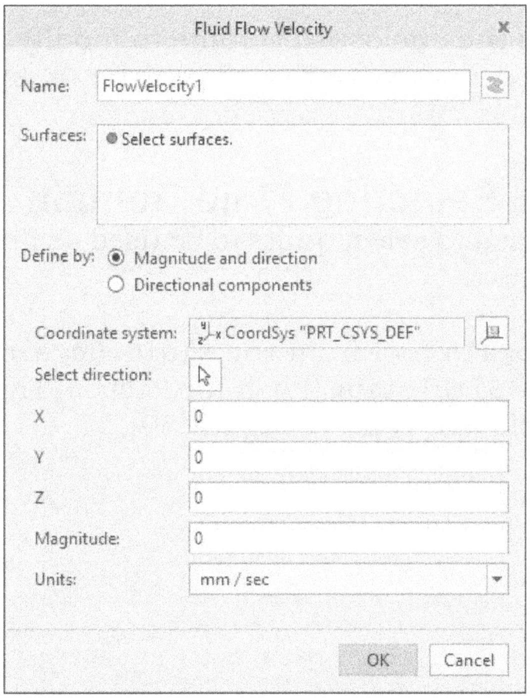

Figure-61. Fluid Flow Velocity dialog box

- Specify desired name for the boundary condition in the **Name** edit box and click on **Change the color** button next to the name edit box if you want to change the color of boundary condition.
- Select the surfaces of the model on which you want to apply the boundary condition; refer to Figure-62.

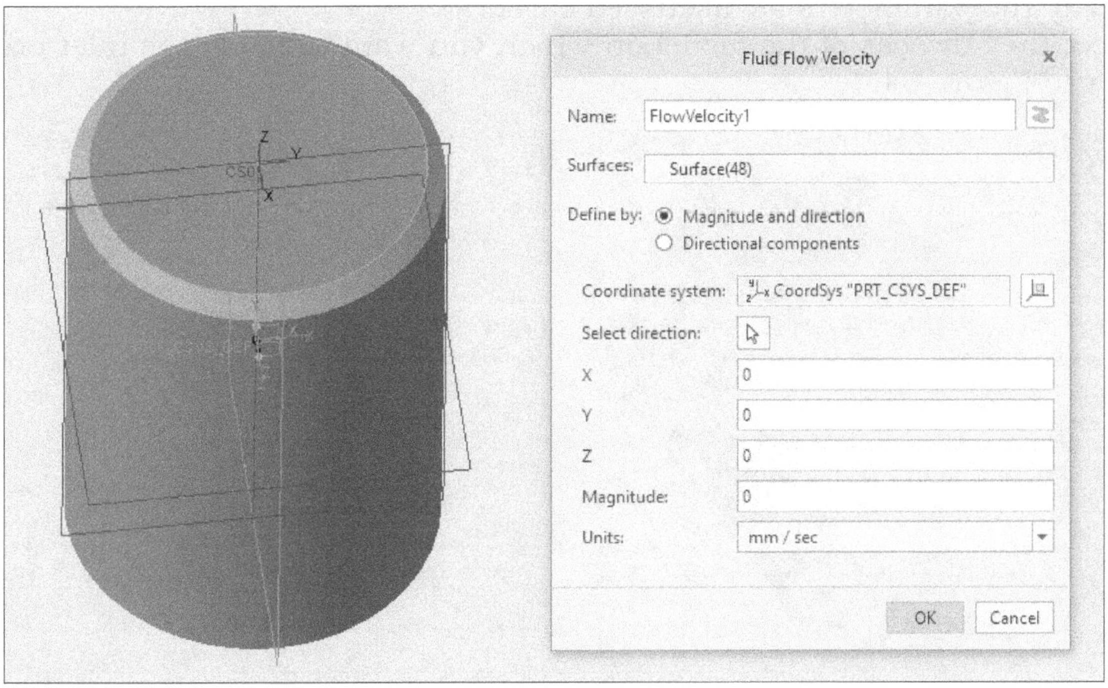

Figure-62. Surface selected for flow velocity boundary condition

- Select the **Magnitude and direction** option from the **Define by** area of the dialog box to specify the direction for velocity in the **X**, **Y**, or **Z** edit box. Alternatively, click on the **Select direction** button and select a linear edge or planar surface to specify the direction of velocity. Specify magnitude of the velocity in the **Magnitude** edit box.
- Select the **Directional components** option from the **Define by** area to specify the components of the velocity for each coordinate direction **X**, **Y**, or **Z** and specify the value of the unit vectors for the direction in the **X**, **Y**, or **Z** edit boxes.
- Select desired units for the flow velocity boundary condition from the **Units** drop-down.
- Click on the **OK** button from the dialog box to create the boundary condition.

Inlet Pressure Boundary Condition

For a fluid flow simulation study, you can define the fluid pressure at the inlet. The procedure to apply inlet pressure boundary condition is discussed next.

- Click on the **Inlet Pressure** button from the **Boundary Conditions** panel of the **Ribbon**. The **Inlet Pressure** dialog box will be displayed; refer to Figure-63.

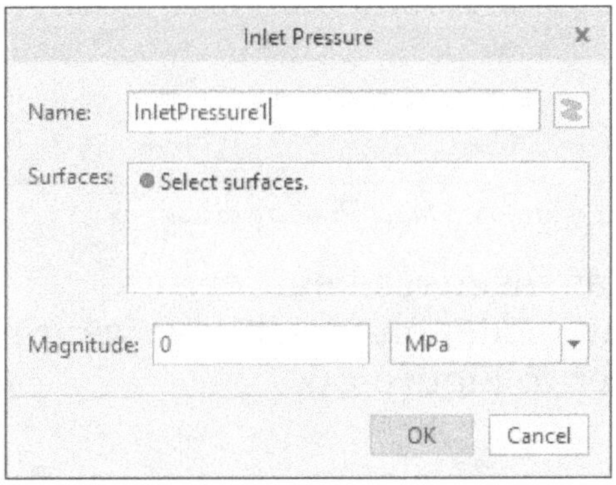

Figure-63. Inlet Pressure dialog box

- Specify the parameters as discussed earlier.
- Select the surfaces of the model on which you want to apply the inlet pressure; refer to Figure-64.

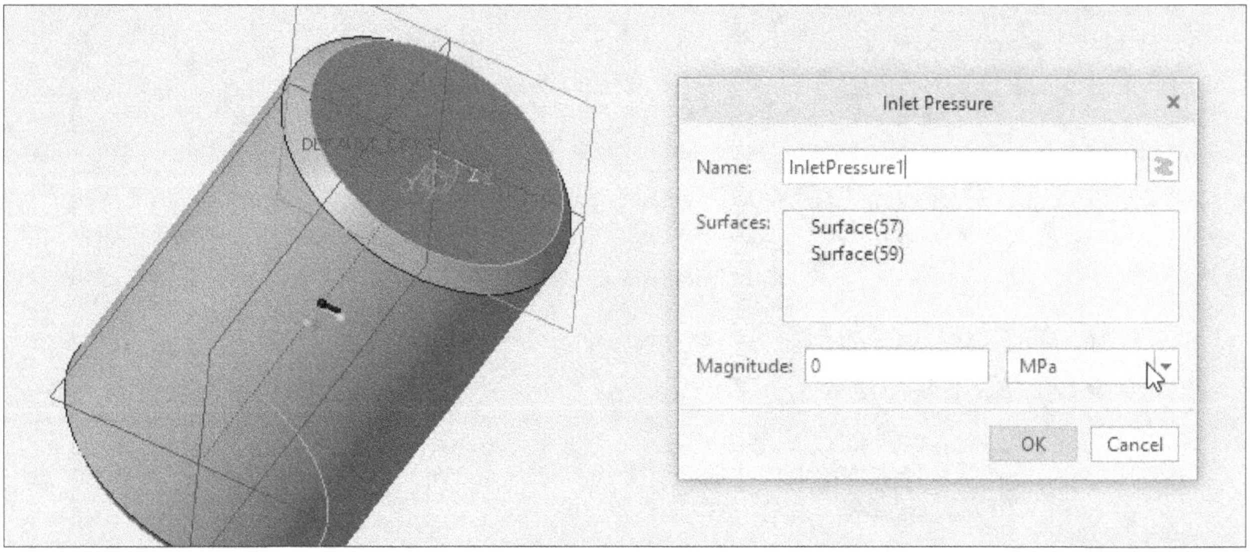

Figure-64. Surface selected for Inlet Pressure

- Specify desired value of pressure in the **Magnitude** edit box and select desired unit of pressure from the drop-down available next to the **Magnitude** edit box.
- Click on the **OK** button from the dialog box to create the inlet pressure boundary condition.

Outlet Pressure Boundary Condition

The outlet pressure is a required boundary condition for a flow simulation study. The outlet pressure must be applied to a surface that is a part of the fluid domain. The procedure to apply the outlet pressure boundary condition is discussed next.

- Click on the **Outlet Pressure** button from the **Boundary Conditions** panel of the **Ribbon**. The **Outlet Pressure** dialog box will be displayed; refer to Figure-65.

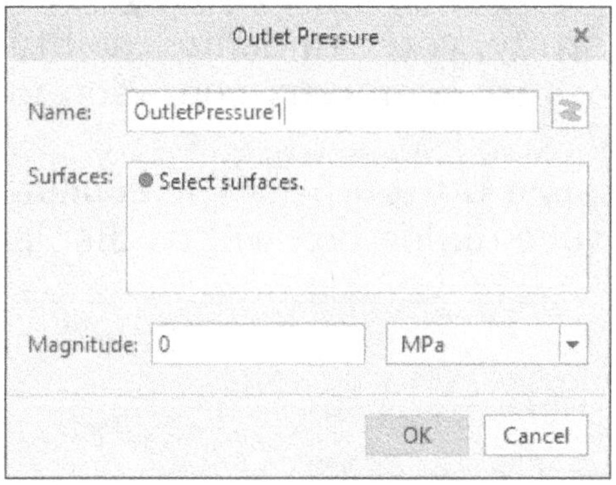

Figure-65. Outlet Pressure dialog box

- Specify the parameters as discussed earlier.
- Select the surfaces of the model on which you want to apply the outlet pressure boundary condition; refer to Figure-66.

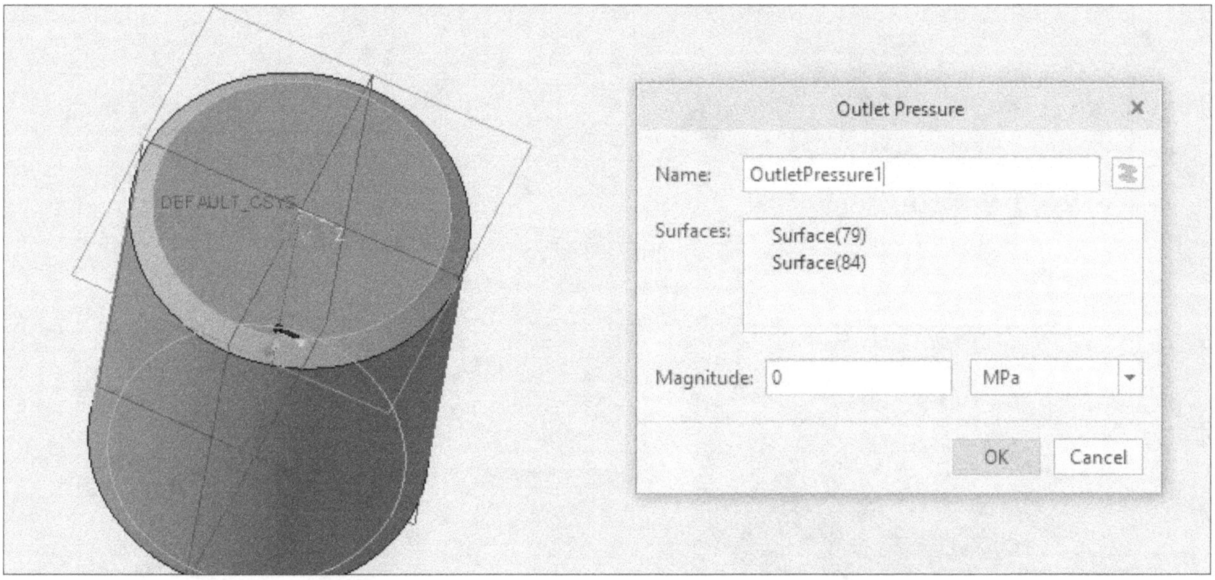

Figure-66. Surface selected for outlet pressure

- Specify desired value of pressure in the **Magnitude** edit box and select desired unit of pressure from the drop-down available next to the **Magnitude** edit box.
- Click on the **OK** button from the dialog box to create the outlet pressure boundary condition.

Mass Flow Boundary Condition

You can specify the mass flow rate as an inlet or outlet boundary condition for a fluid flow simulation study. The procedure to create mass flow boundary condition is discussed next.

- Click on the **Mass Flow** button from the **Boundary Conditions** panel of the **Ribbon**. The **Mass Flow** dialog box will be displayed; refer to Figure-67.

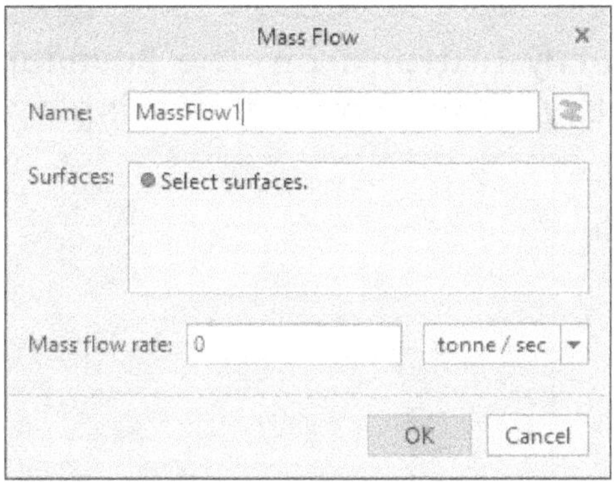

Figure-67. Mass Flow dialog box

- Specify the parameters as discussed earlier.
- Select the surfaces on which you want to apply the mass flow boundary condition; refer to Figure-68.

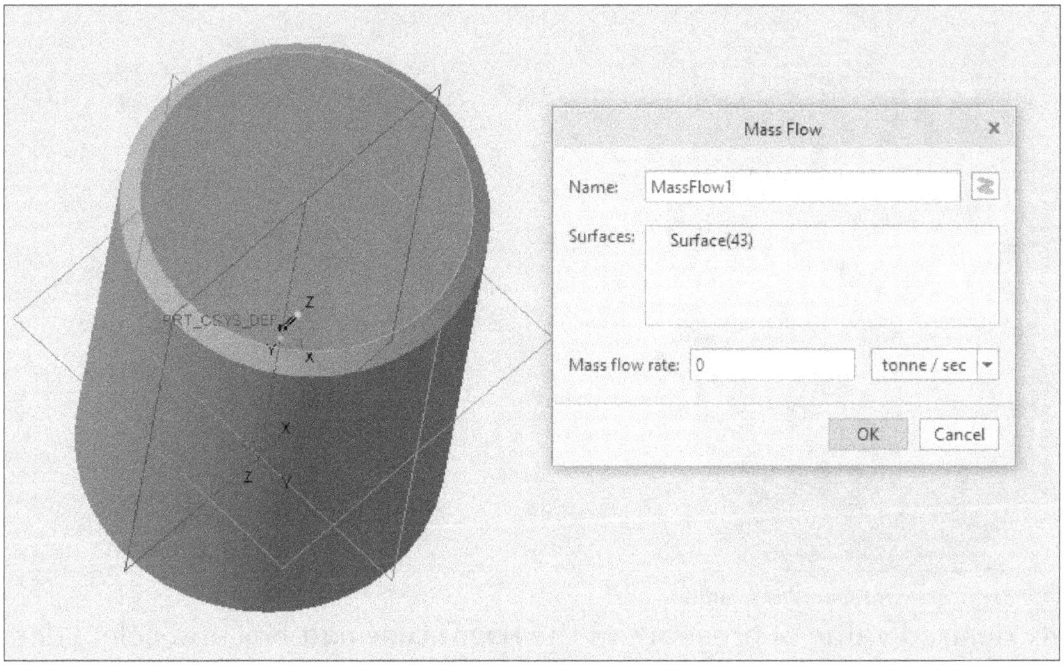

Figure-68. Surface selected for mass flow boundary condition

- Specify desired rate of mass flow in the **Mass flow rate** edit box and select desired unit for the mass flow from the drop-down available next to the edit box.
- Click on the **OK** button from the dialog box to create the mass flow boundary condition.

Slip Symmetry Boundary Condition

A slip symmetry boundary condition can be applied to surfaces, sets of surfaces, or an entire part or body in a fluid simulation study. When slip symmetry is applied to a wall, the fluid flows along the wall without friction, instead of stopping at the wall. The procedure to apply slip symmetry boundary condition will be discussed next.

- Click on the **Slip Symmetry** button from the **Boundary Conditions** panel of the **Ribbon**. The **Slip Symmetry** dialog box will be displayed; refer to Figure-69.

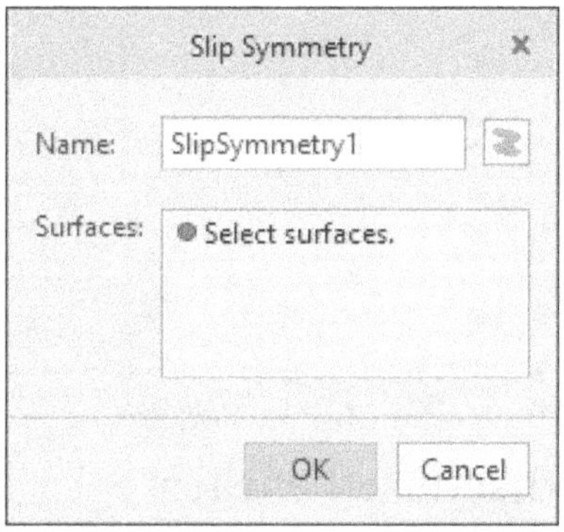

Figure-69. Slip Symmetry dialog box

- Specify the parameters as discussed earlier.
- Select the surfaces of the model on which you want to apply the slip symmetry boundary condition; refer to Figure-70.

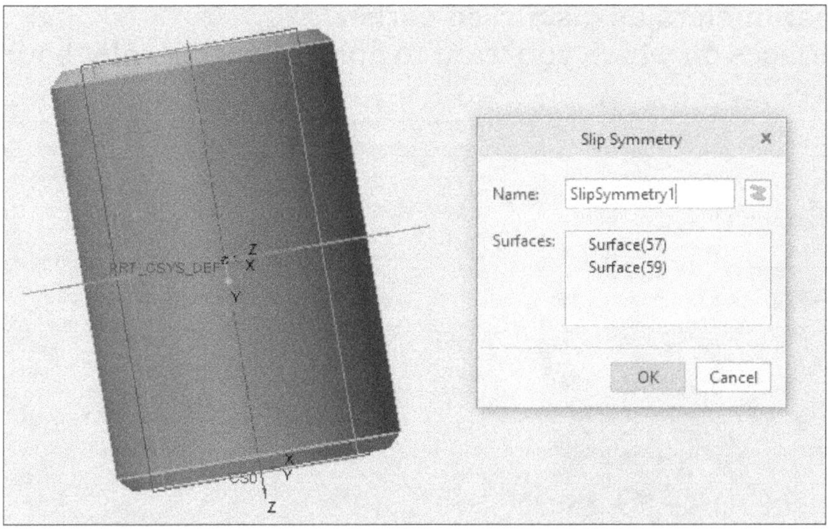

Figure-70. Surface selected for slip symmetry

- Click on the **OK** button from the dialog box to create the slip symmetry boundary condition.

Swirl Inlet Boundary Condition

The swirl inlet boundary condition is available on the expanded **Boundary Conditions** group when a fluid simulation study is the active study. The swirl inlet specifies the inlet velocity as the sum of two separate components, a component normal to the boundary (axial velocity), and a component with a radial velocity. The procedure to create **Swirl Inlet Boundary Condition** is discussed next.

- Click on the **Swirl Inlet** button from the expanded **Boundary Conditions** panel of the **Ribbon**. The **Swirl Inlet** dialog box will be displayed; refer to Figure-71.

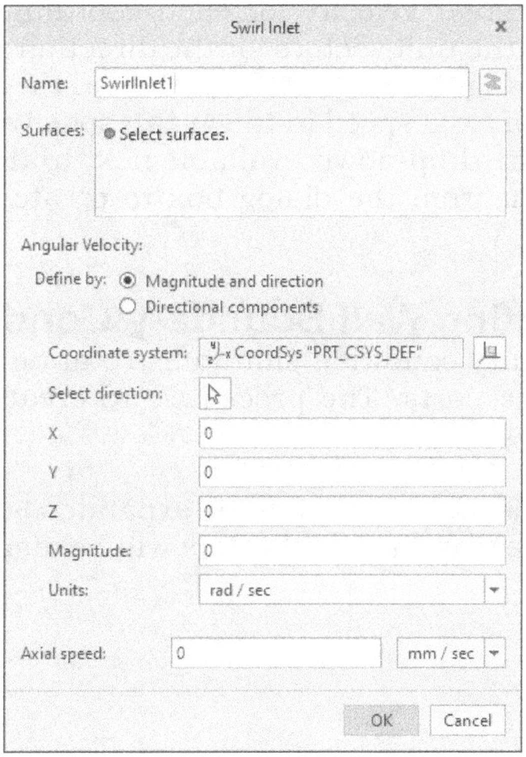

Figure-71. Swirl Inlet dialog box

- Specify the parameters as discussed earlier.
- Select the surfaces on which you want to apply the swirl inlet boundary condition; refer to Figure-72.

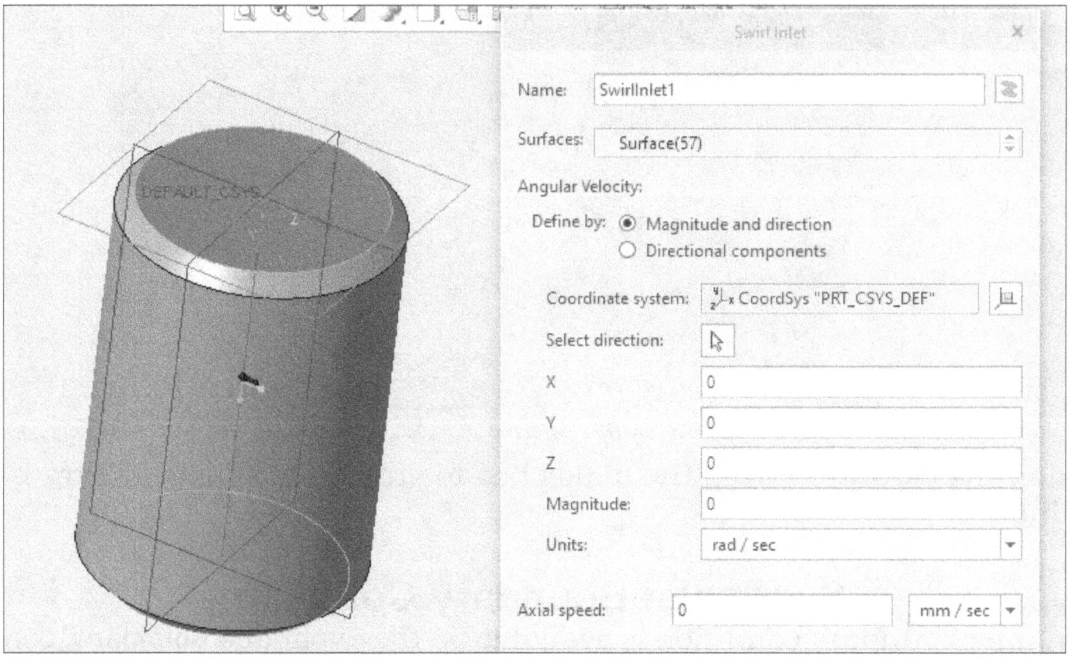

Figure-72. Surfaces selected for Swirl Inlet boundary condition

- Select the **Magnitude and direction** option from the **Define by** area of the dialog box to specify the direction of the angular velocity in the **X**, **Y**, or **Z** edit box. Alternatively, click on the **Select direction** button and select a linear edge or planar surface to specify the direction of angular velocity. Specify the magnitude of the angular velocity in the **Magnitude** edit box.
- Select the **Directional components** option from the **Define by** area to specify the components of the angular velocity for each coordinate direction **X**, **Y**, or **Z** by specifying the value of the unit vectors for the direction in the **X**, **Y**, or **Z** edit boxes.
- Select desired unit of angular velocity from the **Units** drop-down.
- Specify desired value of axial speed in the **Axial speed** edit box and select desired unit of velocity from the drop-down available next to the axial speed edit box.
- Click on the **OK** button from the dialog box to create the swirl inlet boundary condition.

Rotating Wall Boundary Condition

The Rotating Wall boundary condition simulates rotating parts without any actual physical movement of the parts. The procedure to create rotating wall boundary condition is discussed next.

- Click on the **Rotating Wall** button from the expanded **Boundary Conditions** panel of the **Ribbon**. The **Rotating Wall** dialog box will be displayed; refer to Figure-73.

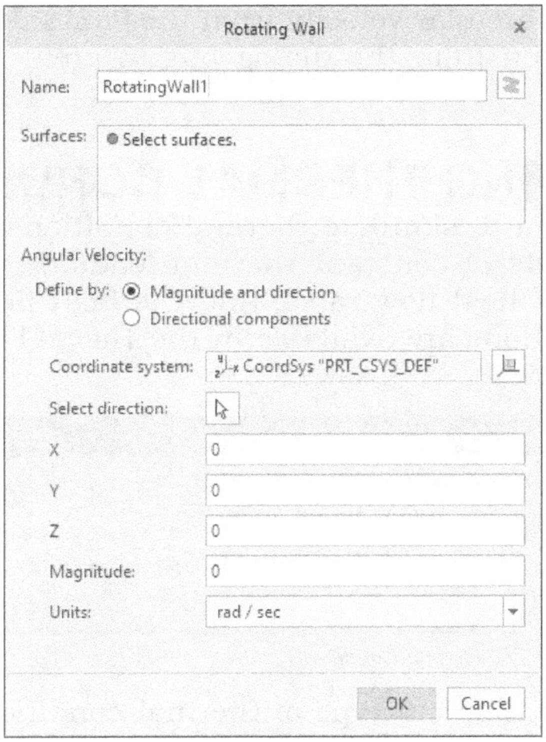

Figure-73. Rotating Wall dialog box

- Specify the parameters as discussed earlier.
- Select the surfaces of the model on which you want to apply the rotating wall boundary condition; refer to Figure-74.

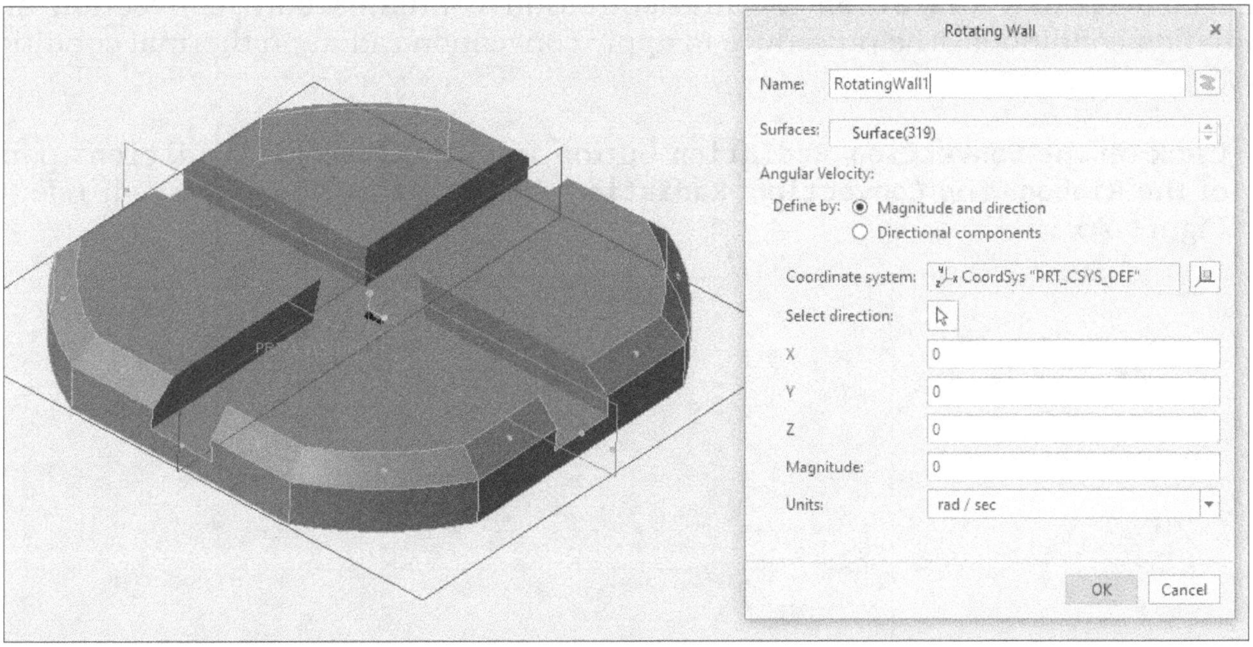

Figure-74. Surfaces selected for rotating wall boundary condition

- Select the **Magnitude and direction** option from the **Define by** area of the dialog box to specify the direction of the angular velocity in the **X**, **Y**, or **Z** edit box. Alternatively, click on the **Select direction** button and select a linear edge or planar surface to specify the direction of angular velocity. Specify the magnitude of the angular velocity in the **Magnitude** edit box.
- Select the **Directional components** option from the **Define by** area to specify the components of the angular velocity for each coordinate direction **X**, **Y**, or **Z** by specifying the value of the unit vectors for the direction in the **X**, **Y**, or **Z** edit boxes.

- Select desired unit of angular velocity from the **Units** drop-down.
- Click on the **OK** button from the dialog box to create rotating wall boundary condition.

APPLYING THERMAL CONDITIONS

Creo Simulate allows you to simulate thermal conditions. A steady state thermal analysis calculates effects of constant thermal loads on a model and is used to determine temperatures, heat flow rates, and the heat fluxes in a part. The tools related to thermal conditions are available in the **Thermal Conditions** panel of the **Ribbon**; refer to Figure-75.

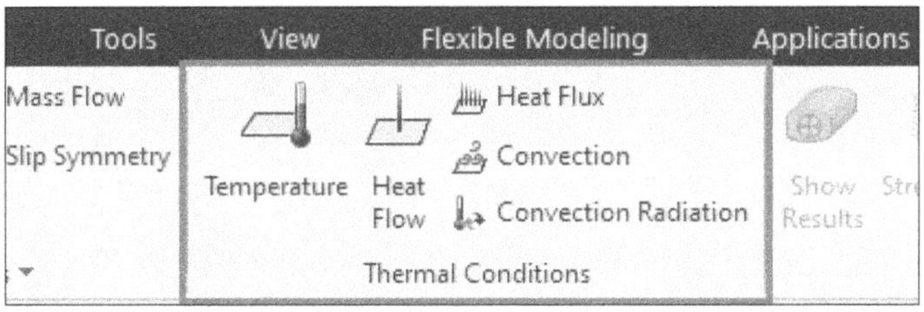

Figure-75. Thermal Conditions panel

The procedures to apply different type of thermal conditions have been discussed earlier in this chapter. Here, we will discuss only about **Convection Radiation Thermal Condition**.

Convection Radiation Thermal Condition

The **Convection Radiation** thermal condition combines both convection and radiation conditions. The procedure to apply convection radiation thermal condition is discussed next.

- Click on the **Convection Radiation** button from the **Thermal Conditions** panel of the **Ribbon**. The **Convection Radiation** dialog box will be displayed; refer to Figure-76.

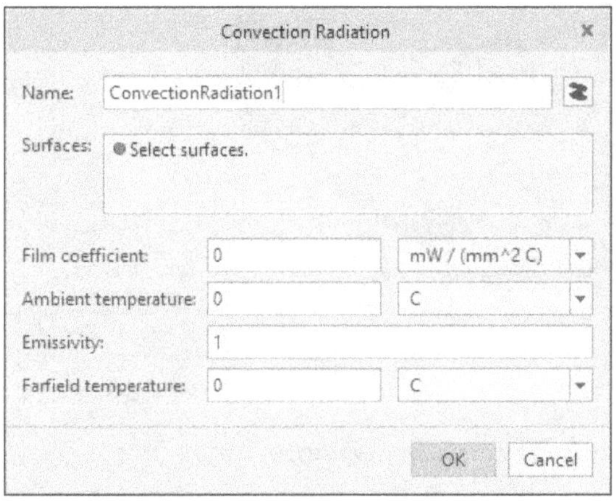

Figure-76. Convection Radiation dialog box

- Specify desired thermal condition name in the **Name** edit box and click on **Change the color** button available next to the edit box if you want to change the color of thermal condition.
- Select the surfaces of the model on which you want to apply the thermal condition; refer to Figure-77.

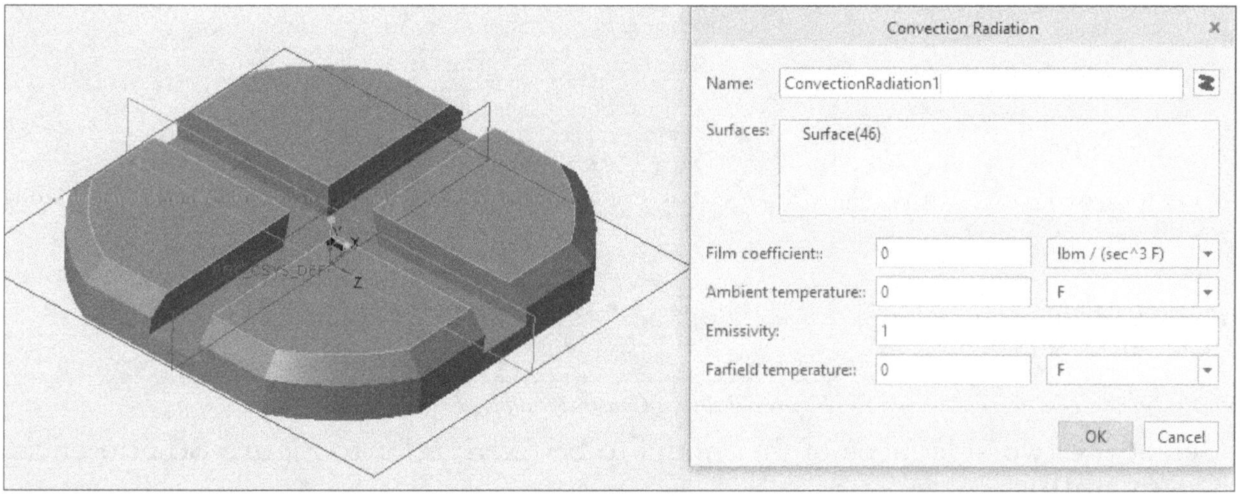

Figure-77. Surfaces selected for convection radiation thermal condition

- Specify desired value for heat transfer coefficient in the **Film coefficient** edit box and **Ambient temperature** edit box.
- Select desired unit from the drop-down available next to the film coefficient and ambient temperature edit boxes.
- Specify desired value for radiative heat transfer in the **Emissivity** edit box and **Farfield temperature** edit box.
- Select desired unit for temperature from the drop-down available next to the **Farfield temperature** edit box.
- Click on the **OK** button from the dialog box to create the convection radiation thermal condition.

PRACTICAL 1 STRUCTURAL SIMULATION STUDY

Perform structural analysis on the model as shown in Figure-78. The model is a rectangular slab of 250mm x 700mm x 50mm.

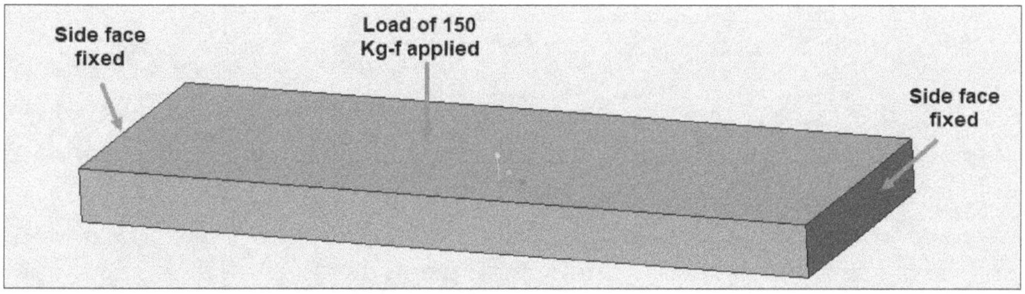

Figure-78. Practical 1 model

Steps:

- Open the model file in Creo Parametric from the downloaded resource kit folder.
- Click on the **Fixed** button from the **Constraints** panel in the **Live Simulation** tab of the **Ribbon**. The **Fixed Constraint** dialog box will be displayed; refer to Figure-79.

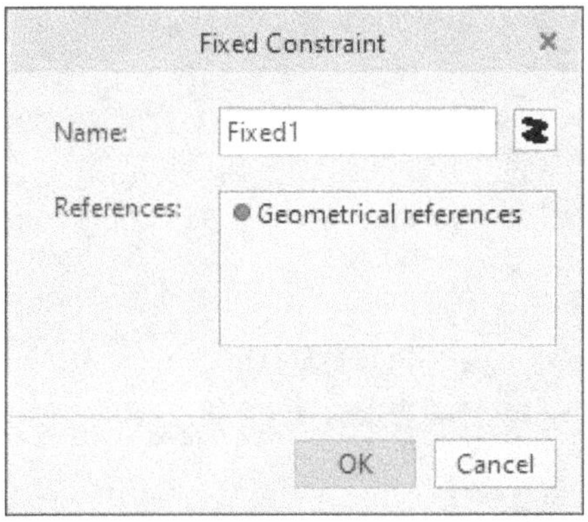

Figure-79. Fixed Constraint dialog box

- Select the two side faces of the model to be fixed; refer to Figure-80 and click on the **OK** button.

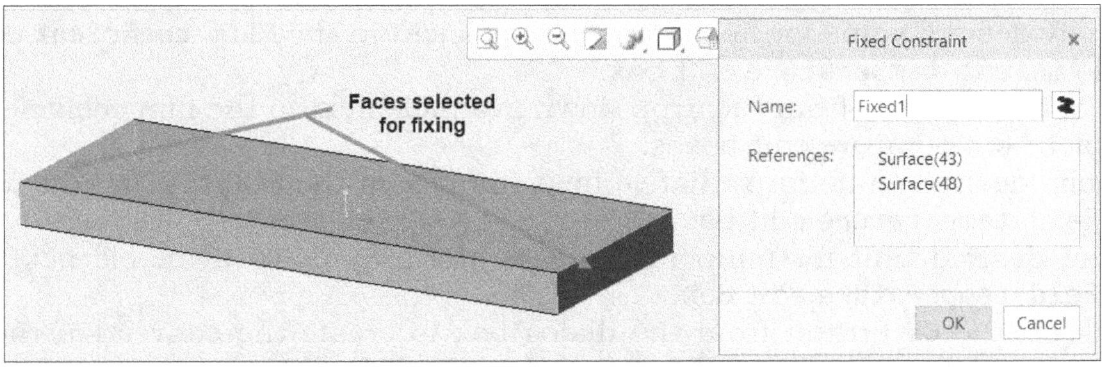

Figure-80. Faces selected for fixing

- Click on the **Force** tool from the **Loads** panel in the **Live Simulation** tab of the **Ribbon**. The **Force Load** dialog box will be displayed.
- Select the face on which you need to apply the load and specify the parameters as shown in Figure-81.

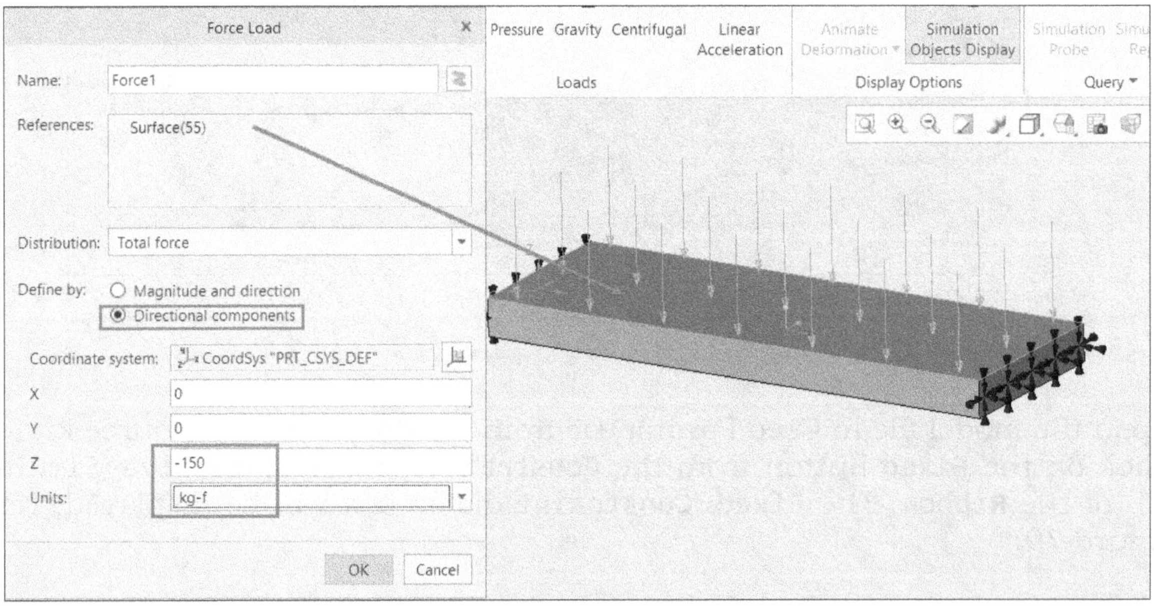

Figure-81. Specifying force load

- After specifying parameters, click on the **OK** button.

- Click on the **Simulate** button from the **Study** panel in the **Live Simulation** tab of **Ribbon** after specifying the parameters. The simulation results will be displayed; refer to Figure-82.

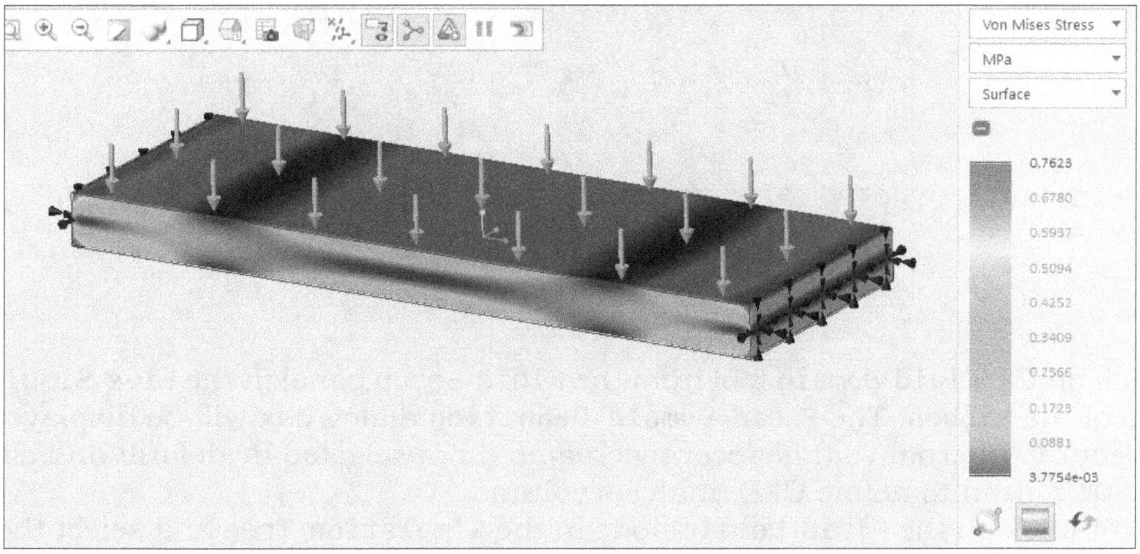

Figure-82. Structure simulation result

PRACTICAL 2 FLUID SIMULATION STUDY

Perform fluid simulation on the model as shown in Figure-83.

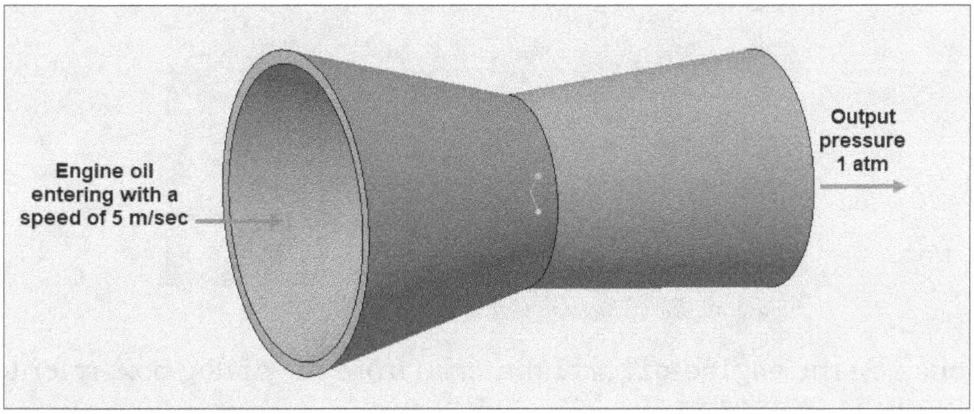

Figure-83. Model for CFD

Steps:

- Open the model file for practical from the resource kit folder.
- Click on the **Fluid Simulation Study** option from the **Add Simulation** drop-down in the **Study** panel of **Live Simulation** tab in the **Ribbon**. A new fluid simulation study will activate.
- Click on the **Internal Volume** tool from the **Fluid Domain** drop-down in the **Fluid Setup** panel of **Live Simulation** tab in the **Ribbon**. The **Internal Volume** contextual tab will be displayed.
- Select the two bounding faces of the model while holding the **CTRL** key as shown in Figure-84. Preview of internal volume will be displayed.
- Click on the **OK** button to create the volume.

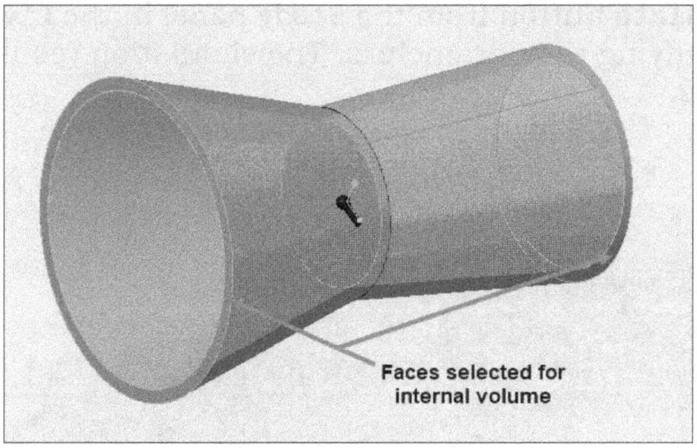

Figure-84. Preview of internal volume

- Click on the **Fluid Domain** tool from the **Fluid Setup** panel in the **Live Simulation** tab of the **Ribbon**. The **Fluid Domain Definition** dialog box will be displayed.
- Select the internal volume recently created if not selected by default and click on the **OK** button to define CFD analysis volume.
- Right-click on the **Fluid Domain** node in the **Simulation Tree** and select the **Edit Materials** option; refer to Figure-85. The **Materials** dialog box will be displayed.

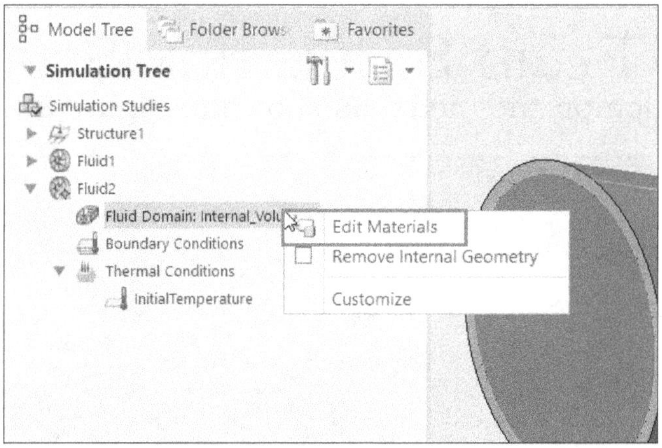

Figure-85. Edit Materials option

- Double-click on the **engine oil.mtl** material from the dialog box; refer to Figure-86 and click on the **OK** button.

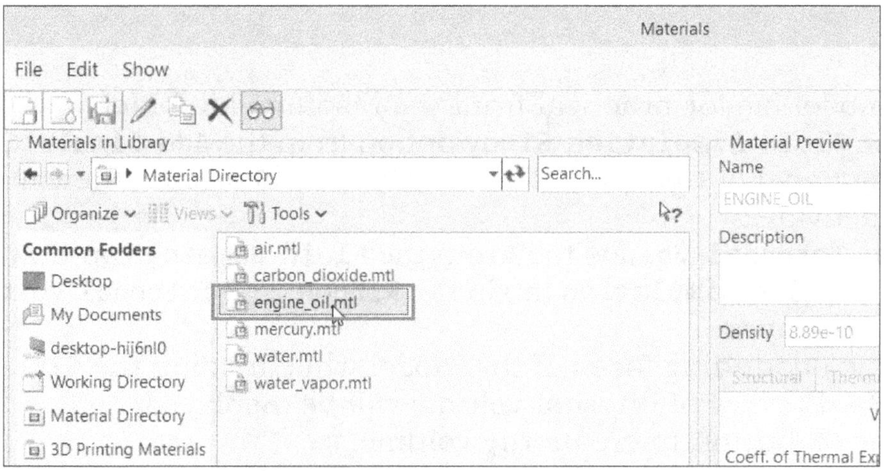

Figure-86. Material selected

- Click on the **Flow Velocity** tool from the **Boundary Conditions** panel in the **Live Simulation** tab of **Ribbon**. The **Fluid Flow Velocity** dialog box will be displayed. Specify desired parameters and select the face as shown in Figure-87.

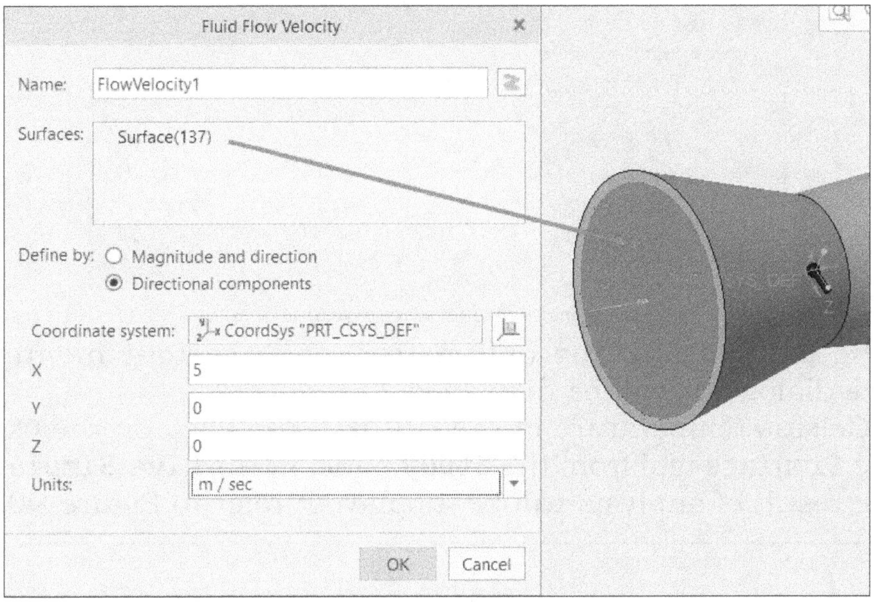

Figure-87. Face selected for applying flow velocity

- After specifying desired parameters, click on the **OK** button from the dialog box.
- Click on the **Outlet Pressure** tool from the **Boundary Conditions** panel in the **Live Simulation** tab of **Ribbon**. The **Outlet Pressure** dialog box will be displayed.
- Select the outlet face of model and specify the parameters as shown in Figure-88.

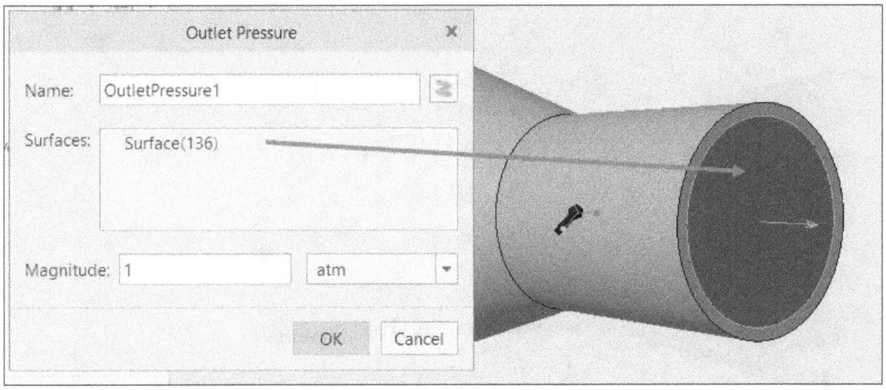

Figure-88. Specifying outlet pressure

- Click on the **OK** button from the dialog box. The outlet pressure will be applied.
- Right-click on the **Initial Temperature** option from the **Thermal Conditions** node in **Simulation Tree**. A shortcut menu will be displayed; refer to Figure-89.

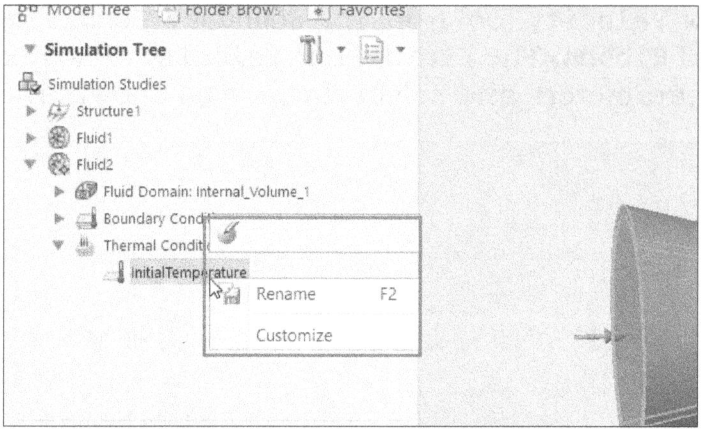

Figure-89. Shortcut menu for initial temperature

- Click on the **Edit Definition** option from the shortcut menu. The **Initial Temperature** dialog box will be displayed.
- Specify **25** Celsius temperature in the edit box and click on the **OK** button.
- Click on the **Simulate** tool from the **Study** panel in the **Live Simulation** tab of the **Ribbon**. The result of analysis will be displayed; refer to Figure-90.

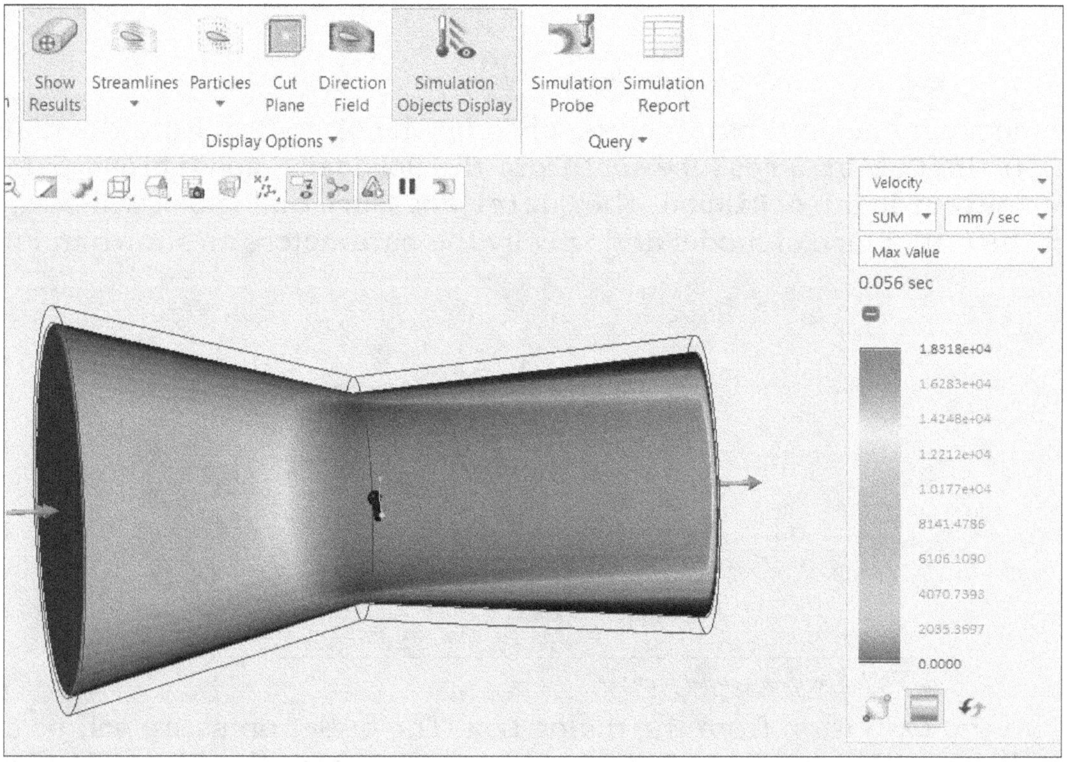

Figure-90. CFD analysis result

- Click on the **Simulate** button from the **In-Graphics Toolbar** to exit simulation.

SELF ASSESSMENT

1. What is Simulation? Give a brief note.

2. Which of the following simulation study is used to evaluate stress and deformation of a solid model?

a) Structure Simulation Study
b) Modal Simulation Study
c) Thermal Simulation Study
d) None of the Above

3. Which of the following loads is used to apply bending load on selected faces of model?

a) Force load
b) Centrifugal load
c) Moment load
d) Linear acceleration load

4. In Fluid Simulation Study, which of the following boundary conditions specifies the inlet velocity as the sum of two separate components, a component normal to the boundary (axial velocity), and a component with a radial velocity?

a) Flow Velocity
b) Inlet Pressure
c) Slip Symmetry
d) Swirl Inlet

5. .... loads simulate local heat sources and sinks of your model. It sets the rate of heat energy transfer of selected surfaces.

6. .... calculates effects of constant thermal loads on a model and is used to determine temperatures, heat flow rates, and the heat fluxes in a part.

7. **Displacement Constraint** prevents selected surface from moving or deforming, that is it removes all degrees of freedom from the surface. (T/F)

8. Select the **Composite** result type from **Results Legend** to see the activity inside the model. (T/F)

9. Which software is integrated with Creo Live Simulation for real-time analysis?

a) SolidWorks
b) Autodesk
c) ANSYS
d) Fusion 360

10. What kind of simulation types can Creo Live Simulation handle?

a) Only structural
b) Only thermal
c) Static structural, thermal, and modal
d) Electrical and thermal only

11. What is the purpose of the Scope tool in simulation?

a) To change color of geometry
b) To specify constraints
c) To define which assembly components are included in the simulation
d) To detect errors in geometry

12. What does the Detect Contacts tool primarily do?

a) Highlights faulty edges
b) Identifies contacts within a specified distance
c) Creates bonded connections
d) Modifies component colors

13. What does a fixed constraint do in Creo simulation?

a) Allows full motion
b) Restricts translation only
c) Removes all degrees of freedom from a surface
d) Locks angular movement only

14. A cylindrical constraint allows:

a) Full movement in all directions
b) Axial movement and fixes radial movement
c) Only translation along Z-axis
d) No movement at all

15. What does a ball constraint simulate?

a) A pin joint
b) A sliding surface
c) A ball joint with fixed translation and free rotation
d) A weld joint

16. Which constraint restricts off-plane displacement but allows movement on the plane?

a) Ball
b) Cylindrical
c) Planar
d) Fixed

17. Gravity load in Creo Parametric simulates:

a) Heat
b) Torque
c) Earth's gravitational effect
d) Surface roughness

18. Which load simulates rigid body rotation effects?

a) Linear acceleration
b) Centrifugal
c) Gravity
d) Pressure

19. The Linear Acceleration load applies to:

a) A single vertex only
b) Edges only
c) A body or multiple bodies
d) Constraints

20. What does the Simulation Results Legend allow you to do?

a) Set units for pressure
b) View result types and rendering options
c) Animate constraints
d) Export to PDF

21. Which rendering method allows viewing inside the model?

a) Surface
b) Composite
c) Max Value
d) Min Value

22. The Inspect Deviation tool is used to:

a) Highlight maximum load areas
b) Display unresolved areas after simulation
c) Remove errors
d) Compare two models

23. What is the main purpose of a Thermal Simulation Study in Creo?

a) To calculate mechanical deformation due to forces
b) To calculate the thermal response to heat loads
c) To determine fluid pressure in a system
d) To measure physical vibration frequency

24. What does a convection boundary condition simulate in a thermal study?

a) Heat generation inside the body
b) Fluid flow rate
c) Cooling or heating at a surface due to convection
d) Vibration of structural components

25. What does a heat flux load represent?

a) Internal temperature of a surface
b) Pressure on a surface
c) Rate of heat transfer per unit area
d) Total mass flow through an object

26. In a Modal Simulation Study, what is "resonance"?

a) Alignment of a body with the X-axis
b) Loss of heat energy during simulation
c) Natural vibration of a structure matching an external frequency
d) Maximum flow of fluid through an enclosure

27. What does a Fluid Simulation Study help predict?

a) Acoustic vibrations
b) Internal and external fluid flow and heat transfer
c) Thermal stress deformation
d) Chemical composition of fluids

28. The Internal Volume tool is used to:

a) Add thermal boundary layers
b) Create internal fluid volume for CFD analysis
c) Convert solid bodies into surfaces
d) Analyze heat flux data

29. What is the use of the Fluid Domain tool in Creo?

a) Apply loads to solid parts
b) Specify domain for boundary condition application
c) Select quilts as fluid domain for CFD
d) Create simulation report

30. The Flow Velocity boundary condition defines:

a) Fluid color and density
b) Inlet fluid velocity and its direction
c) Surface temperature
d) Ambient air pressure

31. Inlet pressure is applied to:

a) Define radiation boundaries
b) Set resistance in a component
c) Specify fluid pressure at the inlet
d) Determine turbulence

32. What condition must be met to apply an Outlet Pressure boundary?

a) Apply to all external bodies
b) Apply to a surface within fluid domain
c) Apply before thermal load
d) Apply to rotating parts

33. What does the Slip Symmetry boundary condition simulate?

a) Frictional flow on rough surfaces
b) Free flow along a wall without friction
c) Complete blockage of flow
d) Turbulence generation at corners

34. Which boundary condition allows defining both radial and axial flow velocity?

a) Flow Velocity
b) Mass Flow
c) Swirl Inlet
d) Slip Symmetry

35. What is a Rotating Wall boundary condition used for?

a) Simulate real-time movement of rotating parts
b) Apply magnetic field to rotating parts
c) Simulate rotation effects without physical movement
d) Restrict fluid flow to rotating components

36. The Convection Radiation condition includes which two forms of heat transfer?

a) Conduction and convection
b) Convection and fluid friction
c) Convection and radiation
d) Vibration and conduction

FOR STUDENT NOTES

Answers to Self Assessment Questions :

2. (a) **3.** (c) **4.** (d) **5.** Heat Flow **6.** Thermal Conditions **7.** F **8.** T

Index

Symbols

A

B

C

E

F

G

H

S

T

Ethics of an Engineer

- Engineers shall hold paramount the safety, health and welfare of the public and shall strive to comply with the principles of sustainable development in the performance of their professional duties.
- Engineers shall perform services only in areas of their competence.
- Engineers shall issue public statements only in an objective and truthful manner.
- Engineers shall act in professional manners for each employer or client as faithful agents or trustees, and shall avoid conflicts of interest.
- Engineers shall build their professional reputation on the merit of their services and shall not compete unfairly with others.
- Engineers shall act in such a manner as to uphold and enhance the honor, integrity, and dignity of the engineering profession and shall act with zero-tolerance for bribery, fraud, and corruption.
- Engineers shall continue their professional development throughout their careers, and shall provide opportunities for the professional development of those engineers under their supervision.

www.ingramcontent.com/pod-product-compliance
Lightning Source LLC
LaVergne TN
LVHW082002200926
848481LV00010B/2787